Tax Advisers' Guide to Trusts

Second Edition

Tax Advisers' Guide to Trusts

Second Edition

by

Nigel Eastaway
of WJB Chiltern Plc, and

Ian Richards BA
Barrister of Pump Court Tax Chambers

with David Garlick

LexisNexis™ UK

Members of the LexisNexis Group worldwide

United Kingdom	LexisNexis UK, a Division of Reed Elsevier (UK) Ltd, Halsbury House, 35 Chancery Lane, LONDON, WC2A 1EL, and 4 Hill Street, EDINBURGH EH2 3JZ
Argentina	LexisNexis Argentina, BUENOS AIRES
Australia	LexisNexis Butterworths, CHATSWOOD, New South Wales
Austria	LexisNexis Verlag ARD Orac GmbH & Co KG, VIENNA
Canada	LexisNexis Butterworths, MARKHAM, Ontario
Chile	LexisNexis Chile Ltda, SANTIAGO DE CHILE
Czech Republic	Nakladatelství Orac sro, PRAGUE
France	Editions du Juris-Classeur SA, PARIS
Germany	LexisNexis Deutschland GmbH, FRANKFURT and MUNSTER
Hong Kong	LexisNexis Butterworths, HONG KONG
Hungary	HVG-Orac, BUDAPEST
India	LexisNexis Butterworths, NEW DELHI
Ireland	LexisNexis, DUBLIN
Italy	Giuffrè Editore, MILAN
Malaysia	Malayan Law Journal Sdn Bhd, KUALA LUMPUR
New Zealand	LexisNexis Butterworths, WELLINGTON
Poland	Wydawnictwo Prawnicze LexisNexis, WARSAW
Singapore	LexisNexis Butterworths, SINGAPORE
South Africa	LexisNexis Butterworths, DURBAN
Switzerland	Stämpfli Verlag AG, BERNE
USA	LexisNexis, DAYTON, Ohio

A CIP Catalogue record for this book is available from the British Library.

ISBN 0 7545 2251 2

Typeset by Columns Design Ltd, Reading, England

Printed and bound in Great Britain by Clays Ltd, St Ives Plc

Visit LexisNexis UK at www.lexisnexis.co.uk

Preface

Many tax advisers seem to feel rather uncomfortable with the concept of trusts, and the purpose of this book is to try to demystify the subject and explain the tax rules and the way in which trusts can be used in practice as a flexible and effective means of wealth accumulation and protection in an uncertain world.

A trust is not a separate legal entity, but a relationship which depends upon the concept of Anglo Saxon common law recognising a distinction between the legal and beneficial ownership of a property. Common law has been developed over the years and much statute law is now involved in the regulation and taxation of trusts. It is assumed that, as this book is aimed at tax advisers, readers will have readily to hand the taxing statutes. However, many tax advisers may not have some of the non-tax legislation, which we feel is essential to consider in effective trust planning, and the appendices therefore reproduce the major trust legislation and extracts relating to trusts from a number of other relevant acts. We hope that practitioners will find this useful.

It is also assumed that readers will be familiar with the general tax rules relating to the computation of income and gains for self-assessment purposes, so this book concentrates on the UK tax rules applicable to trusts, resident in the UK or abroad, and the resultant tax liabilities of the trustees, settlors and beneficiaries, and opportunities for reducing those liabilities where possible. The law is stated as at 1 November 2003.

We would like to thank Liz Te Puia for typing the manuscript and dealing with our many alterations, David Hughes for checking the draft, and Suzie Stamei for her comments on the first edition.

Nigel Eastaway and Ian Richards
October 2003

Nigel Eastaway and David Garlick
WJB Chiltern Plc
3 Sheldon Square
Paddington
London W2 6PS
Tel: 020 7339 9000
Fax: 020 7339 9010
E-mail: eastawayn@wjbchiltern.com

Ian Richards
Pump Court Tax Chambers
16 Bedford Row
London WC1R 4EB
Tel: 020 7414 8080
Fax: 020 7414 8099
E-mail: ianir@pumptax.com

Contents

Abbreviations and References

AA 1870	=	Apportionment Act
ACT	=	Advance Corporation Tax
AEA 1925	=	Administration of Estates Act
AJA 1985	=	Administration of Justice Act
BA 1914	=	Bankruptcy Act
CA 1985, 1989	=	Companies Acts
CA 1993	=	Charities Act
CAA 1990, 2001	=	Capital Allowances Acts
CGT	=	Capital Gains Tax
CTO	=	Capital Taxes Office
CTVA 1954	=	Charitable Trusts (Validation) Act
DMPA 1973	=	Domicile and Matrimonial Proceedings Act
EBT	=	Employee Benefit Trust
ESC	=	Extra Statutory Concession
EPAA 1985	=	Enduring Powers of Attorney Act
ESOP	=	Employee Share Ownership Plan
ESOT	=	Employee Share Ownership Trust
FA	=	Finance Acts
FLRA 1969	=	Family Law Reform Act
FRS	=	Finance Reporting Standard
FSA 1986	=	Finance Services Act
IA 1986	=	Insolvency Act
ICTA 1988	=	Income and Corporation Taxes Act
IEA 1952	=	Intestate Estates Act
IHT	=	Inheritance Tax
IHTA 1984	=	Inheritance Tax Act
IPFDA 1975	=	Inheritance (Provision for Family and Dependants) Act
ITEPA 2003	=	Income Tax (Earnings and Pensions) Act
LA 1980	=	Limitation Act
LCA 1925	=	Land Charges Act
LPA 1925	=	Law of Property Act
LP(MP)A 1989	=	Law of Property (Miscellaneous Provisions) Act
MCA 1973	=	Matrimonial Causes Act
MLR 2003	=	Money Laundering Regulations
MLRO	=	Money Laundering Reporting Officer
MHA 1983	=	Mental Health Act
MPPA 1970	=	Matrimonial Proceedings and Property Act
MWPA 1882	=	Married Women's Property Act
NCIS	=	National Criminal Intelligence Service
PA 1890	=	Partnership Act
PAA 1964	=	Perpetuities and Accumulations Act
PAA 1971	=	Powers of Attorney Act
PCA 2002	=	Proceeds of Crime Act

PTA 1906	=	Public Trustee Act
RCA 1958	=	Recreational Charities Act
RI	=	Revenue Interpretation
RTA 1987	=	Recognition of Trusts Act
SLA 1882'90, 1925	=	Settled Land Acts
SP	=	Statement of Practice
SSCBA 1992	=	Social Security Contributions and Benefits Act
TA 1925, 2000	=	Trustee Acts
TCGA 1992	=	Taxation of Chargeable Gains Act
TDA 1999	=	Trustee Delegation Act
TIA 1961	=	Trustee Investment Act
TLATA 1996	=	Trusts of Land and Apportionment of Trustees Act
UITF	=	Urgent Issues Task Force
VAT	=	Value Added Tax
VATA 1994	=	Value Added Tax Act
VTA 1958	=	Variation of Trusts Act
WA 1837, 1963, 1968	=	Wills Acts

Table of Statutes

Paragraph numbers and appendices in bold indicate that the legislation is set out in part or in full.

Table of Statutory Instruments

Table of Cases

B

D

E

F

G

H

I

J

K

L

M

N

O

P

R

S

U

V

Y

Z

Chapter 1

A Useful Relationship

Introduction

1.1 A common view of the origin of trusts rests with the landed knight in shining armour rushing off to the crusades to fight for Christendom. Before leaving, however, he would transfer the family estates to his loyal brother for the use of his wife and family. It not infrequently happened that the loyal brother turned into a wicked uncle and took the estate for himself and if the remains of our trusty knight were rusting away on some foreign field his wife and family were destitute. The only hope was an appeal to the King, or, in due course, to the Lord Chancellor as keeper of the King's conscience to give them back the use of the family estate, even though the legal title to the land remained with the brother.

1.2 The reality, of course, was rather less romantic and, in fact, the holding of land by one person for the use of another was not unknown prior to the Norman conquest, but the common law did not recognise the use and it was not actually until about 1400 that the Lord Chancellor was acting to enforce uses, appointing the legal owner the *feoffee to uses* and the intended occupier or beneficiary the *cestui que use*. One of the consequences of holding land for the use of another, by the relatively simple device of vesting the land in a number of *feoffees to uses* as joint tenants, was that the legal estate passed by survivorship to the remaining joint tenants on the death of one of the *feoffees* and the feudal dues payable on assets passing on death did not apply. The rights of the *cestui que use* continued to be enforced under the law of equity in what in due course became the Chancery Division of the courts and could be passed to successive *cestui que use* without incurring a tax charge. The exploitation of the English system of equity for tax avoidance therefore has a long pedigree. One of the earliest anti-avoidance provisions was the Statute of Uses, introduced in 1535, which was designed to extinguish most of the uses and transfer the legal estate to the *cestui que use*, which helped to raise increased feudal dues arising on death for Henry VIII and his successors. However, the tax avoidance industry of the day came up with the solution whereby the land was transferred to the *feoffees* (A) for the use of the *cestui que use* (B) to hold in trust for the intended beneficiary (C). Thus the use upon a use turned into a trust, as the statute of uses merely transferred the legal estate from A to B but equity would still enforce the rights of the beneficiary C. In due course it was only necessary to transfer the property to the trustee who held the legal estate for the benefit of the beneficiary who held the equitable estate. The Court of Chancery was there to remind the trustee that although he may hold the legal estate his conscience ought not to allow him to treat it as if it were his own property, rather, it was entrusted to him for the beneficiary. Equity would not permit him to do the unconscionable and ignore the beneficiary's interests.

A matter of conscience

1.3 The concept of acting in accordance with the conscience of the alleged trustee is still fundamental to trusts, as is shown by the House of Lords in *Westdeutsche Landesbank Girozentrale v Islington London Borough Council* [1996] AC 669 at 705 where Browne-Wilkinson LJ summarised the basic requirements of a valid trust as follows:

'(i) equity operates on the conscience of the owner of the legal interest. In the case of a trust the conscience of the legal owner requires him to carry out the purposes for which the property was vested in him (express or implied trust) or which the law imposes on him by reason of his unconscionable conduct (constructive trust);

(ii) since the equitable jurisdiction to enforce trusts depends upon the conscience of the holder of the legal interest being affected he cannot be a trustee of the property if and so long as he is ignorant of the facts alleged to affect his conscience ie until he is aware that he is intended to hold the property for the benefit of others, in the case of an express or implied trust, or in the case of a constructive trust of the factors which are alleged to affect his conscience;

(iii) in order to establish a trust there must be identifiable trust property. The only apparent exception to this rule is a constructive trust imposed on a person who dishonestly assists in a breach of trust who may come under fiduciary duties even if he does not receive identifiable trust property;

(iv) once a trust is established, as from the date of its establishment the beneficiary has in equity a proprietary interest in the trust property which proprietary interest will be enforceable in equity against any subsequent holder of the property (whether the original property or substituted property into which it can be traced) other than a purchaser for value of the legal interest without notice.'

1.4 Although the Judicature Acts of 1873–75 abolished the requirement to take separate actions under common law or equity by allowing courts to apply legal or equitable remedies where appropriate, the dual thread of law and equity, with the consequent legal interests of the trustee and equitable interests of the beneficiary in a trust situation, with its inevitable consequence of two enforceable interests in the same property at the same time, continues to the present day. It also continues to confuse those familiar with civil law jurisdictions where an equitable interest distinct from a legal interest is unknown.

The nature of a trust

1.5 A trust is not in any sense a separate legal entity in the same way as a company or building society is a separate legal person created by statute. It is a relationship enforceable at law which arises when the owner of property, the settlor, transfers the legal estate in that property to trustees who become the legal owners, for the benefit of the beneficiaries. These beneficiaries, or others on their behalf, may enforce their rights under the trust, which are usually encompassed in a trust deed or deed of settlement or implied by a statute or jurisprudence. A trust of land is often referred to as a settlement and a trust, usually of a landed estate, created under SLA 1925 as a strict settlement. However, for tax purposes the term settlement or settled property includes any trust whether or not the assets include land, and as this book is aimed at tax advisers rather than trust lawyers the terms trust and settlement will be treated as synonymous except where a contrary intention is indicated.

1.6 A trust requires a settlor, but the settlor can be a trustee, even the sole trustee, and can be a beneficiary, even the sole beneficiary. There must, however, be other interests or potential beneficiaries as otherwise there is full retention of the legal title which includes all proprietorial rights over the assets. An equitable interest does not arise until another party is involved. In *Westdeutsche Landesbank Girozentrale v Islington London Borough Council* [1996] AC 669 Browne-Wilkinson LJ stated that a person solely entitled to the full beneficial ownership of money or property both at law and in equity does not enjoy an equitable interest in that property. The legal title carries with it all rights. Unless and until there is a separation of the legal and equitable estates there is no separate equitable title.

Types of trust

Bare trusts

1.7 The simplest type of trust is the bare trust, under which assets are transferred by the settlor to the legal ownership of the trustee, or nominee, for the benefit of the settlor absolutely. The bare trust is often used in share dealings where the investment manager is appointed the shareholder, as nominee, to enable shares to be bought and sold expeditiously. It is sometimes used to make the beneficial owner less conspicuous, although nowadays CA 1985 s 208 requires certain nominee holdings to be disclosed to the company. It is not unusual for a group of shareholders and members of the same family to transfer their shares to the same trustees to hold as nominees for them, enabling the combined shareholding to be voted as a single block of shares, which, in turn, enables the influence of the individual shareholdings to be maximised.

1.8 In the case of land, the number of joint owners is limited to four and it is common practice where real estate is owned in a partnership, to hold the legal estate in the names of four of the more senior partners as nominees for all the equity partners interested in the property, for the time being. In some cases the land is held through a company acting as nominee for the partners for the same purpose.

Discretionary trusts

1.9 A discretionary trust is one where at least some of the beneficiaries are identified but the precise interests of each beneficiary, including that of any future beneficiary appointed by the trustees, is left to the discretion of the trustees. In some cases the trustees are required to refer to the settlor for guidance before exercising their discretion, in other cases at the time of creating the trust the settlor indicates to the trustees how he would like the discretion to be exercised and this is recorded in a trustees' minute. In other cases the settlor may write to the trustees setting out his wishes in a letter which, although not binding on the trustees, is likely to be followed by them in most circumstances. The Inland Revenue regards a settlor's letter of wishes as part of the trust documentation. Whether the Revenue is right is a moot point in the light of *Re Londonderry's Settlement* [1965] Ch 918.

1.10 The wide powers to add potential beneficiaries to a discretionary trust have been explored in *Re Manisty's Settlement* [1974] Ch 17 and in *Abrahams Wills Trust* [1969] 1 Ch 463. *Nova Scotia Trust v Barletta*, Bahamas Supreme Court, EG No 550 of 1984, confirms that a letter of wishes is in no way binding on the trustees and any circumscription of the trustees' powers has to be included in the trust deed itself.

Interest in possession trusts

1.11 An interest in possession exists where a beneficiary has a present entitlement to the present income of the trust, after deduction of proper trust expenses (*Pearson v IRC* [1980] STC 318). The beneficiary with an interest in possession for life is usually known as the life tenant. A beneficiary may be entitled to an interest in possession in the whole or any part of the trust fund.

Accumulation and maintenance trusts

1.12 An accumulation and maintenance trust is a discretionary trust for minors, where the trustees are empowered to use the trust income for the maintenance, education or benefit of the beneficiaries, with any balance being accumulated and added to the trust capital. The term is usually confined to those trusts within the definition in IHTA 1984 s 71, which in turn is based on the statutory trusts for infants in the Trustee Act 1925 s 31. As well as the requirement that there is no interest in possession in the settlement while it is an accumulation and maintenance settlement, there is also the requirement that one or more of the beneficiaries will become entitled to an interest in possession on or before reaching the age of 25. A requirement to have an interest in possession at age 25 or earlier is not a requirement to have any entitlement to the trust capital at that stage, although the beneficiary's share of the trust fund has become vested. It is quite common to provide that a beneficiary's share of the trust capital should be paid to his estate on death, or advanced to him at an earlier age as specified in the trust deed, or left to the trustees' discretion.

Protective trusts

1.13 A protective trust, or spendthrift trust, is one in which the beneficiary's interest in the trust, which is usually a life interest, is determinable upon his bankruptcy or attempted alienation of his rights under the trust. On determination of the life interest the trust usually reverts to being a discretionary trust in favour of the former life tenant and his spouse and children, if any. TA 1925 s 33 provides a model form of protective trust.

Disabled persons' trusts

1.14 A disabled person's trust is a discretionary trust, although for IHT purposes under IHTA 1984 s 89 it is treated as an interest in possession trust in which the disabled person has the life tenancy. In order to qualify, the trust must be for someone incapable of looking after their own affairs within the meaning of MHA 1983 or in receipt of an attendance allowance or disability living allowance under SSCBA 1992. Normally the true interest in possession trust or the straightforward discretionary trust is used in preference to a disabled person's trust in these situations.

Charitable trusts

1.15 A charitable trust is a purpose trust which is given a number of taxation privileges and is exempt from the normal perpetuity period applied to a trust, and can therefore last indefinitely. Charitable purposes were summarised by MacNaughten LJ in *Income Tax Special Purposes Comrs v Pemsel* [1891] AC 531 as falling into four principle divisions:

(a) trusts for the relief of poverty;

(b) trusts for the advancement of education;

(c) trusts for the advancement of religion; and

(d) trusts for other purposes beneficial to the community and not falling under any of the other preceding heads.

Purpose trusts

1.16 It is generally considered under English law that purpose trusts for non-charitable purposes will only be enforced in very limited cases such as trusts for the erection or maintenance of monuments or graves, trusts for the saying of masses, trusts for the maintenance of particular animals, trusts for the benefit of unincorporated associations and miscellaneous cases. This classification in the rule against perpetuities by *Morris & Leach* (1956) was endorsed by Lord Evershed MR in *Re Endacott* [1960] Ch 232. Some commentators argue that the perceived prohibition of most purpose trusts that are not charitable under English law is misconceived, and many foreign jurisdictions specifically allow purposes trusts for either public or private purposes. Where purpose trusts are created they are usually discretionary in nature.

Resulting trusts

1.17 The trusts so far described have been created by the settlor as a result of consciously transferring assets to trustees to hold on trust for the beneficiaries. Trusts, however, can also arise as a result of law without there being any express trust. A resulting trust arises where the settlor and beneficiary are the same person. For example, if property is transferred into the name of the third party, in the absence of consideration or any evidence of donative intent by the transferor, the transferee is presumed to hold the legal estate in trust for the transferor who retains the absolute beneficial interest. There is therefore a presumed resulting bare trust, with the transferee being treated as mere nominee for the transferor (*Re Vandervells Trust (No 2)* [1974] Ch 269). A second type of resulting trust arises where there is a transfer to a trustee of the legal estate but some or all of the beneficial interests are undisposed of and automatically held on resulting trusts for the settlor. *Barclays Bank Ltd v Quistclose Investments Ltd* [1970] AC 567 and *Westdeutsche v Islington London Borough Council [1996] AC 669* would seem to confirm that these are the only two types of resulting trust acceptable to the law.

Implied trusts

1.18 Implied trusts arise where the court infers the settlor's intentions from his actions. For example if an author were to send copies of a number of aircraft books to the librarian of an aviation trust, the implication would be that these were an addition to the trust archives, not to the librarian in his personal capacity, although, as with all presumptions, this is capable of being rebutted by appropriate evidence to the contrary.

Constructive trusts

1.19 A constructive trust is imposed by the court contrary to the wishes of the person identified as the trustee in circumstances where his acquisition of the legal title was subject to the equitable interests of some third party beneficiary. This may apply, for example, in the case of co-habitees who acquire a house in the name of one of the parties, which is occupied by both. In order to show a constructive trust of part of the property in favour of the non-legal owner it is necessary to show either that there was some prior agreement, however informal, for them to share the beneficial interest and that the beneficiary has altered his or her position to his or her detriment in reliance on the presumed equitable interest.

1.20 Alternatively the trust may be construed as a result of both parties' contribution to the original purpose or the repayment of the mortgage on the property acquired. (*Lloyds Bank Plc v Rosset* [1991] 1 AC 107).

1.21 Constructive trusts can also be imposed as a result of fraud by the transferee, as in *McCormick v Grogan* (1869) LR 4 HL 82, or to give effect to a secret trust, eg *Ottaway v Norman* [1972] Ch 698, where a property was left in A's will to B on terms that she would leave it in her own will to A's son C.

Statutory trusts

1.22 Under LPA 1925 s 19 the conveyance of a legal estate to an infant is held on statutory trust until he reaches the age of 18. Under LPA 1925 s 36 where a legal estate is held as joint tenants it is treated as held on a trust of land under TLATA 1996.

1.23 Under LPA 1925 s 34 land held in undivided shares, eg, for the members of a partnership, will vest in the first four named joint owners as a trust of land for all the partners. Under AEA 1925 s 33 the property of an intestate vests in his personal representatives on trusts for sale, and to the extent that this includes real property as a trust of land. AEA 1925 s 47 sets out the statutory trusts which apply on intestacy.

Strict and Settled Land Act settlements

1.24 Prior to the Settled Land Acts of 1882 to 1890 it was not uncommon for land to be settled for generations which prevented it being freely transferable. This stultified its development, leading to general decay for both the landed families and the workers on the land. The reform of settled land and the rule against perpetuities allowed a person to appoint real estate on a strict settlement for himself for life with remainder to his son for life, followed by an entailed interest for his son's eldest son as, in practice, land was settled in entail male, with daughters being excluded. When the grandson became the life tenant entail in possession, he could bar the entail and create for himself a freehold interest of the fee simple absolute in possession, which would allow him to sell the land.

1.25 In order to keep the property within the settlement it became common practice to grant an income from the land to the entailed beneficiary before he came into possession, on condition that, on barring the entail to create a freehold, which could only be done with his father's consent because he was not yet in possession, he resettled the land on his father and himself for life and would then entail it for his own eldest son. When the son came into possession on the death of his father he would be life tenant not tenant entail in possession, because of the existence of the new entail to his own son. The land was then kept in the family for generations. The Settled Land Acts of 1882, 1884, 1887, 1889, 1890 and 1925 effectively gave the life tenant in possession power to sell the freehold interest, although the proceeds of sale had to be paid to the trustees of the settlement. SLA 1925 separated the trust instrument on which the land, or any proceeds of sale, would be held from the deed vesting the legal estate in the land in the life tenant as the statutory owner. Unfortunately the 1925 Act applied wherever there was a succession of equitable interests, sometimes with unforeseen consequences. TLATA 1996 s 24 has prevented the formation of any further strict settlements and prospectively abolishes such settlements under SLA 1925 by providing that if there ceases to be any relevant property which is or is deemed to be subject to the settlement, the settlement permanently ceases at that time to be a settlement for the purposes of SLA 1925.

Trusts for sale

1.26 Various statutory trusts, as referred to above, and express trusts provide that assets are to be held on trusts for sale with or without powers of postponement. Where such trusts relate to real property TLATA 1996 s 4 implies, despite any provisions in the trust deed to the contrary, a power for the trustees to postpone sale of the land for an indefinite period. The trustees of a trust of land therefore have no duty to sell the land. Section 6 gives trustees power to convey the land to beneficiaries who are *sui juris* and to acquire land for the purposes of the trust. TLATA 1996 came into effect on 1 January 1997.

Three certainties of a valid trust

1.27 In order to create a valid trust there must, except in the case of a constructive trust, be an intention on the part of the settlor to create in the trust 'the certainty of intention'. Secondly, there is the requirement actually to transfer the assets to the trustees or identify the assets held by the settlor as trustee, which is the 'certainty of subject matter'. Thirdly, there is the necessity to be able to identify the beneficiaries, ie the 'certainty of objects'. It is not necessary to identify all possible beneficiaries because a discretionary trust may be drafted widely enough to include beneficiaries unborn at the time of creation or otherwise unidentified. It is necessary to have at least one beneficiary and to identify whether or not someone falls within the class of beneficiaries. In the case of a purpose trust, rather than identifying specific beneficiaries the requirement is to be able to identify the charitable objects or other valid purpose of the trust.

1.28 These three certainties may be traced back to the judgment given by Langdale LJ in *Knight v Knight* (1840) 3 Beav 148. If there is a valid transfer of property but there is no certainty as to the intention to create a trust, the transferee would hold the legal estate absolutely, ie for his own benefit. If, however, for any reason the subject matter of the trust or the object could not be identified, the transferee would hold on a resulting trust for the settlor.

Certainty of intention

1.29 Although it is not necessary for a trust to be in writing it is necessary that the settlor intended to create a trust. It was held in *Re Adams and Kensington Vestry* (1884) 27 Ch D 394 that a bequest to a widow 'in full confidence that she would do what was right as to the disposal thereof between my children either in her lifetime or by will after her decease', was insufficient to create a trust in favour of the children and the widow was 'entitled to the assets absolutely'. It is necessary, however, to look at the entire document, in *Re Hamilton* [1895] 2 Ch 370 and in *Comiskey v Bowring-Hanbury* [1905] AC 84 it was held that the bequest made 'absolutely in full confidence that she (the widow) will make such use of (the property) as I would have made myself and that on her death she will devise it to such one or more of my nieces as she may think fit', created a trust for the nieces. Where there is no doubt as to the intention to make the transfer but the trust itself fails for uncertainty, the transferee takes the assets absolutely not subject to the failed trust (*Hancock v Watson* [1902] AC 14).

Certainty of subject matter

1.30 In *Palmer v Simmonds* (1854) 2 Drew 221 a trust of the 'bulk' of the residue was insufficient to identify that portion of the residue subject to trust and therefore the residuary legatee took absolutely. Similar uncertainty was found in the reference to 'blue chip securities' in *Re Kolb's Will Trust* [1962] Ch 531 as the term was not sufficiently precise to determine the actual securities to which it was intended to refer. Surprisingly, in *Re Golay's Will Trust* [1965] 1 WLR 969 a reference to 'reasonable income from my other properties' was accepted as something which could be determined by the court. Certainty of subject matter does not necessarily require the asset to be segregated and in *Hunter v Moss* [1994] 3 All ER 215 a declaration that a settlor held 50 of his 950 shares on trust for an individual was sufficient identification.

1.31 Further cases on certainty of intention include *Re Challoner Club Ltd (in liquidation)*, (1997) Times, 4 November in which a mere transfer of additional funds received into a separate bank account did not create a trust in favour of the contributors, as this did not sufficiently identify the terms of the trust, unlike *Re Kayford Ltd* [1975] 1 WLR 279 where a company in financial difficulties set up a specific customers' trust bank deposit account into which deposits paid by customers pending delivery were placed, and in this case the terms of the trust were sufficiently clear to enable it to be upheld by the court.

Certainty of objects

1.32 Under the concept of a trust, a settlor, having passed the legal title in the trust assets to the trustees, will normally cease to have anything to do with the trust unless the trust deed specifically provided otherwise, or unless he was also a beneficiary. It is the beneficiaries who are empowered to enforce the trust and it is therefore essential for the trustees to know who the beneficiaries are, so that they can ensure that their interests are properly taken into account and so the court can determine, if necessary, who it is who can take action against the trustees.

1.33 Where trustees are given wide discretionary powers it may not be practicable to identify everybody who could be entitled at any one time, and in *Re Gestetner Settlement, Barnett v Blumka* [1953] Ch 672, it was confirmed that the inability to classify the entire class would not cause the trust to fail for lack of certainty of objects. All that is necessary is to be able to determine with certainty whether an individual is or is not a member of the class (*Whishaw v Stephens* [1970] AC 508). It is, however, necessary for trustees contemplating a distribution to take into account, so far as possible, the interests of all the beneficiaries and if necessary the court would itself exercise discretion if the trustees refused to do so (*McPhail v Doulton* [1971] AC 424). A trust for the benefit of any or all or some of the inhabitants of the county of West Yorkshire failed for lack of certainty of objects in *R v District Auditor (No 3) Audit District of West Yorkshire Metropolitan County Council, ex p West Yorkshire Metropolitan County Council* [1986] RVR 24.

1.34 A discretion given to trustees has to be exercised even if that discretion is exercised by deciding to accumulate income within the permissible accumulation period and not to distribute. A power of appointment, be it a general or specific power, given to trustees is different from a discretion in that there is no requirement to exercise a power, and in the absence of exercising it the trust will normally provide for a trust to other beneficiaries or in some cases a resulting trust in favour of a settlor. Therefore a power to benefit anyone in the world, apart from excluded persons, was upheld in *Re Mainsty's Settlement* [1974] Ch 17 and *Re Hay's Settlement Trusts* [1982] 1 WLR 202.

1.35 A provision in a will enabling 'any members of my family and any friends of mine who wish to do so to purchase paintings at their catalogue price or probate value whichever was the lower' was upheld as not void for lack of certainty, as family could be defined as a blood relation, and a friend merely had to prove that he had been a friend of the testatrix and it was not necessary to know who all the friends were (*Re Barlow's Will Trusts* [1979] 1 WLR 278).

1.36 Although powers are contained within trusts it is perfectly possible for a donee to be given assets with the power of appointment to a specific class of beneficiaries. If he fails to exercise that power, the deed of gift will probably provide for a giftover in favour of a trust or, in the absence of such a clause, the assets would revert to the settlor on a resulting trust. However, the donee of a general power of appointment may, by definition, appoint anybody, including himself, as beneficiary as he has no fiduciary duty to exercise the power in any particular way, or indeed at all. His position is therefore analogous to that of an absolute owner (*Melville v IRC* [2001] STC 1271).

Agency relationships and entities with trust-like characteristics

1.37 A principal and agent relationship is a fiduciary relationship in that the agent must not make secret profits and has a duty of good faith to his principal, and to that limited extent such relationship may be compared with that of the trustee to a beneficiary (*Sorrell v Finch* [1977] AC 728).

1.38 A beneficiary has a proprietary equitable interest in property owned legally by the trustee and on the trustee's insolvency could recover the trust property held by the trustees, which would not be available for the trustee's own creditors. If the trustee had misapplied the money in breach of trust, equity would allow the beneficiary to trace the money and recover it (*Chase Manhattan Bank v Israel-British Bank* [1981] Ch 105). An agency relationship is a personal one between the principal and agent and the agent's duties cannot therefore be delegated further; *delegatus non potest delegare*. To the extent that an agent has his principal's property vested in him he will normally only be in possession of it and not have legal title to it (*Cave v MacKenzie* (1877) 46 LJ Ch 564; *Montgomerie v United Kingdom Mutual Steamship Association Ltd* [1891] 1 QB 370). It is possible for an agency agreement to require an agent to keep funds belonging to his principal separately from those of his own, in which case he would be trustee of those funds (*Burdick v Garrick* (1870) 5 Ch App 233). The principal will therefore merely be a creditor of the agent and able to claim accordingly; *Lister & Co v Stubbs* (1890) 45 Ch D 1 followed *Re A-G's Reference (No 1) of 1985* [1986] 2 All ER 219. However, where the agent has acted in breach of his fiduciary duty, the Privy Council imputed a constructive trust in favour of the principal which would allow equitable tracing (*A-G for Hong Kong v Reid* [1994] 1 AC 324).

Bailments

1.39 Under a bailment the property involved has to be a chattel, it cannot be land or an intangible asset. Legal title remains with the bailor but the bailee acquires possession and the right to use the asset for his own benefit (*Tappenden v Artus* [1964] 2 QB 185). If the bailee were fraudulently to sell the chattel, the purchaser, even the purchaser for value without notice, would not obtain good title because the transferor had no title and could not pass on what he did not have, *nemo dat quad non habet* (*Cundy v Lindsay* (1878) 3 App Cas 459), except in rare cases such as estoppel or under the Factors Act 1889 by a mercantile agent. This compares with a situation where a trustee who has legal title but not beneficial ownership sells an asset to a bona fide purchaser for value; in those circumstances the purchaser would obtain good title.

Contracts

1.40 A contract requires offer and acceptance and consideration passing from the offeree to the offeror (*Carhill v Carbolic Smoke Ball Co* [1893]

1 QB 256; *Moss v Hancock* [1899] 2 QB 111). It is enforceable at law or in some cases in equity, e g specific performance as in *Phillips v Lamdin* [1949] 2 KB 33. Only in the case of a contract under seal is it possible to do without the consideration, although the adequacy or otherwise of consideration is not a factor. In the absence of consideration the offeree is a mere volunteer and has no rights in common law. Neither does he normally have rights in equity as equity will not assist a volunteer (*Re Plumptre's Marriage Settlement* [1910] 1 Ch 609).

1.41 The beneficiary under a trust, however, who is also normally a volunteer, has an enforceable proprietary right under the trust (*Fletcher v Fletcher* (1844) 4 Hare 67). It is possible to have a valid contract with consideration or under seal under which the offeror binds himself to settle assets upon trust.

Interests under a will or intestacy

1.42 Where a person dies and the assets pass to his personal representatives, either the executors under the will or administrators returning letters of administration, they are acting in a fiduciary capacity even though they are not trustees as such. TA 1925, however, governs the fiduciary relationship of the personal representatives to beneficiaries, as it does that of trustees and beneficiaries, with a number of differences. A trustee is entitled to retire under TA 1925 s 36 or s 39, whereas an executor holds office for life and can only relinquish office with leave of the court. The power to appoint new trustees under TA 1925 s 40 does not apply to executors. A trustee is only a trustee of the trust of which he is appointed, whereas if an executor dies his executor may have to deal not only with the deceased executor's estate but also with the estates for which he was acting as executor, under the chain of representation applied by AEA 1925 s 7. The limitation period for actions of a breach of trust under the Limitation Act 1980 is six years, whereas that for claims against executors may be twelve years. A single executor can pass title to a chattel but trustees must act jointly (*Attenborough v Solomon* [1913] AC 76). A beneficiary under a will cannot directly enforce a legacy or bequest as the personal representatives take the full legal title, albeit in a fiduciary capacity, and there is no external equitable interest (*Stamp Duties Comr (Queensland) v Livingston* [1965] AC 694). The beneficiaries' right under a will or intestacy is for the estate to be properly administered, which is a chose in action which is assignable (*Re Leigh's Will Trusts* [1970] Ch 277).

1.43 The precise relationship of the personal representatives and the beneficiaries may change in that the will itself may create a trust and may appoint the personal representatives as trustees. At the termination of the administration, the personal representatives cease to hold the assets as personal representatives and hold them as trustees, at which point the beneficiaries have the normal rights to have their interests as beneficiaries enforced under the trust. It is not always clear when the administration of the estate ceases and the will trust becomes established, but it will normally be when the specific and pecuniary bequests have been paid, the assets collected and the liabilities paid.

1.44 Statutory will trusts may arise on intestacy in favour of minor beneficiaries under AEA 1925 s 47. Where, however, a person dies intestate without having made a will, or where the will is wholly or partly invalid or does not cover the entire estate, the personal representatives hold the assets on trust for sale under AEA 1925 s 33 except in the case of land which becomes a trust of land under TLATA 1996 s 1. A beneficiary on intestacy therefore has the normal rights to enforce the trust as a proprietorial right in equity.

Powers

1.45 The use of powers within a trust has already been referred to above. Powers of appointment only exist under trust under LPA 1925 s 1 (7). There is no obligation or duty on the donee of a power to exercise it (*Re Combe* [1925] Ch 210).

1.46 The most common area where powers arise outside a trust are powers of attorney under which the attorney is specifically appointed to act on behalf of the appointee either generally or for a specific purpose. The power of attorney may be a legal power, eg to convey land.

Usufruct

1.47 *Usufruct* is the assignment, for consideration or by way of gift, of income arising from an asset without disposing of the asset itself. It is commonly met with in civil law jurisdictions but is unusual under English law, where the same effect would normally be achieved by transferring the asset to trustees for the benefit of the beneficiary for life or for a period of years with a revision in favour of the transferor. This is not very tax efficient under UK law, as the income remains that of the settlor. [ICTA 1988 s 660A or s 730]. A more common arrangement is for the settlor to create a life interest trust or discretionary trust from which the settlor and his spouse are entirely excluded from benefit. In some jurisdictions the income arising on the asset is only taxable on the *usufructee* who receives the income, not on the *usufructor* who retains ownership of the asset.

Deeds of covenant

1.48 A covenant is essentially a contract under seal enforceable at common law. It may be used to provide an income to an intended donee not normally possible under equity, which would not allow specific performance, except in the limited case of a contract made in contemplation of, and in consideration of, marriage to a specific individual.

1.49 Historically, covenants paid out of income were deductible for tax purposes by the payer as a charge on income and taxable on the payee. They were therefore used as a tax-effective means of transferring income from wealthier to less wealthy members of a family. In this sense they are no longer effective and the income remains that of the donor. They can, however, still have a place, eg in persuading an elderly person to part with assets in return for an assured income provided by the donee or a third party under covenant. Until recently, covenants were also used for charitable donations but for UK tax purposes charitable covenants have been subsumed into the Gift Aid scheme. Covenants are still met with in partnerships, where unfunded pensions may be paid to former partners by way of covenant, which because of the consideration given are treated as charges on the income of the donor under ICTA 1988 s 347A(2)(c) as a payment made for bona fide commercial reasons in connection with the individual's, trade, profession or vocation.

Foundations

1.50 A foundation is often used in civil law jurisdictions where a trust would be used in a common law jurisdiction. A foundation differs fundamentally from a trust in that it is a separate legal entity to which assets are transferred by a donor and which is then managed, as a company would be, by a board of directors. It is common for the donor to retain wide powers of control over the appointment and dismissal of the directors and a foundation may be either revocable or irrevocable. In UK fiscal terms a revocable foundation might be regarded as a nomineeship of the donor, and still regarded as his property. An irrevocable foundation may be regarded as a company.

Anstalts

1.51 An *anstalt*, or establishment, is an entity peculiar to Liechtenstein. It is a separate legal entity, usually used for the purposes of managing family interests, and can be compared with a private family purpose trust set up in those common law jurisdictions which allow valid purpose trusts more readily than England.

Trust enterprises

1.52 A trust enterprise is known to a number of civil law jurisdictions, such as Louisiana in the USA and Liechtenstein, as being very close to an English trading trust except that it has the distinction of being a separate legal entity and not merely an enforceable relationship like an English trust. Apart from this aspect, a trust enterprise has so many of the characteristics of an English trust that it is likely to be classified in similar way for UK tax purposes.

Hybrid companies

1.53 A hybrid company is one limited by shares and guarantee and may be so structured that the guarantee members are entitled to the majority of the profits and assets, but only when distributed to them by the directors who are appointed by the shareholder members. The effect is to create a vehicle with many of the characteristics of a trust but which may not be classified as such for tax purposes. Hybrid companies are still popular in the Isle of Man and certain other former British jurisdictions but no longer exist under UK company law. The articles of a hybrid company may provide that on the death or resignation of a guarantee member the assets may be retained within the company for the remaining guarantee members and there may be power to add new members.

1.54 It is probable that the UK Revenue would regard a hybrid company as being an arrangement equivalent to a settlement for UK tax purposes under ICTA 1988 s 660G(1).

Unincorporated associations

1.55 An unincorporated association such as a club or society has, by definition, no legal personality and therefore cannot itself own property. On the basis that a purpose trust is invalid, property cannot, under English law, be held for the purposes of the club or society (*Re Rechers Will Trust* [1972] Ch 526; *Leahy v A-G for New South Wales* [1959] AC 457).

1.56 *Neville Estates v Madden* [1962] Ch 832 suggested the contractual solution of a gift to the existing members, not as joint tenants but subject to their respective contractual rights and liabilities towards one another as members of the association. In such a case, a member cannot sever his share. It will accrue to the other members on his death or resignation even though such members include persons who became members after the gift took effect. If this is the effect of the gift, it will not be open to objection on the score of perpetuity or uncertainty unless there is something in its terms or circumstances, or in the rules of the association, which precludes the members at any given time from dividing the subject of the gift between them on the footing that they are solely entitled to it in equity. In order for this to work, the club rules must be sufficient to give the club suitable autonomy, which was a problem in *Re Grant's Will Trusts* [1980] 1 WLR 360 in respect of a donation to the Chertsey and Walton Constituency Labour Party, which did not have control over its own property, being bound by the rules of the Labour Party nationally. As a result the gift failed.

1.57 An unincorporated association may be wound up under its rules or, if all the interested parties agree, if a court so orders or if its substratum has gone (*Re William Denby & Sons Ltd, Sick and Benevolent Fund* [1971] 1 WLR 973; *Re St Andrews Allotment Association* [1969] 1 WLR 229). On this contractual analysis, each member's subscription or any donation to the club is to the members for the time being absolutely, which means that on dissolution only the existing members share in the surplus on winding-up, and they do so equally (*Re Bucks Constabulary Widows' and Orphans' Fund Friendly Society (No 2)* [1979] 1 WLR 936). Because, on the contractual basis, the members for the time being are those entitled to the assets, a gift cannot be conditional on being used for a particular purpose (*Re Lipinski's Will Trust* [1976] Ch 235).

1.58 It is because of these problems that many non-charitable associations for particular purposes, such as professional societies, are incorporated as companies limited by guarantee, which gives them a legal persona and enables the society to serve its non-charitable purpose. In some cases a charity may properly be formed as, say, an educational charity, as a charitable trust or have a separate legal entity under Royal Charter.

The civil law approach to trusts

1.59 A number of civil law and non-common law jurisdictions have actually introduced trust law, including Scotland, Quebec, Sri Lanka, South Africa, Liechtenstein, Panama and Mexico. Even France toyed with the idea of introducing '*La Fiducie*', although this proposal seems to be permanently stalled.

1.60 In the USA, Louisiana has a largely civil law-based state code but has enacted legislation for trusts and trust enterprises. Mauritius and Vanuatu, with their legal systems based originally on French and English law, nonetheless have fully developed trust legislation. Most other territories which recognise trusts have a legal system originally based on English common law and equity.

1.61 In the absence of specific trust legislation, the problem for a civil law jurisdiction is that the civil code does not recognise more than one interest in property and cannot therefore readily conceive of legal title being held by the trustees with the beneficiaries having a proprietorial right over the same assets enforceable in equity. This potentially gives rise to a host of problems. If the settlor transfers assets to trustees in an Anglo-Saxon style trust for the benefit of his children, what are the consequences? The settlor has no intention of benefiting the trustees to whom he has given the property, therefore should he be treated as if he had made no such disposition and the property was still his? However, the trustees own the property and have full legal title to it. Does this mean that they are to be treated as the owners and that the assets are part of their own estate, in insolvency or on death, with the consequence that the trust assets would be available for creditors and subject to estate and gifts taxes on the death of a trustee? Is the settlor to be regarded as making a disposition to the trustees, or indirectly to his children, and how is this dealt with where there are different rates of tax payable, as there are in many civil law jurisdictions, for gifts to close family at lower rates than those applicable to gifts to third parties, such as the trustees? Where there is an acquisitions tax do the trustees become liable to pay tax at third party rates, or is the trustee ignored and the asset treated as passing directly to the beneficiaries, and taxable accordingly? Is the income arising in the trust, and any trust capital gains, to be that of the settlor, the trustees, or the beneficiary? Where the trust is a discretionary trust does the income, and the tax liability arising thereon, go into limbo until a distribution is made, and is the distribution taxed as income or as a capital gain or as a gift of capital or a mixture of these, on the distributee beneficiary?

1.62 There is also a problem in many civil law jurisdictions in that the surviving spouse and children are entitled to a minimum pre-ordained share of the overall estate, and if much of the property has already been passed into an Anglo-Saxon style trust the estate may be substantially reduced. There have been a number of actions by disappointed heirs who feel that their forced heirship rights under the civil code were undermined by the *inter vivos* trust, eg the Cayman Island cases of *Lemos v Coutts & Co* (1992/3) CILR 5/460 and *Re Lemos Trust Settlement* (1992/3) CILR 26 and the Bermudan case of *Schindler v Garner and Bermuda Trust*, EQ No 318 of 1991/94 of 1992. In the Jersey case of *Rahman v Chase Bank* [1991] JLR 103 the Jersey trust was successfully attacked by the heirs on the grounds that it was a sham, as a result of the way the trustees allowed the settlor to continue to manage the trust assets that had ostensibly been transferred to them, in precisely the same way as if he had retained legal ownership of them.

1.63 In relatively few cases have trusts been considered by the courts in civil law jurisdictions, and even where they have the treatment has not been clear and consistent even within a single jurisdiction. In any event, prior jurisprudence is not binding as precedent in a civil law jurisdiction in the same way as it is under the English legal system. The difficulties, in many civil law jurisdictions, of dealing with trusts can be both a trap for the unwary and an opportunity for tax arbitrage, to take advantage of the different rules in different jurisdictions.

The Hague Convention

1.64 In order to try and deal with some of the problems created by trusts within civil law jurisdictions, on 1 July 1985 the Hague Convention on the Law Applicable to Trusts and on Their Recognition [Appendix 1] was entered into. The Convention was signed by most of the main civil law and common law jurisdictions but has actually been ratified by relatively few. However, it is a starting point for the interpretation of trusts in a civil law jurisdiction, although the Convention is by no means all-embracing. It only applies to trusts created voluntarily and evidenced in writing and does not address the validity of the trust in the first instance, eg whether the settlor or testator had power to create the trust. [Art 3]. The applicable law is, usually, that chosen by the settlor, which obviously has to be related to a system of law, which in the UK is England and Wales, Northern Ireland or Scotland and in the USA is the law of each state. Where for some reason the proper law is not referred to in the trust instrument or is inapplicable, eg because it is in a jurisdiction which does not recognise the trust, the proper law has to be determined under Art 6 by reference to:

(a) the place of administration of the trust designated by the settlor;

(b) the *situs* of the assets of the trust;

(c) the place of residence or business of the trustee; and

(d) the objects of the trust and the places where they are to be fulfilled.

Only if these tests lead to a trust jurisdiction does the convention apply at all. Article 9 allows different legal systems to apply to different aspects of the trust.

1.65 Article 11 is extremely important because this recognises a trust as a separate fund, and therefore not part of the trustees' own assets, for insolvency purposes and allows the trustee to sue and be sued in his capacity as such. However, Art 13 specifically provides that no state is bound to recognise the trust where significant elements of it are closely connected with a jurisdiction which does not know the trust concept. Therefore a German resident and national could not settle German assets in favour of his German beneficiaries on a Jersey trust and expect it to be recognised in Germany. It is also provided in Art 19 that nothing in the Convention shall prejudice the powers of states in fiscal matters, which effectively means that the convention is of no direct assistance in sorting out the fiscal consequences of a trust in a civil law jurisdiction. However, the mere fact that there is an international convention on the recognition of trusts does help with their classification for fiscal purposes, and a number of civil law jurisdictions have recognised trusts, particularly as far as they relate to foreign nationals and assets outside the jurisdiction.

1.66 In some cases civil law trusts in those states where there is specific legislation enabling them to be formed can have advantages. Liechtenstein and Panama, for example, have statutory trust legislation, which follows typical English trust law in many ways but does not have any rule against accumulations or perpetuities and which will recognise purpose trusts in nearly all circumstances.

1.67 It is sometimes possible to avoid some of the problems of a trust owning assets in a civil law jurisdiction by owning the asset through a company owned by the trustees. However, this is not always a practical solution as some countries, eg France and Spain, levy a capital tax on the value of real estate held by a company in a jurisdiction with which there is no appropriate double taxation treaty, so ownership by a foreign trust through a company in a low tax jurisdiction such as Jersey or the British Virgin Islands would be ineffective in avoiding the annual capital tax.

1.68 It is outside the scope of this book to provide a detailed coverage of the treatment of trusts in other jurisdictions but the practitioner needs to be aware that it is unsafe to assume that the treatment by foreign fiscal authorities will in any way follow that adopted under UK law.

Scotland

1.69 This book is based on the law in England and Wales, although the taxation provisions apply to the whole of the UK, occasionally with modification to take account of the Scottish Legal System. This system is based on Roman law, canon law in relation to marriage, wills, succession and contract and feudal law in relation to land. There is no concept of different legal and equitable interests in Scottish law. Scottish trusts are now largely governed by the Trusts (Scotland) Act 1961, the rights of beneficiaries and duties of trustees under Scottish law may differ from those under English law. The settlor is called the trustor.

1.70 Property, under Scottish law is corporeal (tangible) heritable property, consisting of land and buildings but including crops and growing timber, or incorporeal (intangible) heritable property, including bonds or securities over land. All other property is either corporeal or incorporeal moveable property.

1.71 A child in Scotland comes of age at 18 but the Trusts (Scotland) Act 1961 s 5 refers to a minor as a person under the age of 21, and governs the maximum accumulation period of 21 years. There is no rule against perpetuities under Scottish law. Under the Age of Legal Capacity (Scotland) Act 1991 a child has full legal capacity from age 16.

1.72 The executor of a valid will is the executor nominate, the personal representative of an intestate is an executor dative and the estate is an executory. Confirmation (probate) of a will is obtained from the Sheriff's Clerk's Office. The surviving spouse and children under Scottish law have specific legal rights, *legitim* or forced heirship entitlements. If there are no surviving children or remoter issue, the surviving spouse can claim one half of the moveable estate, otherwise one third. Conversely, children can claim, between them, one third of the net moveable estate if there is a surviving spouse, otherwise one half. A life rent (life interest) in an estate can be created for a life in being and a trust can arise under the doctrine of equitable compensation.

1.73 The Inland Revenue has a trust office (IR Trusts) in Edinburgh dealing with Scottish trust and estate matters. Readers are referred to specialist books on Scottish trusts such as Wilson and Duncan, *Trusts, Trustees and Executors* and Norrie and Scabbie, *Trusts.*

Northern Ireland

1.74 Northern Ireland has its own legal system and legislation, but it follows closely the law of England and Wales.

Chapter 2

Main Trust Legislation

2.1 In this chapter the main statutory provisions which impact on trusts and trustees, other than the taxes acts, are summarised. However no such summary should be regarded as a substitute for the actual wording of the statue where relevant to an actual case.

2.2 In Appendix 1 the main trust legislation is reproduced together with extracts from other important legislation, other than on taxation, affecting trusts.

The Trust Acts

Trustee Act 1925 (TA 1925)

2.3 There has been no recent consolidation of trust legislation and much of TA 1925 remains in force, although Part I (dealing with investments) has been replaced by TA 2000. TA 1925 sets out the general powers of trustees, including their appointment and discharge, the powers of the court and various general provisions.

Part II General Powers of Trustees and Personal Representatives

12 Power of trustees for sale to sell by auction etc
Where trustees have a trust for sale or power to sell trust property, they may do so in whole or part, subject to prior charges such as mortgages or with unencumbered title, by public auction or by private contract, subject to such conditions as to the title as the trustees think fit. Trustees also have power to vary a contract for sale and buy in at an auction or rescind the contract for sale and resell, without being liable for any loss.

13 Power to sell subject to depreciatory conditions
Beneficiaries cannot complain about any conditions imposed on the sale by reason of their being unnecessarily depreciatory, unless this results in the sale proceeds being rendered inadequate, or it appears that the purchaser was acting in collusion with the trustee when the contract was made.

14 Power of trustees to give receipts
Where a person transfers personal property such as money or investments to trustees a receipt in writing exonerates the transferor from any responsibility

for loss arising on the application by the trustees of such assets. A sole trustee, other than a trust corporation, cannot give a valid receipt for the proceeds of sale or other capital money under a trust of land.

Where there was more than one trustee however the receipt to be valid must be given by all the trustees.

15 Power to compound liabilities
Trustees may accept property, real or personal, sever and apportion mixed trust funds, pay or allow claims on what they consider to be sufficient evidence, accept any composition or security for any debt, allow time for the payment of a debt or compromise or compound claims or submit them to arbitration, abandon or settle them. In such cases the trustee is not responsible for any loss so long as he has discharged the duty of care under TA 2000 s 1(1).

16 Power to raise money by sale, mortgage etc
Trustees are authorised to mortgage trust property except for charitable trusts, or strict settlements under SLA 1925 unless the statutory owner.

17 Protection to purchasers and mortgagees dealing with trustees
No purchaser or mortgagee is responsible for the application of funds transferred to the trustees on purchase or mortgage.

18 Devolution of powers or trusts
Where two or more trustees hold powers or trusts and a trustee dies the survivor or survivors may act until the appointment of new trustees. Where a sole trustee dies the personal representatives of the trustee act, although this is subject to the trustee's power to give receipts in section 14.

19 Power to insure
This section was substituted by TA 2000 s 34 and now provides that the trustee may insure any property which is subject to the trust against risks of loss or damage due to any event, and to pay the premiums out of the trust fund. In the case of property held on a bare trust this power is subject to any direction from the beneficiary that the property not be insured or as to the conditions upon which it may be insured.

It should be noted, however, that not only does the trustee now have a wide power to insure he also has, by TA 2000 Sch 1 para 5, a duty of care in relation to insurance and must therefore exercise such care and skill as is reasonable in the circumstances, under TA 2000 s 1(1). Subject to any directions in the trust deed, a prudent trustee should normally ensure that all the trust property not held merely as nominee is fully insured for its current market value.

20 Application of insurance money for a policy kept up under any trust power or obligation
This section deals with the application of proceeds of insurance where property is subject to a trust as a strict settlement under the SLA 1925.

22 Reversionary interests, valuations and audit
Where the trust assets include a reversionary interest, on it falling into possession, or becoming payable or transferable, the trustees may agree the amount to which they are entitled, accept any authorised investments in or towards satisfaction of their rights, and allow deductions for reasonable duties, costs, charges and expenses and execute releases to the transferors. The trustees are not responsible for any loss so long as they have discharged their duty of care under TA 2000 s 1(1). Trustees are not obliged to charge such property or take proceedings unless instructed to do so by or on behalf of a beneficiary, and with an indemnity for the costs, although they do have a general responsibility to ensure that they collect everything due to them as trustees, so far as it is possible to do so. Trustees are empowered to ascertain and fix the value of any trust property which is then binding on the beneficiaries, so long as the trustees have exercised their duty of care under TA 2000 s 1(1).

The trustees may have trust accounts audited but not more than once every three years unless the nature of the trust or any special dealings in the trust property make a more frequent audit reasonable. The trustees may determine whether the audit costs are to be paid out of capital or income but in the absence of such exercise of their discretion the costs attributable to capital will be borne by capital, and those attributable to income, by income. A beneficiary may insist on an audit not more than once every three years, unless he bears the costs, provided the proposed auditor is a solicitor or accountant who is acceptable to the trustees and in the absence of such agreement the audit is carried out by the Public Trustee. [PTA 1906 s 13].

24 Power to concur with others
Where a trust is entitled to an undivided share in any property, the trustees may act in conjunction with persons having an interest in other shares in the property, even if they have an interest in another fiduciary capacity or in their own right in other shares in the property.

25 Delegation of trustee's functions by power of attorney
A trustee may by power of attorney delegate all or any of the trusts, powers and directions vested in him as trustee for a period of up to twelve months. The donor of the power of attorney must give written notice to any person entitled to appoint a new trustee and each of the existing trustees, although failure to comply will not invalidate the attorney's act so far as a third party is concerned. The required form of the power of attorney to delegate the trustee's functions is as follows:

> 'This general trustee power of attorney is made on ....[date] by ....[name of one donor] of ....[address of donor] as trustee of ....[name or details of one trust].
>
> I appoint ....[name of one donee] of .... [address of donee] to be my attorney [if desired the date on which the delegation commences or the period for which it continues (or both)] in accordance with section 25(5) of the Trustee Act 1925.'

(To be executed as a deed.)

The donor remains liable for the attorney's acts or defaults as if they were his own. The attorney may exercise the powers of the trustee; when the attorney has been appointed under SLA 1925 notices have to be given to the personal representatives and tenant for life as well as the trustees.

26 Protection against liability in respect of rents and covenants
Where a trustee is liable for any rent, covenant or agreement under a lease or rent charge, or under an authorised guarantee agreement under the Landlord and Tenant (Covenants) Act 1995, and everything due is paid for or provided for up to date, he may, without incurring any personal liability, distribute to the beneficiaries. This does not affect the lessor's right to trace any claim through to the recipients of the trust property.

27 Protection by means of advertisements
The trustees of a settlement contemplating a distribution to the beneficiaries may give notice by advertisement in the (London) *Gazette* and in the local newspaper of the area in which the land is situated requiring any person claiming an interest in the property to give the details of his claim within a stated time period, being not less than two months. Such a notice protects the trustees from any claim of which they were unaware, on making a distribution after the time fixed by the notice, but trustees still have to make the usual diligent searches and a person with a valid claim may follow the property into the hands of the beneficiary to whom it has been distributed.

28 Protection in regard to notice
A trustee is not deemed to have received notice in respect of one trust or estate merely because he has received notice in relation to another trust for which he acts.

Maintenance, advancement and protective trusts

31 Power to apply income for maintenance and to accumulate surplus income during a minority
The statutory power of maintenance and accumulation under this section is very often incorporated into a trust deed with or without modification. It provides that during the infancy of a beneficiary the trustees may, at their sole discretion, pay to his parent or guardian any income of the trust for the beneficiary's maintenance, education or benefit, so long as it is reasonable, notwithstanding that the beneficiary may also be entitled under another trust fund or if some other person is bound by law to provide for his maintenance or education. Once the beneficiary has reached the age of 18 the trustees must pay him the income to which he is entitled even if his interest is not yet vested. This is subject to the proviso in sub-section (1) that the trustees have to have regard to the age of the infant and his requirements and generally to the circumstances of the case, and in particular where income is available from more than one fund to ensure that a proportionate part only of the income of each fund is used for the child's maintenance, education or benefit. As this could be an onerous task it is common for the proviso to be disapplied in the trust deed. A common form of wording is:

'Section 31 of the Trustee Act 1925 will have effect as if:

(a) The words in sub-section 1(1) "as may in all the circumstances be reasonable" were deleted and in their place the words "as my Trustees shall in their absolute discretion think fit" were substituted

(b) The words from "Provided that" to the end of sub-section 1 were deleted.'

Income not distributed has to be accumulated by investing it, and the profits from so investing it until the child reaches the age of 18 or marries under that age, if his interest then becomes vested, or where he becomes absolutely entitled to the property from which the income arose, it will be held for the beneficiary absolutely but if he only acquires a vested interest at that date or later. Otherwise the accumulations of income are held as an accretion to capital. During infancy accumulations from one period may be treated as income for a subsequent period as if it were income arising in the current year, so that, for example, income might be accumulated during the child's early years and then used to pay school fees where these are in excess of the current year's income. Where the child has only a contingent interest he is only entitled to the intermediate income if the trust deed so specified. This section also applies to a vested annuity as if it were income of property held by the trustees to pay the income to the annuitant although in this case the accumulations of income during infancy are held for the annuitant absolutely.

As these provisions only apply to vested or contingent interests they do not apply to discretionary beneficiaries.

32 Power of advancement
Trustees may advance capital from the trust in such manner as they may in their absolute discretion see fit, to any person entitled to an interest in the trust capital whether absolutely or contingently. It does not matter that the beneficiary's interest might be defeated by a subsequent power of appointment or reallocation or be diminished if further beneficiaries are born or appointed. There is a proviso, which is often excluded by the trust deed, which limits the amount of the advancement to one half of the presumptive or vested share of the beneficiary in the trust property. The money so advanced is brought into account as part of his entitlement. An advancement must not prejudice the life tenant or other beneficiaries unless they are of full age and consent in writing nor does it apply to capital money arising under SLA 1925. The advance must be for the benefit of the beneficiary (*Re Pauling's Settled Trust* [1964] Ch 303) but benefit is widely construed and can include a potential saving in taxation (*Pilkington v IRC* [1964] AC 612).

33 Protective trusts
Under these provisions it is possible to draft a trust deed under which the principal beneficiary has a protected life interest, which means that if he were to become bankrupt or compound with his creditors his entitlement to the income ceases, and the trustees then hold the trust funds on discretionary trusts for the maintenance or support or otherwise for the benefit of the principal beneficiary and his or her spouse and children or remoter issue, or the principal beneficiary and the persons who would benefit under the trust

deed on his death. Such trusts were originally aimed at spendthrift beneficiaries or those involved in high-risk businesses. It is not possible for the settlor of a protective trust also to be the principal beneficiary, and it is important that the life interest is determinable upon the bankruptcy or other relevant event, in order not to be considered a device to defeat creditors.

Part III Appointment and Discharge of Trustees

34 Limitation of the number of trustees
Where there is a settlement creating trusts of land there must not be more than four persons who are named as trustees except in the case of charitable or other purpose trusts.

35 Appointments of trustees of settlements and trustees of land
Under subs (1), in the case of a strict settlement under SLA 1925 the trustees of the land shall, unless the court orders otherwise, also be the trustees of the proceeds of sale of the land.

36 Power of appointing new or additional trustees
Where a trustee dies or remains out of the UK for more than twelve months or wishes to be discharged from his duties, or refuses to act, or is incapable of acting or is unfit to act he may be replaced by whoever is nominated for the purpose of appointing new trustees in the trust instrument, or if there is no such person by the continuing trustee or trustees or by the personal representative of the last surviving or continuing trustee. This also applies where the trustee is removed under a power contained in the trust instrument or where a trust corporation has been dissolved.

Where a trust has no more than three trustees, the person nominated to appoint new trustees in the trust deed, or if there is no such a person the existing trustees, may appoint additional trustees. An additional trustee acts in exactly the same way as if he had originally been appointed by the trust deed. Where a trustee becomes incapable by reason of mental disorder within the meaning of MHA 1983 he can only be replaced with the leave of the Court of Protection.

37 Supplemental provisions as to appointment of trustees
Subject to any statutory limitation on the number of trustees, further trustees may be appointed. It is possible to have a separate set of trustees, not exceeding four, for the purpose of holding trust real estate. It is possible to have a single trustee to replace a sole trustee where land is not involved. In other cases a sole trustee must be a trust corporation in order for the retiring trustee to be discharged or there must be at least two trustees. This can be a trap when a trust is exported, as an overseas trust company is not a trust corporation. A trust corporation is the Public Trustee or a corporation either appointed by the court to act as trustee or automatically entitled to do so because it is incorporated in the UK and has issued capital of at least £250,000 of which at least £100,000 has been paid up in cash [Public Trustee Rules 1912 (SR and O 1912 No 348) rule 30, as amended]. It is therefore

necessary in such cases to ensure there are at least two trustees in the new jurisdiction, either personal or corporate [TA 1925 s 37(1)(c)], otherwise the change in trustees would be invalid and the trust would remain resident in the UK.

The necessary steps have to be taken to vest the trust property in the new trustees. A sole trustee other than a trust corporation cannot be appointed unless able to give valid receipts for all capital money arising under the trust, ie where the trust does not contain any land. [TA 1925 s 14(2)(a)].

38 Evidence as to a vacancy in a trust
The deed appointing the new trustee, containing a statement to the effect that the previous trustee has remained out of the UK for more than twelve months, or refuses or is unfit to act, or is incapable of acting, or that he is entitled to a beneficial interest in the property in possession, shall be conclusive evidence of that fact, in favour of the purchaser of the legal estate in land, and any appointment or vested declaration consequent on the appointment shall be valid in favour of such a purchaser.

39 Retirement of trustee without a new appointment
A trustee who wishes to retire and does not have to be replaced may be discharged provided there are at least two other trustees or a trust corporation remaining.

40 Vesting of trust property in new or continuing trustees
It is normally possible in the deed of appointment of a new trustee to include a declaration to the effect that any trust property shall vest in the trustees, including the new trustee, by virtue of the deed without requiring any further conveyance or assignment. Interestingly, even if it does not contain such a declaration it operates as if it had. Similarly, a deed by which a retiring trustee is discharged under TA 1925 s 39 or TLATA 1996 s 19 may contain a declaration by the retiring and continuing trustees, or other person empowered to appoint trustees, that the deed shall operate to vest the trust property in the continuing trustees and this will also apply even where the deed does not specifically include such a declaration. These provisions do not normally apply to lands conveyed by way of mortgage for securing money or to land held under a lease which contains covenants against assignment without consent, or stocks or shares and other property only transferable in accordance with statutory rules.

Part IV Powers of the Court

Appointment of new trustees

41 Power of court to appoint new trustees
The court has an overriding power to appoint new trustees (but not an executor or administrator) where it is found inexpedient, difficult or impractical so to do without the assistance of the court.

42 Power to authorise remuneration
The court may fix the remuneration where it appoints a corporation other than the Public Trustee to be a trustee, either solely or jointly with another person.

43 Powers of new trustee appointed by the court
The court appointee shall be treated in all respects as if it were an original trustee appointed by the trust instrument.

Vesting orders

44 Vesting orders of land
The court may make an order vesting any interest in land in trustees appointed by the court, or where trustees are otherwise unable to act, or where it appears to the court expedient so to do.

45 Orders as to contingent rights of unborn persons
The court may make an order releasing an interest in land from the contingent rights of unborn persons, who, on coming into existence, would be beneficiaries, or may vest such interest in any person on behalf of future beneficiaries.

46 Vesting order in place of conveyance by infant mortgagee
The court may make a vesting order releasing or disposing of an interest in land where a mortgagee is an infant.

47 Vesting order consequential on order for sale or mortgage of land
Where a court directs the sale or mortgage of any land, the person with the legal estate is treated as if he were a trustee and the court may vest the land in a purchaser or mortgagee or any other person.

48 Vesting order consequential on judgment for specific performance etc
Where a judgment is given for specific performance on a contract for the sale of land the court may declare the legal owner to be a trustee, and may make a vesting order taking into account the rights of unborn persons.

49 Effect of vesting order
A vesting order made by the court has the same effect as if the land had been duly conveyed to the trustees.

50 Power to appoint person to convey
The court may, instead of making a vesting order, appoint a person to convey the land or release a contingent right, which has the same effect.

51 Vesting orders as to stock and things in action
Where a trustee is unable or unwilling to transfer stocks and shares, shares in registered ships or choses in action the court may make an appropriate vesting order.

52 Vesting orders of charity property
The court may make vesting orders over interests in land, stocks and shares and choses in action held by a charity.

53 Vesting orders in relation to infant's beneficial interest
The court may, in looking after the interests of an infant, appoint a person to whom to convey property or transfer assets or hold the income thereof for the benefit of the infant.

54 Jurisdiction in regard to mental patients
The High Court, not the authority having jurisdiction under Part VII of MHA 1983, will make appropriate orders where a trustee becomes of unsound mind. A receiver has concurrent authority to implement such court orders.

55 Orders made up on certain allegations to be conclusive evidence
Vesting orders properly made based on a trustee's alleged incapacity are conclusive evidence of the allegation upon any question as to the validity of the order.

56 Application of vesting order to property out of England
The court may make a vesting order extending to any part of 'Her Majesty's dominions' except Scotland.

57 Power of court to authorise dealings with trust property
Where the court considers it expedient to do so, and the trust deed does not contain the appropriate powers, the court may empower the trustees to deal with the trust property and direct the manner in which it is to be dealt with.

58 Persons entitled to apply for orders
An order for the appointment of a new trustee, or in relation to trust property, may be brought by or on behalf of any beneficiary.

59 Power to give judgment in the absence of a trustee
Where a trustee defendant cannot be found, the court may give judgment as if he had been duly served and represented in the action.

60 Power to charge costs on trust estate
The court may order the costs and expenses of any application to be paid out of the trust funds or by other persons that the court thinks just.

61 Power to relieve trustee from personal liability
A trustee who may be in breach of trust but who has acted honestly and decently and ought fairly to be excused may be relieved of personal liability by the court. In practice, a trustee contemplating legal action on behalf of the trust should obtain the leave of the court or be at risk for the costs of the action (*Re Beddoe* [1893] 1 Ch 547).

62 Power to make beneficiary indemnify for breach of trust
Where a trustee commits a breach of trust at the request of or with the consent in writing of a beneficiary, the court may, if it thinks fit, require the beneficiary to indemnify the trustee.

63 Payment into court by trustees
The trustees may, by a majority, vote to pay trust funds into court, which might be the only option where trustees are required to act unanimously but

cannot agree. The court may order such a payment into court at the request of the majority, without the concurrence of the others. The court may order payment or delivery of money or securities held by third parties into court.

63A Jurisdiction of county court
The county court has jurisdiction for various provisions, as listed, within the applicable county court monetary limits.

Part V General Provisions

64 Application of Act to Settled Land Act Trustees
TA 1925 applies also to trustees of a strict settlement for the purposes of SLA 1925.

66 Indemnity to banks etc
Banks and others may rely on court orders without making further enquiry.

67 Jurisdiction of the court
Court means the High Court or a county court.

68 Definitions
Various terms are defined.

69 Application of Act
TA 1925 applies not only to trusts but also where appropriate to executorships and administrationships.

70 Enactments repealed

71 Short title, commencement, extent
TA 1925 applies to England and Wales only.

Variation of Trusts Act 1958 (VTA 1958)

2.4 The court has very wide powers under VTA 1958 to deal with real or personal property held on trust, arising at any time, under any will, settlement or other disposition, and to approve any arrangement varying or revoking all or any of the trusts or enlarging the powers of the trustees or managing or administering any of the trust property on behalf of any person incapable of assenting by reason of infancy or other incapacity, or any person who may become entitled under the trusts at a future date, or on the happening of a future event or any person unborn, or any discretionary beneficiary under protective trusts where the interests of the principal beneficiary have not failed or determined. Except in the last case the court must be satisfied that the arrangements are for the benefit of the beneficiary. These powers do not limit the general power to authorise dealings in trust property under SLA 1925 s 64 or TA 1925 s 57 or under Part VII of MHA 1983.

Trustee Investments Act 1961 (TIA 1961)

2.5 This Act has at last been repealed so far as England and Wales is concerned by TA 2000. The remaining sections are interpretations of references to trust property and trust funds. Property includes real and personal property of any description including money and things (choses) in action but it does not include an expectancy until it falls into possession. Property in the hands of the trustees shall constitute of one trust fund only so far as it is held on trusts which are not identical to those on which any other property is held. TIA 1961 divided trust investments into narrower range investments not requiring advice, narrower range investments requiring advice, both of which are basically fixed interest securities, and wider range investments, basically UK equities.

Perpetuities and Accumulations Act 1964 (PAA 1964)

2.6 As a general matter of public policy it is not possible in the UK to put money into a private trust, ie in practice a non-charitable trust, for an unlawful period or to accumulate income indefinitely. This started as a common law rule and developed into the concept of lives in being plus 21 years as the maximum period for a private trust. This was normally worded on the basis of all vesting of an interest taking place within '21 years of the death of the last survivor of all the descendants of King George V now living', usually known as the life in being provision. PAA 1964, which applied to instruments taking effect on or after 16 July 1964, substituted definite periods for a number of common law rules.

1 Power to specify perpetuity period
A trust may specify a perpetuity period not exceeding 80 years.

2 Presumptions and evidence as to future parenthood
It is presumed for perpetuity periods based on the ability of a person to have a child that a male can have a child at the age of 14 or over but not under that age and that a female can have a child at the age of 12 or over but not under that age, and is to be presumed to be incapable of bearing a child once over the age of 55. This extends to adopted children, legitimisation or other means of acquiring a child. The court has an overriding ability to make such orders as it thinks fit if in any particular case a person does have a child outside these age ranges.

3 Uncertainty as to remoteness
Where a trust would otherwise be void on the ground that an interest might not become vested until too remote a time, it is not void until it becomes obvious that the vesting must in fact occur beyond the permitted period, at which time any vesting beyond the permitted period becomes void. This applies also to powers of appointment, powers, options or other rights.

4 Reduction of age and exclusion of class members to avoid remoteness
Where a beneficiary becomes entitled at a specified age greater than 21, which would fall outside the perpetuity period, the required age is reduced so

that the greatest age that falls within the perpetuity period is substituted. Class members who could cause the trust to fail for remoteness are automatically excluded by section 4(4).

5 Condition relating to death of surviving spouse
Early vesting also takes place where a disposition is limited by reference to the death of the survivor of a person in being at the start of the perpetuity period and any spouse of that person.

6 Saving and acceleration of expectant interests
A disposition is not void for remoteness merely because it is dependent on a prior void interest and may be accelerated accordingly.

7 Powers of appointment
A power of appointment is usually treated as a special power.

8 Administrative powers of trustees
The rule against perpetuities does not prevent trustees dealing with trust property or otherwise in the administration of the trust.

9 Options relating to land
The rule against perpetuities does not apply to an option over a reversionary interest.

10 Avoidance of contractual and other rights in cases of remoteness
The purchaser of an interest void for remoteness has no remedy for its lack of effect.

11 Rights for enforcement of rentcharges
The rule against perpetuities does not apply to powers or remedies nor for recovering the payment of annual sums which are rentcharges under LPA 1925 s 121 or s 122.

12 Possibilities of reverter, conditions subsequent, exceptions and reservations
The rule against perpetuities does apply to certain reversions and resulting trusts.

13 Amendments of section 164 of Law of Property Act 1925
The period for which income may be accumulated within the trust is 21 years from the date of making the trust, or the date of the testator's death in a will trust, and the minority of any person in being at the date of the trust creation. A person attains full age at 18 under FLRA 1969 s 1(1). These periods are in addition to those provided by LPA 1925 s 164 which allows accumulation periods for one, but only one, of the following:

(a) the life of the settlor;

(b) 21 years from the death of the settlor;

(c) the minority of any person living or *en ventre sa mere* at the death of the settlor; or

(d) the minority or respective minorities of beneficiaries who, if of full age, would be entitled to the income whether living at the date of creation of the trust or not.

14 Right to stop accumulations
Beneficiaries where all are *sui jurice* can, under the rule in *Saunders v Vautier* (1841) 4 Beav 115, bring an accumulation period to an end, but where future born children could be beneficiaries this could prevent such an action. In determining whether any future children are to be taken into account, the assumptions of possible parenthood in s 2 are applied.

The restrictions on accumulations apply wherever there is a power to accumulate income whether or not there is a duty to exercise that power and whether or not it extends to income arising on the investment of accumulated income.

15 Short title interpretation and extent

Recognition of Trusts Act 1987 (RTA 1987)

2.7 This Act brings into UK law the Hague Convention of 1 July 1985 on the Law Applicable to Trusts and on Their Recognition. It is extended to include any trusts arising under the law of any part of the UK or by virtue of a judicial decision whether in the UK or elsewhere. In Arts 15 and 16 the UK confirms that the usual conflict of law provisions take precedence over the Convention. The UK ratified the convention on 17 November 1989 and it came into force on 1 January 1992. The UK ratification was on behalf of the United Kingdom of Great Britain and Northern Ireland, the Isle of Man, Bermuda, the British Antarctic Territory, the British Virgin Islands, the Falkland Islands, Gibraltar, St Helena, the St Helena dependencies, South Georgia and the South Sandwich Islands and the United Kingdom sovereign base areas of Akrotiri and Dhekelia on the island of Cyprus. On 30 March 1990 the UK extended the convention to Hong Kong, the bailiwick of Jersey, the island of Guernsey (but not the islands of Alderney and Sark) and the Turks and Caicos Islands. The Convention continues to apply to Hong Kong from 1 July 1997 as the Hong Kong Special Administration of the Peoples Republic of China. The UK construes the Convention as applying to any country or territory which has its own system of law whether a party to the Convention or not.

2.8 The Schedule to the Act reproduces Arts 1–15, para 1 of Art 16, and Arts 17, 18 and 22 of the Convention.

Hague Convention of 1 July 1985 on the Law Applicable to Trusts and on Their Recognition

2.9 The Hague Convention arises from the Hague Conference on Private and International Law and is intended to deal with the institution of the trust, which is known to certain member states of the Conference, most often states of common law, but which is unknown in the majority of the civil law states of the members of the Conference. For the states which have trusts, the principle interest is obviously to have the trusts created under their laws recognised in the countries which do not have this institution. However, the common law states would also find the conflict rules of the Convention useful, given that their national systems of private international law differ in this field.

2.10 There has never been any intention to introduce the trust into the civil law countries but simply to furnish their judges with the instruments which are appropriate to grasp this legal device. Since the institution is not provided for in their substantive laws they do not have rules of private international law to govern it, and they are therefore reduced to seeking laboriously to introduce the elements of trusts into their own concepts. The Convention puts at their disposal conflict of laws rules for trusts, it then indicates what the recognition of a trust should consist of but also the limits of this recognition. The Hague Convention has been ratified by Australia, Canada, Italy, Malta, Netherlands and the UK and originally came into force on 1 January 1992.

2.11 Although it has not been widely ratified, the Hague Convention is useful in determining the likely treatment of trusts in foreign jurisdictions, but it should be remembered that Art 19 provides that nothing in the convention shall prejudice the powers of states in fiscal matters.

Chapter 1 Scope

Article 1
This convention specifies the law applicable to trusts and governs their recognition.

Article 2
The term 'trust' refers to the legal relationships created *inter vivos* or on death by a settlor when assets have been placed under the control of a trustee for the benefit of a beneficiary, or for a specific purpose. A trust has the following characteristics:

(a) The assets constitute a separate fund and are not a part of the trustees' own estate.

(b) Title to the trust assets is in the name of the trustee or nominee for the trustee.

(c) The trustee has the power and the duty, in respect of which he is accountable, to manage, employ or dispose of the assets in accordance with the terms of the trust and by law. The settlor may retain certain rights and powers and the trustee may have rights as a beneficiary, which are not necessarily inconsistent with the existence of a trust.

Article 3

The Convention only applies to trusts created voluntarily and evidenced in writing and therefore does not extend to trusts created by operation of law or by judicial decision unless so extended under Art 20. The UK, through RTA 1987 s 1, has extended the Convention in this manner so far as the UK is concerned. The explanatory report by Alfred E Von Overbeck on the Hague Convention suggests at para 51 that the Convention would extend to a resulting trust which arises in favour of the settlor where the purposes of an express trust have been fulfilled, but the trustees continue to hold certain assets under a resulting trust. The trust instrument does not have to be in writing, but if not itself written down must be evidenced in writing.

Article 4

The Convention does not deal with the initial validity of a trust and whether or not it meets the requirements of a valid trust under the laws of the jurisdiction in which it is established. Nor does it deal with whether or not assets have been properly transferred to the trustees. Any problems of this nature will be dealt with under the law in which the trust is established and the asset transferred and, if different, dealt with under the normal conflict of laws rules.

Article 5

The Convention does not apply where the applicable law specified by Chapter 2 does not provide for trusts of the type involved.

Chapter 2 Applicable law

Article 6

The settlor is free to choose the law under which the trust is to be governed expressly or by implication. In the unlikely event that the law chosen by the settlor does not provide for trusts or the category of trust involved the choice is ineffective and Art 7 applies.

Article 7

Where no applicable law has been chosen a trust should be governed by the law with which it is most closely connected. This is ascertained from the place of administration designated by the settlor, the *situs* of the trust assets, the place of residence or business of the trustee and the objects of the trust and the places where they are to be fulfilled.

Article 8

The law specified by Art 6 or 7 governs the validity of the trust, its construction, its effect and the administration of the trust including the appointment, resignation and removal of trustees, the capacity to act as a trustee and the rights and duties of trustees, the right to delegate, the power to administer and deal with trust assets and grant security.

It covers powers of investment, restrictions on the duration of the trust under a rule against perpetuities or the power to accumulate income. It also governs relationships between trustees and beneficiaries and their personal liabilities, variation or termination of the trust, the distribution of trust assets and the duties of the trustees to account for their administration.

Article 9
It is possible for a separable aspect of the trust such as administration to be governed by a different law so that, for example, a trust established in the British Virgin Islands may be administered from Jersey.

Article 10
Such a dual law aspect of a trust is only available where the law applicable to the validity of the trust so allows.

Chapter 3 Recognition

Article 11
A trust properly constituted under the applicable law is to be recognised as a trust. This implies, as a minimum, that the trust property constitutes a trust fund, but the trustees may sue and be sued and appear before a notary or public official in their capacity as trustees. It also implies that the personal creditors of a trust have no recourse against the trust assets and that the trust assets do not form part of the trustee's estate on his insolvency or bankruptcy, and do not form part of his or his spouse's matrimonial property nor part of his estate on death. It also means that trust assets may be recovered from the trustee following a breach of trust where trust assets have been mingled with the trustee's own assets. Rights and obligations of any third party holder of trust assets depend on the law applicable to an asset under the ordinary conflict of law rules and will often be the law of the territory where the asset is situated. A trustee should be able to register trust assets in his capacity as trustee, so that the existence of the trust is disclosed so far as this is not inconsistent with the law of the state where registration is sought.

Article 13
No state is bound to recognise a trust where the significant elements, such as the habitual residence or nationalities of the settlor or beneficiaries or location of the assets, are more closely connected with the state which does not have the institution of the trust, or the category of trust involved, even though the choice of applicable law of the place of administration and the habitual residence of the trustee are in a valid trust jurisdiction. For example, France would not be bound to recognise a trust created in, say, the Isle of Man where the beneficiaries and the trust assets were both in France.

Article 14
The Convention is not intended to prevent states from recognising trusts and they may introduce laws favourable to the recognition of trusts, as Monaco has done.

Chapter 4 General clauses

Article 15
The Convention does not overrule the ordinary conflict of law rules on, for example, the protection of minors and incapable parties, the effects of

marriage, succession rights, forced heirship rules, the transfer of title and security interests in property, the protection of creditors and of third parties acting in good faith. If these rules prevent the trust from being recognised, the courts will try to give effect to the object of the trust by other means.

Article 16
Certain laws of immediate application, such as those which are intended to protect the cultural heritage of a country, public health, certain vital economic interests, the protection of employees or of the weaker party to another contract, will be dealt with under the laws of the appropriate jurisdictions such as where real estate is sited, irrespective of rules of conflict of laws, and the Convention makes no attempt to override these provisions. In some cases it may be appropriate for the laws of immediate application of a third state to have effect where there is a sufficiently close connection with such a state. Countries are allowed to disapply the third state for laws of immediate application and the UK has done so in its ratification of 17 November 1989 and RTA 1987 Sch 2.

Article 17
In the Convention the word 'law' means the domestic law of a state.

Article 18
The Convention is disregarded when it is manifestly incompatible with public policy.

Article 19
The Convention does not prejudice the powers of states in fiscal matters. It was necessary to state in the Convention that tax law would not be affected. Indeed, if the Convention appeared to allow the evasion of certain taxes by means of trusts, its chances of ratification would have been seriously compromised.

Article 20
Any contracting state may, at any time, declare that the provisions of the Convention would extend to trusts declared by judicial decisions and the UK has done so under RTA 1987 s 1(2).

Article 21
Recognition of trusts may be confined to those governed by the law of a contracting state. For example, a trust in Bermuda or the British Virgin Islands would be in a contracting state for this purpose. But one in the Bahamas or the Cayman Islands would not.

Article 22
The Convention applies to trusts regardless of the date on which they were created, although a contracting state may reserve the right not to apply the Convention to trusts created before the date on which, in relation to that state, the Convention enters into force.

Article 23
References to applicable law for a federal state are to the law in force in the territorial unit in question. For example, in the British Isles the relevant laws are those of England and Wales, Scotland, Northern Ireland, the Isle of Man, Jersey and Guernsey.

Article 24
If a federal state has territorial units with different trust laws it is not bound to apply the Convention to any internal conflict of laws.

Article 25
The Convention does not affect any other international agreement to which a contracting state becomes a party even if it contains provisions on matters governed by the Convention.

Chapter 5 Final clauses

Article 26
The only reservations allowed are under Arts 16, 21 and 22, as explained above, although a reservation may subsequently be withdrawn.

Article 27
The Convention may be signed by members of the Hague Conference on Private International Law at the time of its 15th session and deposited with the Ministry of Foreign Affairs of the Netherlands.

Article 28
Any other state may accede to the Convention after it has entered into force, and Malta did so on 31 December 1995 with effect from 1 March 1996.

Article 29
States with two or more territorial units may, at the time of signature, declare that the Convention shall extend to all their territorial units or only to one or more of them, and may modify this declaration by submitting a further declaration at any time. If a state makes no such a declaration the Convention extends to all territorial units of that state. The territories for which the UK has ratified the Convention are set out in the summary to RTA 1987.

Article 30
The Convention entered into force on 1 January 1992.

Thereafter the Convention enters into force for states ratifying it on the first day of the third calendar month after deposit of the notice of ratification etc.

Article 31
A contracting state may denounce the Convention by formal notification to the Ministry of Foreign affairs in the Netherlands which then takes effect six months after the notification is received or such later date as is specified in the notification.

Article 32
The Ministry of Foreign Affairs of the Netherlands must notify the member states of signatures and ratifications etc.

Trusts of Land and Appointment of Trustees Act 1996 (TLATA 1996)

2.12 Under LPA 1925 and SLA 1925 land could only be held by more than one person as a trust for sale or a strict settlement. Joint ownership either as tenants in common or joint tenants, where the interests are concurrent, was held on a trust for sale. Under a trust for sale the land has to be sold unless the trustees unanimously agree to postpone the sale, which meant in practice that if, for example, two co-owners fell out, either could effectively enforce the sale of the property by refusing to agree to the postponement. [LPA 1925 ss 34 and 36].

2.13 One of the problems of leaving land to persons in succession is that SLA 1925 would automatically apply unless it was specifically stated that the land was to be held on trust for sale. [SLA 1925 s 1]. Strict settlements were therefore not infrequently created purely by accident, often through home-made wills, resulting unintentionally in the highly complex and expensive to run strict settlement (*Bannister v Bannister* [1948] 2 All ER 133). Problems could arise in relation to a trust for sale where property was put into the name of one of the purchasers (*Bull v Bull* [1955] 1 All ER 253). *Williams and Glyns Bank v Boland* [1981] AC 487 confirmed that an undivided share in land can only take effect in equity behind a trust for sale. Bare trusts where land was held by one person for another absolutely are not dealt with as trusts under LPA 1925 or SLA 1925.

2.14 LPA 1925 s 2 allowed a purchaser of land to acquire good title without enquiring into the equitable interests in detail, by providing that a conveyance to a purchaser of a legal estate of land shall overreach any equitable interest or power affecting the estate. Under LPA 1925 s 27 a purchaser was not concerned with any trusts affecting the land, provided that the capital money was paid to at least two persons or a trust corporation, as trustees, although payment to a sole personal representative was sufficient. [LPA 1925 s 27(2)]. This overreaching machinery did not, however, apply to a bare trust. The effect of overreaching is to transfer the rights of beneficiaries from the land itself to the proceeds of sale of the land. TA 1925 s 14 prevents a single trustee other than a trust corporation from giving a valid receipt for the proceeds of sale of land. The ability of the overreaching provisions to defeat all equitable interests arose in *City of London Building Society v Flegg* [1988] AC 54 where property was held in a single name. However, the beneficiary in occupation could defeat the purchaser following *Hodgson v Marks* [1971] 2 All ER 684. TLATA 1996 substitutes the concept of a trust of land instead of a trust for sale, and prevents the creation of any further strict settlements under SLA 1925.

2.15 The new concept of a trust of land is very widely defined and would include bare trusts, statutory trusts and implied, resulting or constructive trusts. A trust of land differs from a trust for sale in that there is no duty to sell, with the power to retain, but an equal power to sell or retain, although this itself could give rise to problems where one co-owner wishes to sell and the other to retain the property. An express trust for sale is still possible, in which there is an implied power to retain. In some cases an express trust for sale would prevent deadlock by requiring the property to be sold in the absence of a unanimous agreement to retain.

2.16 TLATA 1996 generally enhances the rights of beneficiaries as compared with trustees, including a consultation process, rights to occupy and the abolition of the doctrine of conversion, which means that beneficial rights in a trust of land consists of real property. Existing strict settlements, under SLA 1925, may continue. The 1996 Act also gives trustees wider powers of investment and management and the opportunity to purchase property for occupation by a beneficiary. Part II of the Act also gives limited powers to beneficiaries to change trustees where they are all *sui juris* and unanimous.

Part I Trusts of Land

Introductory

1 Meaning of 'trust of land'
Trusts of land are defined as any trust or property which consists of or includes land and 'trustees of land' are trustees of a trust of land. The definition includes all trusts whenever created except land to which the Universities and College Estates Act 1925 applies.

Settlements and trusts for sale as trusts of land

2 Trusts in place of settlements
The Act came into force on 1 January 1997 under the Trusts of Land and Appointment of Trustees Act 1996 (Commencement) Order 1996 SI 1996/2974 and thereafter it became impossible to create a strict settlement under SLA 1925, but this does not outlaw existing strict settlements nor any changes to them, or settlements derived therefrom unless the deed otherwise provides. If there is no relevant property in a strict settlement, i e land and heirlooms within SLA 1925 s 67(1) then it ceases to be a strict settlement and becomes a normal trust. Under Sch 1 an attempt to create a strict settlement by transferring land to minors does not pass legal title but creates a trust in favour of the purported transferees. Land held on charitable, ecclesiastical or public trusts is not deemed to be settled land under SLA 1925 even if it was prior to 1 January 1997. It is not possible to create an entailed interest after 1 January 1997 and an attempt to do so results in the property being held in trust absolutely for the intended beneficiary. Where a strict settlement ceases to be so because of lack of relevant property, any subsequent property required under the settlement is held in trust for the beneficiaries. Schedule 1 introduces consequential provisions.

3 Abolition of doctrine of conversion
Other than in the case of a pre-existing will trust, where land is held by trustees subject to a trust for sale it is not regarded as personal property.

4 Express trusts for sale as trusts of land
In spite of anything to the contrary in the trust deed, trustees are given an absolute right to postpone the sale of land, and are not personally liable as a result of postponing the sale of land in the exercise of their discretion for an indefinite period.

5 Implied trusts for sale as trusts of land
Schedule 2 is introduced to treat land held on trusts for sale as a trust of land without a duty to sell and modifies LPA 1925 ss 31, 32, 34 and 36; LPA 1925 Sch 1; and AEA 1925 s 33.

Functions of trustees of land

6 General powers of trustees
The trustees of land have all the powers of an absolute owner, including the power to convey the land to beneficiaries of full age and capacity, and the beneficiaries or the court shall do whatever is necessary to secure that the land so vests. The trustees of land have power to acquire land under TA 2000 s 8, having regard to the rights of the beneficiaries and not in contravention of any order made under any other statute or rule of law or equity, which includes any order of any court or the Charity Commissioners. Trustees of land must exercise a duty of care under TA 2000 s 1 when exercising their powers to acquire or dispose of land.

7 Partition by trustees
Trustees may partition land among beneficiaries absolutely entitled, and may convey the partitioned land either absolutely or in trust, and whether or not subject to any legal mortgage raised to providing equality money for the partition, but the trustees require the consent of the beneficiaries to the partition. Trustees must discharge any liability encumbering the land or otherwise give effect to it. Where land is absolutely vested in a minor, the trustees may act on his behalf and hold the land in trust for him.

8 Exclusion and restriction of powers
The powers in sections 6 and 7 above can be disapplied by the trust deed, or made conditional on consent, except in the case of charitable, ecclesiastical or public trusts and subject to any restriction in any other act.

9 Delegation by trustee
The trustees may delegate any of their functions as trustees of the land to an adult beneficially entitled to an interest in possession, by way of power of attorney. Interests of third parties dealing with the beneficiary are protected and the power of attorney must be given by all the trustees jointly, but may be revoked by any one of them or on the appointment of a new trustee. The power of attorney is automatically revoked if the donee ceases to be a beneficiary. Delegation under these provisions may be for any period or indefinite but cannot be an enduring power within the meaning of the EPAA 1985. When exercising the functions of the trustees the beneficiary has the same duties and liabilities as a trustee.

9A Duties of trustees in connection with delegation etc
Trustees, in delegating their functions over the land, must exercise a duty of care under TrA 2000 s 1 and, unless the delegation is irrevocable, they must keep it under review and if appropriate give directions to the beneficiary or revoke the delegation. A trustee of land, provided that he has exercised the duty of care, is not liable for any act or default of the beneficiary.

Consents and consultation

10 Consents
Where a consent is required by the trustees in respect of a trust of land, any two beneficiaries giving consent will be sufficient. This does not apply to trustees of land held on charitable, ecclesiastical or public trusts. Where the beneficiary required to give a consent is under age, his consent is not required so far as the purchaser is concerned, but the trustees have to obtain the consent of the parent or guardian.

11 Consultation with beneficiaries
Adult beneficiaries should be consulted by the trustees in exercise of any function relating to the land and so far as is consistent with the general interest of the trust, the trustees must give effect to the wishes of the majority of the beneficiaries by value.

This does not apply to a pre-1 January 1997 will trust, or where the trust deed provides otherwise or where the land is to be conveyed to the beneficiaries under section 6(2). Nor does it apply to a trust created prior to 1 January 1997 unless so provided in a supplemental deed executed by the settlor.

Right of beneficiaries to occupy trust land

12 The right to occupy
A beneficiary entitled to an interest in possession in land subject to a trust of land is entitled to occupy the land if so provided by the trust deed, or if the trustees are holding the land for his occupation, although these provisions do not apply if the land is either unavailable or unsuitable for occupation and is subject to section 13.

13 Exclusion and restriction of right to occupy
Where two or more beneficiaries are *prima facie* entitled to occupy the land under section 12, the trustees may restrict the entitlement of one or more but not all of them, provided that they are acting reasonably. They have to take into account the intentions of the person who created the trust, the purpose for which the land is held and the circumstances and wishes of each of the beneficiaries. The trustees may impose obligations on the beneficiary such as paying the expenses in respect of the land, or assume other obligations in relation to any activity on the land, or to pay compensation to excluded beneficiaries or cause them to forego other benefits to which they would otherwise be entitled. They cannot, however, dispossess a beneficiary in occupation without the consent of that beneficiary or the court.

Powers of court

14 Applications for order
A trustee or beneficiary of a trust of land may apply to the court for an order relating to the exercise by the trustees of their functions, or declaring the nature or extent of a person's interest in property.

15 Matters relevant in determining application
The court, in making an order under section 14 must have regard to the intentions of the settlor, the purpose for which the property is held, the welfare of any minor who is or might occupy the land as his home, and the interests of any secured creditor or beneficiary. On an application under section 13 the court must have regard to the circumstances and wishes of each of the beneficiaries except in the case of a transfer of the land to beneficiaries under section 6(2), or an application by a trustee in bankruptcy under IA 1986 s 335A (inserted by Sch 3).

Purchaser protection

16 Protection of purchasers
The purchaser of land which has been subject to a trust is not concerned to see that the trustees have complied with any requirement imposed on them unless the purchaser has actual notice of a contravention. Where the powers of the trustees are limited by the trust deed the trustees must take all reasonable steps to bring the limitation to the notice of the purchaser, but if they fail to do so it does not invalidate the conveyance to the purchaser who has no actual notice of the limitation. Where land is conveyed to the beneficiaries the trustees must execute a deed declaring that they are discharged from the trust in relation to the land, and if they fail to do so the court may make an order requiring them to do so, but the purchaser is entitled to assume that the land is not subject to the trust unless he has actual notice that the trustees were mistaken in believing that the beneficiaries were of full age and entitled to the property, although this section does not apply to registered land.

Supplementary

17 Application of provisions to trusts and proceeds of sale
The application for a court order applies to a trust and proceeds of sale of land as it applies to a trust of land. A trust of proceeds of sale of land is property which includes the proceeds of a sale of land or property representing such proceeds, which excludes a strict settlement (including heirlooms) but includes other trusts.

18 Application of parts to personal representatives
Provisions relating to trustees, apart from sections 10, 11 and 14 apply with appropriate modification to personal representatives.

Part II Appointment and Retirement of Trustees

19 Appointment and retirement of trustee at instance of beneficiary
Where there are adult beneficiaries absolutely entitled to the property subject to a trust, and there is no person nominated for the purpose of appointing new

trustees by the trust deed, the beneficiaries may direct a trustee or trustees to retire and to appoint a new trustee or trustees as directed provided that reasonable arrangements have been made for the protection of the retired trustee and there will, after his retirement, be either a trust corporation or at least two trustees to perform the trust, and either another person is to be appointed on his retirement or the continuing trustees consent to his retirement. The retiring trustee makes a deed declaring his retirement and he is deemed to have retired and be discharged from the trust. The remaining trustees will do whatever is necessary to vest the trust property in the ongoing trustees, subject to the limitation of the trustees to four in the case of a trust of land.

20 Appointment of substitute for incapable trustees
A notice directing a trustee to retire may be given to the receiver of a trustee incapable by reason of mental disorder from exercising his functions as trustee, or to his attorney, or to person authorised under Part VII of MHA 1983.

21 Supplementary
The administrative arrangements for directions being given by beneficiaries are set out.

Part III Supplementary

22 Meaning of beneficiary
Beneficiary is defined.

23 Other interpretation provisions
Various terms are defined by reference to LPA 1925.

24 Application to Crown
The Act applies to the Crown but not to affect or alter the descent, devolution or nature of the estates and interest of land vested in the Crown, the Duchy of Lancaster or the Duchy of Cornwall.

25 Amendments, repeals etc
Schedule 3 sets out the minor or consequential amendments, Sch 4, the repeals.

27 Short title commencement and extent
The Trusts of Land and Appointment of Trustees Act 1996 came into effect on 1 January 1997.

Trustee Delegation Act 1999 (TDA 1999)

2.17 TDA 1999 enables a trustee of a trust of land to appoint his co-owner his attorney, either under a trustee power of attorney under TA 1925 s 25, an enduring power of attorney under EPAA 1985, or a general power of attorney under PAA 1971 s 10, overruling *Walia v Michael Noughton Ltd* [1985] 1 WLR 1115. It also prevents EPAA 1985 being used to usurp the functions of a trustee. It also replaces the trustee power of attorney under TA 1925 s 25 and gives limited rights to attorneys to appoint new trustees, but protects the two-trustee rule for the receipt for capital monies to overreach equitable interests.

Attorney of trustee with beneficial interest in land

1 Exercise of trustee functions by attorney
A co-owner as trustee can appoint his co-owner as his attorney. The donee of a power of attorney can act in relation to land or the sale proceeds of land or income from land provided that the donor had a beneficial interest in the land, proceeds or income, unless the instrument creating the power of attorney provides otherwise. This only applies whether the attorney is regarded as exercising a trustee function not where he is acting under a trustee delegation power. These provisions only apply where the power of attorney has been entered into after the commencement of the Act, on 1 March 2000 by the Trustee Delegation Act 1999 (Commencement) Order SI 2000/216.

2 Evidence of beneficial interest
An appropriate statement signed by the attorney is conclusive evidence of the donor's beneficial interest in the property and therefore the attorney's ability to act as against a purchaser.

3 General powers and specified forms
The general prohibition under PAA 1971 s 10(2) for an attorney exercising a function as trustee etc is made subject to TDA 1999 s 1.

4 Enduring Powers
EPAA 1985 s 3(3), which enables the attorney to exercise the donor's functions as trustee does not apply to enduring powers created on or after 1 March 2000 or to earlier powers where the registration is cancelled or refused.

Trustee delegation under section 25 of the Trustee Act 1925

5 Delegation under section 25 of the Trustee Act 1925
A new section replaces the original TA 1925 s 25, *qv*.

6 Section 25 powers as enduring powers
Powers of attorney created after 1 March 2000 may be enduring powers.

Miscellaneous provisions about attorney acting for trustee

7 Two-trustee rules
Where two or more trustees are required to give a valid receipt for capital monies or to overreach an interest or power it is not satisfied by a relevant attorney, who is an attorney of two or more trustees, acting alone, unless the relevant entity is a trust corporation.

8 Appointment of additional trustee by attorney
An attorney acting under a registered power under the Enduring Powers of Attorney Act 1985 s 6 may appoint an additional trustee or trustees where he intends to exercise any function of the trustees under TDA 1999 s 1(1) or substituted TA 1925 s 25.

9 Attorney acting for incapable trustee
A new trustee may be appointed, or an incapable trustee discharged, by an attorney acting under an enduring power of attorney.

Authority of attorney to act in relation to land

10 Extent of attorney's authority to act in relation to land
The attorney appointed on or after 1 March 2000 may act in relation to land unless the deed appointing him provides otherwise.

Supplementary

11 Interpretation

12 Repeals, in accordance with the Schedule

13 Commencement etc

Trustee Act 2000 (TA 2000)

2.18 TA 2000 imposes a statutory duty of care on trustees, and although it can be disapplied it is unlikely that many trust deeds will actually do so. It also provides a number of default powers of investment, which are particularly useful where, for example, a statutory trust arises on intestacy or a new settlement fails to incorporate a full range of express powers of the trustees or where an old settlement incorporates limited and unsatisfactory powers. A well-drafted express trust is likely to continue to give the trustees all the powers included in TA 2000, e g see *Society of Trust and Estate Practitioners Standard Provisions*, first edition. The Act does not outlaw trustee exculpation clauses; although the Trust Law Committee produced a consultation paper against clauses exonerating professional trustees from negligence or, in many cases, anything other than fraud, such clauses remain effective (*Armitage v Nurse* [1988] Ch 241).

Part I The Duty of Care

1 The duty of care
A trustee in carrying out his duties must exercise such care and skill as is reasonable in the circumstances having regard in particular to any special knowledge or experience that he has or claims to have and, if a professional trustee, to any special knowledge or experience that it is reasonable to expect such a person to have. This is referred to as the duty of care, and came into effect on 1 February 2001. [SI 2001/49].

2 Application of duty of care
Schedule 1 provides when the duty of care applies to a trustee, i e when exercising the powers of investment or review of investments, when exercising power to acquire land or in relation to land, and on the appointment of agents, nominees or custodians, and in reviewing their actions, in particular

selecting who is to act and in determining the terms on which he is to act, and in the preparation of a policy statement governing asset management functions. It applies generally to asset management functions and insurance. It also applies to trustees valuing reversionary interests or other trust property. The duty of care does not apply if it appears from the trust instrument that it is not meant to apply.

Part II Investment

3 General power of investment
A trustee may make any kind of investment that he could make if he was absolutely entitled to the assets of the trust, which is called the general power of investment. This general power does not permit a trustee to make investments in land, other than in loans secured on land, as the acquisition of land is dealt with in Part III below.

4 Standard investment criteria
When exercising any power of investment a trustee must have regard to the standard investment criteria, ie the suitability to the trust of proposed investments, and the need for diversification in so far as is appropriate to the circumstances of the trust. The trustee must from time to time review the investments of the trust and consider whether they should be varied.

5 Advice
A trustee must obtain and consider proper advice before exercising any power of investment or when reviewing whether the investment should be varied unless he reasonably concludes that in all the circumstances it is unnecessary or inappropriate to do so. Proper advice is from a person reasonably believed by the trustee to be qualified to give it.

6 Restriction or exclusion of this Part etc
The general power of investment is in addition to the trustees' existing powers and subject to any restriction or exclusion imposed by the trust deed or by law.

7 Existing trusts
Trustees' investment powers contained in a deed made before 3 August 1961 do not restrict the trustees' general power of investment nor does a provision in the trust authorising investments under TIA 1961.

Part III Acquisition of Land

8 Power to acquire
A trustee may acquire freehold or leasehold land in the UK as an investment for occupation by a beneficiary or for any other reason.

9 Restriction or exclusion of this Part etc
The power to acquire land is in addition to powers otherwise conferred on trustees but is subject to any restriction imposed by the trust deed or by law.

10 Existing trusts
The power to acquire land applies to all trusts other than strict settlements under SLA 1925 or a trust to which the Universities and College Estates Act 1925 applies.

Part IV Agents, Nominees and Custodians

Agents

11 Power to employ agents
Trustees may delegate to any person as their agent matters other than (except in the case of a charitable trust) decisions as to whether or in what way any assets of the trust should be distributed, whether trust expenses should be borne by income or capital, or the appointment of a new trustee or the power to delegate or appoint a person as nominee or custodian, which must be done by the trustees themselves.

In a charitable trust, the trustees delegable functions are carrying out the trustees' decisions, the investment of assets, the raising of funds, other than by means of a trade which is an integral part of the trust's charitable purposes, or any other function prescribed by an order made by the Secretary of State.

12 Persons who may act as agents
Trustees may authorise a trustee to be an agent but may not authorise two or more persons to exercise the same function, unless they act jointly, but a beneficiary cannot be an agent. The agent can also be a nominee or custodian.

13 Linked functions etc
An agent must abide by the statutory rules applicable to his task, so that investment agent must follow the standard investment criteria relating to the trust. An agent who is an expert does not have to take advice in his area of expertise and an agent dealing with trust land has no duty to consult beneficiaries or give effect to their wishes, but the terms of his appointment must not prevent the trustees from complying with their statutory duties to consult, under TLATA 1996 s 11(1).

14 Terms of agency
Trustees can fix the terms of engagement and remuneration of the agent but unless it is reasonably necessary must not permit the agent to appoint a substitute or restrict his liability or to have a conflict of interest.

15 Asset management: special restrictions
Agents carrying out asset management functions must have an agreement which is evidenced in writing and the trustee must have prepared a policy statement that gives evidence as to how the function should be exercised, and the agent must agree to follow the policy statement or any revision or replacement thereof. The policy statement must ensure that the asset management will be in the best interests of the trust, and must be in, or evidenced in, writing. Asset management functions are those relating to the investment of the trust assets and the acquisition, management or disposing of trust property.

Nominees and custodians

16 Power to appoint nominees
Trustees may hold trust assets, other than settled land under SLA 1925, in the name of a nominee whose appointment must be in, or evidenced in, writing. These provisions do not apply to the trust having a custodian trustee or assets vested in the official custodian for charities.

17 Power to appoint custodians
Trustees have an unfettered right to appoint a person to act as a custodian in relation to trust assets, to undertake the safe custody of the assets, or of any documents or records concerning the assets. The appointment must be in or evidenced in writing but does not apply to a custodian trustee.

18 Investment in bearer securities
The trustees must appoint a person to act as custodian of bearer securities, unless the trust deed provides otherwise, and such appointment must be in, or evidenced in, writing. This section does not apply where there is a custodian trustee.

19 Persons who may be appointed as nominees or custodians
A nominee or custodian must be a person carrying on a business which includes such activities, or be a body corporate controlled by the trustees, or one recognised under AJA 1985 s 9. The company is controlled by trustees if they have voting control or have powers to secure that the affairs of the company are conducted in accordance with their wishes under ICTA 1988 s 840. The trustees of a charitable trust must follow the advice of the Charity Commissioners concerning the selection of a custodian or nominee. Appointees may include a trustee if it is a trust corporation, or two or more trustees to act as joint nominees or joint custodians. Nominees may also be custodians or agents and vice versa.

20 Terms of appointment of nominees and custodians
The trustees may fix the remuneration and terms of engagement of a nominee or custodian but must not, unless it is reasonably necessary to do so, permit a nominee or custodian to appoint a substitute or restrict their liability or have a conflict of interest.

Review of and liability for agents, nominees and custodians etc

21 Application of sections 22 and 23
Sections 22 and 23 apply where trustees have appointed an agent, nominee or custodian unless these are inconsistent with the trust instrument.

22 Review of agents, nominees and custodians etc
The trustees must keep under the review the arrangements under which an agent, nominee or custodian acts, and to exercise any power of intervention they may have, if necessary. They must also keep the policy statement under review.

23 Liability for agents, nominees and custodians etc
A trustee is not liable for any act or default of an agent, nominee or custodian, unless he has failed to comply with his duty of care, and the same applies to any duly appointed substitute.

Supplementary

24 Effect of trustees exceeding their powers
The fact that a trustee has exceeded his power in authorising an agent or appointing a nominee or custodian does not invalidate the authorisation or appointment.

25 Sole trustees
These provisions also apply to sole trustees except that a trust corporation does not need to appoint a custodian for bearer securities.

26 Restriction or exclusion of this Part etc
The ability of trustees to appoint agents, nominees or custodians is in addition to any other powers they have at law, or under the trust instrument, but may be restricted or excluded by the trust deed.

27 Existing trusts
These provisions apply to trusts whenever created.

Part V Remuneration

28 Trustee's entitlement to payment under trust instrument
Provided that the instrument provides for trustees to be paid, a trust corporation or professional trustee is entitled to receive payment for his services.

A trustee of a charitable trust who is not a trust corporation and is not a sole trustee can only be paid to the extent that a majority of the other trustees have agreed that he should be paid. A payment to a trustee is treated as a remuneration for services and not as a gift from the trust for the purposes of WA 1837 s 15 and AEA 1925 s 34(3).

29 Remuneration of certain trustees
A trust corporation that is not a trustee of a charitable trust is entitled to receive reasonable remuneration out of the trust funds, as is a professional trustee, unless the trust instrument deals with his entitlement to remuneration or it is covered by any other legislation. It also applies where a trustee has appointed an agent, nominee or custodian.

30 Remuneration of trustees of charitable trusts
The Secretary of State may make regulations to provide for the remuneration of trustees of charitable trusts who are trust corporations or act in a professional capacity. At the time of writing no such regulations have yet been produced.

31 Trustee's expenses
A trustee is entitled to be reimbursed from the trust funds, or may use the trust funds, to pay expenses properly incurred by him when acting on behalf of the trust, whether or not an agent, nominee or custodian has been appointed.

32 Remuneration and expenses of agents, nominees and custodians
Trustees are authorised to pay reasonable remuneration to, and reimburse the expenses of, an agent, nominee or custodian whose terms of engagement entitle him to be remunerated.

33 Application
The provisions relating to trustees' remuneration apply to trusts whenever created, but not to the administration of estates where the death occurred before the Act came into force on 1 February 2001.

Part VI Miscellaneous and Supplementary

34 Power to insure
This section substitutes a new power to insure in TA 1925 s 19, and is dealt with there.

35 Personal representatives
This Act applies to personal representatives administering an estate, as well as to trustees with appropriate modifications, such as references to the trust instrument being references to the will, and to beneficiaries, the persons interested in the due administration of the estate, or in relation to the occupation of trust property by a beneficiary under TA 2000 s 8(1)(b) to a person beneficially interested in the estate. The remuneration of the personal representative is treated as an administration expense and takes priority over preferential debts in an insolvent estate under the Insolvency Act 1986 Sch 6, except in the case of a death occurring before 1 February 2001.

36 Pension schemes
Pension schemes established under a trust, and subject to the law of England and Wales, are within only some of the provisions of this Act. The duty of care in Part I and the provisions relating to acquisitions and investment in land in Parts II and III do not apply. The provisions relating to the appointment of agents exclude the employer or associate of an employer from being an agent. The provisions relating to nominees and custodians do not apply to the trustees of a pension scheme.

37 Authorised unit trusts
Parts II, III and IV do not apply to authorised unit trusts under FSA 1986 s 78.

38 Common investment schemes for charities etc
Parts II, III and IV do not normally apply to common investment schemes under CA 1993 ss 24 or s 25.

39 Interpretations
Various terms are defined.

40 Minor and consequential amendments etc
Schedules 2 (minor and consequential amendments), 3 (transitional provisions and savings) and 4 (repeals) are enacted.

41 Power to amend other Acts
A Minister of the Crown may make such amendments to any Act, including an Act extending to places outside England and Wales, as appears to him appropriate in connection with the investment and acquisition of land provisions in Part II or III. Before doing so, in relation to a local, personal or private Act, the Minister must consult any person who appears to be affected. Such an order is exercisable by statutory instrument.

42 Commencement and extent
The Act came into force on 1 February 2001 by order made by the Trustee Act 2000 (Commencement) Order 2001 SI 2001/49. Generally the Act applies to England and Wales only.

43 Short title
This Act may be cited as the Trustee Act 2000. The alterations to existing statutes made by Sch 2 are included in the commentary on those Acts, where appropriate, or are otherwise outside the scope of this book.

Wills, families and estates

2.19 Acts dealing with family and inheritance law are set out below.

Wills Act 1837 (WA 1837)

2.20 Important provisions of the WA 1837 that are still in force include section 9, which provides that no will shall be valid unless it is in writing and signed by the testator, or by some other person in his presence and by his direction, and it appears that the testator intended by his signature to give effect to the will and the signature is made or acknowledged by the testator in the presence of two or more witnesses present at the same time, and each witness either attests and signs the will or acknowledges his signature in the presence of the testator but not necessarily in the presence of any other witness, but no formal attestation shall be necessary. It is, however, common to have an attestation clause such as 'signed by the said … [testator] in our joint presence and attested by us in his/her presence and that of each other'; together with the signature, address and occupational status of the witnesses.

2.21 Other sections still in force are as follows.

11 Soldiers and mariners wills excepted
A soldier on actual military service and a mariner at sea even if aged under 18 may dispose of his personal estate through a hand-written (holograph) but unwitnessed will, see Wills (Soldiers and Sailors) Act 1918.

15 Gifts to an attesting witness to be void
A person who attests the execution of a will cannot take any benefit from the will and nor can his or her spouse although it does not invalidate any other aspect of the will. This provision is modified by WA 1968 s 1, which provides that if the will is duly executed without the potential beneficiary's attestation and without that of any other such beneficiary, the intended beneficiary's attestation can be ignored and he or his spouse can benefit under the will.

18 Wills to be revoked by marriage, except in certain cases
A will is automatically revoked by the testator's marriage but a power of appointment is not. A will made in contemplation of a marriage which subsequently takes place is valid.

18A Effect of dissolution or annulment of marriage on wills
Where a testator is divorced or his marriage annulled after he has made a will, it takes effect as if the former spouse had died on the date the marriage was dissolved or annulled.

20 No will to be revoked by another will or codicil or by a writing executed like a will or by destruction
A will can only be revoked or amended by a formal revocation, new will or codicil executed in accordance with section 9 or 11.

21 No alteration in a will shall have any effect unless executed as a will
A will can only be altered by a proper codicil executed in accordance with section 9 or 11.

22 No will revoked to be reviewed otherwise than by re-execution or a codicil to revive it
Execution in accordance with section 9 or 11 is necessary.

24 A will shall be construed to speak from the death of the testator

25 A residuary devise shall include estates comprised in lapsed and void devises
Where property is devised but fails as a result of the prior death of the devisee or for some other reason, such property is included in the residuary devise contained in the will or otherwise falls into residue. This applies subject to any contrary intention in the will.

26 A general devise of the testator's lands shall include … leasehold as well as freehold interests
Unless a contrary intention appears in the will.

27 A general gift shall include estates over which the testator has a general power of appointment

33 Gifts to children or other issue who leave issue living at the testator's death shall not lapse
Where a child dies before the testator his or her issue will share their deceased parent's inheritance, known as taking *per stirpes* (through the stem). This includes illegitimate and posthumous children *en ventre sa mere* at the testator's death.

Apportionment Act 1870 (AA 1870)

2.22 This Act provides that rents, annuities, dividends and other periodical payments in the nature of income shall, like interest on money lent, be considered as accruing from day to day and shall be apportionable in respect of time accordingly. The apportionment of such income on death or on a beneficiary becoming absolutely entitled to income or capital, or where a beneficiary is born or dies can become an administrative nightmare and expensive in terms of trust administration. Fortunately AA 1870 s 7 allows a will or trust deed to disapply the apportionment rules by expressly providing that they shall not apply and most well drawn wills and trusts take advantage of this provision. There can also be cases where equitable apportionment applies, see **4.53–4.55**.

Married Women's Property Act 1882 (MWPA 1882)

2.23 This Act originally gave married women the right to own property and to sue in their own name, for the first time. The main practical effect these days is in relation to insurance policies effected by a husband in favour of his wife under MWPA 1882 s 11, enabling her to claim on a policy on her husband's death even though not a contractual party to it.

2.24 MWPA 1882 s 17 enables the court to ascertain the property rights of spouses or of couples who were previously engaged to be married. In such cases it would be normal for resulting trust principles to determine the beneficial interest of the spouse based on her contribution to the purchase price of the matrimonial home. There may also be arguments under constructive trust principles which would take into account non-financial contributions to the marriage. See MPPA 1970 ss 37 and 39.

Domicile And Matrimonial Proceedings Act 1973 (DMPA 1973)

2.25 The portion of this Act which is of relevance is Part I, which deals with domicile.

Husband and Wife

Abolition of wife's dependant domicile
The domicile of a married woman, after the coming into force of this section, by s 17(5) on 1 January 1974, is ascertained by reference to the same factors as in the case of any individual capable of having an independent domicile as opposed to one the same as that of her husband by virtue only of marriage.

However where a woman was married on or before 1 January 1974 and had acquired her husband's domicile by dependence she is treated as retaining that domicile as a domicile of choice until it is changed by acquisition or revival of another domicile, ie her domicile prior to marriage does not automatically revive. This section extends to England and Wales, Scotland and Northern Ireland.

Minors and pupil

3 Age at which independent domicile can be acquired
A person becomes capable of having an independent domicile when he attains the age of 16 or marries before that age. This section applies to England and Wales and Northern Ireland but not to Scotland, where the age of independent domicile is 12 for a girl and 14 for a boy. Prior to this section and until 31 December 1970, the age of independent domicile was 21. Subsequently, under the Family Law Reform Act 1969 s 1(1) it was 18 until 31 December 1973 in England and Wales and Northern Ireland. A child aged between 16 and 18 on 1 January 1974 became capable of an independent domicile on that date.

4 Dependent domicile of child not living with his father
Where the father and mother are alive but living apart, the child's domicile while dependant shall be that of his mother if he has his home with her and no home with his father or has had a home with her and has not since had a home with his father. If the mother dies, the child retains her domicile at death if he had acquired his mother's domicile and has not since had a home with his father. Illegitimate and posthumous children still have their mother's domicile while dependent. Where the child has been adopted, the father and mother are the adoptive father and mother. This section applies to England, Wales, Scotland and Northern Ireland.

2.26 The remainder of this Act deals with jurisdiction in matrimonial proceedings and is therefore outside the scope of this book.

Inheritance (Provision for Family and Dependants) Act 1975 (IPFDA 1975)

2.27 Under this Act certain dependants of the deceased (including spouses, ex-spouses who have not remarried, children and long-term partners) have a right to claim, within six months of the grant of probate, that the deceased has not made reasonable provision in his or her will or under the intestacy rules. The court may order income or capital of the deceased's estate to be paid or transferred to the claimant if and so far as it thinks fit. Any such order is effective as from the date of death and effectively amends the will or intestacy rules for all purposes including taxation.

Matrimonial Proceedings and Property Act 1970 (MPPA 1970)

2.28 Two sections of this Act are of relevance.

37 Contributions by a spouse in money or money's worth to the improvement of property
Substantial contributions to the improvement of property in money or money's worth by a husband or wife may increase the proportionate beneficial interest in the property to an extent that may seem just, unless there is an express or implied agreement to the contrary.

39 Extension of section 17 of the Married Woman's Property Act 1882
An application for a share in the former matrimonial home can be made within three years of the marriage being dissolved or annulled.

Administration of Estates Act 1925 (AEA 1925)

2.29 AEA 1925 is still the main Act which deals with the administration of deceaseds' estates, whether testate or intestate.

Part III Administration of Assets

32 Real and personal estate of deceased are assets for payment of debt
The real and personal estate whether legal or equitable of the deceased including any property over which he has a general power of appointment are assets for the payment of his debts. Any person to whom such assets are transferred and who disposes of them in good faith passes good title but is liable to the value of the assets disposed of.

33 Trust for sale
Where a person dies intestate as to any part of his estate it should be held in trust by his personal representatives with power to sell it under AEA 1925 s 33(1) and (2), as amended by TLATA 1996 s 5 and Sch 2 para 5. Personal representatives should use any money from the proceeds of disposal of assets to pay funeral, testamentary and administration expenses, debts and other liabilities and any balance should be used to pay any pecuniary legacies bequeathed by the will. Pending payment the trustees may invest the monies which become the residuary estate of the intestate and subject to the provisions contained in the will if any.

34 Administration of assets
Where the estate is solvent, assets are applied in payment of liabilities in accordance with AEA 1925 Sch 1 para 2 in the following order:

(i) property undisposed of by will, subject to a retention to fund any pecuniary legacies;

(ii) property not specifically devised or bequeathed, subject to retention of underpaid pecuniary legacies so far as not already provided for;

(iii) property specifically appropriated, devised or bequeathed for the payment of debt;

(iv) property charged with or devised or bequeathed, subject to a charge for the payment of debt;

(v) the fund, if any, retained to meet pecuniary legacies;

(vi) property specifically devised or bequeathed rateably according to value;

(vii) property appointed by will under a general power rateably according to value;

(viii) the will may vary this order of application.

41 Powers of personal representative as to appropriation
A personal representative may appropriate any part of the real or personal estate towards satisfaction of any legacy which does not prejudice the interests of any specific legatee or devisee. Consent of the donee or his trustees is required.

42 Powers to appoint trustees of infant's property
Where an infant becomes absolutely entitled under a will or an intestacy to a devise or legacy or share of the residue, the personal representatives may appoint trustees to hold the assets for the benefit of the infant.

Part IV Distribution of Residuary Estate

46 Succession to real and personal estate on intestacy
This section, as amended by the IEA 1952 and other legislation, sets out the manner in which the residuary estate of an intestate shall be distributed absolutely or on statutory trusts. The corresponding provisions in Scotland are given by the Succession (Scotland) Act 1964. The intestacy rules as they are usually known are reproduced below.

47 Statutory trusts in favour of issue and other classes of relatives of intestates
The statutory trusts referred to for intestates under AEA 1925 s 46, as amended, are held in trust in equal shares for any child or children of the intestate living at the date of death who obtain the age of 18 years or marry under that age and, if they predecease the intestate, their issue taking their parent's share equally *per stirpes*. The statutory powers of advancement and maintenance and accumulation of surplus income under TA 1925 ss 31 and 32 apply, although when an infant marries he is entitled to give a valid receipt for the income of his share or interest.

Personal representatives may permit any infant with a contingent interest who would inherit on reaching the age of 18, or marrying under that age, to have the use and enjoyment of any personal chattels subject to such conditions as the personal representatives may consider reasonable.

If the children of the intestate fail to obtain a vested interest by dying without issue before their parent, the intestate is treated as having died without leaving issue and the intestacy rules applied accordingly. Where part of the residuary estate of the intestate is held on statutory trusts for relatives other than issue, the residuary estate is shared equally among the members of the class with similar statutory powers of advancement and maintenance and accumulation of surplus income and ability to allow a beneficiary to have the use and enjoyment of any personal chattels as it applies to children of the intestate.

47A Right of surviving spouse to have own life interest redeemed
A surviving spouse entitled to a life interest in part of the residuary estate under the intestacy rules may elect that the personal representatives shall purchase or redeem the life interest for the capital value of the life interest. The election can only be made over such part of the residuary estate as consists of property in possession and is calculated under the intestate succession (Interest and Capitalisation) Order 1977 (SI 1977/1491) as amended by the Intestate Succession (Interest and Capitalisation) Order 1977 (Amendment) Order 1983 (SI 1983/1374).

An election to redeem the life interest must be made within twelve months from the date on which representation with respect to the intestate is first taken out unless the court determines that this would operate unfairly, e g because there was a will subsequently revoked for invalidity or there was a dispute as to the spouse's entitlement. An election is made in writing to the personal representatives and is irrevocable. Where the surviving spouse is also the sole personal representative, an election must be made in writing to the Senior Registrar of the Family Division of the High Court.

48 Powers of a personal representative in respect of interests of surviving spouse
Personal representatives may raise the money to redeem the surviving spouse's life interest by using the remainder of the estate, other than personal chattels, as security in the same way as they are permitted to charge the residue to raise the fixed sum due to the surviving spouse under the intestacy rules.

49 Application to cases of partial intestacy
The personal representative under the will becomes a trustee for the assets undisposed of by will to hold them in accordance with the beneficiary's rights under the intestacy rules.

Intestates Estates Act 1952 (IEA 1952)

2.30 Section 5 states that under IEA 1952 Sch 2, where the residuary estate of the intestate comprises the matrimonial home, the surviving spouse may require the personal representative to appropriate the property *in specie* under AEA 1925 s 41 in or towards satisfaction of the surviving spouse's interest in the estate of the intestate. This right may be exercised within twelve months of representation being taken out in respect of the intestate's estate but not after the death of the surviving spouse and must be notified to the personal representatives in writing or to the court in the same way as to redeem the statutory life interest under the intestacy rules. During this twelve month period the personal representative cannot sell or dispose of the matrimonial home without the surviving spouse's written consent unless it is needed to pay debts of the deceased.

Wills Act 1963 (WA 1963)

2.31 Sections 1 and 2 of this Act are of interest.

1 General rule as to formal validity
A will is also treated as valid if executed in accordance with the law in force in the territory where at the time of its execution or the testator's death he was domiciled, had his habitual residence or was a national.

2 Additional rules
A will executed on board a vessel or aircraft is valid if executed in accordance with the law in force where the vessel or aircraft is registered or most closely connected and, if it relates to immovable property such as real estate, if it is executed in accordance with the law in force in the territory where the property was situated. Such a will may include a power of appointment if it conformed to the law governing the essential validity of the power.

Intestacy rules

England and Wales

2.32 The applicable statute is AEA 1925 s 46 as amended, for deaths on or after 1 December 1993.

Surviving relative(s)	**Person(s) entitled to the estate**	**Person(s) entitled to grant of letters of administration**
1 Spouse only[1]	Surviving spouse[1] absolutely	Surviving spouse[1]
2 Spouse[1]and issue	(a) Surviving spouse[1] takes: (i) personal chattels (ii) £125,000 (iii) Life interest in half residuary estate (b) Issue[2] take residuary estate at age 18 subject to life interest in half of surviving spouse in equal shares *per stirpes*	Surviving spouse[1] and one other person[4]
3 Spouse[1] and parent(s)	(a) Surviving spouse[1] takes: (i) personal chattels (ii) £200,000[3] (iii) half residuary estate absolutely	Surviving spouse[1]

Surviving relative(s)	**Person(s) entitled to the estate**	**Person(s) entitled to grant of letters of administration**
	(b) Parent(s) take half residuary estate in equal shares	
4 Spouse[1] and and brother(s) and/or sister(s) of the whole blood and/or issue of such who predeceased the intestate	(a) Surviving spouse[1] takes (i) personal chattels (ii) £200,000[3] (iii) half residuary estate absolutely (b) Brother(s) and sister(s) and/or issue takes half residuary estate at age 18[6] in equal shares *per stirpes*	Surviving spouse (one other person)[4]
5 Issue	Issue at age 18[6] in equal shares *per stirpes*	Issue
6 Parent(s)	Parent(s) in equal shares	Parent
7 Brother(s) and/or sister(s) of the whole blood and/or issue of such who predeceased the intestate	Parent(s) in equal shares Brother(s) and sister(s) and or issue at age 18[6] in equal shares *per stirpes*	Brother or sister or issue etc (and one other person)
8 Brother(s) and/or sister(s) of the half blood and/or issue of such who predeceased the intestate	Half brother(s) and sister(s) and/or issue at age 18[6] in equal shares *per stirpes*	Half brother or sister or issue etc (and one other person)
9 Grandparent(s)	Grandparent(s) in equal shares	Grandparent
10 Uncle(s) and/or aunt(s) of the whole blood and/or issue of such who predeceased the intestate	Uncle(s) and aunt(s) and/or issue at age 18 in equal shares *per stirpes*	uncle or aunt or issue etc (and one other person)
11 Uncle(s) and/or aunt(s) of the half blood and/or issue of such who predeceased intestate	Such uncle(s) and aunt(s) and/or issue at age 18 equal shares *per stirpes*	Such uncle, aunt or issue etc (and one other person)[4]

Surviving relative(s)	Person(s) entitled to the estate	Person(s) entitled to grant of letters of administration
12 No relative as mentioned above	The Crown as *bona vacantia*	The Crown

Notes

1 Where a decree of judicial separation is in force and the separation is continuing at the date of death the estate of the intestate devolves as if his or her surviving spouse were dead.

2 'Issue' includes issue through all degrees:

(a) Illegitimate children took no interest before 1926; between 1926 and 1970 on the death of his or her mother, provided no legitimate issue survived her, an illegitimate child took such interest as if he or she had been born legitimate; after 1970, an illegitimate child has the same right of inheritance of his or her parent's estate as a legitimate child.

(b) Adopted children: from 1949 on the death of the adopter his or her estate devolves as if the adopted person had been born in wedlock and was not the child of any person other than his or her adopters. An adopted person is deemed to become the brother or sister of the whole blood of the other lawful or adopted children of the adopters; of the half blood, in other cases.

(c) Legitimated children take as if legitimate save as to real or personal property devolving with a dignity or title of honour.

3 The sum payable to the surviving spouse must be paid out of capital. Interest at the rate of 6 per cent a year being the current rate with effect from 1 October 1983 up to the date of payment should if possible be paid out of income. For deaths in earlier years the relevant lump sums were as follows:

Date of death	Issue surviving (£)	No issue surviving (£)
1.1.26 to 31.12.52	1,000	1,000*
1.1.53 to 31.12.66	5,000	20,000
1.1.67 to 30.6.72	8,750	30,000
1.7.72 to 14.3.77	15,000	40,000
15.3.77 to 30.4.81	25,000	55,000
1.5.81 to 31.5.87	40,000	85,000
1.6.87 to 30.11.93	75,000	125,000

* *Up to 1952 where no issue survived, in place of the larger capital sum the surviving spouse took a life interest in the whole estate, subject to which the residue was held on the statutory trusts for the other relatives in classes 6 to 11 in the table above. If no such relatives survived, the surviving spouse took the whole estate absolutely.*

4 If there is a minority or life interest arising under the distribution of the estate of the intestate there must be at least two (but not more than four) administrators.

5 The surviving spouse may elect under AEA 1925 s 47A to have his or her life interest redeemed for a capital sum.

6

(i) Age 21 if the death was before 1 January 1970.

(ii) In the event that a minor beneficiary under the distribution of aforesaid dies before attaining the age of 18 and without leaving issue capable of taking his share by substitution, the distribution of the estate is completed as if such deceased beneficiary had predeceased the intestate.

(iii) TA 1925 ss 31 and 32 will apply to any fund in which under the foregoing rules there subsist minority or life interests.

Scotland

2.33 The relevant statute is the Succession (Scotland) Act 1964 as amended, for deaths on or after 26 November 1993.

1 Spouse and issue survive
Spouse receives, as a prior right, the dwelling house owned by the predeceasing spouse if the surviving spouse was ordinarily resident there. Where house value exceeds £110,000 (net of any securities) the surviving spouse would instead receive that amount. Also the furniture and plenishings within the dwelling house up to a value of £20,000.

Note
In either case, if the property is jointly owned then relevant values are halved, eg a jointly owned house and contents worth £220,000 and £40,000 respectively would remain with a surviving spouse.

(1) Prior right: £30,000

(2) Legal rights: one third share of any remaining moveable estate

Issue receives residue remaining after satisfaction of surviving spouse's prior and legal rights

2 Spouse survives without issue
Spouse receives:

(1) Prior right: as above

(2) Prior right: £50,000

(3) Legal rights: one half share of any remaining moveable estate.

Remainder distributed to:

(1) Parents, and brothers/sisters or their issue; half to each class; or

(2) Brothers/sisters or their issue if no surviving parents; or

(3) Parents if no surviving brothers/sisters.

3 Spouse survives but no issue, parents, brothers or sisters or their issue
Whole estate to surviving spouse.

4 No spouse survives
Estate held for the following in the order given, with no class of beneficiaries participating unless all those in a prior class have predeceased.

(i) Issue of deceased

(ii) Parents, and brothers/sisters or their issue: half to each class

(iii) Brothers/sisters or their issue if no surviving parents; half blood postponed to full blood

(iv) Parents if no surviving brothers/sisters

(v) Uncles/aunts or their issue

(vi) Grandparents

(vii) Great uncles/aunts or their issue

(8) No limit of remoteness in succession although in practice if impossible to trace any relative of intestate then whole estate falls to Crown as *ultimus haeres* administered by Queen's and Lord Treasurer's Remembrancers.

Interests in land

Law of Property Act 1925 (LPA 1925)

2.34 LPA 1925, as amended, still forms the foundation for the purchase and sale of land in England and Wales. Only those sections which have a bearing on trusts have been summarised.

1 Legal estates and equitable interests
The only possible legal interests in land are freehold, 'an estate in fee simple absolute in possession' or leasehold, 'a term of years absolute'. The only interests or charges in or over land which may exit are an easement, a right or privilege in or over land indefinitely or for a fixed term, a rent charge, either perpetual or for a fixed term, a charge by way of legal mortgage, any other similar charge on land not created by an instrument, such as an equitable mortgage arising from the deposit of title deeds, rights of entry by a landlord or holder of a rent charge. All other interests are equitable interests. A legal estate cannot exist in an undivided share in land where there are joint tenants as opposed to tenants in common and cannot be held by an infant.

2 Conveyances overreaching certain equitable interests and powers
A conveyance to a purchaser of a legal estate in land overreaches any equitable interest or power if the conveyance is made under SLA 1925 or is made by trustees approved or appointed by the court or a trust corporation or the conveyance is made by a mortgagee or personal representative or the conveyance is made under an order of the court. Equitable interests which cannot be overreached are an equitable mortgage protected by a deposit of documents, benefit of any covenant or restriction of user, any equitable easement, liberty or privilege, the benefit of any contract and an equitable interest protected by registration under the Land Charges Act 1925, subject to exceptions.

3 Manner of giving effect to equitable interests and powers
Equitable interests and powers in or over land are enforceable against the owner of the legal estate either under this section or under SLA 1925 subject

to the rights of a legal mortgagee or powers of a personal representative. The holder of an equitable interest may be entitled to the legal estate and require the legal owner to convey the land to him, which can be enforced by the court and, in the case of refusal, a court may make a vesting order transferring or creating a legal estate in favour of the holder of the equitable interest. This does not affect a purchaser of a legal estate taking free from an equitable interest or power.

4 Creation and disposition of equitable interests
Interests in land validly created, which are not legal estates, are equitable interests and may be disposed of, including a contingent, executory or future equitable interest in land, a possibility coupled with an interest in land, or a right of entry.

20 Infants not to be appointed trustees
Infants cannot be appointed trustees of any settlement or trust and any such purported appointment is void.

24 Appointment of trustees of land
A person having power to appoint new trustees of land must appoint the same trustees as those of any trust of the proceeds of sale of the same land. The purchaser, however, is not concerned to see that this has been complied with.

27 Purchaser not to be concerned with the trusts of the proceeds
The purchaser of a legal estate from trustees of land is not concerned to see that the trusts are duly complied with. However, the sale proceeds can only be paid to at least two persons as trustees, or to a trust corporation as trustee. Although a sole personal representative can give a valid receipt for other capital money not related to the sale.

31 Trust of mortgaged property where right of redemption is barred
Where the mortgagor's right of redemption is lost through foreclosure or otherwise, the mortgagee applies the income from the property in the same manner as interest paid on the mortgage debt would have been applicable, and if the property is sold to apply the net proceeds of sale after payment of costs and expenses in the same manner as repayment of the mortgage debt would have been applied, in other words to repay the loan plus outstanding interest and account to the mortgagor for the balance.

33 Application of Part I to personal representatives
The provisions relating to trustees of land apply also to personal representatives holding land in trust but without prejudice to their rights and powers for purposes of administration.

34 Effect of future dispositions to tenants in common
Where land is conveyed to persons in undivided shares and those persons are of full age the conveyance shall operate as if the land had been expressly conveyed to the grantees or the first four grantees named in the conveyance as joint tenants in trust for all the persons interested in the land.

36 Joint tenancies
Where a legal estate in land is held in trust for persons as joint tenants it would be held in like manner as if the persons were tenants in common, but not so as to sever the joint tenancy in equity. No severance of a joint tenancy of a legal estate, so as to create a tenancy in common, is permissible although this does not affect the rights of a joint tenant to release his interest to the other joint tenants, or to sever a joint tenancy in an equitable interest.

52 Conveyances to be by deed
Conveyances of a legal estate in land must be made by deed.

53 Instruments required to be in writing
An equitable interest in land can only be created or disposed of by writing signed by the person creating or conveying it or his duly authorised agent. A declaration of trust relating to land must be evidenced in writing by the settlor or by his will, and a disposal of an equitable interest must be in writing signed by the disponor or his duly authorised agent. These requirements do not affect the creation or operation of resulting implied or constructive trusts.

136 Legal assignment of things in action
An absolute assignment by writing signed by the assignor of any debt or other legal thing (chose) in action of which express notice in writing has been given to the debtor, trustee or other person from whom the assignor would have been entitled to claim such debt or thing in action, is effectual in law to pass and transfer the legal right to such debt or thing in action or legal and other remedies.

137 Dealing with life interests, reversions and other equitable interests
In dealing with an equitable interest in settled land or a trust of land or the proceeds of sale of such land the persons to be served with notice shall be the trustees.

164 General restrictions on accumulation of income
The provisions in LPA 1925 have been amended and extended by PAA 1964 s 13 *qv.*

175 Contingent and future testamentary gifts to carry the intermediate income
The contingent or future specific devise or bequest of property, whether real or personal, and contingent residuary devise of freehold land or residuary devise of freehold land to trustees on trust for persons whose interests are contingent or executory shall, subject to the maximum accumulation period, carry the intermediate income of that property from the date of death of the testator, unless the income or any part of it is otherwise expressly disposed of.

198 Registration under the Land Charges Act 1925 to be notice
Registration of any instrument or matter on a register kept under LCA 1972 or any local land charges register is deemed to constitute actual notice of such instrument or matter.

Settled Land Act 1925 (SLA 1925)

2.35 SLA 1925 was mainly aimed at landed estates which tend to pass from generation to generation within a single family.

2.36 Under SLA 1925 a settlement was created by executing two deeds, namely a vesting deed and a trust instrument. The legal estate in the land is vested in the equitable life tenant who therefore becomes the statutory owner, and the sole trustee of the legal estate in trust for himself and other persons beneficially interested under the settlement. However, all capital monies arising from the estate are paid to a second set of trustees called the Settled Land Act Trustees who hold them on similar trusts for the statutory owner and other beneficiaries. The object of SLA 1925 was to enable the beneficial owner to have a free hand in the development and management of the property for the benefit of the beneficiaries and tenants of the estate, but with the protection of the *corpus* of the fund by the requirement that any capital monies be paid to the Settled Land Act trustees.

2.37 Under TLATA 1996 s 2 no further Settled Land Act settlements can be set up after 1 January 1997, although existing settlements may continue.

Powers of Attorney Act 1971 (PAA 1971)

2.38

1 Execution of powers of attorney
A power of attorney must be created by the donor executing a deed.

3 Proof of instruments creating powers of attorney
Photocopies duly certified by a solicitor, notary public or stockbroker and signed by the donor are valid.

4 Powers of attorney given as security
The power of attorney may be irrevocable and may be given to secure a proprietary interest of the donee of the power, or the performance of an obligation owed to the donee. A power of attorney may also be given to a person entitled to a proprietary interest. The company's articles commonly create the company as attorney for the shareholders to enforce pre-emption rights on sale.

5 Protection of donee and third persons where power of attorney is revoked
A donee of a power of attorney who acts after it has been revoked does not incur any liability if at the time he did not know that the power had been revoked, and any dealings with a third party who does not have knowledge of the revocation will be binding.

6 Additional protection for transferees under Stock Exchange transactions
It is conclusively presumed in favour of the transferee of quoted securities that the power had not been revoked if a statutory declaration to that effect is made by the donee on or within three months of the date of transfer.

7 Execution of instruments by donee of power of attorney
The donee of a power of attorney who is an individual may execute any instrument with his own signature and do other things in his own name and anything so done shall be as effective as if it had been done by the donor.

10 Effective general power of attorney in specified form
A general power of attorney in the form set out in Sch 1 or to the like effect, shall operate to confer authority on the donee on behalf of the donor to do anything that can lawfully be done by an attorney, which excludes functions which the donor does as trustee or personal representative or as life tenant or statutory owner under SLA 1925, subject to TDA 1999, *qv*.

Sch 1 Form of general power of attorney for purposes of s 10

The statutory form is:

By this general power of attorney made this ...... day of 200X

I...[the donor] of..[address] appoint ....[the attorney] of ....[address] to be my attorney in accordance with section 10 of the Powers of Attorney Act 1971.

Signed as a deed by the said ....[donor]

Signature of witness

Name of witness

Address

Enduring Powers of Attorney Act 1985 (EPAA 1985)

2.39 The problem with the power of attorney is that if the donor of the power becomes of unsound mind the power of attorney is automatically revoked. However, under EPAA 1985 an enduring power of attorney may continue.

1 Enduring power of attorney to survive mental incapacity of the donor
Where an individual creates a power of attorney which is an enduring power under the Act then it will not be revoked by the subsequent mental incapacity of the donor, however, the donee cannot act under the power once the donor has become mentally incapacitated until the power has been registered or as directed or authorised by the court. There is an exception for action taken to maintain the donor or prevent loss to his estate or to maintain himself or others to the extent that the donor might be expected to provide for their needs.

2 Characteristics of an enduring power
An enduring power has to be in the prescribed form and executed in the prescribed manner by the donor and attorney and incorporating at the time of execution by the donor the prescribed explanatory information. The form of the enduring power of attorney is set out by regulations. This section sets out some of the requirements for an enduring power and those instruments which cannot create an enduring power.

3 Scope of authority of attorney under enduring power
An enduring power may confer general authority to do on behalf of the donor anything which can lawfully be done by an attorney, except that the power to make gifts is limited. Such authority may, however, be limited to enable the attorney to act only in relation to part of the donor's property and to do specified things on the donor's behalf.

4 Duties of attorney in event of actual or impending incapacity of donor
This section sets out the actions which the attorney has to take if he has reason to believe that the donor is becoming mentally incapable, in particular to make an application to the court for the registration of the instrument creating the power.

5 Functions of the court prior to registration
The court may anticipate registration and exercise any power which would become exercisable on registration.

6 Functions of the court on application to registration
The procedure for registration is set out in this section. Where a receiver has been appointed under Part VII of MHA 1983 registration will be refused.

7 Effect and proof of registration etc
The effect of the registration is that the power of the attorney continues as previously.

8 Functions of court with respect to registered powers
The court may determine any question as to the meaning or effect of the instrument and give directions and otherwise oversee the operation of the power.

9 Protection of attorney and third persons where power invalid or revoked
An attorney acting under a power that has been revoked is not liable if he did not know of its revocation and any transactions with third parties, without notice of any defect, remain valid.

Supplementary
Sections 10–13 deal with the applications of the MHA 1983 provisions, the application to joint and several attorneys and the power of the Lord Chancellor to modify pre-registration requirements and interpretations and definitions.

Schedule 1 sets out the procedure for notification prior to registration, the duty to give notice to relatives and the donor, the contents of notices etc.

Schedule 2 sets out further protection of the attorney and third persons and Sch 3 deals with joint and joint and several attorneys.

Partnership Act 1890 (PA 1890)

2.40 A partnership, which is the relation which subsists between persons carrying on a business in common with a view of profit, can result in partners becoming trustees in certain cases.

13 Improper employment of trust property for partnership purposes
If a trustee who is also a partner employs trust property in the business, his fellow partners are not liable for the trust property to the beneficiaries unless they have notice of the breach of trust, although the beneficiaries can trace the assets diverted and recover them from the firm if still in its possession or under its control.

20 Partnership property
Partnership property must be held exclusively for the purposes of the partnership and in accordance with the partnership agreement. A legal estate or interest in land cannot be held by more than four persons and is therefore held by those partners who are legal owners in trust for the partners generally, according to their rights. Merely because land is owned by one or more of the partners it is not necessarily partnership property and may be dealt with for the benefit of the co-owners.

29 Accountability of partners for private profits
Partners must account to the firm for any benefit derived without the consent of the other partners for any transaction concerning the partnership or the use of the partnership name or business connection.

30 Duty of partner not to compete with firm
If a partner without the consent of the other partners carries on a competing business he must account for and pay over all the profits of that business.

Bankruptcy Act 1914 (BA 1914)

2.41 This act has been repealed and replaced by the Insolvency Act 1985 consolidated into the Insolvency Act 1986. Where a trustee has been made bankrupt as a result of a breach of trust he will not have any further liability when he obtains his discharge from the bankruptcy unless the breach of trust was fraudulent.

2.42 Section 42, which prevented debtors transferring assets to a trust to avoid creditors, has been repealed and replaced by IA 1986 ss 339–342 and ss 342–425 *qv*.

Insolvency Act 1986 (IA 1986)

2.43 IA 1986 provides a number of situations in which the transactions may be set aside by the court in the interests of creditors.

339 Transactions at an undervalue
Where an individual is adjudged bankrupt and has within the relevant time, as defined by section 341, entered into a transaction at an undervalue the trustee in bankruptcy may apply to the court for an order to restore the position to what it would have been if the individual had not entered into the transaction. A transaction at undervalue includes a transaction with a person in consideration of marriage, which in other circumstances would be valuable consideration. An undervalue is defined as a gift for no consideration or a transaction for inadequate consideration where the value in money or money's worth is significantly less than the value in money or money's worth provided by the transferor.

340 Preferences
Where a bankrupt has given a preference to any person, the trustee in bankruptcy may apply to the court for an order restoring the position to what it would have been had that preference not been given. A preference is widely defined as anything done in favour of the creditor of the bankrupt or a surety of guarantee of his debts or other liabilities which puts that person in a better position in the event of the debtor's bankruptcy than he would have been in had that action not been taken, and with the intention of so doing. There is a presumption that there is an intention of preferring a creditor or surety who is associated with the bankrupt. The fact that the action was taken in pursuance of a court order does not of itself prevent it constituting a preference.

341 Relevant time under sections 339–340
A transaction at an undervalue is made at a relevant time if it is made within five years prior to the day of the presentation of the bankruptcy petition on which the individual is adjudged bankrupt. A preference which is not a transaction at an undervalue is given at a relevant time if to an associate within two years prior to the day of presentation of the petition and in other cases within six months prior to that day. Where a transaction at undervalue is given more than two years before the day of presentation of the bankruptcy petition, or it is potentially a preference, it is not within a relevant time unless at the time of the transaction or preference the bankrupt was insolvent or became insolvent in consequence of the transaction or preference. There is a presumption of insolvency in relation to any transaction at an undervalue with an associate other than one whose only association is by reason of being an employee. A person is insolvent if he is unable to pay his debts as they fall due or the value of his assets is less than the amount of his liabilities taking into account contingent and prospective liabilities.

342 Orders under sections 339 and 340
A court order under these provisions may provide for any property transferred or acquired out of the proceeds of the sale of property so transferred to be vested in the trustee in bankruptcy. It may also release or discharge any

security given by the bankrupt or sums paid or to be repaid to his trustee in bankruptcy to reimpose the obligations of any surety or guarantor which were released or discharged by the transaction or preference, or the discharge of any obligation imposed as a result of his actions. The beneficiary of the transaction or preference may as a result of such order prove in the bankruptcy. A court order, however, cannot prejudice the interests of a purchaser in good faith and for value, nor will it require a beneficiary of a transaction or preference in good faith and for value, who was at the time a creditor of the individual, to repay unless he was party to the transaction or payment at a time when he was a creditor of the subsequent bankrupt. There is a presumption of lack of good faith where the recipient had notice of the fact that the individual entered into the transaction at an undervalue, or it amounted to a preference, and that the bankruptcy petition had been presented or the individual had been adjudged bankrupt or was an associate of, or connected with, the recipient of the transaction or preference.

These provisions replace those of BA 1914 s 42 and there is no requirement to prove any intention to defraud creditors.

423 Transactions defrauding creditors
Where a person enters into a transaction for the purpose of putting assets beyond the reach of a person who is making or may at some time make a claim against him, or of otherwise prejudicing the interests of such a person in relation to the claim which he is making or may make, and there is a transaction at undervalue, the court may make such order as it thinks fit for restoring the position to what it would have been had the transaction not been entered into and protecting the interests of the victims of the transactions. It is this provision which makes asset protection trusts difficult to sustain in the UK. A victim of a transaction is a person who is capable of being prejudiced by it.

424 Those who may apply for an order under section 423
An application for an order under section 423 will only be made where the debtor has been adjudged bankrupt or is a company being wound up or subject to administration by the Official Receiver, the trustee in bankruptcy or the liquidator or administrator of the company, but only with leave of the court by a victim of the transaction. Where there is a voluntary arrangement, the supervisor of that arrangement may apply for an order as may a victim of the transaction, whether or not bound by the arrangement. In any other case the application for an order may only be made by a victim of the transaction. Any application is treated as made on behalf of every victim of the transaction.

425 Provision which may be made by order under section 423
The remedial order the court may make is similar to that under section 432.

Charitable trusts

Charities Act 1601 (CA 1601)

2.44 CA 1993 defines a charity as an institution established for charitable purposes and charitable purposes means purposes which are exclusively charitable according to the law of England and Wales. For the statute law on what are charitable purposes it is necessary to go back to the preamble to the CA 1601 which provides as follows:

> 'Whereas Lands, Tenements, Rents, Annuities, Profits, Hereditaments, Goods, Chattels, Money and Stocks of Money, have been heretofore given, limited, appointed and assigned, as well by the Queen's most excellent Majesty, and her most noble Progenitors, as by sundry other well-disposed Persons; some for Relief of aged, impotent and poor People, some for Maintenance of sick and maimed Soldiers and Mariners, Schools of Learning, Free Schools, and Scholars in Universities, some for Repair of Bridges, Ports, Havens, Causways, Churches, Sea-banks and Highways, some for Education and Preferment of Orphans, some for or towards Relief, Stock, or Maintenance for House of Correction, some for Marriages of poor Maids, some for Supportation, Aid and Help of young Tradesmen, Handicraftsmen and Persons decayed, and others for Relief or Redemption of Prisoners or Captives, and for Aid or Ease of any poor Inhabitants concerning Payments of Fifteens, setting out of Solders and other Taxes; which Lands, Tenements, Rents, Annuities, Profits, Hereditaments, Goods, Chattels, Money and Stocks of Money, nevertheless have not been employed according to the charitable Intent of the Givers and Founders thereof, by reason of Frauds, Breaches of Trust and Negligence in those that should pay, deliver and employ the same …'

Charities Act 1993 (CA 1993)

2.45 The contents of Parts VI–IX are summarised below.

Part VI Charities accounts, reports, returns

41–49
These sections give the charity trustees the duty of maintaining adequate accounting records and preparing an annual statement of account, which may require to be audited and to produce an annual report subject to exemptions for very small charities. These provisions provide for public inspection of annual reports and annual returns to be made to the Charity Commissioners and provide offences for failure to comply.

Part VII Incorporation of charity trustees

50 Incorporation of trustees of a charity
Provision is made for the trustees of a charity to apply to the Charity Commissioners for a certificate of incorporation of the trustees as a body

corporate usually limited by guarantee. Once incorporated, the trustees act as any other board of directors and the charity may sue and be sued in its corporate name.

51 Estate to vest in body corporate
A certificate of incorporation vests all the assets of the charity in the corporation except for any property vested in the official custodian.

The Commissioners are also given power by section 61 to dissolve an incorporated charity which has ceased to function.

Part VIII Charitable companies

63 Winding-up
A charitable company may be wound up under IA 1986 in the same way as any other company or on petition of the Attorney-General or the Charity Commissioners.

64 Alteration of objects clause
The charitable objects clause must not be altered without the prior written consent of the Charity Commissioners. The Commissioners are also given power to investigate the accounts of a charity under section 69.

Part IX Miscellaneous

72 Persons disqualified from being trustees of a charity
A person is normally disqualified from being a trustee of a charity on being convicted of any offence involving dishonesty or deception, being adjudged bankrupt or making a composition with his creditors, or has been removed by the Charity Commissioners on the grounds of misconduct or mismanagement in the administration of the charity or is subject to a disqualification order under the Company Directors Disqualification Act 1986. A trustee *prima faecie* disqualified under these provisions may continue to act with the consent of the Charity Commissioners who have power to waive disqualification.

74 Power to transfer all property, modify objects etc
As many very small charities continue to exist, power is given to the trustees of small, unincorporated charities to modify their objects to transfer the assets to other registered charities, except where the charity holds land on trusts which stipulate that the land is to be used for the purposes of the charity.

75 Power to spend capital
A charity with permanent endowment can also supplement its gross income if this did not exceed £1,000 in the last financial year by dipping into capital so long as the charity is neither an exempt charity nor a charitable company. Before taking such a step the trustees must consider transferring the assets to other charities under section 74.

Exempt charities are those specified in CA 1993 Sch 2 such as certain universities, grant-maintained schools, trustees of major national museums etc.

Charitable Trusts (Validation) Act 1954 (CTVA 1954)

2.46 This Act enabled charities in existence before 16 December 1952 to achieve their charitable objects if these would not otherwise have been exclusively charitable.

Recreational Charities Act 1958 (RCA 1958)

2.47 This Act provides that the provision of facilities for recreation or other leisure-time occupation provided in the interests of social welfare for the public benefit may be regarded as charitable, provided that the facilities are primarily intended for the disabled or the disadvantaged or are to be made available to the members or female members of the public at large. In particular these provisions apply to the provision of facilities at village halls, community centres and women's institutes.

Chapter 3

Trust Formalities

Legal capacity

3.1 Under FLRA 1969 s 1(1) a person acquires legal capacity on reaching the age of 18, provided that he is not suffering from mental incapacity. He becomes *sui juris* and capable of creating a trust over any assets which he owns. Even where an asset is non-assignable so that the legal ownership cannot be transferred to trustees it may nonetheless be possible to create a trust of the beneficial ownership under a declaration by which the owner declares that he holds the asset in trust for the beneficiaries. A common example is a personal pension policy, retirement annuity policy or occupational pension scheme, the rights to which are non-assignable but which are commonly held in trust for the surviving spouse or children.

3.2 Where a receiver has been appointed under MHA 1983 ss 94 and 99 this would prevent the patient creating a trust (*Re Marshall* [1920] 1 Ch 284), but the court could create a trust over the patient's property under MHA 1983 s 96(1)(d) and, under ss 96(1)(e) and 97, it could create a will on behalf of the patient. A purported trust can be set aside if the settlor did not understand what he was doing (*Re Beaney* [1978] 1 FLR 770; *Simpson v Simpson* [1992] 1 FLR 601).

3.3 A minor can create a valid trust over assets which he holds legally or beneficially but he must be old enough to understand what he is doing, otherwise the trustees merely hold the assets on a resulting trust for the settlor, not under the terms of the purported trust. A trust created by a minor is, however, voidable at any time until he becomes 18 and for a short period thereafter, and if he does not repudiate the trust it becomes binding (*Edwards v Carter* [1893] AC 360).

3.4 A trust of personal property held outright can be created orally by a simple declaration that the owner is holding the assets in trust for a beneficiary (*Petty v Petty* (1853) 22 LJ Ch 1065). The obvious problem with an oral declaration of trust is evidencing the clear intention to create a trust, which is a prerequisite of a valid trust (*Re Kayford* [1975] 1 WLR 279), and a trust is normally created by a trust deed under which the settlor specifically transfers assets to trustees to hold in accordance with the trusts set out in the deed for the beneficiaries specified therein. A trust is usually created by way of a deed, as it is a gift with no consideration but, following LP(MP)A 1989 s 1, no longer has to be under seal. The normal wording is 'signed and delivered as a deed by the said (settlor) in the presence of (Witness, name, address and occupation)'. It is quite common to transfer only a nominal sum to the trustees in the first instance with the intention of adding further property to the trust in due course. In some cases, however, the trust will contain a schedule of assets transferred to the trustees. Although most trusts are created by way of a deed signed by the settlor some are evidenced by a declaration of trust signed by the trustees under which they acknowledge receipt of assets, normally as specified in a schedule, to hold on the trusts specified in the deed. A declaration of trust does not identify the settlor on the face of the document, although the trustees will need to know the source of the funds and the identity of the settlor in order to avoid breaching the money laundering regulations under PCA 2002 and MLR 2003.

3.5 It is not unusual for a settlor to decide to transfer assets into trusts for beneficiaries and to make a formal declaration to that effect, appoint trustees, and create a written trust instrument and then transfer the assets to the trustees. The question then arises as to whether the formal written trust is preceded by an oral trust of personalty which could be important for taxation purposes in determining the date at which the assets ceased to be beneficially owned by the settlor.

3.6 A testamentary trust can only be created by a valid will, which under WA 1837 s 9 is normally required to be in writing and duly attested.

Trusts of land

3.7 LPA 1925 s 53 provides as follows:

'Instruments required to be in writing

(1) Subject to the provisions hereinafter contained with respect to the creation of interests in land by parole—

(a) no interest in land can be created or disposed of except by writing signed by the person creating or conveying the same, or by his agent thereunto lawfully authorised in writing, or by will, or by operation of law;

(b) a declaration of trust respecting any land or any interest therein must be manifested and proved by some writing signed by some person who is able to declare such trust or by his will;

(c) a disposition of an equitable interest or trust subsisting at the time of the disposition, must be in writing signed by the person disposing of the same, or by his agent thereunto lawfully authorised in writing or by will.

(2) This section does not affect the creation or operation of resulting, implied or constructive trusts'.

3.8 Under LPA 1925 s 53(1)(a) an interest in land can only be transferred in writing and section 52 of that Act normally requires a transfer of legal estate in land to be by deed. Unregistered land is transferred by deed, registered land by the appropriate land transfer form under the Land Registration Rules 1925 r 98. The absence of the necessary document causes the transfer to be void, although if the transfer is to trustees the writing need not extend to the particulars of the trusts on which it is to be held (*Re Tyler's Fund Trusts* [1967] 1 WLR 1269).

3.9 LPA 1925 s 53(1)(b) requires a trust over land, which under LPA 1925 s 205 would include leasehold property as well as freehold, easements and other interests in land, to be evidenced in writing. For this purpose the trust itself does not have to be in writing and an oral trust is sufficient provided that there is the appropriate written evidence, eg as in *Childers v Childers* (1857) 1 De G & J 482 where the evidence was contained in a letter, and in *McBlain v Cross* (1871) 25 LT 804 in a telegram. The trust dates from the oral declaration, not from the date of the evidence (*Foster v Hale* (1798) 3 Ves 676). The absence of written evidence in this case, however, does not make the transfer void but merely unenforceable, which means it remains valid unless and until the absence of writing is specifically raised by one of the parties involved. It also means that the necessary written evidence can be provided at any time, it does not have to be contemporary but it must emanate from the settlor.

3.10 Section 53(1)(c) requires a transfer of an equitable interest to be in writing and the question arises as to whether this refers to an equitable interest in land or generally. It seems from *Grey v IRC* [1960] AC 1 that a verbal direction of an equitable interest in pure personalty is insufficient, as it was required to be in writing. This decision was followed in *Oughtred v IRC* [1960] AC 206.

3.11 Section 53(1)(c) only applies on the transfer of an existing equitable interest not on the creation of an equitable interest by a declaration of trust (*Stamp Duties Comr v Livingstone* [1965] AC 694). It is not always easy to see whether there is an assignment of an existing equitable interest required to be in writing under section 53(1)(c) or the creation of a new interest, eg a beneficiary creating a subtrust over his beneficial interest in favour of a third party, as in *Grainge v Wilberforce* (1889) 5 TLR 436.

3.12 Section 53(2) provides that the requirement for writing does not apply to the creation or operation of resulting, implied or constructive trusts, which would seem to apply to an oral assignment of an equitable interest under contract, which would result in a constructive trust in favour of the purchaser (*Lysaght v Edwards* (1876) 2 Ch D 499) and a disclaimer (*Re Paradise Motor Co* [1968] 1 WLR 1125).

3.13 The sort of problems that can arise where insufficient attention is given to the trust formalities is vividly illustrated in *Vandervell v IRC* (1966)

43 TC 519 and in *Re Vandervell's Trusts* (1970) 46 TC 341. Mr Vandervell wanted to endow a Chair in Pharmacology at the Royal College of Surgeons, and did so by transferring shares to the College, subject to the College granting an option to repurchase the shares for a nominal £5,000. Substantial dividends were paid on the shares, and the court decided that because the option had not been transferred to a specific trust it was held on a resulting trust for Mr Vandervell and he was therefore still liable to surtax on the dividends received by the Royal College of Surgeons. The Revenue had argued that, because the shares were actually in the legal name of the bank to whom they had been transferred as security, there had been a transfer of an equitable interest that was void under LPA 1925 s 53(1)(c). The House of Lords held that this was not so as Mr Vandervell actually controlled both the legal and beneficial interest in the shares and there was therefore no separate equitable interest, the bank being his mere nominee. There was no transfer of a separate equitable interest required to be in writing. Although the trustees of the Childrens' Trust exercised the option in 1961, on behalf of the Childrens' Trust, there was no express declaration of the trusts on which the shares were to be held and there was therefore still a resulting trust in favour of Mr Vandervell who was charged to surtax until January 1965 when there was a formal transfer of his interests to his Childrens' Trust. The absence of writing cannot be relied upon to support a fraud. In *Bannister v Bannister* [1948] 2 All ER 133 two cottages were sold on the basis that the vendor could continue to occupy one of them rent free for as long as she wished. As the conveyance did not refer to this right of occupation the owner sought to have her evicted, but failed, the court holding that his conduct was fraudulent and upheld the vendor's claim that the plaintiff held the cottage in which she was living on trust for her for her lifetime.

Incomplete trusts

3.14 Where a trust has been created, either by a valid declaration of trust by the settlor or a transfer to trustees, it becomes binding on all the parties. The settlor therefore cannot change his mind and request the return of the trust property (*Re Bowden* [1936] Ch 71) and a beneficiary can take the necessary steps to enforce the trust *Fletcher v Fletcher* (1844) 4 Hare 67).

3.15 If, however, a trust is incompletely constituted, the mere fact that the settlor had intended to benefit the beneficiary is not enough unless he has given valuable consideration, as equity will not assist a volunteer, i e someone who has not given consideration for the benefit that was to have been conferred upon him. Money or money's worth amounts to valuable consideration. In the case of a marriage settlement there is valuable consideration if it is made before, and in consideration of, the marriage or in pursuance of an ante-nuptial agreement conditional on the marriage taking place, with a view to encouraging or facilitating the marriage. This then becomes valuable consideration (*Re Densham* [1975] 1 WLR 1519). The marriage consideration includes the children of the marriage and their issue (*Pullan v Koe* [1913] 1 Ch 9), and the children of former marriages of either party living with the children of the marriage (*A-G v Jacobs-Smith* [1895] 2 QB 341). A contractual agreement to assign subsequently acquired property may be enforced (*Collyer v Isaacs* [1881] 19 Ch D 342).

3.16 As the majority of trusts involve gratuitous acts by the settlor in favour of the beneficiary, it is important that all necessary actions are taken to transfer the ownership of the trust assets to the trustees, as the beneficiaries, being mere volunteers, cannot take action to remedy any defects (*Milroy v Lord* (1862) 4 De GF & J 264). What constitutes a proper transfer of the property depends on its nature. Land, or any interest therein, must be transferred either by deed (in the case of unregistered land under LPA 1925 s 52(1)), or by the appropriate land transfer form, and duly registered in the name of the trustees (in the case of registered land, under the Land Registration Rules 1925 r 98). Leaseholds must also be transferred by deed, except in the case of leases for less than three years within LPA 1925 s 54(2). Chattels may be transferred by delivery, being an unequivocal transfer to the trustees to hold on the specified trust, (*Re Cole* [1964] Ch 175). A physical transfer is not necessary where the asset is specified in the trust deed (*Jaffa v Taylor Gallery Ltd* (1990) Times, 21 March). Stocks and shares must be transferred by way of a properly executed share transfer form with the shares registered in the trustee's name, under CA 1985 s 183, except in the case of bearer shares transferred by delivery.

3.17 Choses in action may be assigned in writing under LPA 1925 s 36, which requires express notice in writing to be given to the debtor, trustee or other person from whom the assignor would have been entitled to claim. Such an assignment is made subject to equities having priority over the right of the assignee, which might enable there to be an effective assignment in equity in appropriate cases. Where the settlor merely declares himself to be holding the assets in trust for the beneficiaries, the intention to create an irrevocable trust must be unequivocally shown (*Jones v Lock* (1865) 1 Ch App 25; *Paul v Constance* [1977] 1 WLR 527).

3.18 An absolute assignment of a chose in action must relate to the entire interest of the settlor (*Harding v Harding* (1886) 17 QBD 442). If the provisions of LPA 1925 s 136 are not followed, it may or may not be an effective transfer in equity, but without consideration the courts cannot perfect an imperfect gift (*Olsson v Dyson* (1969) 120 CLR 365). If, however, the assignment is of part of the debt or other chose in action and therefore not within LPA 1925 s 136, it may still be effective in equity following *Re McArdle* [1951] Ch 669. Absence of notice to the assignor, as required by LPA 1925 s 136, is not fatal in equity as it is not part of the transfer and under the rule in *Re Rose*, below, it would not prevent the assignment being enforced in equity (*Millroy v Lord* (1862) 4 De GF & J 264). In *Re Ralli's Will Trust* [1964] Ch 288 a covenant to transfer after acquired property into trust was not assigned in accordance with the covenant but came into the possession of the trustee in his capacity as executor, and it was held that this completed the gift into settlement and was not held as part of the covenant or estate.

3.19 Under the rule in *Re Rose* [1952] Ch 499 the transfer becomes completed in equity once the transferor has done everything required by him to complete the transfer of title to the trustees. If therefore a share transfer is submitted to a company for registration, the transfer will be effective in equity from the date of submission even though the company may take several weeks or months to register the transfer, thereby passing legal title to the trustees. *Re Rose* was followed in *Mascall v Mascall* [1984] LS Gaz R 2218 although these decisions are difficult to reconcile with the earlier case of *Re Fry* [1946] Ch 312. Interestingly, it appears that a gift can be perfected on death by appointing the intended donee as executor (*Strong v Bird* (1874) LR 18 Eq 315; *Re Stewart* [1908] 2 Ch 251).

3.20 A covenant under seal to settle property into trust is enforceable (*Hall v Palmer* (1844) 3 Hare 532) but specific performance, which is an equitable remedy, would not be awarded (*Jeffreys v Jeffreys* (1841) Cr & Ph 138). The remedy for an actual breach of covenant in such circumstances is therefore damages (*Re Parkin* [1892] 3 Ch 510). It would appear, however, that following *Re Pryce* [1917] 1 Ch 234 a covenant to settle after acquired property or similar assets would not give rise to a claim for damages (*Re Kay's Settlement* [1939] Ch 329), although it is by no means certain that had the trustees merely claimed damages for breach of covenant they would have succeeded (*Cannon v Hartley* [1949] Ch 213). A trust of a promise may be enforceable if there is an intention to create such a trust (*Fletcher v Fletcher* (1844) 4 Hare 67). A voluntary covenant to assign future property was not enforceable (*Re Ellenborough* [1903] 1 Ch 697). This contrasts with the case where there is a covenant to transfer future property for value, which is enforceable (*Tailby v Official Receiver* (1888) 13 App Cas 523).

Donatio mortis causa

3.21 A gift in contemplation of death is given on terms that the donee only becomes absolutely entitled to the property on the donor's death on which it is conditional. If the donor does not die but survives, he may recover the property given away. The personal representatives may be required to perfect a *donatio mortis causa* following the donor's death (*Birch v Treasury Solicitor* [1951] Ch 298). A *donatio mortis causa* must be intended to be conditional on death (*Gardner v Parker* (1818) 3 Madd 184). It must be made in contemplation of death (*Agnew v Belfast Banking Co* [1896] 2 IR 204). The property must actually be passed to the donee and accepted by him (*Bunn v Markham* (1816) 7 Taunt 224). The property must be capable of passing by way of *donatio mortis causa*, ie normally personalty. Land is now considered to be capable of being the subject of a *donatio mortis causa* (*Sen v Headley* [1991] Ch 425). A cheque that has not been cashed cannot be *donatio mortis causa*, as the cheque is automatically revoked on the drawer's death (*Re Beaumont* [1902] 1 Ch 889). Stocks and shares may constitute a valid *donatio mortis causa* (*Staniland v Willott* (1852) 3 Mac & G 664) although there are contrary decisions. For the transfer of a chose in action the deposit of documents may be sufficient (*Birch v Treasury Solicitor* [1951] Ch 298). A gift of car keys was sufficient to transfer title in *Woodard v Woodard* [1991] Fam Law 470.

Secret trusts

3.22 A secret trust arises when a person leaves property in a will on the strength of an undertaking by the donee that he will hold the property in trust for another beneficiary (*McCormick v Grogan* (1869) LR 4 HL 82). Secret trusts can also arise on intestacy (*Sellack v Harris* (1708) 5 Vin Arb 512 PL 31). On the face of it a fully secret trust appears to be an absolute gift to the donee, but may be enforced by the beneficiary if its existence can be proven, which is not always easy. By definition a secret trust depends on evidence contrary to that required for a normal testamentary gift and is therefore contrary to WA 1837 (*Re Fleetwood* (1880) 15 Ch D 594).

3.23 A half secret trust is where the will refers to the gift being in trust but does not identify the beneficiary or the terms of the trust (*Blackwell v Blackwell* [1929] AC 318).

3.24 The normal rules of probate govern the vesting of the assets to the secret trustee, who is then governed by trust law in the application of the legacy held in trust for the beneficiaries. The existence of the secret trust must be communicated to the legatee who must accept that he will hold the property on trust for a third party, and he will be deemed to agree unless he positively refuses (*Paine v Hall* (1812) 18 Ves 475). If the existence of the secret trust has not been communicated to the legatee who is to hold the legacy on trust prior to the death of the donor, the trustee takes the legacy beneficially (*Wallgrave v Tebbs* (1855) 2 K & J 313).

3.25 In the case of a half secret trust, the legatee is identified as taking the property as trustee by the will. The legatee must have agreed to hold the legacy on trust before the will is made or at the time of it being made, on the authority of *Re Keen* [1937] Ch 236, although this does not make any sense in the light of the situation with the fully secret trust where it is held that the legatee only has to agree prior to the testator's death. The onus on proving the existence of a secret trust rests on the beneficiary (*Re Snowden* [1979] Ch 528).

Precatory trusts

3.26 A precatory trust is where assets are left to a beneficiary in such circumstances that it is clear from the will, read as a whole, that a trust was intended. A mere desire, wish, recommendation, hope or expression of confidence that a donee will use the gift in a certain way does not imply a trust unless, on construing the will as a whole, the court comes to the conclusion that a trust was intended (*Re Williams* [1933] Ch 244; *Re Green* [1935] WN 151). The importance of looking at the precatory words in context was emphasised in *Comiskey v Bowring-Hanbury* [1905] AC 84. It is common to leave certain assets to the executors to hold in trust for beneficiaries in accordance with a letter of wishes left by the testator, which is treated as giving rise to an enforceable trust under which the executors hold as the trustees to distribute the said assets to the named beneficiaries in accordance with the letter of wishes. This is convenient, particularly in larger estates.

Co-ownership

3.27 Land, and indeed other assets, may be held by a number of owners on terms whereby each co-owner owns a specified proportion of the total, ie the property is held jointly as tenants in common. Each such co-owner has an interest in the property, which is part of his estate and may be sold or transferred as if it were a separate asset. Alternatively the property may be held as co-owners on a joint tenancy, which means that the co-owners do not have an asset which can be separately disposed of, and which on the death of one of the joint tenants passes to the other or others by survivorship, *jus accrescendi*, and does not form part of the estate dealt with by will or under the rules of intestacy. A joint tenancy held by the joint tenants beneficially may be severed very simply by serving a notice on the other joint tenants under LPA 1925 s 36(2).

3.28 Prior to 1 January 1997 real property held jointly, whether as tenants in common or as joint tenants, was held on a statutory trust for sale, but under TLATA 1996 s 5 and Sch 2 such holdings are now held as trusts of land with a power to sell and a power to retain. Only if there is an express trust to that effect may land be held on trusts for sale, with a statutory power to postpone the sale under TLATA 1996 s 4. As there is no duty to sell without an express trust to that effect, the possibility of deadlock, with one party wishing to sell and the other wishing to retain the property, is substantial; there may, therefore, still be advantages in having an express trust for sale for jointly owned property.

3.29 LPA 1925 s 34 provides that where land is expressed to be conveyed to any persons in undivided shares, then it is deemed to be held as joint tenants for the grantees, or the first four named in the conveyance if there are more than four grantees. Where the co-owners are not holding beneficially because they are holding in trust, it is not possible to sever the joint tenancy but one of the co-owners can release his interest to the other joint tenants. [LPA 1925 s 36(2)].

3.30 Where property is bought, and the purchase proceeds are provided by two or more parties, even though the property is acquired in the name of only one of them, they are deemed to be equitable tenants in common in proportion to the amount paid by each of them (*Bull v Bull* [1955] 1 QB 234: *Williams & Glyns Bank v Boland* [1981] AC 487). Contributions to income rather than capital do not give the payer any interest in the property (*Savage v Dunningham* [1974] Ch 181).

3.31 A claim to be equitable tenants in common fails where the property is actually conveyed into the names of the owners as joint tenants, in which each joint holder was entitled to an equal share in the proceeds of the sale of the property, irrespective of their initial contributions (*Goodman v Gallant* [1986] Fam 106).

Resulting trusts

3.32 A resulting trust arises where the settlor has made a transfer of property, but does not divest himself of his entire interest in that property. Resulting trusts were considered in *Westdeutsche Landesbank Girozentrale v Islington London Borough Council* [1996] 2 All ER 961. Brown-Wilkinson LJ identified two sets of circumstances where a resulting trust arises:

(i) Where A makes a voluntary transfer to B, or pays (wholly or in part) for the purchase of property which is vested either in B alone or in the joint names of A and B. There is a presumption that A did not intend to make a gift to B, and the money or property is held on trust for A (if he is the sole provider of the money) or in the case of a joint purchase by A and B in shares proportionate to their contributions.

(ii) Where A transfers property to B on express trusts, but the trusts declared do not exhaust the whole beneficial interest (*Re Vandervell's Trusts (No 2)* [1974] Ch 269). If, however, the settlor had expressly or by necessary implication abandoned any interest in the trust property there may be no resulting trust, the undisposed equitable interest vesting in the Crown as *bona vacantia* (*Re West Sussex Constabulary's, Widows, Children and Benevolent (1930) Fund Trusts* [1971] Ch 1).

3.33 In cases where there is an apparent resulting trust this is only a presumption which can be rebutted if, for example, there is evidence to show that a gift was intended. The mere purchase in the name of another, in the absence of any intention to the contrary, is sufficient to give rise to a resulting trust in favour of the provider of the purchase consideration (*Dyer v Dyer* (1788) 2 Cox Eq Cas 92). It also applies where the property is purchased in joint names as in *Bull v Bull* [1955] 1 QB 234 and in *Fowkes v Pascoe* (1875) 10 Ch App 343). Stock purchased in the joint names of a woman and the son of her widowed daughter-in-law was held, in the circumstances, to have been intended as a gift of the property held as joint tenants, not held on a resulting trust. Where a husband and wife buy a property on mortgage, which is paid off by their joint efforts, then the property, if held in the sole name of the husband, would be held partly on a resulting trust for the wife *Cowcher v Cowcher* [1972] 1 WLR 425). The transfer of property into the name of another implies a resulting trust for the transferor in the absence of evidence of there being a gift to the transferee (*Re Vinogradoff* [1935] WN 68). However, in the case of land there is no presumption of a resulting trust where property is conveyed by one party into the name of another, in view of LPA 1925 s 60(3). This again is a rebuttable presumption, and in *Hodgson v Marx* [1971] Ch 892 a resulting trust was held to exist.

3.34 A failure to dispose of the entire beneficial interest gave rise to a resulting trust in *Re Abbott Trusts Fund* [1900] 2 Ch 326. Failure of an express trust because, for example, of a beneficiary failing to survive to obtain a vested interest, can give rise to a resulting trust in favour of the settlor. Similar results follow where surplus funds remain after the objects of the trust have been covered (*Re Gillingham Bus Disaster Fund* [1958] Ch 300). In cases where a surplus exists but there is no resulting trust, the surplus becomes *bona vacantia* and belongs to the Crown (*Cunnack v Edwards* [1896] 2 Ch 679). If a loan is made for a specific purpose which is frustrated there is a resulting trust in favour of the lender (*Barclays Bank v Quistclose Investments* [1970] AC 567).

Advancement

3.35 There may, however, be a presumption of advancement, i e that there is an outright gift in favour of the transferee. This is likely to apply where a husband conveys property to a wife (*Thornley v Thornley* [1893] 2 Ch 229; *Dunbar v Dunbar* [1909] 2 Ch 639) but not vice versa (*Mercier v Mercier* [1903] 2 Ch 98), although such presumption is very easily rebutted in these egalitarian days (*Pettitt v Pettitt* [1970] AC 777). A transfer of property from a father to a child carries with it a presumption of gift (*Shephard v Cartwright* [1955] AC 431; *Re Roberts* [1946] Ch 1), but not from mother to child (*Bennet v Bennet* (1879) 10 Ch D 474). It does not normally apply to more remote relatives unless the donee is standing *in loco parentis*, as in *Ebrand v Dancer* [1680] 2 Cas in Ch 26, which was a transfer to a grandchild where the child's father was dead. The doctrine of advancement is now regarded as a doctrine of last resort, following *Magarth v Wallis* (1995) Times, 13 April. An illegal purpose cannot be used to rebut a presumption of advancement (*Re Emery's Investment Trusts* [1959] Ch 410; *Gascoigne v Gascoigne* [1918] 1 KB 223).

Constructive trusts

3.36 It is arguable that a fully secret trust is a constructive trust; indeed in *Ottaway v Norman* [1972] Ch 698 an oral, fully secret, trust of land was enforced in spite of the fact that LPA 1925 s 53(1)(b) requires express trusts to be in writing, which does not apply under LPA 1925 s 53(2) to resulting, implied or constructive trusts. Most constructive trusts, however, arise by operation of law, not as a result of any intention of the settlor as in an express trust. In normal circumstances such trusts arise because of some act on the part of a person as a result of which he acquires property which in all conscience was due to somebody else. In such circumstances there may well be a constructive trust in favour of the dispossessed.

3.37 One of the bases of a constructive trust is where a statute is used to perpetrate a fraud in the equitable rather than the criminal sense. For example, a purchaser of land subject to a mortgage (as trustee for the mortgagor) who subsequently treated the land as his own, was bound by the trust, notwithstanding the absence of the appropriate writing required by law (*Rochefoucauld v Boustead* [1897] 1 Ch 196). However, in *Midland Bank Trust Co Ltd v Green* [1981] AC 153 there was no constructive trust where a husband sold a farm to his wife to defeat their son's option, which had not been properly registered under LCA 1925, as the purchaser had not made any representation to the son.

3.38 The existence of a constructive trust enables the beneficiary to recover the property if still held by the trustee (*Boardman v Phipps* [1967] 2 AC 46). This would not be possible where their asset had been sold to a bona fide purchaser for value without notice (*Bassett v Nosworthy* (1673) Cas temp Finch 102) but it would allow the proceeds to be traced (*Re Halletts Estate* (1880) 13 Ch D 696). If tracing is unsuccessful, a personal action may be brought against the constructive trustee (*Re Montagu* [1987] Ch 264).

3.39 Where a person acts in breach of a fiduciary relationship, such as a trustee in making a profit which should have gone to the trust, he would be accountable under a constructive trust (*Ex p Lacey* (1802) 6 Ves 625). This would also apply where there was a solicitor client relationship (*Finers v Miro* [1991] 1 WLR 35), a director in relation to a company (*Regal (Hastings) Ltd v Gulliver* [1942] 1 All ER 378), principal and agent, or partnership (*Clegg v Edmondson* (1857) 8 De GM & G 787). Employees owe a fiduciary duty to their employers (*Canadian Aero Services v O'Malley* (1973) 40 DLR (3d) 371). Agents, however, are only constructive trustees if they are merely negligent (*Williams-Ashman v Price* [1942] Ch 219). An innocent donee of trust property is not a constructive trustee, but is subject to the true beneficiaries' rights of tracing (*Re Diplock* [1948] Ch 465). A third party who knowingly receives trust property may be responsible for its proper application, as a constructive trustee (*Baden Delvaux v Société Générale* [1993] 1 WLR 509n). A common form of constructive trust arises on unauthorised remuneration of trustees (*Robinson v Pett* (1734) 3 P Wms 249) or a secret commission (*Williams v Barton* [1927] 2 Ch 9). A bona fide purchaser for value without notice of the beneficiaries' interest would acquire a proper title to the assets (*Bassett v Nosworthy* (1673) Cas temp Finch 102) but not if he had actual or constructive notice (*Nelson v Larholt* [1948] 1 KB 339).

3.40 The proceeds of crime, direct or indirect, may be held on constructive trust, e g property obtained by theft (*Westdeutsche Landesbank Girozentrale v Islington London Borough Council* [1996] 2 All ER 961).

3.41 Where parties, usually a husband and wife, enter into reciprocal wills on the understanding that neither will revoke the will without the other's consent, this would not give rise to a constructive trust, although there could be a breach of contract if one of them revokes while both are alive (*Stone v Hoskins* [1905] P 194), but if one party has died the other may not subsequently revoke his will and a constructive trust arises for the benefit of those entitled under the mutual wills (*Re Cleever* [1981] 1 WLR 939).

3.42 A constructive trust can arise on the sale of land from the date contracts are exchanged until completion, and if, contrary to the contracts, the vendor sells the land to a third party, the displaced purchaser may claim the proceeds as held on constructive trust for him and retain any profit over and above the original contract price (*Lake v Bayliss* [1974] 1 WLR 1073). The doctrine of proprietary estoppel can apply where the owner of land can be held to be subject to a constructive trust in favour of a third party, who has acted to his detriment in the belief that he would have an interest in the property, eg where a person works without wages for a landowner on the understanding that he will inherit the estate (*Re Basham* [1987] 1 All ER 405). In the absence of evidence of some agreement to acquire a proprietary right, however, no constructive trust arises (*Lloyds Bank Plc v Rosset* [1991] 1 AC 107). Where there is a constructive trust, the basis on which the parties share in the property is by no means clear (*Drake v Whipp* [1996] 1 FLR 826).

Perpetuities

3.43 In England the common law developed to prevent property being tied up for many generations to come by introducing a rule against perpetuities, ie to prevent property being held in trust forever. Under common law, it was originally the situation that the trust could not continue for more than the life of someone alive at the time of the disposition (*Duke of Norfolk's case* (1681–5) 22 ER 931 and other citations). This was in due course amended to allow the life in being to reach majority, and became 21 years after the death of someone alive at the time of the creation of the trust. Obviously one practical problem was to determine on which life the rules should be based and it became common practice to refer to the last to die of the descendants of George V alive at the time of the disposition, on the assumption that this would be relatively easily ascertained in practice, it presumably being assumed that the assassination of the entire Royal family, as happened in Russia in 1917, was unthinkable in England and Wales.

3.44 The rule against perpetuities is generally not considered unreasonable, although not all trust jurisdictions have such a rule. The common law rules often gave rise to problems in practice, particularly as they assumed that anyone alive was capable of procreating, and class gifts, say, to children, could fail on the theoretical possibility, however practically unlikely, that another member of the class could be born. The rules therefore were substantially amended by PAA 1964 which came into force on 16 July 1964 and applied to every trust or similar instrument taking effect on or after that date.

3.45 PAA 1964 s 1 allowed the trust instrument to specify the number of years, not exceeding 80, for the duration of the trust, except in the case of an option relating to land, which is limited to 21 years by PAA 1964 s 9. It also provides presumptions as to future parenthood, ie that a male can have a child at the age of 14 or over, a female at the age of 12 or over but not over the age of 55 years, subject to evidence to the contrary. If, in spite of this, the child is born outside these age ranges the High Court may make such order as it thinks fit for justice to be done.

3.46 Instead of a gift being void for remoteness under the rule against perpetuities, as applied to common law, PAA 1984 s 3 adopts a 'wait and see' approach, and a gift is therefore assumed to be valid until it becomes established that the vesting would not occur, or a general power of appointment would not be exercisable within the perpetuity period. Where a number of years up to 80 is not used in the trust deed, or it is not valid under common law, e g by adopting the royal lives in being plus 21 years approach, reference may be had to the life of the donor if living, the donees, the parents or grandparents of donees or anyone having a prior interest, such as a life tenant. [PAA 1964 s 3(5)]. In the absence of any such a person the perpetuity period is 21 years. [PAA 1964 s 3(4)(b)].

3.47 Where a disposition is limited by reference to a person obtaining an age exceeding 21 years, which would make it void for remoteness, the age is reduced to such lesser age in excess of 21 which would cause a disposition to be valid. [PAA 1964 s 4]. Similarly a disposition relating to the death of a surviving spouse is limited to a period which would come to an end immediately before becoming void for remoteness. [PAA 1964 s 5]. An interest expectant on an interest which has become void is not itself void automatically [PAA 1964 s 6] and a power of appointment is treated as a special power unless it is a general power given to one person. [PAA 1964 s 7]. The power of trustees to act in spite of the rule against perpetuities is enshrined in PAA 1964 s 8. The rule does not apply to rent charges and does not give rise to a contractual right to restitution for its lack of effect, if void. [PAA 1964 ss 11 and 10].

3.48 The Law Commission has proposed a reform of the rule against perpetuities by introducing a fixed period of 125 years during which equitable interest must vest which will apply not only to instruments made after the introduction of the change of law but to appointments made under existing powers of appointment. The accumulation period is likely to be the same as the perpetuity period, i e 125 years instead of 21 years. It is understood that these changes will be introduced when parliamentary time permits (Law Commission Report on the Rules against Perpetuities and Excessive Accumulations No 251 (1998)).

Accumulations

3.49 Accumulation is reinvesting the income within the trust rather than distributing it to beneficiaries. If the income is to be accumulated longer than the perpetuity period it is *void ab initio*, but otherwise the periods for which accumulations can validly be made are prescribed by LPA 1925 s 164 as:

(a) the life of the settlor;

(b) 21 years from the death of the settlor;

(c) the minority or respective minorities of the beneficiaries living or *en ventre sa mere* at the death of the settlor;

(d) the minorities or respective minorities of the persons directing the accumulation;

(e) 21 years from the making of the disposition, or the minority of any person in being at that date (added by PAA 1964 s 13).

The trust instrument can choose the accumulation period which is normally limited to 21 years under PAA 1964 s 13(1)(a).

3.50 As with the perpetuity period, the accumulations period is not the same in all jurisdictions which recognise trusts. Jersey, for example, has both a perpetuity and accumulation period of 100 years from the date of the trust, whereas other jurisdictions, such as Panama, have no perpetuity or accumulation periods at all. If the assets were situated outside the UK, such as shares in foreign companies, the foreign perpetuity and accumulation periods would apply, even if the companies own assets in the UK which could be used by a UK resident settlor, as there is no requirement for him to settle a trust under English law.

3.51 Historically, the perpetuity and accumulation periods of a life in being plus 21 years and 21 years equated to the age of majority. Although this was reduced to 18 by FLRA 1969 s 1, there has been no change in the perpetuity or accumulation period.

Vesting

3.52 Property is vested in someone if they have an absolute entitlement to it, now or at some specific time in the future.

Contingent interests

3.53 A contingent interest is one which may occur but has not yet occurred and is not absolutely certain to occur, as opposed to a future vested interest, which is certain to occur. Death is not a contingency because it is bound to occur, so that a settlement on A for life and then to B for life with remainder to C is a vested interest of A, who is currently in possession, and C who has a vested interest in the remainder, but B has a contingent interest which will only become a vested interest if he outlives A. A vested interest can, at least in theory, be sold, even if it is a future interest and not in possession, but a contingent interest may not happen at all and therefore is normally unmarketable.

3.54 A vested interest merely requires a beneficiary to be in existence and identifiable as such, and the extent of his interest must be ascertainable, and nothing further needs to happen before he becomes entitled to that interest, whether in possession or in the future. If, however, an interest is contingent on marriage, which may never happen, it is not vested until the event occurs.

3.55 A gift to a class, such as to children or to grandchildren, is contingent until no future members of the class could arise, taking into account the statutory assumptions on parenthood in PAA 1964 s 2. Normally an interest becomes vested on reaching a specified age, such as 18 or 25, although it is not uncommon to have a vested interest in the income of the trust and leave the appointment of capital to the discretion of the trustees, which may, in turn, be subject to a minimum age.

3.56 A contingency is anything which is not absolutely bound to occur such as surviving to the vesting age. What the rule against perpetuities requires is that the contingency in question could not possibly occur after the end of the perpetuity period. There can obviously be no requirement that the contingency actually occurs or it would not be contingent. If the beneficiary has a contingent interest and the contingency does not occur the interest merely fails. The interest may be conditional, e g in *Re Tuck's Settled Trust* [1978] Ch 49 the Court of Appeal upheld a condition that the beneficiary's interest would be forfeited on a marriage to a person other than an approved wife of Jewish blood, as this could be precisely determined. This contrasts with *Clayton v Ramsden* [1943] AC 320 where forfeiture on marriage to a person not of Jewish parentage and of the Jewish faith was void for uncertainty. In *Blathwayt v Lord Cawley* [1976] AC 397 the Court upheld a forfeiture clause which applied if a beneficiary became a Roman Catholic, in the sense that it was not held to be void on grounds of public policy, but it was not actually applicable on the proper construction of the clause. A condition that the beneficiary continues to use the names and arms of a particular family was upheld in *Re Neeld* [1962] Ch 643.

3.57 A conditional interest is usually regarded as a contingency which is under the control of the beneficiary, e g on condition that he marries. Other conditions not contrary to public policy are also likely to be enforced by the courts.

Variation of trusts

3.58 The court has an inherent jurisdiction to vary a trust, which is likely to be used to give the trustees greater administrative or management powers, if required, for the proper running of the trust (*Re New, Re Leavers* [1901] 2 Ch 534). It will not, however, rearrange beneficial interests (*Chapman v Chapman* [1954] AC 429) except to the extent of allowing the trustees to use income required to be accumulated for the maintenance of the settlor's minor children. There is statutory power given to the court in TA 1925 s 57 to widen the powers of investment, which was used in *Trustees of the British Museum v A-G* [1984] 1 All ER 337. The Court approved an extension of trustee's powers under TA 1925 s 57 in *Anker-Petersen v Anker-Petersen* (1991)

16 LS Gaz R32. The statutory power of advancement can be used to resettle on new trusts for the beneficiaries (*Pilkington v IRC* (1962) 40 TC 416).

3.59 Where all the beneficiaries are *sui juris*, and are in agreement, they can bring the trust to an end under the rule in *Saunders v Vautier* (1841) Cr & Ph 240. All the beneficiaries have to agree, whether their interests are vested or contingent, but if any of the beneficiaries are minors or mentally incapacitated it is not possible to vary the trust. Prior to TLATA 1996 s 19 beneficiaries could not, even if all were *sui juris* and in agreement, force the resignation of a trustee and the appointment of one of their choice without bringing the trust to an end under the rule in *Saunders v Vautier (Re Brockbank* [1948] Ch 206).

3.60 The court is empowered to make a vesting order for the maintenance, education or benefit of an infant beneficially entitled to any trust property. [TA 1925 s 53]. The court also has a power in the case of a strict settlement under SLA 1925 s 64 to authorise the tenant for life to effect any transaction which, in the opinion of the court would be for the benefit of the settled land or for the persons interested under the settlement.

3.61 The court has power under VTA 1958 s 1 to give consent to a trust variation on behalf of an underage beneficiary and possible future beneficiaries, but it does not have a general discretionary power to vary trusts (*Re Hoult's Settlement* [1969] 1 Ch 100; *Goulding v James* [1997] 2 All ER 239).

3.62 The court also has jurisdiction under MHA 1983 and MCA 1973 to vary trusts. The court would normally be unwilling to approve the variation in a trust to the financial detriment of a person not *sui juris* (*Re Tinker's Settlement* [1960] 3 All ER 85n) except in exceptional circumstances where a person was wealthy but mentally ill and would be likely to have approved the variation had she been *sui juris* (*Re CL* [1969] 1 Ch 587) or in the interests of family harmony (*Re Remnant's Settlement Trusts* [1970] 2 All ER 554).

3.63 An attempt to move the jurisdiction of the trust to Jersey for tax avoidance purposes failed in *Re Weston's Settlements* [1969] 1 Ch 223. It has been held that it was to an individual's benefit to have a guaranteed income from the trust instead of merely remaining a discretionary beneficiary (*Re Clitheroe's Settlement Trusts* [1959] 3 All ER 789). However, variations for tax avoidance purposes have been approved in a number of cases, including in relation to capital taxes (*Re Drewe's Settlement* [1966] 2 All ER 844n; *Re Lloyd's Settlement* [1967] 2 All ER 314n), or in respect of income (*Re Sainsbury's Settlement* [1967] 1 All ER 878). The court has approved a change in the jurisdiction of trusts, where the beneficiaries have already moved to the new jurisdiction (*Re Seale's Marriage Settlement* [1961] 3 All ER 136; *Re Windeatt's Will Trusts* [1969] 2 All ER 324). A move to Guernsey was approved in *Re Chamberlain* (1976) 126 New Law Journal 104 where the beneficiaries had no connection with Guernsey but were not domiciled or resident in England. However, where the proposed arrangements amounted to a conspiracy to defraud the Inland Revenue the court, not surprisingly, refused to approve the arrangements (*Re Michelham's Will Trusts* [1964] Ch 550).

Proper law

3.64 A well drafted trust deed will normally state explicitly the governing law, although it may be implicit in the fact that reference is made to English trust law that the proper law of the trust is English. As has been shown above, the courts will only approve a change in the proper law of the trust where they think it appropriate to do so. It is, however, often considered appropriate to have a specific clause in the trust deed allowing the trustees to resign in favour of foreign trustees and to change the proper law of the trust to a new jurisdiction. This may well have tax implications, as explained in Chapter 10, and it is important to remember that a transfer to a single foreign corporate trustee will almost certainly fall foul of TA 1925 s 37(2), as it would probably not be a trust corporation and a sole trustee is prohibited. It is therefore necessary to transfer to at least two overseas trustees to secure a valid emigration of a trust.

3.65 Some trusts, particularly foreign trusts, contain what is known as a flee clause which provides that if an attempt is made by the trust jurisdiction to change the law to expropriate property or introduce or increase taxes in relation to the trust the jurisdiction of the trust automatically passes to trustees in another jurisdiction. This is quite common with Hong Kong trusts prior to 1997, when the terms of the transfer of the colony to the People's Republic of China had not been finalised. It is also said that a number of trusts automatically fled from Bermuda on the assassination of the Governor some years ago, and it took months before they could be returned, as the assassination was actually an isolated incident not the beginning of civil unrest, which was one of the triggering factors in a number of flee clauses being used.

3.66 A flee clause makes sense only where the assets are not in the jurisdiction of the existing proper law, as there is not much point in having the automatic appointment of trustees in another jurisdiction if the assets themselves are left behind to be expropriated. However, where the assets are investments it may well be possible to have the trust and trustees in one jurisdiction automatically fleeing to another, although it may be necessary to ensure that the new trustees' ability to deal with the assets has already been established. This could be done, for example, through the assets being vested in nominees, or through an investment company which need not be situated in either of the trust jurisdictions.

Protectors

3.67 Another method for the settlor to try and ensure that the trustees carry out his wishes, while still preserving the considerable flexibility of a discretionary trust, is to include a protector whose powers and duties are set out in the trust deed. The protector is not himself a trustee but is frequently a personal friend of the settlor, with an intimate knowledge of the family and the settlor's wishes. The protector's powers are usually those of veto under which the appointment or advancement to a particular beneficiary may require his consent. In some cases this veto extends to the disposal of certain trust assets such as shares in the family company or family estates. In some cases, the protector is given power to remove or appoint trustees. Protectors are particularly common in overseas discretionary trusts where the trustees are unlikely to be known personally to the settlor. The nature of a protector was considered in the Isle of Man case of *Steele v Paz* (1993–5) MLR 102 in which it was stated:

> '... nevertheless his (the protector's) role in my opinion is that of assisting in the administration of the trust. He is there to express to the trustees the settlor's wishes as to how the trust is operated ... It is clear as regards his powers he would owe a fiduciary duty to the beneficiaries (and not to the settlor) as to how those powers would be exercised. Thus it was accepted by all parties that the protector could not refuse to exercise a power because the settlor wished this to happen. The protector must bona fide consider the exercise of his powers from the point of view of the beneficiaries under the trust.'

3.68 In this particular case the problem was that the trust deed had not named the protector and it was held that this deficiency was curable and 'the court could, and if necessary should, appoint a protector just in the same circumstances as it would appoint a trustee, if a trustee was neither appointed or declined to act'. It has long been accepted that the court will not allow a trust to fail for want of a trustee (Underhill & Hayton, *Law of Trusts and Trustees*, 15th edition, p 60).

3.69 A protector's power to appoint and remove trustees is a fiduciary power which means it cannot be exercised in his favour to appoint himself a trustee. This was confirmed by the Bermuda Supreme court in *Von Knieriem v Bermuda Trust and Grosvenor Trust* EG Nos 154 and 162 of 1994 following the English case of *Re Skeats' Settlement* (1889) 42 Ch D 522. A protector must not have any responsibility for the day-to-day management, otherwise his fiduciary position may be construed to be enlarged into that of the trustee – JG Goldsworth, *The Nature and Use of Trusts, Trusts and Trustees*, Vol 2, No 5.

Elections

3.70 A donee to whom property is left under a will, which also leaves assets already owned by the donee to a third party, must elect whether to take the legacy under the will and give up the property already owned, to the third party, or renounce the legacy and keep the existing property (*Re Mengel's Will Trust* [1962] 2 All ER 490). An election often arises because of joint ownership of property where one of the joint owners purports to dispose of the entire property (*Re Gordon's Will Trust* [1978] 2 All ER 969). If the electee decides to keep the property which he already had, the legacy or gift is used to benefit the third party instead of the legatee or donee. An election can also arise in connection with a joint tenancy where, on the death of one of the joint tenants, it passes to the other by survivorship. If, as not infrequently happens, the joint tenant misunderstands the law and purports to leave by will his joint interest in the property to a third party and also leaves a legacy to the joint tenant taking the property under survivorship, the joint tenant would have to chose between the legacy and giving a joint interest in the property to a third party (*Re Dicey* [1957] Ch 145). If, however, the testator merely gives the asset away during life and omits to amend his will, there is no question of election as the gift causes the legacy to adeem, ie the legacy is cancelled because it is not part of the testator's estate.

Mistake and rectification

3.71 The courts have a general power to rectify documents where there has been a common mistake by both parties, *Frederick E Rose (London) Ltd v William H Pimm & Co Ltd* [1953] 2 QB 450. Rectification only relates to what is actually in the document and the true intentions of the parties must remain, *Green v Cobham* [2002] STC 820. If there is a mistake, eg by the trustees in executing a deed of appointment on the wrong day, it may be possible to apply to the court to have the document declared *void ab initio*, as happened in the case of *Abacus Trust Co (Isle of Man) Ltd v National Society for the Prevention of Cruelty to Children* [2001] STC 1344, where the trustees were entering into a tax-avoidance flip-flop scheme, the final part of which had to take place after 5 April 1998. The deed of appointment was executed by the trustee on 3 April 1998, contrary to the advice of counsel, and the court held that as the trustees were obliged to take into account the fiscal consequences of their actions they could not have meant to sign the deed of appointment on 3 April, and it was therefore void. This followed the principle in *Re Hastings-Bass (dec'd), Hastings v IRC* [1974] STC 211. The relief is not, however, automatic (*Breadner v Granville-Grossman* [2001] Ch 523, [2000] 4 All ER 705). The court may hold the appointment to be voidable instead of void, which may have different tax consequences (*Abacus Trust Co (Isle of Man) Ltd and Colyb Ltd v Barr* [2003] EWHC 114 (Ch), [2003] WTLR 149).

3.72 It has long been recognised that monies paid under a mistake of fact could be recovered (*Admiralty Comrs v National Provincial and Union Bank Ltd* (1922) 127 LT 452) and the House of Lords has now held that money paid under a mistake of law, previously considered on the authority of earlier cases at first instance to be irrecoverable could in fact be recovered (*Kleinwort Benson Ltd v Lincoln City Council* [1999] 2 AC 349).

3.73 The court has a wide power to order the delivery and cancellation of void documents to avoid confusion (*Hayward v Dimsdale* (1810) 17 Ves 111).

Receivers

3.74 Where money has been lent to a trust, normally on mortgage, the mortgagee would normally have a right to foreclose on the land, and in some cases appoint a receiver or administrative receiver over the trust assets. Alternatively a creditor could apply to the court for the appointment of a receiver (*Owen v Holmon* (1853) 4 HL Cas 997) or on the suit of a beneficiary where an executor or trustee is apparently misapplying or mismanaging assets.

3.75 Trustees themselves may apply to the court for the appointment of a receiver, eg to assist the orderly realisation of assets in a partnership in which they have been partners, with other parties or where they themselves are mortgagees over property or debenture holders in a company.

Chapter 4

Powers and Duties of Trustees

Money Laundering

4.1 Before a trustee can accept assets into a trust it is necessary to consider the provisions of the Proceeds of Crime Act 2002 (PCA 2002) and, in particular, the money laundering provisions contained therein. PCA 2002 is a substantial piece of legislation containing 462 sections and 12 schedules, which was enacted on 24 July 2002.

4.1A Part 1, in sections 1 to 5 and Schedule 1, establishes the Assets Recovery Agency under the control of a director appointed by the Home Secretary. The director has wide powers to exercise his functions the way he considers is best calculated to attribute to the reduction of crime, including setting up a system for the accreditation and training of financial investigators, some of whom will be employed by the ARA, and to cooperate with other law enforcement agencies. The courts on their own behest, or at the instigation of the ARA, may, if they decide that on a balance of probabilities a defendant has a criminal lifestyle and has been convicted of a specified offence, make a confiscation order allowing civil proceedings for the forfeiture of assets. These provisions are contained in Part 2, ss 6–91 relating to England and Wales, Part 3, ss 92–155 relating to confiscation in Scotland and Part 4, ss 156–239 relating to confiscation in Northern Ireland. The civil recovery of proceeds of unlawful conduct are set out in Part 5, ss 240–316.

4.1B PCA 2002, Part 6, ss 317–326, allows the director of the ARA to serve a notice on the Inland Revenue taking over the rights and duties of the Revenue to collect tax, interest and penalties in relation to direct taxes and inheritance tax, where the benefit of unlawful conduct remains in the hands of a criminal and is not already covered by a confiscation order. The intention seems to be to enable the ARA to collect tax, interest or penalties on unidentified funds thought to have a criminal source without identifying the source in question, so to this extent the powers are greater than those of the Inland Revenue. There is a right of appeal to the Special Commissioners under PCA 2002 s 320. The ARA can also serve a notice of withdrawal from the case, effectively handing back the tax gathering powers to the Inland Revenue. PCA 2002 s 322 specifically allows the director to collect inheritance tax from the trustees of a discretionary trust where he has reasonable grounds to suspect that the relevant property is in whole or part, criminal property. Where the ARA takes over the Revenue's functions the Revenue's powers are nonetheless retained by PCA 2002 s 317(7) which could, in theory, lead to double taxation. However, in committee, Mr Ainsworth for the Government stated: *"I assure the committee that we do not intend to double tax ... only the director will collect the tax, interest and penalties due. If the subject of the inquiry demonstrates that tax on the investigated income and gain was paid to the Inland Revenue, the director will not raise an assessment and he will serve notice of withdrawal"* (Hansard 15 January 2002, column 936).

4.1C The money laundering provisions are set out in PCA 2002 Part 7. The offences are: concealing (ss 327–329), failure to disclose (ss 330–332), and tipping-off (s 333). The penalties are in s 334.

4.1D The offence of concealing, disguising, converting or transferring criminal property includes concealing or disguising the ownership, source, location or disposition of property unless appropriate disclosure has been made and consent given under ss 335 or 336. The disclosure procedures are set out in ss 337–339 and the interpretation in s 340. PCA 2002 s 328 makes it an offence to be involved in an arrangement knowing or suspecting that it facilitates the use or acquisition of criminal property by another person, unless the appropriate disclosure has been made. A criminal dealing with his ill-gotten gains is likely also to commit the offence of acquisition, use and possession of criminal property, within s 329, unless the appropriate disclosure has been made. It is up to the defendant to prove his innocence on the balance of probabilities. It seems probable that the challenges will be made to these provisions on the basis of the Human Rights Act 1998.

4.1E Money laundering now applies not just to drug money but the laundering of the proceeds of any criminal conduct. Failure to disclose does not require an active decision not to do so, mere negligence where there are reasonable grounds to suspect that an offence has been committed is sufficient. It should be noted that criminal conduct for these purposes is conduct which (a) constitutes an offence in any part of the United Kingdom or (b) would constitute an offence in any part of the United Kingdom if it occurred there, under PCA 2002 s 340(2). If, therefore, a potential client was setting up a trust and there were reasonable grounds to suspect that he was or had been evading foreign taxes, it would be an offence not to disclose to a constable, customs officer or nominated officer, ie his employer's money laundering reporting officer (MLRO). If it were merely suspected that the client had been guilty of a foreign exchange control offence this would not be reportable, as there is no longer any such offence within the UK. In practice disclosure is normally made to the National Criminal Intelligence Service (NCIS) by the employer's MLRO.

4.1F One of the problems arising from the money laundering offences is that they carry a severe penalty of a fine and/or up to 14 years imprisonment. There is no de minimis limit, so a reasonable suspicion that even the smallest sums come within the wide definition of criminal property in PCA 2002 s 340(3) is reportable. This could easily lead to NCIS being overwhelmed by disclosures of petty amounts.

4.1G Disclosure is required where the business is in the regulated sector as defined by PCA 2002 Sch 9, which includes managing, safeguarding and administering investments which would therefore encompass most of the activities of trustees. A person appointed to give advice about the tax affairs of another person is included within the regulated sector by MLR 2003 para 2(h)(ii).

4.1H The remaining provisions of PCA 2002 relate to investigations into money laundering, in Part 8, ss 341–416; insolvency and the interrelationship between confiscation and insolvency proceedings is in Part 9, ss 417–434. The disclosure and exchange of information provisions are in Part 10, ss 435–442 and cooperation with other enforcement agencies is covered in Part 11, ss 443–447, with Part 12 dealing with miscellaneous and general matters in ss 448–462.

4.1I The easiest way for professional advisors to try and avoid running into problems under these draconian provisions is by having strict compliance procedures and ensuring that partners and staff are fully trained as to their responsibilities under these provisions.

4.1J The offence of tipping-off under PCA 2002 s 333 or prejudicing an investigation under s 342 occurs where a person knows or suspects that a disclosure has been made and passes that information to another party in circumstances likely to prejudice any investigation arising from the disclosure. This does not apply to a professional legal advisor giving advice in relation to actual or complicated legal proceedings. The maximum penalty for tipping-off is five years imprisonment, a fine or both.

4.1K Revenue advice on PCA 2002 and the Proceeds of Crime Act 2002 (Failure to Disclose Money Laundering: Specified Training) Order 2003 (SI 2003 No 171) is contained in Working Together Bulletin, issue 13, June 2003, pages 7–9 (see Appendix 8). An example of typical money laundering procedures is illustrated in Appendix 9. Further advice is available in the form of the British Bankers' Association Joint Money Laundering Steering Group guidance notes (www.jmlsg.org.uk). The CCAB Anti Money Laundering (Proceeds of Crime and Terrorism) Guidance notes (www.icaew.co.uk/ccab/documents) and the Chartered Institute of Taxation and Association of Taxation Technicians Anti-Money Laundering (Proceeds of Crime and Terrorism) Guidance on Dealing with Tax Offences (www.tax.org.uk).

Vesting trust property

4.2 The whole basis of a trust is that the settlor passes the legal title to trust assets to the trustees and the manner in which this is done depends on the assets. It is quite common to start the trust with a nominal transfer of funds, say £100, which is passed to the trustees by cheque, the trustees open a bank account in the name of the trust for which they are the signatories and the trust is now in existence. Further assets may be transferred to the trustees, which may be:

(a) physical assets such as works of art transferred by delivery;

(b) stocks and shares transferred by a stock transfer form duly stamped and registered with the company or issuer;

(c) a leasehold interest in property where the lease is assigned to the trustees, which may require the consent of the landlord; or

(d) a freehold property conveyed to the trustees in the normal manner.

The tax consequences of such transfers into trust will be considered in later chapters.

4.2A Once the transfer has been made to the original trustees there is no need to revest the assets on a change in trustees as this is effected by operation of law, under TA 1925 s 40. Under this section a new trustee is appointed by deed, which automatically vests the trust property in the new trustee in addition to the continuing trustees. Conversely, where a retiring trustee is discharged under TA 1925 s 39 or TLATA 1996 s 19 without a new trustee being appointed, the trust property is automatically vested in the continuing trustees whether or not the deed of retirement contains a specific declaration to that effect. In either a deed of appointment or retirement it is possible to insert an express provision that the trust assets shall not vest in this way, but this would be most unusual. The automatic vesting does not apply to land conveyed by way of mortgage, a lease requiring the landlord's consent, or to any assignment of registered stocks and shares. [TA 1925 s 40(4)]. In these cases it will be necessary to re-register in the names of the new trustees.

4.3 The court also has powers to make vesting orders under TA 1925 ss 44–56, as summarised in Chapter 2.

Appointment of trustees

4.4 In most cases the settlor will appoint the trustees in the trust deed, or will creating the trust, and the deed itself will normally contain instructions as to how existing trustees may retire or be replaced, or how new trustees may be appointed. This power is sometimes reserved to the settlor during his life, or may be given to the continuing trustees (with or without the permission of the protector, if there is one) or to the protector. If a trustee dies, as the trustees hold trust property as joint tenants the trust property vests in the continuing trustees automatically, and on the death of the last trustee the trust assets vest in his personal representatives under AEA 1925 s 1(2) and he, or they, may take on the trusteeship under TA 1925 s 18. If the personal representative does not take on the trusteeship, then the court has the power to appoint new trustees under TA 1925 s 41.

4.5 TA 1925 s 36 supplements the provisions in the trust deed where necessary and, subject to any provisions to the contrary, provides that a new trustee may be appointed where a trustee is dead, or remains outside the UK for an uninterrupted period of more than twelve months (*Re Walker* [1901] 1 Ch 259) or desires to be discharged from all or any of his trusts or powers, or refuses to act, or is unfit to act, e g because of bankruptcy (*Re Roche* [1842] 2 Dr & War 287), is incapable, e g because of a mental disorder (*Re East* (1873) 8 Ch App 735) or is an infant. It should be remembered that these provisions are subject to the trust deed and where a deed only referred to a trustee becoming incapable of acting this did not include bankruptcy (*Turner v Maule* (1850) 15 Jur 761), although the court might substitute a new trustee in place of a bankrupt trustee under TA 1925 s 41(1). The power of appointing trustees under TA 1925 s 36(1) is given to those so nominated in the trust deed, or to the surviving or continuing trustees or to the personal representatives of the last surviving or continuing trustee. A trustee who has been removed under a power contained in the deed is treated as having died. [TA 1925 s 36(2)].

4.6 A sole or last surviving executor intending to renounce may nonetheless accept the trusteeship, and will have to prove his title by reference to a grant of probate or letters of administration with the will annexed (*Re Crowhurst Park* [1974] 1 All ER 991). TA 1925 s 36 was modified by TLATA 1996 s 25 and Sch 3 and power to appoint new trustees is given to a person nominated in the trust instrument or, if there is no such person, the other trustees where there are no more than three trustees. This power may be delegated to an attorney under TDA 1999 s 1. Where a trustee is incapable within the meaning of MHA 1983 and is also a beneficiary, he may not be replaced without leave of the authority having jurisdiction under Part VII of the 1983 Act. Supplementary provisions as to the appointment of trustees allow additional trustees and separate trustees for parts of the trust property held on particular trusts. The appointment of a sole trustee other than a trust corporation is not permitted where the trustee would not be able to give valid receipts for all capital monies arising under the trust. A sole trustee is therefore only possible where the trust is of pure personalty and does not contain English or Welsh land. [LPA 1925 s 27(2)].

4.7 The court's power to appoint new trustees under TA 1925 s 41 extends to cases where there never were any original trustees (*Re Williams' Trusts* (1887) 36 Ch D 231). This confirms the maxim 'equity will not want for a trustee', which was extended to a protector in *Steele v Paz* (1993–5) MLR 102.

4.8 The court also has power to authorise remuneration where it appoints a corporation other than the public trustee to act solely or jointly with other trustees. [TA 1925 s 42]. A trustee appointed by the court has, under TA 1925 s 43, the same powers as if he were appointed by the trust instrument.

4.9 The maximum number of trustees allowed is four in the case of trusts of land, except in the case of charitable and other such trusts. [TA 1925 s 34]. Where the trust instrument does not nominate a person to appoint new trustees, who is capable of doing so? The beneficiaries, if unanimous and *sui juris*, may give a direction to the trustees to retire and to appoint new trustees as specified. A trustee so directed is entitled to an appropriate indemnity under TLATA s 19(3) and is required to do whatever is necessary to vest the trust property in the continuing and new trustees. In practice it is likely that any such written direction will be by deed in order to take advantage of the vesting provisions in TA 1925 s 40.

4.10 Broadly similar powers are given to the beneficiaries to replace a mentally incapable trustee under TLATA 1996 s 20 and the supplementary provisions in section 21. The trust instrument may specifically exclude the beneficiaries' powers to replace trustees under TLATA 1996 ss 19 and 20 and, for trusts created before 1 January 1997, the settlor, if still of full capacity, may exclude them by irrevocable deed.

Qualification of trustees

4.11 Any trustee needs only to be *sui juris*. The appointment of an infant as trustee in relation to a trust of land is void under LPA 1925 s 20. A trustee may be an individual or a company. Many trusts have a custodian trustee, usually a substantial trust corporation, which holds the legal title to the trust assets, while the management is handled by individual trustees. A trust corporation must be incorporated under the law of the UK or another Member State of the EU, and be empowered to undertake trust business in England and Wales, and to have an issued capital of at least £250,000, of which at least £100,000 has been paid up in cash, or be incorporated by a special Act or Royal Charter.

Disqualification of trustees

4.12 The normal reason for disqualifying a trustee is discussed above under TA 1925 ss 36 and 41. The trustee need not accept the appointment and may disclaim at any time before taking up the appointment (*Re Tryon* (1844) 7 Beav 496) but not afterwards (*Re Lister* [1926] Ch 149).

Disclaimer

4.13 A disclaimer would normally be by deed, but this is not essential. Termination obviously occurs on death of the trustee, with the property passing automatically to the remaining trustees as joint tenants. Any powers given to the trustees automatically pass to the survivors under TA 1925 s 18. Ultimately, if further trustees are not appointed, the trusteeship passes to the personal representatives of the last surviving trustee and if they do not take up the appointment themselves they may appoint new trustees. A trustee may also retire by deed with the consent of the continuing trustees, under TA 1925 s 39.

4.14 In addition to its statutory powers, the court has an inherent jurisdiction to remove a trustee with or without appointing a new one in his place, which is rarely exercised but has been used where the relationship between the trustees and the beneficiaries has broken down or become acrimonious (*Letterstedt v Broers* (1884) 9 App Cas 371).

4.15 A trustee is in a position of trust and has a fiduciary duty not to permit a conflict with his own interests (*Bray v Ford* [1896] AC 44). If a conflict arises which is not of his own making different considerations may apply (*Sargeant v National Westminster Bank plc* (1990) 61 P & CR 518).

Trustees' remuneration

4.16 A trustee other than the public trustee, a custodian trustee or an independent trustee of a pension scheme, is not entitled to charge for his time and trouble (*Robinson v Pett* (1734) 3 P Wms 249) unless the settlement so provides (*Willis v Kibble* (1839) 1 Beav 559). Exceptions to this general rule are where a trustee has entered into a legally binding agreement with the beneficiaries who are *sui juris* or, exceptionally, by a trustee solicitor in court (*Cradock v Piper* (1850) 1 Mac & G 664) or where a court has specifically authorised remuneration or the trust property is abroad and the local courts customarily allow remuneration to trustees (*Re Northcote's Will Trusts* [1949] 1 All ER 442). The trustees' right to reimbursement of properly incurred expenses is now enshrined in TA 2000 s 31.

4.17 Most trust deeds provide for the remuneration of professional trustees; such powers being governed by TA 2000 s 28. This only applies to a charitable trust if the trustee is not a sole trustee and a majority of the other trustees have agreed that he should be paid. A payment to the trustee is regarded as remuneration for services, not as a pecuniary legacy. [TA 2000 s 28(4)]. A trustee acts in a professional capacity if he does so in the course of a professional business which includes the provision of services in connection with the management or administration of trusts or any aspect thereof. [TA 2000 s 28(5)]. A lay trustee is not entitled to remuneration unless specifically so authorised by the trust instrument; a lay trustee being a trustee who is not a trust corporation and who does not act in a professional capacity. [TA 2000 s 28(6)]. Remuneration authorised under TA 2000 s 28 applies to services rendered on or after 1 February 2001.

4.18 A trust corporation or trustee acting in a professional capacity other than the trustee of a charitable trust is entitled to receive reasonable remuneration, but in the latter case only if the other trustees have agreed in writing that he may be remunerated for his services or it is specifically provided for in the trust instrument or another enactment. [TA 2000 s 29]. This section reverses the previous rule that a trustee could only be remunerated if the trust deed specifically so authorised. It now means that a trust corporation or professional trustee can be remunerated unless the trust deed specifically prohibits this or the trust is a charitable trust. A sole professional trustee would not, under this provision, be entitled to remuneration as it requires the consent of another trustee or trustees. TA 2000 s 30 gives power to the Secretary of State to make regulations for the remuneration of trustees of charitable trusts who are trust corporations or act in a professional capacity, but no such regulations have yet been made or appear to be in contemplation.

4.19 Trustees appointing agents, nominees and custodians may pay their remuneration and expenses (TA 2000 s 32) in respect of services rendered or expenses incurred after 1 February 2001. [TA 2000 s 33].

4.20 The trustees' right to reimbursement of expenses under TA 2000 s 31 was previously contained in TA 1925 s 30. The right includes expenses paid on behalf of the trust (*Dowse v Gorton* [1891] AC 190). The trustees' expenses are a first charge on the income and capital of the trust (*Stott v Milne* (1884) 25 Ch D 710). Such expenses include the cost of renewing leases (*Ex p Grace* (1799) 1 Bos & P 376), damages awarded against the trustees as owners of trust property (*Re Raybould* [1900] 1 Ch 199), and litigation costs (*Walters v Woodbridge* (1878) 7 ChD 504). It is, however, imperative to obtain permission from the court to engage in litigation in order to obtain indemnity for costs (*Re Beddoe* [1893] 1 Ch 547). Failure to do so could leave the trustees personally liable for costs if they lost (*Re England's Settlement Trusts, Dobb v England* [1918] 1 Ch 24). Exceptionally the trustees indemnity extends beyond the trust assets where there is a single beneficiary of full age and absolutely entitled (*Hardoon v Belilios* [1901] AC 118).

4.21 In the case of the renewal of a lease in *Keech v Sandford* (1726) Sel Cas Ch 61 a lease was renewed by a trustee personally and in *Protheroe v Protheroe* [1968] 1 WLR 519 a lease held as beneficial joint tenants gave rise to an opportunity to purchase the freehold reversion which was acquired by one of the joint tenants personally. In each case the benefit of the acquisition was held in trust for beneficiaries of the trust or the joint tenants.

4.22 A trustee must not make a secret profit from his position as trustee (*Boardman v Phipps* [1967] 2 AC 46) or by way of directors' fees from a company owned by the trust (*Re Macadam* [1946] Ch 73) unless so authorised by the trust instrument or otherwise so authorised. A trustee may have to account for profits where he competes with a business carried on by the trust (*Industrial Development Consultants Ltd v Cooley* [1972] 1 WLR 443). Trustees also have to account for profits made from receipt of information, commission or even selling at normal commercial rates to a trust business (*Barrett v Hartley* (1866) LR 2 Eq 789). A trustee cannot acquire trust property for himself, whether or not for full value (*Tito v Waddell (No 2)* [1977] Ch 106). This would also naturally apply to a purchase in the name of a nominee or company owned by the trustee (*Re Sherman* [1954] Ch 653; *Re Thompson' Settlement* [1986] Ch 99). These prohibitions are subject to anything to the contrary in the trust instrument, but a trustee cannot immediately retire and then buy trust property (*Wright v Morgan* [1926] AC 788); although this does not apply to the tenant for life acquiring property from a strict settlement under SLA 1925 s 68. A trustee's purchase of a beneficiary's beneficial interest can be set aside if he abused his position in making the purchase (*Dougan v MacPherson* [1902] AC 197).

Voting

4.23 Unless the trust deed specifically authorises trustees to act by majority, they must act unanimously (*Re Butlin's Settlement Trust* [1976] 2 All ER 483) except in the case of a charitable trust. This means that where assts are held on trusts for sale they must be sold unless the trustees unanimously favour postponement (*Re Roth* (1896) 74 LT 50). Similarly power to retain existing investments has to be exercised unanimously (*Re Hilton* [1909] 2 Ch 548).

4.24 Trust investments should be in joint names (*Lewis v Nobbs* (1878) 8 ChD 591). All trustees must, unless the settlement authorises otherwise, join in receipt for capital monies (*Walker v Symonds* (1818) 3 Swan 1). Receipts for capital monies on the sale of land must be made by two trustees or a trust corporation, LPA 1925 s 27(2). The ability of a trustee to delegate either under TDA 1999 s 1 or TA 1925 s 25, as substituted by TDA 1999 s 5, does not enable him to delegate to a co-trustee who thereby acts as a sole trustee, to avoid the requirement that a receipt for capital monies on the sale of land must be given by two separate trustees. [TDA 1999 s 7]. Two trustees are required where capital monies are paid to the trustees arising from the sale of land under LPA 1925 s 27(2) or SLA 1925 ss 18(1)(c) and 94(1). The value of receipts for such capital monies cannot be given by a sole trustee, TA 1925 s 14(2) and a conveyance must be made by at least two trustees under LPA 1925 s 2(1)(ii). A trust corporation may act alone.

Trustees' powers

4.25 Where power is given to the trustees to do certain things, it is up to the trustees to decide whether or not to exercise that power. Powers differ from duties, which the trustees must carry out. The trustees normally have a power of sale over land held as a trust of land under TLATA 1996. In the case of a strict settlement the power of sale belongs to the life tenant under SLA 1925 s 1. The trustees may hold land subject to an express trust for sale under TLATA 1996 s 11, with an implied power to postpone sales. Chattels are usually held by trustees on a trust for sale under the terms of a will, or on the death of a person intestate under AEA 1925 s 33, or on the trustees carrying out their duty of conversion into income-producing assets under *Howe v Earl of Dartmouth* (1802) 7 Ves 137. In the case of settled land, heirlooms settled to devolve with the settled land can only be sold by the life tenant with the consent of the court under SLA 1925 s 67. Chattels that are not heirlooms may be held on a trust for sale under LPA 1925 s 130, but may be sold only with the consent of the *usufructuary*, ie the user for the time being, if of full age. [LPA 1925 s 130(5)]. Obviously, trust investments are held under an implied power of sale, in view of the requirement to follow standard investment criteria. A trust of land under TLATA 1996 s 6 gives the trustees all the powers of an absolute owner, which obviously includes the power to sell or not to sell. TA 1925 gives trustees the power to sell trust property by public auction or by private contract and to raise money by sale, mortgage etc. [TA 1925 s 16]. Trustees have the power under TA 1925 s 14 to give receipts and under section 19 of that Act the power to insure trust properties including property held on a bare trust, subject to a contrary direction from a beneficiary, who must be *sui juris*. Trustees have the power to compound liabilities under TA 1925 s 15. Trustees' powers devolve to the survivor on the death of a trustee under TA 1925 s 18, although a sole trustee cannot give a valid receipt for capital monies on the sale of land. [TA 1925 s 14(2)].

4.26 Trustees are given wide powers to deal with reversionary interests under TA 1925 s 22, including having them valued and sold before falling in. The trustees' power, individually, to appoint attorneys to act in their stead is given by TDA 1999 and the power to employ agents, nominees or custodians is given in TA 2000 ss 11–26. The delegation of a trustee's functions by a power of attorney in TA 1925 s 25 has been substituted by TDA 1999 s 5. Trustees have a power to concur with other joint owners under TA 1925 s 24.

Administrative powers

4.27 A well drafted trust deed sets out the powers which the trustees need to administer the trust effectively. These will normally determine the trustees' power of investment and management of property. They may wish to hold joint property, to avoid holding a balance between income and capital, they may wish to accumulate income, permit a beneficiary to occupy trust property, apply trust capital, trade, borrow money, insure trust property, delegate their powers, deposit documents, appoint nominees, carry on the administration of the trust outside the UK, pay tax, give indemnities and security, invest in unquoted companies without getting involved in the management, appropriate trust property, accept receipts for charitable gifts, release powers, amended the statutory powers of maintenance and advancement in TA 1925 ss 31 and 32 dealing with minors. They may wish to make disclaimers, avoid apportionment of income, deal with conflicts of interest, trust powers, obtaining remuneration for trustees, limiting the liability of trustees, the manner in which trustees are to be appointed when they retire and ensure that the trustees administrative powers do not prevent the beneficiary obtaining an interest in possession in an accumulation and maintenance settlement.

4.28 Standard wording for administrative powers is available from the Society of Trust and Estate Practitioners, based on drafts by James Kessler. It is sufficient to put in a trust deed or will the following reference 'Administrative provisions, the standard provisions of the Society of Trust and Estate

Practitioners (First Edition) shall apply with the deletion of paragraph 5. S11 of the Trusts of Land and Appointment of Trustees Act 1996 (Consultation with beneficiaries) shall not apply'.

4.29 Paragraph 5, which is deleted, referred to holding land on trusts for sale which has now been overtaken by TLATA 1996. Section 11 of the 1996 Act imposes duties of consultation inappropriate to a substantive trust. The standard provisions are included in Tolley's *Administration of Trusts* and are included in Appendix 1. The powers to manage trust property are needed both to repair and maintain existing property and develop or improve it as appropriate.

Delegation

4.30 The power of delegation refers to delegation by an individual trustee which is now dealt with in considerable detail in TDA 1999, which came into effect on 1 March 2000, and is summarised in Chapter 2. In the absence of specific powers to delegate, by statute or in the trust deed, the trustees may not do so. The agency concept of delegation prevents this, '*delegatus non potest delegare*'; a person to whom a power or duty is delegated may not himself delegate this to others.

Control over trustees' powers

4.31 A beneficiary who is dissatisfied with the trustees' actions may apply to the court for an order under TLATA 1996 ss 14 and 15. Alternatively a beneficiary with an absolute vested interest in trust property may, under the rule in *Saunders v Vautier* (1841) 4 Beav 115, call for his share of the trust property to be distributed to him (*Berry v Green* [1938] AC 575). Although the court will not interfere with the trustees' discretion, exceptionally, with a discretionary trust, if all the discretionary beneficiaries band together, they could require the trustees to distribute the whole of the trust income to them jointly (*Re Nelson* [1928] Ch 920). The court will not interfere with the trustees' bona fide exercise of their discretion (*Gisborne v Gisborne* (1877) 2 App Cas 300; *Whishaw v Stephens* [1970] AC 508). Where the trustees act perversely (*Re Lofthouse* (1885) 29 Ch D 921) or irrationally (*Re Manisty's Settlement* [1974] Ch 17, or fail to consider whether or not to exercise a discretionary power (*Klug v Klug* [1918] 2 Ch 67) the court may require the trustees to reconsider the exercise of their discretion (*Wain v Earl of Egmont* (1843) 3 My & K 445). In *Stannard v Fisons Pension Trust Ltd* (1992) 1 IRIR 27 the Court invalidated the exercise of a discretion where the trustees had based their decision on an out of date valuation.

4.32 Because of the importance of the tax treatment of interest in possession and accumulation and maintenance settlements, it is not unusual to find an overriding provision that the life tenant must not be deprived of an interest in possession for IHT purposes. [IHTA 1984 ss 49–57A]. An interest in possession is a present right to the present enjoyment of something, and a power of accumulation is inconsistent with an interest in possession (*Pearson v IRC* [1980] STC 318). Similar provisions apply to a trust ceasing to be an accumulation and maintenance trust under IHTA 1984 s 71(1), or would cause a settlement to be an accumulation and maintenance or discretionary settlement under TCGA 1992 s 5. Previously, a similar override was used to prevent a settlement becoming an accumulation or discretionary settlement within TCGA 1992 s 5, which was repealed by FA 1998 s 165 when the CGT distinction between interest in possession trusts and other trusts as to the rate of CGT ceased to apply. Such a provision therefore is no longer needed.

4.33 The trustees, in addition to their statutory duty of care under TA 2000 s 1, must take control of the trust property and understand and follow the terms of the trust. They must also act impartially among the beneficiaries (*Lloyds Bank v Duker* [1987] 1 WLR 1324) and in the best interests of beneficiaries, not, for example, using the trust to promote some other cause (*Cowan v Scargill* [1985] Ch 270). Trustees must keep proper accounts and produce them to the beneficiaries when requested (*Chaine-Nickson v Bank of Ireland* [1976] IR 393). Beneficiaries who want copies of the accounts must pay for them (*Re Watson* (1904) 49 Sol Jo 54). Trustees may have the accounts audited; this is normally done no more than once every three years. [TA 1925 s 22 (4)]. Apart from the trust accounts, beneficiaries are entitled to other trust documents only if they contain information about the trust which the beneficiaries are entitled to know, in which they have a proprietary interest, and which are in the possession of the trustees, but this does not extend to confidential information as to the exercise of the trustees' discretion, such as minutes or correspondence (*Re Londonderry's Settlement* [1965] Ch 918).

4.34 Trustees, in following the requirements of the trust, have a duty to distribute the trust property to those entitled to it. If in doubt they should take professional advice and only apply to the court if all other avenues have failed (*Re Allan Meyrick Will Trusts* [1966] 1 WLR 499).

4.35 In cases of doubt as to who may be members of a class of beneficiaries, TA 1925 s 27 allows trustees to advertise in the *London Gazette* or, where there is land in the trust, to advertise in a newspaper circulating in the district where the land is situated, or to place such other advertisements or notices as would have been directed by a court, giving at least two months' notice of an intended distribution. The court's directions should normally be sought on the advertisement. If such actions fail to flush out all the beneficiaries, the trustees can go ahead and distribute to those known to them (*Re Aldhous* [1955] 1 WLR 459). A beneficiary deprived of his share in such circumstances may seek to trace the property into the hands of those to whom it was distributed and try and recover it.

4.36 If the trustees are due to distribute to a named beneficiary who cannot be found, they may apply to the courts for a presumption of death (*Re Benjamin* [1902] 1 Ch 723; *Re Green's Will Trusts* [1985] 3 All ER 455).

Trustees' liabilities

4.37 A trustee's breach of trust is measured at common law by reference to what would be expected from an honest, diligent and prudent man of business dealing with his own affairs (*Speight v Gaunt* (1883) 9 App Cas 1). A professional trustee is expected to apply an even higher level of expertise to trust affairs (*National Trustees Co of Australasia Ltd v General Finance Co of Australasia Ltd* [1905] AC 373; *Bartlett v Barclays Bank Trust Co Ltd* [1980] Ch 515). Where the statutory duty of care applies under TA 2000 s 1, a trustee is expected to exercise such care and skill as is reasonable in the circumstances, having regard in particular to any special knowledge or experience that he has or holds himself out as having, and if he acts as trustee in the course of a business or profession, to any special knowledge or experience that it is reasonable to expect of a person acting in the course of that kind of business or profession. Where the trustee falls below these standards he may be liable to make good the loss, measured as the difference between what is left in the trust fund and what would have been had it not been for the trustee's breach of duty, (*Nestlé v National Westminster Bank plc* [1994] 1 All ER 118. In TA 1925 s 9 there is a limitation in respect of an advance of trust money on mortgage for inadequate security, where the liability is limited to making good the excess advance (not the whole amount), together with interest, but this only applies in respect of an advance made before 1 February 2000. Where the trustee, in breach of trust, has used trust money for his own private purposes, he must replace the capital appropriated together with the actual profit he has made by the use of the money, or, at the option of the beneficiaries, pay interest, simple or compound depending on the mood of the court, which fairly represents the profit usually made if invested in the manner in which it was actually used. This is a simple option, the beneficiaries cannot cherrypick (*Wallersteiner v Moir* (No 2) [1975] 1 All ER 849). The loss continues until the trust fund is properly reinvested (*Lander v Weston* (1855) 3 Drew 389).

4.38 Where the settlor acts as trustee he is still liable for breach of trust (*Drosier v Brereton* (1851) 15 Beav 221). The trustee is also liable for costs, on the standard non-indemnity basis (*Bartlett v Barclays Bank Trust Co Ltd (No 2)* [1980] 2 All ER 92). The trustee is therefore liable for compensation, not damages. The trustees' liability for compensation may be greater than their liability for damages for tort or breach of contract in that, for example, it is not limited by the concept of remoteness (*Re Dawson* [1966] 2 NSWR 211; *Target Holdings Ltd v Redferns* [1994] 2 All ER 337). The trustees' defence may be that they were not responsible for the loss caused by their negligence, as it was not a direct or immediate consequence of that negligence. But in *Caffrey v Darby* (1801) 6 Ves 488 the court was not impressed by this argument, as in its view, if the trustees had not been negligent the assets would not have been exposed to the loss which occurred. Beneficiaries suing for breach of trust are seeking compensation for the trust fund, not on behalf of themselves. A discretionary beneficiary may therefore sue, even though he himself has as yet suffered no loss. A trustee's liability continues until restitution has been made (*Bartlett v Barclays Bank Trust Co Ltd (No 2)*

[1980] 2 All ER 92). Again, unlike in damages, the fiscal effects of compensation are ignored (*Re Bell's Indenture* [1980] 3 All ER 425 and *Bartlett v Barclays Bank Trust Co Ltd (No 2)* [1980] 2 All ER 92; contrasted with the damages case of *British Transport Commission v Gourley* [1956] AC 185). Where the trustees are in breach of trust, the fact that the loss is exacerbated by a collapse in the property market or negligent valuation of the property may be irrelevant if the breach of trust was the cause of the change in circumstances giving rise to the loss. The claimant has to show that the loss would not have happened had it not been for the breach of trust (*Target Holdings Ltd v Redferns* [1996] AC 421). There has, however, to be a causal link between the loss and the breach of trust (*Bishopsgate Investment Management Ltd v Maxwell (No 2)* [1994] 1 All ER 261). The measure of compensation in *Nestlé v National Westminster Bank* [1994] 1 All ER 118 was the difference between what the fund of investments would have been worth had it been properly invested and had it achieved an average return over the period, compared with what it actually achieved as a result of being improperly invested. A beneficiary is entitled to trust his trustee, although if he continues to do so once he becomes aware of dishonesty he has only himself to blame for any further losses if he takes no action (*Lipkin Gorman v Karpnale* [1992] 4 All ER 331). The trustees' liability for breach of trust is to compensate the trust for the loss, and does not contain any element of penalty (*Guardian Ocean Cargoes v Banco de Brazil* [1992] 2 Lloyd's Rep 193). A trustee is not liable where the loss was inevitable, except to the extent that his action has increased the loss (*Lord Gainsborough Watcombe Terra Cotta Co* (1885) 54 LJ Ch 991; *Re Miller's Deed Trusts* [1978] LS Gaz R 454).

4.39 It appears that the rate of interest implied in calculating compensation for negligence is based on the special investment account under the Court Funds Rules 1987, which is generally in line with that offered by National Savings (*Jaffray v Marshall* [1994] 1 All ER 143). Where, however, the trustee has misapplied the funds, he is deemed to have borrowed the money from the trust and is liable to pay the commercial rate of 1 per cent above the bank base rate (*Wallersteiner v Moir (No 2)* [1975] QB 373). However, if the trustee had actually received a higher rate he would be accountable for the profit (*Re Emmets Estate* (1881) 17 Ch D 142). If as a result of breach of trust the trustee makes an unauthorised profit, he is accountable to the trust for that profit (*Warman International Ltd v Dwyer* (1995) 69 Al Jr 362; *Movitex Ltd v Bulfield* [1988] BCLC 104).

4.40 The liability of trustees is joint and several, where there is a joint default, whatever their individual levels of blame (*Re Biddulph* (1869) 4 Ch App 280). All the trustees would be sued (*Re Jordan* [1904] 1 Ch 260), although the liability, being several as well as joint, may be enforced against any one or more of them (*A-G v Wilson* (1840) Cr & Ph 1). Trustees are only liable for the net loss caused by a particular transaction, but a loss on one transaction cannot be compensated by gain on another separate one (*Wiles v Gresham* (1854) 2 Drew 258).

4.41 Where a trustee intermixes his own funds and trust funds and acquires property, the beneficiaries may elect to trace the funds into whatever they may have been converted (*Re Hallett's Estate* (1880) 13 Ch D 696), see **4.48–4.50**. Where part of the funds came from the trustee's own resources the beneficiaries and the trustees are treated as if they were co-owners (*Re Tilley's Will Trusts* [1967] Ch 1179). The right to trace ceases where the property can no longer be identified, or is traceable into the hands of a third-party, bona fide purchaser of a legal interest for value without notice.

4.42 Where a court is satisfied that trust property is in danger, by reason of the active or passive misconduct of the trustees (*Bell Talbot v Hope-Scott* (1858) 4 K & J 139; *Foley v Burnell* (1783) 1 Bro cc 274), or where the trustees are residing outside the jurisdiction of the court (*Dickins v Harris* (1866) 14 LT 98), a beneficiary may apply to the court for an injunction compelling the trustees to do their duty, or restraining them from interfering with the trust property. A receiver may be appointed by the court in appropriate cases (*Bennett v Colley* (1832) 5 Sims 182). A trustee who admits to holding trust monies personally may be ordered to pay them into court (*London Syndicate v Lord* (1878) 8 Ch D 84).

4.43 A trustee who dishonestly misappropriates trust property could be guilty of theft under the Theft Act 1968, and if convicted could be ordered to pay compensation under the Powers of Criminal Courts Act 1973 s 35. The test of dishonesty is whether the accused trustee must have realised that, by the standards of ordinary and decent people, what he was doing was dishonest (*R v Ghosh* [1982] QB 1053).

4.44 Theft is an offence under the Theft Act 1968 s 1. Other potential offences of a dishonest trustee dealt with under the Theft Act 1968 are:

(a) obtaining property by deception [section 15];

(b) obtaining a pecuniary advantage by deception [section 16];

(c) false accounting [section 17];

(d) publication of false, deceptive or misleading statements by officers of a body corporate or incorporated association [section 19]; and

(e) suppression of documents [section 20].

If two or more co-trustees are involved they may be guilty of conspiracy under the Criminal Law Act 1977 ss 1–5 or the common law offence of conspiracy to defraud (*Scott v Metropolitan Police Comr* [1975] AC 819).

4.45 A trustee is not generally responsible for breaches of trust caused by his co-trustees (*Townley v Sherborne* (1634) Bridg J 35). If, however, he:

(a) hands property to a co-trustee without seeing to its proper application (*Walker v Symonds* (1818) 3 Swan 1); or

(b) allows his co-trustee to receive trust property without making due inquiry into what he does with it (*Wyne v Tempest* (1897) 13 Tlr 360); or

(c) becomes aware of a co-trustees breach of trust and does nothing about it (*Miller's Trustees v Polson* (1897) 34 SLR 798);

he is himself guilty of breach of trust. The statutory indemnity in TA 1925 s 30 was abolished by TA 2000 s 40. The trustee's liability may be limited by the trust deed itself. A new trustee is not liable for breaches of trust committed before he became a trustee, but if he becomes aware of a breach he must take steps to remedy it (*Re Strahan* (1856) 8 De GM & G 291). Similarly, a trustee is not liable for breaches committed by his successors unless he retired in order to facilitate a breach (*Head v Gould* [1898] 2 Ch 250).

4.46 The court has specific power in TA 1925 s 61 to relieve a trustee from personal liability if it appears to the court that he acted honestly and reasonably and ought fairly to be excused from the breach of trust, and for omitting to obtain the directions of the court in the matter in which he committed such a breach. The court may relieve him either wholly or partly from personal liability. A trustee must not merely be honest but must have acted reasonably (*Re Turner* [1897] 1 Ch 536).

4.47 A beneficiary who participated in a breach of trust, or subsequently affirmed it, acquiesced in it, or released the trustees from the breach, cannot make a claim against the trustees' (*Fletcher v Collis* [1905] 2 Ch 24; *Re Deane* (1889) 42 Ch D 9). A deed of release in connection with the trustees' breach of trust is only effective if the beneficiaries knew what they were giving up under the deed (*Re Garnett* (1885) 31 Ch D 1). Mere knowledge of a breach by a beneficiary is not acquiescence, although if it continues for a long period it is likely to be presumed acquiescence (*Sleeman v Wilson* (1871) LR 13 Eq 36). Where the breach was instigated by a beneficiary, the trustee may claim to have the beneficiary's interest impounded to rectify the breach (*Chillingworth v Chambers* [1896] 1 Ch 685). Where the instigation is in writing the impoundment may be made under TA 1925 s 62. The beneficiary must have known that what he was instigating was in breach of trust (*Re Pauling's Settlement Trust (No 2)* [1963] Ch 576). Claims against trustees may be statute barred under the Limitation Act 1980 s 21, which provides a limitation period of six years from the date on which the right of action accrued. It does not apply in cases of fraud or fraudulent breach of trust or property converted by the trustee. [LA 1980 s 21(1)(a) and (b)]. The conversion provisions are limited, in the case of a trustee beneficiary, by Limitation Act 1980 s 21(2) to the excess over his proper share. Time runs from the date of the breach of trust not from the date the loss occurred (*Re Somerset* [1894] 1 Ch 231), except where fraud is involved, in which case time runs from when the fraud is reasonably discoverable. [LA 1980 s 32]. In the case of a remainderman, the limitation period does not commence until his interest falls into possession (*Mara v Browne* [1896] 1 Ch 199). A beneficiary under a disability, such as minority, has the limitation period extended to cover the period of disability. [LA 1980 s 28]. Where a claim is made against one trustee, contribution may be awarded in his favour against other trustees under the Civil Liability (Contributions) Act 1978, in such proportion as the court thinks just. Trustees who rely on a solicitor trustee to advise them may be given indemnity by the court, if reliance on the advice caused a breach of trust (*Re Turner* [1897] 1 Ch 536).

Tracing

4.48 A beneficiary's right to trace trust property is appropriate if he is unable to recover from the trustees (*Re Diplock* [1948] Ch 465). Tracing at common law may make it possible to recover assets but it only applies to somebody with legal ownership or the right of possession under a contract for bailment or hire purchase, and has no application in enforcing a beneficiary's equitable interest under a trust. At common law the right to trace only exists as long as the asset remains identifiable and does not become part of a mixed fund, although precisely why the Court of Appeal in *Re Diplock* (1948) was unwilling to apply the identification rules in *Devaynes v Noble, Clayton's Case* (1816) 1 Mer 572 is not clear. The much wider relief of equitable tracing applies where there is the appropriate fiduciary relationship, the property remains in a traceable form, and tracing it would not give rise to inequity. An ordinary contractual commercial relationship is not in any sense fiduciary (*Goldcorp Exchange* [1995] 1 AC 74; *Westdeutsche Landesbank Girozentrale v Islington London Borough Council* [1996] 2 All ER 961). Where the money passes from the trustee, other than to a bona fide purchaser for value without notice, the assets can be traced into the hands of the donee (*Agip (Africa) Ltd v Jackson* [1991] Ch 547). If the donee has disposed of the property and received nothing in exchange, ie he has consumed or spent it, tracing is not possible, but where the property has been mixed, equitable tracing is permitted (*Re Tilley's Will Trust* [1967] Ch 1179). In effect, the beneficiaries have a claim over the whole of a mixed fund, and anything purchased with it, until the trust fund is repaid in full (*Re Oatway* [1903] 2 Ch 356). Where funds are mixed by an innocent donee, tracing may be applied *pari passu* with the donee's own funds, or the first in first out rule in *Devaynes v Noble, Clayton's Case* (1816) 1 Mer 572 may be applied (*Re Stenning* [1895] 2 Ch 433), unless this produces an inequitable result.

4.49 Where the funds of two or more trusts are mixed, in breach of trust, it is assumed that the trustee spent his own money first leaving the remaining balance available to the trustees (*Re Hallelt's Estate* (1880) 13 Ch D 696). If, on the other hand, the assets are traced into assets which have appreciated in value, the trustee holds them on constructive trust for the beneficiary (*Boardman v Phipps* [1967] 2 AC 46). The innocent volunteer investing funds subsequently traced by a beneficiary is only required to return the amount he received in breach of trust, no account is required for any profit he may have made on it. Monies paid into an overdrawn account cannot be traced further (*Bishopsgate Investment Management Ltd (in liquidation) v Homan* [1995] Ch 211). Similarly, if the money is used by the volunteer to repay debts, there is nothing further to trace (*Re Diplock* [1948] Ch 465).

4.50 Tracing cannot be enforced against a bona fide purchaser for value of the legal estate without notice (*Re J Leslie Engineers Co Ltd* [1976] 2 All ER

85). Tracing will also be refused where it would result in hardship or injustice, eg where the money had been spent on improvements to property (*Re Diplock* [1948] Ch 465). An action against the recipient, instead of tracing to recover money wrongly paid, can only be made in connection with the administration of estates, eg to enable a creditor to recover from legatees (*Harrison v Kirk* [1904] AC 1).

Income and capital

4.51 The STEP administrative provisions do not require trustees to keep a balance between the conflicting interests of persons entitled to trust property in order to give the maximum flexibility in looking after the interests of the beneficiaries as a whole, without a redistribution of incoming monies and expenses between income and capital. Many trusts require just such a division which can give rise to innumerable problems. If a company issues bonus shares they are treated as part of the trust capital (*Re Wright's Settlement Trusts* [1945] Ch 211; *IRC v Blott* [1921] 2 AC 171). Dividends applied in paying up share capital may be capital or income depending on the intention of the company, and were capital in *Re Evans* [1913] 1 Ch 23; *IRC v Blott* [1921] 2 AC 171; *Bouch v Sproule* (1887) 12 App Cas 385; *Re Ogilvie* (1919) 35 TLR 218; and *IRC v Wright* [1927] 1 KB 333, where it was the company's intention to capitalise profits.

4.52 Any payment from a company to its shareholders, other than as a repayment of share capital or other payment so treated by company law is likely to be an income dividend (*Hill v Permanent Trustee Co of New South Wales* [1930] AC 720), although nowadays there can be exceptions to this general rule, as explained below. However, dividends paid out of capital profits are income (*Re Doughty* [1947] Ch 263). An English company making a distribution from a share premium account through a reduction of capital, under CA 1985 s 130, is a return on capital not a dividend. However, in some jurisdictions such as the Isle of Man and the Cayman Islands dividends can be paid out of the share premium account as income. Payments on company restructuring sanctioned by the court, under CA 1985 s 425, may contain an interest element to the extent they relate to arrears of interest (*Re Morris's Will Trust* [1960] 3 All ER 548). In *Rae v Lazard Investments Co Ltd* [1963] 1 WLR 555 it was held that 'every distribution of money or money's worth by an English company must be treated as income in the hands of the shareholders unless it is either a distribution in a liquidation, a repayment in respect of a reduction of capital (or a payment out of a special premium account) or an issue of bonus shares (or it may be, bonus debentures)'. Capital treatment would also appear to apply to the purchase by a company of its own shares and declaration of a dividend immediately used to satisfy a contemporaneous call on unpaid share capital (*Re Hatton* [1917] 1 Ch 357).

Apportionment

4.53 Most trust deeds avoid statutory apportionment of income on a time basis under AA 1870 by providing that income and expenditure shall be treated as arising when payable and does not accrue from day to day. In addition to apportionment under AA 1870 there are a number of rules relating to equitable apportionment which apply in particular to trusts created by will, unless they are excluded by the will or trust instrument, as they usually are when these have been properly drafted.

4.54 These rules include, where there is a duty to convert, the proceeds of sale of the unauthorised investment, which will be apportioned between income and capital on the basis of the current yield on unauthorised investments. This was fixed at 4 per cent in *Re Baker* [1924] 2 Ch 271 and followed in *Re Berry* [1962] Ch 97. Where the trustees decide to postpone conversion, the property has to be valued at the date of death in order to fix the return to the life tenant (*Re Parry* [1947] Ch 23). In other cases where there is no power to postpone conversion, the investment would be valued one year from the testator's death (*Re Fawcett* [1940] Ch 402). The life tenant's income is taken from the actual income so far as possible, and if there is a shortfall it is made up from capital when the investment is sold. Conversely any capital profit over and above the 4 per cent accrues to the benefit of capital. It is not clear to what extent the 4 per cent figure is cast in stone as, at various times, it has been well out of line with current yields on authorised investments.

4.55 Where the investment is an investment in expectancy, i e a reversionary interest which will fall into the estate on the death of the life tenant, it is probably a speculative asset which would be regarded as one where the trustees had a duty to convert, except that purely on the basis of investment criteria it might be better to wait until the life tenant dies and the interest falls in. The life tenant is compensated, on the authority of *Re Earl of Chesterfield's Trusts* (1883) 24 Ch D 643, by giving him 4 per cent per annum compound interest, less income tax at the basic rate, on an amount which, together with that interest, would equal the amount actually received, from the date of death. This rule applies to other non-income producing assets, such as a debt (*Re Duke of Cleveland's Estate* [1895] 2 Ch 542) or compensation for a refusal to grant planning permission (*Re Chance* [1962] Ch 593). The rule in *Allhusen v Whittell* (1867) LR 4 Eq 295 is designed to deal with the perceived inequality between a life tenant and remainderman where debts are paid some time after the date of death out of the residuary estate left in trust. If the debts were paid entirely out of capital, say a year after the date of death, the life tenant would have received excessive income, whereas if the income had been used to pay the debts the remainderman would have benefited at the life tenant's expense. The rule therefore provides that the sum used to pay the debts has to be apportioned between income and capital on an equitable basis using the actual rate of interest, net of basic rate tax, for the years succeeding death (*Re Oldham* [1927] WN 113). These equitable apportionment rules are complex in their calculation and capricious in their effect and are normally excluded by any well drafted will or trust deed.

Scrip (stock) dividends

4.56 An enhanced scrip dividend, as opposed to a mere alternative of taking a scrip or cash dividend of the same value, normally gives rise to a capital receipt under trust law (*Hawkins v Hawkins* (1920) SRNSW 550). The trustees may have power to pay out a capital sum to an income beneficiary corresponding to the amount of a cash dividend foregone in taking the enhanced scrip dividend. The Revenue has accepted, in SP4/94, that *Re Malam* [1894] 3 Ch 578 may apply to such capital profits and the trustees can elect to allow the life tenant a lien over the bonus shares equivalent to the amount of the cash dividend, and then satisfy that lien out of cash from the capital account (see **4.60**). If, however, the trustees take the view that the enhanced scrip dividend is no more than an ordinary dividend paid in a way regarded as beneficial to the company, and therefore outside *Bouch v Sproule* (1887) 12 App Cas 385, the entire distribution would be income (*Re Northage* (1891) 60 LJ Ch 488; *Re Tindal* (1892) 9 TLR 24; *Re Despard* (1901) 17 TLR 478; *Re Hume Nisbet's Settlement* (1911) 27 TLR 461, and would be taxable under ICTA 1988 ss 249–251.

4.57 Scrip dividends, referred to as stock dividends in the Taxes Acts, are not treated as distributions (ICTA 1988 s 230) but are taxable as income of the shareholder or of the life tenant of an interest in possession trust, on the 'appropriate amount in cash', grossed up at the Schedule F ordinary rate (10 per cent for 2003/04), which is then taxed at the taxpayer's marginal rate with a non-payable tax credit at the Schedule F ordinary rate. [ICTA 1988 s 249(4)]. The 'appropriate amount in cash' is the amount of the cash dividend which could have been taken instead of the scrip dividend, unless this is substantially different (15 per cent, SP/A8) from the market value of the shares, in which case it is the market value. [ICTA 1988 s 251(2)].

4.58 Where the scrip dividend is received by a discretionary or accumulation and maintenance trust the 'appropriate amount in cash' grossed up at the Schedule F ordinary rate, with a corresponding non-payable tax credit, will be subject to tax at the Schedule F trust rate (25 per cent for 2003/04). [ICTA 1988 ss 249(6) and 686(1A)(a)].

4.59 Scrip dividends are treated as acquired by the recipient at the appropriate amount in cash, as calculated for income tax under ICTA 1988 s 25 and for CGT purposes under TCGA 1992 s 142.

4.60 Enhanced scrip dividends are dividends where the bonus shares are issued at a price substantially below the market value. They were popular before the abolition of ACT but are no longer common. Arguably scrip dividends are entirely capital, on the basis of *Bouche v Sproule* (1887) 12 App Cas 385, but there are arguments both for income treatment (*Re Northage* (1891) 60 LJ Ch 488) or a fair apportionment under which the life tenant is advanced a capital sum equivalent to the value of the cash dividend foregone. In such a case of apportionment the payment to the life tenant should be a capital receipt, but the Revenue treats such compensation payments as annual payments, subject to deduction of tax by the trustees at the basic rate and taxable on the life tenant as income. [SP 4/94]. If shares are transferred to the life tenant *in specie*, the CGT base value is the *pro rata* cost of the original shares under TCGA 1992 ss 126–128. ICTA 1988 s 249 (4) and TCGA 1992 s 142 have no application in such circumstances. However, the amount distributed would be an income distribution taxable on the trustee at the rate applicable to trusts (34 per cent for 2003/04), with no credit to the tax pool. [ICTA 1988 s 687].

4.61 Capitalised enhanced scrip dividends received by discretionary or accumulation and maintenance trusts are deemed to have been taxed at the Schedule F ordinary rate, under ICTA 1988 s 249(6), but are not treated as accumulated income, being added to capital, and are therefore outside the provisions of ICTA 1988 s 686 which subjects such income to the tax rates applicable to trusts. As ICTA 1988 s 249(6) applies, TCGA 1992 ss 126–128 are disapplied by TCGA 1992 s 142 and the trustees base value for CGT is the appropriate amount in cash under ICTA 1988 s 251(2).

Demergers

4.62 A direct demerger, which involves the distributing company hiving off part of its business to a subsidiary and then distributing the shares by way of a dividend *in specie*, gives rise to an income receipt following *Re Kleinwort's Settlements* [1951] Ch 860 and *Re Sechiari* [1950] 1 All ER 417, which may, however, be tax exempt under ICTA 1988 s 213(3)(a) subject to the anti-avoidance provisions and meeting the requirements of sections 214–217 of the 1988 Act. Although there is no income tax charge where the demerged shares are transferred to a life tenant (ICTA 1988 s 213(3)(a)), there is a problem where the demerged shares are distributed to beneficiaries of an accumulation and maintenance or discretionary trust. The trustees will have to pay tax at the rate applicable to trusts under ICTA 1988 s 687 but there is no credit to the tax pool arising from the demerger.

4.63 Although a demerger is normally treated as a reorganisation under TCGA 1992 ss 126–130, by TCGA 1992 s 192(2) the life tenant and the trustees are not the same person and therefore TCGA 1992 s 127 prevents the tax-free reorganisation rules applying. The life tenant therefore acquires the shares at market value for CGT purposes under TCGA 1992 s 17(1)(a).

4.64 In an indirect demerger, under ICTA 1988 s 213(3)(b) according to which shares in the new company are issued direct to the shareholders of the old companies, the receipt would normally be capital (*Sinclair v Lee* [1993] Ch 497). Where in an indirect demerger the shares are classified as capital, it is treated as a reconstruction for CGT purposes under TCGA 1992 ss 135 and 136, subject to TCGA 1992 ss 137 and 138. The reorganisation of share capital provisions in TCGA 1992 ss 126–130 apply, and under TCGA 1992 s 127 the original cost of the shares is apportioned to the holdings in the demerged companies in proportion to their market values. If, exceptionally, the shares are distributed to a life tenant of an interest in possession trust, he would have a nil base value of his shares as there has been no disposal of the shares on his acquisition.

Purchase of own shares

4.65 A purchase by a company of its own shares under CA 1985 ss 159–181 is capital for trust purposes, by analogy with a redirection of share capital under CA 1985 ss 135–141 (*Rae v Lazard Investments Co Ltd* [1963] 1 WLR 555). However, it is a distribution for tax purposes under ICTA 1988 s 209(2)(a) except for the amount paid on the shares, including any share premium [ICTA 1988 s 209(2)(b)], unless it qualifies for capital treatment under ICTA 1988 ss 219–229. As a distribution, any income element is dealt with under Schedule F. [ICTA 1988 s 20].

4.66 In order to qualify for capital treatment for tax purposes the company has to be a trading company or member of a trading group and the repurchase has to be for the benefit of the trade, not for a tax avoidance purpose or to discharge an IHT liability. [ICTA 1988 s 219(1)]. Capital treatment is not available to non-resident trustees. [ICTA 1988 s 220(1)]. There are a number of conditions which have to be met under ICTA 1988 ss 220–224 and clearance is available under section 225 of the 1988 Act. Revenue guidance is provided by SP 2/82 and *Tax Bulletin*, Issue 21, February 1996, p 280.

4.67 The share sale proceeds are chargeable gains of the vendor shareholders, except to the extent that they have been treated as an income distribution and therefore excluded under TCGA 1992 s 37(1). As the capital element is usually small, the original subscription price, compared with the proceeds, most of which is charged as income, often produces a loss for CGT purposes in these cases. It is frequently possible to have a share buy-back treated as an income distribution by deliberately breaching the conditions in ICTA 1988 ss 220–224, with little additional tax under Schedule F, followed later by a buy-back which qualifies for capital treatment giving rise to a capital gain covered by the capital loss on the earlier distribution. The introduction of taper relief and the reduction in the tax credit makes this less advantageous than it was, but it is still useful in suitable cases.

Reduction of share capital

4.68 For tax purposes a formal reduction of share capital under CA 1985 ss 135–141 is a part disposal of shares for the capital element under TCGA 1992 s 122 (1), ie the amount subscribed for the shares including any share premium, and the balance is an income distribution under ICTA 1988 s 209(2)(b) and is dealt with under the usual Schedule F rules in ICTA 1988 s 20.

4.69 Obviously, a profit on the disposal of investments accrues to capital. Where shares are purchased cum dividend, on receipt the dividend is carried to capital not paid as income (*Re Sir Robert Peel's Settled Estates* [1910] 1 Ch 389), but conversely there is no apportionment of income where shares are *sold* cum dividend (*Scholefield v Redfern* (1863) 2 Drew & Sm 173; *Re Henderson* [1940] 1 All ER 623). A STEP clause enables the trustees to take a broader view of their responsibilities in providing the maximum amount to the income beneficiaries while preserving the real value of capital for the remaindermen.

Payment of tax

4.70 The ability of the trustees to pay tax should extend to liabilities not enforceable against them. Foreign tax claims would not normally be enforceable in the UK following *Government of India v Taylor* [1955] 1 All ER 292 and *Brokaw and Shaheen v Seatrin UK Ltd and US Government* [1971] 2 All ER 98. Within the European Union collection of foreign tax claims may be made under the Mutual Assistance Recovery Directive (76/308/EEC) as amended by Council Directive 2001/44/EC and applied by FA 2002 s 134 and Sch 39. It might, however, be a problem for beneficiaries living in the overseas jurisdiction if the tax was not paid. There are also provisions under UK legislation, eg TCGA 1992 ss 77 and 86, where chargeable gains are assessed on the settlor who has a right of recovery under TCGA 1992 s 78 or Sch 5 para 6. If, for example, the trust has emigrated, there may be no legal requirement to reimburse the settlor but not to do so would be unreasonable, and the trustees could justify the payment provided that they had power to do so, even where it was not in practice enforceable against them.

4.71 There are similar provisions for income tax where the settlor is charged in cases where he retains an interest in the trust or payments are made to his minor children under ICTA 1988 s 660A or 660B. The right of recovery arises under ICTA 1988 s 660D.

Maintenance and advancement

4.72 With regard to the statutory powers of maintenance and advancement in TA 1925 ss 31 and 32, the deletions contained in most trust deeds refer to the proviso to section 31(1), which requires the trustees (before applying money for a minor beneficiary's maintenance, education or benefit) to have regard to the age of the infant and his requirements and generally to the circumstances of the case and in particular to whatever income, if any, is applicable for the same purposes; which potentially causes the trustees to have to make substantial enquiries generally regarded as inappropriate. The deletion in TA 1925 s 32(1)(a) is the limitation to one half of the beneficiary's presumptive or vested share in determining the maximum advancement or benefit which can be paid to him. Again, this is normally regarded as unduly restrictive and best deleted and left to the discretion of the trustees.

4.73 As explained at **4.37** *et seq* the conflict of interest provisions, which apply to trustees on the basis of case law, are extremely onerous and a limitation on these rules is often considered reasonable, provided that there is an independent trustee to make sure that any potential conflict is not abused.

Investment policy

4.74 Investment policy needs to be considered by the trustees in the light of the terms of the trust and their investment powers by statute and under the trust deed. Trustees must act fairly where there are different classes of beneficiaries, eg a life tenant interested in maximising his income and a remainderman interested in maximising the capital left for his benefit on the death of the life tenant (*Nestlé v National Westminster Bank plc* [1994] 1 All ER 118). There has been a gradual move away from the prescriptive investment powers originally contained in TA 1925 ss 1–11, which were relaxed by TIA 1961 and further relaxed by TA 2000 ss 3–10.

4.75 TA 2000 ss 1 and 2 and Sch 1 introduced a statutory duty of care on trustees when considering investments and the acquisition of land, as well as in other areas, although how in practise this duty of care differs from the previous obligation on trustees to act as prudent men of business remains to be seen. Trustees claiming special knowledge or professional trustees have a higher standard of care, but this has always been the case (*Bartlett v Barclays Bank Trust Co Ltd* [1980] Ch 515). The duty of care is expressed in terms of requiring a trustee to exercise such care and skill as is reasonable in the circumstances. [TA 2000 s 1(1)]. The trustees may have a duty to convert investments of a wasting, hazardous or reversionary nature into less hazardous investments (*Howe v Earl of Dartmouth* (1802) 7 Ves 137). This duty to convert does not apply in all cases, and specifically where there is an express provision in the trust deed that the rule in *Howe v Earl of Dartmouth* shall not apply, or where the property was expressly settled with the stated or implied intention that it be enjoyed *in specie* (*Re Van Straubenzee* [1901] 2 Ch 779; *Marshall v Bremner* (1854) 2 Sm & G 237).

4.76 TA 2000 s 3 gives trustees a general power of investment and provides standard investment criteria in TA 2000 s 4. These criteria basically require the trustees to review the investments in the light of their suitability to the trust, and diversification insofar as is appropriate to the circumstances of the trust. This requirement to have regard to standard investment criteria cannot be avoided by any provision in the trust instrument, but it is doubtful whether this does more than codify the previous law (*Nestlé v National Westminster Bank plc* [1994] 1 All ER 118). A trustee must normally obtain proper investment advice under TA 2000 s 5, but is subject to any restriction imposed by the trust deed and applies to existing trusts. [Sections 6 and 7]. The general powers of investment do not give the trustees power to invest in land and buildings, freehold or leasehold, which is given specifically by TA 2000 s 8 and applies to land acquired as an investment, for occupation by a beneficiary, or for any other reason, such as development. A power is given to acquire land throughout the UK and is not restricted to land in England and Wales. There is therefore no statutory default power to invest in land overseas, although investment in a land-owning company would be covered by TA 2000 s 3. The trust deed itself may allow investment in overseas real estate either expressly or by implication where, for example, the trustees may invest trust property in any manner as if they were beneficial owners, as in the *Society of Trust and Estate Practitioners standard provisions* 1st edition, para 3(1)(a).

Chapter 5

Residence and Domicile

5.1 Two cornerstones of UK taxation are residence and domicile, which may affect the UK tax liabilities of the settlor, the beneficiaries and the trustees. Residence is based on physical presence in a territory and there may be different rules for different persons for different tax purposes. Domicile is a concept of international private law which identifies the jurisdiction with which a person has the closest connection, and governs the law relating to marriage and divorce, the legitimacy of children and devolution of the estate on death. Domicile is also important for UK tax purposes and again there are different rules for different taxes. Nationality in the UK is not normally important for tax purposes, except under certain double taxation agreements. Questions relating to residence and domicile are normally dealt with by Revenue specialists at the Centre for Non-Residents (CNR), formerly the Financial Intermediaries and Claims Office (FICO). The CNR is at St John's House, Merton Road, Bootle, Merseyside L69 9BB, tel: 0151 472 6000, fax: 0151 472 6124 (www.inlandrevenue.gov.uk/cnr). The Inland Revenue practice in relation to residence and domicile is published in booklet IR20. This guidance is not statutory and the Revenue reserves the right not to apply the rules where it considers that they are being exploited for tax avoidance purposes. At the time of writing the law on residence and domicile for taxation purposes is under review by the Government (see **5.23**).

Individuals

Residence

5.2 There is no statutory definition of residence in the Taxes Acts and the Revenue practice (published in IR20) is largely based on case law. It is normally necessary to be physically present in the UK at some time in the tax year in order to be resident (IR20 1.2). However, in *Rogers v Inland Revenue* (1879) 1 TC 255 a mariner who had a home in the UK was held resident even though he was not present in the UK at any time during the fiscal year. At law, a person resident in the UK for any part of the year is resident for the entire year (*Neubergh v IRC* [1978] STC 181; *Mitchell v IRC* (1933) 18 TC 108; *Gubay v Kington* [1984] STC 99).

5.3 Although it is possible to be resident in the UK in a year in which there was no physical presence; where the taxpayer was actually living abroad (in California) during the entire fiscal year he was held not to be resident in the UK (*Reed v Clark* [1985] STC 323). The Revenue rule of thumb is that any person physically present in the UK for 183 days or more in the tax year is resident and there are no exceptions to this rule. However, in such circumstances the taxpayer could still be dual resident, if resident under the rules in another country, e g under US rules, a period of 183 days in the USA in a calendar year makes the person resident but the 183 days is calculated on the basis of 100 per cent of the days in the calendar year, a third of the days in the preceding calendar year and a sixth of the days in the year before that. Where there is residence in two countries the taxpayer is either dual resident or treated as resident in one country and not the other for the purposes of a double taxation treaty (see below). A person resident in the UK under the 183 day rule could therefore be treated as non-resident under a double taxation treaty.

5.4 In counting the 183 days, days of arrival and departure are normally ignored, except in the case of the concessionary split-year treatment under extra-statutory concession (ESC) A11 or D2 (IR20 1.2). A person is ordinarily resident where he or she normally lives. If this is outside the UK, the taxpayer may be UK resident in the tax year through spending more than 183 days in the UK during the fiscal year, but not ordinarily resident as not normally living in the UK.

5.5 A British subject who returned to the UK after living abroad for many years was held to be ordinarily resident on his return in *Elmhurst v IRC* (1937) 21 TC 381. Ordinarily resident means that a person must be habitually and normally resident in the UK apart from temporary or occasional absences of long or short duration (*Shah v Barnet London Borough Council* [1983] 1 All ER 226).

5.6 A woman who was outside the UK from July 1919 until summer 1921, apart from four months staying in a hotel in 1920, was held to have remained ordinarily resident in the UK throughout (*Reid v IRC* (1926) 10 TC 673). A British subject who had no fixed abode but lived in the UK in hotels for between four and five months each year, was held to be both resident and ordinarily resident in the UK (*Levene v IRC* (1928) 13 TC 486). A widow who spent varying periods in the UK, from 40 to 177 days in each fiscal year, had been accepted as neither resident nor ordinarily resident for 1924/25 but for 1926/27 she was held to be both resident and ordinarily resident (*Kinloch v IRC* (1929) 14 TC 736). A director of a UK company who lived with his family in the Republic of Ireland was held to be resident in the UK in years in which he visited for 101 and 94 days respectively, generally staying at a hotel (*Lysaght v IRC* (1928) 13 TC 511). In *Peel v IRC* (1927) 13 TC 443 an average of 139 days spent in the UK each year by a British subject made him ordinarily resident, and a foreign national at school in the UK was held to be ordinarily resident in *Miesegaes v IRC* (1957) 37 TC 493.

5.7 The case law on those held to be resident includes a foreigner living in a yacht anchored in the UK (*Bayard Brown v Burt* (1911) 5 TC 667) and a foreigner with a hunting box available for his use in the UK, who stayed less than six months in any one tax year (*Loewenstein v De Salis* (1926) 10 TC 424). Conversely, a British subject living in hotels in the UK and abroad was held not to be resident in the UK in *IRC v Zorab* (1926) 11 TC 289. A similar decision was reached in *IRC v Brown* (1926) 11 TC 292 where the taxpayer had spent only two months in the tax year in the UK. A British actress making a temporary visit to the UK was held not to be resident in *Withers v Wynyard* (1938) 21 TC 724 but an Irish peer serving in the British Army and who lived in the UK in the course of his military duties was held to be resident in *Lord Inchiquin v IRC* (1948) 31 TC 125.

5.8 ESC A11 applies where an individual comes to the UK to take up permanent residence, or to stay for at least two years, or ceases to reside in the UK if he has left for permanent residence abroad. Liability to UK tax, which is affected by residence, is computed by reference to the period of his residence here during the year, provided that he was, prior to his arrival or after his departure, not ordinarily resident in the UK, except where on intended permanent emigration he actually returns to the UK before the end of the tax year following the tax year of departure. Under ESC A11 the fiscal year is split into two parts, a period of residence for the part of the year spent in the UK and a period of non-residence up to the day before the day of arrival or from the day following the day of departure.

5.9 ESC A11 also applies where an individual goes abroad under a contract of employment, and both the absence from the UK and the employment extend over a period covering a complete tax year and interim visits do not exceed 183 days or more in any tax year, or an average 91 days or more in a tax year (the average is taken over the period of absence up to a maximum of four years). In these circumstances the split-year treatment may be applied. The limit on income chargeable on a non-resident individual under FA 1995 s 128 does not apply to split year periods. Leaving for permanent residence abroad implies a period of at least three years (IR20 1.6).

5.10 Short absences by somebody resident and ordinarily resident in the UK do not affect their resident status. This also applies to mobile workers in the UK who make frequent and regular trips abroad in the course of their employment or business (see *Tax Bulletin*, Issue 52, April 2001, pp 836 and 837). A simple count of days of absence, including travelling days, is insufficient in these circumstances.

5.11 In order to be regarded as non-resident through working abroad, a taxpayer has to leave the UK to work full time under a contract of employment. In looking at the average number of days spent in the UK because of exceptional circumstances are not counted. (IR20 2.2). In such circumstances the split year conditions in ESC A11 are also met and the taxpayer is treated as non-resident and not ordinarily resident from the day after leaving to the day before return. ICTA 1988 s 334 provides that a Commonwealth citizen or citizen of the Republic of Ireland, who has been ordinarily resident in the UK, continues to be taxed as resident and ordinarily resident in the UK if he has left the UK for the purpose only of occasional residence abroad. In this connection *Reed v Clark* [1985] STC 323 confirmed that an individual living and working abroad for a complete tax year was not, in such circumstances, absent for the purpose only of occasional residence abroad, and a similar decision was arrived at in *IRC v Combe* (1932) 17 TC 405 where a British subject was on a three-year apprenticeship with a US firm.

5.12 The meaning of full-time employment abroad is dependent on the circumstances and the nature of the employment (IR20 2.5). The Revenue normally regards an employment as being full time if it is the sole or main source of income. An accompanying spouse may, under ESC A78, be treated as not-resident and not ordinarily resident in the same way as a working spouse (IR20 2.6).

Leaving the UK permanently or indefinitely

5.13 An emigrant who continues to visit the UK for 91 days or more a year, on average, unless for exceptional circumstances, remains resident and ordinarily resident (IR20 2.7). A taxpayer intending to live abroad permanently, or for at least three years, will be treated as not resident from the day after the date of departure. If sufficient evidence of intention can be shown, non-resident treatment may be granted after the absence from the UK has covered at least a whole tax year, and the visits to the UK since leaving amount to fewer than 183 days in any tax year and average fewer than 91 days a year. Other evidence of going abroad for a settled purpose may be accepted and if non-resident status is not granted initially it may be reviewed after evidence becomes available, or the taxpayer has actually spent three years away from the UK (IR20 2.8, 2.9).

5.14 The annual average visit is calculated by reference to the total visits to the UK, in days, since departure, divided by the total period in days since departure and multiplied by 365. The average is calculated over a rolling period not exceeding four years (IR20 2.10). A taxpayer leaving the UK will normally complete Inland Revenue form P85 and one arriving in the UK, form P86.

5.15 Crown employees are normally subject to UK tax on their earnings, wherever they are stationed. There are special rules for EU employees, employees working in oil and gas exploration and extraction industries and merchant navy seafarers (IR20 2.14). A person coming to the UK is regarded as UK resident if he comes to live in the UK permanently, or for three years or more, and is regarded as resident and ordinarily resident from the date of arrival (IR20 3.1). Short-term visitors will be treated as resident for a tax year if present in the UK for 183 days or more in the tax year, or if there are regular visits to the UK which, after four tax years, average 91 days or more in a tax year, in which case residence commences from the beginning of the fifth tax year. The average ignores days spent in the UK for exceptional purposes. Residence arises from 6 April in the first year if there is a clear intention to spend more than 91 days a year in the UK, which is actually carried out. If a decision is made to commence regular visits to the UK of 91 days or more in a tax year, residence normally starts from 6 April in the year in which the decision is made (IR20 3.3). ICTA 1988 s 336 gives statutory authority to the exemption from taxation for a temporary visitor to the UK, who has not actually resided for a total period equal to six months in any year of assessment. Temporary purpose is considered without regard to any living accommodation available in the UK for the taxpayer's use. The section, conversely, gives authority for the taxation as a resident, of someone who has actually resided in the UK for six months in the year of assessment. In computing six calendar months, hours and minutes can be taken into account (*Wilkie v IRC* (1951) 32 TC 495). The current Revenue practice is that 183 days or more constitutes six months.

5.16 In *Cooper v Cadwalader* (1904) 5 TC 101 a taxpayer spending about two months a year in the UK, having rented a house and shooting rights in Scotland for a period of three years, was held to be resident in the UK. The Revenue appears to consider that *Cooper v Cadwalader* has been overridden by ICTA 1988 s 336(3) and ignores accommodation available in the UK for people spending on average fewer than 91 days a year in the UK, even when such visits continue year after year. It is not easy to reconcile this with the wording in ICTA 1988 s 336(3) but such treatment is unlikely to be challenged by a taxpayer.

5.17 The Revenue treatment of longer-term visitors is confined to those who come to the UK with the intention of remaining for at least two years, and who own or lease accommodation in the UK, or spend 183 days or more in the UK in the tax year (IR20 3.7). A visitor will also be treated as ordinarily resident in the UK from the date of arrival where they come with the intention of staying for at least three years. A person coming as a student is not ordinarily resident if staying for less than four years, where accommodation is not bought or acquired on a lease for three years or more, and on leaving he does not contemplate regular visits to the UK which average 91 days or more (IR20 3.8, 3.13). In other cases a taxpayer is only treated as ordinarily resident from the beginning of the tax year after the third anniversary of arrival, where a taxpayer did not originally intend to stay for at least three years, and did not buy accommodation or acquire a lease of three years or more. A decision to stay for at least three years after arrival results in ordinary residence from the beginning of the tax year in which the decision is made (IR20 3.9, 3.10). A person coming to, and remaining in, the UK, is treated as ordinarily resident from the day of the arrival, if they already own accommodation, buy accommodation in the tax year of arrival or acquire accommodation on a lease of three years or more during the tax year of arrival or from 6 April in the tax year in which accommodation becomes available when this occurs after the year of arrival (IR20 3.11). If the accommodation is disposed of and the UK is left within three years of arrival, non-ordinary resident status is available throughout (IR20 3.12).

5.18 People working abroad with a home in the UK were normally treated as resident except in a year where the taxpayer lived entirely abroad, as in

Turnbull v Foster (1904) 6 TC 206. Cases where this applied include *Re Young* (1875) 1 TC 57 and *Lloyd v Sulley* (1884) 2 TC 37. ICTA 1988 s 335 provided a statutory escape route in such circumstances where a person was working full time in a trade, profession, vocation, office or employment and no part of those duties was carried on in the UK. In such cases, a place of abode maintained in the UK for his use was ignored in determining his residence, as were incidental duties carried on in the UK. Incidental was held to be a qualitative (not a quantitative) test in *Robson v Dixon* (1972) 48 TC 527. Current Revenue policy seems to be to ignore property available in the UK in determining residence in all cases, not only those covered by ICTA 1988 ss 335(1) and 336(3). SP 2/91 relaxes the period where the stay in the UK exceeds the permitted 91-day average due to exceptional circumstances, and this relaxation is incorporated in IR20 3.4.

Dual residence

5.19 Tax laws around the world are not identical, or even in many cases broadly similar. For instance, the UK taxes on the basis of residence and domicile; the USA by reference to citizenship; others purely by reference to time spent in the country; while yet others have a test akin to consistent presence taking into account available accommodation, family and business interests. Some countries would treat people as resident if they consistently spend substantial periods of time in the country, so that the UK will tax people who spend 91 days or more a year on average in the UK, and the US system counts as resident a person who spends a consistent 123 days a year in the USA, so it is quite possible to be resident in more than one jurisdiction in the same tax year. There is often a mismatch in the tax year itself, the UK being unusual in having a fiscal year ending on 5 April; most other countries have the calendar year as the fiscal year; some have year ends of 31 March or some other date. Where a taxpayer is resident in the UK and another country, his tax liability will be determined either on the basis of the UK rules alone or under the provisions of a double taxation agreement. Most UK treaties follow the OECD model agreement, in general terms, and the 2000 version of the model agreement in Art 4 para 2 has what is usually called a tie-breaker clause. This states:

> '... where by reason of the provisions of paragraph 1 an individual is a resident of both contracting states, then his status shall be determined as follows:
>
> (a) he shall be deemed to be a resident only of the state in which he has a permanent home available to him, if he has a permanent home available to him in both states he shall be deemed to be a resident only of the state with which his personal and economic relations are closer (centre of vital interest).
>
> (b) if the state in which he has his centre of vital interests cannot be determined, or if he has no permanent home available to him in either state, he shall be deemed to be a resident only of the state in which he has an habitual abode.

(c) if he has an habitual abode in both states or in neither of them he shall be deemed to be a resident only of the state of which he is a national.

(d) if he is a national of both states or of neither of them the competent authorities of the contracting state shall settle the question by mutual agreement.'

In these definitions, permanent home is where the taxpayer would normally live, his centre of vital interests is where his business and social connections are most closely allied and a place of abode is somewhere which can be used as a residence.

Domicile

5.20 Domicile, for the purposes of this book, is the concept of English law used to determine the system of law with which a person is most closely connected in his private capacity and governs, for example, the legitimacy of children, marriage, divorce and the devolution of the estate on death by will or on intestacy. As such it is a concept of private international law and, unlike residence, a person can have only one domicile at any time, for any particular purpose. Domicile is a very important concept of UK taxation because a territorial system of taxation is applied to UK resident domiciled outside the United Kingdom of Great Britain and Northern Ireland, ie England and Wales, Scotland and Northern Ireland, each of which has its own system of law. (There is no separate system of law for Wales.) The UK does not include the other British isles, ie the Isle of Man or the Channel Islands, Jersey and the Bailiwick of Guernsey. Where the tax legislation refers to domicile in the UK, eg ICTA 1988 ss 65(4) and ITEPA 2003 s 22 or IHTA 1984 ss 18, 48 and 267, it is generally thought that this refers to domicile in any of the constituent territories of the UK and does not create a separate transnational domicile in the UK itself.

5.21 Domicile is not the same as nationality and a person can be domiciled outside the UK and still be a British citizen under the British Nationality Act 1981. British citizenship may be acquired by birth or adoption, descent, registration or naturalisation but is not normally of importance for UK tax purposes except in the case of the tie-breaker clause on residence in certain double taxation treaties. Other countries may not attach any importance to domicile, in the English law sense, for taxation treaties, but instead rely on either residence or citizenship or a combination of the two.

5.22 Domicile is linked to a system of law rather than a particular country so that a person is domiciled in, for example, Texas or California not the USA and New South Wales or Queensland not Australia; although there are exceptions in that, for example, divorce may be governed by federal law in some jurisdictions, such as Australia and Canada, not by state or provincial law. The cornerstone of domicile is the place where a person has their permanent home (*Winans v A-G* [1904] AC 287):

> 'A person may be said to have his home in a country if he resides in it without any intention of, at present removing from it permanently or for an indefinite period. But a person does not cease to have his home in a country merely because he is temporarily resident elsewhere, and a person who has formed the intention of leaving a country does not cease to have his home in it until he acts according to that intention …'
>
> *Dicey & Morris on the Conflict of Laws* (13th edition, Sweet & Maxwell, 2000), p 108.

5.23 The English law of domicile is a common law concept, modified in the case of married women and children by Part I of DMPA 1973. There have been proposals to reform the law of domicile following the English and Scottish Law Commissions' reports (Nos 168 and 107) in 1987. However, none of the proposed changes has yet been implemented, although the Chancellor of the Exchequer ordered a review of the residence and domicile laws in his 2002 Budget.

5.24 Just as a person cannot have more than one domicile for the same purpose at any one time, he cannot be without a domicile (*Udny v Udny* (1869) LR 1 Sc & Div 441 *et seq*; *Bell v Kennedy* (1868) LR 1 Sc & Div 307).

5.25 Once determined, a person's domicile remains until a new domicile is acquired. Therefore the burden of proving a change of domicile lies on those who assert it (*Wynans v A-G* [1904] AC 287; *Ramsey v Liverpool Royal Infirmary* [1930] AC 588; *Re Estate of Fuld (No 3)* [1968] P 675). It appears that the change of a domicile of origin must be proved beyond reasonable doubt while the change of a domicile of choice may be proved on the balance of probabilities (*Re Cartier* [1952] SASR 280 at 291). Domicile for English purposes is determined in accordance with English law, not that of the foreign country involved (*Collier v Rivaz* (1841) 2 Curt 855; *Re Annelsey* [1926] Ch 692).

Domicile of origin

5.26 A legitimate child whose father is alive at birth takes his father's domicile at the time of his birth (*Udny v Udny* (1869) LR 1 Sc & Div 441; *Forbes v Forbes* (1854) Kay 341). If the father has died at the date of birth, or if the child is illegitimate, he takes his mother's domicile of origin at the time of the birth (*Udny v Udny* (1869) LR 1 Sc & Div 441; *Urquhart v Butterfield* (1887) 37 Ch D 357. A foundling has his domicile of origin in the country in which he was found (*Re McKenzie* (1951) 51 SRNSW 293). The domicile of origin can only be changed by adoption in which case the adoptive father's domicile displaces the birth domicile, which otherwise remains throughout life, although it may be displaced by a domicile of choice. It will be appreciated that if a domicile of origin is not displaced, it may pass from generation to generation, such that the person in question need have no direct contact with the place of his domicile (*Peal v Peal* (1930) 46 TLR 645; *Re O'Keefe* [1940] Ch 124).

5.27 If a legitimate child is born after his parent's divorce it is unclear whether his domicile of origin is that of his father or mother. Where the parents are separated the child has, as his domicile of origin, that of his father, but immediately acquires his mother's domicile as a domicile of dependence. [DMPA 1973 s 4]. If the father has died at the time of the birth, it is assumed that the child acquires his mother's domicile as a domicile of origin at birth. The adopted child is statutorily deemed to be a legitimate child of the adopters under the Adoption Act 1976 s 39(1)(5). A domicile of origin is more difficult to displace than a domicile of choice (*Douglas v Douglas* (1871) LR 12 Eq 617; *Re James* (1908) 98 LT 438). A person who leaves the country of his domicile of origin with the intention not to return, nonetheless retains his domicile of origin until it is displaced by a domicile of choice.

Domicile of choice

5.28 A person who is legally capable of doing so, may acquire a domicile of choice in a territory by actually residing there and having the intention of staying permanently or indefinitely (*IRC v Duchess of Portland* [1982] Ch 314). There is no particular requirement as to length of residence in order to establish a domicile of choice, physical presence and intention being sufficient (*Bell v Kennedy* (1868) LR 1 Sc & Div 307; *Fasbender v A-G* [1922] 2 Ch 850; *Miller v Teale* (1954) 92 ChR 406). There is no requirement to own property in a territory in order to become domiciled there (*Levine v IRC* [1928] AC 217; *Stone v Stone* [1958] 1 WLR 1287; *IRC v Lysaght* [1928] AC 234). Physical presence as a visitor, rather than as an inhabitant, is insufficient to support a new domicile of choice (*IRC v Duchess of Portland* [1982] Ch 314).

5.29 The question of retaining property in the country of origin while maintaining a new domicile of choice is difficult, in that it may not be easy to show the requisite intention to reside permanently or indefinitely elsewhere while retaining a place of abode in the territory of the domicile of origin. If, however, the main residence is in the new territory and only a *pied à terre* is retained in the territory of the previous domicile, it may still be possible to prove the necessary intention to reside permanently or indefinitely in the new territory (*Udny v Udny* (1869) LR 1 Sc & Div 441). A domicile of choice cannot be acquired, by illegal residence (*Re Abdul Manan* [1971] 1 WLR 859; *R v Governor of Pentonville Prison, ex p Azam* [1974] AC 18.

5.30 An intention to stay in a country for a fixed period or for a definite purpose is insufficient to support a change in domicile (*Gulbenkian v Gulbenkian* [1937] 4 All ER 618). If a person leaves the country of the domicile of choice without having the intention to return, his domicile of origin revives unless or until a new domicile is acquired (*Udny v Udny* (1869) LR 1 Sc & Div 441; *Bradfield v Swanton* [1931] IR 446). Domicile of choice is not lost merely by giving up the residence without having the intention not to return (*Bradford v Young* (1885) 29 Ch D 617), nor is a domicile of choice lost merely by giving up the intention to remain permanently or indefinitely without actually leaving (*Zanelli v Zanelli* (1948) 64 TLR 556). A vague intention to move is ignored (*Re Estate of Fuld (No 3)* [1968] P 675; *IRC v Bullock* [1976] 1 WLR 1178; *Re Furse* [1980] 3 All ER 838). A domicile of choice is not acquired where there is a definite intention to leave the country at some time, even though the date of leaving may be indeterminate (*Jopp v Wood* (1865) 4 De GJ & Sm 616; *IRC v Bullock* [1976] 1 WLR 1178).

5.31 Where a person becomes a naturalised citizen, this may be an indication of an intention to reside permanently or indefinitely, but it is not decisive. It is therefore possible to acquire a domicile of choice without becoming a naturalised citizen (*Brunel v Brunel* (1871) LR 12 Eq 298; *Winans v A-G* [1904] AC 287). Conversely taking up citizenship by means of naturalisation does not necessarily result in the acquisition of a domicile of choice (*Wahl v A-G* (1932) 147 LT 382; *Re Estate of Fuld (No 3)* [1968] P 675; *Re Adams* [1967] IR 424). Naturalisation, however, cannot be ignored in determining domicile (*Bheekhun v Williams* [1999] 2 FLR 229, *Tolley's Tax Cases 2001* 46.39). However, in Mrs F and S2, personal representatives of *F v IRC* [2000] STC (SCD) 1 naturalisation, in the circumstances of the case, did not point to an intention to live in the UK permanently or indefinitely. It should be appreciated that statements made to the Home Office on naturalisation are available to the Revenue, sometimes appearing inconsistent with a claim for the retention of a foreign domicile. In this case it was decided that the statements to the Home Office were fuelled by a desperation to obtain a British passport and did not represent the deceased's true intentions.

5.32 In determining whether a person has acquired a domicile of choice in a new territory every aspect of his lifestyle is potentially relevant in determining his intention. Residence by itself is unlikely to be sufficient to confirm the intention of remaining permanently or indefinitely (*Ramsay v Liverpool Royal Infirmary* [1930] AC 588). Case law on what may or may not give rise to a domicile of choice is extensive but merely shows that each case has to be judged on its merits and no one factor is decisive. An individual who is alive and capable may give evidence as to his intention, but such statements are likely to be regarded by the court with a degree of scepticism. If, however, the declaration is entirely consistent with the facts it could even be decisive (*Wilson v Wilson* (1872) LR 2 P & D 435). The motive in moving may itself give an indication of the intention.

5.33 A person may be physically present in a country through circumstances beyond his control, eg, as a member of the armed forces or a diplomat, a prisoner or refugee, an employee seconded to the territory or an invalid or person liable to deportation. In each case physical presence in the territory is one part of the requirement for acquiring a domicile of choice, but the reasons for being there may make it unlikely that the intention has been formed to remain in the territory permanently or indefinitely, implying continued residence, once the requirement to be there has ceased.

5.34 A dependant person, normally a child, has the domicile of the person on whom he is dependent. Under DMPA 1973 s 3(1), the age at which a child ceased to have a domicile of dependence was reduced to 16 with effect from 1 January 1974. Before 1 January 1970 the age at which a child had a dependent domicile extended to 21 and was reduced to 18 by FLRA 1969 s 1(1). Prior to DMPA 1973, a married woman acquired her husband's domicile on marriage. From 1 January 1974 this domicile could be retained as a domicile of choice and could therefore be changed independently of that of her husband. Mentally disordered people may also have a domicile of dependence. If there is no person on whom a child or mentally disordered person is legally dependent, then their existing domicile remains until or unless they are able to exercise an independent domicile of choice. If a woman married after 1 January 1974, she may acquire her husband's domicile as a domicile of choice or she may not, depending on the circumstances. Obviously the marriage to the husband and where she is living is relevant to, but not determinative of, her domicile. Where spouses have different domiciles it can lead to both tax advantages and disadvantages. The main disadvantage is the IHT restriction in IHTA 1984 s 18(2), which restricts the exempt transfer from a UK domiciled to a non-UK domiciled spouse to £55,000 in addition to the nil rate band, if unused.

5.35 Legitimate unmarried children under 16 follow their father's domicile as a domicile of dependence (*Re Duleep Singh* (1890) 6 TLR 385; *Henderson v Henderson* [1967] P 77). Children legitimated by their parent's marriage would originally have the mother's domicile as an illegitimate child, but acquire the father's domicile on the parent's marriage.

5.36 Where the child is illegitimate or the father is dead, the domicile of dependence is usually the same as that as the mother; orphans appear to be fixed with a domicile of dependence at the time of the last to die of their parents until they reach the age of 16 or marry. An adopted child is treated in law as the legitimate child of his adoptive parents and therefore acquires his adoptive father's domicile of origin on adoption and follows his father's domicile as a domicile of dependence.

5.37 Where the parents split up and the child has his home with his mother, and no home with his father, the child's domicile is that of the mother. If the mother dies the child retains her domicile at the date of death. In other cases, e g where the child spends part of the time with each parent, he retains the father's domicile as a domicile of dependence. [DMPA 1973 s 4].

5.38 A mentally disordered person cannot acquire a domicile of choice while he remains mentally disordered, and retains the domicile which he had when he began to be treated. A mentally disordered, dependent child retains his domicile of dependence beyond the age of 16.

5.39 The difficulty of displacing a domicile of origin with a domicile of choice is emphasised by cases such as *Earl of Iveagh v Comrs* [1930] IR 386; *IRC v Cohen* (1937) 21 TC 301; (*Re Clore (No 2), Official Solicitor v Clore* [1984] STC 609; *Re Lawton* (1958) 37 ATC 216; *Plummer v IRC* [1987] STC

698; *IRC v Duchess of Portland* [1982] STC 149; *Buswell v IRC* [1974] STC 266; and *Anderson v IRC* [1998] STC (SCD) 43. Cases where an English domicile of choice was held to be acquired include *Steiner v IRC* [1973] STC 547 and *Re Furse, Furse v IRC* [1980] STC 596.

5.40 If a domicile of choice outside the UK is acquired and someone in such a situation then returns to the UK, the domicile of origin is likely to revive unless there is an intention not to return to the UK permanently or indefinitely. In *Fielden v IRC* (1965) 42 TC 501 the English domicile of origin revived, but only several years after the return to the UK.

5.41 A domicile of origin or choice acquired on marriage is not automatically displaced, with the domicile of origin reviving, on the death of the husband or the dissolution of the marriage (*Re Wallach, Weinschenck v Treasury Solicitor* [1950] 1 All ER 199; *Faye v IRC* (1961) 40 TC 103).

Deemed domicile

5.42 For IHT purposes only, there is a concept known as deemed domicile under which a person not domiciled in the UK at the relevant time, under the ordinary rules of domicile explained above, is nonetheless treated as domiciled in the UK, and not elsewhere, under IHTA 1984 s 267. This applies if he was domiciled in the UK within the three years immediately preceding the relevant time [IHTA 1984 s 267(1)(a)] or he was resident in the UK for no fewer than 17 of the 20 years of assessment ending with the year of assessment in which the relevant time falls. [IHTA 1984 s 267(1)(b)]. Note that in the first case the three-year period commences with the loss of a domicile within the UK under the ordinary rules, and ends with the third anniversary of that date, whereas the 17 out of 20-year period is by reference to years of assessment. Split-year treatment would have no application here, and a person resident at any time in a fiscal year would be deemed to be resident in that year, so the period of stay in the UK could be little more than 15 years for this provision to bite. Similarly, in order to escape this provision a period of non-residence of four complete fiscal years would suffice to start the clock again.

5.43 The deemed domicile provisions do not apply to certain UK securities held by non-domiciliaries under IHTA 1984 s 6(2) and (3) or such securities held by an interest in possession trust under IHTA 1984 s 48(4). Nor do they extend to the interpretation of certain old estates and gifts tax double taxation treaties under IHTA 1984 s 158(6). [IHTA 1984 s 267(2)]. There is a specific exemption for non-domiciliaries at 9 December 1974 who have not subsequently acquired a UK domicile. [IHTA 1984 s 267(3)]. The ordinary income tax rules of residence apply. [IHTA 1984 s 267(4)]. The deemed domicile rules may be overridden by certain of the UK's estate and gifts tax double taxation treaties.

Companies

Company residence

5.44 A company incorporated in the UK is regarded for tax purposes as resident there under FA 1988 s 66(1). This also applies to a company which is no longer carrying on any business or is being wound up outside the UK, if it was previously regarded as resident in the UK prior to cessation. [FA 1988 s 66(2)]. FA 1988 Sch 7 provides exceptions to this general rule, which came into force on 15 March 1988. [FA 1988 s 66(4)]. These apply where a company was carrying on business but was not resident in the UK, either with Treasury consent or under the general consents under ICTA 1988 s 765. If the company ceased to carry on business outside the UK, or ceased to be taxable in a territory outside the UK if it was resident abroad under a general consent, then it is treated as UK resident on the happening of either of those events. [FA 1988 Sch 7 para 1]. Similarly, where a company was carrying on a trade before the commencement date, and emigrated pursuant to a Treasury consent, it may be brought back into the UK tax net and treated as UK resident under FA 1988 s 66(1) on cessation. [FA 1988 Sch 7 para 2].

5.45 There was a general transitional provision for a company carrying on business before the commencement date, which was then not resident in the UK, under which FA 1988 s 66 did not apply until the end of the transitional period of five years from 15 March 1988, ie 15 March 1993. [FA 1988 Sch 7 paras 3 and 5]. A similar provision applied to companies ceasing to be resident with Treasury consent, but not within FA 1988 Sch 7 para 2. [FA 1988 Sch 7 para 5].

5.46 However, the rule was again modified under FA 1994 s 249(3) under which a UK incorporated company, which would not otherwise be regarded as resident in the UK for tax purposes, is treated as resident in another territory with which the UK has a double taxation agreement, where there is a tie-breaker clause giving priority to the company's central management and control or place of effective management in the other territory. [FA 1994 s 249(1)]. In determining whether a company falls within these provisions and, although incorporated in the UK, is treated as resident outside the UK, it is assumed that the relevant claim for relief is made under the double taxation treaty and that such claim would give precedence to the overseas country. [FA 1994 s 249(2)]. These provisions override FA 1988 s 66 with effect from 30 November 1993. [FA 1994 s 249(3)–(5)]. FA 1994 s 250 ensures that where a company becomes non-resident under FA 1994 s 249, the provisions for securing payment of outstanding tax, or for a company leaving a group, will not be triggered by reason of the fact that it ceases to be UK resident under FA 1994 s 249. Companies regarded as non-resident under section 249 are known as treaty non-resident.

5.47 The Revenue practice on company residence is given in SP 1/90, which provides as follows:

'Company residence

1 Residence has always been a material factor, for companies as well as individuals, in determining tax liability. But statute law has never laid down comprehensive rules for determining where a company is resident, and, until 1988, the question was left solely to the courts to decide. FA 1988 s 66 introduced the rule that a company incorporated in the UK is resident here for the purposes of the Taxes Acts. Case law still applies in determining the residence of companies excepted from the incorporation rule or which are not incorporated in the UK.

2 The incorporation rule applies to companies incorporated in the UK subject to the exceptions in FA 1988 Sch 7 for some companies incorporated before 15 March 1988. Paragraphs 3 to 8 below explain how the Revenue interpret various terms used in the legislation.

Carrying on business

3 The exceptions from the incorporation test in Sch 7 depend in part on the company carrying on business at a specified time or during a relevant period. The question whether a company carries on business is one of fact to be decided according to the particular circumstances of the company. Detailed guidance is not practicable but the Revenue take the view that "business" has a wider meaning than "trade"; it can include transactions, such as the purchase of stock, carried out for the purposes of a trade about to be commenced and the holding of investments including shares in a subsidiary company. Such a holding could consist of a single investment from which no income was derived.

4 A company such as a shelf company whose transactions have been limited to those formalities necessary to keep the company on the register of companies will not be regarded as carrying on business.

5 For the purposes of the case law test the residence of a company is determined by the place where its real business is carried on. A company which can demonstrate that in these terms it is or was resident outside the UK will have carried on business for the purposes of Sch 7.

"Taxable in a territory outside the UK"

6 A further condition for some companies for exception from the incorporation test is provided by Sch 7 paras 1(1)(c), 5(1). The company has to be taxable in a territory outside the UK. "Taxable" means that the company is liable to tax on income by reason of domicile, residence or place of management. This is similar to the approach adopted in the residence provisions of many double-taxation agreements. Territories which impose tax on companies by reference to incorporation or registration or similar criteria are covered by the term "domicile". Territories which impose tax by

reference to criteria such as "effective management", "central administration", "head office" or "principal place of business" are covered by the term "place of management".

7 A company has to be liable to tax on income so that a company which is, for example, liable only to a flat rate fee or lump sum duty does not fulfil the test. On the other hand a company is regarded as liable to tax in a particular territory if it is within the charge there even though it may pay no tax because, for example, it makes losses or claims double taxation relief.

"Treasury Consent"

8 Before 15 March 1988 it was unlawful for a company to cease to be resident in the UK without the consent of the Treasury. Companies which have ceased to be resident in pursuance of a Treasury consent, as defined in Sch 7 para 5(1), are excepted from the incorporation rule subject to certain conditions. A few companies ceased to be resident without Treasury consent but were informed subsequently by letter that the Treasury would take no action against them under the relevant legislation. Such a letter is not a retrospective grant of consent and the companies concerned cannot benefit from the exceptions which depend on Treasury consent.

9 This test of company residence is that enunciated by Lord Loreburn in *De Beers Consolidated Mines v Howe* ((1905) 5 TC 198) at the beginning of this century—"A company resides, for the purposes of income tax, where its real business is carried on … I regard that as the true rule; and the real business is carried on where the central management and control actually abides."

10 The "central management and control" test, as set out in *De Beers*, has been endorsed by a series of subsequent decisions. In particular, it was described by Lord Radcliffe in the 1959 case of *Bullock v Unit Construction Co* (1959) 38 TC 712 at 738 as being—"as precise and unequivocal as a positive statutory injunction … I do not know of any other test which has either been substituted for that of central management and control, or has been defined with sufficient precision to be regarded as an acceptable alternative to it. To me … it seems impossible to read Lord Loreburn's words without seeing that he regarded the formula he was propounding as constituting the test of residence."

Nothing which has happened since has in any way altered this basic principle for a company, the residence of which is not governed by the incorporation rule; under current UK case law such a company is regarded as resident for tax purposes where central management and control is to be found.

Place of "central management and control"

11 In determining whether or not an individual company outside the scope of the incorporation test is resident in the UK, it thus becomes necessary to locate its place of "central management and control". The case law concept of central management and control is, in broad terms, directed at the highest level of control of the business of a company. It is to be distinguished from the place where the main operations of a business are to be found, though those two places may often coincide. Moreover, the exercise of control does not necessarily demand any minimum standard of active involvement: it may, in appropriate circumstances, be exercised tacitly through passive oversight.

12 Successive decided cases have emphasised that the place of central management and control is wholly a question of fact. For example, Lord Radcliff in *Unit Construction* said that "the question where control and management abide must be treated as one of fact or 'actuality'" (1959) 38 TC 712 at 741. It follows that factors which together are decisive in one instance may individually carry little weight in another. Nevertheless the decided cases do give some pointers. In particular a series of decisions has attached importance to the place where the company's board of directors meet. There are very may cases in which the board meets in the same country as that in which the business operations take place, and central management and control is clearly located in that one place. In other cases central management and control may be exercised by directors in one country though the actual business operations may, perhaps under the immediate management of local directors, take place elsewhere.

13 But the location of board meetings, although important in the normal case, is not necessarily conclusive. Lord Radcliffe in *Unit Construction* pointed out (1959) 38 TC 712 at 738 that the site of the meetings of the directors' board had not been chosen as "the test" of company residence. In some cases, for example, central management and control is exercised by a single individual. This may happen when a chairman or managing director exercises powers formally conferred by the company's Articles and the other board members are little more than cyphers, or by reason of a dominant shareholding or for some other reason. In those cases the residence of the company is where the controlling individual exercises his powers.

14 In general the place of directors' meetings is significant only insofar as those meetings constitute the medium through which central management and control is exercised. If, for example, the directors of a company were engaged together actively in the UK in the complete running of a business which was wholly in the UK, the company would not be regarded as resident outside the UK merely because the directors held formal meetings outside the UK. While it is possible to identify extreme situations in which central management and control plainly is, or is not, exercised by directors in formal meetings, the conclusion in any case is wholly one of fact depending on the relative weight to be given to various factors. Any attempt to lay down rigid guidelines would only be misleading.

15 Generally, however, where doubts arise about a particular company's residence status, the Revenue adopt the following approach—

(i) they first try to ascertain whether the directors of the company in fact exercised central management and control;

(ii) if so, they seek to determine where the directors exercise this central management and control (which is not necessarily where they meet);

(iii) in cases where the directors apparently do not exercise central management and control of the company, the Revenue then look to establish where and by whom it is exercised.

Parent/subsidiary relationship

16 It is particularly difficult to apply the "central management and control" test in the situation where a subsidiary company and its parent operate in different territories. In this situation, the parent will normally influence, to a greater or lesser extent, the actions of the subsidiary. Where that influence is exerted by the parent exercising the powers which a sole or majority shareholder has in general meetings of the subsidiary, for example to appoint and dismiss members of the board of the subsidiary and to initiate or approve alterations to its financial structure, the Revenue would not seek to argue that central management and control of the subsidiary is located where the parent company is resident. However, in cases where the parent usurps the functions of the board of the subsidiary (such as *Unit Construction* itself) or where that board merely rubber stamps the parent company's decisions without giving them any independent consideration of its own, the Revenue draw the conclusion that the subsidiary has the same residence for tax purposes as its parent.

17 The Revenue recognise that there may be many cases where a company is a member of a group having its ultimate holding company in another country which will not fall readily into either of the categories referred to above. In considering whether the board of such a subsidiary company exercises central management and control of the subsidiary's business, they have regard to the degree of autonomy which those directors have in conducting the company's business. Matters (among others) that may be taken into account are the extent to which the directors of the subsidiary take decisions on their own authority as to investment, production, marketing and procurement without reference to the parent.

Conclusion

18 In outlining factors relevant to the application of the case law test, this statement assumes that they exist for genuine commercial reasons. Where, however, as may happen, it appears that a major objective underlying the existence of certain factors is the obtaining of tax benefits from residence or non-residence, the Revenue examine the facts particularly closely in order to see whether there has been an attempt to create the appearance of central management and control in a particular place without the reality.

19 The case law test examined in this Statement is not always easy to apply. The courts have recognised that there may be difficulties where it is not possible to identify any one country as the seat of central management and control. The principles to apply in those circumstances have not been fully developed in case law. In addition, the last relevant case was decided almost 30 years ago, and there have been many developments in communications since then, which in particular may enable a company to be controlled from a place far distant from where the day-to-day management is carried on. As the Statement makes clear, while the general principle has been laid down by the courts, its application must depend on the precise facts.

20 In general our double taxation agreements do not affect the UK residence of a company as established for UK tax purposes. But where the partner country adopts a different definition of residence, it may happen that a UK resident company is treated, under the partner country's domestic laws, as also resident there. In these cases, the agreement normally specifies what the tax consequences of this "double" residence shall be.

21 Under the double taxation agreement with the United States, for example, the UK residence of a company for UK tax purposes is unaffected. But where that company is also a US corporation it is excluded from some of the reliefs conferred by the agreement. On the other hand, under a double taxation agreement which follows the 1977 OECD Model Taxation Convention, a company classed as resident by both the UK and the partner country is, for the purposes of the agreement, treated as resident where its "place of effective management" is situated.

22 The commentary in Art 4 para 3 of the OECD Model records the UK view that in agreements (such as those with some Commonwealth countries) which treat a company as resident in a state in which "its business is managed and controlled", this expression means "the effective management of the enterprise". More detailed consideration of the question in the light of the approach of Continental legal systems and of Community law to the question of company residence has led the Revenue to revise this view. It is now considered that effective management may, in some cases, be found at a place different from the place of central management and control. This could happen, for example, where a company is run by executives based abroad, but the final directing power rests with non-executive directors who meet in the UK. In such circumstances the company's place of effective management might well be abroad but, depending on the precise powers of the non-executive directors, it might be centrally managed and controlled (and therefore resident) in the UK.

23 The incorporation rule in FA 1988 s 66(1) determines a residence which supersedes a different place "given by any rule of law". This incorporation rule determines residence under UK domestic law and is subject to the provisions of any applicable double taxation agreement. It does not override the provisions of a double taxation agreement which may make a UK incorporated company a resident of an overseas territory for the purposes of the agreement (see paras 20 and 21 above).'

5.48 The central management and control test is also applied in cases such as *Calcutta Jute Mills Co Ltd v Nicholson* (1876) 1 TC 83; *Cesena Sulphur Co Ltd v Nicholson* (1876) 1 TC 83; *Imperial Continental Gas Association v Nicholson* (1877) 1 TC 138; *New Zealand Shipping Co Ltd v Stephens* (1907) 5 TC 553 and *New Zealand Shipping Co Ltd v Thew* (1922) 8 TC 208; and *Untelrab Ltd v McGregor* (and related appeals) [1996] STC (SCD 1). This last case is interesting in that, what were previously non-UK incorporated and resident companies, were brought into the UK tax net by the appointment of UK directors and the resolution to hold future board meetings in the UK.

5.49 The place where shareholders meetings are held is not necessarily the country of residence (*A-G v Alexander* (1874) LR 10 Exch 20. UK companies with overseas boards for specific purposes were held to be UK resident in *American Thread Co v Joyce* (1913) 6 TC 163 and in *Egyptian Hotels Ltd v Mitchell* (1915) 6 TC 542, although the overseas activities controlled by the foreign board in that case were held to be a foreign possession within Schedule D Case V. It all depends on the relevance of the activities carried on by the directors in the UK or abroad *Aramyo Frincke Mines Ltd v Eccott* (1925) 9 TC 445; *John Hood & Co Ltd v Magee* (1918) 7 TC 327 and *Todd v Egyptian Delta Land and Investment Co Ltd* (1928) 14 TC 119). In the latter case, the company's only association with the UK was the appointment of a company secretary to comply with the requirements of the Companies Acts in the UK, and it was held to be non-UK resident. Companies can, under the central management and control test, be resident in more than one country (*Swedish Central Rly Co Ltd v Thompson* (1925) 9 TC 342; *Union Corpn Ltd v IRC* (1953) 34 TC 207). Most commonly, however, a company is dual resident by reason of being incorporated in a country which, as the UK now does, deems the place of incorporation to be determinative as to residence but is actually managed and controlled from another territory which, under the local rules or a double taxation treaty, treats the company as resident in that other territory. Dual residence can give opportunities for claiming deductions in both territories; conversely some double taxation treaties do not apply to dual resident companies.

5.50 A company resident in the UK is in practice regarded as both resident and ordinarily resident (CT 3365). The only way in which a UK incorporated company can now become non-resident is under FA 1994 s 249. CT 3373 includes the flowchart below

Flowchart for residence of a UK incorporated company with central management and control abroad

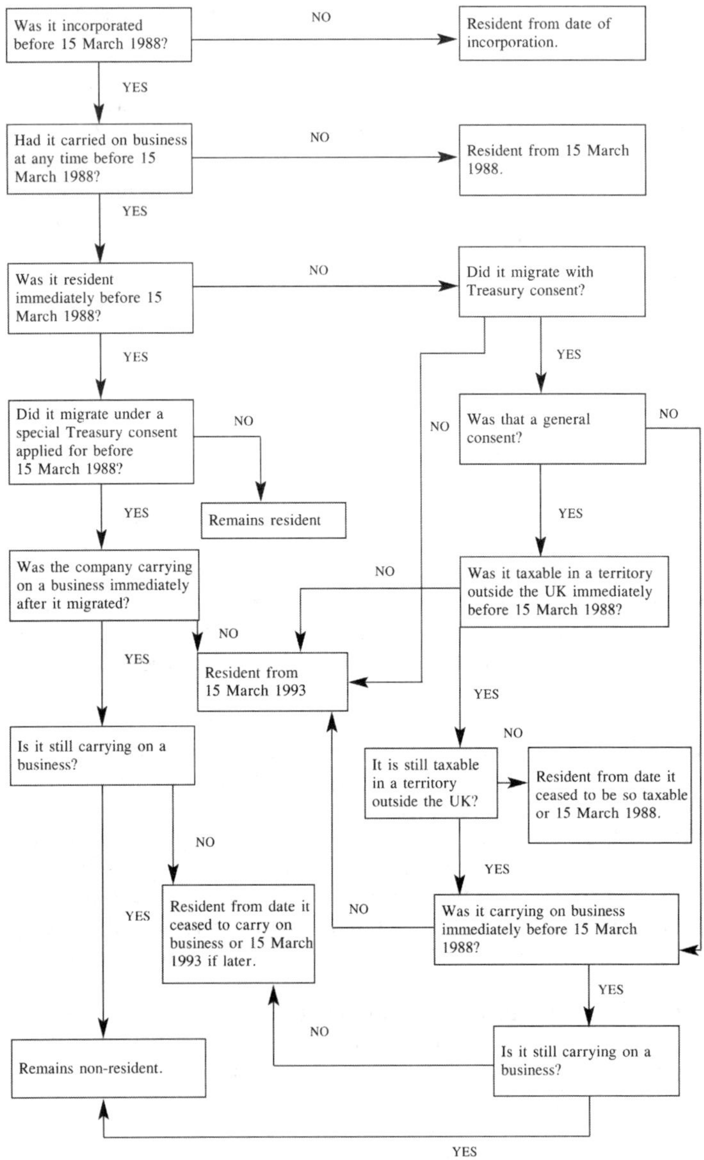

5.51 In the view of the Revenue, a shelf company formed by a company registration agent or professional firm and registered at their address has not yet established central management and control of their business anywhere, and has no residence other than under the incorporation rules, which would make a UK incorporated company resident in the UK (CT 3378). 'Nowhere companies' are those incorporated under a regime that recognises residence by reference to central management and control or some similar test, and which on this test are not resident in any particular country. UK incorporated nowhere companies have not been possible since 15 March 1993, under the incorporation rule, except for companies which became non-resident with Treasury consent under ICTA 1988 s 765 (CT 3382).

5.52 Many double taxation treaties to which treaty non-residence may apply under FA 1994 s 249, refer to place of effective management rather than central management and control. *Tax Bulletin*, Issue 14, 14 December 1994 stated:

> 'The term "place of effective management" has not been considered by UK courts. The commentary to the OECD model tax convention explains that it is the place where the company is actually managed. In practice, effective management is normally found in the same place as central management and control, but that is not always the case. In considering the place where the company is effectively managed, it is necessary to have regard to all the relevant facts including the organisation of the company and the nature of its business and to decide where it is, in substance, actually managed. In particular where the central management and control of a company was transferred from or to the UK, for instance by changing the place where decisions of the Board were made, it would not necessarily follow that the place of effective management would also be transferred, for instance if the place from which the company was actually managed remained the same.'
>
> (CT 3397.)

5.53 There is nothing to stop a company incorporated outside the UK becoming resident in the UK under the central management and control rule, subject to any double taxation treaty provisions (CT 3430).

5.54 There are still provisions which inhibit the issue of shares by non-resident subsidiaries of UK resident companies under ICTA 1988 s 765, except within the EU under ICTA 1988 s 765A; these are subject to criminal sanctions under ICTA 1988 s 766. There are also tax charges that may arise on a company ceasing to be UK resident, as a capital gains exit charge is imposed by TCGA 1992 s 185, and there may be charges arising under ICTA 1988 s 100 or s 337, and arrangements have to be made for paying any tax that may be due under FA 1988 ss 130–132. These provisions are, however, outside the scope of this book.

5.55 There are also restrictions on dual resident companies as regards setting off losses by way of group relief under ICTA 1988 s 404 and Sch 17, and carrying forward losses under ICTA 1988 s 343(2). Group chargeable gains may be chargeable under TCGA 1992 s 171(2) or s 175(2) and there may be capital allowance charges, e g under the Capital Allowances Act 2001 s 61(2). These and other related provisions are outside the scope of this book.

Impact of company residence on trusts

5.56 The main importance of company residence for the purposes of trusts is two-fold. First, where the company is a trustee it is obviously relevant for the purposes of determining the residence of the trust; second, many trusts hold investments through underlying investment companies, and the tax liability of the trustees, the settlor and the beneficiaries can depend on the residence of such companies.

5.57 In many cases the company owning such investments is fairly passive and it becomes extremely important to see whether the board has real control over the company, or is made up of what the Revenue calls 'stooge directors' recruited simply to give the appearance of control (CT 3389).

5.58 Stooge or nominee directors can give rise to serious trouble and there have been a number of recent criminal cases where taxpayers and their professional advisers, resident both in the UK and abroad, have been successfully prosecuted by the Inland Revenue under the common law offence of cheating the Public Revenue which was specifically preserved by the Theft Act 1968 s 32. The offence of cheating the Public Revenue can be committed by an omission to act as well as a positive act of deception (*R v Redford* [1988] STC 845). In *R v Charlton* [1996] STC 1418 the professional advisers were charged and convicted and were duly imprisoned. The scheme depended on an independent Jersey resident company buying tyres and selling them at an uplifted price to the UK dealer. The success of the scheme depended on the Jersey company being resident in Jersey for tax purposes. However, the control of the Jersey companies had been retained by the potential beneficiaries, the directors of the UK companies. The companies that were supposed to be Jersey resident were therefore actually resident in the UK and had not complied with their responsibilities under the Corporation Tax Acts, as defined by ICTA 1988 s 831(1)(a). In the circumstances this amounted to cheating the Public Revenue.

5.59 More recently, in *R v Dimsey* [2001] STC 1520 and *R v Allen* [2001] STC 1537, The Jersey-based accountant and the UK resident taxpayer were convicted of cheating the Public Revenue. The facts were not dissimilar to those in *R v Charlton* and the question of whether or not the Jersey companies were resident in the UK was considered by the Court of Appeal (in *R v Dimsey; R v Allen* [1999] STC 846) where Laws LJ stated at 861:

> '… the factual issues in the case centred on the question of whether it was Dimsey who managed and controlled the companies with Chipping merely acting as a consultant who undertook work in England on behalf of the company. The Jury were presented with a simple choice, there was no

subtle distinction between the functions of Dimsey and the functions of Chipping. So long as the prosecution could satisfy the Jury so that it was sure that Chipping was not a consultant but in fact not only undertook the day to day running of the business but made all the decisions, while Dimsey carried out the functions of the administration in Jersey, no sophisticated or difficult questions of central management and control arise.'

On this basis the jury's view that the Jersey companies were managed and controlled in the UK and were therefore liable to corporation tax secured the conviction on the grounds of conspiracy to cheat the Public Revenue.

5.59A In the House of Lords in *R v Allen* [2001] UKHL 45, [2001] STC 1537, the Hansard procedure under which the Revenue agree not to prosecute if the taxpayer makes a full confession was considered at 1556. To the extent that there was an inducement contained in the Hansard statement the inducement was to give true and accurate information to the Revenue but the accused in both cases did not respond to that inducement and instead of giving true and accurate information gave false information. Therefore, in the authors' opinion, the appellant's argument in this case that he was induced by hope of non-institution of criminal proceedings held out by the Revenue to provide the schedule and that its provisions were therefore involuntary is invalid . However in *R v Gill* [2003] EWCA Crim 2256, [2003] STC 1229 it was held by the Court of Appeal that a Hansard interview was governed by the Police and Criminal Evidence Act 1984 s 69, and should have been given under caution and recorded. The Court in this case held that this procedural breach had not had any adverse effect on the fairness of the proceedings. However it caused the Inland Revenue to suspend Hansard interviews for a time while new procedures were being worked out. The result of this review appears to be that a caution will be given and interviews tape-recorded in future. The Hansard procedure was explained in its latest guise in Tax Bulletin Issue 62, December 2002, pages 979–981 (Appendix 3).

5.60 In the case of *R (on the application of IRC) v Crown Court at Kingston* [2001] STC 1615 Stanley Burton J stated at 1622:

'Before coming to the documents some general comments are called for. The first relates to the use of so called "nominee" directors, usually in offshore jurisdictions [the expression nominee director is to be avoided since it confuses directors who are nominated by shareholders and who properly carry out their responsibility as directors and those who are appointed by shareholders and only do as they are instructed by the person who appointed them]. It is a feature of modern commercial life that many companies have their place of residence in offshore jurisdictions purely in order to avoid tax which would be payable if the company were located in the UK. Corporate residence depends on the location of the central management and control of the company. Inevitably, persons who live onshore wish to own companies that reside offshore. For this purpose they may arrange for the appointment of directors of the company who themselves reside in the offshore jurisdiction in question. Notwithstanding the ultimate foreign ownership of the shares of the company, it will be resident for tax purposes in the offshore jurisdiction in question if the appointed directors generally determine its affairs in that jurisdiction. If however they simply obey the instructions of the ultimate owner of the company's shares who remains in another jurisdiction the central management and control and therefore the residence of the company for the purposes of its tax liabilities will be the location of the ultimate owner of its shares. The difficulty here is to distinguish between the situation in which the directors act as mere ciphers simply doing as they are told by the ultimate owner of the company and the situation in which the directors have explained to them by the ultimate owner of the company's shares that certain transactions are in the interests of the company and decide on the basis of the information given to them that the company should enter into them. In the latter situation the company can genuinely claim to be resident offshore; in the former situation its offshore residence is not genuine but a false sham. The line between them is a very nice one as the Revenue no doubt appreciate and as do those involved in the minimising of tax by locating companies in offshore jurisdictions including the professional directors of offshore companies. That line features large in the case against Mr John. It may be impossible for someone who is not present at the board meetings of a company and who is not told how the Board in fact takes its decisions to know on which side of the line the company operates. It is not alleged that Mr John attended board meetings of the target companies in Guernsey or that he was informed by their directors how they took their decisions.

It is also necessary to comment on the use of pre-prepared minutes of Board meetings. Minutes of both Board and General meetings are often drafted in advance of the meetings to which they relate. There is nothing improper in the use of such drafts provided the meeting does deal with the business before it in the manner indicated in the draft and that in the case of board meetings the directors present do have the discussion and make the decisions indicated by the drafts. It is one thing for directors to take into account the wishes of the ultimate shareholder of the company or the advice of its advisers as indicated by a draft resolution; it is another for them to act without regard to the company's interests or in their own judgement but solely because they are instructed to do so by their ultimate shareholder.'

5.61 A much more sophisticated structure was considered in *R v Hunt* [1994] STC 819 where again the charge of conspiracy to cheat the Public Revenue was upheld on the basis that this time the offshore companies were shams purporting to carry out numerous functions which, in fact, were carried out by other entities and that the documentation included false invoices and manufactured correspondence. While it appeared probable that the residence of the offshore companies was equally in doubt it was not a point that featured in the case.

Company domicile

5.62 The domicile of a company is not normally relevant for tax purposes, but is the country of incorporation (*Gasque v IRC* (1940) 23 TC 210).

Partnerships

5.63 A general partnership in England and Wales governed by PA 1890 is not a separate legal entity, although it is in Scotland. This also applies to a limited partnership under the Limited Partnerships Act 1907. A limited liability partnership under the Limited Liability Partnerships Act 2000 is actually a corporate body but, like all partnerships in the UK, is fiscally transparent. This means that each partner is liable for taxation on his own share of profits, the self-assessment being at partner level not at the level of the partnership. It is quite common for trustees to be partners in a partnership, in which case the trustees would be taxed on their share of the partnership profits.

5.64 Residence is therefore normally attached to the partners personally rather than to the partnership; the exception being a partnership controlled abroad under ICTA 1988 s 112. Under section 112(1) a non-resident partner is taxable in the UK on partnership profits made in the UK, so that if the partnership is trading worldwide, the non-UK profits are not subject to UK tax in the hands of a non-resident partner.

5.65 Where a trade, profession or business is carried on in partnership wholly or partly outside the UK, and the control and management of the trade, profession or business is situated outside the UK, then any UK resident non-UK domiciled partners are taxed on their share of the partnership profits under Schedule D Case V as if it were a possession outside the UK. [ICTA 1988 s 112(1A)]. Where a partner changes his residence he is treated as if he had ceased to be and then immediately again became a partner. [Section 112(1B)].

Trusts

5.66 The residence of a trust would normally follow that of the residence of the trustees, but there are specific rules for income tax and CGT purposes.

Income tax residence

5.67 The residence rules for income tax purposes are set out in FA 1989 s 110 . If all the trustees are resident in one jurisdiction that is the residence of the trust. However, where at least one of the trustees is resident in the UK and one of them is non-UK resident, then the non-resident trustee is deemed to be resident in the UK, and therefore the whole trust is resident in the UK, if the settlor is resident in the UK, ordinarily resident in the UK, or domiciled in the

UK. If the settlor is neither resident, ordinarily resident nor domiciled in the UK, the UK resident trustee is treated as non-resident in the UK, and therefore the trust is resident outside the UK.

5.68 In the case of a will trust, the relevant time for considering the residence and domicile status of the settlor is the time of his death, and in other cases it is where the settlor was resident and domiciled at any time where he provided funds, directly or indirectly, to the settlement. [FA 1989 s 110(3)]. 'Settlor' is defined as including any person who has provided, or undertaken to provide, funds directly or indirectly for the purposes of the settlement. [FA 1989 s 110(4). For most purposes these income tax rules applied from 1989/90. [FA 1989 s 110(6)–(9)].

5.69 Personal representatives of a deceased person are treated on a broadly similar basis to trustees so that where the person died resident in the UK, ordinarily resident in the UK, or domiciled in the UK, a foreign personal representative is treated as UK resident. If the deceased was at the time of his death neither resident, ordinarily resident nor domiciled in the UK, then any UK resident personal representative would be regarded as non-UK resident. [FA 1989 s 111(1) and (2)]. Personal representative is defined by section 111(3) and the starting date was normally 1989/90. [FA 1989 s 111(5)–(8)].

Capital gains tax residence

5.70 For CGT purposes the residence of a trustee is governed by TCGA 1992 s 69. Under TCGA 1992 s 69(1) trustees are treated as a single and continuing body of persons which is treated as being resident and ordinarily resident in the UK, unless the general administration of the trusts is ordinarily carried on outside the UK and the trustees, or a majority of them, are not resident or not ordinarily resident in the UK. A professional trustee carrying on a business which consists of or includes the management of trusts, and acting as trustee in the course of that business, is treated as not resident in the UK provided that the settled property derives from a person who is neither domiciled, resident nor ordinarily resident in the UK at the time of the transfer into trust or in the case of a will trust or trust arising on intestacy, at the date of the settlor's death. [TCGA 1992 s 69(2)]. The claim that the general administration of a settlement was carried out in the Republic of Ireland, for the purposes of chargeable gains under TCGA 1992 s 69(1) failed in *Wensleydale's Settlement Trustees v IRC* [1996] STC (SCD) 241. The interpretation of a single and continuing body of persons in TCGA 1992 s 69(3) was considered in *Roome v Edwards* [1981] STC 96 and *Bond v Pickford* [1983] STC 517 and SP 7/84. In the case of a strict settlement under SLA 1925, the tenant for life and the capital money trustees are treated as a single body of trustees. [TCGA 1992 s 69(3)].

5.71 Where the trustees have not paid CGT within six months of the due date, and transfer the asset to a beneficiary absolutely entitled to it, the

Revenue may at any time within two years from the time when the tax became payable, assess and charge the beneficiary in the name of the trustees and collect from him the CGT due in respect of the gain attributable to the sale proceeds passed to him. [TCGA 1992 s 69(4)].

5.72 It will be appreciated that it is possible, e g by having foreign trustees, a single UK resident trustee and a UK resident or domiciled settlor, to have a trust resident in the UK for income tax purposes under FA 1989 s 110 but, because the majority of the trustees are non-UK resident and the general administration of the trust is carried on abroad, the trust could be non-resident for capital gains purposes under TCGA 1992 s 69(1). Such trusts are often known as 'home and away' trusts and can be useful, for example, to avoid the income tax attribution rules for non-resident trusts in ICTA 1988 ss 739 *et seq* by having the trust UK resident for income tax purposes while still preserving a CGT exemption for a non-resident trust. However, the attribution rules in TCGA 1992 ss 86 *et seq* have to be considered and home and away trusts are now largely confined to non-UK domiciled settlors about to become UK resident and ordinarily resident.

5.73 It is equally possible to have dual resident trusts that are resident in the UK under the rules described above, but are also resident in some other jurisdiction under that country's rules of residence. Whether or not this dual residence can be avoided under a double taxation treaty will depend on the treaties involved. There are special CGT rules for dual resident settlements in TCGA 1992 s 88. For settlements which move from being resident to non-resident or vice versa, and therefore become migrant settlements within TCGA 1992 s 89, see Chapter 10. There is also an exit charge on trustees ceasing to be resident in the UK. [TCGA 1992 s 80].

5.74 There are special rules for CGT in TCGA 1992 s 81 where the death of a trustee causes a settlement to cease to be resident in the UK, provided that, within the period of six months beginning with the trustee's death, the trustees again become resident and ordinarily resident in the UK, normally by the appointment of a new UK resident trustee. [TCGA 1992 s 81(1)]. In such circumstances the exit charge under TCGA 1992 s 80 is limited to assets disposed of by the trustees in the period between the date of the trustee's death and the trustees subsequently becoming once more resident and ordinarily resident in the UK. [Section 81(2) and (3)]. The exemption also applies to assets covered by a double taxation treaty, which constitutes settled property, and any gain would be treaty exempt. [Section 81(4)]. There is also an exemption for assets acquired under the rollover relief provisions in TCGA 1992 s 165 as a gift of business assets, or under TCGA 1992 s 260 as a gift on which IHT is chargeable. [Section 81(5)–(7)].

5.75 Where the exit charge applies, past trustees may remain liable for the tax under TCGA 1992 s 82. The exit charge also applies to trustees becoming treaty non-resident under section 83. Rollover relief for the replacement of business assets under TCGA 1992 s 152 is not available where the acquisition is by dual resident trustees under section 84.

5.76 Where trustees become resident in the UK there is no corresponding rebasing to market value or deemed disposal and reacquisition, equivalent to the exit charge under TCGA 1992 s 80. In such circumstances the trustees should consider whether it would be appropriate to dispose of assets on which any substantial gains have accrued but not realised, before a trust becomes UK resident.

5.77 Where a trust becomes non-resident by the appointment of foreign trustees, TA 1925 s 37(2) would apply, and therefore if a single corporate overseas trustee is appointed, which is not a trust corporation for UK purposes, the appointment would be invalid and the trust would remain resident in the UK.

Inheritance tax residence

5.78 For IHT purposes, the residence of the trustees is not a relevant factor.

Domicile of trustees

5.79 There does not appear to be any jurisprudence on the domicile of trustees as a body of persons and it does not appear to be relevant for any tax purposes. Where the beneficiary has an interest in possession as a life tenant or annuitant of a UK trust, the trustees' income tax liability is based on the beneficiary's domicile. The remittance basis applies to the share of income from abroad, apart from the Republic of Ireland. [ICTA 1988 s 68]. Only income remitted to the UK is included in the trust and estate tax return under ICTA 1988 ss 65 and 65A (*Williams v Singer* (1920) 3 TC 387; *Archer-Shee v Baker* (1927) 11 TC 749; TSM 3165). Similarly, where a UK trust has a non-resident beneficiary with an interest in possession the trustees exclude from their foreign income the amount payable to the non-resident beneficiary (TSM 3160). The same reasoning applies to a beneficiary who is resident, in the UK but not ordinarily resident, in that the trustee's income tax liability is based on the beneficiary's non-ordinarily resident status. Therefore the share of the income from abroad, apart from the Republic of Ireland, payable to the non-resident beneficiary is limited to amounts remitted to the UK provided that the beneficiary is a citizen of the Commonwealth or the Republic of Ireland (TSM 3170). [ICTA 1988 s 65(4)]. Trustees will also exclude from the trust and estate tax return, income from exempt gilt edged securities, to the extent that this becomes the income of a beneficiary with an interest in possession who is not ordinarily resident in the UK. This contrasts with the situation with regard to discretionary trusts where the trustees must include the income on the trust return and pay tax at the rate applicable to trusts unless, exceptionally, the Revenue accepts that there is no liability after referral to the Centre for Non Residents (TSEM 3185).

5.80 A non-UK will trust with trustees resident in the UK, was liable to UK tax on the income arising in *Kelly v Rogers (Willme's Trustee)* (1935) 19 TC 692.

5.81 It would seem arguable that a trust is domiciled in the country under the laws of which it is established. The charitable exemption under ICTA 1988 s 505(1)(c) only applies to charities established in the UK (*IRC v Gull* (1937) 21 TC 374; *Camille & Henry Dreyfus Foundation Inc v IRC* (1955) 36 TC 126). In the case of an American will trust, it was assumed that the US law followed the UK law and that a beneficiary with an interest in possession became entitled to the income of the trust fund as it arose and was not assessable on a remittance basis (*Archer-Shee v Baker* (1927) 11 TC 749). An attempt to adduce late evidence on the actual US legal position was rejected in *Archer-Shee v Baker (No 2)* (1928) 15 TC 1, but in the following year evidence on the relevant US law was given, and it was held that the life tenant's income was from a single foreign possession and therefore taxable on the remittance basis, which then applied (*Garland v Archer-Shee* (1930) 15 TC 693). *Archer-Shee v Baker* was followed in *Nelson v Adamson* (1941) 24 TC 36 in respect of an Australian will trust, in *Drummond v Collins* (1915) 6 TC 525. The mother of a UK resident child was assessed as guardian under Schedule D Case V on amounts remitted to her for the child. An American will trust was treated as a single source in *Lord Inchyra v Jennings* (1965) 42 TC 388.

Chapter 6

Main Taxation Rules Applicable to Trusts

6.1 This chapter deals with the taxation rules which apply to trusts generally. The specific rules applicable to trusts with discretionary beneficiaries are dealt with in Chapter 7; bare trusts and trusts where the beneficiaries have an interest in possession in Chapter 8; and accumulation and maintenance trusts in Chapter 9. Other more specialised trusts are dealt with in Chapters 10 to 14.

Definition of settlement

6.2 A settlement includes any disposition, trust, covenant, agreement, arrangement or transfer of assets, and a settlor in relation to a settlement means any person by whom the settlement was made. [ICTA 1988 s 660G(1)]. A person is deemed to have made a settlement if he has provided, or undertaken to provide, funds directly or indirectly for the purposes of the settlement, or has made, with another person, a reciprocal arrangement for that other person to enter into the settlement.

Income tax

6.3 If A agrees to settle £10,000 on trust for B and B settles a similar sum in trust for A, each would be deemed to be the settlor of the trust for themselves, which would consequently be ineffective for income tax purposes under ICTA 1988 s 660A which assesses the income of a trust on a settlor who has retained an interest in the settlement, see **6.17** et seq. Income arising under the settlement includes any income chargeable to income tax by deduction or otherwise, or which would be chargeable if had been received in the UK by a person domiciled, resident and ordinarily resident in the UK. [ICTA 1988 s 660G(3)]. However, where the settlor is not UK domiciled, not UK resident or not ordinarily resident in the UK in the year of assessment, the settlor is not chargeable if he would not have been subject to UK tax had he actually been entitled to that income. Where he is resident in the UK but not UK domiciled, for certain income he is only assessed on remittances to the UK. [ICTA 1988 s 660G(4)].

6.4 Settlement is widely defined but does require an element of bounty (*IRC v Plummer* [1979] STC 793; *IRC v Levy* [1982] STC 442). An arrangement involving shares of different classes was held to be a settlement in *IRC v*

Morton (1941) 24 TC 259 and *Dalgeaty v IRC* (1941) 24 TC 280. A covenant to pay certain dividends to a controlled company was held to be a settlement in *Burston v IRC* and *Halperin v IRC* (1942) 24 TC 285. Other occasions where different classes of shares in a company amounted to an arrangement, and therefore a settlement, include *IRC v Prince-Smith* (1943) 25 TC 84; *Young v Pearce*; *Young v Scrutton* [1996] STC 743; and *Copeman v Coleman* (1939) 22 TC 594. The arrangement of a loan to a trust for the benefit of children to enable shares to be purchased, was an arrangement amounting to a settlement in *Jenkins v IRC*; *Mason v IRC* (1944) 26 TC 265 and *IRC v Wachtel* (1970) 46 TC 543. A sale of shares at an undervalue to prevent a takeover had a commercial purpose, without an element of bounty, and was therefore not a settlement (*Bulmer v IRC* (1966) 44 TC 1).

6.5 The provision of services to a company owned by a trust makes the service provider a potential settlor, unless such service provider is fully remunerated at market rates (*Crossland v Hawkins* (1961) 39 TC 493; *IRC v Mills* [1974] STC 130). A gift of shares subject to a third party option amounted to an arrangement, and therefore a settlement, in *Vandervell v IRC* (1966) 43 TC 519, as did a trust created by a settlor who then borrowed the trust funds on mortgage in *IRC v Pay* (1955) 36 TC 109.

6.6 A case where two brothers set up a company and issued shares direct to their children amounted to a settlement on the grounds that the brothers provided all the entrepreneurial skills and the opportunity for the company to be profitable, and therefore created an arrangement which amounted to a settlement, in *Butler v Wildin* [1989] STC 22. This followed the earlier case of *Hood-Barrs v IRC* (1946) 27 TC 385; *Hood-Barrs v IRC (No 3)* (1960) 39 TC 209. These cases were distinguished from *Chamberlain v IRC* (1943) 25 TC 317 where the arrangements for different classes of shares did not amount to a settlement. A settlement also arose in *Copeman v Coleman* (1939) 22 TC 594.

6.7 The Revenue believes that a partnership can amount to a settlement:

> '... it is quite likely that an artificial partnership (that is one where the spouse taken into the partnership receives a share of profits out of all proportion to the contribution made to the partnership and probably set up to take advantage of independent taxation) would be vulnerable to challenge under [ICTA 1988] Part XV. For a partnership to exist there must be an agreement, either expressed or implied, by which two or more persons carry on business in common with a view of profit. A partnership is a settlement using the extended definition found at [ICTA 1988 s 660G(1)]. This defines settlement as including any agreement or arrangement. A partnership agreement can therefore be brought within the legislation found at [ICTA 1988] Part XV provided that the agreement involves an element of bounty see *IRC v Plummer* [1979] STC 793. Bounty entails giving something away without receiving a quid pro quo. Partnerships where the incoming partner receives a share of profits out of all proportion to the contribution made to the partnership would therefore include an element of bounty. This approach would be appropriate where it is not possible to

challenge the existence of the partnership and the amount of the tax at risk is significant. All such cases must be referred to IR Trusts – Bootle, formerly FICO (Trusts and Charities) before the question of the settlements legalisation is raised. They will either advise or mount the challenge under [ICTA 1988] Part XV.'

(IM 263).

6.7A The Revenue's view of the wide definition of a settlement for tax purposes is illustrated in Tax Bulletin, Issue 64, April 2003, pages 1011–1016 (Appendix 3). The tax advisers' professional bodies responded to this in a commentary dated 11 September 2003 (Appendix 7) expressing a rather different view, and the Revenue has been asked to reconsider and clarify its views.

6.8 In the Irish case of *O'Dwyer v Cafolla & Co* (1948) 2 ITC 374 a bona fide partnership was upheld. The allegation that a partnership is a settlement is an alternative to an allegation that the partnership does not in fact exist as such (*Hawker v Compton* (1922) 8 TC 306; *Dickenson v Gross* (1927) 11 TC 614; *IRC v Williamson* (1928) 14 TC 335), or that some of the partners were not actually partners (*Alexander Bulloch & Co v IRC* [1976] STC 514).

Stamp duty and stamp duty land tax

6.9 No stamp duty or stamp duty land tax should normally arise on the creation of a settlement because by its very nature it is a gift to the trustees for the benefit of the beneficiaries. The stamp duty charge on gifts *inter vivos*, under F(1909–10)A 1910 s 74 was abolished by FA 1985 s 82, and a similar exemption applies for stamp duty land tax under FA 2003 s 49 and Sch 3 para 1.

6.9A FA 2003 s 48(1)(a) includes as a chargeable interest in land for stamp duty land tax, an estate, interest, right or power over land in the UK. This could include an interest in a non-discretionary trust such that the purchase of a reversionary interest and an interest in possession in such a trust, where the asset is land, could be a land transaction, whatever the proper law of the trust. [FA 2003 s 105 and Sch 16].

6.10 Transfers from trustees to beneficiaries should normally qualify for stamp duty and stamp duty land tax exemption, under the same provisions, and transfers in connection with divorce etc are normally exempt under FA 1985 s 83 and FA 2003 s 49 and Sch 3 para 3. Variations arising on a will or intestacy are normally exempt from stamp duty under FA 1985 s 84. A sale by trustees of trust assets may well attract stamp duty as a conveyance or transfer on sale, under FA 1999 s 112. The rates of stamp duty are given by FA 2000 s 114. On the sale of stocks and marketable securities the rate is 0.5 per cent.

6.11 On the sale of other property the rate of stamp duty or, from 1 December 2003, stamp duty land tax, depends on the consideration.

£0–£60,000	0%
£60,001–£250,000	1%
£250,001–£500,000	3%
Over £500,000	4%

6.12 There are no special rules for trusts or trustees in relation to stamp duty. For a general commentary on stamp duty, including stamp duty reserve tax, see *WJB Chiltern's Orange Tax Guide 2003–04*.

Income tax liability of settlor

Settlements of income

6.13 Where the owner of securities transfers the right to receive any interest payable in respect of those securities, without selling or transferring the securities themselves, he remains taxable on the income under ICTA 1988 s 730(1) and the recipient of the income is not chargeable to tax on it.

6.14 The inability to alienate such income for tax purposes is one of the reasons why a *usufruct*, where the right to income is transferred but the asset retained, is unusual in the UK although it is quite common on the Continent and in other civil law jurisdictions. The alienation of income by way of deed of covenant, although ineffective for tax purposes except to a charity under the Gift Aid regime, or for commercial purposes, such as a pension to a former partner, can still serve a purpose, e g to guarantee an elderly relative's income to enable him to transfer assets to other family members in the knowledge that his income is assured.

6.15 An attempted sale of the right to dividends in order to avoid tax was defeated by invoking the *Ramsay* principle (*W T Ramsay Ltd v IRC* [1981] STC 174) in *IRC v McGuckian* [1997] STC 908. The charge was actually made under ICTA 1988 s 739, *not* s 730, as a result of the taxpayer allegedly keeping material facts and documents from the Revenue. ICTA 1988 s 730 was initially introduced by FA 1938 to overturn the effect of *Paget v IRC* (1938) 21 TC 677. The *usufruct* principle was successfully applied to a sale of a five-year rental stream in return for a lump sum payment in *John Lewis Properties plc v IRC* [2000] STC (SCD) 494, which was in turn stopped by ICTA 1988 s 43B. This applies to a transfer of a right to receive rent other than by means of the grant of a lease, unless it is a finance agreement with a term which exceeds 15 years. [Section 43C]. These rent factoring anti-avoidance provisions are included in sections 43A–43G.

Part XV

6.16 The main income tax settlement provisions are set out in ICTA 1988 Part XV, ss 660A–694.

Settlor's retained interest

6.17 If the settlor retains any interest in the trust property, eg as a beneficiary or potential beneficiary under the trust, the income of the settlement remains his for income tax purposes under ICTA 1988 s 660A(1). This applies where any income from the property put into trust may become payable to, or applicable for the benefit of, the settlor, or his spouse 'in any circumstances whatsoever'. [Section 660A(2)]. There are, however, exceptions. Spouse does not include an intended future spouse until the parties marry, nor a separated spouse under a court order or separation agreement where the separation is likely to be permanent, nor where the settlor has died and the former spouse becomes a beneficiary as widow or widower. [Section 660A(3)(a)–(c)]. There are also exceptions for the settlor whose interest in the property only becomes payable to, or applicable for his benefit, in the event of the bankruptcy of a beneficiary, or the assignment or charging of property by a beneficiary. [Section 660A(4)(a) and (b)]. Further exceptions apply, in the case of a marriage settlement, on the death of both parties to the marriage and all or any of the children of the marriage, or the death of a child of the settlor who had become beneficially entitled to the property at an age not exceeding 25. [Section 660A(4)(c) and (d)]. If, therefore, the income is distributed to, or accumulated for the benefit of, a child under 25 and it can only become payable to the settlor on the bankruptcy or assigning or charging of the child's interest in the property, the settlor is not regarded as having an interest. [Section 660A(5)]. Settlement for these purposes does not include an outright gift to a spouse, unless the gift does not carry a right to the income from the property transferred, or it is merely a gift of income. [Section 660A(6)].

6.18 The restrictions do not apply to divorce settlements or separation agreements. [ICTA 1988 s 660A(8)]. Nor do they apply to annual payments under covenant made by an individual for bona fide commercial reasons in connection with his trade, profession or vocation, eg pension payments to a former partner; qualifying donations to charities under the Gift Aid scheme in FA 1990 s 25; or benefits under an approved pension arrangement. [Section 660A(9)(a)–(c), (11) and (12)]. Provisions apply not only to property originally placed into the trust but also any derived property directly or indirectly representing proceeds of, or income from, the property settled. [Section 660A(10)].

6.19 By definition a revocable settlement is ineffective for tax purposes because the settlor, by revoking the settlement, can benefit and is therefore within ICTA 1988 s 660A. Revocable settlements are therefore unusual in the UK, except where the settlor is the main beneficiary. Revocable settlements are not uncommon in certain overseas jurisdictions, such as the USA, and are frequently used by non-UK domiciliaries to hold assets prior to becoming resident in the UK for a period. They have also been used in artificial tax avoidance schemes (*Melville v IRC* [2001] STC 1271). This case would seem to confirm that the power of revocation, like a general power of appointment, is a separate asset which would be a UK asset if the holder of the power were

UK resident. This could defeat the object of creating the settlement offshore and such powers are now ignored for IHT purposes under FA 2002 s 119. A limited power of revocation, which excludes the appointment of the settlor as beneficiary, could nonetheless be caught if it would enable a future spouse to be included as beneficiary (*IRC v Tennant* (1942) 24 TC 215; SP A30). However, in view of ICTA 1988 s 660A(3)(a) the trust would only be treated as one where the settlor retains an interest if the settlor marries and the spouse becomes a possible beneficiary of the trust. The possibility of the settlor becoming a beneficiary at some future time was considered in the case of an overseas trust in *IRC v Botnar* [1999] STC 711. In this case, although the settlor was excluded from the initial trust, the trustees had power to resettle on terms that may not have excluded the settlor. Although the assessment was made under ICTA 1988 s 739, it would appear that a similar line of reasoning could apply to a domestic trust as a retention of interest by the settlor under ICTA 1988 s 660A. The exclusion of the settlor and his spouse has to be absolute.

6.20 The income of a revocable settlement remained that of the taxpayer in *IRC v Payne* (1940) 23 TC 610, but not where the settlement was irrevocable as in *IRC v Rainsford-Hannay* (1941) 24 TC 273; *Wolfson v IRC* (1949) 31 TC 141; *Chamberlain v IRC* (1943) 25 TC 317; and *Clark v IRC* (1947) 28 TC 55. The unlikelihood of the settlor benefiting was no protection from a charge under ICTA 1988 s 660A in *Barrs Trustees v IRC* (1943) 25 TC 72, which was a settlement on the settlor's grandchildren such that the settlor could only have benefited had his grandchildren all predeceased him. In *Glyn v IRC* (1948) 30 TC 321 a jointly held power of appointment was sufficient to give the settlor a retained interest in the settlement. The right to determine a lease in favour of the trustees was not a retention of interest in the settlement in *Lord Vestey's Executors and Vestey v IRC*; *Lord Vestey's Executors and Vestey v Colquhoun* (1949) 31 TC 1.

6.21 Another revocable settlement was *IRC v Countess of Kenmare* (1957) 37 TC 383. The statutory power of advancement under TA 1925 s 32 in favour of the trustee's wife was not a retention of interest as the terms of the settlement overrode the statutory power of advancement (*IRC v Bernstein* (1960) 39 TC 391). In *IRC v Cookson* [1977] STC 140 where the trust deed failed to dispose of all the income, it was held that the settlor held an interest (*Hannay's Executors v IRC* (1956) 37 TC 217). Other revocable settlement cases include *IRC v Warden* (1939) 22 TC 416; *IRC v Lord Delamere* (1939) 22 TC 525; *Eastwood v IRC* (1943) 25 TC 100; *Hood Barrs v IRC (No 3)* (1960) 39 TC 209; *Jamieson v IRC*; and *Wills v IRC* (1963) 41 TC 43.

6.22 It is often difficult to cure a defect in an original settlement by a supplemental deed, as is shown in *Taylor v IRC* (1946) 27 TC 93 and *IRC v Nicholson and Bartlett* (1953) 34 TC 354. A trust that was effective following a deed of appointment is illustrated by *Blausten v IRC* (1971) 47 TC 542.

6.23 Where assets are put into trust which are subject to IHT, both the settlor and the trustees are liable for any IHT payable under IHTA 1984 s 199.

If the trustees had power to pay the IHT, or in fact paid IHT, on the transfer of assets into the settlement, this is not regarded as a retention of the settlor's interest in the trust for the purposes of ICTA 1988 s 660A (SP 1/82).

6.24 Section 660A of ICTA 1988 states that, where the settlor has retained an interest, the income is that of the settlor and not the income of any other person. The income is shown as income of the settlor in his personal tax return, normally as investment income in Q10, and to the extent that management expenses have been deducted by the trustees in Q13, as other income, because the management expenses are not allowable where the income is deemed to be that of the settlor, under section 660A (see Helpsheet IR270). Although the income is ultimately taxed on the settlor and not on the trustees, the trustees have a liability to tax in the first instance at the rate applicable to trusts under ICTA 1988 s 686, in view of section 660D(3). The tax paid or suffered by the trustees becomes a credit available to the settlor to set against his tax liability on the income deemed to be his under these provisions. To the extent that the income is accumulated, the normal rules apply to charge a trustee at the rate applicable to trusts, and when ultimately distributed give the appropriate pool credit to the beneficiary under ICTA 1988 s 687 (see Chapter 7).

6.25 The statutory authority for the nature of the charge on the settlor under these provisions is contained in ICTA 1988 s 660C, which effectively treats the income as if it were the savings income of the settlor within ICTA 1988 s 1A, ie in particular income chargeable under Schedule F, or equivalent foreign income taxable under Schedule D Case V, distributions from a company within ICTA 1988 s 233(1) including both qualifying and non-qualifying distributions within section 233(1A) and (1B), stock dividends treated as income within section 249 or deemed income arising on the release of a loan from a close company to a participator under section 421(1)(a). [ICTA 1988 ss 660C(1) and (1A) (a)–(g)]. Any other income is taxable under Schedule D Case VI. [Section 660C(1)(b)]. The settlor is entitled to the same deductions as if the income had been received by him directly under ICTA 1988 s 660C(2) and is deemed to be the highest part of his income except for top-slicing relief under ICTA 1988 s 833(3). Therefore the starting rate, basic rate and savings rate are given first to the settlor's own income and then to the deemed income arising in the trust. Income deemed to be that of a settlor is treated as investment income (*Ang v Parrish* [1980] STC 341).

6.26 Where the income of the trust is chargeable on the taxpayer under ICTA 1988 s 660A or s 660B the settlor has a right of recovery against the trustees under ICTA 1988 s 660D(1)(a). He can require the Revenue to furnish him with a certificate specifying the amount of tax he has paid in order to evidence the amount recoverable. [Section 660D(1)(b)]. If, however, the settlor obtains a repayment of tax that he would otherwise not have been entitled to, this has to be accounted for to the trustees. [Section 660D(2)]. Any question of apportionment shall be decided by the General Commissioners whose decision shall be final. The fact that it is deemed to be the income of the settlor does not prevent the trustees being liable to tax as the original recipients of the income. See further **6.20**. [Section 660D(3)].

Example

Mr Boris Bisnovat, who is unmarried and UK resident, but not UK domiciled, settled an accumulation and maintenance trust for his two children, Natasha aged five and Anna aged three. He was excluded from benefit and the income was accumulated.

Boris married his children's mother Lavinia, with whom he had been living for several years, on 22 September 2002.

The trust's net income from a let property in 2002/03 amounted to £12,540 of which £6,810 arose after 21 September 2002. On 5 April 2003 the trustees passed a resolution to exclude Lavinia, and any spouse for the time being, from benefit, under powers in the trust deed.

Boris was assessed to tax on the post-21 September rental income of £6,810 at his marginal rate of tax of 40 per cent, £2,724, under ICTA 1988 s 660A, as his spouse was not excluded from benefit, and the trustees were assessed to tax on the total trust income of £12,540, taxed at the rate applicable to trusts of 34 per cent, £4,263.60. Boris claimed a credit for the tax paid by the trustees on his income of £6,810 at 34 per cent, £2,315.40, and paid the difference of £408.60, which he reclaimed from the trustees under ICTA 1988 s 660D(1)(a).

Settlements on children

6.27 Where a person creates a settlement in favour of his unmarried minor children, and distributions are made to the children which would otherwise be their income, these are treated as income of the settlor and not the income of any other person. [ICTA 1988 s 660B(1)]. Where, however, the income is retained or accumulated by the trustees, only actual distributions made to minor children of the settlor will be deemed to be the settlor's income. The charge on the settlor can therefore be avoided by accumulating the income until the children reach the age of 18, rather than distributing it. [Section 660B(2)]. Most accumulation and maintenance settlements for children allow the trustees to make distributions for the maintenance, education and benefit of the child, but this does not prevent any such distributions being treated as the settlor's income to the extent that it is paid to an unmarried child under the age of 18. The income available to be taxed as that of the settlor is the entire income of the settlement since creation, less any income which has been treated as income of the settlor or distributed to any beneficiary who is not an unmarried minor child of the settlor, or treated as income of an unmarried minor child and subject to tax in 1995/96 to 1997/98, or applied in defraying trustees' expenses, properly chargeable to income. [Section s 660B(3)].

6.28 The taxable income of the child in 1995/96 to 1997/98 is the excess of the child's total income for tax purposes over the personal and other allowances that may be set against it. The amount of the income covered by the child's allowances is taxed as income arising under the settlement. [ICTA 1988 s 660B(3A)]. These particular provisions were introduced by FA 1999 s 64 to close a loophole under which a parent could create a bare trust for his minor unmarried child, but accumulate the income until the child attained the age of 18 or married under that age. Because it was a bare trust it was the child's income absolutely and was not within section 660B because it was accumulated not distributed.

6.29 With effect from 9 March 1999, bare trusts are now caught by ICTA 1988 s 660B(1)(b). Parental gifts producing income of no more than £100 in aggregate are excluded by section 660B(5). These amendments applied to income arising under a settlement made or entered into on or after 9 March 1999, or in respect of funds provided on or after that date. [FA 1999 s 64(5) and (6)]. A further loophole allowed the untaxed part of the income under a bare trust, ie that amount covered by the child's personal and other tax allowances, to be applied for the child's benefit as it had already been treated as the child's income. ICTA 1988 s 660B(3) and (3A) prevent this benefit continuing in relation to payments or applications for a child's benefit made after 8 March 1999, irrespective of when the settlement itself was made. [FA 1999 s 64(6)]. The anti-avoidance provisions apply not only to the bare trust but also to interest in possession trusts where the child is entitled to the income, where TA 1925 s 31 is excluded.

6.30 Where an offshore income gain accrues to a trust for the settlor's children, it is treated as paid to the child under ICTA 1988 s 661(1) and therefore taxed on the parent under section 660B(1)(a). [Section 660B(4)]. Payments include payments in money or money's worth; child includes a step-child or illegitimate child; and minor means a person under the age of 19 years. [Section 660B(6)(a), (b) and (c)].

6.31 These provisions only apply to settlements made by parents on their own children and not, for example, to settlements created by grandparents. However, reciprocal arrangements between the parents and grandparents, perhaps where funds were passed by the parents to the grandparents to enable them to create the settlement on the grandchildren, would cause the parents to be treated as settlors under ICTA 1988 s 660G(2). Similarly, where there is a waiver of dividends by some shareholders so that increased dividends can be paid to trustees, this could constitute an arrangement and if the waiving shareholders were parents of the child beneficiaries, they would become additional settlors under section 660G(1). This would apply even though the divided waiver is specifically not regarded as a chargeable transfer for IHT purposes under IHTA 1984 s 15.

Example

Boris Bisnovat's children's trust had net rental income in 2003/04 of £13,270 and interest from a bank deposit account in Jersey of £615, ie £13,885, which was taxable on the trustees at the rate applicable to trusts of 34 per cent, £4,720.90. In the year the trustees paid Boris's five year old daughter Natasha's school fees of £2,250 and, from the Jersey bank account, £520 to a French travel agent in respect of a skiing holiday for her. The payment of school fees is taxable on Boris under ICTA 1988 s 660B, and he is liable for tax of £2,250 at his marginal rate of, say, 40 per cent, £900, less a credit of £2,250 at 34 per cent, £765, for the tax paid by the trustees, and he paid £135, which he reclaimed from the trustees under ICTA 1988 s 660D(1)(a).

He was not, in view of his non-UK domicile, taxed on Natasha's skiing holiday as he would not have been taxed on any interest on a Jersey bank account of his own if it had been used by him to pay the French travel agent for the holiday, and was therefore not taxable on him, in view of ICTA 1988 s 660G(4).

Multiple settlors

6.32 In view of the definition of settlement and settlor in ICTA 1988 s 660G(1) it will be appreciated that anyone who transfers, directly or indirectly, assets into a settlement or is party to an arrangement constituting a settlement, will be regarded as a settlor. Where there is more than one settlor a settlement is effectively treated as a number of different settlements with each settlor's liability to tax being related back to his contribution to the settlement. [Section 660E(1)–(6)]. Where there are reciprocal arrangements, the assets provided by the other party to the settlement are deemed to be those of the settlor, and the settlor's reciprocal transfers are ignored in calculating the property in the settlement emanating from him. [Section 660E(7)].

Example

Anthony Beriev had discovered that if he settled funds on his own children he would remain taxable on the income distributed to them in respect of education, maintenance or benefit, until they reached the age of 18. He was explaining the position to his friend Timothy Bartini over lunch and they thought it would be a good idea if Anthony settled £25,000 on trust for Tim's children and Tim settled a roughly similar amount on Anthony's children. Tim thought that this was a great idea and suggested that he settled £24,800 and paid for lunch. They were disappointed to find that, had they proceeded to do so, Anthony would be deemed to have settled £24,800 on the trust for his own children and Tim to have settled £25,000 on trust for his own children, and taxed accordingly.

Power to obtain information

6.33 ICTA 1988 s 660F allows the Revenue, by notice, to require any party to a settlement to furnish them within such time as may be directed, being not less than 28 days, with such particulars as is thought necessary for the purposes of section 660A–660G inclusive. One of several trustees was held to be a 'party to a settlement' in *Cutner v IRC* [1974] STC 259. An attempt to argue that the amount of information required by the Revenue was too wide and oppressive failed in *Wilover Nominees Ltd v IRC* [1974] STC 467.

Inheritance tax paid

6.34 Where a settlor transfers assets to a trust on condition that any IHT due in respect of the gift is payable by the trustees this is no longer regarded as the settlor retaining an interest in the settlement within ICTA 1988 s 660A, because IHTA 1984 s 199 provides that both the settlor and the trustees are liable for any IHT payable. The Revenue practice in this connection changed in 1982 and the current practice was confirmed by SP 1/82.

Capital sums paid to settlor

6.35 It is not possible to avoid the provisions of ICTA 1988 ss 660A– 660G by the settlor taking out capital instead of income. ICTA 1988 s 677(1) provides that any capital sum paid directly or indirectly to a settlor shall be treated as his income up to the amount of the available income received, and not otherwise distributed, in the trust to the end of the tax year. If the capital sum exceeds the available income it is treated as the settlor's income up to the amount of the available income in the trust in any of the ten following years.

6.36 The available income is the income received in the year in which the capital sum is paid, and in any previous year, less amounts distributed to beneficiaries – unless the amount has already been charged on the settlor in previous years or applied against an earlier capital sum or already treated as the settlor's income, less provision for tax at the rate applicable to trusts. [ICTA 1988 s 667(2)]. There is also a deduction where the capital sum amounts to the release of a loan under ICTA 1988 s 421 in respect of a loan by an associated close company within section 419. Capital sum includes any amount paid by way of a loan until it has been repaid. [Section 677(4)(a)]. Where a capital sum has previously been lent and repaid but some of the income of the trust has been taxed as the settlor's income under this section, the amount of any further loan is reduced by the amount on which the settlor has already paid tax as a result of previous loans. [Section 677(4)(b)]. Capital sum includes any amount paid to the settlor by way of a loan or the repayment of a loan, which the settlor had previously lent to the trust, and any other sum paid otherwise than as income, unless paid for full consideration in money or money's worth. [Section 677(9)(a)]. However, it does not include an amount paid to the settlor on the death of a beneficiary under the age of 25. [Section 660A(4) and (5)]. Sums paid to the settlor include sums paid to his spouse or to the settlor or his spouse jointly with another person. [Section 677(9)(b)]. A capital sum includes a sum paid to a third party at the settlor's direction, or otherwise applied for the benefit of the settlor. [Section 677(10)].

6.37 Although the capital sum is paid by the trustees in repayment of a loan from the settlor, the treatment of income as that of the settlor ceases if another loan, at least equal to the repayment of the loan, is paid by the settlor, to the trustees. [ICTA 1988 s 667(5)]. The amount taxable on the settlor is the amount of the capital sum grossed up at the rate applicable to trusts.

[Section 667(6)]. The charge on the gross equivalent of the capital sum is under Schedule D Case VI and the settlor is given credit for tax at the rate applicable to trusts, or the amount of tax due if less. [Section 677(7)]. The settlor is entitled to the same allowances and reliefs as if the amount of tax imposed on him had actually been his income. [Section 677(8)].

6.38 These provisions can be a major trap for the unwary settlor. In *De Vigier v IRC* (1964) 42 TC 24 one of the trustees, who was married to the settlor, lent £7,000 to the trustees to acquire some shares. The loan was repaid in two amounts within twelve months and the Revenue successfully assessed the settlor to surtax on the grossed-up equivalent of the capital sum under what is now ICTA 1988 s 677 (see, however, **6.39**). The mere guaranteeing of an overdraft by the settlor was not treated as a capital sum within section 677 in *IRC v Wachtel* (1970) 46 TC 543, although in that case the Revenue won on the alternative argument that the guarantee amounted to an arrangement under which the settlor had retained an interest in the settlement. A loan by the trustees to the settlor was caught by section 677 in *McCrone v IRC* (1967) 44 TC 142.

Example

Vladimir Lebedev settled £100,000 on a discretionary trust from which he and his spouse were excluded from benefit. The trust had undistributed income of £10,000 at 5 April 2002, £3,500 in 2002 and £4,500 in 2003/04. On 20 December 2002 Vladimir borrowed £20,000 from the trustees, to take up a rights issue, at interest of 10 per cent per annum. He sold the shares in April 2003 and repaid the loan on 20 April 2003.

Vladimir was advised that he had assessable income to declare, as follows:

2002/03	£
Loan	20,000
Income up to and including 2002/03	(13,500)
Loan carried forward	6,500
2003/04	
Income for year	(4,500)
Balance of loan	2,000

The balance was not taxable as a result of repaying the loan in 2003/04.

Taxable income of Vladimir 2002/03	
£13,500 grossed up at rate applicable to trusts, 34%	20,454.00
Taxed at Vladimir's marginal rate of 40%	8,181.16
Less credit for tax paid by trust at 34%	(6,954.36)
Tax payable by Vladimir	1,226.80
Taxable income of Vladimir 2003/04	
£4,500 grossed up at rate applicable to trusts, 34%	6,818.00

Taxed at Vladimir's marginal rate of 40%	2,727.20
Less credit for tax paid by trust at 34%	(2,318.12)
Tax payable by Vladimir	409.08
Interest paid by Vladimir to trustees, 10% pa for 4 months	666.67
Cost to Vladimir of borrowing £20,000 for four months £1,266.80+£409.08+£666.67= (which made even a credit card loan look cheap.)	2,342.55

However, Vladimir borrowed a further £25,000 at 10 per cent per annum on 1 August 2004 which he repayed on 31 October 2004. The trust income for 2004/05 was £9,000.

	£
Amount of loan	25,000
Less previous loan charged as income £13,500+£4,500=	(18,000)
	7,000
Available income	9,000
Taxable income of Vladimir 2004/05	
£7,000 grossed up at rate applicable to trusts, 34%	10,606.00
Taxed at Vladimir's marginal rate of 40%	4,242.40
Less credit for tax paid by trust at 34%	(3,606.04)
Tax payable by Vladimir	636.36
Interest paid 10% for 3 months	625.00
Cost to Vladimir of borrowing £25,000 for three months £636.36+£625.00	£1,261.36

Connected companies

6.39 Capital sums, as defined by ICTA 1988 ss 677(5) and 678(5), paid to the settlor include those paid by a company connected with the settlement provided that an associated payment is being made directly or indirectly by the trustees. [Section 678(1)]. The capital sum is the lower of the amount paid to the settlor or the associated payment made to the company by the trustees. [Section 678(2)(a)]. If, however, it is greater than the associated payments made in the year of assessment it will be treated as income of the settlor in a later year, up to the amount of associated payments made during the next ten years. [Section 678(2)(b)]. An associated payment means any capital sum paid by the trustees to the company or any other sum paid or asset transferred to the company by the trustees, which is not paid or transferred for full consideration in money or money's worth but limited to funds paid or assets transferred in the five years from the date of payment of the capital sum to the settlor. Note that the associated payment can be made before or after the date of the capital payment. [Section 678(3)]. A company is connected with a settlement for these purposes if it is a close company, or would be if it were resident in the UK, and the participators include the trustees of the settlement; or it is controlled by such a company under section 682A(2) or is an associated company within the close company definition of section 416. [Section 678(4)].

6.40 The normal definition provisions relating to settlements in ICTA 1988 ss 660E–660G apply for the provisions relating to capital sums paid to settlors. [ICTA 1988 s 682A]. Sums withdrawn by the settlor on his current account with the company were treated as falling within these provisions in *Piratin v IRC* [1981] STC 441. Sums paid by a company to clear a settlor's bank overdraft were also caught in *IRC v Bates* (1966) 44 TC 225. However, payments made to third parties debited to the settlor's current account were not capital sums within these provisions (*Pott's Executors v IRC* (1950) 32 TC 211). However, this ploy is no longer available in view of the extended definition of capital sum to include sums paid to a third party at the settlor's direction. [ICTA 1988 ss 678(5) and 677(10)]. Short-term loans are, however, now allowed under section 678(6) if the loan is repaid within twelve months and the total loans outstanding within a five-year period do not exceed twelve months.

Example

On 1 January 2004 Vladimir Lebedev borrowed £25,000 at interest of 10 per cent per annum from Lavochkin Ltd, a company wholly owned by a discretionary trust which he had settled and from which he and his spouse were excluded from benefit.

The loan was repaid on 31 March 2004 together with interest of £625. This would, in isolation, not be taxable under ICTA 1988 s 678 by virtue of ICTA 1988 s 678(6)(a), as the loan was repaid within 12 months. However, ICTA 1988 s 678(6)(b) aggregates the loan from Lavochkin Ltd with any other loans made by that company, or any other company connected with the settlement, but not by the settlement itself, so the loan is not aggregated with the loans in the previous example at **6.38**, which were direct from the trustees not a connected company.

However, Vladimir was a director of Lavochkin Ltd, and on 1 June the company bought a new car for Vladimir, at a cost of £45,000, which in view of the company car benefit provisions, was charged to his current account, which was then overdrawn by £5,000 and remained so until his remuneration was credited soon after the company's year end, which was on 31 March 2005. This counted as a loan within ICTA 1988 s 677(9)(a)(ii) (COT 6637) as a result of which loans from Lavochkin exceeded 12 months within five years and both loans were caught and taxed as if made by the trustees by virtue of ICTA 1988 s 678(1), because Lavochkin Ltd was partly financed by an interest free loan of £50,000 from the settlement, made on 30 June 1999.

6.41 Rules for ascertaining the undistributed income are set out in ICTA 1988 s 682. Income arising under a settlement in any tax year is deemed not to have been distributed to the extent that it exceeds the aggregate of:

(a) distributions to beneficiaries which would be taxable were they domiciled, resident and ordinarily resident in the UK;

(b) trust expenses properly chargeable to income; and

(c) the amount by which the exempt income of a charitable trust exceeds expenses properly chargeable against that income.

[ICTA 1988 s 682(1)].

Expenses include interest paid by the trustees except to the extent that distributions were made to the settlor or his spouse, in which case there is an apportionment applying the fraction:

$$\frac{A-B}{B}$$

where A is the whole of the income of the settlement less expenses properly charged to income and B is the distributions to beneficiaries other than the settlor or his spouse. [Section 682(2)–(4)]. These provisions do not apply to interest that is statutorily allowable under the Taxes Acts, or to interest payable to the settlor or his spouse living with him, nor do they affect the taxability of the interest on the recipient. [Section 682(5) and (6)].

6.42 The transactions in security provisions in ICTA 1988 ss 703–709 may also have to be considered and clearance obtained under ICTA 1988 s 707.

Clearances under ICTA 1988 s 707

6.43 In *Working Together*, Issue 6, August 2001, the Revenue published the following comments in relation to clearance applications under ICTA 1988 s 707:

> 'S 703 is concerned with the cancellation of tax advantages from certain transactions in securities.
>
> S 707 – a person who has carried out, or proposes to carry out, certain transactions in securities may apply to the Board for a clearance that the transactions are not caught by the provisions of ICTA 1988 s 703.
>
> We receive around 6,000 s 707 clearance applications each year. We try to deal with all such applications within the shortest possible time. But sometimes the transactions are so complex that we need to consider the matter in depth and on occasion we need to request further information before we are able to reach a decision.
>
> However, many agents need to make applications infrequently and in some cases we find that applications do not include information which, had it been given, would have enabled us to issue clearance quicker or possibly avoid issuing a conditional clearance.
>
> The following aide-memoire will help you avoid the most common causes of delay:

Information

The application should include:

— The latest accounts for companies involved in the transaction(s)

— The names of all parties to the transaction(s).

Mergers and acquisitions

If the transaction involves the acquisition by one company of another, the applications should show:

— The nature and extent of any interest held by the vendors in the purchasing company (both before and after the transaction(s)).

— The form and amount of the sale consideration.

If the consideration includes the issue of shares

The application should state:

— Whether they are redeemable or irredeemable.

Liquidations

Where the transaction involves liquidation or informal striking off, the application should state:

— Whether the company's trade has ceased, or

— Whether the trade will be carried on in non-corporate form and if so by whom.

— If the transactions include a s 110 liquidation the application should show what the members receive in addition to consideration shares.

Trusts

Where shares are being sold by a trust the application should state:

— The identities of the trustees, settlor and beneficiaries.

— The family relationship or connection between those persons and the continuing shareholders.

— The date of birth of any beneficiaries who are minors.

— How the trustees intend to apply the sale proceeds.

In the case of a purchase of own shares, if none of the continuing shareholders has any interest in a trust a statement to that effect will suffice.

Layout of application

In many applications we receive, the details of the transactions are combined with narrative explanation as to why they are being undertaken.

It would help us if a schedule of the transactions were provided (say, as an appendix to the application) with any explanation e g as to the commercial reasons being given separately in the covering letter.

Where no Market sensitive information is contained within the application it should be sent to Swaren Sethi at the following address:

Inland Revenue
5th Floor
22 Kingsway
London WC2B 6NR

We take the security of all applications very seriously. Where the information contained within the application is Stock Market sensitive the application should be sent to Ray McCann at the address above.'

6.44 One of the most common problems in a clearance application is where the paper issued on a paper-for-paper transaction by the acquiring company includes redeemable preference shares or loan stock. In the Revenue view, *IRC v Cleary* (1967) 44 TC 399 will cause the relief to be denied. Making the paper irredeemable will often assist in spite of the ability of a company to buy its own shares. A CGT avoidance motive, such as the availability of taper relief, is not normally regarded as a reason for refusing clearance. Potential double taxation may arise where counteraction is taken under ICTA 1988 s 703 where there is a disposal subject to CGT. There is no adjustment of the chargeable gain under TCGA 1992 s 37 in these circumstances but in practice the Revenue will have regard to the CGT payable on any consideration that is subject to counteraction under ICTA 1988 s 703. In *IRC v Laird Group plc* [2003] STC 1349 the Revenue failed to apply section 703 to dividends.

Trustees' expenses

6.45 Trustees who are partners in a trading partnership or who own property through the trust may incur expenses which are wholly and exclusively incurred for the purposes of the trade and are deducted in calculating the profits assessable under Schedule D Case I or are wholly and exclusively incurred in connection with the property business and therefore deductible in calculating the income assessable under Schedule A. Trust management expenses, however, are paid out of net taxed income. Expenses properly charged against income reduce the additional tax charge at the rate applicable to trusts on discretionary and accumulation and maintenance trusts and are deducted when calculating the income of a beneficiary of other trusts, such as where the beneficiary has an interest in possession. Relief is therefore, to an extent, given indirectly to the beneficiaries because it reduces the income that would otherwise be taxable on them. The rules do occasionally have peculiar side effects as in *Aikin v Macdonald Trustees* (1894) 3 TC 306 where the trustees were not allowed to deduct any trust expenses from Schedule D Case V income assessable on the remittance basis. The beneficiaries of a bare trust have the right to take actual possession of the trust property and cannot deduct any expenses of the bare trustees (*Lord Tollemach v IRC* (1926) 11 TC 277; TSEM 3520).

6.46 Where some beneficiaries have an interest in possession and some are discretionary, it is necessary to apportion the expenses rateably between the income of the discretionary and the non-discretionary elements (TSEM 3525). Trust expenses are payable out of net trust income and are grossed up in computing the income available to beneficiaries. If the trustees receive any untaxed income, they are taxable on that income in full and cannot in any way frank it with trust expenses paid (TSEM 3535). If the admissiblc trust expenses in the year exceed that year's statutory income, the trustees can carry the balance forward to the following year to set against that year's income provided that they can do so under the appropriate trust law (TSEM 3540).

6.47 Where trust income is deemed to belong to the settlor under the anti-avoidance provisions in, for example, ICTA 1988 ss 660A, 660B, 677, 678, 739 etc it is the income before any expense is incurred by the trustees which is deemed to be that of the settlor (*Lord Chetwode v IRC* [1977] STC 64). Trust expenses chargeable to income, as opposed to capital, are all ordinary expenses of a recurrent nature such as rates and taxes and interest on charges and encumbrances. Capital should bear all costs, charges and expenses incurred for the benefit of the whole estate (*Carver v Duncan; Bosanquet v Allan* [1985] STC 356). The income of beneficiaries with an interest in possession is the income received by the trustees less the expenses properly charged to income (*IRC v Lord Hamilton of Dalzell* (1926) 10 TC 406; *Murray v IRC* (1926) 11 TC 133; *MacFarlane v IRC* (1929) 14 TC 532).

6.48 If a trust instrument allows trustees to meet normal capital expenses from income, they still reduce the income otherwise payable to the beneficiaries. The Revenue cannot tax a beneficiary on more income than he is entitled to demand from the trustees (*IRC v Dewar* (1935) 19 TC 561). Where, however, the trustees pay expenses on behalf of a beneficiary, he is taxed on the gross equivalent of amounts paid by the trustees at his direction (*IRC v Miller* (1930) 15 TC 25; *Shanks v IRC* (1929) 14 TC 249; *Donaldson's Executors v IRC* (1927) 13 TC 461; *Sutton v IRC* (1929) 14 TC 662; *Sterling Trust Ltd v IRC* (1925) 12 TC 868; TSEM 3510).

6.49 The Inland Revenue, at TSEM 3515, used to list some examples of trust management expenses:

(a) telephone, stationery and postage;

(b) the cost of collecting and distributing income;

(c) accountancy fees – including the cost of preparing trust accounts and returns, arguably these are for the benefit of the trust as a whole; there is a long-standing practice that allows them;

(d) interest on unpaid IHT under IHTA 1984 s 233(3), which is not allowable in computing income for income tax purposes, but trustees can claim it as a trust management expense if they properly pay it from income – this will reduce the income of beneficiaries (TSEM 3760 onwards) or the amount chargeable under ICTA 1988 s 686 (TSEM 3015);

(e) interest paid on overdue income tax – the provisions are similar to those for interest on unpaid IHT;

(f) Interest paid under TMA 1970 s 88 – trustees must have an indemnity under the terms of the trust document.

The latest version, however, merely refers to the expenses being necessarily incurred and properly charged to income.

6.50 Expenses that are not allowable are as follows (TSEM 3515):

(a) capital gains tax;

(b) the costs of creating the trust;

(c) the costs of appointing new trustees;

(d) legal fees – including the costs of legal advice or the cost of preparing supplementary deeds;

(e) the costs of employing an investment adviser, including the costs of making or changing investments;

(f) premiums on life or other insurance policies forming part of the trust fund;

(g) expenses allowable in some other context, eg expenses the trustees deducted to arrive at the taxable Schedule A income.

6.51 Expenses paid by the trustees to a beneficiary as an allowance for the upkeep of trust property is likely to be the income of the beneficiary (*Shanks v IRC* (1928) 14 TC 249; *Waley Cohen v IRC* (1945) 26 TC 471) unless the money is held in a constructive trust for the upkeep of the property (*Marchioness Conyngham v Revenue Comrs* (1928) 1 ITC 259).

6.52 The proliferation of different tax rates for different types of income has necessitated a statutory order of set-off of trust expenses which are treated as paid out of income in the following order under ICTA 1988 s 689B:

(a) dividends and other distributions taxable under Schedule F and carrying a non-payable tax credit;

(b) foreign dividends payable under Schedule D Case V at the Schedule F ordinary rate under ICTA 1988 s 1A(1A)(b) and (3)(b);

(c) other savings income bearing tax of 20 per cent; and

(d) income chargeable at the basic rate of 22 per cent.

6.53 Non-resident trustees have to apportion expenses rateably between income that pays UK tax and that which does not under ICTA 1988 s 686(2A). Only the proportion of expenses applicable to the UK income can be taken into account in calculating the tax payable by the trustees and beneficiaries.

6.54 Where a UK trust has non-UK resident beneficiaries to whom income is distributed, the management expenses incurred by the trustees in the year have to be proportionately disallowed where the beneficiary is not liable to income tax on distributions because of his non-UK residence, or deemed non-UK residence under a double taxation treaty. [ICTA 1988 s 689A(1)]. The disregarded expenses are the amount which bears the same proportion to all the expenses as the untaxed income payable to the non-resident bears to the distributed income payable to all the beneficiaries. [Section 689A(2)]. The proportion of income distributed is the actual income not grossed up for tax purposes. [Section 689A(3) and (4)]. Excluded income taxable on a non-resident under FA 1995 s 128(3), which has not borne tax by deduction at source, is treated as income not liable to tax in the UK by reason of the non-UK resident beneficiary's non-residence. [Section 689A(5)].

6.55 So far as interest paid by the trustees is concerned, interest on unpaid tax, including IHT under IHTA 1984 s 233(3), is not allowable in computing income for income tax purposes, but the trustees can claim it as a trust management expense if the trust deed allows them to pay this properly from income (TSEM 3515). TMA 1970 s 90 disallows tax relief on interest. The general interest deduction provisions in ICTA 1988 ss 353–379 apply to trusts. This includes a loan to pay IHT under ICTA 1988 s 364, although the interest is only deductible for the first year. [Section 364(1)]. Mortgage interest relief at source (MIRAS), which was abolished after 5 April 2000, applied to trusts as well as individuals. Trustees use the gross equivalent of the interest paid in calculating the tax at the rate applicable to trusts and the income of the beneficiary who is entitled to the trust income (TSEM 3605).

6.56 Where income is mandated to a life tenant so that the trustees have no income, any trust expenses would, of necessity, have to be paid from capital and would not serve to reduce the life tenant's taxable income.

Example

The trustees of the Grushin trust were required to pay £500 per annum out of the trust income to maintain the grave of Rover, the settlor's Labrador dog, now deceased, and half the remaining income to Peter, with the balance at their discretion to distribute among a number of beneficiaries or to accumulate.

The trust income consisted of UK dividends of £900, net rents received of £6,000 and bank interest of £400. The trustees incurred fees and expenses chargeable to income of £2,000.

		Dividends	Interest	Rent
	£	£	£	£
Income received		900	400	6,000
Tax credit 1/9		100		
Tax deducted of 20%			100	
		1,000	500	6,000
Less income allocated for specific purposes (Rover's grave) allocated pro rata		(67)	(33)	(400)
		933	467	5,600
Less income allocated to Peter (½) as life tenant		(467)	(233)	(2,800)
		466	234	2,800
Expenses	2,000			
Less allocated for specific purposes $£2,000 \times \frac{500}{7,500}$	(133)			
	1,867			
Less allocated to life tenant £1,867 x ½ =	933			
Less allocated to income taxable at rate applicable to trusts	934			
Grossed up at dividend rate £419 x 10/9		(466)		
Grossed up at lower rate £187 x 100/80			(234)	
Grossed up at basic rate £328 x 100/78				(420)
Amount taxable at rate applicable to trusts		NIL	NIL	2,380
Tax payable by trustees at 34%				809.20

Peter's taxable income from the trust was:

		Dividends	Interest	Rent
	£	£	£	£
Gross income		467	233	2,800
Tax paid by trustees				
10%		(47)		
20%			(46)	
22%				(616)
Net		420	187	2,184

Less management expenses	933			
Allocated to dividends	420	(420)		
Allocated to interest	187		(187)	
Allocated to rents			(326)	
Net income liable to higher rates		NIL	NIL	1,858
Grossed $^{100}/_{78}$				2,382
Tax payable by Peter at 18% (40%–22%)				428.76

Liability to pay tax

6.57 Trustees are persons receiving or entitled to income, and are therefore subject to tax under Schedule D on that income. [ICTA 1988 s 59(1)]. They are charged in the name of the trust. For CGT purposes, trustees are treated as being a single and continuing body of persons distinct from the persons who may from time to time be the trustees. [TCGA 1992 s 69(1)]. Although there is no similar provision for income tax, it is generally assumed that trustees are bodies of persons within TMA 1970 s 71 and subject to tax accordingly. Personal representatives are made responsible for tax under TMA 1970 s 74 and trustees of incapacitated persons by section 72 of that Act. A trustee who has properly delegated to an agent, who actually received the income, is not liable to do anything other than make a trust return in respect of that income under TMA 1970 s 76. These provisions are extended to CGT by TMA 1970 s 77.

Trust income

Trading income

6.58 Trustees may carry on a trade in the UK or throughout the world assessable under Schedule D Case I or II, or entirely abroad assessable under Schedule D Case V. They could also be partners in a trading partnership in their capacity as trustees. They are entitled to the normal reliefs of any other taxpayer such as loss relief under ICTA 1988 s 380 and relief for errors or mistakes under TMA 1970 s 33, and can claim capital allowances. However, but as they are not (when acting as trustees) individuals, they cannot claim personal reliefs under ICTA 1988 ss 256–278.

6.59 It is unusual for trustees to trade for the benefit of the trust because they could be personally liable for *devastavit*, or loss to the trust, if their commercial activities were unsuccessful. This may be covered by indemnities in the trust deed or guaranteed by adult beneficiaries. It is, however, quite common for trustees to be partners in family partnerships, particularly farming partnerships, although again the question of the trustees' personal liability may pose a problem. In some cases it may be possible to arrange for the trustees to be companies with no other assets specifically formed for this purpose. The Limited Partnerships Act 1907 prevented trustee partners from taking part in the management of the partnership but a partnership formed under the Limited Liability Partnerships Act 2000 could enable the trustees to participate in the business yet limit the risks to the assets used in the business.

6.60 The trading profits of a business carried on by the trustees are not classified as earned income but investment income when distributed to the beneficiaries (*Fry v Shiels' Trustees* (1915) 6 TC 583; *M'Dougal v Smith* (1919) 7 TC 134). The profits are only earned income if the beneficiary actively conducts the business (TSEM 3233).

6.61 Where the trustees own land on which there are mines, quarries or similar concerns within ICTA 1988 s 55, the rent is subject to tax under Schedule D under ICTA 1988 s 119, subject to relief for mineral royalties under section 122 of the Act. Rent payable in respect of electric line wayleaves is taxable under Schedule D under section 120. Management expenses incurred by the trustees wholly, exclusively and necessarily as expenses of management or supervision of mineral rights are allowable under section 121 subject to relief under section 122.

6.62 ICTA 1988 s 122 treats one-half of the mineral royalties receivable by the trustees, less one-half of the management expenses as income. The remaining half of the mineral royalties is taxed as a capital gain under TCGA 1992 s 201. No deductions are allowed against the capital element, not even the remaining half of the management expenses. [TCGA 1992 s 122(3)]. The requirement for deduction of tax at source from mineral royalties under ICTA 1988 s 119 is removed with effect from 1 May 1995 by FA 1995 s 145 (CG 71705; TSEM 3235).

Income from abroad

6.63 Trustees will normally be subject to UK tax on income from abroad, although this will depend on the circumstances. Where the foreign income has suffered overseas tax and is liable to tax in the UK, credit for the foreign tax suffered will normally be available under the unilateral relief provisions in ICTA 1988 s 790. This will normally be restricted to withholding taxes, as relief for underlying tax is normally restricted to companies owning at least 10 per cent of the voting power in the company paying the dividend. [ICTA 1988 s 790(6)].

6.64 It is interesting to consider whether if a trust has a corporate trustee it can claim unilateral relief under these provisions on the grounds that as legal owner of the shares it is legally entitled to the required voting control and that the dividend is paid to it, albeit in its capacity as trustee rather than as beneficial owner. Unilateral relief is only available where relief is not available under a double taxation treaty negotiated in accordance with ICTA

1988 s 788. The question as to whether a trust is able to benefit under a double taxation treaty will depend on the precise terms of the relevant treaty. Under some treaties a trust is specifically included in the definition of a resident of the contracting state, whereas other treaties do not mention trusts and the question then to be considered is whether trustees can claim treaty protection as an individual in the case of non-corporate trustees, or as a company in the case of a corporate trustee, or whether they are precluded from claiming any treaty relief as not being the beneficial owners of the income in question.

6.65 Where the beneficiary has an interest in possession and is therefore entitled to the income as it arises, subject only to the trustee's expenses, it might be possible to argue that the beneficiary is entitled to claim relief under the double taxation treaty in respect of that income.

6.66 The only reference in the Taxes Acts to double taxation relief in respect of trusts is found in ICTA 1988 s 809 where the trustees of a discretionary trust have made a distribution to a beneficiary of net income under section 687(2) of the Act, which will be treated as having suffered tax at the rate applicable to trusts. The trustees may certify, if that be the case, that the income (including taxed overseas income of an amount and from a source stated in the certificate) and the amount arose to the trustees not earlier than six years before the end of the year of assessment in which the distribution is made. The beneficiary may claim that the distribution, up to the certified amount, should be treated as his income from the overseas source held by the trustees, and claim double taxation relief accordingly. [ICTA 1988 s 809(1)]. However, taxed overseas income is defined as income in respect of which the trustees are entitled to credit for overseas tax either under a treaty or as unilateral relief. [Section 809(2)].

Deposit interest

6.67 Under ICTA 1988 s 480A a deposit taker making a payment of interest in respect of a relevant deposit, has to deduct tax at the savings rate for the year of assessment in which the payment is made, which is then paid over to the Inland Revenue on a quarterly basis under ICTA 1988 Sch 16. Certain deposit holders, such as non-residents, may qualify to have the interest paid gross under section 480B. A liability to tax on interest from a relevant deposit is on the full amount arising under Schedule D Case III. [Section 480C]. Deposit taker includes an authorised bank, the Post Office or the local authority, or is so prescribed by statutory instrument. [Section 481(2)]. A relevant deposit only arises where the deposit holder is an individual, a Scottish partnership of individuals, a personal representative or the trustees of a discretionary or accumulation and maintenance trust. [Section 481(4)]. A trust is a discretionary or accumulation trust if some or all of the income accruing to the trustees, unless treated as income of the settlor, is taxable under ICTA 1988 s 686. [Section 481(4A)]. Various deposits which do not qualify as relevant deposits are identified in ICTA 1988 s 481(5), (5A) and

(5B), and there are supplementary provisions in section 482. There are broadly similar provisions in relation to building society interest under section 477A.

6.68 Bank or building society interest can be paid to trustees gross if all the beneficiaries are not ordinarily resident in the UK and the appropriate declaration to the deposit taker is given on form R105, so long as each beneficiary has an interest in possession and the income therefore belongs to him as it arises. [ICTA 1988 s 481(4)(a) and (5)(k)(i)]. Trustees of a discretionary trust can also make such a declaration and receive the income gross, but only if the trustees themselves are non-UK resident as well as the beneficiaries (TSEM 3245). [ICTA 1988 s 481(4)(d) and (5)(k)(iii)].

Relevant discounted securities

6.69 Relevant discounted securities are taxable in accordance with FA 1996 s 102 and Sch 13. These are securities where the amount payable on redemption is an amount which is likely to produce a deep gain, ie where the amount payable on redemption exceeds the issue price by more than the lower of 0.5 per cent of the redemption amount for each year between the date of issue and the date of redemption or 15 per cent of the redemption amount. [FA 1996 Sch 13 para 3]. The question of whether a deep gain is likely is determined by looking at the position at redemption or on any occasion before maturity on which it could be redeemed at the option of the holder or in certain other cases. [Sch 13 para 3(1A)]. Gilt strips are included as relevant discounted securities. [Sch 13 para 14]. FA 2003 s 182 and Sch 39 restricted relief for most relevant discounted securities and gilt strips after 26 March 2003.

6.70 The profit on redemption is chargeable as income under Schedule D Case III or in the case of a non-UK relevant discounted security under Schedule D Case IV. [Sch 13 para 1]. Relevant discounted securities are not subject to CGT because they are qualifying corporate bonds. [TCGA 1992 s 117(2AA)]. It is chargeable on the trustees at the rate applicable to trusts (TSEM 3250) [FA 1996 Sch 13 para 6(1)(c)]. Gilt strips are deemed to be disposed of on 5 April each year whether they are or not and any excess over the market value a year earlier or the price paid for them if they are acquired during the year is taxable at the rate applicable to trusts (TSEM 3255). [FA 1996 Sch 13 para 14].

Exempt income

6.71 Certain income is exempt from UK tax and should not be included on the trust and estate tax return. This includes premium bonds, National Lottery and gaming prizes, interest and terminal bonuses under Save as You Earn schemes, accumulated interest on National Savings certificates including index-linked certificates, interest on National Savings children's bonus bonds, interest awarded by a UK court as part of an award of damages for personal injuries or death, and dividends on ordinary shares in venture capital trusts (TSEM 3190).

Non-qualifying policies

6.72 Non-qualifying UK life assurance policies, life annuities and capital redemption policies may give rise to a chargeable event taxable as income under the provisions of ICTA 1988 ss 539–554. Although the tax is usually charged on the settlor, where the policies are held in trust and the settlor is not resident in the UK or is dead at the time of the chargeable event, the trustees may be subject to income tax on the gain. [ICTA 1988 s 547(1)(a) and (d)]. This also applies where the settlor was a company which was not UK resident or had been wound up at the time of a chargeable event. A gift of such a policy, outright or into trust, is not a chargeable event. [ICTA 1988 s 540(1)].

6.73 If the trustees are holding as bare trustees, the income is that of the beneficiary. In other cases, where the deemed income is that of the trustees it is taxable on them at the rate applicable to trusts. A gain is not deemed to be income of the trustees if the policy or life annuity was made before 17 March 1998 and not subsequently enhanced by paying further non-contractual premiums, or in any other way, and the trust was created before that date (TSEM 3200). [FA 1998 Sch 14 para 7(1)(b)]. Similar provisions apply to non-resident policies under ICTA 1988 s 553 (TSEM 3210).

6.74 Where the gain on the chargeable event is taxed on the settlor under ICTA 1988 s 547(1)(a) or (b) the settlor has a right of recovery from the trustees who actually realise the gain under ICTA 1988 s 551 or 551A. The chargeable calculation on non-qualifying insurance policies may result in a deficiency for which relief may be claimed under section 549 of the 1988 Act. In certain cases where a loan is taken it may be treated as a partial surrender under section 548. The insurance company has a duty under section 552 to provide the Inland Revenue with details of the computation of the gain arising on the chargeable event.

6.75 The tax liability arising on personal portfolio bonds can be particularly swingeing as there is a yearly charge to tax under ICTA 1988 s 553C on the deemed income of the bond, which could well exceed the bond's actual performance. Borrowings on life policies can, in certain cases, be treated as income under section 554.

Offshore funds

6.76 Anti-avoidance legislation aimed at offshore roll-up funds is contained in ICTA 1988 ss 757–764. These provisions apply to a non-qualifying offshore fund, which is a fund which is not certified by the Revenue as a distributing fund, i e one which distributes at least 85 per cent of its income as computed under section 760 and Sch 27. If there is a disposal of a material interest in a non-qualifying offshore fund the profit on disposal is treated as income under section 757. A material interest in an offshore fund is defined by section 759 as an interest in a non-resident collective investment scheme constituted as a company, normally an open-ended investment company, a unit trust or similar arrangement.

6.77 Where a trust holds an investment in an offshore fund which is certified as having distributing fund status, any gain on disposal is subject to CGT and is entered as a chargeable gain on the trust return. However, where the fund operates equalisation arrangements under ICTA 1988 s 758, there will be both an income and a capital element in the equalisation adjustments and the income element is taxed as such and the capital element as a capital gain. The income element, because it is actually a capital gain, is chargeable at the rate applicable to trusts. The gain on the disposal of a material interest in a non-qualifying offshore fund held by a UK trust is treated in its entirety as income for tax purposes and is taxable at the rate applicable to trusts (TSEM 3215). [Sections 761(1) and 764]. A disposal by trustees of a non-UK resident trust, however, will be taxed as a capital gain under ICTA 1988 s 761(7). The offshore income gain is deducted from the capital gain on disposal under section 763.

Scrip dividends, demergers etc

6.78 The tax consequences of scrip dividends, enhanced scrip dividends, demergers, reconstructions and companies buying their own shares are dependent on the treatment under trust law and are dealt with in Chapter 4 at **4.30–4.43** (TSEM 3220, 3225).

Estate income

6.79 Estate income from the estate of a deceased person in the course of administration, taxable under ICTA 1988 ss 695–702, may become payable to trustees, and under section 701(3A) it is paid under the deduction of tax at the applicable rate which means the basic rate, the lower rate for savings income or the Schedule F ordinary rate according to the income of the residue of the estate out of which it is paid. Where the income is received by the trustees of a discretionary or accumulation and maintenance settlement, it is grossed up at the rate applicable to trusts or the trust Schedule F rate under section 686 with credit for the applicable rate tax suffered (TSEM 3240).

Premiums etc

6.80 Premiums treated as rent under ICTA 1988 s 34 are capital profits received by the trustees, taxable as income but not at the rate applicable to trusts. Although the premium is taxable partly as rent where the lease does not exceed 50 years, and therefore brought within the Schedule A charge, it is actually a capital profit under trust law and therefore subject to tax at the basic rate, but it is not savings income within ICTA 1988 s 1A and as it is capital it is not subject to the rate applicable to trusts under ICTA 1988 s 686 and TSEM 3260.

6.80A Profits on the sale of certificates of deposit within section 56 of the Act are taxable as income under Schedule D Case VI, although they are capital profits and are therefore taxable at the basic rate, as not within the definition of savings income under section 1A, but are not liable at the rate applicable to trusts as they are actually capital profits (TSEM 3265). Uncertificated deposits are also treated similarly under ICTA 1988 s 56A.

6.81 Company distributions that are in fact capital but deemed to be income under ICTA 1988 s 209 are subject to tax at the Schedule F ordinary rate under sections 1A, 1B and 20 of the Act but as they are capital under trust law they are not taxable at the rate applicable to trusts under ICTA 1988 s 686 (TSEM 3270).

6.82 A loan by a close company to a trust which is written off and treated as income under ICTA 1988 s 421, is taxable on the trustees at the Schedule F lower rate under section 233(1B). However, as this is a capital receipt at law, the Schedule F trust rate under ICTA 1988 s 686(1A)(a) is not charged (TSEM 3275).

6.83 Certain capital profits from transactions in land other than trading transactions are taxable as income under ICTA 1988 s 776 where land is acquired with the sole or main object of realising a gain from disposing of it, or is held as trading stock or developed for the sole or main object of realising a gain from disposing of the land when developed. [Section 776(2)]. A capital profit is taxable under Schedule D Case VI at the basic rate as it is not savings income under ICTA 1988 s 1A. As it is a capital receipt taxed as income it is not subject to the rate applicable to trusts under ICTA 1988 s 686 (TSEM 3280).

6.84 In *Page v Lowther* [1983] STC 799 the trustees of settled land leased the land for 99 years to a development company and were entitled to a premium on the development company granting underleases to tenants as the properties were developed and let. This was sufficient to bring the trustees within the charge to tax under ICTA 1988 s 776 (TESM 3280). Under these provisions an individual providing the gain to other parties, such as trustees, could be taxable (*Sugarwhite v Budd* [1988] STC 533; *Yuill v Wilson* [1980] STC 460; *Yuill v Fletcher* [1984] STC 401). [Section 776(5)(a)].

Annuities

6.85 In *Re Pettit, Le Fevre v Pettit* [1922] 2 Ch 765 it was held that an annuity payable free of tax meant that the annuitant was to receive the stated annuity. It was held that the annuitant had to refund to the trustees part of the tax refund in relation to her personal allowances proportionate to the annuity.

In *Re Maclellan, Few v Byrne* [1939] 3 All ER 81 and *Re Eves, Midland Bank Executor and Trustee Co Ltd v Eves* (1939) 18 ATC 401 a similar decision was reached as it was in *Re Jubb* (1941) 20 ATC 297; *Re Tatham, National Provincial Bank Ltd v MacKenzie* [1945] 1 All ER 29 and a number of other cases. The refund which the annuitant makes to the trustees in these circumstances is taxable on them as additional trust income unless the annuitant is not resident or ordinarily resident in the UK and it does not relate to personal reliefs, for example, as it relates to a repayment of tax on foreign stock (TSEM 3285). In some cases the wording of the annuity is such that the annuitant could retain any tax refund (*Re Jones, Jones v Jones* [1933] Ch 842).

Accrued income scheme

6.86 The accrued income scheme in ICTA 1988 ss 710–728 applies to trustees as it applies to other taxpayers. The scheme applies to gilt-edged securities, company loan stocks and similar investments and is designed to prevent bond-washing, ie buying securities ex-interest and selling them cum interest just before the interest is paid. The aim of the scheme is to tax the purchaser and seller on their share of the interest as it accrues from day to day.

6.87 There is a *de minimis* provision under which an individual escapes a charge where the nominal value of securities held by him does not exceed £5,000. [ICTA 1988 s 715(1)(b)]. This is extended to trustees of a disabled person's trust under section 715(1)(e), as defined by section 715(8) by reference to TCGA 1992 Sch 1 para 1(1). These trust secure that at least half of the property and income of the trust is applied during the lifetime of a mentally disabled person or a person in receipt of attendance relief or of a disability living allowance by virtue of entitlement to the care component at the highest or middle rate for his benefit. Trustees are not liable where they hold merely as bare trustees under section 720 (TSEM 3320), but the settlor remains chargeable. The accrued income charge on the trustees is not the income of a beneficiary but taxable on the trustees at the rate applicable to trusts. [Section 720(5)]. Where there is an accrued interest scheme allowance under section 714(5) it is available to the trustees, unless the income has been mandated to a beneficiary in which case he should claim the allowance against the income (TSEM 3325). Putting securities into trust in the first instance is a transfer from the settlor to the trustee under ICTA 1988 s 710(5)(a).

6.88 A mere change of beneficiaries, eg on the death of a life tenant, is not a transfer unless the assets pass absolutely to another beneficiary, in which case a transfer simply produces self-cancelling, deemed sums and reliefs to the trustees. Where, however, the trustees use their power of advancement to appoint property to a beneficiary, this can amount to a transfer within the scheme. It is possible for the trustees to end up with stranded or unusable accrued interest scheme allowances where, for example, securities are bought cum interest and shortly afterwards transferred to a beneficiary following the death of a life tenant. The allowance cannot be transferred to the beneficiary and may become unusable.

6.89 A transfer to new trustees simply produces self-cancelling deemed sums and reliefs unless the new trustees are non-resident, in which case there is a deemed transfer of the securities by the resident trustees. The accrued income scheme can be applied to non-resident trustees through the anti-avoidance provisions in ICTA 1988 ss 739 and 740 by section 742(4)–(7) of the Act. Where non-resident trustees transfer to resident trustees, there is a transfer for accrued interest scheme purposes (TSEM 3340). The accrued income scheme may also apply to unauthorised unit trusts held by trustees which would be income or an allowance to set against income by the trustees (TSEM 3345). Where the unit trust treats accrued interest as income by adopting a strict, daily, full accruals basis or 'clean price accounting', which strips out the income, the trustees are not charged at the rate applicable to trusts (TSEM 3350). Tax payable under the accrued income scheme goes into the trust tax pool to frank payments to beneficiaries under ICTA 1988 s 687 (TSEM 3360). The accrued income scheme calculations for non-resident trustees assume they are UK resident under section 720(7).

Trustees' liability for tax

6.90 The income of a settlement is received by the trustees jointly, not jointly and severally (*Dawson v IRC* [1989] STC 473). Tax is chargeable on one or more of the relevant trustees under FA 1989 s 151, relevant trustees being those to whom the income or gains arise and any subsequent trustees of the settlement. [Section 151(2)]. This section was deemed always to have had effect, under FA 1989 s 151(4), thus validating the Revenue practice of assessing a single trustee.

6.91 The trustees have a statutory obligation under TMA 1970 s 8A to make and deliver to the Revenue a return containing such information as may reasonably be required in pursuance to a notice given to a relevant trustee, and to deliver with the return such accounts, statements and documents relating to information contained in the return as may reasonably be so required. [Section 8A(1)].

6.92 Payments made by trustees out of capital to beneficiaries may become income in the beneficiaries' hands and the trustees would have to deduct tax under ICTA 1988 s 349 as annual payments (*Brodie's Trustees v IRC* (1933) 17 TC 432; *Lindus and Hortin v IRC* (1933) 17 TC 442; *Jackson's Trustees v IRC* (1942) 25 TC 13; *Cunard's Trustees v IRC; Mcpheeters v IRC* (1945) 27 TC 122; *John Morant Settlement Trustees v IRC* (1948) 30 TC 147; *Milne's Executors v IRC* (1956) 37 TC 10; *Williamson v Ough* (1936) 20 TC 194; *Esdaile v IRC* (1936) 20 TC 700; *Trustees of Pierse-Duncombe Trust v IRC* (1940) 23 TC 199).

6.93 Interestingly, the above cases are all rather old and in *Stevenson v Wishart (Levy's Trustees)* [1987] STC 266 it was held that payments out of capital to defray a beneficiary's medical and nursing home expenses were not annual payments as they were for emergency expenditure to look after a very elderly beneficiary and not part of her normal income. Fixed annuities payable out of trust income would not normally be made these days, although trustees might be instructed to purchase an annuity for a beneficiary, which would be much more tax- effective as part of it would be treated as capital under ICTA 1988 ss 656–658.

Benefits in kind

6.94 Where a beneficiary enjoys trust assets in kind, either land or chattels or a loan from the trust, there is no chargeable benefit if the trust is resident in the UK. There is no question of any deemed income arising to the beneficiary. There may be IHT implications by giving the beneficiary an interest in possession over part of the trust property (SP 10/79; see **6.166** below and there could be CGT implications where the property concerned is occupied by a beneficiary as their main residence (*Sansom (Ridge Settlement Trustees) v Paye* [1976] STC 494; see **6.127** below).

6.95 The use of trust property by beneficiaries where the trustees are non-UK resident, however, could give rise to a benefit in kind under ICTA 1988 ss 739(2)(c) and 740(1)(b) or a charge to CGT under TCGA 1992 s 87 by virtue of TCGA 1992 s 97(2). This was applied to an interest-free loan in *Billingham v Cooper* [2000] STC 122 (see Chapter 10, **10.27**).

Capital gains tax

6.96 For CGT purposes, settled property means any property held in trust other than by nominees or bare trustees. [TCGA 1992 ss 68 and 60]. A transfer into settlement whether revocable or irrevocable is a disposal of the entire property by the settlor, whether or not he is a beneficiary under the settlement or a trustee. (*Berry v Warnett* [1982] STC 396). [TCGA 1992 s 70]. The trustees of a settlement are treated as being a single and continuing body of persons distinct from the persons who may from time to time be the trustees. Trustees shall be treated as being resident and ordinarily resident in the UK unless the general administration of the trust is ordinarily carried on outside the UK and the trustees or a majority of them for the time being are not resident or ordinarily resident in the UK. [TCGA 1992 s 69(1)]. A UK resident professional trustee may be regarded as non-UK resident if, when the settlement was created, the settlor was neither domiciled, resident nor ordinarily resident in the UK and the majority of the trustees are not UK resident and the general administration of the trust is ordinarily carried on outside the UK. [Section 69(2)]. In a strict settlement under SLA 1925, the life tenant, as trustee, and the capital trustees are treated as constituting and acting on behalf of a single body of trustees. [TCGA 1992 s 69(3)]. Where tax is assessed on the trustees in respect of a chargeable gain and is not paid within six months from the due date, the Revenue may collect the tax from any transferee of the trust assets who has become absolutely entitled as against the trustees within two years of the time when the tax became payable. [Section 69(4)].

6.97 The rate of CGT for a settlement is the rate applicable to trusts under ICTA 1988 s 686, as a result of TCGA 1992 s 4(1AA) from 1998/99. For earlier years of assessment, interests in possession trusts were chargeable to CGT at the basic rate of income tax.

6.98 In the case of a trust where the settlor and the trustee are resident and ordinarily resident in the UK and the settlor has retained an interest, chargeable gains are taxed not on the trustees but on the settlor under TCGA 1992 s 77(1) and (7). The settlor has a right of recovery from the trustees on the basis of a certificate from the Revenue confirming the tax paid, under section 78, and rules for determining who is the settlor for these purposes are contained in section 79 of the 1992 Act. In the case of a non-resident settlement, the gains may be assessed on the settlor under TCGA 1992 s 86, or the beneficiaries when capital gains are distributed to them under section 87 (see Chapter 10, 10.60 et seq). The CGT charge on the settlor does not apply in the year of assessment in which the settlor dies or where the interest in the settlement is that of the settlor's spouse in the year in which the spouse dies or the settlor and the spouse divorce (CG 34721). [TCGA 1992 s 77(6)]. From 2000/01 settlors may elect for their personal capital losses to be set against gains attributed to them under TCGA 1992 ss 77, 86, 87 and 89(2) as a result of the removal of the ring fence by FA 2002 s 51 and Sch 11. From 2003/04 no election is necessary.

6.99 A settlor is regarded as having an interest in a settlement if any property comprised in the settlement, or any property derived therefrom, may at any time in any circumstances whatsoever become payable to or applicable for the benefit of the settlor or his spouse, or either of them enjoys a benefit directly or indirectly from any property comprised in the settlement or any derived property. These provisions do not apply where the settlor can only be regarded as having an interest in the settlement on the bankruptcy of a beneficiary or a beneficiary seeking to assign or charge property or, in the case of a marriage settlement, the death of both parties to the marriage, all or any of the children of the marriage, or on the death of a child of the settlor who had become beneficially entitled to the property in the settlement or any derived property at an age not exceeding 25 [TCGA 1992 s 77(4) and (5)]. Any chargeable gains apportioned to the settlor are computed net of taper relief before being regarded as the settlor's gains and are therefore not eligible for taper relief in his hands, otherwise relief would effectively be given twice. [Section 77(6A)].

6.100 A benefit available to the settlor and his spouse includes an interest-free loan, rent-free occupation of trust property or the forgiveness of a loan to the settlor as well as outright appointments of trust income or capital (CG 34751). Any small incidental benefits to the settlor are disregarded as *de* *minimis* (*Taw and Torridge Festival Society Ltd v IRC* (1959) 38 TC 603; *IRC v National Book League* (1957) 37 TC 455; CG 34752). Spouse does not include the person the settlor intends to marry or a spouse from whom the settlor is separated under a court order, a separation agreement or other circumstances such that the separation is likely to be permanent or a widow or widower of the settlor (CG 34753). [TCGA 1992 s 77(3)].

6.101 In determining who is the settlor when charging CGT on the settlor with an interest in the settlement, TCGA 1992 s 79 provides that a person is a settlor if the settlement consists of or includes property originating from him, ie which he provided directly or indirectly for the purposes of the settlement, and any property representing that property. Where there is more than one settlor, there are provisions for apportioning property in order to ascertain the amount provided by the settlor with the interest in the settlement. [TCGA 1992 ss 1–3]. These include property provided to the settlement by a third party under a reciprocal arrangement but not property provided by the settlor to the third party as a result of those arrangements, in order to avoid double counting. [TCGA 1992 s 79(5)]. An attempt to use these provisions for tax avoidance failed in *De Rothschild v Lawrenson* [1995] STC 623 on the grounds that TCGA 1992 s 77 only applied where the trustees were in fact chargeable to tax on the realised gains in the first instance. Interestingly, section 77, which was brought in to protect the Revenue as an anti-avoidance measure, is in fact a relieving provision where the settlor is taxable at no more than the basic rate. Otherwise the trustees would be subject to CGT at the rate applicable to trusts, currently 34 per cent. In the case of a higher rate taxpayer the section still has an anti-avoidance element where the settlor pays tax at the higher rate and the Revenue collects an extra 6 per cent on the gains compared with the rate applicable to trusts.

6.102 There are no provisions to allocate losses made by the trust through to the settlor where he has an interest in the settlement and such losses remain in the trust to set against future trust gains and thereby reduce the amount that may be taxable on the settlor in future years.

6.103 The Revenue has information gathering powers in relation to the settlor interested settlements requiring a settlor trustee or beneficiary to provide the Revenue with particulars necessary for the taxation of the settlor under these provisions. [TCGA 1992 s 79(6)]. Gains or losses of non-resident companies in which the trust holds more than 10 per cent of the shares, which may be apportioned through to the trustees under TCGA 1992 s 13, are further apportioned through to the settlor under section 79(7). Maintenance funds for historic buildings within ICTA 1988 s 619(2) are excluded from treatment as settlor interested settlements by section 79(8).

6.104 Trustees are entitled to an annual exemption equal to half that of an individual. [TCGA 1992 Sch 1 para 2(2)]. In respect of pre-7 June 1978 trusts, the trustees merely have to state on the trust return that the gains do not exceed half the exempt amount for the year and that the consideration does not exceed the exempt amount. Other trusts have to return a full computation of chargeable gains. [Sch 1 para 2(3)]. Where there are several trusts made by the same settlor after 6 June 1978, the annual exempt amount available of one-half of an individual's annual exemption is divided by the number of trusts in the group, subject to the minimum allowance of one-tenth of the annual exemption for each trust. [Sch 1 para 2(4) and (5)]. The income tax definition of 'settlor' in ICTA 1992 s 660G(1) and (2) (see 6.2) is adopted.

6.105 An excluded settlement is defined as one where the trustees are not UK resident or which is a charitable trust or approved superannuation fund. [TCGA 1992 Sch 1 para 2(7) and (8)]. The Inspector is given power to demand information in relation to a settlement in order to determine the entitlement to the proportionate annual allowance under Sch 1 para 2(9). The annual exempt amount for an individual under TCGA 1992 s 3(2) is £7,900 for 2003/04 by virtue of the CGT (Annual Exempt Amount) Order 2001 (SI 2003/842). Where the settlement is for disabled persons, the full annual exempt amount is allowed apportioned among such settlements made by the same settlor if relevant. [TCGA 1992 Sch 1 para 1].

6.106 Because trustees are taxable on disposals of trust assets, including on transfer to beneficiaries, the beneficiaries' interest in the trust, which is in itself an asset, is normally exempt for CGT purposes under TCGA 1992 s 76(1) unless it was acquired for money or money's worth. The exemption is also lost where the trustees were at any time not resident or ordinarily resident in the UK or treated as such for double taxation relief purposes under a double taxation treaty. [Section 76(1A) and (1B)]. The purchaser of an interest in settled property who then becomes absolutely entitled as against the trustee is treated as disposing of the interest he purchased for the value of the property transferred to him. [Section 76(2) and (3)].

6.107 Although the definition of settlor is the same for CGT and income tax purposes, it may not always be the same person. For example, a beneficiary may have assigned the right of income to another party, thus creating a further trust of which he is the settlor which will not affect his position as beneficiary for capital gains purposes. Variation to a deceased testamentary disposition may cause the deceased to be the deemed settlor for CGT purposes under TCGA 1992 s 62(6) but this would not have any effect for income tax purposes and the original legatee would become the settlor. This also applied for the non-resident trust capital gains legislation in TCGA 1992 s 87 (*Marshall v Kerr* [1994] STC 638).

6.108 It is often necessary to determine whether there is more than one settlement which affects not only the annual allowance available to the trust but also the fact that losses cannot be transferred between settlements. The transfer of assets within a settlement would not be a disposal but a transfer to a different settlement would be, at a market valuation (CG 33290). The starting point is that a single settlement deed implies a single settlement even though it may be divided into a number of funds or sub-trusts. The leading case on whether or not a separate trust has been created is *Roome v Edwards* [1981] STC 96. Where a trust was divided into two but the trustees remained the same and were subject to the administrative powers of the main settlement this was just an internal division, not a deemed disposal under TCGA 1992 s 71 (*Bond v Pickford* [1983] STC 517).

6.109 SP 7/84 provides as follows:

> **'Exercise of a power of appointment or advancement over settled property**
>
> The Board's Statement of Practice SP 9/81, which was issued on 23 September 1981 following discussions with the Law Society, set out the Revenue's views on the capital gains tax implications of the exercise of a power of appointment or advancement when continuing trusts are declared, in the light of the decision of the House of Lords in *Roome v Edwards* [1981] STC 96. Those views have been modified to some extent by the decision of the Court of Appeal in *Bond v Pickford* [1983] STC 517.
>
> In *Roome v Edwards* the House of Lords held that where a separate settlement is created there is a deemed disposal of the relevant assets by the old trustees for the purposes of TCGA 1992 s 71(1) (CGTA 1979 s 54(1)). But the judgements emphasised that, in deciding whether or not a new settlement has been created by the exercise of a power of appointment or advancement, each case must be considered on its own facts, and by applying established legal doctrine to the facts in a practical and common-sense manner. In *Bond v Pickford* the judgements in the Court of Appeal explained that the consideration of the facts must include examination of the powers which the trustees purported to exercise, and determination of the intention of the parties, viewed objectively.
>
> It is now clear that a deemed disposal under TCGA 1992 s 71(1) cannot arise unless the power exercised by the trustees, or the instrument conferring the power, expressly or by necessary implication, confers on the trustees authority to remove assets from the original settlement by subjecting them to the trusts of a different settlement. Such powers (which may be powers of advancement or apportionment) are referred to by the Court of Appeal as "powers in the wider form". However, the Board considers that a deemed disposal will not arise when such a power is exercised and trusts are declared in circumstances such that—
>
> (a) the apportionment is revocable, or
>
> (b) the trusts declared of the advanced or appointed funds are not exhaustive so that there exists a possibility at the time when the advancement or apportionment is made that the funds covered by it will on the occasion of some event cease to be held upon such trusts and once again came to be held upon the original trusts of the settlement.
>
> Further, when such a power is exercised the Board considers it unlikely that a deemed disposal will arise when trusts are declared if duties in regard to the appointed assets still fall to the trustees of the original settlement in their capacity as trustees of that settlement, bearing in mind the provisions

in TCGA 1992 s 69(1) (CGTA 1979 s 52(1)) that the trustees of a settlement form a single and continuing body (distinct from the persons who may from time to time be the trustees).

Finally, the Board accept that a power of appointment or advancement can be exercised over only part of the settled property and that the above consequences would apply to that part.'

6.110 A sub-trust of the existing trust was also held to arise in *Swires v Renton* [1991] STC 490, separate trusts were created in *Ewart v Taylor* [1983] STC 721 but not in *Eilbeck v Rawling* [1981] STC 174 although the scheme failed on the grounds of interposed artificial transactions in that case.

6.111 The Revenue analysis of one or more settlements is contained in CG 33295–33323. The Revenue view is that a conventional marriage settlement with funds coming from two families creates two distinct trusts in most cases (CG 33306). Where the original settled funds are purely nominal and funds are added by somebody else, the original named settlor is effectively ignored (CG 33320). Funds added to a substantial settlement by another party may create a new settlement unless the intention is clear that the additional funds are intended to be added to the existing trust property and mingled with it (CG 33321 and CG 33323).

6.112 The trustees are normally the party chargeable to CGT. Because the remittance basis only applies to individuals not domiciled in the UK and trustees are not regarded as individuals the remittance basis cannot apply to capital gains made by trusts. [TCGA 1992 s 65 (2)]. The trustees chargeable are those who were trustees at any time during the year of assessment in which the chargeable gain accrues and any subsequent trustees of the settlement. Where tax is chargeable on trustees who migrate within TCGA 1992 s 80(2) a former trustee is not liable if he can show that at the time he ceased to be a trustee there was no proposal that the trustees should become neither resident nor ordinarily resident in the UK. [Section 65(3) and (4)].

Trustee's expenses deductible for capital gains tax

6.113 TCGA 1992 s 38 allows relief for the incidental costs of making a disposal for CGT purposes. This includes, in the case of a trust, the legal and actuarial services including stamp duty on transfers and auxiliary expenses incurred on varying or ending a settlement, including the termination of an interest in possession under TCGA 1992 s 72 (*IRC v Chubb's Trustee* (1941) 47 TC 353). Relief extends to the expenses of obtaining probate of the deceased's estate (*IRC v Richards' Executors* (1971) 46 TC 626) but not to insurance premiums paid as part of a trust variation (*Allison v Murray* [1975] STC 524). Other fees in respect of discharges and commission on the transfer of assets to beneficiaries would be deductible. Expenditure should be apportioned between chargeable and non-chargeable assets by reference to value (CG 33521).

6.114 Where costs are borne by a beneficiary to whom the assets are transferred, that would be an allowable cost to the transferee on any subsequent disposal unless the trustees have claimed a deduction for the costs on the transfer. TCGA 1992 s 52(1) prevents a double claim (CG 33523). Expenses incurred by corporate trustees for the transfer of assets to beneficiaries are deductible in accordance with SP 8/94 para 6, which allows a basic cost of £20 per holding of stocks or shares with the addition of any exceptional expenditure for unquoted shares or other assets. For quoted stocks and shares the investment fee charged by the trustee is allowed with the addition of actual valuation costs in the case of unquoted shares. The maximum fee for other assets is £60 plus actual valuation costs. In the case of deemed disposals the allowance is £6 per holding, except for unquoted shares and other assets where the actual valuation costs are allowed. Where a comprehensive annual management fee is charged the allowance is 0.25 per cent on the sale or purchase monies (CG 33524–33527). Withdrawal fees charged by the trust departments of banks etc on termination of their trusteeship are not normally deductible, except for the actual work done on valuation or transfer of assets (CG 33522). The normal scale fees of a professional trustee would usually be allowable (CG 33528).

6.115 Although original valuation costs are deductible under TCGA 1992 s 38(2)(b) this does not extend to the costs of appealing against the valuation of unquoted shares (*Caton's Administrators v Couch* [1997] STC 970). However, the cost of defending title to an asset such as partnership goodwill is deductible under section 38(1)(b) (*Lee v Jewitt* [2000] STC (SCD) 517).

Holdover relief

6.116 Where an individual transferor makes a disposal of a business asset other than at arm's length he and the transferee may jointly elect, or the transferor may on his own also elect where the transferees are the trustees of a settlement, that the gain which would otherwise accrue to the transferor be held over and the transferee's base value shall each be reduced by an amount equal to the heldover gain on the disposal. [TCGA 1992 s 165(1) and (4)]. A business asset is, or is an interest in, an asset used for the purposes of a trade, profession or vocation carried on by the transferor or his personal company or member of a trading group or consists of shares or securities of a trading company or the holding company of a trading group which is unlisted, or the transferor's personal company. [Section 165(2)]. It does not apply where the gain is covered by retirement relief under TCGA 1992 Sch 6, or a disposal of qualifying corporate bonds, or a disposal to which IHT applies where relief is given under TCGA 1992 s 260. [Section 165(3)]. Relief also applies to agricultural property under TCGA 1992 s 165(5) and Sch 7, and to settled property where the trade, profession or vocation is carried on by the trustees making the disposal, or by a beneficiary with an interest in possession, or consists of assets or securities in a trading company, or holding company of a trading group where the shares or securities are not listed on a recognised stock exchange, or not less than 25 per cent of the voting rights are exercisable by the trustees. [Sch 7 para 2]. An interest in agricultural property under IHTA 1984 ss 115–124C also qualifies for business asset holdover relief [Sch 7 para 3]. The rules for the calculation of the holdover gain on a gift of business assets within TCGA 1992 s 165 are given in Sch 7 paras 4–8.

Example

James Borokov decided to retire at age 61 on 31 October 2002 and transferred his business into trust for his daughter and two sons equally, as life tenants, which was a potentially exempt transfer not liable to inheritance tax, unless James were to die within seven years. Goodwill was valued at £250,000 (base cost nil on commencement, 1 January 1983) and a freehold property, half used for the purposes of the trade and half let, which was valued at £480,000 and had an indexed cost, including expenses of £200,000.

	£	£
Retirement relief		
Gain on goodwill		250,000
Gains on property		280,000
Total gains		530,000
Less retirement relief full relief	50,000	
50% of excess over £50,000 up to £200,000	75,000	
		(125,000)
Chargeable gain		405,000
Holdover relief		
Restriction for non trading gain on property (½)		(140,000)
Heldover gain		265,000
Chargeable gain on property let to unincorporated business		140,000
Less taper relief, including bonus year 5 years, 15%		(21,000)
Chargeable gain		119,000
Trustees base cost		
Market value at 31 October 2002		
Goodwill	250,000	
Freehold property		480,000
Less heldover gain		
$£265{,}000 \times \frac{250}{530}$	(125,000)	
$£265{,}000 \times \frac{280}{530}$		(140,000)
Adjusted base value	125,000	340,000

On 1 January 2003 the trustees transfer the freehold property to the life tenants and again claim holdover relief. There is no taper relief as the

property has been held for less than one year, so each of the three beneficiaries takes over a share of the property which is valued at £550,000 on the transfer date.

	£
Total value of property	550,000
Less 10% discount for joint interest	(55,000)
	495,000
Less base value	(340,000)
	155,000
Less gain in respect of non-business use (½)	(77,500)
Heldover gain	77,500
Gain chargeable on trustees at rate applicable to trusts, 34%	26,350
Base value for each beneficiary	
⅓ market value £495,000	165,000
Less heldover gain ⅓ £77,500	(25,833)
	139,167

6.117 The retirement relief definitions in TCGA 1992 Sch 6 para 1 are applied and a personal company is therefore any company the voting rights in which are exercisable as to not less than 5 per cent by the individual transferor. A trading company is one whose business consists wholly or mainly of the carrying on of a trade or trades. [TCGA 1992 s 165(8)]. Trade includes the occupation of woodlands managed on a commercial basis. [Section 165(9)]. The heldover gain on disposal is the amount by which the unrelieved gain on the disposal exceeds the actual consideration less allowable expenses. [Section 165(7). If IHT is payable on the transfer, it is allowed as a deduction in computing the chargeable gain for CGT purposes up to the amount of the gain, in other words it cannot create a loss. If the IHT paid varies, for example, on the transferor's death within seven years, the capital gain is recalculated. [Section 165(10) and (11)]. Holdover relief is not available where the transferee is not ordinarily resident in the UK or is an individual treated under a double tax treaty as non-UK resident. [Section 166]. Similarly relief is not available on a gift to foreign controlled companies. [Section 167].

6.118 The holdover gain crystallises if the transferee was a limited liability partnership which has ceased to trade, or if the donee emigrates within six years, unless he becomes temporarily non-resident through working abroad and resumes UK residence within three years without having disposed of the asset. [TCGA 1992 ss 168(4) and (5) and 169A]. Where the trustee emigrates and has not paid the tax within twelve months, the transferor may be charged in the name of the transferee within six years of the end of the year of assessment in which the disposal was made. In such a case the transferor has a right of recovery against the transferee. [Section 168(7)–(9)].

6.119 Where there is a heldover gain on a transfer of business assets within TCGA 1992 s 165 or on a transfer chargeable to inheritance tax within TCGA 1992 s 260, the relief is denied where the transferee trustees are UK resident, but treated by any double taxation agreement as not resident in the UK. [TCGA 1992 s 169]. The heldover gain is also crystallised on the termination of a life interest, or the death of a life tenant, where holdover relief has been given for business assets under TCGA 1992 s 165, or on a chargeable transfer for IHT purposes under TCGA 1992 s 260 by section 74 of the Act. However, the gain so crystallised can itself be heldover under section 260 where there would be a chargeable transfer for IHT purposes. There would not be such a chargeable transfer where, on the death of a life tenant, his or her spouse acquires an interest in possession or becomes absolutely entitled to the trust property (CG 3352). [TCGA 1992 s 58]. Where there is holdover claim on a gift it may not be necessary to have a formal valuation of the property transferred (SP 8/92).

6.120 Gifts on which IHT is chargeable, made by an individual or the trustees of a settlement to an individual or the trustees of a settlement, may be heldover where the appropriate claim is made. The relief is also available where the transfer is exempt from IHT, eg as a transfer to a political party or to maintenance funds for historic buildings etc within TCGA 1992 s 260(2). It does not apply to potentially exempt transfers. [Section 260(2)(a)]. The rollover relief is calculated in the same way as for TCGA 1992 s 165 on a gift of business assets. [Section 260(3)–(5)]. Gifts to non-residents are excluded by TCGA 1992 s 261 and this includes residents deemed to be non-resident under a double taxation treaty. The anti-avoidance provisions on the emigration of a donee, gift into a dual resident trust or cessation of trade by a limited liability partnership in TCGA 1992 ss 168, 169 and 169A apply to gifts on which IHT is chargeable as they apply to gifts of business assets under TCGA 1992 s 165.

6.121 Holdover relief is available under TCGA 1992 s 260(2)(d) where a beneficiary becomes absolutely entitled to trust property, provided that the income and capital vest simultaneously. TA 1925 s 31 gives entitlement to income at the age of 18 unless the trust instrument provides otherwise (*Begg-MacBrearty v Stilwell* [1996] STC 413, so that the beneficiary has an interest in possession from age 18. CGT is payable on a subsequent transfer of assets to the beneficiary under TCGA 1992 s 71 as section 260(2)(d) of that Act does not apply where the IHT-free occasion for charge under IHTA 1984 s 71(4) has already taken place. Relief under TCGA 1992 s 260 is given in preference to the holdover relief on business assets under TCGA 1992 s 165 and must be claimed within six years by the transferor and trustee jointly, unless the transfer is to trustees when only the transferor need make a claim. The death of a life tenant can crystallise capital gains tax on a heldover gain where assets were transferred to a trust under TCGA 1992 s 74 (see Chapter 8).

6.122 If the gift consists of EIS shares or venture capital trust shares on which reinvestment relief has been given, the deferred gain is brought into charge by reason of the transfer under TCGA 1992 s 260(6A) and (6B). Gifts on which IHT is chargeable include those covered by the nil rate band or 100 per cent business property relief or agricultural property relief, as there is no requirement that IHT is actually payable. These provisions were used in a successful avoidance scheme in *Melville v IRC* [2001] STC 1271. In this case the settlor transferred assets to a discretionary settlement, which is not a potentially exempt transfer. The terms of the trust gave to him, after 90 days, a power which amounted in effect to a general power of appointment to direct the trustees to exercise their discretionary powers including the transfer of all or part of the trust fund to the settlor absolutely. This meant that the reduction in the estate on which IHT was payable was minimal in view of the value of the right given to the settlor. The asset could therefore be transferred into trust at negligible IHT cost and with holdover relief for CGT purposes under TCGA 1992 s 260. The settlor's power of appointment only arose after 90 days because there would be no IHT charge if the property were to leave the settlement within the first quarter [IHTA 1984 s 65(4)] and therefore the transfer would not have been chargeable to IHT [TCGA 1992 s 260] holdover relief would not have been available.

6.123 *Melville* has a number of implications in relation to non-domiciliaries obtaining an interest in settlements of excluded property which they created. These are considered in Chapter 10.

6.124 The deferred gain is, in certain cases, halved where it is held over under the gift of business asset rules in TCGA 1992 s 165 and other rollover provisions to compensate for the loss of rebasing. This applies where the deferred gain is deducted from allowable expenditure on a later disposal, other than a no gain/no loss disposal, of an asset acquired after 31 March 1982 and a deduction is attributable directly or indirectly, in whole or in part, to gains accruing on the disposal before 6 April 1988 of an asset acquired before March 1982 by the person making that disposal. This relief is really designed to give a rough and ready solution to cases where pre-March 1982 gains were rolled over or heldover and lost out on rebasing at 31 March 1982. [TCGA 1992 Sch 4].

Example

Guennadi Sloutsky held 24 per cent of the shares in an unlisted trading company which he had formed with a share capital at £2 in 1969. He transferred the shares into a life interest settlement for his son, who did not work in the business, on 31 December 1987, when the shares were worth £400,000.

The gain heldover was:

	£
Market value	400,000
Less cost and indexation	(3)
	399,997

On 31 December 2002 the trustees sold the shares for £1,600,000		
Sale proceeds		1,600,000
Acquisition value 31 December 1987	400,000	
Less half heldover gain	(199,999)	
	200,001	
Indexation to 5/4/98, say		
	115,375	(315,376)
Gain before taper relief		1,284,624

Less taper relief
Relevant period of ownership from 6/4/98 to 31/12/2002 4 years 8 months (56 months)
Business asset from 6/4/2000 to 31/12/2002 2 years 8 months (32 months)
Non-business asset from 6/4/1998 to 5/4/2000 (24 months)

	Business Asset		*Non-business Asset*	*Total*
	£		£	£
Chargeable gain 32/56	734,071	(24/56)	550,553	1,284,624
Less taper 75%/5%	(550,553)		(27,528)	(578,081)
	183,518		523,025	706,543
Less annual exemption				(3,850)
				202,693

6.125 Trustees who are carrying on a trade may claim rollover relief on the replacement of business assets under TCGA 1992 s 152 with proportionate relief for assets only partly replaced under section 153 (*Temperley v Visibell Ltd* [1974] STC 64; *Campbell Connelly & Co Ltd v Barnett* [1994] STC 50; *Watton v Tippett* [1996] STC 101; *Steibelt v Paling* [1999] STC 594; *Tod v Mudd* [1987] STC 141; SP/D11; and ESCs D16; D22; D24; D25; and D30; SP 8/81; SP/D6). Trustees could make a self-assessment declaration that rollover is intended under TCGA 1992 s 152 and rollover into depreciating assets under TCGA 1992 s 154. Rollover relief is only available for specific classes of assets, ie land and buildings, including fixed plant or machinery and occupied for the purpose of the trade (*Anderton v Lamb* [1981] STC 43; *Temperley v Visibell Ltd* [1974] STC 64; *Williams v Evans* [1982] STC 498). Other classes of assets are ships, aircraft and hovercraft, satellites, space stations and space craft, goodwill, milk quotas and other similar quotas and Lloyd's syndicate assets. Goodwill and quotas will be taken out of the corporation tax chargeable gains rollover provisions and brought into the income rollover provisions as replacement of intangibles under FA 2002 s 84 and Sch 29. This will not affect the relief for unincorporated businesses.

[TCGA 1992 s 155]. Assets used for a trade of dealing in or developing land do not qualify for rollover relief. [Section 156]. Where the trade is carried on by a limited liability partnership of which the trustees are members, a gain crystallises on the cessation of trade under section 156A. Relief is available in respect of commercial woodlands. [Section 158(1)(b)] but not to non-residents who replace a business asset within the UK tax regime with a business asset outside it. [Section 159].

Retirement relief

6.126 Retirement relief is still available under TCGA 1992 ss 163, 164 and Sch 6 until 2002/03. This is extended to trustees of a settlement who dispose of shares or securities of a company or an asset used or previously used for the purposes of a business, which is part of the trust fund, and a beneficiary who has an interest in possession other than for a fixed term, in the whole or part of the settled property provided that a number of further conditions are met. [Section 164(3)]. These conditions are that the company was the qualifying beneficiary's personal company, i e he held at least 5 per cent of the voting rights and it was a trading company or the holding company of a trading group and he was a full-time working officer or employee of the company or companies in the group or commercial association of companies and had reached the age of 50 or retired on ill-health grounds below that age (*Palmer v Maloney* [1999] STC 890; CG 63621 and 33560). [Section 164(4) and (5)].

Private residence relief

6.127 Trustees are entitled to private residence relief where a trust property is occupied by a beneficiary of the trust (*Sansom v Peay* [1976] STC 494). [TCGA 1992 s 225]. Relief is extended to personal representatives who dispose of a house which, before and after the deceased's death, has been used as their only or main residence by individuals who, under the will or intestacy, are entitled to the whole or substantially the whole (75 per cent) of the proceeds of the house either absolutely or for life, ESC D5 (*Tax Bulletin*, Issue 12, August 1994, p 148).

6.128 The relief is the same as that available to an individual. The main residence can include a mobile home (*Makins v Elson* [1977] STC 46) but see *Moore v Thompson* [1986] STC 170. The main residence includes grounds of up to 0.5 of a hectare, or such larger area as is required for the reasonable enjoyment of the dwelling-house (*Wakeling v Pearce* [1995] STC (SCD) 96; *Goodwin v Curtis* [1998] STC 475; *Longson v Baker* [2001] STC 6; *Green v IRC* [1982] STC 485). [TCGA 1992 s 222(3)]. A caretaker's lodge was within the definition in *Batey v Wakefield* [1981] STC 521 and *Williams v Merrylees* [1987] STC 445 but not a gardener's cottage in *Lewis v Rook* [1992] STC 171. A bungalow was not part of the same premises as the main building in *Markey v Sanders* [1987] STC 256 nor were separate flats in one building in *Honour v Norris* [1992] STC 304. An election within two years of the beginning of the period of ownership may be made to determine which of two or more residences is an individual's main residence for any period, which has to be given jointly with the trustees (*Griffin v Craig-Harvey* [1994] STC 54). [Section 222(5)(a) and (b)]. Where the residence was not used as the main residence throughout the perod of ownership relief is available in respect of the period of use as the main residence together with the last three years as a fraction of the total period of ownership since 31 March 1982. [Section 223]. The exemption dos not apply where the house was acquired or expenditure was incurred on it with a view to realising the gain on its disposal (*Goodwin v Curtis* [1996] STC 1146; *Jones v Willcock* [1996] STC (SCD) 389). [Section 224(3)].

Taper relief

6.129 CGT is payable by any person resident or ordinarily resident in the UK for the year of assessment. [TCGA 1992 s 2(1)]. Companies are specifically excluded and charged to corporation tax under ICTA 1988 s 6, by TCGA 1992 s 1(2). Taper relief is available to trustees in accordance with TCGA 1992 s 2A and Sch A1. Taper relief will be available at the rate applicable to non-business assets unless the trust qualifies for business asset treatment. A disposal made by trustees of a settlement qualifies for business asset taper relief if the asset was a business asset, ie if it was being used wholly or partly for the purpose of a trade carried on by the trustees of the settlement or by a partnership whose members included the trustees of the settlement, or at least one of the trustees of the settlement, or where the trade was carried on by an eligible beneficiary, alone or in partnership, or the trade was carried on by a company which at the time of the disposal was a qualifying company by reference to the trustees of the settlement, or an eligible beneficiary, or the trade was carried on by a company which was a member of a trading group, the holding company of which was a qualifying company by reference to the trustees of the settlement or an eligible beneficiary, or for the purposes of an office or employment held by an eligible beneficiary for the person carrying on a trade. [Sch A1 para 5(3)]. Similarly, where the disposal was made by an individual's personal representative the asset is a business asset if it was, at that time, being used wholly or partly for the purpose of a trade carried on by the personal representative or by a company which was a qualifying company by reference to the deceased's personal representatives or the trade was carried on by a company which was a member of a trading group, the holding company of which was a qualifying company by reference to the deceased's personal representatives. [Sch A1 para 5(4)]. Where the asset was a business asset of the personal representative, but not the legatee who makes the disposal, business asset relief can be given for the personal representatives' qualifying period. [Sch A1 para 5(5)].

6.130 Where the settled property originates from more than one settlor, each part is treated as a separate and distinct settlement for the property originating from each settlor; TCGA 1992 s 79(1)–(5) applies accordingly. [TCGA 1992 Sch A1 para 20].

6.131 Business asset taper relief is not available where the settlor is a company and the company has an interest in the settlement at the time of the disposal. [TCGA 1992 Sch A1 para 17]. This is an anti-avoidance provision to prevent companies putting assets in trust for the benefit of a company or an associated company directly or indirectly in order to qualify for business asset taper relief instead of the indexation which would be available to the company. [Sch A1 para 17(2)–(7)]. Business asset taper relief is not available for assets held in an ancillary trust fund of a member of Lloyd's. [Sch A1 para 19].

6.132 An eligible beneficiary will enable the trust to qualify for business asset taper relief if the beneficiary had a relevant interest in possession under the settlement in either the whole of the settled property or a part of the settled property that is, or includes, that asset. [TCGA 1992 Sch A1 para 7(1)]. Relevant interest in possession excludes an entitlement to receive an annuity or a fixed-term entitlement as opposed to a life tenancy. [Sch A1 para 7(2) and (3)]. Where the asset was a business asset by reference to one or more beneficiaries, but the asset would not otherwise have been a business asset, ie it is not a case where the trustees were carrying on the trade alone or in partnership, and there is a non-qualifying part of the relevant income or there would be if there were any such income, eg if there are discretionary beneficiaries, and the life tenant is entitled to only part of the income there is a proportionate loss of business asset taper relief. This is measured by reference to the relevant fraction of the income in any period of ownership by the trustees subject to apportionment under these provisions, known as the sharing period, which is not applicable to qualifying eligible beneficiaries. A non-qualifying eligible beneficiary is a life tenant by reference to whom the asset would not qualify as a business asset, eg because he did not work in the appropriate business or company. [Sch A1 para 8(2)–(7)].

6.133 The rate of taper relief is given by TCGA 1992 s 2A(5), as follows:

Gains on disposals of business assets after 5 April 2002

No of whole years in qualifying holding period	*Percentage reduction available*	*Percentage of gain chargeable*
0	–	100.0
1	50.0	50.0
2	75.0	25.0

Gains on disposals of business assets after 5 April 2000 (and before 6 April 2002)

No of whole years in qualifying holding period	*Percentage reduction available*	*Percentage of gain chargeable*
0	–	100.0
1	12.5	87.5
2	25.0	75.0
3	50.0	50.0

Gains on disposals of business assets after 5 April 1998 and before 6 April 2000

*No of whole years in qualifying holding period**	*Percentage reduction available*	*Percentage of gain chargeable*
0	–	100.0
1	7.5	92.5
2	15.0	85.0

Gains on disposals of non-business assets after 5 April 1998

*No of whole years in qualifying holding period**	*Percentage reduction available*	*Percentage of gain chargeable*
0	–	100
1	–	100
2	–	100
3	5	95
4	10	90
5	15	85
6	20	80
7	25	75
8	30	70
9	35	65
10 or more	40	60

**Including bonus year added for assets held on 17 March 1998.*

6.134 Taper relief normally starts from 5 April 1998, but there is a bonus year for a non-business asset held prior to 17 March 1998. [TCGA 1992 s 2A(8) and Sch A1 para 2]. Where an asset qualifies as a business asset for part only of the period of ownership, apportionment is necessary under Sch A1 para 3. The definition of business asset was extended by FA 2000 s 67 in respect of disposals made on or after 6 April 2000, but the changes were not retrospective, so that some assets are investment assets up to 5 April 2000 and business assets thereafter. Apportionment may also be necessary under TCGA 1992 Sch A1 para 9 where the asset is used at the same time for different purposes. Shares qualify as business assets from 5 April 2000 where the company was a qualifying company by reference to the trustees of the settlement, personal representatives, or legatee, under Sch A1 para 4(3)–(5). A qualifying company by reference to the trustees under a settlement is one where the company was a trading company or the holding company of a trading group and it was unlisted; or, if listed, an eligible beneficiary was an officer or employee of the company, or of a company having a relevant connection with it, such as a joint venture company or associated company within Sch A1 para 24, or a company in which the trustees are able to exercise not less than 5 per cent of the voting rights. [Sch A1 para 6(2)]. A company can also qualify where it was a non-trading company, or the holding company of a non-trading group, and an eligible beneficiary was an officer or employee of the company or connected company and the trustees did not have a material interest in the company or its controlling company. [Sch A1 para 6(2A)].

Example A

The trustees of the Antonov discretionary trust bought an investment property on 15 March 1985 for £120,000 and sold it on 14 April 2003 for £280,000.

	£	£
Proceeds (net)		280,000
Less cost	120,000	
Indexation from 15/3/1985 to 5/4/1998		
75.2 x £120,000	90,240	
		(210,240)
Gain before taper relief		69,760
Less taper relief 5 years plus bonus year, 6 years 20%		(13,952)
		55,808
Less annual exemption, say		(3,950)
Taxable gain		51,858
Tax payable at, say, 34%		£17,631.72

Example B

The trustees of the Antonov discretionary trust also bought a farm on 1 June 1999 for £750,000 which they farmed, using subcontractors, until 31 March 2005. It was then let until 31 July 2007 when it was sold for £975,000.

	Business	*Non-business*	*Total*
	£	£	£
Proceeds, net			975,000
Less cost			(750,000)
Gain			225,000
Use	5 years 10 months	2 years 4 months	8 years 2 months
	70/98	28/98	
	£	£	£
Apportioned gain	160,714	64,286	225,000
Taper relief (75%)	(120,535)	(30%) (19,286)	(139,821)
	40,179	45,000	85,179

Less annual exemption, say,	(4,500)
	80,679
Tax payable at, say 34%,	£27,430.86

6.135 A material interest is more than 10 per cent of the issued shares of the company, or of any particular class of shares or of the voting rights, or of the distributed income, or assets available for distribution to participators on a winding-up. [TCGA 1992 Sch A1 para 6A]. Similar provisions apply to personal representatives for holding shares in an unquoted trading company or holding company of a trading group with not less than 5 per cent of the voting rights in any company. [Sch A1 para 6(3)]. In determining whether the trustees have a material interest, connected persons have to be included, under Sch A1 para 6(5), and rights under options etc are to be taken into account under Sch A1 para 6A(2)–(8). The definition of material interest in Sch A1 para 6A(1)(a) as holding more than 10 per cent of the shares of any particular class is a potential trap because shares includes any securities, and could therefore apply to a special class of loan stock issued to shareholders of the target company on an acquisition. [Sch A1 para 22(1)].

6.136 There are swingeing anti-avoidance provisions which can cause the reduction or total loss of business asset taper relief under TCGA 1992 Sch A1 para 10 in the case of arrangements to limit exposure to fluctuations in value, under Sch A1 para 11 where there is a relevant change of activity by the company, which has been replaced for disposals after 16 April 2002 by the much more reasonable provisions in Sch A1 para 11A which merely ignore dormant periods or under Sch A1 para 12 in the case of value shifting. These anti-avoidance rules and the rules for options, assets derived from other assets, special rules for postponed gains, assets acquired on a reconstruction, and joint ventures in Sch A1 paras 13, 14, 16, 18 and 23 apply to trustees of settlements, as does the general rule for apportionment on a just and reasonable basis and on the assumption that gains accrued equally over time in Sch A1 para 21, and the interpretation provisions in Sch A1 para 2. The chattel exemption and marginal relief in TCGA 1992 s 262 applies to trustees as do the rules on valuation under sections 272–274, the *situs* of assets under section 275, double taxation relief under section 277 giving treaty or unilateral relief. Where such relief is not available, an allowance for foreign tax as an expense is given by section 278 and relief for remittances by section 279.

Reinvestment relief

6.137 Trustees are entitled to reinvestment relief under the Enterprise Incentive Scheme (EIS). [TCGA 1992 Sch 5B para 17]. Relief applies to trust assets in the same way as for an individual, provided that the settled property is held in trust for beneficiaries all of whom are individuals if they do not have interests in possession, or any of whom are individuals if they do have an interest in possession. [Sch 5B para 17(1) and (2)]. There is an apportionment to exclude the proportion of the gain held for non-individual beneficiaries. [Sch 5B para 17(3)–(6)]. Trustees are not eligible for Venture Capital Trust (VCT) relief.

6.138 The definition of an interest in possession excludes an interest for a fixed term but the reference to an individual includes a charity. [TCGA 1992 Sch 5B para 17(7) and (8)]. The anti-avoidance provisions which claw back relief where an investor receives value, or where there is an investment linked loan, under Sch 5B paras 13–13C and 15, are extended to trustees, individual beneficiaries and their associates, and charitable beneficiaries and persons connected with them by Sch 5A para 18. These provisions replace the rollover relief on reinvestment by trustees previously available under TCGA 1992 s 164B.

Connected persons

6.139 Transfers between connected persons in TCGA 1992 s 18 are normally treated as made at market value under section 17. A person in his capacity as trustee of a settlement is connected with any individual who (in relation to the settlement) is a settlor, any person who is connected with such individual and any body corporate which is connected with that settlement. [TCGA 1992 s 286(3)]. A person is connected with an individual if that person is the individual's spouse or a relative, or the spouse of a relative of the individual, or of the individual's spouse. [Section 286(2)]. A company is connected with a settlement if it is a close company or would be if it were resident in the UK and the participators include the trustees of the settlement, or is controlled by such a company, and a person is connected with a partner, and with the spouse or relative of a partner, except in relation to bona fide commercial dealings in partnership assets. [Section 286(3A) and (4)]. Companies are connected if they are under common control. [Section 286(5)–(7)]. A relative means brother, sister, ancestor or lineal descendant but not uncle, aunt, nephew, niece or cousin, TCGA 1992 s 286(8). *Tax Bulletin*, Issue 6, February 1993, p56 clarifies the Revenue interpretation of settlements and connected persons. Losses are ring-fenced under TCGA 1992 s 18(3) where the disposal is to a connected person, and can only be set against gains in the same or subsequent fiscal years with the same connected person. The Revenue interpretation (RI38) is as follows:

> 'Where a loss accrues to a person on making a disposal to a connected person, under TCGA 1992 s 18(3) that loss may only be deducted from gains on other disposals by that person to the same connected person, unless exceptionally s 18(4) applies (gifts to certain associations).
>
> The Revenue have been asked several questions about the application and interpretation of the rules in TCGA 1992 ss 18, 286, in cases involving the trustees of settlements.

Are the settlor and the trustees connected at the moment when the settlement comes into existence and the initial property is transferred to the trustees?

Yes. TCGA 1992 s 18(3) applies to a disposal which brings the settlement into existence. It is not restricted to situations where the parties are already connected before the disposal in question.

Are the trustees and beneficiaries connected after the settlor is dead?

No. If the settlor dies, the connection between the trustees and the relatives and spouse of the settlor is broken. Therefore if, for instance, the beneficiaries of the settlement are the children of the late settlor, the trustees are not connected with those beneficiaries, even if one or more of the children are trustees. The basic rule is that the trustees of a settlement are connected with the settlor, and also with any person connected with the settlor (TCGA 1992 s 286(3)). Under TCGA 1992 s 69(1), the trustees are treated as a single and continuing body distinct from the persons who may be the trustees. Therefore in determining whether s 286(3) applies, the identity of the trustees is disregarded.

If the trustees and beneficiaries are connected, does this affect the transfer of losses under TCGA 1992 s 71(2)?

No. On legal advice, the Revenue no longer consider the transfer of losses from trustees to beneficiaries under s 71(2) to be inhibited by s 18(3). Therefore where a beneficiary becomes absolutely entitled against the trustees under TCGA 1992 s 71(1) all the unused losses which have arisen to the trustees in respect of property which is or is represented by the property to which the beneficiary becomes entitled, including any loss accruing on the deemed disposal to the beneficiary, are transferred to the beneficiary under s 71(2).'

Losses

6.140 Losses for CGT are normally calculated in the same way as profits under TCGA 1992 s 16. Losses have to be claimed [section 16(2A)] and losses in 1996/97 or subsequent years of assessment are relieved prior to losses for an earlier period. [FA 1995 s 113(2)(a)]. Losses are deducted before calculating taper relief but may be allocated in the most beneficial manner possible. [TCGA 1992 s 2A(6)].

Death

6.141 Normally on death the personal representatives acquire the assets at market value and there is no charge to CGT, although there could well be an IHT charge. [TCGA 1992 s 62(1)]. It is possible to change the distribution on death under the will or intestacy by an instrument in writing made by the persons who would benefit under the original dispositions. In this case, the variation or disclaimer does not constitute a disposal for CGT purposes and the variation is deemed to have been effected by the deceased or on a disclaimer the claimed benefit is deemed not to have been conferred. [Section 62(6)]. It used to be necessary in such a variation to elect by notice given to the Revenue within six months of the date of the instrument, or such longer time as the Board may allow, for the variation to have an effect for CGT purposes. From 1 August 2002 TCGA 1992 s 62(7) was modified by FA 2002 s 52 to require the deed to specify that it is to apply for capital gains tax, if that is the intention, and no election is required. These provisions do not apply to a variation or disclaimer made for a consideration in money or money's worth other than a consideration consisting of the making of a variation or disclaimer in respect of another of the dispositions. [Section 62(8)]. It does not matter if the administration of the estate is complete or the property distributed in accordance with the original will or intestacy. [Section 62(9)].

6.142 A variation would allow a settlement to be created or a statutory settlement avoided as if it had been made by the deceased, which has the effect of making the disposal by the person entitled under the will or intestacy a CGT-free disposal and the trustees would take the assets at the probate value. It does not, however, mean that the deceased becomes the settlor for CGT purposes and the settlor remains the legatee or person entitled on intestacy (*Marshall v Kerr* [1994] STC 638). There is no similar provision for income tax purposes and any income received by or on behalf of the original legatees or persons entitled on intestacy is taxable as their income, it is not deemed to be that of the trustees or persons in whose favour the dispositions are varied.

Remittances

6.143 Trustees do not apply the remittance basis on gains arising on the disposal of assets situated outside the UK, irrespective of the residence or domicile of the beneficiary (CG 33502). [TCGA 1992 s 65(2)]. The CGT is assessed and charged in the name of one or more of the relevant trustees or the relevant personal representatives. [Section 65].

Deemed disposals

6.144 When a beneficiary becomes absolutely entitled as against the trustees under the terms of the settlement, the appropriate trust assets are deemed to have been disposed of at market value by the trustees and reacquired by them as nominees for the beneficiary within TCGA 1992 s 60(1) (*Crowe v Appleby* [1975] STC 502; *Pexton v Bell* [1976] STC 301; *Stephenson v Barclays Bank Trust Co Ltd* [1975] STC 151; *Hoare v Gardner* [1978] STC 89; *Chinn v Collins* [1981] STC 1; *Roome v Edwards* [1981] STC 96; *Hart v Briscoe* [1978] STC 89). [TCGA 1992 s 71(1)]. These cases demonstrate that whether or not a resettlement amounts to the trustees of the new settlement becoming absolutely entitled as against the trustees of the old settlement, giving rise to a deemed disposal and reacquisition, or is merely a sub-settlement of the original settlement, is a question of fact and degree. Where a power of appointment is exercised to create a new settlement, the settlor of the original settlement is also the settlor of the new settlement for CGT purposes (*Pilkington v IRC* (1962) 40 TC 416; CG 34802). The Revenue view is contained in SP 7/84 which is set out **6.107**.

6.145 Where, on a person becoming absolutely entitled to settled property as against the trustee, an allowable loss would have accrued to the trustees on the deemed disposal at market value, the loss, to the extent that it cannot be deducted from pre-entitlement gains of the trustee, may be treated as an allowable loss accruing to the beneficiary instead of to the trustees, which is a ring-fenced loss deductible only from any gain on the subsequent disposal of the asset giving rise to the loss to the trustees, or, where the asset is an estate, interest or right in or over land, any asset deriving from that asset. [TCGA 1992 s 71(2) and (2B)]. Pre-entitlement gain for this purpose is the loss accruing to the trustees on the deemed disposal at market value on the beneficiary becoming absolutely entitled or any other disposal taking place before that occasion but in the same year of assessment. [Section 71(2A)].

6.146 In computing whether the loss on the deemed disposal can be used by the trustee, it is deductible from trust gains in priority to any other allowable losses accruing to the trustee in that year. The ring-fenced losses of the beneficiary under these provisions can be carried forward indefinitely and are used in priority to any other losses. [TCGA 1992 s 71(2C) and (2B)]. An infant or mentally disabled person is treated as becoming absolutely entitled even though the assets remain held in a bare trust for them, in view of their legal incapacity. [Section 71(3)].

6.147 An asset derives from another asset if its value is wholly or partly derived from the other asset as a result of a merger or division of assets, a change in the nature of the assets or the creation or extinguishment of rights in or over an asset or any combination. [TCGA 1992 s 71(2B)].

6.148 A remainderman, becoming absolutely entitled on the death of a life tenant during the period of administration, takes the assets on the date of death as if he were a legatee (CCAB Press Release, June 1967). Where TA 1925 s 31 is not disapplied by the trust deed, infants acquire an interest in possession at age 18 (*Begg-MacBrearty v Stillwell* [1996] STC 413; *Swires v Renton* [1991] STC 490; *Figg v Clarke* [1997] STC 247; *Bond v Pickford* [1983] STC 517; *Ewart v Taylor (and related appeals)* [1983] STC 721). Where assets have to be valued on a beneficiary becoming absolutely entitled as against the trustees, the valuation would be on the basis of a single unit of property, the total allocated among the relevant assets (*IRC v Gray (Executor of Lady Fox) v IRC* [1994] STC 360). The Inland Revenue interpretation of the situation was given in the *Tax Bulletin* of August 1996 (RI 152):

'Valuations for capital gains tax: applying Gray v IRC

The Revenue have been asked whether the decision of the Court of Appeal in *IRC v Gray (Surviving Executor of Lady Fox deceased)* [1994] STC 360 has any implications for the valuation of assets for the purposes of capital gains tax.

The *Gray* case concerned the valuation of assets for what is now inheritance tax but was at the material time capital transfer tax. IHTA 1984 s 4 deems a transfer of value to have been made for the purpose of capital transfer tax/inheritance tax immediately before death equal to the value of the deceased's estate at that time. IHTA 1984 s 5 defines a person's estate as "the aggregate of all the property to which he is beneficially entitled". And IHTA 1984 s 160 provides that "... the value of any property at any time is ... the price which the property might reasonably be expected to fetch if sold in the open market at that time ...". The main question in *Gray* was whether two items of property comprised in the deceased's estate must be taken separately or whether they could be treated as one unity for valuation under IHTA 1984 s 160.

The principle that emerged from *Gray* is that two or more different assets comprised in an estate can be treated as a single unit of property if disposal as one unit was the course that a prudent hypothetical vendor would have adopted in order to obtain the most favourable price without undue expenditure of time and effort.

This principle will be applicable to capital gains tax valuations in which the statutory hypothesis on which the valuation is based deems two or more assets to be disposed of together. Examples will include—

— an acquisition by personal representatives or legatees under TCGA 1992 s 62 of assets of which a deceased person was competent to dispose;

— an acquisition of settled property under TCGA 1992 s 71(1) on the occasion of a person becoming absolutely entitled to that settled property.

Where the principle established in *Gray* is followed, so as to value a number of assets collectively to produce a total valuation in excess of the value of the assets valued separately, an apportionment will be required in accordance with TCGA 1992 s 52(4). The apportionment is to be made on a just and reasonable basis and so must reflect the value of each of the assets. Commonly this will require an apportionment of the total value in proportion to the value of each asset.

Where the statutory hypothesis requiring a valuation proceeds on the assumption of a disposal of a single asset by itself the principle established in *Gray* cannot apply, for example in *Henderson v Karmel's Executors* [1984] STC 572 the court held that even though at 6 April 1965 Mrs Karmel owned both the freehold interest in a farm and controlled the tenant company, so having the power one way or another to terminate the company's interest, that was insufficient to value the freehold interest on a vacant possession basis for capital gains tax rebasing to 6 April 1965.

Other examples of valuation hypotheses for which assets will continue to be valued singly include—

— TCGA 1992 s 17 where there is a disposal of an asset for consideration deemed to be equal to its market value;

— TCGA 1992 s 35 when a valuation of an asset is required for the purpose of rebasing to 31 March 1982.

The single asset valuation for TCGA 1992 s 17 is modified by TCGA 1992 s 19 where there is a series of linked transactions between connected persons. Each disposal in the series may be treated as being made for consideration equal to a proportion of the aggregate value of all the assets in the series.'

Disposal of interest in settled property

6.149 As the trustees are, in most circumstances, liable to CGT and the beneficiaries should not be, and in order to avoid a double charge on basically the same appreciation in value, a disposal of an interest under a settlement by the person for whose benefit the interest was created by the terms of the settlement does not normally result in a gain being charged on the vendor beneficiary. [TCGA 1992 s 76(1)]. This does not apply where the interest was acquired directly or indirectly for money or money's worth other than consideration consisting of another interest under the settlement, or where the settlement has, at any time, been not resident or ordinarily resident in the UK, or treated as resident elsewhere under a double taxation treaty, or the property in the settlement includes property derived directly or indirectly from such a settlement. [Section 76(1)(1A) and (1B)]. When the purchaser or donee, who has acquired the interest in the settled property, including in particular a reversion or annuity or life interest, becomes absolutely entitled as against the trustees, he is deemed to dispose of his acquired interest for the market value of the settled property received. This does not affect the charge on the trustees. [Section 76(2)].

6.150 TCGA 1992 s 76A and Sch 4A apply where an interest in settled property, i e any interest created by or arising under a settlement, is disposed of for consideration other than another interest in the same settlement, i e actual consideration, and the relevant conditions are met. The trustees are deemed to have disposed of and immediately reacquired the underlying assets in the settlement, thus crystallising a CGT charge. [Sch 4A paras 1–4]. The preconditions are that the trustees must be resident in the UK and not treated as resident elsewhere under a double taxation treaty. [Sch 4A para 5]. The settlor must have been resident or ordinarily resident in the UK in the relevant year of assessment or any of the previous five years. [Sch 4A para 6]. The trust must be a settlor interested settlement where the chargeable gains would otherwise be charged on the settlor under TCGA 1992 s 77, or property derived from such a settlement. It must be a settlor interested settlement at any time in the period beginning two years before the beginning of the year of assessment of the deemed disposal, but not before 6 April 1999. [Sch 4A para 7]. The relevant underlying assets to be deemed disposed of is the whole or part of each of the assets comprised in the settled property or a defined part of the settled property. Where the interest disposed of is a specific fraction of the income or capital of the settled property or defined part, the deemed disposal is of a corresponding part of each asset in the trust or defined part. [Sch 4A para 8].

6.151 The deemed disposal takes place at market value. [TCGA 1992 Sch 4A para 9]. If the disposal is already caught under TCGA 1992 s 76(1) as a disposal of an actual interest in settled property, the deemed disposal provisions do not normally apply. If the gain would be greater or the loss smaller under the deemed disposal provisions, however, they take precedence over the actual gain or loss on the disposal of the interest. [Sch 4A para 10]. If CGT is payable by the trustees, or is recovered by the settlor from the trustees under TCGA 1992 s 78, the trustees have a right of recovery against whoever disposed of the interest in the settlement, thereby causing the trustees a tax charge. The trustees may obtain from the Revenue a certificate specifying the amount of the gains in question and the amount of tax paid. [Sch 4A para 11]. Settlor is defined as for a settlor interested settlement under TCGA 1992 s 79, by Sch 4A para 12. Where the beginning of the disposal, ie the exchange of contracts under TCGA 1992 s 28 or in the case of an option being exercised, when the option is granted, and the effective completion, is in a different tax year, the deemed disposal takes place in the year of completion and the conditions as to residence of trustees, residence of settlor or settlor interest are met if they apply for any of the relevant years. [Sch 4A para 13]. There is an exception for maintenance funds for historic buildings under ICTA 1988 s 691(2); such buildings are treated as non-settlor interested settlements. [Sch 4A para 14].

6.152 These anti-avoidance provisions were introduced to prevent a taxpayer from putting assets into a trust in which he retains an interest and then selling the interest in the trust relying on the exemption on the sale of such an interest provided in TCGA 1992 s 76. Anti-avoidance legislation was introduced in respect of the sale of an interest in a settlor interested settlement after 20 March 2000. [FA 2000 s 91(3)]. The settlor would have rolled over the gain into the trust as a gift of business assets under TCGA 1992 s 165 or s 260 as a gift of non-business assets to trustees where an IHT charge would arise. This would mean that for the first quarter the assets would be held on discretionary trusts, with the settlor being granted the life interest to make it a settlor interested trust after three months (*Melville v IRC* [2001] STC 1271). [TCGA 1992 ss 77 and 65(4)]. There is no motive test to prevent these provisions applying and therefore an innocent sale by a beneficiary of his life interest could be caught (CG 35101). The purpose of the anti-avoidance legislation in TCGA 1992 Sch 4A is explained in the Revenue *Capital Gains Manual* at CG 35101 as follows:

'The main purpose of the legislation is to counteract a number of tax avoidance schemes which exploited the exemption under TCGA 1992 s 76 which applies to disposals of interests in settlements which have always been UK resident, whether by an original beneficiary, or by anyone else, if the interest had never been acquired for money or money's worth. A simple scheme would have been something like this:

- A owns a valuable holding of unlisted shares in a trading company which he wishes to sell to B.
- He creates a settlement under which he has the life interest and his son C has the remainder.
- He transfers the shares to the settlement, claiming hold-over relief under TCGA 1992 s 165.
- He sells his life interest to B and C sells his remainder to D, B's son. The price would be based on the current market value of the shares, with some discount for potential future liability.
- B and D are appointed trustees of the settlement.
- B and D now have full control as beneficiaries and as trustees. They could get the shares out of the trust, using a TCGA 1992 s 165 claim to prevent liability. But this would involve some liability under TCGA 1992 s 76. Alternatively they can simply leave the assets in the settlement.

There is no motive test in the legislation. So, for example, a straightforward sale by a long-term beneficiary to raise money could result in the application of this Schedule.'

See also Tax Bulletin, Issue 66, August 2003, pages 1048–1049 (Appendix 3).

Transfers linked with trustee borrowing

6.153 TCGA 1992 s 76B and Sch 4B introduced legislation to counter the flip-flop scheme. The scheme worked by trustees borrowing against the security of the trust assets in year one and advancing the money borrowed to a new settlement which was created. In the next fiscal year the trustees realised the gains and used the proceeds to pay off the loan. Distributions to the beneficiaries could then be made from the new settlement free of CGT. In a UK-based scheme to avoid the settlor interest charge under TCGA 1992 s 77 the settlor and spouse were excluded from the original settlement after the advance but in year one and was approved by the Special Commissioners in *Tee v Inspector of Taxes* [2002] STC (SCD) 370. The scheme was, however, largely aimed at the foreign trust provisions and taxing the settlor on distributions to beneficiaries under TCGA 1992 ss 86 and 87. These provisions are dealt with in Chapter 10.

Restriction on set-off of trust losses

6.154 In order to enable valuable business assets or unquoted shares to be sold it was possible to find a trust with substantial genuine CGT losses. The beneficial interests of the existing beneficiaries would be purchased and the valuable assets transferred into the trust under a holdover relief claim under TCGA 1992 s 165. The trust losses would be realised, if they had not already been realised, and the valuable assets disposed of with the gain covered by the trust losses. The anti-avoidance provisions apply where a claim for gifts relief has been made under TCGA 1992 s 165 or s 260 in relation to gifts of business assets, or a gift on which IHT is chargeable, and the transferor in respect of the gift has acquired an interest in settled property or entered into an arrangement to acquire such an interest for consideration. [TCGA 1992 s 79A(1)]. The gain on the assets subject to the claim to gifts relief realised by the trustees, is subject to CGT without relief for allowable losses which would otherwise be available (CG 33553). [Section 79A(2)–(4)].

6.155 TCGA 1992 s 275 provides the following rules applicable for CGT purposes for the location of assets:

(a) Rights or interests, in or over immovable property, other than by way of security are situated where the property is.

(b) Rights or interests, other than by way of security, in or over tangible movable property is where the property is.

(c) A debt secured or unsecured is situated in the UK if the creditor is resident in the UK.

(d) Shares or securities issued by any municipal or government authority or by anybody created by such an authority are situated in the country of that authority.

(e) Registered shares or securities are situated where they are registered and if registered in more than one register where the principal register is situated.

(f) A ship or aircraft is situated in the UK if the owner is resident in the UK, and any interest or right in or over a ship or aircraft is situated in the UK if the person entitled to that right or interest is resident in the UK.

(g) The situation of goodwill as a trade, business or professional asset is the place where the trade, business or profession is carried on.

(h) Patents, trademarks and registered designs are situated where they are registered and if registered in more than one register where each register is situated and the rights or licences to use a patent, trademark or registered design are situated in the UK if they, or any rights derived therefrom are exercisable in the UK.

(i) Copyright, design right and franchisees and rights or licences to use any copyright work or design are situated in the UK if they or any rights derived from them are exercisable in the UK.

(j) A judgment debt is situated where the judgment is recorded.

(k) A debt which is owed by a bank and is not in sterling and is represented by a sum standing to the credit of an account in a bank of an individual who is not domiciled in the UK is situated in the UK only if the individual is resident in the UK and the branch of the bank at which the account is maintained is itself situated in the UK.

Inheritance tax

6.156 A chargeable transfer is a transfer of value which is made by an individual which is not an exempt transfer or is exempt only to a limited extent. [IHTA 1984 s 2(1) and (2)]. A chargeable transfer also arises when tax is chargeable under the provisions relating to discretionary trusts under IHTA 1984 ss 58–85. [Section 2(3)].

6.157 IHT is charged on the value transferred by a chargeable transfer. [IHTA 1984 s 1]. A transfer of value is a disposition which results in the fall in value of the estate immediately after the transfer, the difference being the value transferred. [Section 3(1)]. Excluded property is not taken into account. [Section 3(2)]. The omission to exercise a right can be a transfer of value. [Section 3(3)]. A potentially exempt transfer is one made by an individual which would otherwise be a chargeable transfer but consists of a gift to another individual, including to a settlement in which that person has an interest in possession under IHTA 1984 s 49(1) or a gift into an accumulation and maintenance trust or a disabled person's trust, unless it is specifically provided that it is not a potentially exempt transfer. [Section 3A(1)].

6.158 A potentially exempt transfer which is made seven years or more before the death of the transferor is an exempt transfer. [IHTA 1984 s 3A(4)]. It is presumed that a potentially exempt transfer will prove to be an exempt transfer until it actually becomes one on the seventh anniversary of the transfer, or the earlier death of the transferor in which case it becomes a chargeable transfer. [Section 3A(4) and (5)].

6.159 A person's estate is that to which he is beneficially entitled before his death, other than excluded property. [IHTA 1984 s 5(1)]. A general power of appointment is treated as an asset of the estate. [Section 5(2)]. A person entitled to an interest in possession in settled property is treated as beneficially entitled to that property. [IHTA 1984 s 49(1)]. Therefore a transfer into a settlement in which there is an interest in possession is treated as a transfer to an individual and may therefore be potentially exempt. Where a beneficial interest in possession arises as a result of a disposition for money or money's worth, the beneficiary is not deemed to be entitled to the whole property but merely the actuarial value of the life interest he acquired, in determining whether there was a reduction in value of his estate. [Section 49(2)].

Excluded property

6.160 Property situated outside the UK is excluded property if the person beneficially entitled to it is an individual domiciled outside the UK. [IHTA 1984 s 6(1)]. Securities that are free of tax for residents abroad are excluded property if they are in the beneficial ownership of a non-resident. [Section 6(2)]. War savings certificates, National Savings certificates, premium savings bonds, deposits with the National Savings Bank or a trustee savings bank or a certified contractual savings scheme within ICTA 1988 s 326 are excluded property if held by a domiciliary of the Channel Islands or the Isle of Man. Emoluments paid to a non-British citizen who is a member of the armed forces of a foreign country stationed in the UK are excluded property, as is any tangible, movable property in the UK solely due to such presence. [IHTA 1984 ss 6(4) and 155(1)].

6.161 The exemption extends to property deemed to be situated outside the UK under a double taxation agreement under IHTA 1984 s 158. A non-domiciliary may leave out of account the balance on any qualifying foreign currency account, including that held by trustees of settled property in which he had an interest in possession on his death, if he was not domiciled in the UK immediately before his death, unless the settlor was domiciled in the UK when he made the settlement or the trustees are domiciled, resident or ordinarily resident in the UK immediately before his death. [Section 157].

6.162 Unlike for CGT under TCGA 1992 s 275, the IHT legislation contains no *situs* rules for determining whether the property is located in the UK or overseas and, consequently, the normal rules will apply:

(i) Registered securities are situated where they are registered, which is generally the place where the share register is kept and where the shares can be dealt with, see *R v Williams* [1942] AC 541; where dealings may take place in two or more countries the *situs* is the country in which the registered owner would ordinarily deal (*Treasurer for Ontario v Aberdein* [1947] AC 24; *Standard Chartered Bank Ltd v IRC* [1978] STC 272).

(ii) Bearer securities are situated in the country in which the title documents are kept (*Winans v A-G* [1910] AC 27. However, where Eurobonds are held through the Euroclear system, the CTO appears to have regard to the location of the broker.

(iii) Renounceable letters of allotment of shares in UK companies were held to have a UK *situs* irrespective of the location of the documents, in the CGT case, *Young v Phillips* [1984] STC 520.

(iv) A simple contract debt is generally situated in the country where the debtor resides. Where there is more than one country, regard will be had to the contract terms to localise the debt (*New York Life Insurance Co Ltd v Public Trustee* [1924] 2 Ch 101; *Kwok Chi Leung (Executor of Lamson Kwok) v Comr of Estate Duty* [1988] STC 728). A specialty debt (ie a debt based on a document under seal), including a mortgage under seal, is located where the document is situated at the time of the disposition by the creditor (*Royal Trust Co v A-G for Alberta* [1930] AC 144).

(v) Freehold and leasehold land is located where the property is situated.

(vi) Movable property is located where it is physically situated. However, see ESC F7 where foreign works of art temporarily in the UK are not charged to tax. Ships are generally situated where registered unless they are within UK territorial or national waters (*Trustees Executors and Agency Co Ltd v IRC* [1973] STC 96).

6.163 From 6 April 1998 all gilt-edged securities have been excluded property, and therefore free of IHT if they are in the beneficial ownership of a non-resident or non-domiciliary or held in trust and such a person has a qualifying interest in possession therein. [IHTA 1984 s 49; FA 1998 s 161(2)(c)].

6.164 It would appear that a non-domiciled, non-ordinarily resident person deemed to be domiciled under IHTA 1984 s 267 could make transfers free of IHT by acquiring gilts and transferring them *in specie* to the proposed beneficiary. In appropriate circumstances trustees might wish to switch investments to hold such securities if the person having a qualified interest in possession qualifies for the exemption, ie is actually a non-domiciled, non-ordinarily resident person.

6.165 A reversionary interest in settled property is a future interest under a settlement, whether vested or contingent, including an interest expectant on the termination of an interest in possession. [IHTA 1984 s 47]. A reversionary interest is excluded property unless it has been acquired at any time for a consideration in money or money's worth, or is one to which either the settlor or his spouse has been beneficially entitled, or is an interest expectant on the determination of a lease for life treated as a settlement under IHTA 1984 s 43(3). [Section 48(1)]. If the settlement was made before 16 April 1976, the exclusion of the reversionary interest belonging to the settlor's spouse is ignored, and for an interest in a post-16 April 1976 trust acquired before 10 March 1981, the reversionary interest is excluded property unless the settlor or his spouse is beneficially entitled at the relevant date. [Section 48(2)]. Where a settlement is situated outside the UK, the property, but not a reversionary interest in the property, is excluded property if the settlor was domiciled outside the UK at the time the settlement was made and the reversionary interest in the property is excluded property if the person beneficially entitled to it is an individual domiciled outside the UK. [Section 48(3)]. Where FOTRA (free of tax for residents abroad) securities are held in trust, the securities are excluded property if the person with the interest in possession is non-resident or if it can be shown that all beneficiaries of a discretionary trust are non-resident (*Montague Trust Co (Jersey) Ltd v IRC* [1989] STC 477; *Von Ernst and Cie SA v IRC* [1980] STC 111. [Section 48(4)].

6.166 Where a close company is entitled to an interest in possession in settled property, the participators are treated, except for the acquisition of a reversionary interest under IHTA 1984 s 55, as being the persons entitled to the interest according to their interests in the company. [IHTA 1984 s 101]. An attempt to use the excluded property provisions for exempt gilts, using a non-resident close company failed in *IRC v Brandenburg* [1982] STC 555. There are provisions covering the transfer of assets from one trust to another in IHTA 1984 s 48(5) and (6). Property is regarded for the purposes of section 48(3) as becoming comprised in the settlement when it, or other property which it represents, is introduced by the settlor (ESC E9). *Tax Bulletin*, Issue 27, February 1997, RI166, provides as follows:

> **'Excluded property settlements by people domiciled overseas [IHTA 1984 ss 43,44, 48]**
>
> [The Revenue] have been asked how the IHT provisions on excluded property apply to the assets of a settlement made by a person domiciled overseas where—
>
> — all, or only some, of the settled assets are situated outside the UK when a chargeable event occurs;
>
> or
>
> — a person domiciled in the UK has also provided property or funds for the purposes of that settlement.
>
> References in this article are to sections of the Inheritance Tax Act 1984.
>
> **Excluded property**
>
> For persons domiciled abroad, IHT generally applies only to their UK assets; it treats their overseas assets as excluded property, that is not within the charge to IHT – s 6(1). For assets owned outright, it is the owner's domicile at the time of a tax charge that is relevant in deciding whether or not the assets are excluded property.
>
> Slightly different rules apply to property held in settlement. An asset is excluded property if it is situated abroad when a chargeable event occurs and if the settlor (defined in s 44) was domiciled outside the UK at the time the settlement was made – s 48(3).
>
> However, an "excluded" asset is not always completely irrelevant for the purposes of IHT. So—
>
> — an "excluded" asset in a person's estate may still affect the valuation of another asset in the estate, for example, an "excluded" holding of shares in an unquoted company may affect the value of a similar holding in the estate which is not "excluded";
>
> — the value of an "excluded" asset at the time the asset becomes comprised in a settlement may be relevant in determining the rate of

any tax charge arising in respect of the settlement under the IHT rules concerning trusts without interests in possession – ss 68(5), 66(4) and 69(3).

Domicile is a concept of general law but, in certain circumstances (s 267), a person with a general law domicile abroad can be treated as having a UK domicile for IHT purposes.

Settlor adds assets to his/her existing settlements

In the light of the definitions of "settlement" and "settled property" in s 43, [the Revenue's] view is that a settlement in relation to any particular asset is made at the time when that asset is transferred to the settlement trustee, to hold on the declared trusts. Thus, assets added to a settlor's own settlement made at an earlier time when the settlor was domiciled abroad will not be "excluded", wherever they may be situated, if the settlor has a UK domicile at the time of making the addition.

In determining the tax treatment of particular assets held in the same settlement it may, therefore, be necessary to consider the settlor's domicile at times other than when the settlement was first made. And if assets added at different times have become mixed, any dealings with the settled fund after the addition(s) may also need to be considered.

Several persons contribute to a single settlement

There are rules (s 44(2)) which provide that assets contributed to a "single" settlement by more than one settlor are to be treated as comprised in separate settlements for IHT purposes if "the circumstances so require". There is no definition of "required circumstances" or statutory guidance on how the assets in the single, actual settlement are to be attributed to the deemed separate settlements.

However, the provision is similar in terms to FA 1975 Sch 5 para 1(8), which was considered by Chadwick J in *Hatton v IRC* [1992] STC 140. In the light of the decision in that case [the Revenue] take the view—

— that the determination of the extent to which overseas assets in a settlement are excluded property by reason of the settlor's domicile is a relevant "required circumstance"; and

— that where a clear, or reasonably sensible, attribution of settled property between the contributions made by several settlors is possible, there will be a separate settlement, with its own attributed assets, for each contribution for IHT purposes;

— if such an attribution is not feasible, each separate settlement will comprise all the assets of the single, actual settlement.

Trust records

It follows from the comments above that the trustees of a settlement should keep adequate records to enable any necessary attribution of the settled property to be made if either—

— the settlor has added further assets to the settlement after it was made; or

— two or more persons have contributed funds for the purposes of the settlement.'

A settlement for inheritance tax purposes means any disposition however effected whereby property is held in trust for persons in succession or for any person subject to a contingency or held by trustees on trust to accumulate the whole or part of the income or with power to make payments out of that income at the discretion of the trustees or some other person with or without power to accumulate surplus income or charged with the payment of an annuity other than for full consideration in money or money's worth IHTA 1984 s 43(2). A lease for life is treated as a settlement unless the lease was granted for a full consideration in money or money's worth IHTA 1984 s 43(3). The definitions in relation to Scotland and Northern Ireland are covered in IHTA 1984 s 43(4) and (5). Settled property is property comprised in a settlement IHTA 1984 s 43(1).

The settlor includes any person by whom the settlement was made directly or indirectly or who has provided funds directly or indirectly for the purpose of or in connection with the settlement or has made a reciprocal arrangement for some other person to make the settlement IHTA 1984 s 44(1). Except in relation to settlements of exempt gilts under IHTA 1984 s 48(4)–(6) where there is more than one settlor of a settlement it is treated for inheritance tax purposes as if the settled property were comprised in separate settlements IHTA 1984 s 44(2). Trustee means any person in whom the settled property or its management is for the time being vested IHTA 1984 s 45.

The question of a lease for life was considered in *IRC v Lloyds Private Banking Ltd* [1998] STC 559. SP 10/79 gives the Revenue view of a power of the trustees to allow a beneficiary to occupy a dwelling house as follows:

> 'Many wills and settlements contain a clause empowering the trustees to permit a beneficiary to occupy a dwelling-house which forms part of the trust property as they think fit. The Board do not regard the existence of such a power as excluding any interest in possession of the property.
>
> When there is no interest in possession in the property in question, the Board do not regard the exercise of a power as creating one if the effect is merely to allow non-exclusive occupation or to create a contractual tenancy for full consideration. The Board also take the view that no interest in possession arises on the creation of a lease for a term or a periodic tenancy for less than full consideration, though this will normally give rise to a charge for tax under IHTA 1984 s 65(1)(b) (formerly FA 1982 s 108(1)(b)). On the other hand if the power is drawn in terms wide enough to cover the creation of an exclusive or joint residence, albeit revocable, for a definite or indefinite period, and is exercised with the intention of providing a particular beneficiary with a permanent home, the Revenue will normally regard the exercise of the power as creating an interest in possession. And if the trustees in exercise of their powers grant a lease for life for less than full

consideration, this will be regarded as creating an interest in possession in view of IHTA 1984 ss 43(3), 50(6) (formerly FA 1975 Sch 5 paras 1(3), 3(6)).

A similar view will be taken where the power is exercised over property in which another beneficiary had an interest in possession up to the time.'

6.167 A right of occupation as a lease for life within IHTA 1984 s 43(3) was also considered in *Woodhall (Woodhalls personal representative) v IRC* [2000] STC (SCD) 558, although in that case the interest was held to be a joint interest and he was therefore regarded as having an interest in possession in half of the house. [IHTA 1984 s 50(5)]. A trustee's annuity that is no more than reasonable remuneration for his services is not regarded as giving him an interest in possession in the property. [IHTA 1984 s 90]. Where a person would have become entitled to an interest in possession in any part of the residue on the completion of the administration period, it is treated as if he had obtained such an interest in the ascertained residue and unadministered estate from the earliest date that income would become attributable to that interest if the residue had been ascertained immediately after the death. [Section 91]. A disposal of an interest by a beneficiary which was not a disclaimer would therefore incur a charge to tax even though he may never legally have had an interest in possession (*Comr of Stamp Duties (Queensland v Livingstone)* [1964] 3 All ER 692). Difficulties can arise in valuing the relevant property of an estate in administration in view of the definition of an unadminstered estate in section 91(2).

6.168 Wills frequently contain a clause under which a person has to survive for a period in order to benefit. A survivorship period of up to six months is allowed under IHTA 1984 s 92. If the beneficiary survives and therefore inherits or dies before surviving the requisite period so that the dependant beneficiaries inherit the dispositions actually made on the circumstances applying at the end of the period are treated as if they had taken effect at the beginning of the period, ie at the date of death. A person who is entitled to an interest in settled property but disclaims that interest other than for a consideration in money or money's worth, is treated as if he had never become entitled to the interest under section 93.

Close companies

6.169 Where a close company makes a transfer of value, IHT is charged on each individual to whom an amount is apportioned as if each individual had made a net of tax transfer of value equal to the amount so apportioned, less any amount by which the value of his estate has increased, excluding any rights or interests in the company. The amount transferred is apportioned among the participators according to their respective rights and interests in the company immediately before the transfer, with sub-apportionment through other corporate holdings, and by close company shareholders. However, distributions taxable as income are not apportioned. The value of property outside the UK which is the subject of the transfer is not apportioned to non-UK domiciled participators. Surrenders of group relief and surplus ACT are ignored, as are apportionments of 5 per cent or less of the value transferred by the company's transfer of value, which avoids apportionment to very small shareholders. [IHTA 1984 s 94]. There are relieving provisions where transfers take place between close companies and a participator is a shareholder in both. [Section 95]. Preference shares are left out of account in determining the respective rights and interests of the participators. [Section 96]. Apportionment is not made to minority shareholders in a subsidiary company of a group where intra-group transfers are made and they would have only a small effect on the value of the minority participator's rights. [Section 97]. Transfers of value can arise through the alteration of a close company's unquoted share or loan capital or an alteration in any rights attaching to unquoted shares in, or unquoted debentures of, a close company. [Section 98].

6.170 Where the participators are trustees and any part of the value transferred by a close company's transfer of value is apportioned to them, the apportionment goes through a person with a qualifying interest in possession, such as a life tenant, under IHTA 1984 s 99(2)(a). Where there is no qualifying interest in possession in the settled property, the value of the settled property is treated as reduced by the amount so apportioned which could give rise to an exit charge under IHTA 1984 s 65. [Section 99(2)(b)]. Qualifying interest in possession is as defined by IHTA 1984 s 59(1). If as a result of the transfer the value of the settled property increases, ignoring the value of any rights or interests in the company, the amounts apportioned under these provisions are reduced accordingly. [Section 99(3)]. There are corresponding provisions where an alteration in a close company's share or loan capital, or of any rights attaching to shares in or debentures of a close company which is treated as a disposition made by the participators, is apportioned through to an individual entitled to an interest in possession who is treated as if his interest is possession had proportionately come to an end, which could give rise to a charge under IHTA 1984 s 52. Where the apportionment is to a close company having an interest in possession in settled property, the apportionment is carried through to the participators of the close company beneficiary, and, where these are trustees of a settlement, through to any beneficiary having an interest in possession in the trust which is treated as terminated, giving rise to a termination charge under section 52 unless the interest reverts to the settlor under section 53(3) (ESC E5).

6.171 In connection with intragroup transfers a dividend from a subsidiary to a parent is not a transfer of value nor are transfers of assets between wholly-owned subsidiaries or between a wholly-owned subsidiary and its parent (ESC E15). For these purposes close company and participator are defined as for corporation tax purposes but expanded to a company which would be a close company if resident in the UK. [IHTA 1984 s 102(1)]. A person's interests in a company include rights and interests in the assets available for distribution among the participators in the event of a winding-up, or in any other circumstances. [Section 102(2)].

Business property relief

6.172 Relevant business property relief at 100 per cent reduces the value transferred by the chargeable transfer to nil, under IHTA 1984 s 104(1)(a), where the property consists of a business or an interest in a business carried on for gain. [Section 105(1)(a) and 103(3)]. Similar relief applies where the assets consist of securities of a company which are unquoted and which, either by themselves or together with other such securities owned by the transferor and any unquoted shares held by the transferor, gave him control of the company immediately before the transfer. [Section 105(1)(b)]. The relief also applies to any unquoted shares in a company. [Section 105(1)(bb)].

6.173 Relevant business property relief is available at 50 per cent under IHTA 1984 s 104(1)(b) in respect of quoted shares or securities that gave the transferor control of the company immediately before the transfer. [Section 105(1)(cc)]. Relief at 50 per cent is also available on any land or building, machinery or plant which immediately before the transfer was used wholly or mainly for the purpose of a business carried on by a company of which the transferor had control, or by a partnership of which he was a partner. [Section 105(1)(d)]. The transferor of a transfer of value includes the trustees of a settlement. [Section 103(1)(b)]. Relief at 50 per cent also applies to any land or building, machinery or plant which immediately before the transfer was used wholly or mainly for the purposes of a business carried on by the transferor which was owned by the trustees of a settlement in which he was beneficially entitled to an interest in possession. [Section 105(1)(e)]. Business property relief is not available where the business consists of dealing in securities, stocks or shares, land or buildings or making or holding investments, except as a market-maker or holding company of qualifying companies. [Section 105(3) and (4)]. Shares or securities cease to qualify where the company is in liquidation other than for a reconstruction or amalgamation. [Section 105(5)]. Cases on relevant business property include *Beckman v IRC* [2000] STC (SCD) 59; *Furness v IRC* [1999] STC (SCD) 232; *Farmer (Executors of Farmer) v IRC* [1999] STC (SCD) 321; *Grimwood Taylor v IRC* [2000] STC (SCD) 39; *Weston (Executor of Weston) v IRC* [2000] STC 1064; *Martin and Horsfall (Moore's Executors) v IRC* [1995] STC (SCD) 5; *Burkinyoung (Burkinyoung's Executor) v IRC* [1995] STC (SCD) 29; *Brown's Executors v IRC* [1996] STC (SCD) 277; *Hall and Hall (Hall's Executors) v IRC* [1997] STC (SCD) 126; *Powell and Halfhide (Pearce's Personal representatives) v IRC* [1997] STC (SCD) 181; *Mallender (Drury-Lowe's Executors) v IRC* [2000] STC (SCD) 574; *Hardcastle and Hardcastle (Vernede's Executors) v IRC* [2000] STC (SCD) 532; and *Barclays Bank Trust Co Ltd v IRC* [1998] STC (SCD) 125. Settled property used by a life tenant for a farming business was specifically confirmed as qualifying for business property relief in *Fetherstonhaugh v IRC* [1984] STC 261.

6.174 Securities on the alternative investment market are not treated as quoted for tax purposes (IR Press Release, 20 February 1995). In order to qualify for business property relief an asset has to have been owned for the two years immediately preceding transfer but that may include replacement property under IHTA 1984 ss 106 and 107. However, in the case of a legacy the asset is treated as acquired when the donor died and if the donor was a spouse his or her period of ownership may be included. [Section 108]. Where the asset was relevant business property on the death of the transferor, a subsequent transfer by the legatee is also of relevant business property; the fact that the legatee had held the property for less than two years does not disqualify him from business property relief. [Section 109].

6.175 The value of a business is the net value, ie the value of the assets including goodwill used in the business, less any liabilities incurred for business purposes (*Finch v IRC* [1983] STC 157). [IHTA 1984 s 110]. In determining whether a person had control of a company it was held that it was theoretical control that was required and the fact that the substantial shareholder was a minor and unable to exercise his voting rights was irrelevant (*Walding's Executors v IRC* [1996] STC 13).

6.176 Where a group of companies consists only partly of qualifying companies, the non-qualifying companies are omitted for the purposes of calculating business property relief. [IHTA 1984 s 111]. Excepted assets are those which have neither been used wholly or mainly for the purpose of the business throughout the whole of the two years ending with the transfer, nor were required at the time of the transfer for future use in the business. [Section 112(2)]. Excepted assets are excluded in calculating business property relief. [Section 112(1)]. Land or buildings, machinery or plant used by a controlled company or partnership must either have been held for the two years immediately preceding the transfer of value or have replaced other assets where the combined period of ownership is at least two years in the five years immediately preceding the transfer of value. [Section 112(3)]. Just apportionments are provided for under section 112(4).

6.177 Where a contract for sale has been entered into, the asset ceases to qualify for business property relief unless it is a sale of a business to a company wholly or mainly for shares or securities or as part of a reconstruction or amalgamation. [IHTA 1984 s 113]. Business relief may be lost where buy and sell agreements have been entered into, eg by partners agreeing to purchase an outgoing partner's interest (SP 12/80).

6.178 Where a transferor dies within seven years of making a potentially exempt transfer of relevant business property which becomes chargeable on his death or a previously chargeable transfer of relevant business property, the tax on which has to be recomputed in accordance with IHTA 1984 s 7, business property relief will only be available where the transferee has retained ownership of the original property from the date of transfer to the date of death and that property would still qualify as relevant business property at the date of death, ignoring the two-year ownership requirement in IHTA 1984 s 106. If the transferee has died before the transferor, the conditions for business property relief must be met at the transferee's death where the original property consisted of shares or securities; business property relief is preserved if the original transfers were made from a controlling shareholding.

6.179 IHTA 1984 s 113A allows the property to be disposed of and replaced by the donee before the transferor's death, provided that all the net sale proceeds are reinvested in the acquisition of replacement business property within three years or such longer period as the Revenue may allow, after the disposal. Both transactions must be at arm's length and it is the replacement property that is owned by the transferee at the date of the transferor's death which qualifies. [Section 113B]. These provisions, which can cause the loss of business property relief, have to be considered by trustees to whom business property is given and they may think it appropriate to insure the donor's life for the amount of any IHT for which they could become liable if the property were to cease to qualify as relevant business property and the transferor were to die within seven years.

6.180 Agricultural property relief takes precedence over business property relief and double relief is excluded by IHTA 1984 s 114. Agricultural assets such as stock and plant not qualifying for agricultural property relief would normally qualify for business property relief.

6.181 A farming business acquired in replacement of a non-farming business, and owned for less than the minimum period required for agricultural relief, could qualify for relevant business property relief. In the Revenue's view, where agricultural property which is a farming business is replaced by non-agricultural business property, the period of ownership of the original property will be included in applying the minimum ownership condition to the replacement property (*Tax Bulletin*, Issue 14, December 1994, RI95).

6.182 Agricultural property relief is also available to trustees. [IHTA 1984 s 115(1)(b)]. Agricultural property means agricultural land or pasture and includes woodland and any buildings used in connection with the intensive rearing of livestock or fish, if the woodland or building is occupied with agricultural land or pasture and the occupation is ancillary to that of the agricultural land or pasture. It also includes such cottages, farm buildings and farmhouses, together with the land occupied with them, as are of a character appropriate to the property. [Section 115(2)]. Agricultural property is valued on the basis that it be subject to a perpetual covenant prohibiting its use otherwise than as agricultural property, which means that the development value of agricultural land does not qualify for the relief but could qualify for business property relief on the excess value. The breeding and rearing of horses on a stud farm and the grazing of horses in connection with those activities shall be taken to be agriculture, as will any buildings used in connection with such activities. Agricultural property relief is only available on such property in the UK, the Channel Islands or the Isle of Man. Agricultural property relief was denied for a farmhouse where the land was held by a farming company (*Starke v IRC* [1995] STC 689). Relief was also denied in *Harrold v IRC* [1996] STC (SCD) 195. Grazing land use by horses was not connected with agriculture in *Wheatley's Executors v IRC* [1998] STC (SCD) 60. Agricultural property relief is 100 per cent of the value transferred if the interest in the agricultural property is with vacant possession or a right to obtain vacant possession within twelve months or let on a tenancy beginning on or after 1 September 1995. The 100 per cent relief also applies in certain cases where the land has been held since 10 March 1981. [Section 116]. Where the agricultural property is let on a tenancy beginning before 1 September 1995 for twelve months or more, the percentage agricultural property relief is 50 per cent [Section 116(2)].

6.183 There is a minimum period of occupation of two years for owner-occupied property or seven years for let property. [IHTA 1984 s 117]. The provisions for replacement property are in section 118 and occupation by a company controlled by the transferor or a partnership in which he is a partner is covered by section 119. There are also provisions for successions and successive transfers which broadly correspond to the business property relief provisions. [Sections 120 and 121]. The relief is extended to the agricultural value attributable to shares in a company which forms part of the company's assets, where the shares gave the transferor control of the company immediately before the transfer and the property was occupied by the company for the purposes of agriculture throughout the period of two years ending with the date of the transfer, or was let for the purposes of agriculture throughout the seven years ending on that date, subject to qualifying replacements of similarly qualifying property. [Sections 122 and 123].

6.184 Where there is a contract for sale of agricultural property or the sale of the shares or securities in an agricultural company, other than for the purposes of reconstruction or amalgamation or the transfer of a business to a company, the relief is lost. [IHTA 1984 s 124]. Where there has been a potentially exempt transfer of agricultural property or a chargeable transfer and within seven years the transferor dies so that tax may have to be recomputed on death, agricultural relief will only be available if the property comprised in the gift is owned by the transferee throughout the period from the date of transfer to the date of death, and the property is agricultural property occupied either by the transferee or another person for the purposes of agriculture. Where the original agricultural property comprised shares in a farming company the company must have owned the agricultural land throughout the relevant period, subject to reinvestment in other agricultural property which is allowed. Where the transferee predeceases the transferor or where the donee sells agricultural property and reinvests in business property, the conditions must be satisfied at the transferee's death (*Tax Bulletin*, Issue 14, December 1994, p 182). [Section 124A]. Provisions relating to replacement property are contained in section 124B. Land which is taken out of farming but dedicated under one of the habitat schemes listed in section 124C remains agricultural property for IHT purposes.

Woodlands

6.185 The woodlands relief in IHTA 1984 ss 125–130, which allows an election to leave out the value of trees or underwood in determining the value of non-agricultural land held at death, is not applicable to trustees except to the extent that land could be left to trustees under a will trust and the tax which crystallises on a subsequent sale could become chargeable on the trustees under the terms of the will.

Written variations

6.186 Within the period of two years after a person's death it is possible, by means of an instrument in writing, to vary any of the dispositions made by will or under the laws relating to intestacy or otherwise or where any benefit so conferred is disclaimed. IHT should be calculated as if the variations had been effected by the deceased or the disclaimed benefit had never been conferred. [IHTA 1984 s 142(1)]. The variation only had effect on giving written notice to the Board of Inland Revenue within six months of the date of the instrument, or so long a time as the Board may allow, by the persons making the instrument, and, where the variation results in the additional IHT being payable, the personal representatives. The personal representatives could decline to join in an election if they have insufficient assets to discharge the additional tax. [Section 142(2)]. However, for deeds of variation made on or after 1 August 2002, the deed itself must state that it is to apply for inheritance tax if that is the case, or a result of FA 2002 s 120. The deed must be lodged with the Revenue within six months of the death under IHTA 1984 s 218A. Variations made for money or money's worth are not included unless the consideration is another variation or disclaimer. [Section 142(3)]. Property eligible for inclusion in a variation includes excluded property but not an interest in possession in settled property which is governed by the trust deed. [Section 142(5)]. It does not matter whether the administration of the estate is complete or the property concerned has been distributed in accordance with the original dispositions. [Section 142(6)]. Section 142 does not require a deed, merely an instrument in writing, although in practice this is usually in the form of a deed (*Law Society's Gazette*, 18 December 1991).

6.187 Where the variation results in property being held in a trust which ends no more than two years after the death for IHT purposes, the property is deemed to have had effect from the date of death except in relation to any distribution or application of property occurring before the transfer into trust. [IHTA 1984 s 142(4)].

6.188 Rectification of deeds of variation was allowed in *Lake v Lake* [1989] STC 865; *Seymour v Seymour* [1989] BTC 8043; *Schnieder v Mills* [1993] STC 430; and *Matthews v Martin* [1991] BTC 8048.

6.189 The Inland Revenue in *Tax Bulletin*, Issue 15, February 1995, in RI101, clarified the position with regard to the variation of inheritances following a death as follows:

> 'The beneficiaries of a deceased person's estate may wish to alter their entitlements under the estate, by changing the terms under which the original inheritance arose, whether by the deceased's will, the laws of

intestacy or otherwise. For example, a daughter inheriting under her father's will may want to pass the inheritance on to her own child.

Not surprisingly everyone who would lose out as a result of the change – called a variation – must agree to it.

There are special rules concerning the consequences of variations in inheritance tax IHTA 1984 s 142. The main ones are set out below.

If a variation is made—

— in a written instrument; and

— within two years of the relevant death; and

— if all those affected give written notice (usually called an election) to the Board of Inland Revenue within six months of the date of the instrument (or such longer time as the Board may allow); and

— where the variation means that additional inheritance tax is payable, the personal representatives of the deceased also sign the election [but see **6.186**],

then the estate will be taxed as if the variation had been made by the deceased at the time of his/her death. In other words inheritance tax will be calculated on the basis of the varied entitlements, not the original ones.

We have recently been asked for guidance in two areas relating to inheritance tax and instruments of variation.

Marshall v Kerr

In June 1994 the House of Lords, in the case of *Marshall v Kerr* [1994] STC 638 found that those provisions of TCGA 1992 s 62 which apply where there is a variation and election, did not mean that the variation of the terms of a deceased person's will was to be treated for all purposes of capital gains tax as made by the deceased. We have been asked whether variations which meet the conditions in IHTA 1984 s 142 will still be treated for inheritance tax purposes as made by the deceased and not by the beneficiary or beneficiaries.

Our view is that, as the relevant inheritance tax legislation differs from the capital gains tax provisions which were considered in *Marshall v Kerr*, that decision has no application to inheritance tax. Variations which meet all the statutory conditions will continue to be treated for inheritance tax purposes as having been made by the deceased.

Variation of inheritances following the death of an original beneficiary within the statutory two-year period

As explained above, for IHTA 1984 s 142 to apply, all beneficiaries affected by the variation must join in a written election to the Board of Inland Revenue. We have been asked how this requirement should be interpreted when one of the beneficiaries dies before a variation is made.

> Our view is that the legal personal representatives of a beneficiary (the second deceased) may enter into a variation and sign an election.
>
> If the variation will reduce the entitlements of the beneficiaries of the second deceased then they, as well as the legal personal representatives of the second deceased, must agree to the variation. The Revenue will require evidence of the consent of the beneficiaries of the second deceased to the variation. If they are not themselves parties to the variation other written evidence of their consent will be sought.
>
> This view applies for capital gains tax purposes also.'

Subsequent interpretation RI127 in Tax Bulletin 19, October 1995 covered the case of post-death variation of inheritance by survivorship as follows:

> 'Beneficiaries of the estate of a deceased person – whether under the will, rules relating to intestacy or otherwise – may wish to change their inheritances. There are special inheritance tax rules for changes or variations made within two years after the deceased's death.
>
> If a variation made within the two-year period satisfies certain other conditions, inheritance tax is charged on the death as though the deceased person had made the variation and the beneficiaries do not have to pay tax on any gift of their inheritance. The main conditions are that the variation is made in writing and that, within six months after the variation, the persons making the variation give written notice to the Revenue electing for the inheritance tax rules to apply [no longer applicable, see **6.186**].
>
> Similar rules apply for certain purposes of capital gains tax.
>
> Recently [The Revenue] have seen suggestions that these rules do not apply to a variation of the deceased's interest in jointly held assets, which passed on the death to the surviving joint owner(s).
>
> For example, the family home was owned by a mother and her son as beneficial joint tenants and on the mother's death, her interest passed by survivorship to the son who then became the sole owner of the property. It has been suggested that, in this example, the son cannot, for inheritance tax/capital gains tax purposes, vary his inheritance of his mother's interest by redirecting it to his children.
>
> [The Revenue] do not share this view.
>
> Both inheritance tax and capital gains tax rules apply not only to dispositions/inheritances arising under will or the law of intestacy but also those effected "otherwise". In [The Revenue's] view, the words "or otherwise" bring within the rules the automatic inheritance of a deceased owner's interest in jointly held assets by the surviving joint owner(s).'

6.190 On 22 May 1985, the *Law Society's Gazette* published the Revenue view on the interpretation of IHTA 1984 s 142 as follows:

'The Revenue have taken further advice on the interpretation of IHTA 1984 s 142 and have indicated that the following conditions must be satisfied by an instrument if it is to be brought within that provision—

1. the instrument in writing must be made by the persons or any of the persons who benefit or would benefit under the dispositions of the property comprised in the deceased's estate immediately before his death;
2. the instrument must be made within two years after the death;
3. the instrument must clearly indicate the dispositions that are the subject of it, and vary their destination as laid down by the deceased's will, or under the law relating to intestate estates, or otherwise;
4. a notice of election must be given within six months of the date of the instrument, unless the Board see fit to accept a late election; and
5. the notice of election must refer to the appropriate statutory provisions [but see **6.186**].

It is likely that the application of these principles will mean that most cases in which there were thought to be technical objections to instruments of variation will now be accepted. It will not be contended that the instrument of variation, to be eligible, has in terms to purport to vary the will or intestacy provisions themselves: it is sufficient if the instrument of variation identifies the disposition to be varied and varies its destination. It is emphasised, however, that the Revenue will continue to require that the provisions of IHTA 1984 s 142 as interpreted above, are satisfied.

There have been some cases in which a number of instruments of variation have been executed in relation to the same will or intestacy. The Revenue emphasise that these cases must be considered on their precise facts, but in broad terms, their views will be as follows—

(a) an election which is validly made is irrevocable;

(b) an instrument will not fall within IHTA 1984 s 142 if it further redirects any item or any part of an item that has already been redirected under an earlier instrument; and

(c) to avoid any uncertainty, variations covering a number of items should ideally be made in one instrument [see **6.186**].'

Double taxation relief

6.191 Double taxation relief for IHT purposes is given by IHTA 1984 s 158 which gives the statutory authority for entering into double taxation agreements in respect of estate and gifts taxes. The UK has double taxation agreements with France [DTR (Estate Duty) (France) Order 1963 (SI 1963/1319)], India [DTR (Estate Duty) (India) Order 1956 (SI 1956/998)], Ireland [DTR (Taxes on estates of deceased persons and inheritances and on gifts)

(Republic of Ireland) Order 1978 (SI 1978/1107)], Italy [DTR (Estate Duty) (Italy) Order 1968 (SI 1968/304)], Pakistan [DTR (Estate Duty) (Pakistan) Order 1957 (SI 1957/1522)], South Africa [DTR (Taxes on Estates of Deceased Persons and on Gifts) (Republic of South Africa) Order 1979 (SI 1979/576)], Sweden [DTR (Taxes on estates of deceased persons and inheritances and on gifts) (Sweden) Order 1981 (SI 1981/840)], Switzerland [DTR (Taxes on estates of deceased persons and inheritances) (Switzerland) Order 1994 (SI 1994/3214)], USA [DTR (Taxes on estates of deceased persons and on gifts) (United States of America) Order 1979 (SI 1979/1454)].

6.192 Under most of these double taxation treaties there are various rules as to the *situs* of assets, to try and reconcile differences in national law as to where an asset is deemed to be situated and, as in all treaties, these rules take precedence over the national law (*Ostime v Australian Mutual Provident Society* (1959) 38 TC 492), unless specifically overridden (*Padmore v IRC (No 2)* [2001] STC 280).

6.193 The treaty may also attempt to deal with different concepts of domicile or where estate and gifts taxes are based on nationality or residence. As such they may provide for a treaty domicile based on nationality or residence. A treaty domicile, for the specific purposes covered by the treaty, would overrule the normal UK rules and could, for example, deem a settlor or beneficiary to be domiciled outside the UK where he would otherwise be treated as UK domiciled. The effect of this could be to prevent anti-avoidance provisions such as IHTA 1984 s 267, deemed UK domicile, from applying. They could also make property excluded where it would not otherwise be so under IHTA 1984 s 6 or in the case of settled property IHTA 1984 s 48(3).

6.194 Most of the treaties will also provide for a credit against tax payable in the other jurisdiction under the treaty *situs* rules. It is important to consider the terms of the particular treaty where relevant. Many of the treaties are rather old and do not reflect either the changes to UK law on the introduction of corporation tax and CGT or changes in foreign laws, such as capital acquisitions tax in Ireland.

6.195 Unilateral relief for double taxation for IHT purposes is given under IHTA 1984 s 159. Overseas taxes which are similar to IHT or chargeable by reference to gifts or on death are relieved as a credit against UK IHT. If the property is situated in the overseas territory and not in the UK the credit is equal to the full overseas tax charge. Where, however, the property is situated neither in the UK nor the overseas territory or in both the UK and the overseas territory and is subject to IHT or a similar tax in both countries, the credit is calculated in accordance with a formula whereby the smaller of the inheritance tax or the overseas tax is multiplied by

$$\frac{A}{A+B}$$

where A is the IHT and B the overseas tax.

In such cases the property may be liable to tax in a third country and, applying the formula, the overseas tax B is the aggregate of the taxes in each of the overseas countries for the calculation, but in determining the smaller of the IHT or the overseas tax it is the aggregate of all except the largest of the UK IHT and each of the overseas taxes. The unilateral relief is the same as the treaty relief for the USA, South Africa, India and Pakistan. In other cases the higher of treaty relief or unilateral relief may be taken. [Section 159].

Liability for inheritance tax

6.196 The persons liable for tax under a transfer *inter vivos* include:

(a) the transferor;

(b) the person whose estate is increased by the transfer;

(c) any person in whom the property is vested whether beneficially or otherwise, which would include the trustees of the settlement; and

(d) where the property becomes comprised in a settlement, any beneficiary for whose benefit any of the property or income from it is applied, or who is beneficially entitled to an interest in possession in the property.

[IHTA 1984 s 199(1)].

So far as trustees are concerned, SP 1/82 confirms that where trustees pay IHT due on assets put into settlement this is not regarded as an interest in the settlement held by the settlor sufficient to make the income taxable on him under ICTA 1988 s 660A.

6.197 Where tax becomes payable as a result of a transfer on death, the persons liable for IHT on the free estate are the personal representatives under IHTA 1984 s 200(1)(a). Where the property was comprised in a settlement, it is the trustees of the settlement who are liable under section 200(1)(b). Trustees can also be liable if a property is vested in them, as may a beneficiary entitled to an interest in possession, under section 200(1)(c). A beneficiary of a settlement for whose benefit any of the property or income is applied may also be liable for IHT under section 200(1)(d). A person with an interest in part only of the property is deemed to be entitled to an interest in the whole of the property for this purpose, except that a purchaser for value is not liable for tax attributable to the value of that property unless it is subject to an Inland Revenue charge under IHTA 1984 s 237.

6.198 Where IHT is due in respect of settled property, the persons liable for the tax are:

(a) the trustees of the settlement;

(b) any person entitled whether beneficially or not to an interest in possession in the settled property;

(c) any person for whose benefit any of the settled property or income from it is applied at or after the time of the transfer; or

(d) in the case of a lifetime gift to non-resident trustees, the settlor.

[IHTA 1984 s 201(1)].

Trustees are non-resident for this purpose unless the general administration of the settlement is ordinarily carried on in the UK and the trustees – or a majority of them, and where there is more than one class of trustees a majority of each class – are for the time being resident in the UK. [Section 201(5)]. Trustees could also be liable for a chargeable transfer apportioned to the participators in a close company under IHTA 1984 s 99(2). [Section 202].

6.199 A settlor's spouse can be made liable for IHT where property is transferred to her under IHTA 1984 s 203. A personal representative of a deceased person is only liable for IHT attributable to the value of the property which he has received as personal representative or might have so received but for his own neglect or default, which includes land in the UK comprised in the settlement which is available in his hands for the payment of tax or might have been so available but for his own neglect or default. [Section 204(1)].

6.200 A trustee is only liable to IHT to the extent of the property he has actually received or disposed of or has become liable to account for to the beneficiaries and any other property for the time being available in his hands as a trustee for the payment of the tax or which might have been so available but for his own neglect or default. [IHTA 1984 s 204(2)]. Where a trustee is liable for tax as a person in whom property is vested, or a beneficiary is liable as a person entitled to a beneficial interest in possession, he is only liable to the extent of that property. [Section 204(3)]. A beneficiary for whose benefit property or income from any settled property is applied is only liable to the extent of that property or income (less tax). [Section 204(5)]. A person other than the transferor or personal representative liable under section 199 or the trustee of a settlement under section 201 is only liable if the tax remains unpaid after it ought to have been paid. [Section 204(6)–(8)].

6.201 Where, on a reservation of benefit, the estate of the deceased person is treated as including property given away, the personal representative is liable for tax only if it remains unpaid twelve months after the end of the month in which the death occurs, and is limited to the assets in his hands. [IHTA 1984 s 204(1) and (9)]. Where more than one person is liable for the tax the liability is joint and several. [Section 205]. Executors liable for payment of tax are also liable for the delivery of accounts under IHTA 1984 s 216 (*Re Clore (No 3), IRC v Stype Trustees (Jersey) Ltd* [1985] STC 394). A personal representative's liability is absolute and the Revenue can raise a notice of determination on him under section 221 of the 1984 Act (*Howarth's Executors v IRC* [1997] STC (SCD) 162). This also applies to a non-resident executor (*IRC v Stannard* [1984] STC 245; *Berry v Gaukroger* [1903] 2 Ch 116) and to an executor *de son tort* intermeddling in a deceased's estate (*IRC v Stype Investments (Jersey) Ltd; Re Clore* [1982] STC 625).

6.202 A person who, in the course of a trade or profession, other than a barrister, has been concerned with the making of a settlement, and knows or has reason to believe that the settlor was domiciled in the UK and the trustees of the settlement are not or will not be resident in the UK, must, within three months of making the settlement, make a return to the Revenue stating the names and addresses of the settlor and of the trustees of the settlement, except where the settlement is made by will or if a return has been made by some other person or an account has been delivered in relation to it under IHTA 1984 s 216. For the purposes of this section, trustees of a settlement shall be regarded as not resident in the UK unless the general administration of the settlement is ordinarily carried on in the UK and the trustees or a majority of them (and where there is more than one class of trustees a majority of each class) are for the time being resident in the UK. [Section 218].

6.203 The Revenue's wide powers to require information, call for documents, inspect property and exchange information with other countries under IHTA 1984 ss 219–228E apply to property held by trustees as they apply to a property held by other persons.

Associated operations

6.204 Associated operations are any two or more operations of any kind which affect the same property directly or indirectly, or income arising from that property, or which represent accumulations of such income or any two operations of which one is affected by reference to the other. Operations may be effected by the same person or different persons, need not be simultaneous and include an omission. [IHTA 1984 s 268(1)]. A lease granted for full consideration in money or money's worth is not associated with any operation effected more than three years after the grant. [Section 268(2)]. Where a transfer of value is made by associated operations carried out at different times, it is treated as made at the time of the last of them. If an earlier transaction was itself a transfer of value, the value transferred by the earlier operations reduces the value transferred by the totality of the associated operations, except where the earlier operation was exempt as a transfer between spouses [Section 268].

6.205 Life assurance policies and annuities are regarded as not being affected by the associated operations rule if the policy was issued on full medical evidence and would have been issued on the same terms if the annuity had not been bought (SP E4). *Hansard* of 10 March 1975, Vol 888, Col 56, quoted the Chief Secretary of the Treasury on associated operations as follows:

> 'I want to explain the reason for the clause [now IHTA 1984 s 268]. As I said in Committee, it is reasonable for a husband to share capital with his

wife when she has no means of her own. If she chooses to make gifts out of the money she has received from her husband, there will be no question of using the associated operation provisions to treat them as gifts made by the husband and taxable as such.

In a blatant case, where a transfer by a husband to a wife was made on condition that the wife should at once use the money to make gifts to others, a charge on a gift by the husband might arise under the clause. The Hon Gentleman fairly recognised that.

I want to give an example of certain circumstances that could mean the clause having to be invoked. There are complex situations involving transactions between husband and wife and others where, for example, a controlling shareholder with a 60 per cent holding in a company wished to transfer his holding to his son. If he gave half to his son the effect would be to pass a controlling shareholding from father to son. The Revenue would then use the associated operations provisions to ensure that the value of a controlling holding was taxed.

There are ordinary, perfectly innocent transfers between husband and wife. For example, where a husband has the money and the wife has no money – or the other way round, which happens from time to time – and the one with the money gives something to the other to enable the spouse to make a gift to a son or a daughter on marriage, that transaction would not be caught by the clause. It would be a reasonable thing to do. I have made that clear in Committee upstairs, and I make it clear again now.'

6.206 The Revenue confirmed (in correspondence with the Institute of Chartered Accountants in England and Wales on 21 September 1985, published as TR 588) that the existence of specific anti-avoidance provisions in IHTA 1984 s 268 did not preclude the application of the decision in *Furniss v Dawson* [1984] STC 153 on artificial transactions imposed purely for tax avoidance purposes.

6.207 A transfer of shares into trust, followed immediately by a purchase by the company of some of its own shares, and a sale by the trustee of others, was not an associated operation within IHTA 1984 s 268 nor an interposed transaction under the rule in *W T Ramsay v IRC* [1981] STC 174; or *Raynaud v IRC* [1999] STC (SCD) 185. When trustees of a discretionary settlement leased valuable trust pictures to a beneficiary's father on commercial terms, which had the effect of devaluing the trusts interest in the assets, the appointment the following day of a protected life interest of the paintings subject to the lease to the beneficiary was an associated operation in *McPherson v IRC* [1988] STC 362.

Gifts with reservation

6.208 Where an individual disposes of property by way of gift, which includes a gift into trust, and either the possession and enjoyment of the property is not bona fide assumed by the donee at or before the beginning of the relevant period, or if at anytime in the relevant period the property is not enjoyed to the entire exclusion or virtually to the entire exclusion of the donor, and of any benefit to him by contract or otherwise, the property remains in the donor's estate for IHT purposes. The relevant period is the period ending on the date of the donor's death and beginning seven years before that date or the date of the gift if later. [FA 1986 s 102(1)–(3)]. If the property ceases to be subject to such a reservation, the donor is treated as disposing of the property as a potentially exempt transfer at that date. [Section 102(4)]. The provisions do not apply to exempt transfers, such as those between spouses or in consideration of marriage, as listed in section 102(5). Nor do they apply to an insurance policy made before 18 March 1986 and not subsequently varied. [Section 102(6) and (7)]. FA 1986 s 102(8) introduces further provisions in FA 1986 Sch 20, including in relation to substitutions of and accretions to property in paras 2–4 of that schedule.

6.209 Where there is a gift into settlement, the property comprised in the settlement at the material date is treated as the gift subject to reservation. If the settlement comes to an end before the settlor's death the property in it at that time is treated as the gift subject to the reservation. If the donee beneficiary subsequently resettles the property subject to the original settlor's reservation the original settlor is treated as if he had made the settlement. Where property is directly or indirectly derived from a loan made by the settlor to the trustees, the property they acquired is treated as the property originally comprised in the gift into settlement. Accumulations of income, however, are not treated as property derived from the gift. [FA 1986 Sch 20 para 5(5)]. Interests in land or chattels are disregarded if the donor pays full consideration in money or money's worth, eg a rack rent. [Sch 20 para 6(1)(a)]. Occupation by the donor of an interest in land is disregarded if there has been a change in circumstances since he gave it away, and it was a gift to a relative who is now providing reasonable provision for the care and maintenance of the donor who has become unable to maintain himself through old age, infirmity or otherwise. [Sch 20 para 6(1)(b)]. The meaning of full consideration was explained in *Tax Bulletin*, Issue 9, November 1993.

6.210 In the case of settled gifts the substitutions and accretions provisions in FA 1986 Sch 20 paras 2–4 do not apply, but the property comprised in the settlement is treated as the property comprised in the gift, and if the settlement comes to an end before the donor's death, or if the property ceases to be subject to a reservation, any property taken absolutely and beneficially by the donor and any consideration given by him for the property so taken shall be treated as comprised in the gift in addition to any other property so comprised. If the gift is not placed into settlement by the donor but is subsequently settled by the donee, subject to the donor's reservation of benefit, the donor is regarded as the settlor for the purpose of the gift with reservation rules. It is not relevant whether the donee's settlement is *inter vivos* or made on death either under the will or under the intestacy rules. Where property is comprised in the settlement at the material date, i e the date of the donor's death, or the property ceased to be subject to a reservation which is derived directly or indirectly from a loan made by the donor to the trustees, it should be treated as property comprised in the gift. [Sch 20 para 5].

6.211 Insurance schemes which consist of a policy of insurance on the life of the donor or his spouse or on their joint lives under which the benefits which accrue to the donee are measured by reference to the benefits accruing to the donor or his spouse under the policy or another policy, are treated as gifts with reservation. [FA 1986 Sch 20 para 7].

6.212 Where the gift with reservation is relevant business property, agricultural property or shares representing agricultural property, business property or agricultural property relief will be given on the death of the donor or on the property ceasing to be subject to a reservation, if earlier, as if the property comprised in the gift was a transfer of value by the donor so far as it relates to shares or securities and of the donee so far as it relates to other property. Where the relief is calculated by reference to the donee, ownership by the donor prior to the disposal with reservation is treated as ownership by the donee, as is occupation by the donor before or after the disposal which should be treated as occupation by the donee in order to determine whether the minimum period of ownership or occupation requirements in IHTA 1984 ss 106–117 have been met. [FA 1986 Sch 20 para 8(1)–(2)].

6.213 In determining whether shares qualify for relief as a controlling shareholding or as an unquoted holding with more than 25 per cent of the votes, the donor is deemed to continue to own the shares at the date of the cessation of the reservation or on his death. This means that shares retained by the donor or his spouse as related property can be added to those comprised in the gift with reservation, in order to determine whether the shareholding requirement is met. The shares subject to the reservation must still be owned by the donee at the material date. If the donee dies before the transfer his personal representative, or the beneficiaries under his estate, stand in the shoes of the donee. [FA 1986 Sch 20 para 8(3)–(5). The lease carve-out scheme, under which the donor created a lease on property occupied by him at a low or nominal rent which he retained and then gave away the reversion, was successfully applied in *Ingram v IRC* [1999] STC 37. The inevitable anti-avoidance provisions were introduced in FA 1986 ss 102A–102C by FA 1999 s 104 in respect to gifts of land made on or after 9 March 1999. FA 1986 s 102A(2) provides that where the donor or his spouse enjoys a significant right or interest in relation to land which is disposed of as property subject to reservation, it will be treated as remaining in his estate under the gifts with reservation provisions in FA 1986 s 102(3) and (4). A right etc is significant if it entitles or enables the donor to occupy all or part of the land or to enjoy some right in relation to it otherwise than for full consideration in money or money's worth. It is not significant if it does not prevent the enjoyment of the land by the donee to the entire exclusion, or virtually the entire exclusion, of the donor or it does not entitle the donor to occupy all or part of the land immediately after the disposal but would do so were it not for the interest disposed of. Nor is a right or interest significant if it was granted or acquired before the period of seven years ending with the date of the gift. [Section 102A(3)–(5)].

6.214 A disposal of more than one interest in land by way of gift is treated separately in relation to each interest. [FA 1986 s 102A(6)]. Where the gift consists of an undivided share of an interest in land, by making the donee a joint tenant, the share disposed of is treated as a gift with reservation within section 102(3) and (4). These provisions do not apply where the donor does not occupy the land or occupies it to the exclusion of the donee for full consideration in money or money's worth. Nor does it apply when the donor and the donee jointly occupy the land, or the donor does not receive any benefit other than a negligible one which is provided by or at the expense of the donee for some reason connected with the gift. This sort of arrangement applies where the land is jointly occupied by the donor and the donee and each pays their own fair share of the outgoings which is therefore an arrangement not regarded as a gift with reservation. [Section 102B].

6.215 FA 1986 s 102C disapplies the provisions of FA 1986 s 102 to gifts with reservation in connection with the interests in land provisions of FA 1986 ss 102A and 102B. Where FA 1986 s 102B applies, sections 102 and 102A of that Act are disapplied. If FA 1986 s 102A applies, section 102 is disapplied. [FA 1986 s 102C(6) and (7)].

6.216 Debts or encumbrances created on or after 18 March 1986 are not deductible from the value of the estate on death to the extent that they arise from a loan-back from a person to whom the deceased had transferred property directly or indirectly. The repayment of a loan in these circumstances is treated as a potentially exempt transfer. Similarly, a loan secured on an insurance policy is not deductible from the estate unless the policy proceeds are included in the estate. [FA 1986 s 103].

6.217 A gift with reservation, eg into a discretionary trust, could also be a chargeable transfer. Regulations have been introduced by statutory instrument to avoid a double charge to IHT, with the higher liability under the original transfer or the reservation of benefit rules applying, under the Inheritance Tax (Double Charges Relief) Regulations 1987 (SI 1987/1130). Unusually, these regulations in the Schedule provide a number of examples of how the calculations proceed in order to avoid a double charge. The gift with reservation rules can, in practice, be a major inhibition to transferring assets into trust. A discretionary beneficiary would have an interest in a trust in respect of which he was the settlor (*IRC v Eversden (Executors of Greenstock)* [2002] EWHC 1360 (Ch), [2002] STC 1109). *IRC v Eversden (Executors of Greenstock)* [2003] EWCA Civ 668, [2003] STC 822 ended up in the Court of Appeal on a further point as to whether a transfer to a trust for the settlor's spouse for life with remainder to discretionary beneficiaries, including the settlor, was, although a gift with reservation as had been held in the High Court under FA 1986 s 102(5)(a), nonetheless an exempt transfer to a spouse under IHTA 1984 s 18. The Court of Appeal held that the inter-spouse exemption took precedence over the gift with reservation rules which therefore did not apply. For a short time this became a popular inheritance tax mitigation device until it was ended by FA 2003 s 185 in respect of disposals made on or after 20 June 2003. This introduced sub-sections 5A, 5B and 5C into IHTA 1984 s 102, which now provides that a gift with reservation charge will apply where a gift is made into trust and the donor's spouse enjoys an interest in possession, which comes to an end in whole or part, whether on the donee's death or otherwise, before the donee dies, and the subsequent use of the gift is such that it would count as a gift with reservation if it had been made at the time when the interest in possession terminates, ie it does not pass to the donee spouse absolutely or under another interest in possession. The beneficiary's interest in the discretionary trust is a right to be considered as a potential recipient of benefit by the trustees and a right to have his interest protected by a court of equity (*Gartside v IRC* [1968] AC 553).

6.218 There has been a number of Revenue press releases and exchanges of correspondence in connection with gifts of reservation including the *Law Society's Gazette* on 10 December 1986, which has examined a number of examples. Confirmation that Director's remuneration at a market value would not be regarded as a gift with reservation was confirmed in Revenue letters of 19 February 1987 and 5 March 1987 and in relation to gifts of land and gifts involving family businesses or farms on 18 May 1987.

6.219 The following exchange of correspondence between Vic Washtell of Touche Ross on 29 August 1986 and the Controller of the Capital Taxes Office on 29 October 1986 was published in *The Law Society's Gazette* on 10 December 1986.

> '[Q]Could you please let us know whether the Inland Revenue intends to issue a statement of practice regarding the Revenue's view on various types of gift which they would treat as gifts with reservation under the new inheritance tax legislation. If not, could you please let us know whether or not the Revenue would regard gifts in the following situations as gifts with reservation.
>
> [A] As you will doubtless appreciate, any question about the existence and/or extent of any future liability to tax can be determined only in accordance with the particular facts on the basis of the law as it is understood to be. However, in order to be as helpful to you as I can at this stage, I would offer the following comments on the situations outlined in your letter.
>
> 1. [Q] A transfers assets into a discretionary settlement. The class of beneficiaries includes A's wife at the trustees' discretion on a regular basis.
>
>   [A] The mere fact that the donor's spouse is a member of the class of potential beneficiaries would not suffice to bring the gift within the provision of FA 1986 s 102 (gifts with reservation). I should, however, draw your attention to Sch 20 paras 6(1)(c) and 7 (associated operations and certain life assurance arrangements).

2. [Q] B transfers assets into a discretionary settlement under which he is not included in the class of beneficiaries (including B) to the class of beneficiaries in future.

   [A] As you probably know the inclusion of the settlor among the class of beneficiaries subject to powers contained in his trust is considered to be sufficient to constitute his gift as a gift with reservation. Where there is a possibility of the settlor becoming included in the class of beneficiaries by exercise of a power in the settlement, it is considered likely that this would again constitute a gift with reservation.

3. [Q] C buys a house and puts it into the name of himself and his wife as tenants in common. On the death of the wife her share of the house passes to the son absolutely. C remains in occupation of the property. On the death of C is the whole or only C's half of the property treated as part of his estate for inheritance tax purposes?

   [A] Having regard to FA 1986 s 102(5)(a) (exempt transfers between spouses) it is not considered that the original gift to C's wife would constitute a gift with reservation. However, the death of C might give rise to a claim for tax on other grounds but this would fall for consideration in the light of the precise facts as they were shown to be at that time.

4. [Q] D owns freehold property and grants a lease to himself and his wife for twenty years at a peppercorn. D then gifts the reversionary interest in the property to his son.

   [A] If the true construction of the transactions here is that the gift to the son is of the reversionary interest only in the property then the gift would not constitute a gift with reservation.

5. [Q] E gifts all of his shares in his family company into an accumulation and maintenance settlement for his children under which E is a trustee.

   [A] The mere fact that E is a trustee of an accumulation and maintenance settlement for his children would not of itself involve a reservation to him.

6. [Q] F owns a home and some adjacent land. F gifts the land but retains the house.

   [A] If the situation is such that the subject matter of the gift is the land only, I do not see that this constitutes a gift with reservation.

7. [Q] G, a non-domiciliary, gifts excluded property into a discretionary settlement under which he is in the class of beneficiaries. G dies domiciled in the UK. Are the 'excluded property' assets in the settlement treated as part of G's estate?

   [A] Here it seems to me that the settled property would be 'property subject to a reservation' in relation to the settlor. Accordingly it would fall within FA 1986 s 102(3) to be treated as property to which he was beneficially entitled immediately before his death. The effect would be to lock the property into the settlor's estate within the meaning of CTTA/IHTA 1984 s 5(1), which is subject to the exception for "excluded property". It would follow that in the case of settled property, relief for foreign assets could continue to be available under ibid, s 48(3) provided that the settlor was domiciled outside the UK at the time the settlement was made.

8. [Q] Kindly confirm that Statement of Practice E10 will apply for inheritance tax purposes (vendor retaining a lease for life).

   [A] As you will know SP E10 applies in the context of the FA 1975 Sch 5 now para 1(3), CTTA/IHTA 1984 (lease for life treated as a settlement). In the context of gifts with reservation, I might perhaps draw your attention to FA 1986 Sch 20 para 6(1)(a) (occupation, enjoyment or possession by the donor to be disregarded if for full consideration).'

The Controller's letter concludes:

> 'I would emphasise that each case must be looked at in the light of its own particular facts. Too much should not be read, therefore, into general comments on the bare situations outlined in your letter which may not, in the event, be found to apply to the facts of an individual case.
>
> In a separate development, the Revenue has confirmed to the Association of British Insurers that the following do NOT constitute gifts with reservation:
>
> (a) a whole life policy effected by the life assured in trusts for X should X survive the life assured, but otherwise for the life assured.
>
> (b) An endowment effected by the life assured in trust for X if living at the death of the life assured before the maturity date but otherwise for the life assured.'
>
> Also, the Revenue has confirmed that if a gift with reservation is made into a pre-Budget day trust, this will not "taint" the whole trust fund so as to make the funds settled before Budget day liable to inheritance tax.'

6.220 This exchange of correspondence is interesting, in particular in paragraph 1 where it is confirmed that the inclusion of a spouse in the class of potential beneficiaries of a discretionary trust would not of itself be a gift with reservation under FA 1986 s 102 if this were not part of an associated operation. This conclusion could have adverse income tax or CGT consequences as being a settlor interested settlement under ICTA 1988 s 606A and TCGA 1992 s 77.

6.221 In paragraph 7 of the reply to Mr Washtell, at **6.219**, it is confirmed that the gifts with reservation rules do not apply to an excluded property settlement of a non-UK domiciled settlor, which remains exempt under IHTA 1984 s 48(3). It is common for non-domiciliaries to create excluded property settlements of assets of which they and their spouses are beneficiaries prior to acquiring a UK domicile or being deemed domiciled in the UK under IHTA 1984 s 267. It is understood that this interpretation is currently under review and that the Revenue's interpretation may change both for discretionary and life interest settlements, under which the gift with reservation rules would continue to apply to deem excluded property to remain in the settlor's estate. At the time of writing it is not clear whether this will involve legislation or a change in Revenue practice and what provisions will be made for taxpayers who have relied on this statement. SP E10 is now obsolete (IR 131 (1996)).

6.222 There have been a number of estate duty cases on gifts with reservation which are likely to apply for IHT purposes. These include *Comrs of Stamp Duties of New South Wales v Permanent Trustee Co of New South Wales Ltd* [1956] 2 All ER 512; *Chick v Comrs of Stamp Duties of New South Wales* [1958] 2 All ER 623; *Munroe v Coms of Stamp Duties of New South Wales* [1933] All ER Rep 185; *Nichols v IRC* [1975] STC 278; *Earl Grey v A-G* [1900] ACT 124; and *A-G v Worrall* [1895] 1 QB 99.

6.223 That the settlor had reserved a benefit by being a beneficiary under a discretionary trust was confirmed by *A-G v Heywood* (1887) 19 QBD 326 and *A-G v Farrell* [1931] 1 KB 81. A gift to a settlement with a resulting trust in favour of the donor, if the child beneficiary failed to obtain a vested interest, was not a reservation of benefit in *Comrs of Stamp Duties of New South Wales v Perpetual Trust Co Ltd* [1943] 1 All ER 525. A settlor remunerated as trustee had retained a benefit (*Oaks v Comrs of Stamp Duties of New South Wales* [1953] 2 All ER 1563).

6.224 Tax Bulletin, Issue 9, November 1993 made the following comments in relation to gifts with reservation:

> 'Under FA 1986 s 102, any property given away on or after 18 March 1986 subject to a reservation is, on the death of the donor, treated as forming part of the donor's estate immediately before his death. Gifts with reservations (GWRs) are defined as gifts where either—
>
> — the donee does not assume bona fide possession and enjoyment of the property at the date of the gift or seven years before the donor's death, if later; or
>
> — at any time in the period ending with the donor's death and beginning seven years before that date or, if later, from the date of gift, the property is not enjoyed to the entire exclusion or virtually to the entire exclusion of the donor.
>
> This note provides some guidance on the Revenue's interpretation of the de minimis rule which is expressed as "virtually to the entire exclusion" and comments on the exclusion from the GWR provisions where the donor pays full consideration for any use of the property. The note also clarifies the position of the annual exemption under IHTA 1984 s 19 where a reservation of benefit ceases.

Interpretation of de minimis rule

The word "virtually" in the de minimis rule in IHTA 1984 s 102(1)(b) is not defined and the statute does not give any express guidance about its meaning. However, the *Shorter Oxford English Dictionary* defines it as, amongst other things, "to all intents" and "as good as". Our interpretation of "virtually to the entire exclusion" is that it covers cases in which the benefit to the donor is insignificant in relation to the gifted property.

It is not possible to reduce this test to a single crisp proposition. Each case turns on its own unique circumstances and the questions are likely to be ones of fact and degree. We do not operate s 102(1)(b) in such a way that donors are unreasonably prevented from having limited access to property they have given away and a measure of flexibility is adopted in applying the test. Some examples of situations in which we consider that IHTA 1984 s 102(1)(b) permits limited benefit to the donor without bringing the GWR provisions into play are given below to illustrate how we apply the de minimis test—

- a house which becomes the donee's residence but where the donor subsequently—
  - stays, in the absence of the donee, for not more than two weeks each year, or
  - stays with the donee for less than one month each year;
- social visits, excluding overnight stays made by a donor as guest of the donee, to a house which he had given away. The extent of the social visits should be no greater than the visits which the donor might be expected to make to the donee's house in the absence of any gift by the donor;
- a temporary stay for some short-term purpose in a house the donor had previously given away, for example—
  - while the donor convalesces after medical treatment;
  - while the donor looks after a donee convalescing after medical treatment;
  - while the donor's own home is being redecorated;
  - visits to a house for domestic reasons, for example baby-sitting by the donor for the donee's children;
- a house together with a library of books which the donor visits less than five times in any year to consult or borrow a book;
- a motor car which the donee uses to give occasional (ie less than three times a month) lifts to the donor;
- land which the donor uses to walk his dogs or for horse riding provided this does not restrict the donee's use of land.

It follows of course, that if the benefit to the donor is, or becomes, more significant, the GWR provisos are likely to apply. Examples of this include gifts of—

— a house in which the donor then stays most weekends, or for a month or more each year;

— a second home or holiday home which the donor and the donee both then use on an occasional basis;

— a house with a library in which the donor continues to keep his own books, or which the donor uses on a regular basis, for example because it is necessary for his work;

— a motor car which the donee uses every day to take the donor to work.

Exclusion of benefit where full consideration paid for use of property

The GWR provisions do not apply where an interest in land is given away and the donor pays full consideration for future use of the property (FA 1986 Sch 20 para 6 (1)(a)). While we take the view that such full consideration is required throughout the relevant period – and therefore consider that the rent paid should be reviewed at appropriate intervals to reflect market changes – we do consider that there is no single value at which consideration can be fixed as "full". Rather, we accept that what constitutes full consideration in any case lies within a range of values reflecting normal valuation tolerances, and that any amount within that range can be accepted as satisfying the para 6(1)(a) test.

Termination of reserved benefits and the annual exemption

Where a reservation ceases, the donor is treated by FA 1986 s 102(4) as having made a potentially exempt transfer (PET) at that time. In that event the PET will only be taxable if the donor dies within the next seven years, but the value of the PET cannot be reduced by an available annual exemption under IHTA 1984 s 19. The statement in para 3.4 of the IHT1 booklet, which indicates that the annual exemption may apply if the reservation ceases to exist in the donor's lifetime and a PET is treated as made at that time, is incorrect. This will be corrected in IHT1 when it is next updated.

A typical outright gift to an individual of an amount exceeding the available annual exemption is partly exempt, with the balance above the available annual exemption being a PET. But a PET itself cannot qualify for the annual exemption. The reason is that a PET is a transfer which, but for the provisions of IHTA 1984 s 3A, would be an immediately chargeable transfer. By definition a chargeable transfer is a transfer of value which is not an exempt transfer – IHTA 1984 s 2(1). So a PET cannot be an exempt transfer at the time it is made. The PET will, of course, escape a charge to IHT if the donor survives the statutory period after making it.

The annual exemption is not necessarily lost by the taxpayer. For example, suppose he makes a gift of his home in August 1991 but continues to reside there. In May 1992 he finally leaves the gifted house and the reservation ceases. In October 1992 he makes a gift into a discretionary trust (an immediately chargeable transfer). He is treated as making a PET of his residence in May 1992 – the annual £3,000 exemption does not reduce its value. But the £3,000 exemption is available for setting off against the immediately chargeable transfer in October, and so is any unused exemption carried forward from the previous year.'

Appeals

6.225 Appeals for IHT purposes are to the Special Commissioners IHTA 1984 s 232(2) by way of an appeal within 30 days under section 222(1) of the 1984 Act against the Notice of Determination under IHTA 1984 s 221. An appeal may be made direct to the High Court where the appeal is substantially confined to questions of law and gives leave for the appeal to be taken direct. [Section 222(3)]. The appeals and questions as to the value of land may be taken to the Lands Tribunal. [Section 222(4)(4a) and (4b)].

6.226 Appeals may be brought out of time with the consent of the Board or the Special Commissioners. [IHTA 1984 s 223]. The procedure before the Special Commissioners is governed by section 224 and the General and the Special Commissioners (Amendment of Enactments) Regulations 1994 (SI 1994/1813). Appeals from the Special Commissioners are made to the High Court. [Section 225]. The regulations governing appeals in TMA 1970 ss 6A, 56B and 56C apply under IHTA 1984 s 225A.

6.227 The powers of the Inland Revenue to require information and call for documents, and appeals against such requirements, the inspection of property and the exchange of information with other countries are dealt with by IHTA 1984 ss 219–220A.

Valuations

6.228 The basic market value rule in IHTA 1984 s 160 is that property should be valued at the price which it might reasonably be expected to fetch if sold in the open market at the appropriate time but that price shall not be assumed to be reduced on the grounds that the whole property is to be placed on the market at the same time.

6.229 In valuation it is necessary to take into account, where appropriate, potential special purchasers (*IRC v Clay; IRC v Buchanan* (1914) [1914–15] All ER Rep 882). Optimum lotting, ie breaking the estate into its most saleable units, was approved in *Earl of Ellesmere* [1918] 2 KB 735; *Duke of Buccleuch v IRC* [1967] 1 All ER 129. This includes notionally selling, for example, a freehold reversion and an interest in a farming partnership together but not to the extent of assuming that land which is in fact tenanted has vacant possession *IRC v Gray (Executor of Lady Fox)* [1994] STC 360).

6.230 Jointly held property would usually be valued on the basis of half vacant possession value less a discount of 15 per cent (*Whight v IRC Lands Tribunal* (1982) 264 EG 935). Hope value is included (*Gajapatiraju v Revenue Divisional Officer Vizagapatam* [1939] 2 All ER 317). Smaller minority interests of land would attract a larger discount (*Charkham v IRC Lands Tribunal* 14 November 1996, *Tolley's Tax Cases 2001* 72.58).

6.231 The theory behind the valuation is to consider the amount which a hypothetical purchaser would pay to stand in the shoes of the transferor and includes all advantages and disadvantages of ownership of those rights (*Alexander v IRC* [1991] STC 112; *IRC v Crossman* [1936] 1 All ER 762). This would include, for example, rights in a building society that was about to demutualise (*Ward Cook and Buckingham (Cook's Executors) v IRC* [1999] STC (SCD) 1).

6.232 There are special valuation rules for related property in IHTA 1984 s 161 where for valuation purposes a person's estate is deemed to include property comprised in the estate of his spouse, or which has, within the preceding five years, been transferred to a charity, political party, housing association or national institution. [Section 161(2)]. The amount comprised in the estate is the appropriate proportion of the aggregate value. This is important in the context of IHTA 1984 s 3(1) which provides that the value transferred by a transfer of value is the amount by which the value of the transferor's estate has fallen as a result of the transfer, which may be more or less than the value of the property transferred in isolation. This is particularly important in the case of assets such as shares where a transfer of say, a 10 per cent interest may reduce the shareholding in the estate from 55 per cent valued as a controlling interest to 45 per cent valued as a minority interest.

6.233 Related property originally included property transferred into a discretionary trust but this is no longer so. Liabilities are taken into account for valuation purposes, as are restrictions on freedom to dispose acquired for consideration and actual but not hypothetical expenses of transfer. [IHTA 1984 ss 162–164]. Where the transfer is also a disposal for CGT purposes the amount of the tax can be deducted from the value of the chargeable transfer under section 165; debtors are valued as if they were good unless it can be shown otherwise, and there are special rules for the valuation of life policies. [Sections 166 and 167]. Unquoted shares and securities are valued as for CGT on the assumption that there is available to a prospective purchaser all the information which a prudent prospective purchaser might reasonably require if he were proposing to purchase them from a willing vendor by a private treaty and at arm's length. [Section 168].

6.234 In the case of trusts, the termination of an interest in possession which is treated as a transfer of the interest under IHTA 1984 ss 51–53 makes it necessary to value any shares held by the trust on the termination of such an interest. The CTO used to take the view that any shares held by the settlement would be aggregated with shares held in the free estate of the beneficiary and with any related property in determining the value for IHT purposes. For example, A holds 40 per cent of the shares in a private company, his wife 20 per cent and A also has an interest in possession in a settlement holding 15 per cent of the share capital. If someone other than A or his wife becomes absolutely entitled to the shares on the termination of the interest the valuation would, on this interpretation, be on the basis of 15/75ths of a controlling interest. However, sections 51–55 specifically state that the termination of an interest in possessions is not a transfer of value, therefore the quantum of the deemed transfer would be the settlement's own 15 per cent shareholding without aggregation with the shares held by A and his wife, a view which the Revenue now accepts.

6.235 The Revenue has confirmed to the Institute of Chartered Accountants in England and Wales, as reported in the May 1990 edition of *Accountancy* magazine, that it takes the view that when the interest in possession comes to an end during the lifetime of a person entitled to it, the settled property in which the interest subsisted will be valued in isolation without reference to any other property, i e in these circumstances it is not treated as a disposal of part of the settlor's estate.

6.236 Where a person entitled to an interest in possession in settled property is entitled to part only of the income of the property and under IHTA 1984 s 50(1)–(3), his interest is taken to subsist in a proportion of part of that property, his estate for IHT purposes is limited to that part of the property in which his interest subsists. [IHTA 1984 ss 5(1) and 49(1)]. If the trust therefore held, say, 60 per cent of the shares and A had an interest in possession in 25 per cent of the trust fund, on termination of that interest in possession it would be necessary to value a 15 per cent interest, being 25 per cent of the trust holding of 60 per cent not a 60 per cent interest of which 25 per cent would be allocated to A's interest. This would have a material effect on the valuation, as a 15 per cent interest is a small minority shareholding whereas a 60 per cent shareholding is a controlling interest.

6.237 In the case of a settlement with no interest in possession within IHTA 1984 ss 58–76, any IHT charge on a distribution of shares to a beneficiary would be on the basis of the reduction in value of the trust fund as a result of the transfer under section 65(2)(a), i e the same valuation basis as if the shares had been held by an individual chargeable on the reduction in value of his estate under IHTA 1984 s 3(1). For a more detailed treatment on the valuation of unquoted shares and securities see Eastaway, Booth and Eamer, *Practical Share Valuation* (Butterworths, 1998).

6.238 Other valuation rules apply to farm cottages which are to be valued without taking account of the fact that the cottages are suitable for residential use by non-farm workers. [IHTA 1984 s 69]. A lease for life treated as a settlement under IHTA 1984 s 43(3) is valued on the proportionate part of the value of the property which the value of the gift element bore to the market value of the lease on grant. [IHTA 1984 s 170].

Chapter 7

Discretionary Trusts

Definition

7.1 A discretionary trust is a trust under which the trustees are given a discretion to pay or apply income for beneficiaries but no beneficiary is able to claim a right to any part of that income unless the trustees think fit to pay it to him or apply it for his benefit. *Gartside v IRC* [1968] 1 All ER 121 held that beneficiaries of a discretionary trust were not entitled either individually or collectively to receive any part of the trust income unless the trustees so decided, and that they did not have an interest in possession. This was confirmed even when there was only a single beneficiary of a discretionary trust (*Moore and Osborne v IRC* [1984] STC 236; see also *Turner v Turner* [1984] Ch 100; *Tankel v Tankel* [1999] 1 FLR 676). It is perfectly possible to have a mixed trust where some of the beneficiaries have a discretionary interest and some have an interest in possession or a contingent interest.

7.2 The trustees may decide to distribute some or all of the income of the discretionary trust to one or more of the beneficiaries and may decide to accumulate income not so distributed. This should normally be decided before the end of the fiscal year, so that timely distributions may be made, but it is possible to defer the decision for a reasonable time, which could in exceptional cases be several years (*Re Gulbenkian's Settlement Trusts (No 2) Stephens v Maun* [1970] Ch 408). Accumulated income may, at the trustees' discretion or as provided under the trust instrument, remain as accumulations of income and be distributed as income at a later date (*Re Berkeley* [1968] 3 All ER 364) or could involve the addition of income to capital, thus increasing the estate in favour of those entitled to capital and against the interests of those entitled to income. Distributions of capital could still be income in the beneficiaries' hands (*Brodie's Trustees v IRC* (1933) 17 TC 432), see **7.14**.

7.3 Although trustees may, in providing for the maintenance of a beneficiary, make advancements of capital (*Re Howarth* (1873) 8 Ch App 415; *Walker v Wetherell* (1801) 6 Ves 473), they would normally only do so under the statutory rights in TA 1925 s 32 or under specific powers in the trust instrument. The power of advancement enables the trustees to pay or apply the trust capital for the advancement or benefit of beneficiaries entitled to a share in the capital of the trust property, whether absolutely or contingently (*Re Garrett, Croft v Ruck* [1934] Ch 477). Unless the trust instrument otherwise so provides it must not exceed one half of the presumptive or vested share of the beneficiary. [TA 1925 s 32]. The power of advancement cannot be used to prejudice any person entitled to a prior life or other interest, whether vested or contingent, and if the advancee becomes absolutely entitled to a share of the trust property, the amount paid or applied under the advancement must be brought into account as part of that share. [TA 1925 s 32(1) proviso].

7.4 Powers of advancement may be used to make distributions of capital to a beneficiary. A power of appointment may be given to the trustees, or a protector, or may be retained by the settlor or otherwise, as specified in the trust deed, to determine who will actually benefit from distributions of income or capital. It is thus a dispositive as opposed to an administrative power. A general power, which would be unusual in a trust, would enable the holder of the power to appoint the assets to anyone, including himself, and is therefore a valuable asset (*Melville v IRC* [2001] STC 1271). Normally the holder of the power will be excluded from benefit as will other members of an excepted class, usually the settlor or his spouse and the trustees (*Re Hay's Settlement Trusts* [1981] 3 All ER 786; *Re Beattie's Will Trusts* [1990] 3 All ER 844). Such a power is a special power of appointment (*Re Penrose* [1933] Ch 793). It is not uncommon in a discretionary trust to give the trustees, often with the consent of the settlor or protector, a power to appoint additional beneficiaries other than those named or defined by the trust instrument.

Income tax

7.5 Discretionary trusts and accumulation and maintenance trusts are taxable at a special rate applicable to trusts instead of the basic rate under ICTA 1988 s 1, the lower or savings rate under section 1A, or the Schedule F ordinary rate under section 1B. [ICTA 1988 s 686]. The rate applicable to trusts is 34 per cent for 2003/04 and the Schedule F trust rate applicable to dividends and other distributions under ICTA 1988 s 20 is 25 per cent. [Section 686(1A)]. These rates apply to income which is accumulated or payable at the discretion of the trustees or any other person, whether or not the trustees have power to accumulate, and is not treated as the income of any person other than the trustees, e g as income of the beneficiary entitled to an interest in possession (see Chapter 8), or is deemed to be the income of the settlor under ICTA 1988 s 660A. [Section 686(2)(a) and (b)]. The rate applicable to trusts does not apply to income arising to a charitable trust, a fund providing relevant benefits within ICTA 1988 s 612 or personal pension schemes providing benefits within ICTA 1988 s 633. [Section 686(2)(c)]. Trust expenses are paid out of trust income subject to tax at the basic rate or ordinary Schedule F rate. Income so utilised is not subject to the rate applicable to trusts or the Schedule F trust rate. [ICTA 1988 s 2AA]. Trustees' management expenses, which would normally be properly chargeable to income, except that the trustees are non-UK resident and therefore have income not subject to UK tax, are reduced proportionately to the proportion of those expenses which equates with the proportion that the UK taxable income bears to the total trust income. [Section 1988 s 686(2A)]. For this purpose, excluded income within FA 1995 s 128 is included, other than that on which income tax has been deducted at source. [Section 686(2B)].

7.6 Schedule F type income, to which the Schedule F trust rate applies, includes both income chargeable under Schedule F and income chargeable under Schedule D Case V, other than distributions to non-residents or non-qualifying distributions chargeable under ICTA 1988 s 233(1A) and (1B), stock dividends under section 249(6)(b), deemed income arising on the release of a loan from a close company under section 421(1)(a) and other distributions within section 686(5A). These include qualifying distributions made to trustees other than trustees of a unit trust scheme, including deemed distributions on the acquisition by a company of its own shares. [ICTA 1988 s 686A]. Trustees do not include personal representatives, but payments by personal representatives to trustees are deemed to have borne tax at the rate applicable to trusts or to the Schedule F trust rate as appropriate. Section 686(6)]. The exemption for pension fund investments in section 686(2)(c) does not extend to income derived from investments, deposits or other property held as a member of a property investment limited liability partnership. [Section 686 (6A)].

Payments to beneficiaries

7.7 Where the trustees pay tax on the income less expenses (at the rate applicable to trusts, or the Schedule F trust rate, as appropriate) on the income for each fiscal year, they may also have a liability on distributions under ICTA 1988 s 687. This applies where a payment is made to a beneficiary under a discretion exercisable by the trustees or any other person, which is the income of the beneficiary and not treated as the income of the settlor or a payment to a minor child of the settlor under ICTA 1988 s 660B. [Section 687(1)]. The payment is treated as a net amount corresponding to a gross amount from which tax has been deducted at the rate applicable to trusts, ie currently 34 per cent, and therefore the gross equivalent is treated as the income of the person to whom the payment is made or the settlor of a settlor interested trust. The beneficiary therefore receives income carrying with it a tax credit of 34 per cent irrespective of the actual source of the distribution, and the beneficiary can therefore reclaim tax overpaid, if any, or is liable for any higher rate tax should he be so liable depending on his personal circumstances. [Section 687(2)(a).] The trustees have to account to the Revenue for any shortfall between the tax that has been paid by them already under ICTA 1988 s 686 and the grossed-up equivalent of net distributions paid to beneficiaries. [Section 687(2)(b)]. This requirement arises from the fact that in the Revenue view the source of the beneficiary's income is the trust itself not, as in the case of a beneficiary with an interest in possession, the underlying investments, and as the beneficiary is given a credit of the 34 per cent it is necessary to ensure that the Revenue has collected the same amount of tax from the trustees. Where the trust income includes dividends which have been subject to tax only at the Schedule F tax rate of 25 per cent there will be a shortfall which can perhaps best be illustrated by an example, which contrasts the position prior to 6 April 1999.

Example

The pre-6 April 1999 rules for a dividend received via a discretionary trust are as follows:

	£
Dividend received by trustees	80.00
Tax credit	20.00
	100.00
Tax thereon at 34% (of which £20 met by tax credit)	(34.00)
	66.00
Distributed to beneficiary	66.00
Grossed up under ICTA 1988, s 687(2) at 34%	34.00
Gross income of beneficiary	100.00
Tax thereon at 40% (of which £34 met by trustees' deemed deduction)	40.00
Net income of beneficiary	60.00

The post-5 April 1999 rules for a dividend received via a discretionary trust are as follows:

	£	£
Dividend received by trustees		80.00
Tax credit (one-ninth)		8.89
		88.89
Tax thereon at 25% Schedule F trust rate:		
Met by tax credit	8.89	
Paid by trustees	13.33	(22.22)
Net income of trust		66.67
Liability of 34% under ICTA 1988 s 687 on gross payment of £80.00	27.20	
(£80 figure determined by formula – maximum possible distribution)		
Met by trustees' payment above	(13.33)	
Remaining liability of trustees, ICTA 1988 s 687(2)(b)		(13.87)
Available for distribution to beneficiary		52.80
Grossed-up under ICTA 1988 s 687(2)(a) at 34%		27.20
Gross income of beneficiary		80.00
Tax thereon at 40% (of which £27.20 met by trustees)		(32.00)
Net income of beneficiary		48.00

The trouble is that because the tax credit under the post-5 April 1999 rules is a non-payable credit it is not treated as paid by the trustees and therefore not taken into the tax pool under ICTA 1988 s 687.

7.8 From the amount of tax due on the grossed-up distributions of 34 per cent under ICTA 1988 s 687(2)(b), may be deducted the cumulative tax payable under ICTA 1988 s 686 at the rate applicable to trusts or the Schedule F trust rate, to the extent that the Schedule F trust rate exceeds the credit at the Schedule F ordinary rate on the distribution. [ICTA 1988 s 687(3)(a)–(c)]. There may also be a credit left over from 1972/73 in some cases which may be deducted under section 687(3)(d); a credit can also be claimed for income tax arising on offshore income gains of trustees taxable at the rate applicable to trusts under ICTA 1988 s 764 by virtue of section 761(1). A similar credit may be claimed for tax payable at the rate applicable to trusts under the accrued income scheme [Section 687(3)(f)] and a credit for development gains tax paid as allowed under section 687(3)(g). Tax payable on deep discount securities, deep gain securities, convertible securities and discounted securities is creditable under section 687(3)(h)–(k).

7.9 Distributions include distributions in kind. [ICTA 1988 s 687(5)]. These tax pool provisions do not apply to personal representatives. [Section 687(4)]. Where a distribution is made from a discretionary trust to a company which is not a charity, a heritage body or a scientific research association, the tax credit cannot be set off against corporation tax payable under ICTA 1988 ss 7–11 or income tax payable on annual payments under ICTA 1988 Sch 16 para 5(1). However, the distribution is left out of account in calculating the profits of the company for the purposes of corporation tax and no repayment may be claimed by the company. [Section 687A(1)–(3)]. If the company is not resident in the UK these provisions only apply so far as the companies are chargeable to corporation tax. [Section 687A(4)].

7.10 Where trustees receive interest from employees or directors under a scheme enabling them to acquire shares under CA 1985 s 153(4)(b), such interest is exempt from tax under Schedule D Case III. [ICTA 1988 s 688].

7.11 Where trustees make a distribution out of overseas income which has borne tax overseas, which is treated as a net amount grossed-up under ICTA 1988 s 687(2), the trustees may certify that the income out of which the payment was made was, or included, taxed overseas income of an amount and from a source stated in the certificate, which arose not earlier than six years from the end of the year of assessment in which the payment was made. [ICTA 1988 s 809]. In such cases the beneficiary may claim repayment of the amount so certified as if he had received the income from the source specified in the year in which the distribution was made to him.

Trust as source

7.12 The Revenue contention that a discretionary trust is itself the source of the income to the beneficiary is not based on any statute. It was stated in *Memec v IRC* [1996] STC 1336, *obiter*, by Robert Walker J:

> 'under an English trust with an interest in possession the life tenant has an equitable interest in the trust property and the trust income as it comes into the trustees' hands even though the trustees have a lien on capital and accruing income for their expenses. Such a trust is transparent for income tax purposes. A discretionary trust on the other hand is not transparent. No beneficiary is entitled unless and until the trustees exercise their discretion in his or her favour and the trustees' exercise of discretion is regarded as having (in Lord Asquith's words in *Stainer's Executors v Purchase* (1952) 32 TC 367) "independent vitality" and creating a new source of income, although the effect of this may be tempered by specific enactment (see ICTA 1988 s 809) or extra-statutory concession (see extra-statutory concession B18 payments out of discretionary trusts). Similarly the rights of an annuitant under a trust are regarded as a source of income distinct from the underlying trust investments. *Garland v Archer-Shee* (1931) 15 TC 693 shows that a foreign trust is not transparent if the life tenant has no equitable interest and no right to the payment to him or her (as opposed to the application for his or her benefit) of even the balance of net income.'

In the subsequent Court of Appeal hearing of [1998] STC 754 at 764 Peter Gibson LJ stated:

> '… the Judge made a comment [Robert Walker J at [1996] STC 1336] on the distinction between a life tenant under an English trust and a beneficiary under an English discretionary trust, there being transparency in the case of the former but, the Judge said, not in the case of the latter. I merely note that this distinction is supported by the Crown but disputed by Mr Venables (by reference to *Drummond v Collins* (1915) 6 TC 525) but it is not necessary for the purposes of this appeal to resolve the dispute.'

7.13 In *Drummond v Collins* (1915) 6 TC 525 Lord Parker of Waddington stated:

> 'the monies transmitted in this case from America were certainly profits and gains arising from property. The property from which they arose was equally clearly a foreign possession within the meaning of Schedule D Case V as interpreted by the decisions of this House'.

Lord Wrenbury stated:

> '… the first matter is to investigate upon the provisions of the will what the remittances in question are. In the events which have happened the Trustees are, by the will, directed to hold the trust estate and to apply the net income for the use and benefit of the children. So far I find a direct and unfettered gift of the income in favour of the children. There follows a direction that out of the net income of the proportionate share held in trust for any child the Trustees make such provision from time to time as they in their uncontrolled discretion think necessary or advisable for the maintenance and education of the child until he is entitled under provisions after contained to receive the income directly from the Trustees … the gifts are each one of them in favour of the children but the dates for payment to the children are fixed with reference to the exercise by the Trustees of their

discretion or the ages from time to time of the children. At the time with which your Lordships have to do there could be no payment except by exercise of the discretion vested in the Trustees; but so soon as their discretion is exercised in favour of the child the resulting payment seems to me upon the language of the will to be a payment of income to which the child is entitled by virtue of the gift made by the testator. I cannot see any grounds upon which such income is not subject to income tax.'

7.14 The Revenue appeared to rely for its authority of the trust itself being the source of the income on *Cunard's Trustees v IRC; McPheeters v IRC* (1945) 27 TC 122 TSEM 3755. However, this case actually related to a will trust under which the trustees had a discretion to supplement income by payments of capital. It is not immediately apparent why a case which taxed the payments of capital at the discretion of the trustees as income in the hands of the recipient, on the authority of cases such as *Brodie's Trustees v IRC* (1933) 17 TC 432 and *Lindus and Hortin v IRC* (1933) 17 TC 442, should be said to be authority for the proposition that the source of the beneficiary's income in a discretionary trust is the trust itself rather than the underlying investments. It is indeed difficult to envisage quite how a relationship such as a trust can be a source of the income. As far as the individual is concerned it is that relationship under which they are entitled to the income, which is rather a different matter. It seems to follow that if the Revenue view is correct, the income of the beneficiaries, in the case of a UK resident trust, is assessable under Schedule D Case III and if the trustees are resident outside the UK the trust presumably becomes a foreign possession, the income for which is taxed under Schedule D Case V. If the trustees are non-resident ICTA 1988 s 686 would not apply and therefore there would be no credit for any UK tax paid under ICTA 1988 s 687(3). This means that the beneficiaries would again be taxed on the income net of UK tax already paid by the trustees, with the tax already paid being treated as an expense rather than as a credit. The worst aspects of this situation are dealt with under ESC B18 which provides as follows:

'UK resident trusts

A beneficiary may receive from trustees payment to which ICTA 1988 s 687(2) applies. Where that payment is made out of the income of the trustees in respect of which, had it been received directly, the beneficiary would—

— have been entitled to exemption in respect of FOTRA securities issued in accordance with FA 1996 s 154; or

— have been entitled to relief under the terms of a double taxation agreement; or

— not have been chargeable to UK tax because of their not resident and/or not ordinarily resident status

the beneficiary may claim that exemption or relief or, where the beneficiary would not have been chargeable, repayment of the tax treated as deducted from the payment (or an appropriate proportion of it). For this purpose, the payment will be treated as having been made rateably out of all sources of income arising to the trustees on a last in first out basis.

Relief or exemption, as appropriate, will be granted to the extent that the payment is out of income which arose to the trustees not earlier than six years before the end of the year of assessment in which the payment was made, provided the trustees—

— have made trust returns giving details of all sources of trust income and payments made to beneficiaries for each and every year for which they are required; and

— have paid all tax due, and any interest, surcharges and penalties arising; and

— keep available for inspection any relevant tax certificates.

Relief or exemption, as appropriate, will be granted to the beneficiary on a claim made within five years and ten months of the end of the year of assessment in which the beneficiary received the payment from the trustees.

Non-resident trusts

A similar concession will operate where a beneficiary receives a payment from discretionary trustees which is not within ICTA 1988 s 687(2) (i.e. where non-resident trustees exercise their discretion outside the UK).

Where a non-resident beneficiary receives such a payment out of income of the trustees in respect of which, had it been received directly, it would have been chargeable to UK tax, then the beneficiary—

— may claim relief under ICTA 1988 s 278 (personal reliefs for certain non-residents); and

— may be treated as receiving that payment from a UK resident trust but claim credit only for UK tax actually paid by the trustees on income out of which the payment is made.

The beneficiary may also claim exemption from tax in respect of FOTRA securities issued in accordance with FA 1996 s 154 to the extent that the payment is regarded as including interest from such securities.

A UK beneficiary of a non-resident trust may claim appropriate credit for tax actually paid by the trustees on the income out of which the payment is made as if the payments out of UK income were from a UK resident trust and within [IC]TA 1988 s 687(1).

This treatment will only be available where the trustees—

— have made trust returns giving details of all sources of trust income and payments made to beneficiaries for each and every year for which they are required; and

— have paid all tax due and any interest, surcharges and penalties arising; and

— keep available for inspection any relevant tax certificates.

Relief or exemption, as appropriate, will be granted to the beneficiary on a claim made within five years and ten months of the end of the year of assessment in which the beneficiary received the payment from the trustees.

No credit will be given for UK tax treated as paid on income received by the trustees which would not be available for set off under s 687(2) if that section applied, and that tax is not repayable (for example on dividends). However, such tax is not taken into account in calculating the gross income treated as taxable on the beneficiary under this concession.'

7.15 If the Revenue view is wrong the effect is merely that the underlying income of the trust, so far as it is distributed to beneficiaries in the exercise of the trustees' discretion, would be treated as the income of the beneficiaries in the same way as it is in an interest in possession trust, following *Archer-Shee v Baker* (1927) 11 TC 749. It is to be hoped that the current review of the taxation of trusts will put the matter on a proper statutory footing.

Capital gains tax

Gifts on which inheritance tax is chargeable

7.16 As a gift into a discretionary trust is not a potentially exempt transfer under IHTA 1984 s 3A it is a chargeable transfer within TCGA 1992 s 260(2) and holdover relief may be available as described at **6.116** et seq. The provisions relating to a person becoming absolutely entitled to settled property under TCGA 1992 s 71 apply to a discretionary trust. These provisions and others relating to trusts generally, which include discretionary trusts, are covered in Chapter 6. There are no CGT provisions which relate specifically to discretionary trusts.

Inheritance tax

7.17 The IHT provisions relating to discretionary trusts are set out in IHTA 1984, Part III, Ch III ss 58–85. For the purposes of these provisions 'relevant property' means settled property in which no qualifying interest in possession subsists. [IHTA 1984 s 58(1)]. There are, however, a number of exceptions. These are:

(a) property held for charitable purposes only;

(b) property held in accumulation and maintenance trusts, pre-1978 protective trusts, pre-1981 trusts for disabled persons and trusts for the benefit of employees under IHTA 1984 ss 71,73,74 or 86;

(c) property held on maintenance funds for historic buildings within IHTA 1984 Sch 4;

(d) pension schemes within IHTA 1984 s 151;

(e) property comprised in a trade or professional compensation fund; and

(f) excluded property, ie property comprised in a settlement which is situated outside the UK where the settlor was domiciled outside the UK at the time the settlement was made. [IHTA 1984 s 48(3); IHTA 1984 s 58].

7.18 A qualifying interest in possession is defined, unhelpfully, by IHTA 1984 s 59(1) as an interest in possession to which an individual, or a company which acquired it in the course of its business for full consideration in money or money's worth from an individual who was beneficially entitled to it, is entitled. [Section 59(2)]. The normal definition of an interest in possession is taken from *Pearson and Others v IRC* [1980] STC 318 as 'a present right to the present enjoyment' of something. Therefore a power of accumulation given to the trustees, whether exercised or not, would be sufficient to make the trust a discretionary not an interest in possession trust. Other cases in which an interest in possession has been considered include *Moore and Osbourne v IRC; Re Trafford's Settlement Trusts* [1984] STC 236; *Miller v IRC* [1987] STC 108; *Gartside v IRC* [1968] AC 553; *A-G v Power* [1906] 2 IR 272; *Swales v IRC* [1984] STC 413; *Re Delamaere's Settlement Trusts; Kenney v Cunningham-Reid* [1984] 1 All ER 584; *IRC v Lloyds's Private Banking Ltd* [1998] STC 559; and *Woodhall (Woodhall's Personal Representative) v IRC* [2000] STC (SCD) 558. An attempt to use the definition of interest in possession in the 'General Franco' avoidance scheme failed in *IRC v Trustees of Sir John Aird's Settlement* [1983] STC 700.

7.19 A reversionary interest in settled property is excluded property unless it has been acquired for a consideration in money or money's worth or is one to which either the settlor or his spouse, is, or has been, beneficially entitled or is an interest expectant on the determination of a lease treated as a settlement under IHTA 1984 s 43(3). [IHTA 1984 s 84(1) and (2)]. A reversionary interest in property situated outside the UK comprised in a settlement, with a non-domiciled settlor, is only excluded property under IHTA 1984 s 48(3)(b) if held by an individual domiciled outside the UK. [IHTA 1984 s 6(1)]. Gilt edged securities within IHTA 1984 s 6(2) are only excluded property if held in trust if a non-UK resident has an interest in possession or all known persons who might become beneficiaries are non-UK resident. [IHTA 1984 s 48(4)].

Ten-year charge

7.20 A discretionary trust commences when property first becomes comprised in it. [IHTA 1984 s 60]. This date is necessary in order to compute the ten-year anniversary, which is the tenth anniversary of the date on which the settlement commenced and subsequent anniversaries at ten-yearly intervals.

[Section 61(1)]. Where, however, the trust is initially one with an interest in possession to the settlor or his spouse, and therefore remains in the estate of the settlor or spouse under IHTA 1984 s 49(1) and it subsequently becomes held on discretionary trusts, it is deemed to result in the commencement of a separate settlement made when the settlor beneficially entitled ceased to have that interest [IHTA 1984 s 80] and the settlement is deemed to commence at that time for the purpose of the ten-year charge. [Section 61(2)]. No date falling before 1 April 1983 was a ten-year anniversary. [Section 61(3)].

7.21 Settlements are related where made by the same settlor if they commenced on the same day, unless held for charitable purposes only. [IHTA 1984 s 62]. For these provisions a payment includes a transfer of assets other than money and a quarter means a period of three months. [Section 63]. Relevant property, as defined by IHTA 1984 s 58(1), comprised in a settlement immediately before a ten-year anniversary is subject to a charge to IHT under IHTA 1984 s 64 on the value of the relevant property, calculated in accordance with IHTA 1984 ss 66 and 67. Trusts settled on nearly consecutive days were held to be separate trusts and not associated operations within IHTA 1984 s 268 (*Rysaffe Trustee Co (CI) Ltd v IRC* [2003] EWCA Civ 356, [2003] STC 536).

7.22 The rate of the ten-yearly charge is 30 per cent of the effective rate which would be charged on the value transferred by a chargeable transfer, as specified in IHTA 1984 s 66(1). Where property has been added to the trust in the ten-year period, its value is reduced by a fortieth for each quarter which expired before it became relevant property comprised in the settlement. [Section 66(2)]. The notional chargeable transfer is made immediately before the ten-year anniversary by a notional transferor deemed to have made a transfer in the preceding seven years to the trust, which is chargeable at the lifetime rate, ie half of the death rate of IHT under IHTA 1984 s 7(2). The maximum rate of IHT with a 40 per cent death rate is therefore 30 per cent of 20 per cent, ie 6 per cent. [Section 66(3)]. This tax is charged on the value at the ten-year anniversary of relevant property under section 66(4)(a), taking into account the value of any excluded property in the settlement, which although not chargeable to the ten-year anniversary charge is nonetheless included in fixing the rate under section 66(4)(b), and the value of property in any related settlement at commencement. [Section 66(4)(c)]. As a result of section 66(4)(b) it is desirable to avoid mixing excluded property and UK property in the same settlement.

7.23 In fixing the rate of the ten-year charge there have to be included any chargeable transfers made by the settlor in the period of seven years ending with the day on which the settlement commenced [IHTA 1984 s 66(5)(a)] and the amount on which any exit charge under section 65 was calculated in the ten years prior to the anniversary. [Section 66(5)(b)]. In the case of a pre-27 March 1974 settlement, any excluded property, or property in related settlements and settlor's transfers are ignored in calculating the rate of the ten-year charge. [Section 66(6)].

Example

On 1 December 1992, Mr Smithwick who had made chargeable transfers of £180,000, in the previous seven years, created a discretionary trust. On that date he settled £300,000. At 30 November 2002 the discretionary trust held investments with a market value of £1,000,000.

30 November 2002
Ten yearly charge

	Gross	*Tax*
	£	£
Chargeable transfers made by settlor in 7 years prior to settlement	180,000	—
Value of relevant property at 30 November 2002	1,000,000	186,000
	1,180,000*	

(**1,180,000–250,000 = 930,000@20% = 186,000*)

Actual rate is 30% of effective rate

$$\frac{186{,}000}{1{,}000{,}000} \times 100 \times 30\% = 5.58\%$$

Tax payable by trustees:
On relevant property
£1,000,000 x 5.58% = £55,800

Added property

7.24 Where after 8 March 1982 the settlor adds further property to the settlement as a result of which the value of the property comprised in the settlement is increased, and this takes place before the next ten-yearly charge, the amount of the charge is abated. [IHTA 1984 s 67(1)]. However, where the transfer was not primarily intended to increase the value and did not result in the value immediately after the transfer increasing by more than 5 per cent, it is ignored. [Section 67(2)]. In the first instance it is necessary to include in the aggregate values for the computation of the rate of ten-yearly charge the greater of the aggregate value of transfers made by the settlor in the seven years ending with the day on which the settlement commenced, disregarding transfers made before 27 March 1974, and tranfers made on the day of commencement of the settlement. [Section 66(5)(a)]. If greater, the transfers made in the seven years prior to the addition to the settlement, excluding the transfers on that day, are included. [Section 67(3)(a)].

7.25 Where the settlement originally commenced before 27 March 1974, transfers made on or before that date are ignored, as are the values attributable to property already taken into account, e g as related property under IHTA 1984 s 66(4), and the amounts included in the settlement on the previous ten-year anniversary. Where the settlor has made more than one addition to the property, that which results in the greatest aggregate amount is to be included in fixing the rate used. [IHTA 1984 s 67(4) and (5)]. There is a deduction for any property taken out of the settlement in respect of which there was an exit charge under section 65 which is equal to the lesser of the amount on which the exit charge was computed or the value at which the relevant property was included prior to leaving the settlement. [Section 67(6)]. If any part of the settlement consisted of relevant property there is a proportionate adjustment. [Section 67(7)].

Example

The facts as for example above at **7.23** (the initial settled fund was £300,000) on 1 December 2000 Mr Smithwick added further funds of £100,000 to the trust which had appreciated to £150,000 at 30 November 2002. No transfers were made in the seven years immediately preceding 1 December 2000.

30 November 2002
Ten yearly charge

	Gross	*Tax*
	£	£
Chargeable transfers made by settlor in prior 7 years*	180,000	—
Value of relevant property at 30 November 2002	1,000,000	186,000
	1,180,000**	

**The original chargeable transfers are included as their value exceeds the value of the transfers made in the seven years prior to the addition to the settlement (£Nil).*

**(*1,180,000–250,000=930,000@20%=186,000*).

Actual rate is 30% of effective rate

$$\frac{186{,}000}{1{,}000{,}000} \times 100 \times 30\% = 5.58\%$$

Tax payable by trustees:	
On relevant property held for 10 years	
£1,000,000–£150,000=£850,000 x 5.58%=	£47,430
On relevant property added on 1 December 2000	
£150,000 x 8/40@5.58%	1,674
	£49,104

Exit charge

7.26 Where property in a settlement ceases to be relevant property, usually on a distribution to a beneficiary or where as a result of a disposition by the trustees the value of the relevant property reduces, there is a potential charge to IHT. [IHTA 1984 s 65(1)]. IHT is charged on the reduction of value in the relevant property in the settlement as a result of the transfer. [Section 65(2)(a)]. Where the IHT is payable out of the remaining relevant property in the settlement the amount on which IHT is charged has to be grossed up by the tax payable. [Section 65(2)(b)]. There is no exit charge if the disposition takes place within the first three months after the commencement of the settlement or a ten-year anniversary. [Section 65(4)]. There is no exit charge in respect of costs or expenses attributable to relevant property or where a transfer is subject to income tax, or would be if the recipient were resident in the UK. [Section 65(5)]. The reduction in value of the relevant property in the settlement under section 65(1)(b) does not apply to transfers at arm's length not intended to confer gratuitous benefit, which in the case of an individual would fall within IHTA 1984 s 10, or the grant of a tenancy of agricultural property in the UK, the Channel Islands or the Isle of Man if for full consideration of money or money's worth, under IHTA 1984 ss 16 and 65(6). There is no charge where property comprised in the settlement ceases to be situated in the UK and therefore becomes excluded property under IHTA 1984 s 48(3)(a). [Section 66(7)]. Where the settlor was not domiciled in the UK when the settlement was made, there is no charge on property ceasing to be relevant property because it is reinvested in exempt gilts treated as excluded property under IHTA 1984 s 48(4)(b). [Section 65(8)]. The deliberate omission to exercise a right by the trustees would be treated as a disposition made at the latest time when they could have exercised that right. [Section 65(9)]. The rate of tax on an exit charge is calculated in accordance with IHTA 1984 ss 68 or 69. [Section 65(3)].

7.27 The augmentation of a beneficiary's income by payments out of capital would not be regarded as liable to an exit charge under IHTA 1984 s 65, even if not taxable as income in the hands of the recipient as not being made on a regular basis within *Brodie's Trustees v IRC* (1933) 17 TC 432, ESC E6. The grant of a lease to a beneficiary for a term or a periodic tenancy for less than full consideration does not create an interest in possession but would normally give rise to a charge to tax under IHTA 1984 s 65(1)(b) (SP10/79). Undistributed and unaccumulated income is not subject to the ten-year charge because it is not treated as a taxable trust asset but it becomes a taxable asset when formally accumulated, see **7.2** (SP 8/86). The reduction in value of the relevant property in the settlement is illustrated in *MacPherson v IRC* [1988] STC 362 where paintings were leased on commercial terms for 14 years and then transferred to a beneficiary subject to the lease.

Rate of exit charge before first ten-year anniversary

7.28 The rate of tax charged on property ceasing to be relevant property before the first ten-year anniversary, for the purposes of IHTA 1984 s 65, is the appropriate fraction of the effective rate of IHT, at half of the death rate under IHTA 1984 s 7(2). [IHTA 1984 s 68(1)]. The appropriate fraction is 30 per cent multiplied by the number of quarters between the commencement of the settlement and the day before the occasion of the charge, divided by 40, which is the number of quarters in the ten-year period. [Section 68(2)]. If the property was not relevant property or not in the settlement for the entire period since commencement, any quarter of which expired before the property became relevant property is ignored but the quarter in which the property became relevant property is counted. The quarter in which the charge arises is not counted as it would not be a complete quarter. [Section 68(3)].

7.29 The amount of the notional transfer on which the tax is charged is the value of the property comprised in the settlement immediately after its creation, together with the value on creation of the property in any related settlement made by the same settlor on the same day [IHTA 1984 s 62], and of any property added to the settlement before the disposition giving rise to the exit charge. [IHTA 1984 s 68(5)]. This is added to the value of the settlor's transfers made in the seven years ending on the date on which the settlement commenced, disregarding transfers made on that day. [Section 68(4)].

Example

Facts are as for the example at **7.23** above, except on 1 December 1999 the trustees appointed £200,000 to a beneficiary.

1 December 1999
Exit charge on Distribution to Beneficiary
Amount chargeable=£200,000
Calculation of rate

	Gross	*Tax*
Chargeable transfers made by settlor	£	£
in prior 7 years	180,000	—
Initial value of settlement	300,000	49,800*
	480,000	

480,000–231,000=£249,000 x 20%=49,800*

***Nil Threshold 1999/2000.*

Actual rate is 30% of effective rate

$$\frac{49{,}800}{300{,}000} \times 100 \times 30\% = 4.98\%$$

Number of complete quarters between 1 December 1992 and 1 December 1999=28

Tax payable by the beneficiary

£200,000 x 4.98% x 28/40=£6,972

Rate between ten-year anniversaries

7.30 After the first, or any subsequent ten-year anniversary, where there is a disposition of relevant property giving rise to an exit charge under IHTA 1984 s 65, the rate of tax is calculated at the appropriate fraction of the rate applicable to the immediately preceding ten-year anniversary. [IHTA 1984 s 69(1)]. The appropriate fraction is the number of complete successive quarters in the period, beginning with the most recent ten-year anniversary and ending with the day before the disposition giving rise to the charge, divided by 40, being the number of quarters in the ten-year period. Where property has been added since the previous ten-year anniversary, quarters prior to the quarter in which the additional property is added are ignored. [Section 69(4)]. This also applies to property that was previously held but was not then relevant property and has become such during the period. [Section 69(2)]. In the case of property becoming comprised in the settlement, it is valued immediately after it became comprised in the settlement or, where appropriate, when it became relevant property. [Section 69(3)].

7.31 Where there is a reduction in the rate of IHT and an exit charge under IHTA 1984 s 65 is determined by reference to the rate that was charged on the previous ten-yearly anniversary under section 64, the reduction in rate is deemed to have applied at that time in order to compute the exit charge. [IHTA 1984 Sch 2 para 3].

7.32 Where an interest in possession in settled property is terminated without reverting to the settlor or his spouse, it is deemed to become a separate settlement at the date of termination. [IHTA 1984 s 80]. The ten-year charge, however, is calculated by reference to the date the settlement actually commenced as an interest in possession settlement. [IHTA 1984 s 61(2)].

Example

Facts are as for the example at **7.23** above except on 1 December 2005, ie three years after the exit charge imposed on 30 November 2002, trustees appointed £200,000 to a beneficiary.

1 December 2005

Exit charge upon distribution to a beneficiary

Rate applying on prior 10 year charge

Revised to reflect 2005/06 nil rate threshold say £300,000

£1,180,000–£300,000=£880,000@20%=£176,000

$$\frac{176{,}000}{1.000{,}000} \times 100 \times 30\% = 5.28\%$$

Number of complete quarters between 1 December 2002 and 1 December 2005=12

Rate of exit charge

5.28% x 12/40=1.58%

Tax payable by trustees £200,000 x 1.58%=£3,160.

Property moving between settlements

7.33 Property which moves from one settlement to another is treated as remaining in the first settlement, unless in the meantime any person has become beneficially entitled to the property, and not merely an interest in possession in the property. [IHTA 1984 s 81(1)]. Property ceasing to be held after 26 March 1974 and before 10 December 1981 is only regarded as remaining in the first settlement where there was a direct transfer between settlements. [Section 81(2)]. Property is not deemed to remain in the first settlement where it was a reversionary interest settled on the second settlement before 10 December 1981 and was subject to a qualifying interest in possession subsisting under the first settlement. [Section 81(3)].

7.34 In the case of a settlement where there is an initial interest in possession held by the settlor or his spouse or property is moving between settlements, the excluded property provisions of IHTA 1984 s 48(3)(a) (under which non-UK property settled by a non-UK domiciled settlor is not regarded as excluded property for these purposes unless the settlor was not domiciled in the UK when settlement was made) is modified to require the settlor also to be non-UK domiciled when the interest in possession terminated under IHTA 1984 s 80 or the second settlement commenced, under IHTA 1984 s 81. [Section 82(3)]. Similarly, for gilts to be exempt, the settlor has to be non-domiciled both at the date when the settlement was made and when the interest in possession ceased, or the transferee settlement was made, under IHTA 1984 s 80 or 81. [Section 82(2)].

Chapter 8

Bare and Interest in Possession Trusts

Bare trusts (or simple trusts)

8.1 Where a person acts as nominee for another person or as trustee for a person who is absolutely entitled as against the trustee to the property held, or would be were he not an infant or under some disability which prevented him holding the legal title to the assets, the acts of the nominee or trustee are treated as the acts of the beneficiary. This also applies where the nominee or trustee is holding assets for two or more persons who would be jointly entitled as against the trustee. Because the beneficiary is deemed to own the assets there is no capital gains charge on a disposal by him of the legal title to the nominee or trustee or vice versa. [TCGA 1992 s 60(1)]. The person absolutely entitled as against the trustee is someone who has the exclusive right (subject only to satisfying any outstanding charge, lien or other right of the trustees to resort to the asset for payment of duty, taxes, costs or other outgoings) to direct how that asset should be dealt with.

8.2 Funds held in court by the Accountant-General are regarded as held by him as nominee for the persons entitled to, or interested in, the funds or their trustees. [TCGA 1992 s 61]. In *Saunders v Vautier* (1841) 4 Beav 115 it was held that where a beneficiary of an accumulation and maintenance trust was the sole beneficiary, and had reached the age of majority so that he had an absolute indefeasible interest in the property held in trust, he could require payment of the trust assets to him as he was capable of giving a valid discharge, i e he was absolutely entitled as against the trustees.

8.3 A number of cases have considered whether beneficiaries are absolutely entitled as against the trustee, including *Tomlinson v Glyn's Executor and Trustee Co Ltd* (1969) 45 TC 600; *Cochrane v IRC* [1974] STC 335; *Crowe v Appleby* [1975] STC 502; *Scott v Scott* (1930) SC 903; *Kidson v Macdonald* [1974] STC 54; *Harthan v Mason* [1980] STC 94; *Jenkins v Brown, Warrington v Sterland* [1989] STC 577; *Frampton (Trustees of the Worthing Rugby Football Club) v IRC* [1985] STC 186; *Figg v Clarke* [1997] STC 247; *IRC v Matthews Executors* [1984] STC 386; *Prest v Bettinson* [1980] STC 607; *Anders Utklens, Rederi v O/Y Lovisa Stevedoring Co A/B* [1985] STC 301; *Stephenson v Barclays Bank Trust Co Ltd* [1975] STC 151; *Hoare Trustees v Gardner* [1978] STC 89; and *Booth v Ellard* [1980] STC 555.

8.4 The base value for a CGT bare trust is the value on the death of the previous owner of the property, if it was inherited. In the case of trust assets, the base value is the value on the date when the beneficiary became absolutely entitled to the asset under TCGA 1992 s 71(3), or the actual cost to the trustees if acquired on behalf of the beneficiary. The base value is the actual cost to the beneficiary where the asset was subsequently transferred to bare trustees. [CG 34363]. CGT assessments must be made on the beneficiaries not on the trustees, and elections must be made by the beneficiaries. [CG 34366]. Partnership property is often held on bare trusts because the maximum number of owners of the legal estate in land is four.

8.5 Where land is held jointly on bare trusts by tenants in common they may exchange their joint interest in the whole property for an absolute interest in part of the property under ESCD 26 [CG 34411], without crystallising a CGT charge.

8.6 Where a person has a general power of appointment as a beneficiary of a trust this does not mean that it is a bare trust until the property has actually been appointed under the general power of appointment to that beneficiary. Once a beneficiary has all the interests under the settlement it is a bare trust, for example, where he has a life interest and a general power of appointment and also the interest in remainder. [CG 34450–34454]. A transfer by way of security is not a disposal for CGT purposes [TCGA 1992 s 26; CG 34460] (*Aspden v Hildesley* [1982] STC 206; *Passant v Jackson* [1985] STC 133). A gift in a will to someone on attaining a particular age is contingent and therefore not held on bare trusts unless there is a direction to pay the income or such part of it as the trustees think fit to the beneficiary, in which case he would be absolutely entitled, unless he is an infant, and it would be a bare trust. [CG 34471].

8.7 The administrative arrangements for bare trusts are explained in the Inland Revenue Press Release of 20 January 1997 which provides as follows:

'1. Prior to 6 April 1996, the trustees of some bare trusts accounted for income tax at the appropriate rate on the income which they paid over to the beneficiaries. These amounts became taxed income in the hands of the beneficiaries, who were required to give full details of that income in their tax returns, but were liable to pay further tax only if they were higher rate taxpayers. Conversely, they were entitled to a repayment of the tax paid by the trustees if they had no personal liability.

2. Under self-assessment, the Revenue will no longer expect trustees to account for tax in such circumstances because there is no entitlement in law for trustees to deduct tax from income arising to bare trusts. Any income which is received gross by the trustees must be paid gross to the beneficiaries. The only exception to this rule is that UK resident trustees may be required under the non-resident landlords scheme, to deduct and account for tax on the rental income of beneficiaries whose usual place of abode is outside the UK.

3. Trustees of bare trusts will not be required to complete self-assessment tax returns, or to make any payments on account. Beneficiaries will still be required to give details of all their income and gains from bare trusts in their own tax returns, and in addition will be required to account to the Revenue for the full amount of any tax due.

4. Although the Revenue are endeavouring to identify those bare trusts where trustees have previously made annual returns and accounted for the tax, in order to notify them of this change, there will be some cases which will not be recognised in time to prevent the 1996–97 payment on account notices and self-assessment tax returns from being issued to the trustees.

5. Any trustees receiving a payment on account notice should return it to the issuing trust office with a brief explanation so that the records can be amended. Any trustees receiving a self-assessment tax return after 6 April 1997 should complete the final three questions on the return form in accordance with the notes given in step 1 on this form.

6. There are a number of collective investment schemes which are constituted as bare trusts, but only two kinds are treated as such for tax purposes. These are enterprise zone property unit trusts (EZPUTs), and pension fund pooling vehicles (PFPVs). The trustees of such schemes will not receive self-assessment tax returns. That is because the income and gains which arise under EZPUTs and PFPVs belong to the unit holders of the schemes, and if any expenditure is incurred by the trustees which gives rise to capital allowances, those allowances are made to the unit holders and not the trustees.

7. The trustees of EZPUTs and PFPVs will, however, remain responsible for agreeing the amounts of the schemes' income, profits, gains, capital expenditure, capital allowances, and balancing adjustments with their own tax inspectors in accordance with the rules laid down in the relevant income tax regulations, and for providing the unit holders of the schemes with certificates giving details of the parts of those amounts that are, in each case, attributable to them.

Notes

1. A "bare trust" also known as a "simple trust" exists where the beneficial owner of the property held in trust is fully entitled to both the capital and income from that property. The property will be held in the name of the trustee, but the trustee will have no discretion over what income to pay the beneficiary. The trustee is in effect a nominee in whose name the property is held. The beneficial owner is the person who benefits from, and is entitled to, the property and any income it produces.

2. EZPUTs, which first became available in 1984, are unauthorised unit trust schemes which provide tax incentives for individuals to invest collectively in properties in enterprise zones.

3. Regulations providing tax rules for PFPVs were announced in an Inland Revenue Press Release on 19 June 1996 and came into force on 11 July (see Simon's Weekly Tax Intelligence 1996 p 1029).

   These vehicles are pooled investment funds specialising in managing the assets of UK exempt approved pension schemes and their overseas equivalents.

4. Further information about the non-resident landlords scheme can be found in leaflet IR 140 'Non-resident landlords, their agents and tenants".'

The text is the same as that in the Inland Revenue's *Tax Bulletin*, Issue 27, February 1997, p 395. This was modified by *Tax Bulletin,* Issue 32, December 1997, p 487.

> 'In the *Tax Bulletin*, Issue 27, (February 1997, page 395) we explained the Revenue's approach to the taxation of bare trusts, ie trusts where the beneficial owner of the trust property is absolutely entitled to both the capital and income from that property. We said that the trustees of bare trusts would not be required to complete self assessment tax returns, or to make payments on account. That remains the Department's position, and we think that the approach set out in the article will simplify the tax affairs of most bare trustees and beneficiaries under self assessment.
>
> Following discussions with representative bodies, we now accept that the trustees of bare trusts are entitled to make a self assessment return of income, but not of capital gains, and to account for tax on it at the appropriate rate. In those cases where the trustees of bare trusts wish to make a return, the appropriate rate of tax will be at basic rate (or lower rate, if the income is savings income). It is emphasised that capital gains and capital losses must not be included on any self assessment return made by a bare trustee. These remain the sole responsibility of the beneficiaries.
>
> If the trustees and all the beneficiaries of a bare trust wish to follow this course of action they should notify the trust district dealing with the trust's tax affairs as soon as possible. We will expect them to follow this course consistently year on year.
>
> Where the trustees of bare trusts do not notify the trust district that they wish to make a return of income and to pay tax, those trustees and their beneficiaries will be dealt with in accordance with the article in Issue 27 of Tax Bulletin. We expect the great majority of bare trustees to fall into this category, as it is only in relatively unusual circumstances that it will be more convenient for the trustees to self assess. Whether or not the trustees decide to self assess and account for tax, the beneficiaries of these trusts remain within self assessment and are obliged to notify the Inland Revenue of their income and gains.'

8.8 The parent, guardian or tutor of an infant may be charged to tax in default of payment by the infant under TMA 1970 s 73. Similarly the trustee, guardian etc of an incapacitated person having the direction, control or management of property of such a person is liable to tax on that income under TMA 1970 s 72 and may recover the tax paid from the money coming into his hands on behalf of that person under section 72(3).

Interest in possession

8.9 A beneficiary has an interest in possession in a settlement if he has a present right to the present enjoyment of the whole or part of the trust property, *Pearson v IRC* [1980] STC 318. Such a beneficiary is the person receiving or entitled to the income within ICTA 1988 s 59 and subject to tax thereon *(Williams v Singer and others* (1921) 7 TC 387; *Archer-Shee v Baker* (1927) 11 TC 749). Although the income is that of the beneficiary with the interest in possession and he is entitled to it as it arises so that, for example, a dividend from ICI remains in the hands of the beneficiary a dividend from ICI, nonetheless if it passes through the trustees they are liable to tax on the income in the first instance. [ICTA 1988 s 660(D)(3)]. Where the income is actually mandated direct to the beneficiaries so that it does not pass through the trustees' hands, it is not necessary for the trustees to include that income on their trust return.

8.10 This general rule, which arises in case law in England and Wales, is extended by statute to Scottish trusts under FA 1993 s 118. In the case of foreign trusts, however, the beneficiary's interest might be in the foreign trust as the source of the income not in the underlying investment even though he has an interest in possession in the sense of being absolutely entitled to the income arising from the trust or some part of it (*Garland v Archer-Shee* (1930) 15 TC 693). Where the investments are outside the UK and the UK resident beneficiary is domiciled outside the UK, no deduction for the trust expenses is allowable from income taxable on a remittance basis (*Aiken v Macdonald Trustees* (1894) 3 TC 306). In spite of the fact that the beneficiary with an interest in possession has an entitlement to the income as it arises, this is subject to the trustees' right to withhold part of that income for the payment of trust expenses which are therefore paid out of net income (*Murray v IRC* (1926) 11 TC 133; *MacFarlane v IRC* (1929) 14 TC 532).

8.11 Where, however, the beneficiary with the interest in possession is a minor or child of the settlor, the income is taxed on the settlor under ICTA 1988 s 660B(1) not on the beneficiary. Similarly, where the spouse of the settlor is entitled to an interest in possession, the income is nonetheless taxable on the settlor under TA 1988 s 660A(1) and (2).

8.12 An annuity is an annual payment within ICTA 1988 s 348(1) and therefore the person paying the annuity should deduct tax at the basic rate and hold it in charge under section 348(1) or pay it over to the Inland Revenue if it is not a business expense under section 349. The use of trust assets by a beneficiary of a UK resident trust does not give rise to a tax charge on the benefit in kind as there is no mechanism for assessing any notional income in these circumstances. This contrasts with the position in relation to overseas trusts dealt with at **10.25**.

Capital gains tax

Termination of life interest

8.13 On the termination of the life interest on the death of a person entitled to an interest in possession in settled property, the value of the property is rebased for CGT purposes by being deemed to be disposed of and immediately reacquired by the trustee for a consideration equal to the market value of the asset but with no chargeable gain accruing on the disposal. [TCGA 1992 s 72(1)]. This corresponds with the general rebasing to market value on death for assets held by the deceased directly, under TCGA 1992 s 62, and is consistent with the fact that the life tenant is deemed to have an absolute interest in the property for IHT purposes under IHTA 1984 s 49(1).

8.14 The rebasing applies on the death of a life tenant even where the interest does not terminate. [TCGA 1992 s 72(2)]. An annuitant is deemed to be a life tenant for these purposes where the annuity is payable out of, or charged on, settled property. [Section 72(3)]. Where property has been appropriated by the trustees to create a fund out of which the annuity is payable, without any right of recourse to the remainder of the settled property or the income therefrom, the rebasing applies to the property so appropriated as if the fund were a separate settlement. [Section 72(4) and (5)]. SP/D10 provides as follows.

'1. Where an interest in part of settled property terminates and the part can properly be identified with one or more specific assets, or where, within a reasonable time, normally three months, of the termination the trustees appropriate specific assets to give effect to the termination, the Board will accept that the deemed disposals and reacquisitions under TCGA 1992 ss 71, 72 apply to those specific assets, and not to any part of the other assets comprised in the settled property. The treatment must be consistent with that adopted for inheritance tax.

2. In particular, inspectors will be prepared to agree with the trustees, lists of assets properly identifiable with the termination of an interest in possession, and any such agreement will be regarded as binding on the Revenue and the trustees.

3. This practice applies on any act or event which terminates an interest in possession whether voluntarily or involuntarily.'

8.15 Where a person becomes absolutely entitled to settled property on the death of the life tenant there is no chargeable gain on the disposal under TCGA 1992 s 71. [TCGA 1992 s 73(1)(a)]. If the property reverts to the settlor the consideration is deemed to be such as to give rise to a no-gain, no-loss disposal, ie normally the settlor's base cost, with no readjustment to market value. [Section 73(1)(b)]. Where the life tenant's interest extended only to part of the settled fund, only that proportion is exempt from CGT under these provisions. [Section 73(2)]. Cases on the apportionment of trust funds on the death of a life tenant include *Pexton v Bell* [1976] STC 301 and *Crowe v Appleby* [1976] STC 301. Similar rules apply on the death of an annuitant. [Section 73(3)].

8.16 Where a chargeable gain has been held over on the transfer of an asset into settlement as a business asset under TCGA 1992 s 165, or one chargeable to IHT under TCGA 1992 s 260, the CGT exemption on the death of the life tenant or annuitant does not apply but the chargeable gain on the trustees is restricted to the heldover gain, or a corresponding part of it, which arose on the transfer of the asset into trust. [TCGA 1992 s 74(1) and (2)]. Proportionate adjustment is made if the life tenant or annuitant had an interest in any part of the trust. [Section 74(3)].

Inheritance tax

8.17 A qualifying interest in possession for IHT purposes is defined in IHTA 1984 s 59(1) as an interest in possession to which an individual is beneficially entitled, which comes back to the present right to the present enjoyment of the trust property under *Pearson v IRC* [1980] STC 318. Under IHTA 1984 s 49(1), a person beneficially entitled to an interest in possession in settled property is deemed to own that property unless it was acquired for money or money's worth. The Scottish equivalent of an interest in possession is included. [IHTA 1984 s 46].

8.18 The converse of treating the person entitled to the interest in possession as if he had the absolute interest in the property under IHTA 1984 s 49(1), is that the reversionary interest, as defined by IHTA 1984 s 47, is excluded property under IHTA 1984 s 48(1) and (2). An interest in possession in part only of the settled property gives rise to an appropriate apportionment under IHTA 1984 s 50(1). The apportionment is made on the basis of the share of the capital being assumed to be equal to the share of the income paid to the beneficiary with the interest in possession. [Section 50(2)]. However, the Treasury has been given power to prescribe a higher and a lower rate which the property is assumed to yield, in order to arrive at the proportion of the capital deemed to belong to the life tenant, although this cannot exceed the whole of the trust property. [Section 50(3)]. In respect of transfers of value after 17 February 2000, these yields are given by the Inheritance Tax (Settled Property Income Yield) Order 2000, SI 2000/174, on the authority of IHTA 1984 s 50(4). The higher rate is the rate of the irredeemable yield shown in the FT Actuaries Government Securities UK Indices for the date on which the value in question is to be determined, or the latest date preceding that date for which those indices were produced. [SI 2000/174 reg 3]. The lower rate is the rate that is equal to the rate of the All Share Index actual dividend yield shown in the indices, which are known as the FT Actuaries Share Indices and are produced either for the date on which the value in question is to be determined or for the latest date preceding that date on which those indices are produced. [SI 2000/174 reg 4]. So long as the actual yield of the trust falls within these parameters, the apportionment is on the basis of the actual income to which the life tenant is entitled as a proportion of the total income. If the actual yield is below the minimum yield, the notional yield is substituted and if it is above the maximum yield, the maximum yield is substituted.

8.19 Where a life tenant is not entitled to income from the trust but is entitled to the use and enjoyment of trust property, his interest is proportionate to the annual value of his interest in the aggregate values of the trust property and those of the other beneficiaries. [IHTA 1984 s 50(5)]. Where a lease for life is treated as a settlement, the lessee's interest in the property is in the whole of the property less the value of the lessor's interest as determined under IHTA 1984 s 170, as if the lease had been granted for full consideration in money or money's worth. [IHTA 1984 ss 43(3) and 50(6); SP 10/79].

Disposal of interest in possession

8.20 The disposal by a beneficiary of his interest in possession is not a transfer of value but is treated as a termination of his interest and charged accordingly, under IHTA 1984 s 51. This does not apply to a disposition for the maintenance of family in favour of his spouse or child or, in the case of a child under the age of 18 or undergoing full-time education or training, for the maintenance, education or training of that child. The relief is also extended to reasonable provision for the care or maintenance of a dependent relative. [IHTA 1984 ss 11 and 51(2)]. Apportionment is provided for in IHTA 1984 s 51(3).

A charge on termination of interest in possession

8.21 Where an interest in possession comes to an end or is deemed to come to an end under IHTA 1984 s 52, then subject to section 53 of the Act, there will be a transfer of value and the value transferred is equal to the value of the property in which the interest in possession subsisted (*IRC v Brandenburg* [1982] STC 555). [IHTA 1984 s 52(1)]. Where it has been sold, the interest in possession is valued ignoring the value of the reversionary interest but reduced by a consideration in money or money's worth received on sale. [Section 52(2)]. Where the trustees enter into a transaction with the person beneficially entitled to an interest in possession, or a person connected with him, or another beneficiary, which results in the termination charge being reduced, the amount accruing to the benefit of the other beneficiaries will also be deemed to be part of the interest terminated unless the transaction would not be a transfer of value if the property were beneficially owned by the trustees. [Section 52(3)]. Apportionment is provided for under section 52(4).

8.22 Exceptions from the IHT charge on termination of an interest in possession apply where the settled property is excluded property as defined by IHTA 1984 ss 272 and 48(3), ie property situated outside the UK where the settlor was domiciled outside the UK at the time the settlement was made.

Under section 48(3)(a) this does not apply to a reversionary interest in such property unless it is held by an individual domiciled outside the UK. [IHTA 1984 s 48(3)(b) and (6)(a)].

8.23 Where a person's interest in possession comes to an end on the same occasion on which he becomes beneficially entitled to the entire property, or to another interest in possession in the property, there is no IHT charge (IHTA 1984 s 53(2)), except where the new interest in possession is less valuable than the old, in which case there is a charge on the difference under IHTA 1984 s 52(4)(b). There is no charge on a termination of an interest in possession where the settlor is still alive and the property then reverts to him (*Hatton v IRC* [1992] STC 140; *Countess Fitzwilliam v IRC* [1993] STC 502). [IHTA 1984 s 53(3)].

Transfers to a spouse

8.24 The exemption for transfers to the transferor's spouse in IHTA 1984 s 18(1), subject to the limitation of £55,000 where the transferee spouse is non-UK domiciled and the transferor spouse is UK domiciled under IHTA 1984 s 18(2), is extended to cases where the property is held in trust for the spouse by IHTA 1984 s 18(4). Therefore tax is not chargeable on the termination of an interest in possession if on that occasion the settlor's spouse becomes beneficially entitled to the settled property and is domiciled in the UK. [IHTA 1984 s 53(4)(a)]. Spouse does not extend to unmarried partners living together (*Holland v IRC* [2003] STC (SCD) 43). This also applies to the settlor's widow or widower where the settlor has died within the previous two years. [Section 53(4)(b)]. The reverter to settlor or spouse exemption does not apply where the settlor acquired a reversionary interest in the property for a consideration in money or money's worth, or it was transferred into a settlement on or after 10 March 1981. [Section 53(5)]. Indirect consideration is included by section 53(6), although these restrictions may not apply where the interest was acquired prior to 12 April 1978. [Section 53(7) and (8)].

8.25 One of the main changes introduced by IHT compared with estate duty, was to charge IHT on the second death where a couple are married, whereas estate duty charged tax on the first death. There was, however, an exemption where assets were left in trust for the surviving spouse for life so that estate duty was not chargeable on the second death, on those assets. There is still a number of surviving spouses alive whose spouse died before 13 November 1974 when what is now IHT was introduced. IHTA 1984 Sch 6 para 2 preserves the surviving spouse exemption which applied for estate duty under FA 1894 s 5(2) to exempt the property in such a settlement from giving rise to a termination charge under IHTA 1984 s 52 on the death of the surviving spouse. Although not chargeable to IHT, the property in the surviving spouse's trust is still deemed to be that of the surviving spouse with an interest in possession under IHTA 1984 s 49(1) and could therefore affect the value of other assets held by the surviving spouse personally, e g where 30 per cent of the shares in a family company were owned by the surviving spouse personally and 30 per cent through a surviving spouse trust exempt under IHTA 1984 Sch 6 para 2, the shares in the free estate would still be valued on the basis of half of a 60 per cent shareholding, ie on the basis of a proportion of a controlling interest valuation.

Exemptions from charge on death

8.26 Where the life tenant dies and the property reverts to the settlor, who is still alive, the value of the property which would otherwise be deemed to be part of the life tenant's estate is left out of account. [IHTA 1984 s 54(1)]. This also applies where on the life tenant's death the property passes to the settlor's spouse or widow or widower, if the settlor has died within the previous two years, so long as the spouse is domiciled in the UK, except where the settlor or spouse acquired a reversionary interest in the property for consideration in money or money's worth, or a reversionary interest was transferred into settlement on or after 10 March 1981. [Section 54(3)]. Where two or more persons have died in circumstances where it is not known which died first they should be assumed to have died at the same instant. [Section 54(4)]. The potentially exempt transfer provisions in IHTA 1984 s 3A were extended by F(No 2)A 1987 s 96 to include transfers into a settlement where there is an interest in possession or on the termination of an interest in possession. As a transfer directly into a discretionary trust is not a potentially exempt transfer, anti-avoidance provisions are needed to prevent an indirect transfer by means of a transfer into a trust with an interest in possession where that interest has shortly afterwards terminated, and the settled property becomes subject to discretionary trusts. These provisions are contained in IHTA 1984 ss 54A and 54B which apply unless the discretionary trusts involved are accumulation and maintenance trusts within IHTA 1984 s 71 (see Chapter 9) which would be potentially exempt transfers under IHTA 1984 s 3A(1)(c) if made direct.

8.27 In appropriate circumstances a charge to IHT arises on the termination of the interest in possession during the life of or on the death of the person beneficially entitled to it, the interest in possession being referred to as the relevant interest. [IHTA 1984 s 54A(1)]. The circumstances arise where the whole or part of the relevant interest arises as a part of a potentially exempt transfer by the settlor on or after 17 March 1987, and within the previous seven years, and the settlor is alive when the interest in possession terminates, and on the termination the settled property is sold or transferred other than to interest in possession or accumulation and maintenance trusts, and does not become subject to interest in possession, or accumulation and maintenance trusts within six months of the termination of the interest in possession. [Section 54A(2)]. Where part only of the property qualifies, apportionment is provided for under section 54A(3). The property remaining on discretionary trusts is known as the special rate property. The IHT on the value transferred is the greater of the charge that would arise on the termination of the interest in possession, ie by reference to the life tenant's cumulative transfers (section 54A(4)) or by reference to the tax that would have been charged on a chargeable transfer of the relevant property plus the cumulative transfers by the settlor made within seven years prior to the date of the potentially exempt transfer to the interest in possession trust, ie the tax that would have been payable had there been a direct transfer by the settlor into discretionary trusts. [Section 54A(5) and (6)].

8.28 It seems that an initial potentially exempt transfer into an accumulation and maintenance trust followed by a beneficiary obtaining an interest in possession, which is then terminated in favour of discretionary trusts, would not be caught under these provisions, nor would a transfer to a trust in which the settlor's spouse had an interest in possession terminated in favour of discretionary trusts, subject to the associated operation provisions in IHTA 1984 s 268. The deemed transfer by the settlor where these provisions apply is charged at the lifetime rate of half of the death rate in IHTA 1984 ss 7(1) and 54A(6)(c). Where tax is payable under IHTA 1984 s 54A by reference to cumulative transfers of the settlor or life tenant, the only adjustment required on death is where this would result in a higher charge in relation to the settlor where section 54A(5) and (6) applies or by reference to the life tenant where section 54A(4) applies. [IHTA 1984 s 54B(1) and (2)]. Where the charge is made by reference to the settlor's previous transfers, this includes previous transfers within section 54A (within the previous seven years). [IHTA 1984 s 54B(3)–(7)].

Acquisition of reversionary interest

8.29 Where a person already entitled as a beneficiary, whether to an interest in possession or not, in any settled property, acquires a reversionary interest in the same settlement he is treated as making a transfer of value, which may be a potentially exempt transfer, equal to the amount of the consideration given for that reversionary interest. This is an anti-avoidance provision to prevent a person reducing the value of his estate when he already holds an interest in the settlement, eg a life tenant, deemed to own the assets of the settlement, could reduce his estate by buying the reversionary interest, cash passing out of the estate and his interest in the settled property would not increase because as a life tenant he is already entitled to the entire interest in the property. The normal exemption for a reversionary interest as excluded property, under IHTA 1984 s 48(1), incorporated in the definition of his estate within IHTA 1984 s 5(1), is disapplied, as is the exemption for arm's length transactions in IHTA 1984 s 10(1).

Exclusion of exemptions

8.30 Exemptions normally available to an individual in respect of transfers between spouses under IHTA 1984 s 18 (IHTA 1984 ss 23 (gifts to charities), 24 (gifts to political parties), 24A (gifts to housing associations), 25 (gifts for national purposes such as museums), 26A (potentially exempt transfers of property subsequently held for national purposes), and 27 (maintenance funds for historical buildings)) do not apply where they are given in exchange for reversionary interest in a settlement, where the reversionary interest would not form part of the estate of the donor under IHTA 1984 s 55. This is an anti-avoidance provision to prevent these exemptions being used for the artificial reduction in the transferor's estate for IHT purposes. [IHTA 1984 s 56(1)].

8.31 The inter-spouse exemption under IHTA 1984 s18 does not apply where the reversionary interest is acquired for money or money's worth. [IHTA 1984 s 56(2)]. Exemptions in IHTA 1984 ss 23–27 do not apply. The interest in possession does not cease on making the transfer of value where the interest under the settlement has been acquired for money or money's worth before being transferred to an exempt body. [IHTA 1984 s 56(3) and (4)]. Partial termination of previously purchased interests in possession do not qualify for a charitable deduction under IHTA 1984 s 23, in view of IHTA 1984 s 56(3) (*Powell-Cotton v IRC* [1992] STC 625).

8.32 A number of exemptions are specifically applied on the termination of an interest in possession in settled property, if this is within the annual exemption under IHTA 1984 s 19 or as a gift in consideration of marriage under IHTA 1984 s 22. [IHTA 1984 s 57]. Where the transfer is a termination of an interest in possession which results in the property ceasing to be settled property, it is treated as an outright gift for the purposes of IHTA 1984 s 22 and is regarded as settled by gift if it remains within the trust. [Section 57(2)]. In order for the exemptions to apply, the transferor must inform the trustees of the availability of the exemption. [Section 57(3) and (4)]. The notice to the trustees must be given to the trustees within six months following the date of the transfer of value. The transfer to a maintenance fund for historic buildings within IHTA 1984 s 27 and Sch 4 is treated as if it had become comprised in the settlement by virtue of the transfer where it remained settled property. [Section 57(5)].

8.33 The fiction under IHTA 1984 s 49(1), whereby the person beneficially entitled to an interest in possession in settled property is treated as if he were the absolute owner of that property rather than the mere beneficiary, has a number of knock-on effects.

8.34 The trust property becomes part of the beneficiary's estate for IHT purposes within IHTA 1984 s 5(1), which means that a gift into settlement where a person has an interest in possession is treated as a gift to that individual, and is a potentially exempt transfer under IHTA 1984 s 3A(1). Similarly, a transfer out of an interest in possession settlement can be a potentially exempt transfer under IHTA 1984 s 3A(6). The whole of the beneficiary's share of the trust in which he has an interest in possession is part of his estate if he dies (within IHTA 1984 s 4) and, as such, any chargeable transfer in relation to the settled property is chargeable either at the death or lifetime rates under IHTA 1984 s 7, including the taper relief on an *inter vivos* transfer within seven years of death under section 7(4) and the indexation of rate bands and transitional provisions on reduction of tax in sections 8 and 9.

8.35 A disposition for the maintenance of a transferor's family in favour of a spouse or child, for the maintenance of the spouse or for the maintenance, education or training of the child under the age of 18 or undergoing full-time education or training, is not a transfer of value for IHT purposes, nor is one in favour of a dependent relative. [IHTA 1984 s 11]. Such dispositions include transfers to trusts in respect of which the spouse, children or dependant relative are beneficiaries. They also include those by a child in favour of his unmarried mother incapacitated by old age or infirmity or generally financially dependent on the child. [ESC F12].

8.36 For valuation purposes, unquoted shares held in a settlement where there is an interest in possession are aggregated with the beneficiary's free estate for valuation purposes under IHTA 1984 ss 160 and 168, as a result of IHTA 1984 ss 49(1) and 5(1). However, a transfer of shares by the trustees, other than on the death of the life tenant, would not be aggregated with the beneficiary's own shareholding for valuation purposes (see **6.234**). In determining the value of the beneficiary's estate or that of his spouse, property held in the trust in which he had an interest in possession would be aggregated as related property under IHTA 1984 s 161.

Chapter 9

Accumulation and Maintenance Trusts

Income tax and capital gains tax

9.1 For trust law purposes, an accumulation and maintenance trust is merely a discretionary trust which gives the trustees powers to distribute income, and, where the trust deed so provides or under TA 1925 s 32, to make advances of capital for the maintenance, education or benefit of one or more beneficiaries, and to accumulate any income not so distributed. There are no particular income tax or CGT rules applying to accumulation and maintenance trusts which are therefore dealt with as ordinary discretionary trusts for such purposes, as described in Chapter 7.

9.2 Where distributions are made out of an accumulation and maintenance settlement to minor beneficiaries the income will be theirs for tax purposes, unless it is a parent's settlement caught by ICTA 1988 s 660B. It will therefore have suffered tax at the rate applicable to trusts and the net distribution can be grossed up at that rate, and an income tax repayment claim made on the minor beneficiaries' behalf. Although a maintenance and accumulation trust can be created by will it can also be established by a deed of variation under IHTA 1984 s 142(1). However, if the children benefiting under an accumulation and maintenance trust set up by variation are the children of the initial beneficiary, any distributions of income would be taxed as that beneficiary's income as the true settlor for income tax purposes, under ICTA 1988 s 660B, as the variation only deems the settlement to be created by the deceased for IHT and CGT purposes (*Marshall v Kerr* [1994] STC 638). [IHTA 1984 s 142(1); TCGA 1992 s 62(6)].

Inheritance tax

Definition

9.3 For IHT purposes the term 'accumulation and maintenance trust' is normally confined to one which meets the specific requirements of IHTA 1984 s 71. The main IHT advantage of a discretionary trust qualifying as an accumulation and maintenance trust under section 71 is that it is not relevant property under IHTA 1984 s 58(1)(b) and therefore there is no IHT charge on a ten-year anniversary and no exit charge on distributions of capital. [IHTA 1984 ss 64 and 65]. The first requirement of an accumulation and maintenance trust is that one or more of the beneficiaries will, under the terms of the trust, on or before obtaining a specified age not exceeding 25, become beneficially entitled to the trust property, or an interest in possession in it. (*Lord Inglewood v IRC* [1983] STC 133). [Section 71(1)]. In this case the powers of revocation and reappointment in the trust deed meant that it could not be said that any child would obtain an interest in possession and therefore it was not an accumulation and maintenance trust within section 71. A conditional appointment that depended on the power of accumulation being valid under the Trusts (Scotland) Act 1961, which both the Revenue and the taxpayer agreed that it was, was effective in *Maitland's Trustees v Lord Advocate* 1982 SLT 483. The remote likelihood of a challenge did not mean that the beneficiaries would not obtain an interest in possession, and the trust qualified as an accumulation and maintenance trust within section 71.

9.4 A beneficiary with a prospective, protected life interest could qualify under IHTA 1984 s 71(1)(a) as this would be treated as an interest in possession under IHTA 1984 s 88(2)(b), even though the interest in possession may be protected by being held on protective trusts similar to those specified in TA 1925 s 33(1). A trust deed does not actually need to mention age 25 if it is obvious that, in fact, the beneficiaries will acquire an interest in possession at that age, e g at the end of the maximum accumulation period of 21 years (see ESC F8). 'Beneficiary' includes an unborn person provided that there is also a living beneficiary. [Section 71(7)]. The definition of a beneficiary to include an unborn child enables the beneficiaries to be described by class such as the children of a particular person. Children include illegitimate, adopted and step-children. [Section 71(8)]. So long as a beneficiary obtains an interest in possession by age 25, at the latest, there is no requirement to obtain a vested interest in capital at any particular age.

9.5 The second requisite of an accumulation and maintenance trust for IHT purposes is that there is no current interest in possession in the trust property, or in the income from it, which has to be accumulated in so far as it is not applied for the maintenance, education or benefit of a beneficiary. [IHTA 1984 s 71(1)(b)]. This requirement follows closely TA 1925 s 31 where the trustees normally have a power to apply the income for the maintenance, education or benefit of a beneficiary and to accumulate the balance of income, although these provisions may be modified by the trust instrument. The requirement is that the income must either be applied for the maintenance, education or benefit of a beneficiary or accumulated; this therefore includes a trust where the trustees must accumulate the income or must use it for the maintenance, education or benefit of the beneficiaries (see *IRC v Berrill* [1981] STC 784, although this case actually concerned ICTA 1988 s 686, as the trust was a discretionary trust). In *Re Clore's Settlement Trusts* [1966] 2 All ER 272 a gift to charity by the trustees through an accumulation and maintenance settlement was held to be for the benefit of a beneficiary from a wealthy family.

9.6 It should be noted that the provisions apply to settled property, not the settlement as such, and it is perfectly possible to have a single trust with an interest in possession in part, which would be identified under IHTA 1984 s 50, and have discretionary beneficiaries as well as accumulation and maintenance trusts. For example, there is no requirement that the accumulations of income are held on trusts which qualify under IHTA 1984 s 71(1). These two conditions are sometimes known as the capital condition under section 71(1)(a) and the income condition under section 71(1)(b). However, this terminology, although convenient, is perhaps misleading in that the capital condition does not require the beneficiary to have a vested interest in capital at any stage so long as he has an interest in possession. An Inland Revenue Press Release of 19 January 1976 stated:

> '... where there is a trust for accumulation and maintenance of a class of persons who become entitled to the property (or to an interest in possession in it) at a specified age not exceeding 25 it would not be disqualified under IHTA 1984 s 71(1)(a) by the existence of a power to vary or determine the respective shares of members of the class (even to the extent of excluding some members altogether) provided the power is exercisable only in favour of a person under 25 who is a member of the class.'

This is also confirmed in similar terms by SP E1 which provides as follows:

'1. It is not necessary for the interests of individual beneficiaries to be defined. They can, for instance, be subject to powers of appointment. In any particular case the exemption will depend on the precise terms of the trust and power concerned, and on the facts to which they apply. In general, however, the official view is that the conditions do not restrict the application of IHTA 1984 s 71 to settlements where the interests of individual beneficiaries are defined and indefeasible.

2. The requirements of IHTA 1984 s 71(1)(a) is that one or more persons will, on or before attaining a specified age not exceeding 25, become beneficially entitled to, or to an interest in possession in, the settled property or part of it. It is considered that settled property would meet this condition if at the relevant time it must vest for an interest in possession in some member of an existing class of potential beneficiaries on or before that member attains 25. The existence of a special power of appointment would not of itself exclude s 71, if neither the exercise nor the release of the power could break the condition. To achieve this effect might, however, require careful drafting.

3. The inclusion of issue as possible objects of a special power of appointment would exclude a settlement from the benefit of section 71 if the power would allow the trustees to prevent any interest in possession in the settled property from commencing before the beneficiary concerned attained the age specified. It would depend on the precise words of the settlement and the facts to which they had to be applied whether a particular settlement satisfied the conditions of s 71(1). In many cases the rules against perpetuity and accumulations would operate to prevent an effective appointment outside those conditions. However the application of s 71 is not a matter for a

once-for-all decision. It is a question that needs to be kept in mind at all times when there is settled property in which no interest in possession subsists.

4. Also, a trust which otherwise satisfied the requirement of s 71(1)(a) would not be disqualified by the existence of a power to vary or determine the respective shares of members of the class (even to the extent of excluding some members altogether) provided the power is exercisable only in favour of a person under 25 who is a member of the class.

Annex to SP E1

Practical illustrations of IHTA 1984 s 71. The examples set out below are based on a settlement for the children of X contingently on attaining 25, the trustees being required to accumulate the income so far as it is not applied for the maintenance of X's children.

Example A

The settlement was made on X's marriage and he has as yet no children.

IHTA 1984 s 71 of Schedule 5 will not apply until a child is born and that event will give rise to a charge for tax under IHTA 1984 s 65.

Example B

The trustees have power to apply income for the benefit of X's unmarried sister.

IHTA 1984 s 71 does not apply because the condition of subsection (1)(b) is not met.

Example C

X has power to appoint the capital not only among his children but also among his remoter issue.

IHTA 1984 s 71 does not apply (unless the power can be exercised only in favour of persons who would thereby acquire interests in possession on or before attaining age 25). A release of the disqualifying power would give rise to a charge for tax under IHTA 1984 s 65. Its exercise would give rise to a charge under IHTA 1984 s 65.

Example D

The trustees have an overriding power of appointment in favour of other persons.

IHTA 1984 s 71 does not apply (unless the power can be exercised only in favour of persons who would thereby acquire interests in possession on or before attaining age 25). A release of that disqualifying power would give rise to a charge for tax under IHTA 1984 s 65. Its exercise would give rise to a charge under IHTA 1984 s 65.

Example E

The settled property has been revocably appointed to one of the children contingently on his attaining 25 and the appointment is now irrevocable.

If the power to revoke prevents IHTA 1984 s 71 from applying, (as it would for example, if the property thereby became made subject to a power of appointment as at C or D) tax will be chargeable under IHTA 1984 s 65 when the appointment is made irrevocable.

Example F

The trust to accumulate income is expressed to be during the life of the settlor.

As the settlor may live beyond the 25th birthday of any of his children the trust does not satisfy the condition in subsection (1)(a) and IHTA 1984 s 71 does not apply.'

9.7 There are a number of further requirements in order to qualify as an accumulation and maintenance trust. These are either that not more than 25 years have elapsed since the commencement of the settlement or since it became an accumulation and maintenance trust, or all the persons who are or have been beneficiaries are, or were, either grandchildren of a common grandparent or children, widows or widowers of such grandchildren who were beneficiaries but died before obtaining an interest in possession or an absolute interest in part of the trust property. [IHTA 1984 s 71(2)(a) and (b)].

Ceasing to qualify

9.8 Where settled property ceases to qualify under the accumulation and maintenance trust rules there is an IHT charge, as there is where the trustees make a disposition reducing the value of the settled property under the accumulation and maintenance trusts. [IHTA 1984 s 71(3)]. The charge to tax in such cases follows that of property leaving temporary charitable trusts, so that the charge is on the value of the property ceasing to qualify, depending on how long the asset has been in the trust, measured in quarters of a year. The rates under IHTA 1984 s 70(6) are:

(a) 0.25 per cent for each of the first 40 complete successive calendar quarters;

(b) 0.20 per cent for each of the next 40;

(c) 0.15 per cent for each of the next 40;

(d) 0.10 per cent for each of the next 40; and

(e) 0.05 per cent for each of the next 40.

This formula means that a charge to IHT on termination of the 25-year period would give rise to a tax charge at 21 per cent with no nil rate band, i e 40 quarters at 0.25 per cent + 40 quarters at 0.20 per cent + 20 quarters at

0.15 per cent. If the settlor does not survive the seven-year gift *inter vivos* period the trustees must deliver an account under IHTA 1984 s 216(1)(bb) and are responsible for paying the tax out of the trust assets.

9.9 There is no charge on ceasing to qualify where a beneficiary becomes absolutely entitled to part of the settled property, or to an interest in possession in it, on or before obtaining the specified age not exceeding 25, or on his death before obtaining that age. [IHTA 1984 s 71(4)]. Section 71(5) provides that there is no exit charge where the property ceasing to qualify is taxed as the beneficiary's income, or would be if he were UK resident.

Resettlement

9.10 In some cases it is found that the beneficiary is entitled to substantial amounts of capital at an early age and it may be sensible to consider resettling on amended trusts for that beneficiary, giving him an interest in possession but deferring the entitlement to capital, as being for the beneficiary's long-term benefit, following *Pilkington v IRC* (1962) 40 TC 416.

Maintenance, education or benefit

9.11 TA 1925 s 31 empowers trustees to apply income for maintenance and to accumulate surplus income during a beneficiary's minority. This is a form of discretionary trust under which the trustees may:

> '… during the infancy of a beneficiary, at their sole discretion, pay to his parent or guardian, if any, or otherwise apply for or towards his maintenance, education or benefit the whole or such part, if any, of the income of that property as may in all the circumstances be reasonable, whether or not there is (a) any other fund applicable to the same purpose or (b) any person bound by law to provide for his maintenance or education. If such a person, on attaining the age of 18 years, has not a vested interest in such income the trustees shall thenceforth pay the income of that property and of any accretion therefore to him until he either retains a vested interest therein or dies, or until failure of his interest.'

The trustees have to have regard to the age of the infant and his requirements and generally to the circumstances of the case and, in particular, to whatever income, if any, is applicable for the same purposes, with the intention, apparently, of spreading the costs of maintaining the infant among the available resources. During the infancy, the trustees accumulate any undistributed income until the beneficiary obtains the age of 18 years or marries under that age. Where the infant has a vested interest on attaining the age of 18 or marrying, the trustees hold the accumulations in trust for him absolutely. Otherwise the accumulated income is added to the trust fund but not so as to prevent the income being used for the maintenance, education or benefit of the child in the later year as if it were income arising in that year. [TA 1925 s 31(2)]. In the case of a contingent interest, which carries the intermediate income into an annuity as if the annuity were trust income, section 31(3) and (4) applies.

9.12 SP 8/86 confirms that the Revenue takes the view that undistributed and unaccumulated income of a discretionary trust should not be taxable as a trust asset and for the purposes of determining the rate of charge on accumulated income the income should be treated as becoming a taxable asset of the trust on the date when the accumulation is made.

Powers of appointment

9.13 An Inland Revenue letter of 8 October 1975 confirms that a special power of appointment would only exclude a settlement from qualifying as an accumulation and maintenance settlement if the power would allow the trustees to prevent any interest in possession in the settled property from commencing before the beneficiary concerned attained the age specified. It also confirms that qualification as an accumulation and maintenance settlement is an ongoing test, not a matter for a once and for all decision. It also confirms that beneficiaries do not need to be identified nor their interests to be quantified in the trust deed, much less equal. The Revenue also confirmed, in a Press Release of 24 September 1975, that where a beneficiary is entitled to income in accordance with TA 1925 s 31(1)(2) on attaining his majority, this would satisfy the provisions of IHTA 1984 s 71(1)(a).

Interest in possession

9.14 The reference to an interest in possession enjoyed by a beneficiary is to a present right to the present enjoyment of trust income, following *Pearson v IRC* [1980] STC 318.

Potentially exempt transfers

9.15 A transfer to an accumulation and maintenance trust has the distinct advantage of being a potentially exempt transfer (PET) under IHTA 1984 s 3A(1)(c) and FA 1986 s 101 and Sch 19 which means that no IHT is payable on the transfer of assets into an accumulation and maintenance settlement unless the settlor dies within a seven-year gift *inter vivos* period. [IHTA 1984 s 7]. It is common for the trustees to insure the settlor's life for the amount of IHT payable, taking account of the taper relief in section 7(4), during the gift *inter vivos* period of seven years. If the settlor's life is to be insured by the trustees, they should make sure that the premiums are charged to capital – as a payment of premiums out of income would not be for the maintenance, education or benefit of the beneficiaries and would not be an accumulation and therefore the trust would be inadvertently taken outside the definition of an accumulation and maintenance trust in IHTA 1984 s 71(1).

9.16 Where assets are being put into a discretionary trust within the nil rate band exemption, it may be worth considering whether the trust should be converted into an accumulation and maintenance trust before the first or next relevant ten-year anniversary. It is sometimes useful to nominate an accumulation and maintenance trust as the recipient of death-in-service life insurance under an occupational pension scheme in order to avoid wasting the spouse exemption. The trustees may use the proceeds to purchase at market value illiquid assets from the deceased's surviving spouse. Non-pension insurance policies may also be held by the accumulation and maintenance trustees.

9.17 To qualify as a potentially exempt transfer on the creation of an accumulation and maintenance trust, it is necessary for there to be an absolute gift to the trustees, not, for example, the payment of a life insurance premium or payment direct to the school for school fees on behalf of the beneficiaries.

Entitlement to capital

9.18 It is common in an accumulation maintenance settlement to provide for the beneficiary to obtain an interest in possession only in income at an age below 25 but not to obtain a right to capital at that time. In such circumstances if capital is subsequently distributed, so that the beneficiary becomes absolutely entitled as against the trustees, there is a disposal for CGT purposes under TCGA 1992 s 71 and it does not escape under section 260(2)(d) of the 1992 Act which only applies where the beneficiary becomes entitled to the capital and income at the same time under IHTA 1984 s 71(4). If it is intended that both the capital and income are distributed at, say, age 25 it is important to make sure that TA 1925 s 31 has been excluded, as otherwise the beneficiary would have a statutory entitlement to the income from age 18 and would not be entitled to the capital until age 25. Although there is no time limit on the duration of an accumulation and maintenance trust where all the beneficiaries are grandchildren of a common grandparent, in other cases the trust can only exist from 25 years from commencement under IHTA 1984 s 71(2)(a).

9.19 The CGT problem on beneficiaries becoming absolutely entitled at a later date is avoided where the trust assets are business or agricultural assets eligible for rollover under TCGA 1992 s 165. A beneficiary may also become absolutely entitled to income on the expiration of the permitted accumulation period under LPA 1925 s 164.

Temporary beneficiaries

9.20 Sometimes the requirement for a living beneficiary in an accumulation and maintenance settlement means that a cousin is included as a beneficiary, as there are no grandchildren yet born, but with the intention of benefiting the grandchildren. This is often known as a 'peg-leg' trust and because not all the beneficiaries are children of a common grandparent the 25-year limit applies, which means that it may be necessary to distribute the trust or resettle it prior to the 25th anniversary to avoid an IHT charge on the termination of the trust with no beneficiaries with an interest in possession. If instead of the cousin being a beneficiary a nephew or niece was appointed there would be a common grandparent and the intended beneficiaries could benefit with the peg-leg beneficiaries merely standing in until the intended beneficiaries are born.

Termination

9.21 The Termination of an accumulation and maintenance trust where there is an interest in possession will be exempt from a charge to IHT under IHTA 1984 s 52 by section 53(2) of that Act. A disposal of an interest in settled property escapes CGT under TCGA 1992 s 76.

Variation

9.22 The trustees may be given power to vary a beneficiary's share after he has taken an interest in possession. Although this would give rise to an IHT occasion of charge it would normally be a potentially exempt transfer by the beneficiary who is deemed to have an absolute interest in the asset under IHTA 1984 s 49. Where a beneficiary has attained an interest in possession, the birth of a beneficiary could reduce his share which would be an occasion of charge for IHT and would normally be a potentially exempt transfer.

9.23 The death of a life tenant would be an occasion of a charge to IHT. A resettlement by the life tenant on discretionary trusts would also give rise to a potential IHT charge. IHTA 1988 s 49 deems a life tenant to own outright the assets in which he has a life interest.

Chapter 10

Foreign Trusts

10.1 For the purposes of this chapter, a foreign trust is one where the trustees are resident outside the UK and the trust is administered outside the UK. The trust may be written under English law, but this would be unusual except where the trust has originally had an English trustee and has subsequently emigrated. In most cases the foreign trust will be written under the trust law of the overseas jurisdiction which may or may not differ from English trust law in material respects. In particular, the rule against perpetuities may not apply or the perpetuity period may be, say, 100 years. Similarly there may not be an accumulation period, or if there is one it may be materially greater than the 21 years allowed under English law, and often allows accumulation for the entire perpetuity period. Some civil law jurisdictions allow trusts by statute, although there appears to be little jurisprudence in such jurisdictions to show how the law is applied in practice. Most foreign trusts are therefore set up in common law-based jurisdictions, which are often colonies or dependencies of the Crown or the UK or previously came under the influence of the English legal system.

10.2 For UK tax purposes, the choice of a foreign jurisdiction is largely irrelevant but it is likely to be important for non-tax considerations such as:

(a) the powers of the trustees and any protector;

(b) the rights of the beneficiaries to enforce the trust;

(c) the right to obtain information; and

(d) the protection given to creditors or to the trustees against creditors.

What is important is that the trust is actually resident in the intended jurisdiction and that the trustees act as trustees making independent decisions for the benefit of the beneficiaries, with or without guidance from the settlor.

10.3 In some jurisdictions, particularly civil law jurisdictions such as Switzerland where a lot of trust administration is carried out, it is important for the trustees to recognise the difference between acting in a fiduciary capacity on the instructions of the founders of a foundation and acting independently as trustees with the advice of, but not following the instructions of, the settlor. In such cases it is often advisable to have at least one of the trustees in a common law jurisdiction. There is no reason why the trust should necessarily be administered in the same jurisdiction as the trustees making their decisions in the interests of the beneficiaries. It is not uncommon to have trustees based in more than one jurisdiction reaching their decisions by telephone or e-mail and communicating them to the administrators for implementation.

Proper law

10.4 The Hague Convention on the law applicable to trusts and on their recognition, of 10 January 1986, which was brought into UK law by RTA 1987, allows the settlor to choose the proper law of the trust which must be expressly stated in or implied from the trust deed. In the absence of a choice of proper law by the settlor, the trust is governed by the law with which it is most closely connected, which would appear to replicate the common law situation (*Perpetual Executors and Trustees Association of Australia Ltd v Roberts* [1970] VR 732; *Iveagh v IRC* [1954] Ch 364). The jurisdiction with which the trust is most closely connected depends on:

(a) the place of administration of the trust designated by the settlor;

(b) the *situs* of the assets of the trust;

(c) the place of residence or business of the trustees;

(d) the objects of the trust; and

(e) the places where they are to be fulfilled.

10.5 The law governing the trust can be changed either by the settlor reserving the power to change the applicable law, or by the trustees, under powers given to them by the trust instrument. Otherwise it may be necessary, in order to move the trust law out of England, to apply to the courts under VTA 1958. The court certainly has power to revoke the trusts of an English settlement and substitute those of a foreign settlement and appoint any foreign trustees (*Re Seale's Marriage Settlement* [1961] Ch 574; *Re Windeatt* [1969] 1 WLR 692). However, it may choose not to do so if it does not consider this to be in the best interests of the beneficiaries (*Re Weston's Settlements* [1969] 1 Ch 223).

Residence and domicile

Trustees

10.6 The rules which govern the residence and domicile of trustees, the settlor and beneficiaries are explained in Chapter 5, and the implications of these factors for UK tax purposes will become apparent from this chapter. The residence of trustees is of fundamental importance in determining their liability to income tax and CGT but the *situs* of assets and, in particular, whether they are in the UK or abroad may also have a bearing on the tax charge.

Settlor

10.7 The residence of the settlor is important in determining the application of anti-avoidance provisions, as is his domicile and, for IHT purposes, his deemed domicile, which itself is based on residence under IHTA 1984 s 267. A number of the anti-avoidance provisions do not apply to non-UK domiciliaries such as deeming the capital gains made by offshore companies or trusts to be those of the shareholder or settlor under TCGA 1992 ss 13 and 86.

Beneficiaries

10.8 A non-UK resident beneficiary is clearly not liable to UK taxation on non-UK source income and the tax liability on UK source income may be limited to tax withheld at source, if any. A non-resident beneficiary is also useful in managing the trusts of an international family because once income has been distributed to a non-resident it may no longer be available to be treated as the income of a UK resident beneficiary. It may also give the opportunity for a non-resident beneficiary to reallocate amounts distributed to him by, for example, resettling part of the funds for the benefit of resident beneficiaries. Obviously this cannot be achieved by conditional distributions to a non-resident beneficiary, because then he would be acting merely as nominee for the resident beneficiaries if he was required to resettle on trust for them. The domicile of a beneficiary can also be important because distributions to a UK resident non-UK domiciled beneficiary from an overseas trust in respect of overseas income may be taxable only on the remittance basis, and in the case of chargeable gains would escape tax entirely even if remitted to the UK under TCGA 1992 s 87(7).

Income tax

UK source income and gains

10.9 Merely because the settlor or trustees are non-UK resident and domiciled does not mean that there is no exposure to UK taxation, because UK source income such as rent will remain liable to tax, and where the trustees carry on a trade in the UK through a branch or agency, not only will the trading profits be subject to UK tax but assets used for the purposes of the trade will be subject to UK CGT under TCGA 1992 s 10.

Anti-avoidance provisions

10.10 One of the problems of dealing with foreign trusts is the complexity of the anti-avoidance legislation, which usually deems that which has not happened to have happened for taxation purposes, and this in turn leads to the question of when the deeming stops and the extent to which the effect of deeming is carried to its logical, or in some cases illogical, conclusion. *Marshall v Kerr* [1994] STC 638 is regarded as authority for the proposition that deeming is only carried through to the extent that it is necessary to achieve the anti-avoidance objective, or to allow the intended relieving provision to operate, without extending the effect of the deeming beyond its immediate purpose. In that case, a deed of family arrangement avoided CGT on the transfers resulting from the arrangement itself under TCGA 1992 s 62(6), on the basis that the reference to the section applying as if the variation had been effected by the deceased or, as the case may be, the disclaimed benefit had never been conferred, section 62(6)(b) did not mean that the deceased was the settlor when the assets were placed into trust as a result of the variation, it merely relieved the CGT that would otherwise have arisen as a result of the variation. This reasoning was followed in *De Rothschild v Lawrenson* [1995] STC 623, when it was held that a charge arose under TCGA 1992 s 87(2) on the amount on which the trustees would have been chargeable to tax if they had been resident or ordinarily resident in the UK, which was assessable on the beneficiary. It did not make the trustees themselves chargeable to tax under TCGA 1992 s 77, as that was confined to gains actually realised by the trustees, who were non-resident and would therefore have no such liabilities. Deeming the gain accruing to the beneficiary to be computed on the assumption that the trustees had been resident or ordinarily resident in the UK was merely the means of quantifying the chargeable amount which, under the anti-avoidance provisions, was then assessable on the beneficiary. The limitation of deeming in this way was approved in *R v Dimsey* [2001] STC 1520 at 1531.

Treaty non-residence

10.11 The deeming provisions are also important in the context of double taxation treaties, which may exempt actual income or gains in the hands of a resident of the treaty country from UK income tax or CGT, so that, for example, a UK domiciliary who moves to Belgium for a period and becomes resident there for treaty purposes may escape UK taxation on chargeable gains realised during the period of non-residence under the treaty, in spite of the fact that there may be no Belgian taxation on those gains. He would not be subject to tax on his return to the UK within five years, under TCGA 1992 s 10A, as the actual gains were treaty protected. If, however, he were a beneficiary of an overseas trust and gains were distributed to him which would have been chargeable under section 87 of the 1992 Act had he been UK resident, or if he was the settlor such that the gains would have been charged on him under section 86 had he been UK resident, there could be a charge on returning to the UK within five years under section 10A, as the gains deemed to be realised while non-resident would not be treaty protected as the treaty only protects actual income and gains (*Bricom Holdings Ltd v IRC* [1997] STC 1179).

Settlement code

10.12 The settlement provisions in ICTA 1988 Part XV, in particular ss 660A–689B, apply to foreign trusts as they apply to UK resident trusts, so that, for example, the settlor remains taxable where he has retained an interest in the settlement under section 660A, or where payments are made to an unmarried minor child of the settlor, the settlor is taxable under section 660B. The provisions relating to capital sums paid to the settlor in section 677, and via a company connected with the settlement under section 678, have no territorial limitation and apply to foreign trusts as well as UK trusts. These provisions are explained in some detail in Chapter 6.

10.13 It should be noted that where the settlor is not domiciled or not resident or not ordinarily resident in the UK in the year of assessment, he cannot be charged under the settlement provisions on income arising under the settlement if, had he received that income directly, he would not have been subject to taxation by reason of being non-UK domiciled, resident or ordinarily resident. However, if the income is remitted to the UK, which would have been chargeable had it been the settlor's own income, on the remittance basis, such remittances will be taxable under the deeming provisions of the settlement legislation. [ICTA 1988 s 660G(4)].

Transfers of assets abroad

10.14 Where the income is not taxable on the settlor under the settlement provisions in ICTA 1988 Part XV, it may be taxable under the transfer of assets abroad anti-avoidance provisions in Part XVII Chap III. [ICTA 1988 ss 739–746]. Section 744 provides that no income should be taken into account more than once in charging tax under the provisions of sections 739 and 740, so that income already taxed, e g under the settlement provisions, cannot be taxed again. However, where there is a choice as to the persons in relation to whom an amount of income can be taxed under section 739 or 740, the income can be taxed on any one of them or apportioned to more than one in such a manner as appears to the Revenue to be just and reasonable. [Section 744(1)(a)]. Such a decision is appealable to the Special Commissioners. [Section 744(1)(b)]. The income to be charged is restricted to the amount chargeable under section 739, 740 or 743(5), to the income arising, the benefit to the beneficiary or the amount of income giving rise to the benefit to the beneficiary, or the amount of income out of which the benefit is provided under section 744(2).

Charge on transferor

10.15 ICTA 1988 s 739 applies where there has been at any time a transfer of assets by an individual ordinarily resident in the UK as a result of which, either alone or in conjunction with associated operations, income becomes payable to persons resident or domiciled outside the UK. Income which has been subject to UK tax under the controlled foreign company legislation is excluded by sections 739 and 747(4)(b). In *IRC v Willoughby* [1997] STC 995 it was held to be necessary for the transferor to have been ordinarily resident in the UK at the time of the transfer, but the legislation was amended by FA 1997 s 81 in respect of income arising on or after 26 November 1996 and there is now no requirement that the taxpayer should have been ordinarily resident in the UK at the time when the transfer was made. [Section 739(1)(a)]. According to section 739(1A)(b), there is no tax avoidance motive required to bring these provisions into effect (*Carvill v IRC* [2002] STC 1167) subject to the possible motive defence under ICTA 1988 s 741 (see **10.36**).

10.16 In order for there to be a charge under ICTA 1988 s 739, the taxpayer must have the power to enjoy, whether presently or in the future, any income of a person resident or domiciled outside the UK which, if it were income received by him in the UK, would have been chargeable to income tax whether by deduction at source or otherwise. That income shall be chargeable on the taxpayer where it arises by virtue of or in consequence of the transfer of assets, either alone or in conjunction with associated operations. [Section 739(2)]. In IM 4620 the Revenue interpretation of these provisions is that any disposal of assets made at any time by the individual to a company, trust or other person abroad is a transfer of assets or, alternatively, an associated operation for the purposes of section 739. If all the necessary conditions are fulfilled the income of the foreign person is deemed to be that of the individual who made the transfer for all the purposes of the Income Tax Acts. Section 739 can potentially apply not only to an individual who transfers assets but to someone who is 'associated with' a transaction (according to the decision of the courts in *Vestey v IRC* [1977] STC 414). The Revenue regards this as including anyone who procured the transfer of assets (*Tax Bulletin*, Issue 40, April 1999).Where the same assets are transferred by several individuals, the Revenue practice is to assess the transferors in proportion to their share of the assets transferred. Thus where, for example, shares of a UK company are held by three shareholders in the proportion 40 per cent, 40 per cent and 20 per cent, and there is a section 739 liability in respect of the income of an overseas person to which the shares are transferred, the liability is assessed on each of the three shareholders in proportion to their respective holdings.

10.17 Where an individual receives, or is entitled to receive, any capital sum at any time, the payment of which is in any way connected with the transfer, or any associated operations, and income (as a result of the transfer directly or indirectly) becomes the income of a person resident and domiciled outside the UK (whether or not it would otherwise be chargeable to income tax), it is deemed to be the income of the transferor for all income tax purposes. [ICTA 1988 s 739]. Capital sum includes any sum payable by way of a loan or the repayment of a loan, and any other sum paid or payable otherwise than as income, except where the sum is paid for full consideration in money or money's worth. [Section 739(4)(a) and (b)]. The right to a capital sum includes the right of a third person entitled to receive it by virtue of the individual's direction, or by virtue of the assignment of his right. [Section 739(5)]. Income is not assessable on the individual under these provisions where the capital sum is a loan which has been repaid before the beginning of the tax year. [Section 739(6)]. Section 739 is one of the earliest targeted anti-avoidance provisions and it has given rise to many cases over the years.

10.18 In the leading case of *Lord Howard de Walden v IRC* (1941) 25 TC 121 an individual transferred a valuable asset to four Canadian companies for a series of promissory notes, which included an income element taxable under Schedule D Case V, as held in *Lord Howard de Walden v Beck* (1940) 23 TC 384. The charge under ICTA 1988 s 739 on Lord Howard de Walden was based on the entire income of the Canadian companies. An argument that he only had powers to enjoy a small proportion of that income was rejected, Lord Green MR commenting 'it scarcely lies in the mouth of the taxpayer who plays with fire to complain of burnt fingers'. A transfer of shares to a Canadian company controlled by the taxpayer for a series of promissory notes also enabled the Revenue to assess him on the entire income of the company in *Lee v IRC* (1941) 24 TC 207. Similar transfers to Canadian companies in return for debentures were successfully assessed by the Revenue under section 739 in *Cottingham's Executors v IRC* (1938) 22 TC 344; *Admiral Earl Beatty's Executors v IRC* (1940) 23 TC 574; and *Beatty v IRC* (1940) 23 TC 574. A transfer in exchange for a credit to a loan account led to a charge to tax on the company's income in *Ramsden v IRC* (1957) 37 TC 619.

10.19 In *IRC v Botnar* [1999] STC 711 a transfer to an overseas trust, which excluded the settlor from benefiting, was not sufficiently tightly drafted to prevent the trustees from resettling at some time in the future on another trust which could include the settlor, and there was evidence that this was indeed the intention. As a result the Revenue were able to tax the trust income on the settlor on the basis that he had power to enjoy the income. The sale of an interest in a partnership in return for debentures in a company led to the income of the company being taxed on the transferor's husband under section 739 in *Latilla v IRC* (1943) 25 TC 107. Other cases involving associated operations include *Corbett's Executrices v IRC* (1943) 25 TC 305 and *Aykroyd v IRC* (1942) 24 TC 515.

10.20 In spite of the title of ICTA 1988 Ch III Part XVII referring to the transfer of assets abroad, there is in fact no requirement for the transfer to be from the UK to overseas. The only requirement is the transfer of an asset, even to a UK resident, if as a result income becomes payable overseas (*Congreve and Congreve v IRC* (1948) 30 TC 163). This case was unusual in that the individual assessed had not made the transfer but had procured that it be made. In *Philippi v IRC* (1971) 47 TC 75 the taxpayer's father who was resident in the Republic of Ireland, had transferred UK securities to an Irish company the income for which was then taxed on the UK resident son under ICTA 1988 s 739.

10.21 The definition of assets involved in a transfer of assets is extremely wide. In *IRC v Brackett; Brackett v Chater* [1986] STC 521 an employment contract with an overseas company amounted to a transfer of assets, namely its rights under the contract, as a result of which the income of the company was assessed on the employee under ICTA 1988 s 739. A complex scheme involving the assignment of dividends was duly caught in *IRC v McGuckian* [1997] STC 908. In this case the intervening sale of dividends for a capital sum was disregarded as having been inserted for the sole purpose of gaining a tax advantage, applying the doctrine in *W T Ramsay Ltd v IRC* [1981] STC 174.

10.22 Where investments had been transferred to an overseas company, the costs of managing the company were disallowed in computing the income assessable under ICTA 1988 s 739 in *Lord Chetwode v IRC* [1977] STC 64, as there would not have been any allowance for managing the investments if they had been retained by the individual. Section 739 is extended to the wife or husband of the individual making the transfer by ICTA 1988 s 742(9)(a) but this does not include a widow (*Lord Vestey's Executors v IRC; Lord Vestey's Executors v Colquhoun* (1949) 31 TC 1). The Revenue originally argued that section 739 applied to beneficiaries of a trust set up by the transferor and had been successful in *Bambridge v IRC* (1955) 36 TC 313. This case was overruled, however, by *Vestey v IRC* [1980] STC 10, although it remains an authority for the definition of 'associated operation' within section 739(2). In the *Vestey* case the Revenue had argued that it was entitled to assess each of the beneficiaries of the trust on the whole of the trust income, although it would not normally do so. As a result, section 739 was extended by legislation to enable non-transferors to be assessed under ICTA 1988 s 740. A case where the Revenue failed to establish an associated operation on the transfer of investments to an Irish company was *Fynn v IRC* (1957) 37 TC 629 and a similar result was reached in *Herdman v IRC* (1969) 45 TC 394. Where the transferors do not control the company to which the assets have been transferred it was held that they did not have power to enjoy the income (*IRC v Pratt* [1982] STC 756). The power to appoint trustees is not, of itself, a power to enjoy the income of the trust (*IRC v Schroder* [1983] STC 480).

10.23 An argument that income was taxable under ICTA 1988 s 739(2) was not successful in avoiding a criminal prosecution for cheating the Public Revenue in *R v Dimsey* [2001] STC 1520 and *R v Allen* [2001] STC 1537. The potential criminal consequences of unsuccessfully trying to avoid tax through the use of overseas companies and trusts is illustrated in these cases and in *R v Charlton* [1996] STC 1418; *R v Hunt* [1994] STC 819; and *R v W* [1998] STC 550.

10.24 The basic provisions in ICTA 1988 s 739 are supplemented to confirm that income tax at the basic rate, the lower rate or Schedule F ordinary rate, shall not be charged under section 739 to the extent that income has already borne tax at that rate by deduction or otherwise, but apart from that the income is taxable under Schedule D Case VI. [ICTA 1988 s 743(1)]. This applies also to income chargeable under Schedule F which would have been assessed if it came from a foreign source and is chargeable under Schedule D Case V; it is a non-qualifying distribution on which Schedule F ordinary rate is deemed to have been paid under section 733(1) or 233(1A) or 233(1B), or a stock dividend under which Schedule F ordinary rate tax is deemed to have been paid under section 249(4), or is tax due on the release of a close company loan in respect of which ordinary rate tax is deemed to have been paid under section 421(1)(a). [Section 743(1A)]. In computing the tax due under section 739, the same deductions and reliefs shall be allowed as would have been allowed if the income deemed to be his had actually been received by him. [Section 743(2)].

10.25 A non-UK domiciliary is not chargeable to tax on any income deemed to be his if it would not have been taxed had it in fact been his income, ie if it had not been remitted to the UK where the remittance basis applies by reason of his non-UK domicile. [ICTA 1988 s 743(3)]. Where the deemed income has been taxed under section 739 and is subsequently received by the individual who is being taxed, it does not again form part of his income for tax purposes. [Section 743(4)]. Where an individual is taxable on a benefit under section 742(2)(c) as a result of a transfer which makes him liable to tax under section 739, the whole amount of the benefit is taxable except to the extent that it can be shown to have been derived from income already charged to tax, notwithstanding the credit for basic rate or Schedule F ordinary rate tax normally available under section 743(1) (*IRC v Botnar* [1999] STC 711). [Section 743(5)].

Associated operations

10.26 Associated operation for these purposes is defined by ICTA 1988 s 742(1) as an operation of any kind effected by any person in relation to any of the assets transferred or any assets representing, whether directly or indirectly, any of the assets transferred, or to the income arising from any such assets, or to any assets representing, whether directly or indirectly, the accumulations of income arising from such assets. As will be appreciated, this is an extremely wide definition. Cases on associated operations mentioned above include *Latilla v IRC* (1943) 25 TC 107; *Corbett's Executrices v IRC* (1943) 25 TC 305; *Bambridge v IRC* (1955) 36 TC 313; and *Congreve and Congreve v IRC* (1948) 30 TC 163 (subject to Viscount Dilhorne's comments in *Vestey v IRC* [1980] STC 10).

Power to enjoy

10.27 Power to enjoy income of a person resident or domiciled outside the UK includes income so dealt with as to be calculated at some point in time, and whether in the form of income or not, to enure for the benefit of the individual. [ICTA 1988 s 742(2)(a)]. Where the receipt or accrual of income increases the value to the individual of any assets held by him or for his benefit, he has power to enjoy within section 742(2)(b). Where the individual actually receives a benefit provided out of the income arising as a result of the transfer of assets he is taxable on the value of the benefit under section 742(c) (*IRC v Botnar* [1999] STC 711). The value of the benefit is the market value which, on the basis of the CGT cases of *Billingham v Cooper* and *Edwards v Fisher* [2001] STC 1177 would seem to be the amount which would be paid by the recipient of the beneficiary if he were in receipt of the benefit on arm's length terms.

10.28 In some cases the value of the benefit is readily ascertainable from the market, eg the rental value of a property or the cost of hiring a yacht or car or the benefit of an interest-free loan. In the Special Commissioners' decision of *IRC v Botnar* [1998] STC 38 concerning the rent-free occupation of a flat, under licence from the trustees, the value of the benefit was held to be the rent which the taxpayer would have had to pay on an arm's length letting. In other cases it may be far harder to find a market value – the benefit of having an Old Master on the wall is difficult to quantify. Many owners of such works lend them to museums and art galleries on the basis that the museum takes responsibility for the painting and makes sure that it is secure and in a properly controlled environment, but no rent is paid for its loan. If the trustees of an offshore settlement lent such a painting to the UK resident beneficiary on condition that the beneficiary insured the painting and provided a proper controlled environment and security it would be quite proper to argue that there was no taxable benefit under ICTA 1988 s 742(2)(c). The non-monetary benefit of the enjoyment of the painting is covered by the actual costs of the insurance and security measures required by the trustees. A similar argument would appear to be equally valid in the case of antique furniture, sculptures and other assets for which there is no rental market.

10.29 If an individual may, on the exercise or successive exercise of one or more powers, with or without the consent of another person, become entitled to the beneficial enjoyment of the income, he is taxable on it under ICTA 1988 s 742(2)(d). Although this is extremely widely drawn it can hardly mean that a discretionary beneficiary who has not benefited from a trust, but could if the trustees were to exercise their discretion in his favour, be taxed on the income of the trust as this would reintroduce the situation identified as unacceptable in *Vestey v IRC* [1980] STC 10. What it is aimed at is a situation where the trustees have power to appoint back to the settlor or to resettle for his benefit, as in *IRC v Botnar* [1999] STC 711.

10.30 If the individual is able to control the application of the income directly or indirectly he has power to enjoy it under ICTA 1988 s 742(2)(e). This was held to apply in the case of a taxpayer who had retained voting shares in a company (*Lee v IRC* (1941) 24 TC 207) but not to fiduciary powers as in *Lord Vestey's Executors v IRC and Vestey's Executors v Colquhoun* (1949) 31 TC 1 and *IRC v Schroder* [1983] STC 480.

10.31 It has been established by the courts (in Lord Howard de Walden v IRC *(1941) 25 TC 121*) that 'power to enjoy' the income of a person resident or domiciled outside the UK is not restricted to the income or benefit actually received. However, it has not been determined by the courts whether all the income of the overseas person should be assessed, or only the income of that person to the extent that it arose by virtue or in consequence of the relevant transfer of assets and any associated operation(s). It has been the Revenue's practice (since the decision in *Vestey v IRC* [1977] STC 414) to assess on the second of those two possible bases (*Tax Bulletin*, Issue 40, April 1999).

10.32 In determining whether an individual has power to enjoy income it is necessary to look at the overall picture, including the effect of the transfer and associated operations and the benefits which he might as a matter of practice enjoy. [ICTA 1988 s 742(3)]. Section 742(4)–(7) ensures that the liability under section 739 takes proper account of charges and allowances under the accrued income scheme by IM 4624. [Sections 710–728]. A number of terms are widely defined by section 742(9), such as references to an 'individual' including the spouse of the individual, 'assets' as including property rights of any kind, 'transfer' including the creation of such rights and 'benefit' including any payment of any kind. Spouse could include a future spouse (*IRC v Tennant* (1942) 24 TC 215), however unlikely the individual is to marry: *Unmarried Settlor v IRC* [2003] STC (SCD) 274.

Potential double charge

10.33 Where a company is incorporated outside the UK it is treated for ICTA 1988 s 739 as if it were resident outside the UK, even though it may be resident in the UK by reason of central management and control being in the UK. [ICTA 1988 s 742(8)]. It is quite common for non-UK domiciliaries to use non-UK companies to trade in the UK for IHT or CGT reasons, even though the company is managed and controlled in the UK and liable to UK corporation tax. It would seem therefore that the income of the company which was subject to UK corporation tax could also be taxed on the individual making a transfer under section 739. The Court of Appeal, in *R v Dimsey* and *R v Allen* [1999] STC 846, accepted that this potential double charge on the same income was possible under the legislation, although the courts might be invited to prohibit it as an abuse of power; in the House of Lords Counsel for the Revenue, in *R v Dimsey* [2001] STC 1520 *per* Scott LJ at 1530, confirmed that if the Revenue were seeking to recover income tax against a transferor on the basis of a foreign incorporated UK resident company under these provisions, credit would always be given for any tax that had been paid on the same income by the company. The courts, however, accepted that profits were liable both to corporation tax on the company and income tax on the transferor under section 739.

Charge on beneficiary

10.34 The extension of the transfer of asset provisions to non-transferors applies where, by virtue or in consequence of a transfer of assets, either alone or in conjunction with associated operations, income becomes payable to a person either domiciled or resident outside the UK, and an individual ordinarily resident in the UK, who is not subject to tax under ICTA 1988 s 739 by reference to the transfer, receives a benefit provided out of assets which is available for the purpose by virtue or in consequence of the transfer or any associated operations. [ICTA 1988 s 740(1)]. The amount of the benefit which is taxable is limited in the first instance to the income arising up to and including the year of assessment in which the benefit is received. [Section 740(2)(a)]. However, if the value of the benefit exceeds the available income the excess is carried forward and treated as income of the individual for future years, to the extent of the income that becomes available in future years. [Section 740(2)(b)]. Where there is no income in the trust because, for example, the only asset is property in the UK owned by the foreign trustees and occupied by the individual as beneficiary, there is no income to deem to be that of the beneficiary under these provisions in spite of the fact that he is in receipt of a benefit. If, however, the property were held through an overseas company of which the individual could be held to be a director or a shadow director, he could be taxed on employment income as receiving a benefit in kind under ITEPA 2003 ss 67, 97–113, 201–210 (*R v Allen* [2001) STC 1537).

10.35 The relevant income tax year of assessment is that in which the benefit is provided, and the assessment on the beneficiary is under Schedule D Case VI. [ICTA 1988 ss 742(3) and 740(4)]. A non-domiciliary is not to be taxed on any benefit not received in the UK if he would not have been subject to tax if he had received it directly, and not through the trust, on account of not being UK domiciled, ie if it would not have been a constructive remittance within ICTA 1988 s 65(5)–(9). [Section 742(5)]. Where a benefit is taxed on a beneficiary under the CGT anti-avoidance provisions in TCGA 1992 ss 87, 89(2) or Sch 4C para 8, he is treated as having been taxed on the benefit for the purposes of future income arising in the trust, which would otherwise be taxable on him under ICTA 1988 s 740(2)(b). [Section 740(6)]. For the purpose of this section, a transfer or associated operations can take place at any time, but it only applies to relevant income arising on or after 10 March 1981, when the legislation to catch non-transferors first became effective, following the Revenue's defeat in *Vestey v IRC* [1980] STC 10.

Non-tax-avoidance motive

10.36 It is possible, although often difficult in practise, to avoid the rigours of ICTA 1988 ss 739 and 740 by showing, to the satisfaction of the Revenue, that the purpose of avoiding liability to taxation was not the purpose or one of the purposes for which the transfer or associated operations or any of them were effected, or that the transfer and any associated operations were bona fide commercial transactions and were not designed for the purpose of avoiding liability to taxation. [ICTA 1988 s 741(a) and (b)]. Any decision of the Revenue on this is subject to appeal to the Special Commissioners. An argument that the avoidance of estate duty was not the avoidance of taxation failed in *Sassoon v IRC* (1943) 25 TC 154. By analogy it also includes the avoidance of CGT. The Special Commissioner rejected a case where 59 per cent of the shares in a UK company, held by a non-domiciliary, were transferred to a Bermudan company (*Carvill v IRC* [1996] STC 126). However, in a subsequent hearing relating to the same company the Special Commissioner, having heard further evidence, came to the conclusion that the transfers were bona fide commercial transactions within section 741(b) (*Carvill v IRC (No 2)* [2000] STC (SCD) 143). In *Beneficiary v IRC* [1999] STC (SCD) 134 it was held that the rearrangement of funds by a Japanese citizen transferring money to Jersey was legitimate tax mitigation, not tax avoidance, within section 741(a), relying on the distinction in *IRC v Challenge Corpn Ltd* [1986] STC 548. This distinction, however, was criticised in *MacNiven v Westmoreland Investments Ltd* [2001] STC 237.

10.37 A defence to a charge under ICTA 1988 s 739 or 740 by section 741 of that Act may not always be a good idea if the alternative leads to a CGT charge under TCGA 1992 s 87, which, because the gains had been rolled up within the trust, becomes subject to a surcharge as notional interest under TCGA 1992 s 91, which at current rates can increase the effective rate of tax from 40 per cent to 64 per cent.

Information powers

10.38 The Revenue is given wide powers to obtain information in connection with transfers of assets abroad by ICTA 1988 s 745. They may issue a notice requiring information to anyone, allowing a minimum of 28 days to respond. Attempts to avoid a notice failed in *Royal Bank of Canada v IRC* (1971) 47 TC 565 and in *Clinch v IRC* [1973] STC 155. The favourite recipients of these notices are banks, as the Revenue has apparently found notes made by bank managers in relation to offshore planning structures refreshingly informative. Solicitors are required only to confirm that they were acting on behalf of a client and to give his name and address and the name and address of any transferor and transferee for whom they have acted and a name and address of any body corporate which they have formed and similarly in connection with any offshore trust. [Section 745(3)]. The companies referred to are those which would be close companies if resident in the UK. Banks are not compelled to furnish particulars of ordinary banking transactions, but the onus of proof is on the bank to show that the transactions were such (*Royal Bank of Canada v IRC* (1971) 47 TC 565).

10.39 A notice under ICTA 1988 s 745(2) may require particulars as to transactions with respect to which the recipient of the notice has acted on behalf of others, whether or not any tax liability is thought to arise for the recipient of the notice, and whether or not the recipient of the notice has taken any part in any transactions of a description specified in the notice.

10.39A The Revenue and HM Customs and Excise are authorised to disclose information relating to the affairs of taxpayers to the authorities of another European Union state under the Mutual Assistance Directive 77/799/EEC, as amended by Council Directive 79/1070/EEC and 92/12/EEC or such amending or replacement provisions as are adopted after 16 April 2003, by FA 2003 s 197. The authorities must be satisfied that the overseas revenue have similar rules of confidentiality to those of the UK and that the information will only be used for tax or tax enforcement purposes by the other states. The mutual assistance provisions in VATA 1994 s 48 are redefined by reference to the Recovery of Taxes in Other Member states provisions in FA 2002 s 134 and Sch 39 and the Exchange of Information provisions in FA

2003 s 197. These may be amended by Treasury Order. Previous Exchange of Information provisions in FA 1978 s 77, FA 1978 s 17, FA 1993 s 22 and parts of FA 1990 s 125 are repealed and replaced by these provisions.

10.39B Exchange of Information provisions in double taxation treaties under TA 1988 s 788 and 815C and IHTA 1984 ss 158 and 220 are amended by FA 2003 s 198 to include any information foreseeably relevant to the administration or enforcement of the tax laws of either territory. The UK is also authorised to enter into exchange of information agreements with countries with whom they do not have double taxation agreements by TA 1988 s 815C and for inheritance tax by IHTA 1984 s 220A. The Revenue's information-gathering powers under TMA 1970 s 20 are extended to enable them to be used to provide information requested by another Competent Authority by FA 2000 s 147 and recovery of taxes in other member states is assisted by FA 2002 s 134.

10.39C The exchange of information among Revenue authorities in connection with taxpayers' affairs has increased substantially in recent years and is likely to continue to do so. Structures are only tax efficient if they will withstand scrutiny by the Revenue authorities in all relevant jurisdictions on the assumption that the full facts are known to the authorities.

10.39D The European Union made a Council Directive of 3 June 2003 on taxation of savings income in the form of interest payments (2003/48/EC 2003 STWI 1/2/05) which will be applied from 1 January 2005 (IP/03/787 STWI 3/6/03). The intention is that EU countries will exchange information on cross-border payments of interest and savings income to Competent Authorities within the EU. However Austria, Belgium and Luxembourg will instead levy a withholding tax for a period, and it is hoped that Switzerland, Liechtenstein, Andorra, Monaco and San Marino will agree to do likewise. FA 2003 s 199 provides the vires for regulations to be made to require paying agents to obtain information about the identity and residence of payees to whom they make savings payments, and to furnish this information to the Inland Revenue for submission to overseas Revenue authorities within the EU. The regulations will be made by Treasury Order and will allow Revenue inspection and will extend and replace the existing requirements in TMA 1970 ss 17 and 18. There will be penalties for non-compliance under TMA 1970 s 98. Paying agents include public officers and government departments.

10.39E The withholding tax arrangements for Austria, Belgium and Luxembourg are available for a period as a result of their banking secrecy laws, to avoid general disclosure of interest payments where competing jurisdictions outside the EU in Europe do not disclose, in order to avoid a flight of capital to the non EU jurisdictions. Switzerland already imposes a withholding tax and if the other countries do likewise there will be an effective alternative of paying a withholding tax or allowing disclosure of information to own country revenue authorities. Jersey, Guernsey and the Isle of Man allow the taxpayer either to suffer a withholding tax or to authorise disclosure. The ultimate aim is full disclosure worldwide but this may take several years to achieve. There may be money laundering disclosure aspects where taxpayers prefer to suffer withholding tax rather than allow the exchange of information.

Republic of Ireland

10.40 Residents of the Republic of Ireland may be brought within these anti-avoidance provisions by ICTA 1988 s 746 in respect of the grant of a lease at a premium, the charge on assignment of a lease granted at an undervalue and a charge on sale of land with a right to reconveyance under ICTA 1988 ss 34–36.

Offshore funds

10.41 Under ICTA 1988 s 761(7) the treatment of an offshore income gain from an offshore fund as income does not apply where the gain accrues to a non-resident trust, which means that it cannot be assessed as the settlor's income under ICTA 1988 s 660A where the settlor has retained an interest in the settlement. The provisions of TCGA 1992 s 86 do not apply to an offshore income gain because, in computing the capital gain, the offshore income gain is deducted. Any payment to a UK resident non-domiciled beneficiary may be paid to the beneficiary and may be remitted to the UK as it will not be chargeable in view of TCGA 1992 s 87(7). However, an offshore income gain could be assessed on a UK resident non-domiciliary under ICTA 1988 ss 739 or 740 as a result of section 762(5) of that Act, but if the capital payment is made in the same year as the capital payment is received by the settlor beneficiary there is no charge to tax under section 739 or 740 as the income has been received in the UK. [Section 762(6)].

Revenue interpretations

10.42 The Revenue interpretation of the operation of ICTA 1988 ss 739–746 was set out in *Tax Bulletin*, Issue 40, April 1999 as follows:

> 'ICTA 1988 ss 739–746 are anti-avoidance provisions aimed at certain transactions involving transfers of assets abroad. These notes provide guidance on how the Inland Revenue interpret various aspects of this legislation at the time of writing, in cases where the courts have not given a definitive interpretation of particular statutory wording.
>
> **Section 739**
>
> [see **10.16** and **10.31**]
>
> **Section 740**
>
> A non-UK domiciled individual who transfers assets but is outside the charge to tax under s 739 by virtue of the provision of s 743(3), is not assessed under s 740.

For the purposes of s 740(1)(b) a benefit is treated as not including either the giving of a life interest to a beneficiary or the receipt by a beneficiary of the proceeds of selling a life interest. But it is otherwise treated as including all benefits taken into account in determining whether an individual has power to enjoy income for the purposes of s 739. It therefore includes for example receipt of a loan at less than a commercial rate of interest, and the use of trust property at less than an open market rental.

For the purposes of s 740(3) the measure of "relevant income" is treated as not including such part of the income as has already been genuinely paid away to a beneficiary or to a bona fide charity.

Once relevant income has arisen and continues to be available to provide a benefit, it must in the Revenue's view be carried forward year by year until extinguished by such a benefit, even if it is capitalised in the accounts of the overseas person.

Section 741

The legislation places the onus on the taxpayer to demonstrate to the satisfaction of the Revenue that the conditions for relief under s 741 are met, or likewise to the satisfaction of the Special Commissioners in a case where the taxpayer has appealed against a decision by the Revenue that relief is not due. In either event the terms of s 741 in effect require the taxpayer to show that the transactions had a non-fiscal purpose, and did not also have a tax avoidance purpose. Where the taxpayer has been able to establish that at least one of the purposes for undertaking the transactions did not entail tax avoidance, the Revenue will regard it as incumbent on them to indicate why in their view tax avoidance may also have been involved. They will explain their reasons to the taxpayer, after considering fully all the documents submitted in support of his or her contentions, and will do so prior to any Special Commissioners' hearing.

Although it is sometimes referred to as a 'motive test', s 741 in fact refers to the 'purpose' of a transfer and any associated operations. Consequently, it is only the purpose of a transaction that the Revenue consider in applying the section. 'Purpose' is taken to be the end it is sought to achieve by the transaction. Furthermore, if a transaction involves tax avoidance, that is considered by the Revenue to be at least one of its purposes even if the transferor did not form the subjective intention of avoiding tax.

The law was amended in 1969 following a decision of the Courts (in *IRC v Herdman* ((1968) 45 TC 394) that only the transfer and any associated operations giving a power to enjoy at the outset were relevant for determining whether the terms of s 741 were satisfied. The amendment to the legislation sought to bring all associated operations into consideration when s 741 was invoked. Because of doubts expressed as to the effectiveness of this amendment, it has been the Revenue's practice in considering whether a defence under s 741 is available to consider only the transfer and any associated operations which directly establish a power to enjoy the income of the overseas person under any particular sub-head in s 742(2).

The role of advisers is taken into account in assessing the purpose of the transaction when considering the application of s 741.

The expression 'bona fide commercial' in s 741(b) is taken to apply only to the furtherance of trade or business, and not to the making or managing of investments.

The Revenue's view is that one of the essential conditions of s 741(b) would not be satisfied where there was a significant element of tax avoidance purpose in the design of the transfer and any associated operations.

Section 742

The wording of s 742(1) is interpreted as meaning that an associated operation does not necessarily have to take place after a transfer of assets. A transaction undertaken 'in relation to' a transfer of assets can precede the transfer.

Section 743

Unless transactions are part of a wider arrangement, Revenue practice is not to seek to assess a UK domiciled individual on the income of a non-UK domiciled spouse, where that income arises from a transfer of assets by that spouse and would be outside the charge to tax under s 739 by virtue of the provisions of s 743(3).

Where a non-UK domiciled individual transfers assets but is not chargeable to tax under the provisions of s 739 owing to s 743(3), there is no bar in the Revenue's view on the application of s 740 to others who did not themselves make the transfer but were beneficiaries of it.

Section 744

Where more than one person can be potentially assessable under ss 739, 740, the Revenue will seek to agree with the taxpayer under the terms of s 744 a "just and reasonable" division of liability.

Section 745

In the Revenue's view the introduction of a client to anyone responsible for establishing an overseas entity does not constitute the giving of professional advice to a client within s 745(3).

Miscellaneous

Where income could be fully assessed under both s 739 and the settlements legislation in ICTA 1988 Part XV, it will not in practice be charged under both. Similarly, income will not in practice be charged on both the beneficiary under s 740 and the settlor under the settlements legislation, where an assessment could in strictness be made on each of them in a case involving income that is accumulated within a discretionary offshore trust in which the settlor retains an interest, and then paid to a beneficiary as capital. However, in both cases this is subject to the proviso that the Revenue may sometimes raise alternative assessments, for example where a taxpayer has not provided full information. Moreover, where income arises in an offshore company underlying a settlement and the income is not paid up immediately to that settlement, the provisions of s 739 will be invoked where necessary to assess the income of the underlying company.

The Revenue's practice is only to allow trading losses in an offshore company to be carried forward to be offset against future trading profits of that company. They cannot be offset against investment income of the same, previous or future years.

Because of their complex and specialised nature the provisions of ss 739–746 are applied in individual cases by the Revenue's Special Compliance Office and (Centre for Non-Residents) (see Inspector's Manual IM 4622). It is incumbent on taxpayers or their advisers to draw the Revenue's attention to the implications of the legislation when submitting details of transactions to which it may potentially apply (in the light of the decision of the courts in *R v IRC ex p MFK Underwriting Agents Ltd* ([1989] STC 873).

Taxpayers are required to disclose clearly in their self-assessment return if there is any income or benefit assessable under s 739 or 740, and whether reliance is being placed on s 741 to exclude income or benefit from assessment. Where such a disclosure has been made and exemption under s 741 claimed, the Revenue will make any necessary enquiries about that exemption in the statutory period allowed, and will not seek to reopen that year's return on discovery grounds if the s 741 exemption has to be reconsidered in later years.'

10.43 Where an overseas trust is in receipt of income which has suffered UK tax where that income is assessable to a parent settlor on a distribution to minor children under ICTA 1988 s 660B, the Revenue will, by concession, allow a credit for the UK tax paid against the settlor's liability provided that the trustees have made trust returns giving details of all sources of trust income and payments made to beneficiaries for all years for which they are required and have paid all the tax due including any interests, penalties and surcharges and have retained the relevant tax certificates (ESC A93).

10.44 The Inspector's Manual (at IM 4622) illustrates some of the circumstances in which a report should be made to the Centre for Non- Residents (Audit and Compliance) where there is reason to suppose that a foreign entity including an overseas company, partnership or trust is being used for avoidance purposes. These are:

'… the taxpayer is found to have a direct interest in—

— an overseas company which may be a private company

or

— a foreign entity with no equivalent in English or Scottish law such as an anstalt, stiftung etc

or

— an overseas trust

or

1. any of the share or loan capital of a private company is held by an overseas trust or by an overseas company which may be a private company

2. the assets of a United Kingdom trust or of a private company are held by an overseas trust or by an overseas company which may be a private company

3. it is apparent that contracts have been made by individuals ordinarily resident in the United Kingdom for the provision of services to overseas companies and the purpose seems to be substantial avoidance of Income Tax by those individuals. In some instances contracts of service are with United Kingdom companies who subsequently assign the right to income arising from such services to overseas tax haven companies (see *IRC v Brackett* (1986) 60 TC 134)

4. returns show any income receivable by a company, trust etc abroad, resulting from a transfer of assets or the receipt of any payment or other benefit from such a source, or a taxpayer or his/her representatives voluntarily disclose liability under ICTA 1988 s 739 or ICTA 1988 s 740

5. a taxpayer (including a company or trust) is known to have acquired or transferred assets abroad from which no income or an abnormally low income is returned, or a taxpayer is known to have received a benefit, in cash or in kind, from an overseas source

6. income such as dividends or interest becomes payable by a person resident in UK to an overseas company, trust or foreign entity in circumstances which suggests that the payment is not for genuine commercial reasons

7. in particular, where in a self-assessment return it is disclosed that the taxpayer is relying on the provisions of ICTA 1988 s 741 (box 6.5A of Foreign Pages).'

Capital gains tax

Non-residents

10.45 Under TCGA 1992 s 2(1) CGT is normally confined to a person, which would include trustees, who is resident in the UK in any part of the year of assessment or during which he is ordinarily resident in the UK. This general rule is alleviated for non-UK residents coming to the UK who have not been resident in the UK during the immediately preceding five years or for temporary residents by allowing a split-year treatment, excluding gains made before arrival or after departure, under ESC D2. Temporary residents are those who have been neither resident nor ordinarily resident for the whole of at least four out of the seven years of assessment immediately preceding the year of departure. Non-residents using assets in a UK trade carried on through a branch or agency are still chargeable to CGT under TCGA 1992 s 10. A long-term UK resident who leaves the UK and returns with fewer than five years of assessment falling between the year of departure and the year of return, is liable to CGT on gains made on assets held at the time of departure and disposed of during the period of non-residence, under section 10A, where the taxpayer was resident in the UK at any time in a fiscal year on or after 17 March 1998. Non-UK domiciled individuals are not chargeable to CGT in respect of assets situated outside the UK, except to the extent that the gains are received in the UK. [TCGA 1992 s 12]. Remittances of the proceeds of capital assets sold at a profit are treated as part return of the original investment and part remitted gain on a proportionate basis. Constructive remittances are included by reference to ICTA 1988 s 65(5)–(9) by reference to TCGA 1992 s 12(2). Capital losses are disallowed by TCGA 1992 s 16(4).

Non-resident companies

10.46 Where a chargeable gain accrues to a company which is not resident in the UK, and which would be a close company if it were so resident, the gain which is not chargeable on the company because it is not resident is apportioned to a UK resident or ordinarily resident individual participator who is domiciled in the UK who is subject to CGT as if the apportioned part of the chargeable gain had been made by him. [TCGA 1992 s 13(2)]. The gain is apportioned by reference to the participator's interest in the company, normally the number of ordinary shares, but no gain is apportioned to a participator to whom no more than 10 per cent of the gain is apportioned [Section 13(3) and (4)]. Apportionment does not apply to gains on assets used by a company carrying on a trade wholly outside the UK or for a non-UK branch or on currency or debts used for the purpose of the non-UK trade or which are applicable to a UK branch or agency taxable under TCGA 1992 s 10(3). [Section 13(5)]. If the gain is distributed within three years, the amount of CGT paid on the apportioned gain can be set against the tax due on the distribution under section 13(5A) and (5B). The gain is computed in accordance with corporation tax rules under section 13(11A) and therefore taper relief is not available. [Section 13(10A)].

10.47 If not otherwise relieved, the CGT paid by the participator is allowed as an expense in computing his ultimate capital gain on the disposal of shares in the company under TCGA 1992 s 7, and the amount apportioned is treated as the highest part of his income or gains under section 13(7A) of the 1992 Act. Limited loss relief is allowed in arriving at the gain to be apportioned under section 13(8). Apportionment through a chain of companies is allowed by section 13(9). Where the participators are trustees who are neither resident nor ordinarily resident in the UK, gains may be apportioned to them where the shares are held either directly or indirectly through a chain of companies under secton 13(10). It is this provision which allows capital gains made by non-resident companies to be apportioned through to UK resident settlors or beneficiaries under the foreign trust apportionment rules in TCGA 1992 s 86 *et seq*, and which can result in a further charge on disposal of the shares in the underlying company which is a double charge, unless this is done within three years and apportioned to the same taxpayer to whom the original gain was apportioned, under section 13(10). [Section 13(5A)].

10.48 Gains are not apportioned if the participation is only sufficient to fall within the 10 per cent threshold as a result of including shares held by pension funds. [TCGA 1992 s 13(10A)]. Section 13(11) allows the non-resident company to pay the CGT on behalf of chargeable participators without it being regarded as a payment to the participator. Participator is defined by reference to the close company definition in ICTA 1988 s 417 and apportionment among participators by reference to their interests is covered in TCGA 1992 s 13(12)–(14) and any appeal is made to the Special Commissioners under section 13(15). The intragroup transfer provisions and company leaving a group provisions are extended to non-resident groups of companies for apportionment purposes by TCGA 1992 s 14. Delayed remittance relief under TCGA 1992 s 279 is not available to a participator where the company does not make a distribution of the gain (*Van Arkadie v Plunket* [1983] STC 54. In *Marshall v Kerr* the gains of the company owned by the trust, Brookside Investments Ltd, were apportioned through to the trustees and taxed on the settlor Mrs Kerr (*Marshall v Kerr* [1991] STC 686 at 692).

10.49 In terms of obtaining information about non-resident companies and trusts it should be remembered that the Revenue may serve a notice on any person holding shares or securities in a non-resident company to provide such particulars as the Revenue may consider are required to determine whether the company falls within TCGA 1992 s 13, and whether any chargeable gain has accrued to the company under TMA 1970 s 28. It has similar powers to require, by notice in writing, that any party to a settlement should furnish it with such particulars as are necessary for CGT purposes within such time as it may direct, being not less than 28 days. [TMA 1970 s 27].

10.50 Rollover relief available for gifts of business assets in TCGA 1992 s 165 does not apply to gifts to non-residents or to individuals treated as non-resident under a double taxation treaty. [Section 166]. Similarly, gifts to foreign-controlled companies are denied rollover relief by section 167. It is also denied where the transfer is to a dual resident trust, by section 169. The holdover relief normally available on a gift on which IHT is chargeable, typically a gift to a discretionary trust, is denied where the transferee is non-resident or an individual deemed to be non-resident under a double taxation treaty, by TCGA 1992 s 261, and for a dual resident trust. [Section 169]. Rollover relief in respect of gifts of business assets under section 165 or on which IHT is payable under section 260 is withdrawn on emigration of the donee within six years. [Section 168].

10.51 Where the non-resident company making the capital gain is resident in a treaty jurisdiction, the treaty may prevent the gain from being chargeable even though it would not be chargeable in any event under UK domestic law, and as such there would be nothing to apportion to participators, who are individuals. In the case of trustees who are participators, however, TCGA 1992 s 79B provides that nothing in any double taxation relief arrangements will prevent the attribution of gains by non-resident close companies to non-resident trustees under TCGA 1992 s 13(10).

Trust emigration

10.52 Where the trustees of a settlement become neither resident nor ordinarily resident in the UK, the trustees are deemed to have disposed of the trust assets and immediately reacquired them at their market value immediately before emigration, which would obviously produce a chargeable gain or loss within the CGT regime, chargeable on the trustees. [TCGA 1992 s 80(1) and (2)]. The assets deemed to be disposed of are all the assets constituting settled property of the settlement immediately prior to emigration, except for assets used in a trade carried on in the UK through a branch or agency which will continue to be so used after emigration of the trustees. Assets protected by a double taxation treaty are excluded from the emigration charge. [Section 80(3)–(5)]. The rollover relief for business assets under TCGA 1992 s 165 is excluded unless the new assets are situated in the UK and used for the purposes of a trade carried on by the trustees through a branch or agency. [Sections 165 and 80(6)–(8)].

10.53 Where the trust becomes non-resident because of the death of a trustee and a new UK resident and ordinarily resident trustee is appointed within six months, the emigration charge under TCGA 1982 s 80 is restricted to any assets disposed of while the trust is temporarily non-resident, or they become treaty protected. [Section 81(2)–(4)]. Conversely, if a non-resident trust becomes resident as a result of the death of a trustee and becomes non-resident within six months, normally on the appointment of another non-resident trustee, the deemed disposal is limited to any assets acquired during the period of temporary UK residence as a result of gifts to the trustees in respect of which rollover relief was claimed under TCGA 1992 s 165 or 260(3). Trustees are normally liable to CGT in the UK if they are resident or ordinarily resident in the UK in the fiscal year (SP 5/92 para 2).

10.54 The obvious problem the Revenue might have on a trust emigrating is that the UK resident trustees may have transferred all the assets to non-resident trustees, against whom the Revenue would find it difficult to enforce the collection of any tax due on emigration under TCGA 1992 s 80(2). Therefore if the tax is not paid within six months of when it became payable, the Revenue may, within three years of the determination of the final tax liability, serve notice on a former trustee of the settlement stating the amount of tax payable, together with interest, and requiring payment within 30 days. [Section 82(1)–(3)].

10.55 If, at the time a trustee ceased to be a trustee prior to the trust emigrating, there was no proposal that the trustees might become neither resident nor ordinarily resident in the UK, he may escape liability under section 82(3). A trustee who has to pay the tax may recover it from the emigrating trustees under section 82(4), and his right of recovery is not in any way chargeable upon him as a capital payment, a distribution from the trust or within ICTA 1988 s 739 or 740 and there are no IHT implications (SP 5/92 para 6). The payment, however, is not allowed as a deduction for tax purposes. The provisions only apply to a trustee who was acting as a trustee within twelve months prior to the emigration of the trust. [Section 82(6)]. The charge cannot be raised on a trustee who dies before the notice of liability has been served on him. The Revenue normally starts with the last serving UK resident trustee in order to hold him responsible but will then consider other trustees within the relevant period of twelve months ending with the emigration as necessary (SP 5/92 paras 4 and 5).

10.56 Trustees who are treated as non-UK resident under a double taxation treaty, so that gains on the disposal of trust assets are treaty protected, are deemed to have emigrated under TCGA 1992 s 83. Rollover relief on reinvestment of business assets is denied where the new assets are acquired by treaty non-resident, dual-resident trustees such that a disposal of the new assets would not be within the charge to UK CGT under section 84.

Interests in settled property

10.57 A disposal of an interest in settled property is normally exempt from CGT under TCGA 1992 s 76, as explained in Chapter 6. However, this exemption does not apply where the trustees are neither resident nor ordinarily resident in the UK. [TCGA 1992 s 85(1)]. Where the trustees cease to be resident in the UK and the trust assets are deemed to have been disposed of and immediately reacquired under TCGA 1992 s 80, and after the emigration there is a deemed disposal of the interest in the settlement created for the benefit of the beneficiary or otherwise acquired by him prior to the emigration, the gain on disposal is treated as if he had, immediately prior to emigration, sold the interest in the trust and immediately reacquired it at market value. This would have been an exempt disposal under section 76(1) and would effectively rebase the interest at the time of the trust emigrating. [Section 85(2) and (3)]. This rebasing does not apply where, prior to their acquisition, the trustees were treaty protected within sections 83 and 85(4).

10.58 In similar circumstances, but where the trustees became treaty protected after creation or acquisition of the interest in the trust, it is treated as having been disposed of and reacquired at market value when the trustees became treaty protected, within TCGA 1992 s 83. [TCGA 1992 s 85(5)–(9)]. Rebasing does not apply where, at the appropriate time, the interest was in a settlement which had relevant offshore gains chargeable on beneficiaries under TCGA 1992 s 89(2) or Sch 4C para 8(3). [Section 85(10) and (11)].

10.59 TCGA 1992 Sch 4C attributes gains to beneficiaries by TCGA 1992 s 85A. This Schedule applies where there was a transfer of value after 20 March 2000 (see below). [FA 2000 s 92(5)].

Attribution of gains to settlors

10.60 TCGA 1992 s 86 will normally deem the gains made by a non-resident trust to have been made by the settlor if a number of conditions are met. First of all the non-resident trust has to be a 'qualifying settlement' as defined by TCGA 1992 Sch 5 para 9, ie it qualifies to have its gains charged to the settlor. This applies to settlements created on or after 19 March 1991 for the year of assessment in which it was created and subsequent years of assessment. [Sch 5 para 9(1)]. A settlement created before 19 March 1991 is a qualifying settlement in 1999/2000 and subsequent years of assessment unless it is a protected settlement. [Sch 5 para 9(1A)]. A protected settlement is where the beneficiaries are confined to children of the settlor or of the spouse of the settlor, who are under the age of 18 at the time of the disposal, or who were under that age at the end of the immediately preceding year of assessment, unborn children of the settlor or spouse or of a future spouse, and future spouses of any such children. A future spouse of the settlor and other persons are outside the defined categories if there is no settlor by reference to whom they can be defined. [Sch 5 paras 9(10A) and 9(10B)]. The beneficiary of a settlement and various other terms are defined in Sch 5 para 9(10C)–(11).

10.61 A settlement created before 19 March 1991, which is a protected settlement at 6 April 1999, is treated as a qualifying settlement only if five conditions are satisfied. [TCGA 1992 Sch 5 para 9(1B)]. The first such condition is that property must be provided to the settlement on or after 19 March 1991, other than under an arm's length transaction or earlier liability incurred ignoring in most cases the trust expenses of administration or taxation [Sch 5 para 9(3)]. The second condition is that the trustees became non-UK resident or were regarded as such under a double tax treaty. [Sch 5 para 9(4)]. The third condition is that the terms of the settlement are varied on or after 19 March 1991 to include unacceptable beneficiaries, known as defined persons. [Sch 5 para 9(5)]. These are the settlor, the spouse of the settlor, the child of a settlor or of a settlor's spouse, the spouse of any such child, any grandchild of the settlor or the settlor's spouse, any spouse of such grandchild, a company controlled by such persons or a company associated with a company controlled by such persons. [Sch 5 para 7]. The close company definition of control and associates in ICTA 1988 s 416 is applied. [Sch 5 para 7(9) and (10)]. The fourth condition is that an unacceptable beneficiary enjoys a benefit from the settlement for the first time who would not have qualified as a beneficiary before 19 March 1991. [Sch 5 para 9(6)]. The fifth condition is that the settlement ceases to be a protected settlement at any time on or after 6 April 1999. [Sch 5 para 9(6A)].

10.62 These provisions are explained further in SP 5/92 paras 11–37. They are also referred to in the ICAEW guidance note of 14 December 1992 and

Tax Bulletin, Issue 8, August 1993 and Issue 16, April 1995. The remarkably easy procedure of inadvertently turning a pre-19 March 1991 protected settlement into a qualifying settlement subject to potential apportionment under TCGA 1992 s 86 is known as tainting. These guidance notes relating to non-resident trusts are reproduced in Appendix 2.

10.63 In addition to being a qualifying settlement, a non-resident trust has to fulfil further conditions before the chargeable gains are apportioned to the settlor. These are that the trustees are not resident or ordinarily resident in the UK during any part of the year, or are treated as such under a double taxation arrangement. [TCGA 1992 s 86(1)(b) and (2)]. The settlor must be domiciled in the UK at some time in the year and be resident in the UK during any part of the year or ordinarily resident in the UK during the year. [Section 86(1)(c)]. The deeming provisions therefore have no application where the settlor is non-UK domiciled or is non-resident or not ordinarily resident for the entire year.

10.64 The settlor has to have an interest in the settlement, which is a rather misleading test because it has a special meaning given to it by TCGA 1992 Sch 5 para 2. It applies where any defined person, as listed in **10.61** is or may become a beneficiary in any circumstances to property or income originating from the settlor, except on bankruptcy or death. [Sch 5 para 2(1)–(6)]. Various terms are defined and close company definitions adopted in Sch 5 para 2(7)–(10). The settlor is not treated as having an interest in a settlement created before 17 March 1998 merely because a grandchild or the spouse of a grandchild was a beneficiary, unless the settlement becomes tainted by, for example, adding property to the trust, the trustees becoming non-resident, varying the terms of the settlement to include a grandchild or allowing them to benefit for the first time after 17 March 1998. [Sch 5 para 2A(1)–(10)].

10.65 In essence, a trust created prior to 17 March 1998 for the benefit of grandchildren, which remains untainted, is not subject to deeming within TCGA 1992 s 86 during the minority of the beneficiaries. For the deeming provisions to apply there must be gain which would be chargeable were the trust to be resident in the UK. [Section 86(1)(e) and (3)]. All of these provisions have to apply before the trust gains are deemed to be those of the settlor, and the provisions must not be prevented from applying by Sch 5 paras 3–5, [Section 86(1)(f)], ie where the settlor dies in the year, where beneficiaries include former spouses of the settlor, child or grandchild, or where the defined person tainting the trust dies in the year. [Sch 5 paras 3–5].

10.66 Where TCGA 1992 s 86 applies, chargeable gains calculated on the basis that the trust was resident in the UK, are treated as accruing to the settlor as the highest part of the gains on which he is chargeable to CGT. [Section 86(4)]. Taper relief is taken into account in computing the trust gains but no further taper relief is allowed to the settlor to whom they are deemed to accrue. [Section 86(4A)]. The settlor is defined as a person from whom trust property originated, and the meaning of originating is explained as property directly or indirectly provided by the settlor or under a reciprocal arrangement, or by a qualifying company controlled by the settlor. [TCGA 1992 Sch 5 paras 7 and 8]. A qualifying company is a close company, or would be if it were resident in the UK, under the close company definitions of control etc in ICTA 1988 ss 416–417.

10.67 The basis of computing the chargeable gains deemed to have accrued to the settlor ignores the annual exempt amount in TCGA 1992 s 3, and the charge on a resident trust where the settlor has an interest, and his right of recovery, in TCGA 1992 ss 77–79. [TCGA 1992 Sch 5 para 1(1)]. Losses may be set against capital gains in accordance with TCGA 1992 s 2(2) including losses that would otherwise be disallowed to a non-resident under TCGA 1992 s 16(3). [Sch 5 para 2]. Gains or losses of companies apportioned to the participators under TCGA 1992 s 13 are included in the gains deemed to be those of the settlor. [Schedule 5 para 1(3)]. Gains from treaty protected assets are excluded by Sch 5 para 1(4).

10.68 Where the conditions necessary for the attribution of chargeable gains to the settlor did not apply in an earlier year, losses brought forward are excluded by TCGA 1992 Sch 5 paras 5 and 6. Pre-19 March 1991 losses are disallowed by Sch 5 para 1(7). Treaty protected assets are defined by Sch 5 para 1(8) and (9).

10.69 Where CGT is assessed on the settlor under these provisions, and paid by him, he has a right of recovery of the tax from the trustees and may require from the Revenue a certificate specifying the amount of the chargeable gains and the amount of tax paid, as conclusive evidence of those facts to confirm his right of recovery. [TCGA 1992 Sch 5 para 6]. However, although the right of recovery is clearly stated it is difficult to see how this can be enforced by the settlor against trustees in a foreign jurisdiction when, as will normally be the case, he is excluded from benefit under the trust and UK tax legislation is unlikely to be binding on the trustees. Many well drafted trusts will actually include a clause allowing the non-resident trustees to pay unenforceable tax liabilities payable in such circumstances. If reimbursement is made to the settlor the Revenue has confirmed that there are no adverse UK tax consequences on him as a result of his being reimbursed (SP 5/92 paras 7–10).

10.70 If the trust is written under English law, the trustees may have a better argument for reimbursing the settlor, although under *Government of India v Taylor* [1955] AC 491 it is difficult to see how – if the Revenue could not require the trustees to pay the tax under UK tax law, if they were so liable – a settlor can exercise the right of indemnity that is also based on UK tax law. If the trustees were to indemnify the settlor in accordance with these provisions it might well be sensible for them to seek a counter indemnity against any action by beneficiaries, binding against the settlor and his estate, in order to avoid possible personal liability if a beneficiary were to object to the trustees' actions needlessly depleting the trust fund. This is particularly relevant where there are minor beneficiaries who cannot approve the trustees' reimbursement of the settlor.

10.71 The Revenue may, by notice, require a person who is, or has been, a trustee or beneficiary to provide information in connection with the settlement for the purposes of TCGA 1992 s 86 and Sch 5, within a specified period of not less than 28 days. [Sch 5 para 10]. There are also general information gathering powers in connection with settlements with a foreign element under Sch 5A.

10.72 In order for gains to be chargeable on the settlor he must be resident or ordinarily resident in the UK during the year. [TCGA 1992 s 86(1)(c)]. However, if he has left the UK since 17 March 1998 and returned within five complete fiscal years, he may be liable to CGT on his return under TCGA 1992 s 10A. While the settlor is non-resident and section 86 does not apply to attribute gains to him, there could have been capital payments made to beneficiaries taxed on them under section 87. If these exceed the 's 87 pool' at the end of the year of departure, in other words if the gains during the non-residence of the settlor have been taxed on the beneficiaries, the tax so paid, as determined under section 86A(1)(b), is deducted from the amount chargeable on the settlor on his return. [Section 86A(2)]. In order to reduce the section 86 charge on the settlor on return the gains have actually to be chargeable to tax on the beneficiaries, so that, for example, a capital payment to a non-domiciled beneficiary, exempt from charge under section 87(7), would not reduce the charge on the settlor on his return. [Section 86A(3)]. The 's 87 pool' is calculated in accordance with section 86A(4) and (5) and, to the extent that the settlor is charged under TCGA 1992 s 10A on his return, there is a corresponding reduction in the amount of the s 87 pool carried forward. [Section 86A(6)–(8)].

Attribution of gains to beneficiaries

10.73 Prior to 1981, capital gains distributed from an overseas trust to beneficiaries where not taxable on them. However, from 10 March 1981 where the settlor was resident and domiciled in the UK, trust gains could be taxable on the beneficiaries. [TCGA 1992 s 87(10)]. Where the settlor was not resident or domiciled in the UK, however, there was no charge to tax on beneficiaries in respect of capital gains made by an overseas trust until 17 March 1998. Gains made by the offshore trust on and after that date may be taxed as capital gains on the beneficiaries when distributed to them in the same way as gains from trusts set up by a UK resident and domiciled settlor. [FA 1998 s 130 (4)]. Where beneficiaries are not domiciled in the UK, however, no tax is charged on capital payments, whether these are brought to the UK or not. [TCGA 1992 s 87(7)].

10.74 Basically the attribution of gains to beneficiaries applies where the trustees of the settlement are not resident or ordinarily resident in the UK, and the trust gains are not attributed to the settlor under TCGA 1992 s 86. [Section 87(1)]. For each year of assessment it is necessary to compute the capital gains made by the trustees as if they were resident in the UK, and that amount together with gains for earlier years since 10 March 1981, or where the settlor was non-UK resident and domiciled, 17 March 1998, are referred to as the trust gains for the year of assessment. [TCGA 1992 s 87(2) and (10); FA 1998 s 130(4)]. Trust gains for the year are reduced by any amounts chargeable on the settlor under TCGA 1992 s 86(4) by section 87(3) of that Act. The trust gains for the year of assessment, as defined by section 87(2), are taxed on beneficiaries who have received capital payments in the year of assessment, or in any earlier year. [Section 87(4)]. It is therefore not possible to make a payment to a beneficiary out of capital and then realise a gain in a subsequent year of assessment, because it then becomes taxable on the beneficiary by reference to the earlier capital payment. A capital payment for these purposes means any payment not chargeable to income tax or, in the case of a non-resident, any payment received otherwise than as income. [TCGA 1992 s 97(1)(a)]. It does not include a payment under an arm's length transaction. [Section 97(1)(b)]. A payment includes a transfer of assets. [Section 97(2)].

10.75 A capital payment to a beneficiary may also be a capital payment taxable as income arising from a transfer of assets under ICTA 1988 s 740. Up to the amount of available income in the year of assessment, a capital payment to a beneficiary is taxable under section 740 as income and not charged as a capital gain. [TCGA 1992 s 97(3)(b)]. Any excess over the available income then becomes a capital payment for capital gains purposes under section 97(1)(a). If there is further income in a subsequent year this would normally be taxed on the recipient of the capital payment received previously under ICTA 1988 s 740(2)(b), but to the extent that it has already been allocated to beneficiaries as a capital payment for CGT purposes under TCGA 1992 s 87(4) it will not again be subject to tax as income under section 740(2)(b) of the 1988 Act as a result of section 740(6).

10.76 Where the capital payment is made by way of a loan, or is not an outright payment of money, it is treated as a capital payment equal to the value of the benefit conferred by it, eg a market rate of interest in the case of an interest-free loan (*Billingham v Cooper; Edwards v Fisher* [2001] STC 1177). A capital payment can be received directly or indirectly. [TCGA 1992 s 27(5)]. Losses made by the trustees are taken into account under section 27(6). The income tax definition of settlor and settlement in ICTA 1988 s 660G(1) and (2) are applied for capital gains purposes by TCGA 1992 s 97(7) and a beneficiary is a person who benefits from the settlement, other than the trustees. [Section 97(8)–(10)].

10.77 Chargeable gains are allocated to beneficiaries in proportion to the capital payments received by them but cannot exceed such payments. [TCGA 1992 s 87(5)]. A capital payment is not included again where it has already been treated as accruing to the beneficiary in an earlier year. [Section 87(6)]. A trust created by will or intestacy is treated as made at the time of death. [Section 87(9)]. The charge on a settlor with an interest in the settlement, which applies to a UK resident trust under TCGA 1992 ss 77–79 is ignored for the purpose of computing the trust gains attributable to beneficiaries under section 87(2). [Section 87(8)].

Taper relief

10.78 Taper relief is deducted in computing the trust gains of the trustees under TCGA 1992 s 2A and is therefore not again allowable to beneficiaries charged under these provisions. [TCGA 1992 s 87(6A)]. Where the trusts are dual resident but treated under a double taxation treaty as resident outside the UK, the provisions relating to the attribution of gains to beneficiaries in section 87 are applied by section 88(1) and (2). The charge is computed as if the double taxation relief did not apply, except to the extent that it relates to protected assets specifically exempted from charge under the treaty. [Section 88(3)–(5)].

Migrant settlements

10.79 A migrant settlement is one where a trust is resident in the UK for a period and then becomes non-resident. Capital payments received by a beneficiary in the resident period are not chargeable under TCGA 1992 s 87, unless made in anticipation of a disposal made by the trustees in the non-resident period. [TCGA 1992 s 89(1)]. Where a non-resident period is succeeded by a resident period, and the trust gains in the non-resident period have not been wholly charged on the beneficiaries, they will be chargeable on the beneficiaries when distributed under section 87. [Section 89(2) and (3)].

10.80 It is not possible to avoid the attribution of gains to beneficiaries rules by the simple expedient of resettling, because where assets are transferred from a transferor settlement to a transferee settlement the trust gains for the year of the transferee settlement are increased by the trust gains for the year of the transferor settlement or a proportionate part where there is partial resettlement. [TCGA 1992 s 90(1)(a)]. A similar transfer takes place where the transfer is to a migrant settlement, where a non-resident period is succeeded by a resident period. [Section 90(1)(b)]. Even if TCGA 1992 s 89(2) does not apply, eg because the trust is a UK resident trust, the transferee settlement is nonetheless deemed to have taken over the trust gains of the transferor settlement under section 90(1)(c). The trust gains are those not already charged to beneficiaries under section 87(4) or 89(2). [Section 90(2) and (3)]. The purchase of an interest in a settlement for consideration in money or money's worth is not within these provisions. [Section 90(4)].

10.81 Where the anti-flip-flop scheme provisions in TCGA 1992 Sch 4B apply there is no charge under TCGA 1992 s 90(5), which was intended to prevent a double charge to tax. However, where a non-resident trust has substantial realised gains, known as stockpiled gains, it can enter into a linked borrowing under which funds are advanced to a new trust to bring it within Sch 4B, and flip-flop the stockpiled gains into the new trust, which are excluded from being trust gains of the transferee settlement by section 90(5). Any unrealised gains will be caught by the proposed transfer unless any further avoiding action is possible.

Surcharge in lieu of interest

10.82 A problem arises where an offshore settlement has realised chargeable gains over several years and not distributed them to beneficiaries, perhaps merely because the beneficiaries have no need of further funds at that time. If the trustees make a capital payment in respect of gains arising in an earlier year of assessment and under the matching rules in TCGA 1992 ss 92–95 the beneficiary is charged to tax under section 87 or 89(2), the tax is payable not merely at the beneficiary's highest rates of CGT but is subject to a surcharge. [TCGA 1992 s 91(1) and (2)]. This surcharge is the amount equal to interest at 10 per cent per annum on the tax in relation to a chargeable period. [Section 91(3)]. A chargeable period begins on the later of 1 December in the year of assessment in the year in which the gain was made by the trust, or 1 December falling six years before 1 December in the year of assessment following that in which the capital payment is made. [Section 91(4) and (5)]. However, under section 91(1)(c) a capital payment is matched with the qualifying amount falling before the immediately preceding year of assessment to the one in which the payment is made and if, therefore, it is made before the end of the fiscal year following that in which the gain arises, no interest charge arises. [Sections 91(5)(b)].

10.83 The maximum surcharge is six years at 10 per cent of the tax currently at 40 per cent, ie a maximum surcharge of 24 per cent, making the effective rate up to 64 per cent. If CGT rates change there is a cap, in that the tax and surcharge cannot exceed the amount of the capital payment. [TCGA 1992 s 91(3)]. The percentage surcharge may be altered by statutory instrument. [Section 91(6) and (7)]. The matching rules in TCGA 1992 ss 92–95 apply. The qualifying amount for 1992/93 and subsequent years of assessment is the net chargeable gain made by the trustees for the fiscal year, as if the trustees had been UK resident, under TCGA 1992 s 87(2).

10.84 For 1990/91 and 1991/92 the qualifying amount is equal to the trust gains for the year, ie the cumulative trust gains from 6 April 1981 less distributions to beneficiaries. [TCGA 1992 s 92(2)]. Where capital payments are made to beneficiaries on or after 6 April 1991, the payments are matched with qualifying amounts in the settlement for 1990/91 onwards. [Section 92(3)].

10.85 Earlier payments are matched with earlier qualifying amounts, ie on a first-in, first-out basis, and excess payments are carried forward to be matched with future trust gains. [TCGA 1992 s 92(4)(a) and (b)]. A payment of less than the qualifying amount is matched to the extent of the payment and the balance is carried forward. A payment in excess of an unmatched amount shall be matched with other unmatched amounts. Where only part of the capital payment is taxable, eg because it is distributed to a non-domiciled beneficiary and is therefore exempt under TCGA 1992 s 87(7), it is not matched until other capital payments made in the same year of assessment have been matched. [Section 92(5)].

10.86 A capital payment made in one fiscal year in favour of a non-UK domiciled beneficiary who may be resident in the UK, can be used to clear out the gains so that on subsequent distributions, chargeable UK resident beneficiaries would not, in the first instance, have any gains matched against their capital distribution although any future gains could be so matched under TCGA 1992 s 92(4)(b). The matching rules need to be modified where a capital payment is made and charged to tax on the beneficiary and is matched with qualifying amounts for different years of assessment. Such a capital payment is treated as split into subsidiary payments, each of which is matched with the qualifying amount for each year on a just and reasonable basis in whole or in part. [TCGA 1992 s 93].

10.87 Where all or part of the settled property is to be transferred from a transferor settlement to a transferee settlement, any unmatched balance from the transferor settlement is treated as part of the transferee settlement's qualifying amount. Apportionments are made as necessary on a just and reasonable basis. [TCGA 1992 s 94]. Matching in these circumstances is made in the transferee settlement by reference to the state of affairs existing immediately before the beginning of the year of assessment in which the transfer is made, ignoring the transfer, and thereafter payments are matched with qualifying amounts in the transferee settlement and transferred from the transferor settlement. [TCGA 1992 s 95].

Capital payments from connected companies

10.88 Where a capital sum is received from a qualifying company controlled by the trustees, it is treated as received directly from the trustees for the purposes of the attribution of gains to beneficiaries. [TCGA 1992 s 96(1)]. A qualifying company is a close company or one which would be if it were resident in the UK. [Section 96(6)]. It is controlled by the trustees of a settlement if it is controlled by the trustees alone or together with the settlor or a person connected with him. [Section 96(7) and (8)]. Where the recipient is a non-resident qualifying company that would have been a close company had it been resident, and it is controlled by a person resident or ordinarily resident in the UK, the capital sum is treated as a capital payment received by that person. [Section 96(2), (3) and (9)]. A person is resident in the UK if the year of assessment is an intervening year while he is temporarily non-UK resident for the purposes of TCGA 1992 s 10. [Section 96(9A) and (9B)]. Where the company is controlled by two or more persons, if one of them is resident or ordinarily resident in the UK it is treated as a capital payment received by that person and if two or more of them are so resident it should be treated as separate capital payments received by each of them, quantified on a just and reasonable basis. [Section 96(4) and (5)]. The close company provisions in ICTA 1988 ss 416 and 417 are used for these provisions. [Section 96(10)].

Information powers

10.89 The Revenue may obtain information for the attribution of gains from overseas trusts by requiring any person to furnish them, within a period of not less than 28 days, such particulars as it thinks necessary. [TCGA 1992 s 98(1)]. The income tax information gathering powers in ICTA 1988 s 745 were imported by section 98(2). Further information powers are contained in TCGA 1992 Sch 5A introduced by section 98A. These additional information provisions apply from 3 May 1994. [TCGA 1992 Sch 5A para 1]. Where a settlement was created before 17 March 1998 and further assets are transferred to it, and the trustees are not resident or ordinarily resident in the UK, the transferor must, within twelve months, deliver a return to the Revenue identifying the settlement and specifying the property transferred, the day on which it was made and the consideration, if any, for the transfer. [Sch 5A para 2]. Where the trust is created on or after 3 May 1994 with non-resident trustees, a UK domiciled and resident or ordinarily resident settlor must, within three months of the creation of the settlement, inform the Revenue of the name and address of the person delivering the return and names and addresses of the trustees. [Sch 5A para 3]. Where the settlement is created on or after 19 March 1991 with non-resident trustees, a settlor who subsequently becomes domiciled and resident in the UK must, within twelve months of so becoming, give particulars to the Revenue of the date on which the settlement was created, the name and address of the person delivering the return and the names and addresses of trustees. [Sch 5A para 4].

10.90 Where the trustees of the settlement become neither resident nor ordinarily resident in the UK, or are deemed to be so under a double taxation treaty, a trustee immediately prior to the trust becoming non-resident must, within twelve months of that date, inform the Revenue of the date on which the settlement was created, the name and address of the settlor and the names and addresses of the trustees. [TCGA 1992 Sch 5A para 5]. Information is not required if it has already been submitted to the Revenue. [Sch 5A para 6].

Flip-flop schemes

10.91 The straightforward flip-flop scheme was usually one where the settlor, and/or his children, were beneficiaries of a non-resident trust with substantial assets. The trustees would borrow an amount equal to practically the whole of the value of the trust fund and advance the money to a new UK settlement in which the original beneficiaries would be beneficiaries. The class of beneficiaries in the offshore settlement would be changed to exclude defined persons under TCGA 1992 Sch 5 para 2(3), ie the settlor and his immediate family, and appoint, for example, a sibling or cousin or parents of the settlor, who are not defined persons, as beneficiaries. In the next fiscal year the trustees would sell the assets and repay the borrowing. The overseas trust would no longer be a qualifying trust within TCGA 1992 s 86, having no beneficiaries who were defined persons, and therefore the gains would not be deemed to be those of the settlor. As the assets were sold to repay the loan there would be no material net assets available to make capital payments to beneficiaries, which would be caught under section 87. The value in the original trust would therefore end up in the new UK trust as free capital, which in due course could be distributed to beneficiaries free of CGT, provided that the courts, in due course, hold that the scheme worked. The first such case was successful before the Special Commissioners in *Tee v Inspector of Taxes* [2002] STC (SCD) 370, but this decision was overturned by the High Court in *West v Trennary* [2003] EWHC 676 (Ch), [2003] STC 580.

10.92 Although in most cases the flip-flop involved a non-UK settlement, the anti-avoidance provisions introduced by TCGA 1992 s 76B and Sch 4B apply to UK settlor interested settlements under TCGA 1992 s 77, as well as non-resident settlements where gains may be attributed to the settlor, or the beneficiaries on making capital distributions to them under TCGA 1992 ss 86 and 87, and there is a transfer of value linked with trustee borrowings. In such a case the trustees are treated as disposing of, and immediately reacquiring, the whole or a proportion of each of the chargeable assets that remain within the settlement. [Sch 4B para 1]. The trustees are deemed to make a transfer of value if they lend money or transfer assets for no consideration or issue a security for no consideration. [Sch 4B para 2]. Where the settlement is within section 77, 86 or 87 it falls within these provisions. [Sch 4B para 3]. See also Tax Bulletin, Issue 66, August 2003, pages 1048–1051 (Appendix 3).

10.93 Trustees are treated as borrowing if money or any other assets are linked to them, or an asset is transferred to them and the trustees incur a contractual obligation to restore or transfer to any person that or any other asset. The proceeds of the borrowing are, in the case of a loan, the market value of the asset and in the case of a transfer the market value reduced by any consideration received from it immediately before the loan is made or the transfer effected. [TCGA 1992 Sch 4B para 4]. A transfer of value by the trustees is linked with the trustee borrowing, as these terms are defined, if at the time of the transfer of value (the material time) there is an outstanding trustee borrowing. [Sch 4B paras 2(2) and (5)].

10.94 There is an exemption for the proceeds of borrowing for normal trust purposes in respect of an ordinary trust asset where:

(a) the transaction is at arm's length;

(b) the asset forms part of the settled property; and

(c) the sum paid would be allowed as a deduction in computing a gain in respect of the disposal of the asset.

[TCGA 1992 Sch 4B para 6].

Ordinary trust assets are shares or securities, tangible property or assets used for the purpose of a trade or profession carried on by the trustees or a beneficiary with an interest in possession. [Sch 4B para 7]. It is possible to meet an alternative condition for exemption under Sch 4B para 6(2)(b) where the asset is treated as having been disposed of on becoming of negligible value within TCGA 1992 s 24 and Sch 4B para 8.

10.95 The Treasury may make regulations to define what is meant by normal trust purposes but no such regulations have yet been tabled. [TCGA

1992 Sch 4B para 9]. The deemed disposal of the remaining chargeable assets, which are treated as having been disposed of and immediately reacquired, is subject to apportionment under Sch 4B paras 10 and 11. The value attributable to trustee borrowing is the value of the assets borrowed except to the extent that they have been applied for normal trust purposes. [Sch 4B para 12]. Assets and transfers are defined Sch 4B para 13.

10.96 Where the trustees of the settlement are UK resident, the deemed disposal and reacquisition is sufficient to crystallise the UK CGT charge. Similarly, where the trust is within TCGA 1992 s 86 the settlor is chargeable on the gains attributed to him.

10.97 Where, however, the settlement is within TCGA 1992 s 87 some further rules are needed to attribute the gains to beneficiaries which are contained in TCGA 1992 Sch 4C. This displaces the normal rules of attribution in TCGA 1992 ss 86A–95. [Sch 4C para 1]. Instead, the trust gains, as calculated in accordance with Sch 4B, are attributed to beneficiaries of the transferor or transferee settlements who have received capital payments from the trustees, and any allowable loss accruing under Sch 4B can only be set against such gains. [Sch 4C para 2].

10.98 The computation of the TCGA 1992 Sch 4B trust gains, under Sch 4C para 3, is the chargeable amount to which the trustees would have been charged had they been resident in the UK, if the settlement is non-resident or dual resident. [Sch 4C paras 4 and 5]. Any gains attributable to the settlor by virtue of TCGA 1992 s 86(4) or 10A, as computed under Sch 4C para 6, are deducted. Losses are allowed under Sch 4C para 7 on the attribution of gains to beneficiaries who receive capital payments, to the extent that they exceed gains already attributed to the beneficiaries under section 87(4) or 89(2). Any surplus of Sch 4B trust gains are carried forward against future capital payments. [Sch 4C paras 8 and 9].

10.99 There is an exemption for non-UK domiciled beneficiaries receiving capital payments under TCGA 1992 Sch 4C para 9(2). The residence of the trustees from whom the capital payment is received is not relevant but any gain received while the trustees are UK resident is ignored for attribution purposes. [Sch 4C para 10]. Taper relief is given in arriving at the trust gains, and no further taper relief is available to the beneficiaries. [TCGA 1992 s 2A and Sch 4C para 11]. To avoid a double charge to tax, any charge on a settlor on his return from a temporary absence from the UK is reduced by the amount charged to the beneficiaries under these provisions in the meantime. [Sch 4C para 12]. A surcharge in lieu of interest as under TCGA 1992 s 91 is applied by Sch 4C para 13, and various terms are defined by para 14.

10.99A With effect from 9 April 2003 the anti flip-flop rules in TCGA 1992 s 85A and Schs 4B and 4C are replaced and amended by FA 2003 s 163 and Sch 29. The original flip-flop scheme aimed to strand unrealised gains on a transfer of gains from one settlement to another and the revised scheme deliberately used the anti-avoidance provisions introduced in TCGA 1992 Schs 4B and 4C to take advantage of the disapplication of the legislation relating to transfers between settlements in TCGA 1992 s 90(5) with the aim of stranding realised gains in one settlement and allowing capital payments to be made by another without incurring a capital gains tax charge. Revised TCGA 1992 s 85A applies the TCGA 1992 Sch 4C anti-avoidance provisions where there has been a transfer of value made by trustees and a trustee borrowing within TCGA 1992 Sch 4B. This extends the Sch 4C charge to all disposals and deemed disposals not chargeable on the settlor under TCGA 1992 s 86. The pool of gains so created can be attributed to beneficiaries of either the transferor or the transferee settlement who receive capital payments within the anti-avoidance provisions, TCGA 1992 ss 86A–95. Gains and losses created by a transfer of value by the trustees are ring-fenced when they have outstanding borrowings within TCGA 1992 Sch 4B. The inter-settlement transfer provisions in TCGA 1992 s 90(5) are disapplied only where the transfer is caught by TCGA 1992 Schs 4B or 4C, so blocking the loophole inadvertently created by the original anti-avoidance provisions. Any unrestricted gains caused by a transfer of value between 21 March 2000 and 8 April 2003 are brought into the TCGA 1992 Sch 4C pool at 9 April 2003.

10.99B FA 2003 Sch 29 amends TCGA 1992 Sch 4C so that it applies where there has been an original transfer of value within the meaning of TCGA 1992 Sch 4B, ie one linked with trustee borrowings. The deemed gains under TCGA 1992 Sch 4B are added to any actual stockpiled gains under TCGA 1992 ss 87–89. These are the Sch 4C gains and go into the Sch 4C pool which may be augmented if there are any further transfers of value under para 7B below. A transfer within Sch 4B includes any transfer of intra-trust borrowings whether or not any chargeable gain or loss arises under Sch 4B. The outstanding TCGA 1992 ss 87–89 gains consist of stockpiled gains computed in accordance with TCGA 1992 s 87(2) together with any gains transferred in under the inter-settlement transfer provisions of TCGA 1992 s 90, or are within the capital gains pool as a result of a settlement migrating under TCGA 1992 s 89, less any gains already treated as accruing to beneficiaries under TCGA 1992 s 87(4) or 89(2) plus any distributions to beneficiaries not chargeable to capital gains tax, for example by reason of their being non-resident or non-UK domiciled. This is designed to prevent the pool being diminished by capital distributions to non-chargeable beneficiaries in order to reduce the stockpiled gains by making tax-free distributions to non-chargeable beneficiaries, which used to be possible. Any subsequent transfer of value linked to trustee borrowings within Sch 4B gets added to the Sch 4C pool, as do any further stockpiled gains. If there is a Sch 4B transfer after the Sch 4C pool has been fully distributed a new Sch 4C pool is created, TCGA 1992 Sch 4C para 7B. The Sch 4C pool at the end of the year of assessment is available to be treated as gains chargeable on beneficiaries who receive capital payments from any relevant settlement in the year of assessment or any earlier year. Gains chargeable on beneficiaries cannot exceed the amount of the capital payments received. Payments to non-chargeable beneficiaries do not reduce the pool. The excess of the pool over distributions in the year is carried forward to the following year, TCGA 1992 Sch 4C para 8.

10.99C A distribution is chargeable if it is made out of a relevant settlement, which is one where there has been a transfer of value linked to a trustee borrowing within Sch 4B and any settlement receiving a transfer of value. Capital payments made to beneficiaries from gains in the Sch 4C pool are chargeable on them. A relevant settlement which engages in either a transfer of value within Sch 4B or a transfer of settled property within TCGA 1992 s 90 will be a relevant settlement for the purposes of the Sch 4C pool, TCGA 1992 Sch 4C para 8.

10.99D Under TCGA 1992 Sch 4C para 8B, gains are attributable to beneficiaries on a first-in, first-out basis, which means that the notional interest surcharge under TCGA 1992 s 91 is maximised where the gains have been stockpiled within the trust. Allocations are made in proportion to the capital payments received by beneficiaries up to the amount of such payments. TCGA 1992 Sch 4C para 8C provides that Sch 4C gains are attributed to beneficiaries before any gains under TCGA 1992 s 87 or 89.

10.99E Capital payments which have already been franked by gains under the provisions of TCGA 1992 Sch 4 paras 8–8C cannot again be charged. Capital payments made before 21 March 2000 or in any year of assessment prior to the year preceding that in which the Sch 4B transfer was made, are excluded from the Sch 4C pool by TCGA 1992 Sch 4C para 9. Where a beneficiary has become temporarily non-resident but is caught by the "return within five years" charge under TCGA 1992 s 10A he is taxable on any capital payments made to him during his period of non-residence, in the year of return to the UK, up to the amount of the gains distributed. However the notional interest charge under TCGA 1992 s 91 only runs to the date of the actual distribution not the date it becomes chargeable, TCGA 1992 Sch 4C para 12A.

Deduction of personal losses from gains treated as accruing to settlors

10.100 TCGA 1992 s 2(5) is amended from 2003/04, by FA 2002 s 51 and Sch 11 so that a settlor can set personal losses against deemed gains attributed to him under TCGA 1992 s 77 or 86. Losses must be set against personal gains first, then against deemed gains. If there are gains from different settlements, personal losses are deducted from each *pro rata*. These provisions also apply where gains during temporary non-residence are attributed to a settlor, except to the extent that these have already been attributed to beneficiaries. [FA 2002 Sch 11 para 2]. A taxpayer may elect, prior to 31 January 2005, for the amended calculation rules to apply for 2000/01, 2001/02 and/or 2002/03. [Sch 11 para 8].

10.101 TCGA 1992 s 86(1)(e) is amended to ensure that the attributed gains are calculated before taper relief, but trust losses are set against trust gains as though taper relief were available, so that losses are first used against gains with no taper relief. Gains attributed to a settlor who retains an interest in the settlement had previously been attributed after taper relief but with no relief for personal losses available against the gain. The new provisions enable the gross gains before taper relief to be attributed to the settlor, who will be allowed to set personal losses against the attributable gains and then apply taper relief to the net gains at the rate available to the trustees if they had been eligible for taper relief. [FA 2002 Sch 11 para 4].

10.102 TCGA 1992 s 86A(2) and (7) is amended to require the trustees to deduct taper relief before attributing gains to a temporary non-resident on return, where chargeable gains have already been attributed to beneficiaries under TCGA 1992 s 87. Under section 86A a settlor may not set losses against gains attributed to him on his return to the UK as the attribution to beneficiaries is from a pool of tapered gains. [FA 2002 Sch 11 para 5]. The pool of gains to be attributed to beneficiaries under section 87 is reduced by gains attributed to the settlor after the deduction of notional taper relief.

Planning

10.103 It might be worth considering sheltering unrealised gains in a non-resident trust by moving the residence of the trust to a suitable treaty-protected jurisdiction, by appointing new trustees and establishing the trust's residence in the other jurisdiction. During this period the trust assets would be disposed of, realising a capital gain which would be treaty protected under the relevant double taxation treaty, and not subject to taxation in the other jurisdiction. In the same fiscal year the trustees would then resign in favour of UK resident trustees bringing the trust, with its now realised gains, into the UK. As the settlor would be resident in the UK during a part of the same fiscal year in which the gain arose there should be no attribution to the settlor under TCGA 1992 s 86(1)(c) and the gains would have been realised while the trust was still not resident and therefore there would be no charge on the settlor with an interest in the settlement under TCGA 1992 s 77. Mauritius used to be a favourite jurisdiction in such cases until a protocol to the UK-Mauritius double taxation treaty was signed on 27 March 2003 which overrode the treaty exemption for capital gains (2003 SWTI 521, SI 2003/2620).

Inheritance tax

10.104 For IHT purposes, the residence of the trustees has no particular significance. A charge on trust assets arises either as though they were the property of the life tenant under IHTA 1984 s 49, or subject to the discretionary trust regime of a ten yearly charge and exit charge under IHTA 1984 ss 64 and 65, unless otherwise exempted. The exemption which is available in respect of trust assets applies where property comprised in a settlement is situated outside the UK, which is treated as excluded property, although a reversionary interest in it is not, provided that the settlor was not domiciled in the UK at the time the settlement was made. [IHTA 1984 s 48(3)(a)]. A reversionary interest in the property is excluded property if it falls within IHTA 1984 s 6(1) under section 48(3)(b). Section 6(1) provides that property situated outside the UK is excluded property if the person beneficially entitled to it is an individual domiciled outside the UK. Such excluded property is taken out of the discretionary trust regime by IHTA 1984 s 58(1)(f).

10.105 So long as the settlor was non-UK domiciled at the time of creation of the settlement it does not matter if he subsequently acquires a UK domicile or is treated as domiciled in the UK for IHT purposes. [IHTA 1984 s 267].

10.106 It is by no means uncommon for an expatriate working abroad for a long time to settle surplus funds earned overseas on trusts in an offshore jurisdiction without giving a thought to the UK IHT liability arising. If, however, he was domiciled in the UK at the time of his departure, and his intention was to return to the UK on his retirement, he has probably retained his UK domicile throughout his period of non-residence, and has therefore remained within the UK IHT net, and may well have made chargeable transfers, say, on settling discretionary trusts (*Civil Engineer v IRC* [2002] STC (SCD) 72).

Disclosure of settlements with a foreign element

10.107 Where a person in the course of a trade or profession carried on by him, other than as a barrister, has been concerned with the making of a settlement, where the settlor was domiciled in the UK and the trustees of the settlement are not resident in the UK, he must within three months of the making of the settlement make a return to the Revenue stating the names and addresses of the settlor and the trustees of the settlement. [IHTA 1984 s 218(1)]. This does not apply to a settlement made by will or a settlement where a return has already been made by another person or an account has been delivered in relation to the death under IHTA 1984 s 216. The trustees should be regarded as not resident in the UK unless the general administration of the settlement is ordinarily carried on in the UK and the trustees, or a majority of them, are for the time being resident in the UK. [Section 218(3)]. Failure to make a return under these provisions results in a liability to a penalty not exceeding £300 and a further penalty not exceeding £60 for every day after the day on which the failure has been declared by a court or the Special Commissioners, and before the day on which the return is made. [IHTA 1984 s 245A(1)].

Similar disclosure requirements apply under the capital gains tax provisions. [TGCA 1992 Sch 5A]. However, under para 6 a return is not required where the information concerned has been given either under Sch 5A or under other provisions.

Chapter 11

Charitable Trusts

Definition

11.1 A charity is an organisation set up for charitable purposes such as the relief of poverty, the advancement of education, the advancement of religion, or for purposes beneficial to the community. A charity is often formed as a company, normally a company limited by guarantee. Such charitable companies are outside the scope of this book.

11.2 Charitable objectives may, however, be achieved through the medium of a charitable trust, which is one of the few types of purpose trust allowed by English law. Trusts normally have human beneficiaries who can be identified and in fact this is one of the so-called three certainties that is necessary for a valid trust. A charitable trust is different in that it is designed to achieve a purpose and that purpose must fall within one of the charitable heads described above (*Income Tax Special Purposes Comrs v Pemsel* (1891) 3 TC 53). A charitable trust does not have to be established in the UK in order to carry out its charitable objects but it needs to be established in the UK in order to qualify for the tax benefits available to charities (*Camille and Henry Dreyfus Foundation Inc v IRC* (1955) 36 TC 126; *IRC v Gull* (1937) 21 TC 374; *Civil Engineer v IRC* [2002] STC (SCD) 72). A charity may carry out its objectives overseas, such as relieving poverty in Third World countries, or as a missionary society.

11.3 The relief of poverty included almshouses (*Mary Clark Home Trustees v Anderson* (1904) 5 TC 48) and societies for the relief of widows or disabled persons, even if limited to people in their particular occupation (*IRC v Society for the Relief of Widows and Orphans of Medical Men* (1926) 11 TC 1; *IRC v Medical Charitable Society for the West Riding of Yorkshire* (1926) 11 TC 1). A mixed trust that makes charitable payments is not exempt from tax as the income is not applicable to charitable purposes only (*Lawrence v IRC* (1940) 23 TC 333).

11.4 There have been a number of tax cases on what is meant by the advancement of education, which includes the running of schools and universities (*Blake v London Corpn* (1887) 2 TC 209; *Cardinal Vaughan Memorial School Trustees v Ryall* (1920) 7 TC 611; *Ereaut v Girls Public Day School Trust Ltd* (1930) 15 TC 529; *R v Income Tax Special Comrs* *(ex p University College of North Wales)* (1909) 5 TC 408; *London Hospital Medical College v IRC* (1976) 51 TC 365; *Scottish Woollen Technical College Galashiels v IRC* (1926) 11 TC 139).

11.5 Education includes the promotion of music and science and the furtherance of craftsmanship (*IRC v Glasgow Musical Festival Association* (1926) 11 TC 154; *Royal Choral Society v IRC* (1943) 25 TC 263; *Institution of Civil Engineers v IRC* (1931) 16 TC 158; *IRC v White (Re Clerkenwell Green Association of Craftsmen)* (1980) 55 TC 651). Education in its widest form has embraced the publication of law reports, the Ethical Society and the Football Association Youth Trust (*Incorporated Council of Law Reporting v A-G* (1971) 47 TC 321; *Barralet (South Place Ethical Society Trustees) v A-G* (1980) 54 TC 446; *IRC v McMullen* (1980) 54 TC 413).

11.6 The advancement of religion includes the support of missionary work (*Income Tax Special Purpose Comrs v Pemsel* (1891) 3 TC 53), and looking after the widows and orphans of ministers (*Baptist Union of Ireland (Northern) Corpn Ltd v IRC* (1945) 26 TC 335). The advancement of religion is fairly widely defined and includes, for example, the Salvation Army (*Re Fowler* (1914) 31 TLR 102) but not Freemasonry (*United Grand Lodge of Ancient Free and Accepted Masons v Holborn Borough Council* [1957] 1 WLR 1080).

11.7 Purposes beneficial to the community include nursing homes and convalescent homes (*IRC v Peeblesshire Nursing Association* (1927) 11 TC 335; *Grand Council of the Royal Antediluvian Order of Buffalos v Owens* (1927) 13 TC 176). The definition encompasses holiday homes, agricultural societies and municipal recreation grounds, (*IRC v Roberts Marine Mansions Trustees* (1927) 11 TC 425; *IRC v Yorkshire Agricultural Society* (1927) 13 TC 58; *IRC v Tayport Town Council* (1936) 20 TC 191). It also includes the Crystal Palace (*Crystal Palace Trustees v Minister of Town and Country Planning* [1950] 2 All ER 857n) and temperance cafés (*IRC v Falkirk Temperance Café Trust* (1926) 11 TC 353; *Dean Leigh Temperance Canteen Trustees v IRC* (1958) 38 TC 315).

11.8 An educational trust for a limited class of beneficiaries is unlikely to be charitable (*IRC v Educational Grants Association Ltd* (1967) 44 TC 93). Professional associations, by and large, do not qualify for charitable status although some do, including, for example, the Chartered Institute of Taxation (*R v Special Comrs, ex p Headmasters Conference* (1925) 10 TC 73; *General Medical Council v IRC* (1928) 13 TC 819; *General Nursing Council for Scotland v IRC* (1929) 14 TC 645; *Midland Counties Institution of Engineers* (1928) 14 TC 285; *Geologists Association v IRC* (1928) 14 TC 271; *Honourable Company of Master Mariners v IRC* (1932) 17 TC 298).

11.9 Similarly, members clubs, societies and other associations are not charitable (*Scottish Flying Club Ltd v IRC* (1935) 20 TC 1; *Sir H J Williams Trust v IRC* (1947) 27 TC 409; *Tennent Plays Ltd v IRC* [1948] 1 All ER 506).

Mixed charitable and non-charitable activities prevent an organisation from being registered as charitable (*IRC v Oldham Training and Enterprise Council* [1996] STC 1218; *IRC v Glasgow Police Athletic Association* (1953) 34 TC 76).

11.10 The Charity Commission for England and Wales emphasises the public character of a charity in its booklet RR8, which states at para 16 'an organisation is not charitable just because one of its purposes is charitable. The organisation must be set up solely for charitable purposes for the benefit of the community or a sufficient section of the community'.

11.11 The Recreational Charities Act 1958 was introduced to clarify the law, following *IRC v Baddeley (Newtown Trust) v IRC* (1955) 35 TC 661, which extended the meaning of 'for the public benefit' to social and physical training and recreation, and made clear that this was charitable.

11.12 The Charity Commission for England and Wales has the responsibility for approving charities under the Charities Act 1993 and can be contacted at www.charity-commission.gov.uk.

11.13 Generally speaking, trusts for the promotion of political or sporting purposes are unlikely to be charitable (*Anglo-Swedish Society v IRC* (1931) 16 TC 34; *Keren Kayemeth Le Jisroel Ltd v IRC* (1932) 17 TC 27; *McGovern v A-G* [1981] 3 All ER 493; *IRC v National Anti-Vivisection Society* (1947) 28 TC 311; *Bonar Law Memorial Trust v IRC* (1933) 17 TC 508; *IRC v Temperance Council of the Christian Churches of England and Wales* (1926) 10 TC 748.

11.14 A disaster fund is unlikely to be charitable. In *Re Gillingham Bus Disaster Fund* [1958] 1 All ER 37 it was suggested that where a fund was contributed to by a large number of anonymous small donors, if the beneficiaries could not be identified, there was nevertheless a resulting trust in favour of the donors, or the Treasury Solicitor could claim the balance as *bona vacantia*. Such funds would normally not be charitable and the trustees would have to pay the surplus into court pending a decision on its distribution or return to the original donors.

11.15 In the case of a charitable trust where the original purpose cannot be carried out, it can be used for other purposes as close as possible to the original purpose, under what is known as the Cy-près doctrine, now encapsulated in CA 1993 ss 13 and 14. In the case of a small charity with an income of less than £5,000, the assets may be transferred to another charity under CA 1993 ss 74 and 75.

11.16 In order to attain charitable status it is necessary to apply to the Charity Commissioners, who publish a booklet, CC21 entitled 'Starting a Charity'. The draft statutes or trust deed of the charity are normally submitted for approval, and if approved the charity is registered and given a registration number. A charity that is accepted as such by the Charity Commissioners will normally be accepted as charitable for taxation purposes.

Taxation on setting up

Stamp duty

11.17 A transfer into a charitable trust of assets or property should not be subject to stamp duty in view of the specific exemption for transfers to charities in FA 1982 s 129. *Inter vivos* gifts generally are exempt under FA 1985 s 82.

Income tax, settlements of income and Gift Aid

11.18 The provisions relating to charitable covenants under F(No 2)A 1992 s 27 and ICTA 1988 s 347(2)(b) were repealed by FA 2000 s 41, which also repealed covenanted subscriptions to charities under FA 1989 s 59 and removed the requirement to deduct tax from such payments under ICTA 1988 s 348(3). Effectively the old deed of covenant system was swept away and replaced by an extended Gift Aid scheme under FA 1990 s 25, which was amended by FA 2000 s 39 in respect of gifts made on or after 6 April 2000 for covenanted payments falling to be made after that date. Where a deed of covenant was executed before 6 April 2000, FA 2000 s 41(8) provides for the covenanted payments to be what they would have been had the payer continued to be entitled to deduct tax at the basic rate from each payment. This reflects the fact that the payment will now be relieved under Gift Aid, which is a net payment grossed up by the recipient charity. [FA 1990 s 25(6)]. Where the covenant is in what used to be a common format of 'such a sum as after deduction of income tax at the basic rate for the time-being is equal to £X' the taxpayer will actually continue to pay the same amount as previously. Covenants made after 5 April 2000 would normally be for a specific sum with no grossing-up formula.

11.19 Millennium Gift Aid under FA 1998 s 48 is repealed by FA 2000 s 42, as it is unnecessary in the light of the extension of Gift Aid to all donations to charity however small after 5 April 2000. In respect of gifts made before 6 April 2000 of less than £100, which was the minimum relief, it is possible to aggregate subsequent gifts which amount in aggregate to £100 or more to enable the earlier gift to qualify for Gift Aid treatment.

11.20 The current Gift Aid rules in FA 1990 s 25, as amended by FA 2000 s 39 for gifts made on or after 6 April 2000, which are not covenanted payments or covenanted payments falling to be made on or after that date, are set out in detail in FA 1990 s 25. A gift to a charity by an individual is a qualifying donation if it takes the form of the payment of a sum of money, is not subject to repayment, is not within the payroll deduction scheme under ICTA 1988 s 202, and neither the donor nor any person connected with him receives a benefit from the donation unless it is small (see **11.22**). The gift must not be conditional on, or associated with, any arrangement involving the acquisition of property by the charity otherwise than by way of gift from the donor or person connected with him, ie it must not be a gift of cash requiring the charity to buy an asset from the donor. The donor must be resident in the UK, or be a Crown employee serving overseas treated as if he were resident in the UK, or if the grossed-up amount of the gift would be payable out of profits or gains brought into charge to income tax or CGT in the hands of a non-resident. The donor must give an appropriate declaration to the charity. [FA 1990 s 25(1) and (2)]. The declaration must be in the prescribed form [FA 1990 s 25(3)], which the Revenue has published on its website www.inlandrevenue.gov.uk/charities as follows:

'Gift Aid declaration

Name of charity ....

Details of donor

Title..........................Forename(s).........................Surname..........................

Address ....

....

....Post code ....

I want the charity to treat

* the enclosed donation of £.................

* the donation(s) of £...............which I made on .../....../......

* all donations I make from the date of this declaration until I notify you otherwise

* all donations I have made since 6 April 2000, and all donations I make from the date of this declaration until I notify you otherwise

as Gift Aid donations.

N.B. Charities do not have to include all these statements on their declarations, but can choose whichever is appropriate.

Notes

1 You must pay an amount of income tax and/or capital gains tax at least equal to the tax that the charity reclaims on your donations in the tax year (currently 28p for each £1 you give).

2 You can cancel this declaration at any time by notifying the charity.

3 If in the future your circumstances change and you no longer pay tax on your income and capital gains equal to the tax that the charity reclaims, you can cancel your declaration (see note 1).

4 If you pay tax at the higher rate you can claim further tax relief in your Self-Assessment tax return.

5 If you are unsure whether your donations qualify for Gift Aid tax relief, ask the charity. Or ask your local tax office for leaflet IR 65.

6 Please notify the charity if you change your name or address.'

11.21 Regulations were introduced by FA 1990 s 25(3A) (The Donations to Charity By Individuals (Appropriate Declarations) Regulations 2000 (SI 2000/2074)). These provisions allow declarations to be given by a donor to a charity to treat a gift as falling under Gift Aid, either in writing, orally or by means of electronic communications, which allows, for example, phone-in donations during a television charity show to be made by credit card, provided that the charity makes a note of the name and address of the donor, the name of the charity, a description of the gift and that they are treated as falling under the Gift Aid provisions. The charity must then send a written copy of the record to the donors. [SI 2000/2074 para 5]. An oral declaration may be cancelled within 30 days of receipt of the notice from the charity by giving notice in writing to the charity, in which case the donation is treated as never having taken effect. [SI 2000/2074 para 6].

11.22 There are provisions for establishing the value of a small benefit, which in aggregate must not exceed £250, and must not exceed 25 per cent of the amount of the gift of up to £100, no more than £25 for a gift between £100 and £1,000 and no more than 2.5 per cent of a gift in excess of £1,000. [FA 1990 s 25(2E), (4)–(5D)]. Section 25(5E) allows free admission to view property, the preservation of which is the sole or main purpose of the charity, or to observe wildlife, the conservation of which is the sole or main purpose of the charity provided that the opportunity to make gifts which attract such rights is available to members of the public generally. [Section 25(5F) and (5G)].

11.23 A gift which is a qualifying donation is treated as a net amount after deduction of income tax at the basic rate. [FA 1990 s 25(6A)(i)]. This enables the charity to recover the tax on the grossed-up equivalent of the amount of the gift. As far as the donor is concerned the basic rate limit is increased by the grossed-up amount of the Gift Aid payment which effectively gives higher rate tax relief for the grossed-up gift. [Section 25(6A)(ii)]. There are a number of anti-avoidance provisions, the most important of which is that where the tax on grossing up a Gift Aid donation exceeds the donor's liability for the year, the excess may be claimed from him under section 25(8). The right of the charity to recover the basic rate tax treated as if it were deducted from the grossed-up equivalent of the gift is given by section 25(10).

11.24 Under FA 2002 s 98, a Gift Aid donation may be carried back to the previous year of assessment on making the appropriate election to the Revenue before the tax return is delivered, and not later than 31 January following the end of the year of assessment to which the gift is to be related back. Such an election can only be made if the donor's income was sufficient to frank the grossed-up donation. Gift Aid relief is then available as if the donation had been made in the previous year of assessment. This does not affect the date of receipt of the donation by the charity. It only applies to gifts made on or after 6 April 2003. It is intended that, from April 2004, taxpayers will be able to nominate all or part of a tax repayment, which is due to them, in favour of a charity.

11.25 There are provisions to allow Gift Aid relief under the pay-roll giving scheme. [ICTA 1988 s 202].

Corporation tax

11.26 Gift Aid payments may be made by companies under FA 2000 s 40 and treated as charges on income under ICTA 1988 s 339, which are deducted from total profits under ICTA 1988 s 338. Gift Aid payments by companies are paid gross under section 338(3), unless they take the form of distributions. [Section 339(1)]. There are restrictions on close company donations which are disguised loans or which provide a benefit in excess of an aggregate of £250. The benefit provisions relating to individuals are applied to company Gift Aid. [Section 339(3B)–(3E)]. The normal connected person definition is applied for these purposes. [Section 339(7A)].

11.27 The amount paid by a company to a charity is treated as an annual payment of the amount actually paid to the charity [ICTA 1988 s 339(4)], which has the effect of making the payment tax free in the hands of the charity as income assessable under Schedule D Case III by way of ICTA 1988 ss 505(1)(c)(ii) and 18(3).

11.28 The corporation tax treatment of charitable donations in ICTA 1988 s 339 is modified in the case of a qualifying donation to a charity made by a company which is wholly owned by a charity. The gift of a sum of money to a charity by a company is an annual payment, and an annual payment is a charge on income. [ICTA 1988 ss 338A(2)(b) and 339(4)]. Charges on income are allowed as deductions from a company's total profits in computing the corporation tax for an accounting period under section 338. However, in the case of a company owned by a charity, the company may claim that a donation paid within nine months of the end of the accounting period should be treated as a charge of income for that accounting period. [Section 339(7AA)].

11.29 This enables the profits of a trading company owned by a charity to be paid up under the Gift Aid regulations to the charity, to eliminate the taxable profit of the trading company, which typically produces Christmas cards or runs charity shops not directly connected with the purposes of the charity and is therefore taxable as a trade. It was previously necessary to pay out the profits by way of a variable deed of covenant immediately prior to the company's accounting year end in order to have a deduction for a charge on income against the company's trading profits, which obviously produced problems of estimating the level of the company's profits in order to make the payment in time. The nine-month leeway should improve the precision of this exercise and enable the charitable company to avoid taxation in most cases by gifting its profits to charity, interestingly not necessarily the charity owning the shares in the company. [ICTA 1988 s 339, Schs 7AB and 7AC].

11.30 Charities for tax purposes include national institutions and scientific research organisations within ICTA 1988 ss 507 and 508 as well as a body of persons or trusts established for charitable purposes only within section 506(1). [ICTA 1988 s 339(9)].

Capital gains tax

11.31 Although in order to qualify for Gift Aid, donations must be in cash [FA 1990 s 25(2A)], gifts of assets to charities, or for national purposes etc to bodies listed in IHTA 1984 Sch 3 (which are not disposals of shares in a venture capital trust already exempt under TCGA 1992 s 151A) are treated as made on a no gain/no loss disposal, with the charity taking over the donor's base value. [TCGA 1992 s 257(1) and (2)]. Relief also applies to a sale for consideration not exceeding the capital gains base cost under TCGA 1992 s 38, which extends to gifts into settlement.

11.32 Where there is a disposal by trustees, other than on the termination of a life interest within TCGA 1992 s 72, the disposal is treated as a no gain/no loss disposal under TCGA 1992 s 257(3) where the donee is a charity or recognised body for gifts for national purposes.

11.33 Where, other than on a bargain made at arm's length, an individual or company disposes of the whole of the beneficial interest in qualifying investments to a charity, a claim may be made to the Revenue and the relevant amount transferred will be treated as a deduction from the total income of the individual, or a charge on income where the donor is a company, provided that it is not a gift of a trading asset exempt under ICTA 1988 s 83(A). [ICTA 1988 s 587B(1) and (2)]. The base value to the charity is reduced accordingly under section 587B(3).

11.34 The relevant amount is the market value of the investment at the time of disposal to the charity or the undervalue where there is consideration below the market value. [ICTA 1988 s 587B(4)]. The relevant amount is reduced by any benefit to the donor and increased by the incidental costs of the disposal to the donor. [Section 587B(5) and (6)]. The incidental costs of making the disposal can be increased where the consideration is less than the donor's base value under TCGA 1992 s 257(2)(a). [ICTA 1988 s 587B(7)]. The relief is modified in the case of a life assurance company by section 587B(8). Qualifying investment means shares or securities listed or dealt in on a recognised stock exchange, authorised unit trusts, shares in an open-ended investment company, interests in an offshore fund or a freehold or leasehold interest in land. [Sections 587B(9)–(9E)].

11.35 Market value is that applicable for CGT purposes, except for offshore funds where TCGA 1992 s 272(5) applies. [ICTA 1988 s 587B(10) and (11)].

In the case of a qualifying interest in land, joint interests are treated as disposals by each of the joint owners and the relief apportioned among them. [Section 587C(1)–(3)]. In order to claim relief for a donation to charity under these provisions it is necessary to obtain a certificate from the donee charity specifying the qualifying interest in land. [Section 587C (4)–(7). There are anti-avoidance provisions to prevent a disposal to a connected person through a charity. [Section 587C(8)–(12)].

Miscellaneous

11.36 A gift in kind to a charity by a person carrying on a trade, profession or vocation which is an article manufactured or sold in the course of trade is allowable for tax purposes by excluding any deemed income based on the value of the stock transferred to the charity. [ICTA 1988 s 83A]. A similar relief is available on the disposal of plant or machinery to a charity, heritage body or educational establishment where no disposal value is to be brought into account for capital allowances purposes under the Capital Allowances Act 2001 s 63(2).

11.37 Gifts of medical supplies or medical equipment from trading stock for human use are given tax relief in that no credit has to be brought into the trading account for the value of the property, and any costs of transporting goods to the beneficiaries is tax deductible, subject to the normal anti-avoidance provisions. There is no requirement for the recipient to be a charity. This applies to gifts made on or after 1 April 2002. [FA 2002 s 55].

11.38 From 1 or 6 April 2002 depending on whether or not the club is incorporated, gifts to community amateur sports clubs qualify for Gift Aid as if the club were a registered charity. [FA 2002 Sch 18 para 9]. CGT and IHT relief for gifts etc to charities is also available as if the sports club were a charity. The requirements to be met by a club entitled to be registered as a community amateur sports club are set out in FA 2002 Sch 18 paras 1–3.

11.39 Where a settlor retains an interest in a settlement, the income is taxable on him under ICTA 1988 s 660A except to the extent that that income is given to a charity, or is income to which the charity is entitled under the terms of the trust. [FA 2000 s 44]. Income partly distributed to charities is apportioned *pro rata* with that not so given, unless the trustees otherwise specify. [Section 44(2) and (3)]. Management expenses are similarly apportioned. [Section 44(4)]. These provisions apply for trust income arising on or after 6 April 2000 and various terms are defined by section 44(5) and (6). The settlement provisions do not apply to loans to charities in respect of income arising on or after 6 April 2000. [Section 45].

Inheritance tax

11.40 IHT relief is available on gifts to charities which are treated as exempt transfers of value. [IHTA 1984 s 23(1)]. Relief is not available for a deferred gift where someone else has use of the property in the meantime, or where the gift is conditional or defeasible within twelve months. [Section 23(2)]. A disposal of an interest in a property to a charity which is less than that held by the donor, or is given for a limited period, is excluded from relief by section 23(3). A transfer subject to a reserved interest by the donor is also excluded unless an arm's length price is paid for the interest retained. [Section 23(4)]. A gift to a charity must become the property of the charity or be held on trust for charitable purposes only. [Section 23(6)]. Relief does not apply to a gift of property if any part of it may become applicable otherwise than for charitable or national purposes, or to a housing association within IHTA 1984 s 24A. [Section 23(5)]. A charitable trust is excluded from being relevant property for the ten-yearly or exit charges under IHTA 1984 ss 64–69 by section 58(1)(a) of that Act.

11.41 Where the loss to the donor's estate exceeds the value of the asset in the hands of the charity, e g a small tranche of shares from a marginal majority shareholding, the charitable exemption nonetheless extends to the whole value transferred (SP E13).

11.42 Property ceasing to be relevant property held in a discretionary trust or leaving a favoured trust or maintenance fund for historic buildings etc, which then becomes held for charitable purposes only or property of a political party within IHTA 1984 s 24 or held for national purposes etc, escapes an exit charge. The exemption does not extend to a charge arising on a conditionally exempt transfer of a work of art etc to a settlement chargeable under IHTA 1984 s 79. [IHTA 1984 s 76(1)]. In the case of a transfer from a settlement where the amount that would otherwise be chargeable exceeds the value of the property transferred to the charity etc or is reduced by any consideration given for the property, the exemption is not available but the amount chargeable to tax is limited to the difference. [Section 76(3) and (4)].

11.43 The relief does not apply where:

(a) the transfer is defeasible within twelve months; or

(b) the property may become applicable for purposes other than charitable purposes; or

(c) the property may become applicable for the purposes of an approved body; or

(d) an interest under the settlement has been sold to a non-exempt body, IHTA 1984 s 76(5)–(8)].

A gift to a charity or on trust for charitable purposes only remains related property of the donor for five years after the gift. [IHTA 1984 s 161(2)(b)].

11.44 Where property is held on charitable trusts only until the end of a period, there is an IHT charge at the end of the period unless the property is then applied for charitable purposes, or where there is a non-charitable disposition from a charity. [IHTA 1984 s 70(1) and (2)]. There is no charge where the disposition relates to proper costs or expenses or which is subject to income tax in the hands of a recipient, or would be if he were resident in the UK. [Section 70(3)]. Nor does it apply to dispositions at arm's length not intended to confer a gratuitous benefit, or the grant of a tenancy of agricultural property. [Section 70(4)]. The charge is on the reduction in value in the settlement as a result of a chargeable event, which has to be grossed up if the tax is payable by the trustees. [Section 70(5)]. The rate at which the tax is payable is the aggregate of:

(a) 0.25 per cent for each of the first 40 complete successive calendar quarters; since the later of the last day on which the property became chargeable property or 13 March 1975;

(b) 0.20 per cent for each of the next 40 quarters;

(c) 0.15 per cent for each of the next 40 quarters;

(d) 0.10 per cent for each of the next 40 quarters; and

(e) 0.05 per cent for each of the next 40.

11.45 If a property was excluded property during the relevant period for an entire quarter, that quarter is left out of account. [IHTA 1984 ss 70(6)–(8)]. In certain cases the starting date may be modified under section 70(9). The deliberate omission to exercise a right is treated as a disposition by section 70(10). Where the terms of a discretionary trust require part of the income to be applied for charitable purposes, a corresponding part of the settled property itself is regarded as held for charitable purposes under IHTA 1984 s 84.

Charity tax relief

Income tax relief

11.46 The taxation of charities is dealt with in England and Wales and Northern Ireland by Inland Revenue (Charities), and claims for the repayment of taxation are made to (Repayments) Unit 361, St John's House, Merton Road, Bootle, Merseyside L69 9BB, tel: 0151 472 6293, fax: 0151 472 6268.

11.47 The repayment claim form R68 (2000), which may be submitted at any time to recover tax deducted at source, covers the period since the commencement of the charity or the previous claim. This is accompanied by schedules, as appropriate, of other income received under deduction of tax, on form R68 (F), a schedule of tax credit compensation in respect of dividend income, on form R68 (TCTR), and a schedule of tax payments under Gift Aid on or after 6 April 2000 on form R68 (New Gift Aid).

11.48 Charities are only exempt from taxation where specifically so provided, under ICTA 1988 s 505, in respect of, in the case of a charitable trust, income tax and under TCGA 1992 s 256 in respect of chargeable gains.

11.49 Income from land taxable under Schedule A or Schedule B, which is held for charitable purposes and applied to charitable purposes only, is exempt from tax under ICTA 1988 s 505(1)(a). The tax on interest, annuities, annual payments, discounts and on gilt-edged securities is within Schedule D Case III where it arises in the UK, and under Schedule D Case IV or V where it arises outside the UK. Dividends or other distributions from companies in the UK are taxable under Schedule F and for foreign companies under Schedule D Case V. Non-trading gains on intangible fixed assets within FA 2002 Sch 29 are taxed under Schedule D Case VI. All such income is exempt in the hands of a charity so far as it is applied for charitable purposes only. [ICTA 1988 s 505(1)(c)]. Public revenue dividends, as defined by section 505(1A), held by trustees which are applicable to and applied only for the repair of a cathedral or other building used for purposes of divine worship are exempt under section 505(1)(d). Where the charity carries on a trade, profits are only exempt if they are applied solely for the purposes of the charity, and the trade is exercised in the course of the actual carrying out of a primary purpose of a charity, such as a school or university, or in connection with a trade carried out by beneficiaries of the charity, such as a disabled persons' workshop. [Section 505(1)(e)]. Where the charity carries on a lottery and the profits are applied solely to the charity's purpose, the profit may be exempt from tax under section 505(1)(f).

11.50 Cases have suggested that where the charity's activities are split between non-taxable charitable activities and an additional trade, the profits of the trade remain taxable even where the overall activities show a loss, which is why charities with material trading activities unconnected with those of the charity carry them on through a wholly-owned trading company (*Religious Trust and Book Society of Scotland v Forbes* (1896) 3 TC 415; *Grove v Young Men's Christian Association* (1903) 4 TC 613; *Governors of Rotunda Hospital, Dublin v Coman* (1920) 7 TC 517; *Davis v Superioress of the Mater Misericordiae Hospital, Dublin* (1933) 2 ITC 1; *British Legion, Peterhead Branch v IRC* (1953) 35 TC 509). In a convent school it was held that the teaching nuns were also beneficiaries of the charity, in view of their vow of poverty, and the trading profits were exempt under ICTA 1988 s 505(1)(e)(ii) (*Brighton Convent of the Blessed Sacrament v IRC* (1933) 18 TC 76).

11.51 A payment received by a charity from another charity other than for full consideration is chargeable to tax under Schedule D Case III, but should be exempt as an annual payment under ICTA 1988 s 505(1)(c) in so far as it is applied for charitable purposes only. [Section 505(2)]. There is a charging provision where the income and gains of a charity exceed £10,000, and exceed the amount of its qualifying expenditure, and it incurs non-qualifying expenditure. The excess, up to the amount of the non-qualifying expenditure, does not qualify for exemption under section 505(1) or exemption from CGT under TCGA 1992 s 256. [ICTA 1988 s 505(3)]. For this purpose the £10,000 is reduced proportionately for a chargeable period of less than twelve months. The relevant income and gains means that which would otherwise be exempt from tax only under ICTA 1988 s 505(1) or TCGA 1992 s 256. [ICTA 1988 s 505(4) and (5)].

11.52 The charity may self-declare the income or gains chargeable under these provisions and must do so if so required within 30 days of receiving the notice to that effect. [ICTA 1988 s 505(6)]. Where two or more charities are acting in concert in respect of tax avoidance transactions, they may lose their charitable exemption, subject to appeal. [Section 505(7) and (8)]. Manipulations of charities and companies could also give rise to a possible charge under the transaction in securities legislation under ICTA 1988 s 703 on the grounds that *Sheppard v IRC (No 2)* [1993] STC 240 was overruled by *IRC v University Superannuation Scheme Ltd* [1997] STC 1. But see *IRC v Laird Group plc* [2003] STC 1349.

11.53 Charity is defined for the purposes of ICTA 1988 s 505 and Sch 20 by ICTA 1988 s 506(1) as any body of persons or a trust established for charitable purposes only. Qualifying expenditure means expenditure incurred in that period for charitable purposes only, and non-qualifying expenditure means expenditure which is not qualifying expenditure under section 506(1). Expenditure can be allocated against income on an accruals basis under section 506(2), payments made to bodies situated outside the UK will not be qualifying expenditure unless the charity has taken reasonable steps to ensure that the payment will be applied for charitable purposes. [Section 506(3)].

11.54 A charity which invests in a non-qualifying investment, or makes a non-qualifying loan under ICTA 1988 Sch 20, is treated as having non-qualifying expenditure of the amount so invested or lent, there is, however, no double charge if the investment or loan is reinvested or loaned. [ICTA 1988 s 506(4) and (5)]. If the amount invested or lent, which amounts to non-qualifying expenditure, exceeds the relevant income and gains for the period, it could be treated as non-qualifying expenditure incurred in earlier periods under section 506(6).

11.55 Charities' qualifying investments under ICTA 1988 Sch 20 include:

(a) approved investments under TIA 1961;

(b) investments in the Charities' Common Investment Fund or deposit fund;

(c) interests in land;

(d) shares or securities of a company enlisted on a recognised stock exchange or dealt in on the unlisted securities market, which may extend to the alternative investment market although this is not so specified;

(e) units of unit trust schemes;

(f) bank deposits;

(g) certificates of deposit; and

(h) loans or other investments approved by the Board of Inland Revenue on a claim by the charity that the loan is made for the benefit of the charity, and not for the avoidance of tax.

[ICTA 1988 Sch 20 paras 1–9].

11.56 Qualifying loans are those made to another charity for charitable purposes only, or to a beneficiary of a charity in the normal course of its charitable activities, money placed on current account with the bank or loans made for the benefit of the charity and not for the avoidance of tax to the satisfaction of the Revenue. [ICTA 1988 Sch 20 para 10]. The attribution of excess non-qualifying expenditure to earlier chargeable periods is dealt with in Sch 20 paras 11–14.

Transitional relief

11.57 The abolition of payable tax credits by F(No 2)A 1997 s 30 resulted in transitional relief for charities in respect of qualifying distributions made on or after 6 April 1999, and before 6 April 2004. Where these are made by a UK resident company to a charity or other ICTA 1988 s 505 body, it is entitled to transitional taper relief for such dividends under F(No 2)A 1997 s 35(1).

11.58 The amount of the relief is:

(a) 21 per cent of the distributions made in 1999/2000;

(b) 17 per cent of those made in 2000/01;

(c) 13 per cent of those made in 2001/02;

(d) 8 per cent of those made in 2002/03; and

(e) 4 per cent of those made in 2003/04.

[F(No 2)A 1997 s 35(2)].

A section 505 body is a charity, heritage body or scientific research organisation as defined by ICTA 1988 ss 506–508. [F(No 2)A 1997 s 35(3)].

11.59 The transaction in security provisions in ICTA 1988 ss 703–709 apply as if the transitional relief was a repayment of tax. [F(No 2)A 1997 s 35(5) and (6)]. A claim must be made within two years of the end of the chargeable period of the charity in which the distribution is made. [Section 35(7)]. Appeals may be made to the Special Commissioners under section 35(8) and (9). The transitional relief is treated as a tax credit for the purposes of excess repayment under ICTA 1988 s 252.

11.60 Where a charity has a small amount of Schedule D Case I or Case VI income, otherwise not exempt from tax, it may be uneconomic for the company to set up a separate trading company which could make a Gift Aid payment to the charity. If the gross income does not exceed the requisite limit it may claim exemption from tax on the income arising under Schedule D Case I or VI, unless specifically excluded from the small income exemption.

[FA 2000 s 46(1)–(3)]. The exemption limit is the greater of £5,000 or 25 per cent of all the charity's income and resources for the chargeable period, up to £50,000, proportionately reduced for a chargeable period of less than twelve months. [Section 46(4)–(7)].

Capital gains tax relief

11.61 CGT relief is given to charities by providing that a gain shall not be a chargeable gain if it accrues to a charity and the proceeds are applicable and applied for charitable purposes. [TCGA 1992 s 256(1)]. Where property held on charitable trust ceases to be so held, the trustees are treated as having disposed of and immediately reacquired the property at market value, any gain on the disposal being treated as not accruing to a charity and therefore chargeable to CGT. Any consideration received for the disposal of assets by trustees in these circumstances is treated as not having accrued to the charity. The CGT assessment may be made within three years of the end of the year of assessment in which the property ceases to be subject to charitable trusts. [Section 256(2)]. Temporary loss of charitable status, where land ceases to be used for charitable purposes and reverts to the original donor, will not crystallise a charge under these provisions if it subsequently becomes again held on charitable trusts or the revertee is identified as a charity (ESC D47).

11.62 A capital payment by a non-UK resident trust to a UK charity, within TCGA 1992 s 87(4), is exempt from CGT under TCGA 1992 s 256(1) under RI 189 (*Tax Bulletin*, Issue 36, September 1998).

11.63 Community amateur sports clubs are exempt from tax on trading income under FA 2002 Sch 18 para 4, and on interest and Gift Aid income and property income under Sch 18 paras 4, 5 and 6. They are also exempt from tax on chargeable gains under Sch 18 para 7. The exemption is reduced where the club incurs non-qualifying expenditure. [Sch 18 para 8].

11.64 There may be a chargeable gain on the club ceasing to qualify, or to hold property for qualifying purposes. [FA 2002 Sch 18 para 10]. A club must be registered with the Inland Revenue under Sch 18 para 11 and provide appropriate information under Sch 18 para 12. It may appeal against non-registration or termination of registration under Sch 18 para 13. There are interpretation provisions in Sch 18 paras 14–16 and the Relief For Community Amateur Sports Clubs (Designation) Order 2002 (SI 2002/1966).

Value added tax

11.65 There is no general charitable relief for VAT and charities or companies owned by charities will have to register in the normal way if carrying on a business with a turnover above the registration limits, ie £55,000 per annum from 25 April 2002.

11.66 There is no general relief from VAT for goods supplied to charities nor is there any such relief for goods supplied by charities. There are, however, a number of exemptions which are particularly applicable to charities such as zero rating in VATA 1994 Sch 8, which includes in Group 4, talking books for the blind and handicapped and wireless sets for the blind; Group 12, drugs, medicines, aids for the handicapped etc; and Group 15, charities etc, which includes the sale or hiring by a charity of goods donated to it, which extends to a similar sale or hire by a trading company which is a 'profits-to-charity person' in respect of the goods, ie it has a written agreement to pay over the profits to the charity as in the case of a charity's wholly-owned trading company. [VATA 1994 Sch 8 Group 15 items 1 and 1A]. This extends to the repair and maintenance of goods owned by a charity, the supply of advertising services, and the supply of medicinal products. [Sch 8 Group 15 items 2–10].

11.67 Fundraising activities of charities are exempt supplies under VATA 1994 Sch 9 Group 12 and the Value Added Tax (Fund-Raising Events By Charities and Other Qualifying Bodies) Order 2000 (SI 2000/802).

11.68 Fundraising bazaars etc would normally be exempt from tax if within the VAT exemption in VATA 1994 Sch 9 Group 12, and the profits are transferred to charities or applied for charitable purposes under ESC C4.

Chapter 12

Protective Trusts and Trusts for the Disabled

12.1 Protective Trusts under TA 1925 s 33 are where the income is held on trust for the principal beneficiary for life, or a shorter period called the trust period, or until he does or attempts to do anything, or an event happens, which would deprive him of his right to receive the trust income, other than where an advance is made to another person under statutory or express powers in the trust. In such circumstances the trust of the income in favour of the principal beneficiary fails or determines, and for the remainder of the trust period income is held upon trust to be applied as the trustees in their absolute discretion think fit for the maintenance, support or otherwise for the benefit of the principal beneficiary and his or her wife or husband, if any, and his or her children or more remote issue if any. If there is no spouse or issue of the principal beneficiary, the income will be held for the benefit of the principal beneficiary and those who would inherit on his death. The principal beneficiary therefore has an interest in possession in the whole or part of the trust property to begin with, and he and the trust are taxed accordingly. However, in the event of a determinative event the trust becomes a discretionary trust and both the trustees and the principal beneficiary are taxed accordingly.

12.2 Where a protective trust failed or was determined before 12 April 1978 there is an IHT charge on the property ceasing to be held on protective trusts, other than by a payment out of the settled property for the benefit of the principal beneficiary, and tax is calculated in the same way as for property leaving a charitable trust under IHTA 1984 s 70. [IHTA 1984 s 73]. SP E7 confirms that the trust has to follow closely the provisions of TA 1925 s 33, apart from minor variations or additional administrative duties or powers of the trustees. This does not include extension of the list of potential beneficiaries to siblings. Pre-1978 protective trusts are taken out of the IHT discretionary trust regime by IHTA 1984 s 58(1)(b).

12.3 Where IHTA 1984 s 73 does not apply, ie where the trust had not failed or determined prior to 12 April 1978 but the property is nonetheless held on protective trusts within TA 1925 s 33, the principal beneficiary is deemed to have retained his interest in possession following the failure or determination of the trust, as a result of which it is actually held on discretionary trusts for him. The trust property remains in his estate for IHT purposes. A deed of advancement to a third party would crystallise an IHT charge as the termination of the interest in possession under IHTA 1984 ss 52 and 53 (*Cholmondeley v IRC* [1986] STC 384).

12.4 Protective trusts under TA 1925 s 33 are nowadays rare, the same effect being achieved by giving the trustees power to revoke a life interest in favour of a beneficiary who would otherwise have been the principal beneficiary, and hold the trust fund on trust for other beneficiaries to whom an interest in possession would be given, or to hold on discretionary trusts. In such cases the normal interest in possession and discretionary trust rules apply, as appropriate.

Trusts for a disabled person

12.5 Property settled on discretionary trusts, before 10 March 1981, which secure that the settled property is applied during the disabled person's life only or mainly for his benefit, are not treated as discretionary trusts for IHT purposes. [IHTA 1984 ss 74(1) and 58(1)(b)]. There is a charge to tax where the property ceases to be held for the benefit of the disabled person by way of an exit charge under IHTA 1984 s 70(3)–(10), in the same way as for property leaving a temporary charitable trust. [Section 74(2)–(4)].

12.6 Where property is transferred to a discretionary trust after 9 March 1981, for the benefit of a disabled person who does not have a life interest and for whose benefit not less than half of the settled property (which is applied during his life), is applied, for IHT purposes, the disabled person is treated as entitled to an interest in possession in the settled property. It is therefore treated as part of his estate [IHTA 1984 s 89(1)]. Trustees' powers of advancement under TA 1925 s 32 are ignored in considering the application of the settled property. [IHTA 1984 s 89(2) and (3)]. Disabled person is defined by section 89(4).

12.7 For income tax purposes, a trust for the disabled is taxed as a discretionary trust, because a beneficiary is only treated as having a life interest for the purposes of IHT under IHTA 1984 s 89. There are no special rules for income tax. Where, however, a person is acting as a bare trustee, guardian, tutor, curator or committee of an incapacitated person the trustee etc is taxed as if the income were that of the incapacitated person, although the trustee is made answerable for compliance with the Income Tax Acts, and has a right of indemnity in respect of any tax paid. [TMA 1970 s 72].

12.8 For CGT purposes, the trust is treated as a discretionary trust and is subject to tax accordingly, except where it is a post-9 March 1981 disabled persons settlement within IHTA 1984 s 89, in which case the CGT annual exemption is the same as that applicable to an individual, not half the normal exempt amount or less depending on the number of associated trusts. [TCGA 1992 Sch 1].

Chapter 13

Employee Trusts

Employee benefit trusts

Inheritance tax

13.1 An employee benefit trust (EBT) is one set up by a company wholly and exclusively for the benefit of employees or former employees of the company, and their spouses and dependants. A trust for the benefit of employees is defined as one which does not permit any of the settled property to be applied otherwise than for the benefit of persons of a class defined by reference to employment in a particular trade or profession or being employed by or holding an office with the body carrying on a trade, profession or undertaking, or persons of a class defined by reference to marriage or relationship to or dependence on persons of a class so defined. [IHTA 1984 s 86(1)(a) and (b)]. Body would seem to exclude a sole trader or English partnership from setting up such a trust (*Customs and Excise Comrs v Glassborrow* [1974] STC 142). Residuary charitable purposes are permitted. [Section 86 (2)]. It must extend to include all or most of the persons employed by, or holding office with, the company or under an approved profit sharing scheme under ICTA 1988 Sch 9 or an employee share incentive plan under ITEPA 2003 Sch 2 [IHTA 1984 s 86(3)]. An interest in possession in any part of the trust is disregarded if it is less than 5 per cent of the whole. [Section 86(4)]. Transfers between employee benefit trusts within this definition are allowed. [Section 86(5)]. If the trust does not comply with IHTA 1984 s 86 it could, as a discretionary trust, be subject to a ten-yearly charge and an exit charge under IHTA 1984 ss 64–69.

13.2 EBTs are normally discretionary trusts, but are excluded from the normal IHT ten-yearly charge and exit charge under IHTA 1984 s 58(1)(b), although there can be an exit charge in certain circumstances under IHTA 1984 s 72 where property leaves the trust other than by a payment or disposition out of the settled property. [Section 72(2)(a) and (c)]. Payment for this purpose includes a transfer of any asset [IHTA 1984 s 63], but such a transfer may not be a payment for other tax purposes (*DTE Financial Services Ltd v Wilson* [2001] STC 777), and could have corporation tax consequences, although a payment in kind could still be wholly and exclusively expended for the purposes of the paying company's trade under ICTA 1988 s 74. An exit charge also applies where a payment is made to a settlor or person connected with him who has settled more than £1,000 in any one year on the trust, or to an employee of a close company who is a participator owning 5 per cent or more of any class of shares in the company or would be entitled to not less than 5 per cent of the assets on a winding-up, or has bought his interest in the trust. [Section 72(3)(a)–(c)]. There are exemptions for disposals in accordance with approved profit sharing schemes and employee share ownership plans. [Section 72(4) and (4A)]. The exit charge is calculated in the same way as for property leaving temporary charitable trusts under IHTA 1984 s 70. [Section 72(5)]. Various terms are defined in section 72(6).

13.3 It will be seen, therefore, that EBTs can include directors and minority shareholders holding less than 5 per cent, but not substantial shareholders holding 5 per cent or more, if an exit charge is to be avoided. However, death in service cover is often provided through an EBT which is not a relevant benefit for the purposes of ITEPA 2003 ss 393, 394, 400 (see para **13.13**) but which allows the trust to qualify as a sponsored superannuation scheme within ICTA 1988 s 624(1), which in turn may bring the EBT within the definition of a pension scheme for the purposes of IHTA 1984 s 151 which means that the trust would not be one of relevant property, in view of IHTA 1984 s 58(1)(d), and therefore not a discretionary trust to which the ten-year anniversary charge or exit charge under IHTA 1984 ss 64 and 65 applies. It can sometimes be a problem in practice to arrange such insurance where the EBT trustees are non-UK resident.

13.4 If the trust is not wholly and exclusively for the benefit of the trade, the contributions would be disallowed for corporation tax purposes and could attract an IHT charge as a gift by a close company apportioned to its shareholders under IHTA 1984 s 94.

13.5 The IHT exemption for the creation of the EBTs contained in IHTA 1984 s 12(1) should apply where the contributions are deductible for income tax or corporation tax purposes. There is also an exemption for dispositions by a close company within IHTA 1984 s 86 for the benefit of employees which may apply, although only where all participators and connected persons are excluded from benefiting from the EBT. [IHTA 1984 s 13(2)–(5)]. The close company IHT provisions in IHTA 1994 s 94 would not require a transfer of value on contributions to the EBT to be apportioned among the participators as it is a commercial transaction where the contributions are allowable for income tax or corporation tax under IHTA 1984 s 12(1). Property coming out of an existing discretionary trust into an EBT within IHTA 1984 s 86(1) may fall within IHTA 1984 s 75(1) and escape the exit charge under IHTA 1984 s 65 provided that the conditions in section 75(2) are complied with, ie that the EBT is for the benefit of all or most of the employees and it is not for the benefit of the settlor or persons connected with him and the same conditions apply as with exemption for transfers by an individual to an employee trust under IHTA 1984 s 28, *mutatis mutandis*. IHTA 1984 s 13(1) could prevent the EBT qualifying under these provisions where the fund is made for the sole benefit of the employees of a small subsidiary, unless the benefits are limited to income benefits within SP E11. Section 28 of the 1984 Act applies to exempt transfers to an EBT where an individual makes a transfer of shares in a company to the trustees of an EBT who, as a result of the transfer or within a year thereafter, hold more than half of the ordinary shares in the company and have voting control. [Section 28(1) and (2)]. The EBT must exclude as beneficiaries, participator settlors holding 5 per cent or more of any class of shares or assets on a winding- up. [Section 28(3)–(7)]. This relief has very limited application.

EBTs in action

Restriction of deductions for employee benefit contributions

13.6 FA 2003 s 143 and Sch 24 was introduced to restrict the deductibility of contributions to an employee benefit trust. An employee benefit contribution is a payment by an employer to a third party to use to provide benefits under an employee benefit scheme, in particular a contribution to an employee benefit trust (EBT). Such a contribution, which would normally be allowed as a deduction under UK GAAP, is deferred and allowed only to the extent that a qualifying benefit or expense is made in the accounting period or within 9 months from the end of it, and any amount so disallowed is deductible in a subsequent period in which a qualifying benefit is provided (Sch 24, para 1).

13.6A The Inland Revenue had argued that FA 1989 s 42(11) could be interpreted to require payments to be made to employees to justify a deduction in the company making the contribution to the EBT, but it was difficult to follow this interpretation of the statute and it was rejected by the Special Commissioners in *Dextra Accessories Ltd v Macdonald* [2002] STC (SCD) 413 and in the High Court, *Macdonald v Dextra Accessories Ltd* [2003] EWHC 872 (Ch), [2003] STC 749, although this case is apparently going to the Court of Appeal.

13.6B A qualifying benefit is a payment of money (excluding a loan) or a transfer of ownership of an asset on which an income tax charge arises, and for which the employer has a liability to pay employer's National Insurance contributions (NIC). It also applies where the employee would have been charged to tax and the employer liable to NICs if the duties had been performed in the UK, or if made in connection with the termination of the recipient's employment, (Sch 24, para 2). Qualifying expenses may be paid out of the contributions, which include costs of a third party such as the EBT trustees in running the employee benefit scheme, other than capital expenditure, (Sch 24, para 3). Qualifying benefits are treated as provided to employees up to the amount of the contributions to the EBT less benefits and expenses previously paid, i e ignoring any income earned by the EBT or other third party (Sch 24, para 4). Where an asset is transferred to an employee which has fallen in value since being acquired by the third party, the deduction is limited to the value at the time of the transfer which would be taxable on the employee, or would be taxable if he worked in the UK. Where a self-assessment tax return is filed by the company prior to the end of the 9 month period, only those qualifying benefits and expenses actually paid out may be deducted in the computation, although this may be adjusted if further amounts are paid out after filing but before the end of the period by making an amended self assessment tax return (Sch 24, paras 5 and 6).

13.6C FA 2003 Sch 24 does not apply to payments made by employers for goods or services, retirement benefits, accident benefits and share related benefits for which relief is given elsewhere in the Taxes Acts (Sch 24 para 8).

Commencement and transitory provisions

13.6D FA 2003 Sch 24 applies to deductions which would otherwise have been allowed for a period ending on or after 27 November 2002, when the restrictions were announced, in respect of employee benefit contributions made on or after that date. There is no anti-forestalling provision for accounting periods shortened in order to end prior to 27 November 2002. References are made to the predecessor sections of ITEPA 2003 for periods prior to 6 April 2003 and the Schedule does not apply to employee share acquisitions within FA 2003 Sch 23 for periods beginning before 1 January 2003.

13.6E Prior to FA 2003 Sch 24, EBTs were used to benefit employees other than by immediate distributions, by, for example, providing cars to employees. This did not avoid the company car scale charge under ICTA 1988 s 157 and Sch 6 but it did provide the company with an immediate deduction for the contribution to the EBT, rather than capital allowances over a period of years, under the Capital Allowances Act 2001 s 74, with a cap on the writing-down allowance of £3,000 per annum under section 75 of that Act. Alternatively, the EBT lent funds interest-free to employees to enable them to buy their own cars either from the company or in the market. The company paid the employee a mileage rate for using the car on business within the limits of the fixed profits car scheme and the car allowances enhanced reporting scheme, under ICTA 1988 ss 197AD–197AH and Sch 12AA (see Inland Revenue Press Release of 14 December 1999). The employee had a benefit in kind on the interest-free loan taxable under ICTA 1988 s 160 and Sch 7 at the official rate of interest under FA 1989 s 178, which was 5 per cent per annum with effect from 6 January 2002 under SI 2001/3860 (see Inland Revenue Press Release of 3 December 2001).

13.7 Interest-free loans can still be made for personal reasons such as the purchase of a property, now that mortgage relief is no longer available. The benefit in kind charge on loan interest, as for a car loan, would apply but tax on the benefit of the interest is considerably less than the full commercial mortgage interest. Loans to directors and persons connected with them may be prohibited by CA 1985 ss 330–347, although it is usually possible to avoid an arrangement under section 330(7) of the Act. Such a loan may be preferable to additional remuneration or a dividend loan without an immediate corporation tax deduction for the contribution to the EBT.

13.8 In spite of the deferral of tax relief for contributions under FA 2003 Sch 24 an EBT may be funded to hold shares in the employing company, perhaps in conjunction with a share option scheme so that an internal market for the shares is created, provided it is for the benefit of employee shareholders generally (*Heather v PE Consulting Group Ltd* (1973) 48 TC 293) and not for the benefit only of controlling shareholders (*Mawsley Machinery Ltd v Robinson* [1998] STC (SCD) 236). The company may grant to employees options under the Enterprise Management Incentive Scheme in ITEPA 2003 Sch 5 under which the effective rate of tax on the subsequent sale of shares following exercise of the option is an effective 10 per cent at the CGT tax rates if full business asset taper relief is available. The EBT could provide the liquidity to enable the shares to be sold. Alternatively, employees could be lent money (as for the purchase of a car or house, to allow them to buy shares), in which case the benefit in kind on the interest-free loan could be reduced to zero because the interest would be allowable under ICTA 1988 s 360(1)(a) provided that individual has worked for the greater part of his time in the actual management or conduct of the company or of an associated company of the company [section 360(3)] and provided that the anti-avoidance provisions are not breached and the company is close, or where the individual has a material interest of 5 per cent of the ordinary share capital. [Sections 360(2) and 360A].

13.9 The actual ownership of the shares enables the employee to claim taper relief under TCGA 1992 Sch A1 after two years in the case of a trading company, and he can then sell the shares to the EBT, which might still be attractive even without a current deduction for the company's contributions to the EBT.

13.10 EBTs can also acquire holiday homes for the use of employees, who would be subject to a benefit in kind charge on the value of the accommodation they occupied, although the company would not be able to claim a deduction for the contributions to the EBT unless the asset was transferred to the employee, or was otherwise taxable as income.

13.11 An EBT is sometimes used to acquire investment property in the UK or abroad which is let commercially. The trust can borrow to acquire such a property and will be taxable under Schedule A on the net rents. EBTs can be set up either in the UK or abroad; if a foreign EBT is used it would normally register under the non-resident landlord scheme to self-assess income tax on the rents, and as a non-UK resident investor it would not be liable to CGT on the eventual profit on the disposal of the property. Such investments are sometimes structured through an underlying non-UK resident company but the effect of the anti-avoidance provisions in TCGA 1992 s 13 – and, in particular, where an EBT is involved section 13(10) – have to be considered. These apportion a capital gain made by the company to non-resident trustees and therefore, potentially, to beneficiaries in receipt of non-taxable benefits under TCGA 1992 s 87, if applicable.

13.12 An EBT, whether resident in the UK or not, should not be a settlement as defined by ICTA 1988 s 660G(1) because it is a commercial arrangement made by the company with no element of bounty (*IRC v Plummer* [1979] STC 793; *IRC v Levy* [1982] STC 442) which means that the anti-avoidance settlement provisions in ICTA 1988 Part XV do not apply and the income is not deemed to be that of the employing company under section 660A. In the anti-avoidance provisions for CGT in TCGA 1992 s 86 there is a requirement that the settlement is a qualifying settlement, under section 86(1)(a), which excludes property provided to a settlement by way of a transaction entered into at arm's length [TCGA 1992 Sch 5 para 9(3)(a)]. For the attribution of gains to beneficiaries under TCGA 1992 s 87, the definition of a settlement is the income tax definition in ICTA 1988 s 660G(1) and (2), by reason of TCGA 1992 s 97(7). Similarly, the offshore trusts anti-avoidance provisions in ICTA 1988 ss 739 and 740 are subject to ICTA 1988 s 741 which exempts bona fide commercial transactions not designed for the purpose of avoiding liability to taxation. The anti-avoidance provisions in section 740 mean that distributions and benefits provided by an offshore EBT could be taxed on the value of the benefit, if they are not already subject to income tax, as would normally be the case (*Billingham v Cooper* [2001] STC 1177). However the loss of corporation tax relief for contributions, or its postponement, possibly for a long period, considerably reduces the attractiveness of EBTs and consideration might be given to buying into established trusts.

Taxation of employees

13.13 If a distribution is made to an employee from an EBT it is likely that the trust would be an intermediary under ITEPA 2003 s 687. Most EBT trust deeds will allow trustees to pay taxes whether enforceable or not, so on making a distribution to an employee the trustees would withhold income tax and national insurance under PAYE as appropriate and may pay it to the Inland Revenue under a PAYE scheme, thereby taking on the liability under section 687(2). Alternatively, it may be more convenient for the trustees to reimburse the company, which in turn will deduct tax on payment to the employee under its usual PAYE scheme. The company is, in any event, liable to the tax and National Insurance under section 687(1) and the employee to tax as employment income, which would enable the contributions to be claimed under FA 2003 Sch 24 (*Brumby v Milner; Day v Quick,* [1976] STC 534). Where the trustees have suffered UK tax on investment income which is distributed and taxed on the recipient as employment income, the trustee may recover part of the trust income tax paid and reduce the tax pool under ICTA 1988 s 687, by claiming relief under ESC A68.

13.14 It is not uncommon for the trustees of an EBT to transfer assets to a sub-trust for a particular employee and his family, including persons other than those in his immediate family or household, ie spouse, sons and daughters and their spouses, parents, servants, dependants and guests. This could include, say, grandchildren which would take the beneficiaries outside ITEPA 2003 s 721(5) and prevent the transfer to the sub-trust being treated as a benefit to the employee under ITEPA 2003 s 71(2). Sub-trusts may also be created for a group of employees, say those employees employed in a particular period, which may have accounting implications under UTIF 32, see **13.21** *et seq*, or to acquire an asset such as a holiday villa for a particular group of employees. The appointment to sub-trusts would normally be revocable and the assets would be held at the trustees' discretion. This type of arrangement was approved in *Macdonald v Dextra Accessories Ltd* [2003] EWHC 872 (Ch), [2003] STC 749.

13.15 It is important to ensure that the contribution by the employer to the EBT is not itself a benefit in kind as a non-approved pension arrangement taxable under ITEPA 2003 s 393(1). It is therefore normal for such trusts to exclude specifically the provision of relevant benefits as defined by ICTA 1988 s 612(1), ie pensions, lump sums, gratuities given on retirement or death or in anticipation thereof, other than benefits afforded solely by reason of the disablement by accident of an employee or of his death by accident. Normal EBT distributions to retiring employees should be outwith ITEPA 2003 s 393 as being outside the definitions in ICTA 1988 s 612(1).

Deductibility of contributions

13.16 The key to an employment benefit trust is to make sure that it is genuinely set up and used for the benefit of employees, as it is only on this basis that the trust could obtain a tax deduction for contributions, on the basis that the expenditure is incurred wholly and exclusively for the purposes of the trade under ICTA 1988 s 74(1)(a) and FA 2003 Sch 24. The leading case on EBTs is *Heather v PE Consulting Group Ltd* (1972) 48 TC 293. PE Consulting Group Ltd was a company of consulting engineers, and the senior professional staff were concerned about the possibility of control of the company passing to outside shareholders with no professional qualifications. An EBT was set up to assist the staff in acquiring shares in the company, which undertook to pay 10 per cent of its annual profits (subject to a minimum of £5,000) to the trust. The company's articles were changed to ensure that shares available for transfer had to be offered to trustees in the first instance. In this case the group pension scheme already owned 41 per cent of the shares and it was intended that the EBT would acquire up to 40 per cent of the shares, which would ultimately be distributed to the employees.

13.17 Although the court confirmed that the distinction between capital and revenue expenditure for tax purposes was a matter of law, accountancy evidence was given and accepted to the effect that the cost of securing and retaining the services of employees is normal revenue expenditure. The commitment to transfer funds to the EBT was open ended and not limited to a specific sum, and support was found from *IRC v Carron Co* (1968) 45 TC 18 and *Anglo-Persian Oil Co v Dale* (1931) 16 TC 253, where the costs of changes to a company's internal organisation were held to be revenue matters. The Revenue had argued that relief for EBT contributions should be deferred until paid to employees, under FA 1989 s 43, but it is difficult to see how these provisions were relevant. However, the law was changed for contributions made on or after 27 November 2002 to achieve just such a deferral of relief in FA 2003 Sch 24.

13.18 This case has to be contrasted with *Atherton v British Insulated and Helsby Cables Ltd* (1925) 10 TC 155, which set up a pension fund for its staff at a time when there was no statutory deduction for such payments, and the House of Lords held that although the payment was wholly and exclusively for trading purposes it was a capital payment not a revenue payment and therefore not deductible. The reason was that it brought into existence a pension fund and in the words of Viscount Cave, 'that expenditure was made not only once and for all but with a view to bringing into existence an asset or an advantage for the enduring benefit of the trade'. The fact that there was now a pension fund where there was not one previously was sufficient to bring such a benefit into existence. Because of this decision an EBT is normally started with a contribution sufficient to cover the trustee's costs of bringing the trust into existence, which is treated as a capital expense. Further contributions should then be treated as a revenue expense under *Heather v PE Consulting Group Ltd* (1972) 48 TC 293.

13.19 In *Jeffs v Ringtons Ltd* [1985] STC 809 a company set up an EBT to invest contributions from the company in shares in itself, and distribute assets to the employees at its discretion. It was envisaged that the company would contribute 5 per cent of its profits to the fund and it made a series of payments. The High Court upheld the Commissioners' decision that the contributions were allowable deductions as each payment was one of a series and not a once and for all payment or an instalment of a larger amount. Although there was an advantage to the company in setting up the fund, the payment in question had not created or acquired an asset of a capital nature for the enduring benefit of the company. In *E Bott Ltd v Price* [1987] STC 100 the employees were concerned that the shares were held by two elderly directors and their wives and the company therefore set up an EBT and made contributions to it which enabled it to acquire 5 per cent of the share capital from the directors. It was held that, on the evidence, that the payments had been incurred wholly and exclusively for the purposes of the company's trade and had not brought an enduring asset into being.

13.20 However, in *Rutter v Charles Sharp & Co Ltd* [1979] STC 711, the EBT was set up to acquire shares in the company, the dividends of which were to be paid to the employees. However, the shares themselves were to be held for the ultimate benefit of the company and therefore each payment used to buy the shares brought into being a capital asset and was not allowed as a revenue deduction. In *Mawsley Machinery Ltd v Robinson* [1998] STC (SCD) 236 the company set up an EBT with the specific purpose of building up a fund to which the controlling director's shares could be sold on his retirement. The contributions were therefore not laid out wholly and exclusively for the purpose of the company's trade, in order to provide a smooth succession on the controlling director's retirement, but so that he could sell his shares without trouble when he retired.

Accounting issues

13.21 A company's taxable profits are normally based on the accounting profits, as adjusted for specific tax disallowables such as depreciation or entertaining expenses (*Odeon Associated Theatres Ltd v Jones* (1971) 48 TC 257; *Herbert Smith v Honour* [1999] STC 173; *Jenners Princes Street Edinburgh Ltd v IRC* [1998] STC (SCD) 196; *Johnston v Britannia Airways Ltd* [1994] STC 763). The accounting profit itself, however, has to be calculated on generally accepted accounting principles (*Threlfall v Jones* [1993] STC 537) which means compliance with the Companies Acts and financial reporting standards etc from the Accounting Standards Board and its predecessors. This requirement is given statutory authority by FA 1998 s 42, which requires the profits of a trade, profession or vocation under Schedule D Case I or II to be computed on an accounting basis which gives a true and fair view subject to any adjustments required or authorised in law, in computing profits for those purposes. The Companies Act requirement for a company to produce accounts on a true and fair basis arises from CA 1985 s 226. The Revenue view on the calculation of profits for tax purposes is given in *Tax Bulletin*, Issue 32, December 1997, p 485; Issue 39, February 1999, p 623; Issue 44, December 1999, p 707; and Issue 53, June 2001, p 859. The Companies Acts give statutory recognition to accounting standards in CA 1985 s 256 and Sch 4, as amended by CA 1989. Mary Arden, in her opinion dated 21 April 1993, included as an appendix to the foreward to the accounting standards, confirms the authority of the standards, including the pronouncements of the Urgent Issues Task Force (UITF), and is consistent with the decision in *Lloyd Cheyham v Littlejohn* [1987] BCLC 303.

13.22 UITF Abstract 13 is entitled 'Accounting for ESOP trusts', ie employee share ownership plans, which 'are designed to facilitate employee shareholdings and are often used as vehicles for distributing shares to employees under remuneration schemes'. Most EBTs are not regarded as employee share ownership plans, as their purposes are very much wider. Statutory employee share ownership trusts (ESOTs) within FA 1989 ss 67–74 and Sch 5 would be within UITF 13. The Accounting Standards Board issued information sheet 29 in June 1998, which indicated that UITF 13 was not confined to employee share ownership plans but extended to similar arrangements, which the Revenue interpreted as applying to EBTs. However, UITF Abstract 32, issued on 13 December 2001, deals with EBTs and other intermediate payment arrangements. This states that although ESOPs are an example of intermediate payment arrangements, UITF 32 does not apply to them because there is already a UITF abstract on the subject (UITF abstract 13, 'Accounting for ESOP trusts') which implies that UITF 13 does not extend to EBTs other than ESOPs. The point is of some importance because UITF 13 states that most ESOP trusts are specifically designed so as to serve the purposes of the sponsoring company and to ensure that there will be minimal risk of any conflict arising between the duties of the trustees and the interests of the companies. Where this is so, the sponsoring company has *de facto* control as there will be nothing to encumber implementation of its wishes in practice. The consequence of this accounting treatment is to defer the corporation tax relief until the EBT assets are distributed to the beneficiaries. It also, suprisingly in view of scandals such as Enron, forces the company to include in its balance sheet assets in which it has no legal interest and which would not be available to creditors.

13.23 FRS 5 requires reporting entities' financial statements to report the substance of transactions. UITF 13 deems the commercial effect to be that the sponsoring company is for all practical purposes in the same position as if it had purchased the shares held by the ESOP directly and that it should account for them as its own assets. Interestingly the shares are not deemed to be cancelled, as would happen if there was an actual purchase by the company of its own shares. UITF 13 does not apply to companies using the Financial Reporting Standard for Smaller Entities (FRSSE). The FRSSE is available for small companies, as defined in CA 1985 ss 247 and 247A. A small company is one which does not exceed two or more of the following criteria, turnover £2.8 million, balance sheet total £1.4 million, average number of employees 50. These conditions must, other than for a newly incorporated company, be exceeded for two consecutive years for it to cease to be a small company. There are certain exceptions, such as for public companies.

13.24 The Revenue Interpretation was given in *Tax Bulletin*, Issue 27, February 1997, p 399 as follows:

> **'Schedule D Cases I & II: Employee Share Ownership Trusts**
>
> This article considers the treatment of an employer's contributions to an Employee Share Ownership Trust (ESOT). It is concerned with situations where:
>
> - the trust is not a statutory ESOT, that is it is not one set up in terms of sections 67 to 74 and Schedule 5 of the Finance Act (FA) 1989;
> - applying ordinary Schedule D Case I/II principles, contributions are revenue in character (not capital);
> - normal accounting practice requires Urgent Issues Task Force abstract No13 (UITF 13) to be applied to treat the making of the contributions as giving rise to an asset in the employer's accounts.
>
> We have been asked to say how contributions made by an employer in these circumstances should be dealt with for tax purposes.
>
> ***Background***
>
> An ESOT is part of the mechanism to give effect to an Employee Share Ownership Plan (ESOP), which has been defined – loosely – as an arrangement whereby an employee benefit trust (the ESOT) acquires a substantial quantity of employer shares or securities for subsequent distribution to some or all employees, with financial assistance provided directly or indirectly by the employer.
>
> Urgent Issues Task Force abstract No13 (UITF 13 – Accounting for ESOP trusts) explains how Financial Reporting Standard No5 (FRS 5: Reporting

the Substance of Transactions) applies to ESOTs. It is beyond the scope of this article to set out in detail the guidance in the UITF. But very briefly, under it, cash held and shares purchased by the trustees will normally remain assets of the employer for accounting purposes (in accordance with the definition of an asset in FRS 5) until the rights in the shares are transferred to employees. Consequently contributions to the trust by the employer will not necessarily be charged against profits as they fall due but in an earlier or later period.

Our view

As a matter of general Case I computational principles it is well established that:

- the starting point for the computation of taxable profits is the accounts of a trader drawn up in accordance with normal accounting practice;
- the profits shown by those accounts are then adjusted to give effect to specific statutory rules or to more general principles, derived by the courts from the need to compute "the full amount of the profits or gains" (Sections 60 and 70 [of the] Income and Corporation Taxes Act 1988).

Unlike statutory ESOTs – for which Section 67 [of] FA 1989 guarantees a Schedule D Case I deduction at the time of the company's contribution to the trustees, no specific statutory rules apply to contributions to non-statutory ESOTs. (Note: FA 1989 s 67 was repealed by FA 2003 s142 for accounting periods beginning on or after 1 January 2003.)

Unless therefore, the treatment in the accounts is over-ridden by such a tax rule, it is followed in computing taxable profit. The point at issue here is whether the time at which contributions to "non-statutory" ESOTs are charged against profits under UITF 13 is overridden by some general tax principle.

Recent cases show that the courts are nowadays reluctant to discern general tax principles which override the time when income and expenses are recognised in accounts drawn up in accordance with normal commercial practice. See *Threlfall v Jones* ((1993) 66 TC 77) and *Johnston v Britannia Airways Ltd* ((1994) 67 TC 99).

We consider that no such principle overrides the accounting treatment required by UITF 13. In particular, the Court of Appeal judgements in *Threlfall* make it clear that there is no general tax principle that an expense should necessarily be deducted for tax when it is incurred or paid. Nor, in our view, should UITF 13 be over-ridden for timing purposes on the grounds that it strays too far from the legal form of the transactions. A similar contention, that Statement of Standard Accounting Practice 21 (Accounting for leases and hire purchase contracts) should not be followed because it treated the hiring of an asset as a loan, failed in *Threlfall* (66 TC at 126I–127F).

By the same token, no general tax principal derived from case-law would, in our view, prevent a deduction for a properly calculated provision included in an employer's trading accounts for a period in respect of future contributions to an ESOT to reflect employees' accruing entitlement to benefits in that period (*Threlfall v Jones* ((1993) 66 TC 77) and *Johnston v Britannia Airways Ltd* ((1994) 67 TC 99).'

13.25 If the inference is right that UITF abstract 32 deals with EBTs and UITF 13 only deals with ESOTs, the Revenue Interpretation, which effectively delays the deduction for corporation tax purposes until distributions are allocated to employees, is incorrect. It is understood that a case will shortly be heard before the Special Commissioners on accounting issues for EBTs.

13.26 UITF 32 was preceded by a discussion document in UITF Information Sheet 48, which led to substantial changes between the draft abstract and UITF 32. It is apparent that the overriding objective of the Accounting Standards Board in producing UITF 32 was to prevent companies obtaining a current year deduction for large contributions to an EBT where these were, in substance, designed to defray employee costs for future years. There was no intention to deny deduction for liabilities relating to employee costs properly referable to a company's current year operation or past performance. If, therefore, the company used the EBT to produce a bonus pool for employees for services rendered in the current year, such that this created a constructive obligation under FRS 12, there would be a proper charge to the company's profit and loss account for the period, which should be deductible for corporation tax in the company's accounts in the year in which the provision is made irrespective of when cash payments were actually made to the EBT.

13.27 Deductibility by reference to a constructive obligation within FRS 12 is confirmed by UITF 32, in particular para 5, relating to the accruals basis; para 6, which confirms that the payment date is irrelevant; and para 7, which confirms that UITF 32 only applies where the constructive liability is not provided for under FRS 12. In order to bring a provision for a liability within FRS 12, it must relate to a past event which has resulted in a present obligation on the part of the company to transfer economic benefits to settle the obligation, and the amount of the obligation can be reliably estimated. It is sufficient that the obligation is a constructive obligation, namely that the company has indicated that it will accept responsibility for it and has created a valid expectation on the part of its employees that it will discharge its responsibilities.

13.28 In order to achieve this it is necessary to ensure that amounts transferred into the EBT benefit the current workforce for work already done, not for work to be done in the future or for future employees. This is often done by the directors resolving, when making a contribution to a company's EBT, that the contribution is in respect of the employees for the current year and the trustees of the EBT will then allocate this to a specific sub-trust for those employees, who can, of course, be identified. The directors, in order to create the necessary valid expectation, will inform the workforce of their decision to make a contribution to the EBT in recognition of the employee's services during that period. This should be a provision for a constructive liability within FRS 12 and accordingly constitutes a deductible expense for accounting purposes. It should also qualify as wholly and exclusively incurred for the purpose of the company's trade for tax purposes and be immediately deductible. The provision for the contribution will be discharged by subsequent payment and UITF 32 only becomes of relevance in relation to contributions to an EBT not previously provided for. Only if the contribution is linked to access to future economic benefits and the company has control of the contributions within UITF 32 para 8(b) and para 9 would a deduction be deferred. In the absence of these requirements the contribution would be immediately deductible for accounting and therefore for tax purposes. UITF 32 para 12 confirms that the abstract is not applicable where assets transferred to the intermediary vest unconditionally in identified beneficiaries. This is the purpose of the sub-trust, which identifies the beneficiaries by reference to a class, ie the employees or some of the employees employed during the accounting period. UITF 32 does not require the beneficiaries to be identified as individuals, nor for the assets to vest in individual employees.

13.29 Where funds are distributed by the trustees to a sub-trust for an individual employee and his family there would normally be a revocable appointment on discretionary trusts so that the employment income charge on the employee is deferred until distributions are made to him or members of his family or household [ITEPA 2003 ss 6, 7, 10, 70 and 721(5)]. Clearly the beneficiaries have to include persons outside this definition, such as grandchildren, siblings, nephews and nieces. The employment income charge now applies to former employees, overruling *Bray v Best* [1989] STC 159 [ITEPA 2003 ss 17, 30].

13.30 Where EBTs have been set up prior to the introduction of UITF 32 it is probably sensible for the directors to confirm that the contributions already made to the EBT are in respect of services already rendered and the trustees would then put the matter beyond doubt by transferring the assets down to a sub-trust for those employees as a class. UITF 32 does not apply to companies reporting under the FRSSE. In order to meet the criteria for an immediate corporation tax deduction it is necessary for each contribution to be 'ring fenced' for employees employed during the year the contribution is made. Figure 13.1 illustrates, over a period of years, how the structure develops. The following definitions apply:

SYST: Single year sub-trust used to 'ring fence' the annual contribution

SEST: Single employee sub-trust for an employee, his family and dependants

SAST: Single asset sub-trust to hold assets such as a holiday home (another form of 'ring fencing').

13.31 There are occasions when it will be desirable to bring an EBT within UITF 32, where there is a group structure. The parent company sets up the

Figure 13.1: Employee Benefit Trust – Example of Structure

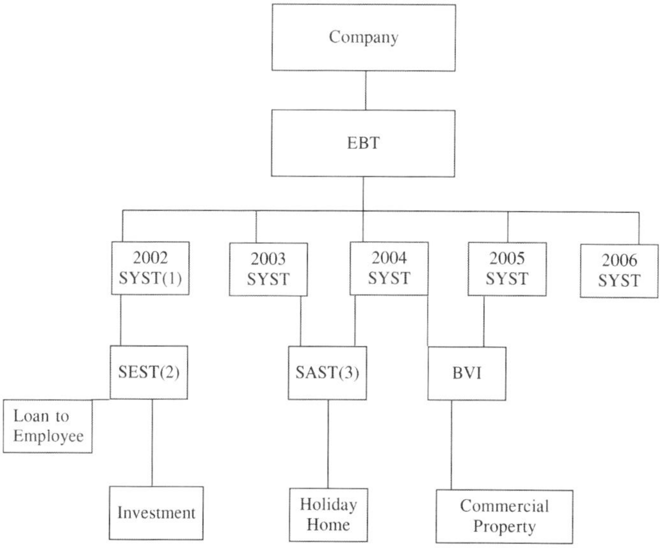

EBT for the benefit of its own employees and those of all the other members of the group, and the other group companies pay a management charge which includes payment for the provision of an EBT to their employees. As far as each of the individual subsidiaries is concerned this management charge is wholly and exclusively for the purposes of the trade and is not within UITF 32. However, so far as the parent is concerned, if the funds remain in the EBT and are not allocated out to sub-trusts, so that the parent company is deemed to have access to future economic benefit, and therefore control within UITF 32, it includes the assets of the trust in its balance sheet. The subsidiaries, however, pay up management charges which are wholly and exclusively incurred for the purpose of the trade, as they have no control over the EBT which the parent company has set up for all the group employees. The tax deduction is therefore obtained at subsidiary level while the asset is still on the parent company balance sheet. Although this is in accordance with UITF 32 the auditors might consider, after Enron, that the true and fair override in CA 1985 ss 226(5) and 227(6) and Sch 8 para 15 precludes the inclusion in the parent company balance sheet of assets which actually belong to the EBT. This is a case where there is considerable tension between the accounting standard and the legal reality, and auditors will have to take a view as to whether they think that in the circumstances of any particular case UITF 32 does produce a true and fair view, in the light of the Enron and WorldCom scandals.

13.32 In another form of group arrangement the parent company offers to extend participation in the group's share option arrangements to employees of a subsidiary, provided that the subsidiary agrees to meet the costs of any option gains. In such cases the trustees would be requested to grant options to the subsidiary's employees under the terms of the parent company's share option arrangements. The parent company grants a call option to the trustees allowing them to subscribe for the shares needed to satisfy the exercise of the share options, at a price equal to the market value of the shares at the date of exercise.

13.33 When the employees of the subsidiary exercise their options they will pay to the trustees the exercise price. The subsidiary pays to the trustees, as agreed, a contribution equal to the difference between the market value and the exercise price of the option shares to enable the trustees to take up their call option with the parent company, acquire the shares and transfer them to the employees exercising their options. The subsidiary's contribution to the EBT should be allowable for corporation tax purposes as a trading expense, under FA 2003 s 142. In the parent company accounts, the shares issued to the trustees are credited to share capital and the share premium account but, on consolidation, the EBT contribution is set against the share premium account, under FRS 5, and there is therefore no charge to the consolidated profit and loss account. These arrangements need to be set in place prior to the grant of the options to the subsidiary's employees to avoid unlawful financial assistance problems. The subsidiary will be liable to the employer's National Insurance contributions on the market value of the shares at the time of exercise, less the exercise price, unless employer and employees had jointly elected for this liability to be borne by the employees under ICTA 1988 s 187A and SSCBA 1992 Sch 1, prior to 5 April 2003, ITEPA 2003 s 722 and Sch 6 paras 1 and 28A.

Offshore EBTs

13.34 Contributions by the company to the EBT are treated as a capital addition to the settled fund and are not as such taxable in the hands of the trustees. When these funds are invested, however, the income may be liable to tax and this may depend where the trust is located. A UK resident trust would be liable to income tax and CGT at the usual rate applicable to trusts, which for 2003/04 is 34 per cent.

13.35 However, the purpose of the EBT is to benefit the employees and if distributions are made to employees in a taxable form, that is subject to tax as employment income in the hands of the employees. To the extent that this represents income on which the trustees have paid tax there is a double charge. This is partially relieved by ESC A68, which enables the trustees to reclaim tax on income which has been taxed in the hands of the beneficiaries. But there is no such concession for the double charge to CGT that could arise from a capital profit made by the trustees which is distributed to the employee beneficiaries and taxed as employment income. ESC D35 exempts the trustees from CGT on the deemed disposal at market value, provided that the employee is taxable on the earnings on that value only in respect of assets transferred *in specie*. ESC D35 is disapplied for employees who are participators entitled to 5 per cent or more of any class of shares, or 5 per cent or more of the assets on a winding-up, nor does it apply in the common situation where the assets are sold by the trustees and cash distributed to the employees. If an employing close company, as defined by ICTA 1988 ss 414 and 415, transfers a chargeable asset *in specie* to an EBT and it is not a transfer of value because of IHTA 1984 s 13, or an exempt transfer is made by an individual under IHTA s 28, it will be deemed to be made on a no gain/ no loss basis for chargeable gains purposes, where the disposal is a gift or a sale of no more than the CGT base value. [TCGA 1992 s 239(1)–(3)]. This relief also applies to disposals to an EBT not at arm's length which is within IHTA 1984 s 86 if participators are excluded. [Section 239(4)–(7)]. Where a transfer of assets to an employee trust is made on a no gain/no loss basis under section 239, relief is automatic and does not have to be claimed. Therefore the relief applies in priority to gifts holdover relief or retirement relief (CG 36010).

13.36 If TCGA 1992 s 239 does not apply, the transfer would be at deemed market value under TCGA 1992 ss 17 and 18. Close company includes a company which would be close if it were UK resident. [TCGA 1992 ss 239(8), 288]. Because of the taxation problems and potential double charges arising for a UK-based EBT, many such trusts are formed overseas in suitable trust jurisdictions such as the Channel Islands, the Isle of Man, Cyprus, Gibraltar or other tax havens with suitable trust legislation. Provided the trust has been properly set up as a genuine EBT, wholly and exclusively for the purpose of the company's trade, with no element of bounty, and with the intention of rewarding employees, not avoiding tax, the main anti-avoidance provisions should not apply.

13.37 Under TCGA 1992 s 125, where a close company transfers an asset otherwise than by way of a bargain made at arm's length or for a consideration of an amount or value less than the market value of the asset, an amount equal to the difference should be apportioned among the issued shares of the company. [Section 125(1)]. The amount so apportioned is deducted from the shareholders' base value of the shares. [Section 125(2)]. Sub-apportionment is possible but the provisions do not apply to intragroup transfers. [Section 125(3) and (4)]. This could apply to a transfer of an asset at undervalue by a close company to an employee trust. Where the asset transfer is within TCGA 1992 s 239(3), the figure to be apportioned among the shareholders under section 125(1) is the lower of the difference in the consideration paid by the trust and the company's allowable acquisition cost or the market value of the asset (CG 57125). These complications are avoided where contributions to the EBT are made in cash.

13.38 Where the company is settlor and any property may revert to the company on failure of the trust for employees TCGA 1992 s 77 could apply so that any capital gains of UK resident trustees could be assessed on the company. Where, however, the contributions are wholly and exclusively for the purpose of the trade and allowed for corporation tax there is no element of bounty and therefore the settlor retained interest provisions should not apply (CG 35020–35022).

Employee share ownership trusts

13.39 A contribution by a company to the trustees of a qualifying employee share trust, usually known as an ESOT or QUEST, is immediately deductible in computing the profits of the trade under Schedule D Case I, or as management expenses of an investment company. [FA 1989 s 67(1)(a) and (2) in respect of accounting periods beginning before 1 January 2003, FA 2003 s 142(1)]. The company, or a company of which it has voting control under ICTA 1988 s 840, must have employees who are eligible to benefit under the terms of the trust deed and be resident in the UK. [FA 1989 s 67(1)(b), (c) and (3)]. A claim has to be made for the relief and the trustees must use the funds in the trust for a qualifying purpose within the expenditure period. [Section 67(1)(d) and (e)]. These trusts are being replaced by share incentive plans (SIPs) under ITEPA 2003 Sch 2. FA 1989 s 69 was modified by FA 2003 s 142(2) to allow a tax-free transfer to a SIP for funds held on 26 November 2002 without losing the corporation tax relief already obtained. However, the ESOT legislation remains unchanged and existing trusts can continue to hold and distribute shares.

13.40 A qualifying purpose for an ESOT is the acquisition of shares in the company which established the trust, the repayment of loans, the payment of interest on sums borrowed, the payment to a beneficiary under the terms of the trust deed or the meeting of trust expenses. [FA 1989 s 67(4)]. The expenditure period is the period of nine months from the end of the period of account in which the contribution is charged as an expense of the company, or such longer period as the Board of Inland Revenue may allow by notice given to the company. [FA 1989 s 69(5)]. The claim for relief under these provisions must be made in the period of two years beginning with the end of the period of account in which the contribution is charged as an expense of the company. [Section 69(6)]. The trustees are deemed to spend the contributions they receive on a first-in, first-out basis. [Section 69(7)]. The trustees may be charged to tax if a chargeable event occurs. [Section 68(1)]. A chargeable event is defined by section 69 (see **13.41**). The calculation of the amount chargeable on the trustees is in accordance with section 70 (see **13.42**) and the charge is under Schedule D Case VI at the rate applicable to trusts for the year of assessment in which the event occurs [Section 68(2)]. If the trustees do not pay within six months, the tax may be collected from the company together with interest, on serving a notice of liability. The Company has a right of recovery against the trustees. [Section 68(3)–(5)]. A qualifying company for recovery purposes is a company which established the trust or has contributed to the trust and claimed a deduction for the contribution. [Section 68(6) and (7)].

13.41 A chargeable event occurs:

(a) if the trustees transfer securities, other than on a qualifying transfer, to a beneficiary under the trust deed; or

(b) where the terms of the transfer are not qualifying terms under the trust deed; or

(c) where securities are retained by the trustees at the expiry of the qualifying period from the date they acquired them; or

(d) where the trustees make a payment for a non-qualifying purpose; or

(e) where the trustees sell the securities but do not spend the proceeds on a qualifying purpose within the qualifying period.

[FA 1989 s 69(1) and (2)].

A transfer at market value to an approved profit sharing scheme under ICTA 1988 Sch 9 is also a qualifying transfer, as is a transfer to an employee share ownership plan under ITEPA 2003 Sch 2 [FA 1989 s 69(3), (3AA), (3AB), (3AC) and (3AD)]. An exchange of securities on a take-over is also a qualifying transfer FA 1989 s 69(3A). A transfer is made on qualifying terms if all the securities are transferred on similar terms and have been offered to all the beneficiaries and transferred to those who have accepted, or it is eligible under a savings-related share option scheme. [ITEPA 2003 Sch 2; FA 1989 s 69(4) and (4ZA)]. The qualifying period during which securities may be held under FA 1989 s 69(1)(c) is seven years for trusts established on or before 3 May 1994 and 20 years in other cases, from the date of the trust deed. [FA 1989 s 70(4)]. The qualifying purposes and any period in which sums must be expended on the acquisition of shares in the company which established the trust etc are specified by FA 1989 s 69(4) and (5) in view of section 70(5) and (5A). The transfer of securities on similar terms may, however, take account of levels of remuneration of beneficiaries, length of service etc. [Section 70(6)]. Securities are treated as being disposed of on a first-in, first-out basis and provision is made for take-overs and share reorganisations. [Section 70(7)–(9)]. An agreement to transfer securities, ie shares or debentures, dates from the date of the agreement not the subsequent transfer. [Section 70(10)–(12)].

13.42 The amount chargeable on the errant trustees is the chargeable gains tax allowable cost, as if the trustees had made a disposal at the time when the chargeable event occurs, or the amount of the expenditure applied for a non-qualifying purpose. [FA 1989 s 70(1)–(3)]. Where the transfer is to trustees of a SIP under ITEPA 2003 Sch 2, the amount of the charge is equal to the undistributed proceeds. [FA 1989 s 70(4)]. Where a chargeable event under FA 1989 s 69 occurs and the trustees have outstanding borrowings, a further chargeable event will occur at the end of any year of assessment in which any part of the principal borrowed is repaid from borrowings, treated as repaid on a first-in, first-out basis. [FA 1989 s 71(1)–(5)]. Where the amount on the initial chargeable event was limited under section 72(2)(b) the overall charge on non-chargeable events does no more than recover the amount originally allowed on contributions to the ESOT. [Section 71(6)–(8)]. There are provisions to prevent a double charge where the borrowings remain outstanding for more than one chargeable event. [Section 71(9)–(11)]. The chargeable amount recovered on the happening of a chargeable event under section 69 or in respect of the repayment of a borrowing under section 71 is limited in total to the deductible amount by way of contributions made by the companies making contributions to the ESOT. [Section 72].

13.43 Where an ESOT has been set up and the Revenue has approved the trust deed under FA 1989 Sch 5 para 1 by a founding company, which is a trading company or holding company of a trading group, CGT rollover relief is available for a person transferring shares to the trustees to avoid crystallising a capital gain in his hands. The shares must be fully paid-up ordinary shares in the founding company, irredeemable and not subject to any restriction not applicable to all shares of that class, or which require, under the company's articles, former directors and employees to sell on specified terms. The ESOT must be entitled to at least 10 per cent of the founding company's ordinary share capital immediately after the sale, or within twelve months thereafter. The vendor must receive consideration and use it to acquire replacement taxable assets within six months of the sale or of the 10 per cent condition becoming satisfied if later. Any chargeable assets qualify for this rollover relief other than securities in the founding company or another company in the same group. There must be no arrangements under which the vendor or other person connected with him is entitled to reacquire some or all of the shares sold within the prescribed period. The ESOT must not be subject to a chargeable event under FA 1989 s 69 in the tax year of sale or the intervening tax year. [TCGA 1992 s 227]. Arrangements are spelt out in more detail in TCGA 1992 s 228. The vendor must be resident and ordinarily resident and the replacement asset must give rise to a chargeable gain if sold, the retirement relief definition is used for a trading company and holding company of a trading group. [TCGA 1992 Sch 6].

13.44 Rollover relief must be claimed by the vendor within two years of acquiring the replacement assets. If all the proceeds are reinvested there is no chargeable gain and the cost of the new asset is reduced by the rolled-over gain. If only part of the proceeds are reinvested, as with other rollover reliefs, that part of the proceeds not reinvested is chargeable to CGT. As the relief is only rolled over and reduces the base value of the new asset it is merely a deferral unless it is rolled over further or the vendor dies. Rollover relief under these provisions is only available up to 5 April 2001 [FA 2000 s 54], but a similar relief is introduced for ESOPs under TCGA 1992 s 236A and Sch 7C. The provisions are still relevant, however, for transfers to ESOTs made prior to 6 April 2001. It was not possible to claim rollover relief for a principal private residence, or where enterprise investment relief was claimed on shares. [TCGA 1992 ss 230 and 231]. A chargeable event in the ESOT can cause the replacement assets to be deemed to be disposed of and immediately reacquired at market value, thus crystallising the gain rolled over. [TCGA 1992 ss 232–234]. Information powers are given to the Revenue and a double charge is avoided where relief is clawed back. [TCGA 1992 s 235 and 236].

13.45 The Revenue has powers to require the trustees of an ESOT to make a tax return and may specify the information to be contained in it including:

(a) details of the sums received, including borrowings by the trustees;

(b) expenditure incurred by them;

(c) assets acquired by them; and

(d) transfers of assets made by them.

[FA 1989 s 73(1)–(3)].

The information required may also include identification of contributions to the ESOT, the purpose of expenditure, the persons from whom the assets were acquired and the consideration provided by the trustees and the transferees of assets and any consideration furnished by them. [Section 73(4)–(7)]. The Revenue may certify the contribution made to the ESOT qualifying for relief as a trading expense under section 73(8) and there are penalties for non-disclosure. [FA 1989 s 73(9); TMA 1970 s 98].

13.46 FA 1989 s 74 introduces FA 1989 Sch 5 which sets out the conditions to be met by an ESOT in order to qualify for relief. [Sch 5 para 1]. It must be established under a trust deed by a UK resident company not controlled by another company, the trustees must be appointed in accordance with the deed, which will specify the conditions under which they operate. [Sch 5 paras 2, 3, 3A, 3B and 3C]. Beneficiaries must be employees or directors of the company. Directors must work for at least 20 hours a week. [Sch 5 para 4]. The trustees' functions and responsibilities to do with sums received and the securities they may require are dealt with in Sch 5 paras 5–9. The trust deed must not contain features which are not essential or reasonably incidental to the purpose of the ESOT. [Sch 5 para 10]. There are further rules about acquisitions and the position of the trust after establishment, and various terms are defined in Sch 5 paras 11–17.

13.47 ESOTs have not been popular, which is hardly surprising in view of the prescriptive nature of the rules which have to be followed, and the fact that the statutory allowance of a trading deduction under FA 1989 s 67(2)(a) would normally be available in any event for such a trust, following *Heather v PE Consulting Group Ltd* (1973) 48 TC 293. For an investment company, the certainty of a deduction as a management expense under FA 1989 s 67(2)(b) could be an advantage.

Approved share option schemes

13.48 Approved share option schemes, including savings-related share option schemes, Save As You Earn (SAYE) option schemes and other Company Share Option Plans (CSOPs) governed by ITEPA 2003 ss 516–526 and Schs 3 and 4, as amended by FA 2003 s 140 and Sch 22 (formerly ICTA 1988 ss 185, 187 and Sch 9), do not involve a trust, although they are sometimes operated in conjunction with an EBT, eg ITEPA 2003 Sch 4 para 13, and are therefore outside the scope of this book.

Share incentive plans (SIPs)

13.49 Share incentive plans, formerly all employee share ownership plans (ESOPs or AESOPs), established under ITEPA 2003 ss 488–515 and Sch 2 as amended by FA 2003 s 140 and Sch 24 (formerly FA 2000 s 47 and Sch 8), do require the establishment of a trust, and the trustees' rights and duties are specified in ITEPA 2003 Sch 2 Part 9, paras 70–80. A SIP is one which provides for free shares which are appropriated to employees without payment (but which may be augmented by partnership shares, which may be paid for out of gross salary), and matching shares provided proportionately to the partnership shares but without payment. A plan is established by a parent company, which may extend to participating companies in a group. Shares are awarded to employees on appropriation as free or matching shares or as partnership shares paid for by a participant. Plans have to be approved by the Revenue and appeals against non-approval are made to the Special Commissioners. [ITEPA 2003 Sch 2 paras 81–85].

13.50 A SIP needs to meet various general requirements in that it is only allowed to provide for benefits to employees through the acquisition of shares, and must be available for all eligible employees taxable on worldwide employment income, although it may be extended to other employees. Employees must be invited to participate on the same terms, although these may vary by reference to remuneration, length of service, hours worked etc. The benefits must not be confined to directors or senior employees, and additional conditions and loan arrangements are prohibited. [ITEPA 2003 Sch 2 paras 6–12]. A SIP can only be made available to eligible employees who may participate in free shares, and matching shares where they have acquired partnership shares. An employee may only belong to one SIP in any tax year. The employees must be employees of the company or a participating company in a group plan and there may be a qualifying period of up to 18 months before they become eligible.

13.51 Employees with a material interest in the company, defined as direct or indirect beneficial ownership of 25 per cent of the share capital, or the right to receive 25 per cent of the assets on a distribution, are not allowed to join the plan. Option shares have to be included in determining a material interest, but shares held under an approved profit sharing scheme under ICTA 1988 Sch 9 may be disregarded where they have not yet been appropriated to or acquired by an individual employee. The interests of associates have to be included in determining a material interest, although these do not include the trustees of an EBT nor a normal beneficiary of a discretionary trust. [ITEPA 2003 Sch 2 paras 14–24].

13.52 Free shares must be limited to those having an initial market value at the day of appropriation not exceeding £3,000, ignoring any restrictions or risks of forfeiture. It is possible to set performance targets in order to qualify for free shares, but all eligible employees must be able to take part in any performance assessment which must be fair and objective. No more than one performance-related award can be made per employee. Employees must be notified of the targets and measures which will determine their allocation of free shares, except where that information is confidential. At least 20 per cent of the free shares must be allocated without reference to performance, and no more than four times this number may be allocated under the performance-related criteria. Alternatively some or all of the free shares may be allocated on the basis of performance within each performance unit. The shares acquired must be held in trust for between three and five years, during which the beneficial interest cannot be assigned, charged or otherwise disposed of. This holding period comes to an end on the employee leaving the employment. The existence of the holding period does not prevent the trustees from participating in a take-over. [ITEPA 2003 Sch 2 paras 34–43].

13.53 Partnership shares must be issued in accordance with the plan by way of purchase, through a deduction of the cost price from the employee's salary under the partnership share agreement. The maximum deduction is £1,500 or 10 per cent of the employee's salary for each tax year, whichever is lower. A minimum of up to £10 may be specified, and the employee must be notified of the possible effect on state benefit entitlements of the reduction in salary. The amount withheld from salary has to be paid over to the trustees and is used for the acquisition of partnership shares within 30 days or twelve months, if the plan so provides [ITEPA 2003 Sch 2 paras 43–50].

13.54 Partnership money not immediately used to purchase shares is to be held on deposit and any money so held must be paid over to an employee on leaving as soon as possible. The plan may authorise a maximum number of shares to be awarded as partnership shares. An employee may give notice to stop the deductions from his salary and may restart them at a later date, but not make up the difference. An employee may withdraw from the partnership share agreement by giving notice and any monies held on his behalf must be returned as soon as possible. If approval of the plan is withdrawn or terminated, partnership share monies must be returned to employees within 60 days. An employee may withdraw all or any of his partnership shares, subject to a possible tax charge under ITEPA 2003 s 506. Salary includes emoluments paid under deduction of tax under PAYE, excluding expenses and benefits in kind. [ITEPA 2003 Sch 2 paras 51–57].

13.55 Matching shares must be of the same class and carry the same rights as the partnership shares to which they relate and must be rewarded on the same day and on the same basis. The partnership share agreement specifies the matching ratio, which must not exceed two matching shares for each partnership share. Similar holding periods to those for free shares apply. [ITEPA 2003 Sch 2 paras 58–61].

13.56 The plan may also provide for dividends to be reinvested. Up to £1,500 from a dividend in any tax year may be used to acquire further shares, with any excess being paid to the employee. Dividend shares must be of the same class as those on which the dividends were paid and dividend shares must be acquired within 30 days of receipt of the cash dividend at the market value. Participants must be treated fairly and equally. The five-year holding period provisions apply to dividend shares as if they were acquired when the shares out of the dividends on which they were paid for were acquired. [ITEPA 2003 Sch 2 paras 62–69]. Eligible shares must be ordinary share capital of the company to which the scheme relates, or its holding company or consortium company. The shares must be in a parent company, a listed company or a subsidiary of a listed company. The shares must be fully paid and not redeemable and must not be subject to restrictions other than being non-voting or having limited voting rights, or be subject to forfeiture, other than as a bad leaver, or on pre-emption, except where it applies to all employees and other shareholders of the same class of share. Shares in an employer company, the business of which is substantially the provision of the services of its employees to persons controlling the company or associated businesses are not eligible shares. [ITEPA 2003 Sch 2 paras 25–33].

13.57 The trustees of a SIP must be required by the plan to acquire free or matching shares and appropriate them to employees and to apply partnership share money or dividend share monies in acquiring shares in accordance with the plan. Trustees must be regulated by the plan trust which is constituted under the law of a part of the UK and which complies with ITEPA 2003 Sch 2 paras 70–80 and does not contain any terms which are neither essential nor reasonably incidental to complying with these provisions. [ITEPA 2003 Sch 2 para 71]. The trustees must retain records of participants who have participated in other SIPs established by the company or a connected company [ITEPA 2003 Sch 2 para 71A, as allowed by para 18A].

13.58 The trustees have power to borrow to acquire shares, or as specified in the trust instrument. [ITEPA 2003 Sch 2 para 76]. The trust instrument must provide that the trustees give notice of the award of free or matching shares to an employee as soon as practicable, specifying the number and description of the shares, the market value at the date of the award and the holding period. Similar notices must be given in respect of partnership or dividend shares and the allocation of the money used to acquire them. [ITEPA 2003 Sch 2 para 75].

13.59 The SIP trust deed must require the trustees to dispose of a participant's plan shares in accordance with the participant's instructions, subject to meeting any PAYE obligations. Trustees must not dispose of shares during the holding period unless the participant leaves the employment, except in the case of a take-over or to subscribe for shares under a rights issue or to meet PAYE obligations or on termination of the plan. Monies due to employees must be handed over as soon as practicable. [ITEPA 2003 Sch 2 paras 72–74].

13.60 Trustees may sell shares in order to subscribe for further shares under a rights issue subject to the participants' directions to the contrary. [ITEPA 2003 Sch 2 para 77]. Trustees must meet any PAYE obligations in respect of the participants' plan shares ceasing to be subject to the plan and may dispose of the participants' plan shares as necessary. A PAYE obligation arises under ITEPA 2003 ss 510–514 and further tax liabilities may arise on the disposal of the participants' plan shares under ITEPA 2003 ss 497–508. The disposal of a participant's beneficial interest in any of his shares, other than on insolvency, is treated as a disposal by the trustees and tax calculated accordingly. [TCGA 1992 s 238A and Sch 7D]. The trust instrument must require the trustees to maintain records necessary for the calculation of their own and the employing company's PAYE obligations in connection with the SIP and must inform the participant if he becomes liable to tax, and provide him with the information to compute his liabilities. [ITEPA 2003 Sch 2 para 80]. Where there is a qualifying transfer of shares to the trustees, those shares must be included in any free or matching shares and not sold as partnership shares. A qualifying transfer of shares refers to shares purchased for money in an ESOT immediately before 21 March 2000 under FA 1989 s 69(3AA).

13.61 Employees under a SIP may be subject to tax as employment income in certain cases. There is no charge on shares being appropriated to the employee or acquired on his behalf under the plan. There is an income tax charge where a participant receives a capital receipt within five years of receiving a free matching or partnerships share or within three years of receiving a dividend share. Capital receipt does not include the proceeds of disposal of the shares or receipts arising on a company reconstruction, rights issue, or after the death of the employee. [ITEPA 2003 ss 489–502]. There is no income tax charge on removal of a forfeiture or restriction or at the end of a holding period or an increase in value of plan shares which could otherwise arise under ITEPA 2003 ss 422–432 as substituted by FA 2003 Sch 24 paras 1 and 3(1). There is, however, an income tax charge where free and matching shares cease to be subject to the plan on a withdrawal within three years. Income tax is charged on the market value of the shares at the time of withdrawal. A withdrawal with between three and five entitlement years is on the lesser of the market value of the shares when awarded and the market value on withdrawal, less any tax on capital receipts. Shares withdrawn after being held in the plan for five or more years are not normally liable to income tax. There could also be an income tax charge on a participant breaching the holding period, which is calculated on the market value of the shares at the time of the withdrawal, less any tax paid on capital receipts. Partnership share money comes out of pre-tax income so effectively tax relief is given on the purchase, but does not reduce the employee's income for calculating pension and annuity contribution limits.

13.62 Partnership share money paid to an employee is normally taxable as employment income as is any money paid on cancelling his partnership share agreement. [ITEPA 2003 ss 497–508]. There is an income tax charge on an employee withdrawing partnership shares within three years, based on the market value of the shares at the time of withdrawal. If the withdrawal is between three and five years, income tax is calculated on the lesser of the amount used to buy the shares and their value on withdrawal. There is no charge after five years. An employee leaving within five years is not subject to income tax if he is leaving because of injury, disability, redundancy, take-over of the company or retirement on reaching normal retirement age of at least 50, or on death. [ITEPA 2003 ss 498 and 506].

13.63 Dividends received by the trustees are exempt from the Schedule F rate applicable to trusts provided that the shares brought from the dividends are appropriated to a participant within two years, or where the shares are not readily convertible assets within five years, identified on a first-in, first-out basis. There is no tax on cash dividends reinvested in dividend shares but the employee is not entitled to a tax credit unless the shares are withdrawn from the plan within three years, in which case the employee is subject to tax under Schedule F with a tax credit. Excess cash dividends which cannot be used to acquire dividend shares are held in bare trusts for the employees who must be informed of the amount so received. Dividends retained for reinvestment by the trustees are not treated as income unless taken out from the plan early or paid over in cash from unreinvested cash dividends received. [ITEPA 2003 ss 493 and 496]. Employees are subject to income tax on shares ceasing to be part of the plan as if they were tradeable assets. The employee must either reimburse the company or the trustees must do so or pay over the PAYE deducted from payments to the employee direct to the Revenue. This also applies to PAYE on capital receipts ITEPA 2003 ss 509–514].

13.64 No CGT is payable by trustees on shares awarded to employees within two years of acquisition or five years if they are not readily convertible assets. Awards are made on a first-in, first-out basis. A participant is treated as absolutely entitled, as against the trustees, to any shares awarded to him in accordance with the plan which means that taper relief runs from the date of the award not the date the shares are actually transferred to the employees. Shares acquired under the SIP are treated as a different class of share from those acquired in any other way, as are any shares acquired from an ESOT. When the shares are no longer subject to the plan they are deemed to have been disposed of and immediately reacquired at market value by the employee, but there is no chargeable gain on the deemed disposal. This also applies to forfeited shares. Shares acquired by trustees from approved profit sharing schemes are acquired on a no gain/no loss transfer for CGT purposes and are deemed to have been acquired at the date they were acquired under the profit sharing scheme. Trustees are not liable to CGT on the sale of rights where these are sold to produce the cash necessary to take up the remaining rights. [TCGA 1992 Sch 7D].

13.65 The issuing company may claim a corporation tax deduction equal to the market value of free or matching shares awarded to employees at the time they were acquired by the trustees. In the case of a group plan the market value of the total number of shares awarded is divided among the participating companies in proportion to the number of shares awarded to the employees of each company. Tax relief is also available for the excess of the market value of partnership shares over the amount paid for them by the participants. No deduction is available where shares are awarded to an individual not chargeable to income tax or the shares are transferred from another plan or trust in respect of which a corporation tax deduction has already been claimed, or where the shares are liable to depreciate substantially for reasons unconnected with the shares in the company generally. There is no corporation tax deduction for dividend shares or where forfeited shares are awarded to other employees. The costs of establishing a SIP are deductible when incurred, provided that approval to the plan is given within nine months of the end of the accounting period, and, if not, relief is given in the accounting period in which the plan is approved. Deduction is allowed for the expenses of running a SIP but these deductions will be withdrawn if approval to the plan itself is withdrawn. In the case of investment companies relief is given as a management expense. [TA 1988 Sch 4AA].

13.66 Rollover is allowed on company reconstructions except where redeemable shares or securities are issued, stock dividends are paid or bonus shares issued following a repayment of share capital. Shares acquired in a rights issue are normally treated as plan shares. [ITEPA 2003 Sch 2 paras 86–88]. The Revenue has power to require information in connection with a SIP and may withdraw approval subject to an appeal to the Special Commissioners. [ITEPA 2003 Sch 2 paras 42, 83–85, 89 and 90]. The company may terminate a plan and notify the Revenue, the trustees, the participants and those who have entered into a partnership share agreement. Thereafter no further shares may be appropriated or acquired on behalf of the participants. The market value of plan shares is determined as for CGT under TCGA 1992 ss 272 and 273. Various terms are defined by ITEPA 2003 paras 91–100.

13.67 The CGT rollover relief for transfers to trustees of SIPs, under TCGA 1992 s 236A and Sch 7C, requires the plan to be approved by the Revenue, the shares to be unquoted and satisfying the requirements of the SIP under ITEPA 2003 ss 488–515 and Sch 2. The SIP must hold at least 10 per cent of the ordinary share capital of the company, including shares held in the plan already awarded to individuals and there must be no unauthorised provisions enabling the claimant of rollover relief or anyone connected with him to acquire shares from the SIP. [TCGA 1992 Sch 7C paras 1 and 2]. The replacement assets into which the gain on the disposal of the shares to the SIP is rolled over do not include shares or debentures in the founding company or any company in the group.

13.68 At least 10 per cent of the ordinary shares must be held within one year of the disposal of shares to the SIP, by the claimant, and the rollover period for reinvestment is six months from the date of the disposal, or when the 10 per cent entitlement is fulfilled, if later. [TCGA 1992 Sch 7C paras 3 and 4]. Rollover relief must be claimed within two years of the acquisition of the replacement asset and, as with other forms of rollover relief, the disposal is treated as taking place as an amount that would give rise to no gain or loss, with the base value of the replacement asset being reduced by the gain which would otherwise have arisen. Where only part of the proceeds are reinvested the non-reinvested part remains chargeable to CGT. [Sch 7C para 5]. Dwelling-houses which become a principal private residence are not eligible for rollover, nor are shares under which enterprise investment scheme (EIS) relief has been claimed under ICTA 1988 ss 289–312. [TCGA 1992 Sch 7C paras 6 and 7]. A chargeable asset is defined as one which would give rise to a chargeable gain on a disposal, and requires the vendor to be resident or ordinarily resident in the UK. [Sch 7C para 8].

Enterprise management incentives

13.69 Enterprise management incentives (EMIs) are qualifying options in qualifying companies carrying on qualifying trades available to eligible employees aimed at small, higher risk trading companies. A scheme does not involve any trust being set up and is therefore outside the scope of this book. [ITEPA 2003 ss 527–541 and Sch 5]. However, shares held by EBTs for the benefit of employees are disregarded, if for the benefit of employees generally, under ITEPA 2003 Sch 5 para 32, in determining whether eligible employees have a material interest in the company.

Chapter 14

Trust Tax Returns

Establishing contact with the Revenue

14.1 When assets are transferred to trustees to hold under the terms of a trust, and there is any liability to income tax or CGT for any year of assessment, the trustees must, within six months of the end of the fiscal year, give notice to the Revenue that they are chargeable, if they have not already received a trust tax return (*Reid's Trustees v IRC* (1929) 14 TC 512) [TMA 1970 s 7(1),(2) and (9); FA 1989 s 151]. In practice this is normally done by informing one of the Inland Revenue trust tax districts of the existence of the trust and the Revenue will normally respond by sending form 41G (Trust) to the trustees. This requests details of the full title of the trust, the names and addresses of the trustees, the first of whom will be the trustee to whom return forms should normally be sent, and the name and address of tax agents acting for the trustees, if any. The form enquires whether the trust is governed by the laws of a country outside the UK and whether its general administration is carried on outside the UK. It also enquires whether the terms of the trust enable the trustees to pay income to beneficiaries at their discretion or to accumulate income, in either of which cases the trustees would be liable to tax at the rate applicable to trusts.

14.2 If the trust is established by a will or intestacy, the Revenue will wish to know the full name and last address of the deceased, the date of the death, the Tax Office dealing with the deceased's last tax return or with the estate, together with a reference number and the deceased's National Insurance number. If the administration period has ended, the date on which it ended is required, and if the will has been altered by a deed of variation or family arrangement, the date of the deed is requested. Details of who will be the settlor for income tax purposes, ie every person who took less under the deed than they would have done under the will, is requested, as is whether the deed created a new trust, additional to that established under the will or intestacy, in which case a form 41G is required for each trust.

14.3 The Revenue also requires to know the date the trust was established, the name, address, Tax District and National Insurance or tax reference number of the settlor or settlors, the assets settled and whether the settlor or his spouse has retained any interest in the capital or income, in any circumstances, at any time, in which case the income would be deemed to be that of the settlor under ICTA 1988 s 660A. The form requires a trustee's signature. What it does not require is the submission of the trust deed which, if sent, will merely be filed by the Revenue unless they decide to enquire into the trust tax return. It is therefore up to the trustees to determine whether any of the beneficiaries has an interest in possession, such that the income is treated as theirs *ab initio* for tax purposes, or whether the trust gives the trustees power to accumulate or gives them a discretion over income, in which case the trust would be subject to tax at the rate applicable to trusts.

14.4 Where an agent is acting on behalf of the trustees it will be necessary for the trustees to authorise the agent to deal with the Revenue on their behalf by completing the form 64–8, signed by one or more of the trustees.

14.5 An agent of trustees of a non-resident trust may have the requirement to provide information to the Revenue under IHTA 1984 s 218 (see Chapter 10). Trustees may also be required to provide details of shareholdings in non-resident companies on receipt of a notice under TMA 1970 s 28. IHT is payable on the creation of a settlement unless it is a potentially exempt transfer as a gift into an accumulation and maintenance trust, or a disabled trust, within IHTA 1984 s 3A(1)(c). A beneficiary with an interest in possession is treated as beneficially entitled to the property, therefore a transfer into such a trust is treated as potentially exempt as if it were a transfer to an individual. In other cases, such as a transfer to a discretionary trust outside the nil rate band, the trustees will have to submit a form IHT100 to the Inland Revenue CTO. This requires details of the agent or trustee who will be dealing with the Revenue, the date of the transfer, the type of transfer, details of the transferor, ie the settlor, and the transferees, who will be the trustees, and details of the assets transferred. Interestingly, the CTO does call for copies of the trust deeds.

14.6 Further details of the transfer and any deductions are requested, together with any exemptions or reliefs claimed, such as agricultural or business property relief, or any other relief such as, for example, gifts in consideration on marriage, together with the annual and any other exemption claimed. There are questions on IHT100 relating to the payment of the tax, and who is to bear the tax, and whether there have been any other transfers of value. The trustees have to sign the account, which is then submitted to the Revenue in accordance with the statutory requirements in IHTA 1984 s 216. If anything is returned incorrectly, a corrected account may be made under section 217. The form of the account, ie the IHT form IHT100, is contained in IHTA 1984 ss 256–261.

Annual trust returns

14.7 The annual trust tax return is a self-assessment tax return, on form SA900, issued under the authority of TMA 1970 s 8A, which is due for submission by 31 January following the end of the year of assessment, or within three months if issued by the Revenue after 31 October following the end of the year of assessment. [TMA 1970 s 8A(1A)]. The normal self-assessment rules apply in that the trust return has to include a self-assessment under TMA 1970 s 9, although in fact the Revenue will calculate the tax if the return is submitted by 30 September following the fiscal year end.

14.8 The trustees return may be amended within twelve months of the filing date under TMA 1970 s 9ZA, and obvious errors or omissions in the return may be corrected by the Revenue under section 9ZB. Information about chargeable gains is included via TMA 1970 s 12. The first step in completing the trust return is to determine to what extent it needs to be completed. Where there is a bare trust, or an interest in possession trust, with the income mandated to the beneficiaries or subject to tax at source, and a number of other conditions are met, it is only necessary to complete questions 19, 20, 21 and 22, ie the trustees' telephone number or the agent's name, address and telephone number, the names and addresses of the trustees and whether the trust has terminated, or whether there have been any tax refunds or provisional figures, and the trustees' declaration.

14.9 The first seven questions on the return enquire whether the trustees had trust and estate income, income from a partnership, income from land and property, foreign income, capital gains, or are claiming non-residence or charitable status. If the answer to any of these questions is in the affirmative, then supplementary pages are needed.

14.10 A number of questions are asked about the status of the trust, to determine whether it is liable to the rate applicable to trusts or the dividend trust rate on any of its income, or whether any of its income or gains should be assessed on the settlor. The main trust return begins at question 9 with interest, dividends, gains on UK life insurance policies and other income. Question 10 enquires about charges on income and other reliefs; question 11, whether any annual payments were made out of capital or income not brought into charge to income tax. Question 12 enquires whether any assets or funds have been added to the trust. Question 13 deals with trust income not liable to tax at the rate applicable to trusts or the dividend trust rate, eg because it is treated as the income of the settlor or is used in payment of trust management expenses. Question 14 enquires about discretionary payments of income made to beneficiaries. Question 15A requires details of any capital payments made for the benefit of minor unmarried children of the settlor during the settlor's lifetime and question 15B requires details of capital transactions between trustees and the settlors. Question 16 deals with trusts which have been at any time non-resident; question 17 deals with the calculation of tax where the Revenue have not been requested to calculate this. Question 18 deals with the destination of any repayment of tax. The trust and estate return guide extends to 29 pages.

14.11 The Trust and Estate Trade supplementary pages are very similar to those applicable to individuals, requesting details of the business, capital allowances and balancing charges, total income and expenses where the three-line account applies, ie where annual turnover is below £15,000, and more detailed income and expenses where the turnover limit is exceeded, when the standard accounts information is required. Tax adjustments to the net profit or loss are dealt with in order to arrive at the taxable profits of the business. Tax paid at source is returned and there is a request for a summary balance sheet where one is available. There are eight pages of notes. There are separate pages for the fairly unusual case where the trust or, more likely, the estate of a deceased underwriter, has income or losses from Lloyd's. The Trust and Estate Partnership return mirrors the normal self-assessment individual partners' pages, with details of the partnership and the share of the partnerships trading or professional income. The notes on Trust and Estate Partnership income include instructions on transferring figures from the partnership statement to the partnership pages in the trust return.

14.12 The Trust and Estate Land and Property pages mirror those of an individual self-assessment return, requiring details of income from furnished holiday lettings in the UK and other property income including chargeable premiums, ie premiums on the grant of leases for less than 50 years, partly taxed as income under ICTA 1988 s 34. The Trust and Estate Foreign pages deal with the foreign income of UK trusts, including interest and other savings income, dividends, income assessed on a remittance basis, ie where a beneficiary has an absolute interest in income and is resident in the UK but not domiciled in the UK. The country from which the income is sourced has to be disclosed, together with the income before tax, the foreign tax paid and the amount chargeable which will normally be the amount before tax, where the foreign tax is claimed as a credit or that amount less the foreign tax where it is treated as an expense under ICTA 1988 s 811. It is normally preferable to claim the foreign tax as a credit where possible. Income reported elsewhere on the return such as on the supplementary pages for trade or partnership income which has suffered foreign tax has to be cross-referred to the foreign supplementary pages in order to claim relief for the foreign tax paid. This also applies to chargeable gains, see Return TF3 and Guidance Notes TFN 11 and 12.

14.13 Other income which might require to be returned includes holdings in offshore funds, gains on foreign life insurance policies, which may or may not have a credit for tax treated as paid. Further details of income and expenses in respect of land and property abroad is required on pages TF4 and TF5, which will normally be required for each overseas property unless all the overseas let properties are in the same country, and all the income is remittable, or they are in different countries but there has been no foreign tax deducted from any of the income and all of it is remittable.

14.14 The supplementary pages for Trust and Estate Capital Gains require particulars of chargeable gains and allowable losses, including those brought forward from earlier years. The basis of the form closely follows that of the personal self-assessment capital gains forms, although there are boxes for where a life tenant has died, where a person has become absolutely entitled to any part of the property during the year, where the trustees have ceased to become UK resident, or become dual resident, or where chargeable gains are chargeable on the settlor. Further information is required for each transaction where the gains arise from the sale of unlisted shares or securities, land and property or other assets such as goodwill or chattels. The Trust and Estate Non-residence pages are used to determine the residence status of the trust for income tax purposes, and separately for CGT purposes in accordance with the residence rules for trustees, as explained in Chapter 5.

14.15 The final supplementary pages are for charitable trusts, specifying the basis of the claim to exemption, the return period, the payments claimed or being claimed, the income for which exemption is claimed and the expenses and assets, as included in the charity accounts, together with the formal claim for exemption.

14.16 There is also a Trust and Estate Tax Calculation Guide for those trustees who wish to calculate the tax payable. As with all the self-assessment tax calculation guides, it is extremely complex, with more than 160 boxes in the twelve-page guide.

14.17 As for individuals and partnerships, the Revenue publishes a very useful reference guide for Inland Revenue staff and tax practitioners entitled *The Self Assessment Trust and Estate Tax Return Guide*, which is available to agents from the Self-Assessment Orderline: tel: 0845 9000 404, fax: 0845 9000 604 or via e-mail on saorderline.ir@gtnet.gov.uk and quoting the agent reference number. The Revenue sometimes issue a tax return and request for information form 50 (FS) to non-UK resident trustees where there is a UK connection. This is a non-statutory form and completion is voluntary (see Appendix 4).

14.18 In *Tax Bulletin*, Issue 27, February 1997, p 395, the Revenue confirmed that trustees of bare trusts would not be required to complete trust tax returns, but in Issue 32, December 1997, p 407, it was accepted that trustees were entitled to make a self-assessment return of income, but not of capital gains, and account for tax at the basic rate, or lower rate if the income is savings income, which is sometimes convenient, for example, if a property is jointly owned. Trustees of bare trusts, in such circumstances, may inform the Trust District that they intend to self-assess on a regular and consistent basis.

Provisional figures and estimates

14.19 The statutory authority for self-assessment tax returns is TMA 1970 s 8 and in the case of trust returns TMA 1970 s 8A. The Revenue has always accepted that it may be necessary in self-assessment returns in certain circumstances to complete the return with provisional figures, or estimates on the authority of *Dunk v Havant Comrs* [1976] STC 460n. The Revenue policy was spelt out at some length in *Tax Bulletin*, Issue 37, October 1998, p 593 and reiterated in *Tax Bulletin*, Issue 53, June 2001, p 847. The Revenue practice originally was to send back the return where it was not satisfied that there was sufficient justification for the use of a provisional or estimated figure, but it no longer does so, although that information will be a factor taken into account in deciding whether to open an enquiry into the return under TMA 1970 s 9A. The Revenue will no longer reject returns containing estimated or provisional figures (*Tax Bulletin*, Issue 57, February 2002, p 916).

14.20 Where provisional figures are concerned if the date on which final figures become available is known or can be anticipated with reasonable accuracy it should be inserted in the white space for additional information on the tax return, as this may avoid an enquiry being commenced.

Valuations

14.21 Where a CGT computation includes valuations, the basis of valuations should be disclosed and professional valuations obtained where necessary. These valuations can be submitted with the trust return in support of the computation or may be submitted to the Revenue immediately after a disposal has taken place together with form CG34, which will enable the valuation agreement procedure with the Shares Valuation Division or the District Valuer as necessary to commence at an earlier date in accordance with the Inland Revenue Press Release of 4 February 1997. The trustees should enclose a capital gains computation for the disposal with an estimate of the CGT liability for the year in respect of which the disposal was made, details of any reliefs due to be claimed with respect to the disposal, a copy of any valuation report obtained if available, the cost and date of acquisition of the assets and details of any improvements made. In the case of share valuations, accounts for the three years up to the valuation should be enclosed, and in the case of land which is let, a copy of the lease or tenancy agreement or a plan showing the location of the land if the valuation is of undeveloped land, together with any other relevant information.

14.22 The CG 34 procedure may enable the valuation to be agreed prior to the due date for the submission of the return and avoid the Revenue having to open an enquiry in order to agree the valuation.

Claims and elections

14.23 The self-assessment system is designed for claims for reliefs to be included in the relevant tax return for the period to which they relate under TMA 1970 s 42, which requires the claim to be quantified. However, the self-assessment system is designed so that each year, once any Revenue enquiry has been completed, it becomes final and events happening in future years should not lead to the re-opening of a closed year. It is therefore possible to make claims outside the tax return under TMA 1970 Sch 1A, and where claims involve relief for two or more years under Sch 1B.

14.24 Claims made outside the tax return may be amended by the trustees or corrected by the Revenue in the same way as if the claim had been included in the return. [TMA 1970 Sch 1A para 3].

Time limits for claims

14.25 Income and Corporation Taxes Act 1988, main claims periods:

(a) Section 62A (Change of basis period – conditions for such a change) – tax return filing date (ie ten months).

(b) Section 84 (Gifts to educational establishments) – one year ten months.

(c) Section 101 (Valuation of work in progress at discontinuance of profession or vocation) – one year ten months.

(d) Section 379A (Schedule A losses) – one year ten months.

(e) Section 380 (Trading losses) – one year ten months.

(f) Section 392 (Case VI losses) – five years ten months.

(g) Section 504 (Letting of furnished holiday accommodation treated as a trade: supplementary provisions) – one year ten months.

(h) Section 524 (Taxation of receipts from sale of patent rights) – one year ten months.

(i) Section 585 (Relief from tax on delayed remittances) – five years ten months.

(j) Section 691 (Maintenance funds for historic buildings – certain income not to be income of settlor) – one year ten months.

(k) Section 700 (Estate of deceased persons in course of administration – adjustments and information) – three years ten months.

(l) Section 781 (Assets leased to traders and others) – five years ten months.

(m) Section 804 (Double taxation relief – relief against income tax in respect of income arising in years of commencement) – five years ten months.

(n) Section 806 (Double taxation relief – time limit for claims etc) – five years ten months.

14.26 Taxation of Chargeable Gains Act 1992:

(a) Section 35 (Computation of gains: general provisions – assets held on 31 March 1982 (including assets held on 6 April 1965)) – one year ten months.

(b) Section 161 (Appropriations to and from stock) – one year ten months.

(c) Section 242 (Small part disposals) – one year ten months.

(d) Section 243 (Part disposal to authority with compulsory powers) – one year ten months.

(e) Section 244 (Part disposal: consideration exceeding allowable expenditure) – one year ten months.

(f) Section 253 (Debts – relief for loans to traders) – five years ten months.

(g) Section 279 (Foreign assets: delayed remittances) – five years ten months.

(h) Sch 2 (Assets held on 6 April 1965) – one year ten months.

(i) Sch 4 (Deferred charges on gains before 31 March 1982) – one year ten months.

14.27 Finance (No 2) Act 1992:

(a) Section 41 (Films – relief for preliminary expenditure) – one year ten months.

(b) Section 42 (Films – relief for production or acquisition expenditure) – one year ten months.

14.28 Capital Allowances Act 2001:

(a) Section 85 (Short-life assets – election for certain machinery or plant to be treated as short-life assets) – one year ten months.

(b) Section 129 (Ships: exclusion of CAA 2001 s 127) – one year ten months.

(c) Section 130 (Ships – first-year and writing-down allowances) – one year ten months.

(d) Section 177 (Fixtures expenditure incurred by equipment lessor) – one year ten months.

(e) Section 382 (Agriculture – balancing events) – one year ten months.

(f) Sch 2 para 82 (FA (No 2) A 1992 s 40D(4)(a)) (Exclusions of certain expenditure relating to films, tapes and discs) – one year ten months.

Error or mistake

14.29 Where the trustees discover that the tax return is incorrect more than twelve months after the due date of submission, and therefore out of time for amendment under TMA 1970 s 9ZA, they may be able to make an error or mistake claim within five years from 31 January following the end of the year of assessment to which the return relates. [TMA 1970 s 33(1)]. On receiving the claim the Revenue have to examine it and, where appropriate, make a just and reasonable repayment. No relief, however, is available where the return was made on the basis of, or in accordance with, the practice generally prevailing at the time when it was made. [Section 33(2A)(a)]. An error or mistake claim cannot be made in respect of a claim which is included in the return, but the trustees may make a supplementary claim within the time limit allowed for the original claim (*Howard v IRC* [2002] SWTI 1264). [Sections 33(2A)(b) and 49(2)]. Where there is an error or mistake in a partnership return, any partner, including trustees where appropriate, may make an error or mistake claim under section 33A. This includes consequential amendments to each partner's own return, which would include the trust return where trustees are partners. [Section 33A(4)].

Enquiries

14.30 The Revenue may open an enquiry into a trust return within one year from the filing date. [TMA 1970 s 9A(2A)]. This gives the Revenue sufficient time to collate information received from third parties and consider whether the return requires further investigation. The Revenue has to give the trustees notice of the intention to enquire into the return, including any amendments or claims which have been made. If the Revenue considers that there is likely to be a loss to the Crown it may amend the self-assessment by making a jeopardy assessment under section 9C during the course of the enquiry. Most enquiries are settled by agreement either by amending an existing self-assessment or by way of a contract settlement. The Inspector will issue a closure notice following the Revenue's enquiries, which must either confirm that no amendment of the return is required or make the amendments of the return required to give effect to the Revenue Officer's conclusions at the end of his enquiry under TMA 1970 s 28A.

14.31 Enquiries into partnership returns, which could have a knock-on effect on a trustee partner, are similarly handled under TMA 1970 s 28B, and where no return has been delivered the Revenue may make a determination of the amount that should have been included in the self- assessment under section 28C. The trustees' right of appeal is defined in section 31 of the 1970 Act and technical disputes may be referred to the Commissioners during the enquiry under sections 28ZA–28ZE.

14.32 The Revenue may, in the course of an enquiry, include an enquiry into a partnership where the trust is a partner. [TMA 1970 s 12AC]. These powers, contained in section 19A of the Act, may require the production of information within the time specified in the notice, which must be at least 30 days. The Revenue has more formal information gathering powers under sections 20–20D. The Revenue may also obtain information from third parties under TMA 1970 ss 13–19 and 22–26. Under section 27 the Board may, by notice in writing, require any person who is party to a trust to provide information within a specified period of not less than 28 days. It may also require a person liable to tax on chargeable gains from a non-resident company under TCGA 1992 s 13 to provide appropriate information under TMA 1970 s 28.

14.33 Although under the self-assessment rules the Revenue is entitled to make a random enquiry into any self-assessment return, the vast majority of enquiries are targeted enquiries as a result of a Revenue risk assessment of the tax at stake and the likelihood of errors. The majority of such focused enquiries are aspect enquiries into a particular entry or entries on the tax return rather than a full enquiry looking closely into the books and records.

Discovery

14.34 Where the time limit for opening an enquiry has expired and the Revenue become aware of a suspected defect in the trustees' self-assessment they may seek to make a discovery under TMA 1970 s 29 in order to make good a loss of tax. No discovery is possible if the return was made in accordance with practice generally prevailing at that time, or unless the underpayment is attributable to fraudulent or negligent conduct, which has been considered in cases such as *Hancock v IRC* [1999] STC (SCD) 287; *King v Walden* [2000] STC (SCD) 179 and [2001] STC 822; and *Last Viceroy Restaurant (a firm) v Jackson* [2000] STC 1093. [Section 29(2) and (4)].

14.35 Alternatively a discovery may be made if the Revenue Officer, at the time he ceased to be entitled to raise an enquiry into a return, could not reasonably be expected to be aware of the tax deficiency on the basis of the information available to him. [TMA 1970 s 29(5)]. Information is treated as having been made available if it is contained in the taxpayer's last tax return or in any accounts, statements or documents accompanying the return, or amended return, for the chargeable period and the two immediately preceding periods, or produced during an enquiry, or which could reasonably be expected to be inferred by the Revenue Officer from such information or which is notified to him in writing. [Section 29(6) and (7)]. Enquiries can be raised into claims outside the return in the same way as for the return itself, and there are similar powers to call for documents and procedures on completion of enquiries into claims under TMA 1970 Sch 1A paras 5–10.

Tax payment dates

14.36 CGT is due for payment on 31 January following the end of the tax year in which the disposal takes place – as is any balance of income tax for that year, being the tax payable less the interim payments on account. On the same date the first instalment of income tax for the current year, being half the income tax for the preceding year, is due for payment, together with a similar amount on 31 July following the end of the year of assessment. [TMA 1970 ss 59A and 59B]. If tax remains unpaid on the day following the expiry of 28 days from the due date, the trustees may be liable for a surcharge of 5 per cent of the unpaid tax and a further 5 per cent surcharge where any tax remains unpaid following the expiry of six months from the due date, ie 31 July following the end of the next fiscal year. [Section 59C(2) and (3)]. The surcharge applies from the due date, which means the date on which the tax becomes due and payable [section 59C(12)], which does not extend to the payments on account required under section 59A(2). Payments on account may be reduced on making a claim under section 59A(3)–(6). An appeal may be lodged against the imposition of a surcharge where the taxpayer had a reasonable excuse other than shortage of money. [Section 59C(7)–(11)]. Unpaid tax, including a surcharge, will also be subject to interest at the rate applicable under FA 1989 s 178 and TMA 1970 s 86.

Liability and collection

14.37 In the case of a trust, the trustees are made responsible for the tax affairs of the trust under FA 1989 s 151, and recovery of the tax, interest surcharge or penalties may be recovered from relevant trustees under TMA 1970 s 107A. Relevant trustees are the trustees of the settlement at the time when the income or gains arose, and any subsequent trustees. [TMA 1970 s 118(1), (7) and (9); FA 1989 s 151(2)].

14.38 Trustees are liable for the IHT on settled property on a chargeable transfer, as are beneficiaries entitled to an interest in possession or who have obtained benefits under the trust, or in the case of non-resident trustees, the settlor. [IHTA 1984 s 201]. A trustee's liability is limited to the property he has actually received, or should have received but for his own neglect or default. [Section 204(2)]. The payment rules for IHT are set out in IHTA 1984 s 226 with the primary liability being six months after the end of the month in which the chargeable transfer is made, or, in the case of a transfer made after 5 April and before 1 October in any year, otherwise than on death, at the end of April in the following year.

14.39 The Revenue powers for collection and recovery of unpaid tax, interest, surcharges or penalties are set out in TMA 1970 ss 60–70. The date of payment by cheque is normally the day on which the cheque is received by the Revenue under section 70A. A trustee who has authorised the receipt of profits arising from trust property by a person entitled to them, or their agent, is only required to make a return of their name, address and the amount of the profits under section 76, except in the case of chargeable gains which are normally assessable on the trustees. [Section 77].

14.40 In the case of IHT, interest on unpaid tax is charged by IHTA 1984 s 233 and on unpaid instalments, where the instalment basis applies under IHTA 1984 s 227. [Section 234]. Interest on overpaid tax is payable to the taxpayer under section 235. The interest provisions may be modified in special cases where, for example, there is an order under the IPFDA 1975 which modifies the disposition on death, or on a gift *inter vivos*. Interest will only run from the date of the order. [Sections 236]. The Revenue may in certain cases secure payment of unpaid tax by imposing an Inland Revenue charge, or mortgage over assets. [Sections 237–244].

14.41 Where income tax or CGT has been overpaid, the excess is refunded together with interest in the form of a repayment supplement under ICTA

1988 s 824 and TCGA 1992 s 283. Interest paid on overdue tax is not deductible for tax purposes and interest or repayment supplements received are not subject to tax.

Inheritance tax returns

14.42 Where there is a transfer of value for IHT purposes, which is not a potentially exempt transfer under IHTA 1984 s 3A, the transferor must submit an IHT return (IHT100) to the Capital Taxes Office giving details of the transfer and any IHT payable.

14.43 In addition to the return IHT100 relating to transfers of value chargeable to IHT, such as a transfer by a settlor to the trustees of a discretionary trust, there will be chargeable events arising on, for example, property being transferred from the trustees to a beneficiary of a discretionary trust, the so-called 'exit charge' under IHTA 1984 s 65, or the ten-yearly charge under section 64 or on the termination of an interest in possession under section 52, unless this is exempt from charge under section 53. In these cases an Inland Revenue account for IHT on the chargeable event has to be submitted on form IHT101. The Revenue may make regulations about accounts for IHT purposes and describe their form and such particulars as may be required. [IHTA 1984 ss 256 and 257].

14.44 For IHT purposes the Revenue may require any person to furnish it with such information as it may require for IHT purposes by written notice specifying a time limit to respond of not less than 30 days, but such a notice can only be given with the consent of a Special Commissioner on being satisfied that in all the circumstances the Board is justified in proceeding under IHTA 1984 s 219(1) and (1A). A notice may be combined with an income tax information notice and a barrister or solicitor is only required to disclose non-privileged information without his client's consent. A solicitor may be obliged to disclose the name and address of his client and, if the client carries on a business outside the UK relating to the formation of trusts and companies or managing or administering them, the name and address of any person in the UK for whom such services or facilities have been provided in the course of his business. [Section 219(2)–(4)].

14.45 The Revenue may call for documents from anyone who has delivered or is liable to deliver an account, by written notice specifying the documents within the recipient's possession or power and requiring him to furnish accounts or particulars which the Revenue may reasonably require. [IHTA 1984 ss 216, 217 and 219A(1)]. This enables the Revenue to enquire into an account to determine whether it is in any way incorrect or incomplete, in order to make a determination under section 221. [Section 219A(2)]. Photocopies of documents are normally satisfactory but originals must be produced on demand. The Revenue may take copies and the notice must allow 30 days for compliance. Documents required for appeals need not be produced pending the appeal. [Section 219A(3)–(7)]. An appeal against a requirement to produce documents may be made under section 219B to the Special Commissioners. The Revenue has powers of inspection in respect of any property for the purposes of ascertaining its value, and may exchange information with other countries under a double taxation or exchange of information agreement. [Sections 220 and 220A].

14.46 The Revenue may give notice in writing to a person who appears to be liable to pay IHT on a transfer of value, specifying the date of the transfer, the value transferred and the property to which it relates, the transferor, the tax chargeable and the persons who are liable to pay the tax, the amount of any overpayment, the interest applicable thereto and any other matter which appears to be relevant. [IHTA 1984 s 221(1) and (2)]. This determination may be made in accordance with an account or return, if thought to be correct, or to the best of the Revenue's judgment. It must also specify the manner in which the appeal may be made but is otherwise determinative of the tax payable. [Section 221(3)–(6)].

14.47 An appeal against the determination can be made to the Special Commissioners under IHTA 1984 s 222, or direct to the High Court, if so agreed with the Revenue or by leave of the court on notification by the appellant. [Section 222(1)–(3)]. An appeal on the question of the value of land may be made to the Lands Tribunal. [Section 222(4)].

14.48 The appeal must be made within 30 days of service of the Notice of Determination, IHTA 1984 s 222(1), but an appeal out of time may be made with the consent of the Board or the Special Commissioners if there is a reasonable excuse and the appeal is made without unreasonable delay. [Sections 222 and 223]. The appeal before the Commissioners is not bound to follow the original grounds of appeal if the Special Commissioners so allow under section 224. An appeal from the Special Commissioners is made in the normal way to the High Court under section 225. The normal regulations in relation to the conduct of appeals in TMA 1970 ss 56B, 56C and 56D are applied by IHTA 1984 s 225A.

14.49 A notice of determination which can no longer be varied or quashed on appeal becomes evidence of the matters determined, and proceedings may take place on the basis of a certificate to that effect by an Officer of the Board that tax or interest is due which has not been paid. [IHTA 1984 s 254]. Where a determination has been made on the basis of a view of the law which then generally prevailed, and the tax paid, any question of whether the right amount has been paid should be determined on the same view, notwithstanding that a subsequent legal decision has indicated that the view of the law being used was or may have been wrong. [IHTA 1984 s 255].

Penalties

14.50 The normal income tax self-assessment penalties which apply to individuals in respect of failures to submit a timeous tax return under TMA

1970 s 8 apply in a similar manner to trustees in respect of a trust return, under TMA 1970 s 8A. The penalty is £100 plus £60 for each day on which the failure continues, if so determined by the General or Special Commissioners on an application by the Revenue. [TMA 1970 s 93(1)–(3)]. A further £100 penalty is levied if the return remains outstanding for a further six months. These fixed penalties may be reduced to the amount of tax actually payable in respect of the return under section 93(7). If the return remains outstanding for more than a year beyond the due date, and tax is payable, the amount of a penalty may be an amount not exceeding such tax liability. [Section 93(5)]. The daily penalty ceases once the completed return is submitted. [Section 93(6)]. The trustees may escape these penalties if they had a reasonable excuse for not delivering the return on time, or may set a determination aside, although in practice this is likely to be very difficult to establish where there are professional trustees. [Section 93(8)]. Various terms are defined by section 93(9) and (10).

14.51 As well as the penalty for the failure to make a return, there is a penalty for an incorrect trust return made fraudulently or negligently, in TMA 1970 s 95, which extends to incorrect returns, statements or declarations in connection with any claim or any allowance, deduction or relief in respect of income tax or CGT or the submission of any incorrect accounts with liability to income tax or CGT. The maximum penalty is the additional tax payable for the year in which the incorrect return etc is delivered, the next following year or any preceding year of assessment. [Section 95(2) and (3)]. Where the return was not submitted fraudulently or negligently but it subsequently becomes apparent that it was incorrect, the error must be remedied without unreasonable delay in order to avoid a penalty. [TMA 1970 s 97].

14.52 There are also penalties for failure to make partnership or corporation tax returns under TMA 1970 ss 93A and 94; for incorrect returns under TMA 1970 s 95A and FA 1998 Sch 18 para 89; for failure to produce documents as required by section 19A, under section 97AA of that Act; and for failure to comply with specific requirements to produce returns etc, under TMA 1970 s 98. PAYE penalties are covered by TMA 1970 s 98A. Further provisions in relation to penalties are given in TMA 1970 ss 100–107. Trustees are potentially liable to penalties and have to be particularly careful that they do not assist in the preparation of an incorrect return under TMA 1970 s 99, or give an incorrect certificate of non-taxability under section 99A. Where two or more tax-geared penalties could be charged these must not, in total, exceed the maximum penalty which can be levied. [TMA 1970 s 97A].

14.53 The penalty provisions in relation to IHT include a £100 fixed penalty on failure to deliver an account, which may be increased by the Commissioners to £60 per day until the account is delivered, with a further penalty if it is more than six months overdue unless there is a reasonable excuse. [IHTA 1984 s 245]. There are penalties for failure to provide information in IHTA 1984 s 245A; providing incorrect information under section 247; or failing to remedy errors under section 248. Proceedings for the recovery of penalties may be made under IHTA 1984 s 249, within the appropriate time limits under section 250. Penalties may be appealed against under IHTA 1984 s 251, to the High Court against a summary determination by the Special Commissioners and if not so appealed may be recoverable as a debt due to the Crown under section 252, subject to the Board's overriding power to mitigate under section 253.

14.54 Where the Revenue took penalty proceedings against a solicitor acting for an estate, for alleged underdeclaration of property values, not only were they held to be wrong in alleging negligence (*Robertson v IRC* [2002] STC (SCD) 182), but to have acted wholly unreasonably (*Robertson v IRC (No 2)* [2002] STC (SCD) 242). The solicitor had put in a provisional valuation on the Inland Revenue account for IHT on the basis of the information which he then had in accordance with normal practice and had acted prudently and properly throughout and fulfilled his statutory duties. The costs of the Special Commissioners hearing were therefore awarded against the Revenue.

Record-keeping

14.55 The requirement for trustees to keep records for the purposes of making proper tax returns under TMA 1970 s 8A are contained in TMA 1970 s 12B and are the same as for individual and partnership returns, i e the requirement is to keep all such records as may be required for the purpose of enabling trustees to make and deliver a correct and complete return for the fiscal year. [TMA 1970 s 12B(1)(a)]. The records have to be kept until the latest of the date the Revenue enquires are completed, or where an Officer of the Revenue no longer has power to make enquiries, i e the first anniversary of 31 January following the end of the year of assessment, except where the trustees are carrying on a trade, alone or in partnership, in which case it is the fifth anniversary of 31 January following the year of assessment. [Section 12B(2)].

14.56 If the notice to make the return is given late, the period for which records need to be kept may also be extended. [TMA 1970 s 12B(2)(a)]. In the case of a trade or profession the records must include particulars of amounts received and expended in the course of the trade, and of the receipts and expenditure and details of all sales and purchases where the trade involves dealing in goods, including supporting documents. [Section 12B(3)]. It is not always necessary to keep original records, except where specifically so required. [Section 12B(4) and (4A)]. Failure to keep proper records will involve a penalty of up to £3,000, except where their only purpose would have been to support a claim or election not included in the return, or are dividend vouchers or tax deduction certificates where details of the income may be proved by other documentary evidence such as bank statements. [Section 12B(5), (5A), (5B) and (6)]. Revenue guidance on record-keeping in SA BK4 'A General Guide to Keeping Records' and SA BK3 'A Guide to Keeping Records for the Self-employed' (which also applies to owners of let property and partners) may be helpful in ensuring that appropriate records are kept.

14.57 Trustees will normally wish to keep records for some time in case of any challenge by beneficiaries becoming entitled at a later date, eg on reaching their maturity. With capital gains records there can be a problem where there are pre-1996/97 capital losses, as there is no power within the Taxes Acts to agree these figures with the Revenue until such time as the losses can be used against subsequent trust gains (*Todd v South Essex Motors (Basildon) Ltd* [1988] STC 392). The records ultimately need to be sufficient to support a possible Revenue challenge in order to convince the Commissioners that the return is correct or the assessment is excessive. [TMA 1970 s 50(6)].

Deduction of tax from distributions

14.58 Where distributions are made to a life tenant from a trust, ie where the income is first of all received by the trustees and not mandated direct to the life tenant, the trustees must, on request, give the beneficiary a tax certificate under ICTA 1988 s 352. This is given on form R185 (non-discretionary trust) which distinguishes between:

(a) untaxed income;

(b) income liable at the Schedule F ordinary rate, eg UK dividends;

(c) income on which tax is treated as paid but is not repayable, other than income liable at the Schedule F rate, eg stock dividends;

(d) income liable at the lower rate or which has a lower rate tax credit, eg bank or building society interest;

(e) income liable at the basic rate, eg Schedule A; and

(f) foreign income where UK tax at less than the basic rate has been deducted when taking into account the overseas tax.

The form should show the gross amount of beneficiary's income, the UK tax or tax credit and the net amount of the beneficiary's share, which is then used by him in completing the trust supplementary pages in his personal tax return.

14.59 Where the trust is a discretionary one the trustees will have paid tax at the rate applicable to trusts, and the certificate of deduction on form R185 will show the nature of the payment, such as a distribution from a discretionary trust, profits, or other source out of which it is paid, eg the trust fund, the gross payment, the income tax deducted at the rate applicable to trusts, and the net payment.

14.60 In the case of a will trust, the trustees will use the form R185 or R185 (non-discretionary trusts) as appropriate once the trust has been established, which if it is a trust of residue may be some time after the date of death. If income is distributed to beneficiaries, form R185 (estate income) would be used for differentiating between income receivable, tax paid, and the taxable amount where it is subject to basic rate tax, lower rate tax, Schedule F ordinary rate tax, non-repayable basic rate tax, non-repayable lower rate tax and non-repayable Schedule F ordinary rate tax.

14.61 There follows over the remaining pages of Chapter 14 a detailed worked example.

General Trust Example

Completed return and calculation of tax payable

The trustees of the Florov trust were determined to complete the Trust and Estate Tax Return for 2002–03 and collected the relevant information, trust return, supplementary pages and tax calculation guide.

The trustees ran a small hotel on behalf of the trust and began by completing the Trust and Estate trade pages, TT1–TT4. They completed the business details and noted the accounting period from 1 January to 31 December 2002 in boxes 1.4 and 1.5.

They calculated the capital allowances and balancing charges for boxes 1.14 to 1.23. Turnover was in excess of £15,000, so they completed the standard accounts information (SAI) boxes, noting that the figures excluded VAT in box 1.28. The figures were extracted from the accounts for the year, which required a certain amount of reallocation of expenses to fit in with the headings in boxes 1.29 to 1.65. The trustees resolved to ask the accountants to change the accounts headings to match the SAI boxes in future to make this task easier. The net profit in 1.65 agreed with the accounts figure and the trustees considered what expenses would be disallowable for tax purposes and inserted speeding fines of £200 in box 1.37, entertaining expenses of £6,870 in box 1.39 and depreciation of £14,750 in box 1.44. The total of boxes 1.30 to 1.45 was inserted in box 1.66, the balancing charges in box 1.68 and the net business profit for tax purposes was calculated for boxes 1.73 and 1.76 at £82,471. There was a loss brought forward from 2001, during which the manager had been replaced, of £26,874, inserted in boxes 1.88 and 1.89, resulting in a taxable profit after losses brought forward, in box 1.90, of £55,597, which was also the figure of total profits from the business in box 1.92. The trustees completed the balance sheet summary figures and decided to submit the audited accounts with the tax return, as these explained the accounting policies used, and noted this in the white space for additional information.

The trustees were not Lloyd's Underwriters and could ignore the Lloyd's pages.

The trustees owned substantial areas of farmland and were partners in a farming partnership which prepared its accounts on a fiscal year basis. The partnership statement had been obtained from the farm accountants and the trustees used this to complete the Trust and Estate partnership pages TP1 and TP2. The trustees share of total taxable profits from this business, in box 2.22, were £42,555. The farming partnership had sold some partnership land during the year and the trustees share of the chargeable gain, after taper relief, was £26,740, in respect of which details were inserted on the capital gains pages TC2, TC3 and TC6.

The trustees owned farmland that was let to the partnership at a market rent, which required completion of the Trust and Estate land and property pages TL1 and TL2. There were no furnished lettings so the gross rent of £18,000 was inserted in box 3.20. As the land was let on a fully repairing lease there were no other expenses to claim and the profit for the year (box 3.42) was also £18,000.

The trust owned foreign shares and the trustees listed on the Trust and Estate foreign pages TF1–TF5 the country of origin, the gross dividend, the foreign tax and the amount chargeable, which was the gross amount; so columns B and E were the same, because the foreign tax at column D was being claimed as a credit and the box in column E was ticked accordingly. The total of column E (box 4.2) was £2,645.

The total of the foreign tax credits in column D, £248, was entered in box 4.9. The trust has a life tenant, Suzie, entitled to one half of the trust income, and three discretionary beneficiaries, Jon, James and Gemma. Therefore, the tax credit relief referable to that part of the net income, after deductions, chargeable at the Schedule F dividend trust rate of 25 per cent under ICTA 1988 s 686(1A)(a) and (5A), was half of £248, ie £124, inserted in box 4.9A.

The only chargeable gain made by the trust in the year was the sale of the partnership land, so the Trust and Estate capital gains pages TC1–TC8 were completed accordingly, the taxable gain for 2002–03, box 5.11, being £22,790 (£26,640 less the annual exempt amount of £3,850 for 2002–03).

The trust is UK-resident, so the Trust and Estate non-residence pages TNR1 and TNR2 are inapplicable.

Having completed the supplementary pages, the trustees turned to the Trust and Estate Tax Return and answered questions 1–5 and 8.16, 13, 14, 17, 18 in the affirmative and 6–7 and 8.1–8.14 and 10, 11, 12, 15A, 15B, 16 and 20 in the negative (or left them unchecked).

Interest from UK banks amounted to £5,420 gross (box 9.4), £1,084 tax deducted at source (box 9.3) and £4,336 net (box 9.2), of which half related to Suzie's life interest (box 13.9).

Dividends from UK companies amounted to £9,000 (box 9.15) with a tax credit of 1/9, £1,000 (box 9.16), totalling £10,000 (box 9.17).

There were no interest payments or annual payments made and no additions to the trust funds.

The trustees incurred trust management expenses of £5,000 (box 13.19), chargeable to income in accordance with the trust deed, of which half are related to Suzie's life interest. The figure of income charged at 10 per cent in box 13.7 being £5,000 (half the UK dividends of £10,000) plus £1,322.50 (half of foreign dividends of £2,645) was therefore £6,322.50, and the management expenses applicable thereto under ICTA 1988 s 689B were £2,500 (boxes 13.8, and 13.20). Income chargeable at the lower rate (box 13.9) was £2,710 (half the bank interest of £5,420).

The basic rate income applicable to Suzie was £27,798.50 (half of trading profits of £55,597) plus £21,277.50 (half of partnership profits of £42,555) and £9,000 (half of rents of £18,000), ie £58,076 (box 13.11).

Discretionary payments of £10,000 each were made to the three discretionary beneficiaries, returned at question 14. The unused tax pool brought forward from 2001–02 (box 14.15) was £19,873.

There were no capital payments to children of the settlor and no capital transactions with the settlor (questions 15A and 15B). The trust has never been non-resident (question 16). The trustees had not been able to submit the trust return by 30 September as they were awaiting the partnership statement from the farm accountants and so had to calculate the tax payable (question 17, see below). No repayment was due (question 18), but the trustees would want to receive any overpayment without delay so completed the relevant boxes.

The trustees' contact number was given at question 19 and their names and addresses at question 20. No other information was required at question 20, so the trustees signed the declaration and submitted the return well before 31 January 2004.

The tax calculation showed tax payable for 2002–03 of £41,198.77 (box 17.1) less paid on account £10,690, which appeared low because of the trading loss in 2001–02 and chargeable gain in 2002–03. The balance of £30,508.77 was paid on 28 January 2004, to be on the safe side, together with the first payment on account for 2003–04 of £16,725.08, a total of £47,233.85.

The calculations, using the Revenue's tax calculation guide, are shown on the following pages. The calculation identifies the different types of income, ie savings type income, dividend type income, other types of income and deemed income. Allowable deductions for interest or losses are shown and tax is calculated at the appropriate rates for each type of income.

Trust management expenses relating to income taxed at the rate applicable to trusts, or the Schedule F trust rate, are calculated and allocated in accordance with ICTA 1988 s 689B. Income liable at the rate applicable to trusts or the dividend (Schedule F) trust rate under ICTA 1988 s 686 is identified and the additional tax calculated. The tax pool under ICTA 1988 s 687 is calculated, together with any additional tax liability, or the tax pool carried forward. The tax due is computed, less foreign tax credits and including chargeable gains, and deducting payments on account. Then the payments on account for the following year are calculated, as is the amount payable or overpaid at 31 January following the end of the fiscal year.

Inland Revenue **Trust and Estate Tax Return** for the year ended 5 April **2003**

Tax reference

Date *6th April 2003*

Inland Revenue office

Area Director
London Trusts District
3rd Floor Charles House
375 Kensington High Street
London
W14 8QS

Issue address

WJB Chiltern plc
3 Sheldon Square
London
W2 6PS

Telephone *020 7605 9800*

For Reference *Florov Trust*

Please read this page first

The green arrows and instructions will guide you through your Tax Return

This Notice requires you by law to send me a Tax Return for the year from 6 April 2002 to 5 April 2003, containing details of the income and capital gains. I've sent you this paper form to fill in, or you could use:

- ***other Inland Revenue approved paper versions, OR***
- ***the Electronic Lodgement Service (available through some tax advisers).***

Make sure the Tax Return, and any documents I ask for, reach me by:

- ***the later of 30 September 2003 and 2 months after the date this notice was given if you want me to calculate the trust or estate's tax, OR***
- ***the later of 31 January 2004 and 3 months after the date this notice was given, at the latest, or you will be liable to an automatic penalty of £100.***

Make sure your payment of any tax the trust or estate owes reaches me by 31 January 2004. Otherwise, you will have to pay interest, and perhaps a surcharge.

The Trust and Estate Tax Return may be checked. Please remember that there are penalties for supplying false information.

Calculating your tax

You can choose to calculate the trust or estate's tax. But if you don't want to, and providing I receive the Return by 30 September, I'll work out the tax for you and I'll also let you know if there's tax to pay by 31 January 2004.

***However,** if you file later than 30 September or 2 months after the date this notice was given, see the Tax Calculation Guide (sent with this Return unless I know you have a tax adviser).*

The Trust and Estate Tax Return - your responsibilities

I have sent you pages 1 to 12 of the Tax Return.

You might need other forms - 'supplementary Pages' - if the trust or estate had particular income or capital gains. Use page 3 to check.

***You** are responsible for sending me a complete and correct return, but **we** are here to help **you** get it right.*

Four ways we can help you

- ***look** at the Trust and Estate Tax Return Guide (sent with this Tax Return, unless I know you have a tax adviser). It should answer most of your questions, **OR***
- ***visit** our website at www.inlandrevenue.gov.uk, **OR***
- ***ring** me on the above number - when the office is closed, call our Helpline on 0845 9000 444, **OR***
- ***call** in to one of our Inland Revenue Enquiry Centres - look under 'Inland Revenue' in the phone book.*

SA900 (Substitute)(LexisNexis UK)

■ Trust and Estate Tax Return: Page 1

INCOME AND CAPITAL GAINS *for the year ended 5 April 2003*

Step 1 You may not have to answer all the questions in this Tax Return. *Tick if this applies*

- see notes on pages 4 and 6 of the Trust and Estate Tax Return Guide

1) **If you are the trustee of a bare trust** (except an unauthorised unit trust), that is, one in which the beneficiary(ies) has/have an immediate and absolute title to both capital and income you can go straight to Question 19 on page 11. ☐

2) **If you are the personal representative of a deceased person,** completing this Tax Return for a period of administration **and all** the points below apply:
   - all the income arose in the UK
   - you do not wish to claim reliefs
   - no annual payments have been made out of capital
   - all income has had tax deducted before you received it (or is UK dividends with tax credit)
   - there are no accrued income charges or reliefs, no income from relevant discounted securities, gilt strips, offshore income gains, or gains on life insurance policies, life annuities or capital redemption policies where no tax is treated as having been paid on the gain.

   Then, **if you have not made any chargeable disposals**, go straight to Question 19 on page 11 ☐

   or, **if you have made chargeable disposals,** answer Questions 5 and 6 at Step 2, Question 8 and then Questions 17 to 22. ☐

3) **If you are the trustee of an interest in possession trust** (one which is exclusively an interest in possession trust), and:
   - no income arose to the trust, **or** ☐
   - you have mandated all the trust income to the beneficiary(ies), **or** ☐
   - all the income arose in the UK and has had tax deducted before you receive it (or is UK dividends with tax credit), **or** ☐
   - you have mandated part of the income to the beneficiary(ies) where the part you have not mandated comprises only income arising in the UK which has had tax deducted before you received it ☐

   and all of the following points apply:
   - the answer will be 'No' in boxes 8.11 and 8.13 of Question 8
   - there are no accrued income charges or reliefs, no income from relevant discounted securities, gilt strips, company buy-backs, offshore income gains, or gains on life insurance policies, life annuities or capital redemption policies
   - you do not wish to claim reliefs (Question 10)
   - no annual payments have been made out of capital (Question 11)
   - no further capital has been added to the settlement (Question 12)
   - no capital payments have been made to or for the benefit of minor unmarried children of the settlor during his/her lifetime (Question 15A)
   - the trust has never been non-resident and has never received any capital from another trust which is, or at any time has been, non-resident (Question 16)

   Then, **if you have not made any chargeable disposals**, go straight to Question 19 on page 11 ☐

   or, **if you have made chargeable disposals,** answer Questions 5 and 6 at Step 2, Question 8 and then Questions 17 to 22. ☐

4) **If you are the trustee of a charitable trust**, and:
   - you are claiming exemption from tax on all your income and gains, you can go straight to Question 7 and then Question 22, **or**
   - you are claiming exemption from tax on only part of your income and gains, you must complete this Return for any income or gains for which you are not claiming exemption.

5) **In any other cases,** including if you are the trustee of an unauthorised unit trust, you should go to Step 2.

Step 2 Answer Questions 1 to 7 on page 3 to check if you need supplementary Pages to give details of particular income or gains. Pages 8 and 9 of the Trust and Estate Tax Return Guide will help. (Ask the Orderline for a Guide if I haven't sent you one with the Tax Return, and you want one.) If you answer **'Yes'**, ask the Orderline for the appropriate supplementary Pages and Notes.

Ring the Orderline on 0845 9000 404 or fax on 0845 9000 604 for any you need (closed Christmas Day, Boxing Day and New Year's Day). Make sure you ask for the supplementary Pages for the Trust and Estate Tax Return.

■ Trust and Estate Tax Return: Page 2

INCOME AND CAPITAL GAINS *for the year ended 5 April 2003* continued

Make sure you have the supplementary Pages you need and then tick the box below when you have filled them in.

Q1 Did the trust or estate make any profit or loss from a sole trade? (Read page 8 of the Trust and Estate Tax Return Guide if you are the personal representative of a deceased Name at Lloyd's.) — Yes ✓ — *Trust and estate trade* ✓

Q2 Did the trust or estate make any profit or loss or have any other income from a partnership? — Yes ✓ — *Trust and estate partnership* ✓

Q3 Did the trust or estate receive any rent or other income from land and property in the UK? — Yes ✓ — *Trust and estate land and property* ✓

Q4 Did the trust or estate receive any income from foreign companies or savings institutions, offshore funds or trusts abroad, land and property abroad, or gains on foreign life insurance policies? — Yes ✓

Is the trust or estate claiming relief for foreign tax paid on foreign income or gains, or relief from UK tax under a Double Taxation Agreement? — Yes ✓ — *Trust and estate foreign* ✓

Q5 Capital gains

- did the trust or estate dispose of assets worth more than £15,400 in total? — Yes ✓
- were the trust's or estate's chargeable gains more than its annual exemption or do you want to make a claim or election for the year? — Yes ✓

Does this Return include the disposal of assets for either a Trust/Settlement with 'separate funds', or for just one of those separate funds? Read page 9 of the Trust and Estate Tax Return Guide. — Yes — *Trust and estate capital gains* ✓

Q6 Is the trust claiming to be not resident in the UK, or dual resident in the UK and another country for all or part of the year for:

- Income Tax? — Yes
- Capital Gains Tax? — Yes — *Trust and estate non-residence etc*

Q7 Is the trust claiming total or partial exemption from tax because of its charitable status? — Yes — *Trust and estate charities*

Q8 **Read pages 10 and 11 of the Trust and Estate Return Guide.**

Are you completing this Tax Return

	No		Yes	
- for a period of administration?	8.1	✓	8.2	
- as the trustee of an unauthorised unit trust?	8.3	✓	8.4	
- as the trustee of an employment related trust?	8.5	✓	8.6	
- as the trustee of an Heritage Maintenance Fund?	8.7	✓	8.8	
Trustees of Funded Unapproved Retirement Benefit Schemes (FURBS): have you provided any non-relevant benefits to any of the scheme's beneficiaries?	8.9	✓	8.10	
If you are a trustee,				
- can any settlor (or living settlor's spouse) benefit from the capital or income?	8.11	✓	8.12	
- are you a participator in an underlying non-resident company (a company that would be a close company if it were resident in the UK)?	8.13	✓	8.14	
- is the trust liable to Income Tax at either or both the rate applicable to trusts (34%) or the dividend trust rate (25%) on any part of the income (for example, it is a discretionary trust)?	8.15		8.16	✓

Now fill in any supplementary Pages BEFORE answering Questions 9 to 21, as directed.
Please use blue or black ink to fill in the Trust and Estate Tax Return.
Please do not include pence. Round down income and gains. Round up tax credits and tax deductions.
Round to the nearest pound.

■ TRUST AND ESTATE TAX RETURN: PAGE 3 — *Please turn over*

INCOME *for the year ended 5 April 2003*

Q9 Did the trust or estate receive any other income not already included on the supplementary Pages? YES ✓ — If yes, fill in boxes 9.1 to 9.40 as appropriate.

You may, **if you wish**, not complete some of the boxes in 9.1 to 9.40 in the following circumstances:

a) **If you are the trustee of an interest in possession trust (one which is exclusively an interest in possession trust)**, you may exclude income which has had tax deducted before you received it (or is UK dividends with tax credit) unless:

(i) that income has not been mandated to the beneficiary and there is accrued income scheme relief to set against the interest or you are claiming losses against general income, **or**

(ii) its exclusion would make you liable to make a payment on account which would not be due if you included it - see page 11 of the Trust and Estate Tax Calculation Guide concerning payments on account **before** following this guidance.

b) **If you are the trustee of a (non-interest in possession) trust where the income is treated as the settlor's for tax purposes** because the settlor has retained an interest (if in doubt ask the Orderline for *Help Sheet IR270: Trusts and settlements - income treated as the settlor's*) you may exclude income which has had tax deducted before you received it (or is UK dividends with tax credit) unless any of the following apply:

- there is accrued income scheme relief to set against the interest, **or**
- you are claiming reliefs (Question 10) which exceed the untaxed income, **or**
- you are claiming losses against general income, **or**
- the exclusion would make you liable to make payments on account which would not be due if you included it – see page 11 of the Trust and Estate Tax Calculation Guide concerning payments on account **before** following this guidance.

c) **If you are the personal representative of a deceased person** you may exclude income which has had tax deducted before you received it (or is UK dividends with tax credit) unless there is accrued income scheme relief to set against the interest. If the reliefs claimed at Question 10 on page 5 exceed untaxed income, you will need to include estate income that has had tax deducted to ensure a repayment can be calculated.

- Have you received any taxed income (or UK dividends with tax credit) which you have not included in this Trust and Estate Tax Return because (a), (b) or (c) above apply? YES

■ *Interest*

- Interest from UK banks, building societies and deposit takers (interest from UK Internet accounts must be included) – *if you have more than one bank or building society etc account enter* **totals** *in the boxes.*

	Amount after tax deducted	Tax deducted	Gross amount before tax / Taxable amount
- where **no tax** has been deducted			9.1 £
- where **tax has** been deducted – *the Working Sheet on page 13 of the Guide will help you to fill in boxes 9.2 to 9.4.*	9.2 £ *4,336.00*	9.3 £ *1,084.00*	9.4 £ *5,420.00*
• Interest distributions from UK authorised unit trusts and open-ended investment companies (dividend distributions go in boxes 9.18 to 9.20)	9.5 £	9.6 £	9.7 £
• National Savings & Investments (other than First Option Bonds and Fixed Rate Savings Bonds)			Taxable amount 9.8 £
• National Savings & Investments First Option Bonds and Fixed Rate Savings Bonds	9.9 £	9.10 £	9.11 £
• Other income from UK savings and investments (except dividends)	9.12 £	9.13 £	9.14 £

■ Trust and Estate Tax Return: Page 4

INCOME *for the year ended 5 April 2003* continued

■ *Dividends*

• Dividends and other qualifying distributions from UK companies	Dividend/distribution 9.15 £ *9,000.00*	Tax credit 9.16 £ *1,000.00*	Dividend/distribution plus credit 9.17 £ *10,000.00*
• Dividend distributions from UK authorised unit trusts and open-ended investment companies	Dividend/distribution 9.18 £	Tax credit 9.19 £	Dividend/distribution plus credit 9.20 £
• Scrip dividends from UK companies	Dividend 9.21 £	Notional tax 9.22 £	Dividend plus notional tax 9.23 £
• Dividends and other qualifying distributions received by unauthorised unit trusts	Amount of dividend only 9.24 £		
• Scrip dividends received by unauthorised unit trusts	Amount of dividend only 9.25 £		
• Non-qualifying distributions and loans written off	9.26 £	Notional tax 9.27 £	Taxable amount 9.28 £

■ *Gains on UK life insurance policies, life annuities and capital redemption policies*

• on which no tax is treated as paid		Amount of gain 9.29 £
• on which tax is treated as paid	Tax treated as paid 9.30 £	Amount of gain 9.31 £

■ *Other income*

• Other income	Amount after tax deducted 9.32 £	Tax deducted 9.33 £	Gross amount before tax 9.34 £
		Losses brought forward 9.35 £	Losses used in 2002-03 9.36 £
		Losses sustained in 2002-03 9.37 £	
• Deemed income etc. *(see page 19 of the Trust and Estate Tax Return Guide)*			Taxable amount 9.38 £
• Company purchase of its own shares		Tax credit 9.39 £	Taxable amount 9.40 £

OTHER INFORMATION *for the year ended 5 April 2003*

Q10 Do you want to claim any reliefs? YES

If yes, fill in boxes 10.1 to 10.4 as appropriate. If not applicable go to question 11.

■ ***Interest eligible for relief on qualifying loans***

	Amount of payment
• Interest on loans to pay Inheritance Tax	10.1 £

■ ***Other charges***

	Amount of payment	Tax deducted	Gross amount
• Annuities and other annual payments	10.2 £	10.3 £	10.4 £

Q11 Were any annual payments made out of capital or out of income not brought into charge to Income Tax? YES

If yes, fill in boxes 11.1 to 11.3 as appropriate. If not applicable go to question 12.

	Amount of payment	Tax deducted	Gross amount
• Annual payments	11.1 £	11.2 £	11.3 £

If you are a personal representative, go to Question 17. There is no need to fill in Questions 12 to 16.

Q12 Have any assets or funds been put into the trust? YES

If yes, fill in boxes 12.1 to 12.9 as appropriate. If not applicable go to question 13.

Settlor's name and address	Description of asset	Value of asset
12.1 Postcode	12.2	12.3 £
12.4 Postcode	12.5	12.6 £
12.7 Postcode	12.8	12.9 £

■ TRUST AND ESTATE TAX RETURN: PAGE 6

OTHER INFORMATION *for the year ended 5 April 2003*

If you ticked box 8.15 in Question 8, page 3, then you do not need to complete this page - please go to Question 16 on page 9 and carry on filling in the Tax Return.
If you have ticked box 8.16 in Question 8, page 3, complete Questions 13 to 15.

13 Is any part of the trust income not liable to tax at the rate applicable to trusts or the dividend trust rate? YES ✓ If yes, fill in boxes 13.1 to 13.22 below. If not applicable, fill in boxes 13.13 to 13.22.

• Amount of income charged at the 10% rate treated as that of the settlor		13.1 £
• Trust management expenses applicable to the income in box 13.1	13.2 £	
• Amount of income chargeable at the lower rate treated as that of the settlor		13.3 £
• Trust management expenses applicable to the income in box 13.3	13.4 £	
• Amount of income chargeable at the basic rate treated as that of the settlor		13.5 £
• Trust management expenses applicable to the income in box 13.5	13.6 £	
• Amount of income charged at the 10% rate applicable to beneficiaries whose entitlement is not subject to the trustees' (or any other person's) discretion		13.7 £ 6,322.50
• Trust management expenses applicable to the income in box 13.7	13.8 £ 2,500.00	
• Amount of income chargeable at the lower rate applicable to beneficiaries whose entitlement is not subject to the trustees' (or any other person's) discretion		13.9 £ 2,710.00
• Trust management expenses applicable to the income in box 13.9	13.10 £	
• Amount of income chargeable at the basic rate applicable to beneficiaries whose entitlement is not subject to the trustees' (or any other person's) discretion		13.11 £ 58,076.00
• Trust management expenses applicable to the income in box 13.11	13.12 £	
• Amount of income charged at the 10% rate allocated to specific purposes		13.13 £
• Trust management expenses applicable to the income in box 13.13	13.14 £	
• Amount of income chargeable at the lower rate allocated to specific purposes		13.15 £
• Trust management expenses applicable to the income in box 13.15	13.16 £	
• Amount of income chargeable at the basic rate allocated to specific purposes		13.17 £
• Trust management expenses applicable to the income in box 13.17	13.18 £	
• Total amount of deductible trust management expenses *(see notes on pages 21 to 24 of the Trust and Estate Tax Return Guide)*		13.19 £ 5,000.00
• Expenses set against income not liable at the rate applicable to trusts	total of column above 13.20 £ 2,500.00	
• Total income not liable to UK Income Tax and not included elsewhere on this Trust and Estate Tax Return (non-resident trusts only)		13.21 £
• Exceptional deductions		13.22 £

■ TRUST AND ESTATE TAX RETURN: PAGE 7 *Please turn over*

OTHER INFORMATION *for the year ended 5 April 2003*

If you ticked box 8.15 in Question 8, page 3, then you do **not** need to complete this page - please go to Question 16 on page 9 and carry on filling in the Tax Return.
If you have ticked box 8.16 in Question 8, page 3, complete Questions 13 to 15.

Q14 Have discretionary payments of income been made to beneficiaries? *Trustees of Heritage Maintenance Funds:* ***do not*** *complete these boxes for expenditure on heritage property.*
See notes on page 24 of the Trust and Estate Tax Return Guide before filling in these boxes.

YES ✓ — **If yes,** fill in boxes 14.1 to 14.15 as appropriate. **If not applicable, fill in box 14.15 only.**

Box	Name of beneficiary	Box	Amount of payment	Tick the box if the beneficiary was a minor and unmarried child of the settlor and the settlor was alive when payment was made.
14.1	*Jon*	14.2	£ *10,000.00*	
14.3	*James*	14.4	£ *10,000.00*	
14.5	*Gemma*	14.6	£ *10,000.00*	
14.7		14.8	£	
14.9		14.10	£	
14.11		14.12	£	
14.13		14.14	£	

- Amount, if any, of unused tax pool brought forward from last year (enter '0' if appropriate) — 14.15 £ *19,873.00*

Q15A Have the trustees made any capital payments to, or for the benefit of, minor, unmarried children of the settlor during the settlor's lifetime?

YES — **If yes,** fill in box 15.1. If not applicable go to question 15B.

- Total capital payments to minor unmarried children — Amount paid 15.1 £

Q15B Were there capital transactions between the trustees and the settlors?

YES — **If yes,** fill in boxes 15.2 to 15.13 as appropriate. If not applicable go to question 16.

■ ***Capital transactions between the trustees and settlors*** *(Read page 24 of the Trust and Estate Tax Return Guide)*

Date	Amount	Name of company (if appropriate)	Registered office
15.2 / /	15.3 £	15.4	15.5 Postcode
15.6 / /	15.7 £	15.8	15.9 Postcode
15.10 / /	15.11 £	15.12	15.13 Postcode

■ Trust and Estate Tax Return: Page 8

OTHER INFORMATION *for the year ended 5 April 2003*

Q16 **Has the trust at any time been non-resident or received any capital from another trust which is, or at any time has been, non-resident?** YES

If YES, have the trustees made any capital payments to, or provided any benefits for, the beneficiaries? YES

If yes, read pages 24 and 25 of the Trust and Estate Tax Return Guide and if appropriate fill in box 16.1. If not applicable go to question 17.

- Total capital payments or value of benefits provided 16.1 £

Please give details of the payments in box 16.1 in the boxes below. If there are insufficient boxes please provide the additional details on a separate sheet.

Name of beneficiary 16.2

Name of beneficiary 16.3

Address of beneficiary 16.4 Postcode

Address of beneficiary 16.5 Postcode

Amount/value of payment/benefit 16.6 £

Amount/value of payment/benefit 16.7 £

Name of beneficiary 16.8

Name of beneficiary 16.9

Address of beneficiary 16.10 Postcode

Address of beneficiary 16.11 Postcode

Amount/value of payment/benefit 16.12 £

Amount/value of payment/benefit 16.13 £

Name of beneficiary 16.14

Name of beneficiary 16.15

Address of beneficiary 16.16 Postcode

Address of beneficiary 16.17 Postcode

Amount/value of payment/benefit 16.18 £

Amount/value of payment/benefit 16.19 £

If you have received capital from any other trust which is, or at any time has been, non-resident please provide the following details:

Name of trust 16.20

Date trust set up 16.21 / /

Address of trustee 16.22 Postcode

Amount of value received 16.23 £

OTHER INFORMATION *for the year ended 5 April 2003*

Q17 Do you want to calculate the tax? YES ✓ — **If yes,** do it now and then fill in boxes 17.1 to 17.9 below. The *Trust and Estate Tax Calculation Guide* will help you.

- Total tax due for 2002-03 **before** you made any payments on account *(put the amount in brackets if an overpayment)* — 17.1 £ *41,198.77*
- Tax due for earlier years — 17.2 £
- Tick box 17.3 if you have calculated tax overpaid for earlier years and enter the amount in box 17.4 — 17.3 — 17.4 £
- Tick box 17.5 if you are making a claim to reduce your payments on account, enter your **reduced** payment in box 17.7 and say why in the 'Additional information' box, box 21.7, on page 12 — 17.5 — Tick box 17.6 if you do not need to make payments on account — 17.6
- Your first payment on account for 2003-04 *(include the pence)* — 17.7 £ *16,725.08*
- Tick box 17.8 if you are claiming a repayment of 2003-04 tax now and enter the amount in box 17.9 — 17.8 — 17.9 £

Q18 Do you want to claim a repayment if the trust or estate has paid too much tax? *(If you do not tick 'Yes', or the tax overpaid is below £10, I will use the amount you are owed to reduce the next tax bill.)* YES ✓ — **If yes,** fill in boxes 18.1 to 18.12 as appropriate. If not applicable go to question 19.

Should the repayment (or payment) be sent:

- to your bank or building society account? *Tick box 18.1 and fill in boxes 18.3 to 18.7* — 18.1

or

- to your nominee's bank or building society account? *Tick box 18.2 and fill in boxes 18.3 to 18.12* — 18.2

We prefer to make repayment direct into a bank or building society account. (But tick box 18.8A or box 18.8B if you would like a cheque to be sent to you or your nominee.)

Name of bank or building society — 18.3

Branch sort code — 18.4

Account number — 18.5

Name of account holder — 18.6

Building society reference. — 18.7

If you would like a cheque to be sent to

- you at the address on page 1, *tick box 18.8A* — 18.8A ✓

or

- your nominee, *tick box 18.8B* — 18.8B

If your nominee is your agent, *tick box 18.9A* — 18.9A

Agent's reference for you (if your nominee is your agent) — 18.9

I authorise

Name of your nominee/agent — 18.10

Nominee/agent address — 18.11

Postcode

to receive on my behalf the amount due

18.12 — *This authority must be signed by you. A photocopy of your signature will not do.*

Signature

■ Trust and Estate Tax Return: Page 10

OTHER INFORMATION *for the year ended 5 April 2003*

19 Trustee or personal representative details

- Your daytime telephone number — **19.1**
- your agent's telephone number, and — **19.2** *020 7339 9000*
- your agent's name and address, and — **19.3** *WJB Chiltern plc*, *3 Sheldon Square*, *London*, Postcode *W2 6PS*
- your agent's reference for you. — **19.4**

20 Have there been any changes to the names and addresses of the trustees or personal representatives?

YES

If yes, fill in boxes 20.1 to 20.12, as appropriate. If not applicable go to question 21.

If the 'acting trustee' has changed, please give details in the 'Additional information' box, box 21.7 on page 12.

- Retiring trustees' or personal representatives' names and addresses

20.1 Postcode

20.2 Postcode

20.3 Postcode

20.4 Postcode

- New trustees' or personal representatives' names and addresses

20.5 Postcode

20.6 Postcode

20.7 Postcode

20.8 Postcode

- Existing trustees' or personal representatives' names and new addresses

20.9 Postcode

20.10 Postcode

20.11 Postcode

20.12 Postcode

Please turn over

OTHER INFORMATION *for the year ended 5 April 2003*

Q21 Other Information

- If you are completing this Trust and Estate Tax Return as a personal representative, please enter in box 21.1 the date of death of the deceased. — 21.1 Date / /
- If the administration period ceased in the year to 5 April 2003, please enter in box 21.2 the date of cessation. — 21.2 Date / /
- Tick box 21.3 if the administration period ceased in the year to 5 April 2003 and there is a continuing trust. — 21.3
- If you are a trustee and the trust was terminated in the year to 5 April 2003 please enter in box 21.4 the date of termination and, in the 'Additional information' box, box 21.7 below, the reason for termination. — 21.4 Date / /
- If this Trust and Estate Tax Return contains any figures that are provisional because you do not yet have final figures, please tick box 21.5. Page 25 of the Trust and Estate Tax Return Guide explains the circumstances in which provisional figures may be used and asks for some additional information to be provided in box 21.7 below. — 21.5
- If any 2002-03 tax was refunded directly by the Inland Revenue office, or (personal representatives only) by the Benefits Agency (in Northern Ireland, the Social Security Agency), please enter the amount in box 21.6. Do **not** include any refunds of excessive payments on account. — 21.6 Amount £

21.7 *Additional information*

Boxes 13.7, 13.9, 13.11: Beneficiaries' income not subject to trustee's discretion
Suzie 50.00%

Q22 Declaration

I have filled in and am sending back to you the following Trust and Estate Tax Return Pages:

Page	Tick	Page	Tick	Page	Tick
1 to 12 of this form	✓	*Trust and estate land and property*	✓		
Trust and estate trade	✓	*Trust and estate foreign*	✓	*Trust and estate non-residence etc*	
Trust and estate partnership	✓	*Trust and estate capital gains*	✓	*Trust and estate charities*	

Before you send the completed Tax Return back to the Inland Revenue office, you must sign the statement below.

If you give false information or conceal any part of trust or estate income or chargeable gains, you may be liable to financial penalties and/or you may be prosecuted.

22.1 **The information I have given in this Tax Return is correct and complete to the best of my knowledge and belief.**

Signature Date

- Please PRINT your name in box 22.2 — 22.2
- Enter the capacity in which you are signing — 22.3

Inland Revenue

Income for the year ended 5 April 2003

TRUST AND ESTATE TRADE

Fill in these boxes first

Name of trust or estate: *The Trustees of Florov Trust*

Tax reference:

The notes on pages TTN1 and TTN2 tell you when you need to complete more than one set of Trust and Estate Trade Pages. You must complete a separate copy of these Pages:

- *for each trade, and*
- *for each set of accounts relating to the basis period.*

Box numbers 1.9, 1.82 and 1.94 to 1.96 are not used on these Pages.

Business details

Name of business **1.1**

Description of business **1.2**

Address of business **1.3**

Accounting period
Read page TTN2 of the Notes before filling in these boxes

Start **1.4** *01/01/2002* End **1.5** *31/12/2002*

- Tick box 1.6 if details in boxes 1.1 or 1.3 have changed since the last Trust and Estate Tax Return **1.6**
- Date of commencement if after 5 April 2000 **1.7** / /
- Date of cessation if before 6 April 2003 **1.8** / /
- Tick box 1.10 if you entered details for all relevant accounting periods on last year's Trust and Estate Tax Return and boxes 1.14 to 1.73 and 1.99 to 1.115 will be blank **1.10**
- Tick box 1.11 if the accounts do not cover the period from the last accounting date (explain why in the 'Additional information' box, box 1.116) **1.11**
- Tick box 1.12 if the accounting date has changed (only if this is a permanent change and you want it to count for tax) **1.12**
- Tick box 1.13 if this is the second or further change (explain in box 1.116 on page TT4 why you have not used the same date as last year) **1.13**

Capital allowances and balancing charges

	Capital allowances	Balancing charges
Cars costing more than £12,000 (A separate calculation must be made for each car)	**1.14** £ *5,200.00*	**1.15** £
Other business plant and machinery	**1.16** £ *8,661.00*	**1.17** £
Agricultural or Industrial Buildings Allowance (A separate calculation must be made for each block of expenditure.)	**1.18** £	**1.19** £
Other capital allowances claimed (Separate calculations must be made.)	**1.20** £ *4,162.00*	**1.21** £
Total capital allowances/balancing charges	total of column above **1.22** £ *18,023.00*	total of column above **1.23** £

- Tick box 1.22A if box 1.22 includes enhanced capital allowances for environmentally friendly expenditure **1.22A**

Income and expenses

If the annual turnover is £15,000 or more, **ignore** *boxes 1.24 to 1.26. Instead fill in Page TT2*

If the annual turnover is below £15,000, **fill in boxes 1.24 to 1.26 instead of Page TT2.** *Read page TTN2 of the Notes*

- Turnover including other business receipts and goods etc. taken for personal use (and balancing charges from box 1.23) **1.24** £
- Expenses allowable for tax (including capital allowances from box 1.22) **1.25** £

Net profit (put figure in brackets if a loss) box 1.24 *minus* box 1.25 **1.26** £

You must now fill in Page TT3

SA901 (Substitute)(LexisNexis UK)

Trust and Estate Tax Return ■ Trade: page TT1

Income and expenses

You must fill in this Page if the annual turnover is £15,000 or more - read page TTN2 of the Notes

If the trust or estate was registered for VAT, do the figures in boxes 1.29 to 1.64 include VAT? **1.27** [ ] or exclude VAT? **1.28** ✓

	Disallowable expenses included in boxes 1.46 to 1.63	Total expenses	Sales/business income (turnover)
			1.29 £ *326,627.00*
• Cost of sales	**1.30** £	**1.46** £ *70,972.00*	
• Construction industry subcontractor costs	**1.31** £	**1.47** £	
• Other direct costs	**1.32** £	**1.48** £	
		Gross profit/(loss)	box 1.29 *minus* (boxes 1.46 + 1.47 + 1.48) **1.49** £ *255,655.00*
		Other income/profits	**1.50** £
• Employee costs	**1.33** £	**1.51** £ *63,275.00*	
• Premises costs	**1.34** £	**1.52** £ *40,820.00*	
• Repairs	**1.35** £	**1.53** £ *15,690.00*	
• General administrative expenses	**1.36** £	**1.54** £ *10,380.00*	
• Motor expenses	**1.37** £ *200.00*	**1.55** £ *11,863.00*	
• Travel and subsistence	**1.38** £	**1.56** £ *4,727.00*	
• Advertising, promotion and entertainment	**1.39** £ *6,870.00*	**1.57** £ *10,870.00*	
• Legal and professional costs	**1.40** £	**1.58** £ *1,250.00*	
• Bad debts	**1.41** £	**1.59** £ *650.00*	
• Interest	**1.42** £	**1.60** £ *220.00*	
• Other finance charges	**1.43** £	**1.61** £	
• Depreciation and loss/(profit) on sale	**1.44** £ *14,750.00*	**1.62** £ *14,750.00*	
• Other expenses	**1.45** £	**1.63** £ *2,486.00*	
	Put the total of boxes 1.30 to 1.45 in box 1.66 below	**Total expenses**	total of boxes 1.51 to 1.63 **1.64** £ *176,981.00*
		Net profit/(loss)	box 1.49 + 1.50 *minus* 1.64 **1.65** £ *78,674.00*

Tax adjustments to net profit or loss

• Disallowable expenses	boxes 1.30 to 1.45 **1.66** £ *21,820.00*	
• Goods etc. taken for personal use and other adjustments (apart from disallowable expenses) that increase profits	**1.67** £	
• Balancing charges (from box 1.23)	**1.68** £	
Total additions to net profit (deduct from net loss)		boxes 1.66 + 1.67 + 1.68 **1.69** £ *21,820.00*
• Capital allowances (from box 1.22)	**1.70** £ *18,023.00*	
• Deductions from net profit (add to net loss)	**1.71** £	boxes 1.70 + 1.71 **1.72** £ *18,023.00*
Net business profit for tax purposes (put figure in brackets if a loss)		boxes 1.65 + 1.69 *minus* 1.72 **1.73** £ *82,471.00*

TRUST AND ESTATE TAX RETURN ■ TRADE: PAGE TT2 *Now fill in Page TT3*

You must fill in boxes 1.74 and 1.75 and all other boxes that apply to the trust or estate on this Page

Adjustments to arrive at taxable profit or loss

Basis period begins	1.74	01 / 01 / 2002
and ends	1.75	31 / 12 / 2002
Profit or loss of this account for tax purposes (box 1.26 or 1.73)	1.76	£ 82,471.00
Adjustment to arrive at profit or loss for this basis period	1.77	£
• Overlap profit brought forward	1.78	£
• Deduct overlap relief used this year	1.79	£
• Overlap profit carried forward	1.80	£
• Averaging for farmers, and creators of literary or artistic works (see the Notes, page TTN6 if you made a loss for 2002-03)	1.81	£
Net profit for 2002-03 (if a loss, enter '0')	1.83	£ 82,471.00
Allowable loss for 2002-03 (if a profit, enter '0')	1.84	£
• Loss offset against other income for 2002-03	1.85	£
• Loss to carry back	1.86	£
• Loss to carry forward (that is an allowable loss not claimed in any other way)	1.87	£
• Losses brought forward from earlier years	1.88	£ 26,874.00
• Losses brought forward from earlier years used this year	1.89	£ 26,874.00
Taxable profit after losses brought forward (box 1.83 *minus* box 1.89)	1.90	£ 55,597.00
• Any other business income	1.91	£
Total taxable profits from this business (box 1.90 + box 1.91)	1.92	£ 55,597.00
• Tick box 1.93 if the figure in box 1.92 is provisional	1.93	

Subcontractors in the construction industry

• Deductions made by contractors on account of tax (please send the CIS25s to us) for the period 6 April 2002 to 5 April 2003	1.97	£

Tax deducted from trading income

• Any tax deducted from trading income (not CIS25 deductions)	1.98	£

Summary of balance sheet

Leave these boxes blank if there is no balance sheet

		Box	£	Box	£
Assets	• Plant, machinery and motor vehicles	1.99	*28,742.00*		
	• Other fixed assets (premises, goodwill, investments etc.)	1.100	*413,850.00*		
	• Stock and work in progress	1.101	*22,667.00*		
	• Debtors/prepayments/other current assets	1.102	*4,250.00*		
	• Bank/building society balances	1.103	*12,897.00*		total of boxes 1.99 to 1.104
	• Cash in hand	1.104	*420.00*	1.105	*482,826.00*
Liabilities	• Trade creditors/accruals	1.106	*25,633.00*		
	• Loans and overdrawn bank accounts	1.107			total of boxes 1.106 to 1.108
	• Other liabilities	1.108	*1,250.00*	1.109	*26,883.00*
Net business assets (put the figure in brackets if there were net business liabilities)					box 1.105 *minus* 1.109
				1.110	*455,943.00*

Represented by

Capital Account

	Box	£	Box	£
• Balance at start of period*	1.111	*437,269.00*		
• Net profit/(loss)*	1.112	*78,674.00*		
• Capital introduced	1.113			
• Drawings	1.114	*60,000.00*		total of boxes 1.111 to 1.113 *minus* box 1.114
• Balance at end of period*			1.115	*455,943.00*

* If the Capital Account is overdrawn, or the business made a net loss, enter the figure in brackets.

1.116 *Additional information*

Now fill in any other supplementary Pages that apply to you. Otherwise, go back to page 3 in the Trust and Estate Tax Return and finish filling it in.

TRUST AND ESTATE TAX RETURN ■ TRADE: PAGE TT4

Inland Revenue

Income for the year ended 5 April 2003

TRUST AND ESTATE PARTNERSHIP

Fill in these boxes first

Name of trust or estate: *The Trustees of Florov Trust*

Tax reference:

You will need to fill in a copy of these Pages for each partnership of which the trust or estate was a member, and for each business the partnership carried on. If you need help, look up the box numbers in the Notes on Trust and Estate Partnership.

Partnership details

Partnership reference number	2.1	
Partnership trade or profession	2.2	*Farming*
• Date started being a partner (if during 2002-03)	2.3	/ /
• Date stopped being a partner (if during 2002-03)	2.4	/ /

The share of the partnership's trading or professional income

Basis period begins	2.5	*06 / 04 / 2002*
and ends	2.6	*05 / 04 / 2003*
• Share of the profit or loss of this year's account for tax purposes	2.7	£ *42,555.00*
• Adjustment to arrive at profit or loss for this basis period	2.8	£
• Overlap profit brought forward	2.9	£
Deduct overlap relief used this year	2.10	£
• Overlap profit carried forward	2.11	£
• Averaging for farmers, and creators of literary or artistic works (or foreign tax deducted if tax credit relief not claimed)	2.12	£
Net profit for 2002-03 (if loss, enter '0' here)	2.13	£ *42,555.00*
Allowable loss for 2002-03 (if profit, enter '0' here)	2.14	£
• Loss offset against other income for 2002-03	2.15	£
• Loss to carry back	2.16	£
• Loss to carry forward (that is allowable loss not claimed in any other way)	2.17	£
• Losses brought forward from last year	2.18	£
• Losses brought forward from last year used this year	2.19	£
Taxable profit after losses brought forward (box 2.13 *minus* box 2.19)	2.20	£ *42,555.00*
• Add amounts **not** included in the partnership accounts which are needed to calculate the taxable profit	2.21	£
Total taxable profits from this business (box 2.20 + box 2.21)	2.22	£ *42,555.00*

SA902 (Substitute)(LexisNexis UK)

TRUST AND ESTATE TAX RETURN ■ PARTNERSHIP: PAGE TP1 — *Please turn over*

Share of partnership investment income

- Please tick box 2.23 if the partnership had any investment income and your share will be returned in boxes 9.1 to 9.40, on pages 4 and 5, of the Trust and Estate Tax Return. **2.23** [ ]

- Share of losses on partnership investments **2.24** £

2.25 ***Additional information***

Now go back to page 3 of the Trust and Estate Tax Return and finish filling it in.

Inland Revenue

Income for the year ended 5 April 2003

TRUST AND ESTATE LAND AND PROPERTY

Name of trust or estate

Fill in these boxes first

The Trustees of Florov Trust

Tax reference

If you want help, look up the box numbers in the Notes on Trust and Estate Land and Property.

Answer this question to help you decide which parts of Pages TL1 and TL2 to fill in.

Is the income from furnished holiday lettings?
If not applicable, turn over and fill in Page TL2 to give details of the property income

YES ☐ If 'Yes', fill in boxes 3.1 to 3.18 before completing Page TL2

Furnished holiday lettings in the UK

- Income from furnished holiday lettings — 3.1 £

■ ***Expenses*** (furnished holiday lettings only)

- Rent, rates, insurance, ground rents etc. — 3.2 £
- Repairs, maintenance and renewals — 3.3 £
- Finance charges, including interest — 3.4 £
- Legal and professional costs — 3.5 £
- Cost of services provided, including wages — 3.6 £
- Other expenses — 3.7 £ — total of boxes 3.2 to 3.7: 3.8 £

Net profit (put figures in brackets if a loss) — box 3.1 *minus* box 3.8: 3.9 £

■ ***Tax adjustments***

- Private use — 3.10 £
- Balancing charges — 3.11 £ — box 3.10 + box 3.11: 3.12 £
- Capital allowances — 3.13 £
- Tick box 3.13A if box 3.13 includes enhanced capital allowances for environmentally friendly expenditure — 3.13A ☐

Profit for the year (copy to box 3.19). If loss enter '0' in box 3.14 and put the loss in box 3.15 — boxes 3.9 + 3.12 *minus* box 3.13: 3.14 £

Loss for the year (if you have entered '0' in box 3.14) — boxes 3.9 + 3.12 *minus* box 3.13: 3.15 £

- Loss offset against 2002-03 total income — 3.16 £
- Loss carried back — see Notes, page TLN4: 3.17 £
- Loss offset against other income from property (copy to box 3.37) — see Notes, page TLN4: 3.18 £

SA903 (Substitute)(LexisNexis UK)

Other property income

Income

		£	Tax deducted	
Furnished holiday lettings profits	3.19 (copy from box 3.14)	£		
Rents and other income from land and property	3.20	£ *18,000.00*	3.21 £	
Chargeable premiums	3.22	£		
Reverse premiums	3.22A	£		3.23 (boxes 3.19 + 3.20 + 3.22 + 3.22A) £ *18,000.00*

Expenses (do not include figures you have already put in boxes 3.2 to 3.7 on Page TL1)

		£	
Rent, rates, insurance, ground rents etc.	3.24	£	
Repairs, maintenance and renewals	3.25	£	
Finance charges, including interest	3.26	£	
Legal and professional costs	3.27	£	
Costs of services provided, including wages	3.28	£	
Other expenses	3.29	£	3.30 (total of boxes 3.24 to 3.29) £

Net profit (put figures in brackets if a loss) — 3.31 (box 3.23 *minus* box 3.30) £ *18,000.00*

Tax adjustments

		£	
Private use	3.32	£	
Balancing charges	3.33	£	3.34 (box 3.32 + box 3.33) £
Capital allowances	3.35	£	
Tick box 3.35A if box 3.35 includes a claim for 100% capital allowances for flats over shops	3.35A		
Tick box 3.35B if box 3.35 includes enhanced capital allowances for environmentally friendly expenditure	3.35B		
10% wear and tear	3.36	£	
Furnished holiday lettings losses (from box 3.18)	3.37	£	3.38 (total of boxes 3.35 to 3.37) £

Adjusted profit (if loss enter '0' in box 3.39 and put the loss in box 3.40) — 3.39 (boxes 3.31 + 3.34 *minus* box 3.38) £ *18,000.00*

Adjusted loss (if you have entered '0' in box 3.39) — 3.40 (boxes 3.31 + 3.34 *minus* box 3.38) £

- Loss brought forward from previous year — 3.41 £

Profit for the year — 3.42 (box 3.39 *minus* box 3.41) £ *18,000.00*

- Loss offset against total income (read the note on page TLN7) — 3.43 £
- Loss to carry forward to following year — 3.44 £

Tick box 3.45 if these Pages include details of property let jointly — 3.45

Now go back to page 3 of the Trust and Estate Tax Return and finish filling it in.

TRUST AND ESTATE TAX RETURN ■ LAND AND PROPERTY: PAGE TL2

Inland Revenue

Income and gains and foreign tax credit relief for the year ended 5 April 2003

TRUST AND ESTATE FOREIGN

Fill in these boxes first

Name of trust or estate: *The Trustees of Florov Trust*

Tax reference:

If you want help, look up the box numbers in the Notes on Trust and Estate Foreign

Foreign savings

Fill in columns A, B, D and E, and tick the box in column E if you want to claim foreign tax credit relief.

	Country A	tick box if income is unremittable	Amount before tax B	Foreign tax D	Amount chargeable E	tick box to claim foreign tax credit relief
▪ *Interest and other savings income* -see Notes, page TFN3			£	£	£	
			£	£	£	
			£	£	£	
			£	£	£	
			£	£	£	
			£	£	£	
			£	£	£	
			£	£	£	
			£	£	£	
			£	£	£	
			£	£	£	
			£	£	£	
					total of column above 4.1 £	
▪ *Dividends* -see Notes, page TFN4			£ *2,645.00*	£ *248.00*	£ *2,645.00*	✓
			£	£	£	
			£	£	£	
			£	£	£	
			£	£	£	
			£	£	£	
			£	£	£	
			£	£	£	
			£	£	£	
			£	£	£	
			£	£	£	
			£	£	£	
					total of column above 4.2 £ *2,645.00*	

SA904 (Substitute)(LexisNexis UK)

Please turn over

Foreign savings income taxable on the remittance basis and foreign income from land and property abroad

Fill in columns A to E, and tick the box in column E if you want to claim foreign tax credit relief.

	Country (tick box if income is unremittable) A	Amount before tax B	UK tax C	Foreign tax D	Amount chargeable (tick box to claim foreign tax credit relief) E
■ *Dividends, interest and other savings income taxable on the remittance basis* -see Notes, page TFN2		£		£	£
		£		£	£
		£		£	£
		£		£	£
		£		£	£
		£		£	£
		£		£	£
		£		£	£
		£		£	£
		£		£	£
		£		£	£
		£		£	£
		£		£	£
■ *Income from land & property* IMPORTANT -see Notes page TFN5		£	£	£	£
■ *Chargeable premiums*		£	£	£	£
			total of column C 4.3 £		total of column E 4.4 £

- Disposals of holdings in offshore funds, income from non-resident trusts and income received by trusts or companies abroad — 4.5 £

- Gains on foreign life insurance policies, life annuities and capital redemption policies - on which no tax is treated as paid — Amount of gain 4.6 £

- Gains on foreign life insurance policies, life annuities and capital redemption policies - on which tax is treated as paid — Tax treated as paid 4.7 £ — Amount of gain 4.8 £

Now fill in Page TF3

Foreign tax credit relief for foreign tax paid on trade, partnership and other income

See Notes, page TFN11

Enter in this column the page number in the Trust and Estate Tax Return from which information is taken. Do this for each item for which you are claiming tax credit	Country A	Foreign tax D	Amount chargeable E tick box to claim foreign tax credit relief
		£	£
		£	£
		£	£
		£	£
		£	£
		£	£
		£	£
		£	£
		£	£

- Enter in box 4.9 the total foreign tax credit relief on the income (if there is an entry in box 4.9, box 4.9A must also be completed) **4.9** £ *248.00*
- Enter in box 4.9A the amount of foreign tax credit relief referable to that part of net income, after deductions, chargeable at the rate applicable to trusts or the dividend trust rate. (Enter zero if appropriate) **4.9A** £ *124.00*

Foreign tax credit relief for foreign tax paid on chargeable gains reported on the Trust and Estate Capital Gains Pages

See Notes, page TFN12

Amount of gain under UK rules	Period over which UK gain accrued	Amount of gain under foreign tax rules	Period over which foreign gain accrued	Foreign tax paid D tick box to claim foreign tax credit relief
£	days	£	days	£
£	days	£	days	£
£	days	£	days	£
£	days	£	days	£
£	days	£	days	£
£	days	£	days	£
£	days	£	days	£
£	days	£	days	£
£	days	£	days	£

- If you are calculating the tax, enter the total foreign tax credit relief on the gains in box 4.10 **4.10** £

Now go back to page 3 in the Trust and Estate Tax Return and finish filling it in

TRUST AND ESTATE TAX RETURN ■ FOREIGN ETC: PAGE TF3

Income from land and property abroad

Fill in one Page TF4 if:
- *there is only **one** overseas let property, **or***
- *there is more than one but all overseas let properties are in the same country **and** all the income is remittable, **or***
- *there is more than one and they are in different countries **but** there has been **no foreign tax deducted** from any of the income **and** all the income is remittable.*

If any of the income is unremittable or the overseas let properties are in different countries and some foreign tax has been deducted you must fill in a copy of Page TF4 for each property letting. (Take copies of TF4 before you start or ask the Orderline for more copies of the Trust and Estate Foreign Pages.) Please put the trust or estate name and tax reference next to the address box on each copy.

If you are using Page TF4 to return income from more than one property please use the address box below for the first property and the 'Additional information' box on Page TF5 for the other addresses.

Address of property

Postcode

Income

- Income - total rents and other receipts (excluding chargeable premiums) — **4.11** £
- Tick box 4.11A if box 4.11 contains income from more than one property — **4.11A**
- Tick box 4.11B if the income in box 4.11 is unremittable — **4.11B**

Expenses - see Notes, page TFN6

- Rent, rates, insurance etc. — **4.12** £
- Repairs, maintenance and renewals — **4.13** £
- Finance charges, including interest — **4.14** £
- Legal and professional costs — **4.15** £
- Costs of services provided including wages — **4.16** £
- Other expenses — **4.17** £ — total of boxes 4.12 to 4.17 **4.18** £

Net profit (or loss) - show loss in brackets — box 4.11 *minus* 4.18 **4.19** £

Tax Adjustments to net profit (or loss) - see Notes, page TFN7

- Private use — **4.20** £
- Balancing charges — **4.21** £ — box 4.20 + box 4.21 **4.22** £
- Capital allowances — **4.23** £
- Tick box 4.23A if box 4.23 includes enhanced capital allowances for environmentally friendly expenditure — **4.23A**
- 10% wear and tear — **4.24** £ — box 4.23 + box 4.24 **4.25** £

Adjusted profit (if loss, enter '0' here, and enter loss in box 4.27) — box 4.19 + box 4.22 *minus* box 4.25 **4.26** £

Adjusted loss (if '0' in box 4.26) — box 4.19 + box 4.22 *minus* box 4.25 **4.27** £

Trust and Estate Tax Return ■ Foreign etc: page TF4

Go to Page TF5

Income from land and property abroad, continued

Fill in boxes 4.28 to 4.32 (if you completed only one Page TF4) or boxes 4.33 to 4.38 if you have completed a separate Page TF4 for each property.

- Taxable profit or allowable loss from box 4.26 or 4.27 (enter a loss in brackets) **4.28** £

minus losses brought forward from earlier years **4.29** £

Total taxable profits (if box 4.28 is a profit and is more than box 4.29) box 4.28 *minus* 4.29 **4.30** £ *Copy to column B on Page TF2*

or loss to carry forward (if box 4.28 is a profit but less than box 4.29, enter box 4.29 minus box 4.28, or, if box 4.28 is a loss, enter box 4.28 plus box 4.29) **4.31** £

- If you have only one property or your properties are all in the same foreign country and foreign tax was deducted, enter the tax paid **4.32** £ *Copy to column D on Page TF2 and fill in columns A and E as appropriate*

If you have filled in more than one Page TF4 enter details below using a separate line for each overseas let property. ***Exclude*** *any unremittable income from the 'Taxable profit or loss' column.*

	Country	Taxable profit or loss (from box 4.26 or 4.27)	Foreign tax	Amount chargeable
1		£	£	£
2		£	£	£
3		£	£	£
4		£	£	£
5		£	£	£
6		£	£	£

total of column above **4.33** £

minus losses brought forward **4.34** £

Total taxable profits **4.35** £ *Copy to column B on Page TF2* **4.36** £ *Copy to column D on Page TF2* **4.37** £ *Copy to column E on Page TF2*

or loss to carry forward **4.38** £

4.39 *Additional information*

Inland Revenue

For the year ended 5 April 2003

TRUST AND ESTATE CAPITAL GAINS

Fill in these boxes first

Name of trust or estate	Tax reference
The Trustees of the Florov Trust	

If you want help, look up the box numbers in the Notes on Trust and Estate Capital Gains.

Chargeable gains and allowable losses

Once you have completed Pages TC2 to TC7 fill in this Page.

Have you ticked any row in Column B 'Tick box if estimate or valuation used' on Page TC2?	YES	
Have you given details in Column G on Pages TC2 and TC3 of any capital gains reliefs claimed or due?	YES	
Are you claiming and/or using any 'clogged losses' (see Notes, page TCN10)?	YES	

Enter the **number** of transactions from column AA on Page TC2, as follows:

• transactions in quoted shares or other securities	box Q	
• transactions in other shares or securities	box U	
• transactions in land and property	box L	*1*
• transactions in other assets	box O	
Total taxable gains from Page TC3	5.7	£ *26,640.00*
Only Trustees need consider boxes 5.8 and 5.9		
If the trust was made after 6 June 1978 how many trusts that were made after 6 June 1978 by the settlor of this trust still existed during the year to 5 April 2003?	5.8	*1*
Is this trust for a disabled person? If yes, tick box 5.9	5.9	
minus Annual exempt amount (see Notes, page TCN6)	5.10	£ *3,850.00*
	box 5.7 *minus* box 5.10	
• Taxable gains for 2002-03 (leave box 5.11 blank if '0' or negative)	5.11	£ *22,790.00*

Capital losses

(Remember, if your loss arose on a transaction with a connected person, see page TCN13, you can only set that loss against gains you make on disposals to that same connected person. See the Notes on clogged losses on page TCN10.)

■ ***This year's losses***	from box 5.2	
• total from Page TC3	5.12	£
• used against gains	5.13	£
• 2002-03 losses transferred to beneficiaries during the year and 2002-03 losses on mineral leases carried back	5.14	£
	box 5.12 *minus* (boxes 5.13 + 5.14)	
• carried forward losses of 2002-03	5.15	£
■ ***Summary of earlier years' losses***		
• unused losses of 1996-97 and later years	5.16	£
• used this year (losses from box 5.16 are used in priority to losses from box 5.17A)	5.16A	£
	box 5.16 *minus* box 5.16A	
• remaining unused losses of 1996-97 and later years	5.17	£
• unused losses of 1995-96 and earlier years	5.17A	£
	from box 5.6 *minus* box 5.16A	
• used this year (losses from box 5.16 are used in priority to losses from box 5.17A)	5.17B	£
■ ***Total of unused losses to carry forward***	box 5.15 + box 5.17	
• Carried forward losses of 1996-97 and later years	5.18	£
	box 5.17A *minus* box 5.17B	
• Carried forward losses of 1995-96 and earlier years	5.18A	£

SA905 (Substitute)(LexisNexis UK)

TRUST AND ESTATE TAX RETURN ■ CAPITAL GAINS: PAGE TC1 *Please turn over*

Your 2002-03 Capital Gains Tax liability

A Brief description of asset	AA* Type of disposal. Enter **Q, U, L or O**	B Tick box if estimate or valuation used	C Tick box if asset held at 31March 1982	D Enter the later of date of acquisition and 16 March 1998	E Enter the date of disposal	F Disposal proceeds	G Enter details of any elections made, reliefs claimed or due and state amounts (£)
Gains on assets which are either wholly business or wholly non-business							
1				*02/12/01*	*01/12/02*	£ *66,640.00*	
2						£	
3						£	
4						£	
5						£	
6						£	
7						£	
8						£	
Gains on assets which are partly business and partly non-business (see the notes on pages TCN17)							
9						£	
10						£	

* For transactions in

- quoted shares or other securities (the definition is on page TCN2), enter **Q**
- other shares or securities, enter **U**
- land and property, enter **L**
- other assets (for example, goodwill or valuable antiques), enter **O**

Complete Pages TC5 to TC7 for all transactions identified as U, L or O

Losses

Description of asset	Type of* disposal. Enter **Q, U, L or O**	Tick box if estimate or valuation used	Tick box if asset held at 31March 1982	Enter the later of date of acquisition and 16 March 1998	Enter the date of disposal	Disposal proceeds	Enter details of any elections made, reliefs claimed or due and state amounts (£)
13						£	
14						£	
15						£	
16						£	

Total losses of

Trust and Estate Tax Return ■ Capital Gains: page TC2

	H Chargeable Gains after reliefs but before losses and taper	I Enter 'Bus' if business asset	J Taper rate	K Losses deducted			L Gains after losses	M Tapered gains (gains from column L x % in column J)
				K1 Allowable losses of the year	K2 Income losses set against gains	K3 Unused losses b/f from earlier years		
	£ *26,640.00*		*100* %	£	£	£	£ *26,640.00*	£ *26,640.00*
	£		%	£	£	£	£	£
	£		%	£	£	£	£	£
	£		%	£	£	£	£	£
	£		%	£	£	£	£	£
	£		%	£	£	£	£	£
	£		%	£	£	£	£	£
	£		%	£	£	£	£	£
	£	Bus	%	£	£	£	£	£
	£		%	£	£	£	£	£
	£	Bus	%	£	£	£	£	£
	£		%	£	£	£	£	£
Total	5.1 £ *26,640.00* Total column H				5.5 £ Total column K2	5.6 £ Total column K3		5.6B £ *26,640.00* Total column M

	Losses arising
	£
	£
	£
	£
year	5.2 £

Boxes 5.3 and 5.4 are not used on these Pages

Amount chargeable on the settlor 5.6A £

Total taxable gains (after allowable losses and taper relief) box 5.6B *minus* box 5.6A £ *26,640.00*

Copy to box 5.7 on Page TC1

Copy to box 5.12 on Page TC1 and, unless you need only complete the totals boxes (see page TCN4), complete column K1

Trust and Estate Tax Return ■ Capital Gains: page TC3

Other events in the year

Ignore this Page if you are a personal representative

Please tick the boxes which apply and provide the information requested.

Has any person holding an interest in possession in settled property died during the year? If yes, tick the box and give details below **5.19**

Name and address of life tenant or liferenter, etc.

Date of death / /

Has any person become absolutely entitled to any part of the property during the year? If yes, tick the box and give details below **5.20**

Name and address of beneficiary

Date beneficiary became absolutely entitled / /

Nature of asset

Value of asset vesting £

Amount of loss transferred to beneficiary **5.20A** £

Have the trustees ceased being resident in the UK, or did they become dual resident? If yes, tick the box and give details below **5.21**

Description of assets held

Date of change / /

Amount of chargeable gains £

Were any chargeable gains chargeable on the settlor? If yes, tick the box and give details below **5.22**

Name and address of settlor

Amount of chargeable gains £

Enter this amount in box 5.6A

If you have used an extra sheet, tick this box **5.23**

Now go back to page 3 of the Trust and Estate Tax Return and finish filling it in.

TRUST AND ESTATE TAX RETURN ■ CAPITAL GAINS: PAGE TC4

Land and property (L) - further information

If you have more than two transactions of this type of asset to return, please photocopy this Page **before** completion and send all completed Pages with your Tax Return.

1st transaction

Full address of land/property affected (attach a copy of any plan if this helps identification)

Mycroft Field
Hartford
Glos.
GL3 1ZS

Description of land/property disposed of, including details of your ownership, for example freehold/leasehold and any tenancies affecting your ownership at the date of disposal and any other date for which a valuation has been made, and except in the case of an outright disposal of all of your interests, the interest which you have disposed of, or granted.

Tick box if you have already submitted form CG34 ☐

Partnership freehold land, sold 01/12/01 for £133,080. Bought 02/12/00 for £80,000, trustee's share, one half.

State any connection between you and the person from whom you acquired the asset or to whom you disposed of the asset (see Notes, page TCN13)

If you have used an estimate or valuation in your capital gains computation but have not submitted form CG34, please enter the date to which the valuation relates, the amount (£) and the reason for the estimate or valuation. Please also attach a copy of any valuation obtained.

2nd transaction

Full address of land/property affected (attach a copy of any plan if this helps identification)

Description of land/property disposed of, including details of your ownership, for example freehold/leasehold and any tenancies affecting your ownership at the date of disposal and any other date for which a valuation has been made, and except in the case of an outright disposal of all of your interests, the interest which you have disposed of, or granted.

Tick box if you have already submitted form CG34 ☐

State any connection between you and the person from whom you acquired the asset or to whom you disposed of the asset (see Notes, page TCN13)

If you have used an estimate or valuation in your capital gains computation but have not submitted form CG34, please enter the date to which the valuation relates, the amount (£) and the reason for the estimate or valuation. Please also attach a copy of any valuation obtained.

TRUST AND ESTATE TAX RETURN ■ CAPITAL GAINS: PAGE TC6

Other assets (O) - further information

If you have more than two transactions involving any other type of asset to return, please photocopy this Page **before** completion and send all completed Pages with your Tax Return.

1st transaction

Full description of the asset (other than shares or land/property) affected and any other information which helps identify the asset

Tick box if you have already submitted form CG34 ☐

State any connection between you and the person from whom you acquired the asset or to whom you disposed of the asset (see Notes, page TCN13)

If you have used an estimate or valuation in your capital gains computation but have not submitted form CG34, please enter the date to which the valuation relates, the amount (£) and the reason for the estimate or valuation. Please also attach a copy of any valuation obtained.

2nd transaction

Full description of the asset (other than shares or land/property) affected and any other information which helps identify the asset

Tick box if you have already submitted form CG34 ☐

State any connection between you and the person from whom you acquired the asset or to whom you disposed of the asset (see Notes, page TCN13)

If you have used an estimate or valuation in your capital gains computation but have not submitted form CG34, please enter the date to which the valuation relates, the amount (£) and the reason for the estimate or valuation. Please also attach a copy of any valuation obtained.

continued over

5.24 ***Additional information***

Working Sheet for Question 13

Income treated as that of the settlor as it arises

	Net income	Share of expenses	Tax	Gross income
• Income charged at 10% rate	G1 £	G2 £ *copy to 13.2*	G3 £	G4 £ *copy to 13.1*
• Income charged at 20% rate	G5 £	G6 £ *copy to 13.4*	G7 £	G8 £ *copy to 13.3*
• Other income	G9 £	G10 £ *copy to 13.6*	G11 £	G12 £ *copy to 13.5*

Income of beneficiary(ies) not subject to trustees' discretion

If more than three beneficiaries, photocopy this section and add the totals in boxes G49 to G54 below.

Beneficiary 1 Suzie — Share of income (% or fraction if appropriate) 50.00 %

	Net income	Share of expenses	Tax	Gross income
Income charged at 10% rate	G13 £ 5,690.25	G14 £ 2,500.00	G15 £ 632.25	G16 £ 6,322.50
Income charged at 20% rate	G17 £ 2,168.00	G18 £	G19 £ 542.00	G20 £ 2,710.00
Other income	G21 £ 45,299.28	G22 £	G23 £ 12,776.72	G24 £ 58,076.00

Beneficiary 2 — Share of income (% or fraction if appropriate)

	Net income	Share of expenses	Tax	Gross income
Income charged at 10% rate	G25 £	G26 £	G27 £	G28 £
Income charged at 20% rate	G29 £	G30 £	G31 £	G32 £
Other income	G33 £	G34 £	G35 £	G36 £

Beneficiary 3 — Share of income (% or fraction if appropriate)

	Net income	Share of expenses	Tax	Gross income
Income charged at 10% rate	G37 £	G38 £	G39 £	G40 £
Income charged at 20% rate	G41 £	G42 £	G43 £	G44 £
Other income	G45 £	G46 £	G47 £	G48 £

• Income charged at 10% rate	Total G14, G26 + G38	G49 £ 2,500.00 *copy to 13.8*	Total G16, G28 + G40	G50 £ 6,322.50 *copy to 13.7*
• Income charged at 20% rate	Total G18, G30 + G42	G51 £ *copy to 13.10*	Total G20, G32 + G44	G52 £ 2,710.00 *copy to 13.9*
• Other income	Total G22, G34 + G46	G53 £ *copy to 13.12*	Total G24, G36 + G48	G54 £ 58,076.00 *copy to 13.11*

Income allocated to specific purposes

	Net income	Share of expenses	Tax	Gross income
• Income charged at 10% rate	G55 £	G56 £ *copy to 13.14*	G57 £	G58 £ *copy to 13.13*
• Income charged at 20% rate	G59 £	G60 £ *copy to 13.16*	G61 £	G62 £ *copy to 13.15*
• Other income	G63 £	G64 £ *copy to 13.18*	G65 £	G66 £ *copy to 13.17*

■ Trust and Estate Tax Return Guide: page 22

Inland Revenue

2002-03 Trust and Estate Tax Calculation Guide

How to calculate your tax

You can use this guide to work out the trust or estate's tax, if you want to, **and** check any calculation we send you.

If you decide not to work out the tax bill, make sure the Trust and Estate Tax Return reaches us by 30 September 2003. If we receive your Tax Return after 30 September 2003 and you haven't calculated the tax we will do it for you but we can't guarantee to let you know what to pay by 31 January 2004. If you don't know exactly what to pay, make an estimate and pay that. If you don't pay enough, you will also have to pay interest, and perhaps a surcharge.

If you need help, ask your Inland Revenue office or the Helpline (0845 9000 444). But we will only be able to do the calculation once we have the Return from you.

Only trustees liable to Income Tax at the special rate applicable to trusts or the dividend trust rate need complete Sections 2, 3 and 4. If this applies to you, you should have ticked 'Yes' in box 8.16 on page 3 of the Return. Pages 10 and 11 of the Trust and Estate Tax Return Guide will help you decide if you are unsure.

Other trustees should complete Section 1 and then go straight to Section 5.

Copy figures from boxes in the Trust and Estate Tax Return, and the supplementary Pages, to boxes in the Calculation Working Sheet. Instructions are alongside each box and there are notes at the beginning of each Section to help you.

SA951 (Substitute)(LexisNexis UK)

***SECTION 1** All trustees and personal representatives should complete this section using information from the Trust and Estate Tax Return and the supplementary Pages*

The calculation will calculate tax at the basic rate of 22% on income except for dividend type income at 10% and other savings income at 20%.

For trustees, certain types of income and deemed income are always chargeable at the rate applicable to trusts or the dividend trust rate. These are accrued income charges, income from relevant discounted securities, gilt strips, offshore income gains, income from companies purchasing their own shares and gains on life insurance policies, life annuities and capital redemption policies (boxes 9.29 to 9.31 and 9.38 to 9.40 on the Trust and Estate Tax Return and boxes 4.6 to 4.8 on the Trust and Estate Foreign Pages).

	Income other than savings or dividend type income			Savings type income 20%	
	Income	**Tax**	**Non-payable tax credit**	**Income**	**Tax**
Trades, professions and vocations	from boxes 1.92, 1L.91 T1.1 £ *55,597.00*	from boxes 1.97, 1.98, 1L.12, 1L.50 and 1L.53 T1.2 £	from boxes 1L.24 and 1L.38 T1.3 £		
Partnership	from box 2.22 T1.4 £ *42,555.00*				
Land and property	from box 3.42 T1.5 £ *18,000.00*	from box 3.21 T1.6 £			
Foreign income				from box 4.1 T1.7 £	
	from boxes 4.4 and 4.5 T1.9 £	from box 4.3 T1.10 £			
Other income				from boxes 9.1, 9.4, 9.7, 9.8, 9.11 and 9.14 T1.14 £ *5,420.00*	from boxes 9.3, 9.6, 9.10 and 9.13 T1.15 £ *1,084.00*
	from box 9.34 T1.21 £	from box 9.33 T1.22 £			
	total column above T1.25 £ *116,152.00*	total column above T1.26 £	from box T1.3 T1.27 £	total column above T1.28 £ *5,420.00*	from box T1.15 T1.29 £ *1,084.00*

TTCG PAGE 2

Trustees of an unauthorised unit trust (abbreviated to UUT in this calculation guide) will, generally, pay tax on their income at the basic rate (22%). Accrued income and income from relevant discounted securities treated as income in the accounts of the unit trust scheme are taxable at the basic rate. Trustees should therefore have included this income in box 9.34. Where such items are not treated as income in the accounts, the trustees are taxable at the rate applicable to trusts and the income should have been included in box 9.38.

If you are the trustee of a trust liable at the rate applicable to trusts or the dividend trust rate complete Sections 2, 3 and 4. Otherwise, ignore those sections and go straight to Section 5.

Dividend type income		Deemed income			Dividend type income	
	10%					
Income	**Non-payable tax credit**	**Income**	**Income**	**Non-payable tax credit**	**Income**	**Non-payable tax credit**
from box 4.2 T1.8 £ *2,645.00*						
		from box 4.6 T1.11 £	from box 4.8 T1.12 £	from box 4.7 T1.13 £		
from boxes 9.17, 9.20, 9.23, 9.24, 9.25 and 9.28 T1.16 £ *10,000.00*	from boxes 9.16, 9.19, 9.22 and 9.27 T1.17 £ *1,000.00*	from boxes 9.29 and 9.38 T1.18 £	from box 9.31 T1.19 £	from box 9.30 T1.20 £		
					from box 9.40 T1.23 £	from box 9.39 T1.24 £
total column above T1.30 £ *12,645.00*	from box T1.17 T1.31 £ *1,000.00*	total column above T1.32 £	total column above T1.33 £	total column above T1.34 £	from box T1.23 T1.35 £	from box T1.24 T1.36 £

TTCG PAGE 3

	Income other than savings or dividend type income			Savings type income 20%	
	Income	Tax	Non-payable tax credit	Income	Tax
	b/f from page 2 T1.25	b/f from page 2 T1.26	b/f from page 2 T1.27	b/f from page 2 T1.28	b/f from page 2 T1.29
DEDUCTIONS Interest on loans, etc.	£ *116,152.11*	£	£	£ *5,420.00*	£ *1,084.00*

from boxes 10.1 and 10.4
T1.37 £

Losses from boxes 1.85, 1L.85, 2.15, 2.24, 3.16, 3.43 and 9.36
T1.38 £

Total deductions T1.37 + T1.38
T1.39 £

CALCULATION HELP
If T1.39 is zero (0), enter zero (0) in boxes T1.40 to T1.49 and go straight to box T1.50. Otherwise, if box T1.32 exceeds box T1.39, enter box T1.39 in box T1.40 and zero ('0') in boxes T1.41 to T1.49. Otherwise, enter box T1.32 in box T1.40 and go to box T1.41.

T1.39 *minus* T1.40
T1.41 £

CALCULATION HELP
If box T1.25 exceeds box T1.41, enter box T1.41 in box T1.42 and zero in boxes T1.43 to T1.49. Otherwise, enter box T1.25 in box T1.42 and go to box T1.43.

T1.42 £

T1.41 *minus* T1.42
T1.43 £

CALCULATION HELP
If box T1.28 exceeds box T1.43, enter box T1.43 in box T1.44 and zero in boxes T1.45 to T1.49. Otherwise, enter box T1.28 in box T1.44 and go to box T1.45.

T1.44 £

T1.43 *minus* T1.44
T1.45 £

CALCULATION HELP
Personal representatives should enter the figure from box T1.45 in box T1.49 and zero in boxes T1.46 to T1.48. Trustees of Settlor Interested Trusts should enter the figure from box T1.45 in box T1.47, and zero in box T1.46. Other trustees, if box T1.35 exceeds box T1.45, enter box T1.45 in box T1.46 and zero in boxes T1.47 to T1.49. Otherwise, trustees should enter box T1.35 in box T1.46 and go to box T1.47.

T1.45 *minus* T1.46
T1.47 £

CALCULATION HELP
If box T1.33 exceeds box T1.47, enter box T1.47 in box T1.48 and zero in box T1.49. Otherwise, enter box T1.33 in box T1.48 and go to box T1.49.

- **Income *minus* deductions. If the result is a *minus* amount, enter zero ('0')**

T1.25 *minus* T1.42 — T1.50 £ *116,152.00*

T1.28 *minus* T1.44 — T1.51 £ *5,420.00*

CALCULATION HELP
All trustees and personal representatives enter T1.50 x 22% in T1.56

CALCULATION HELP
Trustees of UUT enter T1.51 x 22% in T1.57
All others enter T1.51 x 20% in T1.57

T1.56 £ *25,553.44*

T1.57 £ *1,084.00*

- **Deduct non-repayable tax. If the result is a *minus* amount, enter zero ('0')**

T1.56 *minus* T1.27 — T1.62 £ *25,553.44*

- **Deduct repayable tax.**

T1.62 *minus* T1.26 — T1.66 £ *25,553.44*

T1.57 *minus* T1.29 — T1.67 £

from box T1.59 and boxes T1.63 to T1.67
Income Tax due T1.68 £ *25,817.94*

TTCG Page **4**

Dividend type income 10%		Deemed income			Dividend type income	
Income	Non-payable tax credit	Income	Income	Non-payable tax credit	Income	Non-payable tax credit
b/f from page 3 T1.30	b/f from page 3 T1.31	b/f from page 3 T1.32	b/f from page 3 T1.33	b/f from page 3 T1.34	b/f from page 3 T1.35	b/f from page 3 T1.36
£ *12,645.00*	£ *1,000.00*	£	£	£	£	£

CALCULATION HELP

The calculation boxes at T1.40 to T1.49 will set off deductions in the order most beneficial for personal representatives and most trustees. In exceptional circumstances another order of set off will be more beneficial. If you need help, or think this applies to you, contact your Inland Revenue office.

T1.40 £

T1.46 £

T1.48 £

T1.47 *minus* T1.48

T1.49 £

T1.30 *minus* T1.49

T1.52 £ *12,645.00*

T1.32 *minus* T1.40

T1.53 £

T1.33 *minus* T1.48

T1.54 £

T1.35 *minus* T1.46

T1.55 £

CALCULATION HELP

Trustees of UUT enter T1.52 x 22% in T1.58

All others enter T1.52 x 10% in T1.58

CALCULATION HELP

Personal representatives enter T1.53 x 22% in T1.59 and T1.54 x 22% in T1.60

All others enter T1.53 x 34% in T1.59 and T1.54 x 34% in T1.60

CALCULATION HELP

Settlor Interested Trusts and personal representatives enter T1.55 x 10%

Other trusts enter T1.55 x 25%

T1.58 £ *1,264.50*

T1.59 £

T1.60 £

T1.61 £

T1.58 *minus* T1.31

T1.63 £ *264.50*

T1.60 *minus* T1.34

T1.64 £

T1.61 *minus* T1.36

T1.65 £

Only complete Sections 2, 3 and 4 if you are liable to Income Tax at the special rate applicable to trusts or the dividend trust rate.

Otherwise go straight to Section 5.

TTCG Page **5**

SECTION 2 Only trustees of a trust liable at the rate applicable to trusts or the dividend trust rate need complete this section

You need to complete this section only if there are expenses to be deducted from income taxable at the rate applicable to trusts or the dividend trust rate (see the notes for the completion of Question 13 on pages 19 and 20 of the Trust and Estate Tax Return Guide). In order to complete part of this section (see boxes T2.7 to T2.9), you will need to complete part of Section 3.

The calculation allocates expenses paid against income (net after tax) chargeable at the rate applicable to trusts or the dividend trust rate in order, firstly against dividend income carrying a non-repayable 10% tax credit, then against other savings income carrying a 20% tax credit and finally against other income.

CALCULATION OF TRUST MANAGEMENT EXPENSES

Total income	box 13.21 + T1.25 + T1.28 + T1.30	T2.1	£ *134,217.00*
Income not liable to UK Income Tax included	from box 13.21	T2.2	£
Total trust management expenses	from box 13.19	T2.3	£ *5,000.00*

- **Deduct expenses applicable to income not liable to UK Income Tax (non-resident trusts only)**

T2.3 x T2.2 *divided by* T2.1	T2.4	£

- **Deduct expenses applicable to income not liable at the rate applicable to trusts**

	from box 13.20	T2.5	£ *2,500.00*
Trust management expenses allowable	T2.3 *minus* (T2.4 + T2.5)	T2.6	£ *2,500.00*

CALCULATION HELP
Now go to section 3 before filling in boxes T2.7 to T2.9

	T3.9 x (78/100) T2.7	T3.10 x (80/100) T2.8	T3.11 x (90/100) T2.9
Notional maximum amount of net trust management expenses which could be allowed against income	£ *45,299.28*	£ *2,168.00*	£ *5,690.25*

CALCULATION HELP
If box T2.9 exceeds box T2.6, enter box T2.6 in box T2.10 and zero ('0') in boxes T2.11 and T2.12.
Otherwise, copy box T2.9 to box T2.10 and follow the guidance for box T2.11.

lower of T2.6 and T2.9 — T2.10 — £ *2,500.00*

CALCULATION HELP
If box T2.8 exceeds (box T2.6 *minus* box T2.9), enter (box T2.6 *minus* box T2.9) in box T2.11 and zero ('0') in box T2.12.
Otherwise, enter box T2.8 in box T2.11 and follow the guidance for box T2.12.

lower of T2.8 and (T2.6 *minus* T2.9) — T2.11 — £

CALCULATION HELP
Enter box T2.6 *minus* (box T2.8 + box T2.9). If a *minus* amount, enter zero ('0').

T2.6 *minus* (T2.8 + T2.9) — T2.12 — £

	T2.12 x (100/78) T2.13	T2.11 x (100/80) T2.14	T2.10 x (100/90) T2.15
Grossed up trust management expenses	£ *0*	£ *0*	£ *2,777.78*

TTCG Page **6**

SECTION 3 Only trustees of a trust liable at the rate applicable to trusts or the dividend trust rate need complete this section.

The calculation deducts from total income any income not chargeable at the rate applicable to trusts or the dividend trust rate, then deducts expenses and calculates the tax due at the rate applicable to trusts or the dividend trust rate.

Credit is then given for tax at the 22% basic rate, 20% lower rate and 10% dividend rate charged on this income as calculated in Section 1.

INCOME LIABLE AT THE RATE APPLICABLE TO TRUSTS OR THE DIVIDEND TRUST RATE

Income *minus* deductions - from Section 1	copy from T1.50 T3.1 £ 116,152.00	copy from T1.51 T3.2 £ 5,420.00	copy from T1.52 T3.3 £ 12,645.00
minus income not chargeable at the rate applicable to trusts or the dividend trust rate	boxes 13.5 + 13.11 + 13.17 T3.4 £ 58,076.00	boxes 13.3 + 13.9 + 13.15 T3.5 £ 2,710.00	boxes 13.1 + 13.7 + 13.13 T3.6 £ 6,322.50
minus exceptional items	box 13.22 *minus* box 9.28 T3.7 £		from box 9.28 T3.8 £
Income liable at the rate applicable to trusts or the dividend trust rate	T3.1 *minus* (T3.4 + T3.7) T3.9 £ 58,076.00	T3.2 *minus* T3.5 T3.10 £ 2,710.00	T3.3 *minus* (T3.6 + T3.8) T3.11 £ 6,322.50
minus grossed up trust management expenses - see Section 2	from T2.13 T3.12 £	from T2.14 T3.13 £	from T2.15 T3.14 £ 2,777.78
Income chargeable at the rate applicable to trusts or the dividend trust rate (if negative, enter zero ('0')	T3.9 *minus* T3.12 T3.15 £ 58,076.00	T3.10 *minus* T3.13 T3.16 £ 2,710.00	T3.11 *minus* T3.14 T3.17 £ 3,544.72
Tax	T3.15 x 34% T3.18 £ 19,745.84	T3.16 x 34% T3.19 £ 921.40	T3.17 x 25% T3.20 £ 886.18
minus tax on this income at basic, savings and dividend rates	T3.15 x 22% T3.21 £ 12,776.72	T3.16 x 20% T3.22 £ 542.00	T3.17 x 10% T3.23 £ 354.47
Tax due	T3.18 *minus* T3.21 T3.24 £ 6,969.12	T3.19 *minus* T3.22 T3.25 £ 379.40	T3.20 *minus* T3.23 T3.26 £ 531.71
		Income Tax due	T3.24 + T3.25 + T3.26 T3.27 £ 7,880.23

TTCG Page 7

SECTION 4 Only trustees of a trust liable at the rate applicable to trusts or the dividend trust rate need complete this section

When you make discretionary payments that are income in the hands of the beneficiaries, those payments carry a tax credit. The tax credits have to be matched as far as possible with the tax payable by you on the trust income or tax credits attached to the income you have received. If the tax credits attaching to the payments to beneficiaries exceed the total of tax credits and tax payments (the tax pool), you have to pay the difference to us.

Relief for foreign tax and notional tax credits on dividends and deemed income are not available for repayment and cannot be used to frank tax credits allowed to beneficiaries.

The calculation excludes from the tax pool the proportion of such foreign tax and notional credits which relates to income which is to be accumulated or is payable at the trustees' discretion.

Any excess of the tax credits attaching to payments to beneficiaries over your available tax credits and tax payments (the tax pool) is carried to Section 5 and added to the tax bill for 2002-03. Any excess in the tax pool is carried forward to the tax pool for the tax year 2003-04.

CALCULATION OF TAX POOL

Amount of tax pool brought forward — from box 14.15 — **T4.1** £ *19,873.00*

Tax charged at the rate applicable to trusts or the dividend trust rate — T1.61 + T3.18 + T3.19 + T3.20 — **T4.2** £ *21,553.42*

Tax charged on deemed income at the rate applicable to trusts — lesser of 9.38 x 34% and T1.59 — **T4.3** £

minus foreign tax credit relief — lower of box 4.9 or 4.9A — **T4.4** £ *124.00*

minus non-repayable tax, etc.:
- lesser of T1.27 and T1.56 — **T4.5** £
- lesser of T1.31 and T1.58 — **T4.6** £ *1,000.00*
- lesser of T1.36 and T1.61 — **T4.7** £

Restrict to proportion of income liable at the rate applicable to trusts etc.:
- T4.5 x T3.15 *divided by* T1.50 — **T4.8** £
- T4.6 x (T1.52 *minus* T3.6) / T1.52 *minus* T2.15 / 10 If negative, enter zero ('0') — **T4.9** £ *222.23*
- from T4.7 — **T4.10** £

Total deduction of non-repayable tax, etc. — T4.8 + T4.9 + T4.10 — **T4.11** £ *222.23*

Pool available — greater of T4.1 + T4.2 + T4.3 *minus* (T4.4 + T4.11) and T4.1 — **T4.12** £ *41,080.19*

Tax on payments to beneficiaries — boxes 14.2, 14.4, 14.6, 14.8, 14.10, 14.12 and 14.14 *multiplied by* 34/66 — **T4.13** £ *15,454.55*

Tax pool to carry forward to next year (if negative, enter zero ('0')) — T4.12 *minus* T4.13 — **T4.14** £ *25,625.64*

Additional tax due (if negative, enter zero ('0')) — T4.13 *minus* T4.12 — **T4.15** £ *0*

Copy to box T5.6 on page 10

TTCG Page **8**

SECTION 5 All trustees and personal representatives should complete this section

The calculation brings together the tax due at dividend rate (10%), lower rate (20%) and basic rate (22%) from Section 1, tax due at the dividend trust rate (25%) and the rate applicable to trusts (34%) from Section 2, any additional tax due for the tax pool from Section 4 and Capital Gains Tax liability from the Capital Gains supplementary Pages. Further adjustments are made for relief given in terms of tax, and for tax on charges and annual payments made, to arrive at the total tax due for the year 2002-03.

box C (Capital Gains) Tax Credit Relief: If you have paid any foreign tax in respect of any gains included in box 5.7 of the Capital Gains Pages, you may be able to claim relief for all or part by way of credit against the Capital Gains Tax payable, see page TCN18 of the Notes for Trust and Estate Capital Gains Pages. Ask the Orderline for *Help Sheet IR261: Foreign tax credit relief and capital gains* to enable you to calculate the amount of the relief to enter in box C. You will also need to have completed Page TF3 of the Trust and Estate Foreign Pages.

box T5.9 Enter in box T5.9 the amount of any repayment of 2002-03 tax in box 21.4 in the Trust and Estate Tax Return. Do not include any repayments from trading losses carried back to an earlier year.

box T5.10 You may have paid too little tax in earlier years because:

- you claim farmers' averaging which has increased the income for last year, **or**
- you claim backwards spreading of literary or artistic income which has increased the income for last year and possibly the year before as well, **or**
- you claim to carry back post cessation receipts to the year the business ceased - increasing the income in that year.

You need to work out the underpayment of tax by reference to the tax rate and circumstances for the earlier year. Recalculate the liability for that year (the equivalent of the figure in box T5.8) taking account of the adjustment. The difference between the recalculated figure and the original figure is the amount of the underpayment. Include any entry in box 1L.79 of the Trust and Estate Lloyd's Underwriters Pages. Enter it in box T5.10. **Copy this figure to box 17.2 in the Trust and Estate Tax Return.** If you need help, ask the Inland Revenue office or your tax adviser.

box T5.12 You may have paid too much tax for an earlier year because:

- you claim that losses are set against income of an earlier year or years, **or**
- you claim farmers' averaging which has reduced the income for last year.

Do not include losses for which you have previously claimed relief. You need to work out how much tax you overpaid by reference to the tax rate and circumstances for the earlier year. Recalculate the liability for that year (the figure in box T5.8), taking account of the adjustment. The difference between the recalculated figure and the original figure is the amount of the overpayment. Enter it in box T5.12. **Copy this figure to box 17.4 and tick box 17.3 in the Trust and Estate Tax Return.**

box T5.13 If you have made payments on account for 2002-03, the payments will be shown on the Statements of Account sent to you. Add up the payments on account that have been used to offset the 2002-03 liability and put the total in box T5.13. You must not include payments which have been set against:

- interest
- penalties
- surcharges
- liabilities arising from earlier years.

If you are in any doubt about how much to include, please ask the Inland Revenue office or your tax adviser for help.

WORKING OUT TAX YOU OWE OR WE OWE YOU, FOR 2002-03

Income Tax due (from Sections 1 and 3)	T1.68 + T3.27	T5.1	£ *33,698.17*
Tax credit relief on foreign income	from box 4.9	T5.2	£ *248.00*
Net Income Tax due (if negative and there is an entry in box T5.2, the negative figure in T5.3 should be restricted to T1.26 + T1.29)	T5.1 *minus* T5.2	T5.3	£ *33,450.17*
Recoverable tax on charges and annual payments made out of capital	box 10.3 + box 11.2	T5.4	£
Chargeable gains for the year	from box 5.11	A	£ *22,790.00*
Capital Gains Tax due (box A x 34%) **or** for UUTs (box A x 20%)		B	£ *7,748.60*
Foreign tax credit relief	from box 4.10	C	£
Tax credit attached to dividends	If (T1.25 + T1.28) exceeds 10.4, enter zero ('0') in box T5.5. Otherwise, enter the lesser of 10% of (box 10.4 *minus* (T1.25 + T1.28)) or box 9.16 + box 9.19	T5.5	£ *0*
Tax pool adjustment (from Section 4)	from T4.15	T5.6	£
Capital Gains Tax (if negative amount, enter zero ('0'))	B *minus* C	T5.7	£ *7,748.60*
Income Tax and Capital Gains Tax due for 2002-03 (copy this figure to box 17.1 in the Trust and Estate Tax Return)	T5.3 + T5.4 + T5.6 + T5.7 *minus* T5.5	T5.8	£ *41,198.77*
2002-03 tax already refunded	from box 21.6	T5.9	£
Tax due for earlier years (see notes and then copy this figure to box 17.2 in the Trust and Estate Tax Return)		T5.10	£
Total amount due	T5.8 + T5.9 + T5.10	T5.11	£ *41,198.77*
Tax overpaid in earlier years (see notes, then, on the Trust and Estate Tax Return, tick box 17.3 and copy T5.12 to box 17.4)		T5.12	£
Payments already made (from your Statements of Account)		T5.13	£ *10,690.00*
Total overpaid and payments made	T5.12 + T5.13	T5.14	£ *10,690.00*
Tax you owe for 2002-03 (if negative, enter zero ('0') and fill in box T5.16)	T5.11 *minus* T5.14	T5.15	£ *30,508.77*
OR			
Tax we owe you for 2002-03	T5.14 *minus* T5.11	T5.16	£

TTCG Page **10**

SECTION 6 All trustees and personal representatives should complete this section

All trustees and personal representatives should complete this section to work out payments on account for 2003-04 and the amount due.

The first payment is due on 31 January 2004, and the second is due on 31 July 2004.

You will not have to make payments on account for 2003-04 if the tax bill for 2002-03 is below a threshold of £500 or if most (80%) of the tax is collected at source.

This section of the calculation will:

- help you decide whether you have to make payments on account
- help you work out the amount of these payments
- tell you what figure to copy to box 17.5 in the Trust and Estate Tax Return.

Reducing payments on account

You might want to make reduced payments on account if:

- you expect the income in 2003-04 to be lower than the income in 2002-03, **or**
- you expect reliefs to be higher, **or**
- you expect that more of the income will be taxed at source in 2003-04, because:
  - it will be covered by subcontractor deductions (CIS25), **or**
  - more of the income will come from savings.

If you want to reduce the payments on account you must make a reasonable estimate on the basis of the information you have now of the difference between the Income Tax you expect to pay for 2003-04 and the Income Tax liability for 2002-03 on this Trust and Estate Tax Return. You can reduce each of the payments on account by half this difference:

- put the amount of each reduced payment on account in box 17.5 **(include the pence)**
- tick box 17.6
- write the reason for reducing the payments on account in the 'Additional information' box, box 21.7 on page 12 of the Trust and Estate Tax Return.

If you decide later that you have reduced the payments on account by too little you should write to the Inland Revenue office giving the reason why you are claiming to reduce your payments further.

You should ensure that the payments you make by 31 January 2004 and by 31 July 2004 add up to your best estimate of the final liability for 2003-04.

If the payments on account turn out to be different from the tax bill for 2003-04 and:

- you have paid more than you needed to, you will be credited with interest
- you have paid less than you needed to, you will be charged interest.

Your two payments on account only need to add up to the smaller of:

- the actual Income Tax due for 2003-04 (net of tax deducted at source and tax credits on dividends)
- the actual Income Tax due for 2002-03 (net of tax deducted at source and tax credits on dividends).

If you have been fraudulent or negligent in claiming a reduction in payments on account, you may be charged a penalty.

If you decide later that you have reduced the payments on account by too much, you can make a claim to revise the amounts upwards and/or pay additional amounts in line with your revised estimate. If you do not make a claim, additional amounts paid may be allocated to other outstanding liabilities.

boxes 17.8 and 17.9 in the Tax Return

If you are claiming now to carry back to 2002-03, a 2003-04 trading loss (write details of your claim in the 'Additional information' box, box 21.7 on page 12 of the Trust and Estate Tax Return), you will need to calculate the amount of the 2003-04 repayment by reference to the tax rates and circumstances for 2002-03.

Recalculate the 2002-03 tax liability taking into account the loss. The difference between that figure and the figure in box T5.8 is the amount of the 2003-04 repayment. **Tick box 17.8 and enter the amount in box 17.9 of the Trust and Estate Tax Return.**

These notes are for guidance only, and reflect the position at the time of writing. They do not affect any rights of appeal.

CALCULATION OF PAYMENT ON ACCOUNT FOR 2003-04

Income Tax bill for 2002-03	T5.8 *minus* T5.7 — T6.1	£ *33,450.17*

If box T6.1 is less than £500, you do not need to make payments on account. Tick box 17.6 in the Trust and Estate Tax Return. Otherwise, leave box 17.6 blank and continue

Tax deducted at source, notional tax, tax credit, etc.	T1.26 + T1.27 + T1.29 + T1.31+ T1.34 + T1.36 — T6.2	£ *2,084.00*
Total Income Tax due	T6.1 + T6.2 — T6.3	£ *35,534.17*
20% of total Income Tax	T6.3 x 20% — T6.4	£ *7,106.83*

If box T6.1 is less than box T6.4, you do not need to make payments on account. Tick box 17.6 in the Trust and Estate Tax Return. Otherwise, leave box 17.6 blank and continue

The amount of each payment on account for 2003-4	T6.1 x 50% — T6.5	£ *16,725.08*

Copy box T6.5, **including pence**, to box 17.7 in the Trust and Estate Tax Return

WORKING OUT THE PAYMENTS DUE ON 31 JANUARY 2004

If you have paid too little tax for 2002-03

The amount you owe for 2002-03	from T5.15 — T6.6	£ *30,508.77*
plus the first payment on account for 2003-04	*plus* from T6.5 — T6.7	£ *16,725.08*
minus any 2003-04 repayment (see notes)	*minus* from box 17.9 — T6.8	£
equals the amount due on 31 January 2004 (or, if negative, the amount you are owed)	*equals* — T6.9	£ *47,233.85*

CALCULATION HELP

If payments on account for 2002-03 were due, but not paid on or before the due dates of 31 January 2003 and 31 July 2003, interest may be due.

If you have paid too much tax for 2002-03

The amount we owe you for 2002-03	from T5.16 — T6.10	£
plus any 2003-04 repayment (see notes)	*plus* from box 17.9 — T6.11	£
minus the first payment on account for 2003-04	*minus* from T6.5 — T6.12	£
equals the amount we owe you (or, if negative, the amount you owe on 31 January 2004)	*equals* — T6.13	£

If you have outstanding liabilities (such as unpaid tax from earlier years, unpaid interest, unpaid surcharges or unpaid penalties), the net overpayment will be used to pay them first. Otherwise, you can claim a repayment. Fill in Question 18 in the Trust and Estate Tax Return as appropriate. If you do not claim a repayment, the net overpayment will be set against the next tax bill.

Suzie's income from the trusts, was shown after settling off her share of management expenses of £2,500 against divided income, reducing her income from this source from £5,689 net of tax credit to £3,189 net, on form R185.

Inland Revenue

Statement of income from trusts

Trustees: use this form to advise beneficiaries about income payments made under discretion, and income entitlement from trusts. For annuities and other annual payments, use form R185.

Beneficiaries: keep this form and refer to it if making a Tax Return or claiming a tax repayment. The box numbers 7.1 to 7.12 below refer to the box numbers on the *Trusts etc.* page of the Tax Return.

I certify that *(Name and address of beneficiary)*

Full name *Suzie Fiddlesticks*
Address *Sherlock, Butchers Place*
Hartford
Glos
Postcode

is a beneficiary of *(name of trust)* *Florov Trust*

Tax reference of trust ______ Agent's/Solicitor's reference ______

The information below is correct.
Signature of trustee *A Trustee* Date / /

Discretionary income payment from a trust

I paid income to the beneficiary as follows:

	Net amount	Tax credit at the rate applicable to trusts	Taxable amount	Year ended 5 April
Total payments in tax year *(see Note 1 overleaf)*	7.1 £	7.2 £	7.3 £	20

Income entitlement under a trust

The beneficiary's income entitlement for year ended 5 April 20 *03* was:

Income taxed at:	Net amount	UK tax or tax credit	Taxable amount	Type of income for a non-resident beneficiary *(see Note 6 overleaf)*
basic rate *(see Note 2 overleaf)*	7.4 £ *45,299 28*	7.5 £ *12,776 72*	7.6 £ *58,076 00*	
lower rate *(see Note 3 overleaf)*	7.7 £ *2,168 00*	7.8 £ *542 00*	7.9 £ *2,710 00*	
non-repayable dividend rate *(see Note 4 or 10 overleaf)*	7.10 £ *3,189 00*	7.11 £ *354 33*	7.12 £ *3,543 33*	

			Taxable amount	Type of income
Untaxed income *(see Note 7 or 11 overleaf)*			£	

	Net amount	UK tax paid	Taxable amount
Foreign income *(see Note 5 or 12 overleaf)*	£	£	£
		Foreign tax paid	
		£	

	Dividend	Notional tax	Dividend + notional tax
Stock/scrip dividends *(see Note 13 overleaf)*	£	£	£

R185(Trust Income) (Substitute)(LexisNexis UK)

Jon's income from the trust was shown on form R185.

Inland Revenue

Statement of income from trusts

Trustees: use this form to advise beneficiaries about income payments made under discretion, and income entitlement from trusts. For annuities and other annual payments, use form R185.

Beneficiaries: keep this form and refer to it if making a Tax Return or claiming a tax repayment. The box numbers 7.1 to 7.12 below refer to the box numbers on the *Trusts etc.* page of the Tax Return.

I certify that *(Name and address of beneficiary)*

Full name *Jon Fiddlesticks*
Address *Sherlock, Butchers Place*
Hartford
Glos
Postcode

is a beneficiary of *(name of trust)* *Florov*

Tax reference of trust

Agent's/Solicitor's reference

The information below is correct.
Signature of trustee *A Trustee*

Date / /

Discretionary income payment from a trust

I paid income to the beneficiary as follows:

	Net amount	Tax credit at the rate applicable to trusts	Taxable amount	Year ended 5 April
Total payments in tax year *(see Note 1 overleaf)*	7.1 £ *10,000 00*	7.2 £ *5,152 52*	7.3 £ *15,151 52*	20 *03*

Income entitlement under a trust

The beneficiary's income entitlement for year ended 5 April 20 was:

Income taxed at:	Net amount	UK tax or tax credit	Taxable amount	Type of income for a non-resident beneficiary *(see Note 6 overleaf)*
basic rate *(see Note 2 overleaf)*	7.4 £	7.5 £	7.6 £	
lower rate *(see Note 3 overleaf)*	7.7 £	7.8 £	7.9 £	
non-repayable dividend rate *(see Note 4 or 10 overleaf)*	7.10 £	7.11 £	7.12 £	

	Taxable amount	Type of income
Untaxed income *(see Note 7 or 11 overleaf)*	£	

	Net amount	UK tax paid	Taxable amount
Foreign income *(see Note 5 or 12 overleaf)*	£	£	£
		Foreign tax paid	
		£	

	Dividend	Notional tax	Dividend + notional tax
Stock/scrip dividends *(see Note 13 overleaf)*	£	£	£

R185(Trust Income) (Substitute)(LexisNexis UK)

The Trustees of Florov Trust

INCOME: YEAR TO 5 APRIL 2003

CLIENT SCHEDULES TO TRADE PAGES

Balance sheet – as at 31 December 2002

Assets		
Plant, machinery and motor vehicles	28,742	
Other fixed assets	413,850	
Stock and work in progress	22,667	
Other current assets	4,250	
Bank/building society balances	12,897	
Cash in hand	420	
		482,826
Liabilities		
Trade creditors/accruals	25,633	
Other liabilities	1,250	
		26,883
		£455,943
Net business assets represented by:		
Capital account		
Balance at start of period	437,269	
Net profit/(loss)	78,674	
Drawings	(60,000)	
		455,943
		£455,943

NI Number: **UTR:**

The Trustees of Florov Trust

INCOME: YEAR TO 5 APRIL 2003

CLIENT SCHEDULES TO TRADE PAGES

Period from 1 January 2002 to 31 December 2002	
Tax adjustments	
Net profit/(loss) per Accounts	78,674
Add: Disallowable Expenses	
	200
	6,780
	14,750
	100,494
Less: Capital Allowances	
Capital allowance	18,023
	82,471
Net business profit/(loss) for tax purposes	£82,471

NI Number: **UTR:**

The Trustees of Florov Trust

INCOME: YEAR TO 5 APRIL 2003

CLIENT SCHEDULES TO TRADE PAGES

Statement of Income and Expenses: Period from 1 January 2002 to 31 December 2002

	£	£
Income		
		326,627
Expenses		
	63,275	
	40,820	
	15,690	
	10,380	
	11,863	
	4,727	
	10,870	
	1,250	
	650	
	220	
	14,750	
	2,486	
	70,972	
		(247,953)
Profit/(Loss)		£78,674

NI Number: **UTR:**

The Trustees of Florov Trust

INCOME: YEAR TO 5 APRIL 2003

CLIENT SCHEDULES TO TAX RETURN Q9, PAGE 3

Interest from UK banks, building societies and deposit takers:

Interest paid net of tax:	**£**	**£**	**£**
	Net Interest	**Tax Deducted**	**Gross Amount**
Banks etc:			
	4,336.00	1,084.00	5,420.00
	£4,336.00	£1,084.00	£5,420.00
Totals per Tax Return	£4,336.00	£1,084.00	£5,420.00

CLIENT SCHEDULE TO TAX RETURN Q9, PAGE 4
Dividends and other qualifying distributions from UK companies:

Company and share description	**Quantity Held**	**Date Paid**	**£ Dividend/ Distribution**	**£ Tax Credit**
			9,000.00	1,000.00
			£9,000.00	£1,000.00

CLIENT SCHEDULE TO WORKING SHEET FOR QUESTION 13

Income of beneficiary(ies) not subject to trustees discretion:

	£ Net income	**£ Share of expenses**	**£ Tax**	**£ Gross Income**
Suzie				
Income charged at 10% rate	5,690.25	2,500.00	632.25	6,322.50
Income charged at 20% rate	2,168.00		542.00	2,710.00
Other income	45,299.28		12,776.72	58,076.00
Total				67,108.50
Total as per Calculation work sheet				
Income charged at 10% rate	5,690.25	2,500.00	632.25	6,322.50
Income charged at 20% rate	2,168.00		542.00	2,710.00
Other income	45,299.28		12,776.72	58,076.00
Total				67,108.50

NI Number: **UTR:**

The Trustees of Florov Trust
INCOME: YEAR TO 5 APRIL 2003
CLIENT SCHEDULES TO TRADE PAGES

Period from 1 January 2002 to 31 December 2002

Reconciliation of detailed Financial Accounts to Tax Form Accounts pro-forma pages: Profit and Loss Account

Tax Form pro-forma description	Financial accounts description	£ Disallowable	£ Total
Sales			326,627
			£326,627
Cost of sales			70,972
		£0	£70,972
[Gross profit/(loss) – amount calculated]			255,655
Employee costs			63,275
		£0	£63,275
Premises costs			40,820
		£0	£40,820
Repairs			15,690
		£0	15,690
General administrative expenses			10,380
		£0	£10,380
Motor expenses		200	11,863
		£200	£11,863
Travel and subsistence			4,727
		£0	£4,727
Advertising, promotion and entertainment		6,870	10,870
		£6,870	£10,870
Legal and professional costs			1,250
		£0	£1,250
Bad debts			650
		£0	£650

NI Number: **UTR:**

The Trustees of Florov Trust

INCOME: YEAR TO 5 APRIL 2003
CLIENT SCHEDULES TO TRADE PAGES

Period from 1 January 2002 to 31 December 2002

Reconciliation of detailed Financial Accounts to Tax Form Accounts pro-forma pages: Profit and Loss Account

Tax Form pro-forma description	Financial accounts description	£ Disallowable	£ Total
Interest			220
		£0	£220
Depreciation and loss/(profit) on sale		14,750	14,750
		£14,750	£14,750
Other expenses			2,486
		£0	£2,486
[Total expenses – amount calculated]			
			£176,981
[Net profit/(loss) – amount calculated]			
			£78,674

NI Number: **UTR:**

The Trustees of Florov Trust

INCOME: YEAR TO 5 APRIL 2003

CLIENT SCHEDULES TO TRADE PAGES

Period from 1 January 2002 to 31 December 2002

Capital allowances claim:

Pooled	**General Pool** £
W.D.V. brought forward	
Additions at cost	
Disposal proceeds	
	—
Balancing charge	
Balancing allowance	
	—
Initial/F.Y. allowance	
Writing down allowance	(8,661)
Amount disclaimed	
Private use	
	—
W.D.V. carried forward	
	—

Assets with private use	**Asset** £
W.D.V. brought forward	
Additions at cost	
Disposal proceeds	
	—
Balancing charge	
Balancing allowance	
	—
Initial/F.Y. allowance	
Writing down allowance	(5,200)
Amount disclaimed	
Private use	
	—
W.D.V. carried forward	
	—

NI Number: **UTR:**

The Trustees of Florov Trust

INCOME: YEAR TO 5 APRIL 2003

CLIENT SCHEDULES TO TRADE PAGES

Period from 1 January 2002 to 31 December 2002

Capital allowances claim:
Other assets

	Other assets £
W.D.V. brought forward	
Additions at cost	
Disposal proceeds	
	—
Balancing charge	
Balancing allowance	
	—
Initial/F.Y. allowance	
Writing down allowance	(4,162)
Amount disclaimed	
Private use	
	—
W.D.V. carried forward	
	—

NI Number: **UTR:**

The Trustees of Florov Trust

INCOME: YEAR TO 5 APRIL 2003

CLIENT SCHEDULE TO LAND AND PROPERTY PAGES, TL2

Income from land and property in the UK:

Income from property (excluding Furnished Holiday Lets)	**£ Expenses**	**£ Income**
Address of property:		
Type of rental: Unfurnished property		
Gross rents and other income:		18,000
		£18,000

NI Number: **UTR:**

The Trustees of Florov Trust

INCOME: YEAR TO 5 APRIL 2003

CLIENT SCHEDULE TO LAND AND PROPERTY PAGES, TL2

Reconciliation of individual property accounts to Land and Property page TL2:

Property	**Accounts Description**	**£**
Rents and other income from land and property		
		18,000
		£18,000

NI Number: **UTR:**

The Trustees of Florov Trust
INCOME: YEAR TO 5 APRIL 2003

CLIENT SCHEDULE TO FOREIGN PAGES, PAGE TF1

Foreign savings taxable on the arising basis:

Dividends	**£ Foreign Tax**	**£ Amount Chargeable**
A	£248.00	2,645.00
Grand Total	£248.00	£2,645.00

Summary

£ Amount before Tax	**£ Foreign Tax**	**£ Amount Chargeable**
£2,645.00	£248.00	£2,645.00

NI Number: **UTR:**

The Trustees of Florov Trust

CAPITAL GAINS: YEAR TO 5 APRIL 2003

CLIENT SCHEDULE TO CAPITAL GAINS PAGES

This fund	**Date**	**Value**	**£ Gain/ (Loss)**
Disposal	01/12/2002	66,640.00	
Acquired	02/12/2000	(40,000.00)	
Personal usage			
Chargeable gains/(allowable loss) after reliefs		26,640.00	
Net gain/(loss)			£26,640.00
Total gains after all reliefs and losses (but before annual exemption)			£26,640.00
Net chargeable gains/(losses)			£26,640.00

NI Number: **UTR:**

Appendix 1

Legislation

Wills Act 1837

1837 CHAPTER 26

An Act for the amendment of the Laws with respect to Wills [3rd July 1837]

Initial Commencement—Specified date: 1 January 1838 (with effect in relation to wills made after that date): see s 34.
Extent—This Act does not extend to Scotland: see s 35.

---

1 Meaning of certain words in this Act

… the words and expressions herein-after mentioned, which in their ordinary signification have a more confined or a different meaning, shall in this Act, except where the nature of the provisions or the context of the Act shall exclude such construction, be interpreted as follows; (that is to say,) the word 'will' shall extend to a testament, and to a codicil, and to an appointment by will or by writing in the nature of a will in exercise of a power, [and also to an appointment by will of a guardian of a child], … and to any other testamentary disposition; and the words 'real estate' shall extend to manors, advowsons, messuages, lands, tithes, rents, and hereditaments, … whether corporeal, incorporeal, or personal, … and to any estate, right, or interest (other than a chattel interest) therein; and the words 'personal estate' shall extend to leasehold estates and other chattels real, and also to monies, shares of government and other funds, securities for money (not being real estates), debts, choses in action, rights, credits, goods, and all other property whatsoever which by law devolves upon the executor or administrator, and to any share or interest therein; and every word importing the singular number only shall extend and be applied to several persons or things as well as one person or thing; and every word importing the masculine gender only shall extend and be applied to a female as well as a male.

Amendment—Repealed in part, in relation to Northern Ireland, by the Statute Law Revision (Northern Ireland) Act 1954, the Statute Law Revision (Northern Ireland) Act 1976, and the Wills and Administration Proceedings (NI) Order 1994, SI 1994/1899, art 38, Sch 3.

First words omitted repealed by the Statute Law Revision Act 1893; words in square brackets substituted by the Children Act 1989, s 108(5), (6), Sch 13, para 1, Sch 14, para 1; second and third words omitted repealed by the Statute Law (Repeals) Act 1969; final words omitted repealed by the Trusts of Land and Appointment of Trustees Act 1996, s 25(2), Sch 4, for savings in relation to entailed interests created before the commencement of that Act, and savings consequential upon the abolition of the doctrine of conversion, see s 25(4), (5) thereof.

---

3 All property may be disposed of by will

< … > it shall be lawful for every person to devise, bequeath, or dispose of, by his will executed in manner herein-after required, all real estate and all personal estate which he shall be entitled to, either at law or in equity, at the time of his death, and which, if not so devised, bequeathed, and disposed of, would devolve < … > upon his executor or administrator; and < … > the power hereby given shall extend < … > to all contingent, executory or other future interests in any real or personal estate, whether the testator may or may not be ascertained as the person or one of the persons in whom the same respectively may become vested, and whether he may be entitled thereto under the instrument by which the same respectively were created, or under any disposition thereof by deed or will; and also to all rights of entry for conditions

broken, and other rights of entry; and also to such of the same estates, interests, and rights respectively, and other real and personal estate, as the testator may be entitled to at the time of his death, notwithstanding that he may become entitled to the same subsequently to the execution of his will.

Amendment—Repealed, in relation to Northern Ireland, by the Wills and Administration Proceedings (NI) Order 1994, SI 1994/1899, art 38, Sch 3.
First and third words omitted repealed by the Statute Law Revision (No 2) Act 1888; second and fourth words omitted repealed by the Statute Law (Repeals) Act 1969.

---

7 No will of a person under age valid

< … > no will made by any person under the age of [eighteen years] shall be valid.

Amendment—Repealed, in relation to Northern Ireland, by the Wills and Administration Proceedings (NI) Order 1994, SI 1994/1899, art 38, Sch 3.
Words omitted repealed by the Statute Law Revision (No 2) Act 1888; words in square brackets substituted by the Family Law Reform Act 1969, s 3(1)(a).

[9 Signing and attestation of wills]

[No will shall be valid unless—

(a) it is in writing, and signed by the testator, or by some other person in his presence and by his direction; and
(b) it appears that the testator intended by his signature to give effect to the will; and
(c) the signature is made or acknowledged by the testator in the presence of two or more witnesses present at the same time; and
(d) each witness either—

 (i) attests and signs the will; or
 (ii) acknowledges his signature,in the presence of the testator (but not necessarily in the presence of any other witness),

but no form of attestation shall be necessary.]

Amendment—Substituted, in relation to England and Wales, by the Administration of Justice Act 1982, s 17.
Repealed, in relation to Northern Ireland, by the Wills and Administration Proceedings (NI) Order 1994, SI 1994/1899, art 38, Sch 3.

---

10 Appointments by will to be executed like other wills, and to be valid, although other required solemnities are not observed

< … > no appointment made by will, in exercise of any power, shall be valid, unless the same be executed in manner herein-before required; and every will executed in manner herein-before required shall, so far as respects the execution and attestation thereof, be a valid execution of a power of appointment by will, notwithstanding it

shall have been expressly required that a will made in exercise of such power should be executed with some additional or other form of execution or solemnity.

Amendment—Repealed, in relation to Northern Ireland, by the Wills and Administration Proceedings (NI) Order 1994, SI 1994/1899, art 38, Sch 3.
Words omitted repealed by the Statute Law Revision (No 2) Act 1888.

11 Saving as to wills of soldiers and mariners

Provided always, … that any soldier being in actual military service, or any mariner or seaman being at sea, may dispose of his personal estate as he might have done before the making of this Act.

Amendment—Words omitted repealed by the Statute Law Revision (No 2) Act 1888.

13 Publication of will not requisite

< … > every will executed in manner herein-before required shall be valid without any other publication thereof.

Amendment—Repealed, in relation to Northern Ireland, by the Wills and Administration Proceedings (NI) Order 1994, SI 1994/1899, art 38, Sch 3.
Words omitted repealed by the Statute Law Revision (No 2) Act 1888.

14 Will not be void on account of incompetency of attesting witness

< … > if any person who shall attest the execution of a will shall at the time of the execution thereof or at any time afterwards be incompetent to be admitted a witness to prove the execution thereof, such will shall not on that account be invalid.

Amendment—Repealed, in relation to Northern Ireland, by the Wills and Administration Proceedings (NI) Order 1994, SI 1994/1899, art 38, Sch 3.
Words omitted repealed by the Statute Law Revision (No 2) Act 1888.

15 Gifts to an attesting witness, or his or her wife or husband, to be void

< … > if any person shall attest the execution of any will to whom or to whose wife or husband any beneficial devise, legacy, estate, interest, gift, or appointment, of or affecting any real or personal estate (other than and except charges and directions for the payment of any debt or debts), shall be thereby given or made, such devise, legacy, estate, interest, gift, or appointment shall, so far only as concerns such person attesting the execution of such will, or the wife or husband of such person, or any person claiming under such person or wife or husband, be utterly null and void, and such person so attesting shall be admitted as a witness to prove the execution of such will, or to prove the validity or invalidity thereof, notwithstanding such devise, legacy, estate, interest, gift, or appointment mentioned in such will.

Amendment—Repealed, in relation to Northern Ireland, by the Wills and Administration Proceedings (NI) Order 1994, SI 1994/1899, art 38, Sch 3.
Words omitted repealed by the Statute Law Revision (No 2) Act 1888.

16 Creditor attesting a will charging estate with debts shall be admitted a witness

< … > in case by any will any real or personal estate shall be charged with any debt or debts, and any creditor, or the wife or husband of any creditor, whose debt is so charged, shall attest the execution of such will, such creditor notwithstanding such charge shall be admitted a witness to prove the execution of such will, or to prove the validity or invalidity thereof.

Amendment—Repealed, in relation to Northern Ireland, by the Wills and Administration Proceedings (NI) Order 1994, SI 1994/1899, art 38, Sch 3.
Words omitted repealed by the Statute Law Revision (No 2) Act 1888.

17 Executor shall be admitted a witness

< … > no person shall, on account of his being an executor of a will, be incompetent to be admitted a witness to prove the execution of such will, or a witness to prove the validity or invalidity thereof.

Amendment—Repealed, in relation to Northern Ireland, by the Wills and Administration Proceedings (NI) Order 1994, SI 1994/1899, art 38, Sch 3.
Words omitted repealed by the Statute Law Revision (No 2) Act 1888.

[18 Will to be revoked by marriage]

[(1) Subject to subsections (2) to (4) below, a will shall be revoked by the testator's marriage.

(2) A disposition in a will in exercise of a power of appointment shall take effect notwithstanding the testator's subsequent marriage unless the property so appointed would in default of appointment pass to his personal representatives.

(3) Where it appears from a will that at the time it was made the testator was expecting to be married to a particular person and that he intended that the will should not be revoked by the marriage, the will shall not be revoked by his marriage to that person.

(4) Where it appears from a will that at the time it was made the testator was expecting to be married to a particular person and that he intended that a disposition in the will should not be revoked by his marriage to that person,—

(a) that disposition shall take effect notwithstanding the marriage; and

(b) any other disposition in the will shall take effect also, unless it appears from the will that the testator intended the disposition to be revoked by the marriage.]

Amendment—Substituted, in relation to England and Wales, by the Administration of Justice Act 1982, s 18(1).
Repealed, in relation to Northern Ireland, by the Wills and Administration Proceedings (NI) Order 1994, SI 1994/1899, art 38, Sch 3.

[18A Effect of dissolution or annulment of marriage on wills]

[(1) Where, after a testator has made a will, *a decree* [an order or decree] of a court [of civil jurisdiction in England and Wales] dissolves or annuls his marriages [or his marriage is dissolved or annulled and the divorce or annulment is entitled to recognition in England and Wales by virtue of Part II of the Family Law Act 1986],—

[(a) provisions of the will appointing executors or trustees or conferring a power of appointment, if they appoint or confer the power on the former spouse, shall take effect as if the former spouse had died on the date on which the marriage is dissolved or annulled, and

(b) any property which, or an interest in which, is devised or bequeathed to the former spouse shall pass as if the former spouse had died on that date,]

except in so far as a contrary intention appears by the will.

(2) Subsection (1)(b) above is without prejudice to any right of the former spouse to apply for financial provision under the Inheritance (Provision for Family and Dependants) Act 1975.

(3) …]

Amendment—Inserted, in relation to England and Wales, by the Administration of Justice Act 1982, s 18(2).
Sub-s (1): first words in italics prospectively repealed with savings and subsequent words in square brackets prospectively substituted with savings by the Family Law Act 1996, s 66(1), Sch 8, para 1, as from a day to be appointed, for savings see s 66(2), Sch 9, para 5 thereof; second words in square brackets inserted, and third words in square brackets substituted, by the Family Law Act 1986, s 53; paras (a), (b) substituted by the Law Reform (Succession) Act 1995, s 3.
Sub-s (3): repealed by the Law Reform (Succession) Act 1995, s 5, Schedule.

19 No will to be revoked by presumption from altered circumstances

< … > no will shall be revoked by any presumption of an intention on the ground of an alteration in circumstances.

Amendment—Repealed, in relation to Northern Ireland, by the Wills and Administration Proceedings (NI) Order 1994, SI 1994/1899, art 38, Sch 3.
Words omitted repealed by the Statute Law Revision (No 2) Act 1888.

20 No will to be revoked otherwise than as aforesaid or by another will or codicil, or by destruction thereof

< … > no will or codicil, or any part thereof, shall be revoked otherwise than as aforesaid, or by another will or codicil executed in manner herein-before required, or by some writing declaring an intention to revoke the same and executed in the manner in which a will is herein-before required to be executed, or by the burning, tearing, or otherwise destroying the same by the testator, or by some person in his presence and by his direction, with the intention of revoking the same.

Amendment—Repealed, in relation to Northern Ireland, by the Wills and Administration Proceedings (NI) Order 1994, SI 1994/1899, art 38, Sch 3.
Words omitted repealed by the Statute Law Revision (No 2) Act 1888.

---

21 No alteration in a will after execution except in certain cases, shall have any effect unless executed as a will

< … > no obliteration, interlineation, or other alteration made in any will after the execution thereof shall be valid or have any effect, except so far as the words or effect of the will before such alteration shall not be apparent, unless such alteration shall be executed in like manner as herein-before is required for the execution of the will; but the will, with such alteration as part thereof, shall be deemed to be duly executed if the signature of the testator and the subscription of the witnesses be made in the margin or on some other part of the will opposite or near to such alteration, or at the foot or end of or opposite to a memorandum referring to such alteration, and written at the end of some other part of the will.

Amendment—Repealed, in relation to Northern Ireland, by the Wills and Administration Proceedings (NI) Order 1994, SI 1994/1899, art 38, Sch 3.
Words omitted repealed by the Statute Law Revision (No 2) Act 1888.

---

22 No revoked will shall be revived otherwise than by re-execution or a codicil, etc

< … > no will or codicil, or any part thereof, which shall be in any manner revoked, shall be revived otherwise than by the re-execution thereof or by a codicil executed in manner herein-before required and showing an intention to revive the same; and when any will or codicil which shall be partly revoked, and afterwards wholly revoked, shall be revived, such revival shall not extend to so much thereof as shall have been revoked before the revocation of the whole thereof, unless an intention to the contrary shall be shown.

Amendment—Repealed, in relation to Northern Ireland, by the Wills and Administration Proceedings (NI) Order 1994, SI 1994/1899, art 38, Sch 3.
Words omitted repealed by the Statute Law Revision (No 2) Act 1888.

---

23 Subsequent conveyance or other act not to prevent operation of will

< … > no conveyance or other act made or done subsequently to the execution of a will of or relating to any real or personal estate therein comprised, except an act by

which such will shall be revoked as aforesaid, shall prevent the operation of the will with respect to such estate or interest in such real or personal estate as the testator shall have power to dispose of by will at the time of his death.

Amendment—Repealed, in relation to Northern Ireland, by the Wills and Administration Proceedings (NI) Order 1994, SI 1994/1899, art 38, Sch 3.
Words omitted repealed by the Statute Law Revision (No 2) Act 1888.

---

24 Wills shall be construed, as to the estate comprised, to speak from the death of the testator

< … > every will shall be construed, with reference to the real estate and personal estate comprised in it, to speak and take effect as if it had been executed immediately before the death of the testator, unless a contrary intention shall appear by the will.

Amendment—Repealed, in relation to Northern Ireland, by the Wills and Administration Proceedings (NI) Order 1994, 1994/1899, art 38, Sch 3.
Words omitted repealed by the Statute Law Revision (No 2) Act 1888.

---

25 Residuary devises shall include estates comprised in lapsed and void devises

< … > unless a contrary intention shall appear by the will, such real estate or interest therein as shall be comprised or intended to be comprised in any devise in such will contained, which shall fail or be void by reason of the death of the devisee in the lifetime of the testator, or by reason of such devise being contrary to law or otherwise incapable of taking effect shall be included in the residuary devise (if any) contained in such will.

Amendment—Repealed, in relation to Northern Ireland, by the Wills and Administration Proceedings (NI) Order 1994, SI 1994/1899, art 38, Sch 3.
Words omitted repealed by the Statute Law Revision (No 2) Act 1888.

---

26 A general devise of the testator's lands shall include copyhold and leasehold as well as freehold lands, in the absence of a contrary intention

< … > a devise of the land of the testator, or of the land of the testator in any place or in the occupation of any person mentioned in his will, or otherwise described in a general manner, and any other general devise which would describe a < … > leasehold estate if the testator had no freehold estate which could be described by it, shall be construed to include the < … > leasehold estates of the testator, or his < … > leasehold estates, or any of them, to which such description shall extend, as the case may be, as well as freehold estates, unless a contrary intention shall appear by the will.

Amendment—Repealed, in relation to Northern Ireland, by the Wills and Administration Proceedings (NI) Order 1994, SI 1994/1899, art 38, Sch 3.
First words omitted repealed by the Statute Law Revision (No 2) Act 1888; other words omitted repealed by the Statute Law (Repeals) Act 1969.

---

27 A general gift of realty or personalty shall include property over which the testator has a general power of appointment

< … > a general devise of the real estate of the testator, or of the real estate of the testator in any place or in the occupation of any person mentioned in his will, or otherwise described in a general manner, shall be construed to include any real estate, or any real estate to which such description shall extend (as the case may be), which he may have power to appoint in any manner he may think proper, and shall operate as an execution of such power, unless a contrary intention shall appear by the will; and in like manner a bequest of the personal estate of the testator, or any bequest of personal property described in a general manner, shall be construed to include any personal estate, or any personal estate to which such description shall extend (as the case may be), which he may have power to appoint in any manner he may think proper, and shall operate as an execution of such power, unless a contrary intention shall appear by the will.

Amendment—Repealed, in relation to Northern Ireland, by the Wills and Administration Proceedings (NI) Order 1994, SI 1994/1899, art 38, Sch 3.
Words omitted repealed by the Statute Law Revision (No 2) Act 1888.

---

28 A devise of real estate without any words of limitation shall pass the fee, etc

< … > where any real estate shall be devised to any person without any words of limitation, such devise shall be construed to pass the fee simple, or other the whole estate or interest which the testator had power to dispose of by will in such real estate, unless a contrary intention shall appear by the will.

Amendment—Repealed, in relation to Northern Ireland, by the Wills and Administration Proceedings (NI) Order 1994, 1994/1899, art 38, Sch 3.
Words omitted repealed by the Statute Law Revision (No 2) Act 1888.

---

29 The words 'die without issue,' or 'die without leaving issue,' etc shall mean a want or failure of issue in the lifetime or at the death of the person, except in certain cases

< … > in any devise or bequest of real or personal estate the words 'die without issue' or 'die without leaving issue,' or 'have no issue,' or any other words which may import either a want or failure of issue of any person in his lifetime or at the time of his death, or an indefinite failure of his issue, shall be construed to mean a want or failure of issue in the lifetime or at the time of the death of such person, and not an indefinite failure of his issue, unless a contrary intention shall appear by the will, by reason of such person having a prior estate tail, or of a preceding gift, being, without any implication arising from such words, a limitation of an estate tail to such person or issue, or otherwise: Provided, that this Act shall not extend to cases where such words as aforesaid import if no issue described in a preceding gift shall be born, or if there shall be no issue who shall live to attain the age or otherwise answer the description required for obtaining a vested estate by a preceding gift to such issue.

Amendment—Repealed, in relation to Northern Ireland, by the Wills and Administration Proceedings (NI) Order 1994, SI 1994/1899, art 38, Sch 3.
Words omitted repealed by the Statute Law Revision (No 2) Act 1888.

---

30 Devise of realty to trustees or executors shall pass the fee, etc, except in certain cases

< … > where any real estate (other than or not being a presentation to a church) shall be devised to any trustee or executor, such devise shall be construed to pass the fee simple or other the whole estate or interest which the testator had power to dispose of by will in such real estate, unless a definite term of years, absolute or determinable, or an estate of freehold, shall thereby be given to him expressly or by implication.

Amendment—Repealed, in relation to Northern Ireland, by the Wills and Administration Proceedings (NI) Order 1994, SI 1994/1899, art 38, Sch 3.
Words omitted repealed by the Statute Law Revision (No 2) Act 1888.

---

31 Trustees under an unlimited devise, where the trust may endure beyond the life of a person beneficially entitled for life, shall take the fee, etc

< … > where any real estate shall be devised to a trustee, without any express limitation of the estate to be taken by such trustee, and the beneficial interest in such real estate, or in the surplus rents and profits thereof, shall not be given to any person for life, or such beneficial interest shall be given to any person for life, but the purposes of the trust may continue beyond the life of such person, such devise shall be construed to vest in such trustee the fee simple, or other the whole legal estate which the testator had power to dispose of by will in such real estate, and not an estate determinable when the purposes of the trust shall be satisfied.

Amendment—Repealed, in relation to Northern Ireland, by the Wills and Administration Proceedings (NI) Order 1994, SI 1994/1899, art 38, Sch 3.
Words omitted repealed by the Statute Law Revision (No 2) Act 1888.

[33 Gifts to children or other issue who leave issue living at the testator's death shall not lapse]

[(1) Where—

(a) a will contains a devise or bequest to a child or remoter descendant of the testator; and
(b) the intended beneficiary dies before the testator, leaving issue; and
(c) issue of the intended beneficiary are living at the testator's death,

then, unless a contrary intention appears by the will, the devise or bequest shall take effect as a devise or bequest to the issue living at the testator's death.

(2) Where—

(a) a will contains a devise or bequest to a class of person consisting of children or remoter descendants of the testator; and
(b) a member of the class dies before the testator, leaving issue, and
(c) issue of that member are living at the testator's death,

then, unless a contrary intention appears by the will, the devise or bequest shall take effect as if the class included the issue of its deceased member living at the testator's death.

(3) Issue shall take under this section through all degrees, according to their stock, in equal shares if more than one, any gift or share which their parent would have taken and so that no issue shall take whose parent is living at the testator's death and that no issue shall take whose parent is living at the testator's death and so capable of taking.

(4) For the purposes of this section—

(a) the illegitimacy of any person is to be disregarded; and
(b) a person conceived before the testator's death and born living thereafter is to be taken to have been living at the testator's death.]

Amendment—Substituted, in relation to England and Wales, by the Administration of Justice Act 1982, s 19.
Repealed, in relation to Northern Ireland, by the Wills and Administration Proceedings (NI) Order 1994, SI 1994/1899, art 38, Sch 3.

Apportionment Act 1870

1870 Chapter 35

An Act for the better apportionment of rents and other periodical payments.

[1 August 1870]

Initial Commencement—Royal Assent: 1 August 1870: (no specific commencement provision).

---

2 Rents, etc to be apportionable in respect of time

… All rents, annuities, dividends, and other periodical payments in the nature of income (whether reserved or made payable under an instrument in writing or otherwise) shall, like interest on money lent, be considered as accruing from day to day, and shall be apportionable in respect of time accordingly.

Amendment—Words omitted repealed by the Statute Law Revision (No 2) Act 1893.

---

7 Nor where stipulation made to the contrary

The provisions of this Act shall not extend to any case in which it is or shall be expressly stipulated that no apportionment shall take place.

Settled Land Act 1925

1925 Chapter 18

An Act to consolidate the enactments relating to settled land in England and Wales.

[9 April 1925]

Initial Commencement—Specified date: 1 January 1926.
Extent—This Act does not extend to Scotland: see s 120(3).

PART I
GENERAL PRELIMINARY PROVISIONS

Settlements and Settled Land

1 What constitutes a settlement

(1) Any deed, will, agreement for a settlement or other agreement, Act of Parliament, or other instrument, or any number of instruments, whether made or passed before or after, or partly before and partly after, the commencement of this Act, under or by virtue of which instrument or instruments any land, after the commencement of this Act, stands for the time being—

(i) limited in trust for any persons by way of succession; or
(ii) limited in trust for any person in possession—

  (a) for an entailed interest whether or not capable of being barred or defeated;
  (b) for an estate in fee simple or for a term of years absolute subject to an executory limitation, gift, or disposition over on failure of his issue or in any other event;
  (c) for a base or determinable fee [(other than a fee which is a fee simple absolute by virtue of section 7 of the Law of Property Act 1925)] or any corresponding interest in leasehold land;
  (d) being an infant, for an estate in fee simple or for a term of years absolute; or

(iii) limited in trust for any person for an estate in fee simple or for a term of years absolute contingently on the happening of any event; or
(iv) ...
(v) charged, whether voluntarily or in consideration of marriage or by way of family arrangement, and whether immediately or after an interval, with the payment of any rentcharge for the life of any person, or any less period, or of any capital, annual, or periodical sums for the portions, advancement, maintenance, or otherwise for the benefit of any persons, with or without any term of years for securing or raising the same;

creates or is for the purposes of this Act a settlement and is in this Act referred to as a settlement, or as the settlement, as the case requires;

Provided that, where land is the subject of a compound settlement, references in this Act to the settlement shall be construed as meaning such compound settlement, unless the context otherwise requires.

(2) Where an infant is beneficially entitled to land for an estate in fee simple or for a term of years absolute and by reason of an intestacy or otherwise there is no instrument under which the interest of the infant arises or is acquired, a settlement shall be deemed to have been made by the intestate, or by the person whose interest the infant has acquired.

(3) An infant shall be deemed to be entitled in possession notwithstanding any subsisting right of dower (not assigned by metes and bounds) affecting the land, and such a right of dower shall be deemed to be an interest comprised in the subject of the settlement and coming to the dowress under or by virtue of the settlement.

Where dower has been assigned by metes and bounds, the letters of administration or probate granted in respect of the estate of the husband of the dowress shall be deemed a settlement made by the husband.

(4) An estate or interest not disposed of by a settlement and remaining in or reverting to the settlor, or any person deriving title under him, is for the purposes of this Act an estate or interest comprised in the subject of the settlement and coming to the settlor or such person under or by virtue of the settlement.

(5) Where—

(a) a settlement creates an entailed interest which is incapable of being barred or defeated, or a base or determinable fee, whether or not the reversion or right of reverter is in the Crown, or any corresponding interest in leasehold land; or
(b) the subject of a settlement is an entailed interest, or a base or determinable fee, whether or not the reversion or right of reverter is in the Crown, or any corresponding interest in leasehold land;

the reversion or right of reverter upon the cesser of the interest so created or settled shall be deemed to be an interest comprised in the subject of the settlement, and limited by the settlement.

(6) Subsection (4) and (5) of this section bind the Crown.

[(7) This section does not apply to land held upon trust for sale.]

Amendment—Sub-s (1): words in square brackets inserted by the Trusts of Land and Appointment of Trustees Act 1996, s 25(1), Sch 3, para 2(2), for savings in relation to entailed interests created before the commencement of that Act, and savings consequential upon the abolition of the doctrine of conversion, see s 25(4), (5) thereof; words omitted repealed by the Married Women (Restraint upon Anticipation) Act 1949, s 1(4), Sch 2.
Sub-s (7): inserted by the Law of Property (Amendment) Act 1926, s 7, Schedule.

---

2 *What is settled land*

Land which is or is deemed to be the subject of a settlement is for the purposes of this Act settled land, and is in relation to the settlement referred to in this Act as the settled land.

3 Duration of settlements

Land [which has been subject to a settlement which is a settlement for the purposes of this Act] shall be deemed for the purposes of this Act to remain and be settled land, and the settlement shall be deemed to be a subsisting settlement for the purposes of this Act so long as—

(a) any limitation, charge, or power of charging under the settlement subsists, or is capable of being exercised; or
(b) the person who, if of full age, would be entitled as beneficial owner to have that land vested in him for a legal estate is an infant.

Amendment—Words in square brackets substituted by the Trusts of Land and Appointment of Trustees Act 1996, s 25(1), Sch 3, para 2(3); for savings in relation to entailed interests created before the commencement of that Act, and savings consequential upon the abolition of the doctrine of conversion, see s 25(4), (5) thereof.

---

4 Authorised method of settling land inter vivos

(1) Every settlement of a legal estate in land inter vivos shall, save as in this Act otherwise provided, be effected by two deeds, namely, a vesting deed and a trust instrument and if effected in any other way shall not operate to transfer or create a legal estate.

(2) By the vesting deed the land shall be conveyed to the tenant for life or statutory owner (and if more than one as joint tenants) for the legal estate the subject of the intended settlement:

Provided that, where such legal estate is already vested in the tenant for life or statutory owner, it shall be sufficient, without any other conveyance, if the vesting deed declares that the land is vested in him for that estate.

(3) The trust instrument shall—

(a) declare the trusts affecting the settled land;
(b) appoint or constitute trustees of the settlement:
(c) contain the power, if any, to appoint new trustees of the settlement;
(d) set out, either expressly or by reference, any powers intended to be conferred by the settlement in extension of those conferred by this Act;
(e) bear any ad valorem stamp duty which may be payable (whether by virtue of the vesting deed or otherwise) in respect of the settlement.

5 Contents of vesting deeds

(1) Every vesting deed for giving effect to a settlement or for conveying settled land to a tenant for life or statutory owner during the subsistence of the settlement (in this Act referred to as a 'principal vesting deed') shall contain the following statements and particulars, namely:—

(a) A description, either specific or general, of the settled land;
(b) A statement that the settled land is vested in the person or persons to whom it is conveyed or in whom it is declared to be vested upon the trusts from time to time affecting the settled Land;

(c) The names of the persons who are the trustees of the settlement;
(d) Any additional or larger powers conferred by the trust instrument relating to the settled land which by virtue of this Act operate and are exercisable as if conferred by this Act on a tenant for life;
(e) The name of any person for the time being entitled under the trust instrument to appoint new trustees of the settlement.

(2) The statements or particulars required by this section may be incorporated by reference to an existing vesting instrument, and, where there is a settlement subsisting at the commencement of this Act, by reference to that settlement and to any instrument whereby land has been conveyed to the uses or upon the trusts of that settlement, but not (save as last aforesaid) by reference to a trust instrument nor by reference to a disentailing deed.

(3) A principal vesting deed shall not be invalidated by reason only of any error in any of the statements or particulars by this Act required to be contained therein.

6 Procedure in the case of settlements by will

Where a settlement is created by the will of an estate owner who dies after the commencement of this Act—

(a) the will is for the purposes of this Act a trust instrument; and
(b) the personal representatives of the testator shall hold the settled land on trust, if and when required so to do, to convey it to the person who, under the will, or by virtue of this Act, is the tenant for life or statutory owner, and, if more than one, as joint tenants.

7 Procedure on change of ownership

(1) If, on the death of a tenant for life or statutory owner, or of the survivor of two or more tenants for life or statutory owners, in whom the settled land was vested, the land remains settled land, his personal representatives shall hold the settled land on trust, if and when required so to do, to convey it to the person who under the trust instrument or by virtue of this Act becomes the tenant for life or statutory owner and, if more than one, as joint tenants.

(2) If a person by reason of attaining full age becomes a tenant for life for the purposes of this Act of settled land, he shall be entitled to require the trustees of the settlement, personal representatives, or other persons in whom the settled land is vested, to convey the land to him.

(3) If a person who, when of full age, will together with another person or other persons constitute the tenant for life for the purposes of this Act of settled land attains that age, he shall be entitled to require the tenant for life, trustees of the settlement, personal representatives or other persons in whom the settled land is vested to convey the land to him and the other person or persons who together with him constitute the tenant for life as joint tenants.

(4) If by reason of forfeiture, surrender, or otherwise the estate owner of any settled land ceases to have the statutory powers of a tenant for life and the land remains settled land, he shall be bound forthwith to convey the settled land to the person who

under the trust instrument, or by virtue of this Act, becomes the tenant for life or statutory owner and, if more than one, as joint tenants.

(5) If any person of full age becomes absolutely entitled to the settled land (whether beneficially, or as personal representative, or as [trustee of land], or otherwise) free from all limitations, powers, and charges taking effect under the settlement, he shall be entitled to require the trustees of the settlement, personal representatives, or other persons in whom the settled land is vested, to convey the land to him, and if more persons than one being of full age become so entitled to the settled land they shall be entitled to require such persons as aforesaid to convey the land to them as joint tenants.

Amendment—Sub-s (5): words in square brackets substituted by the Trusts of Land and Appointment of Trustees Act 1996, s 25(1), Sch 3, para 2(4); for savings in relation to entailed interests created before the commencement of that Act, and savings consequential upon the abolition of the doctrine of conversion, see s 25(4), (5) thereof.

Tenants for Life and Persons with Powers of Tenant for Life

19 Who is tenant for life

(1) The person of full age who is for the time being beneficially entitled under a settlement to possession of settled land for his life is for the purposes of this Act the tenant for life of that land and the tenant for life under that settlement.

(2) If in any case there are two or more persons of full age so entitled as joint tenants, they together constitute the tenant for life for the purposes of this Act.

(3) If in any case there are two or more persons so entitled as joint tenants and they are not all of full age, such one or more of them as is or are for the time being of full age is or (if more than one) together constitute the tenant for life for the purposes of this Act, but this subsection does not affect the beneficial interests of such of them as are not for the time being of full age.

(4) A person being tenant for life within the foregoing definitions shall be deemed to be such notwithstanding that, under the settlement or otherwise, the settled land, or his estate or interest therein, is incumbered or charged in any manner or to any extent, and notwithstanding any assignment by operation of law or otherwise of his estate or interest under the settlement, whether before or after it came into possession, other than an assurance which extinguishes that estate or interest.

20 Other limited owners having powers of tenant for life

(1) Each of the following persons being of full age shall, when his estate or interest is in possession, have the powers of a tenant for life under this Act, (namely):—

(i) A tenant in tail, including a tenant in tail after possibility of issue extinct, and a tenant in tail who is by Act of Parliament restrained from barring or defeating his estate tail, and although the reversion is in the Crown, but not including such a tenant in tail where the land in respect whereof he is so restrained was purchased with money provided by Parliament in consideration of public services;

(ii) A person entitled to land for an estate in fee simple or for a term of years absolute with or subject to, in any of such cases, an executory limitation, gift, or disposition over on failure of his issue or in any other event;

(iii) A person entitled to a base or determinable fee, although the reversion or right of reverter is in the Crown, or to any corresponding interest in leasehold land;

(iv) A tenant for years determinable on life, not holding merely under a lease at a rent;

(v) A tenant for the life of another, not holding merely under a lease at a rent;

(vi) A tenant for his own or any other life, or for years determinable on life, whose estate is liable to cease in any event during that life, whether by expiration of the estate, or by conditional limitation, or otherwise, or to be defeated by an executory limitation, gift, or disposition over, or is subject to a trust for accumulation of income for any purpose;

(vii) A tenant by the curtesy;

(viii) A person entitled to the income of land under a trust or direction for payment thereof to him during his own or any other life, whether or not subject to expenses of management or to a trust for accumulation of income for any purpose, or until sale of the land, or until forfeiture, cesser or determination by any means of his interest therein, unless the land is subject to [a trust of land];

(ix) A person beneficially entitled to land for an estate in fee simple or for a term of years absolute subject to any estates, interests, charges, or powers of charging, subsisting or capable of being exercised under a settlement;

(x) …

(2) In every such case as is mentioned in subsection (1) of this section, the provisions of this Act referring to a tenant for life, either as conferring powers on him or otherwise, shall extend to each of the persons aforesaid, and any reference in this Act to death as regards a tenant for life shall, where necessary, be deemed to refer to the determination by death or otherwise of the estate or interest of the person on whom the powers of a tenant for life are conferred by this section.

(3) For the purposes of this Act the estate or interest of a tenant by the curtesy shall be deemed to be an estate or interest arising under a settlement made by his wife.

(4) Where the reversion of right or reverter or other reversionary right is in the Crown, the exercise by a person on whom the powers of a tenant for life are conferred by this section of his powers under this Act, binds the Crown.

Amendment—Sub-s (1): words in square brackets in para (viii) substituted by the Trusts of Land and Appointment of Trustees Act 1996, s 25(1), Sch 3, para 2(8), for savings in relation to entailed interests created before the commencement of that Act, and savings consequential upon the abolition of the doctrine of conversion, see s 25(4), (5) thereof; para (x) repealed by The Married Women (Restraint upon Anticipation) Act 1949, s 1(4), Sch 2.

---

21 Absolute owners subject to certain interests to have the powers of tenant for life

(1) Where a person of full age is beneficially entitled in possession to a legal estate subject to any equitable interests or powers, then, for the purpose of overreaching such interests or powers, he may, notwithstanding any stipulation to the contrary, by deed (which shall have effect as a principal vesting deed within the meaning of this Act) declare that the legal estate is vested in him on trust to give effect to all equitable interests and powers affecting the legal estate, and that deed shall be executed by two

or more individuals approved or appointed by the court or a trust corporation, who shall be stated to be the trustees of the settlement for the purposes of this Act.

Thereupon so long as any of the equitable interests and powers are subsisting the following provisions shall have effect:—

(a) The person so entitled as aforesaid and each of his successors in title being an estate owner shall have the powers of a tenant for life and the land shall be deemed to be settled land;

(b) The instrument (if any) under which his estate arises or is acquired, and the instrument (if any) under which the equitable interests or powers are subsisting or capable of taking effect shall be deemed to be the trust instrument:Provided that where there is no such instrument as last aforesaid then a deed (which shall take effect as a trust instrument) shall be executed contemporaneously with the vesting deed, and shall declare the trusts affecting the land;

(c) The persons stated in the principal vesting deed to be the trustees of the settlement for the purposes of this Act shall also be the trustees of the trust instrument for those purposes; and

(d) Capital money arising on any disposition of the land shall be paid to or by the direction of the trustees of the settlement or into court, and shall be applicable towards discharging or providing for payment in due order of any principal money payable in respect of such interests or charges as are overreached by such disposition, and until so applied shall be invested or applied as capital money under the trust instrument, and the [resultant profits] shall be applied as the income of such capital money, and be liable for keeping down in due order any annual or periodical sum which may be overreached by the disposition.

(2) The following equitable interests and powers are excepted from the operation of subsection (1) of this section namely—

(i) an equitable interest protected by a deposit of documents relating to the legal estate affected;

(ii) the benefit of a covenant or agreement restrictive of the user of land;

(iii) an easement, liberty or privilege over or affecting land and being merely an equitable interest;

(iv) the benefit of a contract to convey or create a legal estate, including a contract conferring either expressly or by statutory implication a valid option of purchase, a right of pre-emption, or any other like right;

(v) any equitable interest protected by registration under the Land Charges Act 1925, other than—

  (a) an annuity within the meaning of Part II of that Act;

  (b) a limited owner's charge or a general equitable charge within the meaning of that Act.

(3) Subject to the powers conferred by this Act on a tenant for life, nothing contained in this section shall deprive an equitable chargee of any of his rights or of his remedies for enforcing those rights.

Amendment—Sub-s (1): in para (d) words 'resultant profits' in square brackets substituted by the Trustee Act 2000, s 40(1), Sch 2, Pt II, para 7. Date in force: 1 February 2001: see SI 2001/49, art 2.

Trustees of Settlement

30 Who are trustees for purposes of Act

(1) Subject to the provisions of this Act, the following persons are trustees of a settlement for the purposes of this Act, and are in this Act referred to as the 'trustees of the settlement' or 'trustees of a settlement', namely—

(i) the persons, if any, who are for the time being under the settlement trustees with power of sale of the settled land (subject or not to the consent of any person), or with power of consent to or approval of the exercise of such a power of sale, or if there are no such persons; then
(ii) the persons, if any, for the time being, who are by the settlement declared to be trustees thereof for the purposes of the Settled Land Acts 1882 to 1890, or any of them, or this Act, or if there are no such persons; then
(iii) the persons, if any, who are for the time being under the settlement trustees with [a power or duty to sell] any other land comprised in the settlement and subject to the same limitations as the land to be sold or otherwise dealt with, or with power of consent to or approval of the exercise of such a power of sale, or, if there are no such persons; then
(iv) the persons, if any, who are for the time being under the settlement trustees with [a future power or duty to sell] the settled land, or with power of consent to or approval of the exercise of such a future power of sale, and whether the power [or duty] takes effect in all events or not, or, if there are no such persons; then
(v) the persons, if any, appointed by deed to be trustees of the settlement by all the persons who at the date of the deed were together able, by virtue of their beneficial interests or by the exercise of an equitable power, to dispose of the settled land in equity for the whole estate the subject of the settlement.

(2) Paragraphs (i) (iii) and (iv) of the last preceding subsection take effect in like manner as if the powers therein referred to had not by this Act been made exercisable by the tenant for life or statutory owner.

(3) Where a settlement is created by will, or a settlement has arisen by the effect of an intestacy, and apart from this subsection there would be no trustees for the purposes of this Act of such settlement, then the personal representatives of the deceased shall, until other trustees are appointed, be by virtue of this Act the trustees of the settlement, but where there is a sole personal representative, not being a trust corporation, it shall be obligatory on him to appoint an additional trustee to act with him for the purposes of this Act, and the provisions of the Trustee Act 1925, relating to the appointment of new trustees and the vesting of trust property shall apply accordingly.

Amendment—Sub-s (1): words in square brackets substituted by the Trusts of Land and Appointment of Trustees Act 1996, s 25(1), Sch 3, para 2(9); for savings in relation to entailed interests created before the commencement of that Act, and savings consequential upon the abolition of the doctrine of conversion, see s 25(4), (5) thereof.

PART II
POWERS OF A TENANT FOR LIFE

Sale and Exchange

38 Powers of sale and exchange.

A tenant for life—

(i) May sell the settled land, or any part thereof, or any easement, right or privilege of any kind over or in relation to the land; and
(ii) …
(iii) May make an exchange of the settled land, or any part thereof, or of any easement, right, or privilege of any kind, whether or not newly created, over or in relation to the settled land, or any part thereof, for other land, or for any easement, right or privilege of any kind, whether or not newly created, over or in relation to other land, including an exchange in consideration of money paid for equality of exchange.

Amendment—Words omitted repealed by the Statute Law (Repeals) Act 1969, s 1, Schedule, Part III.

Leasing Powers

41 Power to lease for ordinary or building or mining or forestry purposes

A tenant for life may lease the settled land, or any part thereof, or any easement, right, or privilege of any kind over or in relation to the land, for any purpose whatever, whether involving waste or not, for any term not exceeding—

(i) In case of a building lease, nine hundred and ninety-nine years;
(ii) In case of a mining lease, one hundred years;
(iii) In case of a forestry lease, nine hundred and ninety-nine years;
(iv) In case of any other lease, fifty years.

Miscellaneous Powers

49 Power on dispositions to impose restrictions and make reservations and stipulations

(1) On a sale or other disposition or dealing under the powers of this Act—

(a) any easement, right, or privilege of any kind may be reserved or granted over or in relation to the settled land or any part thereof or other land, including the land disposed of, and, in the case of an exchange, the land taken in exchange; and
(b) any restriction with respect to building on or other user of land, or with respect to mines and minerals, or with respect to or for the purpose of the more beneficial working thereof, or with respect to any other thing, may be imposed and made binding, as far as the law permits, by covenant, condition or otherwise, on the tenant for life or statutory owner and the settled land or any part thereof, or on the other party and any land disposed of to him; and
(c) the whole or any part of any capital or annual sum (and in the case of an annual sum whether temporary or perpetual) charged on or payable out of the land

disposed of, or any part thereof, and other land subject to the settlement, may as between the tenant for life or statutory owner and his successors in title, and the other party and persons deriving title under or in succession to him (but without prejudice to the rights of the person entitled to such capital or annual sum) be charged exclusively on the land disposed of, or any part thereof, or such other land as aforesaid, or any part thereof, in exoneration of the rest of the land on or out of which such capital or annual sum is charged or payable.

(2) A sale of land may be made subject to a stipulation that all or any of the timber and other trees, pollards, tellers, underwood, saplings and plantations on the land sold (in this section referred to as 'timber') or any articles attached to the land (in this section referred to as 'fixtures') shall be taken by the purchaser at a valuation and the amount of the valuation shall form part of the price of the land, and shall be capital money accordingly.

(3) Where on a sale the consideration attributable to any timber or fixtures is by mistake paid to a tenant for life or other person not entitled to receive it, then, if such person or the purchaser or the persons deriving title under either of them subsequently pay the aforesaid consideration, with such interest, if any, thereon as the court may direct to the trustees of the settlement or other persons entitled thereto or into court, the court may, on the application of the purchaser or the persons deriving title under him, declare that the disposition is to take effect as if the whole of the consideration had at the date thereof been duly paid to the trustees of the settlement or other persons entitled to receive the same.

The person, not entitled to receive the same, to whom the consideration is paid, and his estate and effects shall remain liable to make good any loss attributable to the mistake.

51 Power to grant options

(1) A tenant for life may at any time, either with or without consideration, grant by writing an option to purchase or take a lease of the settled land, or any part thereof, or any easement, right, or privilege over or in relation to the same at a price or rent fixed at the time of the granting of the option.

(2) Every such option shall be made exercisable within an agreed number of years not exceeding ten.

(3) The price or rent shall be the best which, having regard to all the circumstances, can reasonably be obtained and either—

(a) may be a specified sum of money or rent, or at a specified rate according to the superficial area of the land with respect to which the option is exercised: or the frontage thereof or otherwise; or
(b) in the case of an option to purchase contained in a lease or agreement for a lease, may be a stated number of years' purchase of the highest rent reserved by the lease or agreement; or
(c) if the option is exercisable as regards part of the land comprised in the lease or agreement, may be a proportionate part of such highest rent;

and any aggregate price or rent may be made to be apportionable in any manner, or according to any system, or by reference to arbitration.

(4) An option to take a mining lease may be coupled with the grant of a licence to search for and prove any mines or minerals under the settled land, or any part thereof, pending the exercise of the option.

(5) The consideration for the grant of the option shall be capital money arising under this Act.

64 General power for the tenant for life to effect any transaction under an order of the court

(1) Any transaction affecting or concerning the settled land, or any part thereof, or any other land (not being a transaction otherwise authorised by this Act, or by the settlement) which in the opinion of the court would be for the benefit of the settled land, or any part thereof, or the persons interested under the settlement, may, under an order of the court, be effected by a tenant for life, if it is one which could have been validly effected by an absolute owner.

(2) In this section 'transaction' includes any sale, ... exchange, assurance, grant, lease, surrender, reconveyance, release, reservation, or other disposition, and any purchase or other acquisition, and any covenant, contract, or option, and any application of capital money ... and any compromise or other dealing, or arrangement ... ; and 'effected' has the meaning appropriate to the particular transaction; and the references to land include references to restrictions and burdens affecting land.

Amendment—Sub-s (2): first words omitted repealed by the Statute Law (Repeals) Act 1969, s 1, Schedule, Part III; other words omitted repealed by the Settled Land and Trustee Acts (Court's General Powers) Act 1943, s 2.

Provisions as to special classes of property

65 Power to dispose of mansion

(1) The powers of disposing of settled land conferred by this Act on a tenant for life may be exercised as respects the principal mansion house, if any, on any settled land, and the pleasure grounds and park and lands, if any, usually occupied therewith:

Provided that those powers shall not be exercised without the consent of the trustees of the settlement or an order of the court—

(a) if the settlement is a settlement made or coming into operation before the commencement of this Act and the settlement does not expressly provide to the contrary; or
(b) if the settlement is a settlement made or coming into operation after the commencement of this Act and the settlement expressly provides that these powers or any of them shall not be exercised without such consent or order.

(2) Where a house is usually occupied as a farmhouse, or where the site of any house and the pleasure grounds and park and lands, if any, usually occupied therewith do not together exceed twenty-five acres in extent, the house is not to be deemed a principal mansion house within the meaning of this section, and may accordingly be disposed of in like manner as any other part of the settled land.

66 Cutting and sale of timber, and capitalisation of part of proceeds

(1) Where a tenant for life is impeachable for waste in respect of timber, and there is on the settled land timber ripe and fit for cutting, the tenant for life, on obtaining the consent of the trustees of the settlement or an order of the court, may cut and sell that timber, or any part thereof.

(2) Three fourth parts of the net proceeds of the sale shall be set aside as and be capital money arising under this Act, and the other fourth part shall go as rents and profits.

67 Sale and purchase of heirlooms under order of court

(1) Where personal chattels are settled so as to devolve with settled land, or to devolve therewith as nearly as may be in accordance with the law or practice in force at the date of the settlement, or are settled together with land, or upon trusts declared by reference to the trusts affecting land, a tenant for life of the land may sell the chattels or any of them.

(2) The money arising by the sale shall be capital money arising under this Act, and shall be paid, invested, or applied and otherwise dealt with in like manner in all respects as by this Act directed with respect to other capital money arising under this Act, or may be invested in the purchase of other chattels of the same or any other nature, which, when purchased, shall be settled and held on the same trusts, and shall devolve in the same manner as the chattels sold.

(3) A sale or purchase of chattels under this section shall not be made without an order of the court.

(4) Any reference in any enactment to personal chattels settled as heirlooms shall extend to any chattels to which this section applies.

Dealings as between tenants for life and the estate

68 Provision enabling dealings with tenant for life

(1) In the manner mentioned and subject to the provisions contained in this section—

(a) a sale, grant, lease, mortgage, charge or other disposition of settled land, or of any easement, right, or privilege over the same may be made to the tenant for life; or
(b) capital money may be advanced on mortgage to him; or
(c) a purchase may be made from him of land to be made subject to the limitations of the settlement; or
(d) an exchange may be made with him of settled land for other land; and
(e) any such disposition, advance, purchase, or exchange as aforesaid may be made to, from, or with any persons of whom the tenant for life is one.

(2) In every such case the trustees of the settlement shall, in addition to their powers as trustees, have all the powers of a tenant for life in reference to negotiating and completing the transaction, and shall have power to enforce any covenants by the tenant for life, or, where the tenant for life is himself one of the trustees, then the other

or others of them shall have such power, and the said powers of a tenant for life may be exercised by the trustees of the settlement in the name and on behalf of the tenant for life.

(3) This section applies, notwithstanding that the tenant for life is one of the trustees of the settlement, or that an order has been made authorising the trustees to act on his behalf, or that he is [suffering from mental disorder] but does not apply to dealings with any body of persons which includes a trustee of the settlement, not being the tenant for life, unless the transaction is either previously or subsequently approved by the court.

Amendment—Sub-s (3): words in square brackets substituted by the Mental Health Act 1959, s 149, Sch 7, Part I.

PART IV
IMPROVEMENTS

Improvements with Capital Money

84 Mode of application of capital money

(1) Capital money arising under this Act may be applied in or towards payment for any improvement authorised by this Act or by the settlement, without any scheme for the execution of the improvement being first submitted for approval to, or approved by, the trustees of the settlement or the court.

(2) Where the capital money to be expended is in the hands of the trustees of the settlement, they may apply that money in or towards payment for the whole or any part of any work or operation comprised in the improvement, on—

(i) a certificate to be furnished by a competent engineer or able practical surveyor employed independently of the tenant for life, certifying that the work or operation comprised in the improvement or some specific part thereof, has been properly executed, and what amount is properly payable in respect thereof, which certificate shall be conclusive in favour of the trustees as an authority and discharge for any payment made by them in pursuance thereof; or
(ii) an order of the court directing or authorising the trustees so to apply a specified portion of the capital money:

Provided that—

(a) In the case of improvements not authorised by Part I of the Third Schedule to this Act or by the settlement, the trustees may, if they think fit, and shall if so directed by the court, before they make any such application of capital money require that that money, or any part thereof, shall be repaid to them out of the income of the settled land by not more than fifty half-yearly instalments, the first of such instalments to be paid or to be deemed to have become payable at the expiration of six months from the date when the work or operation, in payment for which the money is to be applied, was completed;
(b) No capital money shall be applied by the trustees in payment for improvements not authorised by Parts I and II of the Third Schedule to this Act, or by the settlement, except subject to provision for the repayment thereof being made in manner mentioned in the preceding paragraph of this proviso.

(3) Where the capital money to be expended is in court, the court may, if it thinks fit, on a report or certificate of the [Secretary of State], or of a competent engineer or able practical surveyor approved by the court, or on such other evidence as the court may think sufficient, make such order and give such directions as it thinks fit for the application of the money, or any part thereof, in or towards payment for the whole or any part of any work or operation comprised in the improvement.

(4) Where the court authorises capital money to be applied in payment for any improvement or intended improvement not authorised by Part I of the Third Schedule to this Act or by the settlement, the court, as a condition of making the order, may in any case require that the capital money or any part thereof, and shall as respects an improvement mentioned in Part III of that Schedule (unless the improvement is authorised by the settlement), require that the whole of the capital money shall be repaid to the trustees of the settlement out of the income of the settled land by a fixed number of periodical instalments to be paid at the times appointed by the court, and may require that any incumbrancer of the estate or interest of the tenant for life shall be served with notice of the proceedings.

(5) All money received by the trustees of the settlement in respect of any instalments under this section shall be held by them as capital money arising from freehold land under the settlement, unless the court otherwise directs.

Amendment—Sub-s (3): words 'Secretary of State' in square brackets substituted by SI 2002/794, art 5(1), Sch 1, para 2. Date in force: 27 March 2002: see SI 2002/794, art 1(2).

PART VI
GENERAL PROVISIONS AS TO TRUSTEES

94 Number of trustees to act

(1) Notwithstanding anything in this Act, capital money arising under this Act shall not be paid to fewer than two persons as trustees of a settlement, unless the trustee is a trust corporation.

(2) Subject as aforesaid the provisions of this Act referring to the trustees of a settlement apply to the surviving or continuing trustees or trustee of the settlement for the time being.

95 Trustees' receipts

The receipt or direction in writing of or by the trustees of the settlement, or where a sole trustee is a trust corporation, of or by that trustee, or of or by the personal representatives of the last surviving or continuing trustee, for or relating to any money or securities, paid or transferred to or by the direction of the trustees, trustee, or representatives, as the case may be, effectually discharges the payer or transferor therefrom, and from being bound to see to the application or being answerable for any loss or misapplication thereof, and, in case of a mortgagee or other person advancing money, from being concerned to see that any money advanced by him is wanted for any purpose of this Act, or that no more than is wanted is raised.

97 Protection of trustees generally

The trustees of a settlement, or any of them—

(a) are not liable for giving any consent, or for not making, bringing, taking, or doing any such application, action, proceeding, or thing, as they might make, bring, take, or do; and

(b) in case of a purchase of land with capital money arising under this Act, or of an exchange, lease, or other disposition, are not liable for adopting any contract made by the tenant for life or statutory owner, or bound to inquire as to the propriety of the purchase, exchange, lease, or other disposition, or answerable as regards any price, consideration, or fine; and

(c) are not liable to see to or answerable for the investigation of the title, or answerable for a conveyance of land, if the conveyance purports to convey the land in the proper mode; and

(d) are not liable in respect of purchase-money paid by them by the direction of the tenant for life or statutory owner to any person joining in the conveyance as a conveying party, or as giving a receipt for the purchase-money, or in any other character, or in respect of any other money paid by them by the direction of the tenant for life or statutory owner on the purchase, exchange, lease, or other disposition.

98 Protection of trustees in particular cases

(1) …

(2) …

(3) The trustees of the settlements shall not be liable in any way on account of any vesting instrument or other documents of title relating to the settled land, other than securities for capital money, being placed in the possession of the tenant for life or statutory owner:

Provided that where, if the settlement were not disclosed, it would appear that the tenant for life had a general power of appointment over, or was absolutely and beneficially entitled to the settled land, the trustees of the settlement shall, before they deliver the documents to him, require that notice of the last or only principal vesting instrument be written on one of the documents under which the tenant for life acquired his title, and may, if the documents are not in their possession, require such notice to be written as aforesaid, but, in the latter case, they shall not be liable in any way for not requiring the notice to be written.

(4) This section applies to dealings and matters effected before as well as after the commencement of this Act.

Amendment—Sub-ss (1), (2): repealed by the Trustee Act 2000, s 40(1), (3), Sch 2, Pt II, para 13, Sch 4, Pt II. Date in force: 1 February 2001: see SI 2001/49, art 2.

---

99 Indemnities to personal representatives and others

Personal representatives, trustees, or other persons who have in good faith, pursuant to this Act, executed a vesting deed, assent, or other conveyance of the settled land, or a deed of discharge of trustees, shall be absolutely discharged from all liability in respect of the equitable interests and powers taking effect under the settlement, and shall be entitled to be kept indemnified at the cost of the trust estate from all liabilities affecting the settled land, but the person to whom the settled land is conveyed (not being a purchaser taking free therefrom) shall hold the settled land upon the trusts, if any, affecting the same.

101 Notice to trustees

(1) Save as otherwise expressly provided by this Act, a tenant for life or statutory owner, when intending to make a sale, exchange, lease, mortgage, or charge or to grant an option—

(a) shall give notice of his intention in that behalf to each of the trustees of the settlement, by posting registered letters, containing the notice, addressed to the trustees severally, each at his usual or last known place of abode in the United Kingdom; and

(b) shall give a like notice to the solicitor for the trustees, if any such solicitor is known to the tenant for life or statutory owner, by posting a registered letter, containing the notice, addressed to the solicitor at his place of business in the United Kingdom;

every letter under this section being posted not less than one month before the making or granting by the tenant for life or statutory owner of the sale, exchange, lease, mortgage, charge, or option, or of a contract for the same:

Provided that a notice under this section shall not be valid unless at the date thereof the trustee is a trust corporation, or the number of trustees is not less than two.

(2) The notice required by this section of intention to make a sale, exchange, or lease, or to grant an option, may be notice of a general intention in that behalf.

(3) The tenant for life or statutory owner is, upon request by a trustee of the settlement, to furnish to him such particulars and information as may reasonably be required by him from time to time with reference to sales, exchanges, or leases effected, or in progress, or immediately intended.

(4) Any trustee, by writing under his hand, may waive notice either in any particular case, or generally, and may accept less than one month's notice.

(5) A person dealing in good faith with the tenant for life is not concerned to inquire respecting the giving of any such notice as is required by this section.

Modification—References to solicitors etc modified to include references to bodies recognised under the Administration of Justice Act 1985, s 9, by the Solicitors' Incorporated Practices Order 1991, SI 1991/2684, arts 4, 5, Sch 1.

Trustee Act 1925

1925 Chapter 19

An Act to consolidate certain enactments relating to trustees in England and Wales.

[9 April 1925]

Initial Commencement—Specified date: 1 January 1926.
Extent—This Act does not exten to Scotlnd: see s 71(3).

PART I

...

Amendment—Repealed by the Trustee Act 2000, s 40(1), (3), Sch 2, Pt II, para 18, Sch 4, Pt II. Date in force: 1 February 2001: see SI 2001/49, art 2.

2

...

Amendment—Repealed by the Trustee Act 2000, s 40(1), (3), Sch 2, Pt II, para 18, Sch 4, Pt II. Date in force: 1 February 2001: see SI 2001/49, art 2.

3

...

Amendment—Repealed by the Trustee Act 2000, s 40(1), (3), Sch 2, Pt II, para 18, Sch 4, Pt II. Date in force: 1 February 2001: see SI 2001/49, art 2.

4

...

Amendment—Repealed by the Trustee Act 2000, s 40(1), (3), Sch 2, Pt II, para 18, Sch 4, Pt II. Date in force: 1 February 2001: see SI 2001/49, art 2.

5

...

Amendment—Repealed by the Trustee Act 2000, s 40(1), (3), Sch 2, Pt II, para 18, Sch 4, Pt II. Date in force: 1 February 2001: see SI 2001/49, art 2.

6

...

Amendment—Repealed by the Trustee Act 2000, s 40(1), (3), Sch 2, Pt II, para 18, Sch 4, Pt II. Date in force: 1 February 2001: see SI 2001/49, art 2.

7

...

Amendment—Repealed by the Trustee Act 2000, s 40(1), (3), Sch 2, Pt II, para 18, Sch 4, Pt II. Date in force: 1 February 2001: see SI 2001/49, art 2.

8

...

Amendment—Repealed by the Trustee Act 2000, s 40(1), (3), Sch 2, Pt II, para 18, Sch 4, Pt II. Date in force: 1 February 2001 (except in relation to loans or investments made before that date): see the Trustee Act 2000, s 40(2), Sch 3, para 2 and SI 2001/49, art 2.

9

...

Amendment—Repealed by the Trustee Act 2000, s 40(1), (3), Sch 2, Pt II, para 18, Sch 4, Pt II. Date in force: 1 February 2001 (except in relation to any advance of trust money made before that date): see the Trustee Act 2000, s 40(2), Sch 3, para 3 and SI 2001/49, art 2.

10

...

Amendment—Repealed by the Trustee Act 2000, s 40(1), (3), Sch 2, Pt II, para 18, Sch 4, Pt II. Date in force: 1 February 2001: see SI 2001/49, art 2.

11

...

Amendment—Repealed by the Trustee Act 2000, s 40(1), (3), Sch 2, Pt II, para 18, Sch 4, Pt II. Date in force: 1 February 2001: see SI 2001/49, art 2.

PART II
GENERAL POWERS OF TRUSTEES AND PERSONAL REPRESENTATIVES

12 Power of trustees for sale to sell by auction, etc

(1) Where [a trustee has a duty or power to sell property], he may sell or concur with any other person in selling all or any part of the property, either subject to prior charges or not, and either together or in lots, by public auction or by private contract, subject to any such conditions respecting title or evidence of title or other matter as the trustee thinks fit, with power to vary any contract for sale, and to buy in at any auction, or to rescind any contract for sale and to re-sell, without being answerable for any loss.

(2) A [duty] or power to sell or dispose of land includes a *trust* [duty] or power to sell or dispose of part thereof, whether the division is horizontal, vertical, or made in any other way.

(3) This section does not enable an express power to sell settled land to be exercised where the power is not vested in the tenant for life or statutory owner.

Amendment—Sub-ss (1), (2): words in square brackets substituted by the Trusts of Land and Appointment of Trustees Act 1996, s 25(1), Sch 3, para 3(2); for savings in relation to entailed interests created before the commencement of that Act, and savings consequential upon the abolition of the doctrine of conversion, see s 25(4), (5) thereof.

---

13 Power to sell subject to depreciatory conditions

(1) No sale made by a trustee shall be impeached by any beneficiary upon the ground that any of the conditions subject to which the sale was made may have been unnecessarily depreciatory, unless it also appears that the consideration for the sale was thereby rendered inadequate.

(2) No sale made by a trustee shall, after the execution of the conveyance, be impeached as against the purchaser upon the ground that any of the conditions subject to which the sale was made may have been unnecessarily depreciatory, unless it appears that the purchaser was acting in collusion with the trustee at the time when the contract for sale was made.

(3) No purchaser, upon any sale made by a trustee, shall be at liberty to make any objection against the title upon any of the grounds aforesaid.

(4) This section applies to sales made before or after the commencement of this Act.

14 Power of trustees to give receipts

(1) The receipt in writing of a trustee for any money, securities, [investments] or other personal property or effects payable, transferable, or deliverable to him under any trust or power shall be a sufficient discharge to the person paying, transferring, or delivering the same and shall effectually exonerate him from seeing to the application or being answerable for any loss or misapplication thereof.

(2) This section does not, except where the trustee is a trust corporation, enable a sole trustee to give a valid receipt for—

[(a) proceeds of sale or other capital money arising under a trust of land;]
(b) capital money arising under the Settled Land Act 1925.

(3) This section applies notwithstanding anything to the contrary in the instrument, if any, creating the trust.

Amendment—Sub-s (1): word 'investments' in square brackets inserted by the Trustee Act 2000, s 40(1), Sch 2, Pt II, para 19. Date in force: 1 February 2001: see SI 2001/49, art 2.
Sub-s (2): para (a) substituted by the Trusts of Land and Appointment of Trustees Act 1996, s 25(1), Sch 3, para 3(3); for savings in relation to entailed interests created before the commencement of that Act, and savings consequential upon the abolition of the doctrine of conversion, see s 25(4), (5) thereof.

---

15 Power to compound liabilities

A personal representative, or two or more trustees acting together, or, subject to the restrictions imposed in regard to receipts by a sole trustee not being a trust corporation, a sole acting trustee where by the instrument, if any, creating the trust, or by statute, a sole trustee is authorised to execute the trusts and powers reposed in him, may, if and as he or they think fit—

(a) accept any property, real or personal, before the time at which it is made transferable or payable; or
(b) sever and apportion any blended trust funds or property; or
(c) pay or allow any debt or claim on any evidence that he or they think sufficient; or
(d) accept any composition or any security, real or personal, for any debt or for any property, real or personal, claimed; or
(e) allow any time of payment of any debt; or
(f) compromise, compound, abandon, submit to arbitration, or otherwise settle any debt, account, claim, or thing whatever relating to the testator's or intestate's estate or to the trust;

and for any of these purposes may enter into, give, execute, and do such agreements, instruments of composition or arrangement, releases, and other things as to him or them seem expedient, without being responsible for any loss occasioned by any act or thing so done by him or them [if he has or they have discharged the duty of care set out in section 1(1) of the Trustee Act 2000].

Amendment—Words 'if he has or they have discharged the duty of care set out in section 1(1) of the Trustee Act 2000' in square brackets substituted by the Trustee Act 2000, s 40(1), Sch 2, Pt II, para 20. Date in force: 1 February 2001: see SI 2001/49, art 2.

---

16 Power to raise money by sale, mortgage, etc.

(1) Where trustees are authorised by the instrument, if any, creating the trust or by law to pay or apply capital money subject to the trust for any purpose or in any manner, they shall have and shall be deemed always to have had power to raise the

money required by sale, conversion, calling in, or mortgage of all or any part of the trust property for the time being in possession.

(2) This section applies notwithstanding anything to the contrary contained in the instrument, if any, creating the trust, but does not apply to trustees of property held for charitable purposes, or to trustees of a settlement for the purposes of the Settled Land Act 1925, not being also the statutory owners.

17 Protection to purchasers and mortgagees dealing with trustees

No purchaser or mortgagee paying or advancing money on a sale or mortgage purporting to be made under any trust or power vested in trustees, shall be concerned to see that such money is wanted; or that no more than is wanted is raised, or otherwise as to the application thereof.

18 Devolution of powers or trusts

(1) Where a power or trust is given to or imposed on two or more trustees jointly, the same may be exercised or performed by the survivors or survivor of them for the time being.

(2) Until the appointment of new trustees, the personal representatives or representative for the time being of a sole trustee, or, where there were two or more trustees of the last surviving or continuing trustee, shall be capable of exercising or performing any power or trust which was given to, or capable of being exercised by, the sole or last surviving or continuing trustee, or other the trustees or trustee for the time being of the trust.

(3) This section takes effect subject to the restrictions imposed in regard to receipts by a sole trustee, not being a trust corporation.

(4) In this section 'personal representative' does not include an executor who has renounced or has not proved.

[19 Power to insure]

[(1) A trustee may—

(a) insure any property which is subject to the trust against risks of loss or damage due to any event, and
(b) pay the premiums out of the trust funds.

(2) In the case of property held on a bare trust, the power to insure is subject to any direction given by the beneficiary or each of the beneficiaries—

(a) that any property specified in the direction is not to be insured;
(b) that any property specified in the direction is not to be insured except on such conditions as may be so specified.

(3) Property is held on a bare trust if it is held on trust for—

(a) a beneficiary who is of full age and capacity and absolutely entitled to the property subject to the trust, or

(b) beneficiaries each of whom is of full age and capacity and who (taken together) are absolutely entitled to the property subject to the trust.

(4) If a direction under subsection (2) of this section is given, the power to insure, so far as it is subject to the direction, ceases to be a delegable function for the purposes of section 11 of the Trustee Act 2000 (power to employ agents).

(5) In this section 'trust funds' means any income or capital funds of the trust.]

Amendment—Substituted by the Trustee Act 2000, s 34(1). Date in force: 1 February 2001 (in relation to trusts created before or after that date): see the Trustee Act 2000, s 34(3) and SI 2001/49, art 2.

---

20 Application of insurance money where policy kept up under any trust, power or obligation

(1) Money receivable by trustees or any beneficiary under a policy of insurance against the loss or damage of any property subject to a trust or to a settlement within the meaning of the Settled Land Act 1925... shall, where the policy has been kept up under any trust in that behalf or under any power statutory or otherwise, or in performance of any covenant or of any obligation statutory or otherwise, or by a tenant for life impeachable for waste, be capital money for the purposes of the trust or settlement, as the case may be.

(2) If any such money is receivable by any person, other than the trustees of the trust or settlement, that person shall use his best endeavours to recover and receive the money, and shall pay the net residue thereof, after discharging any costs of recovering and receiving it, to the trustees of the trust or settlement, or, if there are no trustees capable of giving a discharge therefor, into court.

(3) Any such money—

(a) if it was receivable in respect of settled land within the meaning of the Settled Land Act 1925, or any building or works thereon, shall be deemed to be capital money arising under that Act from the settled land, and shall be invested or applied by the trustees, or, if in court, under the direction of the court, accordingly;
(b) if it was receivable in respect of personal chattels settled as heirlooms within the meaning of the Settled Land Act, 1925, shall be deemed to be capital money arising under that Act; and shall be applicable by the trustees, or, if in court, under the direction of the court, in like manner as provided by that Act with respect to money arising by sale of chattels as heirlooms as aforesaid;
(c) if it was receivable in respect of [land subject to a trust of land or personal property held on trust for sale], shall be held upon the trusts and subject to the powers and provisions applicable to money arising by a sale under such trust;
(d) in any other case, shall be held upon trusts corresponding as nearly as may be with the trusts affecting the property in respect of which it was payable.

(4) Such money, or any part thereof, may also be applied by the trustees, or, if in court, under the direction of the court, in rebuilding, reinstating, replacing, or replacing the property loss or damaged, but any such application by the trustees shall be subject to the consent of any person whose consent is required by the instrument, if

any, creating the trust to the investment of money subject to the trust, and, in the case of money which is deemed to be capital money arising under the Settled Land Act 1925, be subject to the provisions of that Act with respect to the application of capital money by the trustees of the settlement.

(5) Nothing contained in this section prejudices or affects the right of any person to require any such money or any part thereof to be applied in rebuilding reinstating, or repairing the property lost or damaged, or the rights of any mortgagee, lessor, or lessee, whether under any statute or otherwise.

(6) This section applies to policies effected either before or after the commencement of this Act, but only to money received after such commencement.

Amendment—Sub-s (1): words omitted repealed by the Trustee Act 2000, ss 34(2), 40(3), Sch 4, Pt II. Date in force: 1 February 2001 (in relation to trusts created before or after that date): see the Trustee Act 2000, s 34(3) and SI 2001/49, art 2.

Sub-s (3): in para (c) words 'land subject to a trust of land or personal property held on trust for sale' in square brackets substituted by the Trusts of Land and Appointment of Trustees Act 1996, s 25(1), Sch 3, para 3(5); for savings in relation to entailed interests created before the commencement of that Act, and savings consequential upon the abolition of the doctrine of conversion, see s 25(4), (5) thereof.

21

. . .

Amendment—Repealed by the Trustee Act 2000, s 40(1), (3), Sch 2, Pt II, para 21, Sch 4, Pt II. Date in force: 1 February 2001: see SI 2001/49, art 2.

---

22 *Reversionary interests, valuations, and audit*

(1) Where trust property includes any share or interest in property not vested in the trustees, or the proceeds of the sale of any such property, or any other thing in action, the trustees on the same falling into possession, or becoming payable or transferable may—

(a) agree or ascertain the amount or value thereof or any part thereof in such manner as they may think fit;
(b) accept in or towards satisfaction thereof, at the market or current value, or upon any valuation or estimate of value which they may think fit, any authorised investments;
(c) allow any deductions for duties, costs, charges and expenses which they may think proper or reasonable;
(d) execute any release in respect of the premises so as effectually to discharge all accountable parties from all liability in respect of any matters coming within the scope of such release;

without being responsible in any such case for any loss occasioned by any act or thing so done by them [if they have discharged the duty of care set out in section 1(1) of the Trustee Act 2000].

(2) The trustees shall not be under any obligation and shall not be chargeable with any breach of trust by reason of any omission—

(a) to place any distringas notice or apply for any stop or other like order upon any securities or other property out of or on which such share or interest or other thing in action as aforesaid is derived, payable or charged; or
(b) to take any proceedings on account of any act, default, or neglect on the part of the persons in whom such securities or other property or any of them or any part thereof are for the time being, or had at any time been, vested;

unless and until required in writing so to do by some person, or the guardian of some person, beneficially interested under the trust, and unless also due provision is made to their satisfaction for payment of the costs of any proceedings required to be taken:

Provided that nothing in this subsection shall relieve the trustees of the obligation to get in and obtain payment or transfer of such share or interest or other thing in action on the same falling into possession.

(3) Trustees may, for the purpose of giving effect to the trust, or any of the provisions of the instrument, if any, creating the trust or of any statute, from time to time (by duly qualified agents) ascertain and fix the value of any trust property in such manner as they think proper, and any valuation so made … shall be binding upon all persons interested under the trust [if the trustees have discharged the duty of care set out in section 1(1) of the Trustee Act 2000].

(4) Trustees may, in their absolute discretion, from time to time, but not more than once in every three years unless the nature of the trust or any special dealings with the trust property make a more frequent exercise of the right reasonable, cause the accounts of the trust property to be examined or audited by an independent accountant, and shall, for that purpose, produce such vouchers and give such information to him as he may require; and the costs of such examination or audit, including the fee of the auditor, shall be paid out of the capital or income of the trust property, or partly in one way and partly in the other as the trustees, in their absolute discretion, think fit, but, in default of any direction by the trustees to the contrary in any special case, costs attributable to capital shall be borne by capital and those attributable to income by income.

Amendment—Sub-s (1): words 'if they have discharged the duty of care set out in section 1(1) of the Trustee Act 2000' in square brackets substituted by the Trustee Act 2000, s 40(1), Sch 2, Pt II, para 22(a). Date in force: 1 February 2001: see SI 2001/49, art 2.

Sub-s (3): words omitted repealed by the Trustee Act 2000, s 40(1), Sch 2, Pt II, para 22(b). Date in force: 1 February 2001: see SI 2001/49, art 2.

Sub-s (3): words 'if the trustees have discharged the duty of care set out in section 1(1) of the Trustee Act 2000' in square brackets inserted by the Trustee Act 2000, s 40(1), Sch 2, Pt II, para 22(b). Date in force: 1 February 2001: see SI 2001/49, art 2.

23

…

Amendment—Repealed by the Trustee Act 2000, s 40(1), (3), Sch 2, Pt II, para 23, Sch 4, Pt II. Date in force: 1 February 2001 (except in so far as it does not affect the operation of an appointment made under this section before that date): see the Trustee Act 2000, s 40(2), Sch 3, para 6 and SI 2001/49, art 2.

24 Power to concur with others

Where an undivided share in [any] property, is subject to a trust, or forms part of the estate of a testator or intestate, the trustees or personal representatives may (without prejudice to the [trust] affecting the entirety of the land and the powers of the [trustees] in reference thereto), execute or exercise any [duty or] power vested in them in relation to such share in conjunction with the persons entitled to or having power in that behalf over the other share or shares, and notwithstanding that any one or more of the trustees or personal representatives may be entitled to or interested in any such other share, either in his or their own right or in a fiduciary capacity.

Amendment—Words in square brackets substituted by the Trusts of Land and Appointment of Trustees Act 1996, s 25(1), Sch 3, para 3(6); for savings in relation to entailed interests created before the commencement of that Act, and savings consequential upon the abolition of the doctrine of conversion, see s 25(4), (5) thereof.

[25 Delegation of trustee's functions by power of attorney]

[(1) Notwithstanding any rule of law or equity to the contrary, a trustee may, by power of attorney, delegate the execution or exercise of all or any of the trusts, powers and discretions vested in him as trustee either alone or jointly with any other person or persons.

(2) A delegation under this section—

(a) commences as provided by the instrument creating the power or, if the instrument makes no provision as to the commencement of the delegation, with the date of the execution of the instrument by the donor; and
(b) continues for a period of twelve months or any shorter period provided by the instrument creating the power.

(3) The persons who may be donees of a power of attorney under this section include a trust corporation.

(4) Before or within seven days after giving a power of attorney under this section the donor shall give written notice of it (specifying the date on which the power comes into operation and its duration, the donee of the power, the reason why the power is given and, where some only are delegated, the trusts, powers and discretions delegated) to—

(a) each person (other than himself), if any, who under any instrument creating the trust has power (whether alone or jointly) to appoint a new trustee; and
(b) each of the other trustees, if any;

but failure to comply with this subsection shall not, in favour of a person dealing with the donee of the power, invalidate any act done or instrument executed by the donee.

(5) A power of attorney given under this section by a single donor—

(a) in the form set out in subsection (6) of this section; or
(b) in a form to the like effect but expressed to be made under this subsection,

shall operate to delegate to the person identified in the form as the single donee of the power the execution and exercise of all the trusts, powers and discretions vested in the donor as trustee (either alone or jointly with any other person or persons) under the single trust so identified.

(6) The form referred to in subsection (5) of this section is as follows—

'THIS GENERAL TRUSTEE POWER OF ATTORNEY is made on [date] by [name of one donor] of [address of donor] as trustee of [name or details of one trust].

I appoint [name of one donee] of [address of donee] to be my attorney [if desired, the date on which the delegation commences or the period for which it continues (or both)] in accordance with section 25(5) of the Trustee Act 1925.

[To be executed as a deed]'.

(7) The donor of a power of attorney given under this section shall be liable for the acts or defaults of the donee in the same manner as if they were the acts or defaults of the donor.

(8) For the purpose of executing or exercising the trusts or powers delegated to him, the donee may exercise any of the powers conferred on the donor as trustee by statute or by the instrument creating the trust, including power, for the purpose of the transfer of any inscribed stock, himself to delegate to an attorney power to transfer, but not including the power of delegation conferred by this section.

(9) The fact that it appears from any power of attorney given under this section, or from any evidence required for the purposes of any such power of attorney or otherwise, that in dealing with any stock the donee of the power is acting in the execution of a trust shall not be deemed for any purpose to affect any person in whose books the stock is inscribed or registered with any notice of the trust.

(10) This section applies to a personal representative, tenant for life and statutory owner as it applies to a trustee except that subsection (4) shall apply as if it required the notice there mentioned to be given—

(a) in the case of a personal representative, to each of the other personal representatives, if any, except any executor who has renounced probate;
(b) in the case of a tenant for life, to the trustees of the settlement and to each person, if any, who together with the person giving the notice constitutes the tenant for life; and
(c) in the case of a statutory owner, to each of the persons, if any, who together with the person giving the notice constitute the statutory owner and, in the case of a statutory owner by virtue of section 23(1)(a) of the Settled Land Act 1925, to the trustees of the settlement.]

Amendment—Substituted by the Trustee Delegation Act 1999, s 5(1), (2). Date in force: 1 March 2000 (in relation to enduring powers created after that date): see SI 2000/216, art 2.

Indemnities

26 Protection against liability in respect of rents and covenants

(1) Where a personal representative or trustee liable as such for—

(a) any rent, covenant, or agreement reserved by or contained in any lease; or
(b) any rent, covenant or agreement payable under or contained in any grant made in consideration of a rentcharge; or
(c) any indemnity given in respect of any rent, covenant or agreement referred to in either of the foregoing paragraphs;

satisfies all liabilities under the lease or grant [which may have accrued and been claimed] up to the date of the conveyance hereinafter mentioned, and, where necessary, sets apart a sufficient fund to answer any future claim that may be made in respect of any fixed and ascertained sum which the lessee or grantee agreed to lay out on the property demised or granted, although the period for laying out the same may not have arrived, then and in any such case the personal representative or trustee may convey the property demised or granted to a purchaser, legatee, devisee, or other person entitled to call for a conveyance thereof and thereafter—

(i) he may distribute the residuary real and personal estate of the deceased testator or intestate, or, as the case may be, the trust estate (other than the fund, if any, set apart as aforesaid) to or amongst the persons entitled thereto, without appropriating any part, or any further part, as the case may be, of the estate of the deceased or of the trust estate to meet any future liability under the said lease or grant;
(ii) notwithstanding such distribution, he shall not be personally liable in respect of any subsequent claim under the said lease or grant.

[(1A) Where a personal representative or trustee has as such entered into, or may as such be required to enter into, an authorised guarantee agreement with respect to any lease comprised in the estate of a deceased testator or intestate or a trust estate (and, in a case where he has entered into such an agreement, he has satisfied all liabilities under it which may have accrued and been claimed up to the date of distribution)—

(a) he may distribute the residuary real and personal estate of the deceased testator or intestate, or the trust estate, to or amongst the persons entitled thereto—

 (i) without appropriating any part of the estate of the deceased, or the trust estate, to meet any future liability (or, as the case may be, any liability) under any such agreement, and
 (ii) notwithstanding any potential liability of his to enter into any such agreement; and

(b) notwithstanding such distribution, he shall not be personally liable in respect of any subsequent claim (or, as the case may be, any claim) under any such agreement.

In this subsection 'authorised guarantee agreement' has the same meaning as in the Landlord and Tenant (Covenants) Act 1995.]

(2) This section operates without prejudice to the right of the lessor or grantor, or the persons deriving title under the lessor or grantor, to follow the assets of the deceased or the trust property into the hands of the persons amongst whom the same

may have been respectively distributed, and applies notwithstanding anything to the contrary in the will or other instrument, if any, creating the trust.

(3) In this section 'lease' includes an underlease and an agreement for a lease or underlease and any instrument giving any such indemnity as aforesaid or varying the liabilities under the lease; 'grant' applies to a grant whether the rent is created by limitation, grant, reservation, or otherwise, and includes an agreement for a grant and any instrument giving any such indemnity as aforesaid or varying the liabilities under the grant; 'lessee' and 'grantee' include persons respectively deriving title under them.

Amendment—Sub-s (1): words in square brackets substituted by the Law of Property (Amendment) Act 1926, ss 7, 8(2), Schedule.
Sub-s (1A): inserted by the Landlord and Tenant (Covenants) Act 1995, s 30(1), Sch 1, para 1.

---

27 Protection by means of advertisements

(1) With a view to the conveyance to or distribution among the persons entitled to any real or personal property, the trustees of a settlement [, trustees of land, trustees for sale of personal property] or personal representatives, may give notice by advertisement in the Gazette, and [in a newspaper circulating in the district in which the land is situated] and such other like notices, including notices elsewhere than in England and Wales, as would, in any special case, have been directed by a court of competent jurisdiction in an action for administration, of their intention to make such conveyance or distribution as aforesaid, and requiring any person interested to send to the trustees or personal representatives within the time, not being less than two months, fixed in the notice or, where more than one notice is given, in the last of the notices, particulars of his claim in respect of the property or any part thereof to which the notice relates.

(2) At the expiration of the time fixed by the notice the trustees or personal representatives may convey or distribute the property or any part thereof to which the notice relates, to or among the persons entitled thereto, having regard only to the claims, whether formal or not, of which the trustees or personal representatives then had notice and shall not, as respects the property so conveyed or distributed, be liable to any person of whose claim the trustees or personal representatives have not had notice at the time of conveyance or distribution; but nothing in this section—

(a) prejudices the right of any person to follow the property, or any property representing the same, into the hands of any person, other than a purchaser, who may have received it; or
(b) frees the trustees or personal representatives from any obligation to make searches or obtain official certificates of search similar to those which an intending purchaser would be advised to make or obtain.

(3) This section applies notwithstanding anything to the contrary in the will or other instrument, if any, creating the trust.

Amendment—Sub-s (1): first words in square brackets substituted by the Trusts of Land and Appointment of Trustees Act 1996, s 25(1), Sch 3, para 3(7), for savings in relation to entailed interests created before the commencement of that Act, and savings consequential upon the abolition of the doctrine of conversion, see s 25(4), (5) thereof; final words in square brackets substituted by the Law of Property (Amendment) Act 1926, ss 7, 8(2), Schedule.

---

28 Protection in regard to notice

A trustee or personal representative acting for the purposes of more than one trust or estate shall not, in the absence of fraud, be affected by notice of any instrument, matter, fact or thing in relation to any particular trust or estate if he has obtained notice thereof merely by reason of his acting or having acted for the purposes of another trust or estate.

30

...

Amendment—Repealed by the Trustee Act 2000, s 40(1), (3), Sch 2, Pt II, para 24, Sch 4, Pt II. Date in force: 1 February 2001: see SI 2001/49, art 2.

Maintenance Advancement and Protective Trusts

31 Power to apply income for maintenance and to accumulate surplus income during a minority

(1) Where any property is held by trustees in trust for any person for any interest whatsoever, whether vested or contingent, then, subject to any prior interests or charges affecting that property—

(i) during the infancy of any such person, if his interest so long continues, the trustees may, at their sole discretion, pay to his parent or guardian, if any, or otherwise apply for or towards his maintenance, education, or benefit, the whole or such part, if any, of the income of that property as may, in all the circumstances, be reasonable, whether or not there is—

  (a) any other fund applicable to the same purpose; or
  (b) any person bound by law to provide for his maintenance or education; and

(ii) if such person on attaining the age of [eighteen years] has not a vested interest in such income, the trustees shall thenceforth pay the income of that property and of any accretion thereto under subsection (2) of this section to him, until he either attains a vested interest therein or dies, or until failure of his interest:

Provided that, in deciding whether the whole or any part of the income of the property is during a minority to be paid or applied for the purposes aforesaid, the trustees shall have regard to the age of the infant and his requirements and generally to the circumstances of the case, and in particular to what other income, if any, is applicable for the same purposes; and where trustees have notice that the income of more than one fund is applicable for those purposes, then, so far as practicable, unless the entire income of the funds is paid or applied as aforesaid or the court otherwise directs, a proportionate part only of the income of each fund shall be so paid or applied.

(2) During the infancy of any such person, if his interest so long continues, the trustees shall accumulate all the residue of that income [by investing it, and any profits from so investing it] from time to time in authorised investments, and shall hold those accumulations as follows:—

(i) If any such person—

(a) attains the age of [eighteen years], or marries under that age, and his interest in such income during his infancy or until his marriage is a vested interest; or

(b) on attaining the age of [eighteen years] or on marriage under that age becomes entitled to the property from which such income arose in fee simple, absolute or determinable, or absolutely, or for an entailed interest;the trustees shall hold the accumulations in trust for such person absolutely, but without prejudice to any provision with respect thereto contained in any settlement by him made under any statutory powers during his infancy, and so that the receipt of such person after marriage, and though still an infant, shall be a good discharge; and

(ii) In any other case the trustees shall, notwithstanding that such person had a vested interest in such income, hold the accumulations as an accretion to the capital of the property from which such accumulations arose, and as one fund with such capital for all purposes, and so that, if such property is settled land, such accumulations shall be held upon the same trusts as if the same were capital money arising therefrom;

but the trustees may, at any time during the infancy of such person if his interest so long continues, apply those accumulations, or any part thereof, as if they were income arising in the then current year.

(3) This section applies in the case of a contingent interest only if the limitation or trust carries the intermediate income of the property, but it applies to a future or contingent legacy by the parent of, or a person standing in loco parentis to, the legatee, if and for such period as, under the general law, the legacy carries interest for the maintenance of the legatee, and in any such case as last aforesaid the rate of interest shall (if the income available is sufficient, and subject to any rules of court to the contrary) be five pounds per centum per annum.

(4) This section applies to a vested annuity in like manner as if the annuity were the income of property held by trustees in trust to pay the income thereof to the annuitant for the same period for which the annuity is payable, save that in any case accumulations made during the infancy of the annuitant shall be held in trust for the annuitant or his personal representatives absolutely.

(5) This section does not apply where the instrument, if any, under which the interest arises came into operation before the commencement of this Act.

Amendment—Sub-s (1): words in square brackets substituted by the Family Law Reform Act 1969, s 1(3), Sch 1, Part I.

Sub-s (2): words 'by investing it, and any profits from so investing it' in square brackets substituted by the Trustee Act 2000, s 40(1), Sch 2, Pt II, para 25. Date in force: 1 February 2001: see SI 2001/49, art 2.

Sub-s (2): in para (i)(a) words 'eighteen years' in square brackets substituted by the Family Law Reform Act 1969, s 1(3), Sch 1, Part I.

Sub-s (2): in para (i)(b) words 'eighteen years' in square brackets substituted by the Family Law Reform Act 1969, s 1(3), Sch 1, Part I.

---

32 Power of advancement

(1) Trustees may at any time or times pay or apply any capital money subject to a trust, for the advancement or benefit, in such manner as they may, in their absolute discretion, think fit, of any person entitled to the capital of the trust property or of any share thereof, whether absolutely or contingently on his attaining any specified age or on the occurrence of any other event, or subject to a gift over on his death under any specified age or on the occurrence of any other event, and whether in possession or in remainder or reversion, and such payment or application may be made notwithstanding that the interest of such person is liable to be defeated by the exercise of a power of appointment or revocation, or to be diminished by the increase of the class to which he belongs:

Provided that—

(a) the money so paid or applied for the advancement or benefit of any person shall not exceed altogether in amount one-half of the presumptive or vested share or interest of that person in the trust property; and

(b) if that person is or becomes absolutely and indefeasibly entitled to a share in the trust property the money so paid or applied shall be brought into account as part of such share; and

(c) no such payment or application shall be made so as to prejudice any person entitled to any prior life or other interest, whether vested or contingent, in the money paid or applied unless such person is in existence and of full age and consents in writing to such payment or application.

[(2) This section does not apply to capital money arising under the Settled Land Act 1925.]

(3) This section does not apply to trusts constituted or created before the commencement of this Act.

Amendment—Sub-s (2): substituted by the Trusts of Land and Appointment of Trustees Act 1996, s 25(1), Sch 3, para 3(8); for savings in relation to entailed interests created before the commencement of that Act, and savings consequential upon the abolition of the doctrine of conversion, see s 25(4), (5) thereof.

---

33 Protective trusts

(1) Where any income, including an annuity or other periodical income payment, is directed to be held on protective trusts for the benefit of any person (in this section called 'the principal beneficiary') for the period of his life or for any less period, then, during that period (in this section called the 'trust period') the said income shall, without prejudice to any prior interest, be held on the following trusts, namely:—

(i) Upon trust for the principal beneficiary during the trust period or until he, whether before or after the termination of any prior interest, does or attempts to do or suffers any act or thing, or until any event happens, other than an advance under any statutory or express power, whereby, if the said income were payable during the trust period to the principal beneficiary absolutely during that period, he would be deprived of the right to receive the same or any part thereof, in any of which cases, as well as on the termination of the trust period, whichever first happens, this trust of the said income shall fail or determine;

(ii) If the trust aforesaid fails or determines during the subsistence of the trust period, then, during the residue of that period, the said income shall be held upon trust for the application thereof for the maintenance or support, or otherwise for the benefit, of all or any one or more exclusively of the other or others of the following persons (that is to say)—

(a) the principal beneficiary and his or her wife or husband, if any, and his or her children or more remote issue, if any; or
(b) if there is no wife or husband or issue of the principal beneficiary in existence, the principal beneficiary and the persons who would, if he were actually dead, be entitled to the trust property or the income thereof or to the annuity fund, if any, or arrears of the annuity, as the case may be;as the trustees in their absolute discretion, without being liable to account for the exercise of such discretion, think fit.

(2) This section does not apply to trusts coming into operation before the commencement of this Act, and has effect subject to any variation of the implied trusts aforesaid contained in the instrument creating the trust.

(3) Nothing in this section operates to validate any trust which would, if contained in the instrument creating the trust, be liable to be set aside.

[(4) In relation to the dispositions mentioned in section 19(1) of the Family Law Reform Act 1987, this section shall have effect as if any reference (however expressed) to any relationship between two persons were construed in accordance with section 1 of that Act.]

Amendment—Sub-s (4): inserted by the Family Law Reform Act 1987, s 33(1), Sch 2, para 2, Sch 3, para 1.

PART III
APPOINTMENT AND DISCHARGE OF TRUSTEES

34 Limitation of the number of trustees

(1) Where, at the commencement of this Act, there are more than four trustees of a settlement of land, or more than four trustees holding land on trust for sale, no new trustees shall (except where as a result of the appointment the number is reduced to four or less) be capable of being appointed until the number is reduced to less than four, and thereafter the number shall not be increased beyond four.

(2) In the case of settlements and dispositions [creating trusts of land] made or coming into operation after the commencement of this Act—

(a) the number of trustees thereof shall not in any case exceed four, and where more than four persons are named as such trustees, the four first named (who are able and willing to act) shall alone be the trustees, and the other persons named shall not be trustees unless appointed on the occurrence of a vacancy;
(b) the number of the trustees shall not be increased beyond four.

(3) This section only applies to settlements and dispositions of land, and the restrictions imposed on the number of trustees do not apply—

(a) in the case of land vested in trustees for charitable, ecclesiastical, or public purposes; or
(b) where the net proceeds of the sale of the land are held for like purposes; or
(c) to the trustees of a term of years absolute limited by a settlement on trusts for raising money, or of a like term created under the statutory remedies relating to annual sums charged on land.

Amendment—Sub-s (2): words in square brackets substituted by the Trusts of Land and Appointment of Trustees Act 1996, s 25(1), Sch 3, para 3(9); for savings in relation to entailed interests created before the commencement of that Act, and savings consequential upon the abolition of the doctrine of conversion, see s 25(4), (5) thereof.

---

35 Appointments of trustees of settlements and [and trustees of land]

[(1) Appointments of new trustees of land and of new trustees of any trust of the proceeds of sale of the land shall, subject to any order of the court, be effected by separate instruments, but in such manner as to secure that the same persons become trustees of land and trustees of the trust of the proceeds of sale.]

(2) Where new trustees of a settlement are appointed, a memorandum of the names and addresses of the persons who are for the time being the trustees thereof for the purposes of the Settled Land Act 1925, shall be endorsed on or annexed to the last or only principal vesting instrument by or on behalf of the trustees of the settlement, and such vesting instrument shall, for that purpose, be produced by the person having the possession thereof of the trustees of the settlement when so required.

[(3) Where new trustees of land are appointed, a memorandum of the persons who are for the time being the trustees of the land shall be endorsed on or annexed to the conveyance by which the land was vested in trustees of land; and that conveyance shall be produced to the persons who are for the time being the trustees of the land by the person in possession of it in order for that to be done when the trustees require its production.]

(4) This section applies only to settlements and dispositions of land.

Amendment—Section heading: words in square brackets substituted by the Trusts of Land and Appointment of Trustees Act 1996, s 25(1), Sch 3, para 3(10)(c); for savings in relation to entailed interests created before the commencement of that Act, and savings consequential upon the abolition of the doctrine of conversion, see s 25(4), (5) thereof.
Sub-ss (1), (3): substituted by the Trusts of Land and Appointment of Trustees Act 1996, s 25(1), Sch 3, para 3(10)(a), (b); for savings in relation to entailed interests created before the commencement of that Act, and savings consequential upon the abolition of the doctrine of conversion, see s 25(4), (5) thereof.

---

36 Power of appointing new or additional trustees

(1) Where a trustee, either original or substituted, and whether appointed by a court or otherwise, is dead, or remains out of the United Kingdom for more than twelve months, or desires to be discharged from all or any of the trusts or powers reposed in or conferred on him, or refuses or is unfit to act therein, or is incapable of acting therein, or is an infant, then, subject to the restrictions imposed by this Act on the number of trustees,—

(a) the person or persons nominated for the purpose of appointing new trustees by the instrument, if any, creating the trust; or
(b) if there is no such person, or no such person able and willing to act, then the surviving or continuing trustees or trustee for the time being, or the personal representatives of the last surviving or continuing trustee;

may, by writing, appoint one or more other persons (whether or not being the persons exercising the power) to be a trustee or trustees in the place of the trustee so deceased remaining out of the United Kingdom, desiring to be discharged, refusing, or being unfit or being incapable, or being an infant, as aforesaid.

(2) Where a trustee has been removed under a power contained in the instrument creating the trust, a new trustee or new trustees may be appointed in the place of the trustee who is removed, as if he were dead, or, in the case of a corporation, as if the corporation desired to be discharged from the trust, and the provisions of this section shall apply accordingly, but subject to the restrictions imposed by this Act on the number of trustees.

(3) Where a corporation being a trustee is or has been dissolved, either before or after the commencement of this Act, then, for the purposes of this section and of any enactment replaced thereby, the corporation shall be deemed to be and to have been from the date of the dissolution incapable of acting in the trusts or powers reposed in or conferred on the corporation.

(4) The power of appointment given by subsection (1) of this section or any similar previous enactment to the personal representatives of a last surviving or continuing trustee shall be and shall be deemed always to have been exercisable by the executors for the time being (whether original or by representation) of such surviving or continuing trustee who have proved the will of their testator or by the administrators for the time being of such trustee without the concurrence of any executor who has renounced or has not proved.

(5) But a sole or last surviving executor intending to renounce, or all the executors where they all intend to renounce, shall have and shall be deemed always to have had power, at any time before renouncing probate, to exercise the power of appointment given by this section, or by any similar previous enactment, if willing to act for that purpose and without thereby accepting the office of executor.

[(6) Where, in the case of any trust, there are not more than three trustees—]

(a) the person or persons nominated for the purpose of appointing new trustees by the instrument, if any, creating the trust; or
(b) if there is no such person, or no such person able and willing to act, then the trustee or trustees for the time being;

may, by writing appoint another person or other persons to be an additional trustee or additional trustees, but it shall not be obligatory to appoint any additional trustee, unless the instrument, if any, creating the trust, or any statutory enactment provides to the contrary, nor shall the number of trustees be increased beyond four by virtue of any such appointment.

[(6A) A person who is either—

(a) both a trustee and attorney for the other trustee (if one other), or for both of the other trustees (if two others), under a registered power; or
(b) attorney under a registered power for the trustee (if one) or for both or each of the trustees (if two or three),

may, if subsection (6B) of this section is satisfied in relation to him, make an appointment under subsection (6)(b) of this section on behalf of the trustee or trustees.

(6B) This subsection is satisfied in relation to an attorney under a registered power for one or more trustees if (as attorney under the power)—

(a) he intends to exercise any function of the trustee or trustees by virtue of section 1(1) of the Trustee Delegation Act 1999; or
(b) he intends to exercise any function of the trustee or trustees in relation to any land, capital proceeds of a conveyance of land or income from land by virtue of its delegation to him under section 25 of this Act or the instrument (if any) creating the trust.

(6C) In subsections (6A) and (6B) of this section 'registered power' means a power of attorney created by an instrument which is for the time being registered under section 6 of the Enduring Powers of Attorney Act 1985.

(6D) Subsection (6A) of this section—

(a) applies only if and so far as a contrary intention is not expressed in the instrument creating the power of attorney (or, where more than one, any of them) or the instrument (if any) creating the trust; and
(b) has effect subject to the terms of those instruments.]

(7) Every new trustee appointed under this section as well before as after all the trust property becomes by law, or by assurance, or otherwise, vested in him, shall have the same powers, authorities, and discretions, and may in all respects act as if he had been originally appointed a trustee by the instrument, if any, creating the trust.

(8) The provisions of this section relating to a trustee who is dead include the case of a person nominated trustee in a will but dying before the testator, and those relative to a continuing trustee include a refusing or retiring trustee, if willing to act in the execution of the provisions of this section.

[(9) Where a trustee is incapable, by reason of mental disorder within the meaning of [the Mental Health Act 1983], of exercising his functions as trustee and is also entitled in possession to some beneficial interest in the trust property, no appointment of a new trustee in his place shall be made by virtue of paragraph (b) of subsection (1) of this section unless leave to make the appointment has been given by the authority having jurisdiction under [Part VII of the Mental Health Act 1983].]

Amendment—Sub-s (6): words in square brackets substituted by the Trusts of Land and Appointment of Trustees Act 1996, s 25(1), Sch 3, para 3(11); for savings in relation to entailed interests created before the commencement of that Act, and savings consequential upon the abolition of the doctrine of conversion, see s 25(4), (5) thereof.

Sub-ss (6A)–(6D): inserted by the Trustee Delegation Act 1999, s 8. Date in force: 1 March 2000 (in relation to powers created after that date): see SI 2000/216, art 2.

Sub-s (9): substituted by the Mental Health Act 1959, s 149(1), Sch 7, Part I; words in square brackets therein substituted by the Mental Health Act 1983, s 148, Sch 4, para 4.

---

37 Supplemental provisions as to appointment of trustees

(1) On the appointment of a trustee for the whole or any part of trust property—

(a) the number of trustees may, subject to the restrictions imposed by this Act on the number of trustees, be increased; and

(b) a separate set of trustees, not exceeding four, may be appointed for any part of the trust property held on trusts distinct from those relating to any other part or parts of the trust property, notwithstanding that no new trustees or trustee are or is to be appointed for other parts of the trust property, and any existing trustee may be appointed or remain one of such separate set of trustees, or, if only one trustee was originally appointed, then, save as hereinafter provided, one separate trustee may be so appointed; and

(c) it shall not be obligatory, save as hereinafter provided, to appoint more than one new trustee where only one trustee was originally appointed, or to fill up the original number of trustees where more than two trustees were originally appointed, but, except where only one trustee was originally appointed, and a sole trustee when appointed will be able to give valid receipts for all capital money, a trustee shall not be discharged from his trust unless there will be either a trust corporation or at least two [persons] to act as trustees to perform the trust; and

(d) any assurance or thing requisite for vesting the trust property, or any part thereof, in a sole trustee, or jointly in the persons who are the trustees, shall be executed or done.

(2) Nothing in this Act shall authorise the appointment of a sole trustee, not being a trust corporation, where the trustee, when appointed, would not be able to give valid receipts for all capital money arising under the trust.

Amendment—Sub-s (1): in para (c) word in square brackets substituted by the Trusts of Land and Appointment of Trustees Act 1996, s 25(1), Sch 3, para 3(12); for savings in relation to entailed interests created before the commencement of that Act, and savings consequential upon the abolition of the doctrine of conversion, see s 25(4), (5) thereof.

---

38 Evidence as to a vacancy in a trust

(1) A statement, contained in any instrument coming into operation after the commencement of this Act by which a new trustee is appointed for any purpose connected with land, to the effect that a trustee has remained out of the United Kingdom for more than twelve months or refuses or is unfit to act, or is incapable of acting, or that he is not entitled to a beneficial interest in the trust property in possession, shall, in favour of a purchaser of a legal estate, be conclusive evidence of the matter stated.

(2) In favour of such purchaser any appointment of a new trustee depending on that statement, and any vesting declaration, express or implied, consequent on the appointment, shall be valid.

39 Retirement of trustee without a new appointment

(1) Where a trustee is desirous of being discharged from the trust, and after his discharge there will be either a trust corporation or at least two [persons] to act as trustees to perform the trust, then, if such trustee as aforesaid by deed declares that he is desirous of being discharged from the trust, and if his co-trustees and such other person, if any, as is empowered to appoint trustees, by deed consent to the discharge of the trustee, and to the vesting in the co-trustees alone of the trust property, the trustee desirous of being discharged shall be deemed to have retired from the trust, and shall, by the deed, be discharged therefrom under this Act, without any new trustee being appointed in his place.

(2) Any assurance or thing requisite for vesting the trust property in the continuing trustees alone shall be executed or done.

Amendment—Sub-s (1): word in square brackets substituted by the Trusts of Land and Appointment of Trustees Act 1996, s 25(1), Sch 3, para 3(13); for savings in relation to entailed interests created before the commencement of that Act, and savings consequential upon the abolition of the doctrine of conversion, see s 25(4), (5) thereof.
Modification—Modified, in relation to the appointment or discharge of trustees in whom any property is vested in trust for a trade union whose name is entered in the list of trade unions, by the Trade Union and Labour Relations (Consolidation) Act 1992, s 13.

---

40 Vesting of trust property in new or continuing trustees

(1) Where by a deed a new trustee is appointed to perform any trust, then—

(a) if the deed contains a declaration by the appointor to the effect that any estate or interest in any land subject to the trust, or in any chattel so subject, or right to recover or receive any debt or other thing in action so subject, shall vest in the persons who by virtue of the deed become or are the trustees for performing the trust, the deed shall operate, without any conveyance or assignment, to vest in those persons as joint tenants and for the purposes of the trust the estate interest or right to which the declaration relates; and
(b) if the deed is made after the commencement of this Act and does not contain such a declaration, the deed shall, subject to any express provision to the contrary therein contained, operate as if it had contained such a declaration by the appointor extending to all the estates interests and rights with respect to which a declaration could have been made.

(2) Where by a deed a retiring trustee is discharged under [section 39 of this Act or section 19 of the Trusts of Land and Appointment of Trustees Act 1996] without a new trustee being appointed, then—

(a) if the deed contains such a declaration as aforesaid by the retiring and continuing trustees, and by the other person, if any, empowered to appoint trustees, the deed shall, without any conveyance or assignment, operate to vest in the continuing trustees alone, as joint tenants, and for the purposes of the trust, the estate, interest, or right to which the declaration relates; and
(b) if the deed is made after the commencement of this Act and does not contain such a declaration, the deed shall, subject to any express provision to the contrary therein contained, operate as if it had contained such a declaration by

such persons as aforesaid extending to all the estates, interests and rights with respect to which a declaration could have been made.

(3) An express vesting declaration, whether made before or after the commencement of this Act, shall, notwithstanding that the estate, interest or right to be vested is not expressly referred to, and provided that the other statutory requirements were or are complied with, operate and be deemed always to have operated (but without prejudice to any express provision to the contrary contained in the deed of appointment or discharge) to vest in the persons respectively referred to in subsections (1) and (2) of this section, as the case may require, such estates, interests and rights as are capable of being and ought to be vested in those persons.

(4) This section does not extend—

(a) to land conveyed by way of mortgage for securing money subject to the trust, except land conveyed on trust for securing debentures or debenture stock;
(b) to land held under a lease which contains any covenant, condition or agreement against assignment or disposing of the land without licence or consent, unless, prior to the execution of the deed containing expressly or impliedly the vesting declaration, the requisite licence or consent has been obtained, or unless, by virtue of any statute or rule of law, the vesting declaration, express or implied, would not operate as a breach of covenant or give rise to a forfeiture;
(c) to any share, stock, annuity or property which is only transferable in books kept by a company or other body, or in manner directed by or under an Act of Parliament.

In this subsection 'lease' includes an underlease and an agreement for a lease or underlease.

(5) For purposes of registration of the deed in any registry, the person or persons making the declaration expressly or impliedly, shall be deemed the conveying party or parties, and the conveyance shall be deemed to be made by him or them under a power conferred by this Act.

(6) This section applies to deeds of appointment or discharge executed on or after the first day of January, eighteen hundred and eighty-two.

Amendment—Sub-s (2): words in square brackets substituted by the Trusts of Land and Appointment of Trustees Act 1996, s 25(1), Sch 3, para 3(14); for savings in relation to entailed interests created before the commencement of that Act, and savings consequential upon the abolition of the doctrine of conversion, see s 25(4), (5) thereof.
Modification—Modified, in relation to the appointment or discharge of trustees in whom any property is vested in trust for a trade union whose name is entered in the list of trade unions, by the Trade Union and Labour Relations (Consolidation) Act 1992, s 13.

PART IV
POWERS OF THE COURT

Appointment of new Trustees

41 Power of court to appoint new trustees

(1) The court may, whenever it is expedient to appoint a new trustee or new trustees, and it is found inexpedient difficult or impracticable so to do without the

assistance of the court, make an order appointing a new trustee or new trustees either in substitution for or in addition to any existing trustee or trustees, or although there is no existing trustee.

In particular and without prejudice to the generality of the foregoing provision, the court may make an order appointing a new trustee in substitution for a trustee who … is [incapable, by reason of mental disorder within the meaning of [the Mental Health Act 1983], of exercising his functions as trustee], or is a bankrupt, or is a corporation which is in liquidation or has been dissolved.

(2) The power conferred by this section may, in the case of a deed of arrangement within the meaning of the Deeds of Arrangement Act 1914, be exercised either by the High Court or by the court having jurisdiction in bankruptcy in the district in which the debtor resided or carried on business at the date of the execution of the deed.

(3) An order under this section, and any consequential vesting order or conveyance, shall not operate further or otherwise as a discharge to any former or continuing trustee than an appointment of new trustees under any power for that purpose contained in any instrument would have operated.

(4) Nothing in this section gives power to appoint an executor or administrator.

Amendment—Sub-s (1): words omitted repealed by the Criminal Law Act 1967, s 10, Sch 3, Part III; first words in square brackets substituted by the Mental Health Act 1959, s 149(1), Sch 7, Part I, words in square brackets therein substituted by the Mental Health Act 1983, s 148, Sch 4, para 4.

---

42 Power to authorise remuneration

Where the court appoints a corporation, other than the Public Trustee, to be a trustee either solely or jointly with another person, the court may authorise the corporation to charge such remuneration for its services as trustee as the court may think fit.

43 Powers of new trustee appointed by the Court

Every trustee appointed by a court of competent jurisdiction shall, as well before as after the trust property becomes by law, or by assurance, or otherwise, vested in him, have the same powers, authorities, and discretions, and may in all respects act as if he had been originally appointed a trustee by the instrument, if any, creating the trust.

Vesting Orders

44 Vesting orders of land

In any of the following cases, namely:

(i) Where the court appoints or has appointed a trustee, or where a trustee has been appointed out of court under any statutory or express power;

(ii) Where a trustee entitled to or possessed of any land or interest therein, whether by way of mortgage or otherwise, or entitled to a contingent right therein, either solely or jointly with any other person—

(a) is under disability; or
(b) is out of the jurisdiction of the High Court; or
(c) cannot be found, or, being a corporation, has been dissolved;

(iii) Where it is uncertain who was the survivor of two or more trustees jointly entitled to or possessed of any interest in land;
(iv) Where it is uncertain whether the last trustee known to have been entitled to or possessed of any interest in land is living or dead;
(v) Where there is no personal representative of a deceased trustee who was entitled to or possessed of any interest in land, or where it is uncertain who is the personal representative of a deceased trustee who was entitled to or possessed of any interest in land;
(vi) Where a trustee jointly or solely entitled to or possessed of any interest in land, or entitled to a contingent right therein, has been required, by or on behalf of a person entitled to require a conveyance of the land or interest or a release of the right, to convey the land or interest or to release the right, and has wilfully refused or neglected to convey the land or interest or release the right for twenty-eight days after the date of the requirement;
(vii) Where land or any interest therein is vested in a trustee whether by way of mortgage or otherwise, and it appears to the court to be expedient;

the court may make an order (in this Act called a vesting order) vesting the land or interest therein in any such person in any such manner and for any such estate or interest as the court may direct, or releasing or disposing of the contingent right to such person as the court may direct:

Provided that—

(a) Where the order is consequential on the appointment of a trustee the land or interest therein shall be vested for such estate as the court may direct in the persons who on the appointment are the trustees; and
(b) Where the order relates to a trustee entitled or formerly entitled jointly with another person, and such trustee is under disability or out of the jurisdiction of the High Court or cannot be found, or being a corporation has been dissolved, the land interest or right shall be vested in such other person who remains entitled, either alone or with any other person the court may appoint.

45 Orders as to contingent rights of unborn persons

Where any interest in land is subject to a contingent right in an unborn person or class of unborn persons who, on coming into existence would, in respect, thereof, become entitled to or possessed of that interest on any trust, the court may make an order releasing the land or interest therein from the contingent right, or may make an order vesting in any person the estate or interest to or of which the unborn person or class of unborn persons would, on coming into existence, be entitled or possessed in the land.

46 Vesting order in place of conveyance by infant mortgagee

Where any person entitled to or possessed of any interest in land, or entitled to a contingent right in land, by way of security for money, is an infant, the court may make an order vesting or releasing or disposing of the interest in the land or the right in like manner as in the case of a trustee under disability.

47 Vesting order consequential on order for sale or mortgage of land

Where any court gives a judgment or makes an order directing the sale or mortgage of any land, every person who is entitled to or possessed of any interest in the land, or entitled to a contingent right therein, and is a party to the action or proceeding in which the judgment or order is given or made or is otherwise bound by the judgment or order, shall be deemed to be so entitled or possessed, as the case may be, as a trustee for the purpose of this Act, and the court may, if it thinks expedient, make an order vesting the land or any part thereof for such estate or interest as that court thinks fit in the purchaser or mortgagee or in any other person:

Provided that, in the case of a legal mortgage, the estate to be vested in the mortgagee shall be a term of years absolute.

48 Vesting order consequential on judgement for specific performance, etc

Where a judgment is given for the specific performance of a contract concerning any interest in land, or for sale or exchange of any interest in land, or generally where any judgment is given for the conveyance of any interest in land either in cases arising out of the doctrine of election or otherwise, the court may declare—

(a) that any of the parties to the action are trustees of any interest in the land or any part thereof within the meaning of this Act; or
(b) that the interests of unborn persons who might claim under any party to the action, or under the will or voluntary settlement of any deceased person who was during his lifetime a party to the contract or transaction concerning which the judgment is given, are the interests of persons who, on coming into existence, would be trustees within the meaning of this Act;

and thereupon the court may make a vesting order relating to the rights of those persons, born and unborn, as if they had been trustees.

49 Effect of vesting order

A vesting order under any of the foregoing provisions shall in the case of a vesting order consequential on the appointment of a trustee, have the same effect—

(a) as if the persons who before the appointment were the trustees, if any, had duly executed all proper conveyances of the land for such estate or interest as the court directs; or
(b) if there is no such person, or no such person of full capacity, as if such person had existed and been of full capacity and had duly executed all proper conveyances of the land for such estate or interest as the court directs;

and shall in every other case have the same effect as if the trustee or other person or description or class of persons to whose rights or supposed rights the said provisions respectively relate had been an ascertained and existing person of full capacity, and had executed a conveyance or release to the effect intended by the order.

50 Power to appoint person to convey

In all cases where a vesting order can be made under any of the foregoing provisions, the court may, if it is more convenient, appoint a person to convey the land or any interest therein or release the contingent right, and a conveyance or release by that person in conformity with the order shall have the same effect as an order under the appropriate provision.

51 Vesting orders as to stock and things in action

(1) In any of the following cases, namely:—

(i) Where the court appoints or has appointed a trustee, or where a trustee has been appointed out of court under any statutory or express power;

(ii) Where a trustee entitled, whether by way of mortgage or otherwise, alone or jointly with another person to stock or to a thing in action—

- (a) is under disability; or
- (b) is out of the jurisdiction of the High Court; or
- (c) cannot be found, or, being a corporation, has been dissolved; or
- (d) neglects or refuses to transfer stock or receive the dividends or income thereof, or to sue for or recover a thing in action, according to the direction of the person absolutely entitled thereto for twenty-eight days next after a request in writing has been made to him by the person so entitled; or
- (e) neglects or refuses to transfer stock or receive the dividends or income thereof, or to sue for or recover a thing in action for twenty-eight days next after an order of the court for that purpose has been served on him;

(iii) Where it is uncertain whether a trustee entitled alone or jointly with another person to stock or to a thing in action is alive or dead;

(iv) Where stock is standing in the name of a deceased person whose personal representative is under disability;

(v) Where stock or a thing in action is vested in a trustee whether by way of mortgage or otherwise and it appears to the court to be expedient;

the court may make an order vesting the right to transfer or call for a transfer of stock, or to receive the dividends or income thereof, or to sue for or recover the thing in action, in any such person as the court may appoint:

Provided that—

(a) Where the order is consequential on the appointment of a trustee, the right shall be vested in the persons who, on the appointment, are the trustees; and

(b) Where the person whose right is dealt with by the order was entitled jointly with another person, the right shall be vested in that last-mentioned person either alone or jointly with any other person whom the court may appoint.

(2) In all cases where a vesting order can be made under this section, the court may, if it is more convenient, appoint some proper person to make or join in making the transfer:

Provided that the person appointed to make or join in making a transfer of stock shall be some proper officer of the bank, or the company or society whose stock is to be transferred.

(3) The person in whom the right to transfer or call for the transfer of any stock is

vested by an order of the court under this Act, may transfer the stock to himself or any other person, according to the order, and the Bank of England and all other companies shall obey every order under this section according to its tenor.

(4) After notice in writing of an order under this section it shall not be lawful for the Bank of England or any other company to transfer any stock to which the order relates or to pay any dividends thereon except in accordance with the order.

(5) The court may make declarations and give directions concerning the manner in which the right to transfer any stock or thing in action vested under the provisions of this Act is to be exercised.

(6) The provisions of this Act as to vesting orders shall apply to shares in ships registered under the [Merchant Shipping Act 1995] as if they were stock.

Amendment—Sub-s (6): words in square brackets substituted by the Merchant Shipping Act 1995, s 314(2), Sch 13, para 13.

---

52 Vesting orders of charity property

The powers conferred by this Act as to vesting orders may be exercised for vesting any interest in land, stock, or thing in action in any trustee of a charity or society over which the court would have jurisdiction upon action duly instituted, whether the appointment of the trustee was made by instrument under a power or by the court under its general or statutory jurisdiction.

53 Vesting orders in relation to infants' beneficial interests

Where an infant is beneficially entitled to any property the court may, with a view to the application of the capital or income thereof for the maintenance, education, or benefit of the infant, make an order—

(a) appointing a person to convey such property; or
(b) in the case of stock, or a thing in action, vesting in any person the right to transfer or call for a transfer of such stock, or to receive the dividends or income thereof, or to sue for and recover such thing in action, upon such terms as the court may think fit.

[54 Jurisdiction in regard to mental patients]

[(1) Subject to the provisions of this section, the authority having jurisdiction under [Part VII of the Mental Health Act 1983], shall not have power to make any order, or give any direction or authority, in relation to a patient who is a trustee if the High Court has power under this Act to make an order to the like effect.

(2) Where a patient is a trustee and a receiver appointed by the said authority is acting for him or an application for the appointment of a receiver has been made but not determined, then, except as respects a trust which is subject to an order for administration made by the High Court, the said authority shall have concurrent jurisdiction with the High Court in relation to—

(a) mortgaged property of which the patient has become a trustee merely by reason of the mortgage having been paid off;
(b) matters consequent on the making of provision by the said authority for the exercise of a power of appointing trustees or retiring from a trust;
(c) matters consequent on the making of provision by the said authority for the carrying out of any contract entered into by the patient;
(d) property to some interest in which the patient is beneficially entitled but which, or some interest in which, is held by the patient under an express, implied or constructive trust.

The Lord Chancellor may make rules with respect to the exercise of the jurisdiction referred to in this subsection.

(3) In this section 'patient' means a patient as defined by [section 94 of the Mental Health Act 1983], or a person as to whom powers are [exercisable under section 98 of that Act and have been exercised under that section or section 104 of the Mental Health Act 1959].]

Amendment—Substituted by the Mental Health Act 1959, s 149(1), Sch 7, Part I.
Sub-ss (1), (3): words in square brackets substituted by the Mental Health Act 1983, s 148, Sch 4, para 4.

---

55 Orders made upon certain allegations to be conclusive evidence

Where a vesting order is made as to any land under this Act or under [Part VII of the Mental Health Act 1983], as amended by any subsequent enactment, or under any Act relating to lunacy in Northern Ireland, founded on an allegation of any of the following matters namely—

(a) the personal incapacity of a trustee or mortgagee; or
(b) that a trustee or mortgagee or the personal representative of or other person deriving title under a trustee or mortgagee is out of the jurisdiction of the High Court or cannot be found, or being a corporation has been dissolved; or
(c) that it is uncertain which of two or more trustees, or which of two or more persons interested in a mortgage, was the survivor; or
(d) that it is uncertain whether the last trustee or the personal representative of or other person deriving title under a trustee or mortgagee, or the last surviving person interested in a mortgage is living or dead; or
(e) that any trustee or mortgagee has died intestate without leaving a person beneficially interested under the intestacy or has died and it is not known who is his personal representative or the person interested;

the fact that the order has been so made shall be conclusive evidence of the matter so alleged in any court upon any question as to the validity of the order; but this section does not prevent the court from directing a reconveyance or surrender or the payment of costs occasioned by any such order if improperly obtained.

Amendment—Words in square brackets substituted by the Mental Health Act 1983, s 148, Sch 4, para 4.

---

56 Application of vesting order to property out of England

The powers of the court to make vesting orders under this Act shall extend to all property in any part of His Majesty's dominions except Scotland.

Jurisdiction to make other Orders

57 Power of court to authorise dealings with trust property

(1) Where in the management or administration of any property vested in trustees, any sale, lease, mortgage, surrender, release, or other disposition, or any purchase, investment, acquisition, expenditure, or other transaction, is in the opinion of the court expedient, but the same cannot be effected by reason of the absence of any power for that purpose vested in the trustees by the trust instrument, if any, or by law, the court may by order confer upon the trustees, either generally or in any particular instance, the necessary power for the purpose, on such terms, and subject to such provisions and conditions, if any, as the court may think fit and may direct in what manner any money authorised to be expended, and the costs of any transaction, are to be paid or borne as between capital and income.

(2) The court may, from time to time, rescind or vary any order made under this section, or may make any new or further order.

(3) An application to the court under this section may be made by the trustees, or by any of them, or by any person beneficially interested under the trust.

(4) This section does not apply to trustees of a settlement for the purposes of the Settled Land Act 1925.

58 Persons entitled to apply for orders

(1) An order under this Act for the appointment of a new trustee or concerning any interest in land, stock, or thing in action subject to a trust, may be made on the application of any person beneficially interested in the land, stock, or thing in action, whether under disability or not, or on the application of any person duly appointed trustee thereof.

(2) An order under this Act concerning any interest in land, stock, or thing in action subject to a mortgage may be made on the application of any person beneficially interested in the equity of redemption, whether under disability or not, or of any person interested in the money secured by the mortgage.

59 Power to give judgment in absence of a trustee

Where in any action the court is satisfied that diligent search has been made for any person who, in the character of trustee, is made a defendant in any action, to serve him with a process of the court, and that he cannot be found, the court may hear and determine the action and give judgment therein against that person in his character of a trustee as if he had been duly served, or had entered an appearance in the action, and had also appeared by his counsel and solicitor at the hearing, but without prejudice to any interest he may have in the matters in question in the action in any other character.

Modification—References to solicitors etc modified to include references to bodies recognised under the Administration of Justice Act 1985, s 9, by the Solicitors' Incorporated Practices Order 1991, SI 1991/2684, arts 4, 5, Sch 1.

---

60 Power to charge costs on trust estate

The court may order the costs and expenses of and incident to any application for an order appointing a new trustee, or for a vesting order, or of and incident to any such order, or any conveyance or transfer in pursuance thereof, to be raised and paid out of the property in respect whereof the same is made, or out of the income thereof, or to be borne and paid in such manner and by such persons as to the court may seem just.

61 Power to relieve trustee from personal liability

If it appears to the court that a trustee, whether appointed by the court or otherwise, is or may be personally liable for any breach of trust, whether the transaction alleged to be a breach of trust occurred before or after the commencement of this Act, but has acted honestly and reasonably, and ought fairly to be excused for the breach of trust and for omitting to obtain the directions of the court in the matter in which he committed such breach, then the court may relieve him either wholly or partly from personal liability for the same.

62 Power to make beneficiary indemnify for breach of trust

(1) Where a trustee commits a breach of trust at the instigation or request or with the consent in writing of a beneficiary, the court may, if it thinks fit, … make such order as to the court seems just, for impounding all or any part of the interest of the beneficiary in the trust estate by way of indemnity to the trustee or persons claiming through him.

(2) This section applies to breaches of trust committed as well before as after the commencement of this Act.

Amendment—Sub-s (1): words omitted repealed by the Married Women (Restraint upon Anticipation) Act 1949, s 1(4), Sch 2.

Payment into Court

63 Payment into court by trustees

(1) Trustees, or the majority of trustees, having in their hands or under their control money or securities belonging to a trust, may pay the same into court; …

(2) The receipt or certificate of the proper officer shall be a sufficient discharge to trustees for the money or securities so paid into court.

(3) Where money or securities are vested in any persons as trustees, and the majority are desirous of paying the same into court, but the concurrence of the other or

others cannot be obtained, the court may order the payment into court to be made by the majority without the concurrence of the other or others.

(4) Where any such money or securities are deposited with any banker, broker, or other depository, the court may order payment or delivery of the money or securities to the majority of the trustees for the purpose of payment into court.

(5) Every transfer payment and delivery made in pursuance of any such order shall be valid and take effect as if the same had been made on the authority or by the act of all the persons entitled to the money and securities so transferred, paid, or delivered.

Amendment—Sub-s (1): words omitted repealed by the Administration of Justice Act 1965, s 36(4), Sch 3.

[63A Jurisdiction of County Court]

[(1) The county court has jurisdiction under the following provisions where the amount or value of the trust estate or fund to be dealt with in the court does not exceed the county court limit—

section 41;
section 42;
section 51;
section 57;
section 60;
section 61;
section 62.

(2) The county court has jurisdiction under the following provisions where the land or the interest or contingent right in land which is to be dealt with in the court forms part of a trust estate which does not exceed in amount or value the county court limit—

section 44;
section 45;
section 46.

(3) The county court has jurisdiction—

(a) under sections 47 and 48 of this Act, where the judgment is given or order is made by the court;
(b) under sections 50 and 56, where a vesting order can be made by the court;
(c) under section 53, where the amount or value of the property to be dealt with in the court does not exceed the county court limit; and
(d) under section 63 (including power to receive payment of money or securities into court) where the money or securities to be paid into court do not exceed in amount or value the county court limit.

(4) Any reference to the court in section 59 of this Act includes a reference to the county court.

(5) In this section, in its application to any enactment, 'the county court limit'

means the amount for the time being specified by an Order in Council under section 145 of the County Courts Act 1984 as the county court limit for the purposes of that enactment (or, where no such Order in Council has been made, the corresponding limit specified by Order in Council under section 192 of the County Courts Act 1959).]

Amendment—Inserted by the County Courts Act 1984, s 148(1), Sch 2, para 1.

PART V
GENERAL PROVISIONS

64 Application of Act to Settled Land Act Trustees

(1) All the powers and provisions contained in this Act with reference to the appointment of new trustees, and the discharge and retirement of trustees, apply to and include trustees for the purposes of the Settled Land Act 1925, and trustees for the purpose of the management of land during a minority, whether such trustees are appointed by the court or by the settlement, or under provisions contained in any instrument.

(2) Where, either before or after the commencement of this Act, trustees of a settlement have been appointed by the court for the purposes of the Settled Land Acts 1882 to 1890, or of the Settled Land Act 1925, then, after the commencement of this Act—

(a) the person or persons nominated for the purpose of appointing new trustees by the instrument, if any, creating the settlement, though no trustees for the purposes of the said Acts were thereby appointed; or
(b) if there is no such person, or no such person able and willing to act, the surviving or continuing trustees or trustee for the time being for the purposes of the said Acts or the personal representatives of the last surviving or continuing trustee for those purposes,

shall have the powers conferred by this Act to appoint new or additional trustees of the settlement for the purposes of the said Acts.

(3) Appointments of new trustees for the purposes of the said Acts made or expressed to be made before the commencement of this Act by the trustees or trustee or personal representatives referred to in paragraph (b) of the last preceding subsection or by the persons referred to in paragraph (a) of that subsection are, without prejudice to any order of the court made before such commencement, hereby confirmed.

66 Indemnity to banks, etc

This Act, and every order purporting to be made under this Act, shall be a complete indemnity to the Bank of England, and to all persons for any acts done pursuant thereto, and it shall not be necessary for the Bank or for any person to inquire concerning the propriety of the order, or whether the court by which the order was made had jurisdiction to make it.

67 Jurisdiction of the 'court'

(1) In this Act 'the court' means the High Court … or the county court, where those courts respectively have jurisdiction.

(2) The procedure under this Act in … county courts shall be in accordance with the Acts and rules regulating the procedure of those courts.

Amendment—Words omitted repealed by the Courts Act 1971, s 56, Sch 11, Part II.

---

68 Definitions

[(1)] In this Act, unless the context otherwise requires, the following expressions have the meanings hereby assigned to them respectively, that is to say:—

(1) 'Authorised investments' mean investments authorised by the instrument, if any, creating the trust for the investment of money subject to the trust, or by law;

(2) 'Contingent right' as applied to land includes a contingent or executory interest, a possibility coupled with an interest, whether the object of the gift or limitation of the interest, or possibility is or is not ascertained, also a right of entry, whether immediate or future, and whether vested or contingent;

(3) 'Convey' and 'conveyance' as applied to any person include the execution by that person of every necessary or suitable assurance (including an assent) for conveying, assigning, appointing, surrendering, or otherwise transferring or disposing of land whereof he is seised or possessed, or wherein he is entitled to a contingent right, either for his whole estate or for any less estate, together with the performance of all formalities required by law for the validity of the conveyance; 'sale' includes an exchange;

(4) 'Gazette' means the London Gazette;

(5) 'Instrument' includes Act of Parliament;

(6) 'Land' includes land of any tenure, and mines and minerals, whether or not severed from the surface, buildings or parts of buildings, whether the division is horizontal, vertical or made in any other way, and other corporeal hereditaments; also a manor, an advowson, and a rent and other incorporeal hereditaments, and an easement, right, privilege, or benefit in, over, or derived from …; and in this definition 'mines and minerals' include any strata or seam of minerals or substances in or under any land, and powers of working and getting the same …; and 'hereditaments' mean real property which under an intestacy occurring before the commencement of this Act might have devolved on an heir;

(7) 'Mortgage' and 'mortgagee' include a charge or chargee by way of legal mortgage, and relate to every estate and interest regarded in equity as merely a security for money, and every person deriving title under the original mortgagee;

(8) …

(9) 'Personal representative' means the executor, original or by representation, or administrator for the time being of a deceased person;

(10) 'Possession' includes receipt of rents and profits or the right to receive the same, if any; 'income' includes rents and profits; and 'possessed' applies to receipt of income of and to any vested estate less than a life interest in possession or in expectancy in any land;

(11) 'Property' includes real and personal property, and any estate share and interest in any property, real or personal, and any debt, and any thing in action, and any other right or interest, whether in possession or not;

(12) 'Rights' include estates and interests;

(13) 'Securities' include stocks, funds, and shares; … and 'securities payable to bearer' include securities transferable by delivery or by delivery and endorsement;

(14) 'Stock' includes fully paid up shares, and so far as relates to vesting orders made by the court under this Act, includes any fund, annuity, or security transferable in books kept by any company or society, or by instrument of transfer either alone or accompanied by other formalities, and any share or interest therein;

(15) 'Tenant for life,' 'statutory owner,' 'settled land,' 'settlement,' 'trust instrument,' 'trustees of the settlement' … 'term of years absolute' and 'vesting instrument' have the same meanings as in the Settled Land Act 1925, and 'entailed interest' has the same meaning as in the Law of Property Act 1925;

(16) 'Transfer' in relation to stock or securities, includes the performance and execution of every deed, power of attorney, act, and thing on the part of the transferor to effect and complete the title in the transferee;

(17) 'Trust' does not include the duties incident to an estate conveyed by way of mortgage, but with this exception the expressions 'trust' and 'trustee' extend to implied and constructive trusts, and to cases where the trustee has a beneficial interest in the trust property, and to the duties incident to the office of a personal representative, and 'trustee' where the context admits, includes a personal representative, and 'new trustee' includes an additional trustee;

(18) 'Trust corporation' means the Public Trustee or a corporation either appointed by the court in any particular case to be a trustee, or entitled by rules made under subsection (3) of section four of the Public Trustee Act 1906, to act as custodian trustee;

(19) 'Trust for sale' in relation to land means an immediate … trust for sale, whether or not exercisable at the request or with the consent of any person …;

(20) 'United Kingdom' means Great Britain and Northern Ireland.

[(2) Any reference in this Act to paying money or securities into court shall be construed as referring to paying the money or transferring or depositing the securities into or in the Supreme Court or into or in any other court that has jurisdiction, and any reference in this Act to payment of money or securities into court shall be construed—

(a) with reference to an order of the High Court, as referring to payment of the money or transfer or deposit of the securities into or in the Supreme Court; and

(b) with reference to an order of any other court, as referring to payment of the money or transfer or deposit of the securities into or in that court.]

Amendment—Sub-s (1): words omitted from paras (6), (19) repealed by the Trusts of Land and Appointment of Trustees Act 1996, s 25(2), Sch 4, for savings in relation to entailed interests created before the commencement of that Act, and savings consequential upon the abolition of the doctrine of conversion, see s 25(4), (5) thereof; para (8) repealed, and words omitted from para (13) repealed, by the Administration of Justice Act 1965, s 17(1), Sch 1; words omitted from para (15) repealed by the Mental Health Act 1959 s 149(2), Sch 8, Part I.

Sub-s (2): inserted by the Administration of Justice Act 1965, s 17(1), Sch 1.

Modification—Definition 'Trust corporation' modified in relation to Charities, by the Charities Act 1993, s 35.

---

69 Application of Act

(1) This Act, except where otherwise expressly provided, applies to trusts including, so far as this Act applies thereto, executorships and administratorships constituted or created either before or after the commencement of this Act.

(2) The powers conferred by this Act on trustees are in addition to the powers

conferred by the instrument, if any, creating the trust, but those powers, unless otherwise stated, apply if and so far only as a contrary intention is not expressed in the instrument, if any, creating the trust, and have effect subject to the terms of that instrument.

(3) ...

Amendment—Sub-s (3): repealed by the Statute Law (Repeals) Act 1978, s 1, Sch 1, Part XVII.

70 Enactments repealed

... without prejudice to the provisions of section thirty-eight of the Interpretation Act 1889:

(a) Nothing in this repeal shall affect any vesting order or appointment made or other thing done under any enactment so repealed, and any order or appointment so made may be revoked or varied in like manner as if it has been made under this Act;
(b) References in any document to any enactment repealed by this Act shall be construed as references to this Act or to the corresponding enactment in this Act.

Amendment—Words omitted repealed by the Statute Law Revision Act 1950.

71 Short title, commencement, extent

(1) This Act may be cited as the Trustee Act, 1925.

(2) ...

(3) This Act, except where otherwise expressly provided, extends to England and Wales only.

(4) The provisions of this Act bind the Crown.

Amendment—Sub-s (2): repealed by the Statute Law Revision Act 1950.

Law of Property Act 1925

1925 Chapter 20

An Act to consolidate the enactments relating to conveyancing and the law of property in England and Wales. [9 April 1925]

Initial Commencement—Specified date: 1 January 1926.
Extent—This Act does not extend to Scotland: see s 209(3).

PART I
GENERAL PRINCIPLES AS TO LEGAL ESTATES, EQUITABLE INTERESTS AND POWERS

1 Legal estates and equitable interests

(1) The only estates in land which are capable of subsisting or of being conveyed or created at law are—

(a) An estate in fee simple absolute in possession;
(b) A term of years absolute.

(2) The only interests or charges in or over land which are capable of subsisting or of being conveyed or created at law are—

(a) An easement, right, or privilege in or over land for an interest equivalent to an estate in fee simple absolute in possession or a term of years absolute;
(b) A rentcharge in possession issuing out of or charged on land being either perpetual or for a term of years absolute;
(c) A charge by way of legal mortgage;
(d) … and any other similar charge on land which is not created by an instrument;
(e) Rights of entry exercisable over or in respect of a legal term of years absolute, or annexed, for any purpose, to a legal rentcharge.

(3) All other estates, interests, and charges in or over land take effect as equitable interests.

(4) The estates, interests, and charges which under this section are authorised to subsist or to be conveyed or created at law are (when subsisting or conveyed or created at law) in this Act referred to as 'legal estates', and have the same incidents as legal estates subsisting at the commencement of this Act; and the owner of a legal estate is referred to as 'an estate owner' and his legal estate is referred to as his estate.

(5) A legal estate may subsist concurrently with or subject to any other legal estate in the same land in like manner as it could have done before the commencement of this Act.

(6) A legal estate is not capable of subsisting or of being created in an undivided share in land or of being held by an infant.

(7) Every power of appointment over, or power to convey or charge land or any interest therein, whether created by a statute or other instrument or implied by law, and whether created before or after the commencement of this Act (not being a power vested in a legal mortgagee or an estate owner in right of his estate and exercisable by him or by another person in his name and on his behalf), operates only in equity.

(8) Estates, interests, and charges in or over land which are not legal estates are in this Act referred to as 'equitable interests', and powers which by this Act are to operate in equity only are in this Act referred to as 'equitable powers'.

(9) The provisions in any statute or other instrument requiring land to be conveyed to uses shall take effect as directions that the land shall (subject to creating or reserving thereout any legal estate authorised by this Act which may be required) be conveyed to a person of full age upon the requisite trusts.

(10) The repeal of the Statute of Uses (as amended) does not affect the operation thereof in regard to dealings taking effect before the commencement of this Act.

Amendment—Sub-s (2): words omitted repealed by the Finance Act 1963, s 73(8)(b), Sch 14, Part IV, and the Tithe Act 1936, s 48(3), Sch 9.

---

2 Conveyances overreaching certain equitable interests and powers

(1) A conveyance to a purchaser of a legal estate in land shall overreach any equitable interest or power affecting that estate, whether or not he has notice thereof, if—

(i) the conveyance is made under the powers conferred by the Settled Land Act 1925 or any additional powers conferred by a settlement, and the equitable interest or power is capable of being overreached thereby, and the statutory requirements respecting the payment of capital money arising under the settlement are complied with;
(ii) the conveyance is made by [trustees of land] and the equitable interest or power is at the date of the conveyance capable of being overreached by such trustees under the provisions of sub-section (2) of this section or independently of that sub-section, and [the requirements of section 27 of this Act respecting the payment of capital money arising on such a conveyance] are complied with;
(iii) the conveyance is made by a mortgagee or personal representative in the exercise of his paramount powers, and the equitable interest or power is capable of being overreached by such conveyance, and any capital money arising from the transaction is paid to the mortgagee or personal representative;
(iv) the conveyance is made under an order of the court and the equitable interest or power is bound by such order, and any capital money arising from the transaction is paid into, or in accordance with the order of, the court.

[(1A) An equitable interest in land subject to a trust of land which remains in, or is to revert to, the settler shall (subject to any contrary intention) be overreached by the conveyance if it would be so overreached were it an interest under the trust.]

(2) [Where the legal estate affected is subject to [a trust of land], then if at the date of a conveyance made after the commencement of this Act [by the trustees], the trustees (whether original or substituted) are either—]

(a) two or more individuals approved or appointed by the court or the successors in office of the individuals so approved or appointed; or
(b) a trust corporation,

[any equitable interest or power having priority [to the trust]] shall, notwithstanding any stipulation to the contrary, be overreached by the conveyance, and shall, according to its priority, take effect as if created or arising by means of a primary trust affecting the proceeds of sale and the income of the land until sale.

(3) The following equitable interests and powers are excepted from the operation of subsection (2) of this section, namely—

(i) Any equitable interest protected by a deposit of documents relating to the legal estate affected;
(ii) The benefit of any covenant or agreement restrictive of the user of land;
(iii) Any easement, liberty, or privilege over or affecting land and being merely an equitable interest (in this Act referred to as an 'equitable easement');
(iv) The benefit of any contract (in this Act referred to as an 'estate contract') to convey or create a legal estate, including a contract conferring either expressly or by statutory implication a valid option to purchase, a right of pre-emption, or any other like right;
(v) Any equitable interest protected by registration under the Land Charges Act 1925 other than—

    (a) an annuity within the meaning of Part II of that Act;
    (b) a limited owner's charge or a general equitable charge within the meaning of that Act.

(4) Subject to the protection afforded by this section to the purchaser of a legal estate, nothing contained in this section shall deprive a person entitled to an equitable charge of any of his rights or remedies for enforcing the same.

(5) So far as regards the following interests, created before the commencement of this Act (which accordingly are not within the provisions of the Land Charges Act 1925), namely—

(a) the benefit of any covenant or agreement restrictive of the user of the land;
(b) any equitable easement;
(c) the interest under a puisne mortgage within the meaning of the Land Charges Act 1925 unless and until acquired under a transfer made after the commencement of this Act;
(d) the benefit of an estate contract, unless and until the same is acquired under a conveyance made after the commencement of this Act;

a purchaser of a legal estate shall only take subject thereto if he has notice thereof, and the same are not overreached under the provisions contained or in the manner referred to in this section.

Amendment—Sub-s (1): words in square brackets substituted by the Trusts of Land and Appointment of Trustees Act 1996, s 25(1), Sch 3, para 4(2)(a); for savings in relation to entailed interests created before the commencement of that Act, and savings consequential upon the abolition of the doctrine of conversion, see s 25(4), (5) thereof.

Sub-s (1A): inserted by the Trusts of Land and Appointment of Trustees Act 1996, s 25(1), Sch 3, para 4(2)(b); for savings in relation to entailed interests created before the commencement of that Act, and savings consequential upon the abolition of the doctrine of conversion, see s 25(4), (5) thereof.

Sub-s (2): first and fourth words in square brackets substituted by the Law of Property (Amendment) Act 1926, s 7, Schedule; other words in square brackets substituted by the Trusts of Land and Appointment of Trustees Act 1996, s 25(1), Sch 3, para 4(2)(c), for savings in relation to entailed interests created before the commencement of that Act, and savings consequential upon the abolition of the doctrine of conversion, see s 25(4), (5) thereof.

3 Manner of giving effect to equitable interests and powers

(1) All equitable interests and powers in or over land shall be enforceable against the estate owner of the legal estate affected in manner following (that is to say):—

(a) Where the legal estate affected is settled land, the tenant for life or statutory owner shall be bound to give effect to the equitable interests and powers in manner provided by the Settled Land Act 1925;

(b) ...

[In any other case], the estate owner shall be bound to give effect to the equitable interests and powers affecting his estate of which he has notice according to their respective priorities. This provision does not affect the priority or powers of a legal mortgagee, or the powers of personal representatives for purposes of administration.

(2) ...

(3) Where, by reason ... of an equitable right of entry taking effect, or for any other reason, a person becomes entitled to require a legal estate to be vested in him, then and in any such case the estate owner whose estate is affected shall be bound to convey or create such legal estate as the case may require.

(4) If any question arises whether any and what legal estate ought to be transferred or created as aforesaid, any person interested may apply to the court for directions in the manner provided by this Act.

(5) If the estate owners refuse or neglect for one month after demand to transfer or create any such legal estate, or if by reason of their being out of the United Kingdom or being unable to be found, or by reason of the dissolution of a corporation, or for any other reason, the court is satisfied that the transaction cannot otherwise be effected, or cannot be effected without undue delay or expense, the court may, on the application of any person interested, make a vesting order transferring or creating a legal estate in the manner provided by this Act.

(6) This section does not affect a purchaser of a legal estate taking free from an equitable interest or power.

[(7) The county court has jurisdiction under this section where the land which is to be dealt with in the court does not exceed [£30,000] in capital value ... .]

Amendment—Sub-s (1): para (b) repealed, and in para (c) words in square brackets substituted, by the Trusts of Land and Appointment of Trustees Act 1996, s 25(1), (2), Sch 3, para 4(3), Sch 4; for savings in relation to entailed interests created before the commencement of that Act, and savings consequential upon the abolition of the doctrine of conversion, see s 25(4), (5) thereof.

Sub-s (2): repealed by the Trusts of Land and Appointment of Trustees Act 1996, s 25(2), Sch 4; for savings in relation to entailed interests created before the commencement of that Act, and savings consequential upon the abolition of the doctrine of conversion, see s 25(4), (5) thereof.

Sub-s (3): words omitted repealed by the Reverter of Sites Act 1987, s 8(2), (3), Schedule.

Sub-s (5): words omitted repealed by the Trusts of Land and Appointment of Trustees Act 1996, s 25(2), Sch 4; for savings in relation to entailed interests created before the commencement of that Act, and savings consequential upon the abolition of the doctrine of conversion, see s 25(4), (5) thereof.

Sub-s (7): inserted by the County Courts Act 1984, s 148(1), Sch 2, para 2; sum in square brackets substituted and words omitted repealed by SI 1991/724, art 2(3)(a), (8), Schedule, Part I.

---

4 Creation and disposition of equitable interests

(1) Interests in land validly created or arising after the commencement of this Act, which are not capable of subsisting as legal estates, shall take effect as equitable interests, and, save as otherwise expressly provided by statute, interests in land which under the Statute of Uses or otherwise could before the commencement of this Act have been created as legal interests, shall be capable of being created as equitable interests:

Provided that, after the commencement of this Act (and save as hereinafter expressly enacted), an equitable interest in land shall only be capable of being validly created in any case in which an equivalent equitable interest in property real or personal could have been validly created before such commencement.

(2) All rights and interests in land may be disposed of, including—

(a) a contingent, executory or future equitable interest in any land, or a possibility coupled with an interest in any land, whether or not the object of the gift or limitation of such interest or possibility be ascertained;
(b) a right of entry, into or upon land whether immediate or future, and whether vested or contingent.

(3) All rights of entry affecting a legal estate which are exercisable on condition broken or for any other reason may, after the commencement of this Act, be made exercisable by any person and the persons deriving title under him, but, in regard to an estate in fee simple (not being a rentcharge held for a legal estate) only within the period authorised by the rule relating to perpetuities.

Infants and Lunatics

20 Infants not to be appointed trustees

The appointment of an infant to be a trustee in relation to any settlement or trust shall be void, but without prejudice to the power to appoint a new trustee to fill the vacancy.

[Trusts of land]

Amendment—Substituted by the Trusts of Land and Appointment of Trustees Act 1996, s 25(1), Sch 3, para 4(7).

[24 Appointment of trustees of land]

[(1) The persons having power to appoint new trustees of land shall be bound to appoint the same persons (if any) who are for the time being trustees of any trust of the proceeds of sale of the land.

(2) A purchaser shall not be concerned to see that subsection (1) of this section has been complied with.

(3) This section applies whether the trust of land and the trust of proceeds of sale are created, or arise, before or after the commencement of this Act.]

Amendment—Substituted by the Trusts of Land and Appointment of Trustees Act 1996, s 25(1), Sch 3, para 4(7); for savings in relation to entailed interests created before the commencement of that Act, and savings consequential upon the abolition of the doctrine of conversion, see s 25(4), (5) thereof.

---

27 Purchaser not to be concerned with the trusts of the proceeds of sale which are to be paid to two or more trustees or to a trust corporation

(1) ...

[(1) A purchaser of a legal estate from trustees of land shall not be concerned with the trusts affecting the land, the net income of the land or the proceeds of sale of the land whether or not those trusts are declared by the same instrument as that by which the trust of land is created.]

[(2) Notwithstanding anything to the contrary in the instrument (if any) creating a [trust] of land or in [any trust affecting the net proceeds of sale of the land if it is sold], the proceeds of sale or other capital money shall not be paid to or applied by the direction of fewer than two persons as [trustees], except where the trustee is a trust corporation, but this subsection does not affect the right of a sole personal representative as such to give valid receipts for, or direct the application of, proceeds of sale or other capital money, nor, except where capital money arises on the transaction, render it necessary to have more than one trustee.]

Amendment—Sub-s (1): substituted by the Trusts of Land and Appointment of Trustees Act 1996, s 25(1), Sch 3, para 4(8)(a); for savings in relation to entailed interests created before the commencement of that Act, and savings consequential upon the abolition of the doctrine of conversion, see s 25(4), (5) thereof.

Sub-s (2): substituted by the Law of Property (Amendment) Act 1926, s 7, Schedule; words in square brackets substituted by the Trusts of Land and Appointment of Trustees Act 1996, s 25(1), Sch 3, para 4(8)(b), for savings in relation to entailed interests created before the commencement of that Act, and savings consequential upon the abolition of the doctrine of conversion, see s 25(4), (5) thereof.

---

31 [Trust] of mortgaged property where right of redemption is barred

(1) Where any property, vested in trustees by way of security, becomes, by virtue of the statutes of limitation, or of an order for foreclosure or otherwise, discharged from the right of redemption, it shall be held by them [in trust—

(a) to apply the income from the property in the same manner as interest paid on the mortgage debt would have been applicable; and

(b) if the property is sold, to apply the net proceeds of sale, after payment of costs and expenses, in the same manner as repayment of the mortgage debt would have been applicable.]

[(2) Subsection (1) of this section] operates without prejudice to any rule of law relating to the apportionment of capital and income between tenant for life and remainderman.

(3) …

[(4) Where—

(a) the mortgage money is capital money for the purposes of the Settled Land Act 1925;
(b) land other than any forming the whole or part of the property mentioned in subsection (1) of this section is, or is deemed to be, subject to the settlement; and
(c) the tenant for life or statutory owner requires the trustees to execute with respect to land forming the whole or part of that property a vesting deed such as would have been required in relation to the land if it had been acquired on a purchase with capital money,

the trustees shall execute such a vesting deed.]

(5) This section applies whether the right of redemption was discharged before or after the first day of January, nineteen hundred and twelve, but has effect without prejudice to any dealings or arrangements made before that date.

Amendment—Section heading: words in square brackets substituted by the Trusts of Land and Appointment of Trustees Act 1996, s 5, Sch 2, para 1(6); for savings in relation to entailed interests created before the commencement of that Act, and savings consequential upon the abolition of the doctrine of conversion, see s 25(4), (5) thereof.

Sub-ss (1), (2): words in square brackets substituted by the Trusts of Land and Appointment of Trustees Act 1996, s 5, Sch 2, para 1(2), (3); for savings in relation to entailed interests created before the commencement of that Act, and savings consequential upon the abolition of the doctrine of conversion, see s 25(4), (5) thereof.

Sub-s (3): repealed by the Trusts of Land and Appointment of Trustees Act 1996, ss 5, 25(2), Sch 2, para 1(4); for savings in relation to entailed interests created before the commencement of that Act, and savings consequential upon the abolition of the doctrine of conversion, see s 25(4), (5) thereof.

Sub-s (4): substituted by the Trusts of Land and Appointment of Trustees Act 1996, s 5, Sch 2, para 1(5); for savings in relation to entailed interests created before the commencement of that Act, and savings consequential upon the abolition of the doctrine of conversion, see s 25(4), (5) thereof.

---

33 Application of Part I to personal representatives

The provisions of this Part of this Act relating to [trustees of land] apply to personal representatives holding [land in trust], but without prejudice to their rights and powers for purposes of administration.

Amendment—Words in square brackets substituted by the Trusts of Land and Appointment of Trustees Act 1996, s 25(1), Sch 3, para 4(9); for savings in relation to entailed interests created before the commencement of that Act, and savings consequential upon the abolition of the doctrine of conversion, see s 25(4), (5) thereof.

Undivided Shares and Joint Ownership

34 Effect of future dispositions to tenants in common

(1) An undivided share in land shall not be capable of being created except as provided by the Settled Land Act 1925 or as hereinafter mentioned.

(2) Where, after the commencement of this Act, land is expressed to be conveyed to any persons in undivided shares and those persons are of full age, the conveyance shall (notwithstanding anything to the contrary in this Act) operate as if the land had been expressed to be conveyed to the grantees, or, if there are more than four grantees, to the four first named in the conveyance, as joint tenants [in trust for the persons interested in the land]:

Provided that, where the conveyance is made by way of mortgage the land shall vest in the grantees or such four of them as aforesaid for a term of years absolute (as provided by this Act) as joint tenants subject to cesser on redemption in like manner as if the mortgage money had belonged to them on a joint account, but without prejudice to the beneficial interests in the mortgage money and interest.

(3) A devise bequest or testamentary appointment, coming into operation after the commencement of this Act, of land to two or more persons in undivided shares shall operate as a devise bequest or appointment of the land to the personal representatives of the testator, and (but without prejudice to the rights and powers of the personal representatives for purposes of administration) [in trust for the persons interested in the land].

[(3A) In subsections (2) and (3) of this section references to the persons interested in the land include persons interested as trustees or personal representatives (as well as persons beneficially interested).]

(4) ...

Amendment—Sub-s (2): words in square brackets substituted by the Trusts of Land and Appointment of Trustees Act 1996, s 5, Sch 2, para 3(2); for savings in relation to entailed interests created before the commencement of that Act, and savings consequential upon the abolition of the doctrine of conversion, see s 25(4), (5) thereof.

Sub-s (3): words omitted repealed and words in square brackets substituted by the Trusts of Land and Appointment of Trustees Act 1996, ss 5, 25(2), Sch 2, para 3(3), Sch 4; for savings in relation to entailed interests created before the commencement of that Act, and savings consequential upon the abolition of the doctrine of conversion, see s 25(4), (5) thereof.

Sub-s (3A): inserted by the Trusts of Land and Appointment of Trustees Act 1996, s 5, Sch 2, para 3(4); for savings in relation to entailed interests created before the commencement of that Act, and savings consequential upon the abolition of the doctrine of conversion, see s 25(4), (5) thereof.

Sub-s (4): repealed by the Trusts of Land and Appointment of Trustees Act 1996, ss 5, 25(2), Sch 2, para 3(5), Sch 4; for savings in relation to entailed interests created before the commencement of that Act, and savings consequential upon the abolition of the doctrine of conversion, see s 25(4), (5) thereof.

---

36 Joint tenancies

(1) Where a legal estate (not being settled land) is beneficially limited to or held in

trust for any persons as joint tenants, the same shall be held [in trust], in like manner as if the persons beneficially entitled were tenants in common, but not so as to sever their joint tenancy in equity.

(2) No severance of a joint tenancy of a legal estate, so as to create a tenancy in common in land, shall be permissible, whether by operation of law or otherwise, but this subsection does not affect the right of a joint tenant to release his interest to the other joint tenants, or the right to sever a joint tenancy in an equitable interest whether or not the legal estate is vested in the joint tenants:

Provided that, where a legal estate (not being settled land) is vested in joint tenants beneficially, and any tenant desires to sever the joint tenancy in equity, he shall give to the other joint tenants a notice in writing of such desire or do such other acts or things as would, in the case of personal estate, have been effectual to sever the tenancy in equity, and thereupon [the land shall be held in trust on terms] which would have been requisite for giving effect to the beneficial interests if there had been an actual severance.

[Nothing in this Act affects the right of a survivor of joint tenants, who is solely and beneficially interested, to deal with his legal estate as if it were not held [in trust].]

(3) Without prejudice to the right of a joint tenant to release his interest to the other joint tenants no severance of a mortgage term or trust estate, so as to create a tenancy in common, shall be permissible.

Amendment—Sub-s (1): words in square brackets substituted by the Trusts of Land and Appointment of Trustees Act 1996, s 5, Sch 2, para 4(2); for savings in relation to entailed interests created before the commencement of that Act, and savings consequential upon the abolition of the doctrine of conversion, see s 25(4), (5) thereof.

Sub-s (2): first words in square brackets substituted by the Trusts of Land and Appointment of Trustees Act 1996, s 5, Sch 2, para 4(3), for savings in relation to entailed interests created before the commencement of that Act, and savings consequential upon the abolition of the doctrine of conversion, see s 25(4), (5) thereof; second words in square brackets inserted by the Law of Property (Amendment) Act 1926, s 7, Schedule, words in square brackets therein substituted by the Trusts of Land and Appointment of Trustees Act 1996, s 5, Sch 2, para 4(3), for savings in relation to entailed interests created before the commencement of that Act, and savings consequential upon the abolition of the doctrine of conversion, see s 25(4), (5) thereof.

PART II
CONTRACTS, CONVEYANCES AND OTHER INSTRUMENTS

41 Stipulations not of the essence of a contract

Stipulations in a contract, as to time or otherwise, which according to rules of equity are not deemed to be or to have become of the essence of the contract, are also construed and have effect at law in accordance with the same rules.

52 Conveyances to be by deed

(1) All conveyances of land or of any interest therein are void for the purpose of conveying or creating a legal estate unless made by deed.

(2) This section does not apply to—

(a) assents by a personal representative;
(b) disclaimers made in accordance with [sections 178 to 180 or sections 315 to 319 of the Insolvency Act 1986] or not required to be evidenced in writing;
(c) surrenders by operation of law, including surrenders which may, by law, be effected without writing;
(d) leases or tenancies or other assurances not required by law to be made in writing;
(e) receipts [other than those falling within section 115 below];
(f) vesting orders of the court or other competent authority;
(g) conveyances taking effect by operation of law.

Amendment—Sub-s (2): words in square brackets in para (b) substituted by the Insolvency Act 1986, s 439(2), Sch 14; words in square brackets in para (e) substituted by the Law of Property (Miscellaneous Provisions) Act 1989, s 1, Sch 1, para 2.

---

53 Instruments required to be in writing

(1) Subject to the provisions hereinafter contained with respect to the creation of interests in land by parol—

(a) no interest in land can be created or disposed of except by writing signed by the person creating or conveying the same, or by his agent thereunto lawfully authorised in writing, or by will, or by operation of law;
(b) a declaration of trust respecting any land or any interest therein must be manifested and proved by some writing signed by some person who is able to declare such trust or by his will;
(c) a disposition of an equitable interest or trust subsisting at the time of the disposition, must be in writing signed by the person disposing of the same, or by his agent thereunto lawfully authorised in writing or by will.

(2) This section does not affect the creation or operation of resulting, implied or constructive trusts.

See Further—Sub-s (1)(c) above shall not apply to any transfer of title to uncertificated units of a security by means of a relevant system and any disposition or assignment of an interest in uncertificated units of a security title to which is held by a relevant nominee: see the Uncertificated Securities Regulations 2001, SI 2001/3755, reg 38(5), (6).

---

56 Persons taking who are not parties and as to indentures

(1) A person may take an immediate or other interest in land or other property, or the benefit of any condition, right of entry, covenant or agreement over or respecting land or other property, although he may not be named as a party to the conveyance or other instrument.

(2) A deed between parties, to effect its objects, has the effect of an indenture though not indented or expressed to be an indenture.

PART IV
EQUITABLE INTERESTS AND THINGS IN ACTION

136 Legal assignments of things in action

(1) Any absolute assignment by writing under the hand of the assignor (not purporting to be by way of charge only) of any debt or other legal thing in action, of which express notice in writing has been given to the debtor, trustee or other person from whom the assignor would have been entitled to claim such debt or thing in action, is effectual in law (subject to equities having priority over the right of the assignee) to pass and transfer from the date of such notice—

(a) the legal right to such debt or thing in action;
(b) all legal and other remedies for the same; and
(c) the power to give a good discharge for the same without the concurrence of the assignor:

Provided that, if the debtor, trustee or other person liable in respect of such debt or thing in action has notice—

(a) that the assignment is disputed by the assignor or any person claiming under him; or
(b) of any other opposing or conflicting claims to such debt or thing in action;

he may, if he thinks fit, either call upon the persons making claim thereto to interplead concerning the same, or pay the debt or other thing in action into court under the provisions of the Trustee Act 1925.

(2) This section does not affect the provisions of the Policies of Assurance Act 1867.

[(3) The county court has jurisdiction (including power to receive payment of money or securities into court) under the proviso to subsection (1) of this section where the amount or value of the debt or thing in action does not exceed [£30,000].]

Amendment—Sub-s (3): inserted by the County Courts Act 1984, s 148(1), Sch 2, para 4; sum in square brackets substituted by SI 1991/724, art 2(5), (8), Schedule, Part I.
See Further—This section shall not apply to any transfer of title to uncertificated units of a security by means of a relevant system and any disposition or assignment of an interest in uncertificated units of a security title to which is held by a relevant nominee: see the Uncertificated Securities Regulations 2001, SI 2001/3755, reg 38(5), (6).

---

137 Dealings with life interests, reversions and other equitable interests

(1) The law applicable to dealings with equitable things in action which regulates the priority of competing interests therein, shall, as respects dealings with equitable interests in land, capital money, and securities representing capital money effected after the commencement of this Act, apply to and regulate the priority of competing interests therein.

This subsection applies whether or not the money or securities are in court.

(2)

(i) In the case of a dealing with an equitable interest in settled land, capital money or securities representing capital money, the persons to be served with notice of the dealing shall be the trustees of the settlement; and where the equitable interest is created by a derivative or subsidiary settlement, the persons to be served with notice shall be the trustees of that settlement.

(ii) In the case of a dealing with an equitable interest in [land subject to a trust of land, or the proceeds of the sale of such land, the persons to be served with notice shall be the trustees.]

(iii) In any other case the person to be served with notice of a dealing with an equitable interest in land shall be the estate owner of the land affected.

The persons on whom notice is served pursuant to this subsection shall be affected thereby in the same manner as if they had been trustees of personal property out of which the equitable interest was created or arose.

This subsection does not apply where the money or securities are in court.

(3) A notice, otherwise than in writing, given to, or received by, a trustee after the commencement of this Act as respects any dealing with an equitable interest in real or personal property, shall not affect the priority of competing claims of purchasers in that equitable interest.

(4) Where, as respects any dealing with an equitable interest in real or personal property—

(a) the trustees are not persons to whom a valid notice of the dealing can be given; or

(b) there are no trustees to whom a notice can be given; or

(c) for any other reason a valid notice cannot be served, or cannot be served without unreasonable cost or delay;

a purchaser may at his own cost require that—

(i) a memorandum of the dealing be endorsed, written on or permanently annexed to the instrument creating the trust;

(ii) the instrument be produced to him by the person having the possession or custody thereof to prove that a sufficient memorandum has been placed thereon or annexed thereto.

Such memorandum shall, as respects priorities, operate in like manner as if notice in writing of the dealing had been given to trustees duly qualified to receive the notice at the time when the memorandum is placed on or annexed to the instrument creating the trust.

(5) Where the property affected is settled land, the memorandum shall be placed on or annexed to the trust instrument and not the vesting instrument.

Where the property affected is land [subject to a trust of land], the memorandum shall be placed on or annexed to the instrument whereby the equitable interest is created.

(6) Where the trust is created by statute or by operation of law, or in any other case where there is no instrument whereby the trusts are declared, the instrument under

which the equitable interest is acquired or which is evidence of the devolution thereof shall, for the purposes of this section, be deemed the instrument creating the trust.

In particular, where the trust arises by reason of an intestacy, the letters of administration or probate in force when the dealing was effected shall be deemed such instrument.

(7) Nothing in this section affects any priority acquired before the commencement of this Act.

(8) Where a notice in writing of a dealing with an equitable interest in real or personal property has been served on a trustee under this section, the trustees from time to time of the property affected shall be entitled to the custody of the notice, and the notice shall be delivered to them by any person who for the time being may have the custody thereof; and subject to the payment of costs, any person interested in the equitable interest may require production of the notice.

(9) The liability of the estate owner of the legal estate affected to produce documents and furnish information to persons entitled to equitable interests therein shall correspond to the liability of a trustee for sale to produce documents and furnish information to persons entitled to equitable interests in the proceeds of sale of the land.

(10) This section does not apply until a trust has been created, and in this section 'dealing' includes a disposition by operation of law.

Amendment—Sub-ss (2), (5): words in square brackets substituted by the Trusts of Land and Appointment of Trustees Act 1996, s 25(1), Sch 3, para 4(15); for savings in relation to entailed interests created before the commencement of that Act, and savings consequential upon the abolition of the doctrine of conversion, see s 25(4), (5) thereof.

PART VI
POWERS

159 Execution of powers not testamentary

(1) A deed executed in the presence of and attested by two or more witnesses (in the manner in which deeds are ordinarily executed and attested) is so far as respects the execution and attestation thereof, a valid execution of a power of appointment by deed or by any instrument in writing, not testamentary, notwithstanding that it is expressly required that a deed or instrument in writing, made in exercise of the power, is to be executed or attested with some additional or other form of execution or attestation or solemnity.

(2) This section does not operate to defeat any direction in the instrument creating the power that—

(a) the consent of any particular person is to be necessary to a valid execution;
(b) in order to give validity to any appointment, any act is to be performed having no relation to the mode of executing and attesting the instrument.

(3) This section does not prevent the donee of a power from executing it in accordance with the power by writing, or otherwise than by an instrument executed and attested as a deed; and where a power is so executed this section does not apply.

(4) This section applies to appointments by deed made after the thirteenth day of August, eighteen hundred and fifty-nine.

PART VII
PERPETUITIES AND ACCUMULATIONS

Accumulations

164 General restrictions on accumulation of income

(1) No person may by any instrument or otherwise settle or dispose of any property in such manner that the income thereof shall, save as hereinafter mentioned, be wholly or partially accumulated for any longer period than one of the following, namely:—

(a) the life of the grantor or settlor; or
(b) a term of twenty-one years from the death of the grantor, settlor or testator; or
(c) the duration of the minority or respective minorities of any person or persons living or en ventre sa mere at the death of the grantor, settlor or testator; or
(d) the duration of the minority or respective minorities only of any person or persons who under the limitations of the instrument directing the accumulations would, for the time being, if of full age, be entitled to the income directed to be accumulated.

In every case where any accumulation is directed otherwise than as aforesaid, the direction shall (save as hereinafter mentioned) be void; and the income of the property directed to be accumulated shall, so long as the same is directed to be accumulated contrary to this section, go to and be received by the person or persons who would have been entitled thereto if such accumulation had not been directed.

(2) This section does not extend to any provision—

(i) for payment of the debts of any grantor, settlor, testator or other person;
(ii) for raising portions for—

  (a) any child, children or remoter issue of any grantor, settlor or testator; or
  (b) any child, children or remoter issue of a person taking any interest under any settlement or other disposition directing the accumulations or to whom any interest is thereby limited;

(iii) respecting the accumulation of the produce of timber or wood;

and accordingly such provisions may be made as if no statutory restrictions on accumulation of income had been imposed.

(3) The restrictions imposed by this section apply to instruments made on or after the twenty-eighth day of July, eighteen hundred, but in the case of wills only where the testator was living and of testamentary capacity after the end of one year from that date.

165 Qualification of restrictions on accumulation

Where accumulations of surplus income are made during a minority under any statutory power or under the general law, the period for which such accumulations are made is not (whether the trust was created or the accumulations were made before or after the commencement of this Act) to be taken into account in determining the periods for which accumulations are permitted to be made by the last preceding section, and accordingly an express trust for accumulation for any other permitted period shall not be deemed to have been invalidated or become invalid, by reason of accumulations also having been made as aforesaid during such minority.

166 Restriction on accumulation for the purchase of land

(1) No person may settle or dispose of any property in such manner that the income thereof shall be wholly or partially accumulated for the purchase of land only, for any longer period than the duration of the minority or respective minorities of any person or persons who, under the limitations of the instrument directing the accumulation, would for the time being, if of full age, be entitled to the income so directed to be accumulated.

(2) This section does not, nor do the enactments which it replaces, apply to accumulations to be held as capital money for the purposes of the Settled Land Act 1925 or the enactments replaced by that Act, whether or not the accumulations are primarily liable to be laid out in the purchase of land.

(3) This section applies to settlements and dispositions made after the twenty-seventh day of June eighteen hundred and ninety-two.

PART X
WILLS

175 Contingent and future testamentary gifts to carry the intermediate income

(1) A contingent or future specific devise or bequest of property, whether real or personal, and a contingent residuary devise of freehold land, and a specific or residuary devise of freehold land to trustees upon trust for persons whose interests are contingent or executory shall, subject to the statutory provisions relating to accumulations, carry the intermediate income of that property from the death of the testator, except so far as such income, or any part thereof, may be otherwise expressly disposed of.

(2) This section applies only to wills coming into operation after the commencement of this Act.

Administration of Estates Act 1925

1925 Chapter 23

An Act to consolidate enactments relating to the administration of the estates of deceased persons. [9 April 1925]

Initial Commencement—Specified date: 1 January 1926.
Extent—This Act does not extend to Scotland: see s 58(3).

PART I
DEVOLUTION OF REAL ESTATE

1 Devolution of real estate on personal representative

(1) Real estate to which a deceased person was entitled for an interest not ceasing on his death shall on his death, and notwithstanding any testamentary disposition thereof, devolve from time to time on the personal representative of the deceased, in like manner as before the commencement of this Act chattels real devolved on the personal representative from time to time of a deceased person.

(2) The personal representatives for the time being of a deceased person are deemed in law his heirs and assigns within the meaning of all trusts and powers.

(3) The personal representatives shall be the representative of the deceased in regard to his real estate to which he was entitled for an interest not ceasing on his death as well as in regard to his personal estate.

2 Application to real estate of law affecting chattels real

(1) Subject to the provisions of this Act, all enactments and rules of law, and all jurisdiction of any court with respect to the appointment of administrators or to probate or letters of administration, or to dealings before probate in the case of chattels real, and with respect to costs and other matters in the administration of personal estate, in force before the commencement of this Act, and all powers, duties, rights, equities, obligations, and liabilities of a personal representative in force at the commencement of this Act with respect to chattels real, shall apply and attach to the personal representative and shall have effect with respect to real estate vested in him, and in particular all such powers of disposition and dealing as were before the commencement of this Act exercisable as respects chattels real by the survivor or survivors of two or more personal representatives, as well as by a single personal representative, or by all the personal representatives together, shall be exercisable by the personal representatives or representative of the deceased with respect to his real estate.

(2) Where as respects real estate there are two or more personal representatives, a conveyance of real estate devolving under this Part of this Act [or a contract for such a conveyance] shall not ... be made without the concurrence therein of all such representatives or an order of the court, but where probate is granted to one or some of two or more persons named as executors, whether or not power is reserved to the other or others to prove, any conveyance of the real estate [or contract for such a

conveyance] may be made by the proving executor or executors for the time being, without an order of the court, and shall be as effectual as if all the persons named as executors had concurred therein.

(3) Without prejudice to the rights and powers of a personal representative, the appointment of a personal representative in regard to real estate shall not, save as hereinafter provided, affect—

(a) any rule as to marshalling or as to administration of assets;
(b) the beneficial interest in real estate under any testamentary disposition;
(c) any mode of dealing with any beneficial interest in real estate, or the proceeds of sale thereof;
(d) the right of any person claiming to be interested in the real estate to take proceedings for the protection or recovery thereof against any person other than the personal representative.

Amendment—Sub-s (2): words in square brackets inserted, and words omitted repealed, by the Law of Property (Miscellaneous Provisions) Act 1994, ss 16(1), 21(2), Sch 2.
See Further—See further, in relation to the application of this section to interests under a trust for sale of land: the Law of Property (Miscellaneous Provisions) Act 1994, s 16(2).

---

3 Interpretation of Part I

(1) In this Part of this Act 'real estate' includes—

(i) Chattels real, and land in possession, remainder, or reversion, and every interest in or over land to which a deceased person was entitled at the time of his death; and
(ii) Real estate held on trust (including settled land) or by way of mortgage or security, but not ... money secured or charged on land.

(2) A testator shall be deemed to have been entitled at his death to any interest in real estate passing under any gift contained in his will which operates as an appointment under a general power to appoint by will, or operates under the testamentary power conferred by statute to dispose of an entailed interest.

(3) An entailed interest of a deceased person shall (unless disposed of under the testamentary power conferred by statute) be deemed an interest ceasing on his death, but any further or other interest of the deceased in the same property in remainder or reversion which is capable of being disposed of by his will shall not be deemed to be an interest so ceasing.

(4) The interest of a deceased person under a joint tenancy where another tenant survives the deceased is an interest ceasing on his death.

(5) On the death of a corporator sole his interest in the corporation's real and personal estate shall be deemed to be an interest ceasing on his death and shall devolve to his successor.

This subsection applies on the demise of the Crown as respects all property, real and personal, vested in the Crown as a corporation sole.

Amendment—Sub-s (1): words omitted from para (ii) repealed by the Trusts of Land and Appointment of Trustees Act 1996, s 25(2), Sch 4; for savings in relation to entailed interests created before the commencement of that Act, and savings consequential upon the abolition of the doctrine of conversion, see s 25(4), (5) thereof.

PART II
EXECUTORS AND ADMINISTRATORS

General Provisions

5 Cesser of right of executor to prove

Where a person appointed executor by a will—

(i) survives the testator but dies without having taken out probate of the will; or
(ii) is cited to take out probate of the will and does not appear to the citation; or
(iii) renounces probate of the will;

his rights in respect of the executorship shall wholly cease, and the representation to the testator and the administration of his real and personal estate shall devolve and be committed in like manner as if that person had not been appointed executor.

6 Withdrawal of renunciation

(1) Where an executor who has renounced probate has been permitted, whether before or after the commencement of this Act, to withdraw the renunciation and prove the will, the probate shall take effect and be deemed always to have taken effect without prejudice to the previous acts and dealings of and notices to any other personal representative who has previously proved the will or taken out letters of administration, and a memorandum of the subsequent probate shall be endorsed on the original probate or letters of administration.

(2) This section applies whether the testator died before or after the commencement of this Act.

7 Executor of executor represents original testator

(1) An executor of a sole or last surviving executor of a testator is the executor of that testator.

This provision shall not apply to an executor who does not prove the will of his testator, and, in the case of an executor who on his death leaves surviving him some other executor of his testator who afterwards proves the will of that testator, it shall cease to apply on such probate being granted.

(2) So long as the chain of such representation is unbroken, the last executor in the chain is the executor of every preceding testator.

(3) The chain of such representation is broken by—

(a) an intestacy; or

(b) the failure of a testator to appoint an executor; or
(c) the failure to obtain probate of a will;

but is not broken by a temporary grant of administration if probate is subsequently granted.

(4) Every person in the chain of representation to a testator—

(a) has the same rights in respect of the real and personal estate of that testator as the original executor would have had if living; and
(b) is, to the extent to which the estate whether real or personal of that testator has come to his hands, answerable as if he were an original executor.

8 Right of proving executors to exercise powers

(1) Where probate is granted to one or some of two or more persons named as executors, whether or not power is reserved to the others or other to prove, all the powers which are by law conferred on the personal representative may be exercised by the proving executor or executors for the time being and shall be as effectual as if all the persons named as executors had concurred therein.

(2) This section applies whether the testator died before or after the commencement of this Act.

[9 Vesting of estate in Public Trustee where intestacy or lack of executors]

[(1) Where a person dies intestate, his real and personal estate shall vest in the Public Trustee until the grant of administration.

(2) Where a testator dies and—

(a) at the time of his death there is no executor with power to obtain probate of the will, or
(b) at any time before probate of the will is granted there ceases to be any executor with power to obtain probate,

the real and personal estate of which he disposes by the will shall vest in the Public Trustee until the grant of representation.

(3) The vesting of real or personal estate in the Public Trustee by virtue of this section does not confer on him any beneficial interest in, or impose on him any duty, obligation or liability in respect of, the property.]

Amendment—Substituted by the Law of Property (Miscellaneous Provisions) Act 1994, s 14(1).
See Further—See further, the Law of Property (Miscellaneous Provisions) Act 1994, s 9(2)–(6), in relation to the vesting of property of a person dying before the commencement of that section.

---

15 Executor not to act while administration is in force

Where administration has been granted in respect of any real or personal estate of a deceased person, no person shall have power to bring any action or otherwise act as executor of the deceased person in respect of the estate comprised in or affected by the grant until the grant has been recalled or revoked.

17 Continuance of legal proceedings after revocation of temporary administration

[(1)] If, while any legal proceeding is pending in any court by or against an administrator to whom a temporary administration has been granted, that administration is revoked, that court may order that the proceeding be continued by or against the new personal representative in like manner as if the same had been originally commenced by or against him, but subject to such conditions and variations, if any, as that court directs.

[(2) The county court has jurisdiction under this section where the proceedings are pending in that court.]

Amendment—Sub-s (1): numbered as such by the County Courts Act 1984, s 148(1), Sch 2, Part III, para 11.
Sub-s (2): inserted by the County Courts Act 1984, s 148(1), Sch 2, Part III, para 11.

---

21 Rights and liabilities of administrator

Every person to whom administration of the real and personal estate of a deceased person is granted, shall, subject to the limitations contained in the grant, have the same rights and liabilities and be accountable in like manner as if he were the executor of the deceased.

[21A Debtor who becomes creditor's executor by representation or administrator to account for debt to estate]

[(1) Subject to subsection (2) of this section, where a debtor becomes his deceased creditor's executor by representation or administrator—

(a) his debt shall thereupon be extinguished; but
(b) he shall be accountable for the amount of the debt as part of the creditor's estate in any case where he would be so accountable if he had been appointed as an executor by the creditor's will.

(2) Subsection (1) of this section does not apply where the debtor's authority to act as executor or administrator is limited to part only of the creditor's estate which does not include the debt; and a debtor whose debt is extinguished by virtue of paragraph (a) shall not be accountable for its amount by virtue of paragraph (b) of that subsection in any case where the debt was barred by the Limitation Act 1939 before he became the creditor's executor or administrator.

(3) In this section 'debt' includes any liability, and 'debtor' and 'creditor' shall be construed accordingly.]

Special Provisions as to Settled Land

22 Special executors as respects settled land

(1) A testator may appoint, and in default of such express appointment shall be

deemed to have appointed, as his special executors in regard to settled land, the persons, if any, who are at his death the trustees of the settlement thereof, and probate may be granted to such trustees specially limited to the settled land.

In this subsection 'settled land' means land vested in the testator which was settled previously to his death and not by his will.

(2) A testator may appoint other persons either with or without such trustees as aforesaid or any of them to be his general executors in regard to his other property and assets.

23 Provisions where, as respects settled land, representation is not granted to the trustees of the settlement

(1) Where settled land becomes vested in a personal representative, not being a trustee of the settlement, upon trust to convey the land to or assent to the vesting thereof in the tenant for life or statutory owner in order to give effect to a settlement created before the death of the deceased and not by his will, or would on the grant of representation to him, have become so vested, such representative may—

(a) before representation has been granted, renounce his office in regard only to such settled land without renouncing it in regard to other property;
(b) after representation has been granted, apply to the court for revocation of the grant in regard to the settled land without applying in regard to other property.

(2) Whether such renunciation or revocation is made or not, the trustees of the settlement, or any person beneficially interested thereunder, may apply to the High Court for an order appointing a special or additional personal representative in respect of the settled land, and a special or additional personal representative, if and when appointed under the order, shall be in the same position as if representation had originally been granted to him alone in place of the original personal representative, if any, or to him jointly with the original personal representative, as the case may be, limited to the settled land, but without prejudice to the previous acts and dealings, if any, of the personal representative originally constituted or the effect of notices given to such personal representative.

(3) The court may make such order as aforesaid subject to such security, if any, being given by or on behalf of the special or additional personal representative, as the court may direct, and shall, unless the court considers that special considerations apply, appoint such persons as may be necessary to secure that the persons to act as representatives in respect of the settled land shall, if willing to act, be the same persons as are the trustees of the settlement, and an office copy of the order when made shall be furnished to the [principal registry of the Family Division of the High Court] for entry, and a memorandum of the order shall be endorsed on the probate or administration.

(4) The person applying for the appointment of a special or additional personal representative shall give notice of the application to the [principal registry of the Family Division of the High Court] in the manner prescribed.

(5) Rules of court may be made for prescribing for all matters required for giving effect to the provisions of this section, and in particular—

(a) for notice of any application being given to the proper officer;

(b) for production of orders, probates, and administration to the registry;
(c) for the endorsement on a probate or administration of a memorandum of an order, subject or not to any exceptions;
(d) for the manner in which the costs are to be borne;
(e) for protecting purchasers and trustees and other persons in a fiduciary position, dealing in good faith with or giving notices to a personal representative before notice of any order has been endorsed on the probate or administration or a pending action has been registered in respect of the proceedings.

Amendment—Sub-ss (3), (4): words in square brackets substituted by the Administration of Justice Act 1970, s 1(6), Sch 2, para 3.

---

24 Power for special personal representatives to dispose of settled land

(1) The special personal representatives may dispose of the settled land without the concurrence of the general personal representatives, who may likewise dispose of the other property and assets of the deceased without the concurrence of the special personal representatives.

(2) In this section the expression 'special personal representatives' means the representatives appointed to act for the purposes of settled land and includes any original personal representative who is to act with an additional personal representative for those purposes.

Duties, Rights and Obligations

[25 Duty of personal representatives]

[The personal representative of a deceased person shall be under a duty to—

(a) collect and get in the real and personal estate of the deceased and administer it according to law;
(b) when required to do so by the court, exhibit on oath in the court a full inventory of the estate and when so required render an account of the administration of the estate to the court;
(c) when required to do so by the High Court, deliver up the grant of probate or administration to that court.]

26 Rights of action by and against personal representative

(1), (2)…

(3) A personal representative may distrain for arrears of a rentcharge due or accruing to the deceased in his lifetime on the land affected or charged therewith, so long as the land remains in the possession of the person liable to pay the rentcharge or of the persons deriving title under him, and in like manner as the deceased might have done had he been living.

(4) A personal representative may distrain upon land for arrears of rent due or accruing to the deceased in like manner as the deceased might have done had he been living.

Such arrears may be distrained for after the termination of the lease or tenancy as if the term or interest had not determined, if the distress is made—

(a) within six months after the termination of the lease or tenancy;
(b) during the continuance of the possession of the lessee or tenant from whom the arrears were due.

The statutory enactments relating to distress for rent apply to any distress made pursuant to this subsection,

(5), (6)...

Amendment—Sub-ss (1), (2), (5), (6): repealed by the Law Reform (Miscellaneous Provisions) Act 1934, s 1(7).

---

27 Protection of persons on probate or administration

(1) Every person making or permitting to be made any payment or disposition in good faith under a representation shall be indemnified and protected in so doing, notwithstanding any defect or circumstance whatsoever affecting the validity of the representation.

(2) Where a representation is revoked, all payments and dispositions made in good faith to a personal representative under the representation before the revocation thereof are a valid discharge to the person making the same; and the personal representative who acted under the revoked representation may retain and reimburse himself in respect of any payments or dispositions made by him which the person to whom representation is afterwards granted might have properly made.

28 Liability of person fraudulently obtaining or retaining estate of deceased

If any person, to the defrauding of creditors or without full valuable consideration, obtains, receives or holds any real or personal estate of a deceased person or effects the release of any debt or liability due to the estate of the deceased, he shall be charged as executor in his own wrong to the extent of the real and personal estate received or coming to his hands, or the debt or liability released, after deducting—

(a) any debt for valuable consideration and without fraud due to him from the deceased person at the time of his death; and
(b) any payment made by him which might properly be made by a personal representative.

29 Liability of estate of personal representative

Where a person as personal representative of a deceased person (including an executor in his own wrong) wastes or converts to his own use any part of the real or personal estate of the deceased, and dies, his personal representative shall to the extent of the available assets of the defaulter be liable and chargeable in respect of such waste or conversion in the same manner as the defaulter would have been if living.

30 Provisions applicable where administration granted to nominee of the Crown

(1) Where the administration of the real and personal estate of any deceased

person is granted to a nominee of the Crown (whether the Treasury Solicitor, or a person nominated by the Treasury Solicitor, or any other person), any legal proceeding by or against that nominee for the recovery of the real or personal estate, or any part or share thereof, shall be of the same character, and be instituted and carried on in the same manner, and be subject to the same rules of law and equity (including, except as otherwise provided by this Act, the rules of limitation under the statutes of limitation or otherwise), in all respects as if the administration had been granted to such nominee as one of the persons interested under this Act in the estate of the deceased.

(2) An information or other proceeding on the part of His Majesty shall not be filed or instituted, and a petition of right shall not be presented, in respect of the real or personal estate of any deceased person or any part or share thereof, or any claim thereon, except ... subject to the same rules of law and equity within and subject to which a proceeding for the like purposes might be instituted by or against a subject.

(3) The Treasury Solicitor shall not be required, when applying for or obtaining administration of the estate of a deceased person for the use or benefit of His Majesty, to deliver, nor shall ... the High Court or the Commissioners of Inland Revenue be entitled to receive in connexion with any such application or grant of administration, any affidavit, statutory declaration, account, certificate, or other statement verified on oath; but the Treasury Solicitor shall deliver and the said Division and Commissioners respectively shall accept, in lieu thereof, an account or particulars of the estate of the deceased signed by or on behalf of the Treasury Solicitor.

(4) References in sections two, four ... and seven of the Treasury Solicitor Act 1876, and in subsection (3) of section three of the Duchy of Lancaster Act, 1920, to 'personal estate' shall include real estate.

Amendment—Sub-s (2): words omitted repealed by the Limitation Act 1939, s 34(4), Schedule.
Sub-s (3): words omitted repealed by the Administration of Justice Act 1970, s 54(3), Sch 11.
Sub-s (4): words omitted repealed by the Statute Law (Repeals) Act 1981.

---

31 Power to make rules

Provision may be made by rules of court for giving effect to the provisions of this Part of this Act so far as relates to real estate and in particular for adapting the procedure and practice on the grant of letters of administration to the case of real estate.

PART III
ADMINISTRATION OF ASSETS

32 Real and personal estate of deceased are assets for payment of debts

(1) The real and personal estate, whether legal or equitable, of a deceased person, to the extent of his beneficial interest therein, and the real and personal estate of which a deceased person in pursuance of any general power (including the statutory power to dispose of entailed interests) disposes by his will, are assets for payment of his debts (whether by specialty or simple contract) and liabilities, and any disposition by will inconsistent with this enactment is void as against the creditors, and the court shall if necessary, administer the property for the purpose of the payment of the debts and liabilities.

This subsection takes effect without prejudice to the rights of incumbrancers.

(2) If any person to whom any such beneficial interest devolves, or is given, or in whom any such interest vests, disposes thereof in good faith before an action is brought or process is sued out against him, he shall be personally liable for the value of the interest so disposed of by him, but that interest shall not be liable to be taken in execution in the action or under the process.

33 Trust for sale

[(1) On the death of a person intestate as to any real or personal estate, that estate shall be held in trust by his personal representatives with the power to sell it.]

(2) [The personal representatives shall pay out of—

(a) the ready money of the deceased (so far as not disposed of by his will, if any); and
(b) any net money arising from disposing of any other part of his estate (after payment of costs),

all] such funeral, testamentary and administration expenses, debts and other liabilities as are properly payable thereout having regard to the rules of administration contained in this Part of this Act, and out of the residue of the said money the personal representative shall set aside a fund sufficient to provide for any pecuniary legacies bequeathed by the will (if any) of the deceased.

(3) During the minority of any beneficiary or the subsistence of any life interest and pending the distribution of the whole or any part of the estate of the deceased, the personal representatives may invest the residue of the said money, or so much thereof as may not have been distributed, [under the Trustee Act 2000].

(4) The residue of the said money and any investments for the time being representing the same, [and any part of the estate of the deceased which remains] unsold and is not required for the administration purposes aforesaid, is in this Act referred to as 'the residuary estate of the intestate.'

(5) The income (including net rents and profits of real estate and chattels real after payment of rates, taxes, rent, costs of insurance, repairs and other outgoings properly attributable to income) of so much of the real and personal estate of the deceased as may not be disposed of by his will, if any, or may not be required for the administration purposes aforesaid, may, however such estate is invested, as from the death of the deceased, be treated and applied as income, and for that purpose any necessary apportionment may be made between tenant for life and remainderman.

(6) Nothing in this section affects the rights of any creditor of the deceased or the rights of the Crown in respect of death duties.

(7) Where the deceased leaves a will, this section has effect subject to the provisions contained in the will.

Amendment—Sub-s (1): substituted by the Trusts of Land and Appointment of Trustees Act 1996, s 5, Sch 2, para 5(1), (2); for savings in relation to entailed interests created before the commencement of that Act, and savings consequential upon the abolition of the doctrine of conversion, see s 25(4), (5) thereof.

Sub-s (2): words from 'The personal representatives' to 'of costs), all' in square brackets substituted by the Trusts of Land and Appointment of Trustees Act 1996, s 5, Sch 2, para 5(1), (3); for savings in relation to entailed interests created before the commencement of that Act, and savings consequential upon the abolition of the doctrine of conversion, see s 25(4), (5) thereof.

Sub-s (3): words 'under the Trustee Act 2000' in square brackets substituted by the Trustee Act 2000, s 40(1), Sch 2, Pt II, para 27. Date in force: 1 February 2001: see SI 2001/49, art 2.

Sub-s (4): words 'and any part of the estate of the deceased which remains' in square brackets substituted by the Trusts of Land and Appointment of Trustees Act 1996, s 5, Sch 2, para 5(1), (4); for savings in relation to entailed interests created before the commencement of that Act, and savings consequential upon the abolition of the doctrine of conversion, see s 25(4), (5) thereof.

34 Administration of assets

(1), (2)…

(3) Where the estate of a deceased person is solvent his real and personal estate shall, subject to rules of court and the provisions hereinafter contained as to charges on property of the deceased, and to the provisions, if any, contained in his will, be applicable towards the discharge of the funeral, testamentary and administration expenses, debts and liabilities payable thereout in the order mentioned in Part II of the First Schedule to this Act.

Amendment—Sub-s (1): repealed by the Insolvency Act 1985, s 235, Sch 10.

Sub-s (2): repealed by the Administration of Estates Act 1971, s 12(2), (4), (6), Sch 2, Part II.

35 Charges on property of deceased to be paid primarily out of the property charged

(1) Where a person dies possessed of, or entitled to, or, under a general power of appointment (including the statutory power to dispose of entailed interests) by his will disposes of, an interest in property, which at the time of his death is charged with the payment of money, whether by way of legal mortgage, equitable charge or otherwise (including a lien for unpaid purchase money), and the deceased has not by will deed or other document signified a contrary or other intention, the interest so charged, shall as between the different persons claiming through the deceased, be primarily liable for the payment of the charge; and every part of the said interest, according to its value, shall bear a proportionate part of the charge on the whole thereof.

(2) Such contrary or other intention shall not be deemed to be signified—

(a) by a general direction for the payment of debts or of all the debts of the testator out of his personal estate, or his residuary real and personal estate, or his residuary real estate; or
(b) by a charge of debts upon any such estate;

unless such intention is further signified by words expressly or by necessary implication referring to all or some part of the charge.

(3) Nothing in this section affects the right of a person entitled to the charge to obtain payment or satisfaction thereof either out of the other assets of the deceased or otherwise.

36 Effect of assent or conveyance by personal representative

(1) A personal representative may assent to the vesting, in any person who (whether by devise, bequest, devolution, appropriation or otherwise) may be entitled thereto, either beneficially or as a trustee or personal representative, of any estate or interest in real estate to which the testator or intestate was entitled or over which he exercised a general power of appointment by his will, including the statutory power to dispose of entailed interests, and which devolved upon the personal representative.

(2) The assent shall operate to vest in that person the estate or interest to which the assent relates, and, unless a contrary intention appears, the assent shall relate back to the death of the deceased.

(3) …

(4) An assent to the vesting of a legal estate shall be in writing, signed by the personal representative, and shall name the person in whose favour it is given and shall operate to vest in that person the legal estate to which it relates; and an assent not in writing or not in favour of a named person shall not be effectual to pass a legal estate.

(5) Any person in whose favour an assent or conveyance of a legal estate is made by a personal representative may require that notice of the assent or conveyance be written or endorsed on or permanently annexed to the probate or letters of administration, at the cost of the estate of the deceased, and that the probate or letters of administration be produced, at the like cost, to prove that the notice has been placed thereon or annexed thereto.

(6) A statement in writing by a personal representative that he has not given or made an assent or conveyance in respect of a legal estate, shall, in favour of a purchaser, but without prejudice to any previous disposition made in favour of another purchaser deriving title mediately or immediately under the personal representative, be sufficient evidence that an assent or conveyance has not been given or made in respect of the legal estate to which the statement relates, unless notice of a previous assent or conveyance affecting that estate has been placed on or annexed to the probate or administration.

A conveyance by a personal representative of a legal estate to a purchaser accepted on the faith of such a statement shall (without prejudice as aforesaid and unless notice of a previous assent or conveyance affecting that estate has been placed on or annexed to the probate or administration) operate to transfer or create the legal estate expressed to be conveyed in like manner as if no previous assent or conveyance had been made by the personal representative.

A personal representative making a false statement, in regard to any such matter, shall be liable in like manner as if the statement had been contained in a statutory declaration.

(7) An assent or conveyance by a personal representative in respect of a legal estate shall, in favour of a purchaser, unless notice of a previous assent or conveyance affecting that legal estate has been placed on or annexed to the probate or administration, be taken as sufficient evidence that the person in whose favour the assent or conveyance is given or made is the person entitled to have the legal estate conveyed to

him, and upon the proper trusts, if any, but shall not otherwise prejudicially affect the claim of any person rightfully entitled to the estate vested or conveyed or any charge thereon.

(8) A conveyance of a legal estate by a personal representative to a purchaser shall not be invalidated by reason only that the purchaser may have notice that all the debts, liabilities, funeral, and testamentary or administration expenses, duties, and legacies of the deceased have been discharged or provided for.

(9) An assent or conveyance given or made by a personal representative shall not, except in favour of a purchaser of a legal estate, prejudice the right of the personal representative or any other person to recover the estate or interest to which the assent or conveyance relates, or to be indemnified out of such estate or interest against any duties, debts, or liability to which such estate or interest would have been subject if there had not been any assent or conveyance.

(10) A personal representative may, as a condition of giving an assent or making a conveyance, require security for the discharge of any such duties, debt, or liability, but shall not be entitled to postpone the giving of an assent merely by reason of the subsistence of any such duties, debt or liability if reasonable arrangements have been made for discharging the same; and an assent may be given subject to any legal estate or charge by way of legal mortgage.

(11) This section shall not operate to impose any stamp duty in respect of an assent, and in this section 'purchaser' means a purchaser for money or money's worth.

(12) This section applies to assents and conveyances made after the commencement of this Act, whether the testator or intestate died before of after such commencement.

Amendment—Sub-s (3): repealed by the Law of Property (Miscellaneous Provisions) Act 1994, s 21(2), Sch 2.

---

37 Validity of conveyance not affected by revocation of representation

(1) All conveyances of any interest in real or personal estate made to a purchaser either before or after the commencement of this Act by a person to whom probate or letters of administration have been granted are valid, notwithstanding any subsequent revocation or variation, either before or after the commencement of this Act, of the probate or administration.

(2) This section takes effect without prejudice to any order of the court made before the commencement of this Act, and applies whether the testator or intestate died before or after such commencement.

38 Right to follow property and powers of the court in relation thereto

(1) An assent or conveyance by a personal representative to a person other than a purchaser does not prejudice the rights of any person to follow the property to which the assent or conveyance relates, or any property representing the same, into the hands of the person in whom it is vested by the assent or conveyance, or of any other person (not being a purchaser) who may have received the same or in whom it may be vested.

(2) Notwithstanding any such assent or conveyance the court may, on the application of any creditor or other person interested,—

(a) order a sale, exchange, mortgage, charge, lease, payment, transfer or other transaction to be carried out which the court considers requisite for the purpose of giving effect to the rights of the persons interested;
(b) declare that the person, not being a purchaser, in whom the property is vested is a trustee for those purposes;
(c) give directions respecting the preparation and execution of any conveyance or other instrument or as to any other matter required for giving effect to the order;
(d) make any vesting order, or appoint a person to convey in accordance with the provisions of the Trustee Act 1925.

(3) This section does not prejudice the rights of a purchaser or a person deriving title under him, but applies whether the testator or intestate died before or after the commencement of this Act.

[(4) The county court has jurisdiction under this section where the estate in respect of which the application is made does not exceed in amount or value the county court limit.]

Amendment—Sub-s (4): inserted by the County Courts Act 1984, s 148(1), Sch 2, Part III, para 12.

---

39 Powers of management

(1) In dealing with the real and personal estate of the deceased his personal representatives shall, for purposes of administration, or during a minority of any beneficiary or the subsistence of any life interest, or until the period of distribution arrives, have—

(i) [as respects the personal estate,] the same powers and discretions, including power to raise money by mortgage or charge (whether or not by deposit of documents), as a personal representative had before the commencement of this Act, with respect to personal estate vested in him …; and
[(ii) as respects the real estate, all the functions conferred on them by Part I of the Trusts of Land and Appointment of Trustees Act 1996;]
(iii) all the powers [necessary] so that every contract entered into by a personal representative shall be binding on and be enforceable against and by the personal representative for the time being of the deceased, and may be carried into effect, or be varied or rescinded by him, and, in the case of a contract entered into by a predecessor, as if it had been entered into by himself.

[(1A) Subsection (1) of this section is without prejudice to the powers conferred on personal representatives by the Trustee Act 2000.]

(2) Nothing in this section shall affect the right of any person to require an assent or conveyance to be made.

(3) This section applies whether the testator or intestate died before or after the commencement of this Act.

Amendment—Sub-s (1): in para (i) words in square brackets inserted and words omitted repealed, para (ii) substituted and word in square brackets in para (iii) substituted by the Trusts of Land and Appointment of Trustees Act 1996, s 25(1), (2), Sch 3, para 6(1), (2), Sch 4; for savings in relation to entailed interests created before the commencement of that Act, and savings consequential upon the abolition of the doctrine of conversion, see s 25(4), (5) thereof.

Sub-s (1A): inserted by the Trustee Act 2000, s 40(1), Sch 2, Pt II, para 28. Date in force: 1 February 2001: see SI 2001/49, art 2.

40 Powers of personal representative for raising money, etc

(1) For giving effect to beneficial interests the personal representative may limit or demise land for a term of years absolute, with or without impeachment for waste, to trustees on usual trusts for raising or securing any principal sum and the interest thereon for which the land, or any part thereof, is liable, and may limit or grant a rentcharge for giving effect to any annual or periodical sum for which the land or the income thereof or any part thereof is liable.

(2) This section applies whether the testator or intestate died before or after the commencement of this Act.

41 Powers of personal representative as to appropriation

(1) The personal representative may appropriate any part of the real or personal estate, including things in action, of the deceased in the actual condition or state of investment thereof at the time of appropriation in or towards satisfaction of any legacy bequeathed by the deceased, or of any other interest or share in his property, whether settled or not, as to the personal representative may seem just and reasonable, according to the respective rights of the persons interested in the property of the deceased:

Provided that—

(i) an appropriation shall not be made under this section so as to affect prejudicially any specific devise or bequest;

(ii) an appropriation of property, whether or not being an investment authorised by law or by the will, if any, of the deceased for the investment of money subject to the trust, shall not (save as hereinafter mentioned) be made under this section except with the following consents:—

 (a) when made for the benefit of a person absolutely and beneficially entitled in possession, the consent of that person;

 (b) when made in respect of any settled legacy share or interest, the consent of either the trustee thereof, if any (not being also the personal representative), or the person who may for the time being be entitled to the income:

 If the person whose consent is so required as aforesaid is an infant or [is incapable by reason of mental disorder within the meaning of [the Mental Health Act 1983], of managing and administering his property and affairs] the consent shall be given on his behalf by his parents or parent, testamentary or other guardian … or receiver, or if, in the case of an infant, there is no such parent or guardian, by the court on the application of his next friend;

(iii) no consent (save of such trustee as aforesaid) shall be required on behalf of a person who may come into existence after the time of appropriation, or who cannot be found or ascertained at that time;

(iv) if no [receiver is acting for a person suffering from mental disorder] then, if the appropriation is of an investment authorised by law or by the will, if any, of the deceased for the investment of money subject to the trust, no consent shall be required on behalf of the [said person];

(v) if, independently of the personal representative, there is no trustee of a settled legacy share or interest, and no person of full age and capacity entitled to the income thereof, no consent shall be required to an appropriation in respect of such legacy share or interest, provided that the appropriation is of an investment authorised as aforesaid.

[(1A) The county court has jurisdiction under proviso (ii) to subsection (1) of this section where the estate in respect of which the application is made does not exceed in amount or value the county court limit.]

(2) Any property duly appropriated under the powers conferred by this section shall thereafter be treated as an authorised investment, and may be retained or dealt with accordingly.

(3) For the purposes of such appropriation, the personal representative may ascertain and fix the value of the respective parts of the real and personal estate and the liabilities of the deceased as he may think fit, and shall for that purpose employ a duly qualified valuer in any case where such employment may be necessary; and may make any conveyance (including an assent) which may be requisite for giving effect to the appropriation.

(4) An appropriation made pursuant to this section shall bind all persons interested in the property of the deceased whose consent is not hereby made requisite.

(5) The personal representative shall, in making the appropriation, have regard to the rights of any person who may thereafter come into existence, or who cannot be found or ascertained at the time of appropriation, and of any other person whose consent is not required by this section.

(6) This section does not prejudice any other power of appropriation conferred by law or by the will (if any) of the deceased, and takes effect with any extended powers conferred by the will (if any) of the deceased, and where an appropriation is made under this section, in respect of a settled legacy, share or interest, the property appropriated shall remain subject to all [trusts] and powers of leasing, disposition, and management or varying investments which would have been applicable thereto or to the legacy, share or interest in respect of which the appropriation is made, if no such appropriation had been made.

(7) If after any real estate has been appropriated in purported exercise of the powers conferred by this section, the person to whom it was conveyed disposes of it or any interest therein, then, in favour of a purchaser, the appropriation shall be deemed to have been made in accordance with the requirements of this section and after all requisite consents, if any, had been given.

(8) In this section, a settled legacy, share or interest includes any legacy, share or

interest to which a person is not absolutely entitled in possession at the date of the appropriation, also an annuity, and 'purchaser' means a purchaser for money or money's worth.

(9) This section applies whether the deceased died intestate or not, and whether before or after the commencement of this Act, and extends to property over which a testator exercises a general power of appointment, including the statutory power to dispose of entailed interests, and authorises the setting apart of a fund to answer an annuity by means of the income of that fund or otherwise.

Amendment—Sub-s (1): in para (ii) words omitted repealed, and first words in square brackets substituted, by the Mental Health Act 1959, s 149(1), Sch 7, Part I, words in square brackets therein substituted by the Mental Health Act 1983, s 148, Sch 4, para 7; in para (iv) words in square brackets substituted by the Mental Health Act 1959, s 149(1), Sch 7, Part I.

Sub-s (1A): inserted by the County Courts Act 1984, s 148(1), Sch 2, Part III, para 13.

Sub-s (6): word 'trusts' in square brackets substituted by the Trusts of Land and Appointment of Trustees Act 1996, s 25(1), Sch 3, para 6(1), (3); for savings in relation to entailed interests created before the commencement of that Act, and savings consequential upon the abolition of the doctrine of conversion, see s 25(4), (5) thereof. Date in force: 1 January 1997: see SI 1996/2974, art 2.

---

42 Power to appoint trustees of infants' property

(1) Where an infant is absolutely entitled under the will or on the intestacy of a person dying before or after the commencement of this Act (in this subsection called 'the deceased') to a devise or legacy, or to the residue of the estate of the deceased, or any share therein, and such devise, legacy, residue or share is not under the will, if any, of the deceased, devised or bequeathed to trustees for the infant, the personal representatives of the deceased may appoint a trust corporation or two or more individuals not exceeding four (whether or not including the personal representatives or one or more of the personal representatives), to be the trustee or trustees of such devise, legacy, residue or share for the infant, and to be trustees of any land devised or any land being or forming part of such residue or share for the purposes of the Settled Land Act 1925, and of the statutory provisions relating to the management of land during a minority, and may execute or do any assurance or thing requisite for vesting such devise, legacy, residue or share in the trustee or trustees so appointed.

On such appointment the personal representatives, as such, shall be discharged from all further liability in respect of such devise, legacy, residue, or share, and the same may be retained in its existing condition or state of investment, or may be converted into money, and such money may be invested in any authorised investment.

(2) Where a personal representative has before the commencement of this Act retained or sold any such devise, legacy, residue or share, and invested the same or the proceeds thereof in any investments in which he was authorised to invest money subject to the trust, then, subject to any order of the court made before such commencement, he shall not be deemed to have incurred any liability on that account, or by reason of not having paid or transferred the money or property into court.

43 Obligations of personal representative as to giving possession of land and powers of the court

(1) A personal representative, before giving an assent or making a conveyance in

favour of any person entitled, may permit that person to take possession of the land, and such possession shall not prejudicially affect the right of the personal representative to take or resume possession nor his power to convey the land as if he were in possession thereof, but subject to the interest of any lessee, tenant or occupier in possession or in actual occupation of the land.

(2) Any person who as against the personal representative claims possession of real estate, or the appointment of a receiver thereof, or a conveyance thereof, or an assent to the vesting thereof, or to be registered as proprietor thereof under the *Land Registration Act 1925* [Land Registration Act 2002], may apply to the court for directions with reference thereto, and the court may make such vesting or other order as may be deemed proper, and the provisions of the Trustee Act 1925, relating to vesting orders and to the appointment of a person to convey, shall apply.

(3) This section applies whether the testator or intestate died before or after the commencement of this Act.

[(4) The county court has jurisdiction under this section where the estate in respect of which the application is made does not exceed in amount or value the county court limit.]

Amendment—Sub-s (2): words 'Land Registration Act 1925' in italics repealed and subsequent words in square brackets substituted by the Land Registration Act 2002, s 133, Sch 11, para 3. Date in force: 13 October 2003: see SI 2003/1725, art 2(1).

Sub-s (4): inserted by the County Courts Act 1984, s 148(1), Sch 2, Part III, para 14.

---

44 Power to postpone distribution

Subject to the foregoing provisions of this Act, a personal representative is not bound to distribute the estate of the deceased before the expiration of one year from the death.

PART IV
DISTRIBUTION OF RESIDUARY ESTATE

45 Abolition of descent to heir, curtesy, dower and escheat

(1) With regard to the real estate and personal inheritance of every person dying after the commencement of this Act, there shall be abolished—

(a) All existing modes rules and canons of descent, and of devolution by special occupancy or otherwise, of real estate, or of a personal inheritance, whether operating by the general law or by the custom of gavelkind or borough english or by any other custom of any county, locality, or manor, or otherwise howsoever; and

(b) Tenancy by the curtesy and every other estate and interest of a husband in real estate as to which his wife dies intestate, whether arising under the general law or by custom or otherwise; and

(c) Dower and freebench and every other estate and interest of a wife in real estate as to which her husband dies intestate, whether arising under the general law or by custom or otherwise: Provided that where a right (if any) to freebench or other like right has attached before the commencement of this Act which cannot be barred by a testamentary or other disposition made by the husband, such right shall, unless released, remain in force as an equitable interest; and

(d) Escheat to the Crown or the Duchy of Lancaster or the Duke of Cornwall or to a mesne lord for want of heirs.

(2) Nothing in this section affects the descent or devolution of an entailed interest.

46 Succession to real and personal estate on intestacy

(1) The residuary estate of an intestate shall be distributed in the manner or be held on the trusts mentioned in this section, namely:—

[(i) If the intestate leaves a husband or wife, then in accordance with the following Table:

If the intestate—	
(1) leaves—	the residuary estate shall be held in trust for the surviving husband or wife absolutely.
(a) no issue, and	
(b) no parent, or brother or sister of the whole blood, or issue of a brother or sister of the whole blood	
(2) leaves issue (whether or not persons mentioned in sub-paragraph (b) above also survive)	the surviving husband or wife shall take the personal chattels absolutely and, in addition, the residuary estate of the intestate (other than the personal chattels) shall stand charged with the payment of a [fixed net sum], free of death duties and costs, to the surviving husband or wife with interest thereon from the date of the death < … > [at such rate as the Lord Chancellor may specify by order] until paid or appropriated, and, subject to providing for that sum and the interest thereon, the residuary estate (other than the personal chattels) shall be held—
	(a) as to one half upon trust for the surviving husband or wife during his or her life, and, subject to such life interest, on the statutory trusts for the issue of the intestate, and
	(b) as to the other half, on the statutory trusts for the issue of the intestate.

(3) leaves one or more of the following, that is to say, a parent, a brother or sister of the whole blood, or issue of a brother or sister of the whole blood, but leaves no issue

the surviving husband or wife shall take the personal chattels absolutely and, in addition, the residuary estate of the intestate (other than the personal chattels) shall stand charged with the payment of a [fixed net sum], free of death duties and costs, to the surviving husband or wife with interest thereon from the date of the death < … > [at such rate as the Lord Chancellor may specify by order] until paid or appropriated, and, subject to providing for that sum and the interest thereon, the residuary estate (other than the personal chattels) shall be held—

(a) as to one half in trust for the surviving husband or wife absolutely, and

(b) as to the other half—

  (i) where the intestate leaves one parent or both parents (whether or not brothers or sisters of the intestate or their issue also survive) in trust for the parent absolutely or, as the case may be, for the two parents in equal shares absolutely

  (ii) where the intestate leaves no parent, on the statutory trusts for the brothers and sisters of the whole blood of the intestate.]

[The fixed net sums referred to in paragraphs (2) and (3) of this Table shall be of the amounts provided by or under section 1 of the Family Provision Act 1966]

(ii) If the intestate leaves issue but no husband or wife, the residuary estate of the intestate shall be held on the statutory trusts for the issue of the intestate;

(iii) If the intestate leaves [no husband or wife and] no issue but both parents, then … the residuary estate of the intestate shall be held in trust for the father and mother in equal shares absolutely;

(iv) If the intestate leaves [no husband or wife and] no issue but one parent, then … the residuary estate of the intestate shall be held in trust for the surviving father or mother absolutely;

(v) If the intestate leaves no [husband or wife and no issue and no] parent, then … the residuary estate of the intestate shall be held in trust for the following persons living at the death of the intestate, and in the following order and manner, namely:—

— First, on the statutory trusts for the brothers and sisters of the whole blood of the intestate; but if no person takes an absolutely vested interest under such trusts; then

— Secondly, on the statutory trusts for the brothers and sisters of the half blood of the intestate; but if no person takes an absolutely vested interest under such trusts; then

— Thirdly, for the grandparents of the intestate and, if more than one survive the intestate, in equal shares; but if there is no member of this class; then

— Fourthly, on the statutory trusts for the uncles and aunts of the intestate (being brothers or sisters of the whole blood of a parent of the intestate); but if no person takes an absolutely vested interest under such trusts; then
— Fifthly, on the statutory trusts for the uncles and aunts of the intestate (being brothers or sisters of the half blood of a parent of the intestate) …

(vi) In default of any person taking an absolute interest under the foregoing provisions, the residuary estate of the intestate shall belong to the Crown or to the Duchy of Lancaster or to the Duke of Cornwall for the time being, as the case may be, as bona vacantia, and in lieu of any right to escheat.The Crown or the said Duchy or the said Duke may (without prejudice to the powers reserved by section nine of the Civil List Act 1910, or any other powers), out of the whole or any part of the property devolving on them respectively, provide, in accordance with the existing practice, for dependents, whether kindred or not, of the intestate, and other persons for whom the intestate might reasonably have been expected to make provision.

[(1A) The power to make orders under subsection (1) above shall be exercisable by statutory instrument subject to annulment in pursuance of a resolution of either House of Parliament; and any such order may be varied or revoked by a subsequent order made under the power.]

(2) A husband and wife shall for all purposes of distribution or division under the foregoing provisions of this section be treated as two persons.

[(2A) Where the intestate's husband or wife survived the intestate but died before the end of the period of 28 days beginning with the day on which the intestate died, this section shall have effect as respects the intestate as if the husband or wife had not survived the intestate.]

[(3) Where the intestate and the intestate's husband or wife have died in circumstances rendering it uncertain which of them survived the other and the intestate's husband or wife is by virtue of section one hundred and eighty-four of the Law of Property Act 1925, deemed to have survived the intestate, this section shall, nevertheless, have effect as respects the intestate as if the husband or wife had not survived the intestate.

(4) The interest payable on [the fixed net sum] payable to a surviving husband or wife shall be primarily payable out of income.]

Amendment—Sub-s (1): para (i) substituted by the Intestates' Estates Act 1952, s 1; in Table, words omitted from paras 2, 3 repealed by the Statute Law (Repeals) Act 1981, first and third words in square brackets substituted and final words in square brackets inserted, by the Family Provision Act 1966, s 1, second and fourth words in square brackets substituted by the Administration of Justice Act 1977, s 28(1)(a); words omitted from paras (iii), (iv), (v) repealed and words in square brackets substituted by the Intestates' Estates Act 1952, s 1.

Sub-s (1A): inserted by the Administration of Justice Act 1977, s 28(1).

Sub-s (2A): inserted by the Law Reform (Succession) Act 1995, s 1(1), (3).

Sub-s (3): inserted by the Intestates' Estates Act 1952, s 1(4).

Sub-s (4): inserted by the Intestates' Estates Act 1952, s 1(4); words in square brackets substituted by the Family Provision Act 1966, s 1.

---

47 Statutory trusts in favour of issue and other classes of relatives of intestate

(1) Where under this Part of this Act the residuary estate of an intestate, or any part thereof, is directed to be held on the statutory trusts for the issue of the intestate, the same shall be held upon the following trusts, namely:—

(i) In trust, in equal shares if more than one, for all or any the children or child of the intestate, living at the death of the intestate, who attain the age of [eighteen] years or marry under that age, and for all or any of the issue living at the death of the intestate who attain the age of [eighteen] years or marry under that age of any child of the intestate who predeceases the intestate, such issue to take through all degrees, according to their stocks, in equal shares if more than one, the share which their parent would have taken if living at the death of the intestate, and so that no issue shall take whose parent is living at the death of the intestate and so capable of taking;
(ii) The statutory power of advancement, and the statutory provisions which relate to maintenance and accumulation of surplus income, shall apply, but when an infant marries such infant shall be entitled to give valid receipts for the income of the infant's share or interest;
(iii) …
(iv) The personal representatives may permit any infant contingently interested to have the use and enjoyment of any personal chattels in such manner and subject to such conditions (if any) as the personal representatives may consider reasonable, and without being liable to account for any consequential loss.

(2) If the trusts in favour of the issue of the intestate fail by reason of no child or other issue attaining an absolutely vested interest—

(a) the residuary estate of the intestate and the income thereof and all statutory accumulations, if any, of the income thereof, or so much thereof as may not have been paid or applied under any power affecting the same, shall go, devolve and be held under the provisions of this Part of this Act as if the intestate had died without leaving issue living at the death of the intestate;
(b) references in this Part of this Act to the intestate 'leaving no issue' shall be construed as 'leaving no issue who attain an absolutely vested interest';
(c) references in this Part of this Act to the intestate 'leaving issue' or 'leaving a child or other issue' shall be construed as 'leaving issue who attain an absolutely vested interest.'

(3) Where under this Part of this Act the residuary estate of an intestate or any part thereof is directed to be held on the statutory trusts for any class of relatives of the intestate, other than issue of the intestate, the same shall be held on trusts corresponding to the statutory trusts for the issue of the intestate (other than the provision for bringing any money or property into account) as if such trusts (other than as aforesaid) were repeated with the substitution of references to the members or member of that class for references to the children or child of the intestate.

[(4) References in paragraph (i) of subsection (1) of the last foregoing section to the intestate leaving, or not leaving, a member of the class consisting of brothers or sisters of the whole blood of the intestate and issue of brothers or sisters of the whole blood of the intestate shall be construed as references to the intestate leaving, or not leaving, a member of that class who attains an absolutely vested interest.]

[(5) ...]

Amendment—Sub-s (1): in para (i) words in square brackets substituted by the Family Law Reform Act 1969, s 3(2); para (iii) repealed by the Law Reform (Succession) Act 1995, ss 1(2)(a), (3), 5, Schedule.

Sub-s (4): inserted by the Intestates' Estates Act 1952, s 1(3)(c).

Sub-s (5): inserted by the Intestates' Estates Act 1952, s 1(3)(c); repealed by the Family Provision Act 1966, ss 9, 10, Sch 2.

[47A Right of surviving spouse to have his own life interest redeemed]

[(1) Where a surviving husband or wife is entitled to the interest in part of the residuary estate, and so elects, the personal representative shall purchase or redeem the life interest by paying the capital value thereof to the tenant for life, or the persons deriving title under the tenant for life, and the costs of the transaction; and thereupon the residuary estate of the intestate may be dealt with and distributed free from the life interest.

(2) ...

(3) An election under this section shall only be exercisable if at the time of the election the whole of the said part of the residuary estate consists of property in possession, but, for the purposes of this section, a life interest in property partly in possession and partly not in possession shall be treated as consisting of two separate life interests in those respective parts of the property.

[(3A) The capital value shall be reckoned in such manner as the Lord Chancellor may by order direct, and an order under this subsection may include transitional provisions.

(3B) The power to make orders under subsection (3A) above shall be exercisable by statutory instrument subject to annulment in pursuance of a resolution of either House of Parliament; and any such order may be varied or revoked by a subsequent order made under the power.]

(4) ...

(5) An election under this section shall be exercisable only within the period of twelve months from the date on which representation with respect to the estate of the intestate is first taken out:

Provided that if the surviving husband or wife satisfies the court that the limitation to the said period of twelve months will operate unfairly—

(a) in consequence of the representation first taken out being probate of a will subsequently revoked on the ground that the will was invalid, or
(b) in consequence of a question whether a person had an interest in the estate, or as to the nature of an interest in the estate, not having been determined at the time when representation was first taken out, or
(c) in consequence of some other circumstances affecting the administration or distribution of the estate,

the court may extend the said period.

(6) An election under this section shall be exercisable, except where the tenant for life is the sole personal representative, by notifying the personal representative (or, where there are two or more personal representatives of whom one is the tenant for life, all of them except the tenant for life) in writing; and a notification in writing under this subsection shall not be revocable except with the consent of the personal representative.

(7) Where the tenant for life is the sole personal representative an election under this section shall not be effective unless written notice thereof is given to the [[Senior Registrar] of the Family Division of the High Court] within the period within which it must be made; and provision may be made by probate rules for keeping a record of such notices and making that record available to the public.

In this subsection the expression 'probate rules' means rules [of court made under section 127 of the Supreme Court Act 1981].

(8) An election under this section by a tenant for life who is an infant shall be as valid and binding as it would be if the tenant for life were of age; but the personal representative shall, instead of paying the capital value of the life interest to the tenant for life, deal with it in the same manner as with any other part of the residuary estate to which the tenant for life is absolutely entitled.

(9) In considering for the purposes of the foregoing provisions of this section the question when representation was first taken out, a grant limited to settled land or to trust property shall be left out of account and a grant limited to real estate or to personal estate shall be left out of account unless a grant limited to the remainder of the estate has previously been made or is made at the same time.]

Amendment—Inserted by the Intestates' Estates Act 1952, s 2.

Sub-ss (2), (4): repealed by the Administration of Justice Act 1977, ss 28(2), 32(4), Sch 5, Part VI.

Sub-ss (3A), (3B): inserted by the Administration of Justice Act 1977, s 28(3).

Sub-s (7): first words in square brackets substituted by the Administration of Justice Act 1970, s 1(6), Sch 2, para 4, words in square brackets therein substituted by the Supreme Court Act 1981, s 152(1), Sch 5; final words in square brackets substituted by the Supreme Court Act 1981, s 152(1), Sch 5.

---

48 Powers of personal representative in respect of interests of surviving spouse

(1) …

(2) The personal representatives may raise—

(a) [the fixed net sum] or any part thereof and the interest thereon payable to the surviving husband or wife of the intestate on the security of the whole or any part of the residuary estate of the intestate (other than the personal chattels), so far as that estate may be sufficient for the purpose of the said sum and interest may not have been satisfied by an appropriation under the statutory power available in that behalf; and

(b) in like manner the capital sum, if any, required for the purchase or redemption of the life interest of the surviving husband or wife of the intestate, or any part thereof not satisfied by the application for that purpose of any part of the residuary estate of the intestate;

and in either case the amount, if any, properly required for the payment of the costs of the transaction.

Amendment—Sub-s (1): repealed by the Intestates' Estates Act 1952, s 2.
Sub-s (2): words in square brackets substituted by the Family Provision Act 1966, s 1.

---

49 Application to cases of partial intestacy

[(1)] Where any person dies leaving a will effectively disposing of part of his property, this Part of this Act shall have effect as respects the part of his property not so disposed of subject to the provisions contained in the will and subject to the following modifications:—

[(aa)], (a) …

(b) The personal representative shall, subject to his rights and powers for the purposes of administration, be a trustee for the persons entitled under this Part of this Act in respect of the part of the estate not expressly disposed of unless it appears by the will that the personal representative is intended to take such part beneficially.

[(2), (3) …

(4) The references in subsection (3) of section forty-seven A of this Act to property are references to property comprised in the residuary estate and, accordingly, where a will of the deceased creates a life interest in property in possession, and the remaining interest in that property forms part of the residuary estate, the said references are references to that remaining interest (which, until the life interest determines, is property not in possession).]

Amendment—Sub-s (1): para (aa) inserted by the Intestates' Estates Act 1952, s 3, repealed, together with para (a), by the Law Reform (Succession) Act 1995, ss 1(2)(b), 5, Schedule.
Sub-ss (2), (3): inserted by the Intestates' Estates Act 1952, s 3; repealed by the Law Reform (Succession) Act 1995, ss 1(2)(b), (3), 5, Schedule.
Sub-s (4): inserted by the Intestates' Estates Act 1952, s 3.

---

50 Construction of documents

(1) References to any Statutes of Distribution in an instrument inter vivos made or in a will coming into operation after the commencement of this Act, shall be construed as references to this Part of this Act; and references in such an instrument or will to statutory next of kin shall be construed, unless the context otherwise requires, as referring to the persons who would take beneficially on an intestacy under the foregoing provisions of this Part of this Act.

(2) Trusts declared in an instrument inter vivos made, or in a will coming into operation, before the commencement of this Act by reference to the Statutes of Distribution, shall, unless the contrary thereby appears, be construed as referring to the

enactments (other than the Intestates' Estates Act 1890) relating to the distribution of effects of intestates which were in force immediately before the commencement of this Act.

[(3) In subsection (1) of this section the reference to this Part of this Act, or the foregoing provisions of this Part of this Act, shall in relation to an instrument inter vivos made, or a will or codicil coming into operation, after the coming into force of section 18 of the Family Law Reform Act 1987 (but not in relation to instruments inter vivos made or wills or codicils coming into operation earlier) be construed as including references to that section.]

Amendment—Sub-s (3): inserted by the Family Law Reform Act 1987, s 33(1), Sch 2, para 3.

---

51 Savings

(1) Nothing in this Part of this Act affects the right of any person to take beneficially, by purchase, as heir either general or special.

(2) The foregoing provisions of this Part of this Act do not apply to any beneficial interest in real estate (not including chattels real) to which a [person of unsound mind] or defective living and of full age at the commencement of this Act, and unable, by reason of his incapacity, to make a will, who thereafter dies intestate in respect of such interest without having recovered his testamentary capacity, was entitled at his death, and any such beneficial interest (not being an interest ceasing on his death) shall, without prejudice to any will of the deceased, devolve in accordance with the general law in force before the commencement of this Act applicable to freehold land, and that law shall, notwithstanding any repeal, apply to the case.

For the purposes of this subsection, a [person of unsound mind] or defective who dies intestate as respects any beneficial interest in real estate shall not be deemed to have recovered his testamentary capacity unless his … receiver has been discharged.

(3) Where an infant dies after the commencement of this Act without having been married [and without issue], and independently of this subsection he would, at his death, have been equitably entitled under a [trust or] settlement (including a will) to a vested estate in fee simple or absolute interest in freehold land, or in any property … to devolve therewith or as freehold land, such infant shall be deemed to have had [a life interest], and the [trust or] settlement shall be construed accordingly.

(4) …

Amendment—Sub-s (2): words in square brackets substituted by the Mental Treatment Act 1930, s 20(5); words omitted repealed by the Mental Health Act 1959, s 149(2), Sch 8.

Sub-s (3): words 'and without issue' and 'trust or' in square brackets inserted by the Trusts of Land and Appointment of Trustees Act 1996, s 25(1), Sch 3, para 6(1), (4)(a), (b); for savings in relation to entailed interests created before the commencement of that Act, and savings consequential upon the abolition of the doctrine of conversion, see s 25(4), (5) thereof. Date in force: 1 January 1997: see SI 1996/2974, art 2.

Sub-s (3): word omitted repealed by the Trusts of Land and Appointment of Trustees Act 1996, s 25(2), Sch 4; for savings in relation to entailed interests created before the commencement of that Act, and savings consequential upon the abolition of the doctrine of conversion, see s 25(4), (5) thereof. Date in force: 1 January 1997: see SI 1996/2974, art 2.

Sub-s (3): words 'a life interest' in square brackets substituted by the Trusts of Land and Appointment of Trustees Act 1996, s 25(1), Sch 3, para 6(1), (4)(c); for savings in relation to entailed interests created before the commencement of that Act, and savings consequential upon the abolition of the doctrine of conversion, see s 25(4), (5) thereof. Date in force: 1 January 1997: see SI 1996/2974, art 2.

Sub-s (4): repealed by the Trusts of Land and Appointment of Trustees Act 1996, s 25(2), Sch 4; for savings in relation to entailed interests created before the commencement of that Act, and savings consequential upon the abolition of the doctrine of conversion, see s 25(4), (5) thereof. Date in force: 1 January 1997: see SI 1996/2974, art 2.

52 Interpretation of Part IV

In this Part of this Act 'real and personal estate' means every beneficial interest (including rights of entry and reverter) of the intestate in real and personal estate which (otherwise than in right of a power of appointment or of the testamentary power conferred by statute to dispose of entailed interests) he could, if of full age and capacity, have disposed of by his will [and references (however expressed) to any relationship between two persons shall be construed in accordance with section 1 of the Family Law Reform Act 1987].

Amendment—Words in square brackets inserted by the Family Law Reform Act 1987, s 33(1), Sch 2, para 4.

PART V
SUPPLEMENTAL

53 General savings

(1) Nothing in this Act shall derogate from the powers of the High Court which exist independently of this Act or alter the distribution of business between the several divisions of the High Court, or operate to transfer any jurisdiction from the High Court to any other court.

(2) Nothing in this Act shall affect any unrepealed enactment in a public general Act dispensing with probate or administration as respects personal estate not including chattels real.

(3) …

Amendment—Sub-s (3): repealed by the Finance Act 1975, ss 52(2), 59(5), Sch 13, Part I.

54 Application of Act

Save as otherwise expressly provided, this Act does not apply in any case where the death occurred before the commencement of this Act.

55 Definitions

In this Act, unless the context otherwise requires, the following expressions have the meanings hereby assigned to them respectively, that is to say:—

(1)

(i) 'Administration' means, with reference to the real and personal estate of a deceased person, letters of administration whether general or limited, or with the will annexed or otherwise:

(ii) 'Administrator' means a person to whom administration is granted:

(iii) 'Conveyance' includes a mortgage, charge by way of legal mortgage, lease, assent, vesting, declaration, vesting instrument, disclaimer, release and every other assurance of property or of an interest therein by any instrument, except a will, and 'convey' has a corresponding meaning, and 'disposition' includes a 'conveyance' also a devise bequest and an appointment of property contained in a will, and 'dispose of' has a corresponding meaning:

[(iiiA) 'the County Court limit', in relation to any enactment contained in this Act, means the amount for the time being specified by an Order in Council under section 145 of the County Courts Act 1984 as the county court limit for the purposes of that enactment (or, where no such Order in Council has been made, the corresponding limit specified by Order in Council under section 192 of the County Courts Act 1959);]

(iv) 'the Court' means the High Court and also the county court, where that court has jurisdiction …

(v) 'Income' includes rents and profits:

(vi) 'Intestate' includes a person who leaves a will but dies intestate as to some beneficial interest in his real or personal estate:

[(via) 'Land' has the same meaning as in the Law of Property Act 1925;]

(vii) 'Legal estates' mean the estates charges and interests in or over land (subsisting or created at law) which are by statute authorised to subsist or to be created at law; and 'equitable interests' mean all other interests and charges in or over land …:

(viii) '[Person of unsound mind]' includes a [person of unsound mind] whether so found or not, and in relation to a [person of unsound mind] not so found; … and 'defective' includes every person affected by the provisions of section one hundred and sixteen of the Lunacy Act 1890, as extended by section sixty-four of the Mental Deficiency Act 1913, and for whose benefit a receiver has been appointed:

(ix) 'Pecuniary legacy' includes an annuity, a general legacy, a demonstrative legacy so far as it is not discharged out of the designated property, and any other general direction by a testator for the payment of money, including all death duties free from which any devise, bequest, or payment is made to take effect:

(x) 'Personal chattels' mean carriages, horses, stable furniture and effects (not used for business purposes), motor cars and accessories (not used for business purposes), garden effects, domestic animals, plate, plated articles, linen, china, glass, books, pictures, prints, furniture, jewellery, articles of household or personal use or ornament, musical and scientific instruments and apparatus, wines, liquors and consumable stores, but do not include any chattels used at the death of the intestate for business purposes nor money or securities for money:

(xi) 'Personal representative' means the executor, original or by representation, or administrator for the time being of a deceased person, and as regards any liability for the payment of death duties includes any person who takes possession of or intermeddles with the property of a deceased person without the authority of the personal representatives or the court, and 'executor' includes a person deemed to be appointed executor as respects settled land:

(xii) 'Possession' includes the receipt of rents and profits or the right to receive the same, if any:

(xiii) 'Prescribed' means prescribed by rules of court …:

(xiv) 'Probate' means the probate of a will:

(xv), (xvi) < ... >:

(xvii) 'Property' includes a thing in action and any interest in real or personal property:

(xviii) 'Purchaser' means a lessee, mortgagee, or other person who in good faith acquires an interest in property for valuable consideration, also an intending purchaser and 'valuable consideration' includes marriage, but does not include a nominal consideration in money:

(xix) 'Real estate' save as provided in Part IV of this Act means real estate, including chattels real, which by virtue of Part I of this Act devolves on the personal representative of a deceased person:

(xx) 'Representation' means the probate of a will and administration, and the expression 'taking out representation' refers to the obtaining of the probate of a will or of the grant of administration:

(xxi) 'Rent' includes a rent service or a rentcharge, or other rent, toll, duty, or annual or periodical payment in money or money's worth, issuing out of or charged upon land, but does not include mortgage interest; and 'rentcharge' includes a fee farm rent:

(xxii) ...

(xxiii) 'Securities' include stocks, funds, or shares:

(xxiv) 'Tenant for life,' 'statutory owner,' ... 'settled land,' 'settlement,' 'trustees of the settlement,' 'term of years absolute,' 'death duties,' and 'legal mortgage,' have the same meanings as in the Settled Land Act 1925, and 'entailed interest' and 'charge by way of legal mortgage' have the same meanings as in the Law of Property Act 1925:

(xxv) 'Treasury solicitor' means the solicitor for the affairs of His Majesty's Treasury, and includes the solicitor for the affairs of the Duchy of Lancaster:

(xxiv) 'Trust corporation' means the public trustee or a corporation either appointed by the court in any particular case to be a trustee or entitled by rules made under subsection (3) of section four of the Public Trustee Act 1906, to act as custodian trustee:

(xxvii) 'Will' includes codicil.

(2) References to a child or issue living at the death of any person include child or issue en ventre sa mere at the death.

(3) References to the estate of a deceased person include property over which the deceased exercises a general power of appointment (including the statutory power to dispose of entailed interests) by his will.

Amendment—Sub-s (1): para (iiiA) inserted by the County Courts Act 1984, s 148(1), Sch 2, Part III, para 15.

Sub-s (1): words omitted from para (iv) repealed by the Courts Act 1971, s 56(4), Sch 11, Part II.

Sub-s (1): para (via) inserted by the Trusts of Land and Appointment of Trustees Act 1996, s 25(1), Sch 3, para 6(1), (5); for savings in relation to entailed interests created before the commencement of that Act, and savings consequential upon the abolition of the doctrine of conversion, see s 25(4), (5) thereof. Date in force: 1 January 1997: see SI 1996/2974, art 2.

Sub-s (1): in para (vii) words omitted repealed by the Trusts of Land and Appointment of Trustees Act 1996, s 25(2), Sch 4; for savings in relation to entailed interests created before the commencement of that Act, and savings consequential upon the abolition of the doctrine of conversion, see s 25(4), (5) thereof. Date in force: 1 January 1997: see SI 1996/2974, art 2.

Sub-s (1): in para (viii) words in square brackets substituted by the Mental Treatment Act 1930, s 20(5).

Sub-s (1): words omitted from para (viii) repealed by the Mental Health Act 1959, s 149(2), Sch 8, Part I.

Sub-s (1): words omitted from para (xiii) repealed by the Supreme Court Act 1981, s 152(4), Sch 7.

Sub-s (1): para (xv) repealed by the Law of Property (Miscellaneous Provisions) Act 1994, s 21(2), Sch 2.

Sub-s (1): paras (xvi), (xxii) repealed by the Supreme Court Act 1980, s 152(4), Sch 7.

Sub-s (1): in para (xxiv) word omitted repealed by the Trusts of Land and Appointment of Trustees Act 1996, s 25(2), Sch 4; for savings in relation to entailed interests created before the commencement of that Act, and savings consequential upon the abolition of the doctrine of conversion, see s 25(4), (5) thereof. Date in force: 1 January 1997: see SI 1996/2974, art 2.

Sub-s (1): para (xxvii) repealed by the Trusts of Land and Appointment of Trustees Act 1996, s 25(2), Sch 4; for savings in relation to entailed interests created before the commencement of that Act, and savings consequential upon the abolition of the doctrine of conversion, see s 25(4), (5) thereof. Date in force: 1 January 1997: see SI 1996/2974, art 2.

Modification—Modification: definition 'Trust corporation' modified in relation to Charities, by the Charities Act 1993, s 35.

---

56 Repeal

The Acts mentioned in the Second Schedule to this Act are hereby repealed to the extent specified in the third column of that Schedule, but as respects the Acts mentioned in Part I of that Schedule only so far as they apply to deaths occurring after the commencement of this Act.

57 Application to Crown

(1) The provisions of this Act bind the Crown and the Duchy of Lancaster, and the Duke of Cornwall for the time being as respects the estates of persons dying after the commencement of this Act, but not so as to affect the time within which proceedings for the recovery of real or personal estate vesting in or devolving on His Majesty in right of His Crown, or His Duchy of Lancaster, or on the Duke of Cornwall, may be instituted.

(2) Nothing in this Act in any manner affects or alters the descent or devolution of any property for the time being vested in His Majesty either in right of the Crown or of the Duchy of Lancaster or of any property for the time being belonging to the Duchy of Cornwall.

58 Short title, commencement and extent

(1) This Act may be cited as the Administration of Estates Act 1925.

(2) …

(3) This Act extends to England and Wales only:

Amendment—Sub-s (2): repealed by the Statute Law Revision Act 1950.

Intestates' Estates Act 1952

1952 Chapter 64

An Act to amend the law of England and Wales, about the property of persons dying intestate; to amend the Inheritance Family Provision) Act 1938; and for purposes connected therewith. [30 October 1952]

Initial Commencement—Specified date: 1 January 1953: see s 9(2).

PART I
AMENDMENTS OF LAW OF INTESTATE SUCCESSION

5 Rights of surviving spouse as respects the matrimonial home

The Second Schedule to this Act shall have effect for enabling the surviving husband or wife of a person dying intestate after the commencement of this Act to acquire the matrimonial home.

Schedule 2:
Rights of Surviving Spouse as respects the Matrimonial Home

1—(1) Subject to the provisions of this Schedule, where the residuary estate of the intestate comprises of interest in a dwelling-house in which the surviving husband or wife was resident at the time of the intestate's death, the surviving husband or wife may require the personal representative in exercise of the power conferred by section forty-one of the principal Act (and with due regard to the requirements of that section as to valuation) to appropriate the said interest in the dwelling-house in or towards satisfaction of any absolute interest of the surviving husband or wife in the real and personal estate of the intestate.

(2) The right conferred by this paragraph shall not be exercisable where the interest is—

(a) a tenancy which at the date of the death of the intestate was a tenancy which would determine within the period of two years from that date; or
(b) a tenancy which the landlord by notice given for that date could determine within the remainder of that period.

(3) Nothing in subsection (5) of section forty-one of the principal Act (which requires the personal representative, in making an appropriation to any person under that section, to have regard to the rights of others) shall prevent the personal representative from giving effect to the right conferred by this paragraph.

(4) The reference in this paragraph to an absolute interest in the real and personal estate of the intestate includes a reference to the capital value of a life interest which the surviving husband or wife has under this Act elected to have redeemed.

(5) Where part of a building was, at the date of the death of the intestate, occupied as a separate dwelling, that dwelling shall for the purposes of this Schedule be treated as a dwelling-house.

2— Where—

(a) the dwelling-house forms part of a building and an interest in the whole of the building is comprised in the residuary estate; or

(b) the dwelling-house is held with agricultural land and an interest in the agricultural land is comprised in the residuary estate; or

(c) the whole or part of the dwelling-house was at the time of the intestate's death used as a hotel or lodging house; or

(d) a part of the dwelling-house was at the time of the intestate's death used for purposes other than domestic purposes,

the right conferred by paragraph 1 of this Schedule shall not be exercisable unless the court, on being satisfied that the exercise of that right is not likely to diminish the value of assets in the residuary estate (other than the said interest in the dwelling-house) or make them more difficult to dispose of, so orders.

3—(1) The right conferred by paragraph 1 of this Schedule.

(a) shall not be exercisable after the expiration of twelve months from the first taking out of representation with respect to the intestate's estate;

(b) shall not be exercisable after the death of the surviving husband or wife;

(c) shall be exercisable, except where the surviving husband or wife is the sole personal representative, by notifying the personal representative (or, where there are two or more personal representatives of whom one is the surviving husband or wife, all of them except the surviving husband or wife) in writing.

(2) A notification in writing under paragraph (c) of the foregoing sub-paragraph shall not be revocable except with the consent of the personal representative; but the surviving husband or wife may require the personal representative to have the said interest in the dwelling-house valued in accordance with section forty-one of the principal Act and to inform him or her of the result of that valuation before he or she decides whether to exercise the right.

(3) Subsection (9) of the section forty-seven A added to the principal Act by section two of this Act shall apply for the purposes of the construction of the reference in this paragraph to the first taking out of representation, and the promise to subsection (5) of that section shall apply for the purpose of enabling the surviving husband or wife to apply for an extension of the period of twelve months mentioned in this paragraph.

4—(1) During the period of twelve months mentioned in paragraph 3 of this Schedule the personal representative shall not without the written consent of the surviving husband or wife sell or otherwise dispose of the said interest in the dwelling-house except in the course of administration owing to want of other assets.

(2) An application to the court under paragraph 2 of this Schedule may be made by the personal representative as well as by the surviving husband or wife, and if, on an application under that paragraph, the court does not order that the right conferred by paragraph 1 of this Schedule shall be exercisable by the surviving husband or wife, the court may authorise the personal representative to dispose of the said interest in the dwelling-house within the said period of twelve months.

(3) Where the court under sub-paragraph (3) of paragraph 3 of this Schedule extends the said period of twelve months, the court may direct that this paragraph shall apply in relation to the extended period as it applied in relation to the original period of twelve months.

(4) This paragraph shall not apply where the surviving husband or wife is the sole personal representative or one of two or more personal representatives.

(5) Nothing in this paragraph shall confer any right on the surviving husband or wife as against a purchaser from the personal representative.

5—(1) Where the surviving husband or wife is one of two or more personal representatives, the rule that a trustee may not be a purchaser of trust property shall not prevent the surviving husband or wife from purchasing out of the estate of the intestate an interest in a dwelling-house in which the surviving husband or wife was resident at the time of the intestate's death.

(2) The power of appropriation under section forty-one of the principal Act shall include power to appropriate an interest in a dwelling-house in which the surviving husband or wife was resident at the time of the intestate's death partly in satisfaction of an interest of the surviving husband or wife in the real and personal estate of the intestate and partly in return for a payment of money by the surviving husband or wife to the personal representative.

6—(1) Where the surviving husband or wife is a person of unsound mind or a defective, a requirement or consent under this Schedule may be made or given on his or her behalf by the committee or receiver, if any, or, where there is no committee or receiver, by the court.

(2) A requirement or consent made or given under this Schedule by a surviving husband or wife who is an infant shall be as valid and binding as it would be if he or she were of age, and, as respects an appropriation in pursuance of paragraph 1 of this Schedule, the provisions of section forty-one of the principal Act as to obtaining the consent of the infant's parent or guardian, or of the court on behalf of the infant, shall not apply.

7—(1) Except where the context otherwise requires, references in this Schedule to a dwelling-house include references to any garden or portion of ground attached to and usually occupied with the dwelling-house or otherwise required for the amenity or convenience of the dwelling-house.

(2) This Schedule shall be construed as one with Part IV of the principal Act.

Variation of Trusts Act 1958

1958 Chapter 53

An Act to extend the jurisdiction of courts of law to vary trusts in the interests of beneficiaries and sanction dealings with trust property. [23 July 1958]

Initial Commencement—Royal Assent: 23 July 1958: (no specific commencement provision).
Extent—This Act does not extend to Scotlan: see s 2(1).

---

1 Jurisdiction of courts to vary trusts

(1) Where property, whether real or personal, is held on trusts arising, whether before or after the passing of this Act, under any will, settlement or other disposition, the court may if it thinks fit by order approve on behalf of—

(a) any person having, directly or indirectly, an interest, whether vested or contingent, under the trusts who by reason of infancy or other incapacity is incapable of assenting, or
(b) any person (whether ascertained or not) who may become entitled, directly or indirectly, to an interest under the trusts as being at a future date or on the happening of a future event a person of any specified description or a member of any specified class of persons, so however that this paragraph shall not include any person who would be of that description, or a member of that class, as the case may be, if the said date had fallen or the said event had happened at the date of the application to the court, or
(c) any person unborn, or
(d) any person in respect of any discretionary interest of his under protective trusts where the interest of the principal beneficiary has not failed or determined,

any arrangement (by whomsoever proposed, and whether or not there is any other person beneficially interested who is capable of assenting thereto) varying or revoking all or any of the trusts, or enlarging the powers of the trustees of managing or administering any of the property subject to the trusts:

Provided that except by virtue of paragraph (d) of this subsection the court shall not approve an arrangement on behalf of any person unless the carrying out thereof would be for the benefit of that person.

(2) In the foregoing subsection 'protective trusts' means the trusts specified in paragraphs (i) and (ii) of subsection (1) of section thirty-three of the Trustee Act 1925, or any like trusts, 'the principal beneficiary' has the same meaning as in the said subsection (1) and 'discretionary interest' means an interest arising under the trust specified in paragraph (ii) of the said subsection (1) or any like trust.

(3) … the jurisdiction conferred by subsection (1) of this section shall be exercisable by the High Court, except that the question whether the carrying out of any arrangement would be for the benefit of a person falling within paragraph (a) of the said subsection (1) shall be determined by order of [the authority having jurisdiction under [Part VII of the Mental Health Act 1983], if that person is a patient within the meaning of [the said Part VII]].

(4) …

(5) Nothing in the foregoing provisions of this section shall apply to trusts affecting property settled by Act of Parliament.

(6) Nothing in this section shall be taken to limit the powers conferred by section sixty-four of the Settled Land Act 1925, section fifty-seven of the Trustee Act 1925, or [the powers of the authority having jurisdiction under [Part VII of the Mental Health Act 1983]].

Amendment—Sub-s (3): words omitted repealed by the County Courts Act 1959, s 204, Sch 3; first words in square brackets substituted by the Mental Health Act 1959, s 149(1), Sch 7, Part I; words in square brackets therein substituted by the Mental Health Act 1983, s 148, Sch 4, para 14.

Sub-s (4): repealed by the County Courts Act 1959, s 204, Sch 3.

Sub-s (6): first words in square brackets substituted by the Mental Health Act 1959, s 149(1), Sch 7, Part I; words in square brackets therein substituted by the Mental Health Act 1983, s 148, Sch 4, para 14.

Trustee Investments Act 1961

1961 Chapter 62

An Act to make fresh provision with respect to investment by trustees and persons having the investment powers of trustees, and by local authorities, and for purposes connected therewith. [3 August 1961]

Initial Commencement—Royal Assent 3 August 1961: (no specific commencement provision).
Extent—see s 17

---

1 New powers of investment of trustees

(1) A trustee may invest any property in his hands, whether at the time in a state of investment or not, in any manner specified in Part I or II of the First Schedule to this Act or, subject to the next following section, in any manner specified in Part III of that Schedule, and may also from time to time vary any such investments.

(2) The supplemental provisions contained in Part IV of that Schedule shall have effect for the interpretation and for restricting the operation of the said Parts I to III.

(3) No provision relating to the powers of the trustee contained in any instrument (not being an enactment or an instrument made under an enactment) made before the passing of this Act shall limit the powers conferred by this section, but those powers are exerciseable only in so far as a contrary intention is not expressed in any Act or instrument made under an enactment, whenever passed or made, and so relating or in any other instrument so relating which is made after the passing of this Act.

For the purposes of this subsection any rule of the law of Scotland whereby a testamentary writing may be deemed to be made on a date other than that on which it was actually executed shall be disregarded.

(4) In this Act 'narrower-range investment' means an investment falling within Part I or II of the First Schedule to this Act and 'wider-range investment' means an investment falling within Part III of that Schedule.

Amendment—Repealed, except in so far as this section is applied by or under any other enactment, by the Trustee Act 2000, s 40(1), (3), Sch 2, Pt I, para 1(1), Sch 4, Pt I. Date in force: 1 February 2001: see SI 2001/49, art 2.

---

2 Restrictions on wider-range investment

(1) A trustee shall not have power by virtue of the foregoing section to make or retain any wider-range investment unless the trust fund has been divided into two parts (hereinafter referred to as the narrower-range part and the wider- range part), the parts being, subject to the provisions of this Act, equal in value at the time of the division; and where such a division has been made no subsequent division of the same fund shall be made for the purposes of this section, and no property shall be transferred from one part of the fund to the other unless either—

(a) the transfer is authorised or required by the following provisions of this Act, or

(b) a compensating transfer is made at the same time.

In this section 'compensating transfer', in relation to any transferred property, means a transfer in the opposite direction of property of equal value.

(2) Property belonging to the narrower-range part of a trust fund shall not by virtue of the foregoing section be invested except in narrower-range investments, and any property invested in any other manner which is or becomes comprised in that part of the trust fund shall either be transferred to the wider-range part of the fund, with a compensating transfer, or be reinvested in narrower-range investments as soon as may be.

(3) Where any property accrues to a trust fund after the fund has been divided in pursuance of subsection (1) of this section, then—

(a) if the property accrues to the trustee as owner or former owner of property comprised in either part of the fund, it shall be treated as belonging to that part of the fund;
(b) in any other case, the trustee shall secure, by apportionment of the accruing property or the transfer of property from one part of the fund to the other, or both, that the value of each part of the fund is increased by the same amount.

Where a trustee acquires property in consideration of a money payment the acquisition of the property shall be treated for the purposes of this section as investment and not as the accrual of property to the trust fund, notwithstanding that the amount of the consideration is less than the value of the property acquired; and paragraph (a) of this subsection shall not include the case of a dividend or interest becoming part of a trust fund.

(4) Where in the exercise of any power or duty of a trustee property falls to be taken out of the trust fund, nothing in this section shall restrict his discretion as to the choice of property to be taken out.

Amendment—Repealed, except in so far as this section is applied by or under any other enactment, by the Trustee Act 2000, s 40(1), (3), Sch 2, Pt I, para 1(1), Sch 4, Pt I. Date in force: 1 February 2001: see SI 2001/49, art 2.
Modification—Sub-s (3) modified, in relation to a trust fund consisting of property held by or in trust for a charity, by the Charities (Trustee Investments Act 1961) Order 1995, SI 1995/1092, art 3.

---

3 Relationship between Act and other powers of investment

(1) The powers conferred by section one of this Act are in addition to and not in derogation from any power conferred otherwise than by this Act of investment or postponing conversion exerciseable by a trustee (hereinafter referred to as a 'special power').

(2) Any special power (however expressed) to invest property in any investment for the time being authorised by law for the investment of trust property, being a power conferred on a trustee before the passing of this Act or conferred on him under any enactment passed before the passing of this Act, shall have effect as a power to invest property in like manner and subject to the like provisions as under the foregoing provisions of this Act.

(3) In relation to property, including wider-range but not including narrower-range investments,—

(a) which a trustee is authorised to hold apart from—

  (i) the provisions of section one of this Act or any of the provisions of Part I of the Trustee Act 1925, or any of the provisions of the Trusts (Scotland) Act 1921, or
  (ii) any such power to invest in authorised investments as is mentioned in the foregoing subsection, or

(b) which became part of a trust fund in consequence of the exercise by the trustee, as owner of property falling within this subsection, of any power conferred by subsection (3) or (4) of section ten of the Trustee Act 1925, or paragraph (o) or (p) of subsection (1) of section four of the Trusts (Scotland) Act 1921,

the foregoing section shall have effect subject to the modifications set out in the Second Schedule to this Act.

(4) The foregoing subsection shall not apply where the powers of the trustee to invest or postpone conversion have been conferred or varied—

(a) by an order of any court made within the period of ten years ending with the passing of this Act, or
(b) by any enactment passed, or instrument having effect under an enactment made, within that period, being an enactment or instrument relating specifically to the trusts in question; or
(c) by an enactment contained in a local Act of the present Session;

but the provisions of the Third Schedule to this Act shall have effect in a case falling within this subsection.

Amendment—Repealed, except in so far as this section relates to a trustee having a power of investment conferred on him under any enactment which was passed before 3 August 1961 and which is not amended by the Trustee Act 2000, Sch 2, by the Trustee Act 2000, s 40(1), (3), Sch 2, Pt I, para 1(2), Sch 4, Pt I. Date in force: 1 February 2001: see SI 2001/49, art 2.

---

4 Interpretation of references to trust property and trust funds

(1) In this Act 'property' includes real or personal property of any description, including money and things in action:

Provided that it does not include an interest in expectancy, but the falling into possession of such an interest, or the receipt of proceeds of the sale thereof, shall be treated for the purposes of this Act as an accrual of property to the trust fund.

(2) So much of the property in the hands of a trustee shall for the purposes of this Act constitute one trust fund as is held on trusts which (as respects the beneficiaries or their respective interests or the purposes of the trust or as respects the powers of the trustee) are not identical with those on which any other property in his hands is held.

(3) Where property is taken out of a trust fund by way of appropriation so as to

form a separate fund, and at the time of the appropriation the trust fund had (as to the whole or a part thereof) been divided in pursuance of subsection (1) of section two of this Act, or that subsection as modified by the Second Schedule to this Act, then if the separate fund is so divided the narrower-range and wider-range parts of the separate fund may be constituted so as either to be equal, or to bear to each other the same proportion as the two corresponding parts of the fund out of which it was so appropriated (the values of those parts of those funds being ascertained as at the time of appropriation), or some intermediate proportion.

(4) …

Amendment—Sub-s (4): applies to Scotland only.
Modification—Sub-s (3) modified, in relation to a trust fund consisting of property held by or in trust for a charity, by the Charities (Trustee Investments Act 1961) Order 1995, SI 1995/1092, art 3.

---

5 Certain valuations to be conclusive for purposes of division of trust fund

(1) If for the purposes of section two or four of this Act or the Second Schedule thereto a trustee obtains, from a person reasonably believed by the trustee to be qualified to make it, a valuation in writing of any property, the valuation shall be conclusive in determining whether the division of the trust fund in pursuance of subsection (1) of the said section two, or any transfer or apportionment of property under that section or the said Second Schedule, has been duly made.

(2) The foregoing subsection applies to any such valuation notwithstanding that it is made by a person in the course of his employment as an officer or servant.

Amendment—Repealed, except in so far as this section is applied by or under any other enactment, by the Trustee Act 2000, s 40(1), (3), Sch 2, Pt I, para 1(1), Sch 4, Pt I. Date in force: 1 February 2001: see SI 2001/49, art 2.

---

6 Duty of trustees in choosing investments

(1) In the exercise of his powers of investment a trustee shall have regard—

(a) to the need for diversification of investments of the trust, in so far as is appropriate to the circumstances of the trust;
(b) to the suitability to the trust of investments of the description of investment proposed and of the investment proposed as an investment of that description.

(2) Before exercising any power conferred by section one of this Act to invest a manner specified in Part II or III of the First Schedule to this Act, or before investing in any such manner in the exercise of a power falling within subsection (2) of section three of this Act, a trustee shall obtain and consider proper advice on the question whether the investment is satisfactory having regard to the matters mentioned in paragraphs (a) and (b) of the foregoing subsection.

(3) A trustee retaining any investment made in the exercise of such a power and in such a manner as aforesaid shall determine at what intervals the circumstances, and in

particular the nature of the investment, make it desirable to obtain such advice as aforesaid, and shall obtain and consider such advice accordingly.

(4) For the purposes of the two foregoing subsections, proper advice is the advice of a person who is reasonably believed by the trustee to be qualified by his ability in and practical experience of financial matters; and such advice may be given by a person notwithstanding that he gives it in the course of his employment as an officer or servant.

(5) A trustee shall not be treated as having complied with subsection (2) or (3) of this section unless the advice was given or has been subsequently confirmed in writing.

(6) Subsections (2) and (3) of this section shall not apply to one of two or more trustees where he is the person giving the advice required by this section to his co-trustee or co-trustees, and shall not apply where powers of a trustee are lawfully exercised by an officer or servant competent under subsection (4) of this section to give proper advice.

(7) Without prejudice to section eight of the Trustee Act 1925, or section thirty of the Trusts (Scotland) Act 1921 (which relate to valuation, and the proportion of the value to be lent, where a trustee lends on the security of property) the advice required by this section shall not include, in the case of a loan on the security of freehold or leasehold property in England and Wales or Northern Ireland or on heritable security in Scotland, advice on the suitability of the particular loan.

Amendment—Repealed, except in so far as this section is applied by or under any other enactment, by the Trustee Act 2000, s 40(1), (3), Sch 2, Pt I, para 1(1), Sch 4, Pt I. Date in force: 1 February 2001: see SI 2001/49, art 2.

---

7 Application of ss 1–6 to persons, other than trustees, having trustee investment powers

(1) Where any persons, not being trustees, have a statutory power of making investments which is or includes power—

(a) to make the like investments as are authorised by section one of the Trustee Act 1925, or section ten of the Trusts (Scotland) Act 1921, or
(b) to make the like investments as trustees are for the time being by law authorised to make,

however the power is expressed, the foregoing provisions of this Act shall with the necessary modifications apply in relation to them as if they were trustees:

Provided that property belonging to a Consolidated Loans Fund or any other fund applicable wholly or partly for the redemption of debt shall not by virtue of the foregoing provisions of this Act be invested or held invested in any manner specified in paragraph 6 of Part II of the First Schedule to this Act or in wider-range investments.

(2) Where, in the exercise of powers conferred by any enactment, an authority to which paragraph 9 of Part II of the First Schedule to this Act applies uses money belonging to any fund for a purpose for which the authority has power to borrow, the

foregoing provisions of this Act, as applied by the foregoing subsection, shall apply as if there were comprised in the fund (in addition to the actual content thereof) property, being narrower-range investments, having a value equal to so much of the said money as for the time being has not been repaid to the fund, and accordingly any repayment of such money to the fund shall not be treated for the said purposes as the accrual of property to the fund:

Provided that nothing in this subsection shall be taken to require compliance with any of the provisions of section six of this Act in relation to the exercise of such powers as aforesaid.

(3) In this section 'Consolidated Loans Fund' means a fund established under section fifty-five of the Local Government Act 1958, and includes a loans fund established under section two hundred and seventy-five of the Local Government (Scotland) Act 1947, and 'statutory power' means a power conferred by an enactment passed before the passing of this Act or by any instrument made under any such enactment.

12 Power to confer additional powers of investment

(1) Her Majesty may by Order in Council extend the powers of investment conferred by section one of this Act by adding to Part I, Part II or Part III of the First Schedule to this Act any manner of investment specified in the Order.

(2) Any Order under this section shall be subject to annulment in pursuance of a resolution of either House of Parliament.

Amendment—Repealed, except in so far as this section is applied by or under any other enactment, by the Trustee Act 2000, s 40(1), (3), Sch 2, Pt I, para 1(1), Sch 4, Pt I. Date in force: 1 February 2001: see SI 2001/49, art 2.

---

13 Power to modify provisions as to division of trust fund

(1) The Treasury may by order made by statutory instrument direct that, subject to subsection (3) of section four of this Act, any division of a trust fund made in pursuance of subsection (1) of section two of this Act during the continuance in force of the order shall be made so that the value of the wider-range part at the time of the division bears to the then value of the narrower- range part such proportion, greater than one but not greater than three to one, as may be prescribed by the order; and in this Act 'the prescribed proportion' means the proportion for the time being prescribed under this subsection.

(2) A fund which has been divided in pursuance of subsection (1) of section two of this Act before the coming into operation of an order under the foregoing subsection may notwithstanding anything in that subsection be again divided (once only) in pursuance of the said subsection (1) during the continuance in force of the order.

(3) If an order is made under subsection (1) of this section, then as from the coming into operation of the order—

(a) paragraph (b) of subsection (3) of section two of this Act and sub- paragraph (b) of paragraph 3 of the Second Schedule thereto shall have effect with the substitution, for the words from 'each' to the end, of the words 'the wider-range part of the fund is increased by an amount which bears the prescribed proportion to the amount by which the value of the narrower-range part of the fund is increased';

(b) subsection (3) of section four of this Act shall have effect as if for the words 'so as either' to 'each other' there were substituted the words 'so as to bear to each other either the prescribed proportion or'.

(4) An order under this section may be revoked by a subsequent order thereunder prescribing a greater proportion.

(5) An order under this section shall not have effect unless approved by a resolution of each House of Parliament.

Amendment—Repealed, except in so far as this section is applied by or under any other enactment, by the Trustee Act 2000, s 40(1), (3), Sch 2, Pt I, para 1(1), Sch 4, Pt I. Date in force: 1 February 2001: see SI 2001/49, art 2.

---

15 Saving for powers of court

The enlargement of the investment powers of trustees by this Act shall not lessen any power of a court to confer wider powers of investment on trustees, or affect the extent to which any such power is to be exercised.

Amendment—Repealed, except in so far as this section is applied by or under any other enactment, by the Trustee Act 2000, s 40(1), (3), Sch 2, Pt I, para 1(1), Sch 4, Pt I. Date in force: 1 February 2001: see SI 2001/49, art 2.

---

16 Minor and consequential amendments and repeals

(1) The provisions of the Fourth Schedule to this Act (which contain minor amendments and amendments consequential on the foregoing provisions of this Act) shall have effect.

(2) < … >

Amendment—Sub-s (1): repealed by the Trustee Act 2000, s 40(1), (3), Sch 2, Pt I, para 1(3)(c), Sch 4, Pt I. Date in force (for certain purposes): 9 January 2001: see SI 2001/49, art 2.
Sub-s (2): repealed by the Statute Law (Repeals) Act 1974.

---

17 Short title, extent and construction

(1) This Act may be cited as the Trustee Investments Act 1961.

(2) Sections eleven and sixteen of this Act shall extend to Northern Ireland, but except as aforesaid and except so far as any other provisions of the Act apply by virtue of subsection (1) of section one of the Trustee Act (Northern Ireland) 1958, or any

other enactment of the Parliament of Northern Ireland, to trusts the execution of which is governed by the law in force in Northern Ireland, this Act does not apply to such trusts.

(3) So much of section sixteen of this Act as relates to [the National Savings Bank] ... shall extend to the Isle of Man and the Channel Islands.

(4) Except where the context otherwise requires, in this Act, in its application to trusts the execution of which is governed by the law in force in England and Wales, expressions have the same meaning as in the Trustee Act 1925.

(5) ...

Amendment—Sub-s (3): words in square brackets substituted by the Post Office Act 1969, ss 94, 114, Sch 6, Part III; words omitted repealed by the Trustee Savings Banks Act 1985, ss 4(3), 7(3), Sch 4.

Sub-s (5): applies to Scotland only.

Modification—Modified, in relation to a trust fund consisting of property held by or in trust for a charity, by the Charities (Trustee Investments Act 1961) Order 1995, SI 1995/1092, art 3.

The Northern Ireland Act 1998 makes new provision for the government of Northern Ireland for the purpose of implementing the Belfast Agreement (the agreement reached at multi-party talks on Northern Ireland and set out in Command Paper 3883). As a consequence of that Act, any reference in this section to the Parliament of Northern Ireland or the Assembly established under the Northern Ireland Assembly Act 1973, s 1, certain office-holders and Ministers, and any legislative act and certain financial dealings thereof, shall, for the period specified, be construed in accordance with Sch 12, paras 1–11 to the 1998 Act.

Schedule 1:
Manner of Investment

PART
NARROWER-RANGE INVESTMENTS NOT REQUIRING ADVICE

1— In Defence Bonds, National Savings Certificates Ulster Savings Certificates, [Ulster Development Bonds] [National Development Bonds], [British Savings Bonds], [National Savings Income Bonds] [National Savings Deposit Bonds] [National Savings Indexed-Income Bonds], [National Savings Capital Bonds] [National Savings FIRST Option Bonds], [National Savings Pensioners Guaranteed Income Bonds].

2— In deposits in [the National Savings Bank], ... and deposits in a bank or department thereof certified under subsection (3) of section nine of the Finance Act 1956.

Amendment—Words in square brackets inserted by SI 1962/2611, SI 1964/703, SI 1968/470, SI 1982/1086, SI 1983/1525, SI 1985/1780, Post Office Act 1969, ss 94, 114, Sch 6, Part III, SI 1988/2254, art 2, SI 1992/1738, art 2 and SI 1994/265, art 2; words omitted repealed by the Trustee Savings Banks Act 1976, s 36(2), Sch 6.

PART II
NARROWER-RANGE OF INVESTMENTS REQUIRING ADVICE

1— In securities issued by Her Majesty's Government in the United Kingdom, the Government of Northern Ireland or the Government of the Isle of Man, not being securities falling within Part I of this Schedule and being fixed-interest securities registered in the United Kingdom or the Isle of Man, Treasury Bills or Tax Reserve Certificates [or any variable interest securities issued by Her Majesty's Government in the United Kingdom and registered in the United Kingdom].

2— In any securities the payment of interest on which is guaranteed by Her Majesty's Government in the United Kingdom or the Government of Northern Ireland.

3— In fixed-interest securities issued in the United Kingdom by any public authority or nationalised industry or undertaking in the United Kingdom.

4— In fixed-interest securities issued in the United Kingdom by the government of any overseas territory within the Commonwealth or by any public or local authority within such a territory, being securities registered in the United Kingdom.

References in this paragraph to an overseas territory or to the government of such a territory shall be construed as if they occurred in the Overseas Service Act, 1958.

[4A— In securities issued in the United Kingdom by the government of an overseas territory within the Commonwealth or by any public or local authority within such a territory, being securities registered in the United Kingdom and in respect of which the rate of interest is variable by reference to one or more of the following:—

(a) the Bank of England's minimum lending rate;
(b) the average rate of discount on allotment on 91-day Treasury bills;
(c) a yield on 91-day Treasury bills;
(d) a London sterling inter-bank offered rate;
(e) a London sterling certificate of deposit rate.

References in this paragraph to an overseas territory or to the government of such a territory shall be construed as if they occurred in the Overseas Service Act 1958.]

5— In fixed-interest securities issued in the United Kingdom by [the African Development Bank, the Asian Development Bank, the Caribbean Development Bank, [the European Bank for Reconstruction and Development,] the International Finance Corporation, the International Monetary Fund or by] the International Bank for Reconstruction and Development, being securities registered in the United Kingdom.

[In fixed-interest securities issued in the United Kingdom by the Inter-American Development Bank],

[In fixed interest securities issued in the United Kingdom by [the European Atomic Energy Community, the European Economic Community,] the European Investment Bank or by the European Coal and Steel Community, being securities registered in the United Kingdom.]

[5A— In securities issued in the United Kingdom by

(i) the International Bank for Reconstruction and Development or by the European Investment Bank or by the European Coal and Steel Community, being securities registered in the United Kingdom or
(ii) the Inter-American Development Bank

being securities in respect of which the rate of interest is variable by reference to one or more of the following:—

(a) the Bank of England's minimum lending rate;
(b) the average rate of discount on allotment on 91-day Treasury bills;
(c) a yield on 91-day Treasury bills;
(d) a London sterling inter-bank offered rate;
(e) a London sterling certificate of deposit rate.]

[5B— In securities issued in the United Kingdom by the African Development Bank, the Asian Development Bank, the Caribbean Development Bank, the European Atomic Energy Community, [the European Bank for Reconstruction and Development,] the European Economic Community, the International Finance Corporation or by the International Monetary Fund, being securities registered in the United Kingdom and in respect of which the rate of interest is variable by reference to one or more of the following:—

(a) The average rate of discount on allotment on 91-day Treasury Bills;
(b) a yield on 91-day Treasury Bills;
(c) a London sterling inter-bank offered rate;
(d) a London sterling certificate of deposit rate.]

6— In debentures issued in the United Kingdom by a company incorporated in the United Kingdom, being debentures registered in the United Kingdom.

7— In stock of the Bank of Ireland.

[In Bank of Ireland 7 per cent. Loan Stock 1968/91].

8— …

9— In loans to any authority to which this paragraph applies charged on all or any of the revenues of the authority or on a fund into which all or any of those revenues are payable, in any fixed-interest securities issued in the United Kingdom by any such authority for the purpose of borrowing money so charged, and in deposits with any such authority by way of temporary loan made on the giving of a receipt for the loan by the treasurer or other similar officer of the authority and on the giving of an undertaking by the authority that, if requested to charge the loan as aforesaid, it will either comply with the request or repay the loan.

This paragraph applies to the following authorities, that is to say—

(a) any local authority in the United Kingdom;
[(aa) the Greater London Authority;
(ab) any functional body, within the meaning of the Greater London Authority Act 1999;]
(b) any authority all the members of which are appointed or elected by one or more local authorities in the United Kingdom;
(c) any authority the majority of the members of which are appointed or elected by one or more local authorities in the United Kingdom, being an authority which by virtue of any enactment has power to issue a precept to a local authority in England and Wales, or a requisition to a local authority in Scotland, or to the expenses of which, by virtue of any enactment, a local authority in the United Kingdom is or can be required to contribute;
(d) …[a police authority established under [section 3 of the Police Act 1996]];
[(da) the Service Authority for the National Criminal Intelligence Service or the Service Authority for the National Crime Squad;]

(e) the Belfast City and District Water Commissioners;
[(f) the Great Ouse Water Authority];
[(g) any district council in Northern Ireland;]
[(h) ...;
(i) any residuary body established by section 57 of the Local Government Act 1985.]

[9A— In any securities issued in the United Kingdom by any authority to which paragraph 9 applies for the purpose of borrowing money charged on all or any of the revenues of the authority or on a fund into which all or any of those revenues are payable and being securities in respect of which the rate of interest is variable by reference to one or more of the following:—

(a) the Bank of England's minimum lending rate;
(b) the average rate of discount on allotment on 91-day Treasury bills;
(c) a yield on 91-day Treasury bills;
(d) a London sterling inter-bank offered rate;
(e) a London sterling certificate of deposit rate.]

10— ...

[10A— In any units of a gilt unit trust scheme.

References in this Schedule to a gilt unit trust scheme are references to a collective investment scheme—

(a) which is an authorised unit trust scheme within the meaning of the Financial Services Act 1986, a recognised scheme within the meaning of that Act or a UCITS; and
(b) whose objective is to invest not less than 90% of the property of the scheme in loan stock, bonds and other instruments creating or acknowledging indebtedness which are transferable and which are issued or guaranteed by—

 (i) the government of the United Kingdom [or of any other country or territory],
 (ii) by a local authority in the United Kingdom or in a relevant state, or
 (iii) by an international organisation the members of which include the United Kingdom or a relevant state;and, in respect of the remainder of the property of the scheme, whose objective is to invest in any instrument falling within any of paragraphs 1 to 3, 5 or 6 of Schedule 1 to the Financial Services Act 1986.]

11— ...

[12— In deposits with a building society within the meaning of the Building Societies Act 1986.]

13— In mortgages of freehold property in England and Wales or Northern Ireland and of leasehold property in those countries of which the unexpired term at the time of investment is not less than sixty years, and in loans on heritable security in Scotland.

14— In perpetual rent-charges charged on land in England and Wales or Northern Ireland and fee-farm rents (not being rent-charges) issuing out of such land, *and in feu-duties or ground annuals in Scotland.*

[15— In Certificates of Tax Deposit.]

[16— In fixed-interest or variable interest securities issued by the government of a relevant state.

17— In any securities the payment of interest on which is guaranteed by the government of a relevant state.

18— In fixed-interest securities issued in any relevant state by any public authority or nationalised industry or undertaking in that state.

19— In fixed-interest or variable interest securities issued in a relevant state by the government of any overseas territory within the Commonwealth or by any public or local authority within such a territory.

References in this paragraph to an overseas territory or to the government of such a territory shall be construed as if they occurred in the Overseas Development and Co-operation Act 1980.

20— In fixed-interest or variable interest securities issued in a relevant state by—

(a) the African Development Bank;
(b) the Asian Development Bank;
(c) the Caribbean Development Bank;
(d) the International Finance Corporation;
(e) the International Monetary Fund;
(f) the International Bank for Reconstruction and Development;
(g) the Inter-American Development Bank;
(h) the European Atomic Energy Community;
(i) the European Bank for Reconstruction and Development;
(j) the European Economic Community;
(k) the European Investment Bank; or
(l) the European Coal and Steel Community.

21— In debentures issued in any relevant state by a company incorporated in that state.

22— In loans to any authority to which this paragraph applies secured on all or any of the revenues of the authority or on a fund into which all or any of those revenues are payable, in fixed-interest or variable interest securities issued in a relevant state by any such authority in that state for the purpose of borrowing money so secured, and in deposits with any authority to which this paragraph applies by way of temporary loan made on the giving of a receipt for the loan by the treasurer or other similar officer of the authority and on the giving of an undertaking by the authority that, if requested to charge the loan as aforesaid, it will either comply with the request or repay the loan.

This paragraph applies to the following authorities, that is to say—

(a) any local authority in a relevant state; or
(b) any authority all the members of which are appointed or elected by one or more local authorities in any such state.

23— In deposits with a mutual investment society whose head office is located in a relevant state.

24— In loans secured on any interest in property in a relevant state which corresponds to an interest in property falling within paragraph 13 of this Part of this Schedule.]

Amendment—Para 1: words in square brackets inserted by SI 1977/831, art 3.

Paras 4A, 5A, 9A: inserted by SI 1977/1878, art 3.

Para 5: first words in square brackets inserted by SI 1983/772, art 2(a), words in square brackets therein inserted by SI 1991/999, art 2; second words in square brackets inserted by SI 1964/1404, art 1; third words in square brackets inserted by SI 1972/1818, art 3, words in square brackets therein inserted by SI 1983/772, art 2(b).

Para 5B: inserted by SI 1983/772, art 2(c); words in square brackets inserted by SI 1991/999, art 2.

Para 7: words in square brackets inserted by SI 1966/401, art 1.

Para 8: repealed by the Agriculture and Forestry (Financial Provisions) Act 1991, s 1, Schedule, Part IV.

Para 9: sub-paras (aa), (ab) inserted by the Greater London Authority Act 1999, s 387(1), (3)(a). Date in force (for the purposes of its application to the Greater London Authority): 8 May 2000: see SI 1999/3434, art 3. Date in force (for remaining purposes): 3 July 2000: see SI 1999/3434, art 4.

Para 9: in sub-para (d) words omitted repealed by the Greater London Authority Act 1999, ss 387(1), (3)(b), 423, Sch 34, Pt I. Date in force (for the purposes of its application to the Greater London Authority): 8 May 2000: see SI 1999/3434, art 3. Date in force (for remaining purposes): 3 July 2000: see SI 2000/801, art 2(2)(c), Schedule, Pt 3.

Para 9: in sub-para (d) words in square brackets beginning with the words 'a police authority' substituted by the Police and Magistrates' Courts Act 1994, s 43, Sch 4, Pt II, para 47.

Para 9: in sub-para (d) words 'section 3 of the Police Act 1996' in square brackets substituted by the Police Act 1996, s 103, Sch 7, para 1(2)(a).

Para 9: sub-para (da) inserted by the Police Act 1997, s 134(1), Sch 9, para 5. Date in force: 1 April 1998: see SI 1998/354, art 2(2)(bb).

Para 9: sub-para (f) inserted by SI 1962/658, art 1.

Para 9: sub-para (g) inserted by SI 1973/1332, art 3.

Para 9: sub-paras (h), (i) inserted by SI 1986/601, art 2.

Para 9: sub-para (h) repealed by the Education Reform Act 1988, s 237, Sch 1, Sch 13, Pt I.

Para 10: repealed by the Water Act 1989, s 190, Sch 25, para 29.

Para 10A: inserted by the Finance Act 1982, s 150; substituted by SI 1994/1908, art 2(1); in sub-para (b)(i) words in square brackets substituted by SI 1995/768, art 3.

Para 11: repealed by the Trustee Savings Bank Act 1976, s 36(2), Sch 6.

Para 12: substituted by the Building Societies Act 1986, s 120, Sch 18, Part I, para 4(2).

Para 14: words ', and in feu-duties or ground annuals in Scotland' in italics repealed by the Abolition of Feudal Tenure etc (Scotland) Act 2000, s 76(2), Sch 13, Pt 1. Date in force: to be appointed: see the Abolition of Feudal Tenure etc (Scotland) Act 2000, ss 71, 77(2).

Para 15: inserted by SI 1975/1710, art 3.

Paras 16–24: inserted by SI 1994/1908, art 2(2).

PART III
WIDER-RANGE INVESTMENTS

1— In any securities issued in the United Kingdom by a company incorporated in the United Kingdom, being securities registered in the United Kingdom and not being securities falling within Part II of this Schedule.

[2— In shares in a building society within the meaning of the Building Societies Act 1986.]

[2A— In any shares in an investment company with variable capital within the meaning of the Open-Ended Investment Companies (Investment Companies with Variable Capital) Regulations 1996.]

[**3**—In any units of an authorised unit trust scheme within the meaning of the Financial Services Act 1986.]

[**4**—In any securities issued in any relevant state by a company incorporated in that state or by any unincorporated body constituted under the law of that state, not being (in either case) securities falling within Part II of this Schedule or paragraph 6 of this Part of this Schedule.

5—In shares in a mutual investment society whose head office is located in a relevant state.

6—In any units of a collective investment scheme which is—

(a) a recognised scheme within the meaning of the Financial Services Act 1986 which is constituted in a relevant state; or
(b) a UCITS;

and which does not fall within Part II of this Schedule.]

Amendment—Para 2: substituted by the Building Societies Act 1986, s 120, Sch 18, Part I, para 4(3).
Para 2A: inserted by SI 1996/2827, reg 75, Sch 8, para 1.
Para 3: substituted by the Financial Services Act 1986, s 212(2), Sch 16, para 2.
Paras 4–6: inserted by SI 1994/1908, art 2(3).

PART IV
SUPPLEMENTAL

1—The securities mentioned in Parts I to III of this Schedule do not include any securities where the holder can be required to accept repayment of the principal, or the payment of any interest, otherwise than in sterling[, in the currency of a relevant state or in the european currency unit (as defined in article 1 of Council Regulation No 3180/78/EEC)].

2—The securities mentioned in paragraphs 1 to 8 of Part II, other than Treasury Bills or Tax Reserve Certificates, securities issued before the passing of this Act by the Government of the Isle of Man, securities falling within paragraph 4 of the said Part II issued before the passing of this Act or securities falling within paragraph 9 of that Part, and the securities mentioned in paragraph 1 of Part III of this Schedule, do not include—

(a) securities the price of which is not quoted on [a recognised investment exchange within the meaning of the Financial Services Act 1986 [or on an investment exchange which constitutes the principal or only market established in a relevant state on which securities admitted to official listing are dealt in or traded]]

(b) shares or debenture stock not fully paid up (except shares or debenture stock which by the terms of issue are required to be fully paid up within nine months of the date of issue).

[2A— The securities mentioned in paragraphs 16 to 21 of Part II of this Schedule, other than securities traded on a relevant money market or securities falling within paragraph 22 of Part II of this Schedule, and the securities mentioned in paragraph 4 of Part III of this Schedule do not include—

(a) securities the price for which is not quoted on a recognised investment exchange within the meaning of the Financial Services Act 1986 or on an investment exchange which constitutes the principal or only market established in a relevant state on which securities admitted to official listing are dealt in or traded;
(b) shares or debenture stock not fully paid up (except shares or debenture stock which by the terms of issue are required to be fully paid up within nine months of the date of issue or shares issued with no nominal value).]

3— The securities mentioned in paragraph 6 [and 21] of Part II and paragraph 1 [or 4] of Part III of this Schedule do not include—

(a) shares or debentures of an incorporated company of which the total issued and paid up share capital is less than one million pounds;
[(ab) shares or debentures of an incorporated company of which the total issued and paid up share capital at any time on the business day before the investment is made is less than the equivalent of one million pounds in the currency of a relevant state (at the exchange rate prevailing in the United Kingdom at the close of business on the day before the investment is made);]
(b) shares or debentures of an incorporated company which has not in each of the five years immediately preceding the calendar year in which the investment is made paid a dividend on all the shares issued by the company, excluding any shares issued after the dividend was declared and any shares which by their terms of issue did not rank for the dividend for that year.

For the purposes of sub-paragraph (b) of this paragraph a company formed—

(i) to take over the business of another company or other companies, or
(ii) to acquire the securities of, or control of, another company or other companies,

or for either of those purposes and for other purposes shall be deemed to have paid a dividend as mentioned in that sub-paragraph in any year in which such a dividend has been paid by the other company or all the other companies, as the case may be.

[For the purposes of sub-paragraph (b) of this paragraph in relation to investment in shares or debentures of a successor company within the meaning of the Electricity (Northern Ireland) Order 1992 the company shall be deemed to have paid a dividend as mentioned in that sub-paragraph—

(iii) in every year preceding the calendar year in which the transfer date within the meaning of Part III of that Order of 1992 falls ('the first investment year') which is included in the relevant five years; and
(iv) in the first investment year, if that year is included in the relevant five years and that company does not in fact pay such a dividend in that year; and

'the relevant five years' means the five years immediately preceding the year in which the investment in question is made or proposed to be made.]

[3A— ...]

4— In this Schedule, unless the context otherwise requires, the following expressions have the meanings hereby respectively assigned to them, that is to say—

'debenture' includes debenture stock and bonds, whether constituting a charge on assets or not, and loan stock or notes;
'enactment' includes an enactment of the Parliament of Northern Ireland;
'fixed-interest securities' means securities which under their terms of issue bear a fixed rate of interest;
'local authority' in relation to the United Kingdom, means any of the following authorities—

(a) in England and Wales, the council of a county, [a county borough,] a ... borough ... an urban or rural district or a parish, the Common Council of the City of London [the Greater London Council] and the Council of the Isles of Scilly;
(b) in Scotland, a local authority within the meaning of the Local Government (Scotland) Act, 1947;
(c) ...

['mutual investment society' means a credit institution which operates on mutual principles and which is authorised by the appropriate supervisory authority of a relevant state;
'relevant money market' means a money market which is supervised by the central bank, or a government agency, of a relevant state;
'relevant state' means Austria, Finland, Iceland, [Liechtenstein,] Norway, Sweden or a member state other than the United Kingdom;]
...
'securities' includes shares, debentures [units within paragraph 3 [or 6] of Part III of this Schedule], Treasury Bills and Tax Reserve Certificates;
'shares' includes stock;
'Treasury Bills' includes ... bills issued by Her Majesty's Government in the United Kingdom and Northern Ireland Treasury Bills.

5— It is hereby declared that in this Schedule 'mortgage', in relation to freehold or leasehold property in Northern Ireland, includes a registered charge which, by virtue of subsection (4) of section forty of the Local Registration of Title (Ireland) Act, 1891, or any other enactment, operates as a mortgage by deed.

6— [In relation to the United Kingdom,] references in this Schedule to an incorporated company are references to a company incorporated by or under any enactment and include references to a body of persons established for the purpose of trading for profit and incorporated by Royal Charter.

[6A— References in this Schedule to a UCITS are references to a collective investment scheme which is constituted in a relevant state and which complies with the conditions necessary for it to enjoy the rights conferred by Council Directive 85/611/EEC co-ordinating the laws, regulations and administrative provisions relating to undertakings for collective investment in transferable securities; and section 86(8) of the Financial Services Act 1986 (meaning of 'constituted in a member state') shall apply for the purposes of this paragraph as it applies for the purposes of that section but as if for references in that section to a member state there were substituted references to a relevant state.]

7— ...

Amendment—Paras 1, 6: words in square brackets inserted by SI 1994/1908, art 3(2), (7).
Para 2: in sub-para (a) words in square brackets substituted by the Financial Services Act 1986, s 212(2), Sch 16, para 2, words in square brackets therein inserted by SI 1994/1908, art 3(3).
Paras 2A, 6A: inserted by SI 1994/1908, art 3(4), (8).
Para 3: first and second words in square brackets and sub-para (ab) inserted by SI 1994/1908, art 3(5); final words in square brackets inserted by SI 1992/232, art 4.
Para 3A: inserted by the Housing (Consequential Provisions) Act 1985, s 4, Sch 2, para 5; repealed by the Building Societies Act 1986, s 120, Sch 19, Part I.
Para 4: in definition 'local authority', in sub-para (a) first words in square brackets inserted by the Local Government (Wales) Act 1994, s 66(6), Sch 16, para 19(2), first words omitted repealed by London Government Act 1963, s 93(1), Sch 18 Part II, final words omitted repealed by the Local Government Act 1972, s 272(1), Sch 30, final words in square brackets inserted by the London Government Act 1963, s 83(1), Sch 17, sub-para (c) repealed by the Statute Law (Repeals) Act 1981; definitions 'mutual investment society', 'relevant money market', 'relevant state' inserted by SI 1994/1908, art 3(6)(a), in definition 'relevant state' word in square brackets inserted by SI 1995/768, art 2; definitions 'ordinary deposits' and 'special investment' repealed by the Trustee Savings Banks Act 1976, s 36(2), Sch 6; in definition 'securities' first words in square brackets inserted by the Financial Services Act 1986, s 212(2), Sch 16, para 2, words in square brackets therein inserted by SI 1994/1908, art 3(6)(b); in definition 'Treasury Bills' words omitted repealed by the National Loans Act 1968, s 24(2), Sch 6, Part 1.
Para 7: repealed by the Building Societies Act 1986, s 120, Sch 19, Part I.
Modification—The Northern Ireland Act 1998 makes new provision for the government of Northern Ireland for the purpose of implementing the Belfast Agreement (the agreement reached at multi-party talks on Northern Ireland and set out in Command Paper 3883). As a consequence of that Act, any reference in this Schedule to the Parliament of Northern Ireland or the Assembly established under the Northern Ireland Assembly Act 1973, s 1, certain office-holders and Ministers, and any legislative act and certain financial dealings thereof, shall, for the period specified, be construed in accordance with Sch 12, paras 1–11 to the 1998 Act.
See Further—See further, in relation to the application of para 3(b) above to companies nominated by the Secretary of State to succeed the National Research Development Corporation and the National Enterprise Board: the British Technology Group Act 1991, s 13.

Schedule 2:
(Modification of s 2 in relation to property falling within s 3(3)

Amendment—Repealed, except in so far as this section relates to a trustee having a power of investment conferred on him under any enactment which was passed before 3 August 1961 and which is not amended by the Trustee Act 2000, Sch 2, by the Trustee Act 2000, s 40(1), (3), Sch 2, Pt I, para 1(2), Sch 4, Pt I. Date in force: 1 February 2001: see SI 2001/49, art 2.

1— In this Schedule 'special-range property' means property falling within subsection (3) of section three of this Act.

2—(1) Where a trust fund includes special-range property, subsection (1) of section two of this Act shall have effect as if references to the trust fund were references to so much thereof as does not consist of special-range property, and the special-range property shall be carried to a separate part of the fund.

(2) Any property which—

(a) being property belonging to the narrower-range or wider-range part of a trust fund, is converted into special-range property, or
(b) being special-range property, accrues to a trust fund after the division of the fund or part thereof in pursuance of subsection (1) of section two of this Act or of that subsection as modified by sub-paragraph (1) of this paragraph,

shall be carried to such a separate part of the fund as aforesaid; and subsections (2) and (3) of the said section two shall have effect subject to this sub-paragraph.

3— Where property carried to such a separate part as aforesaid is converted into property other than special-range property,—

(a) it shall be transferred to the narrower-range part of the fund or the wider-range part of the fund or apportioned between them, and
(b) any transfer of property from one of those parts to the other shall be made which is necessary to secure that the value of each of those parts of the fund is increased by the same amount.

Amendment—Repealed, except in so far as this section relates to a trustee having a power of investment conferred on him under any enactment which was passed before 3 August 1961 and which is not amended by the Trustee Act 2000, Sch 2, by the Trustee Act 2000, s 40(1), (3), Sch 2, Pt I, para 1(2), Sch 4, Pt I.

Date in force: 1 February 2001: see SI 2001/49, art 2.

Modification—Para 3 modified, in relation to a trust fund consisting of property held by or in trust for a charity, by the Charities (Trustee Investments Act 1961) Order 1995, SI 1995/1092, art 3.

Schedule 3: Provisions Supplementary to s 3(4)

Amendment—Repealed, except in so far as this section relates to a trustee having a power of investment conferred on him under any enactment which was passed before 3 August 1961 and which is not amended by the Trustee Act 2000, Sch 2, by the Trustee Act 2000, s 40(1), (3), Sch 2, Pt I, para 1(2), Sch 4, Pt I.

1— Where in a case falling within subsection (4) of section three of this Act, property belonging to the narrower-range part of a trust fund—

(a) is invested otherwise than in a narrower-range investment, or
(b) being so invested, is retained and not transferred or as soon as may be reinvested as mentioned in subsection (2) of section two of this Act,

then, so long as the property continues so invested and comprised in the narrower-range part of the fund, section one of this Act shall not authorise the making or retention of any wider-range investment.

2— Section four of the Trustee Act 1925, or section thirty-three of the Trusts (Scotland) Act, 1921 (which relieve a trustee from liability for retaining an investment which has ceased to be authorised), shall not apply where an investment ceased to be authorised in consequence of the foregoing paragraph.

Amendment—Repealed, except in so far as this section relates to a trustee having a power of investment conferred on him under any enactment which was passed before 3 August 1961 and which is not amended by the Trustee Act 2000, Sch 2, by the Trustee Act 2000, s 40(1), (3), Sch 2, Pt I, para 1(2), Sch 4, Pt I.

Schedule 4: Minor and Consequential Amendments

1—(1) …

(2) References in the Trusts (Scotland) Act 1921, to section ten or eleven of that Act, or to provisions which include either of those sections, shall be construed respectively as references to section one of this Act and as including references to that section.

2–6—< … >

Amendment—Para 1: sub-para (1) repealed by the Trustee Act 2000, s 40(1), (3), Sch 2, Pt I, para 1(3)(b), Sch 4, Pt I. Date in force: 1 February 2001: see SI 2001/49, art 2.

Para 2: repealed by the Building Societies Act 1962, s 131, Sch 10, Part I.

Paras 4, 5: repealed by the National Savings Bank Act 1971, s 28, Sch 2.

Para 6: repealed by the Housing (Consequential Provisions) Act 1985, s 3, Sch 1, Part I.

Perpetuities and Accumulations Act 1964

1964 Chapter 55

An Act to modify the law of England and Wales relating to the avoidance of future interests in property on grounds of remoteness and governing accumulations of income from property. [16 July 1964]

Initial Comment—Royal Assent : 16 july 1964: (no specific commencement provisions).
Extent—This Act does not extend to Scotland: see s 15(9).

Perpetuities

1 Power to specify perpetuity period

(1) Subject to section 9 (2) of this Act and subsection (2) below, where the instrument by which any disposition is made so provides, the perpetuity period applicable to the disposition under the rule against perpetuities, instead of being of any other duration, shall be of a duration equal to such number of years not exceeding eighty as is specified in that behalf in the instrument.

(2) Subsection (1) above shall not have effect where the disposition is made in exercise of a special power of appointment, but where a period is specified under that subsection in the instrument creating such a power the period shall apply in relation to any disposition under the power as it applies in relation to the power itself.

2 Presumptions and evidence as to future parenthood

(1) Where in any proceedings there arises on the rule against perpetuities a question which turns on the ability of a person to have a child at some future time, then—

(a) subject to paragraph (b) below, it shall be presumed that a male can have a child at the age of fourteen years or over, but not under that age, and that a female can have a child at the age of twelve years or over, but not under that age or over the age of fifty-five years; but
(b) in the case of a living person evidence may be given to show that he or she will or will not be able to have a child at the time in question.

(2) Where any such question is decided by treating a person as unable to have a child at a particular time, and he or she does so, the High Court may make such order as it thinks fit for placing the persons interested in the property comprised in the disposition, so far as may be just, in the position they would have held if the question had not been so decided.

(3) Subject to subsection (2) above, where any such question is decided in relation to a disposition by treating a person as able or unable to have a child at a particular time, then he or she shall be so treated for the purpose of any question which may arise on the rule against perpetuities in relation to the same disposition in any subsequent proceedings.

(4) In the foregoing provisions of this section references to having a child are references to begetting or giving birth to a child, but those provisions (except

subsection (1)(b)) shall apply in relation to the possibility that a person will at any time have a child by adoption, legitimation or other means as they apply to his or her ability at that time to beget or give birth to a child.

3 Uncertainty as to remoteness

(1) Where, apart from the provisions of this section and sections 4 and 5 of this Act, a disposition would be void on the ground that the interest disposed of might not become vested until too remote a time, the disposition shall be treated, until such time (if any) as it becomes established that the vesting must occur, if at all, after the end of the perpetuity period, as if the disposition were not subject to the rule against perpetuities; and its becoming so established shall not affect the validity of anything previously done in relation to the interest disposed of by way of advancement, application of intermediate income or otherwise.

(2) Where, apart from the said provisions, a disposition consisting of the conferring of a general power of appointment would be void on the ground that the power might not become exercisable until too remote a time, the disposition shall be treated, until such time (if any) as it becomes established that the power will not be exercisable within the perpetuity period, as if the disposition were not subject to the rule against perpetuities.

(3) Where, apart from the said provisions, a disposition consisting of the conferring of any power, option or other right would be void on the ground that the right might be exercised at too remote a time, the disposition shall be treated as regards any exercise of the right within the perpetuity period as if it were not subject to the rule against perpetuities and, subject to the said provisions, shall be treated as void for remoteness only if, and so far as, the right is not fully exercised within that period.

(4) Where this section applies to a disposition and the duration of the perpetuity period is not determined by virtue of section 1 or 9 (2) of this Act, it shall be determined as follows:—

(a) where any persons falling within subsection (5) below are individuals in being and ascertainable at the commencement of the perpetuity period the duration of the period shall be determined by reference to their lives and no others, but so that the lives of any description of persons falling within paragraph (b) or (c) of that subsection shall be disregarded if the number of persons of that description is such as to render it impracticable to ascertain the date of death of the survivor;
(b) where there are no lives under paragraph (a) above the period shall be twenty-one years.

(5) The said persons are as follows:—

(a) the person by whom the disposition was made;
(b) a person to whom or in whose favour the disposition was made, that is to say—

(i) in the case of a disposition to a class of persons, any member or potential member of the class;
(ii) in the case of an individual disposition to a person taking only on certain conditions being satisfied, any person as to whom some of the conditions are satisfied and the remainder may in time be satisfied;

(iii) in the case of a special power of appointment exercisable in favour of members of a class, any member or potential member of the class;

(iv) in the case of a special power of appointment exercisable in favour of one person only, that person or, where the object of the power is ascertainable only on certain conditions being satisfied, any person as to whom some of the conditions are satisfied and the remainder may in time be satisfied;

(v) in the case of any power, option or other right, the person on whom the right is conferred;

(c) a person having a child or grandchild within sub-paragraphs (i) to (iv) of paragraph (b) above, or any of whose children or grandchildren, if subsequently born, would by virtue of his or her descent fall within those sub-paragraphs;

(d) any person on the failure or determination of whose prior interest the disposition is limited to take effect.

4 Reduction of age and exclusion of class members to avoid remoteness

(1) Where a disposition is limited by reference to the attainment by any person or persons of a specified age exceeding twenty-one years, and it is apparent at the time the disposition is made or becomes apparent at a subsequent time—

(a) that the disposition would, apart from this section, be void for remoteness, but

(b) that it would not be so void if the specified age had been twenty-one years,

the disposition shall be treated for all purposes as if, instead of being limited by reference to the age in fact specified, it had been limited by reference to the age nearest to that age which would, if specified instead, have prevented the disposition from being so void.

(2) Where in the case of any disposition different ages exceeding twenty-one years are specified in relation to different persons—

(a) the reference in paragraph (b) of subsection (1) above to the specified age shall be construed as a reference to all the specified ages, and

(b) that subsection shall operate to reduce each such age so far as is necessary to save the disposition from being void for remoteness.

(3) Where the inclusion of any persons, being potential members of a class or unborn persons who at birth would become members or potential members of the class, prevents the foregoing provisions of this section from operating to save a disposition from being void for remoteness, those persons shall thenceforth be deemed for all the purposes of the disposition to be excluded from the class, and the said provisions shall thereupon have effect accordingly.

(4) Where, in the case of a disposition to which subsection (3) above does not apply, it is apparent at the time the disposition is made or becomes apparent at a subsequent time that, apart from this subsection, the inclusion of any persons, being potential members of a class or unborn persons who at birth would become members or potential members of the class, would cause the disposition to be treated as void for remoteness, those persons shall, unless their exclusion would exhaust the class, thenceforth be deemed for all the purposes of the disposition to be excluded from the class.

(5) Where this section has effect in relation to a disposition to which section 3

above applies, the operation of this section shall not affect the validity of anything previously done in relation to the interest disposed of by way of advancement, application of intermediate income or otherwise.

(6) ...

[(7) For the avoidance of doubt it is hereby declared that a question arising under section 3 of this Act or subsection (1)(a) above of whether a disposition would be void apart from this section is to be determined as if subsection (6) above had been a separate section of this Act.]

Amendment—Sub-s (6): repeals the Law of Property Act 1925, s 163.
Sub-s (7): inserted by the Children Act 1975, s 108(1)(a), Sch 3, para 43.

---

5 Condition relating to death of surviving spouse

Where a disposition is limited by reference to the time of death of the survivor of a person in being at the commencement of the perpetuity period and any spouse of that person, and that time has not arrived at the end of the perpetuity period, the disposition shall be treated for all purposes, where to do so would save it from being void for remoteness, as if it had instead been limited by reference to the time immediately before the end of that period.

6 Saving and acceleration of expectant interests

A disposition shall not be treated as void for remoteness by reason only that the interest disposed of is ulterior to and dependent upon an interest under a disposition which is so void, and the vesting of an interest shall not be prevented from being accelerated on the failure of a prior interest by reason only that the failure arises because of remoteness.

7 Powers of appointment

For the purposes of the rule against perpetuities, a power of appointment shall be treated as a special power unless—

(a) in the instrument creating the power it is expressed to be exercisable by one person only, and
(b) it could, at all times during its currency when that person is of full age and capacity, be exercised by him so as immediately to transfer to himself the whole of the interest governed by the power without the consent of any other person or compliance with any other condition, not being a formal condition relating only to the mode of exercise of the power:

Provided that for the purpose of determining whether a disposition made under a power of appointment exercisable by will only is void for remoteness, the power shall be treated as a general power where it would have fallen to be so treated if exercisable by deed.

8 Administrative powers of trustees

(1) The rule against perpetuities shall not operate to invalidate a power conferred

on trustees or other persons to sell, lease, exchange or otherwise dispose of any property for full consideration, or to do any other act in the administration (as opposed to the distribution) of any property, and shall not prevent the payment to trustees or other persons of reasonable remuneration for their services.

(2) Subsection (1) above shall apply for the purpose of enabling a power to be exercised at any time after the commencement of this Act notwithstanding that the power is conferred by an instrument which took effect before that commencement.

9 Options relating to land

(1) The rule against perpetuities shall not apply to a disposition consisting of the conferring of an option to acquire for valuable consideration an interest reversionary (whether directly or indirectly) on the term of a lease if—

(a) the option is exercisable only by the lessee or his successors in title, and
(b) it ceases to be exercisable at or before the expiration of one year following the determination of the lease.

This subsection shall apply in relation to an agreement for a lease as it applies in relation to a lease, and 'lessee' shall be construed accordingly.

(2) In the case of a disposition consisting of the conferring of an option to acquire for valuable consideration any interest in land, the perpetuity period under the rule against perpetuities shall be twenty-one years, and section 1 of this Act shall not apply:

Provided that this subsection shall not apply to a right of pre-emption conferred on a public or local authority in respect of land used or to be used for religious purposes where the right becomes exercisable only if the land ceases to be used for such purposes.

10 Avoidance of contractual and other rights in cases of remoteness

Where a disposition inter vivos would fall to be treated as void for remoteness if the rights and duties thereunder were capable of transmission to persons other than the original parties and had been so transmitted, it shall be treated as void as between the person by whom it was made and the person to whom or in whose favour it was made or any successor of his, and no remedy shall lie in contract or otherwise for giving effect to it or making restitution for its lack of effect.

11 Rights for enforcement of rentcharges

(1) The rule against perpetuities shall not apply to any powers or remedies for recovering or compelling the payment of an annual sum to which section 121 or 122 of the Law of Property Act 1925 applies, or otherwise becoming exercisable or enforceable on the breach of any condition or other requirement relating to that sum.

(2) …

Amendment—Sub-s (2): amends the Law of Property Act 1925, s 121(6).

---

12 Possibilities of reverter, conditions subsequent, exceptions and reservations

(1) In the case of—

(a) a possibility of reverter on the determination of a determinable fee simple, or
(b) a possibility of a resulting trust on the determination of any other determinable interest in property,

the rule against perpetuities shall apply in relation to the provision causing the interest to be determinable as it would apply if that provision were expressed in the form of a condition subsequent giving rise, on breach thereof, to a right of re-entry or an equivalent right in the case of property other than land, and where the provision falls to be treated as void for remoteness the determinable interest shall become an absolute interest.

(2) Where a disposition is subject to any such provision, or to any such condition subsequent, or to any exception or reservation, the disposition shall be treated for the purposes of this Act as including a separate disposition of any rights arising by virtue of the provision, condition subsequent, exception or reservation.

Accumulations

13 Amendment of s 164 of Law of Property Act 1925

(1) The periods for which accumulations of income under a settlement or other disposition are permitted by section 164 of the Law of Property Act 1925 shall include—

(a) a term of twenty-one years from the date of the making of the disposition, and
(b) the duration of the minority or respective minorities of any person or persons in being at that date.

(2) It is hereby declared that the restrictions imposed by the said section 164 apply in relation to a power to accumulate income whether or not there is a duty to exercise that power, and that they apply whether or not the power to accumulate extends to income produced by the investment of income previously accumulated.

14 Right to stop accumulations

Section 2 above shall apply to any question as to the right of beneficiaries to put an end to accumulations of income under any disposition as it applies to questions arising on the rule against perpetuities.

Supplemental

15 Short title, interpretation and extent

(1) This Act may be cited as the Perpetuities and Accumulations Act 1964.

(2) In this Act—

'disposition' includes the conferring of a power of appointment and any other disposition of an interest in or right over property, and references to the interest disposed of shall be construed accordingly;

'in being' means living or en ventre sa mere;
'power of appointment' includes any discretionary power to transfer a beneficial interest in property without the furnishing of valuable consideration;
'will' includes a codicil;

and for the purposes of this Act a disposition contained in a will shall be deemed to be made at the death of the testator.

(3) For the purposes of this Act a person shall be treated as a member of a class if in his case all the conditions identifying a member of the class are satisfied, and shall be treated as a potential member if in his case some only of those conditions are satisfied but there is a possibility that the remainder will in time be satisfied.

(4) Nothing in this Act shall affect the operation of the rule of law rendering void for remoteness certain dispositions under which property is limited to be applied for purposes other than the benefit of any person or class of persons in cases where the property may be so applied after the end of the perpetuity period.

(5) The foregoing sections of this Act shall apply (except as provided in section 8 (2) above) only in relation to instruments taking effect after the commencement of this Act, and in the case of an instrument made in the exercise of a special power of appointment shall apply only where the instrument creating the power takes effect after that commencement;

Provided that section 7 above shall apply in all cases for construing the foregoing reference to a special power of appointment.

(6) This Act shall apply in relation to a disposition made otherwise than by an instrument as if the disposition had been contained in an instrument taking effect when the disposition was made.

(7) This Act binds the Crown.

(8) Except in so far as the contrary intention appears, any enactment of the Parliament of Northern Ireland passed for purposes similar to the purposes of this Act shall bind the Crown.

(9) This Act shall not extend to Scotland or (apart from subsection (8) above) to Northern Ireland.

Modification—The Northern Ireland Act 1998 makes new provision for the government of Northern Ireland for the purpose of implementing the Belfast Agreement (the agreement reached at multi-party talks on Northern Ireland and set out in Command Paper 3883). As a consequence of that Act, any reference in this section to the Parliament of Northern Ireland or the Assembly established under the Northern Ireland Assembly Act 1973, s 1, certain office-holders and Ministers, and any legislative act and certain financial dealings thereof, shall, for the period specified, be construed in accordance with Sch 12, paras 1–11 to the 1998 Act.

Powers of Attorney Act 1971

1971 Chapter 27

An Act to make new provision in relation to powers of attorney and the delegation by trustees of their trusts, powers and discretions. [12 May 1971]

Initial Commencement—Specified date: 1 October 1971: see s 11(4).
Extent—This section does not extend to Scotland: see s 11(5).

---

1 Execution of powers of attorney

(1) An instrument creating a power of attorney shall be [executed as a deed by] the donor of the power.

(2) ...

(3) This section is without prejudice to any requirement in, or having effect under, any other Act as to the witnessing of instruments creating powers of attorney and does not affect the rules relating to the execution of instruments by bodies corporate.

Amendment—Sub-s (1): words in square brackets substituted by the Law of Property (Miscellaneous Provisions) Act 1989, s 1, Sch 1, para 6(a).
Sub-s (2): repealed by the Law of Property (Miscellaneous Provisions) Act 1989, ss 1, 4, Sch 1, para 6(b), Sch 2.

2

...

Amendment—Repealed by the Supreme Court Act 1981, s 152(4), Sch 7.

---

3 Proof of instruments creating powers of attorney

(1) The contents of an instrument creating a power of attorney may be proved by means of a copy which—

(a) is a reproduction of the original made with a photographic or other device for reproducing documents in facsimile; and
(b) contains the following certificate or certificates signed by the donor of the power or by a solicitor [duly certificated notary public] or stockbroker, that is to say—

 (i) a certificate at the end to the effect that the copy is a true and complete copy of the original; and
 (ii) if the original consists of two or more pages, a certificate at the end of each page of the copy to the effect that it is a true and complete copy of the corresponding page of the original.

(2) Where a copy of an instrument creating a power of attorney has been made

which complies with subsection (1) of this section, the contents of the instrument may also be proved by means of a copy of that copy if the further copy itself complies with that subsection, taking references in it to the original as references to the copy from which the further copy is made.

(3) In this section ['duly certificated notary public' has the same meaning as it has in the Solicitors Act 1974 by virtue of section 87(1) of that Act and] 'stockbroker' means a member of any stock exchange within the meaning of the Stock Transfer Act 1963 or the Stock Transfer Act (Northern Ireland) 1963.

(4) This section is without prejudice to section 4 of the Evidence and Powers of Attorney Act 1940 (proof of deposited instruments by office copy) and to any other method of proof authorised by law.

(5) For the avoidance of doubt, in relation to an instrument made in Scotland the references to a power of attorney in this section and in section 4 of the Evidence and Powers of Attorney Act 1940 include references to a factory and commission.

Amendment—Sub-ss (1), (3): words in square brackets inserted by the Courts and Legal Services Act 1990, s 125(2), Sch 17, para 4.
Modification—References to solicitors etc modified to include references to bodies recognised under the Administration of Justice Act 1985, s 9, by the Solicitors' Incorporated Practices Order 1991, SI 1991/2684, arts 4, 5, Sch 1.

---

4 Powers of attorney given as security

(1) Where a power of attorney is expressed to be irrevocable and is given to secure—

(a) a proprietary interest of the donee of the power; or
(b) the performance of an obligation owed to the donee,

then, so long as the donee has that interest or the obligation remains undischarged, the power shall not be revoked—

(i) by the donor without the consent of the donee; or
(ii) by the death, incapacity or bankruptcy of the donor or, if the donor is a body corporate, by its winding up or dissolution.

(2) A power of attorney given to secure a proprietary interest may be given to the person entitled to the interest and persons deriving title under him to that interest, and those persons shall be duly constituted donees of the power for all purposes of the power but without prejudice to any right to appoint substitutes given by the power.

(3) This section applies to powers of attorney whenever created.

5 Protection of donee and third persons where power of attorney is revoked

(1) A donee of a power of attorney who acts in pursuance of the power at a time when it has been revoked shall not, by reason of the revocation, incur any liability (either to the donor or to any other person) if at that time he did not know that the power had been revoked.

(2) Where a power of attorney has been revoked and a person, without knowledge of the revocation, deals with the donee of the power, the transaction between them shall, in favour of that person, be as valid as if the power had then been in existence.

(3) Where the power is expressed in the instrument creating it to be irrevocable and to be given by way of security then, unless the person dealing with the donee knows that it was not in fact given by way of security, he shall be entitled to assume that the power is incapable of revocation except by the donor acting with the consent of the donee and shall accordingly be treated for the purposes of subsection (2) of this section as having knowledge of the revocation only if he knows that it has been revoked in that manner.

(4) Where the interest of a purchaser depends on whether a transaction between the donee of a power of attorney and another person was valid by virtue of subsection (2) of this section, it shall be conclusively presumed in favour of the purchaser that that person did not at the material time know of the revocation of the power if—

(a) the transaction between that person and the donee was completed within twelve months of the date on which the power came into operation; or
(b) that person makes a statutory declaration, before or within three months after the completion of the purchase, that he did not at the material time know of the revocation of the power.

(5) Without prejudice to subsection (3) of this section, for the purposes of this section knowledge of the revocation of a power of attorney includes knowledge of the occurrence of any event (such as the death of the donor) which has the effect of revoking the power.

(6) In this section 'purchaser' and 'purchase' have the meaning specified in section 205 (1) of the Law of Property Act 1925.

(7) This section applies whenever the power of attorney was created but only to acts and transactions after the commencement of this Act.

6 Additional protection for transferees under stock exchange transactions

(1) Without prejudice to section 5 of this Act, where—

(a) the donee of a power of attorney executes, as transferor, an instrument transferring registered securities; and
(b) the instrument is executed for the purposes of a stock exchange transaction,

it shall be conclusively presumed in favour of the transferee that the power had not been revoked at the date of the instrument if a statutory declaration to that effect is made by the donee of the power on or within three months after that date.

(2) In this section 'registered securities' and 'stock exchange transaction' have the same meanings as in the Stock Transfer Act 1963.

7 Execution of instruments etc by donee of power of attorney

[(1) If the donee of a power of attorney is an individual, he may, if he thinks fit—

(a) execute any instrument with his own signature, and]
(b) do any other thing in his own name,

by the authority of the donor of the power; and any document executed or thing done in that manner shall be as effective as if executed or done by the donee with the signature … , or, as the case may be, in the name, of the donor of the power.

(2) For the avoidance of doubt it is hereby declared that an instrument to which subsection (3) … of section 74 of the Law of Property Act 1925 applies may be executed either as provided in [that subsection] or as provided in this section.

(3) This section is without prejudice to any statutory direction requiring an instrument to be executed in the name of an estate owner within the meaning of the said Act of 1925.

(4) This section applies whenever the power of attorney was created.

Amendment—Sub-ss (1), (2): words omitted repealed and words in square brackets substituted by the Law of Property (Miscellaneous Provisions) Act 1989, ss 1, 4, Sch 1, para 7, Sch 2.

---

8 Repeal of s 129 of Law of Property Act 1925

…

Amendment—This section repeals the Law of Property Act 1925, s 129.

9

…

Amendment—Repealed by the Trustee Delegation Act 1999, s 12, Schedule. Date in force: 1 March 2000 (in relation to powers of attorney created after that date): see SI 2000/216, art 2.

---

10 Effect of general power of attorney in specified form

(1) Subject to subsection (2) of this section, a general power of attorney in the form set out in Schedule 1 to this Act, or in a form to the like effect but expressed to be made under this Act, shall operate to confer—

(a) on the donee of the power; or
(b) if there is more than one donee, on the donees acting jointly or acting jointly or severally, as the case may be,

authority to do on behalf of the donor anything which he can lawfully do by an attorney.

(2) [Subject to section 1 of the Trustee Delegation Act 1999, this section] does not

apply to functions which the donor has as a trustee or personal representative or as a tenant for life or statutory owner within the meaning of the Settled Land Act 1925.

Amendment—Sub-s (2): words 'Subject to section 1 of the Trustee Delegation Act 1999, this section' in square brackets substituted by the Trustee Delegation Act 1999, s 3. Date in force: 1 March 2000: see SI 2000/216, art 2.

Schedule 1
Form of General Power of Attorney for Purposes of Section 10

THIS GENERAL POWER OF ATTORNEY is made this … day of … 19 … by AB of

I appoint CD of (*or* CD of … … … … .. and EF of … … … … .. jointly *or* jointly and severally) to be my attorney(s) in accordance with section 10 of the Powers of Attorney Act 1971.

IN WITNESS etc,

Domicile and Matrimonial Proceedings Act 1973

1973 Chapter 45

An Act to amend the law relating to the domicile of married women and persons not of full age, to matters connected with domicile and the jurisdiction in marriage proceedings including divorces and legal separations; and for purposes connected therewith.

[25 July 1973]

Initial Commencement—Specified date: 1 January 1974: see s 17(5).
Extent—See s 17

PART I
DOMICILE

Husband and wife

1 Abolition of wife's dependent domicile

(1) Subject to subsection (2) below, the domicile of a married woman as at any time after the coming into force of this section shall, instead of being the same as her husband's by virtue only of marriage, be ascertained by reference to the same factors as in the case of any other individual capable of having an independent domicile.

(2) Where immediately before this section came into force a woman was married and then had her husband's domicile by dependence, she is to be treated as retaining that domicile (as a domicile of choice, if it is not also her domicile of origin) unless and until it is changed by acquisition or revival of another domicile either on or after the coming into force of this section.

(3) This section extends to England and Wales, Scotland and Northern Ireland.

Minors and pupils

3 Age at which independent domicile can be acquired

(1) The time at which a person first becomes capable of having an independent domicile shall be when he attains the age of sixteen or marries under that age; and in the case of a person who immediately before 1st January 1974 was incapable of having an independent domicile, but had then attained the age of sixteen or been married, it shall be that date.

(2) This section extends to England and Wales and Northern Ireland (but not to Scotland).

4 Dependent domicile of child not living with his father

(1) Subsection (2) of this section shall have effect with respect to the dependent domicile of a child as at any time after the coming into force of this section when his father and mother are alive but living apart.

(2) The child's domicile as at that time shall be that of his mother if—

(a) he then has his home with her and has no home with his father; or
(b) he has at any time had her domicile by virtue of paragraph (a) above and has not since had a home with his father.

(3) As at any time after the coming into force of this section, the domicile of a child whose mother is dead shall be that which she last had before she died if at her death he had her domicile by virtue of subsection (2) above and he has not since had a home with his father.

(4) Nothing in this section prejudices any existing rule of law as to the cases in which a child's domicile is regarded as being, by dependence, that of his mother.

(5) In this section, 'child' means a person incapable of having an independent domicile; …

(6) This section extends to England and Wales, Scotland and Northern Ireland.

CONVENTION ON THE LAW APPLICABLE TO TRUSTS AND ON THEIR RECOGNITION

(Concluded July 1st, 1985)

The States signatory to the present Convention,

Considering that the trust, as developed in courts of equity in common law jurisdictions and adopted with some modifications in other jurisdictions, is a unique legal institution,

Desiring to establish common provisions on the law applicable to trusts and to deal with the most important issues concerning the recognition of trusts,

Have resolved to conclude a Convention to this effect, and have agreed upon the following provisions –

CHAPTER I – SCOPE

Article 1— This Convention specifies the law applicable to trusts and governs their recognition.

Article 2— For the purposes of this Convention, the term 'trust' refers to the legal relationships created – inter vivos or on death – by a person, the settlor, when assets have been placed under the control of a trustee for the benefit of a beneficiary or for a specified purpose.

A trust has the following characteristics –

a) the assets constitute a separate fund and are not a part of the trustee's own estate;
b) title to the trust assets stands in the name of the trustee or in the name of another person on behalf of the trustee;
c) the trustee has the power and the duty, in respect of which he is accountable, to manage, employ or dispose of the assets in accordance with the terms of the trust and the special duties imposed upon him by law.

The reservation by the settlor of certain rights and powers, and the fact that the trustee may himself have rights as a beneficiary, are not necessarily inconsistent with the existence of a trust.

Article 3— The Convention applies only to trusts created voluntarily and evidenced in writing.

Article 4— The Convention does not apply to preliminary issues relating to the validity of wills or of other acts by virtue of which assets are transferred to the trustee.

Article 5— The Convention does not apply to the extent that the law specified by Chapter II does not provide for trusts or the category of trusts involved.

CHAPTER II – APPLICABLE LAW

Article 6— A trust shall be governed by the law chosen by the settlor. The choice must be express or be implied in the terms of the instrument creating or the writing evidencing the trust, interpreted, if necessary, in the light of the circumstances of the case.

Where the law chosen under the previous paragraph does not provide for trusts or the category of trust involved, the choice shall not be effective and the law specified in Article 7 shall apply.

Article 7— Where no applicable law has been chosen, a trust shall be governed by the law with which it is most closely connected.

In ascertaining the law with which a trust is most closely connected reference shall be made in particular to –

a) the place of administration of the trust designated by the settlor;
b) the situs of the assets of the trust;
c) the place of residence or business of the trustee;
d) the objects of the trust and the places where they are to be fulfilled.

Article 8— The law specified by Article 6 or 7 shall govern the validity of the trust, its construction, its effects, and the administration of the trust.

In particular that law shall govern –

a) the appointment, resignation and removal of trustees, the capacity to act as a trustee, and the devolution of the office of trustee;
b) the rights and duties of trustees among themselves;
c) the right of trustees to delegate in whole or in part the discharge of their duties or the exercise of their powers;
d) the power of trustees to administer or to dispose of trust assets, to create security interests in the trust assets, or to acquire new assets;
e) the powers of investment of trustees;
f) restrictions upon the duration of the trust, and upon the power to accumulate the income of the trust;
g) the relationships between the trustees and the beneficiaries including the personal liability of the trustees to the beneficiaries;
h) the variation or termination of the trust;
i) the distribution of the trust assets;
j) the duty of trustees to account for their administration.

Article 9— In applying this Chapter a severable aspect of the trust, particularly matters of administration, may be governed by a different law.

Article 10— The law applicable to the validity of the trust shall determine whether that law or the law governing a severable aspect of the trust may be replaced by another law.

CHAPTER III – RECOGNITION

Article 11— A trust created in accordance with the law specified by the preceding Chapter shall be recognized as a trust.

Such recognition shall imply, as a minimum, that the trust property constitutes a separate fund, that the trustee may sue and be sued in his capacity as trustee, and that he may appear or act in this capacity before a notary or any person acting in an official capacity.

In so far as the law applicable to the trust requires or provides, such recognition shall imply, in particular –

a) that personal creditors of the trustee shall have no recourse against the trust assets;
b) that the trust assets shall not form part of the trustee's estate upon his insolvency or bankruptcy;
c) that the trust assets shall not form part of the matrimonial property of the trustee or his spouse nor part of the trustee's estate upon his death;
d) that the trust assets may be recovered when the trustee, in breach of trust, has mingled trust assets with his own property or has alienated trust assets. However, the rights and obligations of any third party holder of the assets shall remain subject to the law determined by the choice of law rules of the forum.

Article 12— Where the trustee desires to register assets, movable or immovable, or documents of title to them, he shall be entitled, in so far as this is not prohibited by or inconsistent with the law of the State where registration is sought, to do so in his capacity as trustee or in such other way that the existence of the trust is disclosed.

Article 13— No State shall be bound to recognize a trust the significant elements of which, except for the choice of the applicable law, the place of administration and the habitual residence of the trustee, are more closely connected with States which do not have the institution of the trust or the category of trust involved.

Article 14— The Convention shall not prevent the application of rules of law more favourable to the recognition of trusts.

CHAPTER IV – GENERAL CLAUSES

Article 15— The Convention does not prevent the application of provisions of the law designated by the conflicts rules of the forum, in so far as those provisions cannot be derogated from by voluntary act, relating in particular to the following matters –

a) the protection of minors and incapable parties;
b) the personal and proprietary effects of marriage;
c) succession rights, testate and intestate, especially the indefeasible shares of spouses and relatives;
d) the transfer of title to property and security interests in property;
e) the protection of creditors in matters of insolvency;
f) the protection, in other respects, of third parties acting in good faith.

If recognition of a trust is prevented by application of the preceding paragraph, the court shall try to give effect to the objects of the trust by other means.

Article 16— The Convention does not prevent the application of those provisions of the law of the forum which must be applied even to international situations, irrespective of rules of conflict of laws.

If another State has a sufficiently close connection with a case then, in exceptional circumstances, effect may also be given to rules of that State which have the same character as mentioned in the preceding paragraph.

Any Contracting State may, by way of reservation, declare that it will not apply the second paragraph of this Article.

Article 17— In the Convention the word 'law' means the rules of law in force in a State other than its rules of conflict of laws.

Article 18— The provisions of the Convention may be disregarded when their application would be manifestly incompatible with public policy (ordre public).

Article 19— Nothing in the Convention shall prejudice the powers of States in fiscal matters.

Article 20— Any Contracting State may, at any time, declare that the provisions of the Convention will be extended to trusts declared by judicial decisions.

This declaration shall be notified to the Ministry of Foreign Affairs of the Kingdom of the Netherlands and will come into effect on the day when this notification is received.

Article 31 is applicable to the withdrawal of this declaration in the same way as it applies to a denunciation of the Convention.

Article 21— Any Contracting State may reserve the right to apply the provisions of Chapter III only to trusts the validity of which is governed by the law of a Contracting State.

Article 22— The Convention applies to trusts regardless of the date on which they were created.

However, a Contracting State may reserve the right not to apply the Convention to trusts created before the date on which, in relation to that State, the Convention enters into force.

Article 23— For the purpose of identifying the law applicable under the Convention, where a State comprises several territorial units each of which has its own rules of law in respect of trusts, any reference to the law of that State is to be construed as referring to the law in force in the territorial unit in question.

Article 24— A State within which different territorial units have their own rules of law in respect of trusts is not bound to apply the Convention to conflicts solely between the laws of such units.

Article 25— The Convention shall not affect any other international instrument containing provisions on matters governed by this Convention to which a Contracting State is, or becomes, a party.

CHAPTER V – FINAL CLAUSES

Article 26— Any State may, at the time of signature, ratification, acceptance, approval or accession, or at the time of making a declaration in terms of Article 29, make the reservations provided for in Articles 16, 21 and 22.

No other reservation shall be permitted.

Any Contracting State may at any time withdraw a reservation which it has made; the reservation shall cease to have effect on the first day of the third calendar month after notification of the withdrawal.

Article 27— The Convention shall be open for signature by the States which were Members of the Hague Conference on Private International Law at the time of its Fifteenth Session.

It shall be ratified, accepted or approved and the instruments of ratification, acceptance or approval shall be deposited with the Ministry of Foreign Affairs of the Kingdom of the Netherlands.

Article 28— Any other State may accede to the Convention after it has entered into force in accordance with Article 30, paragraph 1.

The instrument of accession shall be deposited with the Ministry of Foreign Affairs of the Kingdom of the Netherlands.

The accession shall have effect only as regards the relations between the acceding State and those Contracting States which have not raised an objection to its accession in the twelve months after the receipt of the notification referred to in Article 32. Such an objection may also be raised by Member States at the time when they ratify, accept or approve the Convention after an accession. Any such objection shall be notified to the Ministry of Foreign Affairs of the Kingdom of the Netherlands.

Article 29— If a State has two or more territorial units in which different systems of law are applicable, it may at the time of signature, ratification, acceptance, approval or accession declare that this Convention shall extend to all of its territorial units or only to one or more of them and may modify this declaration by submitting another declaration at any time.

Any such declaration shall be notified to the Ministry of Foreign Affairs of the Kingdom of the Netherlands and shall state expressly the territorial units to which the Convention applies.

If a State makes no declaration under this Article, the Convention is to extend to all territorial units of that State.

Article 30— The Convention shall enter into force on the first day of the third calendar month after the deposit of the third instrument of ratification, acceptance or approval referred to in Article 27.

Thereafter the Convention shall enter into force –

a) for each State ratifying, accepting or approving it subsequently, on the first day of the third calendar month after the deposit of its instrument of ratification, acceptance or approval;
b) for each acceding State, on the first day of the third calendar month after the expiry of the period referred to in Article 28;
c) for a territorial unit to which the Convention has been extended in conformity with Article 29, on the first day of the third calendar month after the notification referred to in that Article.

Article 31— Any Contracting State may denounce this Convention by a formal notification in writing addressed to the Ministry of Foreign Affairs of the Kingdom of the Netherlands, depositary of the Convention.

The denunciation takes effect on the first day of the month following the expiration of six months after the notification is received by the depositary or on such later date as is specified in the notification.

Article 32—The Ministry of Foreign Affairs of the Kingdom of the Netherlands shall notify the States Members of the Conference, and the States which have acceded in accordance with Article 28, of the following –

a) the signatures and ratifications, acceptances or approvals referred to in Article 27;
b) the date on which the Convention enters into force in accordance with Article 30;
c) the accessions and the objections raised to accessions referred to in Article 28;
d) the extensions referred to in Article 29;
e) the declarations referred to in Article 20;
f) the reservation or withdrawals referred to in Article 26;
g) the denunciations referred to in Article 31.

In witness whereof the undersigned, being duly authorized thereto, have signed this Convention.

Done at The Hague, on the first day of July, 1985, in English and French, both texts being equally authentic, in a single copy which shall be deposited in the archives of the Government of the Kingdom of the Netherlands, and of which a certified copy shall be sent, through diplomatic channels, to each of the States Members of the Hague Conference on Private International Law at the date of its Fifteenth Session.

CONVENTION OF 1 JULY 1985 ON THE LAW APPLICABLE TO TRUSTS AND ON THEIR RECOGNITION

Last update: 6 June 2000

Member States	*Signature*	*Ratification, acceptance, approval or accession*	*Entry into force*
Australia	17 October 1991	17 October 1991	1 January 1992
Canada	11 October 1988	20 October 1992	1 January 1993

With the following declarations and reservation:

'Declarations

1. The Government of Canada declares, in accordance with Article 29 of the Convention, that the Convention shall extend to the following provinces:

- Alberta
- British Columbia
- New Brunswick
- Newfoundland
- Prince Edward Island

and that Canada may modify this declaration by submitting another declaration at any time.

2. The Government of Canada also declares, in accordance with Article 20 of the Convention, that the provisions of the Convention will be extended to trusts declared by judicial decisions in Alberta, British Columbia, New Brunswick, Newfoundland and Prince Edward Island.

Reservation

The Government of Canada further declares, by way of reservation, in accordance with Article 26 of the Convention and pursuant to Article 16, that the Province of Alberta will not apply the second paragraph of Article 16.'

Extensions

(1) On 14 April 1994, the Government of Canada extended the Convention to the Province of Manitoba.

Entry into force for the Province of Manitoba: 1 July 1994.

With the following declaration:

'Extension of the Convention

1. In accordance with the provisions of Article 29, the Government of Canada declares that, in addition to the Provinces of Alberta, British Columbia, New Brunswick, Newfoundland and Prince Edward Island, the Convention shall extend to the Province of Manitoba.

Declaration

2. In accordance with the provisions of Article 20, the Government of Canada declares that, in addition to trusts declared by judicial decisions in the Provinces of Alberta, British Columbia, New Brunswick, Newfoundland and Prince Edward Island, the provisions of the Convention shall extend to trusts declared by judicial decisions in the Province of Manitoba.

Other reservations and declarations

The Government of Canada further declares that it may at any time submit other declarations or reservations, pursuant to Article 29 of the Convention, with respect to other territorial units.'

(2) On 8 June 1994, the Government of Canada extended the Convention to the Province of Saskatchewan.

Entry into force for the Province of Saskatchewan: 1 September 1994.

With the following declaration:

'Extension of the Convention

1. In accordance with the provisions of Article 29, the Government of Canada declares that, in addition to the Provinces of Alberta, British Columbia, Manitoba, New Brunswick, Newfoundland and Prince Edward Island, the Convention shall extend to the Province of Saskatchewan.

Declaration

2. In accordance with the provisions of Article 20, the Government of Canada declares that, in addition to trusts declared by judicial decisions in the Provinces of Alberta,

British Columbia, Manitoba, New Brunswick, Newfoundland and Prince Edward Island, the provisions of the Convention shall extend to trusts declared by judicial decisions in the Province of Saskatchewan.

Other reservations and declarations

The Government of Canada further declares that it may at any time submit other declarations or reservations, pursuant to Article 29 of the Convention, with respect to other territorial units.'

Member States	*Entry into force*
CHINA, Hong Kong Special Administrative Region only	1 January 1992

The Ministry of Foreign Affairs of the Kingdom of the Netherlands, depositary of the Convention, gave notice that on 16 June 1997, the Minister for Foreign Affairs of the Kingdom of the Netherlands received a Note dated 11 June 1997 from the Ambassador of the United Kingdom of Great Britain and Northern Ireland at The Hague and a Note dated 3 June 1997 from the Ambassador of the People's Republic of China at The Hague concerning Hong Kong.

The Note from the Ambassador of the United Kingdom reads as follows:

'Your Excellency,

I am instructed by Her Britannic Majesty's Principal Secretary of State for Foreign and Commonwealth Affairs to refer to the Convention on the Law Applicable to Trusts and on their Recognition done at The Hague on 1 July 1985 (hereinafter referred to as the Convention) which applies to Hong Kong at present.

I am also instructed to state that, in accordance with the Joint Declaration of the Government of the United Kingdom of Great Britain and Northern Ireland and the Government of the People's Republic of China on the Question of Hong Kong signed on 19 December 1984, the Government of the United Kingdom will restore Hong Kong to the People's Republic of China with effect from 1 July 1997. The Government of the United Kingdom will continue to have international responsibility for Hong Kong until that date. Therefore, from that date the Government of the United Kingdom will cease to be responsible for the international rights and obligations arising from the application of the Convention to Hong Kong.

I should be grateful if the contents of this Note could be placed formally on record and brought to the attention of the other Parties of the Convention.

(…)

(signed Rosemary Spencer)'.

The Note from the Ambassador of the People's Republic of China reads as follows:

Translation

'Your Excellency,

Convention on the Law Applicable to Trusts and on Their Recognition

In accordance with the Joint Declaration of the Government of the People's Republic of China and the Government of the United Kingdom of Great Britain and Northern Ireland on the Question of Hong Kong signed on 19 December 1984 (hereinafter referred to as the 'Joint Declaration'), the People's Republic of China will resume the exercise of sovereignty over Hong Kong with effect from 1 July 1997. Hong Kong will, with effect from that date, become a Special Administrative Region of the People's Republic of China and will enjoy a high degree of autonomy, except in foreign and defence affairs which are the responsibilities of the Central People's Government of the People's Republic of China.

It is provided both in Section XI of Annex I to the Joint Declaration, 'Elaboration by the Government of the People's Republic of China of its Basic Policies Regarding Hong Kong', and Article 153 of the Basic Law of the Hong Kong Special Administrative Region of the People's Republic of China, which was adopted on 4 April 1990 by the National People's Congress of the People's Republic of China, that international agreements to which the People's Republic of China is not a Party but which are implemented in Hong Kong may continue to be implemented in the Hong Kong Special Administrative Region.

In accordance with the above provisions, I am instructed by the Minister of Foreign Affairs of the People's Republic of China to make the following notification:

The Convention on the Law Applicable to Trusts and on Their Recognition done at The Hague on 1 July 1985 (hereinafter referred to as the 'Convention'), by which the Government of the Kingdom of the Netherlands is designated as the depositary, which applies to Hong Kong at present, will continue to apply to the Hong Kong Special Administrative Region with effect from 1 July 1997. The Government of the People's Republic of China also makes the following declarations:

1. Paragraph 2 of Article 16 of the Convention will not apply to the Hong Kong Special Administrative Region.
2. In accordance with Article 20 of the Convention, the provisions of the Convention will be extended to trusts declared by judicial decisions in the Hong Kong Special Administrative Region.

Within the above ambit, responsibility for the international rights and obligations of a Party to the Convention will be assumed by the Government of the People's Republic of China.

It would be appreciated if the contents of this Note could be placed formally on record and brought to the other Parties to the Convention.

(...)

(signed Zhu Manli, Ambassador Extraordinary and Plenipotentiary of the People's Republic of China to the Kingdom of the Netherlands)'.

Member States	*Signature*	*Ratification acceptance, approval or accession*	*Entry into force*
Cyprus	11 March 1998		
France	26 November 1991		
Italy	1 July 1985	21 February 1990	1 January 1992
Luxembourg	1 July 1985		

Member States	*Signature*	*Ratification acceptance, approval or accession*	*Entry into force*
Malta	(accession) 7 December 1994	31 December 1995	1 March 1996
Netherlands (the Kingdom in Europe)	1 July 1985	28 November 1995	1 February 1996
United Kingdom of Great Britain and Northern Ireland	10 January 1986	17 November 1989	1 January 1992

The Convention is ratified on behalf of: the United Kingdom of Great Britain and Northern Ireland, the Isle of Man, Bermuda, British Antarctic Territory, British Virgin Islands, Falkland Islands, Gibraltar, Saint Helena, Saint Helena Dependencies, South Georgia and the South Sandwich Islands, United Kingdom Sovereign Base Areas of Akrotiri and Dhekelia in the Island of Cyprus, and with the following reservation and declaration:

'The United Kingdom, by way of reservation, declares that it will not apply the second paragraph of Article 16.'

'The United Kingdom declares, in accordance with Article 20, that the provisions of the Convention will be extended to trusts declared by judicial decisions.'

Extensions

Subject to the reservation under Article 16 and the declaration under Article 20 made by the United Kingdom on ratification of the Convention, on 30 March 1990 the United Kingdom of Great Britain and Northern Ireland extended the Convention to Hong Kong * (entry into force: 1 January 1992); on 10 January 1992 to Montserrat (entry into force: 1 January 1992); on 20 December 1991 to the Bailiwick of Jersey (entry into force: 1 March 1992); on 28 April 1993 to the Island of Guernsey (but not the Islands of Alderney and Sark) and to the Turks and Caicos (entry into force: 1 July 1993).

* On 1 July 1997, the Government of the United Kingdom of Great Britain and Northern Ireland restored Hong Kong to the People's Republic of China. See supra, under 'CHINA, Hong Kong Special Administrative Region'.

Member States	*Signature*
United States of America	13 June 1988

Enduring Powers of Attorney Act 1985

1985 Chapter 29

An Act to enable powers of attorney to be created which will survive any subsequent mental incapacity of the donor and to make provision in connection with such powers.
[26 June 1985]

Initial Commencment—To be appointed: see s 14(2).
Appointment—Commencement order: SI 1986/125.
Extent—See s 14(3)

Enduring powers of attorney

1 Enduring power of attorney to survive mental incapacity of donor

(1) Where an individual creates a power of attorney which is an enduring power within the meaning of this Act then—

(a) the power shall not be revoked by any subsequent mental incapacity of his; but
(b) upon such incapacity supervening the donee of the power may not do anything under the authority of the power except as provided by subsection (2) below or as directed or authorised by the court under section 5 unless or, as the case may be, until the instrument creating the power is registered by the court under section 6; and
(c) section 5 of the Powers of Attorney Act 1971 (protection of donee and third persons) so far as applicable shall apply if and so long as paragraph (b) above operates to suspend the donee's authority to act under the power as if the power had been revoked by the donor's mental incapacity.

(2) Notwithstanding subsection (1)(b) above, where the attorney has made an application for registration of the instrument then, until the application has been initially determined, the attorney may take action under the power—

(a) to maintain the donor or prevent loss to his estate; or
(b) to maintain himself or other persons in so far as section 3(4) permits him to do so.

(3) Where the attorney purports to act as provided by subsection (2) above then, in favour of a person who deals with him without knowledge that the attorney is acting otherwise than in accordance with paragraph (a) or (b) of that subsection, the transaction between them shall be as valid as if the attorney were acting in accordance with paragraph (a) or (b).

2 Characteristics of an enduring power

(1) Subject to subsections (7) to (9) below and section 11, a power of attorney is an enduring power within the meaning of this Act if the instrument which creates the power—

(a) is in the prescribed form; and
(b) was executed in the prescribed manner by the donor and the attorney; and
(c) incorporated at the time of execution by the donor the prescribed explanatory information.

(2) The Lord Chancellor shall make regulations as to the form and execution of instruments creating enduring powers and the regulations shall contain such provisions as appear to him to be appropriate for securing—

(a) that no document is used to create an enduring power which does not incorporate such information explaining the general effect of creating or accepting the power as may be prescribed; and
(b) that such instruments include statements to the following effect—

  (i) by the donor, that he intends the power to continue in spite of any supervening mental incapacity of his;
  (ii) by the donor, that he read or had read to him the information explaining the effect of creating the power;
  (iii) by the attorney, that he understands the duty of registration imposed by this Act.

(3) Regulations under subsection (2) above—

(a) may include different provision for cases where more than one attorney is to be appointed by the instrument than for cases where only one attorney is to be appointed; and
(b) may, if they amend or revoke any regulations previously made under that subsection, include saving and transitional provisions.

(4) Regulations under subsection (2) above shall be made by statutory instrument which shall be subject to annulment in pursuance of a resolution of either House of Parliament.

(5) An instrument in the prescribed form purporting to have been executed in the prescribed manner shall be taken, in the absence of evidence to the contrary, to be a document which incorporated at the time of execution by the donor the prescribed explanatory information.

(6) Where an instrument differs in an immaterial respect in form or mode of expression from the prescribed form the instrument shall be treated as sufficient in point of form and expression.

(7) A power of attorney cannot be an enduring power unless, when he executes the instrument creating it, the attorney is—

(a) an individual who has attained eighteen years and is not bankrupt; or
(b) a trust corporation.

(8) …

(9) A power of attorney which gives the attorney a right to appoint a substitute or successor cannot be an enduring power.

(10) An enduring power shall be revoked by the bankruptcy of the attorney whatever the circumstances of the bankruptcy.

(11) An enduring power shall be revoked on the exercise by the court of any of its powers under Part VII of the Mental Health Act 1983 if, but only if, the court so directs.

(12) No disclaimer of an enduring power, whether by deed or otherwise, shall be valid unless and until the attorney gives notice of it to the donor or, where section 4(6) or 7(1) applies, to the court.

(13) In this section 'prescribed' means prescribed under subsection (2) above.

Amendment—Sub-s (8): repealed by the Trustee Delegation Act 1999, s 12, Schedule. Date in force: 1 March 2000 (in relation to powers of attorney created after that date): see SI 2000/216, art 2.
Subordinate Legislation—Enduring Powers of Attorney (Welsh Language Prescribed Form) Regulations 2000, SI 2000/289.

---

3 Scope of authority etc of attorney under enduring power

(1) An enduring power may confer general authority (as defined in subsection (2) below) on the attorney to act on the donor's behalf in relation to all or a specified part of the property and affairs of the donor or may confer on him authority to do specified things on the donor's behalf and the authority may, in either case, be conferred subject to conditions and restrictions.

(2) Where an instrument is expressed to confer general authority on the attorney it operates to confer, subject to the restriction imposed by subsection (5) below and to any conditions or restrictions contained in the instrument, authority to do on behalf of the donor anything which the donor can lawfully do by an attorney.

(3) ...

(4) Subject to any conditions or restrictions contained in the instrument, an attorney under an enduring power, whether general or limited, may (without obtaining any consent) act under the power so as to benefit himself or other persons than the donor to the following extent but no further, that is to say—

(a) he may so act in relation to himself or in relation to any other person if the donor might be expected to provide for his or that person's needs respectively; and
(b) he may do whatever the donor might be expected to do to meet those needs.

(5) Without prejudice to subsection (4) above but subject to any conditions or restrictions contained in the instrument, an attorney under an enduring power, whether general or limited, may (without obtaining any consent) dispose of the property of the donor by way of gift to the following extent but no further, that is to say—

(a) he may make gifts of a seasonal nature or at a time, or on an anniversary, of a birth or marriage, to persons (including himself) who are related to or connected with the donor, and
(b) he may make gifts to any charity to whom the donor made or might be expected to make gifts,

provided that the value of each such gift is not unreasonable having regard to all the circumstances and in particular the size of the donor's estate.

Amendment—Sub-s (3): repealed by the Trustee Delegation Act 1999, s 12, Schedule, with effect in accordance with the provisions contained in s 4 thereof. Date in force: 1 March 2000: see SI 2000/216, art 2.

Action on actual or impending incapacity of donor

4 Duties of attorney in event of actual or impending incapacity of donor

(1) If the attorney under an enduring power has reason to believe that the donor is or is becoming mentally incapable subsections (2) to (6) below shall apply.

(2) The attorney shall, as soon as practicable, make an application to the court for the registration of the instrument creating the power.

(3) Before making an application for registration the attorney shall comply with the provisions as to notice set out in Schedule 1.

(4) An application for registration shall be made in the prescribed form and shall contain such statements as may be prescribed.

(5) The attorney may, before making an application for the registration of the instrument, refer to the court for its determination any question as to the validity of the power and he shall comply with any direction given to him by the court on that determination.

(6) No disclaimer of the power shall be valid unless and until the attorney gives notice of it to the court.

(7) Any person who, in an application for registration, makes a statement which he knows to be false in a material particular shall be liable—

(a) on conviction on indictment, to imprisonment for a term not exceeding two years or to a fine, or both; and
(b) on summary conviction, to imprisonment for a term not exceeding six months or to a fine not exceeding the statutory maximum, or both.

(8) In this section and Schedule 1 'prescribed' means prescribed by rules of the court.

5 Functions of court prior to registration

Where the court has reason to believe that the donor of an enduring power may be, or may be becoming, mentally incapable and the court is of the opinion that it is necessary, before the instrument creating the power is registered, to exercise any power with respect to the power of attorney or the attorney appointed to act under it which would become exercisable under section 8(2) on its registration, the court may exercise that power under this section and may do so whether the attorney has or has not made an application to the court for the registration of the instrument.

6 Functions of court on application for registration

(1) In any case where—

(a) an application for registration is made in accordance with section 4(3) and (4), and
(b) neither subsection (2) nor subsection (4) below applies,

the court shall register the instrument to which the application relates.

(2) Where it appears to the court that there is in force under Part VII of the Mental Health Act 1983 an order appointing a receiver for the donor but the power has not also been revoked then, unless it directs otherwise, the court shall not exercise or further exercise its functions under this section but shall refuse the application for registration.

(3) Where it appears from an application for registration that notice of it has not been given under Schedule 1 to some person entitled to receive it (other than a person in respect of whom the attorney has been dispensed or is otherwise exempt from the requirement to give notice) the court shall direct that the application be treated for the purposes of this Act as having been made in accordance with section 4(3), if the court is satisfied that, as regards each such person—

(a) it was undesirable or impracticable for the attorney to give him notice; or
(b) no useful purpose is likely to be served by giving him notice.

(4) If, in the case of an application for registration—

(a) a valid notice of objection to the registration is received by the court before the expiry of the period of five weeks beginning with the date or, as the case may be, the latest date on which the attorney gave notice to any person under Schedule 1, or
(b) it appears from the application that there is no one to whom notice has been given under paragraph 1 of that Schedule, or
(c) the court has reason to believe that appropriate inquiries might bring to light evidence on which the court could be satisfied that one of the grounds of objection set out in subsection (5) below was established,

the court shall neither register the instrument nor refuse the application until it has made or caused to be made such inquiries (if any) as it thinks appropriate in the circumstances of the case.

(5) For the purposes of this Act a notice of objection to the registration of an instrument is valid if the objection is made on one or more of the following grounds, namely—

(a) that the power purported to have been created by the instrument was not valid as an enduring power of attorney;
(b) that the power created by the instrument no longer subsists;
(c) that the application is premature because the donor is not yet becoming mentally incapable;
(d) that fraud or undue pressure was used to induce the donor to create the power;
(e) that, having regard to all the circumstances and in particular the attorney's relationship to or connection with the donor, the attorney is unsuitable to be the donor's attorney.

(6) If, in a case where subsection (4) above applies, any of the grounds of objection in subsection (5) above is established to the satisfaction of the court, the

court shall refuse the application but if, in such a case, it is not so satisfied, the court shall register the instrument to which the application relates.

(7) Where the court refuses an application for registration on ground (d) or (e) in subsection (5) above it shall by order revoke the power created by the instrument.

(8) Where the court refuses an application for registration on any ground other than that specified in subsection (5)(c) above the instrument shall be delivered up to be cancelled, unless the court otherwise directs.

Legal position after registration

7 Effect and proof of registration, etc

(1) The effect of the registration of an instrument under section 6 is that—

(a) no revocation of the power by the donor shall be valid unless and until the court confirms the revocation under section 8(3);
(b) no disclaimer of the power shall be valid unless and until the attorney gives notice of it to the court;
(c) the donor may not extend or restrict the scope of the authority conferred by the instrument and no instruction or consent given by him after registration shall, in the case of a consent, confer any right and, in the case of an instruction, impose or confer any obligation or right on or create any liability of the attorney or other persons having notice of the instruction or consent.

(2) Subsection (1) above applies for so long as the instrument is registered under section 6 whether or not the donor is for the time being mentally incapable.

(3) A document purporting to be an office copy of an instrument registered under this Act [or under the Enduring Powers of Attorney (Northern Ireland) Order 1987] shall, in any part of the United Kingdom, be evidence of the contents of the instrument and of the fact that it has been so registered.

(4) Subsection (3) above is without prejudice to section 3 of the Powers of Attorney Act 1971 (proof by certified copies) and to any other method of proof authorised by law.

Amendment—Sub-s (3): words in square brackets inserted by the Enduring Powers of Attorney (Northern Ireland Consequential Amendment) Order 1987, SI 1987/1628, art 2.

---

8 Functions of court with respect to registered power

(1) Where an instrument has been registered under section 6, the court shall have the following functions with respect to the power and the donor of and the attorney appointed to act under the power.

(2) The court may—

(a) determine any question as to the meaning or effect of the instrument;
(b) give directions with respect to—

(i) the management or disposal by the attorney of the property and affairs of the donor;

(ii) the rendering of accounts by the attorney and the production of the records kept by him for the purpose;

(iii) the remuneration or expenses of the attorney, whether or not in default of or in accordance with any provision made by the instrument, including directions for the repayment of excessive or the payment of additional remuneration;

(c) require the attorney to furnish information or produce documents or things in his possession as attorney;

(d) give any consent or authorisation to act which the attorney would have to obtain from a mentally capable donor;

(e) authorise the attorney to act so as to benefit himself or other persons than the donor otherwise than in accordance with section 3(4) and (5) (but subject to any conditions or restrictions contained in the instrument);

(f) relieve the attorney wholly or partly from any liability which he has or may have incurred on account of a breach of his duties as attorney.

(3) On application made for the purpose by or on behalf of the donor, the court shall confirm the revocation of the power if satisfied that the donor has done whatever is necessary in law to effect an express revocation of the power and was mentally capable of revoking a power of attorney when he did so (whether or not he is so when the court considers the application).

(4) The court shall cancel the registration of an instrument registered under section 6 in any of the following circumstances, that is to say—

(a) on confirming the revocation of the power under subsection (3) above or receiving notice of disclaimer under section 7(1)(b);

(b) on giving a direction revoking the power on exercising any of its powers under Part VII of the Mental Health Act 1983;

(c) on being satisfied that the donor is and is likely to remain mentally capable;

(d) on being satisfied that the power has expired or has been revoked by the death or bankruptcy of the donor or the death, mental incapacity or bankruptcy of the attorney or, if the attorney is a body corporate, its winding up or dissolution;

(e) on being satisfied that the power was not a valid and subsisting enduring power when registration was effected;

(f) on being satisfied that fraud or undue pressure was used to induce the donor to create the power; or

(g) on being satisfied that, having regard to all the circumstances and in particular the attorney's relationship to or connection with the donor, the attorney is unsuitable to be the donor's attorney.

(5) Where the court cancels the registration of an instrument on being satisfied of the matters specified in paragraph (f) or (g) of subsection (4) above it shall by order revoke the power created by the instrument.

(6) On the cancellation of the registration of an instrument under subsection (4) above except paragraph (c) the instrument shall be delivered up to be cancelled, unless the court otherwise directs.

Protection of attorney and third parties

9 Protection of attorney and third persons where power invalid or revoked

(1) Subsections (2) and (3) below apply where an instrument which did not create a valid power of attorney has been registered under section 6 (whether or not the registration has been cancelled at the time of the act or transaction in question).

(2) An attorney who acts in pursuance of the power shall not incur any liability (either to the donor or to any other person) by reason of the non-existence of the power unless at the time of acting he knows—

(a) that the instrument did not create a valid enduring power; or
(b) that an event has occurred which, if the instrument had created a valid enduring power, would have had the effect of revoking the power; or
(c) that, if the instrument had created a valid enduring power, the power would have expired before that time.

(3) Any transaction between the attorney and another person shall, in favour of that person, be as valid as if the power had then been in existence, unless at the time of the transaction that person has knowledge of any of the matters mentioned in subsection (2) above.

(4) Where the interest of a purchaser depends on whether a transaction between the attorney and another person was valid by virtue of subsection (3) above, it shall be conclusively presumed in favour of the purchaser that the transaction was valid if—

(a) the transaction between that person and the attorney was completed within twelve months of the date on which the instrument was registered; or
(b) that person makes a statutory declaration, before or within three months after the completion of the purchase, that he had no reason at the time of the transaction to doubt that the attorney had authority to dispose of the property which was the subject of the transaction.

(5) For the purposes of section 5 of the Powers of Attorney Act 1971 (protection of attorney and third persons where action is taken under the power of attorney in ignorance of its having been revoked) in its application to an enduring power the revocation of which by the donor is by virtue of section 7(1)(a) above invalid unless and until confirmed by the court under section 8(3) above, knowledge of the confirmation of the revocation is, but knowledge of the unconfirmed revocation is not, knowledge of the revocation of the power.

(6) Schedule 2 shall have effect to confer protection in cases where the instrument failed to create a valid enduring power and the power has been revoked by the donor's mental incapacity.

(7) In this section 'purchaser' and 'purchase' have the meanings specified in section 205(1) of the Law of Property Act 1925.

Supplementary

10 Application of Mental Health Act provisions relating to the court

(1) The provisions of Part VII of the Mental Health Act 1983 (relating to the Court

of Protection) specified below shall apply to persons within and proceedings under this Act in accordance with the following paragraphs of this subsection and subsection (2) below, that is to say—

(a) section 103 (functions of Visitors) shall apply to persons within this Act as it applies to the persons mentioned in that section;
(b) section 104 (powers of judge) shall apply to proceedings under this Act with respect to persons within this Act as it applies to the proceedings mentioned in subsection (1) of that section;
(c) section 105(1) (appeals to nominated judge) shall apply to any decision of the Master of the Court of Protection or any nominated officer in proceedings under this Act as it applies to any decision to which that subsection applies and an appeal shall lie to the Court of Appeal from any decision of a nominated judge whether given in the exercise of his original jurisdiction or on the hearing of an appeal under section 105(1) as extended by this paragraph;
(d) section 106 except subsection (4) (rules of procedure) shall apply to proceedings under this Act and persons within this Act as it applies to the proceedings and persons mentioned in that section.

(2) Any functions conferred or imposed by the provisions of the said Part VII applied by subsection (1) above shall be exercisable also for the purposes of this Act and the persons who are 'within this Act' are the donors of and attorneys under enduring powers of attorney whether or not they would be patients for the purposes of the said Part VII.

(3) In this section 'nominated judge' and 'nominated officer' have the same meanings as in Part VII of the Mental Health Act 1983.

11 Application to joint and joint and several attorneys

(1) An instrument which appoints more than one person to be an attorney cannot create an enduring power unless the attorneys are appointed to act jointly or jointly and severally.

(2) This Act, in its application to joint attorneys, applies to them collectively as it applies to a single attorney but subject to the modifications specified in Part I of Schedule 3.

(3) This Act, in its application to joint and several attorneys, applies with the modifications specified in subsections (4) to (7) below and in Part II of Schedule 3.

(4) A failure, as respects any one attorney, to comply with the requirements for the creation of enduring powers, shall prevent the instrument from creating such a power in his case without however affecting its efficacy for that purpose as respects the other or others or its efficacy in his case for the purpose of creating a power of attorney which is not an enduring power.

(5) Where one or more but not both or all the attorneys makes or joins in making an application for registration of the instrument then—

(a) an attorney who is not an applicant as well as one who is may act pending the initial determination of the application as provided in section 1(2) (or under section 5);

(b) notice of the application shall also be given under Schedule 1 to the other attorney or attorneys; and
(c) objection may validly be taken to the registration on a ground relating to an attorney or to the power of an attorney who is not an applicant as well as to one or the power of one who is an applicant.

(6) The court shall not refuse under section 6(6) to register an instrument because a ground of objection to an attorney or power is established if an enduring power subsists as respects some attorney who is not affected thereby but shall give effect to it by the prescribed qualification of the registration.

(7) The court shall not cancel the registration of an instrument under section 8(4) for any of the causes vitiating registration specified in that subsection if an enduring power subsists as respects some attorney who is not affected thereby but shall give effect to it by the prescribed qualification of the registration.

(8) In this section—

'prescribed' means prescribed by rules of the court; and
'the requirements for the creation of enduring powers' means the provisions of section 2 other than subsections (10) to (12) and of regulations under subsection (2) of that section.

12 Power of Lord Chancellor to modify pre-registration requirements in certain cases

(1) The Lord Chancellor may by order exempt attorneys of such descriptions as he thinks fit from the requirements of this Act to give notice to relatives prior to registration.

(2) Subject to subsection (3) below, where an order is made under this section with respect to attorneys of a specified description then, during the currency of the order, this Act shall have effect in relation to any attorney of that description with the omission of so much of section 4(3) and Schedule 1 as requires notice of an application for registration to be given to relatives.

(3) Notwithstanding that an attorney under a joint or joint and several power is of a description specified in a current order under this section, subsection (2) above shall not apply in relation to him if any of the other attorneys under the power is not of a description specified in that or another current order under this section.

(4) The power to make an order under this section shall be exercisable by statutory instrument which shall be subject to annulment in pursuance of a resolution of either House of Parliament.

13 Interpretation

(1) In this Act—

'the court', in relation to any functions under this Act, means the authority having jurisdiction under Part VII of the Mental Health Act 1983;
'enduring power' is to be construed in accordance with section 2;

'mentally incapable' or 'mental incapacity', except where it refers to revocation at common law, means, in relation to any person, that he is incapable by reason of mental disorder of managing and administering his property and affairs and 'mentally capable' and 'mental capacity' shall be construed accordingly;
'mental disorder' has the same meaning as it has in the Mental Health Act 1983;
'notice' means notice in writing;
'rules of the court' means rules under Part VII of the Mental Health Act 1983 as applied by section 10;
...
'trust corporation' means the Public Trustee or a corporation either appointed by the High Court or a county court (according to their respective jurisdictions) in any particular case to be a trustee or entitled by rules under section 4(3) of the Public Trustee Act 1906 to act as custodian trustee.

(2) Any question arising under or for the purposes of this Act as to what the donor of the power might at any time be expected to do shall be determined by assuming that he had full mental capacity at the time but otherwise by reference to the circumstances existing at that time.

Amendment—Sub-s (1): definition omitted repealed by the Statute Law (Repeals) Act 1993.

---

14 Short title, commencement and extent

(1) This Act may be cited as the Enduring Powers of Attorney Act 1985.

(2) This Act shall come into force on such day as the Lord Chancellor appoints by order made by statutory instrument.

(3) This Act extends to England and Wales only except that section 7(3) and section 10(1)(b) so far as it applies section 104(4) of the Mental Health Act 1983 extend also to Scotland and Northern Ireland.

Schedule 1: Notification Prior to Registration

PART I:
DUTY TO GIVE NOTICE TO RELATIVES AND DONOR

Duty to give notice to relatives

1—Subject to paragraph 3 below, before making an application for registration the attorney shall give notice of his intention to do so to all those persons (if any) who are entitled to receive notice by virtue of paragraph 2 below.

2—(1) Subject to the limitations contained in sub-paragraphs (2) to (4) below, persons of the following classes (referred to in this Act as 'relatives') are entitled to receive notice under paragraph 1 above—

(a) the donor's husband or wife;
(b) the donor's children;
(c) the donor's parents;
(d) the donor's brothers and sisters, whether of the whole or half blood;

(e) the widow or widower of a child of the donor;
(f) the donor's grandchildren;
(g) the children of the donor's brothers and sisters of the whole blood;
(h) the children of the donor's brothers and sisters of the half blood;
(i) the donor's uncles and aunts of the whole blood; and
(j) the children of the donor's uncles and aunts of the whole blood.

(2) A person is not entitled to receive notice under paragraph 1 above if—

(a) his name or address is not known to the attorney and cannot be reasonably ascertained by him; or
(b) the attorney has reason to believe that he has not attained eighteen years or is mentally incapable.

(3) Except where sub-paragraph (4) below applies, no more than three persons are entitled to receive notice under paragraph 1 above and, in determining the persons who are so entitled, persons falling within class (a) of sub-paragraph (1) above are to be preferred to persons falling with class (b) of that sub-paragraph, persons falling within class (b) are to be preferred to persons falling within class (c) of that sub-paragraph; and so on.

(4) Notwithstanding the limit of three specified in sub-paragraph (3) above, where—

(a) there is more than one person falling within any of classes (a) to (j) of sub-paragraph (1) above, and
(b) at least one of those persons would be entitled to receive notice under paragraph 1 above,

then, subject to sub-paragraph (2) above, all the persons falling within that class are entitled to receive notice under paragraph 1 above.

3—(1) An attorney shall not be required to give notice under paragraph 1 above to himself or to any other attorney under the power who is joining in making the application, notwithstanding that he or, as the case may be, the other attorney is entitled to receive notice by virtue of paragraph 2 above.

(2) In the case of any person who is entitled to receive notice under paragraph 1 above, the attorney, before applying for registration, may make an application to the court to be dispensed from the requirement to give him notice; and the court shall grant the application if it is satisfied—

(a) that it would be undesirable or impracticable for the attorney to give him notice; or
(b) that no useful purpose is likely to be served by giving him notice.

Duty to give notice to donor

4—(1) Subject to sub-paragraph (2) below, before making an application for registration the attorney shall give notice of his intention to do so to the donor.

(2) Paragraph 3(2) above shall apply in relation to the donor as it applies in relation to a person who is entitled to receive notice under paragraph 1 above.

PART II:
CONTENTS OF NOTICES

5— A notice to relatives under this Schedule—

(a) shall be in the prescribed form;
(b) shall state that the attorney proposes to make an application to the Court of Protection for the registration of the instrument creating the enduring power in question;
(c) shall inform the person to whom it is given that he may object to the proposed registration by notice in writing to the Court of Protection before the expiry of the period of four weeks beginning with the day on which the notice under this Schedule was given to him;
(d) shall specify, as the grounds on which an objection to registration may be made, the grounds set out in section 6(5).

6— A notice to the donor under this Schedule—

(a) shall be in the prescribed form;
(b) shall contain the statement mentioned in paragraph 5(b) above; and
(c) shall inform the donor that, whilst the instrument remains registered, any revocation of the power by him will be ineffective unless and until the revocation is confirmed by the Court of Protection.

PART III:
DUTY TO GIVE NOTICE TO OTHER ATTORNEYS

7—(1) Subject to sub-paragraph (2) below, before making an application for registration an attorney under a joint and several power shall give notice of his intention to do so to any other attorney under the power who is not joining in making the application; and paragraphs 3(2) and 5 above shall apply in relation to attorneys entitled to receive notice by virtue of this paragraph as they apply in relation to persons entitled to receive notice by virtue of paragraph 2 above.

(2) An attorney is not entitled to receive notice by virtue of this paragraph if—

(a) his address is not known to the applying attorney and cannot reasonably be ascertained by him; or
(b) the applying attorney has reason to believe that he has not attained eighteen years or is mentally incapable.

PART IV:
SUPPLEMENTARY

8—(1) For the purposes of this Schedule an illegitimate child shall be treated as if he were the legitimate child of his mother and father.

(2) Notwithstanding anything in section 7 of the Interpretation Act 1978 (construction of references to service by post), for the purposes of this Schedule a notice given by post shall be regarded as given on the date on which it was posted.

Schedule 2: Further Protection of Attorney and Third Persons

1—Where—

(a) an instrument framed in a form prescribed under section 2(2) creates a power which is not a valid enduring power; and
(b) the power is revoked by the mental incapacity of the donor, paragraphs 2 and 3 below shall apply, whether or not the instrument has been registered.

2— An attorney who acts in pursuance of the power shall not, by reason of the revocation, incur any liability (either to the donor or to any other person) unless at the time of acting he knows—

(a) that the instrument did not create a valid enduring power; and
(b) that the donor has become mentally incapable.

3— Any transaction between the attorney and another person shall, in favour of that person, be as valid as if the power had then been in existence, unless at the time of the transaction that person knows—

(a) that the instrument did not create a valid enduring power; and
(b) that the donor has become mentally incapable.

4— Section 9(4) shall apply for the purpose of determining whether a transaction was valid by virtue of paragraph 3 above as it applies for the purpose of determining whether a transaction was valid by virtue of section 9(3).

Schedule 3: Joint and Joint and Several Attorneys

PART I: JOINT ATTORNEYS

1— In section 2(7), the reference to the time when the attorney executes the instrument shall be read as a reference to the time when the second or last attorney executes the instrument.

2— In section 2(9) and (10), the reference to the attorney shall be read as a reference to any attorney under the power.

3— In section 5, references to the attorney shall be read as including references to any attorney under the power.

4— Section 6 shall have effect as if the ground of objection to the registration of the instrument specified in subsection (5)(e) applied to any attorney under the power.

5— In section 8(2), references to the attorney shall be read as including references to any attorney under the power.

6— In section 8(4), references to the attorney shall be read as including references to any attorney under the power.

PART II: JOINT AND SEVERAL ATTORNEYS

7— In section 2(10), the reference to the bankruptcy of the attorney shall be construed as a reference to the bankruptcy of the last remaining attorney under the power; and the bankruptcy of any other attorney under the power shall cause that person to cease to be attorney, whatever the circumstances of the bankruptcy.

8— The restriction upon disclaimer imposed by section 4(6) applies only to those attorneys who have reason to believe that the donor is or is becoming mentally incapable.

Recognition of Trusts Act 1987

1987 Chapter 14

An Act to enable the UK to ratify the Convention on the law applicable to trusts and on their recognition which was signed on behalf of the UK on 10 January 1986.

[9 April 1987]

Initial Commencement—To be appointed: see s 3(2).
Appointment—1 August 1987: see SI 1987/1177, art 2.
Extent—See s 2.

---

1 Applicable law and recognition of trusts

(1) The provisions of the Convention set out in the Schedule to this Act shall have the force of law in the United Kingdom.

(2) Those provisions shall, so far as applicable, have effect not only in relation to the trusts described in Articles 2 and 3 of the Convention but also in relation to any other trusts of property arising under the law of any part of the United Kingdom or by virtue of a judicial decision whether in the United Kingdom or elsewhere.

(3) In accordance with Articles 15 and 16 such provisions of the law as are there mentioned shall, to the extent there specified, apply to the exclusion of the other provisions of the Convention.

(4) In Article 17 the reference to a State includes a reference to any country or territory (whether or not a party to the Convention and whether or not forming part of the United Kingdom) which has its own system of law.

(5) Article 22 shall not be construed as affecting the law to be applied in relation to anything done or omitted before the coming into force of this Act.

Schedule:
Convention on the Law Applicable to Trusts and on Their Recognition

CHAPTER I:
SCOPE

Article 1

This Convention specifies the law applicable to trusts and governs their recognition.

Article 2

For the purposes of this Convention, the term 'trust' refers to the legal relationship created— inter vivos or on death— by a person, the settlor, when assets have been placed under the control of a trustee for the benefit of a beneficiary or for a specified purpose.

A trust has the following characteristics—

(a) the assets constitute a separate fund and are not a part of the trustee's own estate;

(b) title to the trust assets stands in the name of the trustee or in the name of another person on behalf of the trustee;
(c) the trustee has the power and the duty, in respect of which he is accountable, to manage, employ or dispose of the assets in accordance with the terms of the trust and the special duties imposed upon him by law.

The reservation by the settlor of certain rights and powers, and the fact that the trustee may himself have rights as a beneficiary, are not necessarily inconsistent with the existence of a trust.

Article 3

The Convention applies only to trusts created voluntarily and evidenced in writing.

Article 4

The Convention does not apply to preliminary issues relating to the validity of wills or of other acts by virtue of which assets are transferred to the trustee.

Article 5

The Convention does not apply to the extent that the law specified by Chapter II does not provide for trusts or the category of trusts involved.

CHAPTER II:
APPLICABLE LAW

Article 6

A trust shall be governed by the law chosen by the settlor. The choice must be express or be implied in the terms of the instrument creating or the writing evidencing the trust, interpreted, if necessary, in the light of the circumstances of the case.

Where the law chosen under the previous paragraph does not provide for trusts or the category of trust involved, the choice shall not be effective and the law specified in Article 7 shall apply.

Article 7

Where no applicable law has been chosen, a trust shall be governed by the law with which it is most closely connected.

In ascertaining the law with which a trust is most closely connected reference shall be made in particular to—

(a) the place of administration of the trust designated by the settlor;
(b) the situs of the assets of the trust;
(c) the place of residence or business of the trustee;
(d) the objects of the trust and the places where they are to be fulfilled.

Article 8

The law specified by Article 6 or 7 shall govern the validity of the trust, its construction, its effects and the administration of the trust. In particular that law shall govern—

(a) the appointment, resignation and removal of trustees, the capacity to act as a trustee, and the devolution of the office of trustee;
(b) the rights and duties of trustees among themselves;
(c) the right of trustees to delegate in whole or in part the discharge of their duties or the exercise of their powers;
(d) the power of trustees to administer or to dispose of trust assets, to create security interests in the trust assets, or to acquire new assets;
(e) the powers of investment of trustees;
(f) restrictions upon the duration of the trust, and upon the power to accumulate the income of the trust;
(g) the relationships between the trustees and the beneficiaries including the personal liability of the trustees to the beneficiaries;
(h) the variation or termination of the trust;
(i) the distribution of the trust assets;
(j) the duty of trustees to account for their administration.

Article 9

In applying this Chapter a severable aspect of the trust, particularly matters of administration, may be governed by a different law.

Article 10

The law applicable to the validity of the trust shall determine whether that law or the law governing a severable aspect of the trust may be replaced by another law.

CHAPTER III:
RECOGNITION

Article 11

A trust created in accordance with the law specified by the preceding Chapter shall be recognised as a trust.

Such recognition shall imply, as a minimum, that the trust property constitutes a separate fund, that the trustee may sue and be sued in his capacity as trustee, and that he may appear or act in this capacity before a notary or any person acting in an official capacity.

In so far as the law applicable to the trust requires or provides, such recognition shall imply in particular—

(a) that personal creditors of the trustee shall have no recourse against the trust assets;
(b) that the trust assets shall not form part of the trustee's estate upon his insolvency or bankruptcy;
(c) that the trust assets shall not form part of the matrimonial property of the trustee or his spouse nor part of the trustee's estate upon his death;
(d) that the trust assets may be recovered when the trustee, in breach of trust, has mingled trust assets with his own property or has alienated trust assets. However, the rights and obligations of any third party holder of the assets shall remain subject to the law determined by the choice of law rules of the forum.

Article 12

Where the trustee desires to register assets, movable or immovable, or documents of title to them, he shall be entitled, in so far as this is not prohibited by or inconsistent with the law of the State where registration is sought, to do so in his capacity as trustee or in such other way that the existence of the trust is disclosed.

Article 14

The Convention shall not prevent the application of rules of law more favourable to the recognition of trusts.

CHAPTER IV:
GENERAL CLAUSES

Article 15

The Convention does not prevent the application of provisions of the law designated by the conflicts rules of the forum, in so far as those provisions cannot be derogated from by voluntary act, relating in particular to the following matters—

(a) the protection of minors and incapable parties;
(b) the personal and proprietary effects of marriage;
(c) succession rights, testate and intestate, especially the indefeasible shares of spouses and relatives;
(d) the transfer of title property and security interests in property;
(e) the protection of creditors in matters of insolvency;
(f) the protection, in other respects, of third parties acting in good faith.

If recognition of a trust is prevented by application of the preceding paragraph, the court shall try to give effect to the objects of the trust by other means.

Article 16

The Convention does not prevent the application of those provisions of the law of the forum which must be applied even to international situations, irrespective of rules of conflict of laws.

Article 17

In the Convention the word 'law' means the rules of law in force in a State other than its rules of conflict of laws.

Article 18

The provisions of the Convention may be disregarded when their application would be manifestly incompatible with public policy.

Article 22

The Convention applies to trusts regardless of the date on which they were created.

Trusts of Land and Appointment of Trustees Act 1996

1996 Chapter 47

An Act to make new provision about trusts of land including provision phasing out the Settled Land Act 1925, abolishing the doctrine of conversion and otherwise amending the law about trusts for sale of land; to amend the law about the apportionment and retirement of trustees of any trust; and for connected purposes.

[24 July 1996].

Initial Commencement—To be appointed : see 27(2).
Appointment—1 January 1997: see SI 1996/2974, art 2.
Extent—This Act does not extend to Scotland: see 27(3).

PART I
TRUSTS OF LAND

Introductory

1 Meaning of 'trust of land'

(1) In this Act—

(a) 'trust of land' means (subject to subsection (3)) any trust of property which consists of or includes land, and
(b) 'trustees of land' means trustees of a trust of land.

(2) The reference in subsection (1)(a) to a trust—

(a) is to any description of trust (whether express, implied, resulting or constructive), including a trust for sale and a bare trust, and
(b) includes a trust created, or arising, before the commencement of this Act.

(3) The reference to land in subsection (1)(a) does not include land which (despite section 2) is settled land or which is land to which the Universities and College Estates Act 1925 applies.

Settlements and trusts for sale as trusts of land

2 Trusts in place of settlements

(1) No settlement created after the commencement of this Act is a settlement for the purposes of the Settled Land Act 1925; and no settlement shall be deemed to be made under that Act after that commencement.

(2) Subsection (1) does not apply to a settlement created on the occasion of an alteration in any interest in, or of a person becoming entitled under, a settlement which—

(a) is in existence at the commencement of this Act, or
(b) derives from a settlement within paragraph (a) or this paragraph.

(3) But a settlement created as mentioned in subsection (2) is not a settlement for

the purposes of the Settled Land Act 1925 if provision to the effect that it is not is made in the instrument, or any of the instruments, by which it is created.

(4) Where at any time after the commencement of this Act there is in the case of any settlement which is a settlement for the purposes of the Settled Land Act 1925 no relevant property which is, or is deemed to be, subject to the settlement, the settlement permanently ceases at that time to be a settlement for the purposes of that Act.

In this subsection 'relevant property' means land and personal chattels to which section 67(1) of the Settled Land Act 1925 (heirlooms) applies.

(5) No land held on charitable, ecclesiastical or public trusts shall be or be deemed to be settled land after the commencement of this Act, even if it was or was deemed to be settled land before that commencement.

(6) Schedule 1 has effect to make provision consequential on this section (including provision to impose a trust in circumstances in which, apart from this section, there would be a settlement for the purposes of the Settled Land Act 1925 (and there would not otherwise be a trust)).

3 Abolition of doctrine of conversion

(1) Where land is held by trustees subject to a trust for sale, the land is not to be regarded as personal property; and where personal property is subject to a trust for sale in order that the trustees may acquire land, the personal property is not to be regarded as land.

(2) Subsection (1) does not apply to a trust created by a will if the testator died before the commencement of this Act.

(3) Subject to that, subsection (1) applies to a trust whether it is created, or arises, before or after that commencement.

4 Express trusts for sale as trusts of land

(1) In the case of every trust for sale of land created by a disposition there is to be implied, despite any provision to the contrary made by the disposition, a power for the trustees to postpone sale of the land; and the trustees are not liable in any way for postponing sale of the land, in the exercise of their discretion, for an indefinite period.

(2) Subsection (1) applies to a trust whether it is created, or arises, before or after the commencement of this Act.

(3) Subsection (1) does not affect any liability incurred by trustees before that commencement.

5 Implied trusts for sale as trusts of land

(1) Schedule 2 has effect in relation to statutory provisions which impose a trust for sale of land in certain circumstances so that in those circumstances there is instead a trust of the land (without a duty to sell).

(2) Section 1 of the Settled Land Act 1925 does not apply to land held on any trust arising by virtue of that Schedule (so that any such land is subject to a trust of land).

Functions of trustees of land

6 General powers of trustees

(1) For the purpose of exercising their functions as trustees, the trustees of land have in relation to the land subject to the trust all the powers of an absolute owner.

(2) Where in the case of any land subject to a trust of land each of the beneficiaries interested in the land is a person of full age and capacity who is absolutely entitled to the land, the powers conferred on the trustees by subsection (1) include the power to convey the land to the beneficiaries even though they have not required the trustees to do so; and where land is conveyed by virtue of this subsection—

(a) the beneficiaries shall do whatever is necessary to secure that it vests in them, and
(b) if they fail to do so, the court may make an order requiring them to do so.

(3) The trustees of land have power to [acquire land under the power conferred by section 8 of the Trustee Act 2000].

(4) …

(5) In exercising the powers conferred by this section trustees shall have regard to the rights of the beneficiaries.

(6) The powers conferred by this section shall not be exercised in contravention of, or of any order made in pursuance of, any other enactment or any rule of law or equity.

(7) The reference in subsection (6) to an order includes an order of any court or of the Charity Commissioners.

(8) Where any enactment other than this section confers on trustees authority to act subject to any restriction, limitation or condition, trustees of land may not exercise the powers conferred by this section to do any act which they are prevented from doing under the other enactment by reason of the restriction, limitation or condition.

[(9) The duty of care under section 1 of the Trustee Act 2000 applies to trustees of land when exercising the powers conferred by this section.]

Amendment—Sub-s (3): words 'acquire land under the power conferred by section 8 of the Trustee Act 2000' in square brackets substituted by the Trustee Act 2000, s 40(1), Sch 2, Pt II, para 45(1). Date in force: 1 February 2001: see SI 2001/49, art 2.
Sub-s (4): repealed by the Trustee Act 2000, s 40(1), (3), Sch 2, Pt II, para 45(2), Sch 4, Pt II. Date in force: 1 February 2001: see SI 2001/49, art 2.
Sub-s (9): inserted by the Trustee Act 2000, s 40(1), Sch 2, Pt II, para 45(3). Date in force: 1 February 2001: see SI 2001/49, art 2.

---

7 Partition by trustees

(1) The trustees of land may, where beneficiaries of full age are absolutely entitled

in undivided shares to land subject to the trust, partition the land, or any part of it, and provide (by way of mortgage or otherwise) for the payment of any equality money.

(2) The trustees shall give effect to any such partition by conveying the partitioned land in severalty (whether or not subject to any legal mortgage created for raising equality money), either absolutely or in trust, in accordance with the rights of those beneficiaries.

(3) Before exercising their powers under subsection (2) the trustees shall obtain the consent of each of those beneficiaries.

(4) Where a share in the land is affected by an incumbrance, the trustees may either give effect to it or provide for its discharge from the property allotted to that share as they think fit.

(5) If a share in the land is absolutely vested in a minor, subsections (1) to (4) apply as if he were of full age, except that the trustees may act on his behalf and retain land or other property representing his share in trust for him.

8 Exclusion and restriction of powers

(1) Sections 6 and 7 do not apply in the case of a trust of land created by a disposition in so far as provision to the effect that they do not apply is made by the disposition.

(2) If the disposition creating such a trust makes provision requiring any consent to be obtained to the exercise of any power conferred by section 6 or 7, the power may not be exercised without that consent.

(3) Subsection (1) does not apply in the case of charitable, ecclesiastical or public trusts.

(4) Subsections (1) and (2) have effect subject to any enactment which prohibits or restricts the effect of provision of the description mentioned in them.

9 Delegation by trustees

(1) The trustees of land may, by power of attorney, delegate to any beneficiary or beneficiaries of full age and beneficially entitled to an interest in possession in land subject to the trust any of their functions as trustees which relate to the land.

(2) Where trustees purport to delegate to a person by a power of attorney under subsection (1) functions relating to any land and another person in good faith deals with him in relation to the land, he shall be presumed in favour of that other person to have been a person to whom the functions could be delegated unless that other person has knowledge at the time of the transaction that he was not such a person.

And it shall be conclusively presumed in favour of any purchaser whose interest depends on the validity of that transaction that that other person dealt in good faith and did not have such knowledge if that other person makes a statutory declaration to that effect before or within three months after the completion of the purchase.

(3) A power of attorney under subsection (1) shall be given by all the trustees

jointly and (unless expressed to be irrevocable and to be given by way of security) may be revoked by any one or more of them; and such a power is revoked by the appointment as a trustee of a person other than those by whom it is given (though not by any of those persons dying or otherwise ceasing to be a trustee).

(4) Where a beneficiary to whom functions are delegated by a power of attorney under subsection (1) ceases to be a person beneficially entitled to an interest in possession in land subject to the trust—

(a) if the functions are delegated to him alone, the power is revoked,
(b) if the functions are delegated to him and to other beneficiaries to be exercised by them jointly (but not separately), the power is revoked if each of the other beneficiaries ceases to be so entitled (but otherwise functions exercisable in accordance with the power are so exercisable by the remaining beneficiary or beneficiaries), and
(c) if the functions are delegated to him and to other beneficiaries to be exercised by them separately (or either separately or jointly), the power is revoked in so far as it relates to him.

(5) A delegation under subsection (1) may be for any period or indefinite.

(6) A power of attorney under subsection (1) cannot be an enduring power within the meaning of the Enduring Powers of Attorney Act 1985.

(7) Beneficiaries to whom functions have been delegated under subsection (1) are, in relation to the exercise of the functions, in the same position as trustees (with the same duties and liabilities); but such beneficiaries shall not be regarded as trustees for any other purposes (including, in particular, the purposes of any enactment permitting the delegation of functions by trustees or imposing requirements relating to the payment of capital money).

(8) …

(9) Neither this section nor the repeal by this Act of section 29 of the Law of Property Act 1925 (which is superseded by this section) affects the operation after the commencement of this Act of any delegation effected before that commencement.

Amendment—Sub-s (8): repealed by the Trustee Act 2000, s 40(1), (3), Sch 2, Pt II, para 46, Sch 4, Pt II. Date in force: 1 February 2001: see SI 2001/49, art 2.

[9A Duties of trustees in connection with delegation etc]

[(1) The duty of care under section 1 of the Trustee Act 2000 applies to trustees of land in deciding whether to delegate any of their functions under section 9.

(2) Subsection (3) applies if the trustees of land—

(a) delegate any of their functions under section 9, and
(b) the delegation is not irrevocable.

(3) While the delegation continues, the trustees—

(a) must keep the delegation under review,

(b) if circumstances make it appropriate to do so, must consider whether there is a need to exercise any power of intervention that they have, and
(c) if they consider that there is a need to exercise such a power, must do so.

(4) 'Power of intervention' includes—

(a) a power to give directions to the beneficiary;
(b) a power to revoke the delegation.

(5) The duty of care under section 1 of the 2000 Act applies to trustees in carrying out any duty under subsection (3).

(6) A trustee of land is not liable for any act or default of the beneficiary, or beneficiaries, unless the trustee fails to comply with the duty of care in deciding to delegate any of the trustees' functions under section 9 or in carrying out any duty under subsection (3).

(7) Neither this section nor the repeal of section 9(8) by the Trustee Act 2000 affects the operation after the commencement of this section of any delegation effected before that commencement.]

Amendment—Inserted by the Trustee Act 2000, s 40(1), Sch 2, Pt II, para 47. Date in force: 1 February 2001: see SI 2001/49, art 2.

Consents and consultation

10 Consents

(1) If a disposition creating a trust of land requires the consent of more than two persons to the exercise by the trustees of any function relating to the land, the consent of any two of them to the exercise of the function is sufficient in favour of a purchaser.

(2) Subsection (1) does not apply to the exercise of a function by trustees of land held on charitable, ecclesiastical or public trusts.

(3) Where at any time a person whose consent is expressed by a disposition creating a trust of land to be required to the exercise by the trustees of any function relating to the land is not of full age—

(a) his consent is not, in favour of a purchaser, required to the exercise of the function, but
(b) the trustees shall obtain the consent of a parent who has parental responsibility for him (within the meaning of the Children Act 1989) or of a guardian of his.

11 Consultation with beneficiaries

(1) The trustees of land shall in the exercise of any function relating to land subject to the trust—

(a) so far as practicable, consult the beneficiaries of full age and beneficially entitled to an interest in possession in the land, and

(b) so far as consistent with the general interest of the trust, give effect to the wishes of those beneficiaries, or (in case of dispute) of the majority (according to the value of their combined interests).

(2) Subsection (1) does not apply—

(a) in relation to a trust created by a disposition in so far as provision that it does not apply is made by the disposition,
(b) in relation to a trust created or arising under a will made before the commencement of this Act, or
(c) in relation to the exercise of the power mentioned in section 6(2).

(3) Subsection (1) does not apply to a trust created before the commencement of this Act by a disposition, or a trust created after that commencement by reference to such a trust, unless provision to the effect that it is to apply is made by a deed executed—

(a) in a case in which the trust was created by one person and he is of full capacity, by that person, or
(b) in a case in which the trust was created by more than one person, by such of the persons who created the trust as are alive and of full capacity.

(4) A deed executed for the purposes of subsection (3) is irrevocable.

Right of beneficiaries to occupy trust land

12 The right to occupy

(1) A beneficiary who is beneficially entitled to an interest in possession in land subject to a trust of land is entitled by reason of his interest to occupy the land at any time if at that time—

(a) the purposes of the trust include making the land available for his occupation (or for the occupation of beneficiaries of a class of which he is a member or of beneficiaries in general), or
(b) the land is held by the trustees so as to be so available.

(2) Subsection (1) does not confer on a beneficiary a right to occupy land if it is either unavailable or unsuitable for occupation by him.

(3) This section is subject to section 13.

13 Exclusion and restriction of right to occupy

(1) Where two or more beneficiaries are (or apart from this subsection would be) entitled under section 12 to occupy land, the trustees of land may exclude or restrict the entitlement of any one or more (but not all) of them.

(2) Trustees may not under subsection (1)—

(a) unreasonably exclude any beneficiary's entitlement to occupy land, or
(b) restrict any such entitlement to an unreasonable extent.

(3) The trustees of land may from time to time impose reasonable conditions on any beneficiary in relation to his occupation of land by reason of his entitlement under section 12.

(4) The matters to which trustees are to have regard in exercising the powers conferred by this section include—

(a) the intentions of the person or persons (if any) who created the trust,
(b) the purposes for which the land is held, and
(c) the circumstances and wishes of each of the beneficiaries who is (or apart from any previous exercise by the trustees of those powers would be) entitled to occupy the land under section 12.

(5) The conditions which may be imposed on a beneficiary under subsection (3) include, in particular, conditions requiring him—

(a) to pay any outgoings or expenses in respect of the land, or
(b) to assume any other obligation in relation to the land or to any activity which is or is proposed to be conducted there.

(6) Where the entitlement of any beneficiary to occupy land under section 12 has been excluded or restricted, the conditions which may be imposed on any other beneficiary under subsection (3) include, in particular, conditions requiring him to—

(a) make payments by way of compensation to the beneficiary whose entitlement has been excluded or restricted, or
(b) forgo any payment or other benefit to which he would otherwise be entitled under the trust so as to benefit that beneficiary.

(7) The powers conferred on trustees by this section may not be exercised—

(a) so as prevent any person who is in occupation of land (whether or not by reason of an entitlement under section 12) from continuing to occupy the land, or
(b) in a manner likely to result in any such person ceasing to occupy the land,

unless he consents or the court has given approval.

(8) The matters to which the court is to have regard in determining whether to give approval under subsection (7) include the matters mentioned in subsection (4)(a) to (c).

Powers of court

14 Applications for order

(1) Any person who is a trustee of land or has an interest in a property subject to a trust of land may make an application to the court for an order under this section.

(2) On an application for an order under this section the court may make any such order—

(a) relating to the exercise by the trustees of any of their functions (including an order relieving them of any obligation to obtain the consent of, or to consult, any person in connection with the exercise of any of their functions), or

(b) declaring the nature or extent of a person's interest in property subject to the trust,

as the court thinks fit.

(3) The court may not under this section make any order as to the appointment or removal of trustees.

(4) The powers conferred on the court by this section are exercisable on an application whether it is made before or after the commencement of this Act.

15 Matters relevant in determining applications

(1) The matters to which the court is to have regard in determining an application for an order under section 14 include—

(a) the intentions of the person or persons (if any) who created the trust,
(b) the purposes for which the property subject to the trust is held,
(c) the welfare of any minor who occupies or might reasonably be expected to occupy any land subject to the trust as his home, and
(d) the interests of any secured creditor of any beneficiary.

(2) In the case of an application relating to the exercise in relation to any land of the powers conferred on the trustees by section 13, the matters to which the court is to have regard also include the circumstances and wishes of each of the beneficiaries who is (or apart from any previous exercise by the trustees of those powers would be) entitled to occupy the land under section 12.

(3) In the case of any other application, other than one relating to the exercise of the power mentioned in section 6(2), the matters to which the court is to have regard also include the circumstances and wishes of any beneficiaries of full age and entitled to an interest in possession in property subject to the trust or (in case of dispute) of the majority (according to the value of their combined interests).

(4) This section does not apply to an application if section 335A of the Insolvency Act 1986 (which is inserted by Schedule 3 and relates to applications by a trustee of a bankrupt) applies to it.

Purchaser protection

16 Protection of purchasers

(1) A purchaser of land which is or has been subject to a trust need not be concerned to see that any requirement imposed on the trustees by section 6(5), 7(3) or 11(1) has been complied with.

(2) Where—

(a) trustees of land who convey land which (immediately before it is conveyed) is subject to the trust contravene section 6(6) or (8), but
(b) the purchaser of the land from the trustees has no actual notice of the contravention,

the contravention does not invalidate the conveyance.

(3) Where the powers of trustees of land are limited by virtue of section 8—

(a) the trustees shall take all reasonable steps to bring the limitation to the notice of any purchaser of the land from them, but
(b) the limitation does not invalidate any conveyance by the trustees to a purchaser who has no actual notice of the limitation.

(4) Where trustees of land convey land which (immediately before it is conveyed) is subject to the trust to persons believed by them to be beneficiaries absolutely entitled to the land under the trust and of full age and capacity—

(a) the trustees shall execute a deed declaring that they are discharged from the trust in relation to that land, and
(b) if they fail to do so, the court may make an order requiring them to do so.

(5) A purchaser of land to which a deed under subsection (4) relates is entitled to assume that, as from the date of the deed, the land is not subject to the trust unless he has actual notice that the trustees were mistaken in their belief that the land was conveyed to beneficiaries absolutely entitled to the land under the trust and of full age and capacity.

(6) Subsections (2) and (3) do not apply to land held on charitable, ecclesiastical or public trusts.

(7) This section does not apply to registered land.

Supplementary

17 Application of provisions to trusts of proceeds of sale

(1) …

(2) Section 14 applies in relation to a trust of proceeds of sale of land and trustees of such a trust as in relation to a trust of land and trustees of land.

(3) In this section 'trust of proceeds of sale of land' means (subject to subsection (5)) any trust of property (other than a trust of land) which consists of or includes—

(a) any proceeds of a disposition of land held in trust (including settled land), or
(b) any property representing any such proceeds.

(4) The references in subsection (3) to a trust—

(a) are to any description of trust (whether express, implied, resulting or constructive), including a trust for sale and a bare trust, and
(b) include a trust created, or arising, before the commencement of this Act.

(5) A trust which (despite section 2) is a settlement for the purposes of the Settled Land Act 1925 cannot be a trust of proceeds of sale of land.

(6) In subsection (3)—

(a) 'disposition' includes any disposition made, or coming into operation, before the commencement of this Act, and

(b) the reference to settled land includes personal chattels to which section 67(1) of the Settled Land Act 1925 (heirlooms) applies.

Amendment—Sub-s (1): repealed by the Trustee Act 2000, s 40(1), (3), Sch 2, Pt II, para 48, Sch 4, Pt II. Date in force: 1 February 2001: see SI 2001/49, art 2.

---

18 Application of Part to personal representatives

(1) The provisions of this Part relating to trustees, other than sections 10, 11 and 14, apply to personal representatives, but with appropriate modifications and without prejudice to the functions of personal representatives for the purposes of administration.

(2) The appropriate modifications include—

(a) the substitution of references to persons interested in the due administration of the estate for references to beneficiaries, and
(b) the substitution of references to the will for references to the disposition creating the trust.

(3) Section 3(1) does not apply to personal representatives if the death occurs before the commencement of this Act.

PART II:
APPOINTMENT AND RETIREMENT OF TRUSTEES

19 Appointment and retirement of trustee at instance of beneficiaries

(1) This section applies in the case of a trust where—

(a) there is no person nominated for the purpose of appointing new trustees by the instrument, if any, creating the trust, and
(b) the beneficiaries under the trust are of full age and capacity and (taken together) are absolutely entitled to the property subject to the trust.

(2) The beneficiaries may give a direction or directions of either or both of the following descriptions—

(a) a written direction to a trustee or trustees to retire from the trust, and
(b) a written direction to the trustees or trustee for the time being (or, if there are none, to the personal representative of the last person who was a trustee) to appoint by writing to be a trustee or trustees the person or persons specified in the direction.

(3) Where—

(a) a trustee has been given a direction under subsection (2)(a),
(b) reasonable arrangements have been made for the protection of any rights of his in connection with the trust,
(c) after he has retired there will be either a trust corporation or at least two persons to act as trustees to perform the trust, and
(d) either another person is to be appointed to be a new trustee on his retirement

(whether in compliance with a direction under subsection (2)(b) or otherwise) or the continuing trustees by deed consent to his retirement,

he shall make a deed declaring his retirement and shall be deemed to have retired and be discharged from the trust.

(4) Where a trustee retires under subsection (3) he and the continuing trustees (together with any new trustee) shall (subject to any arrangements for the protection of his rights) do anything necessary to vest the trust property in the continuing trustees (or the continuing and new trustees).

(5) This section has effect subject to the restrictions imposed by the Trustee Act 1925 on the number of trustees.

20 Appointment of substitute for incapable trustee

(1) This section applies where—

(a) a trustee is incapable by reason of mental disorder of exercising his functions as trustee,
(b) there is no person who is both entitled and willing and able to appoint a trustee in place of him under section 36(1) of the Trustee Act 1925, and
(c) the beneficiaries under the trust are of full age and capacity and (taken together) are absolutely entitled to the property subject to the trust.

(2) The beneficiaries may give to—

(a) a receiver of the trustee,
(b) an attorney acting for him under the authority of a power of attorney created by an instrument which is registered under section 6 of the Enduring Powers of Attorney Act 1985, or
(c) a person authorised for the purpose by the authority having jurisdiction under Part VII of the Mental Health Act 1983,

a written direction to appoint by writing the person or persons specified in the direction to be a trustee or trustees in place of the incapable trustee.

21 Supplementary

(1) For the purposes of section 19 or 20 a direction is given by beneficiaries if—

(a) a single direction is jointly given by all of them, or
(b) (subject to subsection (2)) a direction is given by each of them (whether solely or jointly with one or more, but not all, of the others),

and none of them by writing withdraws the direction given by him before it has been complied with.

(2) Where more than one direction is given each must specify for appointment or retirement the same person or persons.

(3) Subsection (7) of section 36 of the Trustee Act 1925 (powers of trustees appointed under that section) applies to a trustee appointed under section 19 or 20 as if he were appointed under that section.

(4) A direction under section 19 or 20 must not specify a person or persons for appointment if the appointment of that person or those persons would be in contravention of section 35(1) of the Trustee Act 1925 or section 24(1) of the Law of Property Act 1925 (requirements as to identity of trustees).

(5) Sections 19 and 20 do not apply in relation to a trust created by a disposition in so far as provision that they do not apply is made by the disposition.

(6) Sections 19 and 20 do not apply in relation to a trust created before the commencement of this Act by a disposition in so far as provision to the effect that they do not apply is made by a deed executed—

(a) in a case in which the trust was created by one person and he is of full capacity, by that person, or
(b) in a case in which the trust was created by more than one person, by such of the persons who created the trust as are alive and of full capacity.

(7) A deed executed for the purposes of subsection (6) is irrevocable.

(8) Where a deed is executed for the purposes of subsection (6)—

(a) it does not affect anything done before its execution to comply with a direction under section 19 or 20, but
(b) a direction under section 19 or 20 which has been given but not complied with before its execution shall cease to have effect.

PART III: SUPPLEMENTARY

22 Meaning of 'beneficiary'

(1) In this Act 'beneficiary', in relation to a trust, means any person who under the trust has an interest in property subject to the trust (including a person who has such an interest as a trustee or a personal representative).

(2) In this Act references to a beneficiary who is beneficially entitled do not include a beneficiary who has an interest in property subject to the trust only by reason of being a trustee or personal representative.

(3) For the purposes of this Act a person who is a beneficiary only by reason of being an annuitant is not to be regarded as entitled to an interest in possession in land subject to the trust.

23 Other interpretation provisions

(1) In this Act 'purchaser' has the same meaning as in Part I of the Law of Property Act 1925.

(2) Subject to that, where an expression used in this Act is given a meaning by the Law of Property Act 1925 it has the same meaning as in that Act unless the context otherwise requires.

(3) In this Act 'the court' means—

(a) the High Court, or
(b) a county court.

24 Application to Crown

(1) Subject to subsection (2), this Act binds the Crown.

(2) This Act (except so far as it relates to undivided shares and joint ownership) does not affect or alter the descent, devolution or nature of the estates and interests of or in—

(a) land for the time being vested in Her Majesty in right of the Crown or of the Duchy of Lancaster, or
(b) land for the time being belonging to the Duchy of Cornwall and held in right or respect of the Duchy.

25 Amendments, repeals etc

(1) The enactments mentioned in Schedule 3 have effect subject to the amendments specified in that Schedule (which are minor or consequential on other provisions of this Act).

(2) The enactments mentioned in Schedule 4 are repealed to the extent specified in the third column of that Schedule.

(3) Neither section 2(5) nor the repeal by this Act of section 29 of the Settled Land Act 1925 applies in relation to the deed of settlement set out in the Schedule to the Chequers Estate Act 1917 or the trust instrument set out in the Schedule to the Chevening Estate Act 1959.

(4) The amendments and repeals made by this Act do not affect any entailed interest created before the commencement of this Act.

(5) The amendments and repeals made by this Act in consequence of section 3—

(a) do not affect a trust created by a will if the testator died before the commencement of this Act, and
(b) do not affect personal representatives of a person who died before that commencement;

and the repeal of section 22 of the Partnership Act 1890 does not apply in any circumstances involving the personal representatives of a partner who died before that commencement.

26 Power to make consequential provision

(1) The Lord Chancellor may by order made by statutory instrument make any such supplementary, transitional or incidental provision as appears to him to be appropriate for any of the purposes of this Act or in consequence of any of the provisions of this Act.

(2) An order under subsection (1) may, in particular, include provision modifying any enactment contained in a public general or local Act which is passed before, or in the same Session as, this Act.

(3) A statutory instrument made in the exercise of the power conferred by this section is subject to annulment in pursuance of a resolution of either House of Parliament.

27 Short title, commencement and extent

(1) This Act may be cited as the Trusts of Land and Appointment of Trustees Act 1996.

(2) This Act comes into force on such day as the Lord Chancellor appoints by order made by statutory instrument.

(3) Subject to subsection (4), the provisions of this Act extend only to England and Wales.

(4) The repeal in section 30(2) of the Agriculture Act 1970 extends only to Northern Ireland.

Schedule 1: Provisions consequential on section 2

Minors

1—(1) Where after the commencement of this Act a person purports to convey a legal estate in land to a minor, or two or more minors, alone, the conveyance—

(a) is not effective to pass the legal estate, but
(b) operates as a declaration that the land is held in trust for the minor or minors (or if he purports to convey it to the minor or minors in trust for any persons, for those persons).

(2) Where after the commencement of this Act a person purports to convey a legal estate in land to—

(a) a minor or two or more minors, and
(b) another person who is, or other persons who are, of full age,

the conveyance operates to vest the land in the other person or persons in trust for the minor or minors and the other person or persons (or if he purports to convey it to them in trust for any persons, for those persons).

(3) Where immediately before the commencement of this Act a conveyance is operating (by virtue of section 27 of the Settled Land Act 1925) as an agreement to execute a settlement in favour of a minor or minors—

(a) the agreement ceases to have effect on the commencement of this Act, and
(b) the conveyance subsequently operates instead as a declaration that the land is held in trust for the minor or minors.

2— Where after the commencement of this Act a legal estate in land would, by reason of intestacy or in any other circumstances not dealt with in paragraph 1, vest in a person who is a minor if he were a person of full age, the land is held in trust for the minor.

Family charges

3— Where, by virtue of an instrument coming into operation after the commencement of this Act, land becomes charged voluntarily (or in consideration of marriage) or by way of family arrangement, whether immediately or after an interval, with the payment of—

(a) a rentcharge for the life of a person or a shorter period, or
(b) capital, annual or periodical sums for the benefit of a person,

the instrument operates as a declaration that the land is held in trust for giving effect to the charge.

Charitable, ecclesiastical and public trusts

4—(1) This paragraph applies in the case of land held on charitable, ecclesiastical or public trusts (other than land to which the Universities and College Estates Act 1925 applies).

(2) Where there is a conveyance of such land—

(a) if neither section 37(1) nor section 39(1) of the Charities Act 1993 applies to the conveyance, it shall state that the land is held on such trusts, and
(b) if neither section 37(2) nor section 39(2) of that Act has been complied with in relation to the conveyance and a purchaser has notice that the land is held on such trusts, he must see that any consents or orders necessary to authorise the transaction have been obtained.

(3) Where any trustees or the majority of any set of trustees have power to transfer or create any legal estate in the land, the estate shall be transferred or created by them in the names and on behalf of the persons in whom it is vested.

Entailed interests

5—(1) Where a person purports by an instrument coming into operation after the commencement of this Act to grant to another person an entailed interest in real or personal property, the instrument—

(a) is not effective to grant an entailed interest, but
(b) operates instead as a declaration that the property is held in trust absolutely for the person to whom an entailed interest in the property was purportedly granted.

(2) Where a person purports by an instrument coming into operation after the commencement of this Act to declare himself a tenant in tail of real or personal property, the instrument is not effective to create an entailed interest.

Property held on settlement ceasing to exist

6— Where a settlement ceases to be a settlement for the purposes of the Settled Land Act 1925 because no relevant property (within the meaning of section 2(4)) is, or is deemed to be, subject to the settlement, any property which is or later becomes subject to the settlement is held in trust for the persons interested under the settlement.

Schedule 2:
Amendments of Statutory Provisions imposing Trust for Sale

Mortgaged property held by trustees after redemption barred

1—(1)–(6) …

(7) The amendments made by this paragraph—

(a) apply whether the right of redemption is discharged before or after the commencement of this Act, but
(b) are without prejudice to any dealings or arrangements made before the commencement of this Act.

Land purchased by trustees of personal property etc

2—(1) …

(2) The repeal made by this paragraph applies in relation to land purchased after the commencement of this Act whether the trust or will in pursuance of which it is purchased comes into operation before or after the commencement of this Act.

Dispositions to tenants in common

3—(1)—(5) …

(6) The amendments made by this paragraph apply whether the disposition is made, or comes into operation, before or after the commencement of this Act.

Joint tenancies

4—(1)–(3) …

(4) The amendments made by this paragraph apply whether the legal estate is limited, or becomes held in trust, before or after the commencement of this Act.

Intestacy

5—(1)–(4) …

(5) The amendments made by this paragraph apply whether the death occurs before or after the commencement of this Act.

Reverter of sites

6—(1)–(5) …

(6) The amendments made by this paragraph apply whether the trust arises before or after the commencement of this Act.

Trusts deemed to arise in 1926

7— Where at the commencement of this Act any land is held on trust for sale, or on the statutory trusts, by virtue of Schedule 1 to the Law of Property Act 1925 (transitional provisions), it shall after that commencement be held in trust for the persons interested in the land; and references in that Schedule to trusts for sale or trustees for sale or to the statutory trusts shall be construed accordingly.

Amendment—Para 1: sub-paras (1)–(6) amend the Law of Property Act 1925, s 31.
Para 2: sub-para (1) repeals the Law of Property Act 1925, s 32.
Para 3: sub-paras (1)–(5) amend the Law of Property Act 1925, s 34.
Para 4: sub-paras (1)–(3) amend the Law of Property Act 1925, s 36(1), (2).
Para 5: sub-paras (1)–(4) amend the Administration of Estates Act 1925, s 33.
Para 6: sub-paras (1)–(5) amend the Reverter of Sites Act 1987, s 1.

Schedule 3:
Minor and Consequential Amendments

< … >

Amendment—This Schedule contains amendments only.
Repealed in part by the Land Registration Act 2002, s 135, Sch 13. Date in force: 13 October 2003: see SI 2003/1725, art 2(1).
Repealed in part by the Trustee Act 2000, s 40(1), (3), Sch 2, Pt II, para 49, Sch 4, Pt II. Date in force: 1 February 2001: see SI 2001/49, art 2.
Repealed in part by the Countryside and Rights of Way Act 2000, s 102, Sch 16, Pt III. Date in force: 30 January 2001: see the Countryside and Rights of Way Act 2000, s 103(2).

Trustee Delegation Act 1999

1999 Chapter 15

An Act to amend the law relating to the delegation of trustee functions by power of attorney and the exercise of such functions by the donee of a power of attorney: and to make provision about the authority of the donee of a power of attorney to act in relation to land. [15 July 1999].

Initial Commencement—To be appointed: see s 13(1).
Appointment—1 March 2000: see SI 2000/216, art 2.
Extent—This Act does not extend to Scotland; see s 13(2).

Attorney of trustee with beneficial interest in land

1 Exercise of trustee functions by attorney

(1) The donee of a power of attorney is not prevented from doing an act in relation to—

(a) land,
(b) capital proceeds of a conveyance of land, or
(c) income from land,

by reason only that the act involves the exercise of a trustee function of the donor if, at the time when the act is done, the donor has a beneficial interest in the land, proceeds or income.

(2) In this section—

(a) 'conveyance' has the same meaning as in the Law of Property Act 1925, and
(b) references to a trustee function of the donor are to a function which the donor has as trustee (either alone or jointly with any other person or persons).

(3) Subsection (1) above—

(a) applies only if and so far as a contrary intention is not expressed in the instrument creating the power of attorney, and
(b) has effect subject to the terms of that instrument.

(4) The donor of the power of attorney—

(a) is liable for the acts or defaults of the donee in exercising any function by virtue of subsection (1) above in the same manner as if they were acts or defaults of the donor, but
(b) is not liable by reason only that a function is exercised by the donee by virtue of that subsection.

(5) Subsections (1) and (4) above—

(a) apply only if and so far as a contrary intention is not expressed in the instrument (if any) creating the trust, and
(b) have effect subject to the terms of such an instrument.

(6) The fact that it appears that, in dealing with any shares or stock, the donee of the power of attorney is exercising a function by virtue of subsection (1) above does not affect with any notice of any trust a person in whose books the shares are, or stock is, registered or inscribed.

(7) In any case where (by way of exception to section 3(1) of the Trusts of Land and Appointment of Trustees Act 1996) the doctrine of conversion continues to operate, any person who, by reason of the continuing operation of that doctrine, has a beneficial interest in the proceeds of sale of land shall be treated for the purposes of this section and section 2 below as having a beneficial interest in the land.

(8) The donee of a power of attorney is not to be regarded as exercising a trustee function by virtue of subsection (1) above if he is acting under a trustee delegation power; and for this purpose a trustee delegation power is a power of attorney given under—

(a) a statutory provision, or
(b) a provision of the instrument (if any) creating a trust,

under which the donor of the power is expressly authorised to delegate the exercise of all or any of his trustee functions by power of attorney.

(9) Subject to section 4(6) below, this section applies only to powers of attorney created after the commencement of this Act.

2 *Evidence of beneficial interest*

(1) This section applies where the interest of a purchaser depends on the donee of a power of attorney having power to do an act in relation to any property by virtue of section 1(1) above.

In this subsection 'purchaser' has the same meaning as in Part I of the Law of Property Act 1925.

(2) Where this section applies an appropriate statement is, in favour of the purchaser, conclusive evidence of the donor of the power having a beneficial interest in the property at the time of the doing of the act.

(3) In this section 'an appropriate statement' means a signed statement made by the donee—

(a) when doing the act in question, or
(b) at any other time within the period of three months beginning with the day on which the act is done,

that the donor has a beneficial interest in the property at the time of the donee doing the act.

(4) If an appropriate statement is false, the donee is liable in the same way as he would be if the statement were contained in a statutory declaration.

3 General powers in specified form

In section 10(2) of the Powers of Attorney Act 1971 (which provides that a general power of attorney in the form set out in Schedule 1 to that Act, or a similar form, does not confer on the donee of the power any authority to exercise functions of the donor as trustee etc), for the words 'This section' substitute 'Subject to section 1 of the Trustee Delegation Act 1999, this section'.

4 Enduring powers

(1) Section 3(3) of the Enduring Powers of Attorney Act 1985 (which entitles the donee of an enduring power to exercise any of the donor's functions as trustee and to give receipt for capital money etc) does not apply to enduring powers created after the commencement of this Act.

(2) Section 3(3) of the Enduring Powers of Attorney Act 1985 ceases to apply to enduring powers created before the commencement of this Act—

(a) where subsection (3) below applies, in accordance with that subsection, and
(b) otherwise, at the end of the period of one year from that commencement.

(3) Where an application for the registration of the instrument creating such an enduring power is made before the commencement of this Act, or during the period of one year from that commencement, section 3(3) of the Enduring Powers of Attorney Act 1985 ceases to apply to the power—

(a) if the instrument is registered pursuant to the application (whether before commencement or during or after that period), when the registration of the instrument is cancelled, and
(b) if the application is finally refused during or after that period, when the application is finally refused.

(4) In subsection (3) above—

(a) 'registration' and 'registered' mean registration and registered under section 6 of the Enduring Powers of Attorney Act 1985, and
(b) 'cancelled' means cancelled under section 8(4) of that Act.

(5) For the purposes of subsection (3)(b) above an application is finally refused—

(a) if the application is withdrawn or any appeal is abandoned, when the application is withdrawn or the appeal is abandoned, and
(b) otherwise, when proceedings on the application (including any proceedings on, or in consequence of, an appeal) have been determined and any time for appealing or further appealing has expired.

(6) Section 1 above applies to an enduring power created before the commencement of this Act from the time when (in accordance with subsections (2) to (5) above) section 3(3) of the Enduring Powers of Attorney Act 1985 ceases to apply to it.

Trustee delegation under section 25 of the Trustee Act 1925

5 Delegation under section 25 of the Trustee Act 1925

(1) For section 25 of the Trustee Act 1925 substitute—

'25 Delegation of trustee's functions by power of attorney

(1) Notwithstanding any rule of law or equity to the contrary, a trustee may, by power of attorney, delegate the execution or exercise of all or any of the trusts, powers and discretions vested in him as trustee either alone or jointly with any other person or persons.

(2) A delegation under this section—

(a) commences as provided by the instrument creating the power or, if the instrument makes no provision as to the commencement of the delegation, with the date of the execution of the instrument by the donor; and
(b) continues for a period of twelve months or any shorter period provided by the instrument creating the power.

(3) The persons who may be donees of a power of attorney under this section include a trust corporation.

(4) Before or within seven days after giving a power of attorney under this section the donor shall give written notice of it (specifying the date on which the power comes into operation and its duration, the donee of the power, the reason why the power is given and, where some only are delegated, the trusts, powers and discretions delegated) to—

(a) each person (other than himself), if any, who under any instrument creating the trust has power (whether alone or jointly) to appoint a new trustee; and
(b) each of the other trustees, if any;

but failure to comply with this subsection shall not, in favour of a person dealing with the donee of the power, invalidate any act done or instrument executed by the donee.

(5) A power of attorney given under this section by a single donor—

(a) in the form set out in subsection (6) of this section; or
(b) in a form to the like effect but expressed to be made under this subsection,

shall operate to delegate to the person identified in the form as the single donee of the power the execution and exercise of all the trusts, powers and discretions vested in the donor as trustee (either alone or jointly with any other person or persons) under the single trust so identified.

(6) The form referred to in subsection (5) of this section is as follows—

"THIS GENERAL TRUSTEE POWER OF ATTORNEY is made on [*date*] by [*name of one donor*] of [*address of donor*] as trustee of [*name or details of one trust*].

I appoint [*name of one donee*] of [*address of donee*] to be my attorney [*if desired, the date on which the delegation commences or the period for which it continues* (*or both*)] in accordance with section 25(5) of the Trustee Act 1925.

[*To be executed as a deed*]".

(7) The donor of a power of attorney given under this section shall be liable for the acts or defaults of the donee in the same manner as if they were the acts or defaults of the donor.

(8) For the purpose of executing or exercising the trusts or powers delegated to him, the donee may exercise any of the powers conferred on the donor as trustee by statute or by the instrument creating the trust, including power, for the purpose of the transfer of any inscribed stock, himself to delegate to an attorney power to transfer, but not including the power of delegation conferred by this section.

(9) The fact that it appears from any power of attorney given under this section, or from any evidence required for the purposes of any such power of attorney or otherwise, that in dealing with any stock the donee of the power is acting in the execution of a trust shall not be deemed for any purpose to affect any person in whose books the stock is inscribed or registered with any notice of the trust.

(10) This section applies to a personal representative, tenant for life and statutory owner as it applies to a trustee except that subsection (4) shall apply as if it required the notice there mentioned to be given—

(a) in the case of a personal representative, to each of the other personal representatives, if any, except any executor who has renounced probate;
(b) in the case of a tenant for life, to the trustees of the settlement and to each person, if any, who together with the person giving the notice constitutes the tenant for life; and
(c) in the case of a statutory owner, to each of the persons, if any, who together with the person giving the notice constitute the statutory owner and, in the case of a statutory owner by virtue of section 23(1)(a) of the Settled Land Act 1925, to the trustees of the settlement.'

(2) Subsection (1) above has effect in relation to powers of attorney created after the commencement of this Act.

(3) In section 34(2)(b) of the Pensions Act 1995 (delegation by trustees of trustee scheme under section 25 of the Trustee Act 1925), for 'during absence abroad' substitute 'for period not exceeding twelve months'.

6 Section 25 powers as enduring powers

Section 2(8) of the Enduring Powers of Attorney Act 1985 (which prevents a power of attorney under section 25 of the Trustee Act 1925 from being an enduring power) does not apply to powers of attorney created after the commencement of this Act.

Miscellaneous provisions about attorney acting for trustee

7 Two-trustee rules

(1) A requirement imposed by an enactment—

(a) that capital money be paid to, or dealt with as directed by, at least two trustees or that a valid receipt for capital money be given otherwise than by a sole trustee, or
(b) that, in order for an interest or power to be overreached, a conveyance or deed be executed by at least two trustees,

is not satisfied by money being paid to or dealt with as directed by, or a receipt for money being given by, a relevant attorney or by a conveyance or deed being executed by such an attorney.

(2) In this section 'relevant attorney' means a person (other than a trust corporation within the meaning of the Trustee Act 1925) who is acting either—

(a) both as a trustee and as attorney for one or more other trustees, or
(b) as attorney for two or more trustees,

and who is not acting together with any other person or persons.

(3) This section applies whether a relevant attorney is acting under a power created before or after the commencement of this Act (but in the case of such an attorney acting under an enduring power created before that commencement is without prejudice to any continuing application of section 3(3) of the Enduring Powers of Attorney Act 1985 to the enduring power after that commencement in accordance with section 4 above).

8 Appointment of additional trustee by attorney

(1) In section 36 of the Trustee Act 1925 (appointment of trustees), after subsection (6) (additional trustees) insert—

'(6A) A person who is either—

(a) both a trustee and attorney for the other trustee (if one other), or for both of the other trustees (if two others), under a registered power; or
(b) attorney under a registered power for the trustee (if one) or for both or each of the trustees (if two or three),

may, if subsection (6B) of this section is satisfied in relation to him, make an appointment under subsection (6)(b) of this section on behalf of the trustee or trustees.

(6B) This subsection is satisfied in relation to an attorney under a registered power for one or more trustees if (as attorney under the power)—

(a) he intends to exercise any function of the trustee or trustees by virtue of section 1(1) of the Trustee Delegation Act 1999; or
(b) he intends to exercise any function of the trustee or trustees in relation to any land, capital proceeds of a conveyance of land or income from land by virtue of its delegation to him under section 25 of this Act or the instrument (if any) creating the trust.

(6C) In subsections (6A) and (6B) of this section 'registered power' means a power of attorney created by an instrument which is for the time being registered under section 6 of the Enduring Powers of Attorney Act 1985.

(6D) Subsection (6A) of this section—

(a) applies only if and so far as a contrary intention is not expressed in the instrument creating the power of attorney (or, where more than one, any of them) or the instrument (if any) creating the trust; and

(b) has effect subject to the terms of those instruments.'

(2) The amendment made by subsection (1) above has effect only where the power, or (where more than one) each of them, is created after the commencement of this Act.

9 Attorney acting for incapable trustee

(1) In section 22 of the Law of Property Act 1925 (requirement, before dealing with legal estate vested in trustee who is incapable by reason of mental disorder, to appoint new trustee or discharge incapable trustee), after subsection (2) insert—

'(3) Subsection (2) of this section does not prevent a legal estate being dealt with without the appointment of a new trustee, or the discharge of the incapable trustee, at a time when the donee of an enduring power (within the meaning of the Enduring Powers of Attorney Act 1985) is entitled to act for the incapable trustee in the dealing.'

(2) The amendment made by subsection (1) above has effect whether the enduring power was created before or after the commencement of this Act.

Authority of attorney to act in relation to land

10 Extent of attorney's authority to act in relation to land

(1) Where the donee of a power of attorney is authorised by the power to do an act of any description in relation to any land, his authority to do an act of that description at any time includes authority to do it with respect to any estate or interest in the land which is held at that time by the donor (whether alone or jointly with any other person or persons).

(2) Subsection (1) above—

(a) applies only if and so far as a contrary intention is not expressed in the instrument creating the power of attorney, and
(b) has effect subject to the terms of that instrument.

(3) This section applies only to powers of attorney created after the commencement of this Act.

Supplementary

11 Interpretation

(1) In this Act—

'land' has the same meaning as in the Trustee Act 1925, and
'enduring power' has the same meaning as in the Enduring Powers of Attorney Act 1985.

(2) References in this Act to the creation of a power of attorney are to the execution by the donor of the instrument creating it.

12 Repeals

The enactments specified in the Schedule to this Act are repealed to the extent specified in the third column, but subject to the note at the end.

13 Commencement, extent and short title

(1) The preceding provisions of this Act shall come into force on such day as the Lord Chancellor may by order made by statutory instrument appoint.

(2) This Act extends to England and Wales only.

(3) This Act may be cited as the Trustee Delegation Act 1999.

Subordinate Legislation—Trustee Delegation Act 1999 (Commencement) Order 2000, SI 2000/216 (made under sub-s (1)).

Schedule: Repeals

Chapter	*Short title*	*Extent of repeal*
1971 c 27	The Powers of Attorney Act 1971	Section 9
1985 c 29	The Enduring Powers of Attorney Act 1985	Section 2(8)
		Section 3(3)

The repeal of section 3(3) of the Enduring Powers of Attorney Act 1985 has effect in accordance with section 4 of this Act and the remaining repeals have effect in relation to powers of attorney created after the commencement of this Act.

Trustee Act 2000

2000 Chapter 29

An Act to amend the law relating to trustees and persons having the investments powers of trustees; and for connected purposes. [23 November 2000]

Initial Commencement—To be appointed: see s 42(2).
Appointment—1 February 2001: see SI 2001/49, art 2.
Extent—See s 42(4).

PART I
THE DUTY OF CARE

1 The duty of care

(1) Whenever the duty under this subsection applies to a trustee, he must exercise such care and skill as is reasonable in the circumstances, having regard in particular—

(a) to any special knowledge or experience that he has or holds himself out as having, and
(b) if he acts as trustee in the course of a business or profession, to any special knowledge or experience that it is reasonable to expect of a person acting in the course of that kind of business or profession.

(2) In this Act the duty under subsection (1) is called 'the duty of care'.

2 Application of duty of care

Schedule 1 makes provision about when the duty of care applies to a trustee.

PART II
INVESTMENT

3 General power of investment

(1) Subject to the provisions of this Part, a trustee may make any kind of investment that he could make if he were absolutely entitled to the assets of the trust.

(2) In this Act the power under subsection (1) is called 'the general power of investment'.

(3) The general power of investment does not permit a trustee to make investments in land other than in loans secured on land (but see also section 8).

(4) A person invests in a loan secured on land if he has rights under any contract under which—

(a) one person provides another with credit, and
(b) the obligation of the borrower to repay is secured on land.

(5) 'Credit' includes any cash loan or other financial accommodation.

(6) 'Cash' includes money in any form.

4 Standard investment criteria

(1) In exercising any power of investment, whether arising under this Part or otherwise, a trustee must have regard to the standard investment criteria.

(2) A trustee must from time to time review the investments of the trust and consider whether, having regard to the standard investment criteria, they should be varied.

(3) The standard investment criteria, in relation to a trust, are—

(a) the suitability to the trust of investments of the same kind as any particular investment proposed to be made or retained and of that particular investment as an investment of that kind, and
(b) the need for diversification of investments of the trust, in so far as is appropriate to the circumstances of the trust.

5 Advice

(1) Before exercising any power of investment, whether arising under this Part or otherwise, a trustee must (unless the exception applies) obtain and consider proper advice about the way in which, having regard to the standard investment criteria, the power should be exercised.

(2) When reviewing the investments of the trust, a trustee must (unless the exception applies) obtain and consider proper advice about whether, having regard to the standard investment criteria, the investments should be varied.

(3) The exception is that a trustee need not obtain such advice if he reasonably concludes that in all the circumstances it is unnecessary or inappropriate to do so.

(4) Proper advice is the advice of a person who is reasonably believed by the trustee to be qualified to give it by his ability in and practical experience of financial and other matters relating to the proposed investment.

6 Restriction or exclusion of this Part etc

(1) The general power of investment is—

(a) in addition to powers conferred on trustees otherwise than by this Act, but
(b) subject to any restriction or exclusion imposed by the trust instrument or by any enactment or any provision of subordinate legislation.

(2) For the purposes of this Act, an enactment or a provision of subordinate legislation is not to be regarded as being, or as being part of, a trust instrument.

(3) In this Act 'subordinate legislation' has the same meaning as in the Interpretation Act 1978.

7 Existing trusts

(1) This Part applies in relation to trusts whether created before or after its commencement.

(2) No provision relating to the powers of a trustee contained in a trust instrument made before 3rd August 1961 is to be treated (for the purposes of section 6(1)(b)) as restricting or excluding the general power of investment.

(3) A provision contained in a trust instrument made before the commencement of this Part which—

(a) has effect under section 3(2) of the Trustee Investments Act 1961 as a power to invest under that Act, or
(b) confers power to invest under that Act,

is to be treated as conferring the general power of investment on a trustee.

PART III
ACQUISITION OF LAND

8 Power to acquire freehold and leasehold land

(1) A trustee may acquire freehold or leasehold land in the United Kingdom—

(a) as an investment,
(b) for occupation by a beneficiary, or
(c) for any other reason.

(2) 'Freehold or leasehold land' means—

(a) in relation to England and Wales, a legal estate in land,
(b) in relation to Scotland—

 (i) the estate or interest of the proprietor of the dominium utile or, in the case of land not held on feudal tenure, the estate or interest of the owner, or
 (ii) a tenancy, and

(c) in relation to Northern Ireland, a legal estate in land, including land held under a fee farm grant.

(3) For the purpose of exercising his functions as a trustee, a trustee who acquires land under this section has all the powers of an absolute owner in relation to the land.

9 Restriction or exclusion of this Part etc

The powers conferred by this Part are—

(a) in addition to powers conferred on trustees otherwise than by this Part, but
(b) subject to any restriction or exclusion imposed by the trust instrument or by any enactment or any provision of subordinate legislation.

10 Existing trusts

(1) This Part does not apply in relation to—

(a) a trust of property which consists of or includes land which (despite section 2 of the Trusts of Land and Appointment of Trustees Act 1996) is settled land, or
(b) a trust to which the Universities and College Estates Act 1925 applies.

(2) Subject to subsection (1), this Part applies in relation to trusts whether created before or after its commencement.

PART IV
AGENTS, NOMINEES AND CUSTODIANS

Agents

11 Power to employ agents

(1) Subject to the provisions of this Part, the trustees of a trust may authorise any person to exercise any or all of their delegable functions as their agent.

(2) In the case of a trust other than a charitable trust, the trustees' delegable functions consist of any function other than—

(a) any function relating to whether or in what way any assets of the trust should be distributed,
(b) any power to decide whether any fees or other payment due to be made out of the trust funds should be made out of income or capital,
(c) any power to appoint a person to be a trustee of the trust, or
(d) any power conferred by any other enactment or the trust instrument which permits the trustees to delegate any of their functions or to appoint a person to act as a nominee or custodian.

(3) In the case of a charitable trust, the trustees' delegable functions are—

(a) any function consisting of carrying out a decision that the trustees have taken;
(b) any function relating to the investment of assets subject to the trust (including, in the case of land held as an investment, managing the land and creating or disposing of an interest in the land);
(c) any function relating to the raising of funds for the trust otherwise than by means of profits of a trade which is an integral part of carrying out the trust's charitable purpose;
(d) any other function prescribed by an order made by the Secretary of State.

(4) For the purposes of subsection (3)(c) a trade is an integral part of carrying out a trust's charitable purpose if, whether carried on in the United Kingdom or elsewhere, the profits are applied solely to the purposes of the trust and either—

(a) the trade is exercised in the course of the actual carrying out of a primary purpose of the trust, or
(b) the work in connection with the trade is mainly carried out by beneficiaries of the trust.

(5) The power to make an order under subsection (3)(d) is exercisable by statutory instrument which shall be subject to annulment in pursuance of a resolution of either House of Parliament.

12 Persons who may act as agents

(1) Subject to subsection (2), the persons whom the trustees may under section 11 authorise to exercise functions as their agent include one or more of their number.

(2) The trustees may not authorise two (or more) persons to exercise the same function unless they are to exercise the function jointly.

(3) The trustees may not under section 11 authorise a beneficiary to exercise any function as their agent (even if the beneficiary is also a trustee).

(4) The trustees may under section 11 authorise a person to exercise functions as their agent even though he is also appointed to act as their nominee or custodian (whether under section 16, 17 or 18 or any other power).

13 Linked functions etc

(1) Subject to subsections (2) and (5), a person who is authorised under section 11 to exercise a function is (whatever the terms of the agency) subject to any specific duties or restrictions attached to the function.

For example, a person who is authorised under section 11 to exercise the general power of investment is subject to the duties under section 4 in relation to that power.

(2) A person who is authorised under section 11 to exercise a power which is subject to a requirement to obtain advice is not subject to the requirement if he is the kind of person from whom it would have been proper for the trustees, in compliance with the requirement, to obtain advice.

(3) Subsections (4) and (5) apply to a trust to which section 11(1) of the Trusts of Land and Appointment of Trustees Act 1996 (duties to consult beneficiaries and give effect to their wishes) applies.

(4) The trustees may not under section 11 authorise a person to exercise any of their functions on terms that prevent them from complying with section 11(1) of the 1996 Act.

(5) A person who is authorised under section 11 to exercise any function relating to land subject to the trust is not subject to section 11(1) of the 1996 Act.

14 Terms of agency

(1) Subject to subsection (2) and sections 15(2) and 29 to 32, the trustees may authorise a person to exercise functions as their agent on such terms as to remuneration and other matters as they may determine.

(2) The trustees may not authorise a person to exercise functions as their agent on any of the terms mentioned in subsection (3) unless it is reasonably necessary for them to do so.

(3) The terms are—

(a) a term permitting the agent to appoint a substitute;

(b) a term restricting the liability of the agent or his substitute to the trustees or any beneficiary;
(c) a term permitting the agent to act in circumstances capable of giving rise to a conflict of interest.

15 Asset management: special restrictions

(1) The trustees may not authorise a person to exercise any of their asset management functions as their agent except by an agreement which is in or evidenced in writing.

(2) The trustees may not authorise a person to exercise any of their asset management functions as their agent unless—

(a) they have prepared a statement that gives guidance as to how the functions should be exercised ('a policy statement'), and
(b) the agreement under which the agent is to act includes a term to the effect that he will secure compliance with—

 (i) the policy statement, or
 (ii) if the policy statement is revised or replaced under section 22, the revised or replacement policy statement.

(3) The trustees must formulate any guidance given in the policy statement with a view to ensuring that the functions will be exercised in the best interests of the trust.

(4) The policy statement must be in or evidenced in writing.

(5) The asset management functions of trustees are their functions relating to—

(a) the investment of assets subject to the trust,
(b) the acquisition of property which is to be subject to the trust, and
(c) managing property which is subject to the trust and disposing of, or creating or disposing of an interest in, such property.

Nominees and custodians

16 Power to appoint nominees

(1) Subject to the provisions of this Part, the trustees of a trust may—

(a) appoint a person to act as their nominee in relation to such of the assets of the trust as they determine (other than settled land), and
(b) take such steps as are necessary to secure that those assets are vested in a person so appointed.

(2) An appointment under this section must be in or evidenced in writing.

(3) This section does not apply to any trust having a custodian trustee or in relation to any assets vested in the official custodian for charities.

17 Power to appoint custodians

(1) Subject to the provisions of this Part, the trustees of a trust may appoint a person to act as a custodian in relation to such of the assets of the trust as they may determine.

(2) For the purposes of this Act a person is a custodian in relation to assets if he undertakes the safe custody of the assets or of any documents or records concerning the assets.

(3) An appointment under this section must be in or evidenced in writing.

(4) This section does not apply to any trust having a custodian trustee or in relation to any assets vested in the official custodian for charities.

18 Investment in bearer securities

(1) If trustees retain or invest in securities payable to bearer, they must appoint a person to act as a custodian of the securities.

(2) Subsection (1) does not apply if the trust instrument or any enactment or provision of subordinate legislation contains provision which (however expressed) permits the trustees to retain or invest in securities payable to bearer without appointing a person to act as a custodian.

(3) An appointment under this section must be in or evidenced in writing.

(4) This section does not apply to any trust having a custodian trustee or in relation to any securities vested in the official custodian for charities.

19 Persons who may be appointed as nominees or custodians

(1) A person may not be appointed under section 16, 17 or 18 as a nominee or custodian unless one of the relevant conditions is satisfied.

(2) The relevant conditions are that—

(a) the person carries on a business which consists of or includes acting as a nominee or custodian;
(b) the person is a body corporate which is controlled by the trustees;
(c) the person is a body corporate recognised under section 9 of the Administration of Justice Act 1985.

(3) The question whether a body corporate is controlled by trustees is to be determined in accordance with section 840 of the Income and Corporation Taxes Act 1988.

(4) The trustees of a charitable trust which is not an exempt charity must act in accordance with any guidance given by the Charity Commissioners concerning the selection of a person for appointment as a nominee or custodian under section 16, 17 or 18.

(5) Subject to subsections (1) and (4), the persons whom the trustees may under section 16, 17 or 18 appoint as a nominee or custodian include—

(a) one of their number, if that one is a trust corporation, or
(b) two (or more) of their number, if they are to act as joint nominees or joint custodians.

(6) The trustees may under section 16 appoint a person to act as their nominee even though he is also—

(a) appointed to act as their custodian (whether under section 17 or 18 or any other power), or
(b) authorised to exercise functions as their agent (whether under section 11 or any other power).

(7) Likewise, the trustees may under section 17 or 18 appoint a person to act as their custodian even though he is also—

(a) appointed to act as their nominee (whether under section 16 or any other power), or
(b) authorised to exercise functions as their agent (whether under section 11 or any other power).

20 Terms of appointment of nominees and custodians

(1) Subject to subsection (2) and sections 29 to 32, the trustees may under section 16, 17 or 18 appoint a person to act as a nominee or custodian on such terms as to remuneration and other matters as they may determine.

(2) The trustees may not under section 16, 17 or 18 appoint a person to act as a nominee or custodian on any of the terms mentioned in subsection (3) unless it is reasonably necessary for them to do so.

(3) The terms are—

(a) a term permitting the nominee or custodian to appoint a substitute;
(b) a term restricting the liability of the nominee or custodian or his substitute to the trustees or to any beneficiary;
(c) a term permitting the nominee or custodian to act in circumstances capable of giving rise to a conflict of interest.

Review of and liability for agents, nominees and custodians etc

21 Application of sections 22 and 23

(1) Sections 22 and 23 apply in a case where trustees have, under section 11, 16, 17 or 18—

(a) authorised a person to exercise functions as their agent, or
(b) appointed a person to act as a nominee or custodian.

(2) Subject to subsection (3), sections 22 and 23 also apply in a case where trustees have, under any power conferred on them by the trust instrument or by any enactment or any provision of subordinate legislation—

(a) authorised a person to exercise functions as their agent, or
(b) appointed a person to act as a nominee or custodian.

(3) If the application of section 22 or 23 is inconsistent with the terms of the trust instrument or the enactment or provision of subordinate legislation, the section in question does not apply.

22 *Review of agents, nominees and custodians etc*

(1) While the agent, nominee or custodian continues to act for the trust, the trustees—

(a) must keep under review the arrangements under which the agent, nominee or custodian acts and how those arrangements are being put into effect,
(b) if circumstances make it appropriate to do so, must consider whether there is a need to exercise any power of intervention that they have, and
(c) if they consider that there is a need to exercise such a power, must do so.

(2) If the agent has been authorised to exercise asset management functions, the duty under subsection (1) includes, in particular—

(a) a duty to consider whether there is any need to revise or replace the policy statement made for the purposes of section 15,
(b) if they consider that there is a need to revise or replace the policy statement, a duty to do so, and
(c) a duty to assess whether the policy statement (as it has effect for the time being) is being complied with.

(3) Subsections (3) and (4) of section 15 apply to the revision or replacement of a policy statement under this section as they apply to the making of a policy statement under that section.

(4) 'Power of intervention' includes—

(a) a power to give directions to the agent, nominee or custodian;
(b) a power to revoke the authorisation or appointment.

23 *Liability for agents, nominees and custodians etc*

(1) A trustee is not liable for any act or default of the agent, nominee or custodian unless he has failed to comply with the duty of care applicable to him, under paragraph 3 of Schedule 1—

(a) when entering into the arrangements under which the person acts as agent, nominee or custodian, or
(b) when carrying out his duties under section 22.

(2) If a trustee has agreed a term under which the agent, nominee or custodian is permitted to appoint a substitute, the trustee is not liable for any act or default of the substitute unless he has failed to comply with the duty of care applicable to him, under paragraph 3 of Schedule 1—

(a) when agreeing that term, or
(b) when carrying out his duties under section 22 in so far as they relate to the use of the substitute.

Supplementary

24 Effect of trustees exceeding their powers

A failure by the trustees to act within the limits of the powers conferred by this Part—

(a) in authorising a person to exercise a function of theirs as an agent, or
(b) in appointing a person to act as a nominee or custodian,

does not invalidate the authorisation or appointment.

25 Sole trustees

(1) Subject to subsection (2), this Part applies in relation to a trust having a sole trustee as it applies in relation to other trusts (and references in this Part to trustees—except in sections 12(1) and (3) and 19(5)—are to be read accordingly).

(2) Section 18 does not impose a duty on a sole trustee if that trustee is a trust corporation.

26 Restriction or exclusion of this Part etc

The powers conferred by this Part are—

(a) in addition to powers conferred on trustees otherwise than by this Act, but
(b) subject to any restriction or exclusion imposed by the trust instrument or by any enactment or any provision of subordinate legislation.

27 Existing trusts

This Part applies in relation to trusts whether created before or after its commencement.

PART V
REMUNERATION

28 Trustee's entitlement to payment under trust instrument

(1) Except to the extent (if any) to which the trust instrument makes inconsistent provision, subsections (2) to (4) apply to a trustee if—

(a) there is a provision in the trust instrument entitling him to receive payment out of trust funds in respect of services provided by him to or on behalf of the trust, and
(b) the trustee is a trust corporation or is acting in a professional capacity.

(2) The trustee is to be treated as entitled under the trust instrument to receive payment in respect of services even if they are services which are capable of being provided by a lay trustee.

(3) Subsection (2) applies to a trustee of a charitable trust who is not a trust corporation only—

(a) if he is not a sole trustee, and
(b) to the extent that a majority of the other trustees have agreed that it should apply to him.

(4) Any payments to which the trustee is entitled in respect of services are to be treated as remuneration for services (and not as a gift) for the purposes of—

(a) section 15 of the Wills Act 1837 (gifts to an attesting witness to be void), and
(b) section 34(3) of the Administration of Estates Act 1925 (order in which estate to be paid out).

(5) For the purposes of this Part, a trustee acts in a professional capacity if he acts in the course of a profession or business which consists of or includes the provision of services in connection with—

(a) the management or administration of trusts generally or a particular kind of trust, or
(b) any particular aspect of the management or administration of trusts generally or a particular kind of trust,

and the services he provides to or on behalf of the trust fall within that description.

(6) For the purposes of this Part, a person acts as a lay trustee if he—

(a) is not a trust corporation, and
(b) does not act in a professional capacity.

29 *Remuneration of certain trustees*

(1) Subject to subsection (5), a trustee who—

(a) is a trust corporation, but
(b) is not a trustee of a charitable trust,

is entitled to receive reasonable remuneration out of the trust funds for any services that the trust corporation provides to or on behalf of the trust.

(2) Subject to subsection (5), a trustee who—

(a) acts in a professional capacity, but
(b) is not a trust corporation, a trustee of a charitable trust or a sole trustee,

is entitled to receive reasonable remuneration out of the trust funds for any services that he provides to or on behalf of the trust if each other trustee has agreed in writing that he may be remunerated for the services.

(3) 'Reasonable remuneration' means, in relation to the provision of services by a trustee, such remuneration as is reasonable in the circumstances for the provision of those services to or on behalf of that trust by that trustee and for the purposes of subsection (1) includes, in relation to the provision of services by a trustee who is an authorised institution under the Banking Act 1987 and provides the services in that capacity, the institution's reasonable charges for the provision of such services.

(4) A trustee is entitled to remuneration under this section even if the services in question are capable of being provided by a lay trustee.

(5) A trustee is not entitled to remuneration under this section if any provision about his entitlement to remuneration has been made—

(a) by the trust instrument, or
(b) by any enactment or any provision of subordinate legislation.

(6) This section applies to a trustee who has been authorised under a power conferred by Part IV or the trust instrument—

(a) to exercise functions as an agent of the trustees, or
(b) to act as a nominee or custodian,

as it applies to any other trustee.

30 Remuneration of trustees of charitable trusts

(1) The Secretary of State may by regulations make provision for the remuneration of trustees of charitable trusts who are trust corporations or act in a professional capacity.

(2) The power under subsection (1) includes power to make provision for the remuneration of a trustee who has been authorised under a power conferred by Part IV or any other enactment or any provision of subordinate legislation, or by the trust instrument—

(a) to exercise functions as an agent of the trustees, or
(b) to act as a nominee or custodian.

(3) Regulations under this section may—

(a) make different provision for different cases;
(b) contain such supplemental, incidental, consequential and transitional provision as the Secretary of State considers appropriate.

(4) The power to make regulations under this section is exercisable by statutory instrument, but no such instrument shall be made unless a draft of it has been laid before Parliament and approved by a resolution of each House of Parliament.

31 Trustees' expenses

(1) A trustee—

(a) is entitled to be reimbursed from the trust funds, or
(b) may pay out of the trust funds,

expenses properly incurred by him when acting on behalf of the trust.

(2) This section applies to a trustee who has been authorised under a power conferred by Part IV or any other enactment or any provision of subordinate legislation, or by the trust instrument—

(a) to exercise functions as an agent of the trustees, or
(b) to act as a nominee or custodian,

as it applies to any other trustee.

32 Remuneration and expenses of agents, nominees and custodians

(1) This section applies if, under a power conferred by Part IV or any other enactment or any provision of subordinate legislation, or by the trust instrument, a person other than a trustee has been—

(a) authorised to exercise functions as an agent of the trustees, or
(b) appointed to act as a nominee or custodian.

(2) The trustees may remunerate the agent, nominee or custodian out of the trust funds for services if—

(a) he is engaged on terms entitling him to be remunerated for those services, and
(b) the amount does not exceed such remuneration as is reasonable in the circumstances for the provision of those services by him to or on behalf of that trust.

(3) The trustees may reimburse the agent, nominee or custodian out of the trust funds for any expenses properly incurred by him in exercising functions as an agent, nominee or custodian.

33 Application

(1) Subject to subsection (2), sections 28, 29, 31 and 32 apply in relation to services provided to or on behalf of, or (as the case may be) expenses incurred on or after their commencement on behalf of, trusts whenever created.

(2) Nothing in section 28 or 29 is to be treated as affecting the operation of—

(a) section 15 of the Wills Act 1837, or
(b) section 34(3) of the Administration of Estates Act 1925,

in relation to any death occurring before the commencement of section 28 or (as the case may be) section 29.

PART VI MISCELLANEOUS AND SUPPLEMENTARY

34 Power to insure

(1) For section 19 of the Trustee Act 1925 (power to insure) substitute—

'19 Power to insure

(1) A trustee may—

(a) insure any property which is subject to the trust against risks of loss or damage due to any event, and
(b) pay the premiums out of the trust funds.

(2) In the case of property held on a bare trust, the power to insure is subject to any direction given by the beneficiary or each of the beneficiaries—

(a) that any property specified in the direction is not to be insured;
(b) that any property specified in the direction is not to be insured except on such conditions as may be so specified.

(3) Property is held on a bare trust if it is held on trust for—

(a) a beneficiary who is of full age and capacity and absolutely entitled to the property subject to the trust, or
(b) beneficiaries each of whom is of full age and capacity and who (taken together) are absolutely entitled to the property subject to the trust.

(4) If a direction under subsection (2) of this section is given, the power to insure, so far as it is subject to the direction, ceases to be a delegable function for the purposes of section 11 of the Trustee Act 2000 (power to employ agents).

(5) In this section "trust funds" means any income or capital funds of the trust.'

(2) In section 20(1) of the Trustee Act 1925 (application of insurance money) omit 'whether by fire or otherwise'.

(3) The amendments made by this section apply in relation to trusts whether created before or after its commencement.

35 Personal representatives

(1) Subject to the following provisions of this section, this Act applies in relation to a personal representative administering an estate according to the law as it applies to a trustee carrying out a trust for beneficiaries.

(2) For this purpose this Act is to be read with the appropriate modifications and in particular—

(a) references to the trust instrument are to be read as references to the will,
(b) references to a beneficiary or to beneficiaries, apart from the reference to a beneficiary in section 8(1)(b), are to be read as references to a person or the persons interested in the due administration of the estate, and
(c) the reference to a beneficiary in section 8(1)(b) is to be read as a reference to a person who under the will of the deceased or under the law relating to intestacy is beneficially interested in the estate.

(3) Remuneration to which a personal representative is entitled under section 28 or 29 is to be treated as an administration expense for the purposes of—

(a) section 34(3) of the Administration of Estates Act 1925 (order in which estate to be paid out), and
(b) any provision giving reasonable administration expenses priority over the preferential debts listed in Schedule 6 to the Insolvency Act 1986.

(4) Nothing in subsection (3) is to be treated as affecting the operation of the provisions mentioned in paragraphs (a) and (b) of that subsection in relation to any death occurring before the commencement of this section.

36 Pension schemes

(1) In this section 'pension scheme' means an occupational pension scheme (within the meaning of the Pension Schemes Act 1993) established under a trust and subject to the law of England and Wales.

(2) Part I does not apply in so far as it imposes a duty of care in relation to—

(a) the functions described in paragraphs 1 and 2 of Schedule 1, or
(b) the functions described in paragraph 3 of that Schedule to the extent that they relate to trustees—

(i) authorising a person to exercise their functions with respect to investment, or
(ii) appointing a person to act as their nominee or custodian.

(3) Nothing in Part II or III applies to the trustees of any pension scheme.

(4) Part IV applies to the trustees of a pension scheme subject to the restrictions in subsections (5) to (8).

(5) The trustees of a pension scheme may not under Part IV authorise any person to exercise any functions relating to investment as their agent.

(6) The trustees of a pension scheme may not under Part IV authorise a person who is—

(a) an employer in relation to the scheme, or
(b) connected with or an associate of such an employer,

to exercise any of their functions as their agent.

(7) For the purposes of subsection (6)—

(a) 'employer', in relation to a scheme, has the same meaning as in the Pensions Act 1995;
(b) sections 249 and 435 of the Insolvency Act 1986 apply for the purpose of determining whether a person is connected with or an associate of an employer.

(8) Sections 16 to 20 (powers to appoint nominees and custodians) do not apply to the trustees of a pension scheme.

37 Authorised unit trusts

(1) Parts II to IV do not apply to trustees of authorised unit trusts.

(2) 'Authorised unit trust' means a unit trust scheme in the case of which an order under section 78 of the Financial Services Act 1986 is in force.

38 Common investment schemes for charities etc

Parts II to IV do not apply to—

(a) trustees managing a fund under a common investment scheme made, or having effect as if made, under section 24 of the Charities Act 1993, other than such a fund the trusts of which provide that property is not to be transferred to the fund except by or on behalf of a charity the trustees of which are the trustees appointed to manage the fund, or

(b) trustees managing a fund under a common deposit scheme made, or having effect as if made, under section 25 of that Act.

39 Interpretation

(1) In this Act—

'asset' includes any right or interest;
'charitable trust' means a trust under which property is held for charitable purposes and 'charitable purposes' has the same meaning as in the Charities Act 1993;
'custodian trustee' has the same meaning as in the Public Trustee Act 1906;
'enactment' includes any provision of a Measure of the Church Assembly or of the General Synod of the Church of England;
'exempt charity' has the same meaning as in the Charities Act 1993;
'functions' includes powers and duties;
'legal mortgage' has the same meaning as in the Law of Property Act 1925;
'personal representative' has the same meaning as in the Trustee Act 1925;
'settled land' has the same meaning as in the Settled Land Act 1925;
'trust corporation' has the same meaning as in the Trustee Act 1925;
'trust funds' means income or capital funds of the trust.

(2) In this Act the expressions listed below are defined or otherwise explained by the provisions indicated—

asset management functions	section 15(5)
custodian	section 17(2)
the duty of care	section 1(2)
the general power of investment	section 3(2)
lay trustee	section 28(6)
power of intervention	section 22(4)
the standard investment criteria	section 4(3)
subordinate legislation	section 6(3)
trustee acting in a professional capacity	section 28(5)
trust instrument	sections 6(2) and 35(2)(a)

40 Minor and consequential amendments etc

(1) Schedule 2 (minor and consequential amendments) shall have effect.

(2) Schedule 3 (transitional provisions and savings) shall have effect.

(3) Schedule 4 (repeals) shall have effect.

41 Power to amend other Acts

(1) A Minister of the Crown may by order make such amendments of any Act,

including an Act extending to places outside England and Wales, as appear to him appropriate in consequence of or in connection with Part II or III.

(2) Before exercising the power under subsection (1) in relation to a local, personal or private Act, the Minister must consult any person who appears to him to be affected by any proposed amendment.

(3) An order under this section may—

(a) contain such transitional provisions and savings as the Minister thinks fit;
(b) make different provision for different purposes.

(4) The power to make an order under this section is exercisable by statutory instrument which shall be subject to annulment in pursuance of a resolution of either House of Parliament.

(5) 'Minister of the Crown' has the same meaning as in the Ministers of the Crown Act 1975.

42 Commencement and extent

(1) Section 41, this section and section 43 shall come into force on the day on which this Act is passed.

(2) The remaining provisions of this Act shall come into force on such day as the Lord Chancellor may appoint by order made by statutory instrument; and different days may be so appointed for different purposes.

(3) An order under subsection (2) may contain such transitional provisions and savings as the Lord Chancellor considers appropriate in connection with the order.

(4) Subject to section 41(1) and subsection (5), this Act extends to England and Wales only.

(5) An amendment or repeal in Part II or III of Schedule 2 or Part II of Schedule 4 has the same extent as the provision amended or repealed.

43 Short title

This Act may be cited as the Trustee Act 2000.

Schedule 1:
Application of Duty of Care

Investment

1— The duty of care applies to a trustee—

(a) when exercising the general power of investment or any other power of investment, however conferred;
(b) when carrying out a duty to which he is subject under section 4 or 5 (duties relating to the exercise of a power of investment or to the review of investments).

Acquisition of land

2— The duty of care applies to a trustee—

(a) when exercising the power under section 8 to acquire land;
(b) when exercising any other power to acquire land, however conferred;
(c) when exercising any power in relation to land acquired under a power mentioned in sub-paragraph (a) or (b).

Agents, nominees and custodians

3—(1) The duty of care applies to a trustee—

(a) when entering into arrangements under which a person is authorised under section 11 to exercise functions as an agent;
(b) when entering into arrangements under which a person is appointed under section 16 to act as a nominee;
(c) when entering into arrangements under which a person is appointed under section 17 or 18 to act as a custodian;
(d) when entering into arrangements under which, under any other power, however conferred, a person is authorised to exercise functions as an agent or is appointed to act as a nominee or custodian;
(e) when carrying out his duties under section 22 (review of agent, nominee or custodian, etc).

(2) For the purposes of sub-paragraph (1), entering into arrangements under which a person is authorised to exercise functions or is appointed to act as a nominee or custodian includes, in particular—

(a) selecting the person who is to act,
(b) determining any terms on which he is to act, and
(c) if the person is being authorised to exercise asset management functions, the preparation of a policy statement under section 15.

Compounding of liabilities

4— The duty of care applies to a trustee—

(a) when exercising the power under section 15 of the Trustee Act 1925 to do any of the things referred to in that section;
(b) when exercising any corresponding power, however conferred.

Insurance

5— The duty of care applies to a trustee—

(a) when exercising the power under section 19 of the Trustee Act 1925 to insure property;
(b) when exercising any corresponding power, however conferred.

Reversionary interests, valuations and audit

6— The duty of care applies to a trustee—

(a) when exercising the power under section 22(1) or (3) of the Trustee Act 1925 to do any of the things referred to there;
(b) when exercising any corresponding power, however conferred.

Exclusion of duty of care

7— The duty of care does not apply if or in so far as it appears from the trust instrument that the duty is not meant to apply.

Schedule 3: Transitional Provisions and Savings

The Trustee Act 1925 (c 19)

1—(1) Sub-paragraph (2) applies if, immediately before the day on which Part IV of this Act comes into force, a banker or banking company holds any bearer securities deposited with him under section 7(1) of the 1925 Act (investment in bearer securities).

(2) On and after the day on which Part IV comes into force, the banker or banking company shall be treated as if he had been appointed as custodian of the securities under section 18.

2— The repeal of section 8 of the 1925 Act (loans and investments by trustees not chargeable as breaches of trust) does not affect the operation of that section in relation to loans or investments made before the coming into force of that repeal.

3— The repeal of section 9 of the 1925 Act (liability for loss by reason of improper investment) does not affect the operation of that section in relation to any advance of trust money made before the coming into force of that repeal.

4—(1) Sub-paragraph (2) applies if, immediately before the day on which Part IV of this Act comes into force, a banker or banking company holds any documents deposited with him under section 21 of the 1925 Act (deposit of documents for safe custody).

(2) On and after the day on which Part IV comes into force, the banker or banking company shall be treated as if he had been appointed as custodian of the documents under section 17.

5—(1) Sub-paragraph (2) applies if, immediately before the day on which Part IV of this Act comes into force, a person has been appointed to act as or be an agent or attorney under section 23(1) or (3) of the 1925 Act (general power to employ agents etc).

(2) On and after the day on which Part IV comes into force, the agent shall be treated as if he had been authorised to exercise functions as an agent under section 11 (and, if appropriate, as if he had also been appointed under that Part to act as a custodian or nominee).

6— The repeal of section 23(2) of the 1925 Act (power to employ agents in respect of property outside the United Kingdom) does not affect the operation after the commencement of the repeal of an appointment made before that commencement.

The Trustee Investments Act 1961 (c 62)

7—(1) A trustee shall not be liable for breach of trust merely because he continues to hold an investment acquired by virtue of paragraph 14 of Part II of Schedule 1 to the 1961 Act (perpetual rent-charges etc).

(2) A person who—

(a) is not a trustee,
(b) before the commencement of Part II of this Act had powers to invest in the investments described in paragraph 14 of Part II of Schedule 1 to the 1961 Act, and
(c) on that commencement acquired the general power of investment,

shall not be treated as exceeding his powers of investment merely because he continues to hold an investment acquired by virtue of that paragraph.

Proceeds of Crime Act 2002

2002 Chapter 29

An Act to establish the Assets Recovery Agency and make provision about the appointment of its Director and his functions (including Revenue functions), to provide for confiscation orders in relation to persons who benefit from criminal conduct and for restraint orders to prohibit dealing with property, to allow the recovery of property which is or represents property obtained through unlawful conduct or which is intended to be used in unlawful conduct, to make provision about money laundering, to make provision about investigations relating to benefit from criminal conduct or to property which is or represents property obtained through unlawful conduct or to money laundering, to make provision to give effect to overseas requests and orders made where property is found or believed to be obtained through criminal conduct, and for connected purposes. [24th July 2002]

Initial Commencement—To be appointed: see s 458(1).
Appointment—Appointment: 13 January 2003: see SI 2002/3055, art 2.

PART 7
MONEY LAUNDERING

Offences

327 Concealing etc

(1) A person commits an offence if he—

(a) conceals criminal property;
(b) disguises criminal property;
(c) converts criminal property;
(d) transfers criminal property;
(e) removes criminal property from England and Wales or from Scotland or from Northern Ireland.

(2) But a person does not commit such an offence if—

(a) he makes an authorised disclosure under section 338 and (if the disclosure is made before he does the act mentioned in subsection (1)) he has the appropriate consent;
(b) he intended to make such a disclosure but had a reasonable excuse for not doing so;
(c) the act he does is done in carrying out a function he has relating to the enforcement of any provision of this Act or of any other enactment relating to criminal conduct or benefit from criminal conduct.

(3) Concealing or disguising criminal property includes concealing or disguising its nature, source, location, disposition, movement or ownership or any rights with respect to it.

328 Arrangements

(1) A person commits an offence if he enters into or becomes concerned in an

arrangement which he knows or suspects facilitates (by whatever means) the acquisition, retention, use or control of criminal property by or on behalf of another person.

(2) But a person does not commit such an offence if—

(a) he makes an authorised disclosure under section 338 and (if the disclosure is made before he does the act mentioned in subsection (1)) he has the appropriate consent;
(b) he intended to make such a disclosure but had a reasonable excuse for not doing so;
(c) the act he does is done in carrying out a function he has relating to the enforcement of any provision of this Act or of any other enactment relating to criminal conduct or benefit from criminal conduct.

329 Acquisition, use and possession

(1) A person commits an offence if he—

(a) acquires criminal property;
(b) uses criminal property;
(c) has possession of criminal property.

(2) But a person does not commit such an offence if—

(a) he makes an authorised disclosure under section 338 and (if the disclosure is made before he does the act mentioned in subsection (1)) he has the appropriate consent;
(b) he intended to make such a disclosure but had a reasonable excuse for not doing so;
(c) he acquired or used or had possession of the property for adequate consideration;
(d) the act he does is done in carrying out a function he has relating to the enforcement of any provision of this Act or of any other enactment relating to criminal conduct or benefit from criminal conduct.

(3) For the purposes of this section—

(a) a person acquires property for inadequate consideration if the value of the consideration is significantly less than the value of the property;
(b) a person uses or has possession of property for inadequate consideration if the value of the consideration is significantly less than the value of the use or possession;
(c) the provision by a person of goods or services which he knows or suspects may help another to carry out criminal conduct is not consideration.

330 Failure to disclose: regulated sector

(1) A person commits an offence if each of the following three conditions is satisfied.

(2) The first condition is that he—

(a) knows or suspects, or

(b) has reasonable grounds for knowing or suspecting,

that another person is engaged in money laundering.

(3) The second condition is that the information or other matter—

(a) on which his knowledge or suspicion is based, or
(b) which gives reasonable grounds for such knowledge or suspicion,

came to him in the course of a business in the regulated sector.

(4) The third condition is that he does not make the required disclosure as soon as is practicable after the information or other matter comes to him.

(5) The required disclosure is a disclosure of the information or other matter—

(a) to a nominated officer or a person authorised for the purposes of this Part by the Director General of the National Criminal Intelligence Service;
(b) in the form and manner (if any) prescribed for the purposes of this subsection by order under section 339.

(6) But a person does not commit an offence under this section if—

(a) he has a reasonable excuse for not disclosing the information or other matter;
(b) he is a professional legal adviser and the information or other matter came to him in privileged circumstances;
(c) subsection (7) applies to him.

(7) This subsection applies to a person if—

(a) he does not know or suspect that another person is engaged in money laundering, and
(b) he has not been provided by his employer with such training as is specified by the Secretary of State by order for the purposes of this section.

(8) In deciding whether a person committed an offence under this section the court must consider whether he followed any relevant guidance which was at the time concerned—

(a) issued by a supervisory authority or any other appropriate body,
(b) approved by the Treasury, and
(c) published in a manner it approved as appropriate in its opinion to bring the guidance to the attention of persons likely to be affected by it.

(9) A disclosure to a nominated officer is a disclosure which—

(a) is made to a person nominated by the alleged offender's employer to receive disclosures under this section, and
(b) is made in the course of the alleged offender's employment and in accordance with the procedure established by the employer for the purpose.

(10) Information or other matter comes to a professional legal adviser in privileged circumstances if it is communicated or given to him—

(a) by (or by a representative of) a client of his in connection with the giving by the adviser of legal advice to the client,
(b) by (or by a representative of) a person seeking legal advice from the adviser, or
(c) by a person in connection with legal proceedings or contemplated legal proceedings.

(11) But subsection (10) does not apply to information or other matter which is communicated or given with the intention of furthering a criminal purpose.

(12) Schedule 9 has effect for the purpose of determining what is—

(a) a business in the regulated sector;
(b) a supervisory authority.

(13) An appropriate body is any body which regulates or is representative of any trade, profession, business or employment carried on by the alleged offender.

331 Failure to disclose: nominated officers in the regulated sector

(1) A person nominated to receive disclosures under section 330 commits an offence if the conditions in subsections (2) to (4) are satisfied.

(2) The first condition is that he—

(a) knows or suspects, or
(b) has reasonable grounds for knowing or suspecting,

that another person is engaged in money laundering.

(3) The second condition is that the information or other matter—

(a) on which his knowledge or suspicion is based, or
(b) which gives reasonable grounds for such knowledge or suspicion,

came to him in consequence of a disclosure made under section 330.

(4) The third condition is that he does not make the required disclosure as soon as is practicable after the information or other matter comes to him.

(5) The required disclosure is a disclosure of the information or other matter—

(a) to a person authorised for the purposes of this Part by the Director General of the National Criminal Intelligence Service;
(b) in the form and manner (if any) prescribed for the purposes of this subsection by order under section 339.

(6) But a person does not commit an offence under this section if he has a reasonable excuse for not disclosing the information or other matter.

(7) In deciding whether a person committed an offence under this section the court must consider whether he followed any relevant guidance which was at the time concerned—

(a) issued by a supervisory authority or any other appropriate body,

(b) approved by the Treasury, and
(c) published in a manner it approved as appropriate in its opinion to bring the guidance to the attention of persons likely to be affected by it.

(8) Schedule 9 has effect for the purpose of determining what is a supervisory authority.

(9) An appropriate body is a body which regulates or is representative of a trade, profession, business or employment.

332 Failure to disclose: other nominated officers

(1) A person nominated to receive disclosures under section 337 or 338 commits an offence if the conditions in subsections (2) to (4) are satisfied.

(2) The first condition is that he knows or suspects that another person is engaged in money laundering.

(3) The second condition is that the information or other matter on which his knowledge or suspicion is based came to him in consequence of a disclosure made under section 337 or 338.

(4) The third condition is that he does not make the required disclosure as soon as is practicable after the information or other matter comes to him.

(5) The required disclosure is a disclosure of the information or other matter—

(a) to a person authorised for the purposes of this Part by the Director General of the National Criminal Intelligence Service;
(b) in the form and manner (if any) prescribed for the purposes of this subsection by order under section 339.

(6) But a person does not commit an offence under this section if he has a reasonable excuse for not disclosing the information or other matter.

333 Tipping off

(1) A person commits an offence if—

(a) he knows or suspects that a disclosure falling within section 337 or 338 has been made, and
(b) he makes a disclosure which is likely to prejudice any investigation which might be conducted following the disclosure referred to in paragraph (a).

(2) But a person does not commit an offence under subsection (1) if—

(a) he did not know or suspect that the disclosure was likely to be prejudicial as mentioned in subsection (1);
(b) the disclosure is made in carrying out a function he has relating to the enforcement of any provision of this Act or of any other enactment relating to criminal conduct or benefit from criminal conduct;
(c) he is a professional legal adviser and the disclosure falls within subsection (3).

(3) A disclosure falls within this subsection if it is a disclosure—

(a) to (or to a representative of) a client of the professional legal adviser in connection with the giving by the adviser of legal advice to the client, or
(b) to any person in connection with legal proceedings or contemplated legal proceedings.

(4) But a disclosure does not fall within subsection (3) if it is made with the intention of furthering a criminal purpose.

334 Penalties

(1) A person guilty of an offence under section 327, 328 or 329 is liable—

(a) on summary conviction, to imprisonment for a term not exceeding six months or to a fine not exceeding the statutory maximum or to both, or
(b) on conviction on indictment, to imprisonment for a term not exceeding 14 years or to a fine or to both.

(2) A person guilty of an offence under section 330, 331, 332 or 333 is liable—

(a) on summary conviction, to imprisonment for a term not exceeding six months or to a fine not exceeding the statutory maximum or to both, or
(b) on conviction on indictment, to imprisonment for a term not exceeding five years or to a fine or to both.

Consent

335 Appropriate consent

(1) The appropriate consent is—

(a) the consent of a nominated officer to do a prohibited act if an authorised disclosure is made to the nominated officer;
(b) the consent of a constable to do a prohibited act if an authorised disclosure is made to a constable;
(c) the consent of a customs officer to do a prohibited act if an authorised disclosure is made to a customs officer.

(2) A person must be treated as having the appropriate consent if—

(a) he makes an authorised disclosure to a constable or a customs officer, and
(b) the condition in subsection (3) or the condition in subsection (4) is satisfied.

(3) The condition is that before the end of the notice period he does not receive notice from a constable or customs officer that consent to the doing of the act is refused.

(4) The condition is that—

(a) before the end of the notice period he receives notice from a constable or customs officer that consent to the doing of the act is refused, and
(b) the moratorium period has expired.

(5) The notice period is the period of seven working days starting with the first working day after the person makes the disclosure.

(6) The moratorium period is the period of 31 days starting with the day on which the person receives notice that consent to the doing of the act is refused.

(7) A working day is a day other than a Saturday, a Sunday, Christmas Day, Good Friday or a day which is a bank holiday under the Banking and Financial Dealings Act 1971 (c 80) in the part of the United Kingdom in which the person is when he makes the disclosure.

(8) References to a prohibited act are to an act mentioned in section 327(1), 328(1) or 329(1) (as the case may be).

(9) A nominated officer is a person nominated to receive disclosures under section 338.

(10) Subsections (1) to (4) apply for the purposes of this Part.

336 Nominated officer: consent

(1) A nominated officer must not give the appropriate consent to the doing of a prohibited act unless the condition in subsection (2), the condition in subsection (3) or the condition in subsection (4) is satisfied.

(2) The condition is that—

(a) he makes a disclosure that property is criminal property to a person authorised for the purposes of this Part by the Director General of the National Criminal Intelligence Service, and
(b) such a person gives consent to the doing of the act.

(3) The condition is that—

(a) he makes a disclosure that property is criminal property to a person authorised for the purposes of this Part by the Director General of the National Criminal Intelligence Service, and
(b) before the end of the notice period he does not receive notice from such a person that consent to the doing of the act is refused.

(4) The condition is that—

(a) he makes a disclosure that property is criminal property to a person authorised for the purposes of this Part by the Director General of the National Criminal Intelligence Service,
(b) before the end of the notice period he receives notice from such a person that consent to the doing of the act is refused, and
(c) the moratorium period has expired.

(5) A person who is a nominated officer commits an offence if—

(a) he gives consent to a prohibited act in circumstances where none of the conditions in subsections (2), (3) and (4) is satisfied, and

(b) he knows or suspects that the act is a prohibited act.

(6) A person guilty of such an offence is liable—

(a) on summary conviction, to imprisonment for a term not exceeding six months or to a fine not exceeding the statutory maximum or to both, or
(b) on conviction on indictment, to imprisonment for a term not exceeding five years or to a fine or to both.

(7) The notice period is the period of seven working days starting with the first working day after the nominated officer makes the disclosure.

(8) The moratorium period is the period of 31 days starting with the day on which the nominated officer is given notice that consent to the doing of the act is refused.

(9) A working day is a day other than a Saturday, a Sunday, Christmas Day, Good Friday or a day which is a bank holiday under the Banking and Financial Dealings Act 1971 (c 80) in the part of the United Kingdom in which the nominated officer is when he gives the appropriate consent.

(10) References to a prohibited act are to an act mentioned in section 327(1), 328(1) or 329(1) (as the case may be).

(11) A nominated officer is a person nominated to receive disclosures under section 338.

Disclosures

337 Protected disclosures

(1) A disclosure which satisfies the following three conditions is not to be taken to breach any restriction on the disclosure of information (however imposed).

(2) The first condition is that the information or other matter disclosed came to the person making the disclosure (the discloser) in the course of his trade, profession, business or employment.

(3) The second condition is that the information or other matter—

(a) causes the discloser to know or suspect, or
(b) gives him reasonable grounds for knowing or suspecting,

that another person is engaged in money laundering.

(4) The third condition is that the disclosure is made to a constable, a customs officer or a nominated officer as soon as is practicable after the information or other matter comes to the discloser.

(5) A disclosure to a nominated officer is a disclosure which—

(a) is made to a person nominated by the discloser's employer to receive disclosures under this section, and
(b) is made in the course of the discloser's employment and in accordance with the procedure established by the employer for the purpose.

338 Authorised disclosures

(1) For the purposes of this Part a disclosure is authorised if—

(a) it is a disclosure to a constable, a customs officer or a nominated officer by the alleged offender that property is criminal property,
(b) it is made in the form and manner (if any) prescribed for the purposes of this subsection by order under section 339, and
(c) the first or second condition set out below is satisfied.

(2) The first condition is that the disclosure is made before the alleged offender does the prohibited act.

(3) The second condition is that—

(a) the disclosure is made after the alleged offender does the prohibited act,
(b) there is a good reason for his failure to make the disclosure before he did the act, and
(c) the disclosure is made on his own initiative and as soon as it is practicable for him to make it.

(4) An authorised disclosure is not to be taken to breach any restriction on the disclosure of information (however imposed).

(5) A disclosure to a nominated officer is a disclosure which—

(a) is made to a person nominated by the alleged offender's employer to receive authorised disclosures, and
(b) is made in the course of the alleged offender's employment and in accordance with the procedure established by the employer for the purpose.

(6) References to the prohibited act are to an act mentioned in section 327(1), 328(1) or 329(1) (as the case may be).

339 Form and manner of disclosures

(1) The Secretary of State may by order prescribe the form and manner in which a disclosure under section 330, 331, 332 or 338 must be made.

(2) An order under this section may also provide that the form may include a request to the discloser to provide additional information specified in the form.

(3) The additional information must be information which is necessary to enable the person to whom the disclosure is made to decide whether to start a money laundering investigation.

(4) A disclosure made in pursuance of a request under subsection (2) is not to be taken to breach any restriction on the disclosure of information (however imposed).

(5) The discloser is the person making a disclosure mentioned in subsection (1).

(6) Money laundering investigation must be construed in accordance with section 341(4).

(7) Subsection (2) does not apply to a disclosure made to a nominated officer.

Interpretation

340 Interpretation

(1) This section applies for the purposes of this Part.

(2) Criminal conduct is conduct which—

(a) constitutes an offence in any part of the United Kingdom, or
(b) would constitute an offence in any part of the United Kingdom if it occurred there.

(3) Property is criminal property if—

(a) it constitutes a person's benefit from criminal conduct or it represents such a benefit (in whole or part and whether directly or indirectly), and
(b) the alleged offender knows or suspects that it constitutes or represents such a benefit.

(4) It is immaterial—

(a) who carried out the conduct;
(b) who benefited from it;
(c) whether the conduct occurred before or after the passing of this Act.

(5) A person benefits from conduct if he obtains property as a result of or in connection with the conduct.

(6) If a person obtains a pecuniary advantage as a result of or in connection with conduct, he is to be taken to obtain as a result of or in connection with the conduct a sum of money equal to the value of the pecuniary advantage.

(7) References to property or a pecuniary advantage obtained in connection with conduct include references to property or a pecuniary advantage obtained in both that connection and some other.

(8) If a person benefits from conduct his benefit is the property obtained as a result of or in connection with the conduct.

(9) Property is all property wherever situated and includes—

(a) money;
(b) all forms of property, real or personal, heritable or moveable;
(c) things in action and other intangible or incorporeal property.

(10) The following rules apply in relation to property—

(a) property is obtained by a person if he obtains an interest in it;
(b) references to an interest, in relation to land in England and Wales or Northern Ireland, are to any legal estate or equitable interest or power;

(c) references to an interest, in relation to land in Scotland, are to any estate, interest, servitude or other heritable right in or over land, including a heritable security;
(d) references to an interest, in relation to property other than land, include references to a right (including a right to possession).

(11) Money laundering is an act which—

(a) constitutes an offence under section 327, 328 or 329,
(b) constitutes an attempt, conspiracy or incitement to commit an offence specified in paragraph (a),
(c) constitutes aiding, abetting, counselling or procuring the commission of an offence specified in paragraph (a), or
(d) would constitute an offence specified in paragraph (a), (b) or (c) if done in the United Kingdom.

(12) For the purposes of a disclosure to a nominated officer—

(a) references to a person's employer include any body, association or organisation (including a voluntary organisation) in connection with whose activities the person exercises a function (whether or not for gain or reward), and
(b) references to employment must be construed accordingly.

(13) References to a constable include references to a person authorised for the purposes of this Part by the Director General of the National Criminal Intelligence Service.

Society of Trust and Estate Practitioners Standard Provisions: 1st Edition

1. Introductory

1(1) These Provisions may be called the standard provisions of the Society of Trust and Estate Practitioners (1st Edition).

1(2) These Provisions may be incorporated in a document by the words:

The standard provisions of the Society of Trust and Estate Practitioners (1st Edition) shall apply

or in any manner indicating an intention to incorporate them.

2. Interpretation

2(1) In these Provisions, unless the context otherwise requires:

(a) **Income Beneficiary**, in relation to Trust Property, means a Person to whom income of the Trust Property is payable (as of right or at the discretion of the Trustees).
(b) **Person** includes a person anywhere in the world and includes a Trustee.
(c) **The Principal Document** means the document in which these Provisions are incorporated.
(d) **The Settlement** means any settlement created by the Principal Document and an estate of a deceased Person to which the Principal Document relates.
(e) **The Trustees** means the personal representatives or trustees of the Settlement for the time being.
(f) **The Trust Fund** means the property comprised in the Settlement for the time being.
(g) **Trust Property** means any property comprised in the Trust Fund.
(h) **A Professional Trustee** means a Trustee who is or has been carrying on a business which consists of or includes the management of trusts or the administration of estates.

2(2) These Provisions have effect subject to the provisions of the Principal Document.

3. Administrative Powers

The Trustees shall have the following powers:

3(1) *Investment*

(a) The Trustees may invest Trust Property in any manner as if they were beneficial owners. In particular the Trustees may invest in unsecured loans.
(b) The Trustees may decide not to diversify the Trust Fund.

3(2) *Management*

The Trustees may effect any transaction relating to the management administration or disposition of Trust Property as if they were beneficial owners. In particular:

(a) The Trustees may repair and maintain Trust Property.
(b) The Trustees may develop or improve Trust Property.

3(3) *Joint Property*

The Trustees may acquire property jointly with any Person.

3(4) *Income and Capital*

The Trustees may decide not to hold a balance between conflicting interests of Persons interested in Trust Property. In particular:

(a) The Trustees may acquire

 (i) wasting assets and
 (ii) assets which yield little or no income for investment or any other purpose.

(b) The Trustees may decide not to procure distributions from a company in which they are interested.
(c) The Trustees may pay taxes and other expenses out of income although they would otherwise be paid out of capital.

3(5) *Accumulated Income*

The Trustees may apply accumulated income as if it were income arising in the current year.

3(6) *Use of Trust Property*

The Trustees may permit an Income Beneficiary to occupy or enjoy the use of Trust Property on such terms as the Trustees think fit. The Trustees may acquire any property for this purpose.

3(7) *Application of Trust Capital*

The Trustees may:

(a) lend money which is Trust Property to an Income Beneficiary without security, on such terms as they think fit,
(b) charge Trust Property as security for debts or obligations of an Income Beneficiary, or
(c) pay money which is Trust Property to an Income Beneficiary as his income, for the purpose of augmenting his income

Provided that:

 (i) the Trustees have power to transfer such Property to that Beneficiary absolutely; or
 (ii) the Trustees have power to do so with the consent of another Person and the Trustees act with the written consent of that Person.

3(8) *Trade*

The Trustees may carry on a trade, in any part of the world, alone or in partnership.

3(9) *Borrowing*

The Trustees may borrow money for investment or any other purpose. Money borrowed shall be treated as Trust Property.

3(10) *Insurance*

The Trustees may insure Trust Property for any amount against any risk.

3(11) *Delegation*

A Trustee may delegate in writing any of his functions to any Person. A Trustee shall not be responsible for the default of that Person (even if the delegation was not strictly necessary or expedient) provided that he took reasonable care in his selection and supervision.

3(12) *Deposit of Documents*

The Trustees may deposit documents relating to the Settlement (including bearer securities) with any Person.

3(13) *Nominees*

The Trustees may vest Trust Property in any Person as nominee, and may place Trust Property in the possession or control of any Person.

3(14) *Offshore administration*

The Trustees may carry on the administration of the trusts of the Settlement outside the United Kingdom.

3(15) *Payment of tax*

The Trustees may pay tax liabilities of the Settlement (and interest on such tax) even though such liabilities are not enforceable against the Trustees.

3(16) *Indemnities*

The Trustees may indemnify any Person for any liability properly chargeable against Trust Property.

3(17) *Security*

The Trustees may charge Trust Property as security for any liability properly incurred by them as Trustees.

3(18) *Supervision of Company*

The Trustees are under no duty to enquire into the conduct of a company in which they are interested, unless they have knowledge of circumstances which call for enquiry.

3(19) *Appropriation*

The Trustees may appropriate Trust Property to any Person or class of Persons in or towards the satisfaction of their interest in the Trust Fund.

3(20) *Receipt by Charities*

Where Trust Property is to be paid or transferred to a charity, the receipt of the treasurer or appropriate officer of the charity shall be a complete discharge to the Trustees.

3(21) *Release of Powers*

The Trustees may by deed release any of their powers wholly or in part so as to bind future trustees.

3(22) *Ancillary Powers*

The Trustees may do anything which is incidental or conducive to the exercise of their functions.

4. Powers of Maintenance and Advancement

Sections 31 and 32 Trustee Act 1925 shall apply with the following modifications:

(a) The Proviso to section 31(1) shall be deleted.
(b) The words one-half of in section 32(1)(a) shall be deleted.

5. Trust for Sale

The Trustees shall hold land in England and Wales on trust for sale.

6. Minors

6(1) Where the Trustees may apply income for the benefit of a minor, they may do so by paying the income to the minor's parent or guardian on behalf of the minor, or to the minor if he has attained the age of 16. The Trustees are under no duty to enquire into the use of the income unless they have knowledge of circumstances which call for enquiry.

6(2) Where the Trustees may apply income for the benefit of a minor, they may do so by resolving that they hold that income on trust for the minor absolutely and:

(a) The Trustees may apply that income for the benefit of the minor during his minority.
(b) The Trustees shall transfer the residue of that income to the minor on attaining the age of 18.
(c) For investment and other administrative purposes that income shall be treated as Trust Property.

7. Disclaimer

A Person may disclaim his interest under the Settlement wholly or in part.

8. Apportionment

Income and expenditure shall be treated as arising when payable, and not from day to day, so that no apportionment shall take place.

9. Conflicts of Interest

9(1) In this paragraph:

(a) A Fiduciary means a Person subject to fiduciary duties under the Settlement.
(b) An Independent Trustee, in relation to a Person, means a Trustee who is not:

(i) a brother, sister, ancestor, descendant or dependent of the Person;
(ii) a spouse of the Person or of (i) above; or
(iii) a company controlled by one or more of any of the above.

9(2) A Fiduciary may:

(a) enter into a transaction with the Trustees, or
(b) be interested in an arrangement in which the Trustees are or might have been interested, or
(c) act (or not act) in any other circumstances

even though his fiduciary duty under the Settlement conflicts with other duties or with his personal interest;

Provided that:

(i) The Fiduciary first discloses to the Trustees the nature and extent of any material interest conflicting with his fiduciary duties, and
(ii) there is an Independent Trustee in respect of whom there is no conflict of interest, and he considers that the transaction arrangement or action is not contrary to the general interest of the Settlement.

9(3) The powers of the Trustees may be used to benefit a Trustee (to the same extent as if he were not a Trustee) provided that there is an Independent Trustee in respect of whom there is no conflict of interest.

10. Powers of Trustees

The powers of the Trustees may be exercised:

(a) at their absolute discretion; and
(b) from time to time as occasion requires.

11. Trustee Remuneration

11(1) A Trustee who is a solicitor or an accountant or who is engaged in a business may charge for work done by him or his firm in connection with the Settlement, including work not requiring professional assistance. This has priority to any disposition made in the Principal Document.

11(2) The Trustees may make arrangements to remunerate themselves for work done for a company connected with the Trust Fund.

12. Liability of Trustees

12(1) A Trustee (other than a Professional Trustee) shall not be liable for a loss to the Trust Fund unless that loss was caused by his own fraud or negligence.

12(2) A Trustee shall not be liable for acting in accordance with the advice of Counsel of at least five years standing, with respect to the Settlement, unless, when he does so:

(a) he knows or has reasonable cause to suspect that the advice was given in ignorance of material facts; or
(b) proceedings are pending to obtain the decision of the court on the matter.

13. Appointment and Retirement of Trustees

13(1) A Person may be appointed trustee of the Settlement even though he has no connection with the United Kingdom.

13(2) A Professional Trustee who is an individual who has reached the age of 65 shall retire if:

(a) he is requested to do so by his co—trustees, or by a Person interested in Trust Property; and
(b) he is effectually indemnified against liabilities properly incurred as Trustee.

On that retirement a new Trustee shall be appointed if necessary to ensure that there will be two individuals or a Trust Corporation to act as Trustee.

In this sub—paragraph Trust Corporation has the same meaning as in them Trustee Act 1925.

This sub-paragraph does not apply to a Professional Trustee who is:

(a) a personal representative
(b) the settlor of the Settlement
(c) a spouse or former spouse of the settlor or testator.

14. Protection for Interest in Possession and Accumulation and Maintenance Settlements

These Provisions shall not have effect:

(a) so as to prevent a Person from being entitled to an interest in possession in Trust Property (within the meaning of the Inheritance Tax Act 1984);
(b) so as to cause the Settlement to be an accumulation or discretionary settlement (within the meaning of section 5 Taxation of Chargeable Gains Act 1992);
(c) so as to prevent the conditions of Section 7 1(1) Inheritance Tax Act 1984 from applying to Trust Property.

Statements of Practice and Press Releases

SP 5/92 (21 May 1992) Non-resident trusts

(See also Inland Revenue Tax Bulletin August 1993 and April 1995.)

I Introduction

1 FA 1991 ss 83–92, Sch 16–18 introduced new rules for capital gains of certain offshore trusts. These are now in TCGA 1992 ss 80–98, Sch 5. This statement explains the practice the Revenue will follow in applying the new rules in the circumstances set out below.

II Charge on migration: residence

2 Under TCGA 1992 s 69, a body of trustees is regarded as capable of changing its residence status part-way through a year of assessment. It must be borne in mind, however, that TCGA 1992 s 2(1) provides that the trustees are liable to tax on all chargeable gains of a tax year during any part of which they are resident or during which they are ordinarily resident in the UK.

3 Trustees who became not resident and not ordinarily resident in the UK between 6 April 1990 and 18 March 1991 (inclusive), and remain so until after 5 April 1991 are not liable to a charge under TCGA 1992 s 80, nor are they regarded as having met the condition in TCGA 1992 Sch 5 para 9(4) for 1990–91.

III Charge on migration: past trustees' liabilities

4 TCGA 1992 ss 80–85 impose a capital gains tax charge on the unrealised gains of a UK trust which ceases to be within the UK tax charge. The charge applies to a trust which migrates on or after 19 March 1991. Where the tax which is due under this charge is not paid by the current trustees, TCGA 1992 s 82 enables the Revenue to look to certain former trustees to meet the liability. No liability can be sought from the personal representatives of a former trustee who dies before a notice of liability has been served on him. Those who can show that there was no proposal, at the time of their resignation, that the trustees might become not resident and not ordinarily resident in the UK are not liable under this section.

5 Payment can only be sought from former trustees where the Revenue is unable to obtain payment from current trustees. In the first instance, payment will generally be sought from those persons who resigned as trustees immediately before the trust migrated and then from earlier trustees. Each case will, however, need to be considered in the light of the relevant facts.

6 An amount recovered from present trustees by a former trustee in respect of capital gains tax under TCGA 1992 s 82 is not regarded as a capital payment under s 97. Further, such amounts do not fall within the provisions of ICTA 1988 Part XV, s 739 or s 740 nor are there any inheritance tax implications.

IV Charge on the settlor: settlor's right to repayment from the trustees

7 TCGA 1992 s 86, Sch 5 charge settlors to capital gains tax where chargeable gains accrue within certain offshore trusts from which the settlor, members of the settlor's immediate family, or companies which they control, can or do benefit. This goes wider than the provisions of ICTA 1988 Part XV eg the settlor could be chargeable on gains realised within a trust from which his adult children could benefit even though there was no possible benefit to the settlor, his spouse or minor children.

8 The settlor's right, under TCGA 1992 Sch 5 para 6, to reimbursement (or any payment in reimbursement) of tax paid under that Schedule is not regarded as creating an interest in a trust for the settlor under the provisions of ICTA 1988 Part XV where the settlor, the settlor's spouse, and any companies in which they are participators cannot otherwise benefit from the trust, eg where the only beneficiaries are the settlor's children. Similarly, this statutory right to, or payment in, reimbursement is not regarded as bringing the settlor within the provisions of ICTA 1988 ss 677, 739, 740, nor as a capital payment for the purposes of TCGA 1992 s 97.

9 Further, this statutory right is not regarded as a reservation of benefit for inheritance tax purposes; nor is a provision in the trust deed either requiring the trustees to recognise the settlor's right to reimbursement under TCGA 1992 Sch 5 para 6 or to reimburse the settlor. But where a settlor does not pursue the statutory right to reimbursement, the failure to exercise this right may give rise to an inheritance tax claim under IHTA 1984 s 3(3), in which case the usual rules for lifetime transfers would apply.

10 A provision written into a settlement deed requiring the trustees to recognise the settlor's right to reimbursement under TCGA 1992 Sch 5 para 6, or to reimburse the settlor, is not, of itself, regarded as giving the settlor an interest in the settlement for the purposes of Sch 5, nor as bringing into play the provisions of ICTA 1988 Part XV, s 739 or s 740.

V Charge on the settlor: trusts created before 19 March 1991

11 All trusts created on or after 19 March 1991 are within the scope of TCGA 1992 Sch 5. Those created before that date will, broadly, fall within the Schedule only where, on or after 19 March 1991, at least one of the following conditions is met—

- subject to certain exclusions, property or income is directly or indirectly provided for the purposes of the trust (Sch 5 para 9(3));
- the trustees become non-resident in the UK or fall to be treated as such for the purposes of a double taxation agreement (Sch 5 para 9(4));
- the terms of the settlement are varied to admit certain new beneficiaries (Sch 5 para 9(5)); or
- a benefit is enjoyed by a defined person who is not a beneficiary under the terms of the trust (Sch 5 para 9(6)).

(*a*) *TCGA 1992 Sch 5 para 9(3): transactions entered into at arm's length*

12 The condition in TCGA 1992 Sch 5 para 9(3) is not met where the property or income is provided to the trust under a transaction entered into at arm's length—see para 9(3)(a). This applies irrespective of whether the parties to the transaction are connected persons under TCGA 1992 s 286. Each case depends on its own facts and circumstances but a transaction is, in general, regarded as being at arm's length where all the facts and circumstances of the transaction are such as might have been expected if the parties to the transaction had been independent persons dealing at arm's length i e dealing with each other in a normal commercial manner unaffected by any special relationship between them.

13 Solely for the purposes of TCGA 1992 Sch 5 para 9(3)(a), a provision in the document governing the transaction for an appropriate adjustment to the consideration where the value agreed by the Revenue differs from the original consideration arrived at by an independent valuer and specified in the sale document is, in general, regarded as falling within the terms of the above definition of an arm's length transaction. The arm's length value of the transaction is to be determined in accordance with the principles set out in para 12 above. This will usually correspond to the value for capital gains tax purposes except, for example, where TCGA 1992 s 19 would apply.

14 It would also be necessary for the terms of the contract to provide for compensating interest at a commercial rate to be paid in either direction once the arm's length value is determined. For this purpose, the official rate of interest for ICTA 1988 s 160 purposes will usually be regarded as equivalent to a commercial rate of interest, although a different rate may be accepted as so equivalent if the circumstances of a particular case warrant this treatment.

15 This practice is, however, subject to the consideration passing on sale being realistically based, i e on a third party valuation by a qualified valuer, all

the other terms of the transaction being at arm's length and the compensating interest being timeously paid. The position in a particular case depends on all the facts and circumstances.

(b) TCGA 1992 Sch 5 para 9(3): close companies

16 The condition in TCGA 1992 Sch 5 para 9(3) may be satisfied where property or income is provided to a company in which the trustees are participators. Where, however, the transaction is carried out with the sole object of leaving funds within the company for the company's purposes and it can be shown that any indirect benefit to the trust is merely incidental to that object, the transaction is disregarded for the purposes of para 9(3).

17 Examples of transactions which may be so disregarded are—

- where another shareholder waives an entitlement to all or part of a dividend; or
- where a director restricts withdrawals of remuneration voted,

in order to assist the company's cash flow, and no payments are made, directly or indirectly, to the trustees as a result of this. All relevant factors will be considered in determining whether it is appropriate to apply this practice in a particular case.

(c) TCGA 1992 Sch 5 para 9(3): transactions with wholly-owned companies

18 In general, transactions between trustees and companies which they, directly or indirectly, wholly own, or between such companies, are outside the scope of TCGA 1992 Sch 5 para 9(3) and are not treated as capital payments within TCGA 1992 s 97. For this purpose, a company is treated as directly wholly owned by the trustees where the whole of its issued share capital is directly owned by the trustees of the settlement for the benefit of the beneficiaries of the settlement. A company is treated as indirectly wholly owned by the trustees where the whole of its issued share capital is directly and beneficially owned by a company which is directly wholly owned by the trustees or it is the 100 per cent subsidiary of such a company, or a chain of companies, which is indirectly wholly owned by the trustees. This approach may not, however, be taken where, on the facts of a particular case, it appears that the transaction has been entered into solely or mainly for the purposes of obtaining a UK tax advantage.

(d) TCGA 1992 Sch 5 para 9(3): loans made to settlements

(i) Loans made before 19 March 1991

19 A fixed-period loan made, directly or indirectly, to a relevant settlement prior to 19 March 1991 on non-commercial terms, e g at a low or nil rate of

interest is, generally, regarded as a provision of property in pursuance of a liability incurred before 19 March 1991, provided the loan remains outstanding on the same terms. As such, it falls within the terms of TCGA 1992 Sch 5 para 9(3)(b) and the first condition set out in para 9(3) is not met.

20 There would, however, be a direct or indirect provision of property for the purposes of the settlement where a fixed-period loan falls to be repaid after 18 March 1991 but repayment is not made and so becomes a repayable on demand loan.

21 An extra-statutory concession D41, which is being published at the same time as this statement, sets out the position in the case of non-commercial, repayable on demand, loans for the purposes of applying TCGA 1992 Sch 5 para 9(3).

(ii) Loans made after 19 March 1991

22 A loan made, directly or indirectly to a relevant settlement after 19 March 1991 on non-commercial terms, e g at a low or nil rate of interest is regarded as a provision of funds for the purposes of TCGA 1992 Sch 5 para 9(3). This is the case whether the loan is for a fixed period or repayable on demand.

(*e*) *TCGA 1992 Sch 5 para 9(3): loans made by trustees*

23 The repayment of any loan made, directly or indirectly, to any person by the trustees is not generally regarded as the provision of funds for the purposes of the settlement under TCGA 1992 Sch 5 para 9(3). This does not, however, apply where more is repaid than is due under the original terms of the loan or, in the case of loans made after 19 March 1991, where the interest charged under the terms of the loan exceeds a commercial rate.

(*f*) *TCGA 1992 Sch 5 para 9(3): failure to exercise rights to reimbursement*

24 Failure, by or on behalf of any relevant person, to exercise statutory rights to reimbursement, e g under ICTA 1988 Part XV may be regarded as the provision of funds for the purposes of the settlement under TCGA 1992 Sch 5 para 9(3). The settlement could remain outside the terms of para 9(3) where the exercise of the right to reimbursement is unsuccessful, provided it could be shown that there had been a genuine attempt to enforce rights to reimbursement.

(*g*) *TCGA 1992 Sch 5 para 9(3): administrative expenses*

25 As provided by TCGA 1992 Sch 5 para 9(3), a trust may remain outside the scope of Sch 5 where funds are provided to pay certain expenses which exceed the income of the trust. These expenses are defined as 'expenses relating to administration and taxation'; and could be chargeable either to the

income or to the capital of the trust. Only sums provided to meet genuine expenses of administration fall within the terms of the proviso: any payments which exceed such expenses are regarded as meeting the condition in para 9(3) and so bringing the trust within the scope of Sch 5.

26 The following items are not regarded as 'expenses relating to administration' within the terms of the proviso to TCGA 1992 Sch 5 para 9(3)—

- loan interest (other than interest on a loan taken out to meet expenses of administration within the terms of the proviso);
- the costs of acquiring, enhancing or disposing of an asset;
- expenses incurred in connection with a particular trust asset to the extent that such expenditure can be set against income arising from that asset. For the purpose of the proviso to para 9(3), the measure of the gross income from such a source is net of expenses.

27 The term 'expenses relating to ... taxation' in TCGA 1992 Sch 5 para 9(3) is regarded as encompassing UK or foreign taxes to which the trustees are liable, along with any interest and penalties due on that tax. It could also include certain costs incurred by the trustees under the terms of the trust in obtaining information regarding the beneficiaries' tax liabilities. One example might be where the trustees, in order to ensure they were acting in a beneficiary's best interests, had to ascertain the tax implications for the beneficiary in adopting a particular course of action.

28 It is only the settlement's expenses relating to administration or taxation which are within the terms of the proviso to TCGA 1992 Sch 5 para 9(3). Expenses of, for example, a company wholly owned by the trustees fall outside its scope.

29 An expense on capital account paid out of trust income is not treated as a provision of income by a beneficiary for the purposes of TCGA 1992 Sch 5 para 9(3) provided that either—

- the trust deed permits payment of capital expenses from income and the beneficiary is entitled only to net income after such payments; or
- the trustees borrow money from the income account which is subsequently restored, along with interest over the period of the loan. The appropriate rate of interest is considered to be that which a Court of Equity would order on the replacement of trust income.

30 Normally the specific date on which the liability to an expense relating to administration or taxation was incurred determines the year into which it falls for the purpose of applying the proviso to TCGA 1992 Sch 5 para 9(3). Where, however, the expense is incurred for a period rather than on a specific date, the basis of allocating expenses adopted by the trustees in preparing trust

accounts or returns is, generally, regarded as acceptable provided that this basis is consistently adopted and is in accordance with conventional trust accounting practice.

31 Additions to meet the difference between expenses relating to administration and taxation and any income arising to the trust do not have to be made by 5 April in the relevant year of assessment. There must, however, be a clear connection between the amount added and the computed shortfall. Additions should, therefore, be made as soon as the relevant figures are available.

32 Income, for the purposes of the proviso to TCGA 1992 Sch 5 para 9(3), is the total income which arises to the trustees in the relevant year, rather than the income which is (or would be if the trust were resident in the UK) subject to UK tax. Usually, items of income will need to be allocated to the year in which they arise for the purposes of the proviso, but, in practice, income arising from a trade carried on by the trustees may be apportioned on a time basis, provided that this basis is consistently followed.

(h) TCGA 1992 Sch 5 para 9(3): life tenants

33 A life tenant is not regarded as having provided income or property for the purposes of the settlement merely because there is an administrative delay in paying out the income that has vested in that beneficiary. If, however, the beneficiary directs the trustees to retain this income on the terms of the settlement, this is regarded as a provision of funds within TCGA 1992 Sch 5 para 9(3).

(i) TCGA 1992 Sch 5 para 9(3): indemnities and guarantees

34 An indemnity given by the new trustees to retiring trustees is not considered as the provision of funds for the purposes of the settlement under TCGA 1992 Sch 5 para 9(3). Other types of indemnity are considered in light of the facts of a particular case.

35 The giving of a guarantee is regarded as an indirect provision of funds under the terms of TCGA 1992 Sch 5 para 9(3). Payment of an obligation under a guarantee given before 9 March 1991 is, in general, regarded as a payment in pursuance of a liability incurred before 19 March 1991 and within para 9(3)(b). This may not, however, apply where—

- the contingent liability under the guarantee cannot be quantified with a sufficient degree of accuracy, e g where the guarantee is open-ended or the contingency is remote; or
- the guarantor does not take reasonable steps to pursue his rights against the debtor.

(j) TCGA 1992 Sch 5 para 9(5): variations

36 This provision is concerned with situations where the terms of the settlement are varied by the beneficiaries or a court to admit new beneficiaries

within the class of persons defined at TCGA 1992 Sch 5 para 9(7) without thereby bringing the settlement to an end and creating a new one. For example, where the terms of the trust include a power to appoint anyone within a specified range to be a beneficiary, exercise of that power after 19 March 1991 will not be regarded as a variation of the settlement. The term 'spouse' in para 9(7) is not considered to include a widow or a widower.

(k) TCGA 1992 Sch 5 para 9(6): ultra vires payments

37 For the purposes of clarification, this condition deals with 'ultra vires' payments, ie cases where one of the persons defined at TCGA 1992 Sch 5 para 9(7) receives a benefit from the trust for the first time and that person is not a beneficiary under the terms of the trust deed. It may also apply where such a person benefits from a transaction with the settlement carried out, for example, under the trustees' investment powers.

VI Charge on beneficiaries: intragroup transfers

38 TCGA 1992 ss 87–89 charge UK resident beneficiaries to capital gains tax on certain capital payments received from non-resident settlements. TCGA 1992 s 96 is concerned with the application of these provisions to capital payments made by companies which are controlled by the trustees and capital payments received by certain non-resident companies.

39 TCGA 1992 s 96 provides that, where the trustees (or a company which they control) make a payment to a closely-controlled non-resident company, the payment is, broadly, treated as made to those who control the company. This may, for example, mean that a payment made by a wholly-owned subsidiary to its holding company (in which the shares are, say, held 50 per cent by the settlor and 50 per cent by the trustees of a non-resident trust) can be treated as being made by the trustees to the settlor.

40 The payment must, however, be a capital payment within TCGA 1992 s 97(1)—ie it must not be chargeable to income tax on the recipient nor be made under a transaction entered into at arm's length. Intragroup payments which are not capital payments, for example a capital distribution on winding up which represents merely a repayment of capital on shares, or a distribution chargeable to corporation tax, do not fall within the ambit of TCGA 1992 s 96.

14 December 1992. ICAEW
Guidance note—non-resident settlements (TAX 20/92)

Introduction

1 FA 1991 ss 83–92, Sch 16–18 introduced new rules for capital gains of certain offshore trusts. The relevant legislation is now in TCGA 1992 ss 80–98, Sch 5.

2 In January 1992 the Inland Revenue invited various professional bodies to comment on a draft statement of practice explaining the practice to be followed in applying the new rules. Comments on the draft statement of practice were submitted by the Tax Faculty in February 1992 following which the statement of practice (SP5/92) and two new extra-statutory concessions (D40 and D41) were issued in May 1992 [Revenue Press Release dated 21 May 1992].

3 This guidance note sets out the text of some of the correspondence between the Tax Faculty and the Inland Revenue in respect of the statement of practice in both draft and final form. Correspondence quoted has been confined to matters which have not been clarified in the statement of practice or the extra-statutory concessions and has been amended to refer to the final version of statement of practice SP5/92 and to TCGA 1992 a consolidating Act which came into force on 6 April 1992.

4 The paragraphs which follow are set out under the relevant headings and paragraph numbers in statement of practice SP5/92. The point made by the Tax Faculty is followed by the Inland Revenue response.

Paragraphs in the Statement of Practice

IV Charge on the settlor: settlor's right to repayment from the trustees

Paragraph 8

5 The reference in para 8 to 'any companies in which they are participators' implies that ICTA 1988 ss 660–694 could apply if a company can benefit from a trust if the settlor/settlor's spouse has a small shareholding in the company. Is this intended?

Revenue response: The reference to which you refer in para 8 is intended to imply that ICTA 1988 ss 660–694 could be invoked in circumstances where a company in which the settlor or the settlor's spouse has a small shareholding is a beneficiary of the trust.

Paragraph 9

6 As regards para 9, we note that a claim under IHTA 1984 s 3 (3) may arise if the settlor does not exercise his right of reimbursement. The drop in value in the settlor's estate will occur when the right to reimbursement expires. We shall therefore be grateful for guidance as to when the right expires.

Revenue response: The duration of the settlor's right to reimbursement is governed by the general law Limitation Act, which prescribes a six-year limit (unless the settlor indicates to the trustees before the expiration of this period that he does not intend to exercise his right to reimbursement, at which point the right would expire). The six-year period would begin when the settlor pays the tax.

V Charge on the settlor: trusts created before 19 March 1991

(*a*) *TCGA 1992 Sch 5 para 9(3): transactions entered into at arm's length*

Paragraphs 13 to 15

7 Paragraphs 13 to 15 deal with adjuster clauses so as to ensure that values are in accordance with what is finally agreed by the Revenue. It may not be appropriate in some circumstances for such a clause to deal only with the provision of compensating interest at a commercial rate but rather for there to be a provision for issued shares to be cancelled (eg in a situation where a company owned by the settlor has acquired shares in a company owned by an offshore trust on a share for share basis).

Revenue response: The practice does not encompass situations to which you refer. It would, of course, be possible for the parties to the transaction to show that the transaction was carried out on arm's length terms.

(*d*) *TCGA 1992 Sch 5 para 9 (3): loans made to settlements*

(i) Loans made before 19 March 1991

Paragraph 19

8 We seek confirmation that the words 'directly or indirectly' in the first line of para 19 covers the position of a loan to an underlying company owned by the trustees.

Revenue response: The phrase 'directly or indirectly' would, inter alia, cover the case of a loan made to a company owned by the trustees.

9 The extra-statutory concession does not deal with the case of a fixed term loan where the period expired after 18 March 1991 but repayment was not made immediately, and this may prove anomalous in a number of cases. There is very little difference between, on the one hand, a loan to trustees which, at 18 March 1991, was repayable on demand and, on the other, a loan which was then fixed term and which fell due shortly thereafter, but where repayment was not made immediately. In both cases, trustees would not have been capable of comprehending the full implications of TCGA 1992 Sch 5 para 9(3). We therefore remain of the view that there are strong grounds for saying that the concessionary treatment should extend to fixed term loans which have become repayable on demand loans at sometime between 18 March 1991 and 31 July 1992.

Revenue response: It is, in our experience, unusual for there to be a fixed-term loan to the trustees on better than commercial terms. But where such loans were in existence at 19 March 1991 and were not prepaid on a subsequent due date, the lender was effectively making a new repayable on demand loan. The extra-statutory concession is concerned only with repayable on demand loans which were entered into before the introduction of the legislation—on the basis that borrowers and lenders entering into such loans after that date were in a position to take the effects of the legislation fully into account. In those circumstances, it would in our view be inequitable to extend the concession to fixed term loans which became repayable on demand loans after 19 March 1991.

10 The Revenue accept in para 19 that a fixed period loan made before 19 March 1991 is generally to be treated as a provision of property in pursuance of a liability incurred before that date, but they do not accept this for a demand loan or similar terms. It is difficult to see the logic of this since a demand loan remains a liability unless and until it is called. There is nothing in the wording of TCGA 1992 Sch 5 para 9(3) to suggest that the failure to exercise a right constitutes the provision of property whether directly or indirectly.

Revenue response: The Revenue considers that the failure to exercise a right is a direct or indirect provision of property within TCGA 1992 Sch 5 para 9(3). The continued provision of the loan on better than commercial terms after it could have been recalled and the 'benefit' to the settlement terminated is clearly within the ambit of para 9(3).

11 As the Revenue have hitherto strongly argued, there can be no such thing as past consideration if, as they now suggest, the terms of an interest-free demand loan be retrospectively amended. What is the status of the 'interest' from the period 6 April 1991 to the date of variation? It cannot be interest and we hesitate to suggest that it is contractually enforceable. It presumably constitutes a distribution of trust assets to the lender. It is not income in his hands: is it therefore a capital payment?

Revenue response: You will note that, as it was not possible to issue the statement before 6 April, this treatment has been reclassified as a concession, and the text has been expanded to spell out how payments made under an arrangement to make the terms of a demand loan fully commercial will be treated in the hands of the recipient. I trust that this answers your comments on the status of such amounts. Similarly, because it was not possible to issue the concession before the end of the last tax year, and because the deadline has been extended to 31 July 1992, we have had to give some further consideration to the possible effects of the treatment of such amounts. As a result, the concessionary treatment has been extended to disapply the provisions of TCGA 1992 ss 92–95, Sch 5 para 9 (6) when considering certain payments for the year ended 5 April 1992.

12 Confirmation is sought that payment of 'interest' or a sum in lieu of interest, will have no inheritance tax implications, and that there is no requirement for any inheritance tax return.

Revenue response: We do not consider the payment of a sum in lieu of interest, such as that envisaged in concession D41, to have any inheritance tax implications.

13 We would also like confirmation that such interest would qualify for a tax deduction where 'real' interest would have been deductible, and that directors' loan accounts in respect of companies underlying trusts would be subject to the same Inland Revenue practice as other loans.

Revenue response: The treatment here will, of course, depend upon whether the sum is paid as interest, or as a sum in lieu of interest. Credit balances on director's loan accounts with underlying companies will be subject to the same treatment as other loans unless, exceptionally, paras 16 and 17 of the redrafted statement apply.

14 Further clarification is sought on five points with regard to the income tax implications of the payment of 'interest'—

(a) This paragraph states that 'the treatment here will, of course, depend upon whether the sum is paid as interest, or as a sum in lieu of interest'. In the circumstances envisaged, there will necessarily have been a loan outstanding at 18 March 1991 which was either interest free, or bearing interest at less than a full rate. Any payment by the trustees to 'make good' the interest must therefore be a payment in lieu of interest. We shall be grateful for confirmation that such payments will qualify for deduction for income tax purposes in determining the amount of income due to a life tenant, and for other income tax purposes (for example ICTA 1988 ss 660–694, 739, 740).

(b) Can the Revenue confirm that where a payment in lieu of interest is made to a lender, who is not a beneficiary, the amount paid will be treated as a capital payment.

(c) The final paragraph of the extra-statutory concession refers to the circumstances where an agreement to pay interest has been entered into by trustees before 6 April 1992 'or in respect of periods after 5 April 1992'. We shall be grateful to have confirmation that the words in parenthesis are intended to refer to interest payable in respect of any period subsequent to the date of the agreement.

(d) If the lender is the settlor, or the settlor's spouse, confirmation is requested that payment of interest in lieu does not bring into play the provisions in ICTA 1988 ss 660–694 or ICTA 1988 ss 739, 740.

(e) What is the tax treatment of a sum in lieu of interest paid by an underlying company?

Revenue response:

(a) I confirm that the payments in lieu of interest will qualify as a deduction, both in determining the income of a life tenant and for the purposes of TA 1988 s 740. Since both ICTA 1988 ss 660–694 and s 739 impose a charge on income arising, no deduction would be due where these provisions are applicable.

(b) I confirm that this is the effect of the concession.

(c) The basic point here is that amounts paid in respect of the fiscal year in which the agreement was made (or in fiscal years after the agreement was made) are treated as interest.

(d) Where funds have been lent to the trustees at less than a commercial rate of interest, it is the Revenue's view that the lender is a settlor and, by virtue of his right to revoke the loan agreement or arrangement by demanding repayment, is taxable under ICTA 1988 ss 672, 674 on income arising from the investment of the loaned monies. These provisions would, therefore, be in point before the question of a repayment in lieu of interest arose. Similarly, as ICTA 1988 s 739(3), (4)(a) specifically include repayments of loans, the provisions of s 739 would also already be in play before any possibility of payments within concession D41 could arise.

(e) The payment would not qualify as a deduction from profits in the hands of the company.

Paragraph 21 and the extra-statutory concession
15 It is suggested in the concession that if the terms of an interest-free demand loan are retrospectively amended so as to impose from 6 April 1991 a commercial rate of interest, that loan will not be treated as tainting the settlement. However, in most circumstances it would be a breach of trust for the trustees to accede to such a variation in the terms.

Revenue response: The other option available to the trustees is, of course, to repay the loan.

(*e*) *TCGA 1992 Sch 5 para 9(3): loans made by trustees*

(ii) Loans made after 19 March 1991

Paragraph 23
16 There are other issues concerning TCGA 1992 Sch 5 para 9(3) where it would be helpful for the statement of practice to provide clarification. Perhaps the most important point is confirmation that if the trustees make a loan to a beneficiary and the beneficiary pays interest at less than an arm's length rate, the payment of such interest does not fall within para 9(3). Similarly if the trustees lease property to a beneficiary and the beneficiary pays less than arm's length rental. While we believe it is clear that this does not fall within para 9(3), albeit that the undercharge of interest/rent is a capital payment within TCGA 1992 s 97, one leading counsel has expressed a contrary view. This is, therefore, a most important point where clarification is required.

Revenue response: Paragraph 23 of the redrafted statement sets out the position under TCGA 1992 Sch 5 para 9(3) where the trustees make a loan on better than commercial terms. The case of other benefits provided by the trustees, e g provision of property on beneficial terms, would be subject to the same principles.

(f) TCGA 1992 Sch 5 para 9(3): failure to exercise rights to reimbursement

Paragraph 24

17 A settlor of a trust may be liable to income tax on income arising to the trustees under, for example, ICTA 1988 ss 672, 674, 674A. Other provisions (such as ICTA 1988 s 675(3)) give the settlor a right of recovery of that income tax from a trustee. It would be helpful if the statement of practice could confirm that a failure by the settlor to exercise such a right of recovery is not regarded as a breach of the TCGA 1992 Sch 5 para 9(3) condition. If this confirmation cannot be given, clarification is needed on how far the settlor would have to go to seek recovery before demonstrating that he had 'done his best' to obtain recovery from overseas trustees.

Revenue response: Paragraph 24 of the statement now covers the position where there is a failure to exercise rights to reimbursement against the settlement. Whether there had been a genuine, but unsuccessful attempt to enforce such rights could only be determined on the facts of the particular case.

18 Paragraph 24 of the statement of practice refers to the rights to reimbursement in ICTA 1988 ss 660–694. Could the Revenue please advise—

(a) when does the time limit for rights to reimbursement under ICTA 1988 ss 661, 667, 675(3), 685(5) expire;

(b) whether the Inland Revenue are operating a concession where the time limit expires after 18 March 1991 and, if so, the period during which the concessionary treatment is to apply.

Revenue response: The main point here is that the failure by the settlor to pursue his right to reimbursement within a reasonable period (and each case must be looked at in the light of its own facts) would, in itself, be a provision of property for the purposes of the settlement.

(g) TCGA 1992 Sch 5 para 9(3): administrative expenses

Paragraph 29

19 Paragraph 29 is rather unhelpful. The first alternative (ie payment of capital expenses out of income) would not normally be permitted where it is sought to have a qualifying interest in possession for inheritance tax purposes. The second alternative (the trustees borrowing money from the income account, which is subsequently restored with notional interest) requires further clarification. In particular, what does 'notional interest' mean? Does it give rise to a liability to income tax on the income beneficiary? In this context, it would also be helpful to have the Revenue's view as to whether such interest constitutes relevant income for the purposes of s 740.

Revenue response: I confirm that interest credited to the income account will constitute taxable income in the hands of the beneficiary (either when it is credited in the case of a life tenant, or when it is paid or applied for the benefit of a discretionary beneficiary). It would also be treated as 'relevant income' for ICTA 1988 s 740 purposes.

20 May we have confirmation that, where such a power exists and is exercised, then the Revenue will not regard the exercise as removing a qualifying interest in possession for inheritance tax purposes.

Revenue response: If the trust deed contains a power to pay capital expenses out of income, exercise of this power will not cause the trust to lose interest in possession status for inheritance tax purposes.

21 Where it becomes necessary to apply income to meet an expense on capital account for a year of assessment (see para 29 in the statement of practice), it of course follows that the income will not be available for distribution to the income beneficiary. Confirmation is sought that, in those circumstances, the income beneficiary is taxable only upon the amount of income, if any, which is available to be distributed to him. An income beneficiary is normally assessable upon the amount of trust income net of expenses charged against that income. If trustees properly apply trust income to meet a shortfall in respect of expenses on capital account relating to administration or taxation, the same reasoning should apply; the beneficiary should be taxed only upon that amount of income to which he is presently entitled. If that is correct, it would seem to follow that when the borrowing from income account is made good in a subsequent year, the relevant amount will become taxable upon the income beneficiary in that year. If the income that originally arose to the trustees had suffered deduction of tax at source, in either the UK or overseas, is credit to be given to the income beneficiary for such tax, when he becomes taxable upon the trust income in a later year?

Revenue response: I confirm that an income beneficiary will only be taxable on the net amount of income available after deduction of any income which has been applied to meet trust expenses on capital account and, when the income account is made good, that income will become taxable on the income beneficiary. The amount which is used to restore the income account is, however, no longer the same item as the income originally borrowed. It would not, therefore, retain the tax credit attached to the original income.

(*i*) *TCGA 1992 Sch 5 para 8*(*3*): *indemnities and guarantees*

Paragraph 35

22 Paragraph 35 of the statement of practice is causing concern. When a private company is being sold, and some or all of the shares in the private company are held by trustees of an offshore trust, it is normal for the purchaser to seek warranties and indemnities (at least in relation to tax) from all the vendors. Normally professional trustees will rightly resist the giving of warranties and indemnities by them, and if they give such warranties/ indemnities, trustees will normally require some protection such as—

(a) a counter indemnity from the other shareholders (if any), or the beneficiaries;

(b) a restriction on the liability of the trust to the assets held in the trust from time to time, whereas there would not be a similar restriction applying to other shareholders who are selling their shares.

The statement of practice does not address this issue, and we shall be grateful to have the Revenue's views on this.

Revenue response: A decision on the issues raised in this paragraph could only be made in the light of all the facts of a particular case. Our general approach however would be on the lines that where the trustees sought to limit their liability on the warranty or indemnity to the value of the trust assets, and the warranty or indemnity was in all other respects identical to that of other vendors, the para 9(3)(a) exception would be regarded as satisfied. But this would not be the case where the trust assets were not exposed to the same risk that the other vendors accept.

(j) TCGA 1992 Sch 5 para 9(5): variations

Paragraph 36

23 Clarification is sought as to whether the Revenue accept that if a trust power is extant before 19 March 1991 any (proper) exercise of that power by the donee will not taint that trust under TCGA 1992 Sch 5 para 9(5).

Revenue response: The practice outlined at para 36 would apply regardless of whether the power was exercisable by the trustees, or by or at the consent or nomination of some other person.

Other Matters

Charge on the settlor: other issues

24 There are a number of further important issues on TCGA 1992 s 86, Sch 5, where it would be helpful for the statement of practice to contain clarification. TCGA 1992 Sch 5 specifies the test as to whether the settlor has an interest. Each of sub-paragraphs 2(1)(a) and(b) uses the words 'may …in any circumstances whatever'. Interpreted literally, it appears virtually impossible to define a trust where the settlor does not have an interest, because any beneficiary may become a relative of the settlor as a result of subsequent marriages (or indeed subsequent births if necessary to imagine all conceivable possibilities). This issue has given rise to litigation in a different context (inheritance tax), and it would be helpful if the Inland Revenue could indicate their practice in this context.

Revenue response: If the terms of a settlement are so framed that a clearly defined person can benefit, e g the class of beneficiaries includes 'any spouse of the settlor' or 'spouses of the settlor's children', or such persons could be added to the class of beneficiaries, then the settlor will be treated as having an 'interest' in the trust. However, where there is no prima facie possibility of a defined person benefiting, the Revenue will not treat the settlor as having an 'interest', unless the terms of the settlement and the circumstances of the case indicate an intention to benefit a person who is likely to become a defined person in the future, e g a settlement in favour of the fiancé of the settlor or of the settlor's child.

25 Also on the question of whether a settlor has an interest in a trust, it would be helpful if the statement of practice could confirm that a separated spouse would not be regarded as the settlor's spouse for this purpose.

Revenue response: A separated spouse would be regarded as a spouse for the purposes of these provisions unless, in accordance with existing practice (see para 13(a) Appendix B of the Resident trusts consultative document [19 March 1991]) on other provisions having a bearing on 'settlor interest' trusts, the separation is permanent.

26 Finally on TCGA 1992 s 86, Sch 5, it would be helpful for the statement of practice to confirm that, in ascertaining the 'amount on which the trustees would be chargeable to tax' as specified in TCGA 1992 s 86(1)(e), the overseas trustees are entitled to make all normal claims and elections available to UK taxpayers.

Revenue response: The trustees are entitled to make all elections and claims where they meet the particular requirements of the legislation. We did not think it necessary to include this in the statement.

Appendix 3

Tax Bulletin Extracts

Tax Bulletin Issue 6, February 1993

Page 56. Capital gains tax: settlements—connected persons and losses

Where a loss accrues to a person on making a disposal to a connected person, under TCGA 1992 s 18(3) that loss may only be deducted from gains on other disposals by that person to the same connected person, unless exceptionally section 18(4) applies (gifts to certain associations).

We have been asked several questions about the application and interpretation of the rules in TCGA 1992 ss 18 and 286, in cases involving the trustees of settlements.

Are the settlor and the trustees connected at the moment when the settlement comes into existence and the initial property is transferred to the trustees?

Yes. Section 18(3) applies to a disposal which brings the settlement into existence. It is not restricted to situations where the parties are already connected before the disposal in question.

Are the trustees and beneficiaries connected after the settlor is dead?

No. If the settlor dies, the connection between the trustees and the relatives and spouse of the settlor is broken. Therefore if, for instance, the beneficiaries of the settlement are the children of the late settlor, the trustees are not connected with those beneficiaries, even if one or more of the children are trustees. The basic rule is that the trustees of a settlement are connected with the settlor, and also with any person connected with the settlor (TCGA 1992 s 286(3). Under TCGA 1992 s 69(1), the trustees are treated as a single and continuing body distinct from the persons who may be the trustees. Therefore in determining whether section 286(3) applies, the identity of the trustees is disregarded.

If the trustees and beneficiaries are connected, does this affect the transfer of losses under TCGA 1992 s 71(2)?

No. On legal advice, we no longer consider the transfer of losses from trustees to beneficiaries under section 71(2) to be inhibited by section 18(3). Therefore where a beneficiary becomes absolutely entitled against the trustees under TCGA 1992 s 71(1) all the unused losses which have arisen to the trustees in respect of property which is or is represented by the property to which the beneficiary becomes entitled, including any loss accruing on the deemed disposal to the beneficiary, are transferred to the beneficiary under section 71(2).

[TCGA 1992 ss 18, 69, 71 and 286]

Tax Bulletin Issue 8, August 1993

Page 82. Capital gains tax: non-resident trusts

A Statement of Practice (SP5/92) and an extra-statutory concession (ESC D41) were issued on 21 May 1992 concerning the provisions in the 1991 Finance Act which impose charges to Capital Gains Tax in respect of the gains of certain offshore trusts. This note offers some guidance on certain points in the Statement and concession.

Rights to reimbursement

Paragraph 24 of the Statement of Practice points out that failure to exercise statutory rights to reimbursement against non- resident trustees may be regarded as the provision of funds for the purposes of the settlement under TCGA 1992 Sch 5 para 9(3). This will not, however, apply in respect of a settlor's non- exercise of statutory rights to reimbursement out of the trust income account where the settlor has a life interest in all the assets of the trust. In such circumstances, failure to exercise the right to reimbursement would, effectively, not add funds to the trust since all income would, in any ease, either be paid to the settlor under the terms of the trust deed or be used to meet expenses chargeable against income.

But even in such cases the settlor may have rights to reimbursement out of the trust capital account, e g in relation to accrued income charges, which if not exercised will be regarded as the provision of funds.

Administrative expenses

Paragraph 29 of the Statement of Practice concerns, inter alia, trust deeds which permit capital expenses to be paid out of the income account. Neither the existence nor the exercise of this power would cause the trust to lose an interest in possession status for IHT purposes.

Where there is no such power, paragraph 29 states that capital expenses may nevertheless be met out of income without the condition in TCGA 1992 Sch 5 para 9(3) being met; provided that the income account is subsequently restored, along with appropriate interest over the period of the loan. The appropriate rate of interest is considered to be equal to the rate payable on the Basic Account administered by the Court Office of the Supreme Courts of

Justice. Such interest will constitute taxable income in the hands of the income beneficiary (either when it is credited in the case of a life tenant, or when it is paid or applied for the benefit of a discretionary beneficiary). It may also be treated as 'relevant income' for ICTA 1988 s 740 purposes.

Income beneficiaries will only be liable on the net amount of income available after deduction of any income which has been applied to meet expenses on capital account. Only when the income account is made good will that income become taxable on the beneficiary.

The original statement will be amended on these lines when it is published in the Statement of Practice booklet later this year.

ESC D41—Detailed points

ESC D41 allowed, inter alia, demand loans made to offshore trustees on better than commercial terms before 19 March 1991 to be put on commercial terms after that date. This enabled a trust to remain outside the condition in TCGA 1992 Sch 5 para 9(3). In order to meet the terms of this concession, it may have been necessary to pay a sum in lieu of interest in respect of periods ended 5 April 1992. Where this was the ease, such a payment would not have any IHT implications and it would qualify as a deduction both in determining the income of the life tenant and for the purposes of ICTA 1988 s 740, provided it was paid out of trust income.

Where the amount in lieu of interest was paid to a person who is not a beneficiary under the terms of the trust, it would nevertheless be treated as a capital payment to that individual under TCGA 1992 s 97. If the amount in lieu of interest was paid by a company underlying the trust, that payment would not qualify for a deduction from the profits of that company.

The payment of such an amount is not considered to trigger the provisions of ICTA 1988 Pt XV or s 739. Our view is that a person making a loan to the trustees on better than commercial terms is already a settlor and transferor and within the provisions of ICTA 1988 Pt XV or s 739(3).

Tax Bulletin Issue 13, October 1994

Page 162. Income tax and capital gains tax: exempt demergers—trustees and beneficiaries

1. Introduction

This article is about demergers and trusts. It looks at the treatment for income tax and capital gains tax purposes of trustees and beneficiaries where the trustees hold shares in a company which carries out an exempt demerger.

We have been asked about the tax treatment of exempt demergers where the shares in the distributing company are held by trustees. The answers vary according to the particular types of interest held by the beneficiaries and also the law which governs the trust.

2. What is a demerger?

A demerger is a series of transactions which has the effect and purpose of dividing the trading activities carried on by a single company or group of companies between two or more companies or groups of companies. ICTA 1988 s 213 and TCGA 1992 s 192 provide special tax treatment if certain conditions are met. Companies may seek advance clearance under ICTA 1988 s 215 from the Board of Inland Revenue that proposed transactions will be an exempt demerger.

3. What kinds of demergers are exempt?

Direct demergers

One type of demerger, which is referred to in this article as a 'direct demerger', falls within ICTA 1988 s 213(3)(a). A direct demerger occurs when

- a company ('the distributing company')
- makes a distribution to its members
- consisting of shares ('the demerged shares')
- in a company ('the demerged company')
- which is a 75% subsidiary of the distributing company.

Indirect demergers

Other types of demerger fall within ICTA 1988 s 213(3)(b). These are referred to in this article as 'indirect demergers'. An indirect demerger occurs when

- a company ('the distributing company')
- makes a distribution
- consisting of the transfer to one or more other companies ('the transferee company or companies') of

  (a) a trade or trades, or

  (b) shares in one or more 75% subsidiaries

  and
- shares ('the issued shares') are issued by the transferee company or companies to shareholders of the distributing company.

4. What is the advance corporation tax and income tax treatment of exempt demergers?

Where there is an exempt demerger, the distribution of the shares of the demerged company in a direct demerger (or the issue of shares by a transferee company in an indirect demerger) is not a distribution by the distributing company for the purposes of advance corporation tax and it is not Schedule F income of the shareholders.

Therefore there is no income tax liability on the shareholders in respect of the receipt of the demerged or issued shares. In certain cases there may however be liabilities under ICTA 1988 s 687 or Case III of Schedule D where the shares or their cash equivalent are distributed as income to beneficiaries (see paragraphs 15 and 17 below).

5. What is the usual capital gains tax treatment of direct demergers?

Company

The fact that the distribution is an exempt demerger does not affect the determination of the company's liability to tax on any chargeable gain arising on the disposal (by distribution) of the shares in the demerged company.

Shareholders

Where persons receive the demerged shares there is no immediate chargeable gain or allowable loss. The distribution is not treated for capital gains tax purposes as a capital distribution. Instead the distributing company shares and the demerged company shares are treated as a single asset acquired when the distributing company shares were acquired (TCGA 1992 s 127, as applied by TCGA 1992 s 192). If a shareholder then sells shares in either of the companies, the original cost of the shares in the distributing company is apportioned between the shares in the distributing company and the shares in the demerged company

- in the case of a quoted company, by reference to the respective values on the first day on which the demerged shares were quoted (TCGA 1992 s 130);
- in other cases, by reference to the respective values at the date of the disposal (TCGA 1992 s 129).

6. What is the usual capital gains tax treatment of indirect demergers?

Company

The transfer of shares or other assets by the distributing company to the transferee company, provided certain conditions are met, is treated as taking place at no gain and no loss (TCGA 1992 s 139).

Shareholders

The transactions normally amount to a reconstruction within TCGA 1992 s 136. See also Statement of Practice SP5/85. The distributing company shares and the issued shares are treated as a single asset in the way described in the previous paragraph, which applies for a direct demerger.

Companies may apply to the Board for clearance under TCGA 1992 ss 138 and 139.

7. Tax treatment: introduction

The rest of this article looks first at the capital gains tax treatment and then at the income tax treatment of exempt demergers where shares are held by trustees.

8. Are the demerged or issued shares capital or income in the hands of the trustees?

The question whether the demerged or issued shares are capital or income of the trust falls to be determined in accordance with the general principles of trust law. The trustees will need to consider the position in the light of all the facts and circumstances.

In the case of a direct demerger we take the view that the demerged shares are received by the trustees as income of the trust, because as a matter of company law they take the form of a dividend paid out of the accumulated profits of the distributing company. This follows principles laid down by Lord Russell of Killowen in the case of *Hill v Permanent Trustee Co of New South Wales* [1930] AC 720 at pages 730–732 in the Privy Council. This case strictly concerned the law of New South Wales, but the principles have been followed by courts in England and Scotland. Because the demerger takes the form of a dividend, the demerged shares are received by the trustees as income for trust purposes.

In the case of an indirect demerger we take the view that, in general, the issued shares are received as an addition to capital. This follows the High Court decision in *Sinclair v Lee* [1993] Ch 497. The court held that the shares to be distributed in the proposed indirect demerger of ICI would be received by the trustees as capital and not as income. The court was dealing with the specific case where the value of the issued shares was over 50% of the value of ICI before the demerger. The decision is not necessarily applicable to all cases involving indirect demergers.

CAPITAL GAINS TAX TREATMENT

9. Shares received as capital: direct demergers

Where, exceptionally, the demerged shares are received by the trustees as capital, or where they are subject to a power of accumulation and become additions to capital, the trustees fall to be treated for capital gains tax purposes in the same way as an individual (see paragraph 5 above).

10. Shares received as capital: indirect demergers

Provided that the issued shares are received as capital, in the case of an indirect demerger, trustees of all kinds are treated for capital gains tax purposes in the same way as individuals. If, exceptionally, the shares are received as income of the trust, then see paragraph 12, particularly the end.

11. Discretionary trusts

Trustees of a discretionary trust are treated for capital gains tax purposes in the same way as individuals (see paragraphs 5 and 6 above). If however they then distribute the demerged (or issued) shares to one or more beneficiaries, there is a disposal of those shares at market value. The chargeable gain or allowable loss is the market value of the shares at the date of distribution, less the appropriate fraction of the original cost of the distributing company shares, apportioned in accordance with paragraph 5 above, less indexation from the date of the original acquisition of the shares in the distributing company. If the shares are income in the hands of the beneficiary that does not affect the computation of the trustees' chargeable gain (see paragraph 18 for the income tax treatment in these circumstances).

Example

Trustees acquire shares in a quoted company X Ltd for £5,000. In due course X Ltd distributes shares in its subsidiary Y Ltd in a direct demerger. The respective values of the holdings at the first date of quotation of the shares in Y Ltd are X Ltd £18,000, Y Ltd £6,000.

The trustees subsequently distribute their shares in Y Ltd to the beneficiaries when their value is £8,000. The allowable expenditure in respect of the Y Ltd shares is

£6,000 × £5,000 = £1,250. £18,000 + £6,000

The chargeable gain is therefore—

Deemed proceeds £8,000

Apportioned cost (£1,250)

Gain £6,750

less indexation on £1,250 calculated from the date on which the X Ltd shares were originally acquired.

12. Shares received as income: English life tenant trusts

In the case of a direct demerger, if the demerged shares are income of the trust, the life tenant (or any other person with an interest in possession) of a trust governed by English Law is immediately entitled to those shares, subject to the right of trustees to meet their expenses. This follows the decision of the

House of Lords in *Archer-Shee v Baker* (1927) 11 TC 749. The shares are therefore never settled property for capital gains tax purposes, and there is no disposal for capital gains tax purposes from the trustees to the life tenant. The allowable cost to the life tenant for any future disposal is the market value of the demerged shares at the date of the distribution, by reason of TCGA 1992 s 17(1), the disposal by the company being the corresponding disposal for the purposes of section 17(2). Practitioners may note that this reflects a change in our thinking. As far as the trustees are concerned, the allowable cost of the shares in the distributing company, which they continue to hold, is unaffected by the demerger.

If the trustees retain the demerged shares, then there has been a disposal by the life tenant to the trustees, and unless the life tenant has been paid the cash value of the shares, he or she is the settlor of them.

If exceptionally there has been an indirect demerger in such circumstances that the issued shares are received as income, the above applies with one difference; because these shares are issued by the transferee company, there is no corresponding disposal and therefore TCGA 1992 s 17 does not apply, and the cost to the life tenant is therefore nil.

13. Shares received as income: Scots liferenter trusts

If the demerged or issued shares are income of a trust governed by Scots Law, however, the position differs. The liferenter (or person with a similar interest in possession) of a trust governed by Scots Law is not immediately entitled to the shares. The right of a liferenter is a personal right to compel the trustees to administer the trust in accordance with the directions of the settler. If the trustees decide to distribute the shares to the liferenter, rather than the cash equivalent, then there is for capital gains tax purposes a disposal by them at market value, and the chargeable gain would fall to be computed in accordance with paragraph 11 above. Although FA 1993 s 118 affected the position for income tax purposes, see paragraph 17, it does not apply for capital gains tax purposes.

14. Other interest in possession trusts

If a trust is governed by neither English nor Scots Law, then the trustees will need to consider the precise interests of the person or persons with an interest in possession. If that person is immediately entitled to the demerged or issued shares, then the trustees and beneficiary fall to be treated in accordance with paragraph 12 above. If, on the other hand, the rights of the beneficiary are similar to those of the taxpayer in *Garland v Archer-Shee* (1931) 15 TC 693 then the trustees and beneficiary fall to be treated in exactly the same way as those of liferenter trusts under paragraph 10 above. The Board will regard trusts established under the Law of Northern Ireland as subject to the same principles as apply to English trusts.

INCOME TAX TREATMENT

15. Introduction

Paragraphs 16–19 are written on the assumption that demerged shares are received as income by the trustees. If exceptionally issued shares are received as income, then the same principles apply. If the shares are received as capital by the trustees:

- no charge to income tax arises on the trustees (ICTA 1988 s 213), and
- paragraphs 16 and 17 do not apply.

Capital received by trustees is not normally distributed under a trust power over income. This may occur at times, (e g where the terms of the trust require or permit capital to be used to augment income distributions), but such situations will be rare.

If they occur, the distribution by the trustees could be annual payments under ICTA 1988 s 349 or, in the case of a discretionary power, ICTA 1988 s 687. The exemption under ICTA 1988 s 213 will not carry through to such distributions.

16. English life tenant trusts

Where under English Law beneficiaries have a life interest or other vested interest in possession in the income of a trust (but not in its capital), shares distributed in a demerger which are income belong to the beneficiary or beneficiaries. No income tax will be charged on that 'income' because of the exemption in ICTA 1988 s 213; nor will liability arise on the trustees under ICTA 1988 ss 686, 687 as they do not have power to accumulate the income within the trust or pay it out at their discretion.

17. Scots liferenter trusts

Under Scots Law, the income of an interest in possession trust arises to the trustees and the liferenter is only entitled to call for an accounting by the trustees for that income. But FA 1993 s 118 deems the life renter to have a right, equivalent to the equitable right in possession enjoyed under English Law, to the income as it arises. This means that Scots liferenters will be treated as receiving income which is exempt under ICTA 1988 s 213 as described in paragraph 16.

18. Discretionary/accumulation trusts

Where there are no vested interests in possession in the trust income, the trustees receive the demerged shares as 'income' exempted from charge to income tax by ICTA 1988 s 213. What happens then depends on the terms of the trust. The trustees may have been given power to distribute the trust income to individual beneficiaries or to a class or classes of beneficiaries at their discretion. They may also be given power to accumulate that income and convert it into additional capital of the trust fund. If so, they have a choice either to:

- accumulate the income as part of the trust fund and then distribute it as capital among the capital beneficiaries (there will not normally be a charge to income tax on those beneficiaries in these circumstances); or
- distribute it as income amongst the income beneficiaries, without exercising the power to accumulate (these beneficiaries will then be liable to income tax on the trust income they receive, but will receive it after deduction of basic rate and additional rate tax (from 6 April 1993, taxed at the rate applicable to Trusts)); or
- accumulate part of the trust income and distribute the other part of it as income to the income beneficiaries. (Each part will then be dealt with according to whether it has become capital, or remained as income.)

Where an income distribution is made by the trustees, they will need to take account of ICTA 1988 ss 686 and 687. Since the demerged shares were exempted from income tax under section 213, they will not have been included in trust income assessed under ICTA 1988 s 686. Liability may therefore arise under section 687 when the income is paid out by the trustees to income beneficiaries. Where the actual shares are distributed to the income beneficiaries by the trustees, their net value for section 687 purposes (before grossing at basic/additional rate or the rate applicable to trusts) would be the lesser of their value at the date of distribution in the demerger to the trustees or at the date of distribution by the trustees to the beneficiaries.

19. Mixed settlements

Where part of the income of a trust vests in a beneficiary or beneficiaries as it arises, and the remainder is payable at the trustees' discretion, the demerged shares will need to be apportioned. The above procedures should then be applied to the appropriate portion.

[ICTA 1988 ss 53, 213, 215, 348, 349, 686 and 687. TCGA 1992 s 17, 127, 129, 130, 136, 138, 139 and 192. FA 1993 s 118

Tax Bulletin Issue 16, April 1995

Page 204. Capital gains tax: non-resident trusts

Tax Bulletin Issue 8 (August 1993) contained guidance on Statement of Practice (SP) 5/92 on pages 82 and 83. Since that article was published we have been asked to give further guidance on that Statement of Practice and on the provisions in FA 1991 concerning the taxation of non-resident trusts. This article offers additional guidance on some of the questions raised.

Settlements

TCGA 1992 s 97(7) imports ICTA 1988 Pt XV definition of 'settlement' for the purposes of the beneficiary charge in TCGA 1992 s 87. Case law has demonstrated that an element of bounty is needed for there to be a settlement within the above definition.

TCGA 1992 Sch 5 para 7 and 8 identify 'settlors' for the purposes of the settlor charge in section 86 of that Act. Paragraph 8(1)(a) refers to property 'provided'. The case of *CIR v Leiner* (1964) 41 TC at page 596 indicates that the word 'provided' must connote 'bounty' in appropriate circumstances.

Therefore, it is accepted that a trust devoid of bounty is not within either the settlor or beneficiary charge legislation. An example would be a genuine commercial arrangement by a company to attract, retain and motivate good quality staff.

Arm's length transactions

Paragraphs 12–15 of SP5/92 cover arm's length transactions. A number of commentators have observed that the 'adjuster clause' suggested in paragraphs 13 and 14 would not be a feature of a normal arm's length transaction. However, its inclusion in appropriate circumstances brings the certainty that the Revenue will not argue that value has been added to the trust provided all necessary steps have been taken. In the absence of such a clause it is always open to the parties concerned to demonstrate that the transaction was on arm's length terms, but it might be more difficult for them to do so.

'One-way' adjuster clauses are satisfactory, provided that the parties are not concerned that they might face a claim that a 'capital payment' had been made by the trustees if more passed out of the trust than was received in return.

Transactions with companies

Paragraphs 16 and 17 of SP5/92 cover certain transactions with companies in which the trustees are participators. Where the trustees hold a large stake in the company, it is almost inevitable that what benefits the company benefits the trust. So the practice described in paragraph 16 of SP5/92 is only likely to be appropriate where the trustees hold a relatively small proportion of the company's issued share capital.

Paragraph 18 of SP5/92 deals with transactions between trustees and any companies they wholly own. The principle underlying that paragraph may also apply in other very limited circumstances where the whole of a company's issued share capital is owned by two or more trusts. However, for this to be so an identical transaction must take place at the same time between the company and each trust and there must be no shift of value from one trust to another.

Trust expenses

The article in Tax Bulletin Issue 8 stated that the appropriate rate of interest for the purposes of paragraph 29 of SP5/92 is considered to be equal to the rate payable on the Basic Account administered by the Court Office of the Supreme Courts of Justice. Only simple interest need be credited.

It is questionable whether a trustee's annual fee should be charged wholly against income. However, if no part of that fee is identifiable as relating to specific duties of a capital nature and it has been the practice to so charge the fee, the Revenue will raise no objection provided this practice is consistently followed.

Guarantees, warranties etc

These are referred to in paragraphs 34 and 35 of SP5/92. Little can be added by way of general guidance as each case needs to be looked at in the light of its own particular facts. However questions which may help to identify potential difficulties in appropriate circumstances are:

Will the giving of the guarantee, warranty etc. by a third party enable the trustees to obtain a better price for what they are selling than would otherwise be the case? Indeed, without that guarantee etc, would the sale go through at all? Are the trust assets to be exposed to the same degree of risk that other vendors will have to accept?

Tainting

Amongst the many situations that the Revenue would regard as satisfying the condition in TCGA 1992 Sch 5 para 9(3), the following are included:

(a) A transfer (on other than arm's length terms) from one settlement to another.

(b) Improvements to a property owned by the trustees, or by an underlying company, paid for by the tenant for which he is not fully reimbursed by those trustees or company as the case may be.

(c) Provision of services to the trustees, or their underlying company, on other than arm's length terms.

(d) Additions to meet liability to interest on unpaid tax that has accrued since 18 March 1991, where the protection of the proviso to TCGA 1992 Sch 5 para 9(3), is not available. Liability to interest on unpaid tax accrues daily.

Enhanced scrip dividends

SP4/94 explains the tax treatment where the trustees of an interest in possession settlement treat enhanced scrip dividends as either wholly capital, or wholly income, or wholly capital but with a compensating payment to the life tenant. It is for the trustees to decide which course to adopt, in the light of advice as to the correct position in trust law in the particular circumstances of the case. Where trustees act in accordance with that advice, the Revenue will not contend that the trust has become tainted solely because they followed that advice.

Company buying own shares

Where payments made by a company on the redemption, repayment or purchase of its own shares are treated as distributions for corporation tax purposes, because the conditions as to residence etc. in ICTA 1988 s 220 are not satisfied, those payments are regarded as 'income arising under a settlement' within section 681. They will therefore be treated as the settlor's income in appropriate cases.

Despite this, the receipts are capital in the trustees' hands. Therefore, if the trust is not to become tainted, the settlor must claim reimbursement of the extra tax he pays even if he is life tenant of the trust—see page 83 of Tax Bulletin Issue 8.

Where a settlor has thus been taxable on the deemed distribution and a payment is made to him in the same year of assessment which is clearly identifiable with the proceeds of the redemption, repayment or purchase, the Revenue will not regard it as falling within the definition of a 'capital payment' for the purposes of TCGA 1992 s 87.

Increase in tax

TCGA 1992 s 91 imposes an increase in tax on liabilities arising under TCGA 1992 s 87 for 1992–93 onwards. For the purpose of calculating such an increase, the gains assessable under TCGA 1992 s 87 are taken to be the lowest slice of the beneficiary's total capital gains for the year.

Benefits to companies

TCGA 1992 s 96 contains rules for attributing benefit where a 'capital payment' is received by a non-resident close company. However, there is no corresponding rule for benefits received by a company resident in the UK. Therefore, such a company receiving a benefit must be treated as a beneficiary of the trust in accordance with TCGA 1992 s 97(8) and can thus have chargeable gains attributed to it under TCGA 1992 s 87.

Page 205. Self-assessment: electronic lodgement system

This year's Finance Bill introduces new provisions to establish an electronic lodgement service (ELS). ELS is being set up to enable the information in respect of certain tax returns to be transmitted to the Inland Revenue by electronic means. We intend to make the service available initially to accept the self-assessment returns issued from April 1997 onwards. We will be looking at the potential to develop the system to handle other returns and documents later.

ELS will enable approved persons (filers) to make use of the latest communications technology to do away with the need to send paper returns. Transmitting returns by ELS will also be much quicker than by post, and will provide agent and taxpayer alike with the certain knowledge that the information has been properly received by the Revenue. In addition, the technology will provide tight security, giving taxpayers the confidence that unauthorised persons will not be able to gain access to information transmitted in this way.

In order to use the system, filers will need enhanced tax return software to enable information on their computer system to be transmitted electronically to the Inland Revenue computer system via a Secure Messaging Gateway. The transmission process will include checks to identify particular errors in the return information and to ensure that they are corrected before the information is accepted on the Inland Revenue's computer system. Once the information is accepted, an automatic acknowledgement will be sent to assure the filer that the return has been successfully lodged.

The legislation provides that the statutory requirement to deliver a return to the Inland Revenue will be deemed to be fulfilled where the relevant information is transmitted electronically and certain conditions are met. These are that—

- the person filing the information is approved to do so,
- the manner of transmission meets the Inland Revenue requirements,
- a hard copy of the information is authenticated by the taxpayer, and
- the formal acceptance of the information is issued by the Inland Revenue.

In response to concerns about the effect on a potential filer of the Revenue's refusal to grant approval, the Government have accepted the need for an appeals procedure. This has now been provided by amendment to the Finance Bill legislation. The Revenue are keen for the system to be widely available, and it is likely that the vast majority of those applying for approval would be successful.

A further amendment to the Finance Bill has removed the requirement for the hard copy to be made shortly before the information is transmitted. Instead, the manner of transmission will include a requirement to supply the date on which the taxpayer authenticated the hard copy.

A trial of the system has been carried out since November last year, and is due to be evaluated shortly. The early results from an interim evaluation report prepared jointly by the Revenue and participants in the trial are encouraging, and demonstrate the viability of the proposed approach to ELS. The results of the trial will be published in due course.

Although the trial was conducted using the Corporation Tax return, ELS will not be made available for the live transmission of these returns for the foreseeable future. This is because the Revenue cannot dispense with the need for company accounts to be submitted, in view of their greater complexity compared to income tax accounts, and at present there is no information technology support to transmit such data. Those involved in consultations on the project have made it clear that unless all the information associated with a return can be transmitted electronically they would have little use for the system.

There are benefits to be gained by the taxpayer and agent in filing electronically, including the greater certainty of lodgement of the return and improvements in the overall efficiency of their operations. We will continue to look at additional ways of making the system attractive to potential users, for example by providing a two-way flow of information, as well as allowing more prompt processing of repayments. But the option of filing returns by paper in the traditional way will of course remain.

We will continue to consult on the development of ELS and will provide in due course further details on the requirements and procedures which are expected to be incorporated into the ELS system.

Tax Bulletin Issue 26, December 1996

Page 373. Trusts—liability at the rate applicable to trusts

We have found that some trustees have wrongly completed returns in the belief that they were liable under ICTA 1988 s 686 to tax at the rate applicable to trusts when they were in fact liable only at the lower or basic rate. The purpose of this article is to help trustees identify any trusts where they may have done this.

Where trustees have powers to pay income at their discretion or to accumulate it, they will generally be liable at the rate applicable to trusts under ICTA 1988 s 686(1). The rate applicable to trusts is 35% for 1995–96 and 34% for 1996–97. However, if the income belongs before distribution to some person other than the trustees, then the trustees will be chargeable only at the basic or lower rate of tax as the persons receiving the income.

The trusts affected are those where a beneficiary has an indefeasibly vested interest in the capital and there is no other person entitled to receive the income. A beneficiary will have an indefeasibly vested interest in capital where he/she has a complete right to receive it without having to satisfy any conditions. When such a beneficiary dies, any income remaining in the hands of the trustees at that date will fall into the beneficiary's estate. It is clear from dicta in the case of *Stanley v CIR* ((1944) 26 TC 12) that income arising to the trust in such circumstances is to be treated as the beneficiary's income so long as he or she is alive. Such income is therefore outside the scope of ICTA 1988 s 686(1) and is not chargeable at the rate applicable to trusts.

This does not apply where a minor beneficiary has a vested interest in income, but not capital, under the law of England and Wales or Northern Ireland. In these circumstances, Trustees Act 1925 s 31 (or its Northern Ireland equivalent) prevents the beneficiary from being entitled to the income as it arises (unless there is some contrary intention expressed in the instrument which creates the interest), and the income is correctly chargeable at the rate applicable to trusts.

Any trustees who think they may have been wrongly assessed and have overpaid tax, because, for example, income over which they had a discretion belonged to the beneficiary, should make a claim for error or mistake relief (subject to the statutory time limit which is 6 years after the end of the year of assessment in which the assessment was made) to their local Trust Office enclosing the trust deed.

[ICTA 1988 s 686]

Page 374. Tax relief for trustees on mineral leases and timber cropping

Under the terms of section 47 of the Settled Land Act (SLA) 1925 a proportion of the rent arising from a mineral lease is allocated to capital. The proportion depends on whether or not the tenant for life is impeachable for waste—in broad terms, whether the tenant is liable to make good any damage caused to the land. There are similar provisions in SLA 1925 s 66 which where a tenant for life sells timber that is ripe and fit for cutting, requires that a proportion of the net proceeds be allocated to capital where the tenant for life is impeachable for waste.

Since the introduction of what is now ICTA 1988 s 686 we have taken the view that the provision for capitalisation in SLA 1925 ss 47 and 66 was an accumulation for the purposes of ICTA 1988 s 686. The effect is that such capitalised income has been charged to tax at what is now the rate applicable to trusts. This view has generally been accepted as being correct.

In the light of recent legal advice, we now accept that the provision for capitalisation in SLA 1925 ss 47 and 66 is not an accumulation for the purposes of ICTA 1988 s 686. We will therefore settle future liabilities on that basis and also deal with any unsettled liabilities in the same way. We do not intend re-opening settled liabilities which were agreed in accordance with the prevailing accepted practice at the time.

[SLA 1925 s 47 and 66 and ICTA 1988 s 686]

Tax Bulletin Issue 27, February 1997

Page 395. Self-assessment: the tax obligations of trustees and beneficiaries of bare trusts

The beneficiaries of certain types of bare trusts must ensure that if they are within self-assessment, all trust income and gains are included in their personal tax returns and any income tax or capital gains tax due, accounted for.

A 'bare trust', also known as a 'simple trust', exists where the beneficial owner of the property is fully entitled to both the capital and income from that property. The property will be held in the name of the trustee, but the trustee will have no discretion over what income to pay the beneficiary. The trustee is in effect a nominee in whose name the property is held. The beneficial owner is the person who benefits from, and is entitled to, the property and any income it produces.

Prior to 6 April 1996, trustees of some bare trusts did in certain situations, deduct and account for tax on trust income received gross. These amounts then became taxed income in the hands of the beneficiaries, and further liability only arose if they were higher rate taxpayers. If however they had no personal liability a repayment would be due.

Under self-assessment, the Inland Revenue will no longer expect trustees to account for tax in such circumstances, because there is no entitlement in law for trustees to deduct tax from income arising to bare trusts. Any income which is received gross by the trustees must be paid gross to the beneficiaries. The only exception to this rule is that UK resident trustees may be required under the Non Resident Landlords Scheme to deduct and account for tax on the rental income of beneficiaries whose usual place of abode is outside the UK.

Trustees of bare trusts will not be required to complete self-assessment tax returns, or to make payments on account. Beneficiaries will still be required to give details of all their income and gains from bare trusts in their own tax returns and in addition, will be required to account to the Inland Revenue for the full amount of any tax due.

Although the Inland Revenue are endeavouring to identify those bare trusts where trustees have previously made annual returns and accounted for tax, in order to notify them of this change, there will be some cases which will not be recognised in time to prevent the 1996–97 payment on account notices and self-assessment tax returns from being issued to the trustees.

Any trustees receiving a payment on account notice should return it to the issuing Trust Office with a brief explanation so that the records can be amended. Any trustees receiving a self-assessment tax return after 6 April 1997 should complete the final three questions on the return form in accordance with the notes given in Step 1 on the form.

There are a number of collective investment schemes which are constituted as bare trusts, but only two kinds of them are treated as such for tax purposes. These are Enterprise Zone Property Unit Trusts (EZPUTs), and Pension Fund Pooling Vehicles (PFPVs). The trustees of such schemes will not receive self-assessment tax returns. That is because the income and gains which arise under EZPUTs and PFPVs belong to the unit holders of the schemes and if any expenditure is incurred by the trustees which gives rise to capital allowances, those allowances are made to the unit holders and not the trustees.

The trustees of EZPUTs and PFPVs will, however, remain responsible for agreeing the amounts of the schemes' income, profits, gains, capital expenditure, capital allowances, and balancing adjustments with their own tax Inspectors in accordance with the rules laid down in the relevant Income Tax Regulations and for providing the unit holders of the schemes with certificates giving details of the parts of those amounts that are, in each case, attributable to them.

Page 398. Inheritance tax (IHT): excluded property settlements by people domiciled overseas

We have been asked how the IHT provisions on excluded property apply to the assets of a settlement made by a person domiciled overseas where:

- all, or only some, of the settled assets are situated outside the UK when a chargeable event occurs; or
- a person domiciled in the UK has also provided property or funds for the purposes of that settlement.

References in this article are to sections of the Inheritance Tax Act 1984.

Excluded property

For persons domiciled abroad, IHT generally applies only to their UK assets; it treats their overseas assets as excluded property, that is: not within the charge to IHT—s 6(1)). For assets owned outright, it is the owner's domicile at the time of a tax charge that is relevant in deciding whether or not the assets are excluded property.

Slightly different rules apply to property held in a settlement. An asset is excluded property if it is situated abroad when a chargeable event occurs and if the settlor (defined in s 44) was domiciled outside the UK at the time the settlement was made—s 48(3).

However, an 'excluded' asset is not always completely irrelevant for the purposes of IHT. So:

- an 'excluded' asset in a person's estate may still affect the valuation of another asset in the estate, for example, an 'excluded' holding of shares in an unquoted company may affect the value of a similar holding in the estate which is not 'excluded';

- the value of an 'excluded' asset at the time the asset becomes comprised in a settlement may be relevant in determining the rate of any tax charge arising in respect of the settlement under the IHT rules concerning trusts without interests in possession—sections 68(5), 66(4) and 69(3).

Domicile is a concept of general law but, in certain circumstances (s 267), a person with a general law domicile abroad can be treated as having a UK domicile for IHT purposes.

Settlor adds assets to his/her existing settlement

In the light of the definitions of 'settlement' and 'settled property' in s 43, our view is that a settlement in relation to any particular asset is made at the time when that asset is transferred to the settlement trustees to hold on the declared trusts. Thus, assets added to a settlor's own settlement made at an earlier time when the settlor was domiciled abroad will not be 'excluded', wherever they may be situated, if the settlor has a UK domicile at the time of making the addition.

In determining the tax treatment of particular assets held in the same settlement it may, therefore, be necessary to consider the settlor's domicile at times other than when the settlement was first made. And if assets added at different times have become mixed, any dealings with the settled fund after the addition(s) may also need to be considered.

Several persons contribute to a single settlement

There are rules (s 44(2)) which provide that assets contributed to a 'single' settlement by more than one settlor are to be treated as comprised in separate settlements for IHT purposes if 'the circumstances so require'. There is no definition of 'required circumstances' or statutory guidance on how the assets in the single, actual settlement are to be attributed to the deemed separate settlements.

However, the provision is similar in terms to FA 1975 Sch 5 para 1(8), which was considered by Chadwick J in *Hatton v IRC* [1992] STC 140. In the light of the decision in that case we take the view

- that the determination of the extent to which overseas assets in a settlement are excluded property by reason of the settlor's domicile is a relevant 'required circumstance'; and
- that
  - where a clear, or reasonably sensible, attribution of settled property between the contributions made by several settlors is possible, there will be a separate settlement, with its own attributed assets, for each contributor for IHT purposes;
  - if such an attribution is not feasible, each separate settlement will comprise all the assets of the single, actual settlement.

Trust records

It follows from the comments above that the trustees of a settlement should keep adequate records to enable any necessary attribution of the settled property to be made if either

- the settlor has added further assets to the settlement after it was made; or
- two or more persons have contributed funds for the purposes of the settlement.

[IHTA 1984 ss 43, 44 and 48 *Hatton v IRC* [1992] STC 140]

Page 399. Schedule D Cases I & II: employee share ownership trusts

This article considers the treatment of an employer's contributions to an Employee Share Ownership Trust (ESOT). It is concerned with situations where:

- the trust is not a statutory ESOT, that is it is not one set up in terms of FA 1989 ss 67 and 74 and Sch 5;
- applying ordinary Schedule D Case I/II principles, contributions are revenue in character (not capital);
- normal accounting practice requires Urgent Issues Task Force abstract No 13 (UITF 13) to be applied to treat the making of the contributions as giving rise to an asset in the employer's accounts.

We have been asked to say how contributions made by an employer in these circumstances should be dealt with for tax purposes.

Background

An ESOT is part of the mechanism to give effect to an Employee Share Ownership Plan (ESOP), which has been defined—loosely—as an arrangement whereby an employee benefit trust (the ESOT) acquires a substantial quantity of employer shares or securities for subsequent distribution to some or all employees, with financial assistance provided directly or indirectly by the employer.

Urgent Issues Task Force abstract No 13 (UITF13—Accounting for ESOP Trusts) explains how Financial Reporting Standard No 5 (FRS 5: Reporting the Substance of Transactions) applies to ESOTs. It is beyond the scope of this article to set out in detail the guidance in the UITF. But very briefly, under it, cash held and shares purchased by the trustees will normally remain assets of the employer for accounting purposes (in accordance with the definition of an asset in FRS 5) until the rights in the shares are transferred to employees. Consequently contributions to the trust by the employer will not necessarily be charged against profits as they fall due but in an earlier or later period.

Our view

As a matter of general Case I computational principle it is well established that:

- the starting point for the computation of taxable profits is the accounts of a trader drawn up in accordance with normal accounting practice;
- the profits shown by those accounts are then adjusted to give effect to specific statutory rules or to more general principles, derived by the courts from the need to compute 'the full amount of the profits or gains' (ICTA 1988 ss 60 and 70).

Unlike statutory ESOTs—for which FA 1989 s 67 guarantees a Schedule D Case 1 deduction at the time of the company's contribution to the trustees, no specific statutory rules apply to contributions to non-statutory ESOTs.

Unless therefore, the treatment in the accounts is over-ridden by such a tax rule, it is followed in computing taxable profit. The point at issue here is whether the time at which contributions to 'non-statutory' ESOTs are charged against profits under UITF 13 is overridden by some general tax principle.

Recent cases show that the courts are nowadays reluctant to discern general tax principles which override the time when income and expenses are recognised in accounts drawn up in accordance with normal commercial practice. See *Threlfall v Jones* ((1993) 66 TC 77) and *Johnston v Britannia Airways Ltd* ((1994) 67 TC 99).

We consider that no such principle overrides the accounting treatment required by UITF 13. In particular, the Court of Appeal judgements in Threlfall make it clear that there is no general tax principle that an expense should necessarily be deducted for tax when it is incurred or paid. Nor, in our view, should UITF 13 be over-ridden for timing purposes on the grounds that it strays too far from the legal form of the transactions. A similar contention, that Statement of Standard Accounting Practice 21 (Accounting for leases and hire purchase contracts) should not be followed because it treated the hiring of an asset as a loan, failed in *Threlfall* ((1993) 66 TC at 126I–127F).

By the same token, no general tax principle derived from case-law would, in our view, prevent a deduction for a properly calculated provision included in an employer's trading accounts for a period in respect of future contributions to an ESOT to reflect employees' accruing entitlement to benefits in that period.

[*Threlfall v Jones* ((1993) 66 TC 77) and *Johnston v Britannia Airways Ltd* ((1994) 67 TC 99)]

Tax Bulletin Issue 32, December 1997

Page 486. Self-assessment—the tax obligations of trustees and beneficiaries of bare trusts

In the Tax Bulletin Issue 27 (February 1997 page 395) we explained the Revenue's approach to the taxation of bare trusts, ie trusts where the beneficial owner of the trust property is absolutely entitled to both the capital and income from that property. We said that the trustees of bare trusts would not be required to complete self-assessment tax returns, or to make payments on account. That remains the Department's position, and we think that the approach set out in the article will simplify the tax affairs of most bare trustees and beneficiaries under self-assessment.

Following discussions with representative bodies, we now accept that the trustees of bare trusts are entitled to make a self-assessment return of income, but not of capital gains, and to account for tax on it at the appropriate rate. In those cases where the trustees of bare trusts wish to make a return, the appropriate rate of tax will be at basic rate (or lower rate, if the income is savings income). It is emphasised that capital gains and capital losses must NOT be included on any self-assessment return made by a bare trustee. These remain the sole responsibility of the beneficiaries.

If the trustees and all the beneficiaries of a bare trust wish to follow this course of action they should notify the trust district dealing with the trust's tax affairs as soon as possible. We will expect them to follow this course consistently year on year.

Where the trustees of bare trusts do not notify the trust district that they wish to make a return of income and to pay tax, those trustees and their beneficiaries will be dealt with in accordance with the article in Issue 27 of Tax Bulletin. We expect the great majority of bare trustees to fall into this category, as it is only in relatively unusual circumstances that it will be more convenient for the trustees to self- assess. Whether or not the trustees decide to self-assess and account for tax, the beneficiaries of these trusts remain within self-assessment and are obliged to notify the Inland Revenue of their income and gains.

Tax Bulletin Issue 36, August 1998

Page 573. Capital payments by offshore trusts to UK resident charities: change in Inland Revenue practice

Following recent legal advice the Inland Revenue are changing their practice on the capital gains tax treatment of capital payments by offshore trusts to UK charities.

Under the provisions of TCGA 1992 s 87, where gains have been realised by the trustees of an offshore settlement, chargeable gains may be treated as accruing to beneficiaries who are resident in the United Kingdom to the extent that they receive capital payments from the trust.

Under TCGA 1992 s 256, gains accruing to charities are not chargeable to tax if they are applicable and applied for charitable purposes. Until now, however, the Inland Revenue have always taken the view that this exemption is not available for gains which are treated by TCGA 1992 s 87 as accruing to a charity as the beneficiary of an offshore settlement.

Following recent representations on the matter, the Inland Revenue have taken legal advice on the application of these provisions and, in the light of that advice, have now concluded that the better view is that TCGA 1992 s 256 may exempt gains which would otherwise be charged on UK charities under TCGA 1992 s 87.

Consequently, where a UK charity, as beneficiary of an offshore settlement, receives a capital payment, in respect of which a chargeable gain would be treated as accruing to it under TCGA 1992 s 87(4), the charity will now be entitled to exemption from tax provided by TCGA 1992 s 256(1) to the extent that the capital payment is applicable and applied for charitable purposes.

This change of practice will apply to capital payments made to charities in the circumstances outlined above on or after 10 August 1998, and to any such payments made before that date where the tax liability is still open.

Tax Bulletin Issue 37, October 1998

Page 593. Self-assessment: (1) incomplete returns (2) the use of provisional figures in returns

We have been asked to clarify our position regarding ‘incomplete returns’ and the use of provisional figures in self-assessment (SA) tax returns.

Statutory background

TMA 1970 s 8(1) allows the Revenue to issue a notice requiring the taxpayer to deliver a return of ‘such information as may reasonably be required’ to establish the tax due for any year of assessment. TMA 1970 s 113(1) provides that any such return shall be ‘in such form’ as the Board prescribe. And TMA 1970 s 8(2) requires that the taxpayer make a declaration to the effect that ‘the return is to the best of his knowledge correct and complete’.

This means that whenever a tax return form is issued the statutory notice incorporated in that form places a obligation on the recipient to make a return of the information required, in the manner specified. If the completed tax return form delivered to the Revenue is not ‘correct and complete’ the statutory notice has not been complied with and the relevant sanctions may apply. The relevant sanctions are penalties under either TMA 1970 s 93 or 95, depending on the nature of the failure and the circumstances in which the failure is identified.

(1) Incomplete returns

In many cases it will be obvious that a tax return form is incomplete when it is received. For example, the signature required to satisfy the mandatory declaration may be missing. Or it may be that there is a tick, or note, to the effect that a particular set of pages have been attached to the form, but in fact they are missing. In such cases the return submitted by the taxpayer is clearly deficient in form and the taxpayer has clearly failed '... to comply with the notice ...' (TMA 1970 s 93(1)(b)). A failure of this sort should be identified during the initial screening of the return and in such cases we will send back the incomplete return almost immediately, to give the taxpayer the opportunity to rectify the omission.

In other cases the fact that the tax return form is incomplete may not come to light until the information in the return is being systematically transferred to our computer database. If so we may try to obtain the missing information from the taxpayer without sending back the return. This would be appropriate where, say, it is clear that there should be an entry in a particular box. But where there is a major omission we send the return back. This might be the case where, for example, we believe the necessary accounts information is incomplete. Whether we send the return back or not, the action we take has but a single purpose—to give the taxpayer the opportunity to rectify the omission.

Giving the taxpayer an opportunity to rectify an omission in such cases is a means of enhancing voluntary compliance. This is because by sending the incomplete tax return form back we are, in effect, opting to help taxpayers meet their obligations rather than penalising them for not doing so.

Incomplete returns delivered to the inland revenue on or before 31 January but sent back close to, or after, the 31 January filing deadline

One of the issues that arose during the first year of self assessment was the treatment of returns delivered to the Inland Revenue on or before 31 January but sent back to taxpayers or their agents, as incomplete close to, or after, the 31 January deadline. If an incomplete return is sent back in these circumstances it may be too late for the omission to be rectified before the filing deadline. If so the taxpayer will face an automatic late filing penalty under TMA 1970 s 93(2).

In the Inland Revenue Press Release of 3 February 1998, Dawn Primarolo, the Financial Secretary to the Treasury announced a concession addressing this issue. The concession provided that taxpayers whose returns were sent back to them (or their agents) in the circumstances described above would still be treated as having met the filing deadline provided they sent back a corrected return within a specified period.

A similar concession will apply for 1997–98 returns. The concession will apply where:

- a return is delivered to the Inland Revenue on or before 31 January 1999, and
- the return is subsequently found to be incomplete, and
- it is sent back to the taxpayer (or agent) for completion on or after 18 January 1999.

In such circumstances the taxpayer will be given 14 days in which to complete the return and deliver it back to the inland revenue if a completed return is delivered to us before the end of this 14-day period the taxpayer will be treated as having met the filing deadline.

The concession will also apply to those who file by electronic lodgement. Any rejection is carried out automatically. Accordingly, if a return is rejected shortly before the filing deadline and resubmitted successfully within the 14-day period, the agent will need to take a print-out of the rejection and send it to the office dealing with the return together with an explanation.

We will be monitoring the operation of the concession this year and, depending on the outcome, may recommend that it is established as a formal Extra Statutory Concession. For the avoidance of doubt it ought to be mentioned that the concession will only apply where the return is incomplete as a result of a genuine oversight. It will not apply where the return is deliberately incomplete, in an attempt to take advantage of the concession. For example, the concession will not apply if a return is deliberately sent in without a relevant set of pages, to buy a little more time to complete those pages. Nor will it apply if a return is deliberately sent in without a signature, to buy a little more time to obtain the signature.

Examples

Return submitted on 20 October 1998 and sent back to taxpayer as incomplete on 10 November 1998. Concession not relevant because taxpayer still has until 31 January 1999 to meet filing deadline.

Return submitted on 20 January 1999 and sent back to taxpayer as incomplete on 21 January 1999. Concession means that providing the completed return is sent back to the Revenue by 4 February 1999 the taxpayer will be treated as having met the filing deadline.

Return submitted on 20 January 1999 and sent back to taxpayer as incomplete on 10 February 1999. Concession means that providing the completed return is sent back to the Revenue by 24 February 1999 the taxpayer will be treated as having met the filing deadline.

Return submitted on 20 February 1999 and sent back to taxpayer as incomplete on 21 February 1999. Concession not relevant because return was not sent in on or before the 31 January 1999 filing deadline.

(2) Use of provisional figures in returns

Given that the purpose of the SA tax return is to establish the tax chargeable for a particular year of assessment it is neither surprising, nor unreasonable, that taxpayers are asked to include correct and final figures of income and gains in their returns.

But it has long been realised that there is an unacceptable tension between an absolute requirement to provide correct and final figures and a requirement to provide such information by a certain date. Prior to self assessment the Courts supported the view that the paramount requirement was to comply with the statutory filing obligation and that this may require the taxpayer to use provisional figures in the return (*Dunk v General Comrs for Havant* (1976) 51 TC 519; *Alexander v General Comrs for Wallington* (1992) 65 TC 777). For example:

> 'If a taxpayer finds particular circumstances that make the best of his knowledge more than usually unreliable, it is open to him to put against his figure for a particular item of income such words as 'estimated—see accompanying memorandum', or something of that kind, and explain the circumstances. If he has done his best, and, of course, he is under a duty to use all proper sources of knowledge—he will not, in my view, be guilty of making a false statement, providing, as I say, he puts in a genuine estimate and, if necessary, explains that it is not very reliable.'
>
> [Goulding J in *Dunk v General Comrs for Havant* (1976) 51 TC at p 521.]

Application of Dunk principles to SA returns

We would argue that the time limits for filing an SA tax return are such that it is reasonable to expect the vast majority of taxpayers to be able to provide correct and final figures by the statutory filing date. Nonetheless, we recognise that there will still be some circumstances in which it is impossible for the taxpayer to provide final figures, despite their best efforts to do so. So it is the Inland Revenue's view that the 'Dunk principles' apply equally well to SA returns. Indeed, these principles are clearly identifiable in the guidance published in 1994, at paragraph 2.53 of SAT 2:

> 'There will be occasions on which some information cannot be finalised within the formal self assessment time limits despite the taxpayers best efforts to do so. In such cases the taxpayer should include a "best estimate" of the information in the return and, if appropriate, a corresponding estimate of the tax due ..... A return containing any such provisional figure will not be regarded as incomplete.'

Our views on the use of the continuing application of the Dunk principles are also reflected in the guidance material provided with the SA tax return. For example, there is general advice on the use of provisional figures at page 27 of the main Tax Return Guide:

> 'Do not delay sending your Tax Return just because you do not have all the information you need. You must do your best to obtain the information, but if you cannot provide final figures by the time you need to send your Tax Return, then estimate the amount.'

Circumstances in which the Inland Revenue could regard a return containing provisional figures as 'incomplete'

Despite the general guidance provided in the 1996–97 tax return there appears to have been some confusion as to the circumstances in which the Inland Revenue could regard a tax return as incomplete simply because it contains provisional figures.

The general guidance in the Tax Return guidance tells the taxpayer that 'You must do your best to obtain the information' and goes on to say that we '... will not normally regard a Tax Return as incomplete simply because it contains provisional figures, provided you have taken all reasonable steps to get the final figures, and you ensure that they are sent as soon as they are available'.

It should be clear from this that we expect the taxpayer to have done all they reasonably can to obtain the final figures, or, in the words of Goulding J the taxpayer must have '... done his best ...'. If a taxpayer has made little or no effort to obtain the final figures before the filing deadline we would argue that a key element of the 'Dunk' principles is absent and the taxpayer has failed to comply with the notice to make a return. Similarly, we would not accept that general pressure of work or the complexity of a taxpayers affairs justify the use of provisional figures. The onus is on the taxpayer (and his agent) to take such factors into account, for example, when considering how long it will take to complete the return.

There is further guidance on the use of provisional figures in the self-employment pages. This guidance (on page SEN3) allows for the return of a single figure of estimated profit, rather than standard accounts information:

> 'If you cannot complete the income and expenses section of your self-employment pages because it is impossible to prepare the figures from which your taxable profit is to be calculated before the latest date for sending your Tax Return, you should provide an estimate of your taxable profit in box 3.88 ...'.

As is made clear this guidance is to be read in conjunction with the general advice on the use of provisional figures in the main Tax Return Guide. It follows that we expect taxpayers to have done all they reasonably can to obtain the final figures. It was certainly not our intention to accept a single figure of profit when, for example, it was only 'impossible' to prepare final figures because the taxpayer had made little or no effort to have the final figures prepared in time to meet the filing deadline. In such circumstances we would argue that a key element of the 'Dunk' principles is absent and the taxpayer has failed to comply with the notice to make a return. In fact we would expect there to be very few circumstances in which, despite the taxpayer's best efforts, it is genuinely 'impossible' for the taxpayer to provide us with accounts information. The only common circumstance would be where, in the case of a newly commenced business, the first accounting period does not end until close to, or after, the statutory filing date. (By 'close to' we mean within 3 months of the filing date, so for the normal 31 January deadline, that means accounting periods ending on or after 1 November.)

Even though there are relatively few circumstances in which it would be acceptable for a single provisional figure of profit to be returned there may be circumstances in which it is acceptable for some, or all, of the standard accounts information to be completed on a provisional basis. For example, there may have been a change of accounting date requiring two sets of accounts to be prepared. If only the earlier set of accounts were final then provisional standard accounts information would be required, pending completion of the second set of accounts. In these and similar circumstances (that is where a provisional figure of profit is estimated by reference to an earlier period of account) we would expect provisional figures for each of the anticipated entries in the standard accounts information.

In practice it is unlikely that we will send back a 1997–98 tax return as incomplete simply because it contains provisional figures. We would prefer to process the return as received and then hold the taxpayer to the obligation to provide final figures as soon as they are available. We will do this by identifying all those returns which contain provisional figures. If the final figures are not provided by the expected date we will take appropriate action to obtain them and in some cases this will mean opening an enquiry. (The guidance in the 1998–99 returns has been clarified along the lines described above).

Tax Bulletin Issue 38, December 1998

Page 620. Offshore trusts: capital gains tax: FA 1998

Finance Act 1998: Definition of 'protected settlement' in new TCGA 1992 Sch 5 paras 9(10A)–(10D).

FA 1998 s 132 brought trusts set up before 19 March 1991 within the scope of a capital gains tax charge, TCGA 1992 s 86, on the settlor of the trust in respect of gains realised by the trust where the settlor, members of the settlor's immediate family, or companies they controlled, could benefit from the trust. For this purpose, 'members of the settlor's immediate family' are the settlor's spouse, children of the settlor or of the settlor's spouse and their spouses. FA 1998 s 132 applies, generally, to chargeable gains realised on or after 6 April 1999.

A category of 'protected settlements' will remain outside the scope of the charge on the settlor under TCGA 1992 s 86. 'Protected settlements' are defined at new TCGA 1992 Sch 5 paras 9(10A)–(10D) as untainted pre-19 March 1991 settlements where the only members of the settlor's immediate family who can benefit from the trust are, broadly:

- unborn children of the settlor or of the settlor's (current or future) spouse, or
- such children who are under the age of 18 at the end of the immediately preceding year of assessment. Future spouses of such children or of the settlor can also be included without jeopardising the 'protected settlement' status, as can persons who are not counted as members of the settlor's immediate family for the purposes of the settlor charge.

However, FA 1998 s 131 treats grandchildren of the settlor or of the settlor's spouse as members of the settlor's immediate family for the purposes of the settlor charge in relation to trusts set up on or after 17 March 1998, or trusts set up before that date which become tainted. There is therefore some question over whether pre-1991 trusts where the beneficiaries, at 6 April 1999, include both children under 18 and grandchildren as the only members of the settlor's immediate family who can benefit from the trust would meet the definition of a 'protected settlement'.

In such cases the Inland Revenue will not regard the existence of the settlor's (or the settlor's spouse's) grandchildren of whatever age as beneficiaries of a relevant settlement as causing the settlement to fall outside the definition of a 'protected settlement' for the purposes of TCGA 1992 Sch 5 paras 9 (10A)–(10D).

Tax Bulletin Issue 39, February 1999

Page 628. Self-assessment and trustees of approved self-administered pension schemes

Background

The tax approval system for pension schemes provides tax reliefs and exemptions totalling nearly £11 billion annually. In 1991, both the Public Accounts Committee and the National Audit Office were critical of the Inland Revenue for not having adequate systems in place for overseeing these reliefs.

In response to that criticism, the Revenue has introduced a series of measures to improve the way it checks that the reliefs and exemptions are properly due. The introduction of self-assessment for trustees of approved self-administered pension schemes is part of that series.

Examination of tax returns completed by trustees of approved self-administered schemes allows the Inland Revenue to check that repayments have been correctly claimed and made; that liability has been correctly notified and tax paid where appropriate. It also helps the Revenue to establish that schemes that neither claim repayment nor notify liability are acting correctly.

Introduction of self-assessment

It was decided that trustees of approved self-administered pension schemes should come within self-assessment from 1996–97. Trustees of approved insured schemes have not been brought within self-assessment.

Self-assessment applies to trustees of approved schemes in the same way as it does to other taxpayers. The same time limits and rules apply. This includes the application of automatic penalties where trustees fail to file their return by 31 January following the end of the year of assessment.

Self-assessment does not apply to administrators of schemes who are required to notify liability on various chargeable events that occur. These include repayment of employee's contributions, commutation of pensions under special circumstances, payments out of surplus funds and payments to employers. In these circumstances, form 1SF should continue to be requested from the local Inspector and an assessment will follow in due course. The administrator and the trustee are two different taxpayers with different responsibilities. The liability of the administrator should not be netted off against repayments due to the trustee.

Returns

There has been a consultation process with the pensions industry and others over the introduction of self-assessment. This has covered the incremental issue of returns, the design of the 1998–99 return and the basis for completion of the return for 1998–99 et seq.

1996–97 returns were issued mainly to those trustees who notified liability for the year. Returns for 1997–98 were issued to trustees of 20% of approved self-administered schemes. 1998–99 will be the first year that trustees of all self-administered schemes will receive a return. If the trustees of an approved self-administered pension scheme do not receive a tax return form for 1998–99 by 30 June 1999, they should contact the scheme's tax office.

The 1998–99 return is considerably different to the returns for earlier years. It follows more closely the format for other returns. It also has a new name: Tax Return for Trustees of Self-Administered Pension Schemes. Trustees of all schemes will receive three forms:

- SA970, the return itself, which starts with a series of questions designed to lead trustees to complete only those questions that are appropriate to them.
- SA975, which are the guidance notes on completing the return.

- SA976, the optional calculation for use by trustees with either a repayment or with liability. Trustees can, of course, ask the Revenue to make the calculation, provided the return is made by 30 September.

As for earlier years' returns accounts will be required to accompany the return. Again, where these are not produced statements of incomings and outgoings and assets and liabilities for the beginning and end of the year will be required.

During the course of the consultations on the return, the Revenue agreed that trustees may, if they wish, complete returns for 1998–99 et seq. on the accounting date basis. This means that where annual accounts are regularly produced, these may form the basis of the return. For example, income shown in the accounts for the year ended 30 June 1998 will be treated as income for the year ended 5 April 1999. Where annual accounts are not produced, the return should be completed on the strict basis of the year ended 5 April 1999.

If trustees are uncertain about where to include particular types of income, they should enter it where it appears to them to be most appropriate. However, they may feel it prudent to provide details of the income and their decision in the Additional Information space. This may apply particularly to trustees who receive sub-underwriting commission and who are uncertain as to how the decision in the High Court case of *Clark v Trustees of British Telecom Pension Scheme* may apply to them.

The vast majority of trustees, who have investment income and capital gains that come from assets held for the purpose of the scheme will only need to complete SA970. Assets held for the purposes of the scheme are assets that will ultimately be used to provide pensions and relevant benefits.

This contrasts with the situation where Pension Schemes Office (PSO) has issued a notice under Schedule 22 para 7 following the declaration of a surplus. This notifies a percentage of income received and capital gains from assets that are held for the purposes of the scheme, and to which exemption from tax shall not apply.

Trustees who have assets that are not held for the purpose of the scheme, or who have received a notice under Schedule 22 from PSO, should ask the Orderline for SA973. These supplementary pages ask for details of income and gains from the same categories that appear in SA970. However, separate totals are required for income received and capital gains from assets that are and that are not held for the purposes of the scheme.

Repayments

The return will form the formal repayment claim for the tax year. The investment income questions ask for details of income, tax deducted, tax repaid and the balance of any income tax still to be repaid. Trustees or their nominees will continue to be able to make provisional in-year repayments on form R63N.

Enquiries into a return

Any return chosen for enquiry will be subject to the normal rules governing all self-assessment enquiries. Local Inspectors will liaise with PSO to ensure that all aspects of a scheme's return are covered. Local Inspectors will concentrate on the repayment and liability aspects. PSO will retain their responsibility for monitoring on-going compliance with the rules under which the scheme was approved.

Page 629. The taxation of Schedule F income received by trustees after 6 April 1999

In his Budget in July 1997 the Chancellor announced a major reform of the corporation tax system including the way in which Schedule F income (dividends, distributions and other similar income) is taxed. The principal legislation is in F (No 2) A 1997 ss 24–36.

We have received a number of enquiries about the effect of these changes on trusts, trustees and beneficiaries. This article provides some general guidance on the changes. It does not cover Schedule F income received by trustees of a United Kingdom unit trust scheme.

All references are to the ICTA 1988 unless otherwise stated.

Bare trustees

Income received by bare trustees is treated as the income of the beneficiary for tax purposes. There have been no changes to that. So Schedule F income arising to such trusts will continue to be treated as the income of the beneficiary and be taxed as if they received the income direct.

Trustees not subject to ICTA 1988 s 686

Such trustees do not generally pay tax at the rate applicable to trusts and likewise will not normally be taxed at the Schedule F trust rate. But they will be liable at the Schedule F trust rate on share buybacks and other similar distributions in accordance with the new section 686A, just as at present they are taxable at the rate applicable to trusts on such distributions.

For other distributions received on and after 6 April 1999 the trustees will be chargeable at the Schedule F ordinary rate (10 per cent). Since the distribution will have a non-payable tax credit of 10 per cent attached to it, there will be no further tax to pay by the trustees just like under the current system.

Trustees liable under ICTA 1988 s 686

At present such trustees are taxed at the rate applicable to trusts (34 per cent) on all income they receive. From 6 April 1999 income falling within Schedule F is to be taxed at a new 'Schedule F trust rate' of 25 per cent.

Schedule F income will have a non-payable tax credit of one-ninth of the amount or value of the dividend. So on a dividend of £900 the non-payable tax credit will be £100.

The Schedule F trust rate of 25 per cent ensures that, in broad terms, the trustees will have to pay the same amount of tax on the same dividend under the new system as they do under the current system. This is demonstrated by the following example.

	Current System £	*New System* £
Dividend	900	900
Tax credit	225	100
Gross income	1,125	1,000
Tax at 34%/25%	382.50	250
Income after tax	742.50	750
Tax due from trustees	382.50	250
Minus tax credit	225	100
Additional tax due	157.50	150

Discretionary payments made by trustees

Where trustees make payments to which section 687 applies, the beneficiary receives an annual payment which is treated as a gross payment from which tax at 34 per cent has been deducted. Thus a payment of £750 is treated as a payment of £1,136.36 from which tax of £386.36 has been deducted. The gross payment of £1,136.36 is treated as the income of the beneficiary with further tax being due from them or tax being repaid to them as appropriate.

From 6 April 1999 as tax credits will be non-payable they cannot go into the section 687(3) 'tax pool'. So, using the example above, whereas at present £382.50 can go into the pool, under the new system only £150 will do so (£250 minus £100).

The example shows that the cash available to the trustees for distribution is £742.50 under the current system and £750 under the new. Under the current system, if the trustees distribute all the available cash (£742.50), the beneficiary's income is £1,125 gross with a tax credit of £382.50. The credit is matched by the amount in the tax pool (see above).

Under the new system from 6 April 1999 if the trustees distribute all the cash available (£750) the beneficiary's income will be £1,136.36 with a tax credit of £386.36. And, as at present, if there is insufficient tax in the tax pool to 'frank' this tax credit there will be further liability on the trustees under section 687(2)(b). In the above example if the only tax in the pool is the £150 paid by the trustees on the dividend then there will be a section 687(2)(b) charge of £236.36 (£386.36 less £150).

If, in the above example, the trustees choose to rely only on the dividend income to fund both the payment to the beneficiary and the section 687(2)(b) liability then they only have sufficient funds to release 66% of the actual dividend, ie £900 x 66% = £594. This will translate to gross income of £900 with a tax credit of £306. The section 687(2)(b) liability will be £156 (£306 minus tax pool of £150). So, the trustees will pay £594 to the beneficiary and £156 to the Inland Revenue. This would equal the £750 cash they have in hand.

It has been suggested that the effect of section 687 has somehow been altered by the changes in legislation. This is incorrect. The current legislation works in exactly the same way where trustees receive a dividend without a tax credit such as a foreign income dividend (FID) as the following example shows. Assume a discretionary trust's only income in 1998–99 is a foreign income dividend of £900.

Dividend	£ 900
Notional tax treated as paid	£ 225
Gross income	£1,125
Tax at 34%	£ 382.50
Income available after tax	£ 742.50

Tax due from trustees	£ 382.50
Minus notional tax treated as paid	£ 225.00
Additional tax due	£ 157.50

So far the computation is identical to that in the previous example.

However, because the notional tax is non-payable it cannot go into the tax pool so only the £157.50 paid by the trustees goes into the pool. If the trustees release the whole of the available cash of £742.50 the beneficiary's income is £1,125 gross with a tax credit of £382.50. As the tax pool is only £157.50 the liability under section 687(2)(b) is £225.

Again if the trustees choose to rely only on the dividend income to fund the payment to the beneficiary and the section 687(2)(b) liability then they only have sufficient funds to release 66% of the actual dividend, ie £900 × 66% = £594. This will translate to gross income of £900 with a tax credit of £306. The section 687(2)(b) liability becomes £148.50 (£306 minus tax pool £157.50). So the trustees will pay £594 to the beneficiary and £148.50 to the Inland Revenue. This equals the £742.50 cash they have in hand.

Trust management expenses

Sections 686(2AA), (2A) and (2B), 689A and 689B contain the rules for trust management expenses. From 6 April 1999 section 689B has been amended so that the new Schedule F income is included in those types of income (ie income not carrying a payable tax credit) against which allowable expenses are set in priority to other income. Therefore allowable expenses will be set against income in the following order from 6 April 1999:

- first against Schedule F income and other income within sections 233(1A) and (1B), 249(6), and 421(1)(a),
- next against foreign dividends as defined in section 1A(3)(b),
- next against savings income within section 1A, and
- finally against other income.

Tax Bulletin Issue 50, December 2000

Page 813. Inheritance tax: accumulation and maintenance trusts

Most practitioners will be familiar with the inheritance tax (IHT) provisions for 'Accumulation and Maintenance' trusts (AMTs). Among other things, these provide exemption from the periodic IHT charge on discretionary trusts either:

- so long as all beneficiaries are grandchildren of a common grandparent (or a surviving spouse of such a grandchild); or
- in other cases, for a maximum period of 25 years since the tests for AMTs were first satisfied.

No IHT charge has arisen yet under this second leg, because the 25-year period has not so far run out for any trust subject to it. But this category includes a significant class of trusts which were already in place when these rules for AMTs were finalised in 1976. So for all those which are still subject to this test, the grace period runs out on the same date 25 years on, at the close of 15 April 2001. Practitioners responsible for pre-75 AMTs may want to note that a charge potentially arises at this point. More generally, they will want to take note that IHT charges at the 25-year point will arise from then on for other trusts set up or modified since the mid-70s, at the particular anniversary dates appropriate to each trust.

In more detail

Trusts are liable to an IHT charge once they fail to qualify under IHTA 1984 s 71 because they no longer meet the conditions for grandparent/grandchildren or a 25 year period has elapsed.

The 25 year period runs from the latest of:

- 15 April 1976;
- the date the settlement commenced; and
- the date of attainment of accumulation and maintenance status.

Settlements not affected are those set up by a common grandparent for grandchildren, whether or not with contingency provision for the widow or widower of any grandchild who dies before becoming entitled to the property.

For those settlements which are affected, IHT is calculated at a flat rate (section 71(5)) which tapers over time on property which ceases to be held on AMTs or when the trustees make a disposition which reduces the value of the property. The tax charge for a 25 year period is 21% calculated as follows:

- 0.25% for each of the first 40 complete successive quarters in the relevant period;
- 0.20% for each of the next 40 complete successive quarters in the relevant period;
- 0.15% for each of the next 40 complete successive quarters in the relevant period.

Thereafter the normal rules for ten-yearly and proportionate charges for discretionary trusts apply to these settlements.

Tax Bulletin Issue 52, April 2001

Page 842. Inland Revenue trusts

As part of the Inland Revenue's drive to provide a better and more responsive service to its customers, we have reorganised work on UK resident trusts and the estates of deceased persons in administration. We have brought together work in these areas within 'Inland Revenue Trusts' (IR Trusts) which now handles operational, compliance, technical and policy work. Some operational work on small estates in administration where there is no resulting trust remains outside IR Trusts in the tax office of the deceased.

IR Trusts aims to provide a high quality service to UK resident trusts and estates and we welcome comments from our customers on how to do things better. Please send any comments to the Customer Service Manager, IR Trusts, Room 112, New Wing, Somerset House, Strand, London, WC2R 1LB.

As part of the reorganisation of IR Trusts, the names of the trust offices will change and some work is being relocated. The table below summarises the new titles and explains what each office now deals with:

Area dealt with	*Inland Revenue Trusts Office*
All trusts established under Scottish law or administered from an address in Scotland and estates in administration valued over £400,000.	Inland Revenue Trusts Meldrum House 15 Drumsheugh Gardens Edinburgh EH3 7UL Tel: 0131 777 4106
UK resident trusts and estates where there is a continuing trust administered from addresses within the Greater London area (broadly within the M25).	Inland Revenue Trusts Charles House 375 Kensington High Street London W14 8QS Tel: 020 7605 9800
UK resident trusts and estates where there is a continuing trust administered from addresses within the Greater Manchester area and trusts and estates with corporate trustees.	Inland Revenue Trusts Albert Bridge House 1 Bridge Street Manchester M60 9AF Tel: 0161 288 6747
UK resident trusts and estates where there is a continuing trust administered from addresses in the South West of England.	Inland Revenue Trusts Lysnoweth Infirmary Hill Truro Cornwall TR1 2JD Tel: 01872 245403
UK resident trusts and estates Inland Revenue Trusts where there is a continuing trust not dealt with by Edinburgh, London, Manchester, or Truro including those administered in Northern Ireland.	Huntingdon Court 90–94 Mansfield Road Nottingham NG1 3HG Tel: 0115 911 6500 DX: 714240 Nottingham 21

Edinburgh office

The Edinburgh office of IR Trusts has taken in the work of FICO (Scotland) on large estates in administration and the trust work of Edinburgh Haymarket TSO.

Tax returns

Unfortunately we have not been able to update all our computer systems so that tax returns issued this April for 2000–01 and most other computer generated forms carry the new names. So you will still see some correspondence from us using the old names. We are sorry about this.

Non-resident trusts

All UK non-resident trusts, and trusts not administered or created under UK law will still be dealt with by the Centre for Non-Residents whose address is: Centre For Non-Residents, Non-Resident Trusts, St John's House, Merton Road, Bootle, Merseyside, L69 9BB. Tel: 0151 472 6001.

Tax Bulletin Issue 53, June 2001

Page 847. Income tax self-assessment (ITSA) returns for 2000–01

As we start to receive the 2000–01 income tax return forms we have tried to identify areas which have caused concern in the past, to see how we can help avoid any problems this year. This article gives a brief outline of our position on three issues:

- signatures on ITSA return (and other) forms;
- using provisional figures in returns;
- rejecting unsatisfactory return forms.

1. Signatures

TMA 1970 s 8(2) requires that every return should include a declaration by the person making the return to the effect that the return is to the best of his knowledge correct and complete. We consider that the obligation to make this declaration is one which the person making the return cannot delegate. Accordingly, it is normal practice to insist that a paper return should be signed by the taxpayer personally. Similarly, where the taxpayer makes a return using the Internet service for self-assessment the return should be personally authenticated by the taxpayer using their confidential password and User ID. Where an agent sends in the return electronically the taxpayer must sign a copy of the return before the electronic version is sent. The exceptions to this are where, because of the age, physical infirmity or mental incapacity of the taxpayer, they are unable to cope adequately with the management of their affairs or where their general health might suffer if they were troubled for a personal signature. In such special circumstances we accept the signature of an attorney who has full knowledge of the taxpayer's affairs.

In all other cases we expect the return to be signed by the taxpayer. If the signature does not appear to be that of the taxpayer we will reject the return form as not satisfying the requirements of TMA 1970 s 8. The form will be sent back to whoever submitted it (taxpayer or agent) with an explanation. If this is close to the filing deadline there is a risk of incurring a late filing penalty (see 'unsatisfactory returns' below). Where the taxpayer is travelling a lot, working or living abroad, we expect them to make arrangements with their agent to ensure that they do sign the return form in time to file by the statutory deadline.

It is worth noting that we also need the taxpayer's signature on the form 64–8, giving an agent authority to receive Revenue documents on their behalf. We cannot pass any information to, or discuss the client's tax matters with, the agent without the taxpayer's signed authority. We may ask for another form 64–8 to be completed if it is not clear that an authority we have already received has been signed by the taxpayer.

2. Provisional figures

Our approach to handling returns containing provisional figures evolved over the first couple of years of income tax self assessment. We explained our position on the use of provisional figures in returns in Tax Bulletins Issue 37 (October 1998) and Issue 44 (December 1999). The first addressed the issue in detail for 1997–98, and TB44 reiterated the message for 1998–99 returns.

We are now in the fifth year of self-assessment. Our view of the legal position has not changed. There are limited circumstances in which we can accept provisional figures as meeting the obligation to file a return and these were set out in detail in TB37 (pages 593–6). But we are now clear that a return containing unjustified provisional figures should be returned to the taxpayer or agent. Our guidance to staff (for example in Enquiry Handbook at EH260) has been updated to explain this approach as appropriate for current and future self-assessment returns.

Where a provisional figure is used we require the taxpayer to tick box 23.3 (for 2000–01 return) and to use the additional information section on the last page of the core return to give:

- an acceptable explanation for the delay in providing final figures, and
- a date by which they expect to provide the final figure.

Unless both of the above are given we will reject the return as not satisfying the requirements of TMA 1970 s 8.

We will not regard pressure of work either on the taxpayer or their tax adviser, or the complexity of the taxpayer's affairs, as reasons for accepting a return containing provisional figures.

3. Rejecting unsatisfactory return forms

In the past we have allowed a 14-day period of grace (when we do not charge a fixed late-filing penalty) where we have sent back an ITSA return form, received on or before the filing deadline, because something is missing. Tax Bulletin 37 said 'we will be monitoring the operation of the concession this year and, depending on the outcome, may recommend that it is established as a formal Extra-Statutory Concession'. We have reviewed the operation of the period of grace and have decided to continue the practice for 2000–01 returns. We have not decided, at this stage, to establish the period of grace as an

Extra-Statutory Concession. Instead we are including this within wider options under consideration to help and encourage people to file on time.

In Tax Bulletin 37, and in other places, we have referred to these returns as 'incomplete returns'. We now believe this could be misleading. A return from which income has been omitted is 'incomplete' but it is still a return under TMA 1970 s 8. We would deal with the omission by opening an enquiry and not by sending the form back to the customer. We are sorry to introduce new terminology but in future we shall refer to returns we reject at the processing stage as 'unsatisfactory returns', because they fail to satisfy section 8.

We will send back a return form when it fails to satisfy the requirements of TMA 1970 s 8. Some examples of an unsatisfactory return form are those:

- not in the prescribed form (standard Revenue form or agreed alternative);
- not signed by the person making the return;
- with a box ticked on page 2 (to say a supplementary page is needed) but the relevant pages not attached;
- containing unjustified provisional figures (see requirements above).

Unsatisfactory returns (those failing to satisfy section 8) will be sent back to whoever submitted them (taxpayer or agent) with an explanatory letter. Where an unsatisfactory return form is received before the filing deadline the customer has until the normal filing date to send back a satisfactory return. In past years we have applied the 14-day period of grace to all unsatisfactory returns received on or before the filing date. We realise this is unnecessary and could be viewed as coercive because until we are within a fortnight of the filing date the customer has longer (up to the filing date) in which to file.

If we receive an unsatisfactory return form on the filing date, or within the previous 13 days we will not charge a late-filing penalty if a satisfactory return is then received within 14 days from the date of our letter sending back the unsatisfactory return. We will also allow a 14-day period of grace where an unsatisfactory return was received earlier but not sent back until on or after the date 13 days before the filing date.

For example: an unsatisfactory return form, to which the 31 January filing date applies, received on any day from 18 January to 31 January will be sent back with a letter allowing the 14 days period of grace. An unsatisfactory return form received on 10 January but not sent back until the 20 January will also be given the benefit of the 14 days. An unsatisfactory return form received and sent back on 11 January would not be given the 14-day period of grace because it is not needed (the customer has 20 days to 31 January). An unsatisfactory return form received on 1 February, or on any day after, is already late and the customer will be asked to send a satisfactory return as soon as possible. We will not give the 14-day period of grace in these cases.

Our aim in doing this is not to penalise someone who has genuinely forgotten something, such as signing the return. The 14-day period of grace will not be given in cases where the taxpayer appears to be using deliberate delaying tactics (for example, unjustified provisional figures put into a last-minute return year on year).

Returns received after the statutory filing date will not have the benefit of any period of grace.

Tax Bulletin Issue 55, October 2001

Page 888. Change of interpretation: non-resident trusts—gains and losses accruing in the transitional period to trusts brought within the settlor charge by FA 1998—treatment for tax year 1999–2000

Summary

This change of view is applicable only to non-resident trusts which were outside the scope of the TCGA 1992 s 86 settlor charge until the enactment of FA 1998 s 132.

As a consequence of recent legal advice, the Revenue has changed its position on the availability of net losses realised by non-resident trustees in the 'transitional period' from 17 March 1998 to 5 April 1999 for set off against capital gains accruing to such trustees during 1999–2000, in respect of which a settlor is chargeable under TCGA 1992 s 86. Until now we have taken the view that net capital losses incurred in the transitional period are not available for set off against 1999–2000 gains. However we now accept that such losses can in fact be set off in this way.

Similarly, the Revenue now accepts that net losses incurred by non-resident trustees in 1999–2000 can be set against gains arising in the transitional period in respect of which a settlor is chargeable under section 86.

Action

Settlors affected by the transitional provisions whose capital gains position for 1999–2000 has been settled on the basis of our previous interpretation may now amend their self assessments for 1999–2000 in order to put into effect our changed interpretation. The amended self-assessment must be submitted before the time limit for amending self-assessments expires. In most cases this will be 31 January 2002.

Background

TCGA 1992 s 86, which charges certain UK domiciled and resident settlors in respect of gains realised by non-resident, or dual resident trustees, was first enacted in FA 1991. This 'settlor charge' taxes settlors of trusts in respect of the capital gains accruing from disposals of trust assets by the trustees, where the settlor or certain members of his family has an interest in the trust and certain other conditions are met. The 1991 legislation excluded from the charge all non-resident trusts created before Budget day, 19 March 1991, subject to certain conditions. Trusts whose gains are within the scope of section 86 are known as 'qualifying settlements'.

Under FA 1998 s 132, all trusts created before 19 March 1991 and otherwise meeting the conditions in Section 86, were brought within the definition of qualifying settlements. This was announced on Budget Day 1998 (17 March) and took effect from 6 April 1999. The period from 17 March 1998 to 5 April 1999 was covered by transitional provisions. These are at FA 1998 Sch 23.

The aim of the transitional provisions was to allow time for trustees not wishing their trusts to become qualifying settlements to remove them from the scope of the settlor charge (e g by removing beneficiaries from the trust, or by certain other means). There were also anti-avoidance provisions to stop trustees realising gains in the transitional period and then removing their trusts from the scope of the settlor charge before 6 April 1999. For those trusts where the requisite steps to remain outside TCGA 1992 s 86 were not taken by 6 April 1999, FA 1998 Sch 23 para 1(2)(a) applied to treat gains and losses arising between 17 March 1998 and 5 April 1999 as accruing on 6 April 1999 for the purposes of the settlor charge.

Until now our interpretation of the transitional provisions has been that a settlor is taxable in 1999–2000 on any net gain arising in the transitional period, but any net loss arising in the transitional period cannot be set off against any actual gains accruing in 1999–2000. Equally, we considered that losses incurred in 1999–2000 were not available for setting off against net gains which arose during the transitional period. This view was seen as consistent with the general basis of the settlor charge, which attributes only net gains, and not losses, to settlors, and with FA 1998 s 132(5), which prohibits gains and losses arising before 6 April 1999 from being taken into account for the purposes of TCGA 1992 s 86.

However, following recent legal advice we now accept that the wording of FA 1998 Sch 23 para 1(2)(a) allows for both net gains, and net losses, to be treated as accruing on 6 April 1999.

Consequences

In cases falling within the provisions of FA 1998 Sch 23 para 1(2)(a)

1. Net capital losses arising on disposals made between 17 March 1998 and 5 April 1999 are available for set off against net capital gains accruing on disposals made between 6 April 1999 and 5 April 2000, for the purposes of calculating the amount on which a settlor is chargeable for 1999–2000 under section 86. To the extent that such losses are not so utilised, they will be available for carry forward in accordance with

TCGA 1992 Sch 5 para 1(6), and so may reduce the amount on which a settlor is charged under TCGA 1992 s 86 for a later year.

2. Net capital losses arising on disposals made between 6 April 1999 and 5 April 2000 are available for set off against net capital gains arising on disposals made between 17 March 1998 and 5 April 1999, for the purpose of calculating the amount on which a settlor is chargeable under TCGA 1992 s 86 for 1999–2000.

This interpretation will apply to all current open and future self-assessments for 1999–2000. As noted above self assessments for 1999–2000 already settled on the basis of our previous view may be reopened, but the amended self-assessment must be submitted to the Revenue before the time limit under TMA 1970 s 9(4)(b) expires.

Further information

This article repeats the one issued in the 'non-residents' pages of the Inland Revenue Internet site on 8 August 2001.

For further advice on how this revised interpretation affects a particular case, write with full details to: Mike Corcoran (Technical Adviser), Centre for Non-Residents 2 (Non-Resident Trusts), Room 310, St John's House, Merton Road, Bootle, Merseyside L69 9BB.

Page 892. Inheritance tax: accumulation and maintenance trusts

An article in Tax Bulletin Issue 50 (December 2000) reminded practitioners that after the relevant period of 25 years has elapsed a settlement will only qualify under IHTA 1984 s 71 so long as all beneficiaries are grandchildren of a common grandparent (or are a surviving spouse or child of such a grandchild).

We have been asked whether the mere existence of a power to appoint (which does not offend the conditions of section 71(1)(a)) in favour of beneficiaries who are not grandchildren of a common grandparent will take the settlement outside the common grandparent rule. We have said that in our opinion the mere existence of such a power, as opposed to its actual exercise, does not take a trust outside the common grandparent category.

Tax Bulletin Issue 57, February 2002

Page 916. Provisional figures in returns

We are sorry to have to address the issue of provisional figures in returns so soon after the article published in June 2001 of Tax Bulletin (Issue 53). Following an appeal against a late filing penalty, we have sought further legal advice about the use of provisional figures. As a result of that advice, on

23 October 2001, we changed our guidance to staff on how to handle ITSA returns containing provisional figures or CTSA returns containing estimated figures. At the same time we put an article onto the Inland Revenue website, explaining the position.

We now accept that a customer has made a return (assuming there are no other problems) where they have used a provisional or estimated figure. We will no longer send back a return that does not have an adequate explanation for why provisional or estimated figures are needed or does not give a date for the supply of final figures. The omission of that information will, however, be a factor we take into account in order to decide whether we need to open an enquiry into the return.

Past Revenue practice on provisional or estimated figures was based on our earlier legal advice and understanding of the law. Any resulting late filing penalties before 23 October 2001 were on this basis and carried the right appeal.

It is possible for the use of provisional or estimated figures to result in an incorrect return for which a penalty may be charged. This can be because the customer did not take reasonable care when they calculated the figures or because final figures could have been obtained before the return was sent to the Revenue.

We will look at the changes we can usefully make to the wording about provisional or estimated figures in ITSA and CTSA returns for 2003 onwards

Page 919. New Form 41G(Trust)—trust details

This is the form trustees can use to provide details of a new trust. We have recently produced a new version. There are no major changes, but minor changes are as follows:

- The form is now described as 'trust details' rather than 'trust enquiry'.
- There are two trustees' details boxes.
- There are new boxes to identify Scots law trusts and employee benefit trusts.
- We have added a box for the date the trust commenced in a will trust.

We have also tried to improve clarity with a view to helping trustees get it right first time. The form is now available from all IR Trusts offices and the Centre for Non-Residents, Bootle.

Trust expenses guidance in IR manual

The Trusts and Settlements Manual (TSM) was published in April 2001 to coincide with the establishment of the new Inland Revenue Trusts business stream. It replaced the Trust Manual. Unfortunately, in carrying across guidance from the old manual, some material about trust expenses in different types of trusts got mixed up, and the TSM guidance was not entirely correct. You should not refer to the affected section of the 2001 manual, TSM3505–3545 'Trust income and gains—Trust Management Expenses'. We have rewritten the guidance to reflect the original position, and to cut out some obsolete (pre-self-assessment) procedures. The new guidance will be incorporated in the TSM from mid-February 2002 as TSM3505–3545 'Trust income and gains—Trust Expenses'.

Tax Bulletin Issue 59, June 2002

Page 937. Trusts

Share scheme trusts

We have recently found that some trustees of share scheme trusts are unaware of their obligation to file a trust tax return if they have income or gains to declare. We require a trust tax return for each share scheme trust, including non-resident trusts with UK source income. These include:

- Qualifying Employee Share Ownership Trusts (QUESTs). That is, plans that comply with the provisions of FA 1989 Sch 5;
- Share Incentive Plan trusts (SIPs), (formerly All Employee Share Ownership Plan trusts (AESOPs)). That is, plans that comply with the provisions of FA 2000 Sch 8 as amended by FA 2001 Sch 13;
- Any other employee share ownership trust.

If you have not notified the appropriate trust office of the existence of the trust, you should complete form 41G(Trust), which is available from any Inland Revenue Enquiry Centre or Tax Office, and return it as soon as possible to the relevant Inland Revenue Trusts Office.

Revised leaflet IR152 'Trusts. An introduction.'

We recently published an updated version of IR152—'Trusts. An introduction.' Part of our Personal Taxpayer Series, the leaflet covers private family trusts and explains how trusts are created, the different sorts of trusts, how they are taxed and when tax is due under self-assessment. Although written with the lay person in mind, we think many practitioners will also find the publication a useful source of reference.

Tax Bulletin Issue 62, December 2002

Page 979. Changes To The 'Hansard' Procedure

Introduction

You may be familiar with the term, the 'Hansard' procedure. For those who are not, this is a process by which the Inland Revenue offers a taxpayer suspected of serious tax fraud an opportunity to confess to all, if any, of the irregularities in their tax affairs. The term 'Hansard' is used, because the practice of the Board of Inland Revenue is set out in a statement by the Chancellor of the Exchequer in the Parliamentary Hansard records.

Hansard is a long established concept and its origins can be traced back to the latter part of the First World War. It first appears in Hansard by way of a lengthy written answer by Sir W. Johnson Hicks, in the House of Commons 19 July 1923. Over the years there have only been minor changes and the Hansard practice has survived a number of challenges in the Courts.

From time to time the Chancellor of the day updates the Hansard statement to reflect the latest practice of the Inland Revenue. This article reports that the Chancellor has recently made a revised statement; it looks at the main changes and the reasons behind these. It also announces changes in the Inland Revenue's Code of Practice number 9, which provides further information about these types of investigations.

Background

The Hansard procedure was last updated by the then Chancellor, the Rt Hon John Major M.P., on 18th October 1990. In answering a Parliamentary Question about the practice of the Board of Inland Revenue with regard to instituting criminal proceedings in case of suspected tax fraud, he gave the following statement:

> 'The practice of the Board of Inland Revenue in cases of tax fraud is as follows:–
>
> The Board may accept a money settlement instead of instituting criminal proceedings in respect of fraud alleged to have been committed by a taxpayer.
>
> They can give no undertaking that they will accept a money settlement and refrain from instituting criminal proceedings even if the case is one in which the taxpayer has made a full confession and has given full facilities for investigation of the facts. They reserve to themselves full discretion in all cases as to the course they pursue.
>
> But in considering whether to accept a money settlement or to institute criminal proceedings, it is their practice to be influenced by the fact that the taxpayer has made a full confession and has given full facilities for investigation into his affairs and for examination of such books, papers, documents or information as the Board may consider necessary'.

This statement includes an indication that a taxpayer who makes a full confession and who co-operates fully with the Inland Revenue during their investigations can expect that the matter will be dealt with on a civil basis, rather than criminal proceedings being taken against them. But the statement is not explicit on the matter and the taxpayer is left with no absolute assurance that the Board of the Inland Revenue will not institute criminal proceedings even in these circumstances.

Statements by the Lords

More recently, the House of Lords has considered the case of 'R v Allen'. In this case the appellant claimed that the admission into evidence of statements made in response to the Hansard procedure breached his right to a fair trial under Article 6(1) of the European Convention of Human Rights. This, he claimed, was because he had been subjected to an inducement at the time when the statements were made. The inducement in question was said to be the assurance implicit in the Hansard statement that if the taxpayer makes a full confession criminal proceedings would not be instituted against him.

There was, however, a flaw in the argument advanced by the appellant. As Lord Hutton explained:

> 'To the extent that there was an inducement contained in the Hansard statement, the inducement was to give true and accurate information to the Revenue, but the accused … did not respond to that inducement and instead of giving true and accurate information gave false information. Therefore, in my opinion, the appellant's argument … that he was induced by the hope of non-institution of criminal proceedings held out by the Revenue to provide the schedule and that its provision was, therefore, involuntary is invalid'.

In other words, the whole basis of the appellant's argument was founded on a false premise. The facts of the appellant's case did not engage the legal argument advanced on his behalf because the appellant had not made full disclosure in accordance with the terms of the Hansard statement.

Lord Hutton pointed out that the position would have been different if the appellant had made full disclosure to the Inland Revenue in response to the Hansard statement.

> 'If, in response to the Hansard statement, the appellant had given true and accurate information which disclosed that he had earlier cheated the Revenue and had been prosecuted for that earlier dishonesty, he would have had a strong argument that the criminal proceedings were unfair and an even stronger argument that the Crown should not rely on evidence of his admission, but that is the reverse of what actually occurred'.

A Full Confession

The conclusion to be drawn from Lord Hutton's remarks is that a taxpayer invited under the Hansard procedure to make a full confession, who unlike the appellant in this case actually did so, would be hard done by if the Revenue then subsequently prosecuted him or her anyway. This would be particularly true if the Revenue used his confession as evidence in court.

These remarks are significant in terms of the Hansard statement. The Board of the Inland Revenue had previously reserved to itself full discretion as to the course of action it would take in any case. Lord Hutton took the view, however, that in cases of a full confession under Hansard, the Revenue would be unfair to prosecute, effectively placing a limit on the full discretion of the Revenue in this matter.

As significant as these points are, in practical terms there is no record of any case in which a taxpayer who has made a full confession under Hansard being prosecuted for these offences later. The substantive point is how assured the taxpayer can be that the Revenue will not prosecute in these circumstances.

It is important to stress that the Hansard procedure invites a full and complete confession. Deliberate failure to disclose errors or omissions may result in criminal prosecution. Depending upon the facts of the particular case and the admissibility of evidence before the Courts, it is possible that someone who only admits to part of the irregularities could face criminal charges not only in relation to the matters undisclosed or misrepresented but also the matters disclosed.

Full Co-operation

A further element to be taken into account according to the previous version of Hansard is whether the taxpayer had given full co-operation to the Revenue during the investigation. This includes the giving of full facilities for investigation into his affairs and for examination of such books, papers, documents or information as the Board may consider necessary. A taxpayer could conclude from this, that even in cases of a full confession, if the right amount of co-operation is not offered, then he or she remains at the risk of prosecution.

Again in practice there have been no cases of the Revenue prosecuting in these circumstances. It has considered instead the fullness of the confession made under Hansard when deciding on subsequent prosecution action. It is a matter for the taxpayer to decide whether or not to co-operate with the investigation and the extent of that co-operation. If the matter remains civil, the Revenue will, however, take the degree of co-operation into account in determining any penalties which may be applicable.

It must however be made clear that the Board does not hold out the opportunity of Hansard indefinitely. So, for example, if a taxpayer who had been given Hansard took an unreasonable amount of time in making their full disclosure, the Inland Revenue may decide to commence its own investigation. Depending upon the information held or obtained by the Inland Revenue, this may lead at any time to the withdrawal of Hansard and the start of an investigation with a view to criminal prosecution. If this happened a full confession subsequently made by the taxpayer would not by itself prevent the Board from continuing to pursue the prosecution.

A Revised Hansard Statement

There has been a revised statement about the Board of the Inland Revenue's policy on these matters. The response to a Parliamentary Question to the Chancellor on 7th November 2002 was:

> 'Further to the statement made on 18th October 1990 at column 882 by the then Chancellor, the Rt. Hon. John Major, the practice of the Board of Inland Revenue in cases of suspected serious tax fraud is as follows:–
>
> The Board reserves complete discretion to pursue prosecutions in the circumstances it considers appropriate.
>
> Where serious tax fraud has been committed, the Board may accept a money settlement instead of pursuing a criminal prosecution.
>
> The Board will accept a money settlement and will not pursue a criminal prosecution, if the taxpayer, in response to being given a copy of this Statement by an authorised officer, makes a full and complete confession of all tax irregularities'.

The significant points to note are that a taxpayer making a full confession under this procedure may now be assured that the Inland Revenue will not pursue a criminal prosecution. The term 'pursue' is used because the Revenue is a prosecuting body in its own right only in England and Wales. In Scotland and in Northern Ireland it refers cases to the Procurator Fiscal and the Director of Public Prosecutions, respectively, for their consideration.

The revised text refers to a copy of the Statement being given by an authorised officer. For these purposes, an authorised officer is a current serving member of the Inland Revenue Special Compliance Office. A copy of the Hansard Statement will normally be given at the first meeting with the taxpayer after the case has been taken up for investigation under Code of Practice 9.

The Hansard procedure is explained in the Inland Revenue Code of Practice 9. This has been substantially updated as a result of the revised Statement. (There have also been some consequential changes to Code of Practice 8, which deals with cases where serious fraud is not suspected). One of the key changes is to make clear that it is for the taxpayer to decide whether to co-operate with the investigation and that in making this decision the taxpayer may seek the help of a professional advisor. The Code of Practice also makes clear that any information that the taxpayer does provide may be used in any subsequent proceedings to determine tax, interest and penalties. As stated above, if the case is concluded by way of a money settlement, the level of co-operation will be one of the factors taken into account in deciding the amount of any penalties.

These changes will have immediate effect and so taxpayers subjected to the Hansard procedure will be read the revised text from now on. Copies of the revised Codes of Practice will be available soon from the Inland Revenue.

Tax Bulletin Issue 64, April 2003

Page 1011. Businesses, Individuals and the Settlements Legislation

Introduction

We have been asked by the Chartered Institute of Taxation (CIOT) if we would provide some further information and examples on the settlements legislation in Part XV of Income and Corporation Taxes Acts (ICTA) 1988 especially in the context of its application to businesses and individuals. We are happy to do so. We have incorporated a number of comments made by the CIOT on a draft of this article and the examples it contains, but the article remains an expression of the views and practice of the Inland Revenue and the CIOT does not necessarily agree with all the points made.

Unless otherwise stated all references are to ICTA 1988 in this article.

The settlements legislation was originally enacted in the 1930's. The legislation was brought up to date in 1995, further amended in 1999 and can now be found at sections 660A to 660G. The legislation not only applies to trusts but can also apply to other situations involving individuals, companies and partnerships. It is these non-trust situations where we have been asked to provide further information.

The existing guidance on the settlements legislation is found in the Inland Revenue's Trusts Estates and Settlements Manual which is available on our website at www.ir.gov.uk/manuals/tsemmanual/. That manual will be updated to incorporate this additional information shortly.

The settlements legislation is intended to prevent an individual from gaining a tax advantage by making arrangements which divert his or her income to another person who is liable at a lower rate of tax or is not liable to income tax.

Definitions

There are two key definitions when considering the settlements legislation, both set out in section 660G(1):

- ***Settlement*** includes any disposition, trust, covenant, arrangement or transfer of assets. Settlement may include a series of transactions which taken together are regarded as an arrangement. The courts have limited the scope of a settlement to where there is some element of bounty, see 'CIR v Plummer [1979] STC 793: 54 TC 1';
- ***Settlor*** means any person by whom the settlement was made.

There are some important statutory exemptions from the legislation:

- Section 660A(6) exempts situations where the property passed to a spouse is an outright gift, unless;

    - the gift does not carry the right to the whole of the income arising, or
    - the property given is wholly or substantially a right to income.
- Section 660A(9)(a) exempts annual payments made by an individual for bona fide commercial reasons in connection with their trade, profession or vocation.
- Section 660A(9)(b) exempts certain donations made to charities.
- Section 660A(9)(c) exempts income consisting of a benefit under approved pension schemes.

So, in general, the settlements legislation can apply where an individual enters into an arrangement to divert income to someone else and in the process tax is saved. So long as those arrangements are:

- bounteous, or
- not commercial, or
- not at arm's length, or
- in the case of a gift between spouses, wholly or substantially a right to income.

Does the legislation only apply to transfers to spouses and minor children?

It is a common misconception that the settlements legislation applies only to arrangements involving a settlor's spouse or minor children. However, section 660A(2) makes it clear the settlor is treated as having an interest in property if 'that property or any derived property is, or will or may become, payable to or applicable for the benefit of the settlor or his spouse in any circumstances whatsoever.' It is not necessary for the settlor's spouse or children to be the people to whom the income is transferred. If the settlor or their spouse retains an interest in the property then the legislation can apply. See example 2 below.

Section 660A applies to arrangements where the settlor, or their spouse, retain an interest in the settlement. Section 660B applies to situations where income not caught by section 660A is paid or made available to a minor unmarried child of the settlor. The 1999 amendments extended the legislation to include income otherwise treated as that of the child with regard to settlements made on or after _9 March 1999. For example a settlor who invests money in a savings scheme which is held on bare trust for their child will find the income treated as theirs under this section if the child's relevant settlement income exceeds £100 (section 660B(5)). There are further examples involving children below at examples 8 and 9.

How does the legislation apply to non-trust situations?

A very small percentage of the enquiries we currently undertake each year involve the settlements legislation and non-trust situations. However we do seek tax, interest and penalties in appropriate cases. It is not possible to provide a definitive list of the issues we look for when deciding which cases to take up for enquiry, but some of the factors that the Revenue is looking for might include:

- Main earner drawing a low salary leading to enhanced profits from which dividends can be paid to shareholders who are friends or family members.
- Disproportionately large returns on capital investments.
- Differing classes of shares enabling dividends to be paid only to shareholders paying lower rates of tax.
- Dividends being waived so that higher dividends can be paid to shareholders paying lower rates of tax.
- Income being transferred from the person making most of the profits of a business to a friend or family member who pays tax at a lower rate.

There are a wide range of arrangements that can potentially be caught by the settlements legislation which do not involve a trust. Each case will depend on the facts but some of the most common situations which we see are:

- Shares subscribed at par that carry only restricted rights.
- Shares given away that carry only restricted rights.
- Shares subscribed at par in a company by someone else where the income of the company derives mainly from a single employee.
- A share in a partnership gifted or transferred below value.
- Dividend waivers.
- Situations where dividends are paid only on certain classes of shares.
- Dividends paid to the settlor's minor children.

These lists are by no means definitive of situations to which the settlements legislation can be applied.

The best way to illustrate how the legislation applies is by using the following examples although it should be noted that these are by no means exhaustive.

Example 1 – Issued shares with restricted rights

An engineering company has 100 ordinary £1 shares. Mr A and Mr B own 50 ordinary shares each. They create a new class of B shares which carry no voting rights and no assets in a winding up. They then issue 50 B shares to each of their wives. Dividends voted on those B shares would be treated as the income of Mr A and Mr B rather than their wives as the B dividends are from shares that are wholly or substantially a right to income and so not exempted from section 660A by section 660A(6). (This example is based on the High Court case of 'Young v Pearce; Young v Scrutton [1996] STC 743').

Example 2 – Gifted shares with restricted rights

Mr C is the sole director and owns all the 1000 ordinary £1 shares in C Limited. His aunt, Mrs D, has always been very kind to him and he wants to thank her for this. He subscribes, at par, for 100 B shares, with no voting rights and restricted rights to capital of £10 per share in the event of winding up. He gifts the shares to Mrs D. Mr C then declares a dividend of £100 per share with Mrs D receiving dividends of £10,000.

This is a bounteous arrangement and we would apply the settlements legislation to the dividends. The property giving rise to the dividends cannot be looked at too narrowly as the shares alone. The wider arrangement must be considered. Because he is in effective control of the company Mr C retains an interest in the underlying property as he could simply pay all future income arising to himself as director's salary or as dividends on the ordinary shares.

Example 3 – Subscribed shares

E Ltd was incorporated in October 1997 to provide the services of Mr E as an IT consultant to a number of clients working in the pharmaceutical industry. The company's share capital is £2 consisting of 2 £1 shares. Mr E is the sole director of the company, and his wife Mrs E is company secretary but takes no other active part in the company. From the beginning each subscribed for one share. The company has no significant capital assets. The figures for the first year's trading are: –

Turnover	100,000
Expenses	5,000
Salary (Mr E)	10,000
Salary (Mrs E)	5,000
Dividends	70,000

In this case Mrs E receives a salary for her duties as company secretary, but the whole arrangement whereby Mrs E invests £1 and in return gets a dividend of £35,000 is bounteous. There is nothing to suggest that the dividend is a commercial return on her investment. As there is no significant capital in the company, what has passed from Mr E to Mrs E is substantially a right to income and the whole of the dividend is taxed on Mr E.

In reaching this conclusion, the legislation allows us to look at the whole arrangement. It is the work that Mr E carries out which creates the company's profits which in turn enable the dividends to be paid. Mrs E's investment of £1 does not enable the company to make profits and the company itself has minimal capital value. In accepting a salary below the market rate from the company, and thereby allowing some of the income earned to pass to Mrs E as a dividend, Mr E has entered into a bounteous arrangement to divert income to his spouse with the aim of avoiding tax.

Example 4 – Subscribed shares with little capital value then gifted

As in example 3 but in October 1997 Mr E was not married and subscribed for both £1 shares himself. Mr E's solicitor was acting as company secretary. A year later he got married and gave his wife one of his shares in the company. At this point Mrs E took over the role of company secretary. In the following year Mrs E receives a wage of £5,000 and the company pays a dividend of £35,000 per share.

Since the capital value of the company is insignificant the gift of the share from Mr E to his wife is not exempt from section 660A by virtue of section 660A(6) as the shares are 'wholly or substantially a right to income'. Accordingly the settlements legislation applies in relation to Mrs E's £35,000 dividend payment and the income would be treated as Mr E's for tax purposes.

Example 5 – Partnerships

Mr F and Mr G are in partnership as second hand car dealers. They do not have any premises but buy and sell cars through auctions and the classified adverts of local papers. The partnership's only assets are some office equipment worth less than £1,000 and they usually have a couple of cars in stock at any one time. They are successful and the profits of £80,000 a year are split equally between them. They decide to admit their wives to the partnership and amend the partnership agreement in order to split profits equally four ways. Mrs F and Mrs G do no work in the partnership and the partnership has no employees.

This is a bounteous arrangement transferring income from one spouse to the other. The settlements legislation will apply and Mr F and Mr G continue to be taxable on half the profits each.

Example 6 – Dividend Waivers

Where a company with few shareholders declares a final dividend when one or more of the shareholders has waived their right to a dividend in circumstances where other shareholders may benefit, it is possible the settlements legislation could apply.

For example Mrs H owns 80 ordinary shares in H Limited. _Mr H owns 20 shares. In 2000 the company made a profit of £25,000. Mrs H waived her right to any dividend. The company then declared a dividend of £1,000 per share, and Mr H, who had no other income, received a dividend of £20,000.

We would apply the settlements legislation in these circumstances. Clearly a dividend of this amount could not have been paid from the company's profits on all the shares, so the waiver arrangement enhanced the dividend paid to Mr H. £16,000 of the dividend paid to Mr H is attributed to Mrs H under section 660A because the waiver was a bounteous arrangement.

Example 7 – Dividends on certain shares

As in example 6, but in this case Mrs I owns A shares and _Mr I owns B shares. Both A and B shares rank equally. Again profits of £25,000 are made and a dividend of £20,000 is voted on the B shares while no dividend is voted on the A shares.

Clearly by not voting dividends on the A shares (which rank equally with the B shares) this is a bounteous arrangement as the dividend paid on the B shares could only be paid if no dividend was declared in respect of the A shares. £16,000 of the dividend paid to Mr I is attributed to Mrs I under section 660A because the decision to only vote dividends on certain shares was a bounteous arrangement.

Example 8 – Children – gift of shares from parent

Mr J owns all 100 issued £1 shares in J Limited. Mr J is the sole company director and is the person responsible for making all the company's profits because of his knowledge, expertise and hard work. Mr J gives each of his four children 10 shares. Dividends are paid.

Section 660B applies and attributes the dividends paid to the children to Mr J for tax purposes. This is because Mr J has paid the income to his unmarried minor children.

Example 9 – Children – gift of shares other than from parent

As in example 8, but the 40 shares held by the children were originally owned by their grandmother who had subscribed for them at par when the company was set up but shortly afterwards had gifted them to her grandchildren.

Section 660B applies and attributes the dividends received by the children to Mr J for tax purposes. Since Mr J is the person responsible for making the company's profits and decides on the level of dividends paid, it is Mr J who is the settlor rather than the children's grandmother.

The legislation could apply in a similar way if the children had subscribed for the shares themselves with money received from a third party or even from bank accounts in their own names.

Where does the legislation not apply?

In most everyday situations involving gifts, dividends, shares, partnerships, etc. the settlements legislation will not apply. If there is no 'bounty' or if the gift to a spouse is an outright gift which is not wholly, or substantially, a right to income, then the legislation will not apply. For example:

Example 10 – An outright gift to a spouse

Mrs L owns 10,000 ordinary shares in a FTSE 100 company. Those shares are worth £40,000. Mrs L gives those shares to her husband. Mr L is now entitled to all the dividends from the shares and can sell the shares if he wants and keep the proceeds. This is an outright gift of shares that are not wholly, or substantially, a right to income since they have a capital value and can be traded, so the settlements legislation does not apply.

Example 11 – Subscribed shares

Mr M is the sole director and owns all the 100 ordinary shares in M Limited, a small manufacturing company. The company employs 10 people and owns a small factory, a high street shop, tools fixtures and fittings and 3 delivery vehicles. Mr M draws a salary of £30,000 each year and receives dividends of £20,000. Mr M then gifts 50 shares to his wife who plays no part in the business. Mr and Mrs M then each receive dividends of £10,000.

We would not seek to apply the settlements legislation to the dividends received by Mrs M. This is because the outright gift of the shares cannot be regarded as wholly or substantially a right to income. The shares have capital rights and the company has substantial assets so on the winding up or sale of the business the shares would have more than an insubstantial value.

Example 12 – Subscribed shares

Mr N wants to set up in business as a bookseller. He needs at least £100,000 to buy premises, equipment and stock. He sets up a company and he and Mrs N each subscribe for 40,000 ordinary £1 shares at par and the company borrows £20,000 from the bank. Mr N draws a salary which after four years is £40,000. Mrs N does not work for the company. Company profits are used to repay debt and expand the business. The business does well and after 6 years the profits are sufficient to pay a dividend of £10,000.

We would not seek to apply the settlements legislation to the dividend of £5,000 received by Mrs N. There is no bounty as Mr N draws a commercial salary for his efforts and the dividend is a commercial return on the initial investment which was vital at the commencement of the business and contained a clear element of risk.

Example 13 – A partnership

Mr and Mrs O and their friend Mr P have a business idea. They want to open a Cycle Repair Shop. Mrs O does not want to work but agrees to invest in the business without taking an active part, that is to say she is a sleeping partner. Each partner invests £10,000 and the £30,000 is used to lease a shop, buy equipment and stock and keep the business going until trade builds up. Under the partnership agreement Mr O and Mr P receive £500 a week with all the remaining profits split three ways between the partners.

The business is a huge success and makes large profits and continues to grow. Within five years Mrs O is receiving £50,000 a year as her share of the partnership profits. Although Mrs O does not work in the business, and her initial investment has turned out to be very successful, the settlements legislation would not apply to treat her share of the partnership profits as Mr O's. Mrs O's original investment was vital to get the business started and she risked losing it if the business failed.

Example 14 – A partnership

Mr P is a self-employed engineer engaged on specialist work for a number of clients in the construction industry. Mr P employs his wife, who plays an active part in the business including ordering and collecting specialist parts. Mrs P is paid a salary of £20,000. The profits of the business are £40,000. Mrs P owns a substantial property inherited from her mother.

Because of a number of claims made against Mr P, his insurers want to raise premiums by £20,000. He doesn't think he can afford this so his insurers agree to not increase the premiums if Mr P agrees to pay the first £25,000 of any claim. Mr P and Mrs P enter into an equal partnership. Accordingly Mrs P no longer draws a salary but is entitled to a share of the profits as well as being exposed to the liabilities of the partnership. The property she owns is therefore potentially at risk.

Mrs P's share of the profits is £30,000. Mrs P therefore has extra overall income of £10,000 because she has taken on the risk of the partnership liabilities including that associated with the £25,000 excess on the insurance policy. There is therefore no bounty and the settlements legislation would not apply.

Example 15 – Gift of shares other than from parent

In 1960 Mr & Mrs Q and Mr & Mrs R set up a small family cleaning company. In total there were, and still are, 100 £1 ordinary shares in the business. Initially Mr Q and Mr R each subscribed at par for 40 shares and Mrs Q and Mrs R each subscribed at par for 10 shares.

When Mr & Mrs Q died they each left their shares in the company (50 in total) to their daughter, Miss Q. When Mr R also died he left his 40 shares in the company to his daughter Mrs S. Miss Q and Mrs S are both directors of the company and carry out its day to day running. The current turnover of the company is approximately £1,000,000 per year and its capital value is over

£250,000. Miss Q and _Mrs S each receive a salary of £60,000 per year. Each year a dividend of £500 per share is paid.

Mrs R has retained her original 10 shares in the company since 1960. Without discussing the matter in advance with either Miss Q or Mrs S, Mrs R decides to give her shares to her five year old granddaughter who is also Mrs S's daughter. Mrs R makes the gift on her granddaughter's next birthday.

The settlements legislation would not apply to this case since Mrs R retains no interest in the shares which she gives to her granddaughter and is therefore not a settlor within the meaning of section 660G. Nor is Mrs R's decision to gift the shares to her granddaughter part of a wider arrangement with Mrs S to settle income on the child.

Summary

Whether or not the settlements legislation applies to an arrangement depends on the particular facts of the case. It is necessary to look at the arrangement as a whole. If there is a bounteous arrangement which effectively transfers income earned by one person to another resulting in a reduction in overall tax liability the arrangement may be liable to challenge under the settlements legislation.

A purely commercial transaction or series of transactions at arms length is outside the meaning of 'settlement'. Most commonly the legislation will apply where individuals seek to divert income to members of their family or to friends. A good test of whether or not the legislation could apply is to consider would the same payments be made to a person who acquired shares in a company or a share of a partnership at arms length. Or whether income is being paid simply because the recipient is your spouse or child or some other individual you might wish to benefit.

If you have any comments on this article and the issues raised you can contact the Editor of Tax Bulletin at the Inland Revenue or at the CIOT contact Liz Lathwood, Technical Officer, Chartered Institute of Taxation, 12 Upper Belgrave Street, London, SW1X 8BB.

Tax Bulletin Issue 66, August 2003

Page 1048. Taxation of Chargeable Gains – Sale of Trust Interests and Transfers Linked to Trustee Borrowing. [Schedules 4A and 4B to the Taxation of Chargeable Gains Act 1992.]

Interpretations

We have been asked by representative bodies and individual firms of tax practitioners to offer guidance on the meaning of certain statutory terms and on the application of the legislation in Schedules 4A and 4B Taxation of

Chargeable Gains Act 1992 ['TCGA']. The relevant legislation was enacted in Finance Act 2000. These schedules are part of a package of measures designed to prevent certain forms of avoidance of capital gains tax involving trusts.

Details: Schedule 4A

Schedule 4A is concerned with certain situations where there is a disposal of an interest in a UK resident settlement for consideration.

A1. Paragraph 3: 'for consideration'.

Under paragraph 3(1) 'A disposal is "for consideration" if consideration is given or received by any person for, or otherwise in connection with, any transaction by virtue of which the disposal is effected'. (Paragraph 3(3) restricts this to actual consideration.) Our view is that 'consideration' in this context does not extend to the incidental costs of the transaction, in particular reasonable fees charged by professional advisers for giving guidance as to the legal and fiscal effects of the transaction or for drafting and executing the relevant paperwork. Therefore, if there are no payments other than in respect of the incidental costs, the transaction does not fall within Schedule 4A.

A2. Paragraph 13(2)(b): 'for practical purposes'

This paragraph is concerned with the situation where there is a period between the beginning of the disposal of the interest in question and the 'effective completion' of it in circumstances where Schedule 4A applies. In this situation the deemed disposal under paragraph 4(1) of the relevant trust assets occurs at the moment of effective completion of the disposal of the interest. This is required for testing the conditions relating to the residence status of the trustees and settlor (paragraphs 5 & 6) and the interest of the settlor in the settlement (paragraph 7). It is also relevant for the purposes of paragraph 8 where the identity of the underlying assets changes during the period, and paragraph 9 where the value changes during the period.

The conditions as to the residence of the settlor and the trustees are met if they applied for

- the tax year in which the disposal of the interest began, or
- the tax year in which it was effectively completed, or
- any tax year in between.

The condition as to the interest of the settlor is met if it applied at any time between

- the beginning of the tax year two years before the tax year in which the disposal of the interest began and

- the date of the effective completion of the disposal.

These two dates are inclusive.

The beginning of the disposal is defined by paragraph 13(2)(a) as, in the case of a disposal involving the exercise of an option, the date of the grant of the option, and in any other case involving a contract, the date the contract was entered into.

The effective completion is defined by paragraph 13(2)(b) as 'the point at which the person acquiring the interest becomes for practical purposes unconditionally entitled to the whole of the intended subject matter of the disposal'. The main purpose of the words 'for practical purposes' is to cover cases where the buyer has the power to compel the trustees to transfer the property to him on giving due notice. Another example would be where the buyer has a right to enjoy the property now, but is not entitled to it until a particular contingency is fulfilled, and there is no real likelihood of its not being fulfilled.

Details: Schedule 4B

Schedule 4B is concerned with situations where the trustees of a settlement falling within section 77, 86 or 87 TCGA make a transfer of value which is treated as linked with trustee borrowing.

B1. Paragraph 2(1)(b): cash distributions which are income.

Where trustees of a discretionary trust make a distribution which is income of the recipient for UK tax purposes, this is not a 'transfer of value' within paragraph 2, which is concerned with capital transactions.

B2. Paragraph 2(1)(a): beneficiary exercising rights under section 12 Trustee etc Act 1996.

In certain circumstances a beneficiary's occupation of property, instead of being the consequence of the volition of the trustees, may result from personal rights under section 12 Trusts of Land and Appointment of Trustees Act 1996. Our view is that if the rights of the beneficiary arise as a consequence of the wording of the deed or will, then the occupation does not give rise to a transfer of value. It may be otherwise where the rights have arisen as a consequence of the exercise by the trustees of a power of appointment or advancement.

B3. Paragraph 2(1)(c): 'issue a security'.

We have been asked what the expression 'issue a security' covers. It caters for those exceptional circumstances where trustees issue to a beneficiary or to the trustees of another trust a document acknowledging liability. Paragraph 13(2) of Schedule 4B provides that references to the transfer of an asset include everything that is or is treated as a disposal of an asset. The issue of a security is not in itself the disposal or part disposal of an asset. Therefore paragraph 2(1)(b) does not apply to it, and it was necessary to have a specific provision to cover this possibility.

B4. Paragraph 4(1): meaning of 'borrowing'.

It is not unusual for the trustees of a non-resident trust to borrow money from a non-resident company which they control. In this situation, if the company were resident in the UK, section 419 of the Income and Corporation Taxes Act 1988 might well be applicable. It has been suggested that in this situation the trustees are effectively 'borrowing' from themselves and therefore outside paragraph 4(1). We consider this incorrect, particularly in the light of *Chamberlain v IRC* (1943) 25 TC 357. It does not matter whether the borrowing is from a company controlled by the trustees or their associates, or from an entirely unconnected company. What matters is the use to which the borrowing is put.

The fact that money was borrowed before 21 March 2000 does not prevent it from being outstanding trust borrowing.

Where trustees are presented with a bill, for example for repairs to trust property, bona fide delay in payment would not convert this into a borrowing for the purposes of paragraph 4.

B5. Paragraph 6(4): application of proceeds to meet current expenses.

We have been asked whether trustee borrowings to meet payments on account or provision for future or past expenses are covered by the expression 'current expenses'. One circumstance in which borrowings are applied for 'normal trust purposes' (paragraph 6) is where they are applied by the trustees in making payments to meet bona fide current expenses incurred by them.

One may note that there are three tests to be met.

- The borrowings have been applied by the moment of the transfer of value (paragraph 5(2)(b)(i)).
- They have been applied to meet bona fide 'current expenses'.
- The expenses are expenses of 'administering' the settlement or any of the settled property.

In the case of borrowing to meet future expenses it is hard to see how the borrowings can be said to have been applied. But the time for making the test is not when the money is borrowed, but the time of the transfer of value (this is 'the material time', as defined in paragraph 2(2)). In the case of payments on account there would be the requisite application and the liability to pay would have been incurred.

We do not regard 'current' as restricting qualification to expenditure which for accounting purposes must fall in the year of borrowing, but we should regard it as excluding borrowing to make a provision for future expenditure or to meet expenditure that was incurred long before but left unpaid. In general where contracts for repairs of an ordinary kind have been entered into, we should regard the expenditure anticipated under those contracts to be current expenses at the moment of borrowing. Where trustees as the owner or tenant of a flat are obliged by contract or under the terms of the lease to make payments into a common fund to meet future maintenance or repair expenditure this would be regarded as a current expense.

The expression 'administering the settlement or any of the settled property' should be construed widely to cover not only those expenses properly chargeable to income, or which would be so chargeable but for express provisions of the trust deed, but also capital expenditure such as capital taxes in the UK or elsewhere, or legal costs of a reorganization, in particular the costs of an application under the Variation of Trusts Act. Other capital expenditure would often be expenditure on the asset itself, and therefore qualify under paragraph 6(2). Contributions to the day-to-day running costs of a nominee company controlled by the trustees would also qualify.

B6. Paragraph 7: 'ordinary trust assets': futures contracts.

We have been asked to say whether a futures contract relating to commodities is an 'ordinary trust asset'. Such a contract is not a tangible asset nor does it give the holder an interest in such an asset. Therefore, it is not an 'ordinary trust asset'.

B7. What happens when trustees put money into a conventional current or deposit account at a bank or building society?

Although in general law this is regarded as a loan from the customer to the bank, in the context of this legislation we do not consider that this comes within the meaning of 'lend' for the purposes of paragraph 2(1)(a). The currency in which the deposit is made is immaterial.

B8. What happens when money is borrowed to purchase the freehold interest of a property which is then rented on a commercial basis?

It is important to appreciate that the expression 'transfer of value' equates to the three types of transaction described in paragraph 2(1). It does not carry the kind of meaning that it has for inheritance tax purposes.

Under paragraph 13(2) references to the transfer of an asset include references to anything that is a disposal, and under section 21(2) TCGA references to a disposal include references to a part disposal. Paragraph 13(3) provides that references to a transfer of an asset do not include the transfer of an asset which is created by the part disposal of another asset. The grant of a lease is a part disposal of the freehold interest and therefore the grant of a lease is a transfer of the freehold interest for the purposes of paragraph 2(1)(b) and is not regarded as the transfer simply of the lease. If the freehold interest was bought with borrowed money it meets the test in paragraph 2(4)(a), and the amount of value transferred equals the market value of the freehold.

Assuming that there is outstanding trustee borrowing at 'the material time', which is defined in paragraph 2(2) as the time the transfer is effectively completed, it is then necessary to consider whether the transfer of value is linked with trustee borrowing. Under paragraph 7 tangible property, and any interest in such property falls within the expression 'ordinary trust assets'. However the property concerned must under paragraph 6(2)(b) either form part of the settled property immediately after the material time, or meet the alternative condition in paragraph 8(1)(b) that it is represented by ordinary trust assets which form part of the settled property immediately after the material time. Paragraph 6(2)(b) and paragraph 8(1)(b) may be looked at together. In this situation we say that the reversion to the lease is still part of the settled property, and the lease itself is represented by the right to the rental stream.

Therefore where trustees borrow money to acquire the freehold interest in a property which is then let commercially and, at the material time, there are no outstanding trustee borrowings other than those which have been applied for normal trust purposes, Schedule 4B does not apply. But the position will be different if at that moment there are outstanding trustee borrowings applied for other purposes.

The same considerations apply where trustees acquire a long lease which is sublet, and where the asset in question is a chattel rather than land or buildings.

B9. What happens when money is spent unproductively, for example on a planning application that fails?

Under paragraph 6(2) there are three conditions that must be met by a payment in respect of 'an ordinary trust asset' if it is to be regarded as applied for normal trust purposes. The third, in paragraph 6(2)(c), is that the sum is allowable under section 38 TCGA (or would be but for section 17 or 39) as a deduction in computing a gain accruing to the trustees on a disposal of the asset. If an application for planning permission fails, then when the land is actually sold the costs relating to the application are generally not allowable; this is because they are not 'reflected in the state or nature of the asset at the time of the disposal'. Paragraph 6(2)(c) however must be referring to a notional disposal not to a real one. In the context of paragraph 6 we consider that the reference can only be to a notional disposal taking place at the time when the expenditure is incurred.

Although one could not lay down as a universal rule that the expenditure would always qualify, the test is whether the existence of the current application for planning permission is reflected in the state or nature of the asset at the time of the notional disposal.

B10. How should we compute the base cost of assets for future disposals?

The trustees are treated as disposing of the whole or a proportion of each of the chargeable assets continuing to form part of the settled property. Suppose that an asset cost £600, the trustees are treated as disposing of two thirds of the asset at the material time (paragraph 10(1)), and the respective values of two thirds and one third immediately after that time are £900 and £450. Leaving aside indexation, if any, the computation is:

Cost	2/3 of 600	400
Deemed Proceeds		900
Gain		500

Remaining original cost	600–400	200
Deemed Acquisition		900
Revised cost		1100

Appendix 4

Forms

Trust details

Inland Revenue

Reference

Please use this reference if you write or call. It will help to avoid delay.

Issued by

Please complete this form and return it to this office. If you pass the form to someone else to complete, please let me know the name and address of that person.

If you have already supplied this information to an Inland Revenue office you do not need to complete this form. Please let me know the name of that office and the reference number quoted.

If the trust is a bare trust - where the beneficiaries have immediate and absolute entitlement to all of the capital and income - and you are the trustee:

- you do not need to complete this form but must let me have written confirmation that this is a bare trust
- you should complete this form if, exceptionally, you intend to submit returns of income as trustees.

Bare trust beneficiaries must show their own income and capital gains on their personal Tax Returns.

Part A Complete in all cases

Trust

1 Full title of the trust

Trustees

2 Full name and address of each trustee

State first the trustee to whom return forms etc. should normally be sent.Continue on a separate sheet if necessary.

Name

Address

Postcode

Name

Address

Postcode

3 Contact details of any professional agent acting

Name

Address

Postcode

Reference

Telephone number

	✓ *as appropriate* Yes	No
4a Is the trust governed by the laws of a country outside the UK?	☐	☐
4b Is the trust's general administration carried on outside the UK?	☐	☐
4c Is the trust established under Scots law?	☐	☐
4d Has the trust been set up for the benefit of employees or is it otherwise employment related, whether set up by an employer or by someone else?	☐	☐

41G(Trust) **(Substitute)(LexisNexis Butterworths Tolley)** BS 3/02

Part B Complete if trust established by a will or intestacy

The deceased

5 Full name and last address of the deceased

Name

Address

Postcode

6a Date of death / /

6b Date trust commenced / /

7a Inland Revenue office that dealt with the deceased's last Tax Return *(or received the probate, letters of administration etc.)*

7b Reference in that office ***or*** National Insurance number

✓as appropriate
Yes No

Administration period

8 Has the administration period ended? ☐ ☐

If yes, give the date it ended / /

Deed of variation or family arrangement

9a Has a deed of variation or family arrangement altered the will or the intestacy provisions? ☐ ☐

If yes, give the date of the deed / /

If you answered 'yes' at question 9a complete Part C to give details of each person who took less under the deed than they would have done under the will. Each such person is a settlor of the amount given up.

9b Did the deed create a trust in addition to the one established under the will or intestacy provisions? ☐ ☐

If yes, refer to Part A and let me have the same information for the additional trust on a separate sheet.

Part C Complete if trust established in settlor's lifetime

10 Date trust established / /

Details of settlor

11a Full name and address of settlor
Where there is more than one settlor you should give details for each, using a separate sheet if necessary.

Name

Address

Postcode

11b Inland Revenue office that deals with the settlor's tax affairs

11c Reference in that office ***or*** National Insurance number

Assets settled

12 Give details of the assets settled, including values.
If land or buildings, state the address.

Part D Complete in all cases

Signature

Capacity in which signed

Full name in CAPITALS

Date / /

Inland Revenue

Trust and Estate Tax Return for the year ended 5 April 2003

Tax reference

Date

Inland Revenue office

Area Director

Issue address

Telephone

For Reference

Please read this page first

The green arrows and instructions will guide you through your Tax Return

This Notice requires you by law to send me a Tax Return for the year from 6 April 2002 to 5 April 2003, containing details of the income and capital gains. I've sent you this paper form to fill in, or you could use:

- ***other Inland Revenue approved paper versions, OR***
- ***the Electronic Lodgement Service (available through some tax advisers).***

Make sure the Tax Return, and any documents I ask for, reach me by:

- ***the later of 30 September 2003 and 2 months after the date this notice was given if you want me to calculate the trust or estate's tax, OR***
- ***the later of 31 January 2004 and 3 months after the date this notice was given, at the latest, or you will be liable to an automatic penalty of £100.***

Make sure your payment of any tax the trust or estate owes reaches me by 31 January 2004. Otherwise, you will have to pay interest, and perhaps a surcharge.

The Trust and Estate Tax Return may be checked. Please remember that there are penalties for supplying false information.

Calculating your tax

You can choose to calculate the trust or estate's tax. But if you don't want to, and providing I receive the Return by 30 September, I'll work out the tax for you and I'll also let you know if there's tax to pay by 31 January 2004.

***However,** if you file later than 30 September or 2 months after the date this notice was given, see the Tax Calculation Guide (sent with this Return unless I know you have a tax adviser).*

The Trust and Estate Tax Return - your responsibilities

I have sent you pages 1 to 12 of the Tax Return.

You might need other forms - 'supplementary Pages' - if the trust or estate had particular income or capital gains. Use page 3 to check.

***You** are responsible for sending me a complete and correct return, but **we** are here to help **you** get it right.*

Four ways we can help you

- ***look** at the Trust and Estate Tax Return Guide (sent with this Tax Return, unless I know you have a tax adviser). It should answer most of your questions, **OR***
- ***visit** our website at www.inlandrevenue.gov.uk, **OR***
- ***ring** me on the above number - when the office is closed, call our Helpline on 0845 9000 444, **OR***
- ***call** in to one of our Inland Revenue Enquiry Centres - look under 'Inland Revenue' in the phone book.*

SA900 (Substitute)(LexisNexis UK)

INCOME AND CAPITAL GAINS *for the year ended 5 April 2003*

Step 1 You may not have to answer all the questions in this Tax Return. *Tick if this applies*

- see notes on pages 4 and 6 of the Trust and Estate Tax Return Guide

1) **If you are the trustee of a bare trust** (except an unauthorised unit trust), that is, one in which the beneficiary(ies) has/have an immediate and absolute title to both capital and income you can go straight to Question 19 on page 11. ☐

2) **If you are the personal representative of a deceased person,** completing this Tax Return for a period of administration **and all** the points below apply:
   - all the income arose in the UK
   - you do not wish to claim reliefs
   - no annual payments have been made out of capital
   - all income has had tax deducted before you received it (or is UK dividends with tax credit)
   - there are no accrued income charges or reliefs, no income from relevant discounted securities, gilt strips, offshore income gains, or gains on life insurance policies, life annuities or capital redemption policies where no tax is treated as having been paid on the gain.

   Then, **if you have not made any chargeable disposals**, go straight to Question 19 on page 11 ☐

   or, **if you have made chargeable disposals,** answer Questions 5 and 6 at Step 2, Question 8 and then Questions 17 to 22. ☐

3) **If you are the trustee of an interest in possession trust** (one which is exclusively an interest in possession trust), and:
   - no income arose to the trust, **or** ☐
   - you have mandated all the trust income to the beneficiary(ies), **or** ☐
   - all the income arose in the UK and has had tax deducted before you receive it (or is UK dividends with tax credit), **or** ☐
   - you have mandated part of the income to the beneficiary(ies) where the part you have not mandated comprises only income arising in the UK which has had tax deducted before you received it ☐

   and all of the following points apply:
   - the answer will be 'No' in boxes 8.11 and 8.13 of Question 8
   - there are no accrued income charges or reliefs, no income from relevant discounted securities, gilt strips, company buy-backs, offshore income gains, or gains on life insurance policies, life annuities or capital redemption policies
   - you do not wish to claim reliefs (Question 10)
   - no annual payments have been made out of capital (Question 11)
   - no further capital has been added to the settlement (Question 12)
   - no capital payments have been made to or for the benefit of minor unmarried children of the settlor during his/her lifetime (Question 15A)
   - the trust has never been non-resident and has never received any capital from another trust which is, or at any time has been, non-resident (Question 16)

   Then, **if you have not made any chargeable disposals**, go straight to Question 19 on page 11 ☐

   or, **if you have made chargeable disposals,** answer Questions 5 and 6 at Step 2, Question 8 and then Questions 17 to 22. ☐

4) **If you are the trustee of a charitable trust**, and:
   - you are claiming exemption from tax on all your income and gains, you can go straight to Question 7 and then Question 22, **or**
   - you are claiming exemption from tax on only part of your income and gains, you must complete this Return for any income or gains for which you are not claiming exemption.

5) **In any other cases,** including if you are the trustee of an unauthorised unit trust, you should go to Step 2.

Step 2 Answer Questions 1 to 7 on page 3 to check if you need supplementary Pages to give details of particular income or gains. Pages 8 and 9 of the Trust and Estate Tax Return Guide will help. (Ask the Orderline for a Guide if I haven't sent you one with the Tax Return, and you want one.) If you answer **'Yes'**, ask the Orderline for the appropriate supplementary Pages and Notes.

Ring the Orderline on 0845 9000 404 or fax on 0845 9000 604 for any you need (closed Christmas Day, Boxing Day and New Year's Day). Make sure you ask for the supplementary Pages for the Trust and Estate Tax Return.

■ TRUST AND ESTATE TAX RETURN: PAGE 2

INCOME AND CAPITAL GAINS *for the year ended 5 April 2003* continued

Make sure you have the supplementary Pages you need and then tick the box below when you have filled them in.

Q1 Did the trust or estate make any profit or loss from a sole trade? (Read page 8 of the Trust and Estate Tax Return Guide if you are the personal representative of a deceased Name at Lloyd's.) — Yes ☐ — Trust and estate trade ☐

Q2 Did the trust or estate make any profit or loss or have any other income from a partnership? — Yes ☐ — Trust and estate partnership ☐

Q3 Did the trust or estate receive any rent or other income from land and property in the UK? — Yes ☐ — Trust and estate land and property ☐

Q4 Did the trust or estate receive any income from foreign companies or savings institutions, offshore funds or trusts abroad, land and property abroad, or gains on foreign life insurance policies? — Yes ☐

Is the trust or estate claiming relief for foreign tax paid on foreign income or gains, or relief from UK tax under a Double Taxation Agreement? — Yes ☐ — Trust and estate foreign ☐

Q5 Capital gains

- did the trust or estate dispose of assets worth more than £15,400 in total? — Yes ☐
- were the trust's or estate's chargeable gains more than its annual exemption or do you want to make a claim or election for the year? — Yes ☐

Does this Return include the disposal of assets for either a Trust/Settlement with 'separate funds', or for just one of those separate funds?
Read page 9 of the Trust and Estate Tax Return Guide. — Yes ☐ — Trust and estate capital gains ☐

Q6 Is the trust claiming to be not resident in the UK, or dual resident in the UK and another country for all or part of the year for:

- Income Tax? — Yes ☐
- Capital Gains Tax? — Yes ☐ — Trust and estate non-residence etc ☐

Q7 Is the trust claiming total or partial exemption from tax because of its charitable status? — Yes ☐ — Trust and estate charities ☐

Q8 **Read pages 10 and 11 of the Trust and Estate Return Guide.**

Are you completing this Tax Return

	No	Yes
- for a period of administration?	8.1 ☐	8.2 ☐
- as the trustee of an unauthorised unit trust?	8.3 ☐	8.4 ☐
- as the trustee of an employment related trust?	8.5 ☐	8.6 ☐
- as the trustee of an Heritage Maintenance Fund?	8.7 ☐	8.8 ☐
Trustees of Funded Unapproved Retirement Benefit Schemes (FURBS): have you provided any non-relevant benefits to any of the scheme's beneficiaries?	8.9 ☐	8.10 ☐
If you are a trustee,		
- can any settlor (or living settlor's spouse) benefit from the capital or income?	8.11 ☐	8.12 ☐
- are you a participator in an underlying non-resident company (a company that would be a close company if it were resident in the UK)?	8.13 ☐	8.14 ☐
- is the trust liable to Income Tax at either or both the rate applicable to trusts (34%) or the dividend trust rate (25%) on any part of the income (for example, it is a discretionary trust)?	8.15 ☐	8.16 ☐

Step 3 **Now fill in any supplementary Pages BEFORE answering Questions 9 to 21, as directed.**
Please use blue or black ink to fill in the Trust and Estate Tax Return.
Please do not include pence. Round down income and gains. Round up tax credits and tax deductions. Round to the nearest pound.

■ Trust and Estate Tax Return: Page 3

Please turn over

INCOME *for the year ended 5 April 2003*

Q9 Did the trust or estate receive any other income not already included on the supplementary Pages? YES [ ] If yes, fill in boxes 9.1 to 9.40 as appropriate.

You may, **if you wish**, not complete some of the boxes in 9.1 to 9.40 in the following circumstances:

a) **If you are the trustee of an interest in possession trust (one which is exclusively an interest in possession trust)**, you may exclude income which has had tax deducted before you received it (or is UK dividends with tax credit) unless:

(i) that income has not been mandated to the beneficiary and there is accrued income scheme relief to set against the interest or you are claiming losses against general income, **or**

(ii) its exclusion would make you liable to make a payment on account which would not be due if you included it - see page 11 of the Trust and Estate Tax Calculation Guide concerning payments on account **before** following this guidance.

b) **If you are the trustee of a (non-interest in possession) trust where the income is treated as the settlor's for tax purposes** because the settlor has retained an interest (if in doubt ask the Orderline for *Help Sheet IR270: Trusts and settlements - income treated as the settlor's*) you may exclude income which has had tax deducted before you received it (or is UK dividends with tax credit) unless any of the following apply:

- there is accrued income scheme relief to set against the interest, **or**
- you are claiming reliefs (Question 10) which exceed the untaxed income, **or**
- you are claiming losses against general income, **or**
- the exclusion would make you liable to make payments on account which would not be due if you included it – see page 11 of the Trust and Estate Tax Calculation Guide concerning payments on account **before** following this guidance.

c) **If you are the personal representative of a deceased person** you may exclude income which has had tax deducted before you received it (or is UK dividends with tax credit) unless there is accrued income scheme relief to set against the interest. If the reliefs claimed at Question 10 on page 5 exceed untaxed income, you will need to include estate income that has had tax deducted to ensure a repayment can be calculated.

- Have you received any taxed income (or UK dividends with tax credit) which you have not included in this Trust and Estate Tax Return because (a), (b) or (c) above apply? YES [ ]

■ *Interest*

- Interest from UK banks, building societies and deposit takers (interest from UK Internet accounts must be included) – *if you have more than one bank or building society etc account enter* ***totals*** *in the boxes.*

	Amount after tax deducted	Tax deducted	Gross amount before tax / Taxable amount
- where **no tax** has been deducted			9.1 £ (Taxable amount)
- where **tax has** been deducted – *the Working Sheet on page 13 of the Guide will help you to fill in boxes 9.2 to 9.4.*	9.2 £	9.3 £	9.4 £
• Interest distributions from UK authorised unit trusts and open-ended investment companies (dividend distributions go in boxes 9.18 to 9.20)	9.5 £	9.6 £	9.7 £
• National Savings & Investments (other than First Option Bonds and Fixed Rate Savings Bonds)			9.8 £ (Taxable amount)
• National Savings & Investments First Option Bonds and Fixed Rate Savings Bonds	9.9 £	9.10 £	9.11 £
• Other income from UK savings and investments (except dividends)	9.12 £	9.13 £	9.14 £

■ TRUST AND ESTATE TAX RETURN: PAGE 4

INCOME *for the year ended 5 April 2003* continued

■ ***Dividends***

• Dividends and other qualifying distributions from UK companies	Dividend/distribution 9.15 £	Tax credit 9.16 £	Dividend/distribution plus credit 9.17 £
• Dividend distributions from UK authorised unit trusts and open-ended investment companies	Dividend/distribution 9.18 £	Tax credit 9.19 £	Dividend/distribution plus credit 9.20 £
• Scrip dividends from UK companies	Dividend 9.21 £	Notional tax 9.22 £	Dividend plus notional tax 9.23 £
• Dividends and other qualifying distributions received by unauthorised unit trusts	Amount of dividend only 9.24 £		
• Scrip dividends received by unauthorised unit trusts	Amount of dividend only 9.25 £		
• Non-qualifying distributions and loans written off	9.26 £	Notional tax 9.27 £	Taxable amount 9.28 £

■ ***Gains on UK life insurance policies, life annuities and capital redemption policies***

• on which no tax is treated as paid			Amount of gain 9.29 £
• on which tax is treated as paid		Tax treated as paid 9.30 £	Amount of gain 9.31 £

■ ***Other income***

• Other income	Amount after tax deducted 9.32 £	Tax deducted 9.33 £	Gross amount before tax 9.34 £
		Losses brought forward 9.35 £	Losses used in 2002-03 9.36 £
		Losses sustained in 2002-03 9.37 £	
• Deemed income etc. *(see page 19 of the Trust and Estate Tax Return Guide)*			Taxable amount 9.38 £
• Company purchase of its own shares		Tax credit 9.39 £	Taxable amount 9.40 £

Please turn over

OTHER INFORMATION *for the year ended 5 April 2003*

Q10 Do you want to claim any reliefs? YES [ ] — **If yes,** fill in boxes 10.1 to 10.4 as appropriate. If not applicable go to question 11.

■ ***Interest eligible for relief on qualifying loans***

	Amount of payment
• Interest on loans to pay Inheritance Tax	10.1 £

■ ***Other charges***

	Amount of payment	Tax deducted	Gross amount
• Annuities and other annual payments	10.2 £	10.3 £	10.4 £

Q11 Were any annual payments made out of capital or out of income not brought into charge to Income Tax? YES [ ] — **If yes,** fill in boxes 11.1 to 11.3 as appropriate. If not applicable go to question 12.

	Amount of payment	Tax deducted	Gross amount
• Annual payments	11.1 £	11.2 £	11.3 £

▶ If you are a personal representative, go to Question 17. There is no need to fill in Questions 12 to 16.

Q12 Have any assets or funds been put into the trust? YES [ ] — **If yes,** fill in boxes 12.1 to 12.9 as appropriate. If not applicable go to question 13.

Settlor's name and address	Description of asset	Value of asset
12.1 Postcode	12.2	12.3 £
12.4 Postcode	12.5	12.6 £
12.7 Postcode	12.8	12.9 £

OTHER INFORMATION *for the year ended 5 April 2003*

If you ticked box 8.15 in Question 8, page 3, then you do **not** need to complete this page - please go to Question 16 on page 9 and carry on filling in the Tax Return.
If you have ticked box 8.16 in Question 8, page 3, complete Questions 13 to 15.

Q13 Is any part of the trust income not liable to tax at the rate applicable to trusts or the dividend trust rate?

YES [ ] **If yes**, fill in boxes 13.1 to 13.22 below. **If not applicable**, fill in boxes 13.13 to 13.22.

- Amount of income charged at the 10% rate treated as that of the settlor — 13.1 £
- Trust management expenses applicable to the income in box 13.1 — 13.2 £
- Amount of income chargeable at the lower rate treated as that of the settlor — 13.3 £
- Trust management expenses applicable to the income in box 13.3 — 13.4 £
- Amount of income chargeable at the basic rate treated as that of the settlor — 13.5 £
- Trust management expenses applicable to the income in box 13.5 — 13.6 £
- Amount of income charged at the 10% rate applicable to beneficiaries whose entitlement is not subject to the trustees' (or any other person's) discretion — 13.7 £
- Trust management expenses applicable to the income in box 13.7 — 13.8 £
- Amount of income chargeable at the lower rate applicable to beneficiaries whose entitlement is not subject to the trustees' (or any other person's) discretion — 13.9 £
- Trust management expenses applicable to the income in box 13.9 — 13.10 £
- Amount of income chargeable at the basic rate applicable to beneficiaries whose entitlement is not subject to the trustees' (or any other person's) discretion — 13.11 £
- Trust management expenses applicable to the income in box 13.11 — 13.12 £
- Amount of income charged at the 10% rate allocated to specific purposes — 13.13 £
- Trust management expenses applicable to the income in box 13.13 — 13.14 £
- Amount of income chargeable at the lower rate allocated to specific purposes — 13.15 £
- Trust management expenses applicable to the income in box 13.15 — 13.16 £
- Amount of income chargeable at the basic rate allocated to specific purposes — 13.17 £
- Trust management expenses applicable to the income in box 13.17 — 13.18 £
- Total amount of deductible trust management expenses *(see notes on pages 21 to 24 of the Trust and Estate Tax Return Guide)* — 13.19 £
- Expenses set against income not liable at the rate applicable to trusts — total of column above — 13.20 £
- Total income not liable to UK Income Tax and not included elsewhere on this Trust and Estate Tax Return (non-resident trusts only) — 13.21 £
- Exceptional deductions — 13.22 £

Please turn over

OTHER INFORMATION *for the year ended 5 April 2003*

If you ticked box 8.15 in Question 8, page 3, then you do **not** need to complete this page - please go to Question 16 on page 9 and carry on filling in the Tax Return.
If you have ticked box 8.16 in Question 8, page 3, complete Questions 13 to 15.

Q14 **Have discretionary payments of income been made to beneficiaries?** *Trustees of Heritage Maintenance Funds:* ***do not*** *complete these boxes for expenditure on heritage property.*
See notes on page 24 of the Trust and Estate Tax Return Guide before filling in these boxes.

YES

If yes, fill in boxes 14.1 to 14.15 as appropriate. **If not applicable, fill in box 14.15 only.**

Name of beneficiary	Amount of payment	Tick the box if the beneficiary was a minor and unmarried child of the settlor and the settlor was alive when payment was made.
14.1	14.2 £	
14.3	14.4 £	
14.5	14.6 £	
14.7	14.8 £	
14.9	14.10 £	
14.11	14.12 £	
14.13	14.14 £	

- Amount, if any, of unused tax pool brought forward from last year (enter '0' if appropriate) 14.15 £

Q15A **Have the trustees made any capital payments to, or for the benefit of, minor, unmarried children of the settlor during the settlor's lifetime?**

YES

If yes, fill in box 15.1. If not applicable go to question 15B.

- Total capital payments to minor unmarried children — Amount paid 15.1 £

Q15B **Were there capital transactions between the trustees and the settlors?**

YES

If yes, fill in boxes 15.2 to 15.13 as appropriate. If not applicable go to question 16.

■ ***Capital transactions between the trustees and settlors*** *(Read page 24 of the Trust and Estate Tax Return Guide)*

Date	Amount	Name of company (if appropriate)
15.2 / /	15.3 £	15.4
		Registered office 15.5 Postcode
15.6 / /	15.7 £	15.8
		Registered office 15.9 Postcode
15.10 / /	15.11 £	15.12
		Registered office 15.13 Postcode

■ Trust and Estate Tax Return: Page 8

OTHER INFORMATION *for the year ended 5 April 2003*

16 **Has the trust at any time been non-resident or received any capital from another trust which is, or at any time has been, non-resident?** YES

If YES, have the trustees made any capital payments to, or provided any benefits for, the beneficiaries? YES

If yes, read pages 24 and 25 of the Trust and Estate Tax Return Guide and if appropriate fill in box 16.1. If not applicable go to question 17.

- Total capital payments or value of benefits provided **16.1** £

Please give details of the payments in box 16.1 in the boxes below. If there are insufficient boxes please provide the additional details on a separate sheet.

Name of beneficiary **16.2**

Address of beneficiary **16.4**

Postcode

Amount/value of payment/benefit **16.6** £

Name of beneficiary **16.3**

Address of beneficiary **16.5**

Postcode

Amount/value of payment/benefit **16.7** £

Name of beneficiary **16.8**

Address of beneficiary **16.10**

Postcode

Amount/value of payment/benefit **16.12** £

Name of beneficiary **16.9**

Address of beneficiary **16.11**

Postcode

Amount/value of payment/benefit **16.13** £

Name of beneficiary **16.14**

Address of beneficiary **16.16**

Postcode

Amount/value of payment/benefit **16.18** £

Name of beneficiary **16.15**

Address of beneficiary **16.17**

Postcode

Amount/value of payment/benefit **16.19** £

If you have received capital from any other trust which is, or at any time has been, non-resident please provide the following details:

Name of trust **16.20**

Address of trustee **16.22**

Postcode

Date trust set up **16.21** / /

Amount of value received **16.23** £

Please turn over

OTHER INFORMATION *for the year ended 5 April 2003*

Q17 Do you want to calculate the tax? YES ☐

If yes, do it now and then fill in boxes 17.1 to 17.9 below. The *Trust and Estate Tax Calculation Guide* will help you.

- Total tax due for 2002-03 **before** you made any payments on account *(put the amount in brackets if an overpayment)* — 17.1 £
- Tax due for earlier years — 17.2 £
- Tick box 17.3 if you have calculated tax overpaid for earlier years and enter the amount in box 17.4 — 17.3 ☐ 17.4 £
- Tick box 17.5 if you are making a claim to reduce your payments on account, enter your **reduced** payment in box 17.7 and say why in the 'Additional information' box, box 21.7, on page 12 — 17.5 ☐

  Tick box 17.6 if you do not need to make payments on account — 17.6 ☐
- Your first payment on account for 2003-04 *(include the pence)* — 17.7 £
- Tick box 17.8 if you are claiming a repayment of 2003-04 tax now and enter the amount in box 17.9 — 17.8 ☐ 17.9 £

Q18 Do you want to claim a repayment if the trust or estate has paid too much tax? YES ☐

(If you do not tick 'Yes', or the tax overpaid is below £10, I will use the amount you are owed to reduce the next tax bill.)

If yes, fill in boxes 18.1 to 18.12 as appropriate. If not applicable go to question 19.

Should the repayment (or payment) be sent:

- to your bank or building society account? *Tick box 18.1 and fill in boxes 18.3 to 18.7* — 18.1 ☐

or

- to your nominee's bank or building society account? *Tick box 18.2 and fill in boxes 18.3 to 18.12* — 18.2 ☐

We prefer to make repayment direct into a bank or building society account. (But tick box 18.8A or box 18.8B if you would like a cheque to be sent to you or your nominee.)

Name of bank or building society — 18.3

Branch sort code — 18.4

Account number — 18.5

Name of account holder — 18.6

Building society reference. — 18.7

If you would like a cheque to be sent to

- you at the address on page 1, *tick box 18.8A* — 18.8A ☐

or

- your nominee, *tick box 18.8B* — 18.8B ☐

If your nominee is your agent, *tick box 18.9A* — 18.9A ☐

Agent's reference for you (if your nominee is your agent) — 18.9

I authorise

Name of your nominee/agent — 18.10

Nominee/agent address — 18.11

Postcode

to receive on my behalf the amount due

18.12 *This authority must be signed by you. A photocopy of your signature will not do.*

Signature

■ Trust and Estate Tax Return: Page 10

OTHER INFORMATION *for the year ended 5 April 2003*

Q19 Trustee or personal representative details

- Your daytime telephone number — 19.1
- your agent's telephone number, and — 19.2
- your agent's name and address, and — 19.3 Postcode
- your agent's reference for you. — 19.4

Q20 Have there been any changes to the names and addresses of the trustees or personal representatives? YES

If yes, fill in boxes 20.1 to 20.12, as appropriate. If not applicable go to question 21.

If the 'acting trustee' has changed, please give details in the 'Additional information' box, box 21.7 on page 12.

- Retiring trustees' or personal representatives' names and addresses

20.1 Postcode | 20.2 Postcode

20.3 Postcode | 20.4 Postcode

- New trustees' or personal representatives' names and addresses

20.5 Postcode | 20.6 Postcode

20.7 Postcode | 20.8 Postcode

- Existing trustees' or personal representatives' names and new addresses

20.9 Postcode | 20.10 Postcode

20.11 Postcode | 20.12 Postcode

Please turn over

OTHER INFORMATION *for the year ended 5 April 2003*

Q21 Other Information

- If you are completing this Trust and Estate Tax Return as a personal representative, please enter in box 21.1 the date of death of the deceased. — 21.1 Date / /
- If the administration period ceased in the year to 5 April 2003, please enter in box 21.2 the date of cessation. — 21.2 Date / /
- Tick box 21.3 if the administration period ceased in the year to 5 April 2003 and there is a continuing trust. — 21.3
- If you are a trustee and the trust was terminated in the year to 5 April 2003 please enter in box 21.4 the date of termination and, in the 'Additional information' box, box 21.7 below, the reason for termination. — 21.4 Date / /
- If this Trust and Estate Tax Return contains any figures that are provisional because you do not yet have final figures, please tick box 21.5. Page 25 of the Trust and Estate Tax Return Guide explains the circumstances in which provisional figures may be used and asks for some additional information to be provided in box 21.7 below. — 21.5
- If any 2002-03 tax was refunded directly by the Inland Revenue office, or (personal representatives only) by the Benefits Agency (in Northern Ireland, the Social Security Agency), please enter the amount in box 21.6. Do **not** include any refunds of excessive payments on account. — 21.6 Amount £

21.7 ***Additional information***

Q22 Declaration

I have filled in and am sending back to you the following Trust and Estate Tax Return Pages:

	Tick		Tick		Tick
1 to 12 of this form		*Trust and estate land and property*			
Trust and estate trade		*Trust and estate foreign*		*Trust and estate non-residence etc*	
Trust and estate partnership		*Trust and estate capital gains*		*Trust and estate charities*	

Before you send the completed Tax Return back to the Inland Revenue office, you must sign the statement below.

If you give false information or conceal any part of trust or estate income or chargeable gains, you may be liable to financial penalties and/or you may be prosecuted.

22.1 **The information I have given in this Tax Return is correct and complete to the best of my knowledge and belief.**

Signature Date

- Please PRINT your name in box 22.2 — 22.2
- Enter the capacity in which you are signing — 22.3

Inland Revenue

Income for the year ended 5 April 2003

TRUST AND ESTATE TRADE

Fill in these boxes first

Name of trust or estate

Tax reference

The notes on pages TTN1 and TTN2 tell you when you need to complete more than one set of Trust and Estate Trade Pages. You must complete a separate copy of these Pages:

- *for each trade, and*
- *for each set of accounts relating to the basis period.*

Box numbers 1.9, 1.82 and 1.94 to 1.96 are not used on these Pages.

Business details

Name of business **1.1**

Description of business **1.2**

Address of business **1.3**

Accounting period
Read page TTN2 of the Notes before filling in these boxes

Start **1.4** / /

End **1.5** / /

- Tick box 1.6 if details in boxes 1.1 or 1.3 have changed since the last Trust and Estate Tax Return **1.6**
- Date of commencement if after 5 April 2000 **1.7** / /
- Date of cessation if before 6 April 2003 **1.8** / /
- Tick box 1.10 if you entered details for all relevant accounting periods on last year's Trust and Estate Tax Return and boxes 1.14 to 1.73 and 1.99 to 1.115 will be blank **1.10**
- Tick box 1.11 if the accounts do not cover the period from the last accounting date (explain why in the 'Additional information' box, box 1.116) **1.11**
- Tick box 1.12 if the accounting date has changed (only if this is a permanent change and you want it to count for tax) **1.12**
- Tick box 1.13 if this is the second or further change (explain in box 1.116 on page TT4 why you have not used the same date as last year) **1.13**

Capital allowances and balancing charges

	Capital allowances	Balancing charges
• Cars costing more than £12,000 (A separate calculation must be made for each car)	1.14 £	1.15 £
• Other business plant and machinery	1.16 £	1.17 £
• Agricultural or Industrial Buildings Allowance (A separate calculation must be made for each block of expenditure.)	1.18 £	1.19 £
• Other capital allowances claimed (Separate calculations must be made.)	1.20 £	1.21 £
Total capital allowances/balancing charges	total of column above 1.22 £	total of column above 1.23 £

- Tick box 1.22A if box 1.22 includes enhanced capital allowances for environmentally friendly expenditure **1.22A**

Income and expenses

If the annual turnover is £15,000 or more, ignore boxes 1.24 to 1.26. Instead fill in Page TT2

If the annual turnover is below £15,000, fill in boxes 1.24 to 1.26 instead of Page TT2. Read page TTN2 of the Notes

- Turnover including other business receipts and goods etc. taken for personal use (and balancing charges from box 1.23) **1.24** £
- Expenses allowable for tax (including capital allowances from box 1.22) **1.25** £

Net profit (put figure in brackets if a loss) box 1.24 *minus* box 1.25 **1.26** £

You must now fill in Page TT3

SA901 (Substitute)(LexisNexis UK)

Income and expenses

You must fill in this Page if the annual turnover is £15,000 or more - read page TTN2 of the Notes

If the trust or estate was registered for VAT, do the figures in boxes 1.29 to 1.64 include VAT? **1.27** or exclude VAT? **1.28**

	Disallowable expenses included in boxes 1.46 to 1.63	Total expenses	Sales/business income (turnover)
			1.29 £
• Cost of sales	1.30 £	1.46 £	
• Construction industry subcontractor costs	1.31 £	1.47 £	
• Other direct costs	1.32 £	1.48 £	
		Gross profit/(loss)	box 1.29 *minus* (boxes 1.46 + 1.47 + 1.48) 1.49 £
		Other income/profits	1.50 £
• Employee costs	1.33 £	1.51 £	
• Premises costs	1.34 £	1.52 £	
• Repairs	1.35 £	1.53 £	
• General administrative expenses	1.36 £	1.54 £	
• Motor expenses	1.37 £	1.55 £	
• Travel and subsistence	1.38 £	1.56 £	
• Advertising, promotion and entertainment	1.39 £	1.57 £	
• Legal and professional costs	1.40 £	1.58 £	
• Bad debts	1.41 £	1.59 £	
• Interest	1.42 £	1.60 £	
• Other finance charges	1.43 £	1.61 £	
• Depreciation and loss/(profit) on sale	1.44 £	1.62 £	
• Other expenses	1.45 £	1.63 £	
	Put the total of boxes 1.30 to 1.45 in box 1.66 below	Total expenses	total of boxes 1.51 to 1.63 1.64 £
		Net profit/(loss)	box 1.49 + 1.50 *minus* 1.64 1.65 £

Tax adjustments to net profit or loss

• Disallowable expenses	boxes 1.30 to 1.45 1.66 £	
• Goods etc. taken for personal use and other adjustments (apart from disallowable expenses) that increase profits	1.67 £	
• Balancing charges (from box 1.23)	1.68 £	
Total additions to net profit (deduct from net loss)		boxes 1.66 + 1.67 + 1.68 1.69 £
• Capital allowances (from box 1.22)	1.70 £	
• Deductions from net profit (add to net loss)	1.71 £	boxes 1.70 + 1.71 1.72 £
Net business profit for tax purposes (put figure in brackets if a loss)		boxes 1.65 + 1.69 *minus* 1.72 1.73 £

Now fill in Page TT3

You must fill in boxes 1.74 and 1.75 and all other boxes that apply to the trust or estate on this Page

Adjustments to arrive at taxable profit or loss

Basis period begins **1.74** / / and ends **1.75** / /

Profit or loss of this account for tax purposes (box 1.26 or 1.73) **1.76** £

Adjustment to arrive at profit or loss for this basis period **1.77** £

- Overlap profit brought forward **1.78** £
- Deduct overlap relief used this year **1.79** £
- Overlap profit carried forward **1.80** £
- Averaging for farmers, and creators of literary or artistic works (see the Notes, page TTN6 if you made a loss for 2002-03) **1.81** £

Net profit for 2002-03 (if a loss, enter '0') **1.83** £

Allowable loss for 2002-03 (if a profit, enter '0') **1.84** £

- Loss offset against other income for 2002-03 **1.85** £
- Loss to carry back **1.86** £
- Loss to carry forward (that is an allowable loss not claimed in any other way) **1.87** £
- Losses brought forward from earlier years **1.88** £
- Losses brought forward from earlier years used this year **1.89** £

Taxable profit after losses brought forward box 1.83 *minus* box 1.89 **1.90** £

- Any other business income **1.91** £

Total taxable profits from this business box 1.90 + box 1.91 **1.92** £

- Tick box 1.93 if the figure in box 1.92 is provisional **1.93**

Subcontractors in the construction industry

- Deductions made by contractors on account of tax (please send the CIS25s to us) for the period 6 April 2002 to 5 April 2003 **1.97** £

Tax deducted from trading income

- Any tax deducted from trading income (not CIS25 deductions) **1.98** £

Summary of balance sheet

Leave these boxes blank if there is no balance sheet

Assets	• Plant, machinery and motor vehicles	1.99	£
	• Other fixed assets (premises, goodwill, investments etc.)	1.100	£
	• Stock and work in progress	1.101	£
	• Debtors/prepayments/other current assets	1.102	£
	• Bank/building society balances	1.103	£
	• Cash in hand	1.104	£
	total of boxes 1.99 to 1.104	1.105	£
Liabilities	• Trade creditors/accruals	1.106	£
	• Loans and overdrawn bank accounts	1.107	£
	• Other liabilities	1.108	£
	total of boxes 1.106 to 1.108	1.109	£
Net business assets (put the figure in brackets if there were net business liabilities)	box 1.105 *minus* 1.109	1.110	£

Represented by

Capital Account

• Balance at start of period*	1.111	£
• Net profit/(loss)*	1.112	£
• Capital introduced	1.113	£
• Drawings	1.114	£
• Balance at end of period* (total of boxes 1.111 to 1.113 *minus* box 1.114)	1.115	£

* If the Capital Account is overdrawn, or the business made a net loss, enter the figure in brackets.

1.116 ***Additional information***

Now fill in any other supplementary Pages that apply to you. Otherwise, go back to page 3 in the Trust and Estate Tax Return and finish filling it in.

Inland Revenue

Income taxable for the year ended 5 April 2003

LLOYD'S UNDERWRITERS: Income from membership of Lloyd's

Name

Tax reference

If you have answered 'Yes' to Question 1, fill in Pages TLU1 to TLU4. If you want help, look up the box numbers in the Trust and Estate Lloyd's Underwriters pages. They will be at the back of your Tax Return guide, if I've sent you one, or you can get them from the Orderline or our website. If you need help, please telephone W. Yorks Personal Tax Unit on 01274 771771 or write to the address given on page TLUN 13.

Part 1 - Income from ancillary or personal funds at Lloyd's - see Notes, page TLUN2

UK interest received in year ended 31 December 2002

• Interest on gilts and from UK banks, building societies, and deposit takers paid **without** tax deducted			Taxable amount 1L.1 £
• Interest from UK banks, building societies, and deposit takers paid **with** tax deducted	Amount after tax deducted 1L.2 £	Tax deducted 1L.3 £	Gross amount before tax 1L.4 £
• National Savings & Investments	Amount after tax deducted 1L.5A £	Tax deducted 1L.5B £	Taxable amount 1L.5 £
• Interest distributions from UK authorised unit trusts and open-ended investment companies - dividends go in boxes 1L.21 to 1L.23	Amount after tax deducted 1L.6 £	Tax deducted 1L.7 £	Gross amount before tax 1L.8 £
• Other income from UK savings and investments including taxed interest on gilts (excluding items covered in boxes 1L.18 to 1L.23)	Amount after tax deducted 1L.9 £	Tax deducted 1L.10 £	Gross amount before tax 1L.11 £
Total UK tax		total of column above 1L.12 £	
Total UK interest before accrued income share			total of column above 1L.13 £
• Accrued Income Scheme and losses on relevant discounted securities	Positive 1L.14 £	Negative 1L.15 £	Aggregate 1L.16 £
Total UK interest			box 1L.13 + or *minus* box 1L.16 1L.17 £

UK dividends and other distributions received in year ended 31 December 2002

• Dividends and other qualifying distributions from UK companies	Dividend/distribution 1L.18 £	Tax credit 1L.19 £	Dividend/distribution *plus* tax credit 1L.20 £
• Dividend distributions from UK authorised unit trusts and open-ended investment companies	1L.21 £	1L.22 £	1L.23 £
Total tax credit		box 1L.19 + 1L.22 1L.24 £	
Total dividends/distributions plus tax credits			box 1L.20 + 1L.23 1L.25 £

SA901L (Substitute)(LexisNexis UK)

Please turn over

Part 1 - Income from ancillary or personal funds at Lloyd's - continued

Stock dividends and non-qualifying distributions received in year ended 31 December 2002

	Dividend	Notional tax	Dividend *plus* notional tax
• Stock (or scrip) dividends from UK companies	1L.26 £	1L.27 £	1L.28 £
		Notional tax	Taxable amount
• Non-qualifying distributions	*Box 1L.35 is not used*	1L.36 £	1L.37 £
		total of column above	
Total notional tax		1L.38 £	
			total of column above
Total stock dividends and non-qualifying distributions plus notional Income Tax			1L.39 £

Foreign source income from assets in personal funds at Lloyd's received in year ended 31 December 2002

	Net income/dividends	Foreign tax deducted	UK tax deducted up to 5 April 2002	Net income *plus* UK/foreign tax
• Non UK interest	1L.40 £	1L.41 £	1L.42 £	1L.43 £
• Other foreign source income (excluding dividends)	1L.44 £	1L.45 £	1L.46 £	1L.47 £
• Dividends from overseas sources	1L.48 £	1L.49 £	1L.50 £	1L.51 £
		total of column above		
Total foreign tax deducted		1L.52 £		
			box 1L.42 + box 1L.46	
Total UK tax deducted (do not include box 1L.50)			1L.53 £	
				total of column above
Total non-UK income before tax				1L.54 £
				boxes 1L.17 + 1L.25 + 1L.39 + 1L.54
Total income from personal funds at Lloyd's				1L.55 £

Part 2 - Other Lloyd's receipts - see Notes, page TLUN5

Receipts

- Refund of Members Special Contributions — 1L.56 £
- Compensation receipts — 1L.57 £
- Other Lloyd's non-syndicate income — 1L.58 £
- Aggregate syndicate profit — 1L.58A £
- Syndicate foreign tax — 1L.58B £ — *Copy this figure to box 1L.76*
- Net withdrawal from Special Reserve Fund — 1L.58C £
- Stop loss recoveries — 1L.58D £
- Repayments of foreign tax previously allowed by deduction — 1L.58E £
- Total other Lloyd's receipts — total of boxes 1L.56 to 1L.58E — 1L.59 £

Total Lloyd's incomings — box 1L.55 + box 1L.59 — 1L.60 £

Part 3 - Outgoings and syndicate losses - see Notes, page TLUN6

Non-syndicate expenditure and syndicate losses

- Fees for bank guarantees/letter of credit — 1L.62 £
- Aggregate syndicate losses — 1L.63 £
- Lloyd's members association expenses — 1L.64 £
- Personal Quota Share premiums — 1L.66 £ — *Boxes 1L.61, 1L.65 and 1L.67 are not used*
- Interest on loans to fund underwriting — 1L.68 £
- Net transfer to Special Reserve Fund — 1L.68A £
- Members' agent profit commission and salaries — 1L.69 £
- Accountancy fees — 1L.70 £
- Other Lloyd's expenses — 1L.71 £

Total Lloyd's outgoings — total of boxes 1L.62 to 1L.71 — 1L.72 £

Part 4 - Lloyd's foreign tax - see Notes, page TLUN7

- Foreign tax on personal fund income — from box 1L.52 — 1L.73 £
- US federal income tax — 1L.74 £
- Canadian federal income tax — 1L.75 £
- Syndicate foreign tax — from box 1L.58B — 1L.76 £
- Additional payments of foreign tax — 1L.77 £

Lloyd's foreign tax pool — total of boxes 1L.73 to 1L.77 — 1L.78 £

- **Refunds of foreign tax for which tax credit relief was given** - if you are calculating the tax yourself, include box 1L.79 in box T5.10 on page 10 of the Tax Calculation Guide — 1L.79 £

Part 5 - Summary of net trading profits/allowable losses - see Notes, page TLUN8

Total of Lloyd's incomings and outgoings

Box numbers 1L.80 and 1L.81 are not used

If total Lloyd's outgoings (box 1L.72) **exceed** incomings (box 1L.60), you have made a net loss. Fill in the column headed 'Loss'.

If total Lloyd's outgoings (box 1L.72) are **less than** incomings (box 1L.60), you have made a net profit. Fill in the column headed 'Profit'.

2002-03 Loss

- Net loss before foreign tax — box 1L.72 *minus* box 1L.60 — 1L.82 £
- If foreign tax claimed as a deduction — from box 1L.78 — 1L.83 £
- 2002-03 loss — box 1L.82 + box 1L.83 — 1L.84 £
- Loss offset against other 2002-03 income — 1L.85 £
- Loss to carry back — 1L.86 £
- Loss to carry forward (that is, allowable loss not claimed in any other way) — 1L.87 £

2002-03 Profit

- Net profit — box 1L.60 *minus* box 1L.72 — 1L.88 £
- Unused Lloyd's trading losses brought forward from earlier years (for use in 2002-03) — 1L.89 £
- If foreign tax claimed as a deduction — from box 1L.78 — 1L.90 £

Total taxable profits from membership of Lloyd's — boxes 1L.88 *minus* box 1L.89 *and* box 1L.90 — 1L.91 £

1L.92 *Additional information*

Now fill in any other supplementary Pages that apply to you.
Otherwise, go back to page 3 in your Tax Return and finish filling it in.

Inland Revenue

Income for the year ended 5 April 2003

TRUST AND ESTATE PARTNERSHIP

Fill in these boxes first

Name of trust or estate

Tax reference

You will need to fill in a copy of these Pages for each partnership of which the trust or estate was a member, and for each business the partnership carried on. If you need help, look up the box numbers in the Notes on Trust and Estate Partnership.

Partnership details

Partnership reference number **2.1**

Partnership trade or profession **2.2**

- Date started being a partner (if during 2002-03) **2.3** / /
- Date stopped being a partner (if during 2002-03) **2.4** / /

The share of the partnership's trading or professional income

Basis period begins **2.5** / / **and ends** **2.6** / /

- Share of the profit or loss of this year's account for tax purposes **2.7** £
- Adjustment to arrive at profit or loss for this basis period **2.8** £
- Overlap profit brought forward **2.9** £ Deduct overlap relief used this year **2.10** £
- Overlap profit carried forward **2.11** £
- Averaging for farmers, and creators of literary or artistic works (or foreign tax deducted if tax credit relief not claimed) **2.12** £

Net profit for 2002-03 (if loss, enter '0' here) **2.13** £

Allowable loss for 2002-03 (if profit, enter '0' here) **2.14** £

- Loss offset against other income for 2002-03 **2.15** £
- Loss to carry back **2.16** £
- Loss to carry forward (that is allowable loss not claimed in any other way) **2.17** £
- Losses brought forward from last year **2.18** £
- Losses brought forward from last year used this year **2.19** £

Taxable profit after losses brought forward box 2.13 *minus* box 2.19 **2.20** £

- Add amounts **not** included in the partnership accounts which are needed to calculate the taxable profit **2.21** £

Total taxable profits from this business box 2.20 + box 2.21 **2.22** £

SA902 (Substitute)(LexisNexis UK)

TRUST AND ESTATE TAX RETURN ■ PARTNERSHIP: PAGE TP1

Please turn over

Share of partnership investment income

- Please tick box 2.23 if the partnership had any investment income and your share will be returned in boxes 9.1 to 9.40, on pages 4 and 5, of the Trust and Estate Tax Return. **2.23**

- Share of losses on partnership investments **2.24** £

2.25 *Additional information*

Now go back to page 3 of the Trust and Estate Tax Return and finish filling it in.

Inland Revenue

Income for the year ended 5 April 2003

TRUST AND ESTATE LAND AND PROPERTY

Fill in these boxes first

Name of trust or estate

Tax reference

If you want help, look up the box numbers in the Notes on Trust and Estate Land and Property.

Answer this question to help you decide which parts of Pages TL1 and TL2 to fill in.

Is the income from furnished holiday lettings?
If not applicable, turn over and fill in Page TL2 to give details of the property income

YES

If 'Yes', fill in boxes 3.1 to 3.18 before completing Page TL2

Furnished holiday lettings in the UK

- Income from furnished holiday lettings — 3.1 £

■ *Expenses* (furnished holiday lettings only)

- Rent, rates, insurance, ground rents etc. — 3.2 £
- Repairs, maintenance and renewals — 3.3 £
- Finance charges, including interest — 3.4 £
- Legal and professional costs — 3.5 £
- Cost of services provided, including wages — 3.6 £
- Other expenses — 3.7 £ — total of boxes 3.2 to 3.7 — 3.8 £

Net profit (put figures in brackets if a loss) — box 3.1 *minus* box 3.8 — 3.9 £

■ *Tax adjustments*

- Private use — 3.10 £
- Balancing charges — 3.11 £ — box 3.10 + box 3.11 — 3.12 £
- Capital allowances — 3.13 £
- Tick box 3.13A if box 3.13 includes enhanced capital allowances for environmentally friendly expenditure — 3.13A

Profit for the year (copy to box 3.19). If loss enter '0' in box 3.14 and put the loss in box 3.15 — boxes 3.9 + 3.12 *minus* box 3.13 — 3.14 £

Loss for the year (if you have entered '0' in box 3.14) — boxes 3.9 + 3.12 *minus* box 3.13 — 3.15 £

- Loss offset against 2002-03 total income — 3.16 £
- Loss carried back — see Notes, page TLN4 — 3.17 £
- Loss offset against other income from property (copy to box 3.37) — see Notes, page TLN4 — 3.18 £

SA903 (Substitute)(LexisNexis UK)

Please turn over

Other property income

■ ***Income***

• Furnished holiday lettings profits	copy from box 3.14 3.19 £		
• Rents and other income from land and property	3.20 £	Tax deducted 3.21 £	
• Chargeable premiums	3.22 £		
• Reverse premiums	3.22A £		boxes 3.19 + 3.20 + 3.22 + 3.22A 3.23 £

■ ***Expenses*** (do not include figures you have already put in boxes 3.2 to 3.7 on Page TL1)

• Rent, rates, insurance, ground rents etc.	3.24 £		
• Repairs, maintenance and renewals	3.25 £		
• Finance charges, including interest	3.26 £		
• Legal and professional costs	3.27 £		
• Costs of services provided, including wages	3.28 £		
• Other expenses	3.29 £		total of boxes 3.24 to 3.29 3.30 £
Net profit (put figures in brackets if a loss)			box 3.23 *minus* box 3.30 3.31 £

■ ***Tax adjustments***

• Private use	3.32 £		
• Balancing charges	3.33 £		box 3.32 + box 3.33 3.34 £
• Capital allowances	3.35 £		
• Tick box 3.35A if box 3.35 includes a claim for 100% capital allowances for flats over shops	3.35A		
• Tick box 3.35B if box 3.35 includes enhanced capital allowances for environmentally friendly expenditure	3.35B		
• 10% wear and tear	3.36 £		
• Furnished holiday lettings losses (from box 3.18)	3.37 £		total of boxes 3.35 to 3.37 3.38 £
Adjusted profit (if loss enter '0' in box 3.39 and put the loss in box 3.40)			boxes 3.31 + 3.34 *minus* box 3.38 3.39 £
Adjusted loss (if you have entered '0' in box 3.39)		boxes 3.31 + 3.34 *minus* box 3.38 3.40 £	
• Loss brought forward from previous year			3.41 £
Profit for the year			box 3.39 *minus* box 3.41 3.42 £
• Loss offset against total income (read the note on page TLN7)		3.43 £	
• Loss to carry forward to following year		3.44 £	
Tick box 3.45 if these Pages include details of property let jointly		3.45	

Now go back to page 3 of the Trust and Estate Tax Return and finish filling it in.

Income and gains and foreign tax credit relief for the year ended 5 April 2003

Inland Revenue

TRUST AND ESTATE FOREIGN

Fill in these boxes first

Name of trust or estate

Tax reference

If you want help, look up the box numbers in the Notes on Trust and Estate Foreign

Foreign savings

Fill in columns A, B, D and E, and tick the box in column E if you want to claim foreign tax credit relief.

	Country A (tick box if income is unremittable)	Amount before tax B	Foreign tax D	Amount chargeable E (tick box to claim foreign tax credit relief)
■ *Interest and other savings income* -see Notes, page TFN3		£	£	£
		£	£	£
		£	£	£
		£	£	£
		£	£	£
		£	£	£
		£	£	£
		£	£	£
		£	£	£
		£	£	£
		£	£	£
		£	£	£
				total of column above 4.1 £
■ *Dividends* -see Notes, page TFN4		£	£	£
		£	£	£
		£	£	£
		£	£	£
		£	£	£
		£	£	£
		£	£	£
		£	£	£
		£	£	£
		£	£	£
		£	£	£
		£	£	£
				total of column above 4.2 £

SA904 (Substitute)(LexisNexis UK)

Please turn over

Foreign savings income taxable on the remittance basis and foreign income from land and property abroad

Fill in columns A to E, and tick the box in column E if you want to claim foreign tax credit relief.

	Country A (tick box if income is unremittable)	Amount before tax B	UK tax C	Foreign tax D	Amount chargeable E (tick box to claim foreign tax credit relief)
■ *Dividends, interest and other savings income taxable on the remittance basis* -see Notes, page TFN2		£		£	£
		£		£	£
		£		£	£
		£		£	£
		£		£	£
		£		£	£
		£		£	£
		£		£	£
		£		£	£
		£		£	£
		£		£	£
		£		£	£
		£		£	£
■ *Income from land & property* IMPORTANT -see Notes page TFN5		£	£	£	£
■ *Chargeable premiums*		£	£	£	£
			total of column C 4.3 £		total of column E 4.4 £

- Disposals of holdings in offshore funds, income from non-resident trusts and income received by trusts or companies abroad — 4.5 £
- Gains on foreign life insurance policies, life annuities and capital redemption policies - on which no tax is treated as paid — Amount of gain 4.6 £
- Gains on foreign life insurance policies, life annuities and capital redemption policies - on which tax is treated as paid — Tax treated as paid 4.7 £ — Amount of gain 4.8 £

Now fill in Page TF3

Foreign tax credit relief for foreign tax paid on trade, partnership and other income

See Notes, page TFN11

Enter in this column the page number in the Trust and Estate Tax Return from which information is taken. Do this for each item for which you are claiming tax credit	Country A	Foreign tax D	Amount chargeable E tick box to claim foreign tax credit relief
		£	£
		£	£
		£	£
		£	£
		£	£
		£	£
		£	£
		£	£
		£	£

- Enter in box 4.9 the total foreign tax credit relief on the income (if there is an entry in box 4.9, box 4.9A must also be completed) **4.9** £
- Enter in box 4.9A the amount of foreign tax credit relief referable to that part of net income, after deductions, chargeable at the rate applicable to trusts or the dividend trust rate. (Enter zero if appropriate) **4.9A** £

Foreign tax credit relief for foreign tax paid on chargeable gains reported on the Trust and Estate Capital Gains Pages

See Notes, page TFN12

Amount of gain under UK rules	Period over which UK gain accrued	Amount of gain under foreign tax rules	Period over which foreign gain accrued	Foreign tax paid D tick box to claim foreign tax credit relief
£	days	£	days	£
£	days	£	days	£
£	days	£	days	£
£	days	£	days	£
£	days	£	days	£
£	days	£	days	£
£	days	£	days	£
£	days	£	days	£
£	days	£	days	£

- If you are calculating the tax, enter the total foreign tax credit relief on the gains in box 4.10 **4.10** £

Now go back to page 3 in the Trust and Estate Tax Return and finish filling it in

TRUST AND ESTATE TAX RETURN ■ FOREIGN ETC: PAGE TF3

Income from land and property abroad

Fill in one Page TF4 if:

- *there is only* **one** *overseas let property,* **or**
- *there is more than one but all overseas let properties are in the same country* **and** *all the income is remittable,* **or**
- *there is more than one and they are in different countries* **but** *there has been* **no foreign tax deducted** *from any of the income* **and** *all the income is remittable.*

If any of the income is unremittable or the overseas let properties are in different countries and some foreign tax has been deducted you must fill in a copy of Page TF4 for each property letting. (Take copies of TF4 before you start or ask the Orderline for more copies of the Trust and Estate Foreign Pages.) Please put the trust or estate name and tax reference next to the address box on each copy.

If you are using Page TF4 to return income from more than one property please use the address box below for the first property and the 'Additional information' box on Page TF5 for the other addresses.

Address of property

Postcode

Income

• Income - total rents and other receipts (excluding chargeable premiums)			4.11 £
• Tick box 4.11A if box 4.11 contains income from more than one property			4.11A
• Tick box 4.11B if the income in box 4.11 is unremittable			4.11B

Expenses - see Notes, page TFN6

• Rent, rates, insurance etc.	4.12 £		
• Repairs, maintenance and renewals	4.13 £		
• Finance charges, including interest	4.14 £		
• Legal and professional costs	4.15 £		
• Costs of services provided including wages	4.16 £		
• Other expenses	4.17 £	total of boxes 4.12 to 4.17 4.18 £	
Net profit (or loss) - show loss in brackets			box 4.11 *minus* 4.18 4.19 £

Tax Adjustments to net profit (or loss) - see Notes, page TFN7

• Private use	4.20 £		
• Balancing charges	4.21 £	box 4.20 + box 4.21 4.22 £	
• Capital allowances	4.23 £		
• Tick box 4.23A if box 4.23 includes enhanced capital allowances for environmentally friendly expenditure	4.23A		
• 10% wear and tear	4.24 £	box 4.23 + box 4.24 4.25 £	
Adjusted profit (if loss, enter '0' here, and enter loss in box 4.27)			box 4.19 + box 4.22 *minus* box 4.25 4.26 £
Adjusted loss (if '0' in box 4.26)		box 4.19 + box 4.22 *minus* box 4.25 4.27 £	

Go to Page TF5

Income from land and property abroad, continued

Fill in boxes 4.28 to 4.32 (if you completed only one Page TF4) or boxes 4.33 to 4.38 if you have completed a separate Page TF4 for each property.

- Taxable profit or allowable loss from box 4.26 or 4.27 (enter a loss in brackets) **4.28** £

minus losses brought forward from earlier years **4.29** £

Total taxable profits (if box 4.28 is a profit and is more than box 4.29) box 4.28 *minus* 4.29 **4.30** £
Copy to column B on Page TF2

or loss to carry forward (if box 4.28 is a profit but less than box 4.29, enter box 4.29 minus box 4.28, or, if box 4.28 is a loss, enter box 4.28 plus box 4.29) **4.31** £

- If you have only one property or your properties are all in the same foreign country and foreign tax was deducted, enter the tax paid **4.32** £
Copy to column D on Page TF2 and fill in columns A and E as appropriate

*If you have filled in more than one Page TF4 enter details below using a separate line for each overseas let property. **Exclude** any unremittable income from the 'Taxable profit or loss' column.*

	Country	Taxable profit or loss (from box 4.26 or 4.27)	Foreign tax	Amount chargeable
1		£	£	£
2		£	£	£
3		£	£	£
4		£	£	£
5		£	£	£
6		£	£	£
		total of column above **4.33** £		
	minus losses brought forward	**4.34** £		
	Total taxable profits	**4.35** £ *Copy to column B on Page TF2*	**4.36** £ *Copy to column D on Page TF2*	**4.37** £ *Copy to column E on Page TF2*
	or loss to carry forward	**4.38** £		

4.39 *Additional information*

Inland Revenue

For the year ended 5 April 2003

TRUST AND ESTATE CAPITAL GAINS

Fill in these boxes first

Name of trust or estate	Tax reference

If you want help, look up the box numbers in the Notes on Trust and Estate Capital Gains.

Chargeable gains and allowable losses

Once you have completed Pages TC2 to TC7 fill in this Page.

Have you ticked any row in Column B 'Tick box if estimate or valuation used' on Page TC2?	YES
Have you given details in Column G on Pages TC2 and TC3 of any capital gains reliefs claimed or due?	YES
Are you claiming and/or using any 'clogged losses' (see Notes, page TCN10)?	YES

Enter the **number** of transactions from column AA on Page TC2, as follows:

• transactions in quoted shares or other securities	box Q
• transactions in other shares or securities	box U
• transactions in land and property	box L
• transactions in other assets	box O
Total taxable gains from Page TC3	5.7 £
Only Trustees need consider boxes 5.8 and 5.9	
If the trust was made after 6 June 1978 how many trusts that were made after 6 June 1978 by the settlor of this trust still existed during the year to 5 April 2003?	5.8
Is this trust for a disabled person? If yes, tick box 5.9	5.9
minus Annual exempt amount (see Notes, page TCN6)	5.10 £
• Taxable gains for 2002-03 (leave box 5.11 blank if '0' or negative)	box 5.7 *minus* box 5.10 5.11 £

Capital losses

(Remember, if your loss arose on a transaction with a connected person, see page TCN13, you can only set that loss against gains you make on disposals to that same connected person. See the Notes on clogged losses on page TCN10.)

■ ***This year's losses***	
• total from Page TC3	from box 5.2 5.12 £
• used against gains	5.13 £
• 2002-03 losses transferred to beneficiaries during the year and 2002-03 losses on mineral leases carried back	5.14 £
• carried forward losses of 2002-03	box 5.12 *minus* (boxes 5.13 + 5.14) 5.15 £
■ ***Summary of earlier years' losses***	
• unused losses of 1996-97 and later years	5.16 £
• used this year (losses from box 5.16 are used in priority to losses from box 5.17A)	5.16A £
• remaining unused losses of 1996-97 and later years	box 5.16 *minus* box 5.16A 5.17 £
• unused losses of 1995-96 and earlier years	5.17A £
• used this year (losses from box 5.16 are used in priority to losses from box 5.17A)	from box 5.6 *minus* box 5.16A 5.17B £
■ ***Total of unused losses to carry forward***	
• Carried forward losses of 1996-97 and later years	box 5.15 + box 5.17 5.18 £
• Carried forward losses of 1995-96 and earlier years	box 5.17A *minus* box 5.17B 5.18A £

SA905 (Substitute)(LexisNexis UK)

TRUST AND ESTATE TAX RETURN ■ CAPITAL GAINS: PAGE TC1

Please turn over

Your 2002-03 Capital Gains Tax liability

A Brief description of asset	AA* Type of disposal. Enter **Q, U, L or O**	B Tick box if estimate or valuation used	C Tick box if asset held at 31March 1982	D Enter the later of date of acquisition and 16 March 1998	E Enter the date of disposal	F Disposal proceeds	G Enter details of any elections made, reliefs claimed or due and state amounts (£)
Gains on assets which are either wholly business or wholly non-business							
1				*02/12/01*	*01/12/02*	£ *66,640.00*	
2						£	
3						£	
4						£	
5						£	
6						£	
7						£	
8						£	
Gains on assets which are partly business and partly non-business (see the notes on pages TCN17)							
9						£	
10						£	

* For transactions in
- quoted shares or other securities (the definition is on page TCN2), enter **Q**
- other shares or securities, enter **U**
- land and property, enter **L**
- other assets (for example, goodwill or valuable antiques), enter **O**

Complete Pages TC5 to TC7 for all transactions identified as U, L or O

Losses

Description of asset	Type of* disposal. Enter **Q, U, L or O**	Tick box if estimate or valuation used	Tick box if asset held at 31March 1982	Enter the later of date of acquisition and 16 March 1998	Enter the date of disposal	Disposal proceeds	Enter details of any elections made, reliefs claimed or due and state amounts (£)
13						£	
14						£	
15						£	
16						£	

Total losses of

TRUST AND ESTATE TAX RETURN ■ CAPITAL GAINS: PAGE TC2

	H Chargeable Gains after reliefs but before losses and taper	I Enter 'Bus' if business asset	J Taper rate	K Losses deducted			L Gains after losses	M Tapered gains (gains from column L x % in column J)
				K1 Allowable losses of the year	K2 Income losses set against gains	K3 Unused losses b/f from earlier years		
	£		%	£	£	£	£	£
	£		%	£	£	£	£	£
	£		%	£	£	£	£	£
	£		%	£	£	£	£	£
	£		%	£	£	£	£	£
	£		%	£	£	£	£	£
	£		%	£	£	£	£	£
	£		%	£	£	£	£	£
	£	Bus	%	£	£	£	£	£
	£		%	£	£	£	£	£
	£	Bus	%	£	£	£	£	£
	£		%	£	£	£	£	£
Total	5.1 £ *Total column H*				5.5 £ *Total column K2*	5.6 £ *Total column K3*		5.6B £ *Total column M*

	Losses arising
	£
	£
	£
	£
year	5.2 £

Boxes 5.3 and 5.4 are not used on these Pages

Amount chargeable on the settlor 5.6A £

Total taxable gains (after allowable losses and taper relief) box 5.6B *minus* box 5.6A £

Copy to box 5.7 on Page TC1

Copy to box 5.12 on Page TC1 and, unless you need only complete the totals boxes (see page TCN4), complete column K1

TRUST AND ESTATE TAX RETURN ■ CAPITAL GAINS: PAGE TC3

Other events in the year

Ignore this Page if you are a personal representative

Please tick the boxes which apply and provide the information requested.

Has any person holding an interest in possession in settled property died during the year? — **If yes,** tick the box and give details below **5.19** ☐

Name and address of life tenant or liferenter, etc.

Date of death   /   /

Has any person become absolutely entitled to any part of the property during the year? — **If yes,** tick the box and give details below **5.20** ☐

Name and address of beneficiary

Date beneficiary became absolutely entitled   /   /

Nature of asset

Value of asset vesting £

Amount of loss transferred to beneficiary **5.20A** £

Have the trustees ceased being resident in the UK, or did they become dual resident? — **If yes,** tick the box and give details below **5.21** ☐

Description of assets held

Date of change   /   /

Amount of chargeable gains £

Were any chargeable gains chargeable on the settlor? — **If yes,** tick the box and give details below **5.22** ☐

Name and address of settlor

Amount of chargeable gains £

Enter this amount in box 5.6A

If you have used an extra sheet, tick this box **5.23** ☐

Now go back to page 3 of the Trust and Estate Tax Return and finish filling it in.

Other shares or securities (U) - further information

If you have more than two transactions of this type of asset to return, please photocopy this Page **before** completion and send all completed Pages with your Tax Return.

1st transaction

Description of shares or securities - including name of company, company registration number (if known), number, class and nominal value of shares. Also, if possible, give a history of the shares disposed of, for instance, if there has been a reorganisation or takeover (give details of the original company and shares held in that company).

Tick box if you have already submitted form CG34 ☐

State any connection between you and the person from whom you acquired the asset or to whom you disposed of the asset (see Notes, page TCN13)

If you have used an estimate or valuation in your capital gains computation but have not submitted form CG34, please enter the date to which the valuation relates, the amount (£) and the reason for the estimate or valuation. Please also attach a copy of any valuation obtained.

2nd transaction

Description of shares or securities - including name of company, company registration number (if known), number, class and nominal value of shares. Also, if possible, give a history of the shares disposed of, for instance, if there has been a reorganisation or takeover (give details of the original company and shares held in that company).

Tick box if you have already submitted form CG34 ☐

State any connection between you and the person from whom you acquired the asset or to whom you disposed of the asset (see Notes, page TCN13)

If you have used an estimate or valuation in your capital gains computation but have not submitted form CG34, please enter the date to which the valuation relates, the amount (£) and the reason for the estimate or valuation. Please also attach a copy of any valuation obtained.

continued over

Land and property (L) - further information

If you have more than two transactions of this type of asset to return, please photocopy this Page **before** completion and send all completed Pages with your Tax Return.

1st transaction

Full address of land/property affected (attach a copy of any plan if this helps identification)

Description of land/property disposed of, including details of your ownership, for example freehold/leasehold and any tenancies affecting your ownership at the date of disposal and any other date for which a valuation has been made, and except in the case of an outright disposal of all of your interests, the interest which you have disposed of, or granted.

Tick box if you have already submitted form CG34 ☐

State any connection between you and the person from whom you acquired the asset or to whom you disposed of the asset (see Notes, page TCN13)

If you have used an estimate or valuation in your capital gains computation but have not submitted form CG34, please enter the date to which the valuation relates, the amount (£) and the reason for the estimate or valuation. Please also attach a copy of any valuation obtained.

2nd transaction

Full address of land/property affected (attach a copy of any plan if this helps identification)

Description of land/property disposed of, including details of your ownership, for example freehold/leasehold and any tenancies affecting your ownership at the date of disposal and any other date for which a valuation has been made, and except in the case of an outright disposal of all of your interests, the interest which you have disposed of, or granted.

Tick box if you have already submitted form CG34 ☐

State any connection between you and the person from whom you acquired the asset or to whom you disposed of the asset (see Notes, page TCN13)

If you have used an estimate or valuation in your capital gains computation but have not submitted form CG34, please enter the date to which the valuation relates, the amount (£) and the reason for the estimate or valuation. Please also attach a copy of any valuation obtained.

Other assets (O) - further information

If you have more than two transactions involving any other type of asset to return, please photocopy this Page **before** completion and send all completed Pages with your Tax Return.

1st transaction

Full description of the asset (other than shares or land/property) affected and any other information which helps identify the asset

Tick box if you have already submitted form CG34 ☐

State any connection between you and the person from whom you acquired the asset or to whom you disposed of the asset (see Notes, page TCN13)

If you have used an estimate or valuation in your capital gains computation but have not submitted form CG34, please enter the date to which the valuation relates, the amount (£) and the reason for the estimate or valuation. Please also attach a copy of any valuation obtained.

2nd transaction

Full description of the asset (other than shares or land/property) affected and any other information which helps identify the asset

Tick box if you have already submitted form CG34 ☐

State any connection between you and the person from whom you acquired the asset or to whom you disposed of the asset (see Notes, page TCN13)

If you have used an estimate or valuation in your capital gains computation but have not submitted form CG34, please enter the date to which the valuation relates, the amount (£) and the reason for the estimate or valuation. Please also attach a copy of any valuation obtained.

continued over

5.24 *Additional information*

Inland Revenue

For the year ended 5 April 2003

TRUST AND ESTATE NON-RESIDENCE

Fill in these boxes first

Name of trust or estate

Tax reference

The Notes on Trust and Estate Non-residence will help you fill in boxes 6.1 to 6.34.

Residence status

The trustees or personal representatives are, as a whole (please tick appropriate box)

- Resident in the UK for Income Tax purposes 6.1
- Not resident in the UK for Income Tax purposes 6.2
- Resident in the UK for Capital Gains Tax purposes 6.3
- Not resident in the UK for Capital Gains Tax purposes 6.4
- Resident in a country other than the UK (under a Double Taxation Agreement) at the same time as being resident in the UK 6.5
- Tick box 6.6 if the deceased whose estate is being administered was domiciled outside the UK at the date of death 6.6

Information required if the trustees or personal representatives claim to be non-resident in the UK for Income Tax purposes

- Did the trustees or personal representatives change during the year to 5 April 2003? Yes 6.7 No 6.8
- Were the trustees or personal representatives resident in the UK for Income Tax purposes in the year to 5 April 2002? Yes 6.9 No 6.10
- Did the trustees or personal representatives have any overseas income during the year to 5 April 2003? Yes 6.11 No 6.12

Information required if the trustees or personal representatives claim to be non-resident in the UK for Capital Gains Tax purposes

- Did the trustees or personal representatives change during the year to 5 April 2003? Yes 6.13 No 6.14
- Were the trustees or personal representatives resident in the UK for Capital Gains Tax purposes in the year to 5 April 2002? Yes 6.15 No 6.16
- Were UK professional trustees acting during the year to 5 April 2003? Yes 6.17 No 6.18
- Did the trustees or personal representatives carry on a trade in the UK through a branch or agency that made disposals for capital gains in the year to 5 April 2003? Yes 6.19 No 6.20

SA906 (Substitute)(LexisNexis UK)

TRUST AND ESTATE TAX RETURN ■ NON-RESIDENCE: PAGE TNR1

Please turn over

Information required if the trustees or personal representatives are resident in the UK and they also claim to be resident in another country for the purposes of a Double Taxation Agreement

- In which country as well as the UK were the trustees or personal representatives regarded as resident for 2002-03? **6.21**
- Were they also regarded as resident in the country in box 6.21 for 2001-02? Yes **6.22** No **6.23**
- Were a majority of the trustees or personal representatives resident in the UK for 2002-03? Yes **6.24** No **6.25**
- Do you consider that in 2002-03 the person(s) who supplied the settled property or funds had close personal and economic relations with *(tick **one** box)*:
  - the UK? **6.26**

  or

  - the country shown in box 6.21? **6.27**

  or

  - neither of these? **6.28**
- Was the general administration of the trust carried out during 2002-03 mainly in *(tick **one** box)*:
  - the UK? **6.29**

  or

  - the country shown in box 6.21? **6.30**

  or

  - neither of these? **6.31**
- Do you consider that, in 2002-03, the trustees or personal representatives have closer personal and economic relations to *(tick **one** box)*:
  - the UK? **6.32**

  or

  - the country shown in box 6.21? **6.33**

  or

  - neither of these? **6.34**

Now go back to page 3 of the Trust and Estate Tax Return and finish filling it in

Inland Revenue

Income for the year ended 5 April 2003

TRUST AND ESTATE CHARITIES

Fill in these boxes first

Name of trust

Name of charity, if different

Tax reference

If you want help, look up the box numbers in the Notes on Trust and Estate Charities.

Claim to exemption

• Charity repayment reference	7.1	
• Charity Commission Registration Number or Scottish Charity Number	7.2	
If the trust is a charity are you claiming exemption from tax on all or part of your income and gains?	YES	
Have all income and gains that you are claiming to be exempt from tax been, or are they to be, applied for charitable purposes?	YES	

Return period

• Are you returning information for the **year ended 5 April 2003?**	YES	
• If not, what period does this Return cover?		
Period begins 7.3 / /	and ends	7.4 / /
• Are accounts to be enclosed with the Return?	YES	
If 'No', explain why	7.5	

Repayments

	Income Tax	Transitional relief
• Amount already claimed on form R68(2000)	7.6 £	7.7 £
• Total repayment/payment due	7.8 £	7.9 £
and		
• further repayment/payment due	7.10 £	7.11 £
or		
• amounts overclaimed	7.12 £	7.13 £
Have any of the amounts in boxes 7.10 or 7.11 been included in any repayment claim on form R68(2000)?	YES	

Income on which you are claiming exemption

Non-exempt amounts should be entered in the appropriate parts of the Return.

• Total turnover from exempt trading activities	7.14	£
• Investment income	7.15	£
• UK land and buildings income	7.16	£
• Gift Aid	7.17	£
• Other charities	7.18	£
• Legacies	7.19	£
• Other donations	7.20	£
• Other, for example, commissions, fees, small fund raising	7.21	£

continued over

SA907 (Substitute)(LexisNexis UK)

Expenses as included in the charity accounts

• Trading costs	7.22	£
• UK land and buildings	7.23	£
• All general administration costs	7.24	£
• All grants and donations made in the UK	7.25	£
• All grants and donations made outside the UK	7.26	£
• Others (not entered elsewhere on the Return)	7.27	£

Assets

	Disposals in year	Held at 5 April 2003
• Tangible fixed assets	7.28 £	7.29 £
• UK investments (excluding controlled companies)	7.30 £	7.31 £
• Shares in, and loans to, controlled companies	7.32 £	7.33 £
• Overseas investments	7.34 £	7.35 £
• Loans and non-trade debtors		7.36 £
• Other current assets		7.37 £
• Were all investments qualifying investments, and were loans made qualifying loans, within Part I or II of Schedule 20 ICTA 1988?		YES
• Value of any non-qualifying investments and loans		7.38 £
• Number of subsidiary or associated companies the charity controls at 5 April 2003		7.39

Claim

I claim exemption from tax

7.40

Signature Date

Print name in full here

Status or capacity in which you are signing

7.41

7.42 ***Additional information***

Inland Revenue

Authorising your agent

It is important that you complete these boxes so we can note our records.

Inland Revenue reference ____________

National Insurance number (individuals only) ____________

Company, Limited Liability Partnership or Limited Partnership registration number ____________

Please read the notes on the back before completing this authority.

This authority overrides any earlier authority given to the Inland Revenue. We will hold the information you give us until you tell us that the details have changed.

I, *(print your name)* ____________

authorise *(print your agent's business name)* ____________

to act on my behalf in connection with any matters within the responsibility of the Inland Revenue.

Signature ____________ *(please see note 1 on the back before signing)* Date ___ / ___ / ___

- ***Please give your details here***

Full address ____________

Postcode ____________

Telephone number ____________
(If you are willing for us to contact you by phone)

- ***Please give your agent's details here***

Full address ____________

Postcode ____________

Telephone number ____________

Fax number ____________

E-mail address ____________

Client reference ____________

Only for Self Assessment customers (not including companies)

We will send your Statement of Account to you, but if you would like us to send it to your agent instead, please tick this box ☐

After you have completed this form, please send it to your Inland Revenue office.

For official use

- Customer's records noted - *please complete the relevant boxes opposite*

	Please ✓	Initials	Date
Tax	☐		/ /
NICs	☐		/ /
Tax credits	☐		/ /
Others	☐		/ /

- Form(s) 64-6A issued ☐ *Please ✓*

Initials ____ *Date* ___ / ___ / ___

64-8 BS7/02

1 Who should sign the form

It depends who the authority is for. See the table below.

Who the authority is for	Who signs the form
You	You.
Company	The secretary or other responsible officer of the company.
Partnership	The partner responsible for the partnership's affairs. It applies only to the partnership. Individual partners need to sign a separate authority for their own affairs.
Trust	One or more of the trustees.

2 What else you should do

- If you have more than one agent acting with us on your behalf, please sign one of these forms for each one and send them to us with a letter telling us which agent deals with what for you. If you deal with more than one Inland Revenue office, please send it to just one office and we will pass on the information.
- If your agent doesn't deal with **all** your Inland Revenue affairs, please send a letter with this form giving us details of those that they do deal with.

3 What this authority means

- This authority allows us to exchange information about you with your agent, and to deal with them on any matters within the responsibility of the Inland Revenue.
- Once we have received your authority we will start sending letters and forms to your agent. But sometimes we need to send them to you as well as, or instead of, your agent. For the latest information on what forms we send automatically visit our website at **www.inlandrevenue.gov.uk/sa/agentlist.htm** or contact any Inland Revenue office.
- You won't receive your Self Assessment Statements of Account if you authorise your agent to receive them instead, but paying any amount due is your responsibility.
- Companies do **not** receive Statements of Account.
- We don't send National Insurance statements and requests for payment to your agent unless you have asked us if you can defer payment.

4 Data Protection Act

The Inland Revenue is a Data Controller under the Data Protection Act. We hold information for the purposes of taxes, social security contributions, tax credits and certain other statutory functions as assigned by Parliament. The information we hold may be used for any of the Inland Revenue's functions.

We may get information about you from others, or we may give information to them. If we do, it will only be as the law permits, to

- check accuracy of information
- prevent or detect crime
- protect public funds.

We may check information we receive about you with what is already in our records. This can include information provided by you as well as by others such as other government departments and agencies and overseas tax authorities. We will not give information about you to anyone outside the Inland Revenue unless the law permits us to do so.

Inland Revenue

Certificate of deduction of income tax

For IR use

'Duty assessed' stamp

Office stamp

This form should be completed by the person making a payment of interest, annual payment or annuity where income tax has been deducted from the payment.

The person receiving the payments should keep this form. It will be needed if a claim for repayment of tax is made.

I certify that on paying to

of

the amount shown in box 2 below I deducted the income tax shown in box 3, and that this tax has been or will be paid by me either directly or by deduction from other income when received by me.

1. Nature of payment, for example, interest, annuity, or annual payment

2. Gross payment £

3. Income tax deducted by me £

4. Net payment £

5. Date payment was made / /

6. Period for which payment was due

from / / to / /

7. Date on which payment due / /

8. Enter in CAPITAL letters your name and address

Name

Address

Postcode

9. Other details

- if you are employed, your employer's name and address
- if a company or if you are in business, the business address

Name

Address

Postcode

10. Office to which your returns or your employer's returns are made

Reference (if known)

Signature

Date

/ /

The person deducting the tax and responsible for accounting for it to the Inland Revenue should sign this form. You should say if you are deducting tax on behalf of your employer, for example as secretary or cashier.

R185

(Substitute)(LexisNexis UK)

Statement of income from trusts

Inland Revenue

Trustees: use this form to advise beneficiaries about income payments made under discretion, and income entitlement from trusts. For annuities and other annual payments, use form R185.

Beneficiaries: keep this form and refer to it if making a Tax Return or claiming a tax repayment. The box numbers 7.1 to 7.12 below refer to the box numbers on the *Trusts etc.* page of the Tax Return.

I certify that
(Name and address of beneficiary)

Full name

Address

Postcode

is a beneficiary of
(name of trust)

Tax reference of trust

Agent's/Solicitor's reference

The information below is correct.

Signature of trustee

Date / /

Discretionary income payment from a trust

I paid income to the beneficiary as follows:

	Net amount	Tax credit at the rate applicable to trusts	Taxable amount	Year ended 5 April
Total payments in tax year *(see Note 1 overleaf)*	7.1 £	7.2 £	7.3 £	20

Income entitlement under a trust

The beneficiary's income entitlement for year ended 5 April 20 was:

Income taxed at:	Net amount	UK tax or tax credit	Taxable amount	Type of income for a non-resident beneficiary *(see Note 6 overleaf)*
basic rate *(see Note 2 overleaf)*	7.4 £	7.5 £	7.6 £	
lower rate *(see Note 3 overleaf)*	7.7 £	7.8 £	7.9 £	
non-repayable dividend rate *(see Note 4 or 10 overleaf)*	7.10 £	7.11 £	7.12 £	

	Taxable amount	Type of income
Untaxed income *(see Note 7 or 11 overleaf)*	£	

	Net amount	UK tax paid	Taxable amount
Foreign income *(see Note 5 or 12 overleaf)*	£	£	£
		Foreign tax paid	
		£	

	Dividend	Notional tax	Dividend + notional tax
Stock/scrip dividends *(see Note 13 overleaf)*	£	£	£

R185(Trust Income)

(Substitute)(LexisNexis UK)

Trustees should read only Notes 1 - 7. Beneficiaries should read only Notes 8 - 13

Notes for Trustees

1 Enter in box 7.1 the actual amount paid, in box 7.2 the amount of tax treated as deducted at the rate applicable to trusts, and in box 7.3 the total of the amounts in boxes 7.1 and 7.2. The rate applicable to trusts is 34%. So, for example, if the discretionary payment to the beneficiary is £660, enter 660 in box 7.1, 340 in box 7.2, and 1000 in box 7.3.

2 Income taxed at the basic rate includes rental income. It does not include interest or dividend income.

3 Income taxed at the lower rate includes savings income such as interest.

4 Income taxed at the dividend rate includes dividends from UK companies.

5 'Foreign tax' is the lower of
- the foreign tax actually withheld
- the amount of tax to which the trust was liable under the terms of a Double Taxation Agreement.

6 If the beneficiary is not resident in the UK, please use the boxes provided to specify the type of income, for example, rent.

7 Use the box on the right to specify the type of income, for example, rent.

Notes for Beneficiaries

8 If you are making a Tax Return, transfer the information from this form to the corresponding boxes on the Tax Return.

9 If you are making a claim for tax repayment, use the information on this form to complete section 6 of form R40.

10 The 10% tax credit on UK dividends is non-repayable from tax year 1999–2000. This means that you will be given credit for the 10% against your income, but we will not repay any excess. If you are making a claim on form R40, mark the entry at section 6 for this income 'non-repayable'.

11 If you are making a Tax Return, include this income in the pages of your Tax Return dealing with that particular type of income, not the *Trusts etc.* page. For example, if the income is rent, include it in the *Land and Property* pages.

12 If you are making a Tax Return, include this information in the *Foreign* pages of your Tax Return if you are resident in the UK, not the *Trusts etc.* page.

13 If you are making a Tax Return, include this in the scrip dividends boxes of the main Tax Return, not the *Trusts etc.* page.

Statement of income from estates

Inland Revenue

Executors/administrators: use this form to advise beneficiaries about income from the estate of a deceased person
- for each year during the administration of the estate if a 'sum' is paid to the beneficiary in that year and
- for the year in which the administration of the estate is completed.

Beneficiaries: keep this form and refer to it if making a Tax Return or claiming a tax repayment. The box numbers 7.13 to 7.31 below refer to the box numbers on the *Trusts etc.* page of the Tax Return.

I certify that

(Name and address of beneficiary)

Full name

Address

Postcode

is a beneficiary of the estate of *(Name of deceased person)* Date of death / /

The information below is correct.

Signature of executor or administrator Date / /

The beneficiary's estate income for the year ended 5 April 20 consisted of the following deemed income:

Income taxed at: *(see Notes 6a to 6f overleaf for tax rates and types of income)*	**Income receivable**	**Tax paid**	**Taxable amount**
basic rate	7.13 £	7.14 £	7.15 £
lower rate	7.16 £	7.17 £	7.18 £
dividend rate	7.19 £	7.20 £	7.21 £
non-repayable basic rate	7.22 £	7.23 £	7.24 £
non-repayable lower rate	7.25 £	7.26 £	7.27 £
non-repayable dividend rate	7.28 £	7.29 £	7.30 £
Total foreign tax for which foreign tax credit relief not claimed		7.31 £	

R185(Estate Income)

Appendix 4 Forms

Notes for Beneficiaries

1 If you normally receive a Tax Return, you should transfer the amounts of income and tax paid shown on the statement overleaf, to the corresponding boxes on the Tax Return, and forward the Tax Return to your Inland Revenue office.

2 If you do not normally receive a Tax Return, you should complete one only if the income you receive from the estate, when added on to any other income, results in you being liable to pay tax at the higher rate.

3 If figures have been entered for tax paid in boxes 7.14, 7.17 or 7.20 overleaf you may be eligible to claim a repayment of the tax paid. If so, use the information from the boxes overleaf to complete section 6 of the R40 claim form. But please note that the tax described overleaf as 'non-repayable' cannot be repaid in any circumstances.

Notes for Executors and Administrators

4 **Please prepare a statement on the form overleaf and give it to the beneficiaries of UK estates**

- for each year during the administration period in which a *sum* is paid to the beneficiary, and
- for the year in which the administration of the estate is completed.

It should not be given to beneficiaries of a foreign estate as none of the tax will be refundable. A schedule of income and UK/foreign tax credit relief claimable may be provided to beneficiaries of a foreign estate.

5 **A 'sum' for this purpose includes cash, assets transferred or appropriated and debts set off or released.**

Tax rates and types of income

6a Income taxed at the basic rate includes rental income and profits from a trade. It does not include savings or dividend income.

b Income taxed at the lower rate includes savings income such as interest received.

c Income taxed at the dividend rate includes dividends from foreign companies.

d Income taxed at the non-repayable basic rate relates to gains realised on certain insurance policies.

e Income taxed at the non-repayable lower rate relates to tax years prior to 5 April 1999, and is only relevant if undistributed income is carried forward from 1998–99 or earlier years.

f Income taxed at the non-repayable dividend rate relates to dividends paid on UK shareholdings from 1999–2000 onwards.

7 You can work out the income which each residuary beneficiary should show in their Tax Return by following four steps. For example, for 2002–03 the steps are:

Step 1 Add to any net amount brought forward from 2001–02 the net amount of the beneficiary's share of the residuary income for 2002–03.

Step 2 Compare the net figures in Step 1 with the sum paid to the beneficiary in 2002–03. If the sum paid is greater than or equal to the result of Step 1, then the beneficiary's income is the amount at Step 1 - that is the aggregate income entitlement.

If the sum paid is less than the result of Step 1, the beneficiary's income is the sum paid. The balance of the aggregate income entitlement is carried forward to the next tax year. This will be the whole of the aggregate income entitlement if no distributions were made.

For the final tax year of the administration period, the residuary beneficiary's aggregate income entitlement will be treated as having been distributed in full.

Step 3 The amount to be treated as income in Step 2 is to be treated as paid in the following order of preference:

1. Income bearing basic rate tax.
2. Income bearing lower rate tax.
3. Income bearing dividend rate tax.
4. Income bearing non-repayable basic rate tax.
5. Income bearing non-repayable lower rate tax.
6. Income bearing non-repayable dividend rate tax.

Step 4 Gross up the income in Step 3. Net income taxed at basic rate should be grossed up at the basic rate of tax for the year in which the distribution is made for example, in 2002–2003 the income should be grossed up by multiplying the net income by the fraction 100/78, because the basic rate of tax is 22%.

Application for post transaction valuation check

Taxpayer Details

Name

Address

Postcode

Reference

National Insurance number *(where appropriate)*

Details of disposal

Date of disposal / /

Name and address of purchaser

Name

Address

Postcode

Reason for valuation

'✓' as appropriate

- [ ] Rebasing to 31 March 1982
- [ ] Market value disposal
- [ ] Other - *please specify*

Valuation required

Description of asset to be valued	Valuation date	Valuation offered

Shares - The description should include the name of the company, the registration number (if known) and the number of shares to be valued. Enter in the table your valuation **per share** and not the total value of your holding.

Land - The description should provide sufficient information to identify the property, with details of your interest in the property and details of any tenancies existing at the valuation date. The term 'land' includes both land and buildings.

Other - The description should provide sufficient information to identify the asset.

Please turn over

CG34 **(Substitute)(LexisNexis Butterworths Tolley)**

BMSD 1/00

1

You should also provide

✓ *to show items enclosed*

☐ A capital gains computation for the disposal with an estimate of your capital gains tax liability for the tax year in which you made the disposal, or for companies the corporation tax liability on chargeable gains

☐ Details of any reliefs due or to be claimed in respect of the disposal

☐ A copy of any valuation report obtained

☐ If available, the cost and date of acquisition of the asset and details of any improvements made

☐ For **share** valuations - accounts for the three years up to the valuation date

☐ For **land** valuations -

- if you held a leasehold interest, a copy of the lease applying at the valuation date
- if the land was let at the valuation date, a copy of any tenancy agreement applying at that date
- a plan showing the location of the land if the valuation is of undeveloped land.

☐ Any other papers you feel may be relevant

Use this space to provide any other information that you consider is relevant to your valuation

2

Inland Revenue

Post-transaction valuation checks for capital gains

Introduction

When working out your Capital Gains Tax liability, or in the case of companies, your Corporation Tax liability on chargeable gains, you sometimes have to value assets. If you use such valuations, we offer a free service to help you complete your Tax Return. You can ask your Inland Revenue office to check valuations after you have made the disposal but before you make your Return. Our service is available to all taxpayers, individuals, trustees and companies.

If we agree your valuations we will not challenge your use of those valuations in your Return unless there are any important facts affecting the valuations that you have not told us about. Agreement to your valuations does not necessarily mean that we agree the gain or loss. We will not consider the other figures you have used until you make your Return.

If we cannot agree your valuations we will suggest alternatives. We use specialist valuers to value some assets, mainly shares, land, goodwill and works of art. You will also be able to discuss your valuations with our valuers. You must file your Return by the filing date printed on it even if we have not been able to agree your valuations or suggest alternatives. Your Return must also tell us about any valuations that we have checked but been unable to agree.

If, after discussion, we cannot reach agreement on any valuations you use in your Return, you will be able to appeal to an independent tribunal.

How to get your valuations checked

If you want us to check your valuations, ask your Inland Revenue office or any Inland Revenue Enquiry Centre for one copy of form *CG34* for each valuation you want us to check. Return the completed form(s) to us together with the information and documents requested on the form. You can also attach any other information that will help us understand your valuations.

If you do not provide all the information requested on the form, we may be unable to check your valuations. If you have difficulty getting all of this information, or you are not sure how to prepare a Capital Gains computation, ask us for help.

How long it will take

Your Inland Revenue office, or our specialist valuers, will contact you as soon as possible after you make your application. Valuation is an exercise of judgement that can sometimes be a difficult and lengthy process, particularly if discussion is necessary.

The sooner you contact us after you have made a disposal, the more likely we will be able to reach agreement with you before you make your Return.

We expect that it will take a minimum of 56 days to agree your valuations or to provide you with an alternative. In more complex cases it may take longer. In a few very complex cases we may not be able to provide you with any alternative valuation before the filing date for your Return. If you want to use our service please send any forms *CG34* to your Inland Revenue office at least two months before you need to make your Return.

Further information

We can give you further information about this scheme at your Inland Revenue office or from your nearest Inland Revenue Enquiry Centre.

3

Inland Revenue Capital Taxes

Inland Revenue Account for Inheritance Tax

Fill in this account to tell us about any of the events listed below. You should read the related guidance notes before filling in any particular box on this or the accompanying forms. Complete all names and addresses in CAPITALS.

A About the Chargeable event

Tick one of the following boxes.

		Tick box	Event form
A1	Gifts and other transfers of value including failed potentially exempt transfers.		IHT100a
A2	Ending of an interest in possession in settled property.		IHT100b
A3	Assets in a discretionary trust ceasing to be relevant property (proportionate charge).		IHT100c
A4	Discretionary trust ten-year anniversary (principal charge).		IHT100d
A5	Assets ceasing to be held on special trusts (flat rate charge). *See page 9 of the notes "How to fill in form IHT100".*		IHT100e
A6	Cessation of conditional exemption and disposal of trees or underwood (recapture charge).		IHT100f

This account must be accompanied by the event form shown against the box you have ticked.

B About the transferor/settlement

Title of transferor/settlor
B1

Surname of the transferor/settlor
B2

Forename(s) of the transferor/settlor
B3

Address, or last usual address of the transferor/settlor
B4

Post Code

Date of birth of the transferor/settlor
B5 / /

Date of death of the transferor/settlor (where appropriate)
B6 / /

IHT reference for the transferor/settlor (where appropriate)
B7

Tax District of the transferor/settlor
B8

Income tax or self assessment reference of the transferor/settlor
B9

National Insurance number of the transferor/settlor
B10

Domicile of the
- settlor when the settlement was made, or
- testator at the date of death, or
- transferor at the date of transfer

B11

Name of the settlement (where appropriate)
B12

IHT reference for the settlement (if known)
B13

Income tax reference for the settlement
B14

(Substitute)(LexisNexis UK)

IHT100 L13/03

C Person we should contact

Name and address of the person to whom communications should be sent

C1

Post code

DX number and exchange C3

Telephone number C4

Reference C5

Contact name C2

Capacity C6

Important. Read the following notes and the more detailed instructions in IHT110 "How to fill in form IHT100" before filling in the rest of this form. One of the event forms IHT100a, IHT100b, IHT100c, IHT100d, IHT100e or IHT100f must be filled in and returned with this form.

Fill in D E and F to tell us about ***the assets included in the chargeable event you are telling us about as follows:***

If you have ticked box

- ***A1*** *tell us about the assets that were given or transferred.*
- ***A2*** *tell us about the assets in respect of which this interest in possession ceased.*
- ***A3*** *tell us about the assets that ceased to be relevant property. (Proportionate charge).*
- ***A4*** *tell us about the relevent property in the settlement. (Principal charge).*
- ***A5*** *tell us about the assets which ceased to be held on special trusts. (Flat rate charge).*
- ***A6*** *tell us about the assets on which a charge to inheritance tax arises. (Recapture charge).*

D Supplementary pages

You must answer all the questions in this section. You should read the notes starting at page 12 of form IHT110 before answering the questions. If you answer **yes** to a question you will need to fill in the supplementary pages shown. If you do not have all of the supplementary pages you should telephone our Orderline on 0845 234 1000.

		Yes	No	
• **Domicile outside the United Kingdom**	Was the transferor domiciled outside the UK at the date of the transfer or the date of the settlement?			D31
• **Stocks and shares**	Do the assets about which you are telling us include stocks and shares?			D32
• **Debts due to the settlement**	Was there any money on loan from the settlement either on mortgage or by personal loan, that had not been repaid at the date of the chargeable event?			D33
• **Insurance**	Were any insurance policies included in the transfer?			D34
• **Household and personal goods**	Do the assets being reported include household and personal goods?			D35
• **Land and buildings: Interests in land: Trees or underwood**	Do the assets being reported include any land, buildings, trees or underwood in the UK?			D36
• **Agricultural relief**	Are you deducting agricultural relief?			D37
• **Business relief**	Are you claiming business relief?			D38
• **Foreign assets**	Do the assets being reported include any assets outside the UK?			D39
• **Other information**	Use this form to provide any additional information.			D40

2

E Assets in the UK where tax may not be paid by instalments

• Quoted stocks, shares and investments *(box SS1 form D32)*	E1	£
• UK Government and municipal securities *(box SS2 form D32)*	E2	£
• Unquoted stocks and shares *(details from form D32)*	E3	£
• Traded unquoted stocks and shares *(details from form D32)*	E4	£
• Dividends or interest *(details from form D32)*	E5	£
• National Savings Investments *(show details on form D40)*	E6	£
• Bank and building society accounts *(show details on form D40)*	E7	£
• Cash	E8	£
• Debts due to the settlement or trust and secured on mortgage *(box DD1 form D33)*	E9	£
• Other debts due to the settlement *(box DD1 form D33)*	E10	£
• Life assurance policies *(box IP1 form D34)*	E11	£
• Capital gains tax repayment	E12	£
• Household and personal goods *(box HG1 form D35)*	E13	£
• Other assets *(show details on form D40)*	E14	£
Total assets *(sum of boxes E1 to E14)*	E15	£

• **Liabilities**

Name of creditor	Description of liability	Amount £

Total liabilities	E16	£
Net total of assets less liabilities *(box E15 less box E16)*	E17	£

• **Exemption and reliefs** *(Do not include any annual exemption)*

Total Exemptions and reliefs	E18	£
Chargeable value of assets in the UK where tax may **not** be paid by instalments *(box E17 less box E18)*	E19	£

3

F Assets in the UK where tax may be paid by instalments

Do you wish to pay the tax on these assets by instalments?

Yes ☐ No ☐ Number of instalments being paid now ☐

• Residential property			F1 £
• Farms			F2 £
• Business property			F3 £
• Woodlands, trees or underwood			F4 £
• Other land and buildings			F5 £
	Interest in a business	Interest in a partnership	
• Farming business	F6.1 £	F6.2 £	F6 £
	Interest in a business	Interest in a partnership	
• Other business interests	F7.1 £	F7.2 £	F7 £
	Farm trade assets	Other business assets	
• Business assets	F8.1 £	F8.2 £	F8 £
• Quoted shares and securities ***(control holding only)***			F9 £
	Control holding	Non-control holding	
• Unquoted shares	F10.1 £	F10.2 £	F10 £
	Control holding	Non-control holding	
• Traded unquoted shares	F11.1 £	F11.2 £	F11 £
		Total assets *(sum of boxes F1 to F11)*	F12 £

Liabilities, exemptions and reliefs

• Name of mortgagee	Property on which mortgage is secured	Amount outstanding £
		F13 £

• Other liabilities

	F14 £

Net total of assets less liabilities *(box F12 less boxes F13 and F14)* F15 £

• Exemptions and reliefs *(do not include any annual exemption)*

	F16 £

Chargeable value of assets in the UK where tax may be paid by instalments *(box F15 less box F16)* F17 £

• Annual exemption being deducted F18 £

4

G Summary of the chargeable event

If you wish to work out the tax yourself you should fill in form IHT100WS so that you can copy the figures to this section and to section H. *You do not have to work out the tax. If you do not wish to do so, leave this section and section H blank and go straight to section J.*
Guidance on how to fill in parts G and H are given on page 25 of the guide - "How to fill in form IHT100". The box number WSA1 etc, refer to the boxes in the worksheet from which the figures come.

Lifetime transfers (event forms IHT100a and IHT100b)

Previous transfers made by the transferor which need to be taken into account *(box WSA1)* G1 £

Threshold at date of transfer *(box TX2)* G2 £

Balance of threshold available *(box TX3)* G3 £

Assets where the tax may not be paid by instalments

- Assets in the UK *(box WSA2)* G4 £
- Foreign assets *(box WSA3)* G5 £

Value of assets where tax may not be paid by instalments *(box WSA4)* G6 £

Assets where the tax may be paid by instalments

- Assets in the UK *(box WSA5)* G7 £
- Foreign assets *(box WSA6)* G8 £

Total assets where tax may be paid by instalments *(box WSA7)* G9 £

Total value of transfer *(box WSA8)* G10 £

Annual exemption *(box WSA9)* G11 £

Chargeable transfer *(box WSA10)* G12 £

Go to box H1 on page 6 to work out the tax.

Non-interest in possession settlements (event forms IHT100c and IHT100d)

Assets where the tax may not be paid by instalments

- Assets in the UK *(box WSB1)* G13 £
- Foreign assets *(box WSB2)* G14 £

Value of assets where tax may not be paid by instalments ***(box WSB3)*** G15 £

Assets where the tax may be paid by instalments

- Assets in the UK *(box WSB4)* G16 £
- Foreign assets *(box WSB5)* G17 £
- Value of assets where tax may be paid by instalments *(box WSB6)* G18 £
- **Total value on which tax is chargeable** *(box WSB7)* G19 £

Go to box H7 on page 6 to work out the tax

5

Flat rate charge and Recapture charge (event forms IHT100e and IHT100f)

- Value of assets where tax may not be paid by instalments *(flat rate charge box WSC3: recapture charge box WSD3)* — G20 £
- Value of assets where tax may be paid by instalments *(flat rate charge box WSC6: recapture charge box WSD4)* — G21 £
- Total value of assets on which tax arises *(flat rate charge box WSC7: recapture charge box WSD5)* — G22 £

H Working out the tax

Lifetime transfers (event forms IHT100a and IHT100b)

- Value chargeable to tax *(box WSA10)* — H1 £
- **Tax** *(box TX9)* — H2 £
- Relief on successive charges *(box TX10)* — H3 £
- Double taxation relief *(box TX11)* — H4 £
- Tax previously paid on this transfer, if any *(box TX12)* — H5 £
- **Tax due on this transfer** *(box TX13)* ***Go to box H13*** — H6 £

Principal and proportionate charges (event forms IHT100c and IHT100d)

Value on which tax is chargeable *(box WSB7)* — H7 £

Rate *(box R24)* — H8 £

Tax *(principal charge box TX39 plus box TX46: proportionate charge box TX59 plus box TX67)* — H9 £

Reduction against tax *(principal charge only box TX40 plus box TX47)* — H10 £

Double taxation relief *(principal charge box TX42 plus box TX49: proportionate charge box TX60 plus box TX68)* — H11 £

Tax payable on this transfer
(principal charge box TX43 plus box TX50: proportionate charge box TX61 plus box TX69) — H12 £

Working out the tax that is payable on this account

- **Lifetime transfers**
- **Principal charge**
- **Proportionate charge**

- Tax which may not be paid by instalments *(lifetime: box TX18, principal: box TX41, proportionate: box TX59)* — H13 £
- Successive charges relief *(lifetime: box TX19)* — H14 £
- Double taxation relief *(lifetime: box TX20, principal: box TX42, proportionate: box TX60)* — H15 £
- Tax previously paid, if any *(box TX21)* — H16 £
- Interest *(lifetime: box TX23, principal: box TX44, proportionate: box TX62)* — H17 £

Tax and interest which may not be paid by instalments
(lifetime: box TX24, principal: box TX45, proportionate: box TX63) — H18 £

6

- Tax which may be paid by instalments *(lifetime box TX29: principal box TX48: proportionate box TX67)* — H19 £
- Successive charges relief *(lifetime box TX30)* — H20 £
- Double taxation relief *(lifetime box TX31: principal box TX49: proportionate box TX68)* — H21 £
- Tax previously paid *(lifetime box TX32)* — H22 £
- Number of instalments being paid now *(lifetime box TX34: principal box TX51: proportionate box TX70)* — H23 / 10
- Tax now payable *(lifetime box TX35: principal box TX52: proportionate box TX71)* — H24 £
- Interest on instalments to be added *(lifetime box TX36: principal box TX53: proportionate box TX72)* — H25 £
- **Tax and interest being paid now which may be paid by instalments** *(lifetime box TX37: principal box TX54: proportionate box TX73)* — H26 £
- **Total tax and interest payable on this account** *(lifetime box TX38: principal box TX55: proportionate box TX74)* — H27 £

Working out the tax. Flat rate charge (event form IHT100e) Recapture charge (event form IHT100f)

- Tax which may not be paid by instalments *(flat rate charge box TX75: recapture charge box TX104 or box TX117)* — H28 £
- Double taxation relief on the tax which may not be paid by instalments *(flat rate charge box TX76)* — H29 £
- Tax not payable by instalments *(flat rate charge box TX77)* — H30 £
- Interest *(flat rate charge box TX78: recapture charge box TX105 or box TX118)* — H31 £
- **Tax which may not be paid by instalments and interest now payable** *(flat rate charge box TX79: recapture charge box TX106 or box TX119)* — H32 £
- Tax which may be paid by instalments *(flat rate charge box TX80: recapture charge box TX110 or box TX120)* — H33 £
- Double taxation relief on the tax which may be paid by instalments *(flat rate charge box TX81)* — H34 £
- Tax which may be paid by instalments *(flat rate charge box TX82)* — H35 £
- Number of instalments due *(flat rate charge box TX83: recapture charge box TX111 or box TX121)* — H36 / 10
- Tax now payable *(flat rate charge box TX84: recapture charge box TX112 or box TX122)* — H37 £
- Interest *(flat rate charge box TX85: recapture charge box TX113 or box TX123)* — H38 £
- **Tax which may be paid by instalments and interest now payable** *(flat rate charge box TX86: recapture charge box TX114 or box TX124)* — H39 £
- **Tax and interest now payable on this account** *(flat rate charge box TX87: recapture charge box TX115 or box TX125)* — H40 £

7

J Authority for repayment of inheritance tax

In the event of any inheritance tax being overpaid the payable order for the overpaid tax and interest in connection with this chargeable event estate should be made out to:

K Declaration

To the best of my/our knowledge and belief, the information I/we have given and the statements I/we have made in this account and in the event form

K1

and the supplementary pages

K2

attached (together called "this account") are correct and complete.

I/We understand that I/we may be liable to prosecution if I/we deliberately conceal any information that affects the liability to inheritance tax arising on the chargeable event OR if I/we deliberately include information in this account which I/we know to be false.

I/We understand that I/we may have to pay financial penalties if this account is incorrect by reason of my/our fraud or negligence OR if I/we fail to remedy anything in this account which is incorrect in any material respect within a reasonable time of it coming to my/our notice.

I/We understand that where we have elected to pay tax by instalments that I/we may have to pay interest on any unpaid tax according to the law.

Each person delivering this account whether as transferor, transferee or trustee, must sign below to indicate that they have read and agreed the statements above.

Full name and address *Signature* *Date* *Capacity: Transferee, transferor, trustee, other(specify)* *Delete the ones that do not apply*	*Full name and address* *Signature* *Date* *Capacity: Transferee, transferor, trustee, other(specify)* *Delete the ones that do not apply*
Full name and address *Signature* *Date* *Capacity: Transferee, transferor, trustee, other(specify)* *Delete the ones that do not apply*	*Full name and address* *Signature* *Date* *Capacity: Transferee, transferor, trustee, other(specify)* *Delete the ones that do not apply*

See notes

8

Inland Revenue
Capital Taxes

Gifts and other transfers of value

Name of transferor

Date of transfer / /

1 About the transfer

1.1

Names and addresses of transferees	Relationship with transferor	Share and/or interest taken

1.2 Is the transferor paying the tax (if any) on this transfer?

Yes No

1.3 Did the transferor receive any assets in return for the assets transferred?

Yes *Answer question 1.4* No *Go to question 1.5*

1.4

Describe the assets received	Value at date of transfer
Total	£

1.5 Was the transfer part of a wider series of transactions or arrangements?

Yes *Answer question 1.6* No *Go to question 1.7*

1.6 Describe the position below

1.7 Were any of the assets included in this transfer subject to any other event, arrangement or transaction connected in any way with this transfer?

Yes *Answer question 1.8* No *Go to question 1.9*

IHT100a (Substitute)(LexisNexis UK) 1 L31/03

1.8 Describe the position below

1.9 If the assets transferred consisted of land or buildings did the transferor retain any land adjacent to the land transferred?

Yes *Answer question 1.10* No *Go to question 1.11*

1.10 Describe the land retained

1.11 If the assets transferred consisted of shares in an unquoted company did the transferor or their spouse retain any shares in the company?

Yes *Answer question 1.12* No *Go to question 1.13*

1.12 Describe the shares retained

1.13 Was the transfer connected in any way with the purchase of or other dealing with an assurance policy or an annuity?

Yes *Answer question 1.14* No *Go to question 2.1*

1.14 Describe the situation below

2 **Earlier transfers**

2.1 Is the transferor alive or did they survive the transfer by more than seven years?

Yes *Answer question 2.2* No *Go to question 2.3*

2.2 Did the transferor make any other gifts or other transfers of value that were chargeable when made during the seven years ending on the date of this transfer?

Yes *Answer questions 2.4 and 2.5*

No *Go to question 2.6*

2

2.3 Did the transferor make any gifts or other transfers of value during the seven years ending on the date of death and before the date of this transfer or any gifts ***or*** other transfers of value that were chargeable at the time they were made during the seven years ending on the date of this transfer?

Yes ☐ *Answer questions 2.4 and 2.5*

No ☐ *Go to question 2.6*

2.4 State the chargeable value of previous transfers £

2.5 State the IHT file reference for the previous transfers (if known)

2.6 Tax threshold £

The tax threshold to be used is normally the threshold applicable at the date of the gift you are telling us about. If this gift occurred within seven years of the date of the transferor's death ***and*** *the threshold at that date is higher, enter the tax threshold applicable at the date of death.*

3 Gifts with reservation

Answer only if the transferor has died

3.1 Did the transferee take full possession of the assets transferred?

Yes ☐ *Go to section 4*

No ☐ *Go to question 3.2*

3.2 If the gift was land, did the transferor or their spouse continue to enjoy any right or interest, or were they party to an arrangement in relation to the land?

Yes ☐ No ☐

3.3 If the gift was any other assets did the deceased continue to have any right or benefit from part of all of the asset(s)?

Yes ☐ No ☐

3.4 If you have answered **yes** to questions 3.2 or 3.3 state the value of the assets at the date of death or the time the rights, benefits or interest came to an end (if earlier) and describe the position below.

£

If you have answered "No" to question 3.1 do not work out the tax yourself. We will work it out for you.

4 Taper relief

Fill in this section if you wish to claim taper relief

4.1 Date of the transferor's death / /

4.2 Rate of relief %

3

5	**Relief on successive charges** *Fill in this section if you wish to claim relief on successive charges*	
5.1	Date of transfer under which the assets which are comprised in this transfer became settled property in which the transferor had an interest in possession *(This is the first transfer)*	/ /
5.2	Net value of the first transfer	£
5.3	Tax paid on the first transfer	£
5.4	Assets from first transfer included in this transfer on which tax may **not** be paid by instalmentss	£
5.5	Assets from first transfer included in this transfer on which tax may be paid by instalments	£
5.6	Rate of relief	%

6	**Double taxation relief** *Fill in this section if you want to claim double taxation relief*	
6.1	Foreign tax paid on assets on which IHT may **not** be paid by instalments	£
6.2	Foreign tax paid on assets on which IHT may be paid by instalments	£
6.3	Total foreign tax paid *(box 6.1 plus box 6.2)*	£

7	**Tax previously paid on this transfer if any**	
7.1	Tax which may **not** be paid by instalments	£
7.2	Tax which may be paid by instalments	£
7.3	Total *(box 7.1 plus box 7.2)*	£

4

Inland Revenue
Capital Taxes

Termination of an interest in possession

Note: If you are telling us about the ending of an interest in possession in settled property on the death of a life tenant do not work out the tax. We will do that for you.

Name of transferor	**Date of transfer**
	/ /

1 About the transfer

1.1

Names and addresses of transferees	Relationship with transferor	Share and/or interest taken

1.2 Name and address of the person who will pay any tax due on this transfer.

Name	Address

1.3 Did the interest in possession come to an end on the death of the life tenant?

Yes ☐ *Go to section 5* No ☐ *Answer question 1.4*

1.4 Did the transferor receive any assets in return for the assets transferred?

Yes ☐ *Answer question 1.5* No ☐ *Go to question 1.6*

1.5

Describe the assets received	Value at date of transfer
Total	£

1.6 Was the transfer part of a wider series of transactions or arrangements?

Yes ☐ *Answer question 1.7* No ☐ *Go to question 1.8*

1

IHT100b (Substitute)(LexisNexis UK) L13/03

1.7 Describe the position below

1.8 Was the transfer connected in any way with the purchase of or other dealing with an assurance policy or an annuity?

Yes *Answer question 1.9* No *Go to question 2.1*

1.9 Describe the situation below

2 Earlier transfers

2.1 Is the transferor alive or did they survive the transfer by more than seven years?

Yes *Answer question 2.2* No *Go to question 2.3*

2.2 Did the transferor make any gifts or other transfers of value that were chargeable to tax at the time they were made during the period of seven years ending on the date of this transfer?

Yes *Answer questions 2.4 and 2.5*

No N/A *Go to question 2.6*

2.3 Did the transferor make any gifts or other transfers of value (including potentially exempt transfers) during the seven years ending on the date of death and before the date of this transfer **or** any gifts or other transfers of value that were chargeable at the time they were made during the seven years ending on the date of this transfer.

Yes *Answer questions 2.4 and 2.5*

No *Go to question 2.6*

2.4 State the chargeable value of the previous transfers. £

2.5 State the IHT file reference for the previous transfers (if known)

2.6 Tax threshold £

The tax threshold to be used is normally the threshold applicable at the date of the gift you are telling us about. If this gift occurred within seven years of the date of the transferor 's death ***and*** *the threshold at that date is higher enter the tax threshold applicable at the date of death.*

2

3 Gift with reservation

Answer only if the transferor has died

3.1 Did the transferor take full possession of the assets transferred?

Yes ☐ *Go to section 4*

No ☐ *Go to section 3.2*

3.2 If the gift was land, did the transferor or their spouse continue to enjoy any right or interest or were they party to any arrangement in relation to the land?

Yes ☐ No ☐

3.3 If the gift was of any other asset(s) did the deceased continue to have any right from all or any part of the asset(s)?

Yes ☐ No ☐

3.4 If you have answered **yes** to questions 3.2 or 3.3 state the value of the assets at the date of death or the time the rights, benefits or interest came to an end (if earlier) and describe the position below.

£

If you have answered 'No' to question 3.1 do not work out the tax yourself. We will work it out for you.

4 Reliefs against tax

Taper relief

Fill in this section if you wish to claim taper relief

4.1 Date of the transferor's death / /

4.2 Rate of relief %

5 Relief on successive charges

Fill in this section if you wish to claim relief on successive charges

5.1 Date of transfer under which the assets which are comprised in this transfer became settled property in which the transferor had an interest in possession (*this is the first transfer*) / /

5.2 Net value of the first transfer £

5.3 Inheritance tax paid on the first transfer £

3

5.4	Assets from first transfer included in this transfer on which tax may not be paid by instalments	£
5.5	Assets from first transfer included in this transfer on which tax may be paid by instalments	£
5.6	Rate of relief	%

6 Double taxation relief

Fill in this section if you wish to claim double taxation relief

6.1	Foreign tax paid on assets on which IHT may **not** be paid by instalments	£
6.2	Foreign tax paid on assets on which IHT may be paid by instalments	£
6.3	Total foreign tax paid (box 6.1 plus box 6.2)	£

7 Tax previously paid on this transfer (if any)

7.1	Tax which may **not** be paid by instalments	£
7.2	Tax which may be paid by instalments	£
7.3	Total (*box 7.1 plus box 7.2*)	£

4

Inland Revenue
Capital Taxes

Assets ceasing to be held on discretionary trusts. Proportionate charge

Note: if the settlement commenced before 27 March 1974 and the event you are telling us about took place before the first ten-year anniversary of the settlement contact our Helpline for advice. See page 2 of the guide 'How to fill in form IHT100' (IHT110).

Name of settlement | **Date of commencement** / /

1 About the chargeable event

1.1 Date of the chargeable event / /

1.2 Describe the chargeable event

1.3 Have the discretionary trusts come to an end? Yes No

About the transferees

1.4 Names and addresses of the transferees

1.5 Share and interest taken

About the payment of tax

1.6 Tick this box if the tax is **not** being paid out of the assets ceasing to be held on discretionary trusts

1.7 Inheritance tax threshold at the date of this transfer £

---

2 ***Answer the questions in this section only if the chargeable event you are telling us about occurred within ten years of the commencement of the discretionary trust.*** *(If the chargeable event you are telling us about took place more than ten years after the settlement commenced go to section 3).*

2.1 Value of the assets comprised in the settlement immediately after it commenced. £

2.2 Have any assets been added to the settlement since it commenced?

Yes *Answer questions 2.3 and 2.4* No *Go to question 2.5*

2.3 Value of any assets added to the settlement after the date on which it commenced at the date they were added. £

2.4 IHT file reference under which the additions were dealt with (if known).

IHT100c (Substitute)(LexisNexis UK) 1 L13/03

2.5 Did the settlor set up any other settlements on the same day as this settlement?

Yes ☐ *Answer question 2.6* No ☐ *Go to question 2.7*

2.6 State the total value of all the settlements made by the settlor on the same date as this settlement at the date on which the settlements were set up. £

2.7 Did the settlor make any other **chargeable** transfers during the seven years prior to the date of this settlement?

Yes ☐ *Answer question 2.8 and 2.9* No ☐ *Go to question 2.10*

2.8 State the total value of chargeable transfers made by the settlor during the seven years immediately before this settlement was set up. £

2.9 State IHT file reference under which the previous transfers have been dealt with (if known).

2.10 Did any of the relevant property on which tax is now being charged become relevant property since the settlement commenced?

Yes ☐ *Answer question 2.11* No ☐ *There are no more questions to answer on this form*

2.11

Description of asset(s)	Date on which the asset(s) last became relevant property	Value at the date the asset(s) last became relevant property
Assets on which the tax may **not** be paid by instalments		
	Total	£
Assets on which the tax may be paid by instalments		
	Total	£

3 ***Answer the following questions if the chargeable event you are telling us about occurred more than ten years after the settlement commenced.***

3.1 Date of the last ten-year anniversary. / /

3.2 What was the value on which the rate of tax was calculated on the last ten-year anniversary of this settlement? £

3.3 State the total value on which proportionate charges arose in the ten years preceding the last ten-year anniversary. £

3.4 State the total value of previous chargeable transfers taken into account in calculating the tax at the last ten-year anniversary. £

2

3.5 Value of the Settlement at the date of the last ten-year anniversary to be taken into account (*box 3.2 minus 3.3 minus box 3.4*). £

3.6 Have there been any additions to this settlement since the last ten-year anniversary?

Yes ☐ *Answer question 3.7*   No ☐ *Go to question 3.8*

3.7 Provide the following details about the additions to this settlement since the last ten-year anniversary.

Description of the asset(s)	Date on which the asset(s) was added to the settlement or if later the date on which it last became relevant property	Value of the asset(s) at the date it was added or if later the date it became relevant property
	Total	£

3.8 Did any assets in the settlement at the date of the last ten-year anniversary which were not relevant property at that time, become relevant property between the date of the last ten-year anniversary and this chargeable event?

Yes ☐ *Answer question 3.9*   No ☐ *Go to question 3.10*

3.9 Provide the following information about the assets in the settlement at the date of the last ten-year anniversary which were not relevant property at that time, which have become relevant property between the date of the last ten-year anniversary and this chargeable event.

Date on which the asset(s) last became relevant property	Description of the asset(s)	Value at the last ten-year anniversary	Value at this chargeable event	Column D minus Column C
A	B	C	D	E
				£
				£
				£
				£
				£
				£
	Totals	£	£	£

3

3.10 Are any assets which became relevant property since the date of the last ten-year anniversary comprised in this chargeable event?

Yes ☐ *Answer question 3.11* **No** ☐ *Go to section 4*

3.11 Provide the following information about the assets comprised in the chargeable event which became relevant property since the last ten-year anniversary.

Assets on which the tax may **not** be paid by instalments		
Asset	Date on which the asset last became relevant property, or, if later the date of the last TYA	Value at this chargeable event
		£

Assets on which the tax may be paid by instalments		
Asset	Date on which the asset last became relevant property, or, if later the date of the last TYA	Value at this chargeable event
		£

4 Double taxation relief

Fill in this section if you wish to claim double taxation relief

4.1	Foreign tax paid on assets on which IHT may **not** be paid by instalments	£
4.2	Foreign tax paid on assets on which IHT may be paid by instalments	£
4.3	Total foreign tax paid *(box 4.1 plus box 4.2)*	£

4

Inland Revenue
Capital Taxes

Non Interest in possession Settlements Principle charge (ten-year anniversary)

Name of settlement

Date of Settlement / /

1.1 Date of ten-year anniversary / /

1.2 Did any of the relevant property in the settlement at the date of the ten-year anniversary become relevant property (1) after the settlement started and (2) during the ten-year period immediately before the ten-year anniversary?

Yes *Answer question 1.3* No *Go to question 1.4*

1.3 Provide the following information about the relevant property in the settlement which became relevant property after the settlement started and during the ten-year period immediately before the ten-year anniversary.

Description of the asset	Date on which the asset last became relevant property	Value at the date of the ten-year anniversary
Assets on which tax may **not** be paid by instalments		
	Total	£

Assets on which tax may be paid by instalments		
	Total	£

1.4 Have any proportionate charges arisen in the period of ten years ending on the anniversary date?

Yes *Answer question 1.5* No *Go to question 1.6*

1.5 State the total value on which proportionate charges arose in the ten years ending on the day before the present ten-year anniversary (*only include the amount taxable*). £

1.6 Did the settlor make any other **chargeable** transfers during the seven years prior to the date of the settlement? (*Answer no if the settlement commenced before 27 March 1974*).

Yes *Answer question 1.7* No *Go to question 1.8*

1.7 State the total of chargeable transfers made by the settlor during the seven years ending immediately before the settlement was set up. *(Disregard any transfers made on or before 27th March 1974).* £

1.8 Did the settlor make any chargeable transfer :

- after the settlement commenced and
- after 8th March 1982 and
- before the present ten-year anniversary

which increased the value of the settlement?

Yes ☐ *Answer question 1.9* No ☐ *Go to question 1.10*

1.9 State the total value of the chargeable transfers made by the settlor during the seven years ending on the date of the transfer referred to in question 1.8. Ignore any transfers made on the date of the transfer referred to in question 1.8 and any transfers made into this settlement. *(If there was more than one such transfer answer the question by reference to the transfer that gives the highest amount. See notes in IHT110).* £

1.10 Enter the higher of 1.7 and 1.9. £

1.11 Have any assets been put into the settlement which are not and never have been relevant property? *(Answer **no** if the settlement commenced before 27 March 1974).*

Yes ☐ *Answer question 1.12* No ☐ *Go to question 1.13*

1.12 Provide the following information in respect of the assets in the settlement which are not and never have been relevant property. *(Ignore if this settlement commenced before 27th March 1974).*

Description of the asset	Date on which the asset was placed in the settlement	Value at the date it was put into the settlement
Assets on which the tax may **not** be paid by instalments		
		£
		£
		£
		£
	Sub Total	£
Assets on which the tax may be paid by instalments		
		£
		£
		£
		£
	Sub Total	£

Total of all assets that are not and never have been relevant property £

2

1.13 Did the settlor make any other settlements on the same day as this settlement?
*(Answer **no** if the settlement commenced before 27 March 1974).*

Yes ☐ *Answer questions 1.14 and 1.15* No ☐ *Go to question 1.16*

1.14 State the total value of all the settlements made by the settlor on the same date as this settlement at the date on which they were set up. £

1.15 State the IHT file reference for the other settlements

1.16 Threshold at the date of the chargeable event £

2 Double taxation relief

Are you claiming double taxation relief?

Yes ☐ *Answer questions 2.1 to 2.3* No ☐ *That completes this form*

2.1 Foreign tax paid on assets on which IHT may **not** be paid by instalments £

2.2 Foreign tax paid on assets on which IHT may be paid by instalments £

2.3 Total foreign tax paid *(box 2.1 plus box 2.2)* £

3

Inland Revenue Capital Taxes

Charges on special trusts

1 Name of settlement | **Date of commencement** / /

1.1 Date of the chargeable event. / /

1.2 Describe the chargeable event.

1.3 If the chargeable event was a gift or other transfer out of the settlement state the name and address of each transferee.

Name	Address

1.4 Do any assets remain held on special trusts in the settlement?

Yes No

1.5 Is the tax being paid out of assets which remain on special trusts after this chargeable event?

Yes No

(Substitute)(LexisNexis UK)

IHT100e 1 L13/03

1.6 Give the following information about each asset included in this chargeable event.

(a) Assets on which the tax may not be paid by instalments

Brief description of the asset*	Date on which the asset last became held on special trusts	Value at the date of the chargeable event
		£

(b) Assets on which the tax may be paid by instalments

		£

**Assets which last became held on special trusts on the same day may be grouped together in one entry.*

2 **Double taxation relief**

2.1 Foreign tax paid on assets on which tax may not be paid by instalments £

2.2 Foreign tax paid on assets on which tax may be paid by instalments £

2.3 Total foreign tax paid *(box 2.1 plus box 2.2)*. £

2

Inland Revenue Capital Taxes

Cessation of conditional exemption. Disposal of timber or underwood

1 Name of transferor/settlement | **Date of chargeable event** / /

1.1 Describe the event

1.2 If the chargeable event was a gift or other transfer of value state the name and address of each transferee.

Name	Address

If you are telling us about the ending of the conditional exemption of heritage property go to section 2. If you are telling us about the disposal of trees or underwood go to section 4.

2 Relevant person

2.1 How many conditionally exempt transfers of the asset have there been?

One — *Go to question 2.5* More than one — *Go to question 2.2*

2.2 Was the last conditionally exempt transfer made more than thirty years before the transfer you are telling us about? *(Ignore any transfers made before 7th April 1976 or before the last chargeable transfer).*

Yes — *Go to question 2.5* No — *Go to question 2.3*

2.3 Was there more than one conditionally exempt transfer in the thirty years before the transfer you are telling us about? *(Ignore any transfers made before 7th April 1976 and before the last chargeable transfer).*

Yes — *Go to question 2.4* No — *Go to question 2.5*

(Substitute)(LexisNexis UK)

IHT100f 1 L13/03

2.4 List the names of the persons who made conditionally exempt transfers in the thirty years before the date of this transfer and if they have died state their date of death.

Name	Date of death (if applicable)

Note: If you have answered question 2.4 do not answer any of the following questions. Do not fill in form IHT100WS to work out the tax yourself. Complete the IHT100 event form and supplementary pages and we will work out the tax for you. (If you are using an electronic version of the IHT100 the tax calculation facility will not be initiated).

2.5 What is the name of the person who made the last conditionally exempt transfer?

☐ **This is the relevant person**

About the assets

3 Rate of tax

3.1 Is the relevant person alive?

Yes ☐ No ☐

3.2 Was the asset settled property at the time of this chargeable event?

Yes ☐ No ☐

3.3 Was the asset relevant property when it became conditionally exempt?

Yes ☐ No ☐

3.4 Was the asset continuously relevant property between the date on which it became conditionally exempt and the date of this chargeable event?

Yes ☐ *Go to question 5.5* No ☐ N/A ☐

3.5 Did the conditionally exempt transfer take place on the death of the relevant person?

Yes ☐ No ☐ N/A ☐

3.6 Is the relevant person deemed to be the settlor because the conditionally exempt transfer which determined the relevant person was an event which affected the discretionary trust

Yes ☐ *Go to question 3.7* No ☐ N/A ☐ *Go to section 5*

3.7 Did this chargeable event occur

(a) before the first ten-year anniversary after the asset became conditionally exempt ☐

(b) between the first and second ten-year anniversaries after the asset became conditionally exempt *(Tick the box that applies)* ☐

Go to section 5.

4 Trees and underwood

Answer questions 4.1 to 4.3 only if you are letting us know about the disposal of trees or underwood which gives rise to an inheritance tax charge.

4.1 State the amount of inheritance tax paid on the deceased's estate. *The deceased is the person from whose estate the value of the trees or underwood was omitted.* £

4.2 On what date did the person from whose estate the value of the trees or underwood was left out die? / /

2

4.3 If the value of the trees or underwood had not been left out of the account would business relief have been allowed on their value?

Yes ☐ Proportion of tax payable 50%. No ☐ Proportion of tax payable 100%.

Answer questions 5.1 and 5.4 below.

5 Other information

5.1 If you are telling us about the disposal of trees or underwood or the relevant person was dead at the date of this chargeable event state the value of their estate at the date of death for inheritance tax purposes. £

5.2 Did the relevant person or the deceased make any transfers of value

(a) If the relevant person is alive, during the seven years ending on the date of the conditionally exempt transfer.

(b) If the relevant person has died, or if you are telling us about the disposal of timber or underwood, during the seven years ending on the date of death

Ignore any failed potentially exempt transfers unless you are telling us about a disposal of trees or underwood.

Yes ☐ No ☐

5.3 State the value of the transfers of value made by the relevant person or the deceased £

Do not include the value of any failed potentially exempt transfers unless you are telling us about the disposal of trees or underwood

5.4 State the inheritance tax threshold at the date of this chargeable event £

5.5 If you have answered **yes** to question 3.4 provide the following information about the conditionally exempt transfers

No	Asset	Date of the last ten-year anniversary before the asset became held on discretionary trusts	Value at the date of the chargeable event
	Column A	Column B	Column C
	Assets on which the tax may not be paid by instalments		
1			
2			
3			
4			
5			
	Assets on which the tax may be paid by instalments		
1			
2			
3			
4			
5			
		Total	£

3

Inland Revenue
Capital Taxes Office

Inland Revenue Account for Inheritance Tax

Account of a Chargeable Event under Inheritance Tax Act 1984 Part III Chapter III

- Please read the notes in IHT 111 before completing this Account. The references in this Account to "notes" are to the note numbers in IHT 111.
- Please send the completed Account, as appropriate, to the Capital Taxes Office, Ferrers House, PO Box 38, Castle Meadow Road, Nottingham NG2 1BB (DX 701201 Nottingham 4); or to the Capital Taxes Office, Meldrum House, 15 Drumsheugh Gardens, Edinburgh EH3 7UG (DX 542001 Edinburgh 14); or to the Capital Taxes Office, Level 3, Dorchester House, 52-58 Great Victoria Street, Belfast BT2 7QL (DX 2001 NR Belfast 2).

1 **Name and date of Settlement / Will Trust** *see note 1*

2 **Date of event** *see note 2*

If date of event is between 9 March 1982 and 24 July 1986 use form Cap C7; if before 9 March 1982 Cap C6

3

Name and address of person to whom any communication should be sent	Reference
	Telephone
Postcode	Capacity

4 **Settlor / Testator** *(delete as appropriate) see note 4*

Surname in CAPITAL letters	
Title and first names in full	
Date of birth (eg 9 September 1988 = 09 SEP 1988)	and if dead, date of death
Usual (or last usual) address	Place of domicile when settlement made or, in the case of a Will trust, at date of death
Please state the Tax District which dealt with the settlement	Tax District reference
If known please state the CTO reference relating to any chargeable transfer made by the settlor/transferor since 26 March 1974	

5 **Beneficiaries** *see note 5*

Full name(s) and address(es)	Extent of interest taken
Postcode	
Postcode	
Postcode	

IHT 101 (Substitute)(LexisNexis Butterworths Tolley) 1 CTO Approval Ref No L24/00 10/93

6 Settlement *see note 6* *Tick and complete as appropriate*

		Yes	Details	No		Not applicable
1	If the settlement was not made by Will has it previously been produced to the Capital Taxes Office?	☐	Under official reference ☐	☐	A copy is attached	☐ Settlement made by Will
2	If the settlement was not made by Will did the settlor make any other settlements on the same day? *This question relates only to settlements made since 26 March 1974*	☐	A copy has been produced under official reference ☐ **or** a copy is attached	☐		☐ Settlement made by Will before 27 March 1974
3	Has there been any other chargeable event in connection with this settlement since 8 March 1982, or were any capital distributions / distribution payments made between 27 March 1974 and 8 March 1982?	☐	Disclosed under official reference ☐ **or** full details and copies of relevant deeds etc attached	☐		
4	Has any property been added to the settlement since 26 March 1974, or has there been any transfer by the settlor since 8 March 1982 which has resulted in an increase in the value of the property comprised in the settlement?	☐	Disclosed under official reference ☐ **or** full details including dates, and by whom the property was added given in attached schedule(s)	☐		
5	Has any property at any time comprised in the settlement become relevant property since the commencement of the settlement or since 26 March 1974 if later?	☐	Disclosed under official reference ☐ **or** copies of relevant deeds etc and other details attached	☐		

7 Chargeable Event *see note 7*

1	Did the chargeable event consist simply of an actual payment or transfer of assets out of the settlement?	☐		☐ Details of chargeable event and copies of relevant deeds attached	
2	Do any funds (apart from assets disclosed in Section 8) remain in this settlement following this chargeable event?	☐	Estimated value £	☐	
3	Where land is included in Section 8 - did the settlement retain land adjacent thereto?	☐	Full details in attached schedule (including estimated values before and after transfer)	☐	☐
4	Where shares in a private company are included in Section 8 -				
	a. did the trustees of the settlement immediately before the event hold other shares or securities in the company?	☐	Details given in attached schedule	☐	☐
	b. did the trustees of the settlement at any time after 26 March 1974 and within 10 years of the event have control of the company?	☐	Details given in attached schedule	☐	☐

2

8 Details of Chargeable event *see note 8* *Attach schedules if necessary*

		Price or basis of valuation		
		Total		

		Total		
		Net value disregarding the tax, reliefs and exemptions		

	3 Reliefs and Exemptions claimed *Complete and give details* **Reliefs** 1 Agricultural			
	2 Business			
	3 Other (specify)			
	Exemptions (specify)			
		Total		
		Total less deductions, reliefs and exemptions		

3

9 Payment of tax *see note 9* *Tick and complete as appropriate*

1 Is the tax chargeable on this event to be provided out of the property included in Section 8?	☐	Yes	
	☐	No	
2 If you are entitled to pay any of the tax by instalments do you elect to do so?	☐	Yes	
	☐	No	
3 Are any deductions against tax claimed?	☐	Yes	
	☐	No	

10 Declaration by the Trustees *see note 10*
To the best of my/our knowledge and belief the statements and particulars in this Account and its accompanying schedules are true and complete. **Agents must *not* sign this declaration.**

Full name and address(es)	Signature(s)	Date(s)
Postcode		
Postcode		
Postcode		
Postcode		

Warning If you fail to verify personally that the statements in this account are true and complete you may make yourself liable to prosecution or penalties.

4

Inland Revenue

Trust gains and capital payments

Inland Revenue office address

Centre for Non-Residents
Non-Resident Trusts (Unit 359)
St. Johns House
Merton Road
BOOTLE
Merseyside L69 9BB
England

Tax Reference	Date of issue
922/CG/	/ /

Name of settlement

Telephone: 0151 472 6384
From abroad: International access code with 44 151 472 6384

Information for the year ended 5 April 2003

Persons may be liable to income tax, capital gains tax, or both, as a result of:

- payments made or benefits provided to them, directly or indirectly by the trustees
- income or gains arising to the trustees
- income or gains arising to any underlying non-resident company.

The law about these liabilities can be found primarily in:

- Sections 739 & 740 Income and Corporation Taxes Act (ICTA) 1988, and
- Sections 86-98 and Schedules 4B, 4C & 5, Taxation of Chargeable Gains Act (TCGA) 1992.

See also Sections 547, 762 and Part XV ICTA 1988.

Important changes were introduced by Sections 130-132 and Schedules 14 & 22/23 Finance Act (FA) 1998, and Sections 92, 94 & 96 and Schedules 25 & 26 FA 2000.

This form is to help us decide if any tax liability arises to a settlor or beneficiary connected with the above settlement. If the information requested in this form is not supplied, we may need to issue a statutory notice requiring similar details.

Any person named in this form, who is resident or ordinarily resident in the United Kingdom, must show on his or her personal Tax Return:

- any payments received
- the value of any benefits received (including assets transferred).

The settlor must show on his or her personal Tax Return

- gains under Section 86 and Schedule 5 TCGA 1992, and
- income under Section 547, Part XV or Section 739 ICTA 1988.

If at any stage this form asks you to go to another part or question, ignore the intervening questions. For all questions requiring an answer 'yes' or 'no', please enter X in the appropriate box.

Part A Is this form needed?

In Part A of this form "treated as" means treated as within the context of Section 69(2) TCGA 1992

1. Were all (or a majority of) the trustees actually, or treated as, not resident or not ordinarily resident in the UK throughout the year ended 5 April 2003? Yes ☐ No ☐

   If the answer is 'No', go to question 3 below

2. Was the general administration of the trust actually, or treated as, carried on outside the UK throughout the year ended 5 April 2003? Yes ☐ No ☐

   If the answer is 'Yes', go to Part B

3. *Only complete this question if you have answered 'No' to either Question 1 or Question 2 above.*

   Did the trustees fall to be regarded for the purposes of any double taxation relief arrangements as resident in a territory outside the UK? Yes ☐ No ☐

   If the answer is 'No' – let me know the names and addresses of the current trustees, and the date they were appointed – send this form to me without completing the rest of it.
   If the answer is 'Yes', go to Part B

50(FS)(2003) 1 BS11/02

Throughout the form, if you need more space please give details separately and enter "see attached" on the form.

Part B General information

1. Please provide a copy of the accounts of the trust and of all companies listed at item 3 below for the accounting period which ended during the year to 5 April 2003. If no accounts have been prepared, please supply a statement of all income arising in that year and a list of assets held on that date.

2. Are the trustees participators in an underlying non-resident company (a company which would be a close company if it were resident in the UK)? Yes ☐ No ☐

   If the answer is 'No', go to Question 4.

   Broadly speaking, a "close company" is one under the control of either the directors or no more than five participators (Section 414 ICTA 1988). "Participator" is defined in Section 417 ICTA 1988.
   In completing this Part of the form, include any non-resident unit trust under the control of five or less participators in which the trustees have invested, as an ***underlying non-resident company****.*

3. State the full name(s) and address(es) of each of the companies referred to at Question 2 above and details of participation, for example percentage and description of shareholdings or of other interests in the company.

Name of company	Address	Description of participation

4. Have the trustees made a transfer of value treated as linked with trustee borrowing, so triggering a deemed disposal within Schedule 4B TCGA 1992, in the year ended 5 April 2003? Yes ☐ No ☐

5. Was the settlor alive on 5 April 2003? Yes ☐ No ☐

   If the answer is 'No', and he or she died in the year ended 5 April 2003, give date of death / / ***then go to Part E***

6. Was the settlor resident or ordinarily resident in the UK for at least part of the year ended 5 April 2003, and domiciled in the UK in that year? Yes ☐ No ☐

   If the answer is 'Yes', go to Part C

   If the answer is 'No', go to Part E

2

Part C Does the settlor charge apply?

Section 86 & Schedule 5 TCGA 1992

1. Do you consider the settlor charge applies (or would have applied if any capital gains had arisen)? Yes ☐ No ☐

If the answer is 'Yes', go to Part D

2. Did a 'defined person' have an interest in the settlement in the year ended 5 April 2003? Yes ☐ No ☐

If the answer is 'No', go to Part E

*A **defined person** is:*

a. the settlor
b. the settlor's husband or wife
c. any child of a person within a. or b.
d. the husband or wife of any child within c.
e. any grandchild of a person within a. or b.
f. the husband or wife of any grandchild within e.
g. a company controlled by one or more of the persons within a. - f.
h. a company associated with a company within g.

A person has "an interest in the settlement" if any income or capital of the settlement has been, or in any circumstances can be, paid to him/her or used for his/her benefit.

In the following questions, a "grandchild settlement" is a settlement where the only 'defined persons' with an interest in it are within e. and f. above, companies controlled by them, and companies associated with such controlled companies.

3. Is this a grandchild settlement, or one in which the only defined persons with an interest in the settlement on 5 April 1999 and on each subsequent 5 April were children within 2c above under age 18? Yes ☐ No ☐

If the answer is 'No', go to Part D

4. Was the settlement created on or after 19 March 1991 or, if a grandchild settlement, on or after 17 March 1998? Yes ☐ No ☐

If the answer is 'Yes', go to Part D

5. Were non-resident trustees first appointed on or after 19 March 1991 or, if a grandchild settlement, on or after 17 March 1998? Yes ☐ No ☐

If the answer if 'Yes', go to Part D

6. Have the terms of the settlement been varied on or after 19 March 1991 or, if a grandchild settlement, on or after 17 March 1998, so that a defined person *(see question 2)* became for the first time a person who will or might benefit from the settlement? Yes ☐ No ☐

If the answer is 'Yes', go to Part D

7. Has any additional capital, income or other value been provided, directly or indirectly for the settlement, on other than arm's length terms, since 18 March 1991 or, if a grandchild settlement, since 16 March 1998? Yes ☐ No ☐

If the answer is 'No', go to Part E

8. Does the value of such additional capital etc exceed the surplus of expenses relating to administration and taxation over the income arising to the settlement for the year ended 5 April to which such additions related? Yes ☐ No ☐

If the answer is 'Yes', go to Part D

If the answer is 'No', and such additional capital etc, has been provided in the year ended 5 April 2003 give details as follows:

Year to which additions relate	Additional capital etc provided for that year	Details of expenses incurred for that year	Net income arising in that year

Then go to Part E

3

Part D Settlor charge for year ended 5 April 2003

Give details below of capital gains/losses arising to the trustees and any underlying non-resident company (as shown at Part B item 3) for the year ended 5 April 2003.
Include any gain deemed to have arisen under Schedule 4B TCGA 1992.
If any part of a gain arising to an underlying company is not considered to fall within the settlor charge, please nevertheless include details together with a full explanation of your reasons for believing that gain to be outside the settlor charge.
Enter X in the end column if the disposal was to a "connected person" (as defined in Section 286 TCGA 1992), or not at arm's length, or of shares/securities not quoted on a "recognised stock exchange" (as defined in Section 841 ICTA 1988)

Gains arising to the trustees

Description of assets	Computation of gains (before taper relief)/losses	Taper relief percentage	Amount of gain after taper/loss £	
		Total (W)	£	

Gains arising to underlying non-resident company(ies)

Enter X in the end column if the disposal was to a "connected person" (as defined in Section 286 TCGA 1992), or not at arm's length, or of shares/securities not quoted on a "recognised stock exchange" (as defined in Section 841 ICTA 1988)

Name of company	Description of assets	Computation of gains/losses	Amount of gain/loss £	
		Total (X)	£	

Amount assessable on settlor	Total (W) + Total (X)	£

Note *if Total (X) is a loss it cannot be set against Total (W) in computing the amount assessable on the settlor.*

Part E Offshore income gains

1. Have the trustees, or any underlying companies shown in Part B, item 3, made offshore income gains within Section 762 ICTA 1988 in the year ended 5 April 2003, or have such income gains arisen in earlier years that have not been wholly treated as those of beneficiaries or of the settlor? Yes ☐ No ☐

   If the answer is 'No' go to Part F

2. Enter the amount of offshore income gains arising to the trustees and to any underlying company shown in Part B, item 3 for the year ended 5 April 2003, plus any such income gains made in earlier years to the extent that they had not, by 6 April 2002, been treated as those of beneficiaries or of the settlor. £ (U)

4

Part F Capital payments for the year ended 5 April 2003

1. Has any person received a payment of capital or a benefit directly or indirectly from the trustees for the year ended 5 April 2003, or were such payments etc. made in earlier years that were not taxed because income/gains were insufficient? Please see the note at the end of this Part if the person who received the payment was the trustee of another settlement. Yes ☐ No ☐

If the answer is 'No', go to Part I

"Benefit" includes loans, transfer or use of assets and accommodation provided (on less than arm's length terms).
"Payment" includes
- *capital vesting absolutely*
- *any payment to a non-resident company under the control of a UK resident person*
- *any payment from a company under the control of the trustees alone or jointly with the settlor or persons connected with the settlor.*

2. Detail below the payment(s) of capital or benefit(s) received for the year ended 5 April 2003. Include such payments brought forward from earlier years which have not been assessed because there was insufficient income/gains.

Name and address of recipient and date of birth if unmarried and under 18		Nature of payment, loan, asset or other benefit and date conferred on the recipient		Amount of payment or value of asset or other benefits £
Recipients who are beneficiaries within the terms of the trust	Date of birth		Date	
Other recipients				
			Total amounts of 'payments' of capital or benefits	£ (Y)

If there have been any transfers, other than on arm's length terms, to the trustees of another settlement enter X in the box. Give full details separately, including your computation of gains to be transferred. ☐

Part G Questions relating to Sections 740 and 762 ICTA 1988 liabilities

1. Is there an amount at (U) of Part E, item 2 and, if so, does it equal or exceed the total payments of capital and benefits at (Y) of Part F, item 2? Yes ☐ No ☐

   If the answer is 'Yes' go to Part I

2. Is the whole of the income arising to the settlement, and to any underlying company shown in Part B, item 3, to be treated as that of the settlor because he/she or his/her spouse has an interest in the settlement? (see Part C, Question 2 for an explanation of "an interest in the settlement") Yes ☐ No ☐

   If the answer is 'Yes' go to Part H

3. State the amount of 'relevant income' as defined at Section 740(3) ICTA 1988 * for years up to and including the year ended 5 April 2003 of
   a. the trustees of the settlement ... ... £
   b. each of the underlying companies shown at Part B item 3 £

   Name of company ______________________ £

   Total 'relevant Income' £ (Z)

   ** broadly speaking undistributed income, but also including life policy gains taxable under Section 547(10) or (11) ICTA 1988, introduced by Schedule 14 FA 1998*

4. Does the total 'relevant income' (see (Z) at question 3 above), together with any offshore income gains (see (U) of Part E, item 2), equal or exceed the total payments of capital and benefits (see (Y) at Part F, item 2)? Yes ☐ No ☐

   If the answer is 'Yes' go to Part I - if the answer is 'No' go to Part H

5

Part H Section 87 TCGA 1992 and Section 91 TCGA 1992

1. Enter full details of capital gains remaining unmatched at 5 April 2002 in respect of any earlier year(s) for the whole of which the trustees were
   - not resident or not ordinarily resident in the UK, or
   - (for any period after 18 March 1991) dual resident.

   If the settlement came within Section 87 TCGA 1992 for the first time because of Section 130 FA 1998, enter only gains arising after 16 March 1998.

"Unmatched" means gains not previously set against payments of capital / benefits nor transferred to another settlement.

Unmatched capital gains arising to trustees and to any underlying company *Part B, item 3*

	Amount £	
Table a. Years 1981-82 to 1996-97* (inclusive)		
Arising to the trustees		
Arising to underlying companies		
	Total	£
Table b. Year to 5 April 1998*		
Arising to the trustees		
Arising to underlying companies		
	Total	£
Table c. Year to 5 April 1999*		
Arising to the trustees		
Arising to underlying companies		
	Total	£
Table d. Year to 5 April 2000*		
Arising to the trustees		
Arising to underlying companies		
	Total	£
Table e. Year to 5 April 2001*		
Arising to the trustees		
Arising to underlying companies		
	Total	£
Table f. Year to 5 April 2002*		
Arising to the trustees		
Arising to underlying companies		
	Total	£

2. Computation of capital gains for the year to 5 April 2003 *

	Amount of gain/loss £	⚬
Arising to the trustees		
Arising to underlying companies		
Name of company		
	Total	£

* *Exclude any gains assessable on settlor under the Settlor Charge (Section 86 TCGA 1992)*

⚬ *Enter X in the end column if the disposal was to a "connected person" (as defined in Section 286 TCGA 1992), or not at arm's length, or of shares/securities not quoted on a "recognised stock exchange" (as defined in Section 841 ICTA 1988)*

Part I Declaration

To the best of my knowledge and belief the particulars given on this form are correct and complete.

Enter X in the appropriate box

☐ I attach a copy of the settlement accounts or a statement and a list as described at Part B item 1 for the accounting period ending in the year to 5 April 2003

☐ I attach a copy of the accounts or a statement and a list as described at Part B item 1 for the underlying non-resident companies mentioned at Part B item 3 for the accounting period ended in the year to 5 April 2003

Your name

Address

Capacity in which completed

Date / /

Postcode

6

Capital Gains Tax—Indexation Allowance for Individuals and Trusts

The indexation allowance is the following percentage of the allowable expenditure or the value at 31 March 1982 for taper relief disposals subject to indexation up to 6 April 1998.

Indexation to 6 April 1998

Month of acquisition	Year of acquisition							
	1982	1983	1984	1985	1986	1987	1988	1989
Jan		96.8	87.2	78.3	68.9	62.6	57.4	46.5
Feb		96.0	86.5	76.9	68.3	62.0	56.8	45.4
Mar	104.7	95.6	85.9	75.2	68.1	61.6	56.2	44.8
Apr	100.6	92.9	83.4	71.6	66.5	59.7	53.7	42.3
May	99.2	92.1	82.8	70.8	66.2	59.6	53.1	41.4
June	98.7	91.7	82.3	70.4	66.3	59.6	52.5	40.9
July	98.6	90.6	82.5	70.7	66.7	59.7	52.4	40.8
Aug	98.5	89.8	80.8	70.3	66.2	59.3	50.7	40.4
Sept	98.7	88.9	80.4	70.4	65.4	58.8	50.0	39.5
Oct	97.7	88.3	79.3	70.1	65.2	58.0	48.5	38.4
Nov	96.7	87.6	78.8	69.5	63.8	57.3	47.8	37.2
Dec	97.1	87.1	78.9	69.3	63.2	57.4	47.4	36.9

	1990	1991	1992	1993	1994	1995	1996	1997	1998
Jan	36.1	24.9	19.9	17.9	15.1	11.4	8.3	5.3	1.9
Feb	35.3	24.2	19.3	17.1	14.4	10.7	7.8	4.9	1.4
Mar	33.9	23.7	18.9	16.7	14.1	10.2	7.3	4.6	1.1
Apr	30.0	22.2	17.1	15.6	12.8	9.1	6.6	4.0	
May	28.8	21.8	16.7	15.2	12.4	8.7	6.3	3.6	
June	28.3	21.3	16.7	15.3	12.4	8.5	6.3	3.2	
July	28.2	21.5	17.1	15.6	12.9	9.1	6.7	3.2	
Aug	26.9	21.3	17.1	15.1	12.4	8.5	6.2	2.6	
Sept	25.8	20.8	16.6	14.6	12.1	8.0	5.7	2.1	
Oct	24.8	20.4	16.2	14.7	12.0	8.5	5.7	1.9	
Nov	25.1	19.9	16.4	14.8	11.9	8.5	5.7	1.9	
Dec	25.2	19.8	16.8	14.6	11.4	7.9	5.3	1.6	

Inheritance Tax Bands

Inheritance tax nil rate bands since 6 April 1990, excess taxable at 20 per cent lifetime rates.

6.4.1990 – 5.4.1991	£128,000
6.4.1991 – 9.3.1992	£140,000
10.3.1992 – 5.4.1995	£150,000
6.4.1995 – 5.4.1996	£154,000
6.4.1996 – 5.4.1997	£200,000
6.4.1997 – 5.4.1998	£215,000
6.4.1998 – 5.4.1999	£223,000
6.4.1999 – 5.4.2000	£231,000
6.4.2000 – 5.4.2001	£234,000
6.4.2001 – 5.4.2002	£242,000
6.4.2002 – 5.4.2003	£250,000
6.4.2003 –	£255,000

Representative Bodies' Response to the Inland Revenue's Interpretation of the Settlement Legislation as it Applies to Business and Individuals

Section 660A, ICTA 1988: Tax, Small Businesses and the Settlements Legislation
Commentary on Tax Bulletin Article

Submitted by CIOT, ICAEW Tax Faculty, ICAS, ACCA, ATT, AAT, FSB & Working Together Representatives

Executive summary

There follows a detailed response to the Inland Revenue's April 2003 Tax Bulletin which gave its interpretation of how the settlements legislation affects small businesses and individual shareholders.

The settlements legislation has been in place for many years, but the Revenue's guidance has identified an issue of great importance to small businesses. Where, for example:

- a husband and wife are in business together, but one spouse is significantly more actively involved in the business than the other; and
- they own an equal number of shares, so that any dividend income arising from the business is divided equally between them

the Revenue said that the settlements legislation gives them the power to reallocate dividend income back to the spouse who does more of the work. Similar issues apply to husband and wife partnerships.

This response to the Bulletin article has been jointly prepared by six key organisations that represent tax professionals, namely:

- The Chartered Institute of Taxation (CIOT);
- The Tax Faculty of the Institute of Chartered Accountants in England and Wales (ICAEW);
- The Institute of Chartered Accountants of Scotland (ICAS);
- The Association of Chartered Certified Accountants (ACCA);
- The Association of Taxation Technicians (ATT); and

- The Association of Accounting Technicians (AAT).

with input from the Federation of Small Businesses (FSB) and representatives from the Working Together programme.

This virtually unprecedented combination of tax representatives issuing a joint response highlights the importance we all place on this matter and reflects the concern expressed by our members as regards the Revenue's interpretation of the settlements legislation.

Our main concerns are:

- Although some aspects of the Revenue's April guidance on the settlements legislation were previously known (for example, where restricted rights shares are used), key elements affecting everyday situations were not. Many taxpayers have taken actions, often with professional advice that reflected best practice, which they believed to be in accordance with the law, but which is now coming into question. The result could be income reallocated to the higher taxpaying spouse, thus leading to taxpayers facing unexpected tax bills running into many thousands of pounds.
- Taxpayers require clear guidance and as much certainty as is possible to ensure they fulfil their tax obligations, particularly in this age of self assessment. We believe that although the Revenue may have always held the views it expressed in the April guidance, for whatever reason this has not been communicated to taxpayers and their advisers.
- We do not accept a number of key technical issues that underpin the Revenue's April guidance. In particular we have concerns about the Revenue's view on the treatment of ordinary shares and its attitude towards partnerships. We believe the Revenue should look again at its view on these issues and reconsider whether its interpretation is correct.
- We have some reservations about a number of the examples provided by the Revenue in its guidance in particular with examples 3, 4 and 5. These relate to typical situations whereby a husband and wife both have shares in the family company or are partners in the family business.

Although publication of the Revenue's guidance is welcome, it has raised worries in the minds of many taxpayers who now need further help to either allay their fears or assist them to meet any tax obligations. The situation is exacerbated by the fact that the Revenue are applying their rules to situations which pre-date the April Bulletin. Our paper is therefore part of what we hope will be a process of developing that further guidance.

Our detailed comments are set out in the Paper we submitted to the Inland Revenue, which follows. The paper is being published by the participating bodies for the use of their members.

Section 660A: Commentary on Tax Bulletin Article

Submitted by CIOT, ICAEW Tax Faculty, ICAS, ACCA, ATT, AAT, FSB & Working Together Representatives

Background

The Inland Revenue published in Tax Bulletin 64 in April 2003 a lengthy article on 'Business, Individuals and the Settlements legislation', revolving round their views on the application of Sections 660A to 660G. This article came about after a series of meetings with the CIOT on the subject of 660A at which CIOT argued that there was a need to get out into the public domain a proper exposition of the Inland Revenue view and practice in this area. CIOT had contended strongly that the Inland Revenue's stance was not widely known about and that, at a minimum, they had a duty to publicise their interpretation. CIOT were able to comment on drafts of the article but the final Tax Bulletin article remained very much the Inland Revenue's statement and CIOT disagreed with aspects of the article.

Subsequent to the publication of the article, there has been a great deal of commentary in the professional press on the subject. In addition there have been various meetings within professional and trade bodies and a degree of conferring between the professional bodies. It seemed sensible for that to lead to some comments on the Tax Bulletin article which might help isolate the areas of particular difficulty that the professions and by extension taxpayers have with the Revenue's position. One particular driver is the taxpayer's obligations under Self Assessment and the requirement for certainty and consistency.

The intention of this paper is to respond to some of the points made in the Tax Bulletin article. It does not of itself constitute the profession's whole response.

Is this a new view?

It needs to be recorded that the professional bodies are deeply concerned about what is seen as a new interpretation by the Revenue. The Revenue maintain that the Tax Bulletin is simply a new exposition of their long-held and consistent view; the appearance is, however that this is a new application of that long-held view. The result does appear to be retrospective taxation to those caught in what have previously been regarded as routine, everyday situations. It is abundantly clear from the responses that the professional bodies have received on the Tax Bulletin article that, to the vast majority of practitioners, the views expressed in the article on the applicability of s660A have come as a considerable surprise. Small family businesses have for decades been organised in a way that now seems to have caused offence to the Revenue.

It is not disputed that the legislation has its origins in the 1930s; it may well be that the Revenue have been consistent in their internal views of it but in the view of the professional bodies there has been no attempt until now to apply the rules widely in the way the Revenue now contend. It is accepted that recent amendments to the Revenue's settlements manual cover some of the more involved aspects but the routine situations now under threat are not dealt with. In any event, the Settlements manual is not exactly mainstream guidance and it is self-evident that the Revenue's views now being expressed have not been widely promulgated.

The Revenue have indicated elsewhere that articles in the professional press (in particular one in Taxation in 1996) showed that the Revenue were known to be looking at the application of the settlements legislation to small family company situations. All tax advisers are aware – or should be – that the settlements legislation can be used to attack certain family company situations (for example the sort of arrangements used in cases such as *Young v Pearce* – see below – or those involving minor children). But it is the alleged scope of the settlements rules now being expressed that was not known nor understood by the profession. In any event, our reading of the Taxation article is that it in fact follows the contentions set out in this response, and does not support the Revenue position.

To practitioners and taxpayers, this approach to s660A is at a minimum a change of practice; leaving aside the possibility of technical challenges to the newly expressed view (explored below), it should surely be the case that the view is only applied from the date that it becomes public – in other words April 2003.

In particular, it seems invidious that within an era of self assessment that taxpayers are expected to self assess in accordance with rules on which the Revenue promoted no guidance and have given no indication that they interpret them in this particular way. If the Revenue's views do prevail on the points which are in contention, interest and penalties should certainly only apply for tax years ending after 6 April 2003.

We also understand that all of the examples 1–9 are based on cases settled by the Revenue with taxpayers. Whilst that may be the case, it does not automatically mean the settlement was based on a correct interpretation of the law. The tax at stake, compared with the cost of litigation, too often forces taxpayers to accept a Revenue view which may well not be followed by a Court had litigation ensued. We find the Revenue attitude that if their interpretation is not accepted the taxpayer can take their case to appeal unacceptable when the cost of that route can be many times the tax at stake. (We suspect that disputes under the settlements rules would probably have to go to the Special Commissioners and may well then proceed at least to the High Court.) It is important to recognise that we are dealing here with family businesses, which have to prepare tax returns in a self assessment environment, and it is essential that Revenue interpretations are both workable and grounded on legal authority

We will now comment on the Tax Bulletin article itself, following the section headings within the article.

Definitions

The statements within Tax Bulletin under this heading are uncontroversial and reasonable summaries of the legislation. However, we would contend that either here or later in the article there should have been some discussion of two other crucial definitions: ordinary shares and partnership.

What is an **ordinary share**? Much of the Revenue's argument seems to rest on it being possible to treat an ordinary share as in effect an income right. That is simply not the case. With ordinary shares come full rights to capital, votes and dividends, together with the responsibility of being a shareholder. Decided Company law cases support this view. In essence, the terms on which a share is issued are the terms of a contract between the individual and the company in question. Thus, prima facie, an ordinary share is not 'wholly or substantially a right to income'. The Revenue have no authority under the tax statute to single out certain terms of the 'share agreement' and consider them in isolation from the other terms thereof. In other contexts, such a share valuations, the Revenue accept and indeed require voting and capital surplus rights to be taken into account for fiscal purpose as well as the right to dividends.

What of an **offer of partnership**? Undoubtedly if the business is profitable, that is a right to income, depending on the profit sharing arrangements. But is it 'wholly or substantially a right to income'? Surely not – if the business runs into difficulty then the partnership is anything but a right to income. There is then the wider issue of the new partner taking on the obligations and burdens of being a partner as well as the rights and benefits, in particular liability for debts etc.

It may well be that these outline definitions are not acceptable to the Inland Revenue or are viewed as too simplistic or out of context but they are at the hub of the professional bodies' concerns with the thrust of the Tax Bulletin article.

There is then the question of what constitutes **a gift within the meaning of s660A(6)**. There is no basis in decided cases for the proposition that either (1) the gift of a shares from one spouse to another; or (2) the admission of a spouse into partnership is a gift of property that 'is wholly or substantially a right to income' (vide TA 1988 s660A(6)).

Decided cases support the view that a gift of ordinary shares, with rights in a winding-up and voting rights are more than 'wholly or substantially a right to income'. The only decided tax case on the point is *Young v Pearce* [1996] STC 743, where Sir John Vinelott considered (at 755e–g) the attributes of particular preference shares that carried no rights in a winding-up, other that the return of the nominal capital and which gave no voting rights. Sir John

Vinelott held that such shares were 'substantially a right to income'. *Per extenso*, if the shares had been ordinary shares with the rights given by Table A, they would have been more (or less?) than a right to income.

The Company Acts give holders of ordinary shares rights that go way beyond a right to income – vide, for example, *Re a Company no 004475 of 1982* [1983] 2 All ER 36 for the rights of a member who is unfairly prejudiced. Matrimonial law is clear that a spouse who owns shares has a capital right.

For the admission of a spouse to partnership, one has to look no further than the analysis of the Privy Council in *Hadlee v IRC* [1993] STC 294. Barry Hadlee purported to transfer to his wife his right to income, while retaining for himself the proprietary interest in the partnership property. In the leading judgement of the Privy Council, Lord Jauncey held that right of a partner is 'a beneficial interest in the entirety of the partnership assets and in each and every particular asset of the partnership' (at 297j).

Does the legislation only apply to transfers to spouses and minor children?

We agree with the two paragraphs under this section of the article – though as our comments below show we do not think the examples on this area are fully valid.

How does the legislation apply to non-trust situations?

It is helpful to have a list such as contained in the article setting out the sort of factors that the Revenue is concerned about. In many ways the professional bodies cannot take issue with this section: it is simply, after all, a list of the sort of issues that trouble the Revenue. However, as will be apparent from our comments on the nature of ordinary shares and partnerships, we have concerns as to the applicability of these brief outlines. In addition, we feel that a number of these factors will need to be present to run the risk of falling foul of the legislation, rather than a single item being the trigger.

We accept that s660A does not contain an 'intent' statement. A settlement can in effect be created accidentally rather than it always being necessary to set out to create a settlement. However, as noted under the definitions section, the Courts have limited the scope of a settlement to where there is some element of bounty. The obvious trigger would thus be for the Revenue to prove that bounty was in the mind of the perceived settlor. But how is this to be applied in a family situation? It is in the nature of family arrangements that there is bounty in many acts. There needs to be an understanding by the Revenue that the arrangements necessary to set up a business often involve sharing of many burdens and issues within a husband/wife unit in a way that would not be paralleled between individuals who are unrelated. Where this is the case, it does not mean that the husband has set out to confer a settlement on the wife. The arrangement needs to be looked at as a whole and it needs to be borne in mind that in the widest sense families are partnerships and the duties and responsibilities accepted by one party may enable the other party to concentrate on the business in a manner which would otherwise not be possible. It is therefore not a question of bounty but a sharing of the risks and rewards of family and business life, which is the essence of most small businesses.

This Revenue approach has overtones of a very narrow view of husband and wife businesses. These may depend on one party, say the husband, to carry out most of the income generating work – for example, he may be an entertainer, plumber or IT specialist. However the wife rarely makes no contribution to the business – she is likely to provide a great deal of support and may organise the husband's engagements, deal with queries and take bookings. Divorce courts certainly recognise the wife's role in business success, including work carried out behind the scenes.

The settlements legislation does, of course, bear more heavily on married couples than unmarried couples because of the provision in s660A(2) that states that 'a settlor shall be regarded as having an interest in property if that property or any derived property is, or will, or may become, payable to or applicable for the benefit of the settlor or his spouse in any circumstances whatsoever.' It is thus much easier for the Revenue to apply s660A(1) because it is easier to show that an 'interest' has been retained. By contrast, where an unmarried couple are working together in a business, the Revenue has to prove, as a question of fact, that one party has retained an interest in the property giving rise to the income received by the other. Thus an unmarried couple can share their income with far less difficulty. This might be described as a tax on marriage and is clearly discriminatory. It has, of course, always been intrinsic in s660A, but the wider use of the section by the Revenue increases the numbers of people affected by this discrimination.

We will now turn to the examples. In what follows, all comments on examples with shares must be read in the context of our understanding that ordinary shares are more than a right to income.

Example 1 – Issued shares with restricted rights

This example is based on the Pearce/Scrutton case and as such we have to accept it. We would merely emphasize that this was very much a case decided on the particular facts of the case and the restricted rights attaching to the (preference) shares – that they were in the circumstances very much a right to income.

Example 2 – Gifted shares with restricted rights

Again the nature of the shares seems important. The restricted nature of the rights attaching to the shares should put all involved on warning that the Settlements legislation could be invoked. As the example suggests, the whole arrangement needs to be looked at together – we endorse the comment within the example that 'the property giving rise to the dividends cannot be looked at too narrowly as the shares alone'. In other words, as we have contended earlier in this article, a number of factors need to be considered. If, for example, the shares did have voting rights and dividends were only paid out of profits after proper remuneration had been paid to the people involved in running the business, then we might well argue that the requirements of s660A are not satisfied.

We would also question the final sentence in the example ('Because he is in effective control of the company ... he could simply pay all future income to himself ...'). This seems a very sweeping statement – does it mean that everyone who controls a company is vulnerable to attack?

In any event, an investment return does not necessarily fail to be commercial simply because it is generous

Example 3 – Subscribed shares

In the 67 years since the settlements legislation was introduced, the Revenue have never stated publicly that they believe it applies to situations like this – where an individual subscribes for shares before the company starts to trade. There has been no public statement, no guidance, no press releases, no Tax Bulletin articles, until this April.

The technical basis for the view is questionable, as a settlement must create rights over some specific property or income. In this situation it is unclear what the 'property' is – it should not be the shares themselves as they have been subscribed for at full value by the spouse.

It seems from standard letters received by taxpayers that the Revenue consider that 'the combination of the granting of the right to subscribe, the shares themselves and the provision of funds to the company by the husband as a result of his work constitutes the "property" ' although this point is not explicitly made in the Bulletin. Assuming this to be the case, then:

1. If husband and wife each subscribe for shares at the same time and out of their own resources it is difficult to say that any 'right to subscribe' exists at all: it is a mutual decision to invest;
2. If this combination is a settlement of property, is it not a gift from husband to wife and thus potentially covered by s660A? In this context we note that in the Young v Pearce case, Sir John Vinelott made no distinction between acquisition on incorporation and where there is a subsequent gift. He indicated that a direct issue of shares was to be regarded as an outright transfer and therefore potentially covered by s660A(6).
3. Assuming that s660A(6) is in point, so that there is only a settlement if the property is 'wholly or mainly a right to income' then it is our understanding that no holder of the Ordinary Shares in E Limited has any right to income by virtue of being a shareholder. Certainly, once the Board of Directors have lawfully resolved to make an interim dividend

payment a 'right' exists until the payment is made (though arguably the directors can rescind an earlier decision before the payment is made). Likewise a valid resolution passed at lawfully convened meeting of the shareholders declaring a final dividend (i.e. in accordance with the powers contained in the Memorandum and Articles of Association), also creates a right to income from the date of the resolution to the date of payment. However, prior to these events coming to pass at best Mrs E will have no more than an expectation of income which surely the courts would distinguish from being a 'right' falling within s660A(6)(b)

4. Any reasonable interpretation of subsection 6(b) is that the right envisaged by the draughtsman is an enduring right in existence at the time of the gift as opposed to merely an expectation that a right to a dividend would arise. For example, if Mr E was the sole director and he decided that the company should diversify into a new business and that neither he nor any other ordinary shareholder should receive a dividend, then Mrs E would not have any entitlement to a continued stream of dividend. Her expectations might well have been dashed but a 'right' would not have been taken away because it would not have existed in the first place.

5. Looking at the work done by the spouse etc, this may be the source from which income is derived, but there is no right to income as such.

6. We wonder if perhaps the Revenue are focusing on what happens after the company has been set up – ie the steps leading to the dividend itself? However in our view the Revenue have no power to ignore some of the steps in an 'arrangement' so as to focus only on one or more steps which they select. It does not seem possible, given the wording of s660G, for the Revenue to focus solely on the one or two steps resulting in the dividend payment while ignoring the very first step in the arrangement, i.e. the acquisition by the spouse of the shares – the very assets giving rise to the income payment. Any such approach appears to have no basis in law. When all is said and done, it is clear that the first step in any arrangement which Mr E might make (in order to gratuitously pay dividends to Mrs E) is to lawfully transfer shares to her. There can be no dividend entitlement without shares. The arrangement must be looked at in the whole and there is case law to support this, see *Crossland v Hawkins* [1961] 2 All ER 812.

In summary, we consider that this example, which is one of the most contentious of those within Tax Bulletin, is not well founded in law and the Revenue should reconsider their position.[1]

1 This case is discussed in more detail by Kevin Slevin in *Taxation* 31 July 2003.

Example 4 – Gifts of shares with little capital value

The Revenue's view here is surprising. As stated above, outright gifts between husband and wife are specifically excluded from the settlements legislation unless the property gifted is 'wholly or substantially a right to income'. The

Revenue argue that because the company has insignificant capital assets the shares are wholly or substantially a right to income and are thus caught by the rules. Many of the arguments against the Revenue position here are the same as those set out in Example 3 so they are not repeated again here.

No court case has ever supported the Revenue interpretation. Mr E gave Mrs E ordinary shares, and these carry a range of rights and not just a right to dividend income. For example, Mrs E is entitled to 50% of the company's assets if it is wound up, and also has the right to vote in general meetings.

And what would happen if the couple split up? Surely Mrs E would demand her half share of the company – which means 50% of any income held within the company as well as 50% of any other assets such as the company's goodwill. It is very doubtful whether a court would agree with the Revenue's view that Mr E's gift of ordinary shares was 'wholly or substantially a right to income'.

In short, we see a fundamental factual difference between examples 3 and 4 and example 1 (based on *Young v Pearce*). In 3 and 4 the wife has full beneficial ownership of half the company. In *Young v Pearce* the wives did not. We do not yet have a case that says the corporate veil can be pierced in the way the Revenue contend.

We are curious as to whether the Revenue feel there is a level of net asset value to the shares that would escape? If so, how can that fit into self assessment?

Example 5 – Partnerships

This example is also surprising. If one of the second hand cars proved to be dangerous and caused serious injury or death, the partnership could have to pay damages. Since partners have unlimited liability, all the partners' assets are at risk – the wives' as well as the husbands'.

Mrs F and Mrs G could thus lose their homes and all they possess as a result of becoming partners in the business. How then can the Revenue say that their share in the business is 'wholly or substantially a right to income' when it brings with it these serious and life-changing risks? As partners, they are automatically identified as part of the business, are held out as such, etc.

And again, what would happen if the couples split up? Surely Mrs F and Mrs G would demand their share of the business – and the divorce courts would be likely to support them. This indicates that they do not have only a 'right to income' and thus should not fall within the settlements legislation.

Example 6 – Dividend waivers

We can accept this example because it is clearly not possible for the dividend in question to be paid without the waiver. If it was an amount that could be paid without the waiver, but one shareholder did decide to waive for perfectly acceptable reasons, we would question whether the Settlements legislation would apply.

Both this example and Example 7 seem to assume a company can only pay dividends out of current profits.

Example 7 – Dividends on certain shares

We can accept much of the principle in this example. However, we are surprised by the suggestion that this is 'clearly a bounteous arrangement'. We are also unclear who is treated as making the settlement. Dividends are proposed by the directors, not by the shareholders. Also, is it correct to reach a view without taking account of the wider issues? What of past patterns of dividends? What if no dividends have been paid out until now on B shares whereas A shares have enjoyed significant dividends over the years? What if dividends are paid only on the A shares the following year?

Example 8 – Children – gift of shares from parent

We have no problem with this example of a Settlement in favour of unmarried minor children.

Example 9 – Children – gift of shares other than from parent

This example does cause us difficulties. Whilst we can understand the Revenue's concern if Mr J was wholly involved in these arrangements, why should not the grandmother subscribe for shares when a company starts up and subsequently gift them to grandchildren? What if grandmother's investment, albeit small, was important in helping the company to get started?

The situation is very different from unmarried minor children using money that they have in bank accounts in their own names to subscribe for shares. Then we could accept that there might be a Settlement by Mr J. But surely grandmother is independent and thus the legislation should not apply? Or are the Revenue open to being convinced in actual circumstances that grandmother was acting independently and the legislation should not apply? The example seems to imply that it matters not whether Mr J is adequately remunerated. Where he is, we question the existence of a Settlement even if one accepted the basic premise of the Revenue's views. In all this, where, then, is the essential certainty required under SA?

Where does the legislation not apply?

As an initial comment, we assume that there would be no question of a settlement being argued for if husband simply made over a bank account to wife, or agreed to make the bank account a joint one. In these cases the wife would have full access to the underlying funds and would be therefore in receipt of far more than simply a right to income.

Example 10 – An outright gift to a spouse

In this situation some shares are given away and the fact that they have a capital value and can be traded is put forward as the reason for the Settlements legislation not applying. Whilst we have no wish to argue with this, it seems to us that the same argument can be applied to basic situations similar to those in examples 3 and 4. There will always be an underlying capital value within a company and there will always be the possibility of trading them – there may not be a daily quote but any unquoted company can be bought and sold. How is it that this is so very different from the basic situations?

Example 11 – Subscribed shares

Similar comments apply – together with our general contention that shares are more than simply a right to income. It seems in this example that the Revenue accept our view.

Example 12 – Subscribed shares

Again we would not wish to argue with this decision. At the same time our concern is what is a 'commercial salary'? Who is to say what it is in a particular situation – this illustrates the difficulty of applying this new Revenue interpretation in a self-assessment regime.

Example 13 – A partnership

We take it that the reason that the Revenue do not see this as a case for applying the Settlements legislation is Mrs O's original investment of £10,000. It is noted that she risked losing it if the business failed. It needs to be stressed that Mrs O risks losing a great deal more than £10,000 if the business fails – as noted at the start of this article, her entire wealth is at risk by the very nature of partnerships. It makes no difference in law whether the partner has subscribed £1 or £100,000. The tax result should not be different either.

Example 14 – A partnership

This seems to us to be a business issue and, correctly, the Settlements legislation is not in point.

Example 15 – Gift of shares other than from parent

Again the nature of the arrangements together with the time lapse means that Settlements is simply not in question in our view.

Summary

We have no concerns with the first paragraph of the summary. The second paragraph does seem to us to be a little biased. In particular the third and fourth sentences seem to ignore the reality that things apply within families that do not apply at arms length – it is simply unrealistic to assume automatically that the arms length test is wholly valid as family support is far more than simply encouragement.

The Chartered Institute of Taxation

Institute of Chartered Accountants in England & Wales

Institute of Chartered Accountants of Scotland

Association of Chartered Certified Accountants

Association of Taxation Technicians

Association of Accounting Technicians

Federation of Small Businesses

with the involvement of and contributions from the above bodies' Working Together representatives.

September 2003

Inland Revenue Response to CIOT, ICAEW Tax Faculty, ICAS, ACCA, ATT, AAT, FSB & Working Together Representatives Paper on Tax Bulletin 64 Article on the Settlements Legislation

In this response the headings used are those from the CIOT, ICAEW Tax Faculty, ICAS, ACCA, ATT, AAT, FSB & Working Together Representatives paper of September 2003.

Background

A clear statement of facts. Nothing to add.

Is this a new view?

There is nothing new in the Tax Bulletin 64 article. This article was published in response to a request from the CIOT for further guidance on our views on the application of the settlements legislation to businesses and individuals. In view of the comments made in the paper it seems that many practitioners were not aware of our views prior to the publication of the article. Nevertheless many practitioners have known about, and had practical experience of, the Revenue's interpretation for many years.

Based on representations made direct to us, and articles in the press (such as 'The Revenue is Right'. The Tax Journal. 22 September 2003. Page 11.), it is clear the views put forward in the paper are not universally accepted by the profession.

Looking specifically at cases like examples 3, 4 & 5 the Inland Revenue has been undertaking enquiries into such cases since about 1992. Prior to that date, and the introduction of Independent Taxation, using the legislation in this way on husband and wife companies or partnerships was unnecessary as all income was taxed on the husband. Ministers made clear during the debates on Independent Taxation during the passage of the 1989 and 1989 Finance Bills that the settlements legislation would be applied in future where there were effectively transfers only of income between husbands and wives. Since 1992 we have undertaken approximately 200 enquiries into cases similar to those in example 3, 4 and 5 and currently have about 50 cases working. We are pleased that the recent publicity is encouraging voluntary compliance in this area and people are seeking to structure their businesses so as not to fall foul of the legislation. We have no plans to significantly increase the number of formal enquires we undertake in this area at this time.

It has been stated by the profession and in the press that two hundred thousand / hundreds of thousands / millions of companies are like example 3 or 4 in the Tax Bulletin article. Based on the publicly available information, we have been able to identify less than 30,000 companies that could be like examples 3 and 4. (Companies with two shareholders, one or two directors and dividends being paid in the year.) We appreciate the publicly available information is incomplete, so the actual answer could be more, but it would appear the various figures quoted by the profession and in the press are pure speculation. Plus, of course, the 30,000 companies we have identified will not all be caught by the legislation due to the particular facts of each individual case.

The Trusts, Settlements and Estates Manual (TSEM) (formerly the Trust Manual) is, like all the other manuals, publicly available. The settlements legislation is also covered in other Inland Revenue guidance and manuals.

Our comments in respect of the article 'To have and to hold' (Taxation 17 October 1996) have been misunderstood. We have not suggested that the article agreed with our interpretation of the legal position, simply that it demonstrated that our views were known outside the Inland Revenue as the following quotation indicates:

> *'It [the Inland Revenue] has been for some time now mounting an attack on the position of married couples conducting business through a private company or a partnership by making use of the settlements legislation in Part XV of the Taxes Act 1988 ... One common misconception is that, where the wife subscribes for shares out of her own resources and purchases them at par, this will not constitute a settlement. This is unfortunately not the case. The Revenue view is that the husband creates the income in the company by virtue of his services and as both shareholder and director he*

> *is able to decide how the company should issue its shares. By allowing the wife to subscribe he is settling the benefit of his income on her and, if she pays less than full market value, dividends paid to her will provide an element of bounty.'*

As it is clear that many practitioners were aware of our views prior to Tax Bulletin 64, and as enquiry cases have been settled on those lines, there can be no question of the interpretation as set out in examples 3, 4 & 5 applying only from April 2003.

The Revenue takes the view that the guidance published in Tax Bulletin 64 should assist taxpayers and their advisors to understand more clearly how the law affects them. The Inland Revenue tries to be as helpful as possible and our Better Guidance Programme is a significant commitment to achieve better, more helpful guidance. However the department is not obliged to provide detailed guidance on every possible set of circumstances in which legislation could apply. The paper seems to be suggesting that before we can use existing legislation in a particular way we must first identify the facts, then publicise that the legislation applies to those facts and finally apply it only from some date in the future. Clearly such an approach would be impractical.

We have said we will look again at examples 3, 4 and 5 and, if appropriate, produce further guidance to help people self assess.

Interest cannot be waived but we have agreed that penalties will not normally be sought for 2002–03 and previous years in cases like examples 3, 4 & 5 involving the settlements legislation.

The settlements legislation requires that appeals are heard by the Special Commissioners in the first instance. They are a long standing and highly respected independent body that exists to resolve tax disputes including those involving the settlements legislation. We do not agree taking an appeal to the Special Commissioners has to be an expensive exercise and we cannot change our view simply because taxpayers do not want to take an appeal to the Special Commissioners. Our legal advice is that our interpretation is correct and we have to apply the legislation in that way until the Special Commissioners or the courts tell us otherwise.

Definitions

We would not disagree with most of the commentary on ordinary shares. We have not suggested that, for the legislation to apply, an ordinary share itself must be wholly or substantially a right to income. We look at the whole arrangement, as the legislation requires. The relevant questions are: What has been invested? What assets, trade, profession have been placed in the company and by whom? Who does what to earn the income of the company? Is the remuneration paid at a commercial rate for the job? Is someone getting a disproportionate return on the capital they have invested because of their relationship with the settlor? All these issues must be considered and if the shares are being used as a vehicle for diverting income then the legislation may apply.

With respect to partnerships the Revenue again looks at the whole arrangement to see whether someone is getting a disproportionate return on their investment because they are related to, or friends with, the settlor.

In the Revenue's view the fact that the shares in *Young v Pearce* [1996] STC 743, were preference shares does not mean that ordinary shares cannot also be caught by the settlements legislation.

Does the legislation apply only to transfers to spouses and minor children?

We note the comments made.

How does the legislation apply to non-trust situations?

We are pleased the list of indicators has proved useful. We do not agree more than one must be present before the legislation could apply. We need to consider the whole arrangement and not all indicators need to be present for there to be a settlement.

The commentary correctly points out that there is no motive test in Section 660A and that there can be no settlement without bounty. However the request for special understanding for family / company arrangements misses the point. An outright gift of money is a bounteous act but does not create a settlement. But an arrangement for one spouse to receive the other's income via dividends is caught by the settlements legislation. There is a substantial body of case law on 'bounty' and the suggestion that the rules should be applied differently in a family situation is not consistent with that case law.

We find the comment that the Revenue approach is 'a very narrow nineteenth century view of husband and wife businesses.' surprising. Because some of the examples state that the wife did no, or little, work does not mean we think all wives in these situations do no work. We have not suggested that a 'non fee-earning' spouse makes no contribution to a business. The question, in the context of the settlements legislation, is 'What contribution does that spouse make and how commercial is the reward for it'? While the settlements legislation does apply where there is a benefit to the settlor's spouse it also applies to any settlement where the settlor retains an interest in the settlement *whoever the beneficiary may be.* In a service company it is usually the person with the specialist knowledge who retains the interest because s/he controls the source of income. Also it should be noted the legislation is neutral, referring to 'settlor' and 'spouse'.

Example 1

We note the comments made.

Example 2

When considering whether the settlements legislation applies to a case the Revenue looks at the whole arrangement and considers all factors so each case will depend on its facts. The level of remuneration paid in relation to the work carried out and the amount of the dividends paid are both relevant factors to be taken into account. Regarding the final comment we accept that investment returns can be both commercial and generous. We are concerned with cases where that generosity is only made possible by the worker accepting an uncommercial rate of remuneration so that enhanced dividends are then paid to someone else – that is where the bounty lies. We note the paper accepts that the settlements legislation applies to the straightforward dividend waiver at example 6 which is based on the same principle.

Example 3

In general we have no problems with the factual analysis. We clearly differ on the interpretation of a 'right' and do not agree that it applies only to the situation where there is a guaranteed income stream. As we have emphasised, we have to look at the whole picture. All factors are relevant and as already stated a key feature of the cases into which the Revenue have raised enquiries is the arrangement whereby a high earning individual agrees to work for a company for a very low rate of remuneration and allows a significant part of the earnings which they generate to be paid to someone else.

Example 4

Here again, we do not say that an ordinary share is solely a right to income so we do not disagree that ordinary shares have other rights as well. Looking at a typical service company scenario we have challenged, we do not accept the argument relating to 'goodwill'. The third party contracts with the company are for a particular individual's expertise. In such circumstances goodwill is personal to that individual and would not be an asset for distribution in the winding up of the company.

Example 5

We agree that the issue of unlimited liability for the partners is a relevant factor. But again, we look at the whole picture. Take the scenario where the jointly held family home has been re-mortgaged to provide further working capital, and the partnership share reflects that contribution. In that case the admission of a spouse into a partnership may well be commercial and is unlikely to be bounteous. At the other extreme, where, because of the nature of the business activity, the partnership has no significant capital base and a spouse who takes no part in the running of the business is made a 50% partner we believe that the settlements legislation can apply.

Examples 6 & 7

We accept that past profits are relevant and TSEM 4225 is a statement of our views. Of course this works both ways – say in year one profits are £100,000 split 80:20 for example and the major shareholder waives but the minor shareholder's dividend is not enhanced – section 660A doesn't apply. In year two the Profit and Loss account brought forward is £80,000 and profits are £20,000 so once again there is £100,000 to distribute and the whole amount is voted. The major shareholder again waives and the minor shareholder receives £20,000. We would look at 2 years together – the minor shareholder has got £40,000 out of £120,000 when his overall share (20%) is £24,000 so £16,000 is only his by virtue of the other shareholder's waiver and that is bounteous.

Example 8

We note the comments made.

Example 9

We would consider all the arguments and facts before reaching a view in a particular case.

Example 10

The difference between this example and those where we consider that the settlements legislation applies is that here the shares have a substantial capital value which we consider is not present in the other cases.

Example 11

We note the comments made .

Example 12

We accept that there are difficulties in determining what the commercial rate for a job is and this is never an exact science. That is one of the reasons our guidance cannot cover every possible set of circumstances. The Tax Bulletin examples were designed to provide some illustration of where the line is drawn.

Example 13

We look at the facts of each case and all the arrangements in deciding whether to apply the settlements legislation.

Examples 14 and 15

We note the comments made .

Summary

Parliament introduced the settlements legislation to prevent individuals transferring their income to a relative or friend in order to avoid tax. It therefore follows that a simple test to indicate whether or not the legislation might apply is to consider whether the same arrangements would have been made with a third party at arms length. To argue otherwise ignores the fundamental purpose of the legislation.

October 2003.

Press Release

17 November 2003

Issued jointly by:

Chartered Institute of Taxation (CIOT)
The Tax Faculty of the Institute of Chartered Accountants in England & Wales (ICAEW)
Institute of Chartered Accountants of Scotland (ICAS)
Association of Chartered Certified Accountants (ACCA)
Association of Taxation Technicians (ATT)
Association of Accounting Technicians (AAT)
Federation of Small Businesses (FSB)
Society of Trust and Estate Practitioners (STEP), and
The non-revenue members of Working Together (WT)

Tax, Accountancy and Business Bodies Criticise 'Secret Husband and Wife Tax'

In an unprecedented show of unity, the heads of the UK's leading tax, accountancy and business bodies have strongly criticised the Revenue's position on Section 660A, characterising it as a secret husband and wife tax.

This obscure but important legislation is commonly known as the 'husband and wife tax' because of its effect on small businesses. If left unchallenged the Revenue's controversial interpretation is likely to leave thousands of small business facing unexpected and hefty tax bills. Whilst the Revenue argues that only 30,000 companies are potentially at risk, the professional bodies believe the figure is much higher (bearing in mind the number of companies started in recent years) and that in any event even 30,000 is too high a number of businesses to be faced with uncertainty.

On 4th November the Revenue published their response to earlier criticism from the professional bodies; the comments of the professional bodies on that response are published today and attached to this press release.

'This is another stealth tax' said Mark Lee, Chairman of the ICAEW Tax Faculty. 'The Revenue did not publish their interpretation of this legislation until 2001, and then only in a technical manual rarely read even by tax specialists. Nevertheless, they are applying their view for at least the last six years, which means many small businesses could face backdated and unexpected tax bills.'

This view was strongly endorsed by Tim Ambrose, President of the CIOT, who said 'we believe that the Revenue have a legal and moral obligation to inform taxpayers of how the legislation is going to be applied. Their current approach is arguably a breach of human rights.'

The professional bodies have suggested a more pragmatic approach, which fits better with self-assessment. 'We believe that taxpayers should normally self-assess on the basis that they are not within these rules, unless the opposite is clearly the case. The Revenue could challenge this self-assessment within the normal time limits, but the onus would be on them to prove their case' suggested Mr Ambrose.

'We are particularly worried that small businesses, which are the engine room of the economy, are being distracted by this unfair tax at a time when they should be concentrating on the market recovery' said John Walker, Policy Chairman of the FSB.

The other professional and business bodies endorsed these comments and called on the Revenue to reconsider their position.

Note for Editors

1. Example of why this issue matters

   Here is a short example of the type of situations affected by the Revenue's guidance:

   Jack and Jill are a married couple who decide to form Hill Limited to exploit Jack's skills in developing new pharmaceutical remedies. The couple own the shares in Hill Ltd equally; the net income of the company is £100,000, derived from Jack's activities. Jill does some work for the company, such as taking phone calls, making bookings and generally supporting Jack.

   Jack is paid a salary of £50,000 and Jill is unpaid despite her general advice and assistance; the net profit after tax of (say) £40,000 is then used to pay the two owners dividends of £20,000 each. Following Example 3 in the Revenue's guidance, Jill's £20,000 dividends are vulnerable to being recharacterised as Jack's income and taxed at his higher rate of income tax. If Jack and Jill are tackled by the Revenue after six years of similar figures, an unexpected tax bill of some £30,000 could result, plus interest and possibly penalties.

2. Section 660A is the relevant section of the Income and Corporations Taxes Act 1988 which provides for the 'husband and wife tax'.

3. The number of new companies formed over the last 3 years per year is:

   2000/1 67,761
   2001/2 175,161
   2002/3 282,207

Participating bodies	**Press Contacts**
Tax Faculty of the Institute of Chartered Accountants in England & Wales	Mark Lee – 020 7153 2495 Francesca Lagerberg – 020 7612 8858
Chartered Institute of Taxation	Anne Redston – 0207 951 2215 John Whiting – 020 7804 4422
Federation of Small Businesses	Simon Sweetman – 01394 274857
Institute of Chartered Accountants of Scotland	Derek Allen – 0131 347 0100.
Association of Chartered Certified Accountants	Chas Roy-Chowdhury 07710 707516
Association of Taxation Technicians	Trevor Johnson – 0151 632 0424 John Kimmer – 01903 821066
Association of Accounting Technicians	Brian Palmer – 01202 524600
Society of Trust and Estate Practitioners	Keith Johnston – 0207 763 7156
Representatives of Working Together are also involved in the process	Richard Shooter – 0116 233 6667 Richard Mannion – 0117 933 3116

Reply to the Inland Revenue's Note to the Professional Bodies, Received on 15 October Concerning the Settlements Legislation and Small Business

Submitted by CIOT, ICAEW Tax Faculty, ICAS, ACCA, ATT, AAT, FSB, STEP & Working Together representatives

We are pleased that the Inland Revenue have considered the points made in our paper, and in particular that they are considering the policy implications of Examples 3 to 5 in Tax Bulletin 64.

We still have serious concerns, however, with the Revenue position. Our specific comments on the Revenue's note to us are set out below, with the Revenue views in italics, and our comments following:

'Nevertheless many practitioners have known about, and had practical experience of, the Revenue's interpretation for many years'

We recognise that some individual practitioners have had past experience of Inspectors raising the arguments set out at Examples 3–5. But this does not mean that the profession as a whole was aware that the position taken by the occasional Inspectors was official Revenue policy. We all do have occasional encounters with Inspectors who take their own views of the legislation, and we know that there are times when they take approaches that do not reflect Head Office policy. As we have frequently stated, there was no official guidance in an accessible form to make us (and still less the unrepresented taxpayer) aware that it was Revenue policy.

Based on representations made direct to us, and articles in the press (such as 'The Revenue is Right'. The Tax Journal. 22 September 2003. Page 11.), it is clear the views put forward in the paper are not universally accepted by the profession.

We are aware that Robert Maas shares the views of the Revenue on this issue and therefore that the profession is not unanimous. But the professional bodies who signed the paper were setting out the views of their members, and thus represent the vast majority of tax professionals. Feedback received from accountants and tax advisers at seminars on this issue since April 2003 has universally expressed surprise at Examples 3–5. It would however be unusual if no-one at all agreed with the Revenue position.

Ministers made clear during the debates on Independent Taxation during the passage of the 1989 and 1989 [sic] Finance Bill that the settlements legislation would be applied in future where there were effectively transfers only of income between husbands and wives.

We have now reviewed the Hansard debates on this issue. We agree that the Minister, Norman Lamont, said that the settlements legislation would be applied when there were transfers only of income between husbands and wives. He also said:

> 'Independent taxation is bound to mean that some couples will transfer assets between them with the result that their total tax bill be reduced. This is an inevitable and acceptable consequence of taxing husbands and wives separately ...we have made it clear that we expect income splitting will occur.'

And:

> 'Provided that a gift of assets between husband and wife is free from conditions and is a complete and irrevocable transfer of the underlying capital as well as the income we see absolutely no case for imposing a tax penalty on the income from those assets.'

He distinguishes this from the limited scenarios where the exemption for gifts between spouses will not apply:

> 'Gifts that do not carry the right to the whole of the income from the property transferred, which are effectively transfers only of income, which are subject to conditions, or under which the donor may benefit directly, will not come within the scope of the provision ... A married couple cannot obtain a tax advantage from a purely artificial transfer of income between them. But if the beneficial ownership of both capital and income is transferred, that genuine change of ownership will be recognised.'

We do not agree that the husband and wife businesses, where the wife owns, as a question of legal right, half of the company or partnership, is 'effectively a transfer only of income'.

We are also of the view that Hansard indicates that tax avoidance and tax planning, in terms of asset allocation between couples, was an expected consequence of independent taxation and was accepted by the government of the time.

These comments of the Minister do also help to explain why tax professionals did not expect that the Revenue were going to take this 'tax avoidance' approach to small businesses – the whole tenor of the debate runs in the other direction.

We have no plans to significantly increase the number of formal enquires we undertake in this area at this time.

At our meeting with you in September we were pleased to receive Revenue confirmation that there was no intention to increase the number of enquiries. However this original straighforward commitment now appears to be suffering from limitation creep. This began with the insertion of 'significant' in the final version of the draft notes of meeting, and now appears to be further restricted by the insertion of the words 'formal' and 'at this time'.

We should be grateful for your confirmation that you have not changed the clear position you set out in September, namely that the Revenue do not intend to increase the number of settlement enquiries beyond the 100 or so per annum which you indicated already occur.

Based on the publicly available information, we have been able to identify less than 30,000 companies that could be like examples 3 and 4. (Companies with two shareholders, one or two directors and dividends being paid in the year.)

Thank you for this information. Clearly the Revenue have access to sources of information which are not available to practitioners, and this is very helpful. We have a few further questions:

- Could you confirm whether this figure represented a single year?
- If so, which year? In particular, we note the very high level of incorporations recently. We assume these are not yet included in 'the publicly available information' and thus the numbers of those affected are likely to be greater than those shown.
- In this context it would be helpful to know, from the information available, how many incorporations there have been in the last three years.
- We are interested to know whether a similar exercise has been carried out for partnerships? It would be our expectation that the number of husband and wife partnerships where only one partner is 'fee-earning' but both partners receive a profit share would be very large.

As it is clear that many practitioners were aware of our views prior to Tax Bulletin 64, and as enquiry cases have been settled on those lines, there can be no question of the interpretation as set out in examples 3, 4 & 5 applying only from April 2003.

We are disturbed by the fact that the Revenue continue to insist that publication of a single example within a Manual which was not made publicly available until 2001, and a single paragraph in an article written by a tax manager, should constitute sufficient public notice of their views on behaviour which they regard as sufficiently reprehensible to warrant reopening of earlier years.

We have now considered this in the context of the Human Rights Act, and our comments are attached as Appendix 1 to this Note.

We are also currently reviewing the common law implications, namely whether the Revenue gave a 'representation by silence' that taxpayers would not be attacked in this manner, and thus prior to the publication of TB64, they had a legitimate expectation that the Revenue would not apply the settlements legislation in these scenarios.

Those of our members who attended the many meetings with the Revenue on the introduction of self-assessment have no record or recollection of this Revenue interpretation being raised at those meetings. In the words of one prominent member of the Self Assessment Consultative Committee (SACC), 'as this interpretation makes self assessment next to impossible I am very surprised that they did not raise it.'

In addition, as mentioned at our meeting, we are concerned that the Revenue are opening enquiries under the self-assessment provisions, and then claiming that they can backdate the amounts claimed for six years. We assume that the Revenue are operating under the 'discovery' provisions of TMA s29(5), namely that 'the officer could not have been reasonably expected, on the basis of the information made available to him before that time, to be aware of the situation', though this is commonly not explicitly stated in the correspondence.

However we would draw your attention to the recent case of *Langham v Veltema* [2002] STC 1557. In that case Mr Justice Park said that:

> 'although the tax return and accompanying documents are obviously the starting point for the question of whether the Inspector could, ''on the basis of'' them, reasonably be expected to be aware that Mr. Veltema's self-assessment was insufficient, the Commissioners and courts are not constrained to proceed on the unreal basis that the tax returns and accompanying documents must have been the only items of information which the Inspector had. If as a matter of common sense and normal administrative procedures it is likely that the Inspector would in fact have other items of information before him the statute does not require the question posed by s 29(5) to be answered on an unrealistic basis'

In our view, taking *Langham v Veltema* into account, 'discovery' will not be appropriate in many of the settlement cases currently being worked by the Revenue.

However the department is not obliged to provide detailed guidance on every possible set of circumstances in which legislation could apply.

Given the Revenue's own identification of 30,000 possibly affected companies (presumably in a single year, and before the great surge in incorporations) plus an unknown number of partnerships which may be affected by this legislation, and which may find themselves with large and unexpected tax bills, we are surprised that this should be dismissed so lightly.

We have said we will look again at examples 3, 4 and 5 and, if appropriate, produce further guidance to help people self assess.

As previously discussed, it is clear that such guidance is needed. For example, in one letter the Revenue have written to the taxpayer as follows:

> 'The provisions in s660A apply to deem the dividends received by Mrs X to be her husband's income for all Income Tax purposes. As he is liable to tax at the higher rates some additional liability will arise. I realise that Mrs X performed her duties for the company without remuneration. I can therefore accept that part of the dividend she received represents a reasonable reward for her services. Given the hours she worked I have taken this part to be equal to 50% of the dividends paid in the accounting period.'

Even if the Revenue are correct in their interpretation of s660A, how, under Self Assessment, is the taxpayer to know how much of the dividend is to be reapportioned back to the higher earner? 50%, as here; or should it be 60%, 40%, or the full 100%?

While we look forward to further guidance, we are nevertheless concerned that this will remain a subjective area and one which is not compatible with self assessment. We suggest that a better approach would be as follows:

- to accept as a matter of practice that the taxpayer can properly self assess on the basis that there is not an arrangement constituting a settlement unless it is clearly within the provisions;
- if the Revenue wish to take a contrary view they may do so but only for the open year and not using it as a basis of the discovery.
- the taxpayer is thus entitled to assume that an arrangement is not a settlement for self assessment purposes unless the Revenue argue otherwise, and that argument is accepted by the taxpayer or it is so held by the Commissioners.

This would give the taxpayer certainty in his self-assessment and be a workable, practical solution.

Such an approach would be similar to that adopted by the Revenue as regards the transactions in securities provisions; these only apply if the Revenue specifically invokes them. It also has parallels with the position (agreed after much discussion at SACC) of financial traders[1].

1 When self assessment was being introduced there was much discussion in SACC about the Crown option where the Revenue has power to determine, in the case of a financial trader, whether the investment income should be assessed under Schedule D Cases 3, 4 or 5 or under Cases 1 or 2.

The option is rarely used and the taxpayer may self asses on the basis he considers appropriate subject to the Revenue making a determination that on exercise of the Crown option a different basis has to be applied.

Interest cannot be waived but we have agreed that penalties will not normally be sought for 2002–03 and previous years in cases like examples 3, 4 & 5 involving the settlements legislation.

We welcome the fact that penalties will not be sought.

We do not agree taking an appeal to the Special Commissioners has to be an expensive exercise

We know that if a taxpayer takes the case himself, and is not represented, that this is not expensive. But it usually results in a David and Goliath battle which the taxpayer loses. A properly argued and prepared case at the Special Commissioners, including prior liaison with the Revenue, preparation of documents, briefing of witnesses etc, is unlikely to cost less than £7,500.

This is a significant sum to most small businesses, who are also facing an unexpected Revenue demand for back tax and interest. In addition, taxpayers are always advised that taking a case to the Commissioners is not necessarily the end of the matter – if they win there is a reasonable chance that the Revenue will appeal, and then the taxpayer has to fund the costs of the case going to the High Court and possibly further. This is a very daunting prospect for the micro-businesses which are under attack.

We look at the whole arrangement, as the legislation requires.

We have a fundamental disagreement here, as to what is required by the legislation. In our view the income flows from the assets, and s660A(6) is sufficient to protect the taxpayer from a reallocation of the dividend income to the higher earner. In our view the Hansard debate supports our interpretation.

With respect to partnerships the Revenue again looks at the whole arrangement to see whether someone is getting a disproportionate return on their investment because they are related to, or friends with, the settlor.

The key question is not whether someone is getting a 'disproportionate return' but whether the partnership arrangements amount to 'wholly or mainly a right to income' – which, because of the unlimited risk taken on, cannot in our view be the case.

In the Revenue's view the fact that the shares in Young v Pearce [1996] STC 743, were preference shares does not mean that ordinary shares cannot also be caught by the settlements legislation.

The concluding judgement of *Young v Pearce* is as follows:

> 'Was the "property given" – the preference shares – "wholly or substantially a right to income"? It seems to me that the answer to that question must be in the affirmative. The preference shares entitled the holders to a preferential dividend if the taxpayers (the only directors and the holders of all the ordinary shares) determined to distribute the whole or part of the profits arising in any given year. Apart from that right to income, the only rights conferred on the preference shareholders were the right to repayment of the nominal sum paid on the allotment of the shares and the right to attend and be heard, but not to vote at, general meetings of the company. As a matter of strict legal principle, the preference shares were assets distinct from the income derived from them, but in reality they could never have been realised. The income was dependent upon the taxpayers determining to distribute part of the profits of the company.'

The factors set out here by Sir John Vinelott do, in terms, distinguish preference shares from ordinary shares, which have a bundle of rights including full rights to capital, votes and dividends.

We have not suggested that a 'non fee-earning' spouse makes no contribution to a business. The question, in the context of the settlements legislation, is 'What contribution does that spouse make and how commercial is the reward for it'?

We are pleased to note that the Revenue appear to accept that the role of the non-fee earning spouse has value. We invite them again to consider the fact that other courts (notably in divorce situations) have fully valued the contribution to building a business made by the non-fee-earning spouse.

We also reiterate the point made extensively in our earlier submission, that the Revenue's emphasis on the contribution made by the spouse ignores the legal reality. The non-fee earning spouse is either an ordinary shareholder or an unlimited partner in a business, and in consequence has rights and obligations. As we said in our earlier paper, the concepts of ordinary shareholder and partner 'are at the hub of the professional bodies' concerns with the thrust of the Tax Bulletin article.'

In a service company it is usually the person with the specialist knowledge who retains the interest because s/he controls the source of income.

We believe that this is a novel interpretation of the well-worn phrase 'retaining an interest'. Where an individual has 50% of the shares in a company, and can sue to obtain her share of the company's value, there are no rights in those shares retained by the spouse.

Looking at a typical service company scenario we have challenged, we do not accept the argument relating to 'goodwill'.

It is our experience, and this is reflected in the actual real-life examples set out in the Tax Bulletin, that the Revenue's attacks on small businesses are not limited to service companies.

Whereby a high earning individual agrees to work for a company for a very low rate of remuneration and allows a significant part of the earnings which they generate to be paid to someone else.

We found the superlatives in this comment helpful in the context of self-assessment, although we have not found this always to be the Revenue's approach in practice. Could they be more specific as to what they will regard as 'very low' and 'significant'?

At the other extreme, where, because of the nature of the business activity, the partnership has no significant capital base and a spouse who takes no part in the running of the business is made a 50% partner we believe that the settlements legislation can apply.

The partnership does not have to have a significant capital base and the partner can be 'sleeping' but still be at risk if the partnership is sued – and can be made bankrupt. Most partnerships are not limited liability partnerships and it is an irrelevance whether the home has actually been mortgaged to provide working capital etc.

Parliament introduced the settlements legislation to prevent individuals transferring their income to a relative or friend in order to avoid tax

We concur with this statement, but would emphasise the fact that Parliament narrowly limited the legislation to deal only with transfers of income. As stated earlier in this paper, the Minister clearly stated that 'if the beneficial ownership of both capital and income is transferred, that genuine change of ownership will be recognised'. Thus a reduction in the family's income tax bill which occurs as a result of transfers of assets was specifically outside the scope of the legislation.

Conclusion

We would welcome the Revenue's further comments in the light of the comments in this paper which we will publish for the benefit of members of all constituent bodies.

As will be apparent from this second joint paper there are a number of areas where the professions consider that the Revenue's views on this subject are novel to say the least.

We have summarised below five key points extracted from the text above:

1. The incompatibility of the Revenue's views with the obligations on taxpayers to self-assess. We have suggested an alternative approach similar to that adopted by the Revenue as regards the transactions in securities provisions.
2. The incompatibility of the Revenue's views with Hansard statements as to the impact of the settlements legislation on transfers between husband and wife.
3. The distinction drawn in the decision of *Young v Pearce* between ordinary and preference shares confirming that ordinary shares are not 'wholly or mainly a right to income'.
4. The significantly wider potential impact of the Revenue's view than is accepted in their 15 October paper.
5. The impact of common law, the decision in *Langham v Veltema* and of the HRA on claims for back taxes and interest.

Comments on Human Rights implications of Revenue approach to guidance on the settlements legislation

Article 1 of Protocol No. 1 to the Human Rights Convention provides that:

> 'Every natural or legal person is entitled to the peaceful enjoyment of his possessions. No one shall be deprived of his possessions except in the public interest and subject to the conditions provided for by law and by the general principles of international law.
>
> The preceding provisions shall not, however, in any way impair the right of a State to enforce such laws as it deems necessary to control the use of property in accordance with the general interest or to secure the payment of taxes or other contributions or penalties.'

Taxation, as an interference with the rights guaranteed in Article 1 of Protocol No. 1, is justified thus under the second paragraph of Article 1. This provision expressly reserves the right of Contracting States to enforce such laws as they may deem necessary to secure the payment of taxes.

The recent case of *Spacek sro v the Czech Republic* (ECHR November 1999) considers the publicity to be given to the law on the computation of a tax liability.

In that case, the requirements were published in a Bulletin put out by the Ministry of Finance. The Bulletin was available to subscribers and through retail outlets. The Court of Human Rights held that in these circumstances this degree of publicity sufficed.

However the decision might have been different if the Bulletin had not been generally available, and the court also pointed out that 'the applicant company, as a legal entity, contrary to an individual taxpayer, could and should have consulted the competent specialists …' [our italics]

This seems to imply that, in the case of an individual taxpayer, it would not have sufficed for the government to say that the taxpayer could consult experts who would know of particular rules.

This case is relevant to the settlements debate because:

- It makes clear that while 'the Convention does not contain any specific requirements as to the degree of publicity to be given to a particular legal provision', nevertheless the Court's decision is founded on the assumption that appropriate publicity was required if the Convention was to be fulfilled;
- In the case of the settlements legislation, it is clear that there was no published guidance from the Revenue on their view that it applied in the circumstances of Examples 3, 4 and 5 before the publication of the Trusts and Settlements Manual in 2001;
- In the light of *Spacek*, it is in our view unlikely that the ECHR would consider that publication in the Trusts and Settlements Manual was sufficient, in the case of an individual taxpayer, to give appropriate notice of the Revenue's view as to how this legislation should be applied;
- Even if we are wrong in this, there was no publication before 2001 and thus this would appear to be the earliest date from which the Revenue can seek to enforce compliance with their view.

The authoritative 'International Tax Law Reports' says of this case 'what seems clear is that taxation based upon unpublished internal rules would be regarded as an unjustified interference with the enjoyment of possessions.'

Appendix 8

Working Together Bulletin Extracts

Working Together Bulletin Issue 13, June 2003

Page 7. Proceeds of Crime Act 2002 and the Money Laundering Regulations 2003

Summary

Home Office legislation, the Proceeds of Crime Act 2002, has been brought into force in stages. This article concerns Part 7 of this Act, which reformed the law on money laundering and is expected to have a significant effect on professional advisers. This article is intended to:

- raise awareness of this new legislation
- cover its interaction with the Inland Revenue in the area of tax evasion.

Other parts of the Act, for example those concerning the establishment and operation of the Asset Recovery Agency, are not dealt with in this article.

Introduction

The Proceeds of Crime Act 2002 requires those in what the legislation terms the 'regulated sector' to report where they know or suspect, or have reasonable grounds for knowing or suspecting, that another person is engaged in laundering the proceeds of crime.

The existing regulated sector, which includes for example banks and investment businesses, is due to be expanded by the Money Laundering Regulations 2003 to include:

- Estate agents
- Casinos
- Insolvency practitioners
- Tax advisers (a person appointed to give tax advice about the tax affairs of another person)
- Accountants and auditors (those providing by way of business accountancy or audit services)

- Legal advisers (those providing by way of business legal services which involves participation in a financial or real property transaction)
- Company formation agents
- Dealers in high value goods, including auctioneers, whenever payment is made in cash, and in an amount of 15,000 euro or more.

These Regulations that expand the regulated sector are expected to be laid around mid June. The Government is however intending to allow a further 3 month period from when they are laid until the Regulations actually come into force. This will allow those affected by the Regulations time to implement training programmes and anti-money laundering procedures.

Previous money laundering legislation has principally concerned the laundering of drug or terrorist funds. The new legislation concerns the proceeds of all crime and this includes all acts of tax evasion and fraud.

For professional advisers (tax advisers, accountants, auditors and legal advisers) this means, as with others in the regulated sector, that if in the course of their business they know or suspect that their clients or others have committed a money laundering offence, including tax evasion, they are required to report their suspicions to the National Criminal Intelligence Service (NCIS).

This is without de minimis limit and thus covers all suspicions irrespective of the amounts involved. The wording in the legislation also captures not just actual knowledge or suspicion, but a more stringent test of whether there were 'reasonable grounds' for such knowledge or suspicion.

Although this is not mandatory upon them yet, some professional advisers have already submitted reports in anticipation of the legislation taking effect.

Requirement for Professional Advisers to Report Knowledge or Suspicion of Tax Evasion

Professional advisers will be required to report their knowledge or suspicion of money laundering (including acts of tax evasion) on a Suspicious Activity Report (SAR) form as soon as is practicable after the information came to them.

The legislation states that a disclosure must be made 'in the prescribed form and manner as set out by the Secretary of State'. The form or forms for this are currently under review. For the time being the existing SAR form should be used which is available from NCIS and can be downloaded from their website at www.ncis.co.uk.

All SAR forms must be submitted direct to NCIS. This is the case whether the report concerns the proceeds of tax evasion or any other form of criminal activity. NCIS is the government body to receive these reports as only they have the information to check whether there are links to wider criminality.

The Inland Revenue is not a receiving body for these reports. Where a voluntary disclosure about unpaid liabilities due to tax evasion is intended to be made to the Revenue the professional adviser is still required to make a SAR to NCIS at the earliest opportunity.

Reports that Concern Tax Evasion

Reports that relate to tax evasion will be referred within NCIS to an Inland Revenue team who will analyse and evaluate them. Where the only criminality identified from this analysis is tax evasion, the reports will be forwarded by NCIS to the Inland Revenue or HM Customs & Excise as appropriate. For offences of evading direct taxes or NICs the Inland Revenue will be the investigating body and, in England and Wales, the prosecuting body for these offences. In Scotland the Procurator Fiscal and in Northern Ireland the Director of Public Prosecutions are the prosecuting bodies. Reports forwarded by NCIS to the Revenue will be received by Special Compliance Office (SCO).

Effect on Inland Revenue Enquiries and Hansard

Any Inland Revenue enquiries that result from or are informed by disclosures forwarded from NCIS will be carried out in the same manner as any other Inland Revenue enquiry.

In particular reporting a case to NCIS ahead of notifying the Revenue will have no bearing on how the Revenue may treat a case, if the taxpayer is actively seeking to set their affairs straight. This also applies to cases dealt with under the Inland Revenue approach to civil settlements known as 'Hansard'.

Confidentiality of information received by the Inland Revenue will of course remain of uppermost importance. In cases other than criminal investigations by SCO, procedures are in place such that investigators receive only the factual information from a SAR with no knowledge of who made the original disclosure.

Tipping Off

The Proceeds of Crime Act also contains an offence referred to in the legislation as 'tipping off'. This makes it an offence for a person who knows or suspects that a SAR has been submitted to NCIS then to make a disclosure likely to prejudice any resulting investigation or to disclose that they suspect that an investigation may be taking place. The most obvious example of this would be where a professional adviser made their client aware that they had sent a SAR to NCIS. This offence, as with others under this legislation, is a criminal offence.

Approaching the Inland Revenue to make a disclosure on behalf of a client about unpaid tax liabilities after the SAR has been sent to NCIS does not constitute tipping off.

Other Aspects of the Legislation

The Act defines the principal money laundering offences of concealing, making arrangements, acquisition, use and possession of what is described as 'criminal property', Criminal property is anything situated anywhere in the world and is defined as money; all forms of property, real or personal, heritable or moveable; other intangible property; property obtained by a person who has an interest in it; things in action.

Where criminal conduct occurs outside the UK it is still within the scope of the Act if it would constitute an offence if it occurred in the UK.

The legislation also contains provisions whereby consent may be necessary from NCIS to proceed with a transaction. Where before a specific transaction takes place it arouses suspicion that it would result in a money laundering offence being committed, consent from NCIS is required before proceeding with that transaction. An example might be where a professional adviser was involved in advising on an arrangement for transferring funds overseas, which the adviser suspected resulted from crime (i.e. from tax evasion).

In such circumstances NCIS have 7 working days from submission of the SAR to give or refuse consent, so early notification to NCIS is vital. If NCIS refuse consent, law enforcement has up to a further 31 days in which to decide what action to take, e.g. to apply for a restraint order.

The legislation also acknowledges professional privilege in certain circumstances where legal advice is given by a professional legal adviser.

Further Information and Help

Further information can be obtained from the Home Office website at www.homeoffice.gov.uk/crimpol/oic/proceeds/index.html and the Treasury website at www.hm-treasury.gov.uk/Documents/Financial_Services/money/fin_money_index.cfm

The legislation itself can be found at http://www.legislation.hmso.gov.uk/acts/acts2002/20020029.htm

In addition the accountancy and taxation bodies are in the process of preparing authoritative guidance in this area for approval by the Treasury. The Revenue is also planning to tell you more on the website.

Appendix 9

WJB Chiltern Group Anti-Money Laundering Procedures (Extract)

The WJB Chiltern group (the 'group') fully accepts its legal and regulatory obligations in respect of the prevention of money laundering and is committed to adopting the highest standards to ensure that the group and its staff, are aware of their respective obligations and have the necessary information and training to enable them to effectively discharge those obligations.

Money laundering is the process by which criminals attempt to conceal the true origin and ownership of the proceeds of their criminal activities. If successful they can maintain control over those proceeds and so provide a legitimate cover for their source of income.

The purpose of these procedures is to codify practices to mitigate the risk of the group and its staff from being used in the process of money laundering.

International Money Laundering Efforts

When dealing with prospective clients, it is important to make a judgment as to the risk of exposure to potential money laundering. FATF, the international Financial Action Task Force, and other agencies such as the International Monetary Fund, have assessed the degree of effectiveness of individual countries' efforts to defeat money laundering.

Non-Cooperative Countries And Territories

FATF publishes a list of jurisdictions that have been identified as non-cooperative in respect of international efforts to combat money laundering-(sometimes known as the 'blacklist'). This is gradually decreasing as countries and territories improve their anti-money laundering legislation.

You are strongly advised, before completing the account opening forms, to discuss with Group Compliance any application to open an account for a prospective client who resides in or has any connection with any of the countries on the blacklist.

Proceeds Of Crime Act 2002

This legislation expands, reforms and consolidates the UK's criminal money laundering offences. The Act makes it an offence to acquire, use, possess, conceal, disguise, convert, transfer or remove criminal property from the jurisdiction, or to facilitate its acquisition, retention, use or control by another person.

Criminal property means any person's benefit, including one's own, from criminal conduct. The maximum penalty for all these offences is 14 years' imprisonment and an unlimited fine.

There is a defence when a person who knows or suspects that property constitutes or represents someone's benefit from criminal conduct, reports his concerns to the National Criminal Intelligence Service (NCIS) or to an appropriate person under approved internal arrangements (i.e., the money laundering reporting officer (MLRO)), either before the prohibited act is carried out or as soon afterwards as is reasonably practical.

The Act makes it a criminal offence for persons working in the regulated financial sector (i.e., anyone who falls within the scope of the Money Laundering Regulations, which now includes all UK group staff) if they fail to report where they have knowledge, suspicion or reasonable grounds for knowledge or suspicion that another person is laundering the proceeds of any criminal conduct, as soon as is reasonably practical after the information came to their attention.

If you have any suspicions regarding any transaction, you MUST report the matter to the MLRO, on the standard form posted in the money laundering section of the group's intranet.

The Offences

There are several money laundering offences covered by the Proceeds of Crime Act 2002. All have a maximum penalty of an unlimited fine, plus a jail term, which varies according to the specific offence as listed below:

Assistance – 14 Years

Assistance occurs where a person is involved in an arrangement with another person and knows or suspects that the other person is or has been involved in or has benefited from criminal conduct if the arrangement helps the other person to retain or control proceeds directly or indirectly or enables the other person to use the proceeds or to invest them for his benefit.

Concealing, Disguising, Converting And Transferring – 14 Years

Concealing, disguising, converting or transferring proceeds of criminal conduct in order to avoid or help someone else to avoid prosecution are all themselves offences. The offence is committed by a person if he knows or has reasonable grounds to suspect the nature of the property.

Acquisition – 14 Years

Acquisition is the offence of use or possession of assets which you know or have reasonable grounds to suspect to be the proceeds of criminal conduct.

Removal Of Property From The Jurisdiction – 14 Years

Facilitating the removal of the proceeds of criminal conduct from the UK is also an offence.

Failure To Disclose – 5 Years

It is a specific and separate offence not to report a suspicion if the information came to the person's attention in the course of his business or employment. Effectively, the duty to report is extended to employees of business institutions where it is the institutions that may become involved in the arrangements and not the employees themselves.

It is expressly provided in the legislation that a disclosure to the MLRO under the reporting procedures described above will not give actionable grounds for a claim for breach of any express or implied duty of confidentiality owed to a client.

Tipping Off – 5 Years

Reporting to the police is not much help if the suspect is tipped off about the investigation. Tipping off, therefore, constitutes an offence when information or any other matter which may prejudice an investigation is disclosed to the subject of the investigation (or anyone else) by someone who knows, suspects or has reasonable cause to suspect that an investigation into money laundering has begun or is about to begin, or law enforcement agencies have been informed of suspicious activities, or a disclosure has been made by another employee under internal reporting procedures.

Money Laundering Regulations 2003

The Second European Money Laundering Directive is enshrined in UK law by the Money Laundering Regulations 2003, which effectively bring the whole of the WJB Chiltern group within the definition of 'regulated sector' for the purposes of the Proceeds of Crime Act 2002.

Accordingly, ALL STAFF are now subject to personal criminal sanction if they fail to report any transaction, which they know or reasonably suspect to be for the purposes of laundering the proceeds of crime.

Preventative Measures

The group is required in a business relationship or a one-off transaction with an applicant for business to maintain certain administrative and training procedures designed to mitigate the risk of money laundering. The four key aspects of the procedures required are:

- Identification,
- Record keeping,
- Reporting, and
- Employee awareness.

In order to minimise the group's exposure it is important to:

- Know our clients,
- Be alert to money arriving from various different sources,
- Be wary of someone who is secretive about his or her identity or background, and
- Keep a look out for transactions that are being conducted in unusual ways or do not 'feel right'.

Identification

One of the group's primary responsibilities with respect to money laundering is the verification of the identity of new clients. It is essential that all new clients be subject to verification of identity in order to:

- Deter money launderers from using our services,
- Provide a defence for the group should a new client pass initial scrutiny but subsequently prove to be involved in money laundering, and
- Protect the reputation and good standing of staff and the group

You must take reasonable steps to find out who the client is by obtaining sufficient evidence of the identity of any client and be able to show that the client is who they claim to be.

If the client is, or appears to be, acting on behalf of another person our obligation extends to obtaining sufficient evidence of identity of the underlying client.

You must obtain the identification from the client as soon as reasonably practicable after your contact with them with a view to either:

- Agreeing with the client to carry out an initial transaction, or
- Reach an understanding (whether binding or not) with the client that you may carry out future transactions.

If the client does not supply evidence of identity within the agreed timescale, you must contact Group Compliance who may recommend that you:

- Discontinue any activity you are conducting for the client and
- Bring to an end any understanding you have reached with the client.

There are some limited exceptions to the general requirement to verify a client's identity contained in the Money Laundering Regulations 2003. At the time of writing, these regulations only exist in draft form, so please contact the MLRO if you think a particular case may be able to rely on an exception.

The verification of identity must be completed when opening a new file. Under the Money Laundering Regulations, evidence must be obtained and filed to verify the identity and the address of all new clients. For corporate clients, evidence is required proving the existence of the legal structure as well as verifying the identity of the directors and the individuals who gave us instructions.

Identity Evidence To Be Obtained

This information is set out in appendix 2 of the client take on form guidance. **You must see the ORIGINAL or properly certified copy documents to verify identity.**

Record Keeping Arrangements

The money laundering regulations require the following records to be kept:

Documents Verifying Identity

- A copy of the evidence of identity,
- A record of where a copy of the evidence of identity can be obtained, or
- When it is not reasonably practicable to comply with either of the above, a record of how the details of the evidence of identity can be obtained.

Transaction Records

You must make a record containing details of every transaction carried out by the regulated company with or for the client in the course of regulated activity. 'Transaction' does not include advice given to a client unless such advice is followed by a transaction with monetary value.

When a client becomes insolvent, and it has taken steps to recover all or part of the debt owed to us by the client, a record of those grounds and those steps is made and kept by Group Credit Control.

Records of internal reports received and NCIS disclosures made (meeting the requirements for the group's FSA-regulated companies under ML 4.1 (Internal reporting) and ML 4.3 (External reporting) respectively) are kept by Group Compliance.

How Long Must The Records Be Kept?

- In relation to evidence of identity, five years from the end of the company's relationship with the client.
- In relation to transactions, five years from the date when the transaction was completed (although, for tax reasons, records should be kept for six years).
- In relation to when a client becomes insolvent, five years from the date of insolvency.
- In any other case, five years from obtaining the information.

Reporting

There is an obligation on all staff to report suspicions of money laundering to the money laundering reporting officer (MLRO). To help ensure that we are not used to launder the proceeds of criminal conduct, all staff should be alert to unusual or suspicious instructions from clients. Any suspicion of money laundering should be reported to the MLRO. All reports should be made on the standard form posted in the money laundering section of the group's intranet. Making a report will itself protect the individual who made it from the risk of criminal prosecution if the client's subsequent activities do turn out to involve money laundering. It is also a criminal offence, known as 'tipping off', to prejudice an investigation by informing the person who is the subject of the suspicion, or any third party, that a disclosure has been made, or that the authorities are acting, or are proposing to act, in connection with an investigation into money laundering.

Suspicion is personal and subjective, and you do not need any proof. Where there is a business relationship, a suspicious transaction will often be one, which is inconsistent with a client's known, legitimate business or personal activities. The first key is, therefore, knowledge about the client's business to enable you to recognise any unusual transaction. Particular care must be taken when dealing with potential tax evasion. Remember, it is often seen as a 'glamorous' offence and one that a client may boast of in order to cover more 'serious' offences, such as drug trafficking. If in doubt, report it to the MLRO.

Be careful not to mention your suspicions to your client. You can, of course, enquire of your client about the transaction, which you are querying; however, you should never advise him that you will be making a money laundering report.

Once a report has been made, the MLRO will evaluate it and give instructions as to the way the client should subsequently be handled. Where clearance is given to continue to act, great care must still be taken not to 'tip off' the client.

Once a report has been made, any transaction in which the company is involved and which results in money being received or paid away by the client must be brought to the attention of the MLRO immediately, before the transaction is effected. Remember, moving criminal assets out of the jurisdiction is an offence.

Employee Awareness

The group is required to take appropriate measures to

- Ensure employees are aware of current policies and procedures to prevent money laundering, and
- Ensure employees are aware of the current legal requirements.

A formal training programme for all staff is in place and you will be advised of training dates when scheduled. Attendance is mandatory.

Throughout the year members of staff will receive continuous training and updating as follows:

- Important developments will be circulated by email.
- The money laundering section of the group's intranet will be regularly updated.

Training courses will be provided on both a scheduled and ad hoc basis as deemed necessary.

The Money Laundering Reporting Officer (MLRO)

The MLRO is there to ensure that the company is able to and does comply with the prevailing legal and regulatory money laundering requirements. He acts as the focal point within the group for the oversight of all activity relating to anti-money laundering.

He is a senior employee, free to act on his own authority, and must be informed if you have any relevant knowledge or suspicion of criminal activity. In turn, he determines which issues he will refer to NCIS. He will also liaise closely with NCIS on any question as to whether to proceed with a specific transaction.

The group has decided that the same person will carry out the three roles of MLRO under the FSA rules, 'nominated officer' under the Proceeds of Crime Act 2002 and 'appropriate person' under the Money Laundering Regulations 2003.

The group and all staff must ensure that the MLRO is able to

- Monitor the day to day operation of its anti-money laundering policies, and

- Respond promptly to any reasonable request for information made by investigating agencies.

The MLRO's responsibilities

The MLRO is responsible for

- Receiving and evaluating internal reports,
- Liaising with and making external reports to NCIS,
- Obtaining and effectively using national and international money laundering data,
- Taking steps to establish and maintain adequate arrangements for awareness and training, and
- Reporting to the Group Compliance Committee and the group's main board.

If the MLRO fails properly to discharge these responsibilities he is personally at risk of criminal prosecution and regulatory sanction.

WJB CHILTERN GROUP / MRI MOORES ROWLAND LLP

MONEY LAUNDERING – SUSPICIOUS CLIENT/MATTER
INTERNAL REPORT TO MONEY LAUNDERING REPORTING OFFICER

Reported by [ ]

Client name [ ] Client no.* [ ]

File name [ ]

File manager* [ ] File no.* [ ]

You can find the information marked with a * on TimeView

Information/detail of transaction(s): 'Routine' TIG disclosure? Tick here ☐

'Routine' TIG disclosure: Only identify tax office dealing and case ref., if known.

Reasons for suspicion:

Signature [ ] Date / /20

Date received / /20 NCIS advised / /20

MLRO ref. [ ] NCIS ref. [ ]

MLRO USE ONLY BELOW LINE Tick box if NCIS not advised ☐

Setting Up a New File for a New Client

All fields are compulsory unless stated otherwise. Completed, approved forms should be sent to Accounts. Forms with missing information will be returned without setting up the client or file.

Client Name and Billing Address

1 Name ______________________

2 Address ______________________
____
____

Postcode ______________

Country ______________

Client Contact Details

3 Contact surname ______________

4 Contact forename and middle initials ______________

5 Contact job title ______________

6 Contact telephone number ______________

7 Contact mobile number (optional) ______________

8 Contact fax number (optional) ______________

9 Contact e-mail (optional) ____________________

Relationship Manager

10 Employee who will be the client relationship manager: ______________

New Client Marketing Information

11 If client was actively won please name the employee who won the client: ______________

12 How did they win the client (Tick one box only)

i) Part of formal targeting programme ☐

ii) Personal networking/direct contact ☐

iii) Brought client with them on joining ☐

iv) Other ☐ Please Explain ______________________

03/12/2003MW xls Version 1 1

13 If the client was ***not actively won by us***, please specify how they came to us:(Tick one box only)

i) Through conference/seminar ☐

ii) MRI referral ☐

iii) Taxline/VATline call ☐

iv) PR/Advertising ☐

v) Referred by existing client ☐ Please specify client: ____________

vi) Website ☐

vii) Other ☐ Please explain: ____________

viii) Don't know ☐

Client Relationships

14 What relationship does this client have to existing clients:

i) Part of existing client group ☐ Existing client group: ____________

ii) None, and the ultimate relationship is with this client ☐

iii) None, and the ultimate relationship is not with this client but with a new client group ☐ New client group: ____________

Relationship manager of new client group: ____________

Contact surname ____________

Contact forename and middle initials ____________

Contact telephone number ____________

Contact mobile number (optional) ____________

Contact fax number (optional) ____________

Contact e-mail (optional) ____________

Client Industry

15 Please enter the client industry (see appendix 1 for options): ____________

Client Type

16 Please enter the client type (see appendix 2 for options): ____________

03/12/2003MW.xls Version 1 2

File Information

17 If work was actively won, which employee won it (if different from 11) __________

18 If winning the work required a formal competitive tender, please tick here: ☐

File Details

19 File name: __________

20 File manager: __________

21 File sub-manager: __________

22 London contact (Jersey files only) __________

23 File profit centre __________

24 Estimated fees in next 12 months: __________

25 Fixed Fee?(Y/N) ☐

26 Jurisdiction __________
(Country of incorporation for a company, residence for an individual)

Billing Information

Billing address (if different from 1 and 2)

27 Name: __________

28 Address: __________

Postcode: __________

Country: __________

29 VAT on invoice? (Y/N) ☐

03/12/2003MW.xls Version 1 3

34 ____________

35 ____________

36 ____________

37 ____________

38 ____________

Compliance Requirements

Please confirm that:

39 A signed engagement letter has been received(Y/N) ☐

40 Appropriate documentation for this client has been obtained
(See appendix 2 for requirements according to type of client)(Y/N) ☐

If you have not ticked either of these boxes, please explain why below.
Please also record what information is missing and when this will be obtained.
Please inform compliance once this information is obtained.

____

____

____

____

____

03/12/2003MW xls   Version 1   4

41

File Manager: ____________ ____________ ____________
Name Signature Date

Profit centre head(Tax) or director of file manager(if Jersey) ____________ ____________ ____________
Name Signature Date

Division Head: ____________ ____________ ____________
Name Signature Date

To be completed by credit control:

Credit limit: [ ] Risk Score: [ ]

Comments by credit control: ____________

____________ ____________ ____________
Name Signature Date

03/12/2003MW.xls Version 1 5

Client Types and Compliance/Due Diligence Requirements

It is always desirable to meet the client face-to-face and see original documents, from which you personally should take and certify copies. If this is not possible, copies certified by a responsible third party (*e.g.*, a qualified professional) can be accepted. However, for non-UK clients, the certification must be by a lawyer or attorney, or by an embassy, consulate, etc. of the issuing country.

Certified copies of identification evidence should be dated, and signed "original seen." The certifier's name and status should also be legible. In situations where a good reproduction of photographic evidence of identity cannot be achieved, the copy should also be certified as providing a good likeness of the applicant.

If the client acts, or appears to act, for another person or entity, then that underlying client's identity will also need to be verified.

Compliance/due diligence requirements

Client Type	**Requirements**
Charitable trust	*See* Charity
Charity	Trust deed or constitutional document Verification on two trustees – *see* Individual Proof of status – print from www.charity-commission.gov.uk/registeredcharities showing relevant entity Proof of contact's authority to act
Church body	*See* Professional body
Foundation	*See* Professional body
Fund	Evidence of domicile of fund Copy of the fund prospectus if the fund is not domiciled within the EU
Government department	Proof of existence – print from www.ukonline.gov.uk showing home page of relevant entity Proof of contact's authority to act

Client Type	**Requirements**
Health authority	Proof of existence – print from www.nhs.uk/localnhsservices showing home page of relevant entity Proof of contact's authority to act
Individual	Passport Two utility bills etc. showing home address Banker's reference showing name and home address *and* Another professional reference
Internal WJB project	None
International body	*See* Professional body
Limited company (*except* Professional regulated entities – *see below*)	*Either* Copy certificate of incorporation, Memorandum & articles of association, List of directors, *and* Copy of latest accounts *Or* Registry search (can be requested centrally) Confirmation of good standing (*e.g.*, not insolvent), or full details if not (can form part of registry check) Verification on two directors – *see* Individual Verification on >=20% (*or >=10% if work to be performed in Private Clients Division*) ultimate beneficial owners – *see* Individual Proof of contact's authority to act if not a director

Client Type	**Requirements**
Limited liability partnership (*except* Professional regulated entities – *see below*)	Latest accounts Verification on two partners – *see* Individual Copy certificate of incorporation Registry search Proof of contact's authority to act if not a member Copy of partnership agreement
Limited partnership (*except* Professional regulated entities – *see below*)	*See* Partnership
Listed company (*except* Professional regulated entities – *see below*)	*Either* Copy certificate of incorporation, Memorandum & articles of association, *and* Copy of latest accounts *Or* Registry search (can be requested centrally) Proof of listing Proof of contact's authority to act
Local authority	*See* Government department
NHS trust	*See* Government department
Offshore partnership	*See* Partnership
Overseas listed company	*See* Listed company, *also* English translations, if applicable
Overseas unlisted company	*See* Limited company, *also* English translations, if applicable
Partnership (*except* Professional regulated entities – *see below*)	Latest accounts Verification on two partners – *see* Individual Proof of contact's authority to act if not a partner Copy of partnership agreement
Police/fire authority	*See* Government department

Client Type	**Requirements**
Professional body	Trust deed or constitutional document Verification on two officers – *see* Individual Proof of contact's authority to act
Professional regulated entities (*e.g.*, solicitor, accountant, IFA) *NB for non-UK professionals please contact group compliance for guidance*	A search on the relevant professional website (ICAEW, FSA, ACCA, Law Society, ICAI, ICAS, CIMA, CIPFA) to verify the existence of the professional entity is sufficient
Sole trader (*except* Professional regulated entities – *see above*)	*See* Individual
Trust – offshore (including foundation)	*See* Trust – onshore
Trust – onshore	Verification on settlor – *see* Individual Verification on adult beneficiaries – *see* Individual Verification on protector (if any) – *see* Individual Proof of contact's authority to act if not a trustee
Unlimited company	*See* Limited company
Unlisted PLC	*See* Limited company

Index

Introduction. The index covers Chapters 1 to 14 and the Appendices. Index entries are generally to paragraph numbers in the form 12.2, indicating paragraph 2 of Chapter 12. In Chapter 2 some index entries are of the form 2.18:10, indicating clause 10 of paragraph 18 of Chapter 2, and in the Appendices, entries are to Appendix numbers in the form App.2. Alphabetical arrangement is word-by-word, where a group of letters followed by a space is filed before the same group of letters followed by a letter, eg 'Share option schemes' will appear before 'Shareholders'.

J

M

S

U